Webster's Vest Pocket Dictionary

D0040408

A Merriam-Webster®

Merriam-Webster Inc., *Publishers*
Springfield, Massachusetts, U.S.A.

A GENUINE MERRIAM-WEBSTER

The name *Webster* alone is no guarantee of excellence. It is used by a number of publishers and may serve mainly to mislead an unwary buyer.

A Merriam-Webster® is the registered trademark you should look for when you consider the purchase of dictionaries or other fine reference books. It carries the reputation of a company that has been publishing since 1831 and is your assurance of quality and authority.

Copyright © 1981 by Merriam-Webster Inc.

Philippines Copyright 1981 by Merriam-Webster Inc.

Library of Congress Cataloging in Publication Data

Main entry under title:

Webster's vest pocket dictionary

    1. English Language—Dictionaries.
PE1628.W567   423   80-29018
ISBN 0-87779-190-2

Made in the United States of America

1213IB8685

Preface

WEBSTER'S VEST POCKET DICTIONARY is a new and extremely concise reference to those words which form the very core of the English vocabulary. It shares many details of presentation with older and more comprehensive members of the Merriam-Webster family of dictionaries, such as Webster's New Collegiate Dictionary, but it also incorporates several features uniquely its own. A few points require special mention.

Main entries follow one another in alphabetical order. Centered periods within the entries show points at which a hyphen may be put at the end of a line. Homographs of closely related origin are run into a single main entry, second and succeeding homographs being represented by a swung dash: ~. Homographs of distinctly different origin (as **1fare** and **2fare**) are given separate entries with preceding raised numerals.

Variant spellings that are quite common appear at the main entry following a comma (as **judg·ment, judge·ment**).

Inflected forms of nouns, verbs, adjectives, and adverbs are shown when they are irregular, when adding the suffix makes a change, or when there might be doubt about their spelling. They are given either in full as **bet·ter . . .; best** at **good**) or cut back to a convenient point of division (as **-ried; -ry·ing** at **hur·ry**).

Common variants of inflected forms are also shown even if they are regular (as **seed** or **seeds** at **seed**). When the inflected forms of a verb involve no irregularity except the doubling of a final consonant, the double consonant is shown instead of full or cutback inflected forms (as **lug . . .** vb **-gg-**).

Several other kinds of entries are also found in this dictionary. A variant or inflected form whose alphabetical place is distant from the main entry is entered at its own place with a cross-reference in small capital letters to the main entry (as **hung** past of HANG). A run-in entry is a term related to a main entry that appears within a definition (as **jet engine** at **jet–propelled**). It is set off by parentheses. An undefined run-on entry appears after all definitions of a main entry set off by a dash (as **—like·ness** at **1like**). Its meaning can be inferred from the meaning of the main entry where it appears and that of another main entry, often a suffix, elsewhere. A run-on phrase is a group of two or more words involving as a major element the main entry where it appears and having a special meaning of its own (as **by way of** at **way** or **come to** at **come**). It always has a definition. Lists of undefined words whose meanings can be inferred from the meaning of a prefix and that of a word entered in the dictionary will be found at the following places: anti–, bi–, co–, counter–, extra–, hyper–, in–, inter–, mini–, multi–, non–, over–, post–, pre–, re–, self–, sub–, super–, un–, and vice–.

Information about the pronunciation of every entry in the dictionary is either given explicitly or implied. A full list of the symbols used is shown on the next page. Pronunciations are placed within slant lines (as \'dabəl\ at **dab·ble**).

Every main entry has an italic label (as vb, n, or prefix) indicating its grammatical function. All abbreviations used in these labels and all other abbreviations used in the dictionary are listed, along with a number of other common abbreviations, in a special section immediately following the dictionary proper. This section is followed in turn by a brief Handbook of Style discussing and illustrating the chief points of English punctuation, italicization, capitalization, and the formation of plurals.

Pronunciation Symbols

ə banana, collide, abut; raised \ə\ in \əl\, \ən\ as in battle, cotton, in \lə\, \mə\, \rə\ as in French table, prisme, titre

'ə, ˌə humbug, abut

ər operation, further

a map, patch

ā day, fate

ä bother, cot, father

à father as pronounced by those who do not rhyme it with *bother*

aú now, out

b baby, rib

ch chin, catch

d did, adder

e set, red

ē beat, nosebleed, easy

f fifty, cuff

g go, big

h hat, ahead

hw whale

i tip, banish

ī site, buy

j job, edge

k kin, cook

ḵ German ich, Buch

l lily, cool

m murmur, dim

n nine, own; raised \ⁿ\ indicates that a preceding vowel or diphthong is pronounced through both nose and mouth, as in French *bon* \bōⁿ\

ŋ sing, singer, finger, ink

ō bone, hollow

ȯ saw, cork

œ French bœuf, German Hölle

œ̄ French feu, German Höhle

ȯi toy, sawing

p pepper, lip

r rarity

s source, less

sh shy, mission

t tie, attack

th thin, ether

th then, either

ü boot, few \'fyü\

ů put, pure \'pyůr\

ue German füllen

ūe French rue, German fühlen

v vivid, give

w we, away

y yard, cue \'kyü\; raised \ʸ\ indicates that a preceding \l\, \n\, or \w\ is modified by the placing of the tongue tip against the lower front teeth, as in French *digne* \dēnʸ\

z zone, raise

zh vision, pleasure

\ slant line used in pairs to mark the beginning and end of a transcription

' mark at the beginning of a syllable that has primary (strongest) stress: \'penmanˌship\

ˌ mark at the beginning of a syllable that has secondary (next-strongest) stress: \'penmanˌship\

( ) indicate that what is symbolized between is present in some utterances but not in others: *factory* \'fakt(ə)rē\

A

¹a \'ā\ *n, pl* **a's** or **as** \'āz\ : 1st letter of the alphabet

²a \ə, (')ā\ *indefinite article* : one or some—used to indicate an unspecified or unidentified individual

aard-vark \'ärd,värk\ *n* : ant-eating African mammal

aback \ə'bak\ *adv* : by surprise

aba-cus \'abəkəs\ *n, pl* **aba-ci** \'abə,sī, -,kē\ or **aba-cus-es** : calculating instrument using rows of beads

abaft \ə'baft\ *adv* : toward or at the stern

ab-a-lo-ne \,abə'lōnē\ *n* : large edible shellfish

¹aban-don \ə'bandən\ *vb* : give up without intent to reclaim —**aban-don-ment** *n*

²abandon *n* : thorough yielding to impulses

aban-doned \ə'bandənd\ *adj* : morally unrestrained

abase \ə'bās\ *vb* **abased; abas-ing** : lower in dignity —**abase-ment** *n*

abash \ə'bash\ *vb* : embarass —**abash-ment** *n*

abate \ə'bāt\ *vb* **abat-ed; abat-ing** : decrease or lessen

abate-ment \ə'bātmənt\ *n* : tax reduction

ab-at-toir \'abə,twär\ *n* : slaughterhouse

ab-bess \'abəs\ *n* : head of a convent

ab-bey \'abē\ *n, pl* **-beys** : monastery or convent

ab-bot \'abət\ *n* : head of a monastery

ab-bre-vi-ate \ə'brēvē,āt\ *vb* **-at-ed; -at-ing** : shorten —**ab-bre-vi-a-tion** \ə,brēvē'āshən\ *n*

ab-di-cate \'abdi,kāt\ *vb* **-cat-ed; -cat-ing** : renounce —**ab-di-ca-tion** \,abdi'kāshən\ *n*

ab-do-men \'abdəmən, ab'dōmən\ *n* 1 : body area between chest and pelvis 2 : hindmost part of an insect —**ab-dom-i-nal** \ab'dämən°l\ *adj* —**ab-dom-i-nal-ly** *adv*

ab-duct \ab'dəkt\ *vb* : kidnap —**ab-duc-tion** \-'dəkshən\ *n* —**ab-duc-tor** \-tər\ *n*

abed \ə'bed\ *adv or adj* : in bed

ab-er-ra-tion \,abə'rāshən\ *n* : deviation or distortion —**ab-er-rant** \a'berənt\ *adj*

abet \ə'bet\ *vb* **-tt-** : incite or encourage —**abet-tor, abet-ter** \-ər\ *n*

abey-ance \ə'bāəns\ *n* : state of inactivity

ab-hor \ab'hȯr, ab-\ *vb* **-rr-** : hate —**ab-hor-rence** \-əns\ *n* —**ab-hor-rent** \-ənt\ *adj*

abide \ə'bīd\ *vb* **abode** \-'bōd\ *or* **abid-ed; abid-ing** 1 : remain, last, or reside 2 : endure

ab-ject \'ab,jekt, ab'-\ *adj* : low in spirit or hope —**ab-jec-tion** \ab'jekshən\ *n* —**ab-ject-ly** *adv* —**ab-ject-ness** *n*

ab-jure \ab'júr\ *vb* 1 : renounce 2 : abstain from —**ab-ju-ra-tion** \,abjə'rāshən\ *n*

ablaze \ə'blāz\ *adj or adv* : on fire

able \'ābəl\ *adj* **abler** \-b(ə)lər\; **ablest** \-b(ə)ləst\ 1 : having sufficient power, skill, or resources 2 : skilled or efficient —**abil-i-ty** \ə'bilətē\ *n* —**ably** \'āblē\ *adv*

-able, -ible \əbəl\ *adj suffix* 1 : capable of, fit for, or worthy of 2 : tending, given, or liable to

ab-lu-tion \ə'blüshən, a'blü-\ *n* : washing of one's body

ab-ne-gate \'abni,gāt\ *vb* **-gat-ed; -gat-ing** 1 : relinquish 2 : renounce —**ab-ne-ga-tion** \,abni'gāshən\ *n*

ab-nor-mal \ab'nȯrmal\ *adj* : deviating from the normal or average —**ab-nor-mal-i-ty** \,abnər'malətē, -(,)nȯr-\ *n* —**ab-nor-mal-ly** *adv*

aboard \ə'bōrd\ *adv* : on, onto, or within a car, ship, or aircraft ~ *prep* : on or within

abode \ə'bōd\ *n* : residence

abol-ish \ə'bälish\ *vb* : do away with —**ab-o-li-tion** \,abə'lishən\ *n*

abom-i-na-ble \ə'bäm(ə)nəbəl\ *adj* : thoroughly unpleasant or revolting

abom-i-nate \ə'bämə,nāt\ *vb* **-nat-ed; -nat-ing** : hate —**abom-i-na-tion** \ə,bämə'nāshən\ *n*

ab·orig·i·nal \\ˌabəˈrij(ə)nəl\\ *adj* **1** : original **2** : primitive

ab·orig·i·ne \\-ˈrijəˌnē\\ *n* : original inhabitant

abort \\əˈbȯrt\\ *vb* : terminate prematurely —**abor·tive** \\-ˈbȯrtiv\\ *adj*

abor·tion \\əˈbȯrshən\\ *n* : removal or induced expulsion of a fetus

abound \\əˈbau̇nd\\ *vb* : be plentiful

about \\əˈbau̇t\\ *adv, prep* **1** : around ~ *prep* **1** : on every side of **2** : on the verge of **3** : having as a subject

above \\əˈbəv\\ *adv* **1** : in or to a higher place ~ *prep* **1** : in or to a higher place than **2** : more than

above·board *adv or adj* : without deception

abrade \\əˈbrād\\ *vb* **abrad·ed; abrad·ing** : wear away by rubbing —**abra·sion** \\-ˈbrāzhən\\ *n*

abra·sive \\əˈbrāsiv\\ *adj* **1** : tending to abrade **2** : causing irritation — *n* : substance for grinding, smoothing, or polishing —**abra·sive·ly** *adv* —**abra·sive·ness** *n*

abreast \\əˈbrest\\ *adv or adj* **1** : side by side **2** : up to a standard or level

abridge \\əˈbrij\\ *vb* **abridged; abridg·ing** : shorten or condense —**abridg·ment, abridge·ment** *n*

abroad \\əˈbrȯd\\ *adv or adj* **1** : over a wide area **2** : outside one's country

ab·ro·gate \\ˈabrəˌgāt\\ *vb* **-gat·ed; -gat·ing** : annul or revoke —**ab·ro·ga·tion** \\ˌabrəˈgāshən\\ *n*

abrupt \\əˈbrəpt\\ *adj* **1** : sudden **2** : so quick as to seem rude —**abrupt·ly** *adv*

ab·scess \\ˈabˌses\\ *n* : collection of pus surrounded by inflamed tissue —**ab·scessed** \\-ˌsest\\ *adj*

ab·scond \\abˈskänd\\ *vb* : run away and hide

ab·sent \\ˈabsənt\\ *adj* : not present ~ **ab·sent** \\abˈsent\\ *vb* : keep oneself away —**ab·sence** \\ˈabsəns\\ *n* —**ab·sen·tee** \\ˌabsənˈtē\\ *n*

ab·sent-mind·ed \\ˌabsəntˈmīndəd\\ *adj* : unaware of one's surroundings or action —**ab·sent-mind·ed·ly** *adv* —**ab·sent-mind·ed·ness** *n*

ab·so·lute \\ˈabsəˌlüt, ˌabsəˈ-\\ *adj* **1** : pure **2** : free from restricton **3** : definite —**ab·so·lute·ly** *adv*

ab·so·lu·tion \\ˌabsəˈlüshən\\ *n* : remission of sins

ab·solve \\əbˈzälv, -ˈsälv\\ *vb* **-solved; -solv·ing** : set free of the consequences of guilt

ab·sorb \\əbˈsȯrb, -ˈzȯrb\\ *vb* **1** : suck up or take in as a sponge does **2** : engage (one's attention) —**ab·sor·ben·cy** \\-ˈsȯrbənsē, -ˈzȯr-\\ *n* —**ab·sor·bent** \\-bənt\\ *adj or n* —**ab·sorb·ing** *adj* —**ab·sorb·ing·ly** *adv*

ab·sorp·tion \\əbˈsȯrpshən, -ˈzȯrp-\\ *n* : process of absorbing —**ab·sorp·tive** \\-tiv\\ *adj*

ab·stain \\əbˈstān\\ *vb* : refrain from doing something —**ab·stain·er** *n* —**ab·sten·tion** \\-ˈstenchən\\ *n* —**ab·sti·nence** \\ˈabstənəns\\ *n*

ab·ste·mi·ous \\abˈstēmēəs\\ *adj* : sparing in use of food or drink —**ab·ste·mi·ous·ly** *adv*

ab·stract \\abˈstrakt, ˈabˌ-\\ *adj* **1** : expressing a quality apart from an object **2** : not representing something specific ~ \\ˈabˌ-\\ *n* : summary ~ \\abˈ-, ˈabˌ-\\ *vb* **1** : remove or separate **2** : make an abstract of —**ab·stract·ly** *adv* —**ab·stract·ness** \\-ˈstrakt(t)nəs, -ˌstrak(t)-\\ *n*

ab·strac·tion \\abˈstrakshən\\ *n* : act of abstracting **2** : abstract idea or work of art

ab·struse \\əbˈstrüs, ab-\\ *adj* : hard to understand —**ab·struse·ly** *adv* —**ab·struse·ness** *n*

ab·surd \\əbˈsərd, -ˈzərd\\ *adj* : ridiculous or unreasonable —**ab·sur·di·ty** \\-ətē\\ *n* —**ab·surd·ly** *adv*

abun·dant \\əˈbəndənt\\ *adj* : more than enough —**abun·dance** \\-dəns\\ *n* —**abun·dant·ly** *adv*

abuse \\əˈbyüz\\ *vb* **abused; abus·ing** **1** : attack with words **2** : misuse **3** : mistreat ~ \\-ˈbyüs\\ *n* **1** : corrupt practice **2** : improper use **3** : mistreatment **4** : coarse and insulting speech —**abu·sive** \\-ˈbyüsiv\\ *adj* —**abu·sive·ly** *adv* —**abu·sive·ness** *n*

abut \\əˈbət\\ *vb* **-tt-** : touch along a border

abut·ment \\əˈbətmənt\\ *n* : structure that supports weight or withstands lateral pressure

abys·mal \\əˈbizməl\\ *adj* : immeasurably deep —**abys·mal·ly** *adv*

abyss \\əˈbis\\ *n* : bottomless pit

-ac \\ˌak\\ *n suffix* : one affected with

aca·cia \\əˈkāshə\\ *n* : leguminous tree or shrub

ac·a·dem·ic \\ˌakəˈdemik\\ *adj* **1** : relating to schools or colleges **2** : theoretical —**ac·a·dem·i·cal·ly** \\-ik(ə)lē\\ *adv*

acad·e·my \\əˈkademē\\ *n, pl* **-mies 1** : private high school **2** : society of scholars or artists

acan·thus \\əˈkanthəs\\ *n* **1** : prickly Mediterranean herb **2** : ornament representing acanthus leaves

ac·cede \\akˈsēd\\ *vb* **-ced·ed; -ced·ing 1** : become a party to an agreement **2**

: express approval **3** : enter upon an office

ac·cel·er·ate \ik'selə₁rāt, ak-\ *vb* **-at·ed; -at·ing 1** : bring about earlier **2** : speed up —**ac·cel·er·a·tion** \-₁selə'rāshən\ *n*

ac·cel·er·a·tor \ik'selə₁rātər, ak-\ *n* : foot-operated pedal for controlling the speed of a motor vehicle

ac·cent \'ak₁sent\ *n* **1** : distinctive manner of pronunciation **2** : prominence given to one syllable of a word **3** : mark (as ˋ, ´, ˆ) over a vowel in writing or printing to indicate pronunciation ~ \'ak-, ₁ak-\ *vb* : emphasize —**ac·cen·tu·al** \ak'sench(ə)wəl\ *adj*

ac·cen·tu·ate \ak'senchə₁wāt\ *vb* **-at·ed; -at·ing** : stress or show off by a contrast —**ac·cen·tu·a·tion** \-₁senchə'wāshən\ *n*

ac·cept \ik'sept, ak-\ *vb* **1** : receive willingly **2** : agree to —**ac·cept·abil·i·ty** \ik₁septə'bilətē, ak\ *n* —**ac·cept·able** \-'septəbəl\ *adj* —**ac·cep·tance** \-'septəns\ *n*

ac·cess \'ak₁ses\ *n* : capability or way of approaching —**ac·ces·si·bil·i·ty** \ik₁sesə'bilətē, ak-\ *n* —**ac·ces·si·ble** \-'sesəbəl\ *adj*

ac·ces·sion \ik'seshən, ak-\ *n* **1** : something added **2** : act of taking office

ac·ces·so·ry \ik'ses(ə)rē, ak-\ *n, pl* **-ries 1** : nonessential addition **2** : one guilty of aiding a criminal —**accessory** *adj*

ac·ci·dent \'aksədənt\ *n* **1** : event occurring by chance or unintentionally **2** : chance —**ac·ci·den·tal** \₁aksə'dent³l\ *adj* —**ac·ci·den·tal·ly** \-'dentlē, -³lē\ *adv*

ac·claim \ə'klām\ *vb or n* : praise

ac·cla·ma·tion \₁aklə'māshən\ *n* **1** : eager applause **2** : unanimous vote

ac·cli·mate \'aklə₁māt, ə'klīmət\ *vb* **-mat·ed; -mat·ing** : accustom to a new climate or situation —**ac·cli·ma·tion** \₁aklə'māshən, ₁ak,lī-\ *n*

ac·cli·ma·tize \ə'klīmə₁tīz\ *vb* **-tized; -tiz·ing** : acclimate —**ac·cli·ma·ti·za·tion** \-₁klīmətə'zāshən\ *n*

ac·co·lade \'akə₁lād\ *n* : award

ac·com·mo·date \ə'kämə₁dāt\ *vb* **-dat·ed; -dat·ing 1** : adapt **2** : provide with something needed **3** : hold without crowding

ac·com·mo·da·tion \ə₁kämə'dāshən\ *n* **1** : quarters —usu. pl. **2** : act of accommodating

ac·com·pa·ny \ə'kəmp(ə)nē\ *vb* **-nied; -ny·ing 1** : go or occur with **2** : play supporting music —**ac·com·pa·ni-**

ment \-mənt\ *n* —**ac·com·pa·nist** \-(ə)nəst\ *n*

ac·com·plice \ə'kämpləs, -'kəm-\ *n* : associate in crime

ac·com·plish \ə'kämplish, -'kəm-\ *vb* : do, fulfill, or bring about —**ac·com·plished** *adj* —**ac·com·plish·er** *n* —**ac·com·plish·ment** *n*

ac·cord \ə'kòrd\ *vb* **1** : grant **2** : agree ~ *n* : agreement —**ac·cor·dance** \-'kòrd³ns\ *n* —**ac·cor·dant** \-³nt\ *adj*

ac·cord·ing·ly \ə'kòrdiŋlē\ *adv* : consequently

according to *prep* **1** : in conformity with **2** : as stated by

ac·cor·di·on \ə'kòrdēən\ *n* : keyboard instrument with a bellows and reeds ~ *adj* : folding like an accordion —**bellows**

ac·cost \ə'kòst\ *vb* : approach and speak to

ac·count \ə'kaunt\ *n* **1** : statement of business transactions **2** : credit arrangement with a vendor **3** : report **4** : worth **5** : sum deposited in a bank ~ *vb* : give an explanation

ac·count·able \ə'kauntəbəl\ *adj* : responsible —**ac·count·abil·i·ty** \-₁kauntə'bilətē\ *n*

ac·coun·tant \ə'kaunt³nt\ *n* : one skilled in accounting —**ac·coun·tan·cy** \-³nsē\ *n*

ac·count·ing \ə'kautiŋ\ *n* : financial record keeping

ac·cou·tre, ac·cou·ter \ə'kütər\ *vb* **-tred** *or* **-tered; -tring** *or* **-ter·ing** \-'kütəriŋ, -'kütriŋ\ : equip

ac·cred·it \ə'kredət\ *vb* **1** : approve officially **2** : attribute

ac·crue \ə'krü\ *vb* **-crued; -cru·ing** : be added by periodic growth —**ac·cru·al** \-əl\ *n*

ac·cu·mu·late \ə'kyümyə₁lāt\ *vb* **-lat·ed; -lat·ing** : collect or pile up —**ac·cu·mu·la·tion** \-₁kyümyə'lāshən\ *n* —**ac·cu·mu·la·tor** \-'kyümyə₁lātər\ *n*

ac·cu·rate \'akyərət\ *adj* : free from error —**ac·cu·ra·cy** \-rəsē\ *n* —**ac·cu·rate·ly** *adv* —**ac·cu·rate·ness** *n*

ac·cursed \ə'kərst, -'kərsəd\, **ac·curst** \ə'kərst\ *adj* **1** : being under a curse **2** : damnable

ac·cuse \ə'kyüz\ *vb* **-cused; -cus·ing** : charge with an offense —**ac·cu·sa·tion** \₁akyə'zāshən\ *n* —**ac·cus·er** *n*

ac·cused \ə'kyüzd\ *n, pl* **-cused** : defendant in a criminal case

ac·cus·tom \ə'kəstəm\ *vb* : cause to treat something as usual or acceptable esp. through repeated experience

ace \'ās\ *n* : one that excels

ac·e·tate \'asə,tāt\ *n* : fast-drying fabric or plastic derived from acetic acid

acetic acid \ə,sētik-\ *n* : acid like that found in vinegar

acet·y·lene \ə'set⁹lən, -⁹l,ēn\ *n* : colorless gas used as a fuel in welding

ache \'āk\ *vb* **ached; ach·ing 1** : suffer a dull persistent pain **2** : yearn —**ache** *n*

achieve \ə'chēv\ *vb* **achieved; achiev·ing** : gain by work or effort —**achieve·ment** *n* —**achiev·er** *n*

ac·id \'asəd\ *adj* **1** : sour or biting to the taste **2** : of or relating to an acid —*n* **1** : sour substance **2** : usu. water-soluble chemical compound —**acid·ic** \ə'sidik\ *adj* —**acid·i·fy** \ə'sidə,fī\ *vb* —**acid·i·ty** \-ətē\ *n*

ac·knowl·edge \ik'nälij, ak-\ *vb* **-edged; -edg·ing 1** : admit as true **2** : admit the authority of **3** : express thanks for —**ac·knowl·edg·ment** *n*

ac·me \'akmē\ *n* : highest point

ac·ne \'aknē\ *n* : skin disorder marked esp. by pimples

ac·o·lyte \'akə,līt\ *n* : one who assists the clergyman in a service

acorn \'ā,kȯrn, -kərn\ *n* : nut of the oak

acous·tic \ə'küstik\ *adj* : relating to hearing or sound —**acous·ti·cal** \-stikəl\ *adj* —**acous·ti·cal·ly** \-k(ə)lē\ *adv*

acous·tics \ə'küstiks\ *n sing or pl* **1** : science of sound **2** : qualities in a room that affect how sound is heard

ac·quaint \ə'kwānt\ *vb* **1** : inform **2** : make familiar

ac·quain·tance \ə'kwānt⁹ns\ *n* **1** : personal knowledge **2** : person with whom one is acquainted —**ac·quain·tance·ship** *n*

ac·qui·esce \,akwē'es\ *vb* **-esced; -esc·ing** : consent —**ac·qui·es·cence** \-'es⁹ns\ *n* —**ac·qui·es·cent** \-⁹nt\ *adj* —**ac·qui·es·cent·ly** *adv*

ac·quire \ə'kwī(ə)r\ *vb* **-quired; -quir·ing** : gain

ac·qui·si·tion \,akwə'zishən\ *n* : a gaining or something gained —**ac·qui·si·tive** \ə'kwizətiv\ *adj*

ac·quit \ə'kwit\ *vb* **-tt- 1** : pronounce not guilty **2** : conduct (oneself) usu. well —**ac·quit·tal** \-⁹l\ *n*

acre \'ākər\ *n* **1** *pl* : lands **2** : 4840 square yards

acre·age \'āk(ə)rij\ *n* : area in acres

ac·rid \'akrəd\ *adj* : sharp and biting —**acrid·i·ty** \ə'kridətē, ə-\ *n* —**ac·rid·ness** *n*

ac·ri·mo·ny \'akrə,mōnē\ *n, pl* **-nies** : harshness of language or feeling —**ac·ri·mo·ni·ous** \,akrə'mōnēəs\ *adj*

ac·ro·bat \'akrə,bat\ *n* : performer of tumbling feats —**ac·ro·bat·ic** \,akrə'batik\ *adj*

across \ə'krȯs\ *adv* : to or on the opposite side ~ *prep* **1** : to or on the opposite side of **2** : on so as to cross

acryl·ic \ə'krilik\ *n* : plastic used for molded parts or in paints

act \'akt\ *n* **1** : thing done **2** : law **3** : main division of a play ~ *vb* **1** : perform in a play **2** : conduct oneself **3** : operate **4** : produce an effect

ac·tion \'akshən\ *n* **1** : legal proceeding **2** : manner or method of performing **3** : activity **4** : thing done over a period of time or in stages **5** : combat **6** : events of a literary plot **7** : operating mechanism

ac·ti·vate \'aktə,vāt\ *vb* **-vat·ed; -vat·ing** : make active or reactive —**ac·ti·va·tion** \,aktə'vāshən\ *n*

ac·tive \'aktiv\ *adj* **1** : causing action or change **2** : lively, vigorous, or energetic **3** : now in operation —**active** *n* —**ac·tive·ly** *adv*

ac·tiv·i·ty \ak'tivətē\ *n, pl* **-ties 1** : quality or state of being active **2** : what one is actively doing

ac·tor \'aktər\ *n* : one that acts —**ac·tress** \-trəs\ *n*

ac·tu·al \'akch(əw)əl\ *adj* : really existing —**ac·tu·al·i·ty** \,akchə'walətē\ *n* —**ac·tu·al·iza·tion** \,akch(əw)ələ-'zāshən\ *n* —**ac·tu·al·ize** \'akch(əw)ə,līz\ *vb* —**ac·tu·al·ly** *adv*

ac·tu·ary \'akchə,werē\ *n, pl* **-ar·ies** : one who calculates insurance risks and premiums —**ac·tu·ar·i·al** \,akchə'werēəl\ *adj*

ac·tu·ate \'akchə,wāt\ *vb* **-at·ed; -at·ing** : put into action —**ac·tu·a·tor** \-,wātər\ *n*

acu·men \ə'kyümən\ *n* : mental keenness

acu·punc·ture \'akyü,pəŋkchər\ *n* : treatment by puncturing the body with needles —**acu·punc·tur·ist** \,akyü'pəŋkchərəst\ *n*

acute \ə'kyüt\ *adj* **acut·er; acut·est 1** : sharp **2** : containing less than 90 degrees **3** : mentally alert **4** : severe —**acute·ly** *adv* —**acute·ness** *n*

ad \'ad\ *n* : advertisement

ad·age \'adij\ *n* : old familiar saying

ad·a·mant \'adəmənt, -,mant\ *adj* : insistent —**ad·a·mant·ly** *adv*

adapt \ə'dapt\ *vb* : adjust to be suitable for a new use or condition

—adapt·abil·i·ty \ə‚daptə'bilətē\ n
—adapt·able adj —ad·ap·ta·tion
\‚ad‚ap'tāshən, -əp-\ n —adap·ter n
—adap·tive \'daptiv\ adj

add \'ad\ vb 1 : join to something else
so as to increase in amount 2 : find a
sum —ad·di·tion \ə'dishən\ n

ad·der \'adər\ n 1 : poisonous European snake 2 : No. American snake

ad·dict \'ad(‚)ikt\ n : one who is psy-
chologically or physiologically dependent (as on a drug) ~ \ə'dikt\ vb
: cause to become an addict —ad·dic-
tion \ə'dikshən\ n —ad·dic·tive
\-'diktiv\ adj

ad·di·tion·al \ə'dish(ə)nəl\ adj : existing as a result of adding —ad·di·tion-
al·ly adv

ad·di·tive \'adətiv\ n : substance added
to another

ad·dle \'ad²l\ vb -dled; -dling : confuse

ad·dress \ə'dres\ vb 1 : direct one's
remarks to 2 : mark an address on ~
\ə'dres, 'ad‚res\ n 1 : formal speech
2 : place where a person may be
reached or mail may be delivered

ad·duce \ə'd(y)üs\ vb -duced; -duc·ing
: offer as proof

ad·e·noid \'ad‚nȯid, -ʰnȯid\ n : enlarged tissue near the opening of the
nose into the throat —usu. pl. —ad·
e·noi·dal \-ȯl\ adj

adept \ə'dept\ adj : highly skilled
—adept·ly adv —adept·ness n

ad·e·quate \'adikwət\ adj : good or
plentiful enough —ad·e·qua·cy
\-kwəsē\ n —ad·e·quate·ly adv

ad·here \əd'hiər, əd-\ vb -hered; -her-
ing 1 : remain loyal 2 : stick fast
—ad·her·ence \-'hirəns\ n —ad·her-
ent \-ənt\ adj or n

ad·he·sion \əd'hēzhən, əd-\ n : act or
state of adhering

ad·he·sive \-'hēsiv, -ziv\ adj : tending
to adhere ~ n : adhesive substance

adieu \ə'd(y)ü\ n, pl adieus or adieux
\ə'd(y)üz\ : farewell

ad·ja·cent \ə'jās²nt\ adj : situated near
or next

ad·jec·tive \'ajiktiv\ n : word that
serves as a modifier of a noun —ad·
jec·ti·val \‚ajik'tīvəl\ adj —ad·jec·ti·
val·ly adv

ad·join \ə'join\ vb : be next to

ad·journ \ə'jərn\ vb : end a meeting
—ad·journ·ment n

ad·judge \ə'jəj\ vb -judged; -judg·ing 1
: think or pronounce to be 2 : award
by judicial decision

ad·ju·di·cate \ə'jüdi‚kāt\ vb -cat·ed;
-cat·ing : settle judicially —ad·ju·di·
ca·tion \ə‚jüdi'kāshən\ n

ad·junct \'aj‚eŋkt\ n : something
joined or added but not essential

ad·just \ə'jəst\ vb : fix, adapt, or set
right —ad·just·er, ad·jus·tor n,
ad·jus·tor \ə'jəstər\ n —ad·just·ment
\ə'jəs(t)mənt\ n

ad·ju·tant \'ajətənt\ n : one who helps
esp. a commanding officer

ad·lib \'ad'lib\ vb -bb- : speak without
preparation —ad·lib n or adj

ad·min·is·ter \əd'minəstər\ vb 1 : manage 2 : give out esp. in doses —ad·
min·is·tra·ble \-strəbəl\ adj —ad·
min·is·trant \-strənt\ n

ad·min·is·tra·tion \əd‚minə'strāshən,
(‚)ad-\ n 1 : process of managing 2
: persons responsible for managing
—ad·min·is·tra·tive \əd'minə‚strā-
tiv\ adj —ad·min·is·tra·tive·ly adv

ad·min·is·tra·tor \əd'minə‚strātər\ n
: one that manages

ad·mi·ra·ble \'adm(ə)rəbəl\ adj : worthy of admiration —ad·mi·ra·bly
\-blē\ adv

ad·mi·ral \'adm(ə)rəl\ n : commissioned officer in the navy ranking
next below a fleet admiral

ad·mire \əd'mī(ə)r\ vb -mired; -mir·ing
: have high regard for —ad·mi·ra·tion
\‚admə'rāshən\ n —ad·mir·er n
—ad·mir·ing·ly adv

ad·mis·si·ble \əd'misəbəl\ adj : that
can be permitted —ad·mis·si·bil·i·ty
\-‚misə'bilətē\ n —ad·mis·si·bly
\-'misəblē\ adv

ad·mis·sion \əd'mishən\ n 1 : acknowledgment of a fact 2 : act of admitting
3 : admittance or a fee paid for this

ad·mit \əd'mit\ vb -tt- 1 : allow to enter 2 : permit 3 : recognize as genuine —ad·mit·ted·ly adv

ad·mit·tance \əd'mit²ns\ n : permission to enter

ad·mix·ture \ad'mikschər\ n 1 : mixture 2 : thing added in mixing

ad·mon·ish \əd'mänish\ vb : rebuke
—ad·mo·ni·tion \‚admə'nishən\ n
—ad·mon·i·to·ry \ad'mänə‚tōrē\ adj

ado \ə'dü\ n 1 : fuss 2 : trouble

ado·be \ə'dōbē\ n : sun-dried building
brick —adobe adj

ad·o·les·cence \‚ad²l'es²ns\ n : period
of growth between childhood and
maturity —ad·o·les·cent \-²nt\ adj
or n

adopt \ə'däpt\ vb 1 : take (a child of
other parents) as one's own child 2
: take up and practice as one's own
—adop·tion \-'däpshən\ n

adore \ə'dȯr\ vb adored; ador·ing 1
: worship 2 : be extremely fond of

—**ador·able** *adj* —**ador·ably** *adv* —**ad·o·ra·tion** \ˌadəˈrāshən\ *n*

adorn \əˈdȯrn\ *vb* : decorate with ornaments —**adorn·ment** *n*

adrift \əˈdrift\ *adv or adj* 1 : afloat without motive power or moorings 2 : without guidance or purpose

adroit \əˈdrȯit\ *adj* : dexterous or shrewd —**adroit·ly** *adv* —**adroit·ness** *n*

adult \əˈdəlt, ˈadˌəlt\ *adj* : fully developed and mature ~ *n* : grown-up person —**adult·hood** *n*

adul·ter·ate \əˈdəltəˌrāt\ *vb* -at·ed; -at·ing : make impure by mixture —**adul·ter·a·tion** \-ˌdəltəˈrāshən\ *n*

adul·tery \əˈdəlt(ə)rē\ *n, pl* -ter·ies : sexual unfaithfulness of a married person —**adul·ter·er** \-tərər\ *n* —**adul·ter·ess** \-t(ə)rəs\ *n* —**adul·ter·ous** \-t(ə)rəs\ *adj*

ad·vance \ədˈvans\ *vb* -vanced; -vanc·ing 1 : bring or move forward 2 : promote 3 : lend ~ *n* 1 : forward movement 2 : improvement 3 : offer ~ *adj* : being ahead of time —**ad·vance·ment** *n*

ad·van·tage \ədˈvantij\ *n* 1 : superiority of position 2 : benefit or gain —**ad·van·ta·geous** \ˌadˌvanˈtājəs, -vən-\ *adj* —**ad·van·ta·geous·ly** *adv*

Ad·vent \ˈadˌvent\ *n* : period before Christmas

ad·ven·ti·tious \ˌadvənˈtishəs\ *adj* : accidental —**ad·ven·ti·tious·ly** *adv* —**ad·ven·ti·tious·ness** *n*

ad·ven·ture \ədˈvenchər\ *n* 1 : risky undertaking 2 : exciting experience —**ad·ven·tur·er** \-ˈvench(ə)rər\ *n* —**ad·ven·ture·some** \-ˈvencharsəm\ *adj* —**ad·ven·tur·ous** \-ˈvench(ə)rəs\ *adj*

ad·verb \ˈadˌvərb\ *n* : word that modifies a verb, an adjective, or another adverb —**ad·ver·bi·al** \adˈvərbēəl\ *adj* —**ad·ver·bi·al·ly** *adv*

ad·ver·sary \ˈadvə(r)serē\ *n, pl* -sar·ies : enemy or rival —**adversary** *adj*

ad·verse \adˈvərs, ˈad-\ *adj* : opposing or unfavorable —**ad·verse·ly** *adv*

ad·ver·si·ty \adˈvərsətē\ *n, pl* -ties : hard times

ad·vert \adˈvərt\ *vb* : refer

ad·ver·tise \ˈadvərˌtīz\ *vb* -tised; -tis·ing : call public attention to —**ad·ver·tise·ment** \ˌadvərˈtīzmənt, ədˈvərtəzmənt\ *n* —**ad·ver·tis·er** *n*

ad·ver·tis·ing \ˈadvərˌtīziŋ\ *n* : business of preparing advertisements

ad·vice \ədˈvīs\ *n* : recommendation with regard to a course of action

ad·vis·able \ədˈvīzəbəl\ *adj* : wise or

prudent —**ad·vis·abil·i·ty** \-ˌvīzəˈbilətē\ *n*

ad·vise \ədˈvīz\ *vb* -vised; -vis·ing : give advice to —**ad·vis·er** or **ad·vi·sor** \-ˈvīzər\ *n*

ad·vise·ment \ədˈvīzmənt\ *n* : careful consideration

ad·vi·so·ry \ədˈvīz(ə)rē\ *adj* : having power to advise

ad·vo·cate \ˈadvəkət, -ˌkāt\ *n* : one who argues or pleads for a cause or proposal ~ \-ˌkāt\ *vb* -cat·ed; -cat·ing : recommend —**ad·vo·ca·cy** \-və-kə-sē\ *n*

adz, adze \ˈadz\ *n* : tool for shaping wood

ae·gis \ˈējəs\ *n* : protection or sponsorship

ae·on \ˈēən, ˈēˌän\ *n* : indefinitely long time

aer·ate \ˈa(ə)rˌāt\ *vb* -at·ed; -at·ing : supply or impregnate with air —**aer·a·tion** \a(ə)rˈāshən\ *n* —**aer·a·tor** \ˈa(ə)rˌātər\ *n*

ae·ri·al \ˈarēəl, āˈirēəl\ *adj* : inhabiting, occurring in, or done in the air ~ *n* : antenna

ae·rie \ˈa(ə)rē, ˈi(ə)rē\ *n* : eagle's nest

aer·o·bic \ˌa(ə)rˈōbik\ *adj* : using or needing oxygen

aero·dy·nam·ics \ˌarōdīˈnamiks\ *n* : science of the motion of gases —**aero·dy·nam·ic** \-ik\, **aero·dy·nam·i·cal** \-ikəl\ *adj* —**aero·dy·nam·i·cal·ly** \-ik(ə)lē\ *adv*

aero·nau·tics \ˌarəˈnȯtiks\ *n* : science dealing with aircraft —**aero·nau·ti·cal** \-ikəl\, **aero·nau·tic** \-ik\ *adj* —**aero·nau·ti·cal·ly** \-ik(ə)lē\ *adv*

aero·sol \ˈarəˌsäl, -ˌsȯl\ *n* 1 : liquid or solid particles suspended in a gas 2 : substance sprayed as an aerosol

aero·space \ˈarōˌspās\ *n* : earth's atmosphere and the space beyond —**aerospace** *adj*

aes·thet·ic \esˈthetik\ *adj* : relating to beauty —**aes·thet·i·cal·ly** \-ik(ə)lē\ *adv*

aes·thet·ics \-ˈthetiks\ *n* : branch of philosophy dealing with beauty

afar \əˈfär\ *adv* : from, at, or to a great distance —**afar** *n*

af·fa·ble \ˈafəbəl\ *adj* : easy to talk to —**af·fa·bil·i·ty** \ˌafəˈbilətē\ *n* —**af·fa·bly** \ˈafəblē\ *adv*

af·fair \əˈfaər\ *n* : something that relates to or involves one

[1]af·fect \əˈfekt, a-\ *vb* : assume for effect —**af·fec·ta·tion** \ˌafˌekˈtāshən\ *n*

[2]affect *vb* : produce an effect on

af·fect·ed \əˈfektəd, a-\ *adj* 1 : pretending to some trait 2 : artificially assumed to impress —**af·fect·ed·ly** adv

af·fect·ing \ə'fektiŋ, a-\ adj : arousing pity or sorrow —**af·fect·ing·ly** adv

af·fec·tion \ə'fekshən\ n : kind or loving feeling —**af·fec·tion·ate** \-sh(ə)nət\ adj —**af·fec·tion·ate·ly** adv

af·fi·da·vit \,afə'dāvət\ n : sworn statement

af·fil·i·ate \ə'filē,āt\ vb -at·ed; -at·ing : become a member or branch —**af·fil·i·ate** \-ēət\ n —**af·fil·i·a·tion** \-,filē'āshən\ n

af·fin·i·ty \ə'finətē\ n, pl -ties : close attraction or relationship

af·firm \ə'fərm\ vb : assert positively —**af·fir·ma·tion** \,afər'māshən\ n

af·fir·ma·tive \ə'fərmətiv\ adj : asserting the truth or existence of something — n : statement of affirmation or agreement

af·fix \ə'fiks\ vb : attach

af·flict \ə'flikt\ vb : cause pain and distress to —**af·flic·tion** \-'flikshən\ n

af·flu·ence \'af,lüən(t)s; ə'flü-, ə-\ n : wealth —**af·flu·ent** \-ənt\ adj

af·ford \ə'fōrd\ vb 1 : manage to bear the cost of 2 : provide

af·fray \ə'frā\ n : fight

af·front \ə'frənt\ vb or n : insult

af·ghan \'af,gan, -gən\ n : crocheted or knitted blanket

afire \ə'fī(ə)r\ adj or adv : being on fire

aflame \ə'flām\ adj or adv : flaming

afloat \ə'flōt\ adj or adv : floating

afoot \ə'füt\ adv or adj 1 : on foot 2 : in progress

afore·said \ə'fōr,sed\ adj : said or named before

afraid \ə'frād, South also ə'fre(ə)d\ adj : filled with fear

afresh \ə'fresh\ adv : anew

aft \'aft\ adv : to or toward the stern or tail

af·ter \'aftər\ adv 1 : at a later time 2 : at the back — prep 1 : behind in place or time 2 : intent on gaining — conj : following the time when — adj 1 : later 2 : located toward the tail

af·ter·life \'aftər,līf\ n : existence after death

af·ter·math \-,math\ n : results

af·ter·noon \,aftər'nün\ n : time between noon and evening

af·ter·thought n : later thought

af·ter·ward \'aftə(r)wərd\, **af·ter·wards** \-wərdz\ adv : at a later time

again \ə'gen, -'gin\ adv 1 : once more 2 : on the other hand 3 : in addition

against \ə'genst\ prep 1 : directly op-

posite to 2 : in opposition to 3 : so as to touch or strike

agape \ə'gāp, -'gap\ adj or adv : having the mouth open in astonishment

ag·ate \'agət\ n : quartz with bands or masses of various colors

age \'āj\ n 1 : length of time of life or existence 2 : particular time in life (as majority or the latter part) 3 : quality of being old 4 : long time 5 : period in history ~ vb : become old or mature

-age \ij\ n suffix 1 : aggregate 2 : action or process 3 : result of 4 : rate of 5 : place of 6 : state or rank 7 : fee

aged adj 1 \'ājəd\ : old 2 \'ājd\ : allowed to mature

age·less \'ājləs\ adj : eternal

agen·cy \'ājənsē\ n, pl -cies 1 : one through which something is accomplished 2 : office or function of an agent 3 : government administrative division

agen·da \ə'jendə\ n : list of things to be done

agent \'ājənt\ n 1 : means 2 : person acting or doing business for another

ag·gran·dize \ə'gran,dīz, 'agrən-\ vb -dized; -diz·ing : make great or greater —**ag·gran·dize·ment** \ə'grandəzmənt, -,dīz-; ,agrən'dīz-\ n

ag·gra·vate \'agrə,vāt\ vb -vat·ed; -vat·ing 1 : make more severe 2 : irritate —**ag·gra·va·tion** \,agrə'vāshən\ n

ag·gre·gate \'agrigət\ adj : formed into a mass ~ \-,gāt\ vb -gat·ed; -gat·ing : collect into a mass ~ \-gət\ n 1 : mass 2 : whole amount

ag·gres·sion \ə'greshən\ n 1 : unprovoked attack 2 : hostile behavior —**ag·gres·sor** \-'gresər\ n

ag·gres·sive \ə'gresiv\ adj 1 : easily provoked to fight 2 : hard working and enterprising —**ag·gres·sive·ly** adv —**ag·gres·sive·ness** n

ag·grieve \ə'grēv\ vb -grieved; -griev·ing 1 : cause grief to 2 : inflict injury on

aghast \ə'gast\ adj : struck with amazement or horror

ag·ile \'ajəl\ adj : able to move quickly and easily —**agil·i·ty** \ə'jilətē\ n

ag·i·tate \'ajə,tāt\ vb -tat·ed; -tat·ing 1 : shake or stir back and forth 2 : excite or trouble the mind of 3 : try to arouse public feeling —**ag·i·ta·tion** \,ajə'tāshən\ n —**ag·i·ta·tor** \'ajə,tātər\ n

ag·nos·tic \ag'nästik, əg-\ n : one who doubts the existence of God

ago \ə'gō\ *adj or adv* : earlier than the present

agog \ə'gäg\ *adj* : full of excitement

ag·o·nize \'agə,nīz\ *vb* -nized; -niz·ing : suffer mental agony —**ag·o·niz·ing·ly** *adv*

ag·o·ny \'agənē\ *n, pl* -nies : extreme pain or mental distress

agrar·i·an \ə'grerēən\ *adj* : relating to land ownership or farming interests —**agrarian** *n* —**agrar·i·an·ism** *n*

agree \ə'grē\ *vb* **agreed; agree·ing** 1 : be of the same opinion 2 : express willingness to agree 3 : get along together 4 : be similar 5 : be appropriate, suitable, or healthful

agree·able \-əbəl\ *adj* 1 : pleasing 2 : willing to give approval —**agree·able·ness** *n* —**agree·ably** *adv*

agree·ment \-mənt\ *n* 1 : harmony of opinion or purpose 2 : mutual understanding or arrangement

ag·ri·cul·ture \'agri,kəlchər\ *n* : farming —**ag·ri·cul·tur·al** \,agri'kəlch(ə)rəl\ *adj* —**ag·ri·cul·tur·ist** \-rəst\, **ag·ri·cul·tur·al·ist** \-(ə)rələst\ *n*

aground \ə'graůnd\ *adv or adj* : on or onto the bottom or shore

ague \'āgyū\ *n* 1 : fever with recurrent chills and sweating 2 : malaria

ahead \ə'hed\ *adv or adj* 1 : in or toward the front 2 : into or for the future 3 : in a more advantageous position

ahead of *prep* 1 : in front or advance of 2 : in excess of

ahoy \ə'hói\ *interj* —used in hailing

aid \'ād\ *vb* : provide help or support ~ *n*: help

aide \'ād\ *n*: helper

ail \'āl\ *vb* 1 : trouble 2 : be ill

ai·le·ron \'ālə,rän\ *n* : movable part of an airplane wing

ail·ment \'ālmənt\ *n* : bodily disorder

aim \'ām\ *vb* 1 : point or direct (as a weapon) 2 : direct one's efforts ~ *n* 1 : an aiming or the direction of aiming 2 : something meant to be achieved —**aim·less** *adj* —**aim·less·ly** *adv* —**aim·less·ness** *n*

air \'aər\ *n* 1 : mixture of gases surrounding the earth 2 : compressed air 3 : travel by or use of aircraft 4 : medium of transmission of radio waves 5 : outward appearance 6 : artificial manner ~ *vb* 1 : expose to the air 2 : broadcast —**air·borne** \-,bórn\ *adj*

air-con·di·tion *vb* : equip with an apparatus (**air conditioner**) for filtering and cooling the air

air·craft *n, pl* **aircraft** : craft that flies

Aire·dale terrier \,aər,dāl-\ *n* : large terrier with a hard wiry coat

air·field *n* : airport or its landing field

air force *n* : military organization for conducting warfare by air

air·lift *n* : a transporting of esp. emergency supplies by aircraft —**airlift** *vb*

air·line *n* : air transportation system —**air·lin·er** *n*

air·mail *n* : system of transporting mail by airplane —**airmail** *vb*

air·man \-mən\ *n* 1 : enlisted man in the air force in one of the 3 ranks below sergeant 2 : enlisted man in the air force ranking below airman first class and above airman basic 3 : aviator

airman basic *n* : enlisted man of the lowest rank in the air force

airman first class *n* : enlisted man in the air force ranking below sergeant and above airman

air·plane *n* : fixed-wing aircraft heavier than air

air·port *n* : place for landing aircraft and receiving passengers

air·ship *n* : propelled lighter-than-air aircraft

air·strip *n* : airfield runway

air·tight *adj* : tightly sealed to prevent flow of air

air·waves \-,wāvz\ *n pl* : medium of transmission of radio waves

airy \'a(ə)rē\ *adj* **air·i·er; -est** 1 : delicate 2 : breezy

aisle \'īl\ *n* : passage between sections of seats

ajar \ə'jär\ *adj or adv* : partly open

akim·bo \ə'kimbō\ *adj or adv* : having the hand on the hip and the elbow turned outward

akin \ə'kin\ *adj* 1 : related by blood 2 : similar in kind

-al \əl\ *adj suffix* : of, relating to, or characterized by

al·a·bas·ter \'alə,bastər\ *n* : white or translucent mineral

alac·ri·ty \ə'lakrətē\ *n* : cheerful readiness

alarm \ə'lärm\ *n* 1 : warning signal 2 : fear at sudden danger ~ *vb* 1 : warn 2 : frighten

al·ba·tross \'albə,tròs, -,träs\ *n, pl* -tross *or* -tross·es : large seabird

al·be·it \ól'bēət, al-\ *conj* : even though

al·bi·no \al'bīnō\ *n, pl* -nos : person or animal with abnormally white skin —**al·bi·nism** \'albə,nizəm\ *n*

al·bum \'albəm\ *n* 1 : book for displaying a collection (as of photographs) 2 : phonograph record

al·bu·men \al'byümən\ n 1 : white of an egg 2 : albumin

al·bu·min \-mən\ n : protein found in blood, milk, egg white, and tissues

al·che·my \'alkəmē\ n : medieval chemistry —**al·chem·ic** \al'kemik\, **al·chem·i·cal** \-ikəl\ adj —**al·che·mist** \'alkəməst\ n

al·co·hol \'alkə,hȯl\ n 1 : intoxicating element in liquor 2 : liquor —**al·co·holic** adj

al·co·hol·ic \,alkə'hȯlik, -'häl-\ n : person affected with alcoholism

al·co·hol·ism \'alkə,hȯl,izəm\ n : addiction to alcoholic beverages

al·cove \'al,kōv\ n : recess in a room or wall

al·der·man \'ȯldərmən\ n : city official

ale \'āl\ n : beerlike beverage —**ale·house** n

alert \ə'lərt\ adj 1 : watchful 2 : quick to perceive and act ~ n : warning signal ~ vb : warn —**alert·ly** adv —**alert·ness** n

ale·wife n : fish of the herring family

al·fal·fa \al'falfə\ n : cloverlike forage plant

al·ga \'algə\ n, pl **-gae** \'al(,)jē\ : any of a group of lower plants that includes seaweed —**al·gal** \-gəl\ adj

al·ge·bra \'aljəbrə\ n : branch of mathematics using symbols —**al·ge·bra·ic** \,aljə'brāik\ adj —**al·ge·bra·ical·ly** \-'brāik(ə)lē\ adv

alias \'ālēəs, 'ālyəs\ adv : otherwise called ~ n : assumed name

al·i·bi \'alə,bī\ n 1 : defense of having been elsewhere when a crime was committed 2 : justification ~ vb **-bied; -bi·ing** : offer an excuse

alien \'ālēən, 'ālyən\ adj : foreign ~ n : foreign-born resident

alien·ate \'ālēə,nāt, 'ālyə-\ vb **-at·ed; -at·ing** : cause to be no longer friendly —**alien·ation** \,ālēə'nāshən, ,ālyə-\ n

alight \ə'līt\ vb : dismount

align \ə'līn\ vb : bring into line —**align·ment** n

alike \ə'līk\ adj : identical or very similar ~ adv : equally

al·i·men·ta·ry \,alə'ment(ə)rē\ adj : relating to or functioning in nutrition

al·i·mo·ny \'alə,mōnē\ n, pl **-nies** : money paid to a separated or divorced spouse

alive \ə'līv\ adj 1 : having life 2 : lively or animated

al·ka·li \'alkə,lī\ n, pl **-lies** or **-lis** : strong chemical base —**al·ka·line** \-kələn, -,līn\ adj —**al·ka·lin·i·ty** \,alkə'linətē\ n

all \'ȯl\ adj 1 : the whole of 2 : greatest possible 3 : every one of ~ adv 1 : wholly 2 : so much 3 : for each side ~ pron 1 : every one 2 : every bit 3 : everything

Al·lah \'alə, ä'lä\ n : supreme being of the Muslims

all-around adj : versatile

al·lay \ə'lā\ vb : relieve or dispel

al·lege \ə'lej\ vb **-leged; -leging** : state as a fact without proof —**al·le·ga·tion** \,ali'gāshən\ n —**al·leg·ed·ly** \ə'lejədlē\ adv

al·le·giance \ə'lējəns\ n : loyalty

al·le·go·ry \'alə,gōrē\ n, pl **-ries** : story in which figures and actions are symbols of general truths —**al·le·gor·i·cal** \,alə'gȯrikəl\ adj

al·le·lu·ia \,alə'lüyə\ interj : hallelujah

al·ler·gen \'alərjən\ n : something that causes allergy —**al·ler·gen·ic** \,alər'jenik\ adj

al·ler·gy \'alərjē\ n, pl **-gies** : abnormal reaction to a substance —**al·ler·gic** \ə'lərjik\ adj —**al·ler·gist** \'alərjəst\ adj

al·le·vi·ate \ə'lēvē,āt\ vb **-at·ed; -at·ing** : relieve or improve —**al·le·vi·a·tion** \ə,lēvē'āshən\ n

al·ley \'alē\ n, pl **-leys** 1 : narrow passage between buildings 2 : place for bowling

al·li·ance \ə'līəns\ n : association

al·lied \ə'līd, 'al,īd\ adj : joined

al·li·ga·tor \'alə,gātər\ n : large aquatic reptile related to the crocodiles

al·lit·er·a·tion \ə,litə'rāshən\ n : repetition of initial sounds of words —**al·lit·er·a·tive** \-'litə,rātiv\ adj

al·lo·cate \'alə,kāt\ vb **-cat·ed; -cat·ing** : assign —**al·lo·ca·tion** \,alə'kāshən\ n

al·lot \ə'lät\ vb **-tt-** : distribute as a share —**al·lot·ment** n

al·low \ə'lau̇\ vb 1 : permit 2 : agree to the truth of —**al·low·able** adj

al·low·ance \-əns\ n 1 : allotted share 2 : money given regularly for expenses

al·loy \'al,ȯi, ə'lȯi\ n : metals fused together —**alloy** vb

all right adv or adj 1 : satisfactorily 2 : yes 3 : certainly

all·spice \'ȯlspīs\ n : berry of a West Indian tree made into a spice

al·lude \ə'lüd\ vb **-lud·ed; -lud·ing** : refer indirectly —**al·lu·sion** \-'lüzhən\ n —**al·lu·sive** \-'lüsiv\ adj —**al·lu·sive·ly** adv —**al·lu·sive·ness** n

al·lure \ə'lu̇r\ vb **-lured; -luring** : attract —**allure** n —**al·lure·ment** n

al·ly \ə'lī, 'al,ī\ vb **-lied; -ly·ing** : unite

in alliance ~ \'al‚ī, ə'lī\ *n, pl* -lies : member of an alliance

al·ly \(ə)lē\ *adv suffix* : -ly

al·ma·nac\'ȯlmə‚nak, 'al-\ *n* : annual information book

al·might·y \ȯl'mītē\ *adj* : having absolute power

al·mond \'ämənd, 'am-; 'ȯlmənd\ *n* : tree with nutlike fruit kernels

al·most \'ȯl‚mōst, ȯl-\ *adv* : only a little less than

alms \'ämz, 'almz\ *n, pl* alms : charitable gift

aloft\ə'lȯft\ *adv* : high in the air

alo·ha \ə'lō‚ä, ä'lōhä\ *interj* : —used to express greeting or farewell

alone \ə'lōn\ *adj* 1 : separated from others 2 : not including anyone or anything else —alone *adv*

along \ə'lȯŋ\ *prep* 1 : on or near in a lengthwise direction 2 : at a point on or during ~ *adv* 1 : forward 2 : as a companion 3 : all the time

along·side \-‚sīd\ *adv* : along or by the side ~ *prep* : side by side with

alongside of *prep* : alongside

aloof \ə'lüf\ *adj* : indifferent and reserved —aloof·ness *n*

aloud \ə'laůd\ *adv* : so that the voice can be heard

al·paca \al'pakə\ *n* 1 : So. American mammal related to the llama 2 : alpaca wool or cloth made of this

al·pha·bet \'alfə‚bet, -bət\ *n* : ordered set of letters of a language —al·pha·bet·ic \‚alfə'betik\, al·pha·bet·i·cal \-ikəl\ *adj* —al·pha·bet·i·cal·ly \-k(ə)lē\ *adv*

al·pha·bet·ize \'alfəbə‚tīz\ *vb* -ized; -iz·ing : arrange in alphabetical order —al·pha·bet·iz·er *n*

al·ready \ȯl'redē\ *adv* : by a given time

al·so \'ȯlsō\ *adv* : in addition

al·tar \'ȯltər\ *n* : structure for rituals

al·ter \'ȯltər\ *vb* : make different —al·ter·a·tion \‚ȯltə'rāshən\ *n*

al·ter·ca·tion \‚ȯltər'kāshən\ *n* : dispute

al·ter·nate \'ȯltərnət, 'al-\ *adj* 1 : arranged or succeeding by turns 2 : every other ~ \-‚nāt\ *vb* -nat·ed; -nat·ing : occur or cause to occur by turns ~ \-nət\ *n* : replacement —al·ter·nate·ly *adv* —al·ter·na·tion \‚ȯltər'nāshən, ‚al-\ *n*

alternating current *n* : electric current that regularly reverses direction

al·ter·na·tive \ȯl'tərnətiv, al-\ *adj* : offering a choice —alternative *n*

al·ter·na·tor \'ȯltər‚nātər, 'al-\ *n* : alternating-current generator

al·though \ȯl'thō\ *conj* : even though

al·tim·e·ter \al'timətər, 'altə‚mētər\ *n* : instrument for measuring altitudes

al·ti·tude \'altə‚t(y)üd\ *n* 1 : distance up from the ground 2 : angular distance above the horizon

al·to\'altō\ *n, pl* -tos : contralto

al·to·geth·er \‚ȯltə'gethər\ *adv* 1 : wholly 2 : on the whole

al·tru·ism \'altru‚izəm\ *n* : concern for others —al·tru·ist \-əst\ *n* —al·tru·is·tic \‚altru'istik\ *adj* —al·tru·is·ti·cal·ly \-tik(ə)lē\ *adv*

al·um \'aləm\ *n* : crystalline compound containing aluminum

alu·mi·num \ə'lümənəm\ *n* : silver-white malleable ductile light metallic element

alum·na \ə'ləmnə\ *n, pl* -nae \-‚(,)nē\ : woman graduate

alum·nus \ə'ləmnəs\ *n, pl* -ni \-‚nī\ : graduate

al·ways \'ȯlwēz, -wəz, -(,)wāz\ *adv* 1 : at all times 2 : forever 3 : without exception

am *pres 1st sing of* BE

amal·gam \ə'malgəm\ *n* 1 : mercury alloy 2 : mixture

amal·gam·ate \ə'malgə‚māt\ *vb* -at·ed; -at·ing : unite —amal·gam·a·tion \-‚malgə'māshən\ *n*

am·a·ryl·lis \‚amə'riləs\ *n* : bulbous herb with clusters of colored flowers like lilies

amass \ə'mas\ *vb* : gather

am·a·teur \'amə‚tər, -ətər, -ə‚t(y)ůr, -ə‚chůr, -əchər\ *n* 1 : person who does something for pleasure rather than for pay 2 : person who is not expert —amateur *adj* —am·a·teur·ish \‚amə'tərish, -'t(y)ůr-\ *adj* —am·a·teur·ism \'amə‚tər‚izəm, -ətə‚riz-, -ə‚t(y)ůr‚iz-, -‚chůr‚iz-, -chə‚riz-\ *n*

am·a·to·ry \'amə‚tōrē\ *adj* : of or expressing sexual love

amaze \ə'māz\ *vb* amazed; amazing : overwhelm with wonder —amaze·ment *n* —amaz·ing·ly *adv*

am·a·zon \'amə‚zän, -əzən\ *n* : tall strong woman —am·a·zo·ni·an \‚amə'zōnēən\ *adj*

am·bas·sa·dor \am'basədər\ *n* : country's representative in a foreign land —am·bas·sa·do·ri·al \-‚basə'dōrēəl\ *adj* —am·bas·sa·dor·ship *n*

am·ber \'ambər\ *n* : yellowish fossil resin or its color

am·ber·gris \'ambər‚gris, -‚grēs\ *n* : waxy substance from certain whales used in making perfumes

am·bi·dex·trous \‚ambi'dekstrəs\ *adj* : equally skilled with both hands —am·bi·dex·trous·ly *adv*

am·big·u·ous \am'bigyəwəs\ *adj* : having more than one interpretation —**am·bi·gu·i·ty** \₁ambə'gyüətē\ *n*

am·bi·tion \am'bishən\ *n* : eager desire for success or power

am·bi·tious \-əs\ *adj* : characterized by ambition —**am·bi·tious·ly** *adv*

am·biv·a·lence \am'bivələns, -ə\ *n* : simultaneous attraction and repulsion —**am·biv·a·lent** \-lənt\ *adj*

am·ble \'ambəl\ *vb* **-bled; -bling** : go at a leisurely gait —**amble** *n*

am·bu·lance \'ambyələns\ *n* : vehicle equipped for carrying injured or sick persons

am·bu·la·to·ry \'ambyələ₁tōrē\ *adj* 1 : relating to or adapted to walking 2 : able to walk about

am·bush \'am₁bùsh\ *n* : trap by which a surprise attack is made from a place of hiding —**ambush** *vb*

ame·lio·rate \ə'mēlyə₁rāt\ *vb* **-rat·ed; -rat·ing** : make or grow better —**ame·lio·ra·tion** \₁mēlyə'rāshən\ *n*

amen \(')ā'men, (')ä-\ *interj* —used esp. at the end of prayers

ame·na·ble \ə'mēnəbəl, -'menə-\ *adj* : ready to yield or be influenced

amend \ə'mend\ *vb* 1 : improve 2 : alter in writing

amend·ment \ə'men(d)mənt\ *n* : change made in a formal document (as a law)

amends \ə'men(d)z\ *n sing or pl* : compensation for injury or loss

ame·ni·ty \ə'menətē, -'mēnət-\ *n, pl* **-ties** 1 : agreeableness 2 : something serving to comfort or convenience 3 *pl* : social conventions

am·e·thyst \'aməthəst\ *n* : blue-purple gemstone

ami·a·ble \'āmēəbəl\ *adj* : easy to get along with —**ami·a·bil·i·ty** \₁āmēə'bilətē\ *n* —**ami·a·bly** \'āmēəblē\ *adv*

am·i·ca·ble \'amikəbəl\ *adj* : friendly —**am·i·ca·bly** \-blē\ *adv*

amid \ə'mid\, **amidst** \-'midst\ *prep* : in or into the middle of

amino acid \ə₁mēnō-\ *n* : any of numerous nitrogen-containing acids some of which are components of proteins

amiss \ə'mis\ *adv* : in the wrong way ~ *adj* : wrong

am·me·ter \'am₁ētər\ *n* : instrument for measuring amperes

am·mo·nia \ə'mōnyə\ *n* 1 : colorless gaseous compound of nitrogen and hydrogen 2 : solution of ammonia in water

am·mu·ni·tion \₁amyə'nishən\ *n* 1

: projectiles fired from guns 2 : explosive items used in war

am·ne·sia \am'nēzhə\ *n* : sudden loss of memory —**am·ne·si·ac** \-z(h)ē₁ak\, **am·ne·sic** \-zik, -sik\ *adj or n*

am·nes·ty \'amnəstē\ *n, pl* **-ties** : a pardon for a group —**amnesty** *vb*

amoe·ba \ə'mēbə\ *n, pl* **-bas or -bae** \-(₁)bē\ : tiny one-celled animal that occurs esp. in water —**amoe·bic** \-bik\ *adj*

amok \ə'mək, -'mäk\ *adv* : in an uncontrolled often murderous way

among \ə'məŋ\ *prep* 1 : in or through 2 : in the number or class of 3 : in shares to each of

am·o·rous \'am(ə)rəs\ *adj* : inclined to love 2 : being in love —**am·o·rous·ly** *adv* —**am·o·rous·ness** *n*

amor·phous \ə'mórfəs\ *adj* : shapeless

amor·tize \'amər₁tīz, ə'mór-\ *vb* **-tized; -tiz·ing** : get rid of (as a debt) gradually with periodic payments —**amor·ti·za·tion** \₁amərt-ə'zāshən, ə₁mórt-\ *n*

amount \ə'maùnt\ *vb* 1 : reach as a total 2 : be equivalent ~ *n* : total number or quantity

amour \ə'mür, ä-, a-\ *n* : love affair

am·pere \'am₁pier\ *n* : unit of electric current

am·per·sand \'ampər₁sand\ *n* : character & used for the word *and*

am·phib·i·ous \am'fibēəs\ *adj* 1 : able to live both on land and in water 2 : adapted for both land and water —**am·phib·i·an** \-ən\ *n*

am·phi·the·ater \'amfə₁thēətər\ *n* : oval or circular structure with rising tiers of seats around an arena

am·ple \'ampəl\ *adj* **-pler** \-plər\; **-plest** \-pləst\ 1 : large 2 : sufficient —**am·ply** \-plē\ *adv*

am·pli·fy \'amplə₁fī\ *vb* **-fied; -fy·ing** : make louder, stronger, or more thorough —**am·pli·fi·ca·tion** \₁amplə-fī'kāshən\ *n* —**am·pli·fi·er** \'amplə₁fī(ə)r\ *n*

am·pli·tude \-₁t(y)üd\ *n* 1 : fullness 2 : extent of a vibratory movement

am·pu·tate \'ampyə₁tāt\ *vb* **-tat·ed; -tat·ing** : cut off (a body part) —**am·pu·ta·tion** \₁ampyə'tāshən\ *n* —**am·pu·tee** \₁ampyə'tē\ *n*

amuck \ə'mək\ *var of* AMOK

am·u·let \'amyələt\ *n* : ornament worn as a charm against evil

amuse \ə'myüz\ *vb* **amused; amusing** 1 : engage the attention of in an interesting and pleasant way 2 : make laugh —**amuse·ment** *n*

an \ən, (')an\ *indefinite article* : a —used before words beginning with a vowel sound

-an \ən\, **-ian** \(ē)ən\, **-ean** \(ē)ən, 'ēən\ *n suffix* **1** : one that belongs to **2** : one skilled in ~ *adj suffix* **1** : of or belonging to **2** : characteristic of or resembling

anach·ro·nism \ə'nakrə,nizəm\ *n* : one that is chronological out of place —**anach·ro·nis·tic** \ə,nakrə'nistik\ *adj*

an·a·con·da \,anə'kändə\ *n* : large So. American snake

ana·gram \'anə,gram\ *n* : word or phrase made by transposing the letters of another word or phrase

anal \'ān°l\ *adj* : relating to the anus

an·al·ge·sic \,an°l'jēzik, -sik\ *n* : pain reliever

anal·o·gy \ə'naləjē\ *n, pl* **-gies** **1** : similarity between unlike things **2** : example of something similar —**ana·log·i·cal** \,an°l'äjikəl\ *adj* —**ana·log·i·cal·ly** \-ik(ə)lē\ *adv* —**anal·o·gous** \ə'naləgəs\ *adj*

anal·y·sis \ə'naləsəs\ *n, pl* **-y·ses** \-,sēz\ **1** : examination of a thing to determine its parts **2** : psychoanalysis —**an·a·lyst** \'an°l,əst\ *n* —**an·a·lyt·ic** \,an°l'itik\, **an·a·lyt·i·cal** \-ikəl\ *adj*

an·a·lyze \'an°l,īz\ *vb* **-lyzed; -lyzing** : make an analysis of

an·ar·chism \'anər,kizəm\ *n* : theory that all government is undesirable —**an·ar·chist** \-kəst\ *n* —**an·ar·chis·tic** \,anər'kistik\ *adj*

an·ar·chy \'anərkē\ *n* : lack of government —**an·ar·chic** \a'närkik\ *adj*

anath·e·ma \ə'nathəmə\ *n* **1** : solemn curse **2** : person or thing accursed or intensely disliked

anat·o·my \ə'natəmē\ *n, pl* **-mies** : science dealing with the structure of organisms —**an·a·tom·ic** \,anə'tämik\, **an·a·tom·i·cal** \-ikəl\ *adj* —**an·a·tom·i·cal·ly** *adv* —**anat·o·mist** \ə'natəmist\ *n*

-ance \əns\ *n suffix* **1** : action or process **2** : quality or state **3** : amount or degree

an·ces·tor \'an,sestər\ *n* : one from whom an individual is descended —**an·ces·tress** \-trəs\ *n*

an·ces·try \-trē\ *n* **1** : line of descent **2** : ancestors —**an·ces·tral** \an'sestrəl\ *adj*

an·chor \'aŋkər\ *n* **1** : heavy device that catches in the sea bottom to hold a ship in place ~ *vb* : hold or become

held in place by or as if by an anchor —**an·chor·age** \-k(ə)rij\ *n*

an·chor·man \'aŋkər,man\ *n* : news broadcast coordinator

an·cho·vy \'an,chōvē, an'chō-\ *n, pl* **-vies** *or* **-vy** : small herringlike fish

an·cient \'ānshənt\ *adj* **1** : having existed for many years **2** : belonging to times long past —**ancient** *n*

-ancy \ənsē\ *n suffix* : quality or state

and \ən(d), (')an(d)\ *conj* —used to indicate connection or addition

and·iron \'an,dī(ə)rn\ *n* : one of 2 metal supports for wood in a fireplace

an·ec·dote \'anik,dōt\ *n* : brief story —**an·ec·dot·al** \,anik'dōt°l\ *adj*

ane·mia \ə'nēmēə\ *n* : blood deficiency —**ane·mic** \ə'nēmik\ *adj*

anem·o·ne \ə'nemənē\ *n* : small herb with showy usu. white flowers

an·es·the·sia \,anəs'thēzhə\ *n* : loss of bodily sensation

an·es·thet·ic \,anəs'thetik\ *n* : agent (as ether) that produces anesthesia —**anesthetic** *adj* —**anes·the·tist** \ə'nesthətəst\ *n* —**anes·the·tize** \-thə,tīz\ *vb*

anew \ə'n(y)ü\ *adv* : over again

an·gel \'ānjəl\ *n* : spiritual being superior to humans —**an·gel·ic** \an'jelik\, **an·gel·i·cal** \-ikəl\ *adj* —**an·gel·i·cal·ly** *adv*

an·ger \'aŋgər\ *n* : strong feeling of displeasure ~ *vb* : make angry

an·gi·na \an'jīnə\ *n* : painful disorder of heart muscles —**an·gi·nal** \an'jīn°l\ *adj*

¹an·gle \'aŋgəl\ *n* **1** : figure formed by the meeting of 2 lines in a point **2** : sharp corner **3** : point of view ~ *vb* **-gled; -gling** : turn or direct at an angle

²angle *vb* **an·gled; an·gling** : fish with a hook and line —**an·gler** \-glər\ *n* —**an·gle·worm** \-,wərm\ *n* —**an·gling** *n*

an·go·ra \aŋ'gōrə, an-\ *n* : yarn or cloth made from the hair of an Angora goat or rabbit

an·gry \'aŋgrē\ *adj* **-gri·er; -est** : feeling or showing anger —**an·gri·ly** \-grəlē\ *adv*

an·guish \'aŋgwish\ *n* : extreme pain or distress of mind

an·gu·lar \'aŋgyələr\ *adj* **1** : having many or sharp angles **2** : thin and bony —**an·gu·lar·i·ty** \,aŋgyə'larətē\ *n*

an·i·line \'an°lən\ *n* : oily poisonous liquid used esp. in making dyes

an·i·mal \'anəməl\ *n* **1** : living being capable of feeling and voluntary motion **2** : lower animal as distinguished from man

an·i·mate \'anəmət\ *adj* : having life ~ \-ˌmāt\ *vb* **-mat·ed; -mat·ing 1** : give life or vigor to **2** : make appear to move —**an·i·mat·ed** *adj*

an·i·ma·tion \ˌanəˈmāshən\ *n* **1** : liveliness **2** : animated cartoon

an·i·mos·i·ty \ˌanəˈmäsətē\ *n, pl* **-ties** : resentment

an·i·mus \'anəməs\ *n* : deep-seated hostility

an·ise \'anəs\ *n* : an herb related to the carrot with aromatic seeds (**aniseed** \-ˌ(ˌ)sēd\) used in flavoring

an·kle \'aŋkəl\ *n* : joint or region between the foot and the leg —**an·kle·bone**

an·nals \'anᵊlz\ *n pl* : chronological record of history —**an·nal·ist** \-ᵊləst\ *n*

an·neal \əˈnēl\ *vb* : make less brittle by heating and then cooling

an·nex \əˈneks, 'anˌeks\ *vb* : assume political control over (a territory) ~ \'anˌeks, -iks\ *n* : added building —**an·nex·a·tion** \ˌanˌekˈsāshən\ *n*

an·ni·hi·late \əˈnīəˌlāt\ *vb* **-lat·ed; -lat·ing** : destroy —**an·ni·hi·la·tion** \-ˌnīəˈlāshən\ *n*

an·ni·ver·sa·ry \ˌanəˈvərs(ə)rē\ *n, pl* **-ries** : annual return of the date of a notable event or its celebration

an·no·tate \'anəˌtāt\ *vb* **-tat·ed; -tat·ing** : furnish with notes —**an·no·ta·tion** \ˌanəˈtāshən\ *n* —**an·no·ta·tor** \'anəˌtātər\ *n*

an·nounce \əˈnauns\ *vb* **-nounced; -nounc·ing** : make known publicly —**an·nounce·ment** *n* —**an·nounc·er** *n*

an·noy \əˈnȯi\ *vb* : disturb or irritate —**an·noy·ance** \-əns\ *n* —**an·noy·ing·ly** \-ˈnȯiŋlē\ *adv*

an·nu·al \'anyə(wə)l\ *adj* **1** : occurring once a year **2** : living only one year —**annual** *n* —**an·nu·al·ly** *adv*

an·nu·ity \əˈn(y)üətē\ *n, pl* **-ities** : amount payable annually or the right to such a payment

an·nul \əˈnəl\ *vb* **-ll-** : make legally void —**an·nul·ment** *n*

an·ode \'anˌōd\ *n* **1** : positive electrode **2** : negative battery terminal —**an·od·ic** \aˌnädik\, **an·od·al** \-ˈnōdᵊl\ *adj* —**an·od·i·cal·ly** \-ik(ə)lē\, **an·od·al·ly** \-ᵊlē\ *adv*

anoint \əˈnȯint\ *vb* : apply oil to as a rite —**anoint·ment** *n*

anom·a·ly \əˈnäməlē\ *n, pl* **-lies** : something abnormal or unusual —**anom·a·lous** \əˈnämələs\ *adj*

anon·y·mous \əˈnänəməs\ *adj* : of unknown origin —**an·o·nym·i·ty** \ˌanəˈnimətē\ *n* —**anon·y·mous·ly** *adv*

an·oth·er \əˈnəthər\ *adj* **1** : any or some other **2** : one more ~ *pron* **1** : one more **2** : one different

an·swer \'ansər\ *n* **1** : something spoken or written in return to a question **2** : solution of a problem ~ *vb* **1** : reply to **2** : be responsible **3** : be adequate —**an·swer·er** *n*

an·swer·able \'ans(ə)rəbəl\ *adj* : subject to taking blame or responsibility

ant \'ant\ *n* : small social insect —**ant·hill** *n*

-ant \ənt\ *n suffix* **1** : one that performs or causes an action **2** : thing that is acted upon ~ *adj suffix* **1** : performing an action or being in a condition **2** : causing an action or process

an·tag·o·nism \anˈtagəˌnizəm\ *n* : active opposition or hostility —**an·tag·o·nist** \-ənəst\ *n* —**an·tag·o·nis·tic** \-ˌtagəˈnistik\ *adj*

an·tag·o·nize \anˈtagəˌnīz\ *vb* **-nized; -niz·ing** : cause to be hostile

ant·arc·tic \antˈärktik, -ˈärtik\ *adj* : relating to the region near the south pole

antarctic circle *n* : circle parallel to the equator approximately 23°27' from the south pole

an·te·bel·lum \ˌantiˈbeləm\ *adj* : existing before the U.S. Civil War

an·te·ced·ent \ˌantəˈsēdᵊnt\ *n* : one that comes before —**antecedent** *adj*

an·te·lope \'antᵊlˌōp\ *n, pl* **-lope** or **-lopes** : deerlike mammal related to the ox

an·ten·na \anˈtenə\ *n, pl* **-nae** \-(ˌ)ē\ or **-nas 1** : one of the long slender paired sensory organs on the head of an arthropod **2** *pl* **-nas** : metallic device for sending or receiving radio waves

an·te·ri·or \anˈtirēər\ *adj* : located before in place or time

an·them \'anthəm\ *n* : song or hymn of praise or gladness

an·ther \'anthər\ *n* : part of a seed plant that contains pollen

an·thol·o·gy \anˈthäləjē\ *n, pl* **-gies** : literary collection

an·thra·cite \'anthrəˌsīt\ *n* : hard coal

an·thro·poid \'anthrəˌpȯid\ *adj* : like humans ~ *n* : large ape

an·thro·pol·o·gy \ˌanthrəˈpäləjē\ *n* : science dealing with humans —**an·thro·po·log·i·cal** \-pəˈläjikəl\ *adj* —**an·thro·pol·o·gist** \-ˈpäləjəst\ *n*

anti- \ˌanti, -ē; ˌanˌtī, ant-, anth-\ *prefix* **1** : opposite in kind, position, or action **2** : opposing or hostile toward **3** : defending against **4** : curing or treating

antiabortion	antidemocratic
antiacademic	antidiscrimina-
antiadministra-	tion
tion	antidrug
antiaggression	antidumping
antiaggressive	antieavesdrop-
antiaircraft	ping
antialien	antiestablishment
antianarchic	antievolution
antianarchist	antievolutionary
antiannexation	antifanatic
antiapartheid	antifascism
antiaristocrat	antifascist
antiaristocratic	antifatigue
antiart	antifemale
antiatheism	antifeminine
antiatheist	antifeminism
antiauthoritarian	antifeminist
antibacterial	antifertility
antibigotry	antiforeign
antiblack	antiforeigner
anti-Bolshevik	antifraud
anti-Bolshevism	antifungus
anti-Bolshevist	antigambling
antibourgeois	antiglare
antiboxing	antigonorrheal
antiboycott	antigovernment
antibureaucratic	antigraft
antiburglar	antiguerrilla
antiburglary	antigun
antibusiness	antihijack
anticancer	antihomosexual
anticapitalism	antihuman
anticapitalist	antihumanism
anticapitalistic	antihumanistic
anti-Catholic	antihumanity
anticensorship	antihunting
anti-Christian	anti-imperialism
anti-Christianity	anti-imperialist
antichurch	anti-inflation
anticigarette	anti-inflationary
anticlerical	anti-institutional
anticollision	anti-integration
anticolonial	anti-intellectual
anticommunism	anti-intellectual-
anticommunist	ism
anticonservation	antijamming
anticonservation-	anti-Japanese
ist	anti-Jewish
anticonsumer	antilabor
anticonventional	antiliberal
anticorrosion	antiliberalism
anticorrosive	antilitter
anticorruption	antilittering
anticrime	antiloitering
anticruelty	antilynching
anticultural	antimale
antidandruff	antimanagement

antimaterialism	antisexual
antimaterialist	antishoplifting
antimaterialis-	antislavery
tic	antismoking
antimicrobial	antismuggling
antimilitarism	antismut
antimilitarist	antispending
antimilitaristic	antistrike
antimilitary	antistudent
antimiscegena-	antisubmarine
tion	antisubversion
antimonopolist	antisubversive
antimonopoly	antisuicide
antimosquito	antisyphilis
antinoise	antitank
antiobesity	antitax
antiobscenity	antitechnologi-
antipapal	cal
antipersonnel	antitechnology
antipolice	antiterrorism
antipollution	antiterrorist
antipornograph-	antitheft
ic	antitobacco
antipornography	antitotalitarian
antipoverty	antitoxin
antiprofiteering	antitraditional
antiprogressive	antitrust
antiprostitution	antituberculo-
antirabies	sis
antiracing	antitumor
antiracketeer-	antityphoid
ing	antiulcer
antiradical	antiunemploy-
antirape	ment
antirealism	antiunion
antirealistic	antiuniversity
antirecession	antiurban
antireform	antivandalism
antireligious	antiviolence
antirepublican	antiviral
antirevolution-	antivivisection
ary	antiwar
antiriot	antiweed
antirobbery	anti-West
antiromantic	anti-Western
antitrust	antiwhite
antisegregation	antiwiretap-
antisex	ping
antisexist	antiwoman

an·ti·bi·ot·ic \ˌantibīˈätik, -bē-\ *n* : substance that inhibits harmful microorganisms —**antibiotic** *adj*
an·ti·body \ˈantiˌbädē\ *n* : bodily substance that counteracts the effects of a foreign substance or organism
an·tic \ˈantik\ *n* : playful act ~ *adj* : playful
an·tic·i·pate \anˈtisəˌpāt\ *vb* **-pat·ed; -pat·ing 1** : be prepared for **2** : look forward to —**an·tic·i·pa·tion** \-ˌtisə-

'pāshən\ n　—an·tic·i·pa·to·ry
\-'tisəpə,tōrē\ adj

an·ti·cli·max \,antī'klī,maks\ n
: something strikingly less important
than what has preceded it —an·ti·cli·
mac·tic \-klī'maktik\ adj

an·ti·dote \'antī,dōt\ n : remedy for
poison

an·ti·freeze \'antī,frēz\ n : substance
to prevent a liquid from freezing

an·ti·mo·ny \'antə,mōnē\ n : brittle
white metallic chemical element

an·tip·a·thy \an'tipəthē\ n, pl -thies
: strong dislike

an·ti·quar·i·an \,antə'kwerēən\ adj
: relating to antiquities or old books
—antiquarian n —an·ti·quar·i·an·ism
n

an·ti·quary \'antə,kwerē\ n, pl -quar-
ies : one who collects or studies antiquities

an·ti·quat·ed \'antə,kwātəd\ adj : out-
of-date

an·tique \an'tēk\ adj : very old or out-
of-date —antique n

an·tiq·ui·ty \an'tikwətē\ n, pl -ties 1
: ancient times 2 pl : relics of ancient
times

an·ti·sep·tic \,antə'septik\ adj : killing
or checking the growth of germs
—antiseptic n —an·ti·sep·ti·cal·ly
\-tik(ə)lē\ adv

an·tith·e·sis \an'tithəsəs\ n, pl -e·ses
\-,sēz\ : direct opposite

ant·ler \'antlər\ n : solid branched
horn of a deer —ant·lered \-lərd\ adj

ant·onym \'antə,nim\ n : word of opposite meaning

anus \'ānəs\ n : the rear opening of the
alimentary canal

an·vil \'anvəl\ n : heavy iron block on
which metal is shaped

anx·i·ety \aŋ'zīətē\ n, pl -eties : uneasiness usu. over an expected misfortune

anx·ious \'aŋkshəs\ adj 1 : uneasy 2
: earnestly wishing —anx·ious·ly adv

any \'enē\ adj 1 : one chosen at random 2 : of whatever number or
quantity ~ pron 1 : any one or ones
2 : any amount ~ adv : to any extent
or degree

any·body \-,bädē, -bəd-\ pron : anyone

any·how \-,hau̇\ adv 1 : in any way 2
: nevertheless

any·more \,enē'mōr\ adv : at the present time

any·one \-(,)wən\ pron : any person

any·place adv : anywhere

any·thing pron : any thing whatever

any·time adv : at any time whatever

any·way adv : anyhow

any·where adv : in or to any place

aor·ta \ā'ȯrtə\ n, pl -tas or -tae \-ē\
: main artery from the heart —aor·tic
\-'ȯrtik\ adj

apart \ə'pärt\ adv 1 : separately in
place or time 2 : aside 3 : to pieces

apart·heid \ə'pär,tāt, -,tīt\ n : racial
segregation

apart·ment \ə'pärtmənt\ n : set of usu.
rented rooms

ap·a·thy \'apəthē\ n : lack of emotion
or interest —ap·a·thet·ic
\,apə'thetik\ adj —ap·a·thet·i·cal·ly
\-ik(ə)lē\ adv

ape \'āp\ n : large tailless primate ~
vb aped; ap·ing : imitate

ap·er·ture \'apə(r),chür, -chər\ n
: opening

apex \'ā,peks\ n, pl apex·es or api·ces
\'āpə,sēz, 'apə-\ : highest point

aphid \'āfəd, 'afəd\ n : small insect
that sucks plant juices

aph·o·rism \'afə,rizəm\ n : short saying stating a general truth —aph·o·
ris·tic \,afə'ristik\ adj

aph·ro·dis·i·ac \,afrə'dizē,ak\ n : substance that excites sexual desire

api·a·rist \'āpēərəst\ n : beekeeper
—api·ary \-pē,erē\ n

apiece \ə'pēs\ adv : for each one

aplomb \ə'pläm, -'pləm\ n : complete
calmness or self-assurance

apoc·a·lypse \ə'päkə,lips\ n : writing
prophesying a cataclysm in which
evil forces are destroyed —apoc·a·
lyp·tic \-,päkə'liptik\, apoc·a·lyp·ti·
cal \-tikəl\ adj

apoc·ry·pha \ə'päkrəfə\ n : writings of
dubious authenticity —apoc·ry·phal
\-fəl\ adj

apol·o·get·ic \ə,pälə'jetik\ adj : expressing apology —apol·o·get·i·cal·ly
\-ik(ə)lē\ adv

apol·o·gize \ə'pälə,jīz\ vb -gized; -giz-
ing : make an apology —apol·o·gist
\-jəst\ n

apol·o·gy \ə'päləjē\ n, pl -gies 1 : formal justification 2 : expression of regret for a wrong

ap·o·plexy \'apə,pleksē\ n : sudden
loss of consciousness caused by rupture or obstruction of an artery of
the brain —ap·o·plec·tic \,apə'plek-
tik\ adj

apos·ta·sy \ə'pästəsē\ n, pl -sies : aban-
donment of a former loyalty
—apos·tate \ə'päs,tāt, -tət\ adj or n

apos·tle \ə'päsəl\ n : disciple or advocate —apos·tle·ship n —ap·os·tol·ic
\,apə'stälik\ adj

apos·tro·phe \ə'pästrə(,)fē\ n : punctuation mark ' to indicate the posses-

sive case or the omission of a letter or figure

apoth·e·cary \ə'päthə,kerē\ *n, pl* **-caries** : druggist

ap·pall \ə'pȯl\ *vb* : fill with horror or dismay

ap·pa·ra·tus \,apə'ratəs, -'rät-\ *n, pl* **-tus·es** *or* **-tus** 1 : equipment 2 : complex machine or device

ap·par·el \ə'parəl\ *n* : clothing

ap·par·ent \ə'parənt\ *adj* 1 : visible 2 : obvious 3 : seeming —**ap·par·ent·ly** *adv*

ap·pa·ri·tion \,apə'rishən\ *n* : ghost

ap·peal \ə'pēl\ *vb* 1 : try to have a court case reheard 2 : ask earnestly 3 : have an attraction —**appeal** *n*

ap·pear \ə'piər\ *vb* 1 : become visible or evident 2 : come into the presence of someone 3 : seem

ap·pear·ance \ə'pirəns\ *n* 1 : act of appearing 2 : outward aspect

ap·pease \ə'pēz\ *vb* **-peased; -peas·ing** : pacify with concessions —**ap·pease·ment** *n*

ap·pel·late \ə'pelət\ *adj* : having power to review decisions

ap·pend \ə'pend\ *vb* : attach

ap·pend·age \ə'pendij\ *n* : something attached

ap·pen·dec·to·my \,apən'dektəmē\ *n, pl* **-mies** : surgical removal of the appendix

ap·pen·di·ci·tis \ə,pendə'sītəs\ *n* : inflammation of the appendix

ap·pen·dix \ə'pendiks\ *n, pl* **-dix·es** *or* **-di·ces** \-də,sēz\ 1 : supplementary matter 2 : narrow closed tube extending from lower right intestine

ap·pe·tite \'apə,tīt\ *n* 1 : natural desire esp. for food 2 : preference

ap·pe·tiz·er \-,tīzər\ *n* : food or drink to stimulate the appetite

ap·pe·tiz·ing \-ziŋ\ *adj* : tempting to the appetite —**ap·pe·tiz·ing·ly** *adv*

ap·plaud \ə'plȯd\ *vb* : show approval esp. by clapping

ap·plause \ə'plȯz\ *n* : a clapping in approval

ap·ple \'apəl\ *n* : rounded fruit with firm white flesh

ap·ple·jack \-,jak\ *n* : brandy made from cider

ap·pli·ance \ə'plīəns\ *n* : household machine or device

ap·pli·ca·ble \'aplikəbəl, ə'plikə-\ *adj* : capable of being applied —**ap·pli·ca·bil·i·ty** \,aplikə'bilətē, ə,plikə-\ *n*

ap·pli·cant \'aplikənt\ *n* : one who applies

ap·pli·ca·tion \,aplə'kāshən\ *n* 1 : act

of applying or thing applied 2 : constant attention 3 : request

ap·pli·ca·tor \'aplə,kātər\ *n* : device for applying a substance

ap·pli·qué \,aplə'kā\ *n* : cut-out fabric decoration —**appliqué** *vb*

ap·ply \ə'plī\ *vb* **-plied; -ply·ing** 1 : place in contact 2 : put to practical use 3 : devote (one's) attention or efforts to something 4 : submit a request 5 : have reference or a connection

ap·point \ə'pȯint\ *vb* 1 : set or assign officially 2 : equip or furnish —**ap·point·ee** \ə,pȯin'tē, ,a-\ *n*

ap·point·ment \ə'pȯintmənt\ *n* 1 : act of appointing 2 : nonelective political job 3 : arrangement for a meeting

ap·por·tion \ə'pȯrshən\ *vb* : distribute proportionately —**ap·por·tion·ment** *n*

ap·po·site \'apəzət\ *adj* : suitable —**ap·po·site·ly** *adv* —**ap·po·site·ness** *n*

ap·praise \ə'prāz\ *vb* **-praised; -prais·ing** : set value on —**ap·prais·al** \'prāzəl\ *n* —**ap·prais·er** *n*

ap·pre·cia·ble \ə'prēshəbəl\ *adj* : considerable —**ap·pre·cia·bly** \-blē\ *adv*

ap·pre·ci·ate \ə'prēshē,āt\ *vb* **-at·ed; -at·ing** 1 : value justly 2 : be grateful for 3 : increase in value —**ap·pre·ci·a·tion** \-,prēshē'āshən\ *n*

ap·pre·cia·tive \ə'prēshətiv, -shē,āt-\ *adj* : showing appreciation

ap·pre·hend \,apri'hend\ *vb* 1 : arrest 2 : look forward to in dread 3 : understand —**ap·pre·hen·sion** \-'henchən\ *n*

ap·pre·hen·sive \-'hensiv\ *adj* : fearful —**ap·pre·hen·sive·ly** *adv* —**ap·pre·hen·sive·ness** *n*

ap·pren·tice \ə'prentəs\ *n* : person learning a craft ~ *vb* **-ticed; -tic·ing** : employ or work as an apprentice —**ap·pren·tice·ship** *n*

ap·prise \ə'prīz\ *vb* **-prised; -pris·ing** : inform

ap·proach \ə'prōch\ *vb* 1 : move nearer or be close to 2 : make initial advances or efforts toward —**approach** *n* —**ap·proach·able** *adj*

ap·pro·ba·tion \,aprə'bāshən\ *n* : approval

ap·pro·pri·ate \ə'prōprē,āt\ *vb* **-at·ed; -at·ing** 1 : take possession of 2 : set apart for a particular use ~ \-'prēət\ *adj* : suitable —**ap·pro·pri·ate·ly** *adv* —**ap·pro·pri·ate·ness** *n* —**ap·pro·pri·a·tion** \ə,prōprē'āshən\ *n*

ap·prov·al \ə'prüvəl\ *n* : act of approving

ap·prove \ə'prüv\ *vb* **-proved; -prov·ing** : accept as satisfactory

ap·prox·i·mate \ə'präksəmət\ adj : nearly correct or exact \-ı̄māt\ vb **-mat·ed; -mat·ing** : come near —**ap·prox·i·mate·ly** adv —**ap·prox·i·ma·tion** \-ı̄präksə'māshən\ n

ap·pur·te·nance \ə'pərt(ə)nəns\ n : accessory —**ap·pur·te·nant** \-'pərtnənt, -ᵊnənt\ adj

apri·cot \'apra,kät, 'āpra-\ n : peach-like fruit

April \'āprəl\ n : 4th month of the year having 30 days

apron \'āprən, -pərn\ n : protective garment

ap·ro·pos \,aprə'pō, 'aprə,pō\ adv : suitably ~ adj : being to the point

apropos of prep : with regard to

apt \'apt\ adj 1 : suitable 2 : likely 3 : quick to learn —**apt·ly** adv —**apt·ness** \'ap(t)nəs\ n

ap·ti·tude \'apta,t(y)üd\ n 1 : capacity for learning 2 : natural ability

aqua \'akwə, 'äk-\ n, pl **aquae** \'ak(,)wē, 'äk,wī\ or **aquas** : light greenish blue color

aquar·i·um \ə'kwareəm\ n, pl **-i·ums** or **-ia** \-ēə\ : container in which aquatic animals and plants are kept (as in the home)

aquat·ic \ə'kwätik, -'kwat-\ adj : of or relating to water —**aquatic** n

aq·ue·duct \'akwə,dəkt\ n : conduit for carrying running water

aq·ui·line \'akwə,līn, -lən\ adj : hooked like an eagle's beak

-ar \ər\ adj suffix 1 : of, relating to, or being 2 : resembling

ar·a·besque \,arə'besk\ n : intricate design

ar·a·ble \'arəbəl\ adj : fit for crops

ar·bi·ter \'ärbətər\ n : final authority

ar·bi·trary \'ärbə,trerē\ adj 1 : selected at random 2 : autocratic —**ar·bi·trari·ly** \,ärbə'trerəlē\ adv —**ar·bi·trari·ness** \'ärbə,trerēnəs\ n

ar·bi·trate \'ärbə,trāt\ vb **-trat·ed; -trat·ing** : settle a dispute as arbitrator —**ar·bi·tra·tion** \,ärbə'trāshən\ n

ar·bi·tra·tor \'ärbə,trātər\ n : one chosen to settle a dispute

ar·bor \'ärbər\ n : shelter under branches or vines

ar·bo·re·al \är'bōrēəl\ adj : living in trees

arc \'ärk\ n 1 : part of a circle 2 : bright streak of an electrical discharge ~ vb : form an arc

ar·cade \är'kād\ n : arched passageway between shops

ar·cane \är'kān\ adj : mysterious or secret

¹arch \'ärch\ n 1 : curved structure

spanning an opening ~ vb : cover with or form into an arch

²arch adj 1 : chief —usu. in combination 2 : mischievous —**arch·ly** adv —**arch·ness** n

ar·chae·ol·o·gy, ar·che·ol·o·gy \,ärkē'äləjē\ n : study of past human life —**ar·chae·o·log·i·cal** \-kēə'läjikəl\ adj —**ar·chae·ol·o·gist** \-kē'äləjəst\ n

ar·cha·ic \är'kāik\ adj : belonging to an earlier time —**ar·cha·i·cal·ly** \-ik(ə)lē\ adv

arch·an·gel \'ärk,ānjəl\ n : angel of high rank

arch·bish·op \ärch'bishəp\ n : chief bishop —**arch·bish·op·ric** \-ə(,)prik\ n

arch·di·o·cese \-'dī-əsəs, -,sēz, -,sēs\ n : diocese of an archbishop

ar·chery \'ärch(ə)rē\ n : shooting with bow and arrows —**ar·cher** \'ärchər\ n

ar·che·type \'ärki,tīp\ n : original pattern or model

ar·chi·pel·a·go \,ärkə'pelə,gō, ,ärchə-\ n, pl **-goes** or **-gos** : group of islands

ar·chi·tect \'ärkə,tekt\ n : building designer

ar·chi·tec·ture \'ärkə,tekchər\ n 1 : building design 2 : style of building —**ar·chi·tec·tur·al** \,ärkə'tekchərəl, -'tekshrəl\ adj —**ar·chi·tec·tur·al·ly** adv

ar·chives \'är,kīvz\ n pl : public records or their storage place —**ar·chi·vist** \'ärkəvəst, -,kī-\ n

arch·way \n\ : passageway under an arch

arc lamp \n\ : lamp that produces light when a current arcs between electrodes

arc·tic \'är(k)tik\ adj 1 : relating to the region near the north pole 2 : frigid

arctic circle \n\ : circle parallel to the equator approximately 23°27' from the north pole

-ard \ərd\ n suffix : one that is

ar·dent \'ärdᵊnt\ adj 1 : characterized by warmth of feeling —**ar·dent·ly** adv

ar·dor \'ärdər\ n : warmth of feeling

ar·du·ous \'ärj(ə)wəs\ adj : difficult —**ar·du·ous·ly** adv —**ar·du·ous·ness** n

are pres 2d sing or pres pl of BE

ar·ea \'arēə\ n 1 : space for something 2 : amount of surface included 3 : region 4 : range covered by a thing or concept

area code \n\ : 3-digit area-identifying telephone number

are·na \ə'rēnə\ n 1 : enclosed exhibition area 2 : sphere of activity

ar·gon \\'är₁gän\\ *n* : colorless odorless gaseous chemical element

ar·got \\'ärgət, -₁gō\\ *n* : special language (as of the underworld)

argu·able \\'ärgyəwabəl\\ *adj* : open to dispute

ar·gue \\'ärgyü\\ *vb* **-gued; -guing 1** : give reasons for or against something **2** : disagree in words

ar·gu·ment \\'ärgyəmənt\\ *n* **1** : reasons given to persuade **2** : dispute with words

ar·gu·men·ta·tive \\₁ärgyə'mentətiv\\ *adj* : inclined to argue

ar·gyle \\'är₁gīl\\ *n* : colorful diamond pattern in knitting

aria \\'ärēə\\ *n* : opera solo

ar·id \\'ärəd\\ *adj* : dry and barren —**arid·i·ty** \\ə'ridətē\\ *n*

arise \\ə'rīz\\ *vb* **arose** \\-'rōz\\; **aris·en** \\-'riz^ə n\\; **aris·ing** \\-'rīziŋ\\ **1** : get up **2** : originate

ar·is·toc·ra·cy \\₁arə'stäkrəsē\\ *n, pl* **-cies** : upper class —**ar·is·to·crat** \\ə'ristə₁krat\\ *n* —**aris·to·crat·ic** \\ə₁ristə'kratik\\ *adj*

arith·me·tic \\ə'rithmə₁tik\\ *n* : mathematics that deals with numbers —**ar·ith·met·ic** \\₁arith'metik\\, **ar·ith·met·i·cal** \\-ikəl\\ *adj*

ark \\'ärk\\ *n* : big boat

¹arm \\'ärm\\ *n* **1** : upper limb **2** : branch —**armed** \\'ärmd\\ *adj* —**arm·less** *adj*

²arm *vb* : furnish with weapons ~ *n* **1** : weapon **2** : branch of the military forces **3** *pl* : family's heraldic designs

ar·ma·da \\är'mädə, -'mād-\\ *n* : naval fleet

ar·ma·dil·lo \\₁ärmə'dilō\\ *n, pl* **-los** : burrowing mammal covered with bony plates

ar·ma·ment \\'ärməmənt\\ *n* : military arms and equipment

ar·ma·ture \\'ärmə₁chúr, -chər\\ *n* : part in an electric generator or motor in which the current is induced

armed forces *n pl* : military

ar·mi·stice \\'ärməstəs\\ *n* : truce

ar·mor \\'ärmər\\ *n* : protective covering —**ar·mored** \\-mərd\\ *adj*

ar·mory \\'ärm(ə)rē\\ *n, pl* **-mor·ies** : factory or storehouse for arms

arm·pit *n* : hollow under the junction of the arm and shoulder

ar·my \\'ärmē\\ *n, pl* **-mies 1** : body of men organized for war esp. on land **2** : great number

aro·ma \\ə'rōmə\\ *n* : usu. pleasing odor —**ar·o·mat·ic** \\₁arə'matik\\ *adj*

around \\ə'raúnd\\ *adv* **1** : in or along a circuit **2** : on all sides **3** : near **4** : in an opposite direction ~ *prep* **1** : surrounding **2** : along the circuit of **3** : to or on the other side of **4** : near

arouse \\ə'raúz\\ *vb* **aroused; arousing 1** : awaken from sleep **2** : stir up —**arous·al** \\-'raúzəl\\ *n*

ar·raign \\ə'rān\\ *vb* **1** : call before a court to answer to an indictment **2** : accuse —**ar·raign·ment** *n*

ar·range \\ə'rānj\\ *vb* **-ranged; -rang·ing 1** : put in order **2** : settle or agree on **3** : adapt (a musical composition) for voices or instruments —**ar·range·ment** *n* —**ar·rang·er** *n*

ar·ray \\ə'rā\\ *vb* **1** : arrange in order **2** : dress esp. splendidly ~ *n* **1** : arrangement **2** : rich clothing **3** : imposing group

ar·rears \\ə'rirəz\\ *n pl* : state of being behind in paying debts

ar·rest \\ə'rest\\ *vb* **1** : stop **2** : take into legal custody —**arrest** *n*

ar·rive \\ə'rīv\\ *vb* **-rived; -riv·ing 1** : reach a destination, point, or stage **2** : come near in time —**ar·riv·al** \\-əl\\ *n*

ar·ro·gant \\'arəgənt\\ *adj* : showing an offensive sense of superiority —**ar·ro·gance** \\-gəns\\ *n* —**ar·ro·gant·ly** *adv*

ar·ro·gate \\'arə₁gāt\\ *vb* **-gat·ed; -gat·ing** : to claim without justification

ar·row \\'arō\\ *n* : slender missile shot from a bow —**ar·row·head** *n*

ar·royo \\ə'róiə, -ō\\ *n, pl* **-royos 1** : watercourse **2** : gully

ar·se·nal \\'ärsnəl, -°nəl\\ *n* **1** : place where arms are made or stored **2** : store

ar·se·nic \\'ärsnik, -°nik\\ *n* : solid gray-ish poisonous chemical element —**ar·sen·i·cal** \\är'senikəl\\ *adj or n* —**ar·se·ni·ous** \\är'sēnēəs\\ *adj*

ar·son \\'ärs°n\\ *n* : malicious burning of property

art \\'ärt\\ *n* **1** : skill **2** : branch of learning **3** : creation of things of beauty or works so produced **4** : ingenuity

art·ful \\-fəl\\ *adj* **1** : ingenious **2** : crafty —**art·ful·ly** *adv* —**art·ful·ness** *n*

ar·te·rio·scle·ro·sis \\är₁tirēōsklə'rōsəs\\ *n* : hardening of the arteries —**ar·te·rio·scle·rot·ic** \\-'rätik\\ *adj or n*

ar·tery \\'ärtərē\\ *n, pl* **-ter·ies 1** : tubular vessel carrying blood from the heart **2** : thoroughfare —**ar·te·ri·al** \\är'tirēəl\\ *adj*

ar·thri·tis \\är'thrītəs\\ *n, pl* **-ti·des** \\-'thrītə₁dēz\\ : inflammation of the joints —**ar·thrit·ic** \\-'thritik\\ *adj or n*

ar·thro·pod \\'ärthrə₁päd\\ *n* : invertebrate animal (as an insect or spider) with segmented body and jointed limbs —**arthropod** adj

ar·ti·choke \'ärtə,chōk\ n : tall thistle-like herb

ar·ti·cle \'ärtikəl\ n 1 : distinct part of a written document 2 : nonfictional published piece of writing 3 : word (as an, the) used to limit a noun 4 : item or piece

ar·tic·u·late \är'tikyələt\ adj : able to speak effectively ~ \-,lāt\ vb -lat·ed; -lat·ing 1 : utter distinctly 2 : unite by joints —**ar·tic·u·late·ly** adv —**ar·tic·u·late·ness** n —**ar·tic·u·la·tion** \-,tikyə'lāshən\ n

ar·ti·fact \'ärtə,fakt\ n : object of human workmanship

ar·ti·fice \'ärtəfəs\ n 1 : trick or trickery 2 : ingenious device or ingenuity

ar·ti·fi·cial \,ärtə'fishəl\ adj 1 : man-made 2 : not genuine —**ar·ti·fi·ci·al·i·ty** \-,fishē'alətē\ n —**ar·ti·fi·cial·ly** adv —**ar·ti·fi·cial·ness** n

ar·til·lery \är'til(ə)rē\ n, pl -ler·ies : large caliber firearms

ar·ti·san \'ärtəzən, -sən\ n : skilled craftsman

art·ist \'ärtəst\ n : one who creates art —**ar·tis·tic** \är'tistik\ adj —**ar·tis·ti·cal·ly** \-ik(ə)lē\ adv —**ar·tis·try** \'ärtəstrē\ n

art·less \'ärtləs\ adj : sincere or natural —**art·less·ly** adv —**art·less·ness** n

arty \'ärtē\ adj art·i·er; -est : pretentiously artistic —**art·i·ly** \'ärtəlē\ adv —**art·i·ness** n

-ary \,erē\ adj suffix : of, relating to, or connected with

as \əz, (,)az\ adv 1 : to the same degree 2 : for example ~ conj 1 : in the same way or degree as 2 : while 3 : because 4 : though ~ pron —used after same or such ~ prep : in the capacity of

as·bes·tos \as'bestəs, az-\ n : fibrous incombustible mineral

as·cend \ə'send\ vb : move upward —**as·cen·sion** \-'senchən\ n

as·cen·dan·cy \ə'sendənsē\ n : domination

as·cen·dant \ə'sendənt\ n : dominant position ~ adj 1 : moving upward 2 : dominant

as·cent \ə'sent\ n 1 : act of moving upward 2 : degree of upward slope

as·cer·tain \,asər'tān\ vb : determine —**as·cer·tain·able** adj

as·cet·ic \ə'setik\ adj : self-denying —**ascetic** n —**as·cet·i·cism** \'setə-,sizəm\ n

as·cribe \ə'skrīb\ vb -cribed; -crib·ing

: attribute —**as·crib·able** adj —**as·crip·tion** \-'skripshən\ n

asep·tic \ā'septik\ adj : free of disease germs

¹**ash** \'ash\ n : tree related to the olives

²**ash** n : matter left when something is burned —**ash·tray** n

ashamed \ə'shāmd\ adj : feeling shame —**asham·ed·ly** \-'shāmədlē\ adv

ash·en \'ashən\ adj : deadly pale

ashore \ə'shōr\ adv : on or to the shore

aside \ə'sīd\ adv 1 : toward the side 2 : out of the way

aside from prep 1 : besides 2 : except for

as·i·nine \'as°n,īn\ adj : foolish —**as·i·nin·i·ty** \,as°n'inətē\ n

ask \'ask\ vb asked \'as(k)t\; ask·ing 1 : call on for an answer or help 2 : utter (a question or request) 3 : invite

askance \ə'skans\ adv 1 : with a side glance 2 : with mistrust

askew \ə'skyü\ adv or adj : out of line

asleep \ə'slēp\ adv or adj 1 : sleeping 2 : numbed 3 : inactive

as long as conj 1 : on condition that 2 : because

as of prep : from the time of

as·par·a·gus \ə'sparəgəs\ n : tall herb related to the lilies or its edible stalks

as·pect \'as,pekt\ n 1 : way something looks to the eye or mind 2 : phase

as·pen \'aspən\ n : poplar

as·per·i·ty \a'sperətē, ə-\ n, pl -ties 1 : roughness 2 : harshness

as·per·sion \ə'spərzhən\ n : remark that hurts someone's reputation

as·phalt \'as,fȯlt\, **as·phal·tum** \as'fȯltəm\ n : tarlike substance used in paving and in paints —**as·phal·tic** \as'fȯltik\ adj

as·phyx·ia \as'fiksēə\ n : lack of oxygen causing unconsciousness

as·phyx·i·ate \-sē,āt\ vb -at·ed; -at·ing : suffocate —**as·phyx·i·a·tion** \-,fiksē'āshən\ n

as·pi·ra·tion \,aspə'rāshən\ n : strong desire to achieve a goal

as·pire \ə'spī(ə)r\ vb -pired; -pir·ing : have an ambition —**as·pi·rant** \'asp(ə)rənt, ə'spīrənt\ n

as·pi·rin \'asp(ə)rən\ n, pl aspirin or aspirins : pain reliever

ass \'as\ n 1 : long-eared animal related to the horse 2 : stupid person

as·sail \ə'sāl\ vb : attack violently —**as·sail·able** adj —**as·sail·ant** n

as·sas·si·nate \ə'sas°n,āt\ vb -nat·ed; -nat·ing : murder esp. for political reasons —**as·sas·sin** \-'sas°n\ n —**as·sas·si·na·tion** \-,sas°n'āshən\ n

as·sault \ə'sȯlt\ n or vb : attack

as·say \'as,ā, a'sā\ n : analysis (as of an ore) to determine quality or properties —**as·say** \a'sā, 'as,ā\ vb

as·sem·ble \ə'sembəl\ vb -**bled; -bling** \-b(ə)liŋ\ **1** : collect into one place **2** : fit together the parts

as·sem·bly \-blē\ n, pl -**blies 1** : meeting **2** cap : legislative body **3** : a fitting together of parts

as·sem·bly·man \-mən\ n : member of a legislative assembly —**as·sem·bly·wom·an** n

as·sent \ə'sent\ vb or n : consent

as·sert \ə'sərt\ vb **1** : declare **2** : defend —**as·ser·tion** \-'sərshən\ n —**as·ser·tive** \-'sərtiv\ adj —**as·sert·ive·ness** n

as·sess \ə'ses\ vb **1** : impose (as a tax) **2** : evaluate for taxation —**as·sess·ment** n —**as·ses·sor** \-ər\ n

as·set \'as,et\ n **1** pl : individually owned property **2** : advantage or resource

as·sid·u·ous \ə'sij(ə)wəs\ adj : diligent —**as·si·du·i·ty** \,asə'd(y)üətē\ n —**as·sid·u·ous·ly** adv —**as·sid·u·ous·ness** n

as·sign \ə'sīn\ vb **1** : transfer to another **2** : appoint to a duty **3** : designate as a task **4** : attribute —**as·sign·able** adj —**as·sign·ment** \-mənt\ n

as·sim·i·late \ə'simə,lāt\ vb -**lat·ed; -lat·ing 1** : absorb as nourishment **2** : understand —**as·sim·i·la·tion** \-,simə'lāshən\ n

as·sist \ə'sist\ vb : help —**assist** n —**as·sis·tance** \-'sistəns\ n —**as·sis·tant** \-tənt\ n

as·so·ci·ate \ə'sōs(h)ē,āt\ vb -**at·ed; -at·ing 1** : join in companionship or partnership **2** : connect in thought —**as·so·ci·ate** \-s(h)ēət, -,shət\ n —**as·so·ci·a·tion** \-,sōs(h)ē'āshən\ n

as soon as conj : when

as·sort·ed \ə'sortəd\ adj : consisting of various kinds

as·sort·ment \-mənt\ n : assorted collection

as·suage \ə'swāj\ vb -**suaged; -suag·ing** : ease or satisfy

as·sume \ə'süm\ vb -**sumed; -sum·ing 1** : take upon oneself **2** : pretend to have **3** : take as granted

as·sump·tion \ə'səmpshən\ n : something assumed

as·sure \ə'shu̇r\ vb -**sured; -sur·ing 1** : give confidence or conviction to **2** : guarantee —**as·sur·ance** \-əns\ n

as·ter \'astər\ n : herb with daisylike flowers

as·ter·isk \'astə,risk\ n : a character * used as a reference mark or as an indication of omission of words

astern \ə'stərn\ adv or adj **1** : behind **2** : at or toward the stern

as·ter·oid \'astə,rȯid\ n : one of thousands of small planets between Mars and Jupiter —**aster·oi·dal** \,astə'rȯid°l\ adj

asth·ma \'azmə\ n : disorder with a cough and difficulty in breathing —**asth·mat·ic** \az'matik\ adj or n

astig·ma·tism \ə'stigmə,tizəm\ n : visual defect —**as·tig·mat·ic** \,astig'matik\ adj

as to prep **1** : concerning **2** : according to

as·ton·ish \ə'stänish\ vb : amaze —**as·ton·ish·ing·ly** adv —**as·ton·ish·ment** n

as·tound \ə'staund\ vb : fill with confused wonder —**as·tound·ing·ly** adv

astrad·dle \ə'strad°l\ adv or prep : so as to straddle

as·tral \'astrəl\ adj : relating to the stars

astray \ə'strā\ adv or adj : off the right way

astride \ə'strīd\ adv : with legs apart or one on each side ~ prep : with one leg on each side of

as·trin·gent \ə'strinjənt\ adj : causing shrinking or puckering of tissues —**as·trin·gen·cy** \-jənsē\ n —**astringent** n

as·trol·o·gy \ə'sträləjē\ n : prediction of events by the stars —**as·trol·o·ger** \-jər\ n —**as·tro·log·i·cal** \,astrə'läjikəl\ adj

as·tro·naut \'astrə,nȯt\ n : space traveler

as·tro·nau·tics \,astrə'nȯtiks\ n : construction and operation of spacecraft —**as·tro·nau·tic** \-ik\, **as·tro·nau·ti·cal** \-ikəl\ adj —**as·tro·nau·ti·cal·ly** adv

as·tro·nom·i·cal \,astrə'nämikəl\, **as·tro·nom·ic** \-ik\ adj **1** : relating to astronomy **2** : extremely large

as·tron·o·my \ə'stränəmē\ n, pl -**mies** : study of the celestial bodies —**as·tron·o·mer** \-əmər\ n

as·tute \ə'st(y)üt, a-\ adj : shrewd —**as·tute·ly** adv —**as·tute·ness** n

asun·der \ə'səndər\ adv or adj **1** : into separate pieces **2** : separated

asy·lum \ə'sīləm\ n **1** : refuge **2** : institution for care esp. of the insane

asym·met·ri·cal \,āsə'metrik\, **asym·met·ri·cal** \-trikəl\ adj : not symmetrical —**asym·me·try** \(')ā'simətrē\ n

at \ət, (')at\ prep **1** —used to indicate a point in time or space **2** —used to indicate a goal **3** —used to indicate condition, means, cause, or manner

at all \at'ol, ə't'ol, at'ol\ *adv* **1** : without restriction or under any circumstances

ate *past of* EAT

-ate \ət, (,)āt\ *n suffix* **1** : office or rank **2** : group of persons holding an office or rank ~ *adj suffix* **1** : brought into or being in a state **2** : marked by having

athe-ist \'āthēəst\ *n* : one who denies the existence of God —**athe-ism** \-,izəm\ *n* —**athe-is-tic** \,āthē'istik\ *adj*

ath-ero-scle-ro-sis \,athərōsklə'rōsəs\ *n* : arteriosclerosis with deposition of fatty substances in the arteries —**ath-ero-scle-rot-ic** \-'rätik\ *adj*

ath-lete \'ath,lēt\ *n* : one trained to compete in athletics

ath-let-ics \ath'letiks\ *n sing or pl* : exercises and games requiring physical skill —**ath-let-ic** \-ik\ *adj*

-a-tion \'āshən\ *n suffix* : action or process

-a-tive \,ātiv, ətiv\ *adj suffix* **1** : of, relating to, or connected with **2** : tending to

at-las \'atləs\ *n* : book of maps

at-mo-sphere \'atmə,sfiər\ *n* **1** : mass of air surrounding the earth **2** : surrounding influence —**at-mo-spher-ic** \,atmə'sfiərik, -'sfer-\ *adj* —**at-mo-spher-i-cal-ly** \-ik(ə)lē\ *adv*

at-oll \'a,tol, -,täl, 'ā-\ *n* : ring-shaped coral island

at-om \'atəm\ *n* **1** : tiny bit **2** : smallest particle of a chemical element that can exist alone or in combination

atom bomb *n* : bomb utilizing the energy released by splitting the atom

atom-ic \ə'tämik\ *adj* : relating to atoms, atom bombs, or atomic energy

atomic energy *n* : energy that can be liberated by changes in the nucleus of an atom

at-om-iz-er \'atə,mīzər\ *n* : device for reducing a liquid to a very fine spray

atone \ə'tōn\ *vb* **atoned**; **aton-ing** : make amends —**atone-ment** *n*

atop \ə'täp\ *prep* : on top of

atro-cious \ə'trōshəs\ *adj* : appalling or abominable —**atro-cious-ly** *adv* —**atro-cious-ness** *n*

atroc-i-ty \ə'träsətē\ *n, pl* **-ties** : savage act

at-ro-phy \'atrəfē\ *n, pl* **-phies** : wasting away of a bodily part or tissue —**at-ro-phy** *vb*

at-ro-pine \'atrə,pēn\ *n* : poisonous drug used esp. to relieve spasms

at-tach \ə'tach\ *vb* **1** : seize legally **2** : bind by personalities **3** : join —**at-tach-ment** *n*

at-ta-ché \,atə'shā, ,a,ta-, ə,ta-\ *n* : technical expert on a diplomatic staff

at-tack \ə'tak\ *vb* **1** : try to hurt or destroy with violence or words **2** : set to work on ~ *n* **1** : act of attacking **2** : fit of sickness

at-tain \ə'tān\ *vb* **1** : achieve or accomplish **2** : reach —**at-tain-abil-i-ty** \ə,tānə'bilətē\ *n* —**at-tain-able** *adj* —**at-tain-ment** *n*

at-tempt \ə'tempt\ *vb* : make an effort toward —**attempt** *n*

at-tend \ə'tend\ *vb* **1** : handle or provide for the care of something **2** : accompany **3** : be present at **4** : pay attention —**at-ten-dance** \-'tendəns\ *n* —**at-ten-dant** \-dənt\ *adj or n*

at-ten-tion \ə'tenchən\ *n* **1** : concentration of the mind on something **2** : notice or awareness —**at-ten-tive** \-'tentiv\ *adj* —**at-ten-tive-ly** *adv* —**at-ten-tive-ness** *n*

at-ten-u-ate \ə'tenyə,wāt\ *vb* **-at-ed**; **-at-ing** **1** : make or become thin **2** : weaken —**at-ten-u-a-tion** \-,tenyə'wāshən\ *n*

at-test \ə'test\ *vb* : certify or bear witness —**at-tes-ta-tion** \,a,tes'tāshən\ *n*

at-tic \'atik\ *n* : space just below the roof

at-tire \ə'tī(ə)r\ *vb* **-tired**; **-tir-ing** : dress —**attire** *n*

at-ti-tude \'atə,t(y)üd\ *n* **1** : posture or relative position **2** : feeling, opinion, or mood

at-tor-ney \ə'tərnē\ *n, pl* **-neys** : legal agent

at-tract \ə'trakt\ *vb* **1** : draw to oneself **2** : have emotional or aesthetic appeal for —**at-trac-tion** \-'trakshən\ *n* —**at-trac-tive** \-'traktiv\ *adj* —**at-trac-tive-ly** *adv* —**at-trac-tive-ness** *n*

at-tri-bute \'atrə,byüt\ *n* : inherent characteristic ~ \ə'tribyət\ *vb* **-trib-ut-ed**; **-ut-ing** **1** : regard as having a specific cause or origin **2** : regard as a characteristic —**at-trib-ut-able** *adj* —**at-tri-bu-tion** \,atrə'byüshən\ *n*

at-tune \ə't(y)ün\ *vb* : bring into harmony

au-burn \'ôbərn\ *adj* : reddish brown

auc-tion \'ôkshən\ *n* : public sale of property to the highest bidder —**auction** *vb* —**auc-tion-eer** \,ôkshə'niər\ *n*

au-dac-i-ty \ô'dasətē\ *n* : boldness or insolence —**au-da-cious** \ô'dāshəs\ *adj*

au·di·ble \'ȯdəbəl\ *adj* : capable of being heard — **au·di·bly** \-blē\ *adv*

au·di·ence \'ȯdēəns\ *n* 1 : formal interview 2 : group of listeners or spectators

au·dio \'ȯdē,ō\ *adj* : relating to sound or its reproduction ~ *n* : television sound

au·dio·vi·su·al \,ȯdēō'vizh(əw)əl\ *adj* : relating to both hearing and sight

au·dit \'ȯdət\ *vb* : examine financial accounts — **audit** *n* — **au·di·tor** \'ȯdətər\ *n*

au·di·tion \ȯ'dishən\ *n* : tryout performance — **au·di·tion** *vb*

au·di·to·ri·um \,ȯdə'tōrēəm\ *n* : room or building used for public gatherings

au·di·to·ry \'ȯdə,tōrē\ *adj* : relating to hearing

au·ger \'ȯgər\ *n* : boring tool

aug·ment \ȯg'ment\ *vb* : enlarge or increase — **aug·men·ta·tion** \,ȯgmən'tāshən\ *n*

au·gur \'ȯgər\ *n* : prophet ~ *vb* : predict — **au·gu·ry** \'ȯg(y)ərē\ *n*

au·gust \ȯ'gəst\ *adj* : majestic

August \'ȯgəst\ *n* : 8th month of the year having 31 days

auk \'ȯk\ *n* : stocky diving seabird

aunt \'ant, 'änt\ *n* 1 : sister of one's father or mother 2 : wife of one's uncle

au·ra \'ȯrə\ *n* 1 : distinctive atmosphere 2 : luminous radiation

au·ral \'ȯrəl\ *adj* : relating to the ear or to hearing

au·ri·cle \'ȯrikəl\ *n* 1 : external ear 2 : chamber of the heart that receives blood from the veins

au·ro·ra bo·re·al·is \ə,rōrə,bōrē'aləs\ *n* : display of light in the night sky of northern latitudes that is held to be of electrical origin

aus·pic·es \'ȯspəsəz, -,sēz\ *n pl* : patronage and protection

aus·pi·cious \ȯ'spishəs\ *adj* : favorable

aus·tere \ȯ'stiər\ *adj* : severe — **aus·tere·ly** *adv* — **aus·ter·i·ty** \ȯ'sterətē\ *n*

au·then·tic \ə'thentik, ȯ-\ *adj* : genuine — **au·then·ti·cal·ly** \-ik(ə)lē\ *adv* — **au·then·tic·i·ty** \,ȯ,then'tisətē\ *n*

au·then·ti·cate \ə'thenti,kāt, ȯ-\ *vb* -cat·ed; -cat·ing : prove genuine — **au·then·ti·ca·tion** \-,thenti'kāshən\ *n*

au·thor \'ȯthər\ *n* 1 : writer 2 : creator — **au·thor·ess** \-th(ə)rəs\ *n* — **au·thor·ship** *n*

au·thor·i·tar·i·an \ə,thärə'terēən, ə-,

-,thȯr-\ *adj* : marked by blind obedience to authority

au·thor·i·ta·tive \ə'thärə,tātiv, ȯ-, -'thȯr-\ *adj* : being an authority — **au·thor·i·ta·tive·ly** *adv*

au·thor·i·ty \ə'thärətē, ȯ-, -'thȯr-\ *n*, *pl* -ties 1 : expert 2 : right, responsibility, or power to influence 3 *pl* : persons in official positions

au·tho·rize \'ȯthə,rīz\ *vb* -rized; -riz·ing : permit or give official approval for — **au·tho·ri·za·tion** \,ȯth(ə)rə'zāshən\ *n*

au·to \'ȯtō\ *n*, *pl* autos : automobile

au·to·bi·og·ra·phy \,ȯtōbī'ägrəfē, -bē-\ *n* : writer's own life story — **au·to·bi·og·ra·pher** \-fər\ *n* — **au·to·bi·o·graph·i·cal** \-,bīə'grafikəl\ *adj*

au·toc·ra·cy \ȯ'täkrəsē\ *n*, *pl* -cies : government by one person having unlimited power — **au·to·crat** \'ȯtə,krat\ *n* — **au·to·crat·ic** \,ȯtə'kratik\ *adj* — **au·to·crat·i·cal·ly** \-ik(ə)lē\ *adv*

au·to·graph \'ȯtə,graf\ *n* : signature ~ *vb* : write one's name on

au·to·mate \'ȯtə,māt\ *vb* -mat·ed; -mat·ing : make automatic — **au·to·ma·tion** \,ȯtə'māshən\ *n*

au·to·mat·ic \,ȯtə'matik\ *adj* 1 : involuntary 2 : designed to function without human intervention ~ *n* : automatic device (as a firearm) — **au·to·mat·i·cal·ly** \-ik(ə)lē\ *adv*

au·tom·a·ton \ȯ'tämətən, -ə'tän\ *n*, *pl* -atons *or* -a·ta \-,atə, -ə,tä\ : robot

au·to·mo·bile \,ȯtəmō'bēl, -'mō,bēl\ *n* : 4-wheeled passenger vehicle with its own power source — **au·to·mo·bil·ist** \-'bēləst, -,mō-\ *n*

au·to·mo·tive \,ȯtə'mōtiv\ *adj* : relating to automobiles

au·ton·o·mous \ȯ'tänəməs\ *adj* : self-governing — **au·ton·o·mous·ly** *adv* — **au·ton·o·my** \-mē\ *n*

au·top·sy \'ȯ,täpsē, 'ȯtəp-\ *n*, *pl* -sies : medical examination of a corpse

au·tumn \'ȯtəm\ *n* : season between summer and winter — **au·tum·nal** \ȯ'təmnəl\ *adj*

aux·il·ia·ry \ȯg'zilyərē, -'zil(ə)rē\ *adj* 1 : being a supplement or reserve 2 : accompanying a main verb form to express person, number, mood, or tense — **auxiliary** *n*

avail \ə'vāl\ *vb* : be of use or make use ~ *n* : use

avail·able \ə'vāləbəl\ *adj* 1 : usable 2 : accessible — **avail·abil·i·ty** \-,vālə-'bilətē\ *n*

av·a·lanche \'avə,lanch\ *n* : mass of sliding or falling snow or rock

av·a·rice \\'av(ə)rəs\\ *n* : greed —**av·a·ri·cious** \\,avə'rishəs\\ *adj*

avenge \\ə'venj\\ *vb* **avenged; aveng·ing** : take vengeance for —**aveng·er** *n*

av·e·nue \\'avə,n(y)ü\\ *n* **1** : way of approach **2** : broad street

av·er·age \\'av(ə)rij\\ *adj* **1** : being about midway between extremes **2** : ordinary ~ *vb* **1** : be usually **2** : find the mean of ~ *n* : mean

averse \\ə'vərs\\ *adj* : feeling dislike or reluctance —**aver·sion** \\-'vərzhən\\ *n*

avert \\ə'vərt\\ *vb* : turn away

avi·ary \\'āvē,erē\\ *n, pl* **-ar·ies** : place where birds are kept

avi·a·tion \\,āvē'āshən, ,avē-\\ *n* : operation or manufacture of airplanes —**avi·a·tor** \\'āvē,ātər, 'avē-\\ *n*

av·id \\'avəd\\ *adj* **1** : greedy **2** : enthusiastic —**avid·i·ty** \\ə'vidətē, a-\\ *n* —**av·id·ly** *adv*

av·o·ca·do \\,avə'kädō, ,äv-\\ *n, pl* **-dos** : tropical fruit

av·o·ca·tion \\,avə'kāshən\\ *n* : hobby

avoid \\ə'vȯid\\ *vb* **1** : keep away from **2** : prevent the occurrence of **3** : refrain from —**avoid·able** *adj* —**avoid·ance** \\-ᵊns\\ *n*

av·oir·du·pois \\,avərdə'pȯiz\\ *n* : system of weight, based on the pound of 16 ounces

avow \\ə'vaŭ\\ *vb* : declare openly —**avow·al** \\-'vaŭ(ə)l\\ *n*

await \\ə'wāt\\ *vb* : wait for

awake \\ə'wāk\\ *vb* **awoke** \\-'wōk\\ *or* **awaked; awaked** *or* **awoke** *or* **awok·en** \\-'wōkən\\; **awak·ing** : wake up —**awake** *adj*

awak·en \\ə'wākən\\ *vb* **-ened; -en·ing** : wake up

award \\ə'wȯrd\\ *vb* : give (something

won or deserved) ~ *n* **1** : judgment **2** : prize

aware \\ə'waər\\ *adj* : having realization or consciousness —**aware·ness** *n*

awash \\ə'wȯsh, -'wäsh\\ *adv or adj* : flooded

away \\ə'wā\\ *adv* **1** : from this or that place or time **2** : out of the way **3** : in another direction **4** : from one's possession —*adj* **1** : absent **2** : distant

awe \\'ȯ\\ *n* : respectful fear or wonder ~ *vb* **awed; aw·ing** : fill with awe —**awe·some** \\-səm\\ *adj* —**awe·struck** *adj*

aw·ful \\'ȯfəl\\ *adj* **1** : inspiring awe **2** : extremely disagreeable **3** : very great —**aw·ful·ly** *adv*

awhile \\ə'hwīl\\ *adv* : for a while

awk·ward \\'ȯkwərd\\ *adj* **1** : clumsy **2** : embarrassing —**awk·ward·ly** *adv* —**awk·ward·ness** *n*

awl \\'ȯl\\ *n* : hole-making tool

aw·ning \\'ȯniŋ\\ *n* : window cover

awry \\ə'rī\\ *adv or adj* : wrong

ax, axe \\'aks\\ *n* : chopping tool

ax·i·om \\'aksēəm\\ *n* : generally accepted truth —**ax·i·om·at·ic** \\,aksēə'matik\\ *adj*

ax·is \\'aksəs\\ *n, pl* **ax·es** \\-,sēz\\ : center of rotation —**ax·i·al** \\-sēəl\\ *adj* —**ax·i·al·ly** *adv*

ax·le \\'aksəl\\ *n* : shaft on which a wheel revolves

aye \\'ī\\ *adv* : yes ~ *n* : a vote of yes

aza·lea \\ə'zālyə\\ *n* : rhododendron with funnel-shaped blossoms

az·i·muth \\'az(ə)məth\\ *n* **1** : arc measured along the horizon **2** : horizontal direction —**az·i·muth·al** \\,azə'məthəl\\ *adj*

azure \\'azhər\\ *n* : blue of the sky —**azure** *adj*

B

b \\'bē\\ *n, pl* **b's** *or* **bs** \\'bēz\\ : 2d letter of the alphabet

bab·ble \\'babəl\\ *vb* **-bled; -bling 1** : utter meaningless sounds **2** : talk foolishly or too much —**babble** *n* —**bab·bler** *n*

babe \\'bāb\\ *n* : baby

ba·bel \\'bābəl, 'bab-\\ *n* : noisy confusion

ba·boon \\ba'bün\\ *n* : large Asian or African ape with a doglike muzzle

ba·by \\'bābē\\ *n, pl* **-bies** : very young child ~ *vb* **-bied; -by·ing** : pamper —**baby** *adj* —**ba·by·hood** *n* —**ba·by·ish** *adj*

ba·by·sit *vb* **-sat; -sit·ting** : care for children while parents are away —**ba·by·sit·ter** *n*

bac·ca·lau·re·ate \\,bakə'lȯrēət\\ *n* : bachelor's degree

bac·cha·na·lia \\,bakə'nālyə\\ *n, pl* **-lia** : drunken orgy —**bac·cha·na·lian** \\-yən\\ *adj or n*

bach·e·lor \\'bach(ə)lər\\ *n* **1** : holder of lowest 4-year college degree **2** : unmarried man —**bach·e·lor·hood** *n*

ba·cil·lus \\bə'siləs\\ *n, pl* **-li** \\-,ī\\ : rod-shaped bacterium —**bac·il·lary** \\'basə,lerē\\ *adj*

back \\'bak\\ *n* **1** : part of a human or

animal body nearest the spine **2** : part opposite the front **3** : player farthest from the opponent's goal ~ *adv* **1** : to or at the back **2** : ago **3** : to or in a former place or state **4** : in reply ~ *adj* **1** : located at the back **2** : not paid on time **3** : moving or working backward ~ *vb* **1** : support **2** : go or cause to go back **3** : form the back of —**back-ache** *n* —**back-er** *n* —**back-ing** *n* —**back-less** *adj* —**back-rest** *n*

back-bite *vb* -**bit**; -**bit-ten**; -**bit-ing** : say spiteful things about someone absent —**back-bit-er** *n*

back-bone *n* **1** : bony column in the back that encloses the spinal cord **2** : firm character

back-drop *n* : painted cloth hung across the rear of a stage

back-fire *n* : explosion in the intake or exhaust passages of an internal-combustion engine —**back-fire** *vb*

back-gam-mon \'bak,gamən\ *n* : board game

back-ground *n* **1** : scenery behind something **2** : sum of a person's experience or training

back-hand *n* : stroke (as in tennis) made with the back of the hand turned forward —**backhand** *adj or vb* —**back-hand-ed** *adj*

back-lash *n* : adverse reaction —**back-lash-er** *n*

back-log *n* **1** : reserve of unfilled orders **2** : accumulation of things to be done —**backlog** *vb*

back-pack *n* : camping pack carried on the back ~ *vb* : hike with a backpack —**back-pack-er** *n*

back-slide *vb* -**slid**; -**slid** *or* -**slid-den** \-,slidᵊn\, -**slid-ing** : lapse in morals or religious practice —**back-slid-er** *n*

back-stage *adv or adj* : in or to an area behind a stage

back-up *n* : substitute

back-ward \'bakwərd\, **back-wards** *adv* **1** : toward the back **2** : with the back foremost **3** : in a reverse direction **4** : toward an earlier or worse state ~ *adj* **1** : directed, turned, or done backward **2** : retarded in development —**back-ward-ness** *n*

back-woods *n pl* : remote or isolated place

ba-con \'bākən\ *n* : salted and smoked meat from a pig

bac-te-ri-um \bak'tirēəm\ *n, pl* -**ria** \-ēə\ : microscopic plant —**bac-te-ri-al** \-ēəl\ *adj* —**bac-te-ri-o-log-ic** \-,tirēə'läjik\, **bac-te-ri-o-log-i-cal** \-əl\ *adj* —**bac-te-ri-ol-o-gist**

\-ē'äləjəst\ *n* —**bac-te-ri-ol-o-gy** \-jē\ *n*

bad \'bad\ *adj* **worse** \'wərs\; **worst** \'wərst\ **1** : not good **2** : naughty **3** : faulty **4** : spoiled —**bad** *n or adv* —**bad-ly** *adv* —**bad-ness** *n*

bade *past of* BID

badge \'baj\ *n* : symbol of status

bad-ger \'bajər\ *n* **1** : burrowing mammal with long claws on the forefeet ~ *vb* -**gered**; -**ger-ing** : harass

bad-min-ton \'bad,mintᵊn\ *n* : tennislike game played with a shuttlecock

baf-fle \'bafəl\ *vb* -**fled**; -**fling** : perplex ~ *n* : device to alter flow (as of liquid or sound)

bag \'bag\ *n* **1** : flexible usu. closable container ~ *vb* -**gg- 1** : bulge out **2** : put in a bag **3** : catch in hunting

bag-a-telle \,bagə'tel\ *n* : trifle

ba-gel \'bāgəl\ *n* : hard doughnut-shaped roll

bag-gage \'bagij\ *n* : traveler's bags and belongings

bag-gy \'bagē\ *adj* -**gi-er**; -**est** : puffed out like a bag —**bag-gi-ly** *adv* —**bag-gi-ness** *n*

bag-pipe *n* : musical instrument with a bag, a tube with valves, and sounding pipes —often pl.

¹**bail** \'bāl\ *n* **1** : security given to guarantee a prisoner's appearance in court **2** : release secured by bail ~ *vb* : bring about the release of by giving bail —**bail-able** *adj* —**bails-man** \'bālzmən\ *n*

²**bail** *n* : container for scooping water out of a boat —**bail** *vb*

bai-liff \'bāləf\ *n* **1** : a British sheriff's aide **2** : minor officer of a U.S. court

bai-li-wick \'bāli,wik\ *n* : one's special field or domain

bait \'bāt\ *vb* **1** : harass with dogs usu. for sport **2** : furnish (a hook or trap) with bait ~ *n* : lure esp. for catching animals

bake \'bāk\ *vb* **baked**; **bak-ing** : cook in dry heat esp. in an oven ~ *n* : party featuring baked food —**bak-er** *n* —**bak-ery** \'bāk(ə)rē\ *n* —**bake-shop** *n*

bal-ance \'baləns\ *n* **1** : weighing device **2** : counter-acting weight, force, or influence **3** : equilibrium **4** : that which remains ~ *vb* -**anced**; -**anc-ing 1** : compute the balance **2** : equalize **3** : bring into harmony or proportion —**bal-anced** *adj*

bal-co-ny \'balkənē\ *n, pl* -**nies** : platform projecting from a wall

bald \'bȯld\ *adj* **1** : lacking a natural or

usual covering (as of hair) **2** : plain —**bald·ing** *adj* —**bald·ly** *adv*

bal·der·dash \'bȯldər,dash\ *n* : nonsense

bale \'bāl\ *n* : large bundle ~ *vb* **baled; bal·ing** : pack in a bale —**bal·er** *n*

bale·ful \'bālfəl\ *adj* **1** : deadly **2** : ominous

balk \'bȯk\ *n* : hindrance ~ *vb* **1** : thwart **2** : stop short and refuse to go on —**balky** *adj*

¹**ball** \'bȯl\ *n* **1** : rounded mass **2** : game played with a ball ~ *vb* : form into a ball

²**ball** *n* : large formal dance —**ball-room** *n*

bal·lad \'baləd\ *n* **1** : narrative poem **2** : slow romantic song —**bal·lad·eer** \,balə'di(ə)r\ *n*

bal·last \'baləst\ *n* : heavy material to steady a ship or balloon ~ *vb* : provide with ballast

bal·le·ri·na \,balə'rēnə\ *n* : female ballet dancer

bal·let \'ba,lā, ba'lā\ *n* : theatrical dancing

bal·lis·tics \bə'listiks\ *n sing or pl* : science of projectile motion —**ballistic** *adj*

bal·loon \bə'lün\ *n* : inflated bag ~ *vb* **1** : travel in a balloon **2** : swell out —**bal·loon·ist** *n*

bal·lot \'balət\ *n* **1** : paper used to cast a vote **2** : system of voting ~ *vb* : vote

bal·ly·hoo \'balē,hü\ *n* : publicity —**ballyhoo** *vb*

balm \'bäm, 'bälm\ *n* **1** : fragrant healing or soothing preparation **2** : spicy fragrant herb

balmy \'bämē, 'bälmē\ *adj* **balm·i·er; -est** : gently soothing —**balm·i·ness** *n*

ba·lo·ney \bə'lōnē\ *n* : nonsense

bal·sa \'bȯlsə\ *n* : very light wood of a tropical tree

bal·sam \'sən\ *n* **1** : aromatic resinous plant substance **2** : balsam-yielding plant

bal·us·ter \'baləstər\ *n* : upright support of a rail

bal·us·trade \-,strād\ *n* : row of balusters topped by a rail

bam·boo \bam'bü\ *n* : tall tropical grass with strong hollow stems

bam·boo·zle \bam'büzəl\ *vb* **-zled; -zling** : deceive

ban \'ban\ *vb* **-nn-** : prohibit ~ *n* : legal prohibition

ba·nal \bə'näl, -'nal; 'bānᵊl\ *adj* : ordinary and uninteresting —**ba·nal·i·ty** \bə-'nal-ət-ē\ *n*

ba·nana \bə'nanə\ *n* : elongated fruit

of a treelike tropical plant or the plant itself

¹**band** \'band\ *n* **1** : something that constrains or restrains **2** : strip that brings or holds together **3** : range of radio wavelengths ~ *vb* **1** : enclose with a band **2** : unite for a common end —**band·ed** *adj* —**band·er** *n*

²**band** *n* **1** : group **2** : musicians playing together

ban·dage \'bandij\ *n* : material used esp. in dressing wounds ~ *vb* : dress or cover with a bandage

ban·dan·na, ban·dana \ban'danə\ *n* : large colored figured handkerchief

ban·dit \'bandət\ *n* : outlaw or robber —**ban·dit·ry** \-dətrē\ *n*

band·stand *n* : stage for band concerts

band·wag·on *n* : candidate, side, or movement gaining support

¹**ban·dy** \'bandē\ *vb* **-died; -dy·ing** : exchange in rapid succession

²**bandy** *adj* : curved outward

bane \'bān\ *n* **1** : poison **2** : cause of woe —**bane·ful** *adj*

bang \'baŋ\ *vb* : strike, thrust, or move usu. with a loud noise ~ *n* **1** : blow **2** : sudden loud noise ~ *adv* : directly

²**bang** *n* : fringe of short hair over the forehead —usu. pl. ~ *vb* : cut in bangs

ban·gle \'baŋgəl\ *n* : bracelet

ban·ish \'banish\ *vb* **1** : force by authority to leave a country **2** : expel —**ban·ish·ment** *n*

ban·is·ter \-əstər\ *n* : upright support of a staircase handrail or the handrail itself

ban·jo \-,jō\ *n, pl* **-jos** : stringed instrument with a drumlike body —**ban·jo·ist** *n*

¹**bank** \'baŋk\ *n* **1** : piled-up mass **2** : rising ground along a body of water **3** : sideways slope along a curve ~ *vb* **1** : form a bank **2** : cover (as a fire) to keep inactive **3** : incline (an airplane) laterally

²**bank** *n* : tier of objects

³**bank** *n* **1** : money institution **2** : reserve supply ~ *vb* : conduct business in a bank —**bank·book** *n* —**bank·er** *n* —**bank·ing** *n*

bank·rupt \-(,)rəpt\ *n* : one required by law to forfeit assets to pay off debts ~ *adj* **1** : legally a bankrupt **2** : lacking something essential —**bankrupt** *vb* —**bank·rupt·cy** \-(,)rəp(t)sē\ *n*

ban·ner \'banər\ *n* : flag ~ *adj* : excellent

banns \'banz\ *n pl* : announcement in church of a proposed marriage

ban·quet \\'baŋkwət\\ *n* : ceremonial dinner —**banquet** *vb*

ban·shee \\'banshē\\ *n* : wailing female spirit that foretells death

ban·tam \\'bantəm\\ *n* : miniature domestic fowl

ban·ter \\-ər\\ *n* : good-natured joking —**banter** *vb*

ban·yan \\'banyən\\ *n* : large tree that grows new trunks from the limbs

bap·tism \\'bap,tizəm\\ *n* : Christian rite signifying spiritual cleansing —**bap·tis·mal** \\bap'tizmal\\ *adj*

bap·tize \\bap'tīz, 'bap,tīz\\ *vb* -**tized; -tiz·ing** : administer baptism to

bar \\'bär\\ *n* 1 : long narrow object used esp. as a lever, fastening, or support 2 : barrier 3 : body of practicing lawyers 4 : wide stripe 5 : food counter 6 : place where liquor is served 7 : vertical line across the musical staff ~ *vb* -**rr**- 1 : obstruct with a bar 2 : shut out 3 : prohibit ~ *prep* : excluding —**barred** *adj* —**bar·room** *n* —**bar·tend·er** *n*

barb \\'bärb\\ *n* : sharp projection pointing backward —**barbed** *adj*

bar·bar·ian \\bär'berēən\\ *adj* 1 : relating to people considered backward 2 : not refined —**barbarian** *n*

bar·bar·ic \\-'barik\\ *adj* : barbarian

bar·ba·rous \\'bärb(ə)rəs\\ *adj* 1 : lacking refinement 2 : mercilessly cruel —**bar·ba·rism** \\-bə,rizəm\\ *n* —**bar·bar·i·ty** \\bär'baratē\\ *n* —**bar·ba·rous·ly** *adv*

bar·be·cue \\'bärbi,kyü\\ *n* : gathering at which barbecued food is served ~ *vb* -**cued; -cu·ing** : cook over hot coals or on a spit often with a highly seasoned sauce

bar·ber \\'bärbər\\ *n* : one who cuts hair

bar·bi·tu·rate \\bär'bichərət\\ *n* : chemical used as a sedative or hypnotic

bard \\'bärd\\ *n* : poet

bare \\'baər\\ *adj* **bar·er; bar·est** 1 : naked 2 : not concealed 3 : empty 4 : leaving nothing to spare 5 : plain ~ *vb* **bared; bar·ing** : make or lay bare —**bare·foot, bare·foot·ed** *adv or adj* —**bare·hand·ed** *adv or adj* —**bare·head·ed** *adv or adj* —**bare·ly** *adv* —**bare·ness** *n*

bare·back, bare·backed *adv or adj* : without a saddle

bare·faced *adj* : open and esp. brazen

bar·gain \\'bärgən\\ *n* 1 : agreement 2 : something bought for less than its value ~ *vb* 1 : negotiate 2 : barter

barge \\'bärj\\ *n* : broad flat-bottomed boat ~ *vb* **barged; barg·ing** : move rudely or clumsily —**barge·man** *n*

bari·tone \\'barə,tōn\\ *n* : male voice between bass and tenor

bar·i·um \\'barēəm\\ *n* : silver-white metallic chemical element

¹bark \\'bärk\\ *vb* 1 : make the sound of a dog 2 : speak in a loud curt tone ~ *n* : sound of a barking dog

²bark *n* : tough corky outer covering of a woody stem or root ~ *vb* : remove bark or skin from

³bark *n* : 3-masted ship

bark·er \\'bärkər\\ *n* : one who calls out to attract people to a sideshow

bar·ley \\-lē\\ *n* : cereal grass or its seeds

barn \\'bärn\\ *n* : building for keeping hay or livestock —**barn·yard** *n*

bar·na·cle \\'bärnikəl\\ *n* : marine crustacean

barn·storm *vb* : tour through rural districts giving performances

ba·rom·e·ter \\bə'rämətər\\ *n* : instrument for measuring atmospheric pressure —**baro·met·ric** \\,barə'metrik\\, **baro·met·ri·cal** \\-əl\\ *adj*

bar·on \\'barən\\ *n* : British peer —**bar·on·age** \\-ij\\ *n* —**ba·ro·ni·al** \\bə'rōnēəl\\ *adj* —**bar·ony** \\'barənē\\ *n*

bar·on·ess \\-ənəs\\ *n* 1 : baron's wife 2 : woman holding a baronial title

bar·on·et \\-ənət\\ *n* : man holding a rank between a baron and a knight —**bar·on·et·cy** \\-sē\\ *n*

ba·roque \\bə'rōk, -'räk\\ *adj* : elaborately ornamented

bar·racks \\'barəks\\ *n sing or pl* : soldiers' housing

bar·ra·cu·da \\,barə'küdə\\ *n, pl* -**da** *or* -**das** : large predatory sea fish

bar·rage \\bə'räzh, -'räj\\ *n* : heavy artillery fire

bar·rel \\'barəl\\ *n* 1 : closed cylindrical container 2 : amount held by a barrel 3 : cylindrical part ~ *vb* -**reled** *or* -**relled; -rel·ing** *or* -**rel·ling** : pack in a barrel —**bar·reled** *adj*

bar·ren \\'barən\\ *adj* 1 : unproductive of life 2 : uninteresting —**bar·ren·ness** \\-ənnəs\\ *n*

bar·rette \\bä'ret, bə-\\ *n* : clasp for a woman's hair

bar·ri·cade \\'barə,kād, ,barə'-\\ *n* : barrier —**barricade** *vb*

bar·ri·er \\'barēər\\ *n* : something that separates or obstructs

bar·ring \\'bäriŋ\\ *prep* : omitting

bar·ris·ter \\'barəstər\\ *n* : British trial lawyer

bar·row \\'barō\\ *n* : wheelbarrow

bar·ter \\'bärtər\\ *vb* : trade by exchange of goods —**barter** *n*

ba·salt \\bə'sȯlt, 'bā-\\ *n* : dark fine-grained igneous rock —ba·sal·tic \bə'sòltik\ adj

¹base \'bās\ n, pl bas·es 1 : bottom 2 : fundamental part 3 : beginning point 4 : supply source of a force 5 : compound that reacts with an acid to form a salt ~ vb based; bas·ing : establish —base·less adj

²base adj bas·er; bas·est 1 : inferior 2 : contemptible —base·ly adv —base·ness n

base·ball n : game played with a bat and ball by 2 teams

base·ment \-mənt\ n : part of a building below ground level

bash \'bash\ vb : strike violently ~ n : heavy blow

bash·ful \-fəl\ adj : self-conscious —bash·ful·ness n

ba·sic \'bāsik\ adj 1 : relating to or forming the base or essence 2 : relating to a chemical base —ba·si·cal·ly adv —ba·sic·i·ty \bā'sisətē\ n

ba·sil \'bazəl, 'bās-\ n : aromatic mint

ba·sil·i·ca \bə'silikə\ n : church or cathedral of high rank

ba·sin \'bāsən\ n 1 : large bowl or pan 2 : depression containing a pond or lake 3 : region drained by a river

ba·sis \'bāsəs\ n, pl ba·ses \-,sēz\ 1 : something that supports 2 : fundamental principle

bask \'bask\ vb : enjoy pleasant warmth

bas·ket \-ət\ n : woven container —bas·ket·ful n

bas·ket·ball n : game played with a ball on a court by 2 teams

bas–re·lief \,bäri'lēf\ n : flat sculpture with slightly raised design

¹bass \'bas\ n, pl bass or bass·es : spiny-finned sport and food fish

²bass \'bās\ n 1 : deep tone 2 : lowest male voice

bas·set hound \'basət-\ n : short-legged dog with long ears

bas·si·net \,basə'net\ n : baby's bed

bas·soon \bə'sün, ba-\ n : low-pitched wind instrument

bas·tard \'bastərd\ n 1 : illegitimate child 2 : offensive person ~ adj 1 : illegitimate 2 : inferior —bas·tard·ize vb —bas·tar·dy n

¹baste \'bāst\ vb bast·ed; bast·ing : sew temporarily with long stitches

²baste vb bast·ed; bast·ing : moisten with liquid at intervals while cooking

bas·tion \'baschən\ n : fortified position —bas·tioned adj

¹bat \'bat\ n 1 : stick or club 2 : sharp blow ~ vb -tt- : hit with a bat

²bat n : small flying mammal

³bat vb -tt- : wink or blink

batch \'bach\ n : quantity used or produced at one time

bate \'bāt\ vb bat·ed; bat·ing : moderate or reduce

bath \'bath, 'bàth\ n, pl baths \'bathz, 'baths, 'bàthz, 'bàths\ 1 : a washing of the body 2 : water for washing the body 3 : liquid in which something is immersed 4 : bathroom —bath·tub n

bathe \'bāth\ vb bathed; bath·ing 1 : wash in liquid 2 : flow against so as to wet 3 : shine light over 4 : take a bath or a swim —bath·er n

bath·robe n : robe worn around the house

bath·room n : room with a bathtub or shower and usu. a washbowl and toilet

ba·tiste \bə'tēst\ n : fine sheer fabric

ba·ton \bə'tän\ n : musical conductor's stick

bat·tal·ion \bə'talyən\ n : military unit composed of a headquarters and two or more companies

bat·ten \'bat²n\ n : strip of wood used to seal or reinforce ~ vb : furnish or fasten with battens

¹bat·ter \'batər\ vb : beat or damage with repeated blows

²batter n : mixture of flour and liquid

³batter n : player who bats

bat·tery \'bat(ə)rē\ n, pl -ter·ies 1 : illegal beating of a person 2 : group of artillery guns 3 : group of electric cells

bat·ting \-iŋ\ n : layers of cotton or wool for stuffing

bat·tle \-³l\ n : military fighting ~ vb -tled; -tling : engage in battle —bat·tle·field n

bat·tle–ax n : long-handled ax formerly used as a weapon

bat·tle·ment \-mənt\ n : parapet on top of a wall

bat·tle·ship n : heavily armed warship

bat·ty \-ē\ adj -ti·er; -est : crazy

bau·ble \'bòbəl\ n : trinket

bawdy \'bòdē\ adj bawd·i·er; -est : obscene or lewd —bawd·i·ly adv —bawd·i·ness n

bawl \'bòl\ vb : cry loudly ~ n : long loud cry

¹bay \'bā\ adj : reddish brown ~ n : bay-colored animal

²bay n : European laurel

³bay n : compartment 2 : area projecting out from a building and containing a window (bay window)

⁴bay vb : bark with deep long tones ~ n 1 : position of one unable to escape danger 2 : baying of dogs

⁵**bay** n : body of water smaller than a gulf that is nearly surrounded by land

bay·ber·ry \-,berē\ n : shrub bearing small waxy berries

bay·o·net \'bānət, ,bā'net\ n : dagger that fits on the end of a rifle ~ vb -net·ed; -net·ing : stab with a bayonet

bay·ou \'bīō, -ū\ n : creek flowing through marshy land

ba·zaar \bə'zär\ n 1 : market 2 : fair for charity

ba·zoo·ka \-'zükə\ n : weapon that shoots armor-piercing rockets

BB n : small shot pellet

be \(')bē\ vb was \(')wəz, 'wäz\, were \(')wər\; been \(')bin\; be·ing \'bēig\; am \əm, (')am\, is \(')iz, əz\, are \ər, (')är\ 1 : equal 2 : exist 3 : occupy a certain place 4 : occur ~ verbal auxiliary —used to show continuous action or to form the passive voice

beach \'bēch\ n : shore of a sea, lake, or river ~ vb : drive ashore

beach·comb·er \-,kōmər\ n : one who searches the shore for useful objects

beach·head n : shore area held by an attacking force

bea·con \'bēkən\ n : guiding or warning light or signal —**beacon** vb

bead \'bēd\ n : small round body esp. strung on a thread ~ vb : form into a bead —**bead·ing** n —**beady** adj

bea·gle \'bēgəl\ n : small short-legged hound

beak \'bēk\ n : bill of a bird —**beaked** adj

bea·ker \'bēkər\ n 1 : large drinking cup 2 : laboratory vessel

beam \'bēm\ n 1 : large long piece of timber or metal 2 : ray of light 3 : directed radio signals for the guidance of pilots ~ vb 1 : send out light 2 : smile 3 : aim a radio broadcast

bean \'bēn\ n : edible plant seed borne in pods

¹**bear** \'baər\ n, pl **bears** 1 or pl **bear** : large heavy mammal with shaggy hair 2 : gruff or sullen person —**bear·ish** adj

²**bear** vb **bore** \'bōr\; **borne** \'bōrn\; **bear·ing** 1 : carry 2 : give birth to or produce 3 : endure 4 : press —**bear·able** adj —**bear·er** n

beard \'biərd\ n 1 : facial hair on a man 2 : tuft like a beard ~ vb : confront boldly —**beard·ed** adj —**beard·less** adj

bear·ing n 1 : way of carrying oneself 2 : supporting object or purpose 3

: significance 4 : machine part in which another part turns 5 : direction with respect esp. to compass points

beast \'bēst\ n 1 : animal 2 : brutal person —**beast·li·ness** n —**beast·ly** adj

beat \'bēt\ vb **beat**; **beat·en** \'bēt⁾n\ or **beat**; **beat·ing** 1 : strike repeatedly 2 : defeat 3 : act or arrive before 4 : throb ~ n 1 : single stroke or pulsation 2 : rhythmic stress in poetry or music ~ adj : exhausted —**beat·er** n

be·atif·ic \,bēə'tifik\ adj : blissful

be·at·i·fy \bē'atə,fī\ vb -**fied**; -**fy·ing** : make happy or blessed —**be·at·i·fi·ca·tion** \-,atəfə'kāshən\ n

be·at·i·tude \-'atə,t(y)üd\ n : saying in the Sermon on the Mount (Matthew 5:3-12) beginning "Blessed are"

beau \'bō\ n, pl **beaux** \'bōz\ or **beaus** : suitor

beau·ty \'byütē\ n, pl -**ties** : qualities that please the senses or mind —**beau·te·ous** \-ēas\ adj —**beau·te·ous·ly** adv —**beau·ti·fi·ca·tion** \,byütəfə'kāshən\ n —**beau·ti·fi·er** \'byütə,fīər\ n —**beau·ti·ful** \-ifəl\ adj —**beau·ti·ful·ly** adv —**beau·ti·fy** \-ə,fī\ vb

bea·ver \'bēvər\ n : large fur-bearing rodent

be·cause \bi'kóz, -'kəz\ conj : for the reason that

because of prep : by reason of

beck \'bek\ n : summons

beck·on \-ən\ vb : summon esp. by a nod or gesture

be·come \bi'kəm\ vb -**came** \-'kām\; -**come**; -**com·ing** 1 : come to be 2 : be suitable —**be·com·ing** adj —**be·com·ing·ly** adv

bed \'bed\ n 1 : piece of furniture to sleep on 2 : flat or level surface ~ vb -**dd**- : put or go to bed —**bed·spread** n

bed·bug n : wingless bloodsucking insect

bed·clothes n pl : bedding

bed·ding n 1 : sheets and blankets for a bed 2 : soft material (as hay) for an animal's bed

be·deck \bi'dek\ vb : adorn

be·dev·il \-'devəl\ vb : harass

bed·lam \'bedləm\ n : uproar and confusion

be·drag·gled \bi'dragəld\ adj : dirty and disordered

bed·rid·den \'bed,rid⁾n\ adj : kept in bed by illness

bed·rock n : solid subsurface rock —**bedrock** adj

bee \'bē\ *n* **1** : 4-winged honey-producing insect **2** : neighborly work session —**bee·hive** *n* —**bee·keep·er** *n* —**bees·wax** *n*

beech \'bēch\ *n, pl* **beech·es** *or* **beech** : tree with smooth gray bark and edible nuts (**beech·nuts**) —**beech·en** \-ən\ *adj*

beef \'bēf\ *n, pl* **beefs** \'bēfs\ *or* **beeves** \'bēvz\ : flesh of a steer, cow, or bull ~ *vb* : strengthen —used with *up* —**beef·steak** *n*

bee·line *n* : straight course

been *past part of* BE

beer \'bir\ *n* : alcoholic drink brewed from malt and hops —**beery** *adj*

beet \'bēt\ *n* : garden root vegetable

bee·tle \'bētəl\ *n* : 4-winged insect

be·fall \bi'fȯl\ *vb* -**fell**; -**fall·en** : happen to

be·fit \bi'fit\ *vb* : be suitable to

be·fore \bi'fōr\ *adv* **1** : in front **2** : earlier ~ *prep* **1** : in front of **2** : earlier than ~ *conj* : earlier than

be·fore·hand *adv or adj* : in advance

be·friend \bi'frend\ *vb* : act as friend to

be·fud·dle \-'fədəl\ *vb* : confuse

beg \'beg\ *vb* -**gg**- : ask earnestly

be·get \bi'get\ *vb* -**got**; -**got·ten** *or* -**got**; -**get·ting** : produce (offspring) as a father

beg·gar \'begər\ *n* : one that begs ~ *vb* : make poor —**beg·gar·ly** *adj* —**beg·gary** *n*

be·gin \bi'gin\ *vb* -**gan** \-'gan\; -**gin·ning** **1** : start **2** : come into being —**be·gin·ner** *n*

be·gone \bi'gȯn\ *vb* : go away

be·go·nia \-'gōnyə\ *n* : tropical herb with waxy flowers

be·grudge \-'grəj\ *vb* **1** : concede reluctantly **2** : envy

be·guile \-'gīl\ *vb* -**guiled**; -**guil·ing** **1** : deceive **2** : amuse

be·half \-'haf, -'häf\ *n* : benefit

be·have \-'hāv\ *vb* -**haved**; -**hav·ing** : act in a certain way

be·hav·ior \-'hāvyər\ *n* : way of behaving —**be·hav·ior·al** \-əl\ *adj*

be·head \-'hed\ *vb* : cut off the head of

be·hest \-'hest\ *n* : command

be·hind \bi'hīnd\ *adv* : at the back ~ *prep* **1** : in back of **2** : less than **3** : supporting

be·hold \-'hōld\ *vb* -**held**; -**hold·ing** : see —**be·hold·er** *n*

be·hold·en \-'hōldən\ *adj* : indebted

be·hoove \-'hüv\, **be·hove** \-'hōv\ *vb* -**hooved** *or* -**hoved**; -**hoov·ing** *or* -**hov·ing** : be necessary for

beige \'bāzh\ *n* : yellowish brown —**beige** *adj*

be·ing \'bēiŋ\ *n* **1** : existence **2** : living thing

be·la·bor \bi'lābər\ *vb* **1** : beat **2** : carry on to absurd lengths

be·lat·ed \-'lātəd\ *adj* : delayed

belch \'belch\ *vb* **1** : expel stomach gas orally **2** : emit forcefully —**belch** *n*

be·lea·guer \bi'lēgər\ *vb* **1** : besiege **2** : harass

bel·fry \'belfrē\ *n, pl* -**fries** : bell tower

be·lie \bi'lī\ *vb* -**lied**; -**ly·ing** **1** : misrepresent **2** : prove false

be·lief \bə'lēf\ *n* **1** : trust **2** : something believed

be·lieve \-'lēv\ *vb* -**lieved**; -**liev·ing** **1** : trust in **2** : accept as true **3** : hold as an opinion —**be·liev·able** *adj* —**be·liev·ably** *adv* —**be·liev·er** *n*

be·lit·tle \bi'litəl\ *vb* -**lit·tled**; -**lit·tling** : make seem unimportant or worthless

bell \'bel\ *n* : hollow metallic device that rings when struck ~ *vb* : provide with a bell

bel·la·don·na \belə'dänə\ *n* : poisonous nightshade yielding a drug used esp. to relieve intestinal spasms

belle \'bel\ *n* : beautiful woman

bel·li·cose \'beli‚kōs\ *adj* : pugnacious —**bel·li·cos·i·ty** \‚beli'käsətē\ *n*

bel·lig·er·ent \bə'lij(ə)rənt\ *adj* **1** : waging war **2** : truculent —**bel·lig·er·ence** \-rəns\ *n* —**bel·lig·er·en·cy** \-rənsē\ *n* —**belligerent** *n*

bel·low \'belō\ *vb* : make a loud deep roar or shout —**bellow** *n*

bel·lows \-ōz, -əz\ *n sing or pl* : device with sides that can be compressed to expel air

bell·weth·er \'welthər, -‚weth-\ *n* : leader

bel·ly \'belē\ *n, pl* -**lies** : abdomen ~ *vb* -**lied**; -**ly·ing** : bulge

be·long \bi'lȯŋ\ *vb* **1** : be suitable **2** : be owned **3** : be a part of

be·long·ings \-iŋz\ *n pl* : possessions

be·loved \bi'ləv(ə)d\ *adj* : dearly loved —**beloved** *n*

be·low \-'lō\ *adv* : in or to a lower place ~ *prep* : lower than

belt \'belt\ *n* **1** : strip (as of leather) worn about the waist **2** : endless band passing around pulleys or cylinders and used to impart motion **3** : distinct region ~ *vb* **1** : put a belt around **2** : thrash

be·moan \bi'mōn\ *vb* : lament

be·muse \-'myüz\ *vb* : confuse

bench \'bench\ *n* **1** : long seat **2** : judge's seat **3** : court

bend \'bend\ *vb* **bent** \'bent\; **bend·ing 1** : curve or cause a change of shape in **2** : turn in a certain direction ~ *n* **1** : act of bending **2** : curve

be·neath \bi'nēth\ *adv or prep* : below

ben·e·dic·tion \,benə'dikshən\ *n* : closing blessing

bene·fac·tor \'benə,faktər\ *n* : one who gives esp. charitable aid —**bene·fac·tion** \,benə'fakshən\ *n* —**bene·fac·tress** \'benə,faktrəs\ *n*

be·nef·i·cence \bə'nefəsəns\ *n* : quality of doing good —**be·nef·i·cent** \-sənt\ *adj*

ben·e·fi·cial \,benə'fishəl\ *adj* : being of benefit —**ben·e·fi·cial·ly** *adv*

ben·e·fi·cia·ry \-'fishē,erē, -'fish(ə)rē\ *n, pl* -**ries** : one who receives benefits

ben·e·fit \'benə,fit\ *n* **1** : something that does good **2** : help **3** : fund-raising event —**benefit** *vb*

be·nev·o·lence \bə'nev(ə)ləns\ *n* **1** : charitable nature **2** : act of kindness —**be·nev·o·lent** \-lənt\ *adj*

be·night·ed \bi'nītəd\ *adj* : ignorant

be·nign \bi'nīn\ *adj* **1** : gentle or kindly **2** : not malignant —**be·nig·ni·ty** \-'nignətē\ *n*

be·nig·nant \-'nignənt\ *adj* : benign

bent \'bent\ *n* : aptitude or interest

be·numb \bi'nəm\ *vb* : make numb esp. by cold

ben·zene, ben·zine \'ben,zēn\ *n* : colorless flammable liquid

be·queath \bi'kwēth, -'kwēth\ *vb* **1** : give by will **2** : hand down

be·quest \bi'kwest\ *n* : something bequeathed

be·rate \-'rāt\ *vb* : scold harshly

be·reaved \-'rēvd\ *adj* : suffering the death of a loved one ~ *n, pl* **bereaved** : one who is bereaved —**be·reave·ment** *n*

be·reft \-'reft\ *adj* : deprived of or lacking something

be·ret \bə'rā\ *n* : round soft visorless cap

beri·beri \,berē'berē\ *n* : thiamine-deficiency disease

ber·ry \'berē\ *n, pl* -**ries** : small pulpy fruit

ber·serk \bə(r)'sərk, -'zərk\ *adj* : crazed —**berserk** *adv*

berth \'bərth\ *n* **1** : place where a ship lies at anchor **2** : place to sit or sleep esp. on a ship **3** : job ~ *vb* : to bring or come into a berth

ber·yl \'berəl\ *n* : light-colored silicate mineral

be·seech \bi'sēch\ *vb* -**sought** \-'sȯt\ or -**seeched**; -**seech·ing** : entreat

be·set \-'set\ *vb* **1** : harass **2** : hem in

be·side \-'sīd\ *prep* **1** : by the side of **2** : besides

be·sides \-'sīdz\ *adv* **1** : in addition **2** : moreover ~ *prep* **1** : other than **2** : in addition to

be·siege \-'sēj\ *vb* : lay siege to —**be·sieg·er** *n*

be·smirch \-'smərch\ *vb* : soil

be·sot \-'sät\ *vb* -**tt-** : become drunk

be·speak \bi-\ *vb* -**spoke**; -**spo·ken**; -**speak·ing** : indicate

best \'best\ *adj, superlative of* GOOD **1** : excelling all others **2** : most productive **3** : largest ~ *adv, superlative of* WELL **1** : in the best way **2** : most ~ *n* : one that is best ~ *vb* : outdo

bes·tial \'beschəl\ *adj* : relating to beasts **2** : brutish —**bes·ti·al·i·ty** \,beschē'alətē\ *n*

be·stir \bi-\ *vb* : rouse to action

best man *n* : chief male attendant at a wedding

be·stow \bi'stō\ *vb* : give —**be·stow·al** \-əl\ *n*

bet \'bet\ *n* **1** : agreement that one whose guess about a result proves wrong will give something to one whose guess proves right **2** : money risked on a bet ~ *vb* **bet; bet·ting 1** : risk (as money) on an outcome **2** : make a bet with

be·tide \bi'tīd\ *vb* : happen to

be·to·ken \bi'tōkən\ *vb* : give an indication of

be·tray \bi'trā\ *vb* **1** : seduce **2** : deliver to an enemy by treachery **3** : prove unfaithful to **4** : reveal unintentionally —**be·tray·al** *n* —**be·tray·er** *n*

be·troth \-'träth, -'trȯth, -'trōth, or with th \-\ *vb* : promise to marry —**be·troth·al** *n* —**be·trothed** *n*

bet·ter \'betər\ *adj, comparative of* GOOD **1** : more than half **2** : improved in health **3** : of higher quality ~ *adv, comparative of* WELL **1** : in a superior manner **2** : more ~ *n* **1** : one that is better **2** : advantage ~ *vb* **1** : improve **2** : surpass —**bet·ter·ment** \-mənt\ *n*

bet·tor, bet·ter \'betər\ *n* : one who bets

be·tween \bi'twēn\ *prep* **1** —used to show two things considered together **2** : in the space separating **3** —used to indicate a comparison or choice ~ *adv* : in an intervening space or interval

bev·el \'bevəl\ *n* : slant on an edge ~ *vb* -**eled** or -**elled**; -**el·ing** or -**el·ling 1** : cut or shape to a bevel **2** : incline

bev·er·age \'bev(ə)rij\ *n* : drink

bevy \'bevē\ *n, pl* **bev·ies** : large group

be·wail \bi'wāl\ *vb* : lament

be·ware \-'waər\ *vb* : be cautious

be·wil·der \-'wildər\ *vb* : confuse —**be·wil·der·ment** *n*

be·witch \-'wich\ *vb* 1 : affect by witchcraft 2 : charm —**be·witch·ment** *n*

be·yond \bē'änd\ *adv* 1 : farther 2 : besides ~ *prep* 1 : on or to the farther side of 2 : out of the reach of 3 : besides

bi- \(')bī, ,bī\ *prefix* 1 : two 2 : coming or occurring every two 3 : twice, doubly, or on both sides

bicolored	bimetal
biconcave	bimetallic
biconcavity	binational
biconvex	binationalism
biconvexity	biparental
bicultural	bipolar
bidirectional	biracial
biethnic	biracially
bifunctional	bitonal

bi·an·nu·al \(')bī-\ *adj* : occurring twice a year —**bi·an·nu·al·ly** *adv*

bi·as \'bīəs\ *n* 1 : line diagonal to the grain of a fabric 2 : prejudice ~ *vb* **-ased** *or* **-assed**; **-as·ing** *or* **-as·sing** : prejudice

bib \'bib\ *n* : protective cover tied under a child's chin

Bi·ble \'bībəl\ *n* 1 : sacred scriptures of Christians 2 : sacred scriptures of Judaism 2 *or* of some other religion —**bib·li·cal** \'biblikəl\ *adj*

bib·li·og·ra·phy \,biblē'ägrəfē\ *n, pl* **-phies** : list of writings on a subject or of an author —**bib·li·og·ra·pher** \-fər\ *n* —**bib·li·o·graph·ic** \-lēə'grafik\, **bib·li·o·graph·i·cal** \-əl\ *adj*

bi·cam·er·al \'bī'kam(ə)rəl\ *adj* : having 2 legislative branches

bi·car·bon·ate \-'käbə,nāt, -nət\ *n* : acid carbonate

bi·cen·ten·ni·al \,bīsen'tenēəl\ *n* : 200th anniversary —**bicentennial** *adj*

bi·ceps \'bī,seps\ *n* : large muscle of the upper arm

bick·er \'bikər\ *vb or n* : squabble

bi·cus·pid \bī'kəspəd\ *n* : double-pointed tooth

bi·cy·cle \'bī,sikəl\ *n* : 2-wheeled vehicle moved by pedaling ~ *vb* **-cled; -cling** : ride a bicycle —**bi·cy·cler** \-(ə)lər\ *n* **bi·cy·clist** \-ləst\ *n*

bid \'bid\ *vb* **bade** \'bad, 'bād\ *or* **bid**; **bid·den** \'bid°n\ *or* **bid**; **bid·ding** 1 : order 2 : invite 3 : express 4 : make a bid ~ *n* 1 : act of bidding 2 : buy-

er's proposed price —**bid·da·ble** \-əbəl\ *adj* —**bid·der** *n*

bide \'bīd\ *vb* **bode** \'bōd\ *or* **bid·ed; bided; bid·ing** 1 : wait 2 : dwell

bi·en·ni·al \bī'enēəl\ *adj* 1 : occurring once in 2 years 2 : lasting 2 years —**biennial** *n* —**bi·en·ni·al·ly** *adv*

bier \'biər\ *n* : stand for a coffin

bifocals \bī'fōkəlz\ *n pl* : eyeglasses that correct for near and distant vision

big \'big\ *adj* **-gg-** : large in size, amount, or scope —**big·ness** *n*

big·a·my \'bigəmē\ *n* : marrying one person while still married to another —**big·a·mist** \-məst\ *n* —**big·a·mous** \-məs\ *adj*

big·horn *n, pl* **-horn** *or* **-horns** : wild mountain sheep

bight \'bīt\ *n* 1 : loop of a rope 2 : bay

big·ot \'bigət\ *n* : one who is intolerant of others —**big·ot·ed** \-ətəd\ *adj* —**big·ot·ry** \-ətrē\ *n*

big·wig *n* : important person

bike \'bīk\ *n* : bicycle or motorcycle

bi·ki·ni \bə'kēnē\ *n* : woman's brief 2-piece bathing suit

bi·lat·er·al \bī-\ *adj* : involving 2 sides —**bi·lat·er·al·ly** *adv*

bile \'bīl\ *n* 1 : greenish liver secretion that aids digestion 2 : bad temper

bi·lin·gual \bī'lingwəl\ *adj* : using 2 languages

bil·ious \'bilyəs\ *adj* : irritable —**bil·ious·ness** *n*

bilk \'bilk\ *vb* : cheat

¹bill \'bil\ *n* : jaws of a bird together with their horny covering ~ *vb* : caress fondly —**billed** *adj*

²bill *n* 1 : draft of a law 2 : list of things to be paid for 3 : printed advertisement 4 : piece of paper money ~ *vb* : submit a bill or account to

bill·board *n* : surface for displaying advertising bills

bil·let \'bilət\ *n* : soldiers' quarters ~ *vb* : lodge in a billet

bill·fold *n* : wallet

bil·liards \'bilyərdz\ *n* : game of driving balls into one another or into pockets on a table

bil·lion \-yən\ *n, pl* **billions** *or* **billion** : 1000 millions —**billion** *adj* —**bil·lionth** \-yənth\ *adj or n*

bil·low \'bilō\ *n* 1 : great wave 2 : rolling mass ~ *vb* : swell out —**bil·lowy** \'biləwē\ *adj*

billy goat *n* : male goat

bin \'bin\ *n* : storage box

bi·na·ry \'bīnərē\ *adj* : consisting of 2 things —**binary** *n*

bind \'bīnd\ *vb* **bound** \'baůnd\; **bind-**

ing 1 : tie **2** : obligate **3** : unite into a mass **4** : bandage **—bind·er** n **—bind·ing** n

binge \'binj\ n : spree

bin·go \'biŋgō\ n, pl **-gos** : game of covering numbers on a card

bin·oc·u·lar \bī'näkyələr, bə-\ adj : of or relating to both eyes — **bin·oc·u·lar optical instrument —usu. pl. bin·oc·u·lar·ly** adv

bio·chem·is·try \ˌbīō-\ n : chemistry dealing with organisms **—bio·chem·i·cal** adj or n **—bio·chem·ist** n

bio·de·grad·able \ˌbīō-\ adj : able to be reduced to harmless products by organisms **—bio·de·grad·abil·i·ty** n **—bio·deg·ra·da·tion** n **—bio·de·grade** vb

bi·og·ra·phy \bī'ägrəfē, bē-\ n, pl **-phies** : written history of a person's life **—bi·og·ra·pher** \-fər\ n **—bio·graph·ic** \ˌbīə'grafik\, **bio·graph·i·cal** \-ikəl\ adj

bi·ol·o·gy \bī'äləjē\ n : science of living beings and life processes **—bio·log·ic** \ˌbīə'läjik\, **bio·log·i·cal** \-əl\ adj **—bi·ol·o·gist** \bī'äləjəst\ n

bio·phys·ics \ˌbīō-\ n : application of physics to biological problems **—bio·phys·i·cal** adj **—bio·phys·i·cist** n

bi·op·sy \'bī,äpsē\ n, pl **-sies** : removal of live bodily tissue for examination

bi·par·ti·san \bī-\ adj : involving members of 2 parties

bi·ped \'bī,ped\ n : 2-footed animal

birch \'bərch\ n : deciduous tree with close-grained wood **—birch, birch·en** \-ən\ adj

bird \'bərd\ n : warm-blooded egg-laying vertebrate with wings and feathers **—bird·bath** n **—bird·house** n **—bird·seed** n

bird's-eye \'bərd,zī\ adj **1** : seen from above **2** : cursory

birth \'bərth\ n **1** : act or fact of being born or of producing young **2** : origin **—birth·day** n **—birth·place** n **—birth·rate** n

birth·mark n : unusual blemish on the skin at birth

birth·right n : something one is entitled to by birth

bis·cuit \'biskət\ n : a bread made with leavening other than yeast

bi·sect \'bī,sekt\ vb : divide into 2 parts **—bi·sec·tion** \'bī-\ n **—bi·sec·tor** \-tər\ n

bish·op \'bishəp\ n **1** : a clergyman higher than a priest or minister **2** : a chess piece

bish·op·ric \-rik\ n **1** : diocese **2** : office of bishop

bis·muth \'bizməth\ n : heavy brittle metallic chemical element

bi·son \'bīs°n, 'bīz-\ n, pl **-son** : large shaggy wild ox of central U.S.

bis·tro \'bēstrō, 'bis-\ n, pl **-tros** : small restaurant or bar

¹bit \'bit\ n **1** : part of a bridle that goes in a horse's mouth **2** : drilling tool **—bit·stock** n

²bit n **1** : small piece or quantity **2** : small degree

bitch \'bich\ n : female dog ∼ vb : complain

bite \'bīt\ vb **bit** \'bit\; **bit·ten** \'bit°n\; **bit·ing** \'bītiŋ\ **1** : to grip or cut with teeth or jaws **2** : dig in or grab and hold **3** : sting **4** : take bait ∼ n **1** : act of biting **2** : bit of food **3** : wound made by biting **—bit·ing** adj

bit·ter \'bitər\ adj **1** : having an acrid lingering taste **2** : intense or severe **3** : extremely harsh or resentful **—bit·ter·ly** adv **—bit·ter·ness** n

bit·tern \'ərn\ n : small heron

bi·tu·men \bə't(y)ümən, bī-\ n : mixture of hydrocarbons (as asphalt or tar)

bi·tu·mi·nous \-mənəs\ adj **1** : resembling or containing bitumen **2** : being coal that yields bituminous matter when heated

bi·valve \'bī-\ n : animal (as a clam) with a shell of 2 parts **—bivalve** adj

biv·ouac \'biv(ə),wak\ n : temporary camp ∼ vb **-ouacked; -ouack·ing** : camp

bi·zarre \bə'zär\ adj : very strange **—bi·zarre·ly** adv

blab \'blab\ vb **-bb-** : talk too much

black \'blak\ adj **1** : of the color black **2** : Negro **3** : soiled **4** : lacking light **5** : wicked or evil **6** : gloomy ∼ n **1** : black pigment or dye **2** : something black **3** : color of least lightness **4** : person of a dark-skinned race ∼ vb : blacken **—black·ing** n **—black·ish** adj **—black·ly** adv **—black·ness** n

black-and-blue adj : darkly discolored from bruising

black·ball n : negative vote **—black·ball** vb

black·ber·ry \-,berē\ n : black or purple fruit of a bramble

black·bird n : bird of which the male is largely or wholly black

black·board n : dark surface for writing on with chalk

black·en \-ən\ vb **1** : make or become black **2** : defame

black·guard \'blagərd, -,ärd\ n : scoundrel

black·head n : small oily mass plugging the outlet of a skin gland

black·jack n 1 : flexible leather-covered club 2 : card game ~ vb : hit with a blackjack

black·list n : list of persons to be punished —**blacklist** vb

black·mail n 1 : extortion by threat of exposure 2 : something extorted by blackmail —**blackmail** vb —**black·mail·er** n

black·out n 1 : darkness due to electrical failure 2 : brief fainting spell —**black out** vb

black·smith n : one who forges iron

black·top n : bituminous material for surfacing roads —**blacktop** vb

blad·der \'bladər\ n : sac into which urine passes from the kidneys

blade \'blād\ n 1 : leaf esp. of grass 2 : something resembling the flat part of a leaf 3 : cutting part of an instrument or tool

blame \'blām\ vb **blamed; blam·ing** 1 : find fault with 2 : hold responsible or responsible for —**blam·able** adj —**blame** n —**blame·less** adj —**blame·less·ly** adv —**blame·wor·thi·ness** n —**blame·worthy** adj

blanch \'blanch\ vb : make or become white or pale

bland \'bland\ adj 1 : smooth in manner 2 : soothing 3 : tasteless —**bland·ly** adv —**bland·ness** n

blan·dish·ment \-ishmənt\ n : flattering or coaxing speech or act

blank \'blaŋk\ adj 1 : showing or causing a dazed look 2 : lacking expression 3 : empty 4 : free from writing 5 : downright ~ n 1 : an empty space 2 : form with spaces to write in 3 : unfinished form (as of a key) 4 : cartridge with no bullet ~ vb : cover or close up —**blank·ly** adv —**blank·ness** n

blan·ket \-ət\ n 1 : heavy covering for a bed 2 : covering layer ~ vb : cover ~ adj : applying to a group

blare \'blaər\ vb **blared; blar·ing** : make a loud harsh sound —**blare** n

blar·ney \'blärnē\ n : skillful flattery

bla·sé \blä'zā\ adj : indifferent to pleasure or excitement

blas·pheme \blas'fēm\ vb **-phemed; -phem·ing** : speak blasphemy

blas·phe·my \'blasfəmē\ n, pl **-mies** : irreverence toward God or anything sacred —**blas·phe·mous** adj

blast \'blast\ n 1 : violent gust of wind 2 : explosion ~ vb 1 : shrivel up 2 : shatter by or as if by explosive —**blast off** vb : take off esp. in a rocket

bla·tant \'blāt³nt\ adj : offensively showy —**bla·tan·cy** \-³nsē\ n

¹blaze \'blāz\ n 1 : fire 2 : intense direct light 3 : strong display ~ vb **blazed; blaz·ing** : burn or shine brightly

²blaze n : white mark on an animal's face 2 : mark made on a tree ~ vb **blazed; blaz·ing** : mark with blazes

blaz·er \-ər\ n : sports jacket

bleach \'blēch\ vb : whiten —**bleach** n

bleach·ers \-ərz\ n sing or pl : uncovered stand for spectators

bleak \'blēk\ adj 1 : desolately barren 2 : lacking cheering qualities —**bleak·ish** adj —**bleak·ly** adv —**bleak·ness** n

blear \'bliər\ adj : dim with water or tears —**blear-eyed** adj

bleary \'bli(ə)rē\ adj : dull or dimmed esp. from fatigue

bleat \'blēt\ n : cry of a sheep or goat or a sound like it —**bleat** vb

bleed \'blēd\ vb **bled** \'bled\; **bleed·ing** 1 : lose or shed blood 2 : feel distress 3 : flow from a wound 4 : draw fluid from 5 : extort money from —**bleed·er** n

blem·ish \'blemish\ vb : spoil by a flaw ~ n : noticeable flaw

¹blench \'blench\ vb : flinch

²blench vb : grow or make pale

blend \'blend\ vb 1 : mix thoroughly 2 : combine into an integrated whole ~ n : product of blending —**blend·er** n

bless \'bles\ vb **blessed** \'blest\; **bless·ing** 1 : consecrate by religious rite 2 : invoke divine care for 3 : make happy —**bless·ed** \'blesəd\, **blest** \'blest\ adj —**bless·ed·ness** n —**bless·ing** n

blew past of BLOW

blight \'blīt\ n 1 : plant disorder marked by withering or an organism causing it 2 : harmful influence ~ vb : affect with or suffer from blight

blimp \'blimp\ n : small airship holding form by pressure of contained gas

blind \'blīnd\ adj 1 : lacking or quite deficient in ability to see 2 : not intelligently controlled 3 : having no way out ~ vb 1 : to make blind 2 : dazzle ~ n 1 : something to conceal or darken 2 : place of concealment —**blind·ly** adv —**blind·ness** n

blind·fold vb : cover the eyes of —**blindfold** n

blink \'bliŋk\ vb 1 : wink 2 : shine intermittently ~ n : wink

blink-er *n* : a blinking light

bliss \'blis\ *n* 1 : complete happiness 2 : heaven or paradise —**bliss-ful** *adj* —**bliss-ful-ly** *adv*

blis-ter \'blistər\ *n* 1 : raised area of skin containing watery fluid 2 : raised or swollen spot ~ *vb* : develop or cause blisters

blithe \'blīth, 'blīth\ *adj* **blith-er; blith-est** : cheerful —**blithe-ly** *adv* —**blithe-some** \-səm\ *adj*

blitz \'blits\ *n* 1 : series of air raids 2 : fast intensive campaign —**blitz** *vb*

bliz-zard \'blizərd\ *n* : severe windy snowstorm

bloat \'blōt\ *vb* : swell

blob \'bläb\ *n* : small lump or drop

bloc \'bläk\ *n* : group working together

block \'bläk\ *n* 1 : solid piece 2 : frame enclosing a pulley 3 : quantity considered together 4 : large building divided into separate units 5 : a city square or the distance along one of its sides 6 : obstruction 7 : interruption of a bodily or mental function ~ *vb* : obstruct or hinder

block-ade \blä'kād\ *n* : the shutting off of a place usu. by troops or ships ~ *vb* **-ad-ed; -ad-ing** : impose a blockade upon

block-head *n* : stupid person

blond, blonde \'bländ\ *adj* 1 : fair in complexion 2 : of a light color —**blond, blonde** *n*

blood \'bləd\ *n* 1 : red liquid that circulates in the heart, arteries, and veins of animals 2 : lifeblood 3 : lineage —**blood-ed** *adj* —**blood-less** *adj* —**blood-stain** *n* —**blood-stained** *adj* —**blood-suck-er** *n* —**blood-suck-ing** *n* —**bloody** *adj*

blood-cur-dling *adj* : terrifying

blood-hound *n* : large hound with a keen sense of smell

blood-mo-bile \-mō,bēl\ *n* : truck for collecting blood from donors

blood-shed *n* : slaughter

blood-shot *adj* : inflamed to redness

blood-stream *n* : blood in a circulatory system

blood-thirsty *adj* : eager to shed blood —**blood-thirst-i-ly** *adv* —**blood-thirst-i-ness** *n*

bloom \'blüm\ *n* 1 : flower 2 : period of flowering 3 : fresh or healthy look ~ *vb* : yield flowers —**bloomy** *adj*

bloo-mers \'blümərz\ *n pl* : woman's underwear of short loose trousers

bloop-er \'blüpər\ *n* : public blunder

blos-som \'bläsəm\ *n or vb* : flower

blot \'blät\ *n* 1 : stain 2 : blemish ~ *vb* **-tt-** 1 : spot 2 : dry with absorbent paper —**blot-ter** *n*

blotch \'bläch\ *n* : large spot —**blotch** *vb* —**blotchy** *adj*

blouse \'blaús, 'blaúz\ *n* : loose garment reaching from the neck to the waist

¹**blow** \'blō\ *vb* **blew** \'blü\; **blown** \'blōn\; **blow-ing** 1 : move forcibly 2 : send forth a current of air 3 : sound 4 : shape by blowing 5 : explode ~ *n* 1 : gale 2 : a blowing from the mouth —**blow-er** *n* —**blowy** *adj*

²**blow** *n* 1 : forcible stroke 2 *pl* : fighting 3 : calamity

³**blow** *vb* **blew; blown; blow-ing** : flower

blow-out *n* : bursting of a tire

blow-torch *n* : small torch that uses a blast of air

¹**blub-ber** \'bləbər\ *n* : fat of whales

²**blubber** *vb* : cry noisily

blud-geon \'bləjən\ *n* : short club ~ *vb* : hit with a bludgeon

blue \'blü\ *adj* **blu-er; blu-est** 1 : of the color blue 2 : melancholy ~ *n* : color of the clear sky —**blu-ish** \-ish\ *adj*

blue-bell *n* : plant with blue bell-shaped flowers

blue-ber-ry \-,berē, -b(ə)rē\ *n* : edible blue or blackish berry

blue-bird *n* : small bluish songbird

blue-fish *n* : bluish marine food fish

blue jay *n* : American crested jay

blue-print *n* 1 : photographic print in white on blue of a mechanical drawing 2 : plan of action —**blueprint** *vb*

blues \'blüz\ *n pl* 1 : depression 2 : music in a usu. melancholy style of American Negro origin

¹**bluff** \'bləf\ *adj* 1 : rising steeply with a broad flat front 2 : frank ~ *n* : cliff

²**bluff** *vb* : deceive by pretense ~ *n* : act of bluffing —**bluff-er** \-ər\ *n*

blu-ing, blue-ing \'blüiŋ\ *n* : dye used in laundering to keep fabrics white

blun-der \'bləndər\ *vb* 1 : move clumsily 2 : make a stupid mistake ~ *n* : bad mistake

blun-der-buss \-,bəs\ *n* : obsolete short-barreled firearm

blunt \'blənt\ *adj* 1 : not sharp 2 : tactless ~ *vb* : make dull —**blunt-ly** *adv* —**blunt-ness** *n*

blur \'blər\ *n* 1 : smear 2 : something vaguely seen ~ *vb* **-rr-** : make or become indistinct —**blur-ry** \-ē\ *adj*

blurb \'blərb\ *n* : short publicity notice

blurt \'blərt\ *vb* : utter suddenly

blush \'bləsh\ *n* : reddening of the face —**blush** *vb* —**blush-ful** *adj*

blus-ter \'bləstər\ *vb* 1 : blow violently

2 : to talk or act with boasts or threats —**blus·ter** n —**blus·tery** adj

boa \'bōə\ n 1 : a large snake (as the **boa con·stric·tor** \-,bōəkən'striktər\) that crushes its prey **2** : fluffy scarf

boar \'bōr\ n : male swine

board \'bōrd\ n **1** : long thin piece of sawed lumber **2** : flat thin sheet esp. for games **3** : daily meals furnished for pay **4** : official body ~ vb **1** : go aboard **2** : cover with boards **3** : supply meals to —**board·er** n

board·walk n : wooden walk along a beach

boast \'bōst\ vb : praise oneself or one's possessions —**boast** n —**boast·er** n—**boast·ful** adj —**boast·ful·ly** adv

boat \'bōt\ n : vessel for traveling on water —**boat** n —**boat·man** \-mən\ n

boat·swain \'bōsᵊn\ n : ship's officer in charge of the hull

¹bob \'bäb\ vb **-bb- 1** : move up and down **2** : appear suddenly

²bob n **1** : float **2** : woman's short haircut ~ vb : cut hair in a bob

bob·bin \'bäbən\ n : spindle for holding thread

bob·ble \'bäbəl\ vb **-bled; -bling** : fumble —**bobble** n

bob·cat n : small American lynx

bob·o·link \'bäbə,liŋk\ n : American songbird

bob·sled \-,sled\ n : racing sled —**bobsled** vb

bob·white \('-)bäb'hwīt\ n : quail

bock \'bäk\ n : dark beer

¹bode \'bōd\ vb **bod·ed; bod·ing** : indicate by signs

²bode past of BIDE

bod·ice \'bädəs\ n : close-fitting top of dress

bod·i·ly \'bädᵊlē\ adj : relating to the body ~ adv **1** : in the flesh **2** : as a whole

body \'bädē\ n, pl **bod·ies 1** : the physical whole of an organism **2** : human being **3** : main part **4** : mass of matter **5** : group —**bod·ied** adj —**bodi·less** \-iləs, -ᵊləs\ adj —**body·guard** n

bog \'bäg, 'bog\ n : swamp ~ vb **-gg-** : sink in or as if in a bog —**bog·gy** adj

bo·gey \'bugē, 'bō-\ n, pl **-geys** : someone or something frightening

bog·gle \'bägəl\ vb **-gled; -gling** : overwhelm with amazement

bo·gus \'bōgəs\ adj : fake

bo·he·mi·an \bō'hēmēən\ n : one living unconventionally —**bohemian** adj

¹boil \'boil\ n : inflamed swelling

²boil vb **1** : heat to a temperature (**boil·ing point**) at which forms vapor forms **2**

: cook in boiling liquid **3** : be agitated —**boil** n

boil·er \'boilər\ n : tank holding hot water or steam

bois·ter·ous \'boistə)rəs\ adj : noisily turbulent —**bois·ter·ous·ly** adv

bold \'bōld\ adj **1** : courageous **2** : insolent **3** : daring —**bold·ly** adv —**bold·ness** n \'bōl(d)nəs\ n

bo·le·ro \bə'le(ə)rō\ n, pl **-ros 1** : Spanish dance **2** : short open jacket

boll \'bōl\ n : seed pod

boll weevil n : a small grayish weevil that infests the cotton plant

bo·lo·gna \bə'lōnē\ n : large smoked sausage

bol·ster \'bōlstər\ n : long pillow ~ vb **-stered; -ster·ing** : support

¹bolt \'bōlt\ n **1** : flash of lightning **2** : sliding bar used to fasten a door **3** : roll of cloth **4** : threaded pin used with a nut ~ vb **1** : move suddenly **2** : fasten with a bolt **3** : swallow hastily

²bolt vb : sift

bomb \'bäm\ n : explosive device ~ vb : attack with bombs —**bomb·proof** adj

bom·bard \bäm'bärd, bəm-\ vb : attack with or as if with artillery —**bom·bard·ment** n

bom·bar·dier \,bämb(r)'diər\ n : one who releases the bombs from a bomber

bom·bast \'bäm,bast\ n : pretentious language —**bom·bas·tic** \bäm'bas·tik\ adj

bomb·er n **1** : one that bombs **2** : airplane for dropping bombs

bomb·shell n **1** : bomb **2** : great surprise

bona fide \'bōnə,fīd, 'bän-; ,bōnə'fīdē\ adj **1** : made in good faith **2** : genuine

bo·nan·za \bə'nanzə\ n : something yielding a rich return

bon·bon \'bän,bän\ n : piece of candy

bond \'bänd\ n **1** pl : fetters **2** : uniting force **3** : obligation made binding by money **4** : interest-bearing certificate **5** : insure **2** : cause to adhere —**bond·hold·er** n

bond·age \'bändij\ n : slavery —**bond·man** \-mən\ n —**bond·wom·an** n

¹bonds·man \'bän(d)zmən\ n : slave

²bondsman n : surety

bone \'bōn\ n : skeletal material ~ vb **boned; bon·ing** : to free from bones —**bone·less** adj —**bony, bon·ey** \'bōnē\ adj

bon·er \'bōnər\ n : blunder

bon·fire \'bän,fi(ə)r\ n : outdoor fire

bo·ni·to \bə'nētō\ n, pl **-tos** or **-to** : medium-sized tuna

bon·net \'bänət\ n : hat for a woman or infant

bo·nus \'bōnəs\ n : extra payment

boo \'bü\ n, pl **boos** : shout of disapproval —**boo** vb

boo·by \'bübē\ n, pl **-bies** : dunce

book \'bùk\ n **1** : paper sheets bound into a volume **2** : long literary work or a subdivision of one ~ vb : reserve —**book·case** n —**book·let** \-lət\ n —**book·mark** n —**book·sell·er** n —**book·shelf** n

book·end n : support to hold up a row of books

book·ie \-ē\ n : bookmaker

book·ish \-ish\ adj : fond of books and reading

book·keep·er n : one who keeps business accounts —**book·keep·ing** n

book·mak·er n : one who takes bets —**book·mak·ing** n

book·worm n : one devoted to reading

¹boom \'büm\ n **1** : long spar to extend the bottom of a sail **2** : beam projecting from the pole of a derrick

²boom vb **1** : make a deep hollow sound **2** : grow rapidly esp. in value ~ n **1** : booming sound **2** : rapid growth

boo·mer·ang \'bümə,raŋ\ n : angular club that returns to the thrower

¹boon \'bün\ n : benefit

²boon adj : congenial

boon·docks \'bün,däks\ n pl : rural area

boor \'bùr\ n : rude person —**boor·ish** adj

boost \'büst\ vb **1** : raise **2** : promote —**boost** n —**boost·er** n

boot \'büt\ n **1** : covering for the foot and leg **2** : kick ~ vb : kick

boo·tee, boo·tie \'bütē\ n : infant's knitted sock

booth \'büth\ n, pl **booths** \'büthz, 'büths\ : small enclosed stall or seating area

boot·leg \'büt,leg\ vb : make or sell liquor illegally —**boot·leg** adj or n —**boot·leg·ger** n

boo·ty \'bütē\ n, pl **-ties** : plunder

booze \'büz\ vb **boozed; booz·ing** : drink liquor to excess ~ n : liquor —**booz·er** n —**boozy** adj

bo·rax \'bōr,aks\ n : crystalline compound of boron

bor·der \'bordər\ n **1** : edge **2** : boundary ~ vb **1** : put a border on **2** : be close

¹bore \'bōr\ vb **bored; bor·ing 1** : pierce **2** : make by piercing ~ n

: cylindrical hole or its diameter —**bor·er** n

²bore past of BEAR

³bore n : one that is dull ~ vb **bored; bor·ing** : tire with dullness —**bore·dom** n

born \'born\ adj **1** : brought into life **2** : being such by birth

borne past part of BEAR

bo·ron \'bōr,än\ n : dark-colored chemical element

bor·ough \'bərō\ n : incorporated town or village

bor·row \'bärō\ vb **1** : take as a loan **2** : take into use

bo·som \'büzəm, 'bü-\ n : breast ~ adj : intimate —**bo·somed** adj

boss \'bòs\ n : employer or supervisor ~ vb : supervise —**bossy** adj

bot·a·ny \'bät(ə)nē\ n : plant biology —**bo·tan·ic** \bō'tanik\, **bo·tan·i·cal** \-əl\ adj —**bot·a·nist** \'bät(ə)nəst\ n —**bot·a·nize** \-ə n,īz\ vb

botch \'bäch\ vb : do clumsily —**botch** n

both \'bōth\ adj or pron : the one and the other ~ conj —used to show each of two is included

both·er \'bäthər\ vb **1** : annoy or worry **2** : take the trouble —**bother** n —**both·er·some** \-səm\ adj

bot·tle \'bät²l\ n : container with a narrow neck and no handles ~ vb **bot·tled; bot·tling** : put into a bottle

bot·tle·neck n : place or cause of congestion

bot·tom \'bätəm\ n **1** : supporting surface **2** : lowest part or place —**bottom** adj —**bot·tomed** adj —**bot·tom·less** adj

bot·u·lism \'bächə,lizəm\ n : acute food poisoning

bou·doir \'büd,wär, 'büd-\ n : woman's private room

bough \'baù\ n : large tree branch

bought past of BUY

bouil·lon \'bü,yän; 'bùl,yän, -yən\ n : clear soup

boul·der \'bōldər\ n : large rounded rock —**boul·dered** adj

bou·le·vard \'bùlə,värd, 'bü-\ n : broad thoroughfare

bounce \'baùns\ vb **bounced; bounc·ing 1** : spring back **2** : make bounce —**bounce** n

¹bound \'baùnd\ adj : intending to go

²bound n : limit or boundary ~ vb : be a boundary of —**bound·less** adj —**bound·less·ness** n

³bound adj **1** : obliged **2** : having a binding **3** : determined **4** : incapable of failing

⁴bound n : leap ~ vb : move by springing

bound-ary \'baund(ə)rē\ n, pl -aries : line marking extent or separation

boun-ty \'bauntē\ n, pl -ties 1 : generosity 2 : reward —**boun-te-ous** \-ēəs\ adj —**boun-te-ous-ly** adv —**boun-ti-ful** \-ifəl\ adj —**boun-ti-ful-ly** adv

bou-quet \bō'kā, bü-\ n 1 : bunch of flowers 2 : fragrance

bour-bon \'bərbən\ n : corn whiskey

bour-geoi-sie \,bùrzh,wä'zē\ n 1 : middle class of society —**bour-geois** \'bùrzh,wä, bùrzh'wä\ n or adj

bout \'baut\ n 1 : contest 2 : outbreak

bou-tique \bü'tēk\ n : specialty shop

bo-vine \'bō,vīn, -,vēn\ adj : relating to cattle —**bovine** n

¹bow \'bau\ vb 1 : submit 2 : bend the head or body ~ n : act of bowing

²bow \'bō\ n 1 : bend or arch 2 : weapon for shooting arrows 3 : knot with loops 4 : rod with stretched horsehairs for playing a stringed instrument ~ vb : curve or bend —**bow-man** \-mən\ n —**bow-string** n

³bow \'bau\ n : forward part of a ship —**bow** adj

bow-els \'bau(ə)ls\ n pl 1 : intestines 2 : inmost parts

bow-er \'bau(ə)r\ n : arbor

¹bowl \'bōl\ n : concave vessel or part —**bowl-ful** \-,fùl\ n

²bowl n : round ball for bowling ~ vb : roll a ball in bowling —**bowl-er** n

bowl-ing n : game in which balls are rolled to knock down pins

¹box \'bäks\ n, pl box or box-es : evergreen shrub —**box-wood** \-,wùd\ n

²box n 1 : container usu. with 4 sides and a cover 2 : small compartment ~ vb : put in a box

³box n : slap ~ vb 1 : slap 2 : fight with the fists —**box-er** n —**box-ing** n

box-car n : roofed freight car

box office n : theater ticket office

boy \'bòi\ n : male child —**boy-hood** n —**boy-ish** adj —**boy-ish-ly** adv —**boy-ish-ness** n

boy-cott \-,kät\ vb : refrain from dealing with —**boycott** n

brace \'brās\ n 1 : crank for turning a bit 2 : something that resists weight or supports ~ vb braced; brac-ing 1 : make taut or steady 2 : invigorate 3 : strengthen

brace-let \'brāslət\ n : ornamental band for the wrist or arm

brack-et \'brakət\ n 1 : projecting support 2 : punctuation mark [or] 3 : class ~ vb 1 : furnish or fasten with

brackets 2 : place within brackets 3 : group

brack-ish \-ish\ adj : salty

brad \'brad\ n : nail with a small head

brag \'brag\ vb -gg- : boast —**brag** n

brag-gart \'bragərt\ n : boaster

braid \'brād\ vb : interweave ~ n : something braided

braille \'brāl\ n : system of writing for the blind using raised dots

brain \'brān\ n 1 : organ of thought and nervous coordination enclosed in the skull 2 : intelligence ~ vb : smash the skull of —**brained** adj —**brain-less** adj —**brainy** adj

braise \'brāz\ vb braised; brais-ing : cook (meat) slowly in a covered dish

brake \'brāk\ n : device for slowing or stopping ~ vb braked; brak-ing : slow or stop by a brake

bram-ble \'brambəl\ n : prickly shrub

bran \'bran\ n : broken grain husks

branch \'branch\ n 1 : division of a plant stem 2 : part ~ vb 1 : develop branches 2 : diverge —**branched** adj

brand \'brand\ n 1 : identifying mark made by burning 2 : stigma 3 : distinctive kind (as of goods from one firm) ~ vb : mark with a brand

bran-dish \'brandish\ vb : wave

brand-new adj : unused

bran-dy \'brandē\ n, pl -dies : liquor distilled from wine

brash \'brash\ adj 1 : impulsive 2 : aggressively self-assertive

brass \'bras\ n 1 : alloy of copper and zinc 2 : brazen self-assurance —**brassy** adj

bras-siere \brə'zir\ n : woman's undergarment to support the breasts

brat \'brat\ n : ill-behaved child —**brat-ty** adj

bra-va-do \brə'vädō\ n, pl -does or -dos : false bravery

¹brave \'brāv\ adj brav-er; brav-est : showing courage ~ vb braved; brav-ing : face with courage —**brave-ly** adv —**brav-ery** \-(ə)rē\ n

²brave n : Indian warrior

bra-vo \'brävō\ n, pl -vos : shout of approval

brawl \'bròl\ n : noisy quarrel or violent fight —**brawl** vb —**brawl-er** n

brawn \'bròn\ n : muscular strength —**brawny** adj

bray \'brā\ n : harsh cry of a donkey —**bray** vb

bra-zen \'brāzⁿn\ adj 1 : made of brass 2 : bold —**bra-zen-ly** adv —**bra-zen-ness** \-(ə)s\ n

bra-zier \'brāzhər\ n : charcoal grill

breach \'brēch\ n 1 : breaking of a law, obligation, or standard 2 : gap ~ vb : make a breach in

bread \'bred\ n : baked food made of flour ~ vb : cover with bread crumbs

breadth \'bredth\ n : width

bread-win-ner n : wage earner

break \'brāk\ vb **broke** \'brōk\; **bro-ken** \'brōkən\; **break-ing** 1 : knock into pieces 2 : transgress 3 : force a way into or out of 4 : exceed 5 : interrupt 6 : fail ~ n 1 : act or result of breaking 2 : stroke of good luck —**break-able** adj or n —**break-age** \'brākij\ n —**break-er** n —**break in** vb 1 : enter by force 2 : interrupt 3 : train —**break out** vb 1 : develop a rash

break-down n : physical or mental failure —**break down** vb

break-fast \'brekfəst\ n : first meal of the day —**breakfast** vb

breast \'brest\ n 1 : milk-producing gland esp. of a woman 2 : front part of the chest

breast-bone n : sternum

breath \'breth\ n 1 : slight breeze 2 : air breathed in or out —**breath-less** adj —**breath-less-ly** adv

breathe \'brēth\ vb **breathed**; **breathing** 1 : draw air into the lungs and expel it 2 : live 3 : utter

breath-tak-ing adj : exciting

breech-es \'brichəz\ n pl : trousers ending near the knee

breed \'brēd\ vb **bred** \'bred\; **breeding** 1 : give birth to 2 : propagate 3 : raise ~ n 1 : kind of plant or animal usu. developed by man 2 : class —**breed-er** n

breeze \'brēz\ n : light wind ~ vb **breezed**; **breez-ing** : move fast —**breezy** adj

breth-ren \'breth(ə)rən, -ərn\ pl of BROTHER

bre-via-ry \'brēv(y)ərē, -vē,erē\ n, pl **-ries** : prayer book used by Roman Catholic priests

brev-i-ty \'brevətē\ n, pl **-ties** : shortness or conciseness

brew \'brü\ vb : make by fermenting or infusing —**brew** n —**brew-er** n —**brew-ery** \'brüərē, 'brú(ə)rē\ n

bribe \'brīb\ vb **bribed**; **brib-ing** n : corrupt or influence by gifts ~ n : something offered or given in bribing —**brib-ery** \-(ə)rē\ n

bric-a-brac \'brikə,brak\ n pl : small ornamental articles

brick \'brik\ n : building block of baked clay —**brick** vb —**brick-lay-er** n —**brick-lay-ing** n

bride \'brīd\ n : woman just married or about to be married —**brid-al** \-ᵊl\ adj

bride-groom n : man just married or about to be married

brides-maid n : woman who attends a bride at her wedding

¹bridge \'brij\ n 1 : structure built for passage over a depression or obstacle 2 : upper part of the nose 3 : platform over the deck of a ship 4 : artificial replacement for missing teeth ~ vb : build a bridge over —**bridge-able** adj

²bridge n : card game for 4 players

bri-dle \'brīdᵊl\ n : headgear to control a horse ~ vb **-dled**; **-dling** 1 : put a bridle on 2 : restrain 3 : show hostility or scorn

brief \'brēf\ adj : short or concise ~ n : concise summary (as of a legal case) ~ vb : give final instructions or essential information to —**brief-ly** adv —**brief-ness** n

brief-case n : case for papers

¹bri-er, bri-ar \'brī(ə)r\ n : thorny plant

²brier n : heath of southern Europe

¹brig \'brig\ n : 2-masted ship

²brig n : jail on a naval ship

bri-gade \brig'ād\ n 1 : a large military unit 2 : a group organized for a special activity

brig-a-dier general \,brigə,diər-\ n : officer ranking next below a major general

brig-and \'brigənd\ n : bandit —**brig-and-age** \-ij\ n

bright \'brīt\ adj 1 : radiating or reflecting light 2 : cheerful 3 : intelligent —**bright-en** \-ᵊn\ vb —**bright-en-er** \'brītnar, -ᵊnar\ n —**bright-ly** adv —**bright-ness** n

bril-liant \'brilyənt\ adj 1 : very bright 2 : splendid 3 : very intelligent —**bril-liance** \-yəns\, **bril-lian-cy** \-yənsē\ n —**bril-liant-ly** adv

brim \'brim\ n : edge or rim —**brim-less** adj —**brimmed** adj

brim-ful \-'fúl\ adj : full to the brim

brim-stone n : sulfur

brin-dled \'brindᵊld\ adj : gray or tawny with dark streaks or flecks

brine \'brīn\ n 1 : salt water 2 : ocean —**brin-i-ness** n —**briny** adj

bring \'briŋ\ vb **brought** \'brót\; **bring-ing** 1 : cause to come with one 2 : persuade 3 : produce 4 : sell for —**bring-er** n —**bring about** vb : make happen —**bring up** vb 1 : care for and educate 2 : cause to be noticed 3 : vomit

brink \\'briŋk\\ n : edge

bri·quette, bri·quet \\brik'et\\ n : pressed mass (as of charcoal)

brisk \\'brisk\\ adj 1 : lively 2 : invigorating —**brisk·ly** adv —**brisk·ness** n

bris·ket \\'briskət\\ n : breast or lower chest of a quadruped

bris·tle \\'brisəl\\ n : short stiff hair ~ vb -tled; -tling 1 : stand erect 2 : show angry defiance 3 : appear as if covered with bristles —**bris·tly** adj

brit·tle \\'brit²l\\ adj -tler, -tlest : easily broken or snapped

broach \\'brōch\\ n : pointed tool (as for opening casks) ~ vb 1 : pierce (as a cask) to open 2 : introduce for discussion

broad \\'brod\\ adj 1 : wide 2 : spacious 3 : clear or open 4 : obvious 5 : liberal in outlook 6 : widely applicable 7 : dealing with essential points —**broad·en** \\-²n\\ vb —**broad·ly** adv —**broad·ness** n

broad·cast n 1 : transmission by radio waves 2 : radio or television program ~ vb -cast; -cast·ing 1 : scatter or sow in all directions 2 : make widely known 3 : send out on a broadcast —**broad·cast·er** n

broad·cloth n : fine cloth

broad·loom adj : woven on a wide loom esp. in solid color

broad·mind·ed adj : free from prejudice —**broad·mind·ed·ly** adv —**broad·mind·ed·ness** n

broad·side n 1 : simultaneous firing of all guns on one side of a ship 2 : verbal attack

bro·cade \\brō'kād\\ n : usu. silk fabric with a raised design

broc·co·li \\'bräk(ə)lē\\ n : green vegetable akin to cauliflower

bro·chure \\brō'shúr\\ n : pamphlet

brogue \\'brōg\\ n : Irish accent

broil \\'bróil\\ vb : cook by radiant heat —**broil** n

broil·er n 1 : utensil for broiling 2 : chicken fit for broiling

¹broke \\'brōk\\ past of BREAK

²broke adj : out of money

bro·ken \\'brōkən\\ adj : imperfectly spoken —**bro·ken·ly** adv

bro·ken·heart·ed \\-'härtəd\\ adj : woeful

bro·ker \\'brōkər\\ n : agent who buys and sells for a fee —**bro·ker·age** \\-k(ə)rij\\ n

bro·mide \\-,mīd\\ n 1 : compound of bromine 2 : trite remark or notion —**bro·mid·ic** \\brō'midik\\ adj

bro·mine \\'brō,mēn\\ n : deep red liquid corrosive chemical element

bron·chi·tis \\brän'kītəs, bräŋ-\\ n : inflammation of the bronchi

bron·chus \\'bräŋkəs\\ n, pl -chi \\-,kī, -,kē\\ : division of the windpipe leading to a lung —**bron·chi·al** \\-kēəl\\ adj

bron·co \\'bräŋkō\\ n, pl -cos : small half-wild horse

bronze \\'bränz\\ vb bronzed; bronz·ing : make bronze in color ~ n 1 : alloy of copper and tin 2 : yellowish brown —**bronzy** \\-ē\\ adj

brooch \\'brōch, 'brüch\\ n : ornamental clasp or pin

brood \\'brüd\\ n : family of young ~ vb 1 : sit on eggs to hatch them 2 : ponder ~ adj : kept for breeding —**brood·er** n

¹brook \\'brúk\\ vb : tolerate

²brook n : small stream

broom \\'brüm, 'brúm\\ n 1 : flowering shrub 2 : implement for sweeping —**broom·stick** n

broth \\'bróth\\ n, pl broths \\'bróths, 'bróthz\\ : liquid in which meat has been cooked

broth·el \\'bräthəl, 'bróth-\\ n : house of prostitutes

broth·er \\'brəthər\\ n, pl brothers also breth·ren \\'breth(ə)rən, 'brethərn\\ 1 : male sharing one or both parents with another person 2 : kindred human being —**broth·er·hood** n —**broth·er·li·ness** n —**broth·er·ly** adj

broth·er·in·law n, pl brothers–in–law : brother of one's spouse or husband of one's sister or of one's spouse's sister

brought past of BRING

brow \\'braú\\ n 1 : eyebrow 2 : forehead 3 : edge of a steep place

brow·beat vb -beat; -beat·en or -beat; -beat·ing : intimidate

brown \\'braún\\ adj 1 : of the color brown 2 : of dark or tanned complexion ~ n : a color like that of coffee ~ vb : make or become brown

browse \\'braúz\\ vb browsed; brows·ing 1 : graze 2 : look over casually —**brows·er** n

bru·in \\'brüən\\ n : bear

bruise \\'brüz\\ vb bruised; bruis·ing 1 : make a bruise on 2 : become bruised ~ n : surface injury to flesh

brunch \\'brənch\\ n : late breakfast, early lunch, or combination of both

bru·net, bru·nette \\brü'net\\ adj : having dark skin, hair, and eyes —**brunet** n

brunt \\'brənt\\ n : main impact

¹brush \\'brəsh\\ n 1 : small cut

branches 2 : coarse shrubby vegetation

²brush n 1 : bristles set in a handle used esp. for cleaning or painting 2 : light touch ~ vb 1 : apply a brush to 2 : remove with or as if with a brush 3 : dispose of in an offhand way 4 : touch lightly —**brush up** : renew one's skill

³brush n : skirmish

brush-off n : abrupt dismissal

brusque \'brəsk\ adj : curt or blunt in manner —**brusque-ly** adv

bru-tal \'brüt³l\ adj : like a brute and esp. cruel —**bru-tal-i-ty** \brü'talətē\ n —**bru-tal-ize** \'brüt³l₁īz\ vb —**bru-tal-ly** \-³lē\ adv

brute \'brüt\ adj 1 : of or typical of beasts 2 : unreasoning 3 : purely physical ~ n 1 : beast 2 : brutal person —**brut-ish** \-ish\ adj

bub-ble \'bəbəl\ vb -bled; -bling : form, rise in, or give off bubbles ~ n : globule of gas in or covered with a liquid —**bub-bly** \-(ə)lē\ adj

bu-bo \'b(y)übō\ n, pl **buboes** : inflammatory swelling of a lymph gland —**bu-bon-ic** \b(y)ü'bänik\ adj

buc-ca-neer \₁bəkə'niər\ n : pirate

buck \'bək\ n, pl **buck** or **bucks** : male animal (as a deer) ~ vb 1 : jerk forward 2 : oppose

buck-et \'bəkət\ n : pail —**buck-et-ful** n

buck-le \-əl\ n 1 : clasp (as on a belt) for two loose ends 2 : bend or fold ~ vb -led; -ling 1 : fasten with a buckle 2 : apply oneself 3 : bend or crumple

buck-ler \-lər\ n : shield

buck-shot n : coarse lead shot

buck-skin n : soft leather (as from the skin of a buck) —**buckskin** adj

buck-tooth n : large projecting front tooth —**buck-toothed** adj

buck-wheat n : herb whose seeds are used as a cereal grain or the seeds themselves

bu-col-ic \byü'kälik\ adj : rural

bud \'bəd\ n 1 : undeveloped plant shoot 2 : partly opened flower ~ vb -dd- 1 : form or put forth buds 2 : be or develop like a bud

Bud-dhism \'bü₁dizəm, 'bud₁iz-\ n : religion of eastern and central Asia —**Bud-dhist** \'büdəst, 'bud-\ n or adj

bud-dy \'bədē\ n, pl -dies : friend

budge \'bəj\ vb budged; budg-ing : move from a place

bud-get \'bəjət\ n 1 : estimate of income and expenses 2 : plan for coordinating income and expenses —**budget** vb —**bud-get-ary** \-ə₁terē\ adj

buff \'bəf\ n 1 : dull yellow-orange color 2 : enthusiast ~ adj : of the color buff —**buff** vb : polish

buf-fa-lo \'bəfə₁lō\ n, pl -lo or -loes also -los : wild ox (as a bison)

¹**buff-er** \'bəfər\ n : one that buffs

²**buffer** n : something that lessens shock

¹**buf-fet** \-ət\ n : blow or slap ~ vb : hit esp. repeatedly

²**buf-fet** \(₁)bə'fā, bü-\ n 1 : sideboard 2 : meal at which people serve themselves

buf-foon \(₁)bə'fün\ n : clown —**buffoon-ery** \-(ə)rē\ n

bug \'bəg\ n 1 : small usu. obnoxious crawling creature 2 : 4-winged sucking insect 3 : disease-producing germ 4 : hidden microphone ~ vb -gg- 1 : pester 2 : conceal a microphone in

bug-a-boo \'bəgə₁bü\ n, pl -boos : bogey

bug-bear n : source of dread

bug-gy \'bəgē\ n, pl -gies : light carriage

bu-gle \'byügəl\ n : trumpetlike brass instrument —**bu-gler** \-glər\ n

build \'bild\ vb built \'bilt\; build-ing 1 : put together 2 : establish 3 : increase ~ n : physique —**build-er** n

build-ing \'bildiŋ\ n 1 : roofed and walled structure 2 : art or business of constructing buildings

bulb \'bəlb\ n 1 : large underground plant bud 2 : rounded or pear-shaped object —**bul-bous** \-əs\ adj

bulge \'bəlj\ n : swelling projecting part ~ vb bulged; bulg-ing : swell out

bulk \'bəlk\ n 1 : magnitude 2 : indigestible fibrous food residues 3 : large mass 4 : major portion ~ vb : have bulk —**bulky** \-ē\ adj

bulk-head n : ship's partition

¹**bull** \'bu̇l\ n : adult male of a bovine or other large animal ~ adj : male

²**bull** n : papal letter

bull-dog n : compact short-haired dog

bull-doze \-₁dōz\ vb 1 : move or level with a tractor (**bull-doz-er**) having a broad blade 2 : force

bul-let \'bu̇lət\ n : missile to be shot from a gun —**bul-let-proof** adj

bul-le-tin \-³n\ n 1 : brief public report 2 : periodical

bull-fight n : sport of taunting and killing bulls —**bull-fight-er** n

bull-finch n : English songbird

bull-frog n : large deep-voiced frog

bull-head-ed adj : stupidly stubborn

bul-lion \'bu̇lyən\ n : gold or silver esp. in bars

bul-lock \-ək\ n 1 : young bull 2 : steer

bull's-eye n, pl **bull's-eyes** : center of a target

bul·ly \'bùlē\ n, pl **-lies** : one who hurts or intimidates others ~ vb **-lied; -ly·ing** : act like a bully toward

bul·rush \'bùl,rəsh\ n : tall coarse rush or sedge

bul·wark \-(,)wȯrk; 'bəl(,)wȯrk\ n 1 : wall-like defense 2 : strong support or protection

bum \'bəm\ vb **-mm-** 1 : wander as a tramp 2 : seek by begging ~ n : idle worthless person ~ adj : worthless

bum·ble·bee \'bəmbəl,bē\ n : large hairy bee

bump \'bəmp\ vb : strike or knock forcibly ~ n 1 : sudden blow 2 : small bulge or swelling **—bumpy** adj

¹bum·per \'bəmpər\ adj : unusually large

²bump·er \'bəmpər\ n : shock-absorbing bar at either end of a car

bump·kin \'bəmpkən\ n : awkward country person

bun \'bən\ n : sweet biscuit or roll

bunch \'bənch\ n : group ~ vb : form into a group **—bunchy** adj

bun·dle \'bənd³l\ n 1 : several items bunched together 2 : something wrapped for carrying 3 : large amount ~ vb **-dled; -dling** : gather into a bundle

bun·ga·low \'bəngə,lō\ n : one-story house

bun·gle \'bəngəl\ vb **-gled; -gling** : do badly **—bungle** n **—bun·gler** n

bun·ion \'bənyən\ n : inflamed swelling of the first joint of the big toe

¹bunk \'bəngk\ n : built-in bed that is often one of a tier ~ vb : sleep

²bunk n : nonsense

bun·ker \'bəngkər\ n 1 : storage compartment 2 : protective embankment

bun·kum, bun·combe \'bəngkəm\ n : nonsense

bun·ny \'bənē\ n, pl **-nies** : rabbit

¹bun·ting \'bəntiŋ\ n : small finch

²bunting n : flag material

buoy \'bū̇ē, 'bȯi\ n : floating marker anchored in water ~ vb 1 : keep afloat 2 : raise the spirits of **—buoy·an·cy** \'bȯiənsē, 'būyən-\ n **—buoy·ant** \-ənt, -yənt\ adj

bur, burr \'bər\ n : rough or prickly covering of a fruit **—bur·ry** adj

bur·den \'bərd³n\ n 1 : something carried 2 : something oppressive 3 : cargo ~ vb : load or oppress **—bur·den·some** \-səm\ adj

bur·dock \'bər,däk\ n : tall coarse herb with prickly flower heads

bu·reau \'byùrō\ n 1 : chest of drawers 2 : administrative unit 3 : business office

bu·reau·cra·cy \byù'räkrəsē\ n, pl **-cies** 1 : body of government officials 2 : unwieldy administrative system **—bu·reau·crat** \'byùrə,krat\ n **—bu·reau·crat·ic** \,byùrə'kratik\ adj

bur·geon \'bərjən\ vb : grow

bur·glary \'bərglərē\ n, pl **-glar·ies** : forcible entry into a building to steal **—bur·glar** \-glər\ n **—bur·glar·ize** \'bərglə,rīz\ vb

bur·gle \'bərgəl\ vb **-gled; -gling** : commit burglary on or in

Bur·gun·dy \'bərgəndē\ n, pl **-dies** : kind of table wine

buri·al \'berēəl\ n : act of burying

bur·lap \'bər,lap\ n : coarse fabric usu. of jute or hemp

bur·lesque \(,)bər'lesk\ n 1 : witty or derisive imitation 2 : broadly humorous variety show ~ vb **-lesqued; -lesqu·ing** : mock

bur·ly \'bərlē\ adj **-li·er, -est** : strongly and heavily built

burn \'bərn\ vb **burned** \'bərnd, 'bȯrnt\ or **burnt** \'bȯrnt\; **burn·ing** 1 : be on fire 2 : feel or look as if on fire 3 : alter or become altered by or as if by fire or heat 4 : cause or make by fire ~ n : injury or effect produced by burning **—burn·er** n

bur·nish \'bərnish\ vb : polish

burp \'bərp\ n or vb : belch

bur·ro \'bərō, 'bùr-\ n, pl **-os** : small donkey

bur·row \'bərō\ n : hole in the ground made by an animal ~ vb : make a burrow **—bur·row·er** n

bur·sar \'bərsər\ n : treasurer esp. of a college

bur·si·tis \(,)bər'sītəs\ n : inflammation of a sac (**bur·sa** \'bərsə\) in a joint

burst \'bərst\ vb **burst** or **burst·ed; burst·ing** 1 : fly apart or into pieces 2 : enter or emerge suddenly ~ n : sudden outbreak or effort

bury \'berē\ vb **bur·ied; bury·ing** 1 : deposit in the earth 2 : hide

bus \'bəs\ n, pl **bus·es** or **bus·ses** : large motor-driven passenger vehicle ~ vb **bused** or **bussed; bus·ing** or **bus·sing** : travel or transport by bus

bus·boy n : waiter's helper

bush \'bùsh\ n 1 : shrub 2 : rough uncleared country 3 : a thick tuft or mat **—bushy** adj

bush·el \'bùshəl\ n : 4 pecks

bush·ing \'bùshiŋ\ n : metal lining used as a guide or bearing

busi·ness \'biznəs, -nəz\ n 1 : vocation 2 : commercial or industrial enterprise 3 : personal concerns —**busi·ness·man** \-,man\ n —**busi·ness·wom·an** \-,wümən\ n

¹**bust** \'bəst\ n 1 : sculpture of the head and upper torso 2 : breasts of a woman

²**bust** vb 1 : burst or break 2 : tame ~ n 1 : punch 2 : failure

¹**bus·tle** \'bəsəl\ vb **-tled; -tling** : move or work briskly ~ n : energetic activity

²**bustle** n : pad or frame formerly worn under a woman's skirt

busy \'bizē\ adj **busi·er; -est** 1 : engaged in action 2 : being in use 3 : full of activity ~ vb **bus·ied; busy·ing** : make or keep busy —**busi·ly** adv

busy·body n : meddler

but \(')bət\ conj 1 : if not for the fact 2 : that 3 : without the accompanying condition 4 : rather 5 : yet nevertheless ~ prep : other than

butch·er \'büchər\ n 1 : one who slaughters animals or dresses their flesh 2 : brutal killer —**butcher** vb —**butch·ery** \-(ə)rē\ n

but·ler \'bətlər\ n : chief male household servant

¹**butt** \'bət\ vb : strike with a butt ~ n : blow with the head or horns

²**butt** n 1 : target 2 : victim

³**butt** vb : join edge to edge

⁴**butt** n : large end or bottom

⁵**butt** n : large cask

butte \'byüt\ n : isolated steep hill

but·ter \'bətər\ n : solid edible fat churned from cream ~ vb : spread with butter —**but·tery** adj

but·ter·cup n : yellow-flowered herb

but·ter·fat n : natural fat of milk and of butter

but·ter·fly n : insect with 4 broad wings

but·ter·milk n : liquid remaining after butter is churned

but·ter·nut n : edible nut of a tree related to the walnut or this tree

but·ter·scotch \-,skäch\ n : candy made from sugar, corn syrup, and water

but·tocks \'bətəks\ n pl : rear part of the hips

but·ton \'bət°n\ n 1 : small knob for fastening clothing 2 : buttonlike object ~ vb : fasten with buttons

but·ton·hole n : hole or slit for a button ~ vb : hold in talk

but·tress \'bətrəs\ n 1 : projecting structure to support a wall 2 : support —**buttress** vb

bux·om \'bəksəm\ adj : full-bosomed

buy \'bī\ vb **bought** \'bȯt\; **buy·ing** : purchase ~ n : bargain —**buy·er** n

buzz \'bəz\ vb : make a low humming sound ~ n : act or sound of buzzing

buz·zard \-ərd\ n 1 : heavy slow-flying hawk 2 : American vulture

buzz·er n : signaling device that buzzes

by \(')bī, bə\ prep 1 : near 2 : through 3 : beyond 4 : throughout 5 : no later than ~ \'bī\ adv 1 : near 2 : farther

by·gone \'bī,gȯn\ adj : past —**bygone** n

by·law, bye·law n : organization's rule

by·line n : writer's name on an article

by·pass n : alternate route ~ vb : go around

by·prod·uct n : product in addition to the main product

by·stand·er n : spectator

by·way \'bī,wā\ n : side road

by·word n : proverb

C

c \'sē\ n, pl **c's** or **cs** \'sēz\ : 3d letter of the alphabet

cab \'kab\ n 1 : light closed horse-drawn carriage 2 : taxicab 3 : compartment for a driver —**cab·by, cab·bie** n —**cab·man** \-mən\ n —**cab·stand** n

ca·bal \kə'bal\ n : group of conspirators ~ vb **-ll-** : plot

ca·bana \kə'ban(y)ə\ n : shelter at a beach or pool

cab·a·ret \,kabə'rā\ n : nightclub

cab·bage \'kabij\ n : vegetable with a dense head of leaves

cab·in \-ən\ n 1 : private room on a

ship 2 : small house 3 : airplane compartment

cab·i·net \-(ə)nət\ n 1 : display case or cupboard 2 : advisory council of a head of state —**cab·i·net·mak·er** n —**cab·i·net·mak·ing** n —**cab·i·net·work** n

ca·ble \'kābəl\ n 1 : strong rope, wire, or chain 2 : cablegram 3 : bundle of electrical wires ~ vb **-bled; -bling** : send a cablegram to

ca·ble·gram \-,gram\ n : message sent by a submarine telegraph cable

ca·boose \kə'büs\ n : crew car on a train

ca·cao \kə'kaů, -'kāō\ n, pl cacaos : So. American tree whose seeds (ca·cao beans) yield cocoa and chocolate

cache \'kash\ n 1 : hiding place 2 : something hidden ~ vb cached; cach·ing : place in a cache

cack·le \'kakəl\ vb -led; -ling : make a cry or laugh like the sound of a hen —cackle n —cack·ler n

ca·coph·o·ny \kə'käfənē\ n, pl -nies : harsh noise —ca·coph·o·nous \-nəs\ adj

cac·tus \'kaktəs\ n, pl cac·ti \-,tī\ or -tus·es : drought-resistant flowering plant with scales or prickles

cad \'kad\ n : ungentlemanly person —cad·dish \-ish\ adj —cad·dish·ly adv —cad·dish·ness n

ca·dav·er \kə'davər\ n : dead body —ca·dav·er·ous \-(ə)rəs\ adj

cad·die, cad·dy \'kadē\ n, pl -dies : golfer's helper —caddie, caddy vb

cad·dy \'kadē\ n, pl -dies : small tea chest

ca·dence \'kādəns\ n : measure of a rhythmical flow —ca·denced \-ənst\ adj

ca·det \kə'det\ n : student in a military academy

cadge \'kaj\ vb cadged; cadg·ing : beg —cadg·er n

cad·mi·um \'kadmēəm\ n : grayish metallic chemical element

cad·re \-rē\ n : nucleus of highly trained people

ca·fé \ka'fā, kə-\ n : restaurant

caf·e·te·ria \,kafə'tirēə\ n : self-service restaurant

caf·feine \ka'fēn, 'ka,fēn\ n : stimulating alkaloid in coffee and tea

cage \'kāj\ n : box of wire or bars for confining an animal ~ vb caged; cag·ing : put or keep in a cage

ca·gey \-ē\ adj -gi·er; -est : shrewd —ca·gi·ly adv —ca·gi·ness n

cais·son \'kā,sän, 'kāsən\ n 1 : ammunition carriage 2 : watertight diving chamber

ca·jole \kə'jōl\ vb -joled; -jol·ing : persuade or coax —ca·jol·ery \-(ə)rē\ n

cake \'kāk\ n 1 : food of baked or fried usu. sweet batter ~ vb caked; cak·ing 1 : form into a cake 2 : encrust

cal·a·bash \'kalə,bash\ n : gourd

cal·a·mine \'kalə,mīn\ n : lotion of oxides of zinc and iron

ca·lam·i·ty \kə'lamətē\ n, pl -ties : disaster —ca·lam·i·tous \-ətəs\ adj —ca·lam·i·tous·ly adv —ca·lam·i·tous·ness n

cal·ci·fy \'kalsə,fī\ vb -fied; -fy·ing : harden —cal·ci·fi·ca·tion \,kalsəfə'kāshən\ n

cal·ci·um \'kalsēəm\ n : silver-white soft metallic chemical element

cal·cu·late \'kalkyə,lāt\ vb -lat·ed; -lat·ing 1 : determine by mathematical processes 2 : judge —cal·cu·la·ble \-ləbəl\ adj —cal·cu·la·bly \-blē\ adv —cal·cu·la·tion \,kalkyə'lāshən\ n —cal·cu·la·tor \'kalkyə,lātər\ n

cal·cu·lat·ing adj : shrewd

cal·cu·lus \'kalkyələs\ n, pl -li \-,lī\ : higher mathematics dealing with rates of change

cal·dron \'kóldrən\ n : large kettle

cal·en·dar \'kaləndər\ n : list of days, weeks, and months

¹calf \'kaf, 'kȧf\ n, pl calves \'kavz, 'kȧvz\ : young cow or related mammal —calf·skin n

²calf n, pl calves : back part of the leg below the knee

cal·i·ber, cal·i·bre \'kaləbər\ n 1 : diameter of a bullet or shell or of a gun bore 2 : degree of mental or moral excellence

cal·i·brate \'kalə,brāt\ vb -brat·ed; -brat·ing : determine, correct, or put measuring marks on —cal·i·bra·tion \,kalə'brāshən\ n —cal·i·bra·tor \'kalə,brātər\ n

cal·i·co \'kali,kō\ n, pl -coes or -cos : printed cotton fabric —calico adj

cal·i·pers, cal·li·pers \'kaləpərz\ n : measuring instrument with two adjustable legs

ca·liph, ca·lif \'kāləf, 'kal-\ n : title of head of Islam —ca·liph·ate \-,āt, -ət\ n

cal·is·then·ics \,kaləs'theniks\ n sing or pl : bending, stretching, and jumping exercises —cal·is·then·ic adj

calk \'kók\ var of CAULK

call \'kól\ vb 1 : shout 2 : summon 3 : demand 4 : telephone 5 : make a visit 6 : name —call n —call·er n —call down vb : reprimand —call off vb : cancel

call·ing n : vocation

cal·li·ope \kə'līə,(,)pē, 'kalē,ōp\ n : musical instrument of steam whistles

cal·lous \'kaləs\ adj 1 : thickened and hardened ~ vb : make callous —cal·los·i·ty \ka'läsətē\ n —cal·lous·ly adv —cal·lous·ness n

cal·low \'kalō\ adj : inexperienced or innocent —cal·low·ness n

cal·lus \'kaləs\ n : callous area on skin or bark ~ vb : form a callus

calm \'käm, 'kälm\ n 1 : period or condition of peacefulness or stillness

~ *adj* : still or tranquil ~ *vb* : make calm —**calm·ly** *adv* —**calm·ness** *n*

ca·lor·ic \kə'lòrik\ *adj* : relating to heat or calories

cal·o·rie \'kal(ə)rē\ *n* : unit for measuring heat and energy value of food

ca·lum·ni·ate \kə'ləmnē,āt\ *vb* -**at·ed**; -**at·ing** : slander —**ca·lum·ni·a·tion** \-,ləmnē'āshən\ *n*

cal·um·ny \'kaləmnē\ *n, pl* -**nies** : false and malicious charge —**ca·lum·ni·ous** \kə'ləmnēəs\ *adj*

calve \'kav, 'kàv\ *vb* **calved**; **calv·ing** : give birth to a calf

calves *pl of* CALF

ca·lyp·so \kə'lipsō\ *n, pl* -**sos** : satirical song of the West Indies

ca·lyx \'kāliks, 'kal-\ *n, pl* -**lyx·es** *or* -**ly·ces** \-lə,sēz\ : sepals of a flower

cam \'kam\ *n* : bump (as on a shaft) for pushing another part

ca·ma·ra·de·rie \,käm(ə)'rädərē, ,kam-, -'rad-\ *n* : fellowship

cam·bric \'kāmbrik\ *n* : fine thin linen or cotton fabric

came *past of* COME

cam·el \'kaməl\ *n* : large hoofed mammal of desert areas

ca·mel·lia \kə'mēlyə\ *n* : shrub or tree grown for its showy roselike flowers or the flower itself

cam·eo \'kamē,ō\ *n, pl* -**eos** : gem carved in relief

cam·era \'kam(ə)rə\ *n* **1** : box with a lens for taking pictures **2** : part of a television transmitter to convert an image to signals —**cam·era·man** \-,man, -mən\ *n*

cam·ou·flage \'kamə,fläzh, -,fläj\ *vb* : hide by disguising —**camouflage** *n*

camp \'kamp\ *n* **1** : place to stay temporarily esp. in a tent **2** : group living in a camp ~ *vb* : make or live in a camp —**camp·er** *n* —**camp·ground** *n* —**camp·site** *n*

cam·paign \kam'pān\ *n* : series of military operations or of activities meant to gain a result —**campaign** *vb* —**cam·paign·er** *n*

cam·pa·nile \,kampə'nēlē, -'nē(ə)l\ *n, pl* -**ni·les** *or* -**ni·li** \-'nēlē\ : bell tower

cam·phor \'kam(p)fər\ *n* : gummy volatile fragrant compound from an evergreen tree (**cam·phor tree**)

cam·pus \'kampəs\ *n* : grounds and buildings of a college or school

¹can \kən, (')kan\ *vb, past* **could** \kəd, (')kùd\; *pres sing & pl* **can 1** : be able to **2** : be permitted to by conscience or feeling **3** : have permission or liberty to

²can \'kan\ *n* : metal container ~ *vb*

-**nn-** : preserve by sealing in airtight cans or jars —**can·ner** *n* —**can·nery** \-(ə)rē\ *n*

ca·nal \kə'nal\ *n* **1** : tubular passage in the body **2** : channel filled with water —**ca·nal·boat** *n*

can·a·pé \'kanəpē, -,pā\ *n* : appetizer

ca·nard \kə'närd\ *n* : false report

ca·nary \-'nē(ə)rē\ *n, pl* -**nar·ies** : yellow or greenish finch

can·cel \'kansəl\ *vb* -**celed** *or* -**celled**; -**cel·ing** *or* -**cel·ling 1** : cross out **2** : destroy, neutralize, or match the force or effect of —**cancel** *n* —**can·cel·la·tion** \,kansə'lāshən\ *n*

can·cer \'kansər\ *n* **1** : malignant tumor that tends to spread **2** : slowly destructive evil —**can·cer·ous** \-(ə)rəs\ *adj* —**can·cer·ous·ly** *adv*

can·de·la·bra \,kandə'läbrə, -'lab-\ *n* : candelabrum

can·de·la·brum \-rəm\ *n, pl* -**bra** \-rə\ : ornamental branched candlestick

can·did \'kandəd\ *adj* **1** : frank **2** : unposed —**can·did·ly** *adv* —**can·did·ness** *n*

can·di·date \'kan(d)ə,dāt, -(d)ədət\ *n* : one who seeks an office or membership —**can·di·da·cy** \-(d)ədəsē\ *n*

can·dle \'kand²l\ *n* : tallow or wax molded around a wick and burned to give light —**can·dle·light** *n* —**can·dle·stick** *n*

can·dor \'kandər\ *n* : frankness

can·dy \-dē\ *n, pl* -**dies** : food made from sugar ~ *vb* -**died**; -**dy·ing** : encrust in sugar

cane \'kān\ *n* **1** : slender plant stem **2** : a tall woody grass or reed **3** : stick for walking or beating ~ *vb* **caned**; **can·ing 1** : beat with a cane **2** : weave or make with cane —**can·er** *n*

ca·nine \'kā,nīn\ *adj* **1** : relating to dogs **2** : being the pointed tooth next to the incisors ~ *n* **1** : canine tooth **2** : dog

can·is·ter \'kanəstər\ *n* : small storage box

can·ker \'kaŋkər\ *n* : mouth ulcer —**can·ker·ous** \-k(ə)rəs\ *adj*

can·na·bis \'kanəbəs\ *n* : dried hemp spikes

can·ni·bal \-əbəl\ *n* : human or animal that eats its own kind —**can·ni·bal·ism** \-bə,lizəm\ *n* —**can·ni·bal·is·tic** \,kanəbə'listik\ *adj*

can·ni·bal·ize \'kanəbə,līz\ *vb* -**ized**; -**iz·ing 1** : take usable parts from **2** : practice cannibalism

can·non \-ən\ *n, pl* -**nons** *or* -**non** : artillery piece —**can·non·ball** *n* —**can·non·eer** \,kanə'niər\ *n*

can·non·ade \‚kanə'nād\ *n* : heavy artillery fire ~ *vb* **-ad·ed; -ad·ing** : bombard

can·not \'kan‚ät; kə'nät\ : can not **—cannot but** : be bound to

can·ny \'kanē\ *adj* **-ni·er; -est** : shrewd **—can·ni·ly** *adv* **—can·ni·ness** *n*

ca·noe \kə'nü\ *n* : narrow sharp-ended boat propelled by paddles **—canoe** *vb* **—ca·noe·ist** *n*

¹can·on \'kanən\ *n* **1** : regulation governing a church **2** : authoritative list **3** : an accepted principle

²canon *n* : clergyman in a cathedral **—can·on·ry** \-rē\ *n*

ca·non·i·cal \kə'nänikəl\ *adj* **1** : relating to or conforming to a canon **2** : orthodox **—ca·non·i·cal·ly** *adv*

can·on·ize \'kanə‚nīz\ *vb* **-ized** \-‚nīzd\; **-iz·ing** : recognize as a saint **—can·on·iza·tion** \‚kanənə'zāshən\ *n*

can·o·py \'kanəpē\ *n, pl* **-pies** : overhanging cover **—canopy** *vb*

¹cant \'kant\ *n* **1** : slanting surface **2** : slant ~ *vb* **1** : tip up **2** : lean to one side

²cant *vb* : talk hypocritically ~ *n* **1** : jargon **2** : insincere talk

can't \'kant, 'känt, 'känt\ : can not

can·ta·loupe \'kant³l‚ōp\ *n* : muskmelon with orange flesh

can·tan·ker·ous \kan'taŋk(ə)rəs\ *adj* : hard to deal with **—can·tan·ker·ous·ly** *adv* **—can·tan·ker·ous·ness** *n*

can·ta·ta \kən'tätə\ *n* : choral work

can·teen \kan'tēn\ *n* **1** : place of recreation for servicemen **2** : water container

can·ter \'kantər\ *n* : slow gallop **—canter** *vb*

can·ti·cle \-ikəl\ *n* : liturgical song

can·ti·le·ver \'kant³l‚ēvər, -‚ev-\ *n* : beam or structure supported only at one end

can·to \'kan‚tō\ *n, pl* **-tos** : major division of a long poem

can·tor \'kantər\ *n* : synagogue official who sings liturgical music

can·vas \'kanvəs\ *n* **1** : strong cloth orig. used for making tents and sails **2** : set of sails **3** : oil painting

can·vass \-vəs\ *vb* : solicit votes, orders, or opinions from ~ *n* : act of canvassing **—can·vass·er** *n*

can·yon \-yən\ *n* : deep valley with steep sides

cap \'kap\ *n* **1** : covering for the head **2** : top or cover like a cap ~ *vb* **-pp-** **1** : provide or protect with a cap **2** : climax **—cap·ful** \-‚fül\ *n*

ca·pa·ble \'kāpəbəl\ *adj* : able to do

something **—ca·pa·bil·i·ty** \‚kāpə'bilətē\ *n* **—ca·pa·bly** \'kāpəblē\ *adv*

ca·pa·cious \kə'pāshəs\ *adj* : able to contain much

ca·pac·i·tance \-'pasətəns\ *n* : ability to store electrical energy

ca·pac·i·tor \-ətər\ *n* : device having capacitance

ca·pac·i·ty \-ətē\ *n, pl* **-ties** **1** : ability to contain **2** : volume **3** : ability **4** : role or job ~ *adj* : equaling maximum capacity

¹cape \'kāp\ *n* : point of land jutting out into water

²cape *n* : garment that drapes over the shoulders

¹ca·per \'kāpər\ *n* : flower bud of a shrub pickled for use as a relish

²caper *vb* : leap or prance about ~ *n* **1** : frolicsome leap **2** : illegal escapade

cap·il·lary \'kapə‚lerē\ *adj* **1** : resembling a hair **2** : having a very small bore ~ *n, pl* **-lar·ies** : tiny thin-walled blood vessel

¹cap·i·tal \-ət³l\ *adj* **1** : punishable by death **2** : being in the series A, B, C rather than a, b, c **3** : relating to capital **4** : excellent ~ *n* **1** : capital letter **2** : seat of government **3** : wealth **4** : total face value of a company's stock **5** : capitalists as a group

²capital *n* : top part of a column

cap·i·tal·ism \-‚izəm\ *n* : economic system of private ownership of capital

cap·i·tal·ist \-əst\ *n* **1** : person with capital invested in business **2** : believer in capitalism ~ *adj* **1** : owning capital **2** : practicing, advocating, or marked by capitalism **—cap·i·tal·is·tic** \‚kapət³l'istik\ *adj* **—cap·i·tal·is·ti·cal·ly** \-k(ə)lē\ *adv*

cap·i·tal·ize \-‚līz\ *vb* **-ized; -iz·ing** **1** : write or print with a capital letter **2** : use as capital **3** : supply capital for **4** : turn something to advantage **—cap·i·tal·iza·tion** \‚kapət³lə'zāshən\ *n*

cap·i·tol \'kapət³l\ *n* : building in which a legislature sits

ca·pit·u·late \kə'pichə‚lāt\ *vb* **-lat·ed; -lat·ing** : surrender **—ca·pit·u·la·tion** \-‚pichə'lāshən\ *n*

ca·pon \'kā‚pän, -pən\ *n* : castrated male chicken

ca·price \kə'prēs\ *n* : whim **—ca·pri·cious** \-'prishəs\ *adj*

cap·size \'kap‚sīz, kap'sīz\ *vb* **-sized; -siz·ing** : overturn

cap·stan \'kapstən, -‚stan\ *n* : upright winch

cap·sule \'kapsəl, -sül\ n 1 : enveloping cover (as for medicine) 2 : small pressurized compartment for astronauts ~ vb -suled : put in compact form ~ adj : very brief or compact —**cap·su·lar** \-sələr\ adj —**cap·su·late** \-sə,lāt, -sələt\ adj —**cap·su·lat·ed** \-,lātəd\ adj

cap·tain \'kaptən\ n 1 : commander of a body of troops 2 : officer in charge of a ship 3 : commissioned officer in the navy ranking next below a rear admiral or a commodore 4 : commissioned officer (as in the army) ranking next below a major 5 : leader ~ vb : be captain of —**cap·tain·cy** n —**cap·tain·ship** n

cap·tion \'kapshən\ n 1 : title 2 : explanation with an illustration —**caption** vb

cap·tious \'kapshəs\ adj : tending to find fault —**cap·tious·ly** adv

cap·ti·vate \'kaptə,vāt\ vb -vat·ed; -vat·ing : attract and charm —**cap·ti·va·tion** \,kaptə'vāshən\ n —**cap·ti·va·tor** \'kaptə,vātər\ n

cap·tive \'kaptiv\ adj 1 : made prisoner 2 : confined or under control —**captive** n —**cap·tiv·i·ty** \kap'tivətē\ n

cap·tor \'kaptər\ n : one that captures

cap·ture \-chər\ n : seizure by force or trickery ~ vb -tured; -tur·ing : take captive

car \'kär\ n 1 : vehicle moved on wheels 2 : cage of an elevator

ca·rafe \kə'raf, -'räf\ n : decanter

car·a·mel \'karəməl, 'kärməl\ n 1 : burnt sugar used for flavoring and coloring 2 : firm chewy candy

car·at var of KARAT

²**car·at** \'karət\ n : unit of weight for precious stones

car·a·van \'karə,van\ n : travelers journeying together (as in a line)

car·a·way \'karə,wā\ n : aromatic herb with seeds used in seasoning

car·bine \'kär,bēn, -,bīn\ n : short-barreled rifle

car·bo·hy·drate \,kärbō'hī,drāt, -drət\ n : compound of carbon, hydrogen, and oxygen

car·bon \'kärbən\ n 1 : chemical element occurring in nature as diamond and graphite 2 : piece of carbon paper or a copy made with it

¹**car·bon·ate** \'kärbə,nāt, -nət\ n : salt or ester of a carbon-containing acid

²**car·bon·ate** \-,nāt\ vb -at·ed; -at·ing : impregnate with carbon dioxide —**car·bon·ation** \,kärbə'nāshən\ n

carbon paper n : thin paper coated with a pigment for making copies

car·bun·cle \'kär,bəŋkəl\ n : painful inflammation of the skin and underlying tissue

car·bu·re·tor \'kärb(y)ə,rātər\ n : device for mixing fuel and air

car·cass \-kəs\ n : dead body

car·cin·o·gen \kär'sinəjən\ n : agent causing cancer —**car·ci·no·gen·ic** \,kärs⁰n⁰'jenik\ adj

car·ci·no·ma \,kärs⁰n'ōmə\ n, pl -mas or -ma·ta \-mətə\ : malignant tumor —**car·ci·no·ma·tous** \-mətəs\ adj

¹**card** \'kärd\ vb : comb (fibers) before spinning ~ n : device for combing fibers —**card·er** n

²**card** n 1 : playing card 2 : game played with playing cards 3 : small flat piece of paper

card·board n : stiff material like paper

car·di·ac \'kärdē,ak\ adj : relating to the heart

car·di·gan \-igən\ n : sweater with an opening in the front

¹**car·di·nal** \'kärdnəl, -⁰nəl\ n 1 : official of the Roman Catholic Church 2 : bright red songbird

²**cardinal** adj : of basic importance

cardinal number n : number (as 1, 82, 357) used in counting

car·dio·gram \'kärdēə,gram\ n : line made by a cardiograph

car·dio·graph \-,graf\ n : instrument that graphically registers movements of the heart —**car·dio·graph·ic** \,kärdēə'grafik\ adj —**car·di·og·ra·phy** \-'ägrəfē\ n

car·di·ol·o·gy \,kärdē'äləjē\ n : study of the heart —**car·di·ol·o·gist** \-jəst\ n

car·dio·vas·cu·lar \-ō'vaskyələr\ adj : relating to the heart and blood vessels

care \'kear\ n 1 : anxiety 2 : watchful attention 3 : supervision ~ vb cared; car·ing 1 : feel anxiety or concern 2 : like 3 : provide care —**care·free** adj —**care·ful** \-fəl\ adj —**care·ful·ly** adv —**care·ful·ness** n —**care·less** adj —**care·less·ly** adv —**care·less·ness** n

ca·reen \kə'rēn\ vb 1 : lean over 2 : sway from side to side

ca·reer \kə'riər\ n : vocation ~ vb : go at top speed

ca·ress \kə'res\ n : tender touch ~ vb : touch lovingly or tenderly

car·et \'karət\ n : mark ∧ showing where something is to be inserted

care·tak·er n : one in charge for another or temporarily

car·go \'kärgō\ n, pl -goes or -gos : transported goods

car·i·bou \'karə,bü\ n, pl -bou or -bous : large No. American deer

car·i·ca·ture \'karikə,chůr\ n : distorted representation for humor or ridicule —**caricature** vb —**car·i·ca·tur·ist** \-əst\ n

car·ies \'ka(ə)rēz\ n, pl caries : tooth decay

car·il·lon \'karə,län\ n : set of tuned bells

car·mine \'kärmən, -,mīn\ n : vivid red

car·nage \'kärnij\ n : slaughter

car·nal \'kärn³l\ adj : sensual —**car·nal·i·ty** \kär'nalətē\ n —**car·nal·ly** adv

car·na·tion \kär'nāshən\ n : showy flower

car·ni·val \'kärnəvəl\ n 1 : festival 2 : traveling enterprise offering amusements

car·ni·vore \-,vȯr\ n : flesh-eating animal —**car·niv·o·rous** \kär'niv(ə)rəs\ adj —**car·niv·o·rous·ly** adv —**car·niv·o·rous·ness** n

car·ol \'karəl\ n : song of joy —**carol** vb

car·om \-əm\ n or vb : rebound

ca·rouse \kə'rauz\ vb -**roused**; -**rous·ing** : drink and be boisterous —**carouse** n —**ca·rous·er** n

car·ou·sel, car·rou·sel \'karə'sel, 'karə,-\ n : merry-go-round

¹carp \'kärp\ vb : find fault

²carp n, pl carp or carps : freshwater fish

car·pel \'kärpəl\ n : modified leaf forming part of the ovary of a flower

car·pen·ter \'kärpəntər\ n : one who builds with wood —**carpenter** vb —**car·pen·try** \-trē\ n

car·pet \-pət\ n : fabric floor covering ~ vb : cover with a carpet —**car·pet·ing** \-iŋ\ n

car·port n : open-sided automobile shelter

car·riage \'karij\ n 1 : conveyance 2 : manner of holding oneself 3 : wheeled vehicle

car·ri·on \-ēən\ n : dead and decaying flesh

car·rot \-ət\ n : root vegetable

car·ry \'karē\ vb -**ried**; -**ry·ing** 1 : move while supporting 2 : hold (oneself) in a specified way 3 : support 4 : keep in stock 5 : reach to a distance 6 : win —**car·ri·er** \-ēər\ n —**carry on** vb 1 : conduct 2 : behave excitedly —**carry out** vb : put into effect

cart \'kärt\ n : wheeled vehicle ~ vb : carry in a cart —**cart·age** \-ij\ n

car·tel \kär'tel\ n : business combination designed to limit competition

car·ti·lage \'kärt³lij\ n : elastic skeletal tissue —**car·ti·lag·i·nous** \,kärt³l'ajənəs\ adj

car·tog·ra·phy \kär'tägrəfē\ n : making of maps —**car·tog·ra·pher** \-fər\ n

car·ton \'kärt³n\ n : cardboard box

car·toon \kär'tün\ n 1 : humorous drawing 2 : comic strip —**cartoon** vb —**car·toon·ist** n

car·tridge \'kärtrij\ n 1 : tube containing powder and a bullet or shot for a firearm 2 : container of material for insertion into an apparatus

carve \'kärv\ vb carved; carv·ing 1 : cut with care 2 : cut into pieces or slices —**carv·er** n

cas·cade \kas'kād\ n : small steep waterfall —vb -**cad·ed**; -**cad·ing** : fall in a cascade

¹case \'kās\ n 1 : particular instance 2 : convincing argument 3 : inflectional form esp. of a noun or pronoun 4 : fact 5 : lawsuit 6 : instance of disease —**in case** : if —**in case of** : in the event of

²case n 1 : box 2 : outer covering ~ vb cased; cas·ing 1 : enclose 2 : inspect

case·ment \-mənt\ n : window opening on hinges

cash \'kash\ n 1 : ready money 2 : money paid at the time of purchase ~ vb : give or get cash for

ca·shew \'kashü, kə'shü\ n : tropical American tree or its nut

¹ca·shier \ka'shiər\ vb : dismiss in disgrace

²cash·ier n : person who handles money

cash·mere \'kazh,miər, 'kash-\ n : fine goat's wool or a fabric of this

ca·si·no \kə'sēnō\ n, pl -nos : place for gambling

cask \'kask\ n : barrel-shaped container for liquids

cas·ket \'kaskət\ n : coffin

cas·se·role \'kasə,rōl, 'kaz-\ n : baking dish or the food cooked in this

cas·sette or **ca·sette** \kə'set, ka-\ n : case containing two reels of magnetic tape

cas·sock \'kasək\ n : long clerical garment

cast \'kast\ vb cast; cast·ing 1 : throw 2 : deposit (a ballot) 3 : assign parts in a play 4 : mold ~ n 1 : throw 2 : appearance 3 : rigid surgical dressing 4 : actors in a play

cas·ta·nets \,kastə'nets\ n pl : shells clicked together in the hand

cast·away \'kastə,wä\ n : survivor of a shipwreck

caste \'kast\ n 1 : social class or rank

cast·er *or* **cas·tor** \\'kastər\ *n* : small wheel on furniture

cas·ti·gate \\'kastə,gāt\ *vb* **-gat·ed; -gat·ing** : chastise severely —**cas·ti·ga·tion** \,kastə'gāshən\ *n* —**cas·ti·ga·tor** \\'kastə,gātər\ *n*

cast iron *n* : hard brittle alloy of iron

cas·tle \\'kasəl\ *n* : fortified building

cast-off *adj* : thrown away —**cast-off** *n*

cas·trate \\'kas,trāt\ *vb* **-trat·ed; -trat·ing** : remove the testes of —**cas·tra·tion** \ka'strāshən\ *n*

ca·su·al \\'kazh(əw)əl\ *adj* **1** : happening by chance **2** : showing little concern **3** : informal —**ca·su·al·ly** \-ē\ *adv* —**ca·su·al·ness** *n*

ca·su·al·ty \-tē\ *n, pl* **-ties 1** : serious or fatal accident **2** : one injured, lost, or destroyed

ca·su·ist·ry \\'kazhəwəstrē\ *n, pl* **-ries** : adroit and esp. false reasoning —**ca·su·ist** \-wəst\ *n*

cat \\'kat\ *n* **1** : small domestic mammal **2** : related animal (as a lion) —**cat·like** *adj*

cat·a·clysm \\'katə,klizəm\ *n* : violent change —**cat·a·clys·mic** \,katə'klizmik\ *adj*

cat·a·comb \\'katə,kōm\ *n* : underground burial place

cat·a·log, cat·a·logue \\'katᵊl,óg\ *n* **1** : list **2** : book containing a description of items ~ *vb* **-loged** *or* **-logued; -log·ing** *or* **-logu·ing 1** : make a catalog of **2** : enter in a catalog —**cat·a·log·er, cat·a·logu·er** *n*

cat·al·pa \kə'talpə\ *n* : tree with broad leaves and long pods

cat·al·y·sis \-əsəs\ *n, pl* **-y·ses** \-,sēz\ : increase in the rate of chemical reaction caused by a substance (**cat·a·lyst** \\'katᵊləst\) that is itself unchanged —**cat·a·lyt·ic** \,katᵊl'itik\ *adj*

cat·a·ma·ran \,katəmə'ran\ *n* : boat with twin hulls

cat·a·mount \\'katə,maúnt\ *n* : cougar

cat·a·pult \-,pəlt, -,púlt\ *n* : device for hurling or launching —**catapult** *vb*

cat·a·ract \-,rakt\ *n* **1** : large waterfall **2** : cloudiness of the lens of the eye

ca·tarrh \kə'tär\ *n* : inflammation of the nose and throat

ca·tas·tro·phe \kə'tastrə(,)fē\ *n* **1** : great disaster or misfortune **2** : utter failure —**cat·a·stroph·ic** \,katə'sträfik\ *adj* —**cat·a·stroph·i·cal·ly** \-ik(ə)lē\ *adv*

cat·bird *n* : American songbird

cat·call *n* : noise of disapproval

catch \\'kach, 'kech\ *vb* **caught** \\'kót\; **catch·ing 1** : capture esp. after pursuit **2** : trap **3** : detect esp. by surprise **4** : grasp **5** : get entangled **6** : become affected with or by **7** : seize and hold firmly ~ *n* **1** : act of catching **2** : something caught **3** : something that fastens **4** : hidden difficulty —**catch·er** *n*

catch·ing \-iŋ\ *adj* : infectious

catch·up \\'kechəp, 'kach-; 'katsəp\ *var of* CATSUP

catch·word *n* : slogan

catchy \-ē\ *adj* **catch·i·er; -est** : likely to catch interest

cat·e·chism \\'katə,kizəm\ *n* : set of questions and answers esp. to teach religious doctrine —**cat·e·chist** \-,kist\ *n* —**cat·e·chize** \-,kīz\ *vb*

cat·e·gor·i·cal \,katə'górikəl\ *adj* : absolute —**cat·e·gor·i·cal·ly** \-k(ə)lē\ *adv*

cat·e·go·ry \\'katə,górē\ *n, pl* **-ries** : group or class —**cat·e·go·ri·za·tion** \,katigərə'zāshən\ *n* —**cat·e·go·rize** \\'katigə,rīz\ *vb*

ca·ter \\'kātər\ *vb* **1** : provide food for **2** : supply what is wanted —**ca·ter·er** *n*

cat·er-cor·ner \,katē'kórnər, ,katə-, ,kitē\, **cat·er-cor·nered** *adv or adj* : in a diagonal position

cat·er·pil·lar \\'katə(r),pilər\ *n* : butterfly or moth larva

cat·er·waul \\'katər,wól\ *vb* : make the harsh cry of a cat —**caterwaul** *n*

cat·fish *n* : big-headed fish with feelers about the mouth

cat·gut *n* : tough cord made usu. from sheep intestines

ca·thar·sis \kə'thärsəs\ *n, pl* **ca·thar·ses** \-,sēz\ : a purging —**ca·thar·tic** \kə'thärtik\ *adj or n*

ca·the·dral \-'thēdrəl\ *n* : principal church of a diocese

cath·e·ter \\'kathətər\ *n* : tube for insertion into a body cavity

cath·ode \\'ka,thōd\ *n* **1** : negative electrode **2** : positive battery terminal —**ca·thod·ic** \ka'thädik\ *adj*

cath·o·lic \\'kath(ə)lik\ *adj* **1** : universal **2** *cap* : relating to Roman Catholics

Cath·o·lic *n* : member of the Roman Catholic Church —**Ca·thol·i·cism** \kə'thälə,sizəm\ *n*

cat·kin \\'katkən\ *n* : long dense flower cluster

cat·nap *n* : short light nap —**catnap** *vb*

cat·nip \-,nip\ *n* : aromatic mint relished by cats

cat's-paw *n, pl* **cat's-paws** : person used as a tool

cat·sup \\'kechəp, 'kach-; 'katsəp\ *n* : spicy tomato sauce

cat·tail n : marsh herb with furry brown spikes

cat·tle \'kat³l\ n pl : domestic bovines —**cat·tle·man** \-mən, -ˌman\ n

cat·ty \'katē\ adj -ti·er, -est : mean or spiteful —**cat·ti·ly** adv —**cat·ti·ness** n

cat·walk n : high narrow walk

Cau·ca·sian \kȯ'kāzhən, -'kazh-\ adj : relating to the white race —**Caucasian** n —**Cau·ca·soid** \'kȯkəˌsȯid\ adj or n

cau·cus \'kȯkəs\ n : political meeting —**caucus** vb

caught past of CATCH

cauldron var of CALDRON

cau·li·flow·er \'kȯliˌflaů(ə)r, 'käl-\ n : vegetable having a compact head of undeveloped flowers

caulk \'kȯk\ vb : make seams watertight —**caulk·er** n —**caulk·ing** n

caus·al \'kȯzəl\ adj : relating to or being a cause —**cau·sal·i·ty** \kȯ'zalətē\ n —**caus·al·ly** \'kȯzəlē\ adv

cause \'kȯz\ n 1 : something that brings about a result 2 : reason 3 : lawsuit 4 : principle or movement to support ~ vb caused; caus·ing : be the cause of —**cau·sa·tion** \kȯ'zāshən\ n —**caus·ative** \'kȯzə-tiv\ adj —**cause·less** adj —**caus·er** n

cause·way n : raised road esp. over water

caus·tic \'kȯstik\ adj 1 : corrosive 2 : sharp or biting —**caustic** n

cau·ter·ize \'kȯtəˌrīz\ vb -ized; -iz·ing : burn to prevent infection or bleeding —**cau·ter·i·za·tion** \ˌkȯtərə'zāshən\ n

cau·tion \'kȯshən\ n 1 : warning 2 : care or prudence ~ vb : warn —**cau·tion·ary** \-shəˌnerē\ adj

cau·tious \'kȯshəs\ adj : taking caution —**cau·tious·ly** adv —**cau·tious·ness** n

cav·al·cade \ˌkavəl'kād\ n 1 : procession on horseback 2 : series

cav·a·lier \ˌ-ə'liər\ n : mounted soldier ~ adj : disdainful or arrogant —**cav·a·lier·ly** adv —**cav·a·lier·ness** n

cav·al·ry \'kavəlrē\ n, pl -ries : troops on horseback or in vehicles —**cav·al·ry·man** \-mən, -ˌman\ n

cave \'kāv\ n : natural underground chamber —**cave in** vb : collapse

cav·ern \'kavərn\ n : large cave —**cav·ern·ous** adj —**cav·ern·ous·ly** adv

cav·i·ar, cav·i·are \'kavēˌär, 'käv-\ n : salted fish roe

cav·il \'kavəl\ vb -iled or -illed; -il·ing or -il·ling : find fault without good reason —**cavil** n —**cav·il·er, cav·il·ler** n

cav·i·ty \-ətē\ n, pl -ties : unfilled place within a mass

ca·vort \kə'vȯrt\ vb : prance or caper

caw \'kȯ\ vb : utter the harsh call of the crow —**caw** n

cay·enne pepper \ˌkīˌen-, ˌkā-\ n : ground dried fruits of a hot pepper

cay·man var of CAIMAN

cease \'sēs\ vb ceased; ceas·ing : stop

cease·less \-ləs\ adj : continuous

ce·dar \'sēdər\ n : cone-bearing tree with fragrant durable wood

cede \'sēd\ vb ced·ed; ced·ing : surrender —**ced·er** n

ceil·ing \'sēliŋ\ n 1 : overhead surface of a room 2 : upper limit

cel·e·brate \'seləˌbrāt\ vb -brat·ed; -brat·ing 1 : perform with appropriate rites 2 : honor with ceremonies 3 : extol —**cel·e·brant** \-brənt\ n —**cel·e·bra·tion** \ˌselə'brāshən\ n —**cel·e·bra·tor** \'seləˌbrātər\ n

cel·e·brat·ed \-əd\ adj : renowned

ce·leb·ri·ty \sə'lebrətē\ n, pl -ties 1 : renown 2 : well-known person

ce·ler·i·ty \sə'lerətē\ n : speed

cel·ery \'sel(ə)rē\ n, pl -er·ies : herb grown for crisp edible stalks

ce·les·ta \sə'lestə\ n : keyboard musical instrument

ce·les·tial \sə'leschəl\ adj 1 : relating to the sky 2 : heavenly

cel·i·ba·cy \'seləbəsē\ n 1 : state of being unmarried 2 : abstention from sexual intercourse —**cel·i·bate** \'seləbət\ n or adj

cell \'sel\ n 1 : small room 2 : tiny mass of protoplasm that forms the fundamental unit of living matter 3 : container holding an electrolyte for generating electricity —**celled** adj

cel·lar \'selər\ n : room or area below ground

cel·lo \'chelō\ n, pl -los : bass member of the violin family —**cel·list** \-əst\ n

cel·lo·phane \'seləˌfān\ n : thin transparent cellulose wrapping

cel·lu·lar \-yələr\ adj : relating to or consisting of cells

cel·lu·lose \-yəˌlōs\ n : complex plant carbohydrate

Cel·sius \'selsēəs\ adj : relating to a thermometer scale on which the freezing point of water is 0° and the boiling point is 100°

ce·ment \si'ment\ n 1 : powdery mixture of clay and limestone that hardens when wetted 2 : binding agent ~ vb : unite or cover with cement —**ce·men·ta·tion** \ˌsēˌmen'tāshən\ n —**ce·ment·er** n

cem·e·tery \'semə,terē\ n, pl **-ter·ies** : burial ground

cen·ser \'sensər\ n : vessel for burning incense

cen·sor \'-sər\ n : one with power to suppress anything objectionable (as in printed matter) ~ vb : be a censor of —**cen·so·ri·al** \sen'sōrēəl\ adj —**cen·sor·ship** \-,ship\ n

cen·so·ri·ous \sen'sōrēəs\ adj : critical —**cen·so·ri·ous·ly** adv —**cen·so·ri·ous·ness** n

cen·sure \'senchər\ n : official reprimand ~ vb **-sured; -sur·ing** : find blameworthy

cen·sus \'-səs\ n : periodic population count

cent \'sent\ n : monetary unit equal to 1/100 of a basic unit of value

cen·taur \'sen,tȯr\ n : mythological creature that is half man and half horse

cen·ten·ni·al \sen'tenēəl\ n : 100th anniversary —**centennial** adj

cen·ter \'sentər\ n 1 : middle point 2 : point of origin or greatest concentration 3 : region of concentrated population 4 : player near the middle of his team ~ vb 1 : place, fix, or concentrate at or around a center 2 : have a center —**cen·tered** adj —**cen·ter·piece** n

cen·ti·grade \'sentə,grād, 'sänt-\ adj : Celsius

cen·ti·me·ter \'sentə,mētər, 'sänt-\ n : 1/100 meter

cen·ti·pede \'sentə,pēd\ n : long flat many-legged arthropod

cen·tral \'sentrəl\ adj 1 : constituting or being near a center 2 : essential or principal —**cen·tral·ly** adv

cen·tral·ize \-trə,līz\ vb **-ized; -iz·ing** : bring to a central point or under central control —**cen·tral·iza·tion** \,sentrələ'zāshən\ n —**cen·tral·iz·er** n

cen·tre chiefly Brit var of CENTER

cen·trif·u·gal \sen'trifyəgəl, -'trifigəl\ adj : acting in a direction away from a center or axis —**cen·trif·u·gal·ly** adv

cen·tri·fuge \'sentrə,fyüj\ n : machine that separates substances by spinning

cen·trip·e·tal \sen'tripət°l\ adj : acting in a direction toward a center or axis —**cen·trip·e·tal·ly** adv

cen·tu·ri·on \sen't(y)ûrēən\ n : Roman military officer

cen·tu·ry \'sench(ə)rē\ n, pl **-ries** : 100 years

ce·ram·ic \sə'ramik\ n 1 pl : art or process of shaping and hardening articles from clay 2 : product of ceramics —**ceramic** adj

ce·re·al \'sirēəl\ adj : made of or relating to grain or to the plants that produce it ~ n 1 : grass yielding edible grain 2 : cereal grain used as food

cer·e·bel·lum \,serə'beləm\ n, pl **-bel·lums** or **-bel·la** \-'belə\ : part of the brain controlling muscular coordination —**cer·e·bel·lar** \-ər\ adj

cerebral palsy n : disorder caused by brain damage and marked esp. by defective muscle control

cer·e·brate \'serə,brāt\ vb **-brat·ed; -brat·ing** : think —**cer·e·bra·tion** \,serə'brāshən\ n

ce·re·brum \sə'rēbrəm, 'serə-\ n, pl **-brums** or **-bra** \-brə\ : part of the brain that contains the higher nervous centers —**ce·re·bral** \'serə-,brəl\ adj —**ce·re·bral·ly** adv

cer·e·mo·ny \'serə,mōnē\ n, pl **-nies** 1 : formal act prescribed by law, ritual, or convention 2 : prescribed procedures —**cer·e·mo·ni·al** \,serə'mōnēəl\ adj or n —**cer·e·mo·ni·ous** \-nēəs\ adj

ce·rise \sə'rēs\ n : moderate red

cer·tain \'sərt°n\ adj 1 : settled 2 : true 3 : specific but not named 4 : bound 5 : assured ~ pron : certain ones —**cer·tain·ly** adv —**cer·tain·ty** \-tē\ n

cer·tif·i·cate \sər'tifikət\ n : document establishing truth or fulfillment

cer·ti·fy \'sərtə,fī\ vb **-fied; -fy·ing** 1 : verify 2 : endorse —**cer·ti·fi·able** \-,fīəbəl\ adj —**cer·ti·fi·ably** \-blē\ adv —**cer·ti·fi·ca·tion** \,sərtəfə'kāshən\ n —**cer·ti·fi·er** n

cer·ti·tude \'sərtə,t(y)üd\ n : state of being certain

cer·vix \'sərviks\ n, pl **-vi·ces** \-və,sēz\ or **-vix·es** 1 : neck 2 : narrow end of the uterus —**cer·vi·cal** \-vikəl\ adj

ce·sar·e·an \si'zarēən\ n : surgical operation to deliver a baby —**cesarean** adj

ce·si·um \'sēzēəm\ n : silver-white soft ductile chemical element

ces·sa·tion \se'sāshən\ n : a halting

ces·sion \'seshən\ n : a yielding

cess·pool \'ses,pül\ n : underground sewage pit

Cha·blis \'shab,lē; sha'blē\ n, pl **Cha·blis** \-,lēz, -'blēz\ : dry white wine

chafe \'chāf\ vb **chafed; chaf·ing** 1 : fret 2 : make sore by rubbing

chaff \'chaf\ n 1 : debris separated from grain 2 : something worthless 3 : banter ~ vb : tease —**chaffy** adj

chaf·ing dish \'chāfiŋ-\ n : utensil for cooking at the table

cha·grin \shə'grin\ n : embarrassment or humiliation ~ vb : cause to feel chagrin

chain \'chān\ n 1 : flexible series of connected links 2 pl : fetters 3 : linked series ~ vb : bind or connect with a chain

chair \'cheər\ n 1 : seat with a back 2 : position of authority or dignity 3 : chairman ~ vb : act as chairman of

chair·man \-mən\ n 1 : presiding officer —**chair·man·ship** n —**chair·wom·an** n

chaise longue \'shāz'lòŋ\ n, pl **chaise longues** \-'lòŋ(z)\ : long couchlike chair

cha·let \sha'lā\ n : Swiss mountain cottage with overhanging roof

chal·ice \'chaləs\ n : eucharistic cup

chalk \'chòk\ n 1 : soft limestone 2 : chalky material used as a crayon ~ vb : mark with chalk —**chalk up** vb 1 : credit 2 : achieve —**chalky** adj

chalk·board n : blackboard

chal·lenge \'chalənj\ vb -**lenged; -leng·ing** 1 : dispute 2 : invite or dare to act or compete —**challenge** n —**chal·leng·er** n

cham·ber \'chāmbər\ n 1 : room 2 : enclosed space 3 : legislative meeting place or body 4 pl : judge's consultation room —**cham·bered** adj

cham·ber·maid n : bedroom maid

chamber music n : music by a small group for a small audience

cha·me·leon \kə'mēlyən\ n : small lizard whose skin changes color

cham·ois \'shamē\ n, pl **cham·ois** \-ē(z)\ 1 : goatlike antelope 2 : soft leather

¹champ \'champ, 'chämp\ vb : chew noisily

²champ \'champ\ n : champion

cham·pagne \sham'pān\ n : sparkling white wine

cham·pi·on \'champēən\ n 1 : advocate or defender 2 : winning contestant ~ vb : protect or fight for

cham·pi·on·ship \-,ship\ n 1 : title of a champion 2 : contest to pick a champion

chance \'chans\ n 1 : unpredictable element of existence 2 : opportunity 3 : probability 4 : risk 5 : raffle ticket ~ vb **chanced; chanc·ing** 1 : happen 2 : encounter unexpectedly 3 : risk —**chance** adj

chan·cel \'chansəl\ n : part of a church around the altar

can·cel·lery, chan·cel·lory \'chans(ə)lərē\ n, pl -**ler·ies** or -**lor-**

ies 1 : position of a chancellor 2 : chancellor's office

chan·cel·lor \-s(ə)lər\ n 1 : chief or high state official 2 : head of a university —**chan·cel·lor·ship** n

chan·cre \'shaŋkər\ n : skin ulcer esp. from syphilis

chan·cy \'chansē\ adj **chanc·i·er; -est** : risky

chan·de·lier \,shandə'liər\ n : hanging lighting fixture

chan·dler \'chandlər\ n : provisions dealer —**chan·dlery** n

change \'chānj\ vb **changed; chang·ing** 1 : make or become different 2 : exchange 3 : give or receive change for ~ n 1 : a changing 2 : excess from a payment 3 : money in smaller denominations 4 : coins —**change·able** adj —**change·less** adj —**chang·er** n

chan·nel \'chan²l\ n 1 : deeper part of a waterway 2 : means of passage or communication 3 : strait 4 : broadcast frequency ~ vb -**neled** or -**nelled; -nel·ing** or -**nel·ling** : make or direct through a channel

chant \'chant\ vb : sing or speak in one tone —**chant** n —**chant·er** n

chan·tey, chan·ty \'shantē, 'chant-\ n, pl -**teys** or -**ties** : sailors' work song

Cha·nu·kah \'känəkə, 'hän-\ var of HANUKKAH

cha·os \'kā,äs\ n : complete disorder —**cha·ot·ic** \kā'ätik\ adj —**cha·ot·i·cal·ly** \-ik(ə)lē\ adv

¹chap \'chap\ n : fellow

²chap vb -**pp-** : dry and crack open usu. from wind and cold

chap·el \'chapəl\ n : private or small place of worship

chap·er·on, chap·er·one \'shapə,rōn\ n : older person who accompanies young people at a social gathering ~ vb -**oned; -on·ing** : act as chaperon at or for —**chap·er·on·age** \-ij\ n

chap·lain \'chaplən\ n : clergyman in a military unit or a prison —**chap·lain·cy** \-sē\ n

chap·ter \'chaptər\ n 1 : main book division 2 : branch of a society

char \'chär\ vb -**rr-** 1 : burn to charcoal 2 : scorch

char·ac·ter \'kariktər\ n 1 : letter or graphic mark 2 : trait or distinctive combination of traits 3 : peculiar person 4 : fictional person —**char·ac·ter·i·za·tion** \,karikt(ə)rə'zāshən\ n —**char·ac·ter·ize** \'kariktə,rīz\ vb

char·ac·ter·is·tic \,kariktə'ristik\ adj : typical ~ n : distinguishing quality —**char·ac·ter·is·ti·cal·ly** \-tik(ə)lē\ adv

cha·rades \shə'rādz\ *n sing or pl* : pantomime guessing game

char·coal \'chär,kōl\ *n* : porous carbon prepared by partial combustion

chard \'chärd\ *n* : leafy vegetable

charge \'chärj\ *vb* **charged; charg·ing** 1 : give an electric charge to 2 : impose a task or responsibility on 3 : command 4 : accuse 5 : rush forward in assault 6 : assume a debt for 7 : fix as a price ~ *n* 1 : excess or deficiency of electrons in a body 2 : tax 3 : responsibility 4 : accusation 5 : cost 6 : attack —**charge·able** *adj*

charg·er \-ər\ *n* : horse ridden in battle

char·i·ot \'chareēət\ *n* : ancient 2-wheeled vehicle —**char·i·o·teer** \,chareēə'tiər\ *n*

cha·ris·ma \kə'rizmə\ *n, pl* **-ris·ma·ta** \kə'rizmətə\ : special ability to lead —**char·is·mat·ic** \,karzí'matik\ *adj*

char·i·ty \'charətē\ *n, pl* **-ties** 1 : love for mankind 2 : generosity or leniency 3 : alms 4 : institution for relief of the needy —**char·i·ta·ble** \-əbəl\ *adj* —**char·i·ta·bly** \-blē\ *adv*

char·la·tan \'shärlətən\ *n* : impostor

charm \'chärm\ *n* 1 : something with magic power 2 : appealing trait 3 : small ornament ~ *vb* : fascinate —**charm·er** *n* —**charm·ing** *adj* —**charm·ing·ly** *adv*

char·nel \'chärnəl\ *n* : place for dead bodies —**charnel** *adj*

chart \'chärt\ *n* 1 : map 2 : diagram ~ *vb* 1 : make a chart of 2 : plan

char·ter \-ər\ *n* 1 : document granting rights 2 : constitution ~ *vb* 1 : establish by charter 2 : rent —**char·ter·er** *n*

char·treuse \shär'trüz, -'trüs\ *n* : brilliant yellow green

char·wom·an *n* : cleaning woman

chary \'cha(ə)rē\ *adj* **chari·er; -est** : cautious —**char·i·ly** \'charəlē\ *adv*

¹chase \'chās\ *vb* **chased; chas·ing** 1 : follow trying to catch 2 : drive away —**chase** *n* —**chas·er** *n*

²chase *vb* **chased; chas·ing** : decorate (metal) by embossing or engraving

chasm \'kazəm\ *n* : gorge

chas·sis \'shasē, 'chas-\ *n, pl* **chas·sis** \-ēz\ : framework

chaste \'chāst\ *adj* **chast·er; chast·est** 1 : abstaining from all or unlawful sexual relations 2 : modest or decent 3 : severely simple —**chaste·ly** *adv* —**chaste·ness** *n* —**chas·ti·ty** \'chastətē\ *n*

chas·ten \'chāsᵊn\ *vb* : discipline

chas·tise \chas'tīz\ *vb* **-tised; -tis·ing** : punish —**chas·tise·ment** \-mənt, 'chastəz-\ *n*

chat \'chat\ *n* : informal talk —**chat** *vb* —**chat·ty** \-ē\ *adj*

châ·teau \sha'tō\ *n, pl* **-teaus** or **-teaux** \-'tō(z)\ 1 : large country house 2 : French vineyard estate

chat·tel \'chatᵊl\ *n* : item of tangible property other than real estate

chat·ter \'chatər\ *vb* 1 : utter rapidly succeeding sounds 2 : talk fast or too much —**chatter** *n* —**chat·ter·er** *n*

chat·ter·box *n* : incessant talker

chauf·feur \'shōfər, shō'fər\ *n* : hired car driver ~ *vb* : work as a chauffeur for

chau·vin·ism \'shōvə,nizəm\ *n* : excessive patriotism —**chau·vin·ist** \-vənəst\ *n* —**chau·vin·is·tic** \,shōvə'nistik\ *adj*

cheap \'chēp\ *adj* 1 : inexpensive 2 : shoddy —**cheap** *adv* —**cheap·en** \'chēpən\ *vb* —**cheap·ly** *adv* —**cheap·ness** *n*

cheap·skate *n* : stingy person

cheat \'chēt\ *n* 1 : act of deceiving 2 : one that cheats ~ *vb* 1 : deprive through fraud or deceit 2 : violate rules dishonestly —**cheat·er** *n*

check \'chek\ *n* 1 : sudden stoppage 2 : restraint 3 : test or standard for testing 4 : written order to a bank to pay money 5 : ticket showing ownership 6 : slip showing an amount due 7 : pattern in squares or fabric in such a pattern 8 : mark placed beside an item noted ~ *vb* 1 : slow down or stop 2 : restrain 3 : compare or correspond with a source or original 4 : inspect or test for condition 5 : mark with a check 6 : leave or accept for safekeeping or shipment 7 : checker —**check in** *vb* : report one's arrival —**check out** *vb* : settle one's account and leave

¹check·er \-ər\ *n* : piece in checkers ~ *vb* : mark with different colors or into squares

²checker *n* : one that checks

check·er·board \-ə(r),bōrd\ *n* : board of 64 squares of alternate colors

check·ers \-ərz\ *n* : game for 2 played on a checkerboard

check·mate *n* : thwart completely —**checkmate** *n*

check·point *n* : place where traffic is checked

check·up *n* : physical examination

ched·dar \'chedər\ *n* : hard smooth cheese

cheek \'chēk\ *n* **1** : fleshy side part of the face **2** : impudence —**cheeked** \'chēkt\ *adj* —**cheeky** *adj*

cheep \'chēp\ *vb* : utter faint shrill sound —**cheep** *n*

cheer \'chiər\ *n* **1** : good spirits **2** : food and drink for a feast **3** : shout of applause or encouragement ~ *vb* **1** : give hope or courage to **2** : make or become glad **3** : urge on or applaud with shouts —**cheer·er** *n* —**cheer·ful** \-fəl\ *adj* —**cheer·ful·ly** *adv* —**cheer·ful·ness** *n* —**cheer·lead·er** *n* —**cheer·less** *adj* —**cheer·less·ly** *adv* —**cheer·less·ness** *n*

cheery \'chi(ə)rē\ *adj* **cheer·i·er; -est** : cheerful —**cheer·i·ly** *adv* —**cheer·i·ness** *n*

cheese \'chēz\ *n* : curd of milk usu. pressed and cured —**cheesy** *adj*

cheese·cloth *n* : light-weight coarse cotton gauze

chee·tah \'chētə\ *n* : spotted swift-moving African cat

chef \'shef\ *n* : chief cook

chem·i·cal \'kemikəl\ *adj* **1** : relating to chemistry **2** : working or produced by chemicals ~ *n* : substance obtained by chemistry —**chem·i·cal·ly** \-k(ə)lē\ *adv*

che·mise \shə'mēz\ *n* **1** : woman's one-piece undergarment **2** : loose dress

chem·ist \'keməst\ *n* **1** : one trained in chemistry **2** *Brit* : pharmacist

chem·is·try \-əstrē\ *n, pl* **-tries** : science that deals with the composition and properties of substances

che·mo·ther·a·py \ˌkēmō-, ˌkemō\ *n* : use of chemicals in treatment of disease —**che·mo·ther·a·peu·tic,** **che·mo·ther·a·peu·ti·cal** *adj*

che·nille \shə'nēl\ *n* : yarn with protruding pile or fabric of such yarn

cheque \'chek\ *chiefly Brit var of* CHECK 5

cher·ish \'cherish\ *vb* : hold dear

cher·ry \'cherē\ *n, pl* **-ries** : small fleshy fruit of a tree related to the roses or the tree or its wood

cher·ub \'chərb\ *n, pl* **-ubs** *or* **-u·bim** \-(y)ə,bim\ **1** : angel **2** : chubby child —**che·ru·bic** \chə'rübik\ *adj*

chess \'ches\ *n* : game for 2 played on a checkerboard —**chess·board** *n* —**chess·man** *n*

chest \'chest\ *n* **1** : boxlike container **2** : part of the body enclosed by the ribs and breastbone —**chest·ed** *adj*

chest·nut \'ches(ˌ)nət\ *n* : nut of a tree related to the beech or the tree

chev·i·ot \'shevēət\ *n* **1** : heavy rough wool fabric **2** : soft-finished cotton fabric

chev·ron \'shevrən\ *n* : V-shaped insignia

chew \'chü\ *vb* : crush or grind with the teeth ~ *n* : something to chew —**chew·able** *adj* —**chew·er** *n* —**chewy** *adj*

chic \'shēk\ *n* : smart elegance of dress or manner ~ *adj* **1** : stylish **2** : currently fashionable

chi·ca·nery \shik'ān(ə)rē\ *n, pl* **-ner·ies** : trickery

chick \'chik\ *n* : young chicken or bird

chick·a·dee \-ə(ˌ)dē\ *n* : small grayish American bird

chick·en \-ən\ *n* **1** : common domestic fowl or its flesh used as food **2** : coward

chicken pox *n* : acute contagious virus disease esp. of children

chi·cle \'chikəl\ *n* : gum from a tropical evergreen tree

chic·o·ry \'chik(ə)rē\ *n, pl* **-ries** : herb used in salad or its dried ground root used to adulterate coffee

chide \'chīd\ *vb* **chid** \'chid\ *or* **chid·ed** \'chīdəd\; **chid** *or* **chid·den** \'chid°n\ *or* **chided; chid·ing** \'chīdiŋ\ : scold

chief \'chēf\ *n* : leader ~ *adj* **1** : highest in rank **2** : most important —**chief·dom** *n* —**chief·ly** *adv*

chief·tain \'chēftən\ *n* : chief —**chief·tain·cy** \-sē\ *n*

chif·fon \shif'än, 'shif-\ *n* : sheer fabric

chig·ger \'chigər\ *n* : bloodsucking mite

chi·gnon \'shēn,yän\ *n* : knot of hair

chil·blain \'chil,blān\ *n* : sore or inflamed swelling caused by cold

child \'chīld\ *n, pl* **chil·dren** \'children\ **1** : unborn or recently born person **2** : son or daughter —**child-bear·ing** *n or adj* —**child-birth** *n* —**child·hood** *n* —**child·ish** *adj* —**child·ish·ly** *adv* —**child·ish·ness** *n* —**child·less** *adj* —**child·less·ness** *n* —**child-like** *adj*

chili, chile, chil·li \'chilē\ *n, pl* **chil·ies** *or* **chil·es** *or* **chil·ies 1** : hot pepper **2** : spicy stew of ground beef, chilies, and beans

chill \'chil\ *vb* : make or become cold or chilly ~ *adj* : moderately cold ~ *n* **1** : feeling of coldness with shivering **2** : moderate coldness

chilly \'chilē\ *adj* **chill·i·er; -est** : noticeably cold —**chill·i·ness** *n*

chime \'chīm\ *n* : set of tuned bells or their sound —*vb* : make bell-like sounds —**chime in** *vb* : break into or join in a conversation

chi·me·ra \kī'mirə, kə-\ or **chi·mae·ra** \ *n* : imaginary monster —**chi·me·ri·cal** \-'merikəl\, **chi·me·ric** \-ik\ *adj*

chim·ney \'chimnē\ *n, pl* **-neys 1** : passage for smoke **2** : glass tube around a lamp flame

chimp \'chimp, 'shimp\ *n* : chimpanzee

chim·pan·zee \,chim,pan'zē, ,shim-; chim'panzē, shim-\ *n* : manlike ape smaller than a gorilla

chin \'chin\ *n* : part of the face below the mouth —**chin·less** *adj*

chi·na \'chīnə\ *n* **1** : porcelain ware **2** : domestic pottery

chin·chil·la \chin'chilə\ *n* : small So. American rodent with soft pearl-gray fur

chink \'chiŋk\ *n* : small crack —*vb* : fill chinks of

chintz \'chints\ *n* : printed cotton cloth

chip \'chip\ *n* **1** : small thin flat piece cut or broken off **2** : thin crisp morsel of food **3** : counter used in games **4** : flaw where a chip came off —*vb* **-pp-** : cut or break chips from —**chip in** *vb* : contribute

chip·munk \-,məŋk\ *n* : small striped ground-dwelling squirrel

chip·per \-ər\ *adj* : lively and cheerful

chi·rop·o·dy \kə'räpədē, shə-\ *n* : podiatry —**chi·rop·o·dist** \-ədəst\ *n*

chirp \'chərp\ *n* : short sharp sound like that of a bird or cricket —**chirp** *vb*

chis·el \'chizəl\ *n* : sharp-edged metal tool —*vb* **-eled** *or* **-elled; -el·ing** *or* **-el·ling 1** : work with a chisel **2** : cheat —**chis·el·er** \-(ə)lər\ *n*

chit \'chit\ *n* : signed voucher for a small debt

chit-chat \-,chat\ *n* : casual conversation

chiv·al·rous \'shivəlrəs\ *adj* **1** : relating to chivalry **2** : honest, courteous, or generous —**chiv·al·rous·ly** *adv* —**chiv·al·rous·ness** *n*

chiv·al·ry \-rē\ *n, pl* **-ries 1** : system or practices of knighthood **2** : spirit or character of the ideal knight —**chi·val·ric** \shə'valrik\ *adj*

chive \'chīv\ *n* : herb related to the onion

chlo·ride \'klōr,īd\ *n* : compound of chlorine

chlo·ri·nate \-ə,nāt\ *vb* **-nat·ed; -nat·ing** : treat or combine with chlorine —**chlo·ri·na·tion** \,klōrə'nāshən\ *n* —**chlo·ri·na·tor** \'klōrə,nātər\ *n*

chlo·rine \-,ēn\ *n* : chemical element that is a heavy strong-smelling greenish yellow irritating gas

chlo·ro·form \'klōrə,fòrm\ *n* : etherlike colorless heavy fluid —*vb* : anesthetize or kill with chloroform

chlo·ro·phyll \-ə,fil\ *n* : green coloring matter of plants

chock \'chäk\ *n* : wedge for blocking the movement of a wheel —**chock** *vb*

chock-full \'chək'fùl, 'chäk-\ *adj* : full to the limit

choc·o·late \'chäk(ə)lət, 'chòk-\ *n* **1** : ground roasted cacao beans or a beverage made from them **2** : candy made of or with chocolate **3** : dark brown

choice \'chòis\ *n* **1** : act or power of choosing **2** : one selected **3** : variety offered for selection —*adj* **choic·er; choic·est 1** : worthy of being chosen **2** : selected with care **3** : of high quality

choir \'kwī(ə)r\ *n* : group of singers esp. in church —**choir·boy** *n* —**choir·mas·ter** *n*

choke \'chōk\ *vb* **choked; chok·ing 1** : hinder breathing **2** : clog or obstruct —*n* **1** : a choking or sound of choking **2** : valve for controlling air intake in a gasoline engine

chok·er \-ər\ *n* : tight necklace

chol·er \'kälər, 'kō-\ *n* : bad temper —**cho·ler·ic** \'kälərik, kə'ler-\ *adj*

chol·era \'kälərə\ *n* : disease marked by severe vomiting and dysentery

cho·les·ter·ol \kə'lestə,ról, -,ról\ *n* : waxy substance in animal tissues

choose \'chüz\ *vb* **chose** \'chōz\; **cho·sen** \'chōz⁰n\; **choos·ing 1** : select after consideration **2** : see fit **3** : decide —**choos·er** *n*

choosy, choos·ey \'chüzē\ *adj* **choos·i·er; -est** : fussy in making choices

chop \'chäp\ *vb* **-pp- 1** : cut by repeated blows **2** : cut into small pieces ~ *n* **1** : sharp downward blow **2** : small cut of meat often with part of a rib

chop·per \-ər\ *n* **1** : one that chops **2** : helicopter

chop·py \-ē\ *adj* **-pi·er; -est 1** : rough with small waves **2** : jerky or disconnected —**chop·pi·ly** *adv* —**chop·pi·ness** *n*

chops \'chäps\ *n pl* : fleshy covering of the jaws

chop-sticks *n pl* : pair of sticks used in eating in oriental countries

cho-ral \'kōrəl\ *adj* : relating to or sung by a choir or chorus or in chorus —**cho-ral-ly** *adv*

cho-rale \kə'ral, -'räl\ *n* 1 : hymn tune or harmonization of a traditional melody 2 : chorus or choir

¹chord \'kȯrd\ *n* 1 : harmonious tones sounded together

²chord *n* 1 : cordlike anatomical structure 2 : straight line joining 2 points on a curve

chore \'chōr\ *n pl* 1 : daily household or farm work 2 : routine or disagreeable task

cho-re-og-ra-phy \kōrē'ägrəfē\ *n, pl* -**phies** : art of dancing or of arranging dances —**cho-reo-graph** \'kōrēə,graf\ *vb* —**cho-re-og-ra-pher** \,kōrē'ägrəfər\ *n* —**cho-reo-graph-ic** \-ēə'grafik\ *adj*

cho-ris-ter \'kōrəstər\ *n* : choir singer

chor-tle \'chȯrt³l\ *vb* -**tled;** -**tling** : laugh or chuckle —**chortle** *n*

cho-rus \'kōrəs\ *n* 1 : group of singers or dancers 2 : part of a song repeated at intervals 3 : composition for a chorus ~ *vb* : sing or utter together

chose *past of* CHOOSE

cho-sen \'chōz³n\ *adj* : favored

¹chow \'chaů\ *n* : food

²chow *n* : thick-coated muscular dog

chow-der \'chaůdər\ *n* : thick soup usu. of seafood and milk

chow mein \-'mān\ *n* : thick stew of shredded vegetables and meat

chris-ten \'kris³n\ *vb* 1 : baptize 2 : name —**chris-ten-ing** *n*

Chris-ten-dom \-dəm\ *n* : areas where Christianity prevails

Chris-tian \'krischən\ *n* : adherent of Christianity ~ *adj* : relating to or professing a belief in Christianity or Jesus Christ —**Chris-tian-ize** \'krischə,nīz\ *vb*

Chris-ti-an-i-ty \,krischē'anətē\ *n* : religion derived from the teachings of Jesus Christ

Christian name *n* : first name

Christ-mas \'krisməs\ *n* : December 25 celebrated as the birthday of Christ

chro-mat-ic \krō'matik\ *adj* 1 : relating to color 2 : proceeding by half steps of the musical scale

chrome \'krōm\ *n* : chromium or something plated with it

chro-mi-um \-ēəm\ *n* : a bluish white metallic element used esp. in alloys

chro-mo-some \-ə,sōm, -,zōm\ *n* : part

of a cell nucleus that contains the genes —**chro-mo-som-al** \,krōmə'sōməl, -'zō-\ *adj*

chron-ic \'kränik\ *adj* : frequent or persistent —**chron-i-cal-ly** \-(ə)lē\ *adv*

chron-i-cle \-əl\ *n* : history ~ *vb* -**cled;** -**cling** : record —**chron-i-cler** \-(ə)lər\ *n*

chro-nol-o-gy \krə'näləjē\ *n, pl* -**gies** : list of events in order of their occurrence —**chron-o-log-i-cal** \,kränə'läjikəl\ *adj* —**chron-o-log-i-cal-ly** \-ik(ə)lē\ *adv*

chro-nom-e-ter \krə'nämətər\ *n* : very accurate timepiece

chrys-a-lis \'krisələs\ *n, pl* **chry-sal-i-des** \kris'alə,dēz\ *or* **chrys-a-lis-es** : insect pupa enclosed in a shell

chrys-an-the-mum \kris'anthəməm\ *n* : plant with showy flowers

chub-by \'chəbē\ *adj* -**bi-er;** -**est** : fat —**chub-bi-ness** *n*

¹chuck \'chək\ *vb* 1 : tap 2 : toss ~ *n* 1 : light pat under the chin 2 : toss

²chuck *n* 1 : cut of beef 2 : machine part that holds work or another part

chuck-le \'chəkəl\ *vb* -**led;** -**ling** : laugh quietly —**chuckle** *n*

chug \'chəg\ *n* : sound of a laboring engine ~ *vb* -**gg-** : work or move with chugs

chum \'chəm\ *n* : close friend ~ *vb* -**mm-** : be chums —**chum-my** \-ē\ *adj*

chump \'chəmp\ *n* : fool

chunk \'chəŋk\ *n* 1 : short thick piece 2 : sizable amount

chunky \-ē\ *adj* **chunk-i-er;** -**est** : stocky 2 : containing chunks

church \'chərch\ *n* 1 : building esp. for Christian public worship 2 : whole body of Christians 3 : denomination 4 : congregation —**church-go-er** *n* —**church-go-ing** *adj or n*

church-yard *n* : cemetery beside a church

churl \'chərl\ *n* : rude ill-bred person —**churl-ish** *adj*

churn \'chərn\ *n* : container in which butter is made ~ *vb* 1 : agitate in a churn 2 : shake violently

chute \'shüt\ *n* : trough or passage

chut-ney \'chətnē\ *n, pl* -**neys** : sweet and sour relish

chutz-pah, chutz-pa \'hůtspə, 'kůt-, -(,)spä\ *n* : nerve or insolence

ci-ca-da \sə'kādə\ *n* : stout-bodied insect with transparent wings

ci-der \'sīdər\ *n* : apple juice

ci-gar \sig'är\ *n* : roll of leaf tobacco for smoking

cig·a·rette \ˌsigəˈret, ˈsigəˌret\ n : cut tobacco rolled in paper for smoking

cinch \ˈsinch\ n 1 : strap holding a saddle or pack in place 2 : sure thing —**cinch** vb

cin·cho·na \sinˈkōnə\ n : So. American tree that yields quinine

cinc·ture \ˈsiŋkchər\ n : belt

cin·der \ˈsindər\ n 1 pl : ashes 2 : piece of partly burned wood or coal

cin·e·ma \ˈsinəmə\ n : movies or a movie theater —**cin·e·mat·ic** \ˌsinəˈmatik\ adj

cin·na·mon \ˈsinəmən\ n : aromatic tree bark used as a spice

ci·pher \ˈsīfər\ n 1 : zero 2 : code

cir·ca \ˈsərkə\ prep : about

cir·cle \ˈsərkəl\ n 1 : closed symmetrical curve 2 : cycle 3 : group with a common tie ~ vb **-cled; -cling** 1 : enclose in a circle 2 : move or revolve around

cir·cuit \ˈsərkət\ n 1 : boundary 2 : regular tour of a territory 3 : complete path of an electric current

cir·cu·itous \ˌsərˈkyüətəs\ adj : circular or winding

cir·cuit·ry \ˈsərkətrē\ n, pl **-ries** : arrangement of an electric circuit

cir·cu·lar \ˈsərkyələr\ adj 1 : round 2 : moving in a circle ~ n : advertising leaflet —**cir·cu·lar·i·ty** \ˌsərkyəˈlaratē\ n

cir·cu·late \ˈsərkyəˌlāt\ vb **-lat·ed; -lat·ing** : move or cause to move in a circle or from place to place or person to person —**cir·cu·la·tion** \ˌsərkyəˈlāshən\ n —**cir·cu·la·to·ry** \ˈsərkyələˌtōrē\ adj

cir·cum·cise \ˈsərkəmˌsīz\ vb **-cised; -cis·ing** : cut off the foreskin of —**cir·cum·ci·sion** \ˌsərkəmˈsizhən\ n

cir·cum·fer·ence \sərˈkəmf(ə)rəns\ n : perimeter of a circle

cir·cum·flex \ˈsərkəmˌfleks\ n : phonetic mark (as ˆ)

cir·cum·lo·cu·tion \ˌsərkəmlōˈkyüshən\ n : excessive use of words

cir·cum·nav·i·gate \ˌsərkəm-\ vb : sail completely around —**cir·cum·nav·i·ga·tion** n

cir·cum·scribe \ˈsərkəmˌskrīb\ vb 1 : draw a line around 2 : limit

cir·cum·spect \ˈsərkəmˌspekt\ adj : careful —**cir·cum·spec·tion** \ˌsərkəmˈspekshən\ n

cir·cum·stance \ˈsərkəmˌstans\ n 1 : fact or event 2 pl : surrounding conditions 3 pl : financial situation —**cir·cum·stan·tial** \ˌsərkəmˈstanchəl\ adj

cir·cum·vent \-ˈvent\ vb : get around esp. by trickery

cir·cus \ˈsərkəs\ n : show with feats of skill, animal acts, and clowns

cir·rho·sis \səˈrōsəs\ n, pl **-rho·ses** \-ˌsēz\ : fibrosis esp. of the liver —**cir·rhot·ic** \-ˈrätik\ adj or n

cir·rus \ˈsirəs\ n, pl **-ri** \-ˌī\ : wispy white cloud

cis·tern \ˈsistərn\ n : underground water tank

cit·a·del \ˈsitədᵊl, - əˌdel\ n : fort

cite \ˈsīt\ vb **cit·ed; cit·ing** 1 : summon before a court 2 : quote 3 : refer to esp. in commendation —**ci·ta·tion** \sīˈtāshən\ n

cit·i·zen \ˈsitəzən\ n : member of a country —**cit·i·zen·ry** \-rē\ n —**cit·i·zen·ship** n

cit·ron \ˈsitrən\ n : lemonlike fruit

cit·rus \ˈsitrəs\ n, pl **-rus** or **-rus·es** : evergreen tree or shrub grown for its fruit (as the orange or lemon)

city \ˈsitē\ n, pl **cit·ies** : place larger or more important than a town

civ·ic \ˈsivik\ adj : relating to citizenship or civil affairs

civ·ics \-iks\ n : study of citizenship

civ·il \ˈsivəl\ adj 1 : relating to citizens 2 : polite 3 : relating to or being a lawsuit —**civ·il·ly** \-(i)lē\ adv

ci·vil·ian \səˈvilyən\ n : person not in a military, police, or fire-fighting force

ci·vil·i·ty \səˈvilətē\ n, pl **-ties** : courtesy

civ·i·li·za·tion \ˌsivələˈzāshən\ n 1 : high level of cultural development 2 : culture of a time or place

civ·i·lize \ˈsivəˌlīz\ vb **-lized; -liz·ing** : raise from a primitive stage of cultural development —**civ·i·lized** adj

civil liberty n : freedom from arbitrary governmental interference —usu. pl.

civil rights n pl : nonpolitical rights of a citizen

civil service n : government service

civil war n : war among citizens of one country

clack \ˈklak\ vb : make or cause a clatter —**clack** n

clad \ˈklad\ adj : covered

claim \ˈklām\ vb 1 : demand or take as the rightful owner 2 : maintain ~ n 1 : demand of right or ownership 2 : declaration 3 : something claimed —**claim·ant** \-ənt\ n

clair·voy·ant \klaərˈvóiənt\ adj : able to perceive things beyond the senses —**clair·voy·ance** \-əns\ n —**clairvoy·ant** n

clam \ˈklam\ n : bivalve mollusk

clam·ber \'klambər\ *vb* : climb awkwardly

clam·my \'klamē\ *adj* **-mi·er; -est** : being damp, soft, and usu. cool **—clam·mi·ness** *n*

clam·or \-ər\ *n* **1** : uproar **2** : protest **—clamor** *vb* **—clam·or·ous** *adj*

clamp \'klamp\ *n* : device for holding things together **—clamp** *vb*

clan \'klan\ *n* : group of related families **—clan·nish** *adj* **—clan·nish·ness** *n*

clan·des·tine \klan'destən\ *adj* : secret

clang \'klaŋ\ *n* : loud metallic ringing **—clang** *vb*

clan·gor \-(g)ər\ *n* : jumble of clangs

clank \'klaŋk\ *n* : brief sound of struck metal **—clank** *vb*

clap \'klap\ *vb* **-pp-** **1** : strike noisily **2** : applaud **~** *n* **1** : loud crash **2** : noise made by clapping the hands

clap·board \'klabərd; 'kla(p),bōrd\ *n* : narrow tapered board used for siding

clap·per \'klapər\ *n* : tongue of a bell

claque \'klak\ *n* : group hired to applaud at a performance

clar·et \'klarət\ *n* : dry red wine

clar·i·fy \'klarə,fī\ *vb* **-fied; -fy·ing** : make or become clear **—clar·i·fi·ca·tion** \,klarəfə'kāshən\ *n*

clar·i·net \,klarə'net\ *n* : woodwind instrument shaped like a tube **—clar·i·net·ist, clar·i·net·tist** \-əst\ *n*

clar·i·on \'klarēən\ *adj* : loud and clear

clar·i·ty \'klarətē\ *n* : clearness

clash \'klash\ *vb* **1** : make or cause a clash **2** : be in opposition or disharmony **~** *n* **1** : crashing sound **2** : hostile encounter

clasp \'klasp\ *n* **1** : device for holding things together **2** : embrace or grasp **~** *vb* **1** : fasten **2** : embrace or grasp

class \'klas\ *n* **1** : group of the same status or nature **2** : social rank **3** : course of instruction **4** : group of students **~** *vb* : classify **—class·less** *adj* **—class·mate** *n* **—class·room** *n*

clas·sic \'klasik\ *adj* **1** : serving as a standard of excellence **2** : classical **~** *n* : work of enduring excellence and esp. of ancient Greece or Rome **—clas·si·cal** \-ikəl\ *adj* **—clas·si·cal·ly** \-k(ə)lē\ *adv* **—clas·si·cism** \'klasə,sizəm\ *n* **—clas·si·cist** \-səst\ *n*

clas·si·fied \'klasə,fīd\ *adj* : restricted for security reasons

clas·si·fy \-,fī\ *vb* **-fied; -fy·ing** : arrange in or assign to classes **—clas·si·fi·ca·tion** \,klasəfə'kāshən\ *n*

clat·ter \'klatər\ *n* : rattling sound **—clatter** *vb*

clause \'klóz\ *n* **1** : separate part of a document **2** : part of a sentence with a subject and predicate

claus·tro·pho·bia \,klóstrə'fōbēə\ *n* : fear of closed or narrow spaces

clav·i·chord \'klavə,kórd\ *n* : early keyboard instrument

clav·i·cle \-ikəl\ *n* : collarbone

claw \'kló\ *n* : sharp curved nail or process (as on the toe of an animal) **~** *vb* : scratch or dig **—clawed** *adj*

clay \'klā\ *n* : plastic earthy material **—clay·ey** \-ē\ *adj*

clean \'klēn\ *adj* **1** : free from dirt or disease **2** : pure or honorable **3** : thorough **~** *vb* : make or become clean **—clean** *adv* **—clean·er** *n* **—clean·ly** \-lē\ *adv* **—clean·ness** *n*

clean·ly \'klenlē\ *adj* **-li·er; -est** : clean **—clean·li·ness** *n*

cleanse \'klenz\ *vb* **cleansed; cleans·ing** : make clean **—cleans·er** *n*

clear \'klir\ *adj* **1** : bright **2** : free from clouds **3** : transparent **4** : easily heard, seen or understood **5** : free from doubt **6** : free from restriction or obstruction **~** *vb* **1** : make or become clear **2** : go away **3** : free from accusation or blame **4** : explain or settle **5** : net **6** : jump or pass without touching **~** *n* : clear space or part **—clear** *adv* **—clear·ance** \'klirəns\ *n* **—clear·ly** *adv* **—clear·ness** *n*

clear·ing \'kli(ə)riŋ\ *n* : land cleared of wood

cleat \'klēt\ *n* : projection that strengthens or prevents slipping

¹**cleave** \'klēv\ *vb* **cleaved** \'klēvd\ *or* **clove** \'klōv\; **cleav·ing** : adhere

²**cleave** *vb* **cleaved** \'klēvd\; **cleav·ing** : split apart **—cleav·age** \'klēvij\ *n*

cleav·er \'klēvər\ *n* : heavy chopping knife

clef \'klef\ *n* : sign on the staff in music to show pitch

cleft \'kleft\ *n* : crack

clem·ent \'klemənt\ *adj* **1** : merciful **2** : temperate or mild **—clem·en·cy** \-ənsē\ *n*

clench \'klench\ *vb* **1** : hold fast **2** : close tightly

cler·gy \'klərjē\ *n* : body of religious officials **—clergy·man** \-jimən\ *n*

cler·ic \'klerik\ *n* : clergyman

cler·i·cal \-ikəl\ *adv* **1** : relating to the clergy **2** : relating to a clerk or office worker

clerk \'klərk, *Brit* 'klärk\ *n* **1** : official responsible for record-keeping **2** : person doing general office work **3**

: salesperson in a store —**clerk** vb —**clerk·ship** n

clev·er \'klevər\ adj 1 : resourceful 2 : marked by wit or ingenuity —**clev·er·ly** adv —**clev·er·ness** n

clew var of CLUE

cli·ché \kli'shā\ n : trite phrase —**cli·chéd** \-'shād\ adj

click \'klik\ n : slight sharp noise ~ vb : make or cause to make a click

cli·ent \'klīənt\ n 1 : person who engages professional services 2 : customer

cli·en·tele \ˌklīən'tel, ˌklē-\ n : body of customers

cliff \'klif\ n : high steep face of rock

cli·mate \'klīmət\ n : average weather conditions over a period of years —**cli·mat·ic** \klī'matik\ adj

cli·max \'klīˌmaks\ n : the highest point ~ vb : come to a climax —**cli·mac·tic** \klī'maktik\ adj

climb \'klīm\ vb 1 : go up or down by use of hands and feet 2 : rise ~ n : a climbing —**climb·er** n

clinch \'klinch\ vb 1 : fasten securely 2 : settle 3 : hold fast or firmly —**clinch** n —**clinch·er** n

cling \'kliŋ\ vb clung \'kləŋ\; **cling·ing** 1 : adhere firmly 2 : hold on tightly

clin·ic \'klinik\ n 1 : facility for diagnosis and treatment of outpatients —**clin·i·cal** \-əl\ adj

clink \'kliŋk\ vb : make a slight metallic sound —**clink** n

clin·ker \'kliŋkər\ n : fused stony matter esp. in a furnace

¹clip \'klip\ vb -pp- : fasten with a clip ~ n : device to hold things together

²clip vb -pp- 1 : cut or cut off 2 : hit ~ n 1 : clippers 2 : sharp blow 3 : rapid pace

clip·per \'klipər\ n 1 pl : implement for clipping 2 : fast sailing ship

clique \'klēk, 'klik\ n : small exclusive group of people

cli·to·ris \'klitərəs, kli'tòrəs\ n : small organ at the anterior part of the vulva

cloak \'klōk\ n 1 : loose outer garment 2 : something that conceals ~ vb : cover or hide with a cloak

clob·ber \'kläbər\ vb : hit hard

clock \'kläk\ n : timepiece not carried on the person ~ vb : record the time of

clock·wise \-ˌwīz\ adv or adj : in the same direction as hands of a clock

clod \'kläd\ n 1 : lump esp. of earth 2 : dull insensitive person

clog \'kläg\ n 1 : restraining weight 2 : thick-soled shoe ~ vb **-gg-** 1 : impede with a clog 2 : obstruct passage through 3 : become plugged up

clois·ter \'klòistər\ n 1 : monastic establishment 2 : covered passage ~ vb : shut away from the world

¹close \'klōz\ vb closed; **clos·ing** 1 : shut 2 : cease operation 3 : terminate 4 : bring or come together n : conclusion or end

²close \'klōs\ adj clos·er; clos·est 1 : confining 2 : secretive 3 : strict 4 : stuffy 5 : having little space between items 6 : fitting tightly 7 : near 8 : intimate 9 : accurate 10 : nearly even —**close** adv —**close·ly** adv —**close·ness** n

clos·et \'kläzət, 'klòz-\ n : small compartment for household utensils or clothing ~ vb : take into a private room for a talk

clo·sure \'klōzhər\ n 1 : act of closing 2 : something that closes

clot \'klät\ n : dried mass of a liquid —**clot** vb

cloth \'klòth\ n, pl cloths \'klòthz, 'klòths\ 1 : fabric 2 : tablecloth

clothe \'klōth\ vb clothed or clad \'klad\; **cloth·ing** : dress

clothes \'klō(th)z\ n pl : clothing

cloth·ier \'klōthyər, -thēər\ n : maker or seller of clothing

cloth·ing \'klōthiŋ\ n : covering for the human body

cloud \'klaůd\ n 1 : visible mass of particles in the air 2 : something that darkens, hides, or threatens ~ vb : darken or hide —**cloud·i·ness** n —**cloud·less** adj —**cloudy** adj

cloud·burst n : sudden heavy rain

clout \'klaůt\ n 1 : blow 2 : influence ~ vb : hit forcefully

¹clove \'klōv\ n : section of a bulb

²clove past of CLEAVE

³clove n : dried flower bud of an East Indian tree used as a spice

clo·ver \'klōvər\ n : leguminous herb with usu. 3-parted leaves

clo·ver·leaf n, pl -leafs or -leaves : highway intersection without left-hand turns or direct crossings

clown \'klaůn\ n : funny costumed entertainer esp. in a circus ~ vb : act like a clown —**clown·ish** adj —**clown·ish·ly** adv —**clown·ish·ness** n

cloy \'klòi\ vb : disgust with excess

club \'kləb\ n 1 : heavy wooden stick 2 : playing card of a suit marked with a black figure like a clover leaf 3 : group associated for a common purpose ~ vb **-bb-** : hit with a club

club·foot n : misshapen foot twisted out

of position from birth —**club·foot·ed** \-'fuṫəd\ *adj*

cluck \'klək\ *n* : sound made by a hen —**cluck** *vb*

clue, clew \'klü\ *n* : piece of evidence that helps solve a problem ∼ *vb* **clued** *or* **clewed; clue·ing** *or* **clu·ing** *or* **clew·ing** : provide with a clue

clump \'kləmp\ *n* **1** : cluster **2** : heavy tramping sound ∼ *vb* : tread heavily

clum·sy \'kləmzē\ *adj* **-si·er; -est 1** : lacking dexterity, nimbleness, or grace **2** : tactless —**clum·si·ly** *adv* —**clum·si·ness** *n*

clung *past of* CLING

clus·ter \'kləstər\ *n* : group ∼ *vb* : grow or gather in a cluster

clutch \'kləch\ *vb* : grasp ∼ *n* **1** : grasping hand or claws **2** : control or power **3** : coupling for connecting two working parts in machinery

clut·ter \'klətər\ *vb* : fill with things that get in the way —**clutter** *n*

co- *prefix* : with, together, joint, or jointly

coact	coinvent
coactor	coinventor
coauthor	coinvestigator
coauthorship	coleader
cocaptain	comanagement
cochairman	comanager
cochampion	co-officiate
cocomposer	co-organizer
coconspirator	co-own
cocreator	co-owner
codefendant	copartner
codesign	copartnership
codesigner	copresident
codevelop	coprincipal
codeveloper	coprisoner
codirect	coproduce
codirector	coproducer
codiscoverer	coproduction
codrive	copromote
codriver	copromoter
coedit	coproprietor
coeditor	coproprietorship
coexecutor	copublish
coexist	copublisher
coexistence	corecipient
coexistent	coresident
cofeature	cosignatory
cofinance	cosigner
cofound	cosponsor
cofounder	costar
coheir	cowinner
coheiress	co-worker
cohost	cowrite
cohostess	

coach \'kōch\ *n* **1** : closed 2-door

4-wheeled carriage **2** : railroad passenger car **3** : bus **4** : 2d-class air travel **5** : one who instructs or trains performers ∼ *vb* : instruct or direct as a coach

co·ag·u·late \kō'agyə‚lāt\ *vb* **-lat·ed; -lat·ing** : clot —**co·ag·u·lant** \-lənt\ *n* —**co·ag·u·la·tion** \-‚agyə'lāshən\ *n*

coal \'kōl\ *n* **1** : ember **2** : black solid mineral used as fuel —**coal-field** *n*

co·alesce \‚kōə'les\ *vb* **-alesced; -alesc·ing** : grow together —**co·ales·cence** \-'lesᵊns\ *n*

co·ali·tion \-'lishən\ *n* : temporary alliance

coarse \'kōrs\ *adj* **coars·er; coars·est 1** : composed of large particles **2** : rough or crude —**coarse·ly** *adv* —**coars·en** \-ᵊn\ *vb* —**coarse·ness** *n*

coast \'kōst\ *n* : seashore ∼ *vb* : move without effort —**coast·al** \-ᵊl\ *adj*

coast guard *n* : military force that guards or patrols a coast —**coast-guards·man** \'kōst‚gärdzmən\ *n*

coast·line *n* : shape of a coast

coat \'kōt\ *n* **1** : outer garment for the upper body **2** : external growth of fur or feathers **3** : covering layer ∼ *vb* : cover with a coat —**coat·ed** *adj* —**coat·ing** *n*

coax \'kōks\ *vb* : move to action or achieve by gentle urging or flattery —**coax·er** *n*

cob \'käb\ *n* : corncob

co·balt \'kō‚bolt\ *n* : shiny silver-white magnetic metallic chemical element

cob·bler \'käblər\ *n* **1** : shoemaker **2** : deep-dish fruit pie —**cob·ble** \'käbəl\ *n*

cob·ble·stone *n* : small round paving stone

co·bra \'kōbrə\ *n* : venomous snake

cob·web \'käb‚web\ *n* : network spun by a spider or a similar filament

co·caine \kō'kān, 'kō‚kān\ *n* : drug obtained from the leaves of a So. American shrub (**co·ca** \'kōkə\)

co·chlea \'kōklēə, 'käk-\ *n, pl* **-chle·as** *or* **-chle·ae** \-lē‚ē, -‚ī\ : the usu. spiral part of the inner ear —**coch·le·ar** \-lēər\ *adj*

cock \'käk\ *n* **1** : male fowl **2** : valve or faucet ∼ *vb* **1** : draw back the hammer of a firearm **2** : tilt to one side —**cock·fight** *n*

cock·ade \kä'kād\ *n* : badge on a hat

cock·a·too \'käkə‚tü\ *n, pl* **-toos** : large Australian parrot

cock·le \'käkəl\ *n* : edible shellfish

cock·pit \-‚pit\ *n* : place for a pilot, driver, or helmsman cock·roach *n* : nocturnal insect often infesting houses

cock·tail \'käk,tāl\ *n* 1 : iced drink of liquor and flavorings 2 : appetizer

cocky \-ē\ *adj* cock·i·er; -est : overconfident —cock·i·ness *n*

co·coa \'kōkō\ *n* 1 : cacao 2 : powdered chocolate or a drink made from this

co·co·nut \-kə(,)nət\ *n* : nutlike fruit of a tropical palm (coconut palm)

co·coon \kə'kün\ *n* : case protecting an insect pupa

cod \'käd\ *n, pl* cod : food fish of the No. Atlantic

cod·dle \'käd°l\ *vb* -dled; -dling : pamper

code \'kōd\ *n* 1 : system of laws or rules 2 : system of signals

co·deine \'kō,dēn, 'kōdēən\ *n* : narcotic drug used in cough remedies

cod·ger \'käjər\ *n* : odd fellow

cod·i·cil \'kädəsəl, -,sil\ *n* : postscript to a will

cod·i·fy \'kädə,fī, 'kōd-\ *vb* -fied; -fying : arrange systematically —cod·i·fi·ca·tion \,kädəfə'kāshən, ,kōd-\ *n*

co·ed \'kō,ed\ *n* : female student in a coeducational institution —coed *adj*

co·ed·u·ca·tion \,kō-\ *n* : education of the sexes together —co·ed·u·ca·tion·al *adj*

co·ef·fi·cient \,kōə'fishənt\ *n* 1 : number that is a multiplier of another 2 : number that serves as a measure of some property

co·erce \kō'ərs\ *vb* -erced; -erc·ing : force —co·er·cion \-'ərzhən, -shən\ *n* —co·er·cive \-'ərsiv\ *adj*

cof·fee \'kȯfē\ *n* : drink made from the roasted and ground seeds (coffee beans) of a tropical shrub —cof·fee·house *n* —cof·fee·pot *n*

cof·fer \'kȯfər\ *n* : box for valuables

cof·fin \-fən\ *n* : box for burial

cog \'käg\ *n* : tooth on the rim of a gear —cogged \'käg\ *adj* —cog·wheel *n*

co·gent \'kōjənt\ *adj* : compelling or convincing —co·gen·cy \-jənsē\ *n*

cog·i·tate \'käjə,tāt\ *vb* -tat·ed; -tat·ing : think over —cog·i·ta·tion \,käjə'tāshən\ *n* —cog·i·ta·tive \'käjə,tātiv\ *adj*

co·gnac \'kōn,yak\ *n* : French brandy

cog·nate \'käg,nāt\ *adj* : related —cognate *n*

cog·ni·tion \käg'nishən\ *n* : act or process of knowing —cog·ni·tive \'kägnətiv\ *adj*

cog·ni·zance \'kägnəzəns\ *n* : notice or awareness —cog·ni·za·ble \-nəzəbəl, käg'nī-\ *adj* —cog·ni·zant \'kägnəzənt\ *adj*

co·hab·it \kō'habət\ *vb* : live together as husband and wife —co·hab·i·ta·tion \-,habə'tāshən\ *n*

co·here \kō'hiər\ *vb* -hered; -her·ing : stick together

co·her·ent \-'hirənt\ *adj* 1 : able to stick together 2 : logically consistent —co·her·ence \-əns\ *n* —co·her·ent·ly *adv*

co·he·sion \-'hēzhən\ *n* : a sticking together —co·he·sive \-siv\ *adj*

co·hort \'kō,hȯrt\ *n* 1 : group of soldiers 2 : companion

coif·fure \kwä'fyu̇r\ *n* : hair style

coil \'kȯil\ *vb* : wind in a spiral ~ *n* : series of loops (as of rope)

coin \'kȯin\ *n* : piece of metal used as money ~ *vb* 1 : make (a coin) by stamping 2 : create —coin·age \-ij\ *n* —coin·er *n*

co·in·cide \,kōən'sīd, 'kōən,sīd\ *vb* -cid·ed; -cid·ing 1 : be in the same place 2 : happen at the same time 3 : be alike —co·in·ci·dence \kō'insədəns\ *n* —co·in·ci·dent \-ənt\ *adj* —co·in·ci·den·tal \-,insə'dent°l\ *adj*

co·itus \'kōətəs\ *n* : sexual intercourse —co·ital \-ət°l\ *adj*

coke \'kōk\ *n* : fuel made by heating soft coal

co·la \'kōlə\ *n* : carbonated soft drink

col·an·der \'kələndər, 'käl-\ *n* : perforated utensil for draining food

cold \'kōld\ *adj* 1 : having a low or below normal temperature 2 : lacking warmth of feeling 3 : suffering from lack of warmth ~ *n* 1 : low temperature 2 : minor respiratory illness —cold·ly *adv* —cold·ness \'kōl(d)nəs\ *n* —in cold blood : with premeditation

cold-blood·ed *adj* 1 : cruel or merciless 2 : having a body temperature that varies with the temperature of the environment

cole·slaw \'kōl,slȯ\ *n* : cabbage salad

col·ic \'kälik\ *n* : sharp abdominal pain —col·icky *adj*

col·i·se·um \,kälə'sēəm\ *n* : arena

col·lab·o·rate \kō'labə,rāt\ *vb* -rat·ed; -rat·ing 1 : work jointly with others 2 : help the enemy —col·lab·o·ra·tion \-,labə'rāshən\ *n* —col·lab·o·ra·tor \-'labə,rātər\ *n*

col·lapse \kə'laps\ *vb* -lapsed; -laps·ing 1 : fall in 2 : break down physically

61

collapsible · come across

or mentally **3** : fold down — *n* : breakdown —**col·laps·ible** *adj*

col·lar \'kälər\ *n* **1** : part of a garment around the neck — by the collar **2** : grab —**col·lar·less** *adj*

col·lar·bone *n* : bone joining the breastbone and the shoulder blade

col·lards \'kälərdz\ *n pl* : kale

col·late \kə'lāt; 'käl,āt, 'kōl-\ *vb* **-lat·ed; -lat·ing 1** : compare carefully **2** : assemble in order

col·lat·er·al \kə'lat(ə)rəl\ *adj* **1** : secondary **2** : descended from the same ancestors but not in the same line **3** : similar — *n* : property used as security for a loan

col·league \'käl,ēg\ *n* : associate

col·lect \kə'lekt\ *vb* **1** : bring, come, or gather together **2** : receive payment of — *adv or adj* : to be paid for by the receiver —**col·lect·ible, collect·able** *adj* —**col·lec·tion** \-'lekshən\ *n* —**col·lec·tor** \-'lektər\ *n*

col·lec·tive \-'tiv\ *adj* : denoting or shared by a group — *n* : a cooperative unit —**col·lec·tive·ly** *adv*

col·lege \'kälij\ *n* : institution of higher learning granting a bachelor's degree —**col·le·gian** \kə'lējən\ *n* —**col·le·giate** \'lējət\ *adj*

col·lide \kə'līd\ *vb* **-lid·ed; -lid·ing** : strike together —**col·li·sion** \-'lizhən\ *n*

col·lie \'kälē\ *n* : large long-haired dog

col·loid \'käl,öid\ *n* : tiny particles in suspension with a fluid —**col·loi·dal** \kə'löid²l\ *adj*

col·lo·qui·al \kə'lōkwēəl\ *adj* : used in informal conversation —**col·lo·qui·al·ism** \-ə,lizəm\ *n*

col·lo·quy \'käləkwē\ *n, pl* **-quies** : formal conversation or conference

col·lu·sion \kə'lüzhən\ *n* : secret cooperation for deceit —**col·lu·sive** \-'lüsiv\ *adj*

co·logne \kə'lōn\ *n* : perfumed liquid

¹co·lon \'kōlən\ *n, pl* **colons** *or* **co·la** \-lə\ : lower part of the large intestine —**co·lon·ic** \kō'länik\ *adj*

²colon *n, pl* **colons** *or* **co·la** \-lə\ : punctuation mark : used esp. to direct attention to following matter

col·o·nel \'kərn²l\ *n* : commissioned officer (as in the army) ranking next below a brigadier general

col·on·nade \,kälə'nād\ *n* : row of supporting columns

col·o·ny \'kälənē\ *n, pl* **-nies 1** : people who inhabit a new territory or the territory itself **2** : animals of one kind (as bees) living together —**co·lo-**

nial \kə'lōnēəl\ *adj or n* —**col·o·nist** \'kälənəst\ *n* —**col·o·nize** \-,nīz\ *vb*

col·or \'kälər\ *n* **1** : quality of visible things distinct from shape that results from light reflection **2** *pl* : flag **3** : liveliness — *vb* **1** : give color to **2** : blush —**col·or·fast** *adj* —**col·or·ful** *adj* —**col·or·less** *adj*

col·or·blind *adj* : unable to distinguish colors —**color blindness** *n*

col·ored \'kälərd\ *adj* **1** : having color **2** : of a race other than the white — *n, pl* **colored** *or* **coloreds** : colored person

co·los·sal \kə'läsəl\ *adj* : very large or great

co·los·sus \-əs\ *n, pl* **-sus·es** *or* **-si** \-'läs,ī\ : something of great size or scope

colt \'kōlt\ *n* : young male horse —**colt·ish** *adj*

col·umn \'käləm\ *n* **1** : vertical section of a printed page **2** : special item (as in a newspaper) **3** : pillar **4** : row (as of soldiers) —**co·lum·nar** \kə'ləmnər\ *adj* —**col·um·nist** \'käləm(n)əst\ *n*

co·ma \'kōmə\ *n* : deep prolonged unconsciousness —**co·ma·tose** \-,tōs, 'kämə-\ *adj*

comb \'kōm\ *n* **1** : toothed instrument for arranging the hair **2** : crest on a fowl's head —**comb** *vb* —**combed** \'kōmd\ *adj*

com·bat \kəm'bat, 'käm,bat\ *vb* **-bat·ed** *or* **-bat·ted; -bat·ing** *or* **-bat·ting** : fight —**com·bat** \'käm,bat\ *n* —**com·bat·ant** \kəm'bat²nt, 'kämbətənt\ *n* —**com·bat·ive** \kəm'bativ\ *adj*

com·bi·na·tion \,kämbə'nāshən\ *n* **1** : process or result of combining **2** : code for opening a lock

com·bine \kəm'bīn\ *vb* **-bined; -bin·ing** : join together — *n* \'käm,bīn\ **1** : association for business or political advantage **2** : harvesting machine

com·bus·ti·ble \kəm'bəstəbəl\ *adj* : apt to catch fire —**com·bus·ti·bil·i·ty** \-,bəstə'bilətē\ *n* —**combustible** *n*

com·bus·tion \-'bəschən\ *n* : process of burning —**com·bus·tive** \-'tiv\ *adj*

come \(')kəm\ *vb* **came** \'käm\; **come; com·ing 1** : move toward or arrive at something **2** : reach a state **3** : originate or exist **4** : amount —**come across** *vb* : meet or find by chance —**come off** *vb* : succeed —**come to** *vb* : regain consciousness —**come to pass** *vb* : happen —**come upon** *vb* : come across

come·back \n 1 : retort 2 : return to a former position —**come back** vb

co·me·di·an \kə'mēdēən\ n 1 : comic actor 2 : funny person —**co·me·di·enne** \-,mēdē'en\ n

com·e·dy \'kämədē\ n, pl -**dies** : an amusing play

come·ly \'kəmlē\ adj -**li·er; -est** : good-looking —**come·li·ness** n

com·et \'kämət\ n : small bright celestial body

com·fort \'kəmfərt\ n 1 : consolation 2 : well-being or something that gives it ~ vb 1 : give hope to 2 : console —**com·fort·able** \'kəm(f)tabəl, 'kəmfərt-\ adj —**com·fort·ably** \-blē\ adv —**com·fort·less** adj

com·fort·er \'kəmfə(r)tər\ n 1 : one that comforts 2 : quilt

com·ic \'kämik\ adj 1 : relating to comedy 2 : funny ~ n 1 : comedian 2 : sequence of cartoons —**com·i·cal** adj

com·ing \'kəmiŋ\ adj : next

com·ma \'kämə\ n : punctuation mark , used esp. to separate sentence parts

com·mand \kə'mand\ vb 1 : order 2 : control ~ n 1 : act of commanding 2 : an order given 3 : mastery 4 : troops under a commander —**com·man·dant** \'kämən,dant, -,dänt\ n

com·man·deer \,kämən'diər\ vb : seize by force

com·mand·er \kə'mandər\ n 1 : officer commanding an army or subdivision of an army 2 : commissioned officer in the navy ranking next below a captain

com·mand·ment \-'man(d)mənt\ n : order

command sergeant major n : noncommissioned officer in the army ranking above a first sergeant

com·mem·o·rate \kə'memə,rāt\ vb -**rat·ed; -rat·ing** : celebrate or honor —**com·mem·o·ra·tion** \-,memə'rāshən\ n —**com·mem·o·ra·tive** \-'mem(ə)rətiv, -'memə,rāt-\ adj

com·mence \kə'mens\ vb -**menced; -menc·ing** : start

com·mence·ment \-mənt\ n 1 : beginning 2 : graduation ceremony

com·mend \kə'mend\ vb 1 : entrust 2 : recommend 3 : praise —**com·mend·able** \-əbəl\ adj —**com·men·da·tion** \,kämən'dāshən, -,men-\ n

com·men·su·rate \kə'mens(ə)rət, -'mench(ə)-\ adj : equal in measure or extent

com·ment \'käm,ent\ n : statement of opinion or remark —**comment** vb

com·men·ta·ry \-ən,terē\ n, pl -**tar·ies** : series of comments

com·men·ta·tor \-ən,tātər\ n : one who discusses news

com·merce \'käm(,)ərs\ n : business

com·mer·cial \kə'mərshəl\ adj : designed for profit or for mass appeal ~ n : broadcast advertisement —**com·mer·cial·ize** \-,īz\ vb —**com·mer·cial·ly** \-ē\ adv

com·min·gle \kə'miŋgəl\ vb : mix

com·mis·er·ate \kə'mizə,rāt\ vb -**at·ed; at·ing** : sympathize —**com·mis·er·a·tion** \-,mizə'rāshən\ n

com·mis·sary \'kämə,serē\ n, pl -**sar·ies** : store esp. for military personnel

com·mis·sion \kə'mishən\ n 1 : order granting power or rank 2 : panel to judge, approve, or act 3 : the doing of an act 4 : agent's fee ~ vb 1 : confer rank or authority to or for 2 : request something be done or made

com·mis·sion·er \-'mish(ə)nər\ n 1 : member of a commission 2 : head of a government department

com·mit \-'mit\ vb -**tt-** 1 : turn over to someone for safekeeping or confinement 2 : perform or do 3 : pledge —**com·mit·ment** n —**com·mit·tal** \-əl\ n

com·mit·tee \-'mitē\ n : panel that examines or acts on something

com·mo·di·ous \kə'mōdēəs\ adj : spacious

com·mod·i·ty \-'mädətē\ n, pl -**ties** : article for sale

com·mo·dore \'kämə,dōr\ n 1 : former commissioned officer in the navy ranking next below a rear admiral 2 : officer commanding a group of merchant ships

com·mon \'kämən\ adj 1 : public 2 : shared by several 3 : widely known, found, or observed 4 : ordinary ~ n : community land —**com·mon·ly** adv —**in common** : shared together

com·mon·place \'kämən,plās\ n : cliché ~ adj : ordinary

common sense n : good judgment

com·mon·weal \-,wēl\ n : general welfare

com·mon·wealth \-,welth\ n : state

com·mo·tion \kə'mōshən\ n : disturbance

¹**com·mune** \kə'myün\ vb -**muned; -mun·ing** : communicate intimately

²**com·mune** \'käm,yün\ n 1 : community that shares all ownership and duties —**com·mu·nal** \-əl\ adj

com·mu·ni·cate \kə'myünə,kāt\ vb -**cat·ed; -cat·ing** 1 : make known 2

: exchange information or opinions —com·mu·ni·ca·ble \-'myünikəbəl\ adj —com·mu·ni·ca·tion \-,myüni'kāshən\ n —com·mu·ni·ca·tive \-'myüni,kātiv, -kət-\ adj

Com·mu·nion \kə-'myünyən\ n : Christian sacrament of partaking of bread and wine

com·mu·ni·qué \kə'myünə,kā, -,myünə'kā\ n : official bulletin

com·mu·nism \'kämyə,nizəm\ n 1 : social organization in which goods are held in common 2 cap : political doctrine based on revolutionary Marxian socialism —com·mu·nist \-nəst\ n or adj, often cap —com·mu·nis·tic \,kämyə'nistik\ adj, often cap

com·mu·ni·ty \kə'myünətē\ n, pl -ties : body of people living in the same place under the same laws

com·mute \kə'myüt\ vb -mut·ed; -mut·ing 1 : reduce (a punishment) 2 : travel back and forth regularly ~ n : trip made in commuting —com·mu·ta·tion \,kämyə'tāshən\ n —com·mut·er n

¹com·pact \kəm'pakt, (')käm-\ adj 1 : hard 2 : small or brief ~ vb : pack together ~ \'käm,pakt\ n 1 : cosmetics case 2 : small car —com·pact·ly adv —com·pact·ness n

²com·pact \'käm,pakt\ n : agreement

com·pan·ion \kəm'panyən\ n 1 : close friend 2 : one of a pair —com·pan·ion·able adj —com·pan·ion·ship n

com·pa·ny \'kəmp(ə)nē\ n, pl -nies 1 : business organization 2 : group of performers 3 : guests 4 : infantry unit

com·par·a·tive \kəm'parətiv\ adj 1 : relating to or being an adjective or adverb form that denotes increase 2 : relative —comparative n —com·par·a·tive·ly adv

com·pare \kəm'paər\ vb -pared; -par·ing 1 : represent as similar 2 : check for likenesses or differences ~ n : comparison —com·pa·ra·ble \'kämp(ə)rəbəl\ adj

com·par·i·son \kəm'parəsən\ n 1 : act of comparing 2 : change in the form and meaning of an adjective or adverb to show different levels of quality, quantity, or relation

com·part·ment \-'pärtmənt\ n : section or room

com·pass \'kəmpəs, 'käm-\ n 1 : scope 2 : device for drawing circles 3 : device for determining direction

com·pas·sion \kəm'pashən\ n : pity —com·pas·sion·ate \-(ə)nət\ adj

com·pat·i·ble \-'patəbəl\ adj : harmonious —com·pat·i·bil·i·ty \-,patə'bilətē\ n

com·pa·tri·ot \kəm'pātrēət, -trē,ät\ n : fellow countryman

com·pel \kəm'pel\ vb -ll- : cause through necessity

com·pen·di·um \kəm'pendēəm\ n, pl -di·ums or -dia \-dēə\ : summary

com·pen·sate \'kämpən,sāt\ vb -sat·ed; -sat·ing 1 : offset or balance 2 : repay —com·pen·sa·tion \,kämpən'sāshən\ n —com·pen·sa·to·ry \kəm'pensə,tōrē\ adj

com·pete \kəm'pēt\ vb -pet·ed; -pet·ing : strive to win —com·pe·ti·tion \,kämpə'tishən\ n —com·pet·i·tive \kəm'petətiv\ adj —com·pet·i·tor \kəm'petətər\ n

com·pe·tent \'kämpətənt\ adj : capable —com·pe·tence \-əns\ n —com·pe·ten·cy \-ənsē\ n

com·pile \kəm'pīl\ vb -piled; -pil·ing : collect or compose from several sources —com·pi·la·tion \,kämpə'lāshən\ n —com·pil·er \kəm'pīlər\ n

com·pla·cence \kəm'plāsəns\ n : self-satisfaction —com·pla·cen·cy \-ənsē\ n —com·pla·cent \-ᵊnt\ adj

com·plain \kəm'plān\ vi 1 : express grief, pain, or discontent 2 : make an accusation —com·plain·ant n —com·plain·er n

com·plaint \-'plānt\ n 1 : expression of grief or discontent 2 : ailment 3 : formal accusation

com·ple·ment \'kämpləmənt\ n 1 : something that completes 2 : full number or amount ~ \-,ment\ vb : complete —com·ple·men·ta·ry \,kämplə'ment(ə)rē\ adj

com·plete \kəm'plēt\ adj -plet·er; -est 1 : having no part lacking 2 : finished 3 : total ~ vb -plet·ed; -plet·ing 1 : make whole 2 : finish —com·plete·ly adv —com·plete·ness n —com·ple·tion \-'plēshən\ n

com·plex \käm'pleks, kəm-; 'käm,pleks\ adj 1 : having many parts 2 : intricate ~ \'käm,pleks\ n : psychological problem —com·plex·i·ty \käm'pleksətē, kəm-\ n

com·plex·ien \kəm'plekshən\ n : hue or appearance of the skin esp. of the face —com·plex·ioned adj

com·pli·cate \'kämplə,kāt\ vb -cat·ed; -cat·ing : make complex or hard to understand —com·pli·cat·ed \-əd\ adj —com·pli·ca·tion \,kämplə-'kāshən\ n com·plic·i·ty \kəm'plisətē\ n, pl -ties : participation in guilt

com·pli·ment \'kämpləmənt\ n 1 : flattering remark 2 pl ~ : greeting — \-,ment\ vb : pay a compliment to

com·pli·men·ta·ry \,kämplə'ment(ə)rē\ adj 1 : praising 2 : free

com·ply \kəm'plī\ vb -plied; -ply·ing : obey —com·pli·ance \-əns\ n —com·pli·ant \-ənt\ n

com·po·nent \kəm'pōnənt, 'käm,pō-\ n : part of something larger ~ adj : serving as a component

com·port \kəm'pōrt\ vb 1 : agree 2 : behave —com·port·ment \-mənt\ n

com·pose \kəm'pōz\ vb -posed; -pos·ing 1 : create (as by writing) or put together 2 : calm 3 : set type —com·pos·er\ n —com·po·si·tion \,kämpə'zishən\ n

com·pos·ite \käm'päzət, kəm-\ adj : made up of diverse parts —composite n

com·post \'käm,pōst\ n : decayed organic fertilizing material

com·po·sure \kəm'pōzhər\ n : calmness

com·pote \'käm,pōt\ n : fruits cooked in syrup

¹com·pound \(')käm'paund, kəm-\ vb 1 : combine or add 2 : pay (interest) on principal and accrued interest ~ \'käm,paund\ adj : made up of 2 or more parts ~ \'käm,paund\ n : something compounded

²com·pound \'käm,paund\ n : enclosure

com·pre·hend \,kämpri'hend\ vb 1 : understand 2 : include —com·pre·hen·si·ble \-'hensəbəl\ adj —com·pre·hen·sion \-'henchən\ n —com·pre·hen·sive \-siv\ adj

com·press \kəm'pres\ vb : squeeze together ~ \'käm,pres\ n : pad for pressing on a wound —com·pres·sion \-'preshən\ n —com·pres·sor \-'presər\ n

compressed air n : air under pressure greater than that of the atmosphere

com·prise \kəm'prīz\ vb -prised; -pris·ing 1 : contain or cover 2 : be made up of

com·pro·mise \'kämprə,mīz\ vb -mised; -mis·ing : settle differences by mutual concessions —compromise n

comp·trol·ler \kən'trōlər, 'kämp,trō-\ n : financial officer

com·pul·sion \kəm'pəlshən\ n 1 : coercion 2 : irresistible impulse —com·pul·sive \-siv\ adj —com·pul·so·ry \-'pəls(ə)rē\ adj

com·punc·tion \-'pəŋkshən\ n : remorse

com·pute \-'pyüt\ vb -put·ed; -put·ing : calculate —com·pu·ta·tion \,kämpyü'tāshən\ n

com·put·er \kəm'pyütər\ n : electronic data processing machine

com·rade \'käm,rad, -,rəd\ n : companion —com·rade·ship n

¹con \'kän\ adv : against ~ n : opposing side or person

²con \'kän\ vb -nn- : swindle

con·cave \(')kän'kāv\ adj : curved like the inside of a sphere —con·cav·i·ty \kän'kavətē\ n

con·ceal \kən'sēl\ vb : hide —con·ceal·ment n

con·cede \-'sēd\ vb -ced·ed; -ced·ing : grant

con·ceit \-'sēt\ n : excessively high opinion of oneself —con·ceit·ed \-əd\ adj

con·ceive \-'sēv\ vb -ceived; -ceiv·ing 1 : become pregnant 2 : think of —con·ceiv·able \-'sēvəbəl\ adj —con·ceiv·ably \-blē\ adv

con·cen·trate \'känsən,trāt\ vb -trat·ed; -trat·ing 1 : gather together 2 : make stronger 3 : fix one's attention on one thing ~ n : something concentrated —con·cen·tra·tion \,känsən'trāshən\ n

con·cen·tric \kən'sentrik\ adj : having a common center

con·cept \'kän,sept\ n : thought or idea

con·cep·tion \kən'sepshən\ n 1 : act of conceiving 2 : idea

con·cern \kən'sərn\ vb 1 : relate to 2 : involve ~ n 1 : affair 2 : worry 3 : business —con·cerned \-'sərnd\ adj —con·cern·ing \-'sərniŋ\ prep

con·cert \-'sərt\ vb 1 : plan together ~ \'kän,(,)sərt\ n 1 : agreement or joint action 2 : public performance of music

con·cer·ti·na \,känsər'tēnə\ n : accordionlike instrument

con·cer·to \kən'chertō\ n, pl -ti \-(,)ē\ or -tos : orchestral work with solo instruments

con·ces·sion \-'seshən\ n 1 : act of conceding 2 : something conceded 3 : right to do business on a property

conch \'käŋk, 'känch\ n, pl conchs \'käŋks\ or conch·es \'känchəz\ : large spiral-shelled marine mollusk

con·cil·i·ate \kən'silē,āt\ vb -at·ed; -at·ing : gain the goodwill of —con·cil·i·a·tion \-,silē'āshən\ n —con·cil·ia·to·ry \-'silyə,tōrē, -'silē-\ adj

con·cise \kən'sīs\ adj : said in few

words —con·cise·ly adv —con·cise·ness n

con·clave \'kän,klāv\ n : private meeting

con·clude \kən'klüd\ vb -clud·ed; -clud·ing 1 : end 2 : decide —con·clu·sion \-'klüzhən\ n —con·clu·sive \-siv\ adj —con·clu·sive·ly adv

con·coct \kən'käkt, kän-\ vb : prepare or devise —con·coc·tion \-'käkshən\ n

con·com·i·tant \-'kämətənt\ adj : accompanying —concomitant n

con·cord \'kän,kord, 'kän-\ n : agreement

con·cor·dance \kən'kordəns\ n 1 : agreement 2 : index of words —con·cor·dant \-ᵊnt\ adj

con·course \'kän,kōrs\ n : open space where crowds gather

con·crete \kän'krēt, 'kän,krēt\ adj 1 : naming something real 2 : actual or substantial 3 : made of concrete ~ \'kän,krēt, kän'krēt\ n : hard building material made of cement, sand, gravel, and water

con·cre·tion \kän'krēshən\ n : hard mass

con·cu·bine \'känkyù,bīn\ n : mistress

con·cur \kən'kər\ vb -rr- : agree —con·cur·rence \-'kərəns\ n

con·cur·rent \-ᵊnt\ adj : happening at the same time

con·cus·sion \kən'kəshən\ n 1 : shock 2 : brain injury from a blow

con·demn \-'dem\ vb 1 : declare to be wrong, guilty, or unfit for use 2 : sentence —con·dem·na·tion \,kän,dem'nāshən\ n

con·dense \kən'dens\ vb -densed; -dens·ing 1 : make or become more compact 2 : express in fewer words —con·den·sa·tion \,kän,den'sāshən, -dən-\ n —con·dens·er n

con·de·scend \,kändi'send\ vb 1 : lower oneself 2 : act haughtily —con·de·scen·sion \-'senchən\ n

con·di·ment \'kändəmənt\ n : pungent seasoning

con·di·tion \kən'dishən\ n 1 : necessary situation or stipulation 2 pl : state of affairs 3 : state of being ~ vb 1 : limit by a condition 2 : put into proper condition —con·di·tion·al \kən'dish(ə)nəl\ adj —con·di·tion·al·ly \-ē\ adv

con·dole \kən'dōl\ vb -doled; -dol·ing : express sympathy —con·do·lence \kən'dōləns, 'kändə-\ n

con·do·min·i·um \,kändə'minēəm\ n, pl -ums : individually owned apartment

con·done \kən'dōn\ vb -doned; -don·ing : overlook or forgive

con·dor \'kändər, -,dór\ n : large western American vulture

con·du·cive \kən'd(y)üsiv\ adj : tending to help or promote

con·duct \'kän(,)dəkt\ n 1 : management 2 : behavior ~ \kən'dəkt\ vb 1 : guide 2 : manage or direct 3 : be a channel for 4 : behave —con·duc·tion \-'dəkshən\ n —con·duc·tive \-'dəktiv\ adj —con·duc·tor \-'dəktər\ n

con·duit \'kän,d(y)üət, -d(w)ət\ n : channel (as for conveying fluid)

cone \'kōn\ n 1 : scaly fruit of pine and related trees 2 : solid figure having a circular base and tapering sides

Con·es·to·ga \,känə'stōgə\ n : covered wagon

con·fec·tion \kən'fekshən\ n : sweet dish or candy —con·fec·tion·er \-sh(ə)nər\ n

con·fed·er·a·cy \kən'fed(ə)rəsē\ n 1 pl -cies : league 2 cap : 11 southern states that seceded from the U.S. in 1860 and 1861

con·fed·er·ate \-rət\ adj 1 : united in a league 2 cap : relating to the Confederacy ~ n 1 : ally 2 cap : adherent of the Confederacy ~ \-'fedə,rāt\ vb -at·ed; -at·ing : unite —con·fed·er·a·tion \-,fedə'rāshən\ n

con·fer \kən'fər\ vb -rr- : give 2 : meet to exchange views —con·fer·ee \,känfə'rē\ n —con·fer·ence \'känf(ə)rəns\ n

con·fess \kən'fes\ vb 1 : acknowledge or disclose one's misdeed, fault, or sin 2 : declare faith in —con·fes·sion \-'feshən\ n —con·fes·sion·al \-'fesh(ə)nəl\ n or adj

con·fes·sor \kən'fesər, 2 also \'kän,fes-\ n 1 : one who confesses 2 : priest who hears confessions

con·fet·ti \kən'fetē\ n : bits of paper or ribbon thrown in celebration

con·fi·dant \'känfə,dant, -,dänt\ n : one to whom secrets are confided

con·fide \kən'fīd\ vb -fid·ed; -fid·ing 1 : share private thoughts 2 : reveal in confidence

con·fi·dence \'känfədəns\ n 1 : trust 2 : self-assurance 3 : something confided —con·fi·dent \-ᵊnt\ adj —con·fi·den·tial \,känfə'denchəl\ adj

con·fig·u·ra·tion \kən,figyə'rāshən\ n : arrangement

con·fine \-'fīn\ vb -fined; -fin·ing 1 : restrain or restrict to a limited area 2 : put in prison confines \'känfīnz\ n *pl* : bounds —**con·fine·ment** *n* —**con·fin·er** *n*

con·firm \kən'fərm\ *vb* 1 : ratify 2 : verify 3 : admit as a full member of a church or synagogue —**con·fir·ma·tion** \ˌkänfər'māshən\ *n*

con·fis·cate \'känfəˌskāt\ *vb* -**cat·ed**; -**cat·ing** : take by authority —**con·fis·ca·tion** \ˌkänfə'skāshən\ *n*

con·fla·gra·tion \ˌkänflə'grāshən\ *n* : great fire

con·flict \'känˌflikt\ *n* 1 : war 2 : clash of ideas ∼ \kən'flikt\ *vb* : clash

con·form \kən'fȯrm\ *vb* 1 : make or be like 2 : obey —**con·for·mi·ty** \kən'fȯrmətē\ *n*

con·found \kən'faund, kän-\ *vb* : confuse

con·front \kən'frənt\ *vb* : oppose or face —**con·fron·ta·tion** \ˌkänfrən'tāshən\ *n*

con·fuse \kən'fyüz\ *vb* -**fused**; -**fus·ing** 1 : make mentally uncertain 2 : jumble —**con·fu·sion** \-'fyüzhən\ *n*

con·fute \-'fyüt\ *vb* -**fut·ed**; -**fut·ing** : overwhelm by argument

con·geal \kən'jēl\ *vb* 1 : freeze 2 : become thick and solid

con·ge·nial \kən-\ *adj* : kindred or agreeable —**con·ge·ni·al·i·ty** *n*

con·gen·i·tal \kən-\ *adj* : existing from birth

con·gest \kən'jest\ *vb* : overcrowd or overfill —**con·ges·tion** \-'jeschən\ *n* —**con·ges·tive** \-'jestiv\ *adj*

con·glom·er·ate \kən'gläm(ə)rət\ *adj* : made up of diverse parts ∼ \-ə-ˌrāt\ *vb* -**at·ed**; -**at·ing** : form into a mass ∼ \-(ə)rət\ *n* 1 : rock composed of fragments and a cementing material 2 : diversified corporation —**con·glom·er·a·tion** \-ˌglämə'rāshən\ *n*

con·grat·u·late \kən'grachəˌlāt\ *vb* -**lat·ed**; -**lat·ing** : express pleasure to for good fortune —**con·grat·u·la·tion** \-ˌgrachə'lāshən\ *n* —**con·grat·u·la·to·ry** \-'grachələˌtȯrē\ *adj*

con·gre·gate \'käŋgriˌgāt\ *vb* -**gat·ed**; -**gat·ing** : assemble

con·gre·ga·tion \ˌkäŋgri'gāshən\ *n* 1 : assembly of people at worship 2 : religious group —**con·gre·ga·tion·al** \-sh(ə)nəl\ *adj*

con·gress \'käŋgrəs\ *n* : assembly of delegates or of senators and representatives —**con·gres·sio·nal** \kən'gresh(ə)nəl, käŋ-\ *adj* —**con·gress·man** \'käŋgrəsmən\ *n* —**con·gress·wom·an** *n*

con·gru·ence \kən'grüəns, 'käŋgrəwəns\ *n* : likeness —**con·gru·ent** \-ənt\ *adj*

con·gru·ity \kən'grüətē, kän-\ *n* : correspondence between things —**con·gru·ous** \'käŋgrəwəs\ *adj*

con·ic \'känik\ *adj* : relating to or like a cone —**con·i·cal** \-ikəl\ *adj*

co·ni·fer \'känəfər, 'kōn-\ *n* : cone-bearing tree —**co·nif·er·ous** \kō'nif(ə)rəs\ *adj*

con·jec·ture \kən'jekchər\ *n or vb* : guess —**con·jec·tur·al** \-əl\ *adj*

con·join \kən-\ *vb* : join together

con·ju·gal \'känjigəl, kən'jü-\ *adj* : relating to marriage

con·ju·gate \'känjəˌgāt\ *vb* -**gat·ed**; -**gat·ing** : give the inflected forms of (a verb) —**con·ju·ga·tion** \ˌkänjə'gāshən\ *n*

con·junc·tion \kən'jəŋkshən\ *n* 1 : combination 2 : occurrence at the same time 3 : a word that joins other words together —**con·junc·tive** \-tiv\ *adj*

con·jure \'känjər, 'kən-\ *vb* -**jured**; -**jur·ing** 1 : summon by sorcery 2 : practice sleight of hand 3 : entreat —**con·jur·er, con·ju·ror** \'känjərər, 'kən-\ *n*

con·nect \kə'nekt\ *vb* : join or associate —**con·nec·tion** \-'nekshən\ *n* —**con·nec·tive** \-tiv\ *n or adj* —**con·nec·tor** *n*

con·nive \kə'nīv\ *vb* -**nived**; -**niv·ing** 1 : pretend ignorance of wrongdoing 2 : cooperate secretly —**con·niv·ance** *n*

con·nois·seur \ˌkänə'sər\ *n* : expert judge esp. of art

con·note \kə'nōt\ *vb* -**not·ed**; -**not·ing** : suggest additional meaning —**con·no·ta·tion** \ˌkänə'tāshən\ *n*

con·nu·bi·al \kə'n(y)übēəl\ *adj* : relating to marriage

con·quer \'käŋkər\ *vb* : defeat or overcome —**con·quer·or** \-kərər\ *n*

con·quest \'kän,kwest, 'käŋ-\ *n* 1 : act of conquering 2 : something conquered

con·science \'känchəns\ *n* : awareness of right and wrong

con·sci·en·tious \ˌkänchē'enchəs\ *adj* : honest and hard-working —**con·sci·en·tious·ly** *adv*

con·scious \'känchəs\ *adj* 1 : aware 2 : mentally awake or alert 3 : intentional —**con·scious·ly** *adv* —**con·scious·ness** *n*

con·script \kən'skript\ *vb* : draft for military service —**con·script** \'kän,skript\ *n* —**con·scrip·tion** \kən'skripshən\ *n*

con·se·crate \'känsəˌkrāt\ *vb* -**crat·ed**; -**crat·ing** 1 : declare sacred 2 : devote to a solemn purpose —**con·se·cra·tion** \ˌkänsə'krāshən\ *n*

con·sec·u·tive \kən'sek(y)ətiv\ *adj*
: following in order —**con·sec·u·tive·ly** *adv*

con·sen·sus \-'sensəs\ *n* 1 : agreement
in opinion 2 : collective opinion

con·sent \-'sent\ *vb* : give permission
or approval —**consent** *n*

con·se·quence \'känsə,kwens\ *n* 1 : result or effect 2 : importance —**con-
se·quent** \-,kwent, -,kwent\ *adj*
—**con·se·quent·ly** *adv*

con·se·quen·tial \,känsə'kwenchəl\ *adj*
: important

con·ser·va·tion \,känsər'vāshən\ *n*
: planned management of natural resources —**con·ser·va·tion·ist**
\-sh(ə)nəst\ *n*

con·ser·va·tive \kən'sərvətiv\ *adj* 1
: disposed to maintain the status quo
2 : cautious —**con·ser·va·tism**
\-və,tizəm\ *n* —**conservative** *n*

con·ser·va·to·ry \kən'sərvə,tōrē\ *n, pl*
-ries : school for art or music

con·serve \-'sərv\ *vb* -**served**; -**serv·ing**
: keep from wasting ~ \'kän,sərv\ *n*
: candied fruit or fruit preserves

con·sid·er \kən'sidər\ *vb* 1 : think
about 2 : give thoughtful attention to
3 : think that —**con·sid·er·ate**
\-'sid(ə)rət\ *adj* —**con·sid·er·ate·ly**
adv —**con·sid·er·ate·ness** *n* —**con-
sid·er·a·tion** \-,sidə'rāshən\ *n*

con·sid·er·able \-'sidər(ə)bəl,
-'sidrabəl\ *adj* 1 : significant 2 : noticeably large —**con·sid·er·a·bly**
\-blē\ *adv*

con·sid·er·ing \-(ə)riŋ\ *prep* : taking
notice of

con·sign \kən'sīn\ *vb* 1 : transfer 2
: send to an agent for sale —**con-
sign·ee** \,känsə'nē, -,sī-; kən,sī-\ *n*
—**con·sign·ment** \kən'sīnmənt\ *n*
—**con·sign·or** \,känsə'nόr, -,sī-;
kən,sī-\ *n*

con·sist \kən'sist\ *vb* 1 : be inherent
—used with *in* 2 : be made up —used
with *of*

con·sis·ten·cy \-'sistənsē\ *n, pl* -**cies** 1
: degree of thickness or firmness 2
: quality of being consistent

con·sis·tent \-tənt\ *adj* : being steady
and regular —**con·sis·tent·ly** *adv*

¹con·sole \kən'sōl\ *vb* -**soled**; -**sol·ing**
: soothe the grief of —**con·so·la·tion**
\,känsə'lāshən\ *n*

²con·sole \'kän,sōl\ *n* : cabinet or part
with controls

con·sol·i·date \kən'sälə,dāt\ *vb* -**dat-
ed**; -**dat·ing** : unite or compact
—**con·sol·i·da·tion** \-,sälə'dāshən\ *n*

con·som·mé \,känsə'mā\ *n* : clear soup

con·so·nance \'käns(ə)nəns\ *n* : agree-

ment or harmony —**con·so·nant**
\-s(ə)nənt\ *adj*

con·so·nant \-s(ə)nənt\ *n* 1 : speech
sound marked by constriction or closure in the breath channel 2 : letter
other than *a, e, i, o,* and *u* —**con·so-
nan·tal** \,känsə'nant?l\ *adj*

con·sort \'kän,sόrt\ *n* : spouse ~
\kən'sόrt\ *vb* : keep company

con·spic·u·ous \kən'spikyəwəs\ *adj*
: very noticeable —**con·spic·u·ous·ly**
adv

con·spire \kən'spī(ə)r\ *vb* -**spired**; -**spir-
ing** : secretly plan an unlawful act
—**con·spir·a·cy** \-'spirəsē\ *n* —**con-
spir·a·tor** \-'spirətər\ *n*

con·sta·ble \'känstəbəl, 'kən-\ *n* : police officer

con·stab·u·lary \kən'stabyə,lerē\ *n, pl*
-lar·ies : police force

con·stant \'känstənt\ *adj* 1 : steadfast
or faithful 2 : not varying 3 : continually recurring ~ *n* : something
unchanging —**con·stan·cy** \-stənsē\
n —**con·stant·ly** *adv*

con·stel·la·tion \,känstə'lāshən\ *n*
: group of stars

con·ster·na·tion \-stər'nāshən\ *n*
: amazed dismay

con·sti·pa·tion \,kän·stə'pāshən\ *n* : difficulty of defecation —**con·sti·pate**
\'känstə,pāt\ *vb*

con·stit·u·ent \kən'stichəwənt\ *adj* 1
: component 2 : having power to
elect ~ *n* 1 : component part 2 : one
who may vote for a representative
—**con·stit·u·en·cy** \-wənsē\ *n*

con·sti·tute \'känstə,t(y)üt\ *vb* -**tut·ed**;
-**tut·ing** 1 : establish 2 : be all or a
basic part of

con·sti·tu·tion \,känstə't(y)üshən\ *n* 1
: physical composition or structure 2
: the basic law of an organized body
or the document containing it —**con-
sti·tu·tion·al** \-əl\ *adj* —**con·sti·tu-
tion·al·i·ty** \-,t(y)üshə'nalətē\ *n*

con·strain \kən'strān\ *vb* 1 : compel 2
: confine 3 : restrain —**con·straint**
\-'strānt\ *n*

con·strict \-'strikt\ *vb* : draw or
squeeze together —**con·stric·tion**
\-'strikshən\ *n* —**con·stric·tive**
\-'striktiv\ *adj*

con·struct \kən'strəkt\ *vb* : build or
make —**con·struc·tion** \-'strəkshən\
n —**con·struc·tive** \-tiv\ *adj*

con·strue \kən'strü\ *vb* -**strued**; -**stru-
ing** : explain or interpret

con·sul \'känsəl\ *n* 1 : Roman magistrate 2 : government commercial official in a foreign country —**con·sul·ar**
\-sələr\ *adj* —**con·sul·ate** \-lət\ *n*

con·sult \kən'səlt\ vb 1 : ask advice or opinion of 2 : confer —con·sul·tant \-ənt\ n —con·sul·ta·tion \ˌkänsəl'tāshən\ n

con·sume \kən'süm\ vb -sumed; -sum·ing : eat or use up —con·sum·able adj —con·sum·er n

con·sum·mate \kən'səmət\ adj : complete or perfect ~ \'känsəˌmāt\ vb -mat·ed; -mat·ing : make complete —con·sum·ma·tion \ˌkänsə'māshən\ n

con·sump·tion \kən'səmpshən\ n 1 : act of consuming 2 : use of goods 3 : tuberculosis —con·sump·tive \-tiv\ adj or n

con·tact \'känˌtakt\ n 1 : a touching 2 : association or relationship 3 : connection or communication ~ vb 1 : come or bring into contact 2 : communicate with

con·ta·gion \kən'tājən\ n 1 : spread of disease by contact 2 : disease spread by contact —con·ta·gious \-jəs\ adj

con·tain \-'tān\ vb 1 : enclose or include 2 : have or hold within 3 : restrain —con·tain·er n —con·tain·ment n

con·tam·i·nate \kən'taməˌnāt\ vb -nat·ed; -nat·ing : soil or infect by contact or association —con·tam·i·na·tion \-ˌtamə'nāshən\ n

con·tem·plate \'käntəmˌplāt\ vb -plat·ed; -plat·ing : view or consider thoughtfully —con·tem·pla·tion \ˌkäntəm'plāshən\ n —con·tem·pla·tive \kən'templətiv; 'käntəmˌplāt-\ adj

con·tem·po·ra·ne·ous \kənˌtempə'rānēəs\ adj : contemporary

con·tem·po·rary \kən'tempəˌrerē\ adj 1 : occurring or existing at the same time 2 : of the same age —contemporary n

con·tempt \kən'tempt\ n 1 : feeling of scorn 2 : state of being despised 3 : disobedience to a court or legislature —con·tempt·ible \-'temptəbəl\ adj

con·temp·tu·ous \-tempchə(wə)s\ adj : feeling or expressing contempt —con·temp·tu·ous·ly adv

con·tend \-'tend\ vb 1 : strive against rivals or difficulties 2 : argue 3 : maintain or claim —con·tend·er n

¹con·tent \kən'tent\ adj : satisfied ~ vb : satisfy ~ n : ease of mind —con·tent·ed adj —con·tent·ed·ly adv —con·tent·ed·ness n —con·tent·ment \-mənt\ n

²con·tent \'känˌtent\ n 1 pl : something contained 2 pl : subject matter (as of a book) 3 : essential meaning 4 : proportion contained

con·ten·tion \kən'tenchən\ n : state of contending —con·ten·tious \-chəs\ adj

con·test \kən'test\ vb : dispute or challenge ~ \'känˌtest\ n 1 : struggle 2 : game —con·test·able \-'testəbəl\ adj —con·test·ably \-blē\ adv —con·tes·tant \-'testənt\ n

con·text \'känˌtekst\ n : words surrounding a word or phrase

con·tig·u·ous \kən'tigyəwəs\ adj : connected to or adjoining —con·ti·gu·i·ty \ˌkäntə'gyüətē\ n

con·ti·nence \'känt²nəns\ n 1 : self-restraint —con·ti·nent \-ənt\ adj

con·ti·nent \'känt²nənt, 'käntnənt\ n : great division of land on the globe —con·ti·nen·tal \ˌkänt²n'ent²l\ adj

con·tin·gen·cy \kən'tinjənsē\ n, pl -cies : possible event

con·tin·gent \-jənt\ adj : dependent on something else ~ n : a quota from an area or group

con·tin·u·al \kən'tinyə(wə)l\ adj 1 : continuous 2 : steadily recurring —con·tin·u·al·ly \-ē\ adv

con·tin·ue \kən'tinyü\ vb -tin·ued; -tin·u·ing 1 : remain in a place or condition 2 : endure 3 : resume after an intermission 4 : extend —con·tin·u·ance \-yəwəns\ n —con·tin·u·a·tion \-ˌtinyə'wāshən\ n

con·tin·u·ous \-'tinyəwəs\ adj : continuing without interruption —con·ti·nu·i·ty \ˌkänt²n'(y)üətē\ n —con·tin·u·ous·ly adv

con·tort \kən'tórt\ vb : twist out of shape —con·tor·tion \-'tórshən\ n

con·tour \'känˌtúr\ n 1 : outline 2 pl : shape

con·tra·band \'käntrəˌband\ n : illegal goods

con·tra·cep·tion \ˌkäntrə'sepshən\ n : prevention of conception —con·tra·cep·tive \-'septiv\ adj or n

con·tract \'känˌtrakt\ n : binding agreement ~ \kən'trakt, 1 usu 'känˌtrakt\ vb 1 : establish or undertake by contract 2 : become ill with 3 : drawn together so as to shorten 4 : shorten (a word) by omission —con·trac·tion \kən'trakshən\ n —con·trac·tor \'känˌtraktər, kən'trak-\ n —con·trac·tu·al \kən'trakchə(wə)l\ adj

con·tra·dict \ˌkäntrə'dikt\ vb : state the contrary of —con·tra·dic·tion

\-'dikshən\ *n* —con·tra·dic·to·ry \-'dikt(ə)rē\ *adj*

con·tral·to \kən'traltō\ *n, pl* -tos : lowest female voice

con·trap·tion \kən'trapshən\ *n* : device or contrivance

con·trary \'kän,trerē; *4 often* kən'tre(ə)rē\ *adj* 1 : opposite in character, nature, or position 2 : mutually opposed 3 : unfavorable 4 : uncooperative or stubborn —con·trari·ly \-'trerəlē, -'trer-\ *adv* —con·trari·wise \-,wīz\ *adv* —con·trary \'kän,trerē\ *n*

con·trast \'kän,trast\ *n* 1 : unlikeness shown by comparing 2 : unlike color or tone of adjacent parts — \kən'trast\ *vb* 1 : show differences 2 : compare so as to show differences

con·tra·vene \,käntrə'vēn\ *vb* -vened; -ven·ing : go or act contrary to

con·trib·ute \kən'tribyət\ *vb* -ut·ed; -ut·ing : give or help along with others —con·tri·bu·tion \,käntrə'byüshən\ *n* —con·trib·u·tor \kən'tribyətər\ *n* —con·trib·u·to·ry \-yə,tōrē\ *adj*

con·trite \'kän,trīt, kən'trīt\ *adj* : repentant —con·tri·tion \kən'trishən\ *n*

con·trive \kən'trīv\ *vb* -trived; -triv·ing 1 : devise or make with ingenuity 2 : bring about —con·triv·ance \-'trīvəns\ *n* —con·triv·er *n*

con·trol \-'trōl\ *vb* -ll- 1 : exercise power over 2 : dominate or rule ~ *n* 1 : power to direct or subordinate 2 : restraint 3 : regulating device —con·trol·la·ble *adj* —con·trol·ler \-'trōlər, 'kän,-\ *n*

con·tro·ver·sy \'käntrə,vərsē\ *n, pl* -sies : clash of opposing views —con·tro·ver·sial \,käntrə'vərshəl, -sēəl\ *adj*

con·tro·vert \'käntrə,vərt, ,käntrə'-\ *vb* : contradict —con·tro·vert·ible *adj*

con·tu·ma·cious \,känt(y)ə'māshəs\ *adj* : stubborn or insubordinate —con·tu·ma·cy \,känt'(y)üməsē, 'känt(y)ə-\ *n*

con·tu·me·ly \,känt'(y)üməlē, 'känt(y)ə,mēlē\ *n* : rudeness

con·tu·sion \kən't(y)üzhən\ *n* : bruise —con·tuse \-'t'(y)üz\ *vb*

co·nun·drum \kə'nəndrəm\ *n* : riddle

con·va·lesce \,känvə'les\ *vb* -lesced; -lesc·ing : gradually recover health —con·va·les·cence \-'les³ns\ *n* —con·va·les·cent \-³nt\ *adj or n*

con·vec·tion \kən'vekshən\ *n* : circulation in fluids due to warmer portions rising and colder ones sinking —con-

vect \-'vekt\ *vb* —con·vec·tion·al \-'veksh(ə)nəl\ *adj* —con·vec·tive \-'vektiv\ *adj*

con·vene \kən'vēn\ *vb* -vened; -ven·ing : assemble or meet

con·ve·nience \-'vēnyəns\ *n* 1 : personal comfort or ease 2 : device that saves work

con·ve·nient \-'nyənt\ *adj* 1 : suited to one's convenience 2 : near at hand —con·ve·nient·ly *adv*

con·vent \'känvənt, -,vent\ *n* : community of nuns

con·ven·tion \kən'venchən\ *n* 1 : agreement esp. between nations 2 : large meeting 3 : body of delegates 4 : accepted usage or way of behaving —con·ven·tion·al \-'vench(ə)nəl\ *adj* —con·ven·tion·al·ly *adv*

con·verge \kən'vərj\ *vb* -verged; -verg·ing : approach a single point —con·ver·gence \-'vərjəns\, con·ver·gen·cy \-jənsē\ *n* —con·ver·gent \-jənt\ *adj*

con·ver·sant \-'vərs³nt\ *adj* : having knowledge and experience

con·ver·sa·tion \,känvər'sāshən\ *n* : an informal talking together —con·ver·sa·tion·al \-sh(ə)nəl\ *adj*

¹con·verse \kən'vərs\ *vb* -versed; -vers·ing : engage in conversation —con·verse \'kän,vərs\ *n*

²con·verse \kən'vərs, 'kän,vərs\ *adj* : opposite —con·verse \'kän,vərs\ *n* —con·verse·ly *adv*

con·ver·sion \kən'vərzhən\ *n* 1 : change 2 : adoption of religion

con·vert \kən'vərt\ *vb* 1 : turn from one belief or party to another 2 : change ~ \'kän,vərt\ *n* : one who has undergone religious conversion —con·vert·er, con·ver·tor \-ər\ *n* —con·vert·ible *adj*

con·vert·ible \kən'vərtəbəl\ *n* : automobile with a removable top

con·vex \kän'veks, 'kän,-, kən-\ *adj* : curved or rounded like the outside of a sphere —con·vex·i·ty \kən'veksətē, kän-\ *n*

con·vey \kən'vā\ *vb* -veyed; -vey·ing : transport or transmit —con·vey·ance \-'vāəns\ *n* —con·vey·er, con·vey·or \-ər\ *n*

con·vict \kən'vikt\ *vb* : find guilty ~ \'kän,vikt\ *n* : person in prison

con·vic·tion \kən'vikshən\ *n* 1 : act of convicting 2 : strong belief

con·vince \-'vins\ *vb* -vinced; -vinc·ing : cause to believe

con·viv·ial \-'vivyəl, -'vivēəl\ *adj* : cheerful or festive —con·viv·i·al·i·ty \-,vivē'alətē\ *n*

con·voke \kən'vōk\ vb -voked; -vok·ing : call together to a meeting —con·vo·ca·tion \,känvə'kāshən\ n

con·vo·lut·ed \'känvə,lütəd\ adj 1 : intricately folded 2 : intricate

con·vo·lu·tion \,känvə'lüshən\ n 1 : a coiling together 2 : convoluted structure

con·voy \'kän,voi, kən'voi\ vb : accompany for protection ~ \'kän,voi\ n : group of vehicles moving together

con·vul·sion \kən'vəlshən\ n : violent involuntary muscle contraction —con·vulse \-'vəls\ vb —con·vul·sive \-'vəlsiv\ adj

coo \'kü\ n : sound of a pigeon —coo vb

cook \'kuk\ n : one who prepares food ~ vb : prepare food —cook·book \-,buk\ n —cook·er n —cook·ery \-(ə)rē\ n —cook·ware n

cook·ie, cooky \'kukē\ n, pl -ies : small sweet flat cake

cool \'kül\ adj 1 : moderately cold 2 : not excited 3 : showing dislike ~ vb : make or become cool ~ n 1 : cool time or place 2 : composure —cool·ant \-ənt\ n —cool·er n —cool·ly \'kül(l)ē\ adv —cool·ness n

coo·lie \'külē\ n : unskilled Oriental laborer

coop \'küp, 'kup\ n : enclosure usu. for poultry ~ vb : confine in or as if in a coop

co-op \'kō,äp\ n : cooperative

coo·per \'küpər, 'kup-\ n : barrel maker —cooper vb

co·op·er·ate \kō'äpə,rāt\ vb : act jointly —co·op·er·a·tion \-,äpə'rāshən\ n

co·op·er·a·tive \kō'äp(ə)rətiv, -'äpə,rāt-\ adj : willing to work with others ~ n : enterprise owned and run by those using its services

co-opt \kō'äpt\ vb 1 : elect as a colleague 2 : take over

co·or·di·nate \kō-'ôrd³nət, -'ôrdnət\ adj : equal esp. in rank ~ n : any of a set of numbers used in specifying the location of a point on a surface or in space ~ \-³n,āt\ vb -nat·ed; -nat·ing 1 : make or become coordinate 2 : work or act together harmoniously —co·or·di·na·tion \-,ôrd³n'āshən\ n —co·or·di·na·tor \-³n,āt-ər\ n

coot \'küt\ n : dark-colored ducklike bird

cop \'käp\ n : police officer

¹cope \'kōp\ n : cloaklike ecclesiastical vestment

²cope vb coped; cop·ing : deal with difficulties

co-pi·lot \'kō-\ n : assistant airplane pilot

cop·ing \'kōpiŋ\ n : top layer of a wall

co·pi·ous \'kōpēəs\ adj : very abundant —co·pi·ous·ly adv —co·pi·ous·ness n

cop·per \'käpər\ n 1 : malleable reddish metallic chemical element 2 : penny —cop·pery adj

cop·per·head n : largely coppery brown venomous snake

co·pra \'kōprə\ n : dried coconut meat

copse \'käps\ n : thicket

cop·u·la \'käpyələ\ n : verb linking subject and predicate —cop·u·la·tive \-,lātiv\ adj

cop·u·late \'käpyə,lāt\ vb -lat·ed; -lat·ing : engage in sexual intercourse —cop·u·la·tion \,käpyə'lāshən\ n

copy \'käpē\ n, pl cop·ies 1 : imitation or reproduction of an original 2 : writing to be set for printing ~ vb cop·ied; copy·ing 1 : make a copy of 2 : imitate —cop·i·er \-ər\ n —copy·ist n

copy·right n : sole right to a literary or artistic work ~ vb : get a copyright on

co·quette \kō'ket\ n : flirt

cor·al \'kôral\ n 1 : skeletal material of colonies of tiny sea polyps 2 : deep pink —coral adj

cord \'kôrd\ n 1 : usu. heavy string 2 : long slender anatomical structure 3 : measure of firewood equal to 128 cu. ft. 4 : small electrical cable ~ vb 1 : tie or furnish with a cord 2 : pile in cords

cor·dial \'kôrjəl\ adj : warmly welcoming ~ n : liqueur —cor·di·al·i·ty \,kôrj(ē)'alətē, kôrd'yal-\ n —cor·dial·ly \'kôrjəlē\ adv

cor·don \'kôrd³n\ n : encircling line of troops or police —cordon vb

cor·do·van \-əvən\ n : soft fine-grained leather

cor·du·roy \'kôrdə,roi\ n 1 : heavy ribbed fabric 2 pl : trousers of corduroy

core \'kōr\ n 1 : central part of some fruits 2 : inmost part ~ vb cored; cor·ing : take out the core of —cor·er n

cork \'kôrk\ n 1 : tough elastic bark of a European oak (cork oak) 2 : stopper of cork ~ vb : stop up with a cork —corky adj

cork·screw \ n : device for drawing corks from bottles

cor·mo·rant \'kôrm(ə)rənt, -ə,rant\ n : dark seabird

¹corn \ˈkȯrn\ n : cereal grass or its seeds ~ vb : cure or preserve in brine —**corn·meal** n —**corn·stalk** n —**corn·starch** n

²corn n : local hardening and thickening of skin

corn-cob n : axis on which the kernels of Indian corn are arranged

cor·nea \ˈkȯrnēə\ n : transparent part of the coat of the eyeball —**cor·ne·al** adj

cor·ner \ˈkȯrnər\ n 1 : point or angle formed by the meeting of lines or sides 2 : place where two streets meet 3 : inescapable position 4 : control of the supply of something ~ vb 1 : drive into a corner 2 : get a corner on 3 : turn a corner

cor·ner·stone n 1 : stone at a corner of a wall 2 : something basic

cor·net \kȯrˈnet\ n : trumpetlike instrument

cor·nice \ˈkȯrnəs\ n : horizontal wall projection

cor·nu·co·pia \ˌkȯrn(y)əˈkōpēə\ n : goat's horn filled with fruits and grain emblematic of abundance

co·rol·la \kəˈrälə\ n : petals of a flower

cor·ol·lary \ˈkȯrəˌlerē\ n, pl -lar·ies 1 : logical deduction 2 : consequence or result

co·ro·na \kəˈrōnə\ n : shining ring around the sun seen during eclipses

cor·o·nary \ˈkȯrəˌnerē\ adj : relating to the heart or its blood vessels ~ n : thrombosis of an artery supplying the heart

cor·o·na·tion \ˌkȯrəˈnāshən\ n : crowning of a monarch

cor·o·ner \ˈkȯrənər\ n : public official who investigates causes of suspicious deaths

¹cor·po·ral \ˈkȯrp(ə)rəl\ adj : bodily

²corporal n : noncommissioned officer ranking next below a sergeant

cor·po·ra·tion \ˌkȯrpəˈrāshən\ n : legal creation with the rights and liabilities of a person —**cor·po·rate** \ˈkȯrp(ə)rət\ adj

cor·po·re·al \kȯrˈpōrēəl\ adj : physical or material —**cor·po·re·al·ly** adv

corps \ˈkȯr\ n, pl corps \ˈkȯrz\ 1 : subdivision of a military force 2 : working group

corpse \ˈkȯrps\ n : dead body

cor·pu·lence \ˈkȯrpyələns\ or **cor·pu·len·cy** \-lənsē\ n : excessive fatness —**cor·pu·lent** \-lənt\ adj

cor·pus \ˈkȯrpəs\ n, pl -po·ra \-pərə\ 1 : corpse 2 : body of writings

cor·pus·cle \ˈkȯr(ˌ)pəsəl\ n : blood cell

cor·ral \kəˈral\ n : enclosure for animals —**corral** vb

cor·rect \-ˈrekt\ vb 1 : make right 2 : chastise ~ adj 1 : true or factual 2 : conforming to a standard —**cor·rec·tion** \-ˈrekshən\ n —**cor·rec·tive** \-ˈrektiv\ adj —**cor·rect·ly** \-ˈrek(t)lē\ adv —**cor·rect·ness** \-ˈrek(t)nəs\ n

cor·re·late \ˈkȯrəˌlāt\ vb -lat·ed; -lat·ing : show a connection between —**cor·re·late** \-lət, -ˌlāt\ n —**cor·re·la·tion** \ˌkȯrəˈlāshən\ n

cor·rel·a·tive \kəˈrelətiv\ adj : regularly used together —**correlative** n

cor·re·spond \ˌkȯrəˈspänd\ vb 1 : match 2 : communicate by letter —**cor·re·spon·dence** \-ˈspändəns\ n

cor·re·spon·dent \-ˈspändənt\ n 1 : person one writes to 2 : reporter

cor·ri·dor \ˈkȯrədər, -əˌdȯr\ n : passageway connecting rooms

cor·rob·o·rate \kəˈräbəˌrāt\ vb -rat·ed; -rat·ing : support with evidence —**cor·rob·o·ra·tion** \-ˌräbəˈrāshən\ n

cor·rode \kəˈrōd\ vb -rod·ed; -rod·ing : wear away by chemical action —**cor·ro·sion** \-ˈrōzhən\ n —**cor·ro·sive** \-ˈrōsiv\ adj or n

cor·ru·gate \ˈkȯrəˌgāt\ vb -gat·ed; -gat·ing : form into ridges and grooves —**cor·ru·ga·tion** \ˌkȯrəˈgāshən\ n

cor·rupt \kəˈrəpt\ vb 1 : change from good to bad 2 : bribe ~ adj : morally debased —**cor·rupt·ible** adj —**cor·rup·tion** \-ˈrəpshən\ n

cor·sage \kȯrˈsäzh, -ˈsäj\ n : bouquet worn by a woman

cor·set \ˈkȯrsət\ n : woman's stiffened undergarment

cor·tege \kȯrˈtezh, kȯrˌ-\ n : funeral procession

cor·tex \ˈkȯrˌteks\ n, pl -ti·ces \ˈkȯrtəˌsēz\ or -tex·es : outer or covering layer of an organism or part (as the brain) —**cor·ti·cal** \ˈkȯrtikəl\ adj

cor·ti·sone \ˈkȯrtəˌsōn, -ˌzōn\ n : adrenal hormone

cos·met·ic \käzˈmetik\ n : beautifying preparation ~ adj : relating to beautifying

cos·mic \ˈkäzmik\ adj 1 : relating to the cosmos 2 : vast or grand

cos·mo·naut \ˈkäzməˌnȯt\ n : Soviet astronaut

cos·mo·pol·i·tan \ˌkäzməˈpälətən\ n : belonging to all the world —**cosmopolitan** adj

cos·mos \ˈkäzməs also -ˌmōs, -ˌmäs\ n : universe

cos·sack \'käs,ak, -ək\ n : Russian czarist cavalryman

cost \'kȯst\ n 1 : amount paid for something 2 : loss or penalty ~ vb cost; cost·ing 1 : require so much in payment 2 : cause to pay, suffer, or lose —cost·li·ness \-lēnəs\ n —cost·ly \-lē\ adv

cos·tume \'käs,t(y)üm\ n : clothing

co·sy \'kōzē\ var of COZY

cot \'kät\ n : small bed

cote \'kōt, 'kät\ n : small shed or coop

co·te·rie \'kōtə,rē, ,kōtə'-\ n : exclusive group of persons

co·til·lion \kō'tilyən\ n : formal ball

cot·tage \'kätij\ n : small house

cot·ton \'kät²n\ n : soft fibrous plant substance or thread or cloth made of it —cot·ton·seed n —cot·tony adj

cot·ton·mouth n : poisonous snake

couch \'kauch\ vb 1 : lie or place on a couch 2 : phrase ~ n : bed or sofa

cou·gar \'kügər, -,gär\ n : large tawny wild American cat

cough \'kȯf\ vb : force air from the lungs with short sharp noises —cough n

could \kəd, (')kud\ past of CAN

coun·cil \'kaunsəl\ n 1 : assembly or meeting 2 : body of lawmakers —coun·cil·lor, coun·cil·or \-s(ə)lər\ n —coun·cil·man \-mən\ n —coun·cil·wom·an n

coun·sel \'kaunsəl\ n 1 : advice 2 : deliberation together 3 pl -sel : lawyer ~ vb -seled or -selled; -sel·ing or -sel·ling 1 : advise 2 : consult together —coun·sel·or, coun·sel·lor \-s(ə)lər\ n

¹count \'kaunt\ vb 1 : name or indicate one by one to find the total number 2 : recite numbers in order 3 : rely 4 : be of value or account ~ n 1 : act of counting or the total obtained by counting 2 : charge in an indictment —count·able adj

²count n : European nobleman

coun·te·nance \'kaunt²nəns, 'kauntnəns\ n : face or facial expression ~ vb -nanced; -nanc·ing : allow or encourage

¹count·er \'kauntər\ n 1 : piece for reckoning or games 2 : surface over which business is transacted

²count·er n : one that counts

³count·er vb 1 : oppose ~ adv : in an opposite direction ~ n : offsetting force or move ~ adj : contrary

counter- prefix 1 : contrary or opposite 2 : opposing 3 : retaliatory

counteraccusation
counteraggression
counterargue
counterassault
counterattack
counterbid
counterblockade
counterblow
countercampaign
counterchallenge
countercharge
counterclaim
countercomplaint
countercoup
countercriticism
counterdemand
counterdemonstration
counterdemonstrator
countereffect
countereffort
counterembargo
counterevidence
counterguerrilla
counterinflationary
counterinfluence
counterintrigue
countermeasure
countermove
countermovement
counteroffer
counterpetition
counterploy
counterpower
counterpressure
counterpropaganda
counterproposal
counterprotest
counterquestion
counterraid
counterrally
counterrebuttal
counterreform
counterresponse
counterretaliation
counterrevolution
counterstrategy
counterstyle
countersuggestion
countersuit
countertendency
counterterror
counterterrorism
counterterrorist
counterthreat
counterthrust
countertrend

coun·ter·act vb : lessen the force of

coun·ter·bal·ance \-,-\ n : balancing influence or weight ~ vb : oppose or balance

coun·ter·clock·wise adv : opposite to the way a clock's hands move —counterclockwise adj

coun·ter·feit \'kauntər,fit\ vb 1 : copy in order to deceive 2 : pretend ~ adj : spurious ~ n : fraudulent copy —coun·ter·feit·er n

coun·ter·mand \-,mand\ vb : supersede with a contrary order

coun·ter·part n : one that is similar or corresponds

coun·ter·point n : music with interwoven melodies

coun·ter·sign n : secret signal ~ vb : add a confirming signature to

count·ess \'kauntəs\ n : wife or widow of a count or an earl or a woman holding that rank in her own right

count·less \-ləs\ adj : too many to be numbered

coun·try \'kəntrē\ n, pl -tries 1 : nation

2 : rural area — adj : rural —**coun-try-man** \-mən\ n

coun-try-side n : rural area or its people

coun-ty \'kaůntē\ n, pl **-ties** : local government division esp. of a state

coup \'kü\ n, pl **coups** \'küz\ 1 : brilliant sudden action or plan 2 : sudden overthrow of a government

cou-pé, coupe \kü'pā, 'küp\ n : 2-door automobile with an enclosed body

cou-ple \'kəpəl\ vb **-pled; -pling** : link together ~ n 1 : pair 2 : two persons closely associated or married

cou-pling \'kəpliŋ\ n : connecting device

cou-pon \'k(y)ü,pän\ n : certificate redeemable for goods or a cash discount

cour-age \'kərij\ n : ability to conquer fear or despair —**cou-ra-geous** \kə'rājəs\ adj

cou-ri-er \'kůrēər, 'kərē-\ n : messenger

course \'kōrs\ n 1 : progress 2 : ground over which something moves 3 : part of a meal served at one time 4 : method of procedure 5 : subject taught in a series of classes ~ vb **coursed; cours-ing** 1 : hunt with dogs 2 : run speedily —**of course** 1 : as might be expected

court \'kōrt\ n 1 : residence of a sovereign 2 : sovereign and his officials and advisers 3 : area enclosed by a building 4 : space marked for playing a game 5 : place where justice is administered ~ vb : woo —**court-house** n —**court-room** n —**court-ship** \-,ship\ n

cour-te-ous \'kərtēəs\ adj : showing politeness and respect for others —**cour-te-ous-ly** adv

cour-te-san \'kōrtəzən, 'kərt-\ n : prostitute

cour-te-sy \'kərtəsē\ n, pl **-sies** : courteous behavior

court-ier \'kōrtēər, 'kōrtyər\ n : person in attendance at a royal court

court-ly \'kōrtlē\ adj **-li-er; -est** : polite or elegant —**court-li-ness** n

court-mar-tial n, pl **courts-martial** : military trial court —**court-martial** vb

court-yard n : enclosure open to the sky that is attached to a house

cous-in \'kəz²n\ n : child of one's uncle or aunt

cove \'kōv\ n : sheltered inlet or bay

cov-e-nant \'kəv(ə)nənt\ n : binding agreement —**cov-e-nant** \-(ə)nənt, -ə,nant\ vb

cov-er \'kəvər\ vb 1 : place something over or upon 2 : clothe 3 : protect or hide 4 : include or deal with ~ n : something that covers —**cov-er-age** \-(ə)rij\ n

cov-er-let \-lət\ n : bedspread

co-vert \'kō(,)vərt, 'kəvərt\ adj : secret ~ \'kəvərt, 'kō-\ n : thicket that shelters animals

cov-et \'kəvət\ vb : desire enviously —**cov-et-ous** adj

cov-ey \'kəvē\ n, pl **-eys** : bird with her young 2 : small flock (as of quail)

¹**cow** \'kaů\ n : adult female of a bovine animal —**cow-hide** n

²**cow** vb : intimidate

cow-ard \'kaů(ə)rd\ n : one who lacks courage —**cow-ard-ice** \-əs\ n —**cow-ard-ly** adv or adj

cow-boy n : a mounted ranch hand who tends cattle —**cow-girl** n

cow-er \'kaů(ə)r\ vb : shrink from fear or cold

cowl \'kaůl\ n : monk's hood

cow-lick \'kaů,lik\ n : turned-up tuft of hair that resists control

cow-slip \-,slip\ n : yellow flower

cox-swain \'käksən, -,swān\ n : person who steers a boat

coy \'kói\ adj : shy or pretending shyness

coy-ote \'kī,ōt, kī'ōt-ē\ n, pl **coy-otes** or **coyote** : small No. American wolf

coz-en \'kəz²n\ vb : cheat

co-zy \'kōzē\ adj **-zi-er; -est** : snug

crab \'krab\ n 1 : short broad shellfish with pincers

crab-by \'krabē\ adj **-bi-er; -est** : cross

¹**crack** \'krak\ vb 1 : break with a sharp sound 2 : fail in tone 3 : break without completely separating ~ n 1 : sudden sharp noise 2 : witty remark 3 : narrow break 4 : sharp blow 5 : try

²**crack** adj : extremely proficient

crack-down n : disciplinary action —**crack down** vb

crack-er \-ər\ n : thin crisp bakery product

crack-le \'krakəl\ vb **-led; -ling** 1 : make snapping noises 2 : develop fine cracks in a surface —**crackle** n

crack-pot \'krak,pät\ n : eccentric

crack-up n : crash

cra-dle \'krād²l\ n : baby's bed ~ vb **-dled; -dling** 1 : place in a cradle 2 : hold securely

craft \'kraft\ n 1 : occupation requiring special skill 2 : craftiness 3 pl usu **craft** : structure designed to provide transportation 4 pl usu **craft** : small boat —**crafts·man** \'kraftsmən\ n —**crafts·man·ship** \-,ship\ n

crafty \'kraftē\ adj **craft·i·er; -est** : sly —**craft·i·ness** n

crag \'krag\ n : steep cliff —**crag·gy** \-ē\ adj

cram \'kram\ vb **-mm-** 1 : eat greedily 2 : pack in tight 3 : study intensely for a test

cramp \'kramp\ n 1 : sudden painful contraction of muscle 2 pl : sharp abdominal pains ~ vb 1 : affect with cramp 2 : restrain

cran·ber·ry \'kran,berē, -b(ə)rē\ n : red acid berry of a trailing plant

crane \'krān\ n 1 : tall wading bird 2 : machine for lifting heavy objects ~ vb **craned; cran·ing** : stretch one's neck to see

cra·ni·um \'krānēəm\ n, pl **-ni·ums** or **-nia** \-nēə\ : skull —**cra·ni·al** \-əl\ adj

crank \'krank\ n 1 : bent lever turned to operate a machine 2 : eccentric ~ vb : start or operate by turning a crank

cranky \'krankē\ adj **crank·i·er; -est** : irritable

cran·ny \'kranē\ n, pl **-nies** : crevice

craps \'kraps\ n : dice game

crash \'krash\ vb 1 : break noisily 2 : fall and hit something with noise and damage ~ n 1 : loud sound 2 : action of crashing 3 : failure

crass \'kras\ adj : crude or unfeeling

crate \'krāt\ n : wooden shipping container —**crate** vb

cra·ter \'krātər\ n : volcanic depression

cra·vat \krə'vat\ n : necktie

crave \'krāv\ vb **craved; crav·ing** : long for —**crav·ing** n

cra·ven \'krāvən\ adj : cowardly —**craven** n

craw·fish \'kro,fish\ n : crayfish

crawl \'krȯl\ vb 1 : move slowly (as by drawing the body along the ground) 2 : swarm with creeping things ~ n : very slow pace

cray·fish \'krā,fish\ n : lobsterlike freshwater crustacean

cray·on \'krā,än, -ən\ n : stick of chalk or wax used for drawing or coloring —**crayon** vb

craze \'krāz\ vb **crazed; craz·ing** : make or become insane ~ n : fad

cra·zy \'krāzē\ adj **cra·zi·er; -est** 1 : mentally disordered 2 : wildly impractical —**cra·zi·ly** adv —**cra·zi·ness** n

creak \'krēk\ vb or n : squeak —**creaky** adj

cream \'krēm\ n 1 : yellowish fat-rich part of milk 2 : thick smooth sauce, confection, or cosmetic 3 : choicest part ~ vb : beat into creamy consistency —**creamy** adj

cream·ery \-(ə)rē\ n, pl **-er·ies** : place where butter and cheese are made

crease \'krēs\ n : line made by folding —**crease** vb

cre·ate \krē'āt\ vb **-at·ed; -at·ing** : bring into being —**cre·ation** \krē'āshən\ n —**cre·ative** \-iv\ adj —**cre·ativ·i·ty** \,krē(,)ā'tivətē, ,krēə'-\ n —**cre·ator** \krē'ātər\ n

crea·ture \'krēchər\ n : lower animal or human being

cre·dence \'krēd²ns\ n : belief

cre·den·tials \kri'denchəlz\ n : evidence of qualifications or authority

cred·i·ble \'kredəbəl\ adj : believable —**cred·i·bil·i·ty** \,kredə'bilətē\ n

cred·it \'kredət\ n 1 : balance in a person's favor 2 : time given to pay for goods 3 : belief 4 : esteem 5 : source of honor ~ vb 1 : believe 2 : give credit to

cred·it·able \-əbəl\ adj : worthy of esteem or praise —**cred·it·ably** \-əblē\ adv

cred·i·tor \-ər\ n : person to whom money is owed

cred·u·lous \'krejələs\ adj : easily convinced —**cre·du·li·ty** \kri'd(y)ülətē\ n

creed \'krēd\ n : statement of essential beliefs

creek \'krēk, 'krik\ n : small stream

creel \'krēl\ n : basket for carrying fish

creep \'krēp\ vb **crept** \'krept\; **creep·ing** 1 : crawl 2 : grow over a surface like ivy —**creep** n —**creep·er** n

cre·mate \'krē,māt\ vb **-mat·ed; -mat·ing** : burn up (a corpse) —**cre·ma·tion** \kri'māshən\ n —**cre·ma·to·ry** \'krēmə,tōrē, 'krem-\ n

cre·o·sote \'krēə,sōt\ n : oily wood preservative

crepe, crêpe \'krāp\ n : light crinkled fabric

cre·scen·do \krə'shendō\ adv or adj : growing louder —**crescendo** n

cres·cent \'kres²nt\ n : shape of the moon between new moon and first quarter

crest \'krest\ n 1 : tuft on a bird's head 2 : top of a hill or wave 3 : part of a coat of arms ~ vb : rise to a crest —**crest·fall·en** adj : sad

cre·tin \'krēt²n\ n : person with marked mental deficiency —**cre·tin·ism** \-,izəm\ n

cre·vasse \kri'vas\ *n* : deep fissure esp. in a glacier

crev·ice \'krevəs\ *n* : narrow fissure

crew \'krü\ *n* 1 : body of workers (as on a ship) —**crew·man** \-mən\ *n*

crib \'krib\ *n* 1 : manger 2 : grain storage bin 3 : baby's bed ~ *vb* -**bb**- : put in a crib

crib·bage \-ij\ *n* : card game scored by moving pegs on a board (**cribbage board**)

crick \'krik\ *n* : muscle spasm

¹**crick·et** \'krikət\ *n* : insect noted for the chirping of the male

²**cricket** *n* : bat and ball game played on a field with wickets

cri·er \'krī(ə)r\ *n* : one who calls out announcements

crime \'krīm\ *n* : serious violation of law

crim·i·nal \'krimən³l\ *adj* : relating to or being a crime or its punishment ~ *n* : one who commits a crime

crimp \'krimp\ *vb* : cause to become crinkled, wavy, or bent —**crimp** *n*

crim·son \'krimzən\ *n* : deep red —**crimson** *adj*

cringe \'krinj\ *vb* **cringed; cring·ing** : shrink in fear

crin·kle \'kriŋkəl\ *vb* -**kled; -kling** : wrinkle —**crinkle** *n* —**crin·kly** \-k(ə)lē\ *adj*

crin·o·line \'krin³lən\ *n* 1 : stiff cloth 2 : full stiff skirt or petticoat

crip·ple \'kripəl\ *n* : disabled person ~ *vb* -**pled; -pling** : disable

cri·sis \'krīsəs\ *n, pl* **cri·ses** \-‚sēz\ : decisive or critical moment

crisp \'krisp\ *adj* 1 : easily crumbled 2 : firm and fresh 3 : lively 4 : invigorating —**crisp** *vb* —**crisp·ly** *adv* —**crisp·ness** *n* —**crispy** *adj*

criss·cross \'kris‚kròs\ *n* : pattern of crossed lines ~ *vb* : mark with or follow a crisscross

cri·te·ri·on \krī'tirēən\ *n, pl* -**ria** \-ēə\ : standard

crit·ic \'kritik\ *n* : judge of literary or artistic works

crit·i·cal \-ikəl\ *adj* 1 : inclined to criticize 2 : being a crisis 3 : relating to criticism or critics —**crit·i·cal·ly** \-ik(ə)lē\ *adv*

crit·i·cize \-ə‚sīz\ *vb* -**cized; -cizing** 1 : judge as a critic 2 : find fault —**crit·i·cism** \-ə‚sizəm\ *n*

cri·tique \krə'tēk\ *n* : critical estimate

croak \'krōk\ *n* : hoarse harsh cry (as of a frog) —**croak** *vb*

cro·chet \krō'shā\ *n* : needlework done with a hooked needle —**crochet**

crock \'kräk\ *n* : thick earthenware pot or jar —**crock·ery** \-(ə)rē\ *n*

croc·o·dile \'kräkə‚dīl\ *n* : reptile of tropical waters

cro·cus \'krōkəs\ *n, pl* -**cus·es** : herb with spring flowers

crone \'krōn\ *n* : ugly old woman

cro·ny \'krōnē\ *n, pl* -**nies** : chum

crook \'krûk\ *n* 1 : bent or curved tool or part 2 : thief ~ *vb* : curve sharply

crook·ed \'krûkəd\ *adj* 1 : bent 2 : dishonest —**crook·ed·ness** *n*

croon \'krün\ *vb* : sing softly —**croon·er** *n*

crop \'kräp\ *n* 1 : pouch in the throat of a bird or insect 2 : short riding whip 3 : something that can be harvested ~ *vb* -**pp**- 1 : trim 2 : appear unexpectedly —used with *up*

cro·quet \krō'kā\ *n* : lawn game of driving balls through wickets

cro·quette \-'ket\ *n* : mass of minced food deep fried

cro·sier \'krōzhər\ *n* : bishop's staff

cross \'kròs\ *n* 1 : figure or structure consisting of an upright and a cross piece 2 : interbreeding of unlike strains ~ *vb* 1 : intersect 2 : cancel 3 : go or extend across 4 : interbreed ~ *adj* 1 : going across 2 : contrary 3 : marked by bad temper —**cross·ing** *n* —**cross·ly** *adv*

cross·bow \-‚bō\ *n* : short bow mounted on a rifle stock

cross·breed *vb* -**bred; -breed·ing** : hybridize

cross·ex·am·ine *vb* : question about earlier testimony —**cross·ex·am·i·na·tion** *n*

cross·eye *n* : abnormality in which the eye turns toward the nose —**cross·eyed** *adj*

cross·re·fer *vb* : refer to another place (as in a book) —**cross·ref·er·ence** *n*

cross·roads *n* : place where 2 roads cross

cross section *n* : representative portion

cross·walk *n* : path for pedestrians crossing a street

cross·ways *adv* : crosswise

cross·wise \-‚wīz\ *adv* : so as to cross something —**crosswise** *adj*

crotch \'kräch\ *n* : angle formed by the parting of 2 legs or branches

crotch·et \'krächət\ *n* : odd notion —**crotch·ety** *adj*

crouch \'kraúch\ *vb* : stoop over —**crouch** *n*

croup \'krüp\ *n* : laryngitis of infants

crou·ton \'krü‚tän\ *n* : bit of toast

crow \'krō\ *n* : large glossy black bird

²**crow** \'krō\ vb **1** : make the loud sound of the cock **2** : gloat ~ n : cry of the cock

crow-bar \'krō-ˌbär\ n : metal bar used as a pry or lever

crowd \'kraȯd\ vb : collect or cram together ~ n : large number of people

crown \'kraȯn\ n **1** : wreath of honor or victory **2** : royal headdress **3** : top or highest part ~ vb **1** : place a crown on **2** : honor —**crowned** \'kraȯnd\ adj

cru·cial \'krüshəl\ adj : vitally important

cru·ci·ble \'krüsəbəl\ n : heat-resisting container

cru·ci·fix \-ˌfiks\ n : representation of Christ on the cross

cru·ci·fix·ion \ˌkrüsə'fikshən\ n : act of crucifying

cru·ci·fy \-ˌfī\ vb **-fied; -fy·ing 1** : put to death on a cross **2** : persecute

crude \'krüd\ adj **crud·er; -est 1** : not refined **2** : lacking grace or elegance ~ n : unrefined petroleum —**crude·ly** adv —**cru·di·ty** \-ətē\ n

cru·el \'krüəl\ adj **-el·er** or **-el·ler; -el·est** or **-el·lest** : causing suffering to others —**cru·el·ly** \-ē\ adv —**cru·el·ty** \-tē\ n

cru·et \'krüət\ n : bottle for salad dressings

cruise \'krüz\ vb **cruised; cruis·ing 1** : sail to several ports **2** : travel at the most efficient speed —**cruise** n

cruis·er \'krüzər\ n **1** : warship **2** : police car

crumb \'krəm\ n : small fragment

crum·ble \'krəmbəl\ vb **-bled; -bling** : break into small pieces —**crum·bly** \-b(ə)lē\ adj

crum·ple \-pəl\ vb **-pled; -pling 1** : crush together **2** : collapse

crunch \'krənch\ vb : chew or press with a crushing noise ~ n : crunching sound —**crunchy** adj

cru·sade \krü'sād\ n **1** cap : medieval Christian expedition to the Holy Land **2** : reform movement —**crusade** vb —**cru·sad·er** n

crush \'krəsh\ vb **1** : squeeze out of shape **2** : grind or pound to bits **3** : suppress ~ n **1** : severe crowding **2** : infatuation

crust \'krəst\ n **1** : hard outer part of bread or a pie **2** : hard surface layer —**crust·al** adj —**crusty** adj

crus·ta·cean \ˌkrəs'tāshən\ n : aquatic arthropod having a firm shell

crutch \'krəch\ n : support for use by the disabled in walking

crux \'krəks, 'krüks\ n, pl **crux·es 1** : hard problem **2** : crucial point

cry \'krī\ vb **cried; cry·ing 1** : call out **2** : weep ~ n, pl **cries 1** : shout **2** : fit of weeping **3** : characteristic sound of an animal

crypt \'kript\ n : underground chamber

cryp·tic \'kriptik\ adj : enigmatic

cryp·tog·ra·phy \krip'tägrəfē\ n : coding and decoding of messages —**cryp·tog·ra·pher** \-fər\ n

crys·tal \'kristʔl\ n **1** : transparent quartz **2** : something (as glass) like crystal **3** : body formed by solidification that has a regular repeating atomic arrangement —**crys·tal·line** \-tələn\ adj

crys·tal·lize \-tə,līz\ vb **-lized; -liz·ing** : form crystals or a definite shape —**crys·tal·li·za·tion** \ˌkristələ'zāshən\ n

cub \'kəb\ n : young animal

cub·by·hole \'kəbē,hōl\ n : small confined space

cube \'kyüb\ n **1** : solid having 6 equal square sides **2** : product obtained by taking a number 3 times as a factor ~ vb **cubed; cub·ing 1** : raise to the 3d power **2** : form into a cube **3** : cut into cubes —**cu·bic** \'kyübik\ adj

cu·bi·cle \-bikəl\ n : small room

cu·bit \-bət\ n : unit of length equal to about 18 inches

cuck·old \'kəkəld, 'kuk-\ n : man whose wife is unfaithful

cuck·oo \'kükü, 'kuk-\ n, pl **-oos** : brown European bird ~ adj : silly

cu·cum·ber \'kyü(ˌ)kəmbər\ n : fleshy fruit related to the gourds

cud \'kəd\ n : food chewed again by ruminating animals

cud·dle \'kədʔl\ vb **-dled; -dling** : lie close

cud·gel \'kəjəl\ n or vb : club

¹**cue** \'kyü\ n **1** : signal —**cue** vb

²**cue** n : stick used in pool

¹**cuff** \'kəf\ n **1** : part of a sleeve encircling the wrist **2** : folded trouser hem

²**cuff** vb or n : slap

cui·sine \kwi'zēn\ n : manner of cooking

cu·li·nary \'kələˌnerē, 'kyülə-\ adj : of or relating to cookery

cull \'kəl\ vb : select

cul·mi·nate \'kəlmə,nāt\ vb **-nat·ed; -nat·ing** : rise to the highest point —**cul·mi·na·tion** \ˌkəlmə'nāshən\ n

cul·pa·ble \'kəlpəbəl\ adj : deserving blame

cul·prit \'kəlprət\ n : guilty person

cult \'kəlt\ n **1** : religious system **2** : faddish devotion —**cult·ist** n

cul·ti·vate \'kəltə,vāt\ vb **-vat·ed; -vat-**

ing 1 : prepare for crops 2 : foster the growth of 3 : refine —**cul·ti·va·tion** \ˌkəltə'vāshən\ n

cul·ture \'kəlchər\ n 1 : cultivation 2 : refinement of intellectual and artistic taste 3 : particular form or stage of civilization —**cul·tur·al** \'kəlch(ə)rəl\ adj —**cul·tured** \'kəlchərd\ adj

cul·vert \'kəlvərt\ n : drain crossing under a road or railroad

cum·ber \'kəmbər\ vb : burden —**cumber·some** adj —**cum·brous** \-brəs\ adj

cu·mu·la·tive \'kyümyələtiv, -,lāt-\ adj : increasing by additions

cu·mu·lus \-ləs\ n, pl -li \-,lī, -,lē\ : massive rounded cloud

cun·ning \'kəniŋ\ adj 1 : crafty 2 : clever 3 : appealing ~ n 1 : skill 2 : craftiness

cup \'kəp\ n 1 : small drinking vessel 2 : contents of a cup ~ vb -pp- : shape like a cup —**cup·ful** n

cup·board \'kəbərd\ n : small storage closet

cup·cake n : small cake

cu·pid·i·ty \kyü'pidətē\ n, pl -ties : excessive desire for money

cu·po·la \'kyüpələ, -,lō\ n : small rooftop structure

cur \'kər\ n : mongrel dog

cu·rate \'kyürət\ n : clergyman —**cu·ra·cy** \-əsē\ n

cu·ra·tor \kyü'rātər\ n : one in charge of a museum or zoo

curb \'kərb\ n 1 : restraint 2 : raised edging along a street ~ vb : hold back

curd \'kərd\ n : coagulated milk

cur·dle \'kərdᵊl\ vb -dled; -dling 1 : form curds 2 : sour

cure \'kyür\ n 1 : recovery from disease 2 : remedy ~ vb cured; cur·ing 1 : restore to health 2 : process for storage or use —**cur·able** adj

cur·few \'kər,fyü\ n : requirement to be off the streets at a set hour

cu·rio \'kyürē,ō\ n, pl -ri·os : rare or unusual article

cu·ri·ous \'kyürēəs\ adj 1 : eager to learn 2 : strange —**cu·ri·os·i·ty** \ˌkyürē'äsətē\ n

curl \'kərl\ vb 1 : form into ringlets 2 : curve ~ n 1 : ringlet of hair 2 : something with a spiral form —**curl·er** n —**curly** adj

cur·lew \-(y)ü\ n, pl -lews or -lew : long-legged brownish bird

curli·cue \'kərli,kyü\ n : fanciful curve

cur·rant \'kərənt\ n 1 : small seedless raisin 2 : berry of a shrub

cur·ren·cy \'kərənsē\ n, pl -cies 1 : general use or acceptance 2 : money

cur·rent \'kərənt\ adj : occurring in or belonging to the present ~ n 1 : swiftest part of a stream 2 : flow of electric charge

cur·ric·u·lum \kə'rikyələm\ n, pl -la \-lə\ : course of study

¹**cur·ry** \'kərē\ vb -ried; -ry·ing : brush (a horse) with a wire brush (**curry-comb**) —**curry favor** : seek favor by flattery

²**curry** n, pl -ries : blend of spices or a food seasoned with this

curse \'kərs\ n 1 : a calling down of evil or harm upon one 2 : afflicton ~ vb cursed; curs·ing 1 : call down injury upon 2 : swear at 3 : afflict

cur·so·ry \'kərs(ə)rē\ adj : hastily done

curt \'kərt\ adj : rudely abrupt —**curt·ly** adv

cur·tail \(,)kər'tāl\ vb : shorten —**cur·tail·ment** n

cur·tain \'kərtᵊn\ n : hanging screen that can be drawn back or raised —**curtain** vb

curt·sy, curt·sey \'kərtsē\ n, pl -sies or -seys : courteous bow made by bending the knees —**curtsy** vb

cur·va·ture \'kərvə,chùr\ n : amount or state of curving

curve \'kərv\ vb curved; curv·ing : bend from a straight line or course ~ n 1 : a bending without angles 2 : something curved

cush·ion \'kùshən\ n 1 : soft pillow 2 : something that eases or protects ~ vb 1 : provide with a cushion 2 : soften the force of

cusp \'kəsp\ n : pointed end

cus·pid \'kəspəd\ n : a canine tooth

cus·pi·dor \'kəspə,dòr\ n : spittoon

cus·tard \'kəstərd\ n : sweetened cooked mixture of milk and eggs

cus·to·dy \'kəstədē\ n, pl -dies : immediate care or charge —**cus·to·di·al** \ˌkəs'tōdēəl\ adj —**cus·to·di·an** \-ēən\ n

cus·tom \'kəstəm\ n 1 : habitual course of action 2 pl : import taxes ~ adj : made to personal order —**cus·tom·ar·i·ly** \ˌkəstə'merəlē\ adv —**cus·tom·ary** \'kəstə,merē\ adj —**cus·tom-built** adj **cus·tom-made** adj

cus·tom·er \'kəstəmər\ n : buyer

cut \'kət\ vb cut; cut·ting 1 : penetrate or divide with a sharp edge 2 : experience the growth of (a tooth) through the gum 3 : shorten 4 : remove by severing 5 : intersect ~ n 1

: something separated by cutting **2** : reduction —**cut in** vb : thrust oneself between others

cu·ta·ne·ous \kyů'tānēǝs\ adj : relating to the skin

cute \'kyüt\ adj **cut·er; -est** : pretty

cu·ti·cle \'kyütikǝl\ n : outer layer (as of skin)

cut·lass \'kǝtlǝs\ n : short heavy curved sword

cut·lery \-lǝrē\ n : cutting utensils

cut·let \-lǝt\ n : slice of meat

cut·ter \'kǝtǝr\ n **1** : tool or machine for cutting **2** : small armed motorboat **3** : light sleigh

cut·throat n : murderer ~ adj : ruthless

-cy \sē\ n suffix **1** : action or practice **2** : rank or office **3** : body **4** : state or quality

cy·a·nide \'sīǝ,nīd, -nǝd\ n : poisonous chemical salt

cy·cle \'sīkǝl, 4 also 'sikǝl\ n **1** : period of time for a series of repeated events **2** : recurring round of events **3** : long period of time ~ vb **-cled; -cling** : ride a cycle

—**cy·clic** \'sīklik, 'sik-\, **cy·cli·cal** \-ǝl\ adj —**cy·clist** \'sīk(ǝ)lǝst, 'sik-\ n

cy·clone \'sī,klōn\ n : tornado —**cy·clon·ic** \sī'klänik\ adj

cy·clo·pe·dia, cy·clo·pae·dia \,sīklǝ-'pēdēǝ\ n : encyclopedia

cyl·in·der \'silǝndǝr\ n **1** : long round body or figure **2** : rotating chamber in a revolver **3** : piston chamber in an engine —**cy·lin·dri·cal** \sǝ'lindrikǝl\ adj

cym·bal \'simbǝl\ n : one of a pair of concave brass plates clashed together

cyn·ic \'sinik\ n : one who attributes all actions to selfish motives —**cyn·i·cal** \-ikǝl\ adj —**cyn·i·cism** \-ǝ,sizǝm\ n

cy·no·sure \'sīnǝ,shůr, 'sinǝ-\ n : center of attraction

cy·press \'sīprǝs\ n : evergreen tree related to the pines

cyst \'sist\ n : abnormal bodily sac —**cys·tic** \'sistik\ adj

czar \'zär\ n : ruler of Russia until 1917 —**czar·ist** n or adj

D

d \'dē\ n, pl **d's** or **ds** \'dēz\ : 4th letter of the alphabet

¹dab \'dab\ n : gentle touch or stroke ~ vb **-bb-** : touch or apply lightly

²dab n : small amount

dab·ble \'dabǝl\ vb **-bled; -bling 1** : splash **2** : work without serious effort

dachs·hund \'däks,hůnt\ : small dog with a long body and short legs

dad \'dad\ n : father

dad·dy \'dadē\ n, pl **-dies** : father

daf·fo·dil \'dafǝ,dil\ n : narcissus with trumpetlike flowers

daft \'daft\ adj : foolish —**daft·ness** n

dag·ger \'dagǝr\ n : knife for stabbing

dahl·ia \'dalyǝ, 'däl-\ n : tuberous herb with showy flowers

dai·ly \'dālē\ adj **1** : occurring, done, or used every day or every weekday **2** : computed in terms of one day ~ n, pl **-lies** : daily newspaper —**daily** adv

dain·ty \'dāntē\ n, pl **-ties** : something delicious ~ adj **-ti·er; -est** : delicately pretty —**dain·ti·ly** adv —**dain·ti·ness** n

dairy \'de(ǝ)rē\ n, pl **-ies** : farm that produces or company that processes milk —**dairy·ing** \'derēin\ n —**dairy-maid** n —**dairy·man** \-mǝn, -,man\ n

da·is \'dāǝs, 'dī-\ n : raised platform (as for a speaker)

dai·sy \'dāzē\ n, pl **-sies** : tall leafy-stemmed plant bearing showy flowers

dale \'dāl\ n : valley

dal·ly \'dalē\ vb **-lied; -ly·ing 1** : flirt **2** : dawdle —**dal·li·ance** \-ǝns\ n

dal·ma·tian \dal'māshǝn\ n : large dog having a spotted white coat

¹dam \'dam\ n : female parent of a domestic animal

²dam n : barrier to hold back water —**dam** vb

dam·age \-ij\ n **1** : loss or harm due to injury **2** pl : compensation for loss or injury ~ vb **-aged; -ag·ing** : do damage to

dam·ask \-ǝsk\ n : firm lustrous figured fabric

dame \'dām\ n : woman of rank or authority

damn \'dam\ vb **1** : condemn to hell **2** : curse —**dam·na·ble** \-nǝbǝl\ adj —**dam·na·tion** \dam'nāshǝn\ n —**damned** adj

damp \'damp\ n : moisture ~ vb **1** : reduce the draft in **2** : restrain **3** : moisten ~ adj : moist —**damp·ness** n

damp·en \'dampǝn\ vb **1** : diminish in

activity or vigor **2** : make or become damp

damp·er \'dampər\ *n* : movable plate to regulate a flue draft

dam·sel \'damzəl\ *n* : young woman

dance \'dans\ *vb* **danced; danc·ing** : move rhythmically to music ~ *n* : act of dancing or a gathering for dancing —**danc·er** *n*

dan·de·li·on \'dand²l₁ən\ *n* : common yellow-flowered herb

dan·der \'dandər\ *n* : temper

dan·druff \'dandrəf\ *n* : whitish scurf on the scalp

dan·dy \'dandē\ *n, pl* **-dies 1** : man too concerned with clothes **2** : something excellent —*adj* **-di·er; -est** : very good

dan·ger \'dānjər\ *n* **1** : exposure to injury or evil **2** : something that may cause injury —**dan·ger·ous** \'dānj(ə)rəs\ *adj*

dan·gle \'dangəl\ *vb* **-gled; -gling 1** : hang and swing freely **2** : be left without support or connection **3** : allow or cause to hang

dank \'daŋk\ *adj* : unpleasantly damp

dap·per \'dapər\ *adj* : neat and stylishly dressed

dap·ple \'-əl\ *vb* **-pled; -pling** : mark with colored spots

dare \'daər\ *vb* **dared; dar·ing 1** : have sufficient courage **2** : urge or provoke to contend —**dare** *n* —**dar·ing** \'da(ə)riŋ\ *n or adj*

dare·dev·il *n* : recklessly bold person

dark \'därk\ *adj* **1** : having little or no light **2** : not light in color **3** : gloomy ~ *n* : absence of light —**dark·en** \-ən\ *vb* —**dark·ly** *adv* —**dark·ness** *n*

dar·ling \'därliŋ\ *n* **1** : beloved **2** : favorite —*adj* **1** : dearly loved **2** : very pleasing

darn \'därn\ *vb* : mend with interlacing stitches —**darn·er** *n*

dart \'därt\ *n* **1** : small pointed missile **2** *pl* : game of throwing darts at a target **3** : tapering fold in a garment **4** : quick movement ~ *vb* : move suddenly or rapidly

dash \'dash\ *vb* **1** : knock or hurl violently or impetuously **2** : smash **3** : ruin **4** : perform or finish hastily **5** : move quickly ~ *n* **1** : sudden burst, splash, or stroke **2** : punctuation mark — **3** : tiny amount **4** : showiness or liveliness **5** : sudden rush **6** : short race

dash·board *n* : instrument panel

dash·ing \'dashiŋ\ *adj* : dapper and charming

das·tard \'dastərd\ *n* : one who sneakingly commits malicious acts

das·tard·ly \-lē\ *adj* : base or malicious

da·ta \'dātə, 'dat-, 'dät-\ *n sing or pl* : factual information

¹date \'dāt\ *n* : edible fruit of a palm

²date *n* **1** : day, month, or year when something is done or made **2** : historical time period **3** : social engagement or the person one goes out with ~ *vb* **dat·ed; dat·ing 1** : determine or record the date of **2** : have a date with **3** : originate —**to date** : up to now

dat·ed \-əd\ *adj* : old-fashioned

da·tum \'dātəm, 'dat-, 'dät-\ *n, pl* **-ta** \-ə\ *or* **-tums** : piece of data

daub \'dob\ *vb* : smear ~ *n* : something daubed on —**daub·er** *n*

daugh·ter \'dotər\ *n* : human female offspring —**daugh·ter·ly** *adj*

daugh·ter-in-law *n, pl* **daugh·ters-in-law** : wife of one's son

daunt \'dont\ *vb* : lessen the courage of

daunt·less \-ləs\ *adj* : fearless

dav·en·port \'davən₁pōrt\ *n* : sofa

daw·dle \'dod²l\ *vb* **-dled; -dling 1** : waste time **2** : loiter

dawn \'don\ *vb* **1** : grow light as the sun rises **2** : begin to appear, develop, or be understood ~ *n* : first appearance (as of daylight)

day \'dā\ *n* **1** : period of light between one night and the next **2** : 24 hours **3** : specified date **4** : particular time or age **5** : period of work for a day —**day·light** *n* —**day·time** *n*

day·break *n* : dawn

day·dream *n* : fantasy of wish fulfillment —**daydream** *vb*

day·light saving time *n* : time one hour ahead of standard time

daze \'dāz\ *vb* **dazed; daz·ing 1** : stun by a blow **2** : dazzle —**daze** *n*

daz·zle \'dazəl\ *vb* **-zled; -zling 1** : overpower with light **2** : impress greatly —**dazzle** *n*

DDT \₁dē(₁)dē'tē\ *n* : long-lasting insecticide

dea·con \'dēkən\ *n* : subordinate church officer —**dea·con·ess** *n*

dead \'ded\ *adj* **1** : lifeless **2** : unresponsive or inactive **3** : exhausted **4** : obsolete **5** : precise ~ *n, pl* **dead 1** : one that is dead—usu. with *the* **2** : most lifeless time —*adv* **1** : completely **2** : directly —**dead·en** \'ded²n\ *vb*

dead·beat *n* : one who will not pay debts

dead end *n* : end of a street with no exit —**dead-end** *adj*

dead heat n : tie in a contest

dead·line n : time by which something must be finished

dead·lock n : struggle that neither side can win —**deadlock** vb

dead·ly \'dedlē\ adj **-li·er; -est** 1 : capable of causing death 2 : very accurate 3 : fatal to spiritual progress 4 : suggestive of death 5 : very great ~ adv : extremely —**dead·li·ness** n

dead·pan adj : expressionless —**dead·pan** n

dead·wood n : something useless

deaf \'def\ adj : unable or unwilling to hear —**deaf·en** \-ən\ vb —**deaf·ness** n

deaf-mute n : deaf person unable to speak

deal \'dēl\ n 1 : indefinite quantity 2 : distribution of playing cards 3 : negotiation or agreement 4 : treatment received 5 : bargain ~ vb **dealt** \'delt\; **deal·ing** \'dēliŋ\ 1 : distribute playing cards 2 : be concerned with 3 : take action 4 : sell —**deal·er** n —**deal·ing** n

dean \'dēn\ n 1 : head of a group of clergymen 2 : university or school administrator 3 : senior member

dear \'dir\ adj 1 : highly valued or loved 2 : expensive ~ n : loved one —**dear·ly** adv —**dear·ness** n

dearth \'dərth\ n : scarcity

death \'deth\ n 1 : end of life 2 : cause of loss of life 3 : state of being dead 4 : destruction or extinction —**death·less** adj —**death·ly** adj or adv

de·ba·cle \di'bäkəl, -'bakəl\ n : disaster or fiasco

de·bar \di'bär\ vb : bar from something

de·bark \-'bärk\ vb : disembark —**de·bar·ka·tion** \,dē,bär'kāshən\ n

de·base \di'bās\ vb : disparage —**de·base·ment** n

de·bate \-'bāt\ vb **-bat·ed; -bat·ing** : discuss a question by argument —**de·bat·able** adj —**debate** n —**de·bat·er** n

de·bauch \-'bóch\ vb : seduce or corrupt —**de·bauch·ery** \-(ə)rē\ n

de·bil·i·tate \-'bilə,tāt\ vb **-tat·ed; -tat·ing** : make ill or weak

de·bil·i·ty \-'bilətē\ n, pl **-ties** : physical weakness

deb·it \'debət\ n : account entry of a payment or debt ~ vb : record as a debit

deb·o·nair \,debə'naər\ adj : gracefully charming

de·bris \də'brē, dā-; 'dā,brē\ n, pl **-bris** \-'brēz, -,brēz\ : remains of something destroyed

debt \'det\ n 1 : sin 2 : something owed 3 : state of owing money —**debt·or** \-ər\ n

de·bunk \dē'bəŋk\ vb : expose as false

de·but \'dā,byü, dā'byü\ n 1 : first public appearance 2 : formal entrance into society —**debut** vb —**deb·u·tante** \'debyù,tänt\ n

de·cade \'dek,ād, -əd; de'kād\ n : 10 years

dec·a·dence \'dekədəns; di'kādᵊns\ n : deterioration —**dec·a·dent** \-ənt; -ᵊnt\ adj or n

de·cal \'dē,kal, di'kal, 'dekəl\ n : picture or design for transfer from prepared paper

de·camp \di'kamp\ vb : depart suddenly

de·cant \-'kant\ vb : pour gently

de·cant·er \-ər\ n : ornamental bottle for decanting and serving

de·cap·i·tate \di'kapə,tāt\ vb **-tat·ed; -tat·ing** : behead —**de·cap·i·ta·tion** \-,kapə'tāshən\ n

de·cay \di'kā\ vb 1 : decline in condition 2 : decompose —**decay** n

de·cease \-'sēs\ n : death —**decease** vb

de·ceit \-'sēt\ n 1 : deception 2 : dishonesty —**de·ceit·ful** \-fəl\ adj —**de·ceit·ful·ly** adv —**de·ceit·ful·ness** n

de·ceive \-'sēv\ vb **-ceived; -ceiv·ing** : trick or mislead —**de·ceiv·er** n

de·cel·er·ate \dē'selə,rāt\ vb **-at·ed; -at·ing** : slow down

De·cem·ber \di'sembər\ n : 12th month of the year having 31 days

de·cent \'dēsᵊnt\ adj 1 : good, right, or just 2 : clothed 3 : not obscene 4 : fairly good —**de·cen·cy** \-ᵊnsē\ n —**de·cent·ly** adv

de·cep·tion \di'sepshən\ n 1 : act or fact of deceiving 2 : fraud —**de·cep·tive** \-'septiv\ adj —**de·cep·tive·ly** adv

de·cide \di'sīd\ vb **-cid·ed; -cid·ing** 1 : make a choice or judgment 2 : bring to a conclusion 3 : cause to decide

de·cid·ed adj 1 : unmistakable 2 : resolute —**de·cid·ed·ly** adv

de·cid·u·ous \di'sijəwəs\ adj : having leaves that fall annually

dec·i·mal \'des(ə)məl\ n : fraction in which the denominator is a power of 10 expressed by a point (**decimal point**) placed at the left of the numerator —**decimal** adj —**dec·i·mal·ly** \-lē\ adv

de·ci·pher \di'sīfər\ vb : make out the meaning of —**de·ci·pher·able** adj

de·ci·sion \-'sizhən\ *n* 1 : act or result of deciding 2 : determination

de·ci·sive \-'sīsiv\ *adj* 1 : having the power to decide 2 : conclusive 3 : showing determination —**de·ci·sive·ly** *adv* —**de·ci·sive·ness** *n*

deck \'dek\ *n* 1 : floor of a ship 2 : pack of playing cards ~ *vb* 1 : array or dress up 2 : knock down

de·claim \di'klām\ *vb* : speak loudly or impressively —**dec·la·ma·tion** \,deklə'māshən\ *n*

de·clare \di'klaar\ *vb* -**clared;** -**clar·ing** 1 : make known formally 2 : state emphatically —**dec·la·ra·tion** \,deklə'rāshən\ *n* —**de·clar·a·tive** \di'klarativ\ *adj* —**de·clar·a·to·ry** \di'klara,tōrē\ *adj* —**de·clar·er** *n*

de·clen·sion \di'klenchən\ *n* : inflectional forms esp. of a noun or pronoun

de·cline \di'klīn\ *vb* -**clined;** -**clin·ing** 1 : turn or slope downward 2 : wane 3 : refuse to accept 4 : inflect ~ *n* 1 : gradual wasting away 2 : change to a lower state or level 3 : a descending slope —**dec·li·na·tion** \,deklə'nāshən\ *n*

de·code \dē'kōd\ *vb* : decipher (a coded message)

de·com·pose \,dēkəm'pōz\ *vb* 1 : separate into parts 2 : decay —**de·com·po·si·tion** \dē,kämpə'zishən\ *n*

de·con·ges·tant \,dēkən'jestənt\ *n* : agent that relieves congestion

de·cor, dé·cor \dā'kòr, 'dā,kòr\ *n* : room design or decoration

dec·o·rate \'dekə,rāt\ *vb* -**rat·ed;** -**rat·ing** 1 : add something attractive to 2 : honor with a medal —**dec·o·ra·tion** \,dekə'rāshən\ *n* —**dec·o·ra·tive** \'dek(ə)rətiv\ *adj* —**dec·o·ra·tor** \'dekə,rātər\ *n*

de·co·rum \di'kōrəm\ *n* : proper behavior —**dec·o·rous** \'dekərəs, di'kōrəs\ *adj* —**dec·o·rous·ly** *adv* —**dec·o·rous·ness** *n*

de·coy \'dē,kòi, di'-\ *n* : something that tempts ~ *vb* : tempt

de·crease \di'krēs\ *vb* -**creased;** -**creas·ing** : grow or cause to grow less —**decrease** \'dē,krēs\ *n*

de·cree \di'krē\ *n* : official order —**decree** *vb*

de·crep·it \di'krepət\ *adj* : impaired by age

de·cre·scen·do \dākrə'shendō\ *adv* or *adj* : with a decrease in volume

de·cry \di'krī\ *vb* : condemn

ded·i·cate \'dedi,kāt\ *vb* -**cat·ed;** -**cat·ing** 1 : set apart for a purpose (as honor or worship) 2 : address to

someone as a compliment —**ded·i·ca·tion** \,dedi'kāshən\ *n* —**ded·i·ca·to·ry** \'dedika,tōrē\ *adj*

de·duce \di'd(y)üs\ *vb* -**duced;** -**duc·ing** : derive by reasoning —**de·duc·ible** *adj*

de·duct \-'dəkt\ *vb* : subtract —**de·duct·ible** *adj*

de·duc·tion \-'dəkshən\ *n* 1 : subtraction 2 : reasoned conclusion —**de·duc·tive** \-'dəktiv\ *adj*

deed \'dēd\ *n* 1 : exploit 2 : document showing ownership ~ *vb* : convey by deed

deem \'dēm\ *vb* : think

deep \'dēp\ *adj* 1 : extending far or a specified distance down, back, within, or outward 2 : occupied 3 : dark and rich in color 4 : low in tone ~ *adv* 1 : deeply 2 : far along in time ~ *n* : deep place —**deep·en** \'dēpən\ *vb* —**deep·ly** *adv*

deep-seat·ed \-'sētəd\ *adj* : firmly established

deer \'diər\ *n, pl* **deer** : ruminant mammal with antlers in the male —**deer·skin** *n*

de·face \di'fās\ *vb* : mar the surface of —**de·face·ment** *n*

de·fame \di'fām\ *vb* -**famed;** -**fam·ing** : injure the reputation of —**def·a·ma·tion** \,defə'māshən\ *n* —**de·fam·a·to·ry** \di'famə,tōrē\ *adj*

de·fault \di'fȯlt\ *n* : failure in a duty —default *vb* —**de·fault·er** *n*

de·feat \di'fēt\ *vb* 1 : frustrate 2 : win victory over ~ *n* : loss of a battle or contest

def·e·cate \'defi,kāt\ *vb* -**cat·ed;** -**cat·ing** : discharge feces from the bowels —**def·e·ca·tion** \,defi'kāshən\ *n*

de·fect \'dē,fekt, di'fekt\ *n* : imperfection —**di'-**\ *vb* : desert —**de·fec·tion** \-'fekshən\ *n* —**de·fec·tor** \-'fektər\ *n*

de·fec·tive \di'fektiv\ *adj* : faulty or deficient —**defective** *n*

de·fend \-'fend\ *vb* 1 : protect from danger or harm 2 : take the side of —**de·fend·er** *n*

de·fen·dant \-'fendənt\ *n* : person charged or sued in a court

de·fense, de·fence \-'fens\ *n* 1 : act of defending 2 : something that defends 3 : party, group, or team that opposes another —**de·fense·less** *adj* —**de·fen·si·ble** *adj* —**de·fen·sive** *adj* or *n*

¹**de·fer** \di'fər\ *vb* -**rr-** : postpone —**de·fer·ment** \di'fərmənt\ *n* —**de·fer·ra·ble** \-əbəl\ *adj*

²de·fer \vb -rr- : yield to the opinion or wishes of another —def·er·ence \'def(ə)rəns\ n —def·er·en·tial \,defə'renchəl\ adj

de·fi·ance \di'fīəns\ n : act or state of defying —de·fi·ant \-ənt\ adj

de·fi·cient \di'fishənt\ adj : lacking something necessary —de·fi·cien·cy \-'fishənsē\ n

def·i·cit \'defəsət\ n : shortage esp. in money

de·file \di'fīl\ vb -filed; -fil·ing : make filthy or corrupt 2 : profane or dishonor —de·file·ment n

de·fine \di'fīn\ vb -fined; -fin·ing 1 : fix or mark the limits of 2 : clarify in outline 3 : set forth the meaning of —de·fin·able adj —de·fin·ably adv —de·fin·er n —def·i·ni·tion \,defə'nishən\ n

def·i·nite \'def(ə)nət\ adj 1 : having distinct limits 2 : clear in meaning, intent, or identity 3 : typically designating an identified or immediately identifiable person or thing —def·i·nite·ly adv

de·fin·i·tive \di'finətiv\ adj 1 : conclusive 2 : authoritative

de·flate \di'flāt\ vb -flat·ed; -flat·ing 1 : release air or gas from 2 : reduce —de·fla·tion \-'flāshən\ n

de·flect \di'flekt\ vb : turn aside —de·flec·tion \-'flekshən\ n

de·fo·li·ate \dē'fōlē,āt\ vb -at·ed; -at·ing : deprive of leaves esp. prematurely —de·fo·li·ant \-lēənt\ n —de·fo·li·a·tion \-,fōlē'āshən\ n

de·form \di'form\ vb 1 : distort 2 : disfigure —de·for·ma·tion \,dē,for'māshən, ,defər-\ n —de·for·mi·ty \di'formətē\ n

de·fraud \di'fród\ vb : cheat

de·fray \-'frā\ vb : pay

de·frost \-'fróst\ vb 1 : thaw out 2 : free from ice —de·frost·er n

deft \'deft\ adj : quick and skillful —deft·ly adv —deft·ness n

de·funct \di'fəŋkt\ adj : dead

de·fy \-'fī\ vb -fied; -fy·ing 1 : challenge 2 : boldly refuse to obey

de·gen·er·ate \di'jen(ə)rət\ adj : degraded or corrupt ~ : degenerate person ~ \-ə,rāt\ vb : become degenerate —de·gen·er·a·cy \-(ə)rəsē\ n —de·gen·er·a·tion \-,jenə'rāshən\ n —de·gen·er·a·tive \-'jenə'rātiv\ adj

de·grade \di'grād\ vb 1 : reduce from a higher to a lower rank or degree 2 : debase —de·grad·able \-'ābəl\ adj —deg·ra·da·tion \,degrə'dāshən\ n

de·gree \di'grē\ n 1 : step in a series 2 : extent, intensity, or scope 3 : title given to a college graduate 4 : a 360th part of the circumference of a circle

de·hy·drate \dē'hī,drāt\ vb 1 : remove water from 2 : lose liquid —de·hy·dra·tion \,dēhī'drāshən\ n

de·i·fy \'dēə,fī\ vb -fied; -fy·ing : make a god of —de·i·fi·ca·tion \,dēəfə'kāshən\ n

deign \'dān\ vb : condescend

de·i·ty \'dēətē\ n, pl -ties 1 cap : God 2 : a god or goddess

de·ject·ed \di'jektəd\ adj : sad —de·jec·tion \-shən\ n

de·lay \di'lā\ n : a putting off of something ~ vb 1 : postpone 2 : stop or hinder for a time

de·lec·ta·ble \di'lektəbəl\ adj : delicious

del·e·gate \'deligət, -,gāt\ n : representative ~ \-,gāt\ vb -gat·ed; -gat·ing 1 : entrust to another 2 : appoint as one's delegate —del·e·ga·tion \,deli'gāshən\ n

de·lete \di'lēt\ vb -let·ed; -let·ing : eliminate something written —de·le·tion \-'lēshən\ n

del·e·te·ri·ous \,delə'tirēəs\ adj : harmful

de·lib·er·ate \di'lib(ə)rət\ adj 1 : determined after careful thought 2 : intentional 3 : not hurried ~ \-ə,rāt\ vb -at·ed; -at·ing vb : consider carefully —de·lib·er·ate·ly adv —de·lib·er·ate·ness n —de·lib·er·a·tion \-,libə'rāshən\ n —de·lib·er·a·tive \-'libə,rātiv, -'lib(ə)rət-\ adj

del·i·ca·cy \'delikəsē\ n, pl -cies 1 : something special and pleasing to eat 2 : fineness 3 : frailty

del·i·cate \'delikət\ adj 1 : subtly pleasing to the senses 2 : dainty and charming 3 : sensitive or fragile 4 : requiring fine skill or tact —del·i·cate·ly adv

del·i·ca·tes·sen \,delikə'tesᵊn\ n : store that sells ready-to-eat food

de·li·cious \di'lishəs\ adj : very pleasing esp. in taste or aroma —de·li·cious·ly adv

de·light \di'līt\ n 1 : great pleasure 2 : source of great pleasure ~ vb 1 : take great pleasure 2 : satisfy greatly —de·light·ful \-fəl\ adj —de·light·ful·ly adv

de·lin·e·ate \di'linē,āt\ vb -eat·ed; -eat·ing : sketch or portray —de·lin·ea·tion \-,linē'āshən\ n

de·lin·quent \-'liŋkwənt\ n : delinquent person ~ adj 1 : violating duty or law **2** : overdue in payment —**de·lin·quen·cy** \-kwənsē\ *n*

de·lir·i·um \di'lirēəm\ *n* : mental disturbance —**de·lir·i·ous** \-ē-əs\ *adj*

de·liv·er \di'livər\ *vb* **1** : set free : hand over **3** : assist in birth **4** : say or speak **5** : send to an intended destination —**de·liv·er·ance** \-(ə)rəns\ *n* —**de·liv·er·er** *n* —**de·liv·ery** \-(ə)rē\ *n*

dell \'del\ *n* : small secluded valley

del·ta \'deltə\ *n* : triangle of land at the mouth of a river

de·lude \di'lüd\ *vb* **-lud·ed; -lud·ing** : mislead or deceive

del·uge \'delyüj\ *n* **1** : flood **2** : drenching rain ~ *vb* **-uged; -ug·ing 1** : flood **2** : overwhelm

de·lu·sion \di'lüzhən\ *n* : false belief

de·luxe \di'lüks, -'ləks, -'lüks\ *adj* : very luxurious or elegant

delve \'delv\ *vb* **delved; delv·ing 1** : dig **2** : seek information in records

dem·a·gogue, dem·a·gog \'demə,gäg\ *n* : politician who appeals to emotion and prejudice —**dem·a·gogu·ery** \-,gäg(ə)rē\ *n* —**dem·a·gogy** \-,gäge, -,gägē\ *n*

de·mand \di'mand\ *n* **1** : act of asking esp. with authority **2** : something claimed as due **3** : ability and desire to buy **4** : urgent need ~ *vb* **1** : ask for with authority **2** : require

de·mar·cate \di'mär,kāt, 'dē,mär-\ *vb* **-cat·ed; -cat·ing** : mark the limits of —**de·mar·ca·tion** \,dē,mär'kāshən\ *n*

de·mean \di'mēn\ *vb* : degrade

de·mean·or \-'mēnər\ *n* : behavior

de·ment·ed \-'mentəd\ *adj* : crazy

de·mer·it \-'merət\ *n* : mark given an offender

demi·god \'demi,gäd\ *n* : mythological being less powerful than a god

de·mise \di'mīz\ *n* : death

demi·tasse \'demi,tas\ *n* : small cup of coffee

de·mo·bi·lize \di-, dē-\ *vb* : disband from military service —**de·mo·bi·li·za·tion** *n*

de·moc·ra·cy \di'mäkrəsē\ *n, pl* **-cies 1** : government in which the supreme power is held by the people **2** : political unit with democratic government

dem·o·crat \'demə,krat\ *n* : adherent of democracy

dem·o·crat·ic \,demə'kratik\ *adj* : relating to or favoring democracy —**dem·o·crat·i·cal·ly** \-ik(ə)lē\ *adv*

de·moc·ra·tize \di'mäkrə,tīz\ *vb*

de·mol·ish \di'mälish\ *vb* **1** : tear down or smash **2** : put an end to —**de·mo·li·tion** \,demə'lishən, ,dē-\ *n*

de·mon \'dēmən\ *n* : evil spirit —**de·mon·ic** \di'mänik\ *adj*

dem·on·strate \'demən,strāt\ *vb* **-strat·ed; -strat·ing 1** : show clearly or publicly **2** : prove **3** : explain —**de·mon·stra·ble** \di'mänstrəbəl\ *adj* —**dem·on·stra·tion** \,demən'strāshən\ *n* —**de·mon·stra·tive** \di'mänstrətiv\ *adj or n* —**dem·on·stra·tor** \'demən,strātər\ *n*

de·mor·al·ize \di'morə,līz\ *vb* : destroy the enthusiasm of

de·mote \-'mōt\ *vb* **-mot·ed; -mot·ing** : reduce to a lower rank

de·mur \-'mər\ *vb* **-rr-** : object —**de·mur** *n*

de·mure \-'myur\ *adj* : modest —**de·mure·ly** *adv*

den \'den\ *n* **1** : animal's shelter **2** : hiding place **3** : cozy private little room

de·na·ture \dē'nāchər\ *vb* **-tured; -tur·ing** : make (alcohol) unfit for drinking

de·ni·al \di'nī(ə)l\ *n* : rejection of a request or of the validity of a statement

den·i·grate \'deni,grāt\ *vb* **-grat·ed; -grat·ing** : speak ill of

den·im \'denəm\ *n* **1** : durable twilled cotton fabric **2** *pl* : pants of denim

den·i·zen \-azən\ *n* : inhabitant

de·nom·i·na·tion \di,nämə'nāshən\ *n* **1** : religious body **2** : value or size in a series —**de·nom·i·na·tion·al** \-sh(ə)nəl\ *adj*

de·nom·i·na·tor \-'nämə,nātər\ *n* : part of a fraction below the line

de·note \di'nōt\ *vb* **1** : mark out plainly **2** : mean —**de·no·ta·tion** \,dēnō'tāshən\ *n* —**de·no·ta·tive** \'dēnō,tātiv, di'nōtətiv\ *adj*

de·noue·ment \,dā,nü'mäⁿ\ *n* : final outcome (as of a drama)

de·nounce \di'nauns\ *vb* **-nounced; -nounc·ing 1** : criticize severely **2** : inform against

dense \'dens\ *adj* **dens·er; -est 1** : thick, compact, or crowded **2** : stupid —**dense·ly** *adv* —**dense·ness** *n* —**den·si·ty** \'densətē\ *n*

dent \'dent\ *n* : small depression —**dent** *vb*

den·tal \-ᵊl\ *adj* : relating to teeth or dentistry

den·ti·frice \'dentəfrəs\ *n* : preparation for cleaning teeth

den·tin \'dentᵊn\, **den·tine** \'den,tēn, ,den'-\ *n* : bonelike component of teeth

den·tist \'dentəst\ *n* : one who cares for and replaces teeth —**den·tist·ry** *n*

den·ture \'denchər\ n : artificial teeth

de·nude \di'n(y)üd\ vb **-nud·ed; -nud·ing** : strip of covering

de·nun·ci·a·tion \di,nənsē'āshən\ n : act of denouncing

de·ny \di'nī\ vb **-nied; -ny·ing 1** : declare untrue **2** : disavow **3** : refuse to grant

de·odor·ant \dē'ōdərənt\ n : preparation to prevent unpleasant odors —**de·odor·ize** \-ˌrīz\ vb

de·part \di'pärt\ vb **1** : go away or away from **2** : die —**de·par·ture** \-'pärchər\ n

de·part·ment \di'pärtmənt\ n **1** : area of responsibility or interest **2** : functional division —**de·part·men·tal** \di,pärt'mentⁱl, ˌdē-\ adj

de·pend \di'pend\ vb **1** : rely for support **2** : be determined by or based on something else —**de·pend·abil·i·ty** \-ˌpendə'bilətē\ n —**de·pend·able** adj —**de·pen·dence** \-'pendəns\ n —**de·pen·den·cy** \-dənsē\ n —**de·pen·dent** \-ənt\ adj or n

de·pict \di'pikt\ vb : show by or as if by a picture —**de·pic·tion** \-'pikshən\ n

de·plete \di'plēt\ vb **-plet·ed; -plet·ing** : use up resources of —**de·ple·tion** \-'plēshən\ n

de·plore \di'plōr\ vb **-plored; -plor·ing** : regret strongly —**de·plor·able** \-əbəl\ adj

de·ploy \di'ploi\ vb : spread out for battle —**de·ploy·ment** \-mənt\ n

de·port \di'pōrt\ vb **1** : behave **2** : send out of the country —**de·por·ta·tion** \ˌdē,pōr'tāshən\ n —**de·port·ment** \di'pōrtmənt\ n

de·pose \di'pōz\ vb **-posed; -pos·ing 1** : remove (a ruler) from office **2** : testify —**de·po·si·tion** \ˌdepə'zishən, ˌdē-\ n

de·pos·it \di'päzət\ vb **-it·ed; -it·ing 1** : put away for safekeeping : give as a pledge **2** : lay or put down ~ n **1** : state of being deposited **2** : something deposited **3** : act of depositing —**de·pos·i·tor** \-'päzətər\ n

de·pos·i·to·ry \di'päzə,tōrē\ n, pl **-ries** : place for deposit

de·pot 1 usu 'depō, 2 usu 'dēpō\ n **1** : place for storage **2** : bus or railroad station

de·prave \di'prāv\ vb **-praved; -prav·ing** : corrupt morally —**de·praved** adj —**de·prav·i·ty** \-'pravətē\ n

dep·re·cate \'depri,kāt\ vb **-cat·ed; -cat·ing 1** : express disapproval of **2** : belittle —**dep·re·ca·tion** \ˌdepri'kāshən\ n —**dep·re·ca·to·ry** \'depri·kə,tōrē\ adj

de·pre·ci·ate \di'prēshē,āt\ vb **-at·ed; -at·ing 1** : lessen in value **2** : belittle —**de·pre·ci·a·tion** \-ˌprēshē'āshən\ n

dep·re·da·tion \ˌdeprə'dāshən\ n : a laying waste or plundering

de·press \di'pres\ vb **1** : press down **2** : lessen the activity or force of **3** : discourage **4** : decrease the market value of —**de·pres·sant** \-ᵊnt\ n or adj —**de·pressed** adj —**de·pres·sive** \-iv\ adj or n —**de·pres·sor** \-ər\ n

de·pres·sion \di'preshən\ n **1** : act of depressing or state of being depressed **2** : period of low economic activity

de·prive \-'prīv\ vb **-prived; -priv·ing** : take or keep something away from —**de·pri·va·tion** \ˌdeprə'vāshən\ n

depth \'depth\ n, pl **depths** \'dep(th)s\ **1** : something that is deep **2** : distance down from a surface **3** : distance from front to back **4** : quality of being deep

dep·u·ta·tion \ˌdepyə'tāshən\ n : delegation

dep·u·ty \'depyətē\ n, pl **-ties** : person appointed to act for another —**dep·u·tize** \-yə,tīz\ vb

de·rail \di'rāl\ vb : run off the rails —**de·rail·ment** n

de·range \-'rānj\ vb **-ranged; -rang·ing 1** : disarrange or upset **2** : make insane —**de·range·ment** n

der·by \'dərbē, Brit 'där-\ n, pl **-bies 1** : horse race **2** : stiff felt hat with dome-shaped crown

der·e·lict \'derə,likt\ adj **1** : abandoned **2** : negligent ~ n **1** : something abandoned **2** : bum —**der·e·lic·tion** \ˌderə'likshən\ n

de·ride \di'rīd\ vb **-rid·ed; -rid·ing** : make fun of —**de·ri·sion** \-'rizhən\ n —**de·ri·sive** \-'rīsiv\ adj

de·rive \di'rīv\ vb **-rived; -riv·ing 1** : obtain from a source or parent **2** : come from a certain source **3** : infer or deduce —**der·i·va·tion** \ˌderə'vāshən\ n —**de·riv·a·tive** \di'rivə,tiv\ adj or n

der·ma·tol·o·gy \ˌdərmə'täləjē\ n : study of the skin and its disorders —**der·ma·tol·o·gist** \-jəst\ n

de·rog·a·to·ry \di'rägə,tōrē\ adj : intended to lower the reputation

der·rick \'derik\ n **1** : hoisting apparatus **2** : framework over an oil well

de·scend \di'send\ vb **1** : move or climb down **2** : come down from a stock or source **3** : extend downward **4** : make a sudden attack —**de·scen·dant, de·scen·dent** \-ənt\ adj or n —**de·scent** \di'sent\ n

de·scribe \di-'skrīb\ *vb* -scribed; -scrib·ing : represent in words —de·scrib·able *adj* —de·scrib·ably *adv* —de·scrip·tion \-'skripshən\ *n* —de·scrip·tive \-'skriptiv\ *adj*

de·scry \di-'skrī\ *vb* -scried; -scry·ing : catch sight of

des·e·crate \'desi,krāt\ *vb* -crat·ed; -crat·ing : treat (something sacred) with disrespect —des·e·cra·tion \,desi'krāshən\ *n*

de·seg·re·gate \dē-\ *vb* : eliminate esp. racial segregation in —de·seg·re·ga·tion *n*

1des·ert \'dezərt\ *n* : dry barren region —desert *adj*

2des·ert \di'zərt\ *n* : what one deserves

3de·sert \di'zərt\ *vb* : abandon —de·sert·er *n* —de·ser·tion \-'zərshən\ *n*

de·serve \-'zərv\ *vb* -served; -serv·ing : be worthy of

des·ic·cate \'desi,kāt\ *vb* -cat·ed; -cat·ing : dehydrate —des·ic·ca·tion \,desi'kāshən\ *n*

de·sign \di'zīn\ *vb* 1 : create and work out the details of 2 : make a pattern or sketch of ~ *n* 1 : mental project or plan 2 : purpose 3 : preliminary sketch 4 : underlying arrangement of elements 5 : decorative pattern —de·sign·er *n*

des·ig·nate \'dezig,nāt\ *vb* -nat·ed; -nat·ing 1 : indicate, specify, or name 2 : appoint —des·ig·na·tion \,dezig'nāshən\ *n*

de·sire \di'zī(ə)r\ *vb* -sired; -sir·ing 1 : feel desire for 2 : request ~ *n* 1 : strong conscious impulse to have, be, or do something 2 : something desired —de·sir·abil·i·ty \-,zīrə'bilətē\ *n* —de·sir·able \-'zīrəbəl\ *adj* —de·sir·ous \-'zīrəs\ *adj*

de·sist \di'zist, -'sist\ *vb* : stop

desk \'desk\ *n* : table esp. for writing and reading

des·o·late \'desələt, 'dez-\ *adj* 1 : lifeless 2 : disconsolate ~ \-,lāt\ *vb* -lat·ed; -lat·ing : lay waste —des·o·la·tion \,desə'lāshən, ,dez-\ *n*

de·spair \di'spaər\ *vb* : lose all hope ~ *n* : loss of hope

des·per·a·do \,despə'rädō, -'rād-\ *n, pl* -does *or* -dos : desperate criminal

des·per·ate \'desp(ə)rət\ *adj* 1 : hopeless 2 : rash 3 : extremely intense —des·per·ate·ly *adv* —des·per·a·tion \,despə'rāshən\ *n*

de·spi·ca·ble \di'spikəbəl, 'despik-\ *adj* : deserving scorn

de·spise \di'spīz\ *vb* -spised; -spis·ing : feel contempt for

de·spite \di'spīt\ *prep* : in spite of

de·spoil \-'spȯil\ *vb* : strip of possessions or value

de·spon·den·cy \-'spändənsē\ *n* : dejection —de·spon·dent \-dənt\ *adj*

des·pot \'despət, -,pät\ *n* : tyrant —des·pot·ic \des'pätik\ *adj* —des·po·tism \'despə,tizəm\ *n*

des·sert \di'zərt\ *n* : sweet food, fruit, or cheese ending a meal

des·ti·na·tion \,destə'nāshən\ *n* : place where something or someone is going

des·tine \'destən\ *vb* -tined; -tin·ing 1 : designate, assign, or determine in advance 2 : direct

des·ti·ny \'destənē\ *n, pl* -nies : that which is to happen in the future

des·ti·tute \'destə,t(y)üt\ *adj* 1 : lacking something 2 : very poor —des·ti·tu·tion \,destə't(y)üshən\ *n*

de·stroy \di'strȯi\ *vb* : kill or put an end to

de·stroy·er \-'strȯi(ə)r\ *n* 1 : one that destroys 2 : small speedy warship

de·struc·tion \-'strəkshən\ *n* : action of destroying 2 : ruin —de·struc·ti·bil·i·ty \-,strəktə'bilətē\ *n* —de·struc·ti·ble \-'strəktəbəl\ *adj* —de·struc·tive \-'strəktiv\ *adj*

de·sul·to·ry \'desəl,tōrē\ *adj* : aimless

de·tach \di'tach\ *vb* : separate

de·tached \-'tacht\ *adj* 1 : separate 2 : aloof or impartial

de·tach·ment \-'tachmənt\ *n* 1 : separation 2 : troops or ships on special service 3 : aloofness 4 : impartiality

de·tail \di'tāl, 'dē,tāl\ *n* : small item or part ~ *vb* : give details of

de·tain \di'tān\ *vb* 1 : hold in custody 2 : delay

de·tect \di'tekt\ *vb* : discover —de·tect·able *adj* —de·tec·tion \-'tekshən\ *n* —de·tec·tor \-tər\ *n*

de·tec·tive \-'tektiv\ *n* : one who investigates crime

dé·tente \dātäⁿt\ *n* : relaxation of tensions between nations

de·ten·tion \di'tenchən\ *n* : confinement

de·ter \-'tər\ *vb* -rr- : discourage or prevent —de·ter·rence \-əns\ *n* —de·ter·rent \-ənt\ *adj or n*

de·ter·gent \di'tərjənt\ *n* : cleansing agent

de·te·ri·o·rate \-'tirēə,rāt\ *vb* -rat·ed; -rat·ing : make or grow worse —de·te·ri·o·ra·tion \-,tirēə'rāshən\ *n*

de·ter·mi·na·tion \di,tərmə'nāshən\ *n* 1 : act of deciding or fixing 2 : firm purpose

de·ter·mine \-'tərmən\ *vb* -mined; -min·ing 1 : decide

on, establish, or settle **2** : find out **3** : be the cause of

de·test \-'test\ *vb* : hate —**de·test·able** *adj* —**de·tes·ta·tion** \₁dē₁tes'tāshən\ *n*

det·o·nate \'detᵊn₁āt, 'detə₁nāt\ *vb* -**nat·ed**; -**nat·ing** : explode —**det·o·na·tion** \₁detᵊn'āshən, ₁detə'nā-\ *n* —**det·o·na·tor** \-ᵊr\ *n*

de·tour \'dē₁túr\ *n* : temporary indirect route —**detour** *vb*

de·tract \di'trakt\ *vb* : take away —**de·trac·tion** \-'trakshən\ *n* —**de·trac·tor** \-'traktər\ *n*

det·ri·ment \'detrəmənt\ *n* : damage —**det·ri·men·tal** \₁detrə'mentᵊl\ *adj* —**det·ri·men·tal·ly** *adv*

deuce \'d(y)üs\ *n* **1** : 2 in cards or dice **2** : tie in tennis **3** : devil—used as an oath

deut·sche mark \₁dóichə-\ *n* : monetary unit of West Germany

de·val·ue \dē-\ *vb* : reduce the value of —**de·val·u·a·tion** *n*

dev·as·tate \'devə₁stāt\ *vb* -**tat·ed**; -**tat·ing** : ruin —**dev·as·ta·tion** \₁devə'stāshən\ *n*

de·vel·op \di'veləp\ *vb* **1** : grow, increase, or evolve gradually **2** : cause to grow, increase, or reach full potential —**de·vel·op·er** *n* —**de·vel·op·ment** *n* —**de·vel·op·men·tal** \-₁veləp'mentᵊl\ *adj*

de·vi·ate \'dēvē₁āt\ *vb* -**at·ed**; -**at·ing** : change esp. from a course or standard —**de·vi·ant** \-vēənt\ *adj or n* —**de·vi·ate** \-vēət, -vē₁āt\ *n* —**de·vi·a·tion** \₁dēvē'āshən\ *n*

de·vice \di'vīs\ *n* **1** : specialized piece of equipment or tool **2** : design

dev·il \'devəl\ *n* **1** : personified supreme spirit of evil **2** : demon **3** : wicked person ~ *vb* -**iled** or -**illed**; -**il·ing** or -**il·ling 1** : pester **2** : mash or chop (food) and season highly —**dev·il·ish** \'dev(ə)lish\ *adj* —**dev·il·ry** \'devəlrē\, **dev·il·try** \-trē\ *n*

de·vi·ous \'dēvēəs\ *adj* : tricky

de·vise \di'vīz\ *vb* -**vised**; -**vis·ing 1** : invent **2** : plot **3** : give by will

de·void \-'vóid\ *adj* : entirely lacking

de·vote \di'vōt\ *vb* -**vot·ed**; -**vot·ing** : set apart for a special purpose —**de·vot·ed** *adj* : ardent

dev·o·tee \₁devə'tē, -'tā\ *n* : zealous follower

de·vo·tion \di'vōshən\ *n* **1** : prayer —usu. pl. **2** : strong affection —**de·vo·tion·al** \-sh(ə)nəl\ *adj*

de·vour \di'vaú(ə)r\ *vb* : consume ravenously —**de·vour·er** *n*

de·vout \-'vaút\ *adj* **1** : devoted to religion **2** : sincere —**de·vout·ly** *adv* —**de·vout·ness** *n*

dew \'d(y)ü\ *n* : moisture condensed at night —**dew·drop** *n* —**dewy** *adj*

dex·ter·ous, dex·trous \'dekst(ə)rəs\ *adj* : skillful with the hands —**dex·ter·i·ty** \dek'sterətē\ *n* —**dex·ter·ous·ly** *adv*

dex·trose \'dek₁strōs\ *n* : plant or blood sugar

di·a·be·tes \₁dīə'bētēz, -'bētəs\ *n* : disorder in which the body has too little insulin and too much sugar —**di·a·bet·ic** \-'betik\ *adj or n*

di·a·bol·ic \-'bälik\, **di·a·bol·i·cal** \-ikəl\ *adj* : fiendish

di·a·crit·ic \-'kritik\ *n* : mark accompanying a letter and indicating a specific sound value —**di·a·crit·i·cal** \-'kritikəl\ *adj*

di·a·dem \'dīə₁dem\ *n* : crown

di·ag·no·sis \₁dīig'nōsəs, -əg-\ *n, pl* -**no·ses** \-₁sēz\ : identifying of a disease from its symptoms —**di·ag·nose** \'dīig₁nōs, -əg-\ *vb* —**di·ag·nos·tic** \₁dīig'nästik, -əg-\ *adj*

di·ag·o·nal \dī'ag(ə)nəl\ *adj* : extending from one corner to the opposite corner ~ *n* : diagonal line, direction, or arrangement —**di·ag·o·nal·ly** \-ē\ *adv*

di·a·gram \'dīə₁gram\ *n* : explanatory drawing or plan ~ *vb* -**gramed** or -**grammed**; -**gram·ing** or -**gram·ming** : represent by a diagram —**di·a·gram·mat·ic** \₁dīəgrə'matik\ *adj*

di·al \'dī(ə)l\ *n* **1** : face of a clock, meter, or gauge **2** : control knob or wheel ~ *vb* -**aled** or **alled**; -**al·ing** or -**al·ling** : turn a dial to call, operate, or select

di·a·lect \'dīə₁lekt\ *n* : variety of language confined to a region or group

di·a·logue, di·a·log \-₁lóg\ *n* : conversation

di·am·e·ter \dī'amətər\ *n* **1** : straight line through the center of a circle **2** : thickness

di·a·met·ric \₁dīə'metrik\, **di·a·met·ri·cal** \-trikəl\ *adj* : completely opposite —**di·a·met·ri·cal·ly** \-(ə)lē\ *adv*

di·a·mond \'dī(ə)mənd\ *n* **1** : hard brilliant mineral that consists of crystalline carbon **2** : flat figure having 4 equal sides, 2 acute angles, and 2 obtuse angles **3** : playing card of a suit marked with a red diamond **4** : baseball field

di·a·per \'dī(ə)pər\ *n* : folded material drawn up between a baby's legs and fastened at the waist ~ *vb* : put a diaper on

di·a·phragm \\'dī(ə)ˌfram\\ *n* **1** : muscular partition between the chest and abdominal cavity **2** : contraceptive device

di·ar·rhea, di·ar·rhoea \\ˌdī'(ə)'rēə\\ *n* : abnormal discharge of loose matter from the bowels

di·a·ry \\'dī(ə)rē\\ *n, pl* **-ries** : daily record of personal experiences —**di·a·rist** \\'dīərəst\\ *n*

di·a·tribe \\'dīəˌtrīb\\ *n* : denunciation

dice \\'dīs\\ *n, pl* **dice** : die or a game played with dice ~ *vb* **diced; dic·ing** : cut into small cubes

dick·er \\'dikər\\ *vb* : bargain

dic·tate \\'dikˌtāt\\ *vb* **-tat·ed; -tat·ing 1** : speak for a person or a machine to record **2** : command ~ *n* : order —**dic·ta·tion** \\dik'tāshən\\ *n*

dic·ta·tor \\'dikˌtātər\\ *n* : person ruling absolutely and often brutally —**dic·ta·to·ri·al** \\ˌdiktətōrēəl\\ *adj* —**dic·ta·tor·ship** \\dik'tātərˌship, 'dikˌ-\\ *n*

dic·tion \\'dikshən\\ *n* **1** : choice of the best word **2** : precise pronunciation

dic·tio·nary \\-shəˌnerē\\ *n, pl* **-nar·ies** : reference book of words with information about their meaning

dic·tum \\'diktəm\\ *n, pl* **-ta** \\-tə\\ : authoritative or formal statement

did *past of* DO

di·dac·tic \\dī'daktik\\ *adj* : intended to teach a moral lesson

¹die \\'dī\\ *vb* **died; dy·ing** \\'dīiŋ\\ **1** : stop living **2** : pass out of existence **3** : stop or subside **4** : long

²die \\'dī\\ *n* **1** *pl* **dice** \\'dīs\\ : small marked cube used in gambling **2** *pl* **dies** \\'dīz\\ : form for stamping or cutting

die·sel \\'dēzəl, -səl\\ *n* : engine in which high compression causes ignition of the fuel

di·et \\'dīət\\ *n* : food and drink regularly consumed (as by a person) ~ *vb* : eat less or according to certain rules —**di·etary** \\'dīəˌterē\\ *adj or n* —**di·et·er** *n*

di·etet·ics \\ˌdīə'tetiks\\ *n sing or pl* : science of nutrition —**di·etet·ic** *adj* —**di·eti·tian, di·eti·cian** \\-'tishən\\ *n*

dif·fer \\'difər\\ *vb* **1** : be unlike **2** : disagree —**dif·fer·ence** \\'difərns, 'dif(ə)rəns\\ *n*

dif·fer·ent \\-ərnt, -(ə)rənt\\ *adj* : not the same —**dif·fer·ent·ly** *adv*

dif·fer·en·ti·ate \\ˌdifə'renchēˌāt\\ *vb* **-at·ed; -at·ing 1** : make or become different **2** : distinguish —**dif·fer·en·ti·a·tion** \\-ˌrenchē'āshən\\ *n*

dif·fi·cult \\'dif(ˌi)ˌkəlt\\ *adj* : hard to do, understand, or deal with

dif·fi·cul·ty \\-(ˌi)kəltē\\ *n, pl* **-ties 1** : difficult nature **2** : great effort **3** : something hard to do, understand, or deal with

dif·fi·dent \\'difədənt\\ *adj* : reserved —**dif·fi·dence** \\-əns\\ *n*

dif·fuse \\dif'yüs\\ *adj* **1** : wordy **2** : scattered ~ \\-'yüz\\ *vb* **-fused; -fus·ing** : pour out or spread widely —**dif·fu·sion** \\-'yüzhən\\ *n*

dig \\'dig\\ *vb* **dug** \\'dəg\\; **dig·ging 1** : turn up soil **2** : hollow out or form by removing earth **3** : uncover by turning up earth **4** : discover **5** : poke ~ *n* **1** : thrust **2** : cutting remark

¹di·gest \\'dīˌjest\\ *n* : body of information in shortened form

²di·gest \\dī'jest, də-\\ *vb* **1** : think over **2** : convert (food) into a form that can be absorbed **3** : summarize —**di·gest·ible** *adj* —**di·ges·tion** \\-'jeschən\\ *n* —**di·ges·tive** \\-'jestiv\\ *adj*

dig·it \\'dijət\\ *n* **1** : any of the figures 1 to 9 inclusive and also the symbol 0 **2** : finger or toe

dig·i·tal \\-ᵊl\\ *adj* : providing information in numerical digits —**dig·i·tal·ly** *adv*

dig·ni·fy \\'dignəˌfī\\ *vb* **-fied; -fy·ing** : give dignity to

dig·ni·tary \\-ˌter-ē\\ *n, pl* **-taries** : person of high position

dig·ni·ty \\'dignətē\\ *n, pl* **-ties 1** : quality or state of being worthy or honored **2** : formal reserve (as of manner)

di·gress \\dī'gres, də-\\ *vb* : wander from the main subject —**di·gres·sion** \\-'greshən\\ *n*

dike \\'dīk\\ *n* : earth bank or dam

di·lap·i·dat·ed \\də'lapəˌdātəd\\ *adj* : fallen into partial ruin —**di·lap·i·da·tion** \\-ˌlapə'dāshən\\ *n*

di·late \\dī'lāt, 'dīˌlāt\\ *vb* **-lat·ed; -lat·ing** : swell or expand —**dil·a·ta·tion** \\ˌdilə'tāshən\\ *n* —**di·la·tion** \\dī'lāshən\\ *n*

dil·a·to·ry \\'diləˌtōrē\\ *adj* **1** : delaying **2** : not prompt

di·lem·ma \\də'lemə\\ *n* : choice between equally undesirable alternatives

dil·et·tante \\'dilə ˌtänt, -ˌtant; ˌdilə'tänt(ē), -'tänt(ē)\\ *n, pl* **-tantes** *or* **-tan·ti** \\-'täntē, -'tant(ē)\\ : one who dabbles in a field of interest

dil·i·gent \\'dilǝjənt\\ *adj* : attentive and busy —**dil·i·gence** \\-jəns\\ *n* —**dil·i·gent·ly** *adv*

dill \'dil\ *n* : herb with aromatic leaves and seeds

dil·ly·dal·ly \'dilē,dalē\ *vb* : waste time by delay

di·lute \dī'lūt, də-\ *vb* **-lut·ed; -lut·ing** : lessen the consistency or strength of by mixing with something else ~ *adj* : weak —**di·lu·tion** \-'lüshən\ *n*

dim \'dim\ *adj* **-mm-** 1 : not bright or distinct 2 : having no luster 3 : not seeing or understanding clearly —**dim** *vb* —**dim·ly** *adv* —**dim·mer** *n* —**dim·ness** *n*

dime \'dīm\ *n* : U.S. coin worth 1/10 dollar

di·men·sion \də'menchən, dī-\ *n* 1 : measurement of extension (as in length, height, or breadth) 2 : extent —**di·men·sion·al** \-'mench(ə)nəl\ *adj*

di·min·ish \də'minish\ *vb* 1 : make less or cause to appear less 2 : dwindle

di·min·u·tive \də'minyətiv\ *adj* : extremely small

dim·ple \'dimpəl\ *n* : small depression esp. in the cheek or chin

din \'din\ *n* : loud noise

dine \'dīn\ *vb* **dined; din·ing** : eat dinner

din·er \'dīnər\ *n* 1 : person eating dinner 2 : railroad dining car or restaurant in the shape of one

din·ghy \'din(k)ē, -gē\ *n, pl* **-ghies** : light rowboat

din·gy \'dinjē\ *adj* **-gi·er; -est** : not fresh, bright, or light —**din·gi·ness** *n*

din·ner \'dīnər\ *n* : main daily meal

di·no·saur \'dīnə,sȯr\ *n* : extinct often huge reptile

dint \'dint\ *n* : force—in the phrase *by dint of*

di·o·cese \'dīəsəs, -,sēz, -,sēs\ *n, pl* **-ces·es** \-əz, -'dīə,sēz\ : territorial jurisdiction of a bishop —**di·o·ce·san** \dī'äsəsən, ,dīə'sēz²n\ *adj or n*

dip \'dip\ *vb* **-pp-** 1 : plunge into a liquid 2 : take out with a ladle 3 : lower and quickly raise again 4 : sink or slope downward suddenly ~ *n* 1 : plunge into water for sport 2 : sudden downward movement or incline —**dip·per** *n*

diph·the·ria \dif'thirēə, dip-\ *n* : acute contagious disease

diph·thong \'dif,thȯn, 'dip-\ *n* : two vowel sounds joined to form one speech sound (as *ou* in *out*)

di·plo·ma \də'plōmə\ *n, pl* **-mas** : record of graduation from a school

di·plo·ma·cy \-məsē\ *n* 1 : business of conducting negotiations between nations 2 : tact —**dip·lo·mat** \'diplə,mat\ *n* —**dip·lo·mat·ic** \,diplə'matik\ *adj*

dire \'dī(ə)r\ *adj* **dir·er; -est** 1 : very horrible 2 : extreme

di·rect \də'rekt, dī-\ *vb* 1 : address 2 : cause to move or to follow a certain course 3 : show (someone) the way 4 : regulate the activities or course of 5 : request with authority ~ *adj* 1 : leading to or coming from a point without deviation or interruption 2 : frank —**direct** *adv* —**di·rect·ly** \-'rek(t)lē\ *adv* —**di·rect·ness** \-'rek(t)nəs\ *n* —**di·rec·tor** \-tər\ *n*

direct current *n* : electric current flowing in one direction only

di·rec·tion \də'rekshən, dī-\ *n* 1 : supervision 2 : order 3 : course along which something moves —**di·rec·tion·al** \-sh(ə)nəl\ *adj*

di·rec·tive \-tiv\ *n* : order

di·rec·to·ry \-t(ə)rē\ *n, pl* **-ries** : alphabetical list of names and addresses

dirge \'dərj\ *n* : funeral hymn

di·ri·gi·ble \'dirəjəbəl, də'rijə-\ *n* : airship

dirt \'dərt\ *n* 1 : mud, dust, or grime that makes something unclear 2 : soil

dirty \'dərtē\ *adj* **dirt·i·er; -est** 1 : not clear 2 : unfair 3 : indecent ~ *vb* **dirt·ied; dirty·ing** : make or become dirty —**dirt·i·ness** *n*

dis·able \dis'ābəl\ *vb* **-abled; -abling** -b(ə-)liŋ\ : make unable to function —**dis·abil·i·ty** \,disə'bilətē\ *n*

dis·abuse \,disə'byüz\ *vb* : free from error

dis·ad·van·tage \,dis-\ *n* : something that hinders success —**dis·ad·van·ta·geous** *adj*

dis·af·fect \,dis-\ *vb* : cause discontent in —**dis·af·fec·tion** *n*

dis·agree \,dis-\ *vb* 1 : fail to agree 2 : differ in opinion —**dis·agree·ment** *n*

dis·agree·able \,dis-\ *adj* : unpleasant

dis·al·low \,dis-\ *vb* : refuse to admit or recognize

dis·ap·pear \,dis-\ *vb* 1 : pass out of sight 2 : cease to be —**dis·ap·pear·ance** *n*

dis·ap·point \,disə'pȯint\ *vb* : fail to fulfill the expectation or hope of —**dis·ap·point·ment** *n*

dis·ap·prove \,dis-\ *vb* 1 : condemn or reject 2 : feel or express dislike or rejection —**dis·ap·prov·al** *n*

dis·arm \dis'ärm\ *vb* 1 : take weapons from 2 : reduce armed forces 3 : make harmless or friendly —**dis·ar·ma·ment** \-'ärməmənt\ *n*

dis·ar·range \,dis-\ *vb* : throw into disorder —**dis·ar·range·ment** *n*

dis·ar·ray \ˌdis-\ *n* : disorder

di·sas·ter \diz'astǝr, dis-\ *n* : sudden great misfortune —**di·sas·trous** \-'astrǝs\ *adj*

dis·avow \ˌdisǝ'vaù\ *vb* : deny responsibility for —**dis·avow·al** \-'vaù(ǝ)l\ *n*

dis·band \dis-\ *vb* : break up the organization of

dis·bar \dis-\ *vb* : expel from the legal profession —**dis·bar·ment** *n*

dis·be·lieve \ˌdis-\ *vb* : hold not to be true or real —**dis·be·lief** *n*

dis·burse \dis'bǝrs\ *vb* -bursed; -bursing : pay out —**dis·burse·ment** *n*

disc *var of* DISK

dis·card \dis'kärd, 'dis,kärd\ *vb* : get rid of as unwanted —**dis·card** \'dis,kärd\ *n*

dis·cern \dis'ǝrn, diz-\ *vb* : discover with the eyes or the mind —**dis·cern·ible** *adj* —**dis·cern·ment** *n*

dis·charge \dis'chärj, 'dis,chärj\ *vb* 1 : unload 2 : shoot 3 : set free 4 : dismiss from service 5 : let go or let off 6 : give forth fluid ~ \'dis,-, dis-\ *n* 1 : act of discharging 2 : a flowing out (as of blood) 3 : dismissal

dis·ci·ple \dis'ipǝl\ *n* : one who helps spread his master's teachings

dis·ci·pli·nar·i·an \ˌdisǝplǝ'nerēǝn\ *n* : one who enforces order

dis·ci·pline \'disǝplǝn\ *n* 1 : field of study 2 : training that corrects, molds, or perfects 3 : punishment 4 : control gained by obedience or training ~ *vb* -plined; -plin·ing 1 : punish 2 : train in self-control —**dis·ci·plin·ary** \'disǝplǝ,nerē\ *adj*

dis·claim \dis'klām\ *vb* : disavow

dis·close \-'klōz\ *vb* : reveal —**dis·clo·sure** \-'klōzhǝr\ *n*

dis·col·or \dis'kǝlǝr\ *vb* 1 : change the color of 2 : stain —**dis·col·or·ation** \dis,kǝlǝ'rāshǝn\ *n*

dis·com·fit \dis'kǝmfǝt\ *vb* : upset —**dis·com·fi·ture** \dis'kǝmfǝ,chùr\ *n*

dis·com·fort \dis'kǝmfǝrt\ *n* : lack of comfort

dis·con·cert \diskǝn'sǝrt\ *vb* : upset

dis·con·nect \diskǝ'nekt\ *vb* : undo the connection of

dis·con·so·late \dis'känsǝlǝt\ *adj* : hopelessly sad

dis·con·tent \diskǝn'tent\ *n* : uneasiness of mind —**dis·con·tent·ed** *adj*

dis·con·tin·ue \ˌdis-\ *vb* : end —**dis·con·tin·u·ance** *n*

dis·cord \'dis,kòrd\ *n* : lack of harmony —**dis·cor·dant** \dis'kòrdᵊnt\ *adj*

dis·count \'dis,kaùnt\ *n* : reduction from a regular price ~ \'dis,-, dis-\ *vb* 1 : reduce the amount of 2 : disregard

dis·cour·age \dis'kǝrij\ *vb* -aged; -ag·ing 1 : deprive of courage, confidence, or enthusiasm 2 : dissuade —**dis·cour·age·ment** *n*

dis·course \'dis,kōrs\ *n* 1 : conversation 2 : formal treatment of a subject ~ \dis'-\ *vb* -coursed; -cours·ing : talk at length

dis·cour·te·ous \dis-\ *adj* : lacking courtesy —**dis·cour·te·ous·ly** *adv* —**dis·cour·te·sy** *n*

dis·cov·er \dis'kǝvǝr\ *vb* 1 : make known 2 : obtain the first sight or knowledge of —**dis·cov·er·er** *n* —**dis·cov·ery** \-(ǝ)rē\ *n*

dis·cred·it \dis'kredǝt\ *vb* 1 : disbelieve 2 : destroy confidence in ~ *n* 1 : loss of reputation 2 : disbelief —**dis·cred·it·able** *adj*

dis·creet \dis'krēt\ *adj* : capable of keeping a secret —**dis·creet·ly** *adv*

dis·crep·an·cy \dis'krepǝnsē\ *n, pl* -cies : difference or disagreement

dis·crete \dis'krēt, 'dis,-\ *adj* : individually distinct

dis·cre·tion \dis'kreshǝn\ *n* 1 : discreet quality 2 : power of decision or choice —**dis·cre·tion·ary** *adj*

dis·crim·i·nate \dis'krimǝ,nāt\ *vb* -nat·ed; -nat·ing 1 : distinguish 2 : show favor or disfavor unjustly —**dis·crim·i·na·tion** \-,krimǝ'nāshǝn\ *n* —**dis·crim·i·na·to·ry** \-'krimǝnǝ,tòrē\ *adj*

dis·cur·sive \dis'kǝrsiv\ *adj* : passing from one topic to another —**dis·cur·sive·ly** *adv* —**dis·cur·sive·ness** *n*

dis·cus \'diskǝs\ *n, pl* -cus·es : disk hurled for distance in a contest

dis·cuss \dis'kǝs\ *vb* : talk about or present —**dis·cus·sion** \-'kǝshǝn\ *n*

dis·dain \dis'dān\ *n* : feeling of contempt ~ *vb* : look upon or reject with disdain —**dis·dain·ful** \-fǝl\ *adj* —**dis·dain·ful·ly** *adv*

dis·ease \diz'ēz\ *n* : condition of a body that impairs its functioning —**dis·eased** \-'ēzd\ *adj*

dis·em·bark \disǝm'bärk\ *vb* : get off a ship —**dis·em·bar·ka·tion** \dis,em,bär'kāshǝn\ *n*

dis·em·bod·ied \ˌdisǝm'bädēd\ *adj* : having no substance or reality

dis·en·chant \disᵊn'chant\ *vb* : to free from illusion —**dis·en·chant·ment** *n*

dis·en·gage \-ᵊn'gāj\ *vb* : release —**dis·en·gage·ment** *n*

dis·en·tan·gle \-ᵊn'tangǝl\ *vb* : free from entanglement

dis·fa·vor \dis-\ n : disapproval

dis·fig·ure \dis-\ vb : spoil the appearance of —**dis·fig·ure·ment** n

dis·fran·chise \dis-\ vb : deprive of the right to vote —**dis·fran·chise·ment** n

dis·gorge \dis'gorj\ vb : spew forth

dis·grace \-'grās\ vb : bring disgrace to ~ n 1 : shame 2 : cause of shame —**dis·grace·ful** \-fəl\ adj —**dis·grace·ful·ly** adv

dis·grun·tle \dis'grənt³l\ vb -tled; -tling : put in bad humor

dis·guise \-'gīz\ vb -guised; -guis·ing : hide the true identity or nature of ~ n : something that conceals

dis·gust \-'gəst\ n : strong aversion ~ vb : provoke disgust in —**dis·gust·ed·ly** adv —**dis·gust·ing·ly** adv

dish \'dish\ n 1 : vessel for serving food or the food it holds 2 : food prepared in a particular way ~ vb : put in a dish —**dish·cloth** n —**dish·rag** n —**dish·wash·er** n —**dish·wa·ter** n

dis·har·mo·ny \dis'härmənē\ n : lack of harmony —**dis·har·mo·ni·ous** \,dis(,)här'mōnēəs\ adj

dis·heart·en \dis'härt³n\ vb : discourage

di·shev·el \dish'evəl\ vb -eled or -elled; -el·ing or -el·ling : throw into disorder —**di·shev·eled, di·shev·elled** adj

dis·hon·est \dis-\ adj : not honest —**dis·hon·est·ly** adv —**dis·hon·es·ty** n

dis·hon·or \dis-\ n or vb : disgrace —**dis·hon·or·able** adj —**dis·hon·or·ably** adj

dis·il·lu·sion \,disə'lüzhən\ vb : to free from illusion —**dis·il·lu·sion·ment** n

dis·in·cli·na·tion \dis-\ n : unwillingness —**dis·in·cline** \,disʔn'klīn\ vb

dis·in·fect \,disʔn'fekt\ vb : destroy disease germs in or on —**dis·in·fec·tant** \-'fektənt\ adj or n —**dis·in·fec·tion** \-'fekshən\ n

dis·in·her·it \,disʔn'herət\ vb : prevent from inheriting property

dis·in·te·grate \dis'intə,grāt\ vb : break into parts or small bits —**dis·in·te·gra·tion** \dis,intə'grāshən\ n

dis·in·ter·est·ed \dis-\ adj 1 : not interested 2 : not prejudiced —**dis·in·ter·est·ed·ness** n

dis·joint·ed \dis'jointəd\ adj 1 : separated at the joint 2 : incoherent

disk \'disk\ n : something round and flat

dis·like \dis'līk\ vb : regard with dislike ~ n : feeling that something is unpleasant and to be avoided

dis·lo·cate \'dislō,kāt, dis'-\ vb : move

out of the usual or proper place —**dis·lo·ca·tion** \,dislō'kāshən\ n

dis·lodge \dis-\ vb : force out of a place

dis·loy·al \dis-\ adj : not loyal —**dis·loy·al·ty** n

dis·mal \'dizməl\ adj : showing or causing gloom —**dis·mal·ly** adv

dis·man·tle \dis'mant³l\ vb -tled; -tling : take apart

dis·may \dis'mā\ vb -mayed; -may·ing : discourage —**dismay** n

dis·mem·ber \dis'membər\ vb : cut into pieces —**dis·mem·ber·ment** n

dis·miss \dis'mis\ vb 1 : send away 2 : remove from service 3 : put aside or out of mind —**dis·miss·al** n

dis·mount \dis-\ vb 1 : get down from something 2 : take apart

dis·obey \,disə'bā\ vb : refuse to obey —**dis·obe·di·ence** \-'bēdēəns\ n —**dis·obe·di·ent** \-ənt\ adj

dis·or·der \dis'ordər\ vb : cause disorder of ~ n 1 : lack of order 2 : breach of public order 3 : abnormal state of body or mind —**dis·or·der·li·ness** n —**dis·or·der·ly** adj

dis·or·ga·nize \dis-\ vb : throw into disorder —**dis·or·ga·ni·za·tion** n

dis·own \dis'ōn\ vb : repudiate

dis·par·age \-'parij\ vb -aged; -ag·ing : say bad things about —**dis·par·age·ment** n

dis·pa·rate \dis'parət, 'disp(ə)rət\ adj : different in quality or character —**dis·par·i·ty** \dis'parətē\ n

dis·pas·sion·ate \dis'pash(ə)nət\ adj : not influenced by strong feeling —**dis·pas·sion** \-ən\ n

dis·patch \dis'pach\ vb 1 : send 2 : kill 3 : attend to rapidly ~ n 1 : message 2 : news item from a correspondent 3 : promptness and efficiency —**dis·patch·er** n

dis·pel \dis'pel\ vb -ll- : clear away

dis·pen·sa·ry \-'pens(ə)rē\ n, pl -ries : place where medical or dental aid is provided

dis·pen·sa·tion \,dispən'sāshən\ n 1 : system of principles or rules 2 : exemption from a rule 3 : act of dispensing

dis·pense \dis'pens\ vb -pensed; -pens·ing 1 : portion out 2 : make up and give out (remedies) —**dis·pens·able** adj —**dis·pens·er** n —**dispense** vb : do without

dis·perse \-'pərs\ vb -persed; -pers·ing : scatter —**dis·per·sal** \-'pərsəl\ n —**dis·per·sion** \-'pərzhən\ n

dis·place \-'plās\ vb 1 : expel or force to flee from home or native land 2

: take the place of —dis·place·ment \-mənt\ n

dis·play \-'plā\ vb : present to view —display n

dis·please \-'plēz\ vb : arouse the dislike of —dis·plea·sure \-'plezhər\ n

dis·port \dis'pōrt\ vb 1 : amuse 2 : frolic

dis·pose \dis'pōz\ vb -posed; -pos·ing 1 : give a tendency to 2 : settle —dispos·able \-'pōzəbəl\ adj —dis·pos·al \-'pōzəl\ n —dis·pos·er n —dispose of 1 : determine the fate, condition, or use of 2 : get rid of

dis·po·si·tion \,dispə'zishən\ n 1 : act or power of disposing of 2 : arrangement 3 : natural attitude

dis·pos·sess \,dispə'zes\ vb : deprive of possession or occupancy —dis·pos·ses·sion \-'zeshən\ n

dis·pro·por·tion \,disprə'pōrshən\ n : lack of proportion —dis·pro·por·tion·ate \-sh(ə)nət\ adj

dis·prove \dis'prüv\ vb : prove false —dis·proof n

dis·pute \dis'pyüt\ vb -put·ed; -put·ing 1 : argue 2 : deny the truth or rightness of 3 : struggle against or over ~ n : debate or quarrel —dis·put·able \-əbəl, 'dispyət-\ adj —dis·put·ably \-blē\ adv —dis·pu·ta·tion \,dispyə'tāshən\ n

dis·qual·i·fy \dis-\ vb : make ineligible —dis·qual·i·fi·ca·tion n

dis·qui·et \dis-\ vb : make uneasy or restless ~ n : anxiety

dis·re·gard \,dis-\ vb : pay no attention to ~ n : neglect

dis·re·pair \,dis-\ n : need of repair

dis·rep·u·ta·ble \dis-\ adj : having a bad reputation

dis·re·pute \,dis-\ n : low regard

dis·re·spect \,dis-\ n : lack of respect —dis·re·spect·ful adj

dis·robe \dis-\ vb : undress

dis·rupt \dis'rəpt\ vb : throw into disorder —dis·rup·tion \-'rəpshən\ n —dis·rup·tive \-'rəptiv\ adj

dis·sat·is·fac·tion \dis,atəs'fakshən\ n : dissatisfied feeling

dis·sat·is·fy \'dis,atəs,fī\ vb : fail to satisfy —dis·sat·is·fied n

dis·sect \dis'ekt, dī'sekt\ vb : cut into parts esp. to examine —dis·sec·tion \-'ekshən, -'sek-\ n

dis·sem·ble \dis'embəl\ vb -bled; -bling : disguise feelings or intention —dis·sem·bler n

dis·sem·i·nate \dis'emə,nāt\ vb -nat·ed; -nat·ing : spread around —dis·sem·i·na·tion \-,em'ənāshən\ n

dis·sen·sion \dis'enchən\ n : discord

dis·sent \dis'ent\ vb : object or disagree ~ n : difference of opinion —dis·sent·er n —dis·sen·tient \-'enchənt\ adj or n

dis·ser·ta·tion \,disər'tāshən\ n : long written study of a subject

dis·ser·vice \dis'ərvəs\ n : injury

dis·si·dent \'disədənt\ n : one who differs openly —dis·si·dence \-əns\ n —dissident adj

dis·sim·i·lar \dis'imələr\ adj : different —dis·sim·i·lar·i·ty \dis,imə'larətē\ n

dis·si·pate \'disə,pāt\ vb -pat·ed; -pat·ing 1 : break up and drive off 2 : squander 3 : drink to excess —dis·si·pa·tion \,disə'pāshən\ n

dis·so·ci·ate \dis'ōs(h)ē,āt\ vb -at·ed; -at·ing : separate from association —dis·so·ci·a·tion \dis,ōs(h)ē'āshən\ n

dis·so·lute \'disə,lüt\ adj : loose in morals or conduct

dis·so·lu·tion \,disə'lüshən\ n : act or process of dissolving

dis·solve \diz'älv\ vb 1 : break up or bring to an end 2 : pass or cause to pass into solution

dis·so·nance \'disənəns\ n : discord —dis·so·nant \-nənt\ adj

dis·suade \dis'wād\ vb -suad·ed; -suad·ing : persuade not to do something —dis·sua·sion \-'wāzhən\ n

dis·tance \'distəns\ n 1 : measure of separation in space or time 2 : reserve

dis·tant \'distənt\ adj 1 : separate in space 2 : remote in time, space, or relationship 3 : reserved

dis·taste \dis'tāst\ n : dislike —dis·taste·ful adj

dis·tem·per \dis'tempər\ n : virus disease of dogs

dis·tend \dis'tend\ vb : swell out —dis·ten·sion, dis·ten·tion \-'tenchən\ n

dis·till \dis'til\ vb : obtain by distillation —dis·til·late \'distə,lāt, -lət\ n —dis·till·er n —dis·till·ery \-'til(ə)rē\ n

dis·til·la·tion \,distə'lāshən\ n : the driving off of gas or vapor from liquids or solids by heating then condensing

dis·tinct \dis'tiŋkt\ adj 1 : distinguished from others 2 : clearly seen or heard —dis·tinct·ly adv —dis·tinct·ness n

dis·tinc·tion \dis'tiŋkshən\ n 1 : act of distinguishing 2 : difference 3 : special recognition

dis·tinc·tive \-'tiŋktiv\ adj 1 : setting one apart 2 : characteristic —dis·tinc·tive·ly adv —dis·tinc·tive·ness n

dis·tin·guish \-'tiŋgwish\ vb 1 : perceive as different 2 : set apart 3 : discern 4 : make outstanding —**dis·tin·guish·able** adj —**dis·tin·guished** \-gwisht\ adj

dis·tort \dis'tòrt\ vb : twist out of shape, condition, or true meaning —**dis·tor·tion** \-'tòrshən\ n

dis·tract \dis'trakt\ vb : divert the mind or attention of —**dis·trac·tion** \-'trakshən\ n

dis·traught \dis'tròt\ adj : agitated with mental conflict

dis·tress \-'tres\ n 1 : suffering 2 : misfortune 3 : state of danger or great need ~ vb : subject to strain or distress —**dis·tress·ful** adj

dis·trib·ute \-'tribyət\ vb -ut·ed; -ut·ing 1 : divide among many 2 : spread or hand out —**dis·tri·bu·tion** \dis-trə'byüshən\ n —**dis·trib·u·tive** \dis'tribyətiv\ adj —**dis·trib·u·tor** \-ər\ n

dis·trict \'dis(,)trikt\ n : territorial division

dis·trust \dis'trəst\ vb or n : mistrust —**dis·trust·ful** \-fəl\ adj

dis·turb \dis'tərb\ vb 1 : interfere with 2 : destroy the peace, composure, or order of —**dis·tur·bance** \-'tərbəns\ n —**dis·turb·er** n

dis·use \-'üs, -'yüs\ n : lack of use

ditch \'dich\ n : trench ~ vb 1 : dig a ditch in 2 : get rid of

dith·er \'dithər\ n : highly nervous or excited state

dit·to \'ditō\ n, pl -tos : more of the same

dit·ty \'ditē\ n, pl -ties : short simple song

di·uret·ic \,dī(y)ə'retik\ adj : tending to increase urine flow —**diuretic** n

di·ur·nal \dī'ərn²l\ adj : daily 2 : of or occurring in the daytime

di·van \'dī,van, di'-\ n : couch

dive \'dīv\ vb dived \'dīvd\ or dove \'dōv\; dived; div·ing 1 : plunge into water headfirst or submerge 2 : descend quickly ~ n 1 : act of diving 2 : sharp decline —**div·er** n

di·verge \də'vərj, dī-\ vb -verged; -verg·ing 1 : move in different directions 2 : differ —**di·ver·gence** \-'vərjəns\ n —**di·ver·gent** \-jənt\ adj

di·vers \'dīvərz\ adj

di·verse \dī'vərs, də-, 'dī,vərs\ adj : involving different forms —**di·ver·si·fi·ca·tion** \də,vərsəfə'kāshən, dī-\ n —**di·ver·si·fy** \-'vərsə,fī\ vb —**di·ver·si·ty** \-sətē\ n

di·vert \də'vərt, dī-\ vb 1 : turn from a

course or purpose 2 : distract 3 : amuse —**di·ver·sion** \-'vərzhən\ n

di·vest \dī'vest, də-\ vb : strip of clothing, possessions, or rights

di·vide \də'vīd\ vb -vid·ed; -vid·ing 1 : separate 2 : distribute 3 : share 4 : subject to mathematical division ~ n : watershed —**di·vid·er** n

div·i·dend \'divə,dend\ n 1 : individual share 2 : bonus 3 : number to be divided by another

div·i·na·tion \,divə'nāshən\ n : practice of trying to foretell future events

di·vine \də'vīn\ adj -vin·er; -est 1 : relating to or being God or a god 2 : supremely good ~ n : clergyman ~ vb -vined; -vin·ing 1 : infer 2 : prophesy —**di·vine·ly** adv —**di·vin·er** n —**di·vin·i·ty** \də'vinətē\ n

di·vis·i·ble \də'vizəbəl\ adj : capable of being divided —**di·vis·i·bil·i·ty** \-,vizə'bilətē\ n

di·vi·sion \-'vizhən\ n 1 : distribution 2 : part of a whole 3 : disagreement 4 : process of finding out how many times one number is contained in another —**di·vi·sion·al** \-'vizh(ə)nəl\ adj

di·vi·sive \də'vīsiv, -'viziv\ adj : creating dissension

di·vi·sor \-'vīzər\ n : number by which a dividend is divided

di·vorce \də'vōrs\ n : legal breaking up of a marriage —**divorce** vb

di·vor·cée \-,vōr'sā, -'sē\ n : divorced woman

di·vulge \də'vəlj, dī-\ vb -vulged; -vulg·ing : reveal

diz·zy \'dizē\ adj -zi·er; -est 1 : having a sensation of whirling 2 : causing or caused by giddiness —**diz·zi·ly** adv —**diz·zi·ness** n

do \'dü\ vb did \(')did\; done \'dən\; do·ing \('dü̇iŋ\; does \(')dəz\ 1 : work to accomplish (an action or task) 2 : behave 3 : prepare or fix up 4 : fare 5 : finish 6 : serve the needs or purpose of 7 : —used as an auxiliary verb —**do away with** 1 : get rid of 2 : destroy —**do by** : act toward in a specified way —**do in** vb 1 : ruin 2 : kill

doc·ile \'däsəl\ adj : easily managed —**do·cil·i·ty** \dä'silətē\ n

¹dock \'däk\ vb 1 : shorten 2 : reduce

²dock n 1 : berth between 2 piers to receive ships 2 : loading wharf or platform ~ vb : bring or come into dock —**dock·hand** n —**dock·work·er** n

³dock n : place in a court for a prisoner

dock·et \'däkət\ *n* **1** : record of the proceedings in a legal action **2** : list of legal causes to be tried —**docket** *vb*

doc·tor \'däktər\ *n* **1** : person holding one of the highest academic degrees **2** : one (as a surgeon) skilled in healing arts ~ *vb* **1** : give medical treatment to **2** : repair or alter —**doc·tor·al** \-t(ə)rəl\ *adj*

doc·trine \'däktrən\ *n* : something taught —**doc·tri·nal** \-trən²l\ *adj*

doc·u·ment \'däkyəmənt\ *n* : paper that furnishes information or legal proof —**doc·u·ment** \-,ment\ *vb* —**doc·u·men·ta·tion** \,däkyəmən-'tāshən\ *n*

doc·u·men·ta·ry \,däkyə'ment(ə)rē\ *adj* **1** : of or relating to documents **2** : giving a factual presentation —**documentary** *n*

dod·der \'dädər\ *vb* : become feeble usu. from age

dodge \'däj\ *vb* **dodged; dodg·ing 1** : move quickly aside or out of the way of **2** : evade —**dodge** *n*

do·do \'dōdō\ *n, pl* -**does** *or* -**dos 1** : heavy flightless extinct bird **2** : stupid person

doe \'dō\ *n, pl* **does** *or* **doe** : adult female deer —**doe·skin** \-,skin\ *n*

do·er \'dü·ər\ *n* : one that does

does *pres 3d sing of* DO

doff \'däf\ *vb* : remove

dog \'dóg\ *n* : flesh-eating domestic mammal ~ *vb* **1** : hunt down or track like a hound **2** : worry as if by dogs —**dog·catch·er** \-,kach-ər\ *n or adj* —**dog·house** *n*

dog-ear \'dóg,iər\ *n* : turned-down corner of a page —**dog-eared** \-,iərd\ *adj*

dog·ged \'dógəd\ *adj* : stubbornly determined

dog·ma \'dógmə\ *n* : tenet or code of tenets

dog·ma·tism \-,tizəm\ *n* : unwarranted stubbornness of opinion —**dog·mat·ic** \dóg'matik\ *adj*

dog·wood *n* : flowering tree

doi·ly \'dóilē\ *n, pl* -**lies** : small decorative mat

do·ings \'düiŋz\ *n pl* : deeds

dol·drums \'dōldrəmz,'däl-\ *n pl* **1** : spell of listlessness or despondency **2** : windless ocean near the equator

dole \'dōl\ *n* : distribution esp. of money to the needy or unemployed ~ *vb* : give out in small portions

dole·ful \'dōlfəl\ *adj* : full of grief —**dole·ful·ly** *adv*

doll \'däll,'dòl\ *n* : small figure of a person used esp. as a child's toy

dol·lar \'dälər\ *n* : any of various basic monetary units (as in the U.S. and Canada)

dol·ly \'dälē\ *n, pl* -**lies** : wheeled frame for moving heavy objects

dol·phin \'dälfən\ *n* **1** : sea mammal related to the whales **2** : saltwater food fish

dolt \'dōlt\ *n* : stupid person —**dolt·ish** *adj*

-**dom** \dəm\ *n suffix* **1** : office or realm **2** : state or fact of being **3** : those belonging to a group

do·main \dō'mān, də-\ *n* **1** : territory over which someone reigns **2** : sphere of activity

dome \'dōm\ *n* : large hemispherical roof

do·mes·tic \də'mestik\ *adj* **1** : relating to the household or family **2** : relating and limited to one's own country **3** : tame ~ *n* : household servant —**do·mes·ti·cal·ly** \-tik(ə)lē\ *adv*

do·mes·ti·cate \-ti,kāt\ *vb* -**cat·ed; -cat·ing** : tame —**do·mes·ti·ca·tion** \-,mesti'kāshən\ *n*

do·mi·cile \'dämə,sīl, 'dō-; 'däməsəl\ *n* : home —**domicile** *vb*

dom·i·nance \'dämənəns\ *n* : control —**dom·i·nant** \-nənt\ *adj*

dom·i·nate \-,nāt\ *vb* -**nat·ed; -nat·ing 1** : have control over **2** : rise high above —**dom·i·na·tion** \,dämə'nā-shən\ *n*

dom·i·neer \,dämə'niər\ *vb* : exercise arbitrary control

do·min·ion \də'minyən\ *n* **1** : supreme authority **2** : governed territory

dom·i·no \'dämə,nō\ *n, pl* -**noes** *or* -**nos** : flat rectangular block used as a piece in a game (**dominoes**)

don \'dän\ *vb* -**nn-** : put on (clothes)

do·nate \'dō,nāt\ *vb* -**nat·ed; -nat·ing** : make a gift of —**do·na·tion** \dō'nāshən\ *n*

1done \'dən\ *past part of* DO

2done *adj* **1** : finished or ended **2** : cooked sufficiently

don·key \'däŋkē, 'dəŋ-\ *n, pl* -**keys** : domestic ass

do·nor \'dōnər\ *n* : one that gives

doo·dle \'düd²l\ *vb* -**dled; -dling** : draw or scribble aimlessly —**doodle** *n*

doom \'düm\ *n* **1** : judgment **2** : fate **3** : ruin —**doom** *vb*

door \'dōr\ *n* **1** : passage for entrance or a movable barrier that can open or close such a passage —**door·jamb** *n* —**door·knob** *n* —**door·mat** *n* —**door·step** *n* —**door·way** *n*

dope \'dōp\ 1 : narcotic preparation 2 : stupid person 3 : information ~ *vb* **doped; dop·ing** : drug

dor·mant \'dormənt\ *adj* : not actively growing or functioning —**dor·man·cy** \-mənsē\ *n*

dor·mer \'dormər\ *n* : window built upright in a sloping roof

dor·mi·to·ry \'dormə̇tōrē\ *n, pl* **-ries** : residence hall (as at a college)

dor·mouse \'dor̩maus\ *n* : squirrellike rodent

dor·sal \'dorsəl\ *adj* : relating to or on the back —**dor·sal·ly** *adv*

do·ry \'dōrē\ *n, pl* **-ries** : flat-bottomed boat

dose \'dōs\ *n* : quantity (as of medicine) taken at one time ~ *vb* **dosed; dos·ing** : give medicine to —**dos·age** \'dōsij\ *n*

dot \'dät\ *n* 1 : small spot 2 : small round mark made with or as if with a pen ~ *vb* **-tt-** : mark with dots

dot·age \'dōtij\ *n* : senility

dote \'dōt\ *vb* **dot·ed; dot·ing** 1 : act feebleminded 2 : be foolishly fond

dou·ble \'dəbəl\ *adj* 1 : consisting of 2 members or parts 2 : being twice as great or as many 3 : folded in two ~ *n* 1 : something twice another 2 : one that resembles another ~ *adv* : doubly ~ *vb* **-bled; -bling** 1 : make or become twice as great 2 : fold or bend 3 : clench

dou·blecross *vb* : deceive by trickery —**dou·ble-cross·er** *n*

dou·bly \'dəblē\ *adv* : to twice the degree

doubt \'daut\ *vb* 1 : be uncertain about 2 : mistrust 3 : consider unlikely ~ *n* 1 : uncertainty 2 : mistrust 3 : inclination not to believe —**doubt·ful** \-fəl\ *adj* —**doubt·ful·ly** *adv* —**doubt·less** \-ləs\ *adv*

douche \'düsh\ *n* : jet of fluid for cleaning a body part

dough \'dō\ *n* : stiff mixture of flour and liquid —**doughy** \'dōē\ *adj*

dough·nut \-(̩)nət\ *n* : small fried ring-shaped cake

dough·ty \'dautē\ *adj* **-ti·er; -est** : able, strong, or valiant

dour \'daúr, 'dúr\ *adj* 1 : severe 2 : gloomy or sullen

douse \'daús, 'daúz\ *vb* **doused; dous·ing** 1 : plunge into or drench with water 2 : extinguish

¹**dove** \'dəv\ *n* : small wild pigeon

²**dove** \'dōv\ *past of* DIVE

dove·tail \'dəv̩tāl\ *n* : flaring tenon and its mortise ~ *vb* 1 : join by dovetails 2 : fit together neatly

dow·a·ger \'daúijər\ *n* : widow with wealth or a title 2 : dignified elderly woman

dowdy \'daúdē\ *adj* **dowd·i·er; -est** : lacking neatness and charm

dow·el \'daú(ə)l\ *n* : peg used for fastening two pieces

dow·er \'daú(ə)r\ *n* : property given a widow for life ~ *vb* : supply with a dower

¹**down** \'daún\ *adv* 1 : toward or in a lower position or state 2 : to a lying or sitting position 3 : as a cash deposit 4 : on paper ~ *adj* 1 : lying on the ground 2 : directed or going downward 3 : being at a low level ~ *prep* : toward the bottom of ~ *vb* 1 : cause to go down 2 : defeat

²**down** *n* : fluffy feathers

down·cast *adj* 1 : sad 2 : directed down

down·fall *n* : ruin or cause of ruin —**down·fall·en** \-̩folən\ *adj*

down·grade *n* : downward slope ~ *vb* : lower in grade or position

down·heart·ed *adj* : sad

down·pour *n* : heavy rain

down·right *adv* : thoroughly ~ *adj* : absolute or thorough

downs \'daúnz\ *n pl* : rolling treeless uplands

down·stairs *adv* : on or to a lower floor and esp. the main floor —**downstairs** *adj or n*

down-to-earth *adj* : practical

down·town *adv* : to, toward, or in the business center of a town —**downtown** *n or adj*

down·trod·den \-'träd³n\ *adj* : abused by superior power

down·ward \'daúnwərd\, **down·wards** \-wərdz\ *adv* : to a lower place or condition —**downward** *adj*

down·wind *adv* : in the direction the wind is blowing

downy \'daúnē\ *adj* **-i·er; -est** : resembling or covered with down

dow·ry \'daú(ə)rē\ *n, pl* **-ries** : property a woman gives her husband in marriage

dox·ol·o·gy \däk'säləjē\ *n, pl* **-gies** : hymn of praise to God

doze \'dōz\ *vb* **dozed; doz·ing** : sleep lightly —**doze** *n*

doz·en \'dəz³n\ *n, pl* **-ens** *or* **-en** : group of 12 —**doz·enth** \-³nth\ *adj*

drab \'drab\ *adj* **-bb-** : dull —**drab·ness** *n*

draft \'draft, 'draft\ *n* 1 : act of drawing or hauling 2 : act of drinking 3 : amount drunk at once 4 : preliminary outline or rough sketch 5 : selection from a pool or the selection process **6** : order for the payment of money **7** : air current ~ *vb* **1** : select usu. on a compulsory basis **2** : make a preliminary sketch, version, or plan of ~ *adj* : drawn from a container —**draft·ee** \draf'tē, dráf-\ *n* —**drafty** \'draftē\ *adj*

drafts·man \'draftsmən, 'dráft-\ *n* : one who draws plans

drag \'drag\ *n* **1** : something dragged over a surface or through water **2** : something that hinders progress or is boring **3** : act or an instance of dragging ~ *vb* **-gg- 1** : haul **2** : move or work with difficulty **3** : pass slowly **4** : search or fish with a drag —**drag·ger** *n*

drag·net \-,net\ *n* **1** : trawl **2** : planned actions for finding a criminal

drag·on \'dragən\ *n* : fabled winged serpent

drag·on·fly *n* : large 4-winged insect

drain \'drān\ *vb* **1** : draw off or flow off gradually or completely **2** : exhaust ~ *n* : means or act of draining —**drain·age** \-ij\ *n* —**drain·er** *n* —**drain·pipe** *n*

drake \'drāk\ *n* : male duck

dra·ma \'drämə, 'dram-\ *n* **1** : composition for theatrical presentation esp. on a serious subject **2** : series of events involving conflicting forces —**dra·mat·ic** \drə'matik\ *adj* —**dra·mat·i·cal·ly** \-ik(ə)lē\ *adv* —**dram·a·tist** \'dramətəst, 'dräm-\ *n* —**dram·a·ti·za·tion** \,dramətə'zāshən, ,dräm-\ *n* —**dra·ma·tize** \'dramə,tīz, 'dräm-\ *vb*

drank *past of* DRINK

drape \'drāp\ *vb* **draped; drap·ing** **1** : cover or adorn with folds of cloth **2** : cause to hang in flowing lines or folds ~ *n* : curtain

drap·ery \'drāp(ə)rē\ *n, pl* **-er·ies** **1** : decorative fabric hung esp. as a heavy curtain

dras·tic \'drastik\ *adj* : extreme or harsh —**dras·ti·cal·ly** \-tik(ə)lē\ *adv*

draught \'dráft\ *chiefly Brit var of* DRAFT

draw \'drȯ\ *vb* **drew** \'drü\; **drawn** \'drȯn\; **draw·ing** **1** : move or cause to move (as by pulling) **2** : attract or provoke **3** : extract **4** : take or receive (as money) **5** : bend a bow in preparation for shooting **6** : leave a contest undecided **7** : sketch **8** : write out **9** : deduce ~ *n* **1** : act, process, or result of drawing **2** : tie —**draw out** *vb* **1** : cause to speak candidly —**draw up** *vb* **1** : write out **2** : pull oneself erect **3** : bring or come to a stop

draw·back *n* : disadvantage

draw·bridge *n* : bridge that can be raised

draw·er \'drȯ(ə)r\ *n* **1** : one that draws **2** : sliding boxlike compartment **3** *pl* : underpants

draw·ing \'drȯiŋ\ *n* **1** : occasion of choosing by lot **2** : act or art of making a figure, plan, or sketch with lines **3** : something drawn

drawl \'drȯl\ *vb* : speak slowly —**drawl** *n*

dread \'dred\ *vb* : feel extreme fear or reluctance ~ *n* : great fear ~ *adj* : causing dread —**dread·ful** \-fəl\ *adj* —**dread·ful·ly** *adv*

dream \'drēm\ *n* **1** : series of thoughts or visions during sleep **2** : dreamlike vision **3** : something notable **4** : ideal ~ *vb* **1** : have a dream **2** : imagine —**dream·er** *n* —**dream·like** *adj* —**dreamy** *adj*

drea·ry \'drir(ē)rē\ *adj* **-ri·er, -est** : dismal —**drea·ri·ly** \'drirəlē\ *adv*

¹dredge \'drej\ *n* : machine for removing earth esp. from under water ~ *vb* **dredged; dredg·ing** : dig up or search with a dredge —**dredg·er** *n*

²dredge *vb* **dredged; dredg·ing** : coat (food) with flour

dregs \'dregz\ *n pl* **1** : sediment **2** : most worthless part

drench \'drench\ *vb* : wet thoroughly

dress \'dres\ *vb* **1** : put clothes on **2** : decorate **3** : prepare (as a carcass) for use **4** : apply dressings, remedies, or fertilizer to ~ *n* **1** : apparel **2** : single garment of bodice and skirt ~ *adj* : suitable for a formal occasion —**dress·mak·er** *n* —**dress·mak·ing** *n*

dress·er \'dresər\ *n* : bureau with a mirror

dress·ing *n* **1** : act or process of dressing **2** : sauce or a seasoned mixture **3** : material to cover an injury

dressy \-ē\ *adj* **dress·i·er, -est** **1** : showy in dress **2** : stylish

drew *past of* DRAW

drib·ble \'dribəl\ *vb* **-bled; -bling** **1** : fall or flow in drops **2** : drool —**dribble** *n*

drier *comparative of* DRY

driest *superlative of* DRY

drift \'drift\ *n* **1** : motion or course of something drifting **2** : mass blown up by wind **3** : general intention or meaning ~ *vb* **1** : float or be driven along (as by a current) **2** : wander without purpose **3** : pile up under force —**drift·er** *n* —**drift·wood** *n*

¹drill \'dril\ *vb* **1** : bore with a drill **2** : instruct by repetition ~ *n* **1** : boring tool **2** : strict training and instruction —**drill-er** n

²drill n : seed-planting implement

³drill n : twill-weave cotton fabric

dri-ly var of DRYLY

drink \'driŋk\ vb **drank** \'draŋk\; **drunk** \'drəŋk\ or **drank**; **drink-ing 1** : swallow liquid **2** : absorb **3** : drink alcoholic beverages esp. to excess ~ n **1** : beverage **2** : alcoholic liquor —**drink-able** adj —**drink-er** n

drip \'drip\ vb **-pp-** : fall or let fall in drops ~ n **1** : a dripping **2** : sound of falling drops

drive \'drīv\ vb **drove** \'drōv\; **driv-en** \'drivən\; **driv-ing 1** : urge or force onward **2** : direct the movement or course of **3** : compel **4** : cause to become **5** : propel forcefully ~ n **1** : trip in a vehicle **2** : driveway **3** : intensive campaign **4** : aggressive or dynamic quality **5** : basic need —**driv-er** n

drive-in adj : accommodating patrons in cars —**drive-in** n

driv-el \'drivəl\ vb **-eled** or **-elled**; **-el-ing** or **-el-ling 1** : drool **2** : talk stupidly ~ n : nonsense

drive-way n : private road from the street to a house

driz-zle \'drizəl\ n : fine misty rain —**drizzle** vb

droll \'drōl\ adj : humorous or whimsical —**droll-ery** n —**drol-ly** \'drō(l)lē\ adv

drom-e-dary \'drämə,derē\ n, pl **-dar-ies** : speedy one-humped camel

drone \'drōn\ n **1** : male honeybee **2** : deep hum or buzz ~ vb **droned**; **dron-ing** : make a dull monotonous sound

drool \'drül\ vb : let liquid run from the mouth

droop \'drüp\ vb **1** : hang or incline downward **2** : lose strength or spirit —**droop** n

drop \'dräp\ n **1** : quantity of fluid in one spherical mass **2** pl : medicine used by drops **3** : decline or fall **4** : distance something drops ~ vb **-pp-1** : fall in drops **2** : let fall **3** : convey **4** : go lower or become less strong or less active —**drop-let** \-lət\ n —**drop back** vb : move toward the rear —**drop behind** vb : fail to keep up —**drop in** vb : pay an unexpected visit

drop-per n : device that dispenses liquid by drops

drop-sy \'dräpsē\ n : abnormal accumulation of serous fluid in the body

dross \'dräs\ n : waste matter

drought, drouth \'draut(h)\ n : long dry spell

¹drove \'drōv\ n : crowd of moving people or animals

²drove past of DRIVE

drown \'draün\ vb **1** : suffocate in water **2** : overpower or become overpowered

drowse \'drauz\ vb **drowsed**; **drows-ing** : doze —**drowse** n

drowsy \'draüzē\ adj **drows-i-er**; **-est** : sleepy —**drows-i-ly** adv —**drows-i-ness** n

drub \'drəb\ vb **-bb-** : beat severely

drudge \'drəj\ vb **drudged**; **drudg-ing** : do hard or boring work —**drudge** n —**drudg-ery** \-(ə)rē\ n

drug \'drəg\ n **1** : substance used as or in medicine **2** : narcotic ~ vb **-gg-** : affect with drugs —**drug-gist** \-əst\ n —**drug-store** n

dru-id \'drüəd\ n : ancient Celtic priest

drum \'drəm\ n **1** : musical instrument that is a skin-covered cylinder beaten with sticks **2** : drum-shaped object (as a container) ~ vb **-mm- 1** : beat a drum **2** : drive, force, or bring about by steady effort —**drum-beat** n —**drum-mer** n

drum-stick n **1** : stick for beating a drum **2** : lower segment of a fowl's leg

drunk \'drəŋk\ adj : having the faculties impaired by alcohol ~ n : one who is drunk —**drunk-ard** \'drəŋkərd\ n —**drunk-en** \-kən\ adj —**drunk-en-ly** adv —**drunk-en-ness** n

dry \'drī\ adj **dri-er** \'drī(ə)r\; **dri-est** \'drīəst\ **1** : lacking water or moisture **2** : thirsty **3** : marked by the absence of alcoholic beverages **4** : uninteresting **5** : not sweet ~ vb **dried**; **dry-ing** : make or become dry —**dry-ly** adv —**dry-ness** n

dry-clean vb : clean (fabrics) chiefly with solvents other than water —**dry cleaning** n

dry-er \'drī(ə)r\ n : device for drying

dry goods n pl : textiles, clothing, and notions

dry ice n : solidified carbon dioxide

du-al \'d(y)üəl\ adj : twofold —**du-al-ism** \-ə,lizəm\ n —**du-al-i-ty** \d(y)ü'alətē\ n

dub \'dəb\ vb **-bb-** : name

du-bi-ous \'d(y)übēəs\ adj **1** : uncertain **2** : questionable —**du-bi-ous-ly** adv —**du-bi-ous-ness** n

du-cal \'d(y)ükəl\ adj : relating to a duke or dukedom

duch-ess \'dəchəs\ n **1** : wife of a duke **2** : woman holding a ducal title

duchy \\'-ē\ *n, pl* **-ies** : territory of a duke or duchess

¹duck \\'dək\ *n, pl* swimming bird related to the goose and swan ~ *vb* 1 : thrust or plunge under water 2 : lower the head or body suddenly 3 : evade —**duck·ling** \-liŋ\ *n*

²duck *n* : cotton fabric

duct \\'dəkt\ *n* : canal for conveying a fluid —**duct·less** \-ləs\ *adj*

duc·tile \\'dəkt³l\ *adj* : able to be drawn out or shaped —**duc·til·i·ty** \,dək'tilətē\ *n*

dude \\'d(y)üd\ *n* : dandy

dudgeon \\'dəjən\ *n* : ill humor

due \\'d(y)ü\ *adj* 1 : owed 2 : appropriate 3 : attributable 4 : expected ~ *n* 1 : something due 2 *pl* : fee ~ *adv* : directly

du·el \\'d(y)üəl\ *n* : combat between 2 persons —**duel** *vb* —**du·el·ist** *n*

du·et \d(y)ü'et\ *n* : musical composition for 2 performers

due to *prep* : because of

dug *past of* DIG

dug·out \\'dəg,aut\ *n* 1 : boat made by hollowing out a log 2 : shelter made by digging

duke \\'d(y)ük\ *n* : nobleman of the highest rank —**duke·dom** *n*

dull \\'dəl\ *adj* 1 : mentally slow 2 : blunt 3 : not brilliant or interesting ~ *vb* : make or become dull —**dull·ard** \\'dələrd\ *n* —**dull·ness, dul·ness** *n* —**dul·ly** \\'dəl(l)ē\ *adv*

du·ly \\'d(y)ülē\ *adv* : in a due manner, time, or degree

dumb \\'dəm\ *adj* 1 : mute 2 : stupid —**dumb·ly** *adv*

dumb·bell \\'dəm,bel\ *n* 1 : short bar with weights on the ends 2 : stupid person

dumb·found, dum·found \,dəm'faund\ *vb* : amaze

dum·my \\'dəmē\ *n, pl* **-mies** 1 : dumb person 2 : imitation of something (as a human figure)

dump \\'dəmp\ *vb* : unload or discard in a mass ~ *n* : place for dumping something (as refuse) —**in the dumps** : sad

dump·ling \\'dəmpliŋ\ *n* : small mass of boiled or steamed dough

dumpy \\'dəmpē\ *adj* **dump·i·er; -est** : short and thick in build

¹dun \\'dən\ *adj* : brownish gray

²dun *vb* **-nn-** : hound for payment of a debt

dunce \\'dəns\ *n* : stupid person

dune \\'d(y)ün\ *n* : hill of sand

dung \\'dəŋ\ *n* : manure

dun·ga·ree \,dəŋgə'rē\ *n* 1 : blue denim 2 *pl* : work clothes made of dungaree

dun·geon \\'dənjən\ *n* : underground prison

dunk \\'dəŋk\ *vb* : dip or submerge temporarily in liquid

duo \\'d(y)ü(,)ō\ *n, pl* **du·os** : pair

du·o·de·num \,d(y)üə'dēnəm, d(y)ü'ädªnəm\ *n, pl* **-na** \-'dēnə, -ªnə\ *or* **-nums** : part of the small intestine nearest the stomach —**du·o·de·nal** \-'dēnªl, -ªnəl\ *adj*

dupe \\'d(y)üp\ *n* : one easily deceived or cheated —**dupe** *vb*

du·plex \\'d(y)ü,pleks\ *adj* : double ~ *n* : 2-level apartment or 2-family house

du·pli·cate \\'d(y)üplikət\ *adj* 1 : consisting of 2 identical items 2 : being just like another ~ *n* : exact copy ~ \-,kāt\ *vb* **-cat·ed; -cat·ing** 1 : make an exact copy of 2 : repeat or equal —**du·pli·ca·tion** \,d(y)üpli'kāshən\ *n* —**du·pli·ca·tor** \\'d(y)üpli,kātər\ *n*

du·plic·i·ty \d(y)ü'plisətē\ *n, pl* **-ties** : deception

du·ra·ble \\'d(y)ürəbəl\ *adj* : lasting a long time —**du·ra·bil·i·ty** \,d(y)ürə'bilətē\ *n*

du·ra·tion \d(y)ü'rāshən\ *n* : length of time something lasts

du·ress \-'res\ *n* : coercion

dur·ing \\'d(y)üriŋ\ *prep* 1 : throughout 2 : at some point in

dusk \\'dəsk\ *n* : twilight —**dusky** *adj*

dust \\'dəst\ *n* : powdered matter ~ *vb* 1 : remove dust from 2 : sprinkle with fine particles —**dust·er** *n* —**dust·pan** *n* —**dusty** *adj*

du·ty \\'d(y)ütē\ *n, pl* **-ties** 1 : action required by one's occupation or position 2 : moral or legal obligation 3 : tax —**du·te·ous** \-əs\ *adj* —**du·ti·able** \-əbəl\ *adj* —**du·ti·ful** \\'d(y)ütifəl\ *adj*

dwarf \\'dwórf\ *n, pl* **dwarfs** \\'dwó(ə)rfs\ *or* **dwarves** \\'dwórvz\ : one that is much below normal size ~ *vb* 1 : stunt 2 : cause to seem smaller —**dwarf·ish** *adj*

dwell \\'dwel\ *vb* **dwelt** \\'dwelt\ *or* **dwelled** \\'dweld, 'dwelt\; **dwell·ing** 1 : reside 2 : keep the attention directed —**dwell·er** *n* —**dwell·ing** *n*

dwin·dle \\'dwind³l\ *vb* **-dled; -dling** : become steadily less

dye \\'dī\ *n* : coloring material ~ *vb* **dyed; dye·ing** : give a new color to

dying *pres part of* DIE

dyke *var of* DIKE

dy·nam·ic \dī'namik\ adj 1 : relating to physical force producing motion 2 : energetic or forceful

dy·na·mite \'dīnə,mīt\ n : explosive made of nitroglycerin —**dynamite** vb

dy·na·mo \-,mō\ n, pl -mos : electrical generator

dy·nas·ty \'dīnəstē, -,nas-\ n, pl -ties : succession of rulers of the same family —**dy·nas·tic** \dī'nastik\ adj

dys·en·tery \'disⁿn,terē\ n, pl -ter·ies : disorder marked by diarrhea

dys·lex·ia \dis'leksēə\ n : disturbance of the ability to read —**dys·lex·ic** \-sik\ adj

dys·pep·sia \-'pepshə, -sēə\ n : indigestion —**dys·pep·tic** \-'peptik\ adj or n

dys·tro·phy \'distrəfē\ n, pl -phies : disorder involving nervous and muscular tissue

E

e \'ē\ n, pl e's or es \'ēz\ : 5th letter of the alphabet

each \'ēch\ adj : being one of the class named ~ pron : every individual one ~ adv : apiece

ea·ger \'ēgər\ adj : enthusiastic or anxious —**ea·ger·ly** adv —**ea·ger·ness** n

ea·gle \'ēgəl\ n : large bird of prey

-ean —see -AN

¹ear \'iər\ n : organ of hearing or the outer part of this —**ear·ache** n —**eared** adj —**ear-lobe** \-,lōb\ n

²ear n : fruiting head of a cereal

ear·drum n : thin membrane that receives and transmits sound waves in the ear

earl \'ərl\ n : British nobleman —**earl·dom** \-dəm\ n

ear·ly \'ərlē\ adj -li·er; -est 1 : relating to or occurring near the beginning or before the usual time 2 : ancient —**early** adv

ear·mark vb : designate for a specific purpose

earn \'ərn\ vb 1 : receive as a return for service 2 : deserve

ear·nest \'ərnəst\ n : serious state of mind —**earnest** adj —**ear·nest·ly** adv —**ear·nest·ness** n

earn·ings \'ərninz\ n pl : something earned

ear·phone n : device that reproduces sound and is worn over or in the ear

ear·ring n : earlobe ornament

ear·shot n : range of hearing

earth \'ərth\ n 1 : soil or land 2 : planet inhabited by man —**earth·li·ness** n —**earth·ly** adj —**earth·ward** \-wərd\, **earth·wards** \-wərdz\ adv

earth·en \'ərthən\ adj : made of earth or baked clay —**earth·en·ware** \-,waər\ n

earth·quake n : shaking or trembling of the earth

earth·worm n : long segmented worm

earthy \'ərthē\ adj earth·i·er; -est 1 : consisting of or resembling soil 2 : practical 3 : coarse —**earth·i·ness** n

ease \'ēz\ n 1 : comfort 2 : naturalness of manner 3 : freedom from difficulty ~ vb eased; eas·ing 1 : relieve from distress 2 : lessen the tension of 3 : make easier

ea·sel \'ēzəl\ n : frame to hold a painter's canvas upright

east \'ēst\ adv : to or toward the east ~ adj : situated toward or at or coming from the east ~ n 1 : direction of sunrise 2 cap : regions to the east —**east·er·ly** \'ēstərlē\ adv or adj —**east·ward** adv or adj —**east·wards** adv

Eas·ter \'ēstər\ n : church feast celebrating Christ's resurrection

east·ern \'ēstərn\ adj 1 cap : relating to a region designated East 2 : lying toward or coming from the east —**East·ern·er** n

easy \'ēzē\ adj eas·i·er; -est 1 : marked by ease 2 : lenient —**eas·i·ly** \'ēz(ə)lē\ adv —**eas·i·ness** \-ēnəs\ n

easy·go·ing adj : taking life easily

eat \'ēt\ vb ate \'āt\; eat·en \'ētⁿn\; eat·ing 1 : take in as food 2 : use up or corrode —**eat·able** adj or n —**eat·er** n

eaves \'ēvz\ n pl : overhanging edge of a roof

eaves·drop vb : listen secretly —**eaves·drop·per** n

ebb \'eb\ n 1 : outward flow of the tide 2 : decline ~ vb 1 : recede from the flood state 2 : wane

eb·o·ny \'ebənē\ n, pl -nies : hard heavy wood of tropical trees ~ (ebony trees) ~ adj 1 : made of ebony 2 : black

ebul·lient \i'bulyənt, -'bəl-\ adj : exuberant —**ebul·lience** \-yəns\ n

ec·cen·tric \ik'sentrik\ adj 1 : odd in behavior 2 : being off center —**eccentric** n —**ec·cen·tri·cal·ly**

\-trik(ə)lē\ *adv* —**ec·cen·tric·i·ty** \,ek,sen'trisətē\ *n*

ec·cle·si·as·tic \ik,lēzē'astik\ *n* : clergyman

ec·cle·si·as·ti·cal \-tikəl\ *adj* : relating to a church —**ecclesiastic** *adj*

ech·e·lon \'eshə,län\ *n* 1 : steplike arrangement 2 : level of authority

echo \'ekō\ *n, pl* **ech·oes** : repetition of a sound caused by a reflection of the sound waves —**echo** *vb*

éclair \ā'klaer\ *n* : custard-filled pastry

eclec·tic \e'klektik, i-\ *adj* : drawing or drawn from varied sources —**eclectic** *n*

eclipse \i'klips\ *n* : total or partial obscuring of one celestial body by another —**eclipse** *vb*

ecol·o·gy \i'käləjē, e-\ *n, pl* **-gies** : science concerned with the interaction of organisms and their environment —**eco·log·i·cal** \,ēkə'läjikəl, ,ek-\ *adj* —**eco·log·i·cal·ly** *adv* —**ecol·o·gist** \i'käləjəst, e-\ *n*

eco·nom·ic \,ekə'nämik, ,ēkə-\ *adj* : relating to the satisfaction of man's material needs

eco·nom·ics \-'nämiks\ *n* : branch of knowledge dealing with goods and services —**econ·o·mist** \i'känəməst\ *n*

econ·o·mize \i'känə,mīz\ *vb* **-mized; -miz·ing** : be thrifty

econ·o·my \-əmē\ *n, pl* **-mies** 1 : thrifty management of resources 2 : economic system —**eco·nom·i·cal** \,ekə'nämikəl, ,ēkə-\ *adj* —**eco·nom·i·cal·ly** *adv* —**economy** *adj*

ecru \'ekrü, 'ākrü\ *n* : beige

ec·sta·sy \'ekstəsē\ *n, pl* **-sies** : extreme emotional excitement —**ec·stat·ic** \ek'statik, ik-\ *adj* —**ec·stat·i·cal·ly** \-ik(ə)lē\ *adv*

ec·u·men·i·cal \,ekyə'menikəl\ *adj* : promoting worldwide Christian unity

ec·ze·ma \ig'zēmə, 'egzəmə, 'eksə-\ *n* : itching skin inflammation

1-ed *d after a vowel or* b, g, j, l, m, n, ŋ, r, <u>th</u>, v, z, zh; *əd, id after* d, t; *t after other sounds*\ *vb suffix or adj suffix* 1 —used to form the past participle of regular verbs 2 : having or having the characteristics of

2-ed *vb suffix* —used to form the past tense of regular verbs

ed·dy \'edē\ *n, pl* **-dies** : whirlpool —**eddy** *vb*

ede·ma \i'dēmə\ *n* : dropsy —**edem·a·tous** \-'demətəs\ *adj*

Eden \'ēd°n\ *n* : paradise

edge \'ej\ *n* 1 : cutting side of a blade 2 : line where something begins or ends ∼ *vb* **edged; edg·ing** 1 : give or form an edge 2 : move gradually —**edg·er** *n*

edgy \'ejē\ *adj* **edg·i·er; -est** : nervous —**edg·i·ness** *n*

ed·i·ble \'edəbəl\ *adj* : fit or safe to be eaten —**ed·i·bil·i·ty** \,edə'bilətē\ *n* —**edible** *n*

edict \'ē,dikt\ *n* : decree

ed·i·fi·ca·tion \,edəfə'kāshən\ *n* : instruction or information —**ed·i·fy** \'edə,fī\ *vb*

ed·i·fice \'edəfəs\ *n* : large building

ed·it \'edət\ *vb* : revise and prepare for publication —**ed·i·tor** \-ər\ *n* —**ed·i·tor·ship** *n*

edi·tion \i'dishən\ *n* 1 : form in which a text is published 2 : total number published at one time

ed·i·to·ri·al \,edə'tōrēəl\ *adj* 1 : relating to an editor 2 : expressing opinion ∼ *n* : article that expresses the views of an editor —**ed·i·to·ri·al·ize** \-ēə,līz\ *vb* —**ed·i·to·ri·al·ly** *adv*

ed·u·cate \'ejə,kāt\ *vb* **-cat·ed; -cat·ing** 1 : give instruction to 2 : develop mentally and morally —**ed·u·ca·ble** \'ejəkəbəl\ *adj* —**ed·u·ca·tion** \,ejə'kāshən\ *n* —**ed·u·ca·tion·al** \-sh(ə)nəl\ *adj* —**ed·u·ca·tor** \-ər\ *n*

-ee *n suffix* 1 : recipient or beneficiary of 2 : person who performs

eel \'ēl\ *n* : snakelike fish

-eer *n suffix* 1 : one that is concerned with, conducts, or produces

ee·rie \'i(ə)rē\ *adj* **-ri·er; -ri·est** : weird —**ee·ri·ly** \'irəlē\ *adv*

ef·face \i'fās, e-\ *vb* **-faced; -fac·ing** : obliterate by rubbing out —**ef·face·ment** *n*

ef·fect \i'fekt\ *n* 1 : result 2 : meaning 3 : influence 4 *pl* : goods or possessions ∼ *vb* : accomplish or produce —**in effect** : in substance

ef·fec·tive \i'fektiv\ *adj* 1 : producing a strong or desired effect 2 : being in operation —**ef·fec·tive·ly** *adv* —**ef·fec·tive·ness** *n*

ef·fec·tu·al \i'fekchə(wə)l\ *adj* : producing an intended effect —**ef·fec·tu·al·ly** *adv* —**ef·fec·tu·al·ness** *n*

ef·fem·i·nate \ə'femənət\ *adj* : unsuitably womanish —**ef·fem·i·na·cy** \-nəsē\ *n*

ef·fer·vesce \,efər'ves\ *vb* **-vesced; -vesc·ing** 1 : bubble and hiss as gas escapes 2 : show exhilaration —**ef·fer·ves·cence** \-'ves°ns\ *n* —**ef·fer-**

ves·cent \-⁹nt\ adj —ef·fer·ves·cent·ly adv

ef·fete \e'fēt\ adj : decadent or worn out

ef·fi·ca·cious \ˌefə'kāshəs\ adj : effective —ef·fi·ca·cy \'efikəsē\ n

ef·fi·cient \i'fishənt\ adj : working well with little waste —ef·fi·cien·cy \-ənsē\ n —ef·fi·cient·ly adv

ef·fi·gy \'efəjē\ n, pl -gies : image of a person

ef·fort \'efərt\ n 1 : a putting forth of strength 2 : use of resources toward a goal 3 : product of effort —ef·fort·less adj —ef·fort·less·ly adv

ef·fron·tery \i'frəntərē\ n, pl -ter·ies : insolence

ef·fu·sion \i'fyüzhən, e-\ n : a gushing forth —ef·fu·sive \i'fyüsiv\ adj —ef·fu·sive·ly adv

¹egg \'eg, 'āg\ vb : urge to action

²egg n 1 : rounded usu. hard-shelled reproductive body esp. of birds and reptiles from which the young hatches 2 : ovum —egg·shell n

egg·nog \-ˌnäg\ n : drink of eggs and cream

egg·plant n : edible purplish fruit of a plant related to the potato

ego \'ēgō\ n, pl egos : self-esteem

ego·cen·tric \ˌēgō'sentrik\ adj : self-centered

ego·tism \'ēgəˌtizəm\ n : exaggerated sense of self-importance —ego·tist \-təst\ n —ego·tis·tic \ˌēgə'tistik\, ego·tis·ti·cal \-tikəl\ adj —ego·tis·ti·cal·ly adv

egre·gious \i'grējəs\ adj : notably bad —egre·gious·ly adv

egress \'ēˌgres\ n : a way out

egret \'ēgrət, i'gret, 'ēgrət\ n : long-plumed heron

ei·der \'īdər\ n : northern sea duck that yields a soft down (eiderdown)

eight \'āt\ n 1 : one more than 7 2 : 8th in a set or series 3 : something having 8 units —eight adj or pron —eighth \'āth\ adj or adv or n

eigh·teen \ā(t)'tēn\ n : one more than 17 —eigh·teen adj or pron —eigh·teenth \-'tēnth\ adj or n

eighty \'ātē\ n, pl eight·ies : 8 times 10 —eight·i·eth \'āteəth\ adj or n —eighty adj or pron

ei·ther \'ēthər, 'ī-\ adj 1 : both 2 : being the one or the other of two ~ pron : one of two or more ~ conj : one or the other

ejac·u·late \i'jakyəˌlāt\ vb -lat·ed; -lat·ing 1 : say suddenly 2 : eject a fluid (as semen) —ejac·u·la·tion \-ˌjakyə'lāshən\ n

eject \i'jekt\ vb : drive or throw out —ejec·tion \i'jekshən\ n

eke \'ēk\ vb eked; ek·ing : barely gain with effort —usu. with out

elab·o·rate \i'lab(ə)rət\ adj 1 : planned in detail 2 : complex and ornate ~ \-əˌrāt\ vb -rat·ed; -rat·ing : work out in detail —elab·o·rate·ly adv —elab·o·rate·ness n —elab·o·ra·tion \-ˌlabə'rāshən\ n

elapse \i'laps\ vb elapsed; elaps·ing : slip by

elas·tic \i'lastik\ adj 1 : springy 2 : flexible ~ n 1 : elastic material 2 : rubber band —elas·tic·i·ty \-ˌlas'tisətē, ˌēˌlas-\ n

elate \i'lāt\ vb elat·ed; elat·ing : fill with joy —ela·tion \-'lāshən\ n

el·bow \'elˌbō\ n 1 : joint of the arm 2 : elbow-shaped bend or joint ~ vb : push aside with the elbow

el·der \'eldər\ adj : older ~ n 1 : one who is older 2 : church officer

el·der·ber·ry \'eldə(r)ˌberē\ n : edible black or red fruit or a tree or shrub bearing these

el·der·ly \'eldərlē\ adj : past middle age

el·dest \'eldəst\ adj : oldest

elect \i'lekt\ adj : elected but not yet in office ~ n elect pl : exclusive group ~ vb : choose esp. by vote —elec·tion \i'lekshən\ n —elec·tive \i'lektiv\ n or adj —elec·tor \i'lektər\ n —elec·tor·al \-t(ə)rəl\ adj

elec·tor·ate \i'lekt(ə)rət\ n : body of persons entitled to vote

elec·tric \i'lektrik\ adj 1 : relating to or run by electricity 2 : thrilling —elec·tri·cal \-trikəl\ adj —elec·tri·cal·ly adv

elec·tri·cian \i·lek'trishən\ n : one who installs or repairs electrical equipment

elec·tric·i·ty \-'tris(ə)tē\ n, pl -ties 1 : fundamental form of energy occurring naturally (as in lightning) or produced artificially 2 : electric current

elec·tri·fy \i'lektrəˌfī\ vb -fied; -fy·ing 1 : charge with electricity 2 : equip for use of electric power 3 : thrill —elec·tri·fi·ca·tion \-ˌlektrəfə'kāshən\ n

elec·tro·car·dio·gram \i·ˌlektrō'kärdēəˌgram\ n : tracing made by an electrocardiograph

elec·tro·car·dio·graph \-ˌgraf\ n : instrument for recording the changes of electrical potential occurring during the heartbeat

elec·tro·cute \i'lektrəˌkyüt\ vb -cut·ed; -cut·ing : kill by an electric shock

—elec·tro·cu·tion \-₁lektrə'kyüshən\ n

elec·trode \i'lek₁trōd\ n : conductor at a nonmetallic part of a circuit

elec·trol·y·sis \i₁lek'träləsəs\ n 1 : production of chemical changes by passage of an electric current through a substance 2 : destruction of hair roots with an electric current —elec·tro·lyt·ic \-₁trə'litik\ adj

elec·tro·lyte \i'lektrə₁līt\ n : nonmetallic electric conductor

elec·tro·mag·net \i₁lektrō'magnət\ n : magnet created with electric current —elec·tro·mag·net·ic \-₁mag'netik\ adj —elec·tro·mag·net·i·cal·ly \-ik(ə)lē\ adv

elec·tron \i'lek₁trän\ n : negatively charged particle within the atom

elec·tron·ic \i₁lek'tränik\ adj : relating to electrons or electronics —elec·tron·i·cal·ly \-ik(ə)lē\ adv

elec·tron·ics \-iks\ n : physics of electrons and their use

elec·tro·plate \i'lektrə₁plāt\ vb : coat (as with metal) by electrolysis

el·e·gance \'eligəns\ n : refined gracefulness —el·e·gant \-gənt\ adj —el·e·gant·ly adv

ele·gi·ac \₁elə'jīak, -₁ak\ adj : expressing grief

el·e·gy \'eləjē\ n, pl -gies : poem expressing grief for one who is dead

el·e·ment \'eləmənt\ n 1 pl : weather conditions 2 : natural environment 3 : constituent part 4 pl : simplest principles 5 : substance not separable by ordinary chemical means —el·e·men·tal \₁elə'ment³l\ adj

el·e·men·ta·ry \₁elə'ment(ə)rē\ adj 1 : simple 2 : relating to the basic subjects of education

el·e·phant \'eləfənt\ n : huge mammal with a trunk and 2 ivory tusks

el·e·vate \'elə₁vāt\ vb -vat·ed; -vat·ing 1 : lift up 2 : exalt

el·e·va·tion \₁elə'vāshən\ n : height or a high place

el·e·va·tor \'elə₁vātər\ n 1 : cage or platform for raising or lowering something 2 : grain storehouse

elev·en \i'levən\ n 1 : one more than 10 2 : 11th in a set or series 3 : something having 11 units —eleven adj or pron —elev·enth \-ənth\ adj or n

elf \'elf\ n, pl elves \'elvz\ : mischievous fairy —elf·in \'elfin\ adj —elf·ish \'elfish\ adj

elic·it \i'lisət\ vb : draw forth

el·i·gi·ble \'eləjəbəl\ adj : qualified to participate or to be chosen —el·i·gi·bil·i·ty \₁eləjə'bilətē\ n —eligible n

elim·i·nate \i'limə₁nāt\ vb -nat·ed; -nat·ing : get rid of —elim·i·na·tion \i₁limə'nāshən\ n

elite \ā'lēt\ n : choice or select group

elix·ir \i'liksər\ n : medicinal solution

elk \'elk\ n : large deer

el·lipse \i'lips, e-\ n : oval —el·lip·tic \-'liptik\, el·lip·ti·cal \-tikəl\ adj

el·lip·sis \i'lipsəs\ n, pl -lip·ses \-₁sēz\ 1 : omission of a word 2 : marks (as . . .) to show omission —el·lip·ti·cal \-tikəl\, el·lip·tic \-'liptik\ adj

elm \'elm\ n : tall shade tree

el·o·cu·tion \₁elə'kyüshən\ n : art of public speaking

elon·gate \i'lȯŋ₁gāt\ vb -gat·ed; -gat·ing : make or grow longer —elon·ga·tion \(₁)ē₁lȯŋ'gāshən\ n

elope \i'lōp\ vb eloped; elop·ing : run away esp. to be married —elope·ment n

el·o·quent \'eləkwənt\ adj : forceful and persuasive in speech —el·o·quence \-kwəns\ n —el·o·quent·ly adv

else \'els\ adv 1 : in a different way, time, or place 2 : otherwise ~ adj 1 : other 2 : more

else·where adv : in or to another place

elu·ci·date \i'lüsə₁dāt\ vb -dat·ed; -dat·ing : explain —elu·ci·da·tion \i₁lüsə'dāshən\ n

elude \ē'lüd\ vb elud·ed; elud·ing : evade —elu·sive \ē'lüsiv\ adj —elu·sive·ly adv —elu·sive·ness n

elves pl of ELF

ema·ci·ate \i'māshē₁āt\ vb -at·ed; -at·ing : become or make very thin —ema·ci·a·tion \i₁mās(h)ē'āshən\ n

em·a·nate \'emə₁nāt\ vb -nat·ed; -nat·ing : come forth —em·a·na·tion \₁emə'nāshən\ n

eman·ci·pate \i'mansə₁pāt\ vb -pat·ed; -pat·ing : set free —eman·ci·pa·tion \i₁mansə'pāshən\ n —eman·ci·pa·tor \i'mansə₁pātər\ n

emas·cu·late \i'maskyə₁lāt\ vb -lat·ed; -lat·ing : castrate 2 : weaken —emas·cu·la·tion \i₁maskyə'lāshən\ n

em·balm \im'bäm, -'bälm\ vb : preserve (a corpse) —em·balm·er n

em·bank·ment \im'baŋkmənt\ n : protective barrier of earth

em·bar·go \im'bärgō\ n, pl -goes : ban on trade —embargo vb

em·bark \-'bärk\ vb 1 : go on board a ship or airplane 2 : make a start —em·bar·ka·tion \₁em₁bär'kāshən\ n

em·bar·rass \im'barəs\ vb : cause distress and self-consciousness —em-bar·rass·ment \ n

em·bas·sy \'embəsē\ n, pl -sies : residence and offices of an ambassador

em·bed \im'bed\ vb -dd- : fix firmly

em·bel·lish \-'belish\ vb : decorate —em·bel·lish·ment \ n

em·ber \'embər\ n : smoldering fragment from a fire

em·bez·zle \im'bezəl\ vb -zled; -zling : steal (money) by falsifying records —em·bez·zle·ment \ n —em·bez·zler \-(ə)lər\ n

em·bit·ter \im'bitər\ vb : make bitter

em·bla·zon \-'blāzᵊn\ vb : display conspicuously

em·blem \'embləm\ n : symbol —em·blem·at·ic \,emblə'matik\ adj

em·body \im'bädē\ vb -bod·ied; -body·ing : give definite form or expression to —em·bodi·ment \-'bädimənt\ n

em·boss \im'bäs, -'bós\ vb : ornament with raised work

em·brace \-'brās\ vb -braced; -brac·ing 1 : clasp in the arms 2 : welcome 3 : include —embrace \ n

em·broi·der \-'bróidər\ vb : ornament with or do needlework —em·broi·dery \-(ə)rē\ n

em·broil \im'bróil\ vb : involve in conflict or difficulties

em·bryo \'embrē,ō\ n : living being in its earliest stages of development —em·bry·on·ic \,embrē'änik\ adj

emend \ē'mend\ vb : correct —emen·da·tion \,ē,men'dāshən\ n

em·er·ald \'em(ə)rəld\ n : green gem ~ adj : bright green

emerge \i'mərj\ vb emerged; emerg·ing : rise, come forth, or appear —emer·gence \-'mərjəns\ n —emer·gent \-jənt\ adj

emer·gen·cy \i'mərjənsē\ n, pl -cies : condition requiring prompt action

em·ery \'em(ə)rē\ n, pl -er·ies : dark granular mineral used for grinding

emet·ic \i'metik\ n : agent that induces vomiting —emetic adj

em·i·grate \'emə,grāt\ vb -grat·ed; -grat·ing : leave a country to settle elsewhere —em·i·grant \-igrənt\ n —em·i·gra·tion \,emə'grāshən\ n

em·i·nence \'emənəns\ n 1 : prominence or superiority 2 : person of high rank

em·i·nent \-nənt\ adj : prominent —em·i·nent·ly adv

em·is·sary \'emə,serē\ n, pl -sar·ies : agent

emit \ē'mit\ vb -tt- : give off or out —emis·sion \-'mishən\ n

emol·u·ment \i'mälyəmənt\ n : salary or fee

emote \i'mōt\ vb emot·ed; emot·ing : express emotion

emo·tion \i'mōshən\ n : intense feeling —emo·tion·al \-sh(ə)nəl\ adj —emo·tion·al·ly adv

em·per·or \'empərər\ n : ruler of an empire

em·pha·sis \'emfəsəs\ n, pl -pha·ses \-,sēz\ : stress

em·pha·size \-,sīz\ vb -sized; -siz·ing : stress

em·phat·ic \im'fatik, em-\ adj : uttered with emphasis —em·phat·i·cal·ly \-'fatik(ə)lē\ adv

em·pire \'em,pī(ə)r\ n : large state or a group of states

em·pir·i·cal \im'pirikəl\ adj : based on observation —em·pir·i·cal·ly \-ik(ə)lē\ adv

em·ploy \im'plói\ vb 1 : use 2 : occupy ~ n : paid occupation —em·ploy·ee, em·ploye \im,pló(i)'ē, -'pló(i),ē\ n —em·ploy·er n —em·ploy·ment \-mənt\ n

em·pow·er \im'pau(ə)r\ vb : authorize

em·press \'empras\ n 1 : wife of an emperor 2 : woman holding an imperial title

emp·ty \'emptē\ adj 1 : containing nothing 2 : not occupied 3 : lacking value, sense, or purpose ~ vb -tied; -ty·ing : make or become empty —emp·ti·ness \-tēnəs\ n

emu \'ēmyü\ n : Australian bird related to the ostrich

em·u·late \'emyə,lāt\ vb -lat·ed; -lat·ing : try to equal or excel —em·u·la·tion \,emyə'lāshən\ n

emul·si·fy \i'məlsə,fī\ vb -fied; -fy·ing : convert into an emulsion —emul·si·fi·ca·tion \-,məlsəfə'kāshən\ n —emul·si·fi·er \-,fī(ə)r\ n

emul·sion \i'məlshən\ n : mixture of mutually insoluble liquids —emul·sive \-'malsiv\ adj

-en \ən, ᵊn\ vb suffix 1 : become or cause to be 2 : cause or come to have

en·able \in'ābəl\ vb -abled; -abling : give power, capacity, or ability to

en·act \in'akt\ vb 1 : make into law. 2 : act out —en·act·ment n

enam·el \in'aməl\ n 1 : glasslike substance used for coating metal or pottery 2 : hard outer layer of a tooth 3 : glossy paint —enamel vb

en·am·or \in'amər\ vb : inflame with love

en·camp \in'kamp\ vb : make camp —en·camp·ment n

en·case \in'kās\ *vb* : enclose in or as if in a case

-ence \əns, ⁿns\ *n suffix* 1 : action or process 2 : quality or state

en·ceph·a·li·tis \in₁sefə'lītəs\ *n, pl -lit·i·des* \-'litə₁dēz\ : inflammation of the brain

en·chant \in'chant\ *vb* 1 : bewitch 2 : fascinate —**en·chant·er** *n* —**en·chant·ment** *n* —**en·chant·ress** \-'chantrəs\ *n*

en·cir·cle \in'sərkəl\ *vb* : surround

en·close \in'klōz\ *vb* 1 : shut up or surround 2 : include —**en·clo·sure** \in'klōzhər\ *n*

en·co·mi·um \en'kōmēəm\ *n, pl -mi·ums or -mia* \-mēə\ : high praise

en·com·pass \in'kəmpəs, -'käm-\ *vb* : surround or include

en·core \'än₁kōr\ *n* : further performance

en·coun·ter \in'kaúntər\ *vb* 1 : fight 2 : meet unexpectedly —**encounter** *n*

en·cour·age \in'kərij\ *vb -aged; -ag·ing* 1 : inspire with courage and hope 2 : foster —**en·cour·age·ment** *n*

en·croach \in'krōch\ *vb* : enter upon another's property or rights —**en·croach·ment** *n*

en·crust \in'krəst\ *vb* : form a crust on

en·cum·ber \in'kəmbər\ *vb* : burden —**en·cum·brance** \-brəns\ *n*

-en·cy \ənsē, ⁿn-\ *n suffix* : -ence

en·cyc·li·cal \in'siklikəl, en-\ *n* : papal letter to bishops

en·cy·clo·pe·dia \in₁sīklə'pēdēə\ *n* : reference work on many subjects —**en·cy·clo·pe·dic** \-'pēdik\ *adj*

end \'end\ *n* 1 : point at which something stops or no longer exists 2 : cessation 3 : purpose ~ *vb* 1 : stop or finish 2 : be at the end of —**end·ed** *adj* —**end·less** *adj* —**end·less·ly** *adv*

en·dan·ger \in'dānjər\ *vb* : bring into danger

en·dear \in'diər\ *vb* : make dear —**en·dear·ment** \-mənt\ *n*

en·deav·or \in'devər\ *vb or n* : attempt

end·ing \'endiŋ\ *n* : end

en·dive \'en₁dīv\ *n* : salad plant

en·do·crine \'endəkrən, -₁krīn, -₁krēn\ *adj* : producing secretions distributed by the bloodstream —**endocrine** *n*

en·dorse \in'dòrs\ *vb -dorsed; -dors·ing* 1 : sign one's name to 2 : approve —**en·dorse·ment** *n*

en·dow \in'daú\ *vb* 1 : furnish with funds 2 : furnish naturally —**en·dow·ment** *n*

en·dure \in'd(y)úr\ *vb -dured; -dur·ing* 1 : last 2 : suffer patiently 3 : tolerate —**en·dur·able** *adj* —**en·dur·ance** \-əns\ *n*

en·e·ma \'enəmə\ *n* : injection of liquid into the rectum

en·e·my \-mē, -n\ *n, pl -mies* : one that attacks or tries to harm another

en·er·get·ic \₁enər'jetik\ *adj* : full of energy or activity —**en·er·get·i·cal·ly** \-i(ə)lē\ *adv*

en·er·gize \'enər₁jīz\ *vb -gized; -giz·ing* : give energy to

en·er·gy \'enərjē\ *n, pl -gies* 1 : capacity for action 2 : vigorous action 3 : capacity for doing work

en·er·vate \'enər₁vāt\ *vb -vat·ed; -vat·ing* : make weak or listless —**en·er·va·tion** \₁enər'vāshən\ *n*

en·fold \in'fōld\ *vb* : surround or embrace

en·force \-'fōrs\ *vb* 1 : compel 2 : carry out —**en·force·able** \-əbəl\ *adj* —**en·force·ment** *n*

en·fran·chise \-'fran₁chīz\ *vb -chised; -chis·ing* : grant voting rights to —**en·fran·chise·ment** \-₁chīzmənt, -chəz-\ *n*

en·gage \in'gāj\ *vb -gaged; -gag·ing* 1 : participate or cause to participate 2 : bring or come into working contact 3 : bind by a pledge to marry 4 : hire 5 : bring or enter into conflict —**en·gage·ment** \-mənt\ *n*

en·gag·ing *adj* : attractive

en·gen·der \in'jendər\ *vb -dered; -der·ing* : create

en·gine \'enjən\ *n* 1 : machine that converts energy into mechanical motion 2 : locomotive

en·gi·neer \₁enjə'niər\ *n* 1 : one trained in engineering 2 : engine operator ~ *vb* : lay out or manage as an engineer

en·gi·neer·ing \-iŋ\ *n* : practical application of science and mathematics

en·grave \in'grāv\ *vb -graved; -grav·ing* : cut into a surface —**en·grav·er** *n* —**en·grav·ing** *n*

en·gross \-'grōs\ *vb* : occupy fully

en·gulf \-'gəlf\ *vb* : swallow up

en·hance \-'hans\ *vb -hanced; -hanc·ing* : improve in value —**en·hance·ment** *n*

enig·ma \i'nigmə\ *n* : puzzle or mystery —**enig·mat·ic** \₁enig'matik, ₁ē-\ *adj*

en·join \in'jóin\ *vb* 1 : command 2 : forbid

en·joy \-'jói\ *vb* : take pleasure in —**en·joy·able** *adj* —**en·joy·ment** *n*

en·large \-'lärj\ *vb -larged; -larg·ing* : make or grow larger —**en·large·ment** *n* —**en·larg·er** *n*

en·light·en \-'līt'n\ *vb* : give knowledge or spiritual insight to —**en·light·en·ment** *n*

en·list \-'list\ *vb* 1 : join the armed forces 2 : get the aid of —**en·list·ee** \-,lis'tē\ *n* —**en·list·ment** \-'lis(t)mənt\ *n*

en·liv·en \in'līvən\ *vb* : give life or spirit to

en·mi·ty \'enmətē\ *n, pl* **-ties** : mutual hatred

en·no·ble \in'ōbəl\ *vb* **-bled; -bling** : make noble

en·nui \'än'wē\ *n* : boredom

enor·mi·ty \i'nörmətē\ *n, pl* **-ties** 1 : great wickedness 2 : huge size

enor·mous \i'nörməs\ *adj* : great in size, number, or degree —**enor·mous·ly** *adv* —**enor·mous·ness** *n*

enough \i'nəf, ²nəf\ *adj* : adequate ~ *adv* 1 : in an adequate manner 2 : in a tolerable degree ~ *pron* : adequate number, quantity, or amount

en·quire \in'kwī(ə)r\, **en·qui·ry** \'in,kwī(ə)rē, in'-; 'inkwərē, 'iŋ-\ *var of* inquire, inquiry

en·rage \in'rāj\ *vb* : fill with rage

en·rich \-'rich\ *vb* : make rich —**en·rich·ment** *n*

en·roll, en·rol \-'rōl\ *vb* **-rolled; -rolling** 1 : enter on a list 2 : become enrolled —**en·roll·ment** *n*

en route \än'rüt, en-, in-\ *adv or adj* : on or along the way

en·sconce \in'skäns\ *vb* **-sconced; -sconc·ing** : settle snugly

en·sem·ble \än'sämbəl\ *n* 1 : small group 2 : complete costume

en·shrine \in'shrīn\ *vb* 1 : put in a shrine 2 : cherish

en·sign \'ensən, *1 also* 'en,sīn\ *n* 1 : flag 2 : commissioned officer in the navy ranking next below a lieutenant junior grade

en·slave \in'slāv\ *vb* : make a slave of —**en·slave·ment** *n*

en·snare \-'snaər\ *vb* : snare

en·sue \-'sü\ *vb* **-sued; -su·ing** : follow as a consequence

en·sure \-'shůr\ *vb* **-sured; -sur·ing** : guarantee

en·tail \-'tāl\ *vb* : involve as a necessary result

en·tan·gle \-'taŋgəl\ *vb* : tangle —**en·tan·gle·ment** *n*

en·ter \'entər\ *vb* 1 : go or come in or into 2 : start 3 : set down (as in a list)

en·ter·prise \'entər,prīz\ *n* 1 : an undertaking 2 : business organization 3 : initiative

en·ter·pris·ing \-,prīziŋ\ *adj* : showing initiative

en·ter·tain \,entər'tān\ *vb* 1 : treat or receive as a guest 2 : hold in mind 3 : amuse —**en·ter·tain·er** *n* —**en·ter·tain·ment** *n*

en·thrall, en·thral \in'thröl\ *vb* **-thralled; -thrall·ing** : hold spellbound

en·thu·si·asm \-'th(y)üzē,azəm\ *n* : strong excitement of feeling or its cause —**en·thu·si·ast** \-,ast, -əst\ *n* —**en·thu·si·as·tic** \-,th(y)üzē'astik\ *adj* —**en·thu·si·as·ti·cal·ly** \-tik(ə)lē\ *adv*

en·tice \-'tīs\ *vb* **-ticed; -tic·ing** : tempt —**en·tice·ment** *n*

en·tire \in'tī(ə)r\ *adj* : complete or whole —**en·tire·ly** *adv* —**en·tire·ty** \-'tīrətē, -'tī(ə)rtē\ *n*

en·ti·tle \-'tīt'l\ *vb* **-tled; -tling** 1 : name 2 : give a right to

en·ti·ty \'entətē\ *n, pl* **-ties** : something with separate existence

en·to·mol·o·gy \,entə'mäləjē\ *n* : study of insects —**en·to·mo·log·i·cal** \-mə'läjikəl\ *adj* —**en·to·mol·o·gist** \-'mäləjəst\ *n*

en·tou·rage \,äntü'räzh\ *n* : retinue

en·trails \'entrəlz, -,trālz\ *n pl* : intestines

¹en·trance \'entrəns\ *n* 1 : act of entering 2 : means or place of entering —**en·trant** \'entrənt\ *n*

²en·trance \in'trans\ *vb* **-tranced; -tranc·ing** : fascinate or delight

en·trap \in'trap\ *vb* : trap —**en·trap·ment** *n*

en·treat \-'trēt\ *vb* : ask earnestly —**en·treaty** \-'trētē\ *n*

en·trée, en·tree \'än,trā\ *n* : principal dish of the meal

en·trench \in'trench\ *vb* : establish in a strong position —**en·trench·ment** *n*

en·tre·pre·neur \,äntrəprə'nər\ *n* : organizer or promoter of an enterprise

en·trust \in'trəst\ *vb* : commit to another with confidence

en·try \'entrē\ *n, pl* **-tries** 1 : entrance 2 : an entering in a record or an item so entered

en·twine \in'twīn\ *vb* : twine together or around

enu·mer·ate \i'n(y)ümə,rāt\ *vb* **-at·ed; -at·ing** 1 : count 2 : list —**enu·mer·a·tion** \i,n(y)ümə'rāshən\ *n*

enun·ci·ate \ē'nənsē,āt\ *vb* **-at·ed; -at·ing** 1 : announce 2 : pronounce —**enun·ci·a·tion** \-,nənsē'āshən\ *n*

en·vel·op \in'veləp\ *vb* : surround —**en·vel·op·ment** *n*

en·ve·lope \'envə,lōp, 'än-\ *n* : paper container for a letter

en·vi·ron·ment \in'vīrənmənt\ *n* : surroundings —**en·vi·ron·men·tal** \-ˌvīrən'ment͡əl\ *adj*

en·vi·ron·men·tal·ist \-ᵊləst\ *n* : one concerned about the human environment

en·vi·rons \in'vīrənz\ *n pl* : vicinity

en·vis·age \in'vizij\ *vb* **-aged; -ag·ing** : have a mental picture of

en·voy \'en,vȯi, 'än-\ *n* : diplomat

en·vy \'envē\ *n* **1** : resentful awareness of another's advantage **2** : object of envy ∼ *vb* **-vied; -vy·ing** : feel envy toward or on account of —**en·vi·able** \-vēəbəl\ *adj* —**en·vi·ous** \-vēəs\ *adj*

en·zyme \'en,zīm\ *n* : complex mostly protein product of living cells

eon \'ēən, ē,än\ *var of* AEON

ep·au·let \,epə'let\ *n* : shoulder ornament on a uniform

ephem·er·al \i'fem(ə)rəl\ *adj* : shortlived

ep·ic \'epik\ *n* : long poem about a hero —**epic** *adj*

ep·i·cure \'epi,kyúr\ *n* : person with fastidious taste esp. in food and wine —**ep·i·cu·re·an** \,epikyú'rēən, -'kyúrē-\ *n or adj*

ep·i·dem·ic \,epə'demik\ *adj* : affecting many persons at one time —**epidemic** *n*

epi·der·mis \,epə'dərməs\ *n* : outer layer of skin

ep·i·gram \'epə,gram\ *n* : short witty poem or saying —**ep·i·gram·mat·ic** \,epəgrə'matik\ *adj*

ep·i·lep·sy \'epə,lepsē\ *n, pl* **-sies** : nervous disorder marked by convulsive attacks —**ep·i·lep·tic** \,epə'leptik\ *adj or n*

epis·co·pal \i'piskəpəl\ *adj* : governed by bishops

ep·i·sode \'epə,sōd, -,zōd\ *n* : occurrence —**ep·i·sod·ic** \,epə'sädik, -'zäd-\ *adj*

epis·tle \i'pisəl\ *n* : letter

ep·i·taph \'epə,taf\ *n* : inscription in memory of a dead person

ep·i·thet \'epə,thet, -thət\ *n* : characterizing often abusive word or phrase

epit·o·me \i'pitəmē\ *n* **1** : summary **2** : ideal example —**epit·o·mize** \-,mīz\ *vb*

ep·och \'epək, 'ep,äk\ *n* : extended period —**ep·och·al** \'epəkəl, 'ep,äkəl\ *adj*

ep·oxy \ep,äksē, ,ep'äksē\ *n* : synthetic resin used esp. in adhesives ∼ *vb* **-ox·ied** *or* **-oxyed; -oxy·ing** : glue with epoxy

equa·ble \'ekwəbəl, 'ēkwə-\ *adj* : free from unpleasant extremes —**equa-**

bil·i·ty \,ekwə'bilətē, ,ē-\ *n* —**equa·bly** \-blē\ *adv*

equal \'ēkwəl\ *adj* : of the same quantity, value, quality, number, or status as another ∼ *n* : one that is equal ∼ *vb* **equaled** *or* **equalled; equal·ing** *or* **equal·ling** : be or become equal to —**equal·i·ty** \i'kwälətē\ *n* —**equal·ize** \'ēkwə,līz\ *vb* —**equal·ly** \'ēkwəlē\ *adv*

equa·nim·i·ty \,ēkwə'nimətē, ek-\ *n, pl* **-ties** : calmness

equate \i'kwāt\ *vb* **equat·ed; equat·ing** : treat or regard as equal

equa·tion \i'kwāzhən, -shən\ *n* : mathematical statement that two things are equal

equa·tor \i'kwātər\ *n* : imaginary circle that separates the northern and southern hemispheres —**equa·to·ri·al** \,ēkwə'tōrēəl, ,ek-\ *adj*

eques·tri·an \i'kwestrēən\ *adj* : relating to horses or horsemanship ∼ *n* : horseback rider

equi·lat·er·al \,ēkwə'lat(ə)rəl\ *adj* : having equal sides

equi·lib·ri·um \-'librēəm\ *n, pl* **-ri·ums** *or* **-ria** \-rēə\ : state of balance

equine \'ē,kwīn, 'ek,wīn\ *adj* : relating to the horse —**equine** *n*

equi·nox \'ēkwə,näks, 'ek-\ *n* : time when day and night are everywhere of equal length

equip \i'kwip\ *vb* **-pp-** : furnish with needed resources —**equip·ment** \-mənt\ *n*

eq·ui·ta·ble \'ekwətəbəl\ *adj* : fair

eq·ui·ty \'ekwətē\ *n, pl* **-ties 1** : justice **2** : value of a property less debt

equiv·a·lent \i'kwiv(ə)lənt\ *adj* : equal —**equiv·a·lence** \-ləns\ *n* —**equivalent** *n*

equiv·o·cal \i'kwivəkəl\ *adj* : ambiguous or uncertain

equiv·o·cate \i'kwivə,kāt\ *vb* **-cat·ed; -cat·ing** : use misleading language —**equiv·o·ca·tion** \-,kwivə'kāshən\ *n*

1-er \ər\ *adj suffix or adv suffix* —used to form the comparative degree of adjectives and adverbs and esp. those of one or two syllables

2-er \ər\, **-ier** \ēər, yər\, **-yer** \yər\ *n suffix* **1** : one that is associated with **2** : one that performs or is the object of an action **3** : one that is

era \'irə, 'erə, 'ērə\ *n* : period of time associated with something

erad·i·cate \i'radə,kāt\ *vb* **-cat·ed; -cat·ing** : do away with —**erad·i·ca·ble** \-əkəbəl\ *adj*

erase \i'rās\ vb **erased; eras·ing** : rub or scratch out —**eras·er** n —**era·sure** \i'rāshər\ n

ere \(,)er\ prep or conj : before

erect \i'rekt\ adj : not leaning or lying down ~ vb 1 : build 2 : bring to an upright position —**erec·tion** \i'rekshən\ n

er·mine \'ərmən\ n : weasel with white winter fur or its fur

erode \i'rōd\ vb **erod·ed; erod·ing** : wear away gradually

ero·sion \i'rōzhən\ n : process of eroding

erot·ic \i'rätik\ adj : sexually arousing —**erot·i·cal·ly** \-ik-(ə)lē\ adv

err \'eər, 'ər\ vb : be or do wrong

er·rand \'erənd\ n : short trip taken to do something often for another

er·rant \-ənt\ adj 1 : traveling about 2 : going astray

er·rat·ic \ir'atik\ adj : irregular or eccentric —**er·rat·i·cal·ly** \-ik(ə)lē\ adv

er·ro·ne·ous \ir'ōnēəs, e'rō-\ adj : wrong —**er·ro·ne·ous·ly** adv

er·ror \'erər\ n 1 : something that is not accurate 2 : state of being wrong

er·satz \'er,zäts\ adj : synthetic or phony

erst·while \'ərst,hwīl\ adv : in the past ~ adj : former

er·u·di·tion \,(er(y)ə'dishən\ n : great learning —**er·u·dite** \'er(y)ə,dīt\ adj

erupt \i'rəpt\ vb : burst forth esp. suddenly and violently —**erup·tion** \i'rəpshən\ n —**erup·tive** \-tiv\ adj

-ery \(ə)rē\ n suffix 1 : character or condition 2 : practice 3 : place of doing

1-es \əz, iz after s, z, sh, ch; z after v or a vowel\ n pl suffix —used to form the plural of some nouns

2-es vb suffix —used to form the 3d person singular present of some verbs

es·ca·late \'eskə,lāt\ vb **-lat·ed; -lat·ing** : become quickly larger or greater —**es·ca·la·tion** \,eskə'lāshən\ n

es·ca·la·tor \'eskə,lātər\ n : moving stairs

es·ca·pade \'eskə,pād\ n : mischievous adventure

es·cape \is'kāp\ vb **-caped; -cap·ing** : get away or get away from ~ n 1 : flight from or avoidance of something unpleasant 2 : leakage 3 : means of escape ~ adj : providing means of escape —**es·cap·ee** \is,kā'pē, ,es(,)kā-\ n

es·ca·role \'eskə,rōl\ n : salad green

es·carp·ment \is'kärpmənt\ n : cliff

es·chew \is'chü\ vb : shun

es·cort \'es,kȯrt\ n : one accompanying another —**es·cort** \is'kȯrt, es-\ vb

es·crow \'es,krō\ n : deposit to be delivered upon fulfillment of a condition

esoph·a·gus \i'säfəgəs\ n, pl **-gi** \-,gī, -,jī\ : muscular tube connecting the mouth and stomach

es·o·ter·ic \,esə'terik\ adj : mysterious or secret

es·pe·cial·ly \is'pesh(ə)lē\ adv : particularly or notably

es·pi·o·nage \'espēə,näzh, -nij\ n : practice of spying

es·pous·al \is'pauzəl\ n 1 : betrothal 2 : wedding 3 : a taking up as a supporter —**es·pouse** \-'pauz\ vb

es·pres·so \e'spresō\ n, pl **-sos** : strong steam-brewed coffee

es·py \is'pī\ vb **-pied; -py·ing** : catch sight of

es·quire \'es,kwī(ə)r\ n —used as a title of courtesy

-ess \əs, ,es\ n suffix : female

es·say \'es,ā\ n : literary composition ~ vb \e'sā, 'es,ā\ : attempt —**es·say·ist** \'es,āəst\ n

es·sence \'es?ns\ n 1 : fundamental nature or quality 2 : extract 3 : perfume

es·sen·tial \i'senchəl\ adj : basic or necessary —**essential** n —**es·sen·tial·ly** adv

-est \əst, ist\ adj suffix or adv suffix —used to form the superlative degree of adjectives and adverbs and esp. those of 1 or 2 syllables

es·tab·lish \is'tablish\ vb 1 : bring into existence 2 : put on a firm basis 3 : cause to be recognized

es·tab·lish·ment \-mənt\ n 1 : business or a place of business 2 : an establishing or being established 3 : controlling group

es·tate \is'tāt\ n 1 : one's possessions 2 : large piece of land with a house

es·teem \i'tēm\ n or vb : regard

es·ter \'estər\ n : organic chemical compound

esthetic var of AESTHETIC

es·ti·ma·ble \'estəməbəl\ adj : worthy of esteem

es·ti·mate \'estə,māt\ vb **-mat·ed; -mat·ing** : judge the approximate value, size, or cost ~ \-mət\ n 1 : rough or approximate calculation 2 : statement of the cost of a job —**es·ti·ma·tion** \,estə'māshən\ n —**es·ti·ma·tor** \'estə,mātər\ n

es·trange \is'trānj\ vb **-tranged; -trang·ing** : make hostile —**es·trange·ment** n

es·tro·gen \'estrəjən\ *n* : hormone that produces female characteristics

es·tu·ary \'eschə,werē\ *n, pl* **-ar·ies** : arm of the sea at a river's mouth

et cet·era \et'setərə, -'setrə\ *n* : and others esp. of the same kind

etch \'ech\ *vb* 1 : make lines on with acid 2 : produce by etching —**etch·er** *n* —**etch·ing** *n*

eter·nal \i'tərnᵊl\ *adj* : lasting forever —**eter·nal·ly** *adv*

eter·ni·ty \-nətē\ *n, pl* **-ties** : infinite duration

eth·ane \'eth,ān\ *n* : gaseous hydrocarbon

eth·a·nol \'ethə,nȯl, -,nōl\ *n* : alcohol

ether \'ēthər\ *n* : light flammable liquid used as an anesthetic

ethe·re·al \i'thirēəl\ *adj* 1 : celestial 2 : exceptionally delicate

eth·i·cal \'ethikəl\ *adj* 1 : relating to ethics 2 : honorable —**eth·i·cal·ly** *adv*

eth·ics \-iks\ *n sing or pl* 1 : study of good and evil and moral duty 2 : moral principles or practice

eth·nic \'nik\ *adj* : relating to races or groups of people with common customs ~ *n* : member of a minority ethnic group

eth·nol·o·gy \eth'näləjē\ *n* : study of the races of mankind —**eth·no·log·ic** \,ethnə'läjik\, **eth·no·log·i·cal** \-ikəl\ *adj* —**eth·nol·o·gist** \eth'näləjəst\ *n*

eth·yl \'ethəl\ *n* : hydrocarbon radical

et·i·quette \'etikət, -,ket\ *n* : good manners

et·y·mol·o·gy \,etə'mäləjē\ *n, pl* **-gies** : history of a word 2 : study of etymologies —**et·y·mo·log·i·cal** \-mə'läjikəl\ *adj* —**et·y·mol·o·gist** \-'mäləjəst\ *n*

eu·ca·lyp·tus \,yükə'liptəs\ *n, pl* **-ti** \-,tī\ *or* **-tus·es** : Australian evergreen tree

Eu·cha·rist \'yükə(ə)rəst\ *n* : Communion —**eu·cha·ris·tic** \,yükə'ristik\ *adj*

eu·lo·gy \'yülōjē\ *n, pl* **-gies** : speech in praise —**eu·lo·gis·tic** \,yülə'jistik\ *adj* —**eu·lo·gize** \'yülə,jīz\ *vb*

eu·nuch \'yünək\ *n* : castrated man

eu·phe·mism \'yüfə,mizəm\ *n* : substitution of a pleasant expression for an unpleasant or offensive one —**eu·phe·mis·tic** \,yüfə'mistik\ *adj*

eu·pho·ni·ous \yü'fōnēəs\ *adj* : pleasing to the ear —**eu·pho·ny** \'yüfənē\ *n*

eu·pho·ria \yü'fōrēə\ *n* : elation —**eu·phor·ic** \-'fȯrik\ *adj*

eu·tha·na·sia \,yüthə'nāzh(ē)ə\ *n* : mercy killing

evac·u·ate \i'vakyə,wāt\ *vb* **-at·ed; -at·ing** 1 : discharge wastes from the body 2 : remove or withdraw from —**evac·u·a·tion** \i,vakyə'wāshən\ *n*

evade \i'vād\ *vb* **evad·ed; evad·ing** : manage to avoid

eval·u·ate \i'valyə,wāt\ *vb* **-at·ed; -at·ing** : appraise —**eval·u·a·tion** \i,valyə'wāshən\ *n*

evan·gel·i·cal \,ē,van'jelikəl, ,evən-\ *adj* : relating to the Christian gospel

evan·ge·lism \i'vanjə,lizəm\ *n* : the winning or revival of personal commitments to Christ —**evan·ge·list** \i'vanjələst\ *n* —**evan·ge·lis·tic** \i,vanjə'listik\ *adj*

evap·o·rate \i'vapə,rāt\ *vb* **-rat·ed; -rat·ing** 1 : pass off in or convert into vapor 2 : disappear quickly —**evap·o·ra·tion** \i,vapə'rāshən\ *n* —**evap·o·ra·tive** \i'vapə,rātiv\ *adj* —**evap·o·ra·tor** \-,rātər\ *n*

eva·sion \i'vāzhən\ *n* : act or instance of evading —**eva·sive** \i'vāsiv\ *adj* —**eva·sive·ness** *n*

eve \'ēv\ *n* : evening

even \'ēvən\ *adj* 1 : smooth 2 : equal or fair 3 : fully revenged 4 : divisible by 2 ~ *adv* 1 : already 2 —used for emphasis ~ *vb* : make or become even —**even·ly** *adv* —**even·ness** *n*

eve·ning \'ēvniŋ\ *n* : early part of the night

event \i'vent\ *n* 1 : occurrence 2 : noteworthy happening 3 : eventuality —**event·ful** *adj*

even·tu·al \i'vench(əw)əl\ *adj* : later —**even·tu·al·ly** *adv*

even·tu·al·i·ty \i,vencha'walətē\ *n, pl* **-ties** : possible occurrence or outcome

ev·er \'evər\ *adv* 1 : always 2 : at any time 3 : in any case

ev·er·green *adj* : having foliage that remains green —**evergreen** *n*

ev·er·last·ing \,evər'lastiŋ\ *adj* : lasting forever

ev·ery \'evrē\ *adj* : being each one of a group 2 : all possible

ev·ery·body \'evri,bädē, -bəd-\ *pron* : every person

ev·ery·day *adj* : ordinary

ev·ery·one \-(,)wən\ *pron* : every person

ev·ery·thing *pron* : all that exists

ev·ery·where *adv* : in every place or part

evict \i'vikt\ *vb* : force (a person) to move from a property —**evic·tion** \i'vikshən\ *n*

ev·i·dence \'evədəns\ *n* **1** : outward sign **2** : proof or testimony

ev·i·dent \-dənt\ *adj* : clear or obvious —**ev·i·dent·ly** \-ədəntlē, -ə,dent\ *adv*

evil \'ēvəl\ *adj* **evil·er** *or* **evil·ler**; **evil·est** *or* **evil·lest** : wicked ~ *n* **1** : sin **2** : source of sorrow or distress —**evil·do·er** \,ēvəl'düər\ *n* —**evil·ly** *adv*

evince \i'vins\ *vb* **evinced; evinc·ing** : show

evis·cer·ate \i'visə,rāt\ *vb* **-at·ed; -at·ing** : remove the viscera of —**evis·cer·a·tion** \i,visə'rāshən\ *n*

evoke \i'vōk\ *vb* **evoked; evok·ing** : call forth or up —**evo·ca·tion** \,ēvō'kāshən, ,evə-\ *n* —**evoc·a·tive** \i'väkətiv\ *adj*

evo·lu·tion \,evə'lüshən\ *n* : process of change by degrees —**evo·lu·tion·ary** \-shə,nerē\ *adj*

evolve \i'välv\ *vb* **evolved; evolv·ing** : develop or change by degrees

ewe \'yü\ *n* : female sheep

ew·er \'yüər\ *n* : vase-shaped jug

ex·act \ig'zakt\ *vb* : compel to furnish ~ *adj* : precisely correct —**ex·act·ing** *adj* —**ex·ac·tion** \-'zakshən\ *n* —**ex·ac·ti·tude** \-'zaktə,t(y)üd\ *n* —**ex·act·ly** *adv* —**ex·act·ness** *n*

ex·ag·ger·ate \ig'zajə,rāt\ *vb* **-at·ed; -at·ing** : say more than is true —**ex·ag·ger·at·ed·ly** *adv* —**ex·ag·ger·a·tion** \-,zajə'rāshən\ *n* —**ex·ag·ger·a·tor** \-'zajərātər\ *n*

ex·alt \ig'zolt\ *vb* : glorify —**ex·al·ta·tion** \,eg,zol'tāshən, ,ek,sol-\ *n*

ex·am \ig'zam\ *n* : examination

ex·am·ine \-ən\ *vb* **-ined; -in·ing 1** : inspect closely **2** : test by questioning —**ex·am·i·na·tion** \-,zamə'nāshən\ *n*

ex·am·ple \-'zampəl\ *n* **1** : representative sample **2** : model **3** : problem to be solved for teaching purposes

ex·as·per·ate \ig'zaspə,rāt\ *vb* **-at·ed; -at·ing** : thoroughly annoy —**ex·as·per·a·tion** \-,zaspə'rāshən\ *n*

ex·ca·vate \'ekskə,vāt\ *vb* **-vat·ed; -vat·ing** : dig or hollow out —**ex·ca·va·tion** \,ekskə'vāshən\ *n* —**ex·ca·va·tor** \'ekskə,vātər\ *n*

ex·ceed \ik'sēd\ *vb* **1** : go or be beyond the limit of **2** : do better than

ex·ceed·ing·ly *adv*, **ex·ceed·ing** *adv* : extremely

ex·cel \ik'sel\ *vb* **-ll-** : do extremely well or far better than

ex·cel·lence \'eks(ə)ləns\ *n* : quality of being excellent

ex·cel·len·cy \-(ə)lənsē\ *n, pl* **-cies** —used as a title of honor

ex·cel·lent \'eks(ə)lənt\ *adj* : very good —**ex·cel·lent·ly** *adv*

ex·cept \ik'sept\ *vb* : omit ~ *prep* **1** : excluding **2** : but ~ *conj* : but —**ex·cep·tion** \-'sepshən\ *n*

ex·cep·tion·al \-'sepsh(ə)nəl\ *adj* : superior —**ex·cep·tion·al·ly** *adv*

ex·cerpt \'ek,sərpt, 'eg,zərpt\ *n* : brief passage ~ \ek'-, eg'-, 'ek,-, 'eg,-\ *vb* : select an excerpt

ex·cess \ik'ses, 'ek,ses\ *n* : amount left over —**excess** *adj* —**ex·ces·sive** \ik'sesiv\ *adj* —**ex·ces·sive·ly** *adv*

ex·change \iks'chānj, 'eks,chānj\ *n* **1** : the giving or taking of one thing in return for another **2** : marketplace esp. for securities ~ *vb* **-changed; -chang·ing** : transfer in return for some equivalent —**ex·change·able** \iks'chānjəbəl\ *adj*

¹ex·cise \'ek,sīz, -,sīs\ *n* : tax

²ex·cise \ik'sīz\ *vb* **-cised; -cis·ing** : cut out —**ex·ci·sion** \-'sizhən\ *n*

ex·cite \ik'sīt\ *vb* **-cit·ed; cit·ing 1** : stir up **2** : kindle the emotions of —**ex·cit·abil·i·ty** \-,sītə'bilətē\ *n* —**ex·cit·able** \-'sītəbəl\ *adj* —**ex·ci·ta·tion** \,ek,sī'tāshən, -sə-\ *n* —**ex·cit·ed·ly** *adv* —**ex·cite·ment** \ik'sītmənt\ *n*

ex·claim \iks'klām\ *vb* : cry out esp. in delight —**ex·cla·ma·tion** \,eks-klə'māshən\ *n* —**ex·clam·a·to·ry** \iks'klamə,tōrē\ *adj*

exclamation point *n* : punctuation mark ! used esp. after an interjection or exclamation

ex·clude \iks'klüd\ *vb* **-clud·ed; -clud·ing** : leave out —**ex·clu·sion** \-'klüzhən\ *n*

ex·clu·sive \-'klüsiv\ *adj* **1** : reserved for particular persons **2** : stylish **3** : sole —**ex·clu·sive·ly** *adv* —**ex·clu·sive·ness** *n*

ex·com·mu·ni·cate \,ekskə-'myünə,kāt\ *vb* : expel from a church —**ex·com·mu·ni·ca·tion** \-,myünə'kāshən\ *n*

ex·cre·ment \'ekskrəmənt\ *n* : bodily waste —**ex·cre·men·tal** \,eks-krə'ment⁰l\ *adj*

ex·crete \ik'skrēt\ *vb* **-cret·ed; -cret·ing** : eliminate wastes from the body —**ex·cre·tion** \-'skrēshən\ *n* —**ex·cre·to·ry** \'ekskrə,tōrē\ *adj*

ex·cru·ci·at·ing \ik'skrüshē,ātiŋ\ *adj* : intensely painful —**ex·cru·ci·at·ing·ly** *adv*

ex·cul·pate \'ek,skəl,pāt\ *vb* **-pat·ed; -pat·ing** : clear from alleged fault

ex·cur·sion \ik'skərzhən\ *n* : pleasure trip

ex·cuse \ik'skyüz\ *vb* **-cused; -cus·ing 1** : pardon **2** : release from an obligation **3** : justify ~ \-'skyüs\ *n* **1** : justification **2** : apology

ex·e·cute \'eksi,kyüt\ *vb* **-cut·ed; -cut·ing 1** : carry to completion **2** : enforce **3** : put to death **—ex·e·cu·tion** \,eksi'kyüshən\ *n* **—ex·e·cu·tion·er** \-sh(ə)nər\ *n*

ex·ec·u·tive \ig'zek(y)ətiv\ *adj* : relating to the carrying out of decisions, plans, or laws ~ *n* **1** : branch of government with executive duties **2** : administrator

ex·ec·u·tor \-(y)ətər\ *n* : one who settles an estate **—ex·ec·u·trix** \-(y)ə,triks\ *n*

ex·em·pla·ry \ig'zemplərē\ *adj* : so commendable as to serve as a model

ex·em·pli·fy \-plə,fī\ *vb* **-fied; -fy·ing** : serve as an example of **—ex·em·pli·fi·ca·tion** \-,zempləfə'kāshən\ *n*

ex·empt \ig'zempt\ *adj* : being free from some liability ~ *vb* : make exempt **—ex·emp·tion** \-'zempshən\ *n*

ex·er·cise \'eksər,sīz\ *n* **1** : a putting into action **2** : exertion to develop endurance or a skill **3** *pl* : public ceremony ~ *vb* **-cised; cis·ing 1** : exert **2** : engage in exercise **—ex·er·cis·er** *n*

ex·ert \ig'zərt\ *vb* : put into action **—ex·er·tion** \-'zərshən\ *n*

ex·hale \eks'hāl\ *vb* **-haled; -hal·ing** : breathe out **—ex·ha·la·tion** \,eks(h)ə'lāshən\ *n*

ex·haust \ig'zȯst\ *vb* **1** : draw out or develop completely **2** : use up **3** : tire or wear out ~ *n* : waste steam or gas from an engine or a system for withdrawing it **—ex·haus·tion** \-'zȯschən\ *n* **—ex·haus·tive** \-'zȯstiv\ *adj*

ex·hib·it \ig'zibət\ *vb* : display esp. publicly ~ *n* **1** : act of exhibiting **2** : something exhibited **—ex·hi·bi·tion** \,eksə'bishən\ *n* **—ex·hib·i·tor** \ig'zibətər\ *n*

ex·hil·a·rate \ig'zilə,rāt\ *vb* **-rat·ed; -rat·ing** : thrill **—ex·hil·a·ra·tion** \-,zilə'rāshən\ *n*

ex·hort \-'zȯrt\ *vb* : urge earnestly **—ex·hor·ta·tion** \,eks,ȯr'tāshən, ,egz-, -ər-\ *n*

ex·hume \igz'(y)üm, iks'(h)yüm\ *vb* **-humed; -hum·ing** : dig up (a buried corpse) **—ex·hu·ma·tion** \,eks(h)yü-māshən, ,egz(y)ü-\ *n*

ex·i·gen·cy \'eksəjənsē, ig'zijən-\ *n, pl* **-cies 1** : urgent need **2** *pl* require-

ments of the 'situation **—ex·i·gent** \'eksəjənt\ *adj*

ex·ile \'eg,zīl, 'ek,sīl\ *n* **1** : banishment **2** : person banished from his country **—exile** *vb*

ex·ist \ig'zist\ *vb* **1** : have real or actual being **2** : live **—ex·is·tence** \-əns\ *n* **—ex·is·tent** \-ənt\ *adj*

ex·it \'egzət, 'eksət\ *n* **1** : departure **2** : way out of an enclosed space **—exit** *vb*

ex·o·dus \'eksədəs\ *n* : mass departure

ex·on·er·ate \ig'zänə,rāt\ *vb* **-at·ed; -at·ing** : free from blame **—ex·on·er·a·tion** \-,zänə'rāshən\ *n*

ex·or·bi·tant \ig'zȯrbətənt\ *adj* : exceeding what is usual or proper

ex·or·cise \'ek,sȯr,sīz, -sər-\ *vb* **-cised; cis·ing** : drive out (as an evil spirit) **—ex·or·cism** \-,sizəm\ *n* **—ex·or·cist** \-,sist\ *n*

ex·ot·ic \ig'zätik\ *adj* **1** : foreign **2** : strange and exciting **—exotic** *n* **—ex·ot·i·cal·ly** \-ik(ə)lē\ *adv* **—ex·ot·i·cism** \-'zätə,sizəm\ *n*

ex·pand \ik'spand\ *vb* : enlarge

ex·panse \-'spans\ *n* : very large area

ex·pan·sion \-'spanchən\ *n* **1** : act or process of expanding **2** : expanded part

ex·pan·sive \-'spansiv\ *adj* **1** : tending to expand **2** : warmly benevolent **3** : of large extent **—ex·pan·sive·ly** *adv* **—ex·pan·sive·ness** *n*

ex·pa·tri·ate \eks'pātrē,āt, -ət\ *n* : exile **—expatriate** \-,āt\ *vb*

ex·pect \ik'spekt\ *vb* **1** : look forward to **2** : consider probable or one's due **—ex·pec·tan·cy** \-ənsē\ *n* **—ex·pec·tant** \-ənt\ *adj* **—ex·pec·tant·ly** *adv* **—ex·pec·ta·tion** \,ek,spek'tāshən\ *n*

ex·pe·di·ent \ik'spēdēənt\ *adj* : convenient or advantageous rather than right or just ~ *n* : convenient often makeshift means to an end

ex·pe·dite \'ekspə,dīt\ *vb* **-dit·ed; -dit·ing** : carry out or handle promptly **—ex·pe·dit·er** *n*

ex·pe·di·tion \,ekspə'dishən\ *n* : long journey for work or research or the people making this

ex·pe·di·tious \-əs\ *adj* : prompt and efficient

ex·pel \ik'spel\ *vb* **-ll-** : force out

ex·pend \-'spend\ *vb* **1** : pay out **2** : use up **—ex·pend·able** *adj*

ex·pen·di·ture \-'spendichər, -də,chùr\ *n* : act of using or spending

ex·pense \ik'spens\ *n* : cost **—ex·pen·sive** \-'spensiv\ *adj* **—ex·pen·sive·ly** *adv*

ex·pe·ri·ence \ik'spirēəns\ *n* **1** : a participating in or living through an event **2** : an event that affects one **3** : knowledge from doing ~ *vb* **-enced; -enc·ing** : undergo

ex·per·i·ment \ik'sperəmənt\ *n* : test to discover something ~ *vb* : make experiments —**ex·per·i·men·tal** \-ˌsperə'ment⁰l\ *adj* —**ex·per·i·men·ta·tion** \-mən'tāshən\ *n* —**ex·per·i·men·ter** \-'sperəˌmentər\ *n*

ex·pert \'ekˌspərt\ *adj* : thoroughly skilled ~ *n* : person with special skill —**ex·pert·ly** *adv* —**ex·pert·ness** *n*

ex·per·tise \ˌek(ˌ)spər'tēz\ *n* : skill

ex·pi·ate \'ekspē,āt\ *vb* : make amends for —**ex·pi·a·tion** \ˌekspē'āshən\ *n*

ex·pire \ik'spī(ə)r, ek-\ *vb* **-pired; -pir·ing** **1** : breathe out **2** : die **3** : end —**ex·pi·ra·tion** \ˌekspə'rāshən\ *n*

ex·plain \ik'splān\ *vb* **1** : make clear **2** : give the reason for —**ex·plain·able** \-əbəl\ *adj* —**ex·pla·na·tion** \ˌeksplə'nāshən\ *n* —**ex·plan·a·to·ry** \ik'splanəˌtōrē\ *adj*

ex·ple·tive \'eksplətiv\ *n* : usu. profane exclamation

ex·pli·ca·ble \ek'splikəbəl, 'ek(ˌ)splik-\ *adj* : capable of being explained —**ex·pli·ca·bly** \-blē\ *adv*

ex·plic·it \ik'splisət\ *adj* : absolutely clear or precise —**ex·plic·it·ly** *adv* —**ex·plic·it·ness** *n*

ex·plode \ik'splōd\ *vb* **-plod·ed; -plod·ing** **1** : discredit **2** : burst or cause to burst violently

ex·ploit \'ekˌsplȯit\ *n* : heroic act ~ \ik'splȯit\ *vb* **1** : utilize **2** : use unfairly —**ex·ploi·ta·tion** \ˌekˌsplȯi'tāshən\ *n*

ex·plore \ik'splōr\ *vb* **-plored; -plor·ing** : examine or range over thoroughly —**ex·plo·ra·tion** \ˌeksplə'rāshən\ *n* —**ex·plor·a·to·ry** \ik'splōrəˌtōrē\ *adj* —**ex·plor·er** *n*

ex·plo·sion \ik'splōzhən\ *n* : process or instance of exploding

ex·plo·sive \-siv\ *adj* **1** : able to cause explosion **2** : likely to explode —**explosive** *n* —**ex·plo·sive·ly** *adv*

ex·po·nent \ik'spōnənt, 'ekˌspō-\ *n* **1** : mathematical symbol showing how many times a number is to be repeated as a factor **2** : advocate —**ex·po·nen·tial** \ˌekspə'nenchəl\ *adj* —**ex·po·nen·tial·ly** *adv*

ex·port \ek'spōrt, 'ekˌspōrt\ *vb* : send to foreign countries —**export** \'ekˌ-\ *n* —**ex·por·ta·tion** \ˌekˌspȯr'tāshən\ *n* —**ex·port·er** \ek'spȯrtər, 'ekˌspȯrt-\ *n*

ex·pose \ik'spōz\ *vb* **-posed; -pos·ing** **1** : deprive of shelter or protection **2** : subject (film) to light **3** : make known —**ex·po·sure** \-'spōzhər\ *n*

ex·po·sé, ex·po·se \ˌekspō'zā\ *n* : exposure of something discreditable

ex·po·si·tion \ˌekspə'zishən\ *n* : public exhibition

ex·pound \ik'spaund\ *vb* : set forth or explain in detail

¹ex·press \-'spres\ *adj* **1** : clear **2** : specific **3** : traveling at high speed with few stops —**express** *adv* or *n* —**express·ly** *adv*

²express *vb* **1** : make known in words or appearance **2** : press out (as juice) —**ex·press·ible** \-əbəl\ *adj* —**ex·press·ibly** \-əblē\ *adv*

ex·pres·sion \-'spreshən\ *n* **1** : utterance **2** : mathematical symbol **3** : significant word or phrase **4** : look on one's face —**ex·pres·sion·less** *adj* —**ex·pres·sive** \-'spresiv\ *adj* —**ex·pres·sive·ness** *n*

ex·press·way \ik'spres,wā\ *n* : high-speed divided highway

ex·pul·sion \-'spəlshən\ *n* : an expelling or being expelled

ex·pur·gate \'ekspərˌgāt\ *vb* **-gat·ed; -gat·ing** : censor —**ex·pur·ga·tion** \ˌekspər'gāshən\ *n*

ex·qui·site \ek'skwizət, 'ek(ˌ)skwiz-\ *adj* **1** : flawlessly beautiful and delicate **2** : keenly discriminating

ex·tant \'ekstənt; ek'stant\ *adj* : existing

ex·tem·po·ra·ne·ous \ekˌstempə-'rānēəs\ *adj* : impromptu —**ex·tem·po·ra·ne·ous·ly** *adv*

ex·tend \ik'stend\ *vb* **1** : stretch forth or out **2** : prolong **3** : enlarge —**ex·tend·able, ex·tend·ible** \-'stendəbəl\ *adj*

ex·ten·sion \-'stenchən\ *n* **1** : an extending or being extended **2** : additional part

ex·ten·sive \-'stensiv\ *adj* : of considerable extent —**ex·ten·sive·ly** *adv*

ex·tent \-'stent\ *n* : size, length, or degree of something

ex·ten·u·ate \ik'stenyəˌwāt\ *vb* **-at·ed; -at·ing** : lessen the seriousness of —**ex·ten·u·a·tion** \-ˌstenyə'wāshən\ *n*

ex·te·ri·or \ek'stirēər\ *adj* : external ~ *n* : external part or surface

ex·ter·mi·nate \ik'stərmə,nāt\ *vb* **-nat·ed; -nat·ing** : destroy utterly —**ex·ter·mi·na·tion** \-ˌstərmə'nāshən\ *n* —**ex·ter·mi·na·tor** \-'stərmə,nātər\ *n*

ex·ter·nal \ek'stərn⁰l\ *adj* : relating to or on the outside —**ex·ter·nal·ly** *adv*

ex·tinct \ik'stiŋkt\ *adj* : no longer existing —**ex·tinc·tion** \-'stiŋkshən\ *n*

ex·tin·guish \-'stiŋgwish\ *vb* : put out (as a fire) —**ex·tin·guish·able** *adj* —**ex·tin·guish·er** *n*

ex·tir·pate \'ekstər,pāt\ *vb* **-pat·ed; -pat·ing** : destroy

ex·tol \ik'stōl\ *vb* **-ll-** : praise highly

ex·tort \-'stȯrt\ *vb* : obtain by force or improper pressure —**ex·tor·tion** \-'stȯrshən\ *n* —**ex·tor·tion·er** *n* —**ex·tor·tion·ist** *n*

ex·tra \'ekstrə\ *adj* **1** : additional **2** : superior —**extra** *n or adv*

extra- *prefix* : outside or beyond

extra-atmospheric	extragalactic
extracampus	extragovernmental
extraclassroom	extrahuman
extracommunity	extralegal
extraconstitutional	extramarital
extracontinental	extranational
extradepartmental	extraplanetary
extradiocesan	extrascholastic
extrafamilial	extrasensory
	extraterrestrial
	extravehicular

ex·tract \ik'strakt\ *vb* **1** : pull out forcibly **2** : withdraw (as a juice) ~ \'ek,-\ *n* **1** : excerpt **2** : product (as a juice) obtained by extracting —**ex·tract·able** *adj* —**ex·trac·tion** \ik'strakshən\ *n* —**ex·trac·tor** \-tər\ *n*

ex·tra·cur·ric·u·lar \,ekstrəkə'rikyələr\ *adj* : lying outside the regular curriculum

ex·tra·dite \'ekstrə,dīt\ *vb* **-dit·ed; -dit·ing** : bring or deliver a suspect to a different jurisdiction for trial —**ex·tra·di·tion** \,ekstrə'dishən\ *n*

ex·tra·ne·ous \ek'strānēəs\ *adj* : not essential or relevant —**ex·tra·ne·ous·ly** *adv*

ex·traor·di·nary \ik'strȯrd²n,erē, ,ekstrə'ȯrd-\ *adj* : notably unusual or exceptional —**ex·traor·di·nari·ly** \ik,strȯrd²n'erəlē, ,ekstrə,ȯrd-\ *adv*

ex·trav·a·gant \ik'stravigənt\ *adj* : wildly excessive, lavish, or costly —**ex·trav·a·gance** \-gəns\ *n* —**ex·trav·a·gant·ly** *adv*

ex·trav·a·gan·za \-,stravə'ganzə\ *n* : spectacular event

ex·tra·vert, ex·tro·vert \'ekstrə,vərt\ *n* : person more interested in the world than in the inner self —**ex·tra·ver·sion** \,ekstrə'vərzhən\ *n* —**extravert** \'ekstrə,vərt\ *adj* —**ex·tra·vert·ed** \-əd\ *adj*

ex·treme \ik'strēm\ *adj* **1** : very great or intense **2** : very severe or drastic **3** : not moderate **4** : most remote ~ *n* **1** : extreme state **2** : something located at one end or the other of a range —**ex·treme·ly** *adv*

ex·trem·i·ty \-'stremətē\ *n, pl* **-ties 1** : most remote part **2** : human hand or foot **3** : extreme degree or state (as of need)

ex·tri·cate \'ekstrə,kāt\ *vb* **-cat·ed; -cat·ing** : set or get free from an entanglement or difficulty —**ex·tri·ca·ble** \ik'strikəbəl, ek-; 'ek(,)strik-\ *adj* —**ex·tri·ca·tion** \,ekstrə'kāshən\ *n*

ex·u·ber·ant \ig'zübə(ə)rənt\ *adj* : joyously unrestrained —**ex·u·ber·ance** \-b(ə)rəns\ *n* —**ex·u·ber·ant·ly** *adv*

ex·ude \ig'züd\ *vb* **-ud·ed; -ud·ing 1** : discharge slowly through pores **2** : give off —**ex·u·date** \'eks(y)ù,dāt\ *n* —**ex·u·da·tion** \,eks(y)ù'dāshən\ *n*

ex·ult \ig'zəlt\ *vb* : rejoice in triumph —**ex·ul·tant** \-'zəlt²nt\ *adj* —**ex·ul·tant·ly** *adv* —**ex·ul·ta·tion** \,ek(,)səl'tāshən, ,eg(,)zəl-\ *n*

-ey —*see* -Y

eye \'ī\ *n* **1** : organ of sight consisting of a globular structure (**eye-ball**) in a socket of the skull with thin movable covers (**eye-lids**) bordered with hairs (**eye-lash·es**) **2** : vision **3** : judgment **4** : something suggesting an eye ~ *vb* **eyed; eye·ing** *or* **ey·ing** : look at —**eye·brow** \-,braù\ *n* —**eyed** \'īd\ *adj* —**eye·strain** *n*

eye·drop·per *n* : dropper

eye·glass·es *n pl* : glasses

eye·let \'īlət\ *n* : small hole (as in cloth) for a lacing or rope

eye·open·er *n* : something startling —**eye·open·ing** *adj*

eye·piece *n* : lens at the eye end of an optical instrument

eye·sight *n* : sight

eye·sore *n* : unpleasant sight

eye·tooth *n* : upper canine tooth

eye·wit·ness *n* : person who actually sees something happen

ey·rie \'ī(ə)rē, *or like* AERIE\ *var of* AERIE

F

f \'ef\ *n, pl* **f's** *or* **fs** \'efs\ : 6th letter of the alphabet

fa·ble \'fābəl\ *n* 1 : legendary story 2 : story that teaches a lesson —**fa·bled** \-bəld\ *adj*

fab·ric \'fabrik\ *n* 1 : structure 2 : material made usu. by weaving or knitting fibers

fab·ri·cate \-ri,kāt\ *vb* -**cat·ed**; -**cat·ing** 1 : construct 2 : invent —**fab·ri·ca·tion** \,fabri'kāshən\ *n*

fab·u·lous \'fabyələs\ *adj* 1 : like, told in, or based on fable 2 : incredible or marvelous —**fab·u·lous·ly** *adv*

fa·cade \fə'säd\ *n* 1 : principal face of a building 2 : false or superficial appearance

face \'fās\ *n* 1 : front or principal surface (as of the head) 2 : presence 3 : facial expression 4 : grimace 5 : outward appearance ~ *vb* **faced**; **fac·ing** 1 : challenge or resist firmly or brazenly 2 : cover with different material 3 : sit or stand with the face toward 4 : front on —**faced** \'fāst\ *adj* —**face·less** *adj* —**face·less·ness** *n* —**fa·cial** \'fāshəl\ *adj or n*

face-down *adv* : with the face downward

fac·et \'fasət\ *n* 1 : surface of a cut gem 2 : phase —**fac·et·ed** *adj*

fa·ce·tious \fə'sēshəs\ *adj* : jocular —**fa·ce·tious·ly** *adv* —**fa·ce·tious·ness** *n*

fa·cile \'fasəl\ *adj* 1 : easy 2 : fluent

fa·cil·i·tate \fə'silə,tāt\ *vb* -**tat·ed**; -**tat·ing** : make easier

fa·cil·i·ty \-'silətē\ *n, pl* -**ties** 1 : ease in doing or using 2 : something built or installed to serve a purpose or facilitate an activity

fac·ing \'fāsiŋ\ *n* : lining or covering or material for this

fac·sim·i·le \fak'siməlē\ *n* : exact copy

fact \'fakt\ *n* 1 : act or action 2 : something that exists or is real —**fac·tu·al** \'fakchə(wə)l\ *adj* —**fac·tu·al·ly** *adv*

fac·tion \'fakshən\ *n* : part of a larger group —**fac·tion·al** *adj* —**fac·tion·al·ism** \-sh(ə)nə,lizəm\ *n*

fac·tious \'fakshəs\ *adj* : causing discord

fac·ti·tious \fak'tishəs\ *adj* : artificial

fac·tor \'faktər\ *n* 1 : something that has an effect 2 : gene 3 : number used in multiplying

fac·to·ry \'fakt(ə)rē\ *n, pl* -**ries** : place for manufacturing

fac·to·tum \fak'tōtəm\ *n* : employee with varied duties

fac·ul·ty \'fakəltē\ *n, pl* -**ties** 1 : ability to act 2 : power of the mind or body 3 : body of teachers or department of instruction

fad \'fad\ *n* : briefly popular practice or interest —**fad·dish** *adj* —**fad·dist** *n*

fade \'fād\ *vb* **fad·ed**; **fad·ing** 1 : wither 2 : lose or cause to lose freshness or brilliance 3 : grow dim 4 : vanish

fag \'fag\ *vb* -**gg**- 1 : drudge 2 : tire or exhaust

fag·ot, fag·got \'fagət\ *n* : bundle of twigs

Fahr·en·heit \'farən,hīt\ *adj* : relating to a thermometer scale with the boiling point at 212 degrees and the freezing point at 32 degrees

fail \'fāl\ *vb* 1 : decline in health 2 : die away 3 : stop functioning 4 : be unsuccessful 5 : become bankrupt 6 : disappoint or abandon 7 : neglect ~ *n* : act of failing

fail·ing *n* : slight defect in character or conduct ~ *prep* : in the absence or lack of

faille \'fīl\ *n* : closely woven ribbed fabric

fail·ure \'fālyər\ *n* 1 : absence of expected action or performance 2 : bankruptcy 3 : deficiency 4 : one that has failed

faint \'fānt\ *adj* 1 : cowardly or spiritless 2 : weak and dizzy 3 : lacking vigor 4 : indistinct ~ *vb* : lose consciousness ~ *n* : act or condition of fainting —**faint-heart·ed** *adj* —**faint·ly** *adv* —**faint·ness** *n*

¹fair \'faər\ *adj* 1 : attractive in appearance 2 : not stormy or cloudy 3 : just or honest 4 : conforming with the rules 5 : open to legitimate pursuit or attack 6 : light in color 7 : adequate —**fair·ness** *n*

²fair *adv* : FAIRLY

³fair *n* : exhibition for judging or selling —**fair·ground** *n*

fair·ly \'fa(ə)rlē\ *adv* 1 : quite 2 : in a fair manner 3 : moderately

fairy \'fa(ə)rē\ *n, pl* **fairies** : imaginary being —**fairy tale** *n*

fairy·land \-,land\ *n* 1 : land of fairies 2 : beautiful or charming place

faith \'fāth\ *n, pl* **faiths** \'fāths, 'fāthz\ **1** : allegiance **2** : belief and trust in God **3** : confidence **4** : system of religious beliefs —**faith·ful** \-fəl\ *adj* —**faith·ful·ly** *adv* —**faith·ful·ness** *n* —**faith·less** *adj* —**faith·less·ly** *adv* —**faith·less·ness** *n*

fake \'fāk\ *vb* **faked; fak·ing 1** : falsify **2** : counterfeit **3** : pretend ~ *n* : copy, counterfeit, or trick ~ *adj* : not genuine —**fak·er** *n*

fa·kir \fə'kiər\ *n* : wandering beggar of India

fal·con \'falkən, 'fȯ(l)-\ *n* : long-winged hawk esp. used for hunting —**fal·con·ry** \-rē\ *n*

fall \'fȯl\ *vb* **fell** \'fel\, **fall·en** \'fȯlən\; **fall·ing 1** : go down by gravity **2** : hang freely **3** : go lower **4** : be defeated or ruined **5** : commit a sin **6** : happen at a certain time **7** : become gradually ~ *n* **1** : act of falling **2** : autumn **3** : downfall **4** *pl* : waterfall **5** : distance something falls

fal·la·cy \'faləsē\ *n, pl* **-cies 1** : false idea **2** : false reasoning —**fal·la·cious** \fə'lāshəs\ *adj*

fal·li·ble \'faləbəl\ *adj* : capable of making a mistake

fall·out *n* : radioactive particles from a nuclear explosion

fal·low \'falō\ *n* : land plowed but not planted —**fallow** *vb or adj*

false \'fȯls\ *adj* **fals·er; fals·est 1** : not genuine, true, faithful, or permanent **2** : misleading —**false·ly** *adv* —**false·ness** *n* —**fal·si·fi·ca·tion** \,fȯlsə-fə'kāshən\ *n* —**fal·si·fy** \'fȯlsə,fī\ *vb* —**fal·si·ty** \'fȯlsətē\ *n*

false·hood \'fȯls,hu̇d\ *n* : lie

fal·set·to \fȯl'setō\ *n, pl* **-tos** : artificially high singing voice

fal·ter \'fȯltər\ *vb* **-tered; -ter·ing 1** : move unsteadily **2** : hesitate —**fal·ter·ing·ly** *adv*

fame \'fām\ *n* : public reputation —**famed** \'fāmd\ *adj*

fa·mil·ial \fə'milyəl\ *adj* : relating to a family

¹fa·mil·iar \fə'milyər\ *n* **1** : companion **2** : guardian spirit

²familiar *adj* **1** : closely acquainted **2** : forward **3** : frequently seen or experienced —**fa·mil·iar·i·ty** \fə,mil-'yaratē, -,milē'(y)ar-\ *n* —**fa·mil·iar·ize** \fə'milyə,rīz\ *vb* —**fa·mil·iar·ly** *adv*

fam·i·ly \'fam(ə)lē\ *n, pl* **-lies 1** : persons of common ancestry **2** : group living together **3** : parents and children **4** : group of related individuals

fam·ine \'famən\ *n* : extreme scarcity of food

fam·ish \-ish\ *vb* : starve

fa·mous \'fāməs\ *adj* : widely known or celebrated

fa·mous·ly *adv* : very well

¹fan \'fan\ *n* : device for producing a current of air ~ *vb* **-nn- 1** : move air with a fan **2** : direct a current of air upon **3** : stir to activity

²fan *n* : enthusiastic follower or admirer

fa·nat·ic \fə'natik\, **fa·nat·i·cal** \-ikəl\ *adj* : excessively enthusiastic or devoted —**fanatic** *n* —**fa·nat·i·cism** \-'natə,sizəm\ *n*

fan·ci·er \'fansēər\ *n* : one devoted to raising a particular plant or animal

fan·cy \'fansē\ *n, pl* **-cies 1** : liking **2** : whim **3** : imagination ~ *vb* **-cied; -cy·ing 1** : like **2** : imagine ~ *adj* **-ci·er, -est 1** : not plain **2** : of superior quality —**fan·ci·ful** \-sifəl\ *adj* —**fan·ci·ful·ly** \-f(ə)lē\ *adv* —**fan·ci·ly** *adv*

fan·dan·go \fan'daŋgō\ *n, pl* **-gos** : lively Spanish dance

fan·fare \'fan,faər\ *n* **1** : a sounding of trumpets **2** : showy display

fang \'faŋ\ *n* : long tooth of a venomous snake

fan·light *n* : semicircular window

fan·ta·sia \fan'tāzhə, -zh(ē)ə; ,fantə'zēə\ *n* : music written to fancy rather than to form

fan·tas·tic \fan'tastik\ *adj* **1** : imaginary or unrealistic **2** : exceedingly or unbelievably great —**fan·tas·ti·cal** \-tikəl\ *adj* —**fan·tas·ti·cal·ly** \-tik(ə)lē\ *adv*

fan·ta·sy \'fantəsē\ *n* **1** : imagination **2** : product (as a daydream) of the imagination **3** : fantasia —**fan·ta·size** \'fantə,sīz\ *vb*

far \'fär\ *adv* **far·ther** \-thər\ *or* **fur·ther** \'fər-\, **far·thest** *or* **fur·thest** \-thəst\ **1** : at or to a distance **2** : much **3** : by a degree **4** : to an advanced point or extent ~ *adv* **farther** *or* **further; farthest** *or* **furthest 1** : remote **2** : long **3** : being more distant

far·away *adj* : distant

farce \'färs\ *n* **1** : satirical comedy with an improbable plot **2** : ridiculous action —**far·ci·cal** \-sikəl\ *adj*

¹fare \'faər\ *vb* **fared; far·ing** : get along

²fare *n* **1** : price of transportation **2** : range of food

fare·well \faər'wel\ *n* **1** : wish of welfare at parting **2** : departure —**farewell** \,faər,wȯl\ *adj*

far·fetched adj : not probable or reasonable

fa·ri·na \fə'rēnə\ n : fine meal made from cereal grains

farm \'färm\ n 1 : place where something is raised — vb 1 : use (land) as a farm 2 : raise something — **farm·er** n — **farm·hand** \-,hand\ n — **farm·house** n — **farm·ing** n — **farm·land** \-,land\ n — **farm·yard** n

farm·stead \'färm,sted\ n : buildings and service areas of a farm

far-off adj : remote in time or space

far·ri·er \'farēər\ n : blacksmith who shoes horses

far·row \'farō\ vb : give birth to a litter of pigs — **farrow** n

far·sight·ed adj 1 : better able to see distant things than near 2 : judicious or shrewd — **far·sight·ed·ness** n

far·ther \'färthər\ adv 1 : at or to a greater distance or more advanced point 2 : more completely ~ adj : more distant

far·ther·most adj : most distant

far·thest \'färthəst\ adj : most distant ~ adv 1 : to or at the greatest distance 2 : to the most advanced point 3 : by the greatest extent

fas·ci·cle \'fasikəl\ n 1 : small bundle 2 : division of a book published in parts — **fas·ci·cled** \-kəld\ adj

fas·ci·nate \'fas^ə n,āt\ vb -nat·ed; -nat·ing : transfix and hold spellbound — **fas·ci·na·tion** \,fas^ə n'āshən\ n

fas·cism \'fash,izəm\ n : dictatorship that exalts nation and race — **fas·cist** \-əst\ n or adj — **fas·cis·tic** \fa'shis·tik\ adj

fash·ion \'fashən\ n 1 : manner 2 : prevailing custom or style ~ vb : form or construct — **fash·ion·able** \-(ə)nəbəl\ adj — **fash·ion·ably** \-blē\ adv

¹**fast** \'fast\ adj 1 : firmly fixed, bound, or shut 2 : faithful 3 : moving or acting quickly 4 : indicating ahead of the correct time 5 : deep and undisturbed 6 : permanently dyed 7 : wild or promiscuous ~ adv 1 : so as to be secure or bound 2 : soundly or deeply 3 : swiftly

²**fast** vb : abstain from food or eat sparingly ~ n : act or time of fasting

fas·ten \'fas^ə n\ vb : attach esp. by pinning or tying — **fas·ten·er** n — **fas·ten·ing** n

fas·tid·i·ous \fas'tidēəs\ adj : hard to please — **fas·tid·i·ous·ly** adv — **fas·tid·i·ous·ness** n

fat \'fat\ adj -tt- 1 : having much fat 2 : thick ~ n : animal tissue rich in greasy or oily matter — **fat·ness** n — **fat·ten** \'fat^ə n\ vb — **fat·ty** adj

fa·tal \'fāt^ə l\ adj : causing death or ruin — **fa·tal·i·ty** \fā'talətē, fə-\ n — **fa·tal·ly** adv

fa·tal·ism \'fāt^ə l,izəm\ n : belief that fate determines events — **fa·tal·ist** \-əst\ n — **fa·tal·is·tic** \,fāt^ə l'istik\ adj

fate \'fāt\ n 1 : cause beyond human control held to determine events 2 : end or outcome — **fat·ed** adj — **fate·ful** \-fəl\ adj — **fate·ful·ly** adv

fa·ther \'fäthər, 'fåth-\ n 1 : male parent 2 cap : God 3 : originator — **father** vb — **fa·ther·hood** \-,hùd\ n — **fa·ther·land** \-,land\ n — **fa·ther·less** adj — **fa·ther·ly** adj

father-in-law n, pl **fa·thers-in-law** : father of one's spouse

fath·om \'fathəm\ n : nautical unit of length equal to 6 feet ~ vb 1 : measure by sounding 2 : understand — **fath·om·able** adj — **fath·om·less** adj

fa·tigue \fə'tēg\ n 1 : weariness from labor or use 2 : tendency to break under repeated stress ~ vb -tigued; -tigu·ing : tire out

fat·u·ous \'fachə)wəs\ adj : foolish or stupid — **fat·u·ous·ly** adv — **fat·u·ous·ness** n

fau·cet \'fòsət, 'fäs-\ n : fixture for drawing off a liquid

fault \'fòlt\ n 1 : weakness in character 2 : something wrong or imperfect 3 : responsibility for something wrong 4 : fracture in the earth's crust ~ vb : find fault in or with — **fault·find·er** n — **fault·find·ing** n — **fault·i·ly** \'fòltəlē\ adv — **fault·less** adj — **fault·less·ly** adv — **faulty** adj

fau·na \'fònə\ n : animals or animal life esp. of a region — **fau·nal** \-^ə l\ adj

faux pas \'fō'pä\ n, pl **faux pas** \-'pä(z)\ : social blunder

fa·vor \'fāvər\ n 1 : approval 2 : partiality 3 : act of kindness ~ vb : regard or treat with favor — **fa·vor·able** \'fāv(ə)rəbəl\ adj — **fa·vor·ably** \-blē\ adv

fa·vor·ite \'fāv(ə)rət\ n : one favored — **favorite** adj — **fa·vor·it·ism** \-,izəm\ n

¹**fawn** \'fòn\ vb : seek favor by groveling

²**fawn** n : young deer

faze \'fāz\ vb **fazed; faz·ing** : disturb the composure of

fear \'fiər\ n : unpleasant emotion caused by expectation or awareness of danger ~ vb : be afraid of — **fear-**

ful \-fəl\ *adj* : **fear·ful·ly** *adv* — **fear·less** *adj* — **fear·less·ly** *adv* — **fear·less·ness** *n* — **fear·some** \-səm\ *adj*

fea·si·ble \'fēzəbəl\ *adj* : capable of being done — **fea·si·bil·i·ty** \ˌfēzə'bilətē\ *n* — **fea·si·bly** \'fēzəblē\ *adv*

feast \'fēst\ *n* 1 : large or fancy meal 2 : religious festival ~ *vb* : eat plentifully

feat \'fēt\ *n* : notable deed

feath·er \'fethər\ *n* : one of the light horny outgrowths that form the external covering of a bird's body — **feather** *vb* — **feath·ered** \-ərd\ *adj* — **feath·er·less** *adj* — **feath·ery** *adj*

fea·ture \'fēchər\ *n* 1 : shape or appearance of the face 2 : part of the face 3 : prominent characteristic 4 : special attraction ~ *vb* : give prominence to — **fea·ture·less** *adj*

Feb·ru·ary \'feb(yə)ˌwerē, 'febrə-\ *n* : 2d month of the year having 28 and in leap years 29 days

fe·ces \'fēˌsēz\ *n pl* : intestinal body waste — **fe·cal** \-kəl\ *adj*

feck·less \'fekləs\ *adj* : irresponsible

fe·cund \'fekənd, 'fē-\ *adj* : prolific — **fe·cun·di·ty** \fi'kəndətē, fe-\ *n*

fed·er·al \'fed(ə)rəl\ *adj* : of or constituting a government with power distributed between a central authority and constituent units — **fed·er·al·ism** \-rəˌlizəm\ *n* — **fed·er·al·ist** \-ləst\ *n or adj* — **fed·er·al·ly** *adv*

fed·er·ate \'fedəˌrāt\ *vb* **-at·ed; -at·ing** : join in a federation

fed·er·a·tion \ˌfedə'rāshən\ *n* : union of organizations

fe·do·ra \fi'dōrə\ *n* : soft felt hat

fed up *adj* : out of patience

fee \'fē\ *n* : fixed charge

fee·ble \'fēbəl\ *adj* **-bler; -blest** : weak or ineffective — **fee·ble·mind·ed** \ˌfēbəl'mīndəd\ *adj* — **fee·ble·mind·ed·ness** *n* — **fee·ble·ness** *n* — **fee·bly** \-blē\ *adv*

feed \'fēd\ *vb* **fed** \'fed\; **feed·ing** 1 : give food to 2 : eat 3 : furnish ~ *n* : food for livestock — **feed·er** *n*

feel \'fēl\ *vb* **felt** \'felt\; **feel·ing** 1 : perceive or examine through physical contact 2 : think or believe 3 : be conscious of 4 : seem esp. to the touch 5 : have sympathy ~ *n* 1 : sense of touch 2 : quality of a thing imparted through touch — **feel·er** *n*

feel·ing \'fēliŋ\ *n* 1 : sense of touch 2 : state of mind 3 *pl* : sensibilities 4 : opinion

feet *pl of* FOOT

feign \'fān\ *vb* : pretend

feint \'fānt\ *n* : mock attack intended to distract attention — **feint** *vb*

fe·lic·i·tate \fi'lisəˌtāt\ *vb* **-tat·ed; -tat·ing** : congratulate — **fe·lic·i·ta·tion** \-ˌlisə'tāshən\ *n*

fe·lic·i·tous \fi'lisətəs\ *adj* : aptly expressed — **fe·lic·i·tous·ly** *adv*

fe·lic·i·ty \-'lisətē\ *n, pl* **-ties** 1 : great happiness 2 : pleasing faculty esp. in art or language

fe·line \'fēˌlīn\ *adj* : relating to cats — **feline** *n*

¹**fell** \'fel\ *vb* : cut or knock down

²**fell** *past of* FALL

fel·low \'felō\ *n* 1 : companion or associate 2 : man or boy — **fel·low·ship** \-ˌship\ *n*

fel·low·man \ˌfelō'man\ *n* : kindred human being

fel·on \'felən\ *n* : one who has committed a felony

fel·o·ny \'felənē\ *n, pl* **-nies** : serious crime — **fe·lo·ni·ous** \fə'lōnēəs\ *adj*

¹**felt** \'felt\ *n* : cloth made of pressed wool and fur

²**felt** *past of* FEEL

fe·male \'fēˌmāl\ *adj* : relating to or being the sex that bears young — **female** *n*

fem·i·nine \'femənən\ *adj* : relating to the female sex — **fem·i·nin·i·ty** \ˌfemə'ninətē\ *n*

fem·i·nism \'feməˌnizəm\ *n* : organized activity on behalf of women's rights — **fem·i·nist** \-nəst\ *n or adj*

fe·mur \'fēmər\ *n, pl* **fe·murs** *or* **fem·o·ra** \'fem(ə)rə\ : long bone of the thigh — **fem·o·ral** \'fem(ə)rəl\ *adj*

fence \'fens\ *n* : enclosing barrier esp. of wood or wire ~ *vb* **fenced; fenc·ing** 1 : enclose with a fence 2 : practice fencing — **fenc·er** *n*

fenc·ing \'fensiŋ\ *n* 1 : combat with swords for sport 2 : material for building fences

fend \'fend\ *vb* : ward off

fend·er \'fendər\ *n* : guard over an automobile wheel

fen·nel \'fen²l\ *n* : herb related to the carrot

fer·ment \fər'ment\ *vb* : cause or undergo fermentation ~ \'fərˌment\ *n* : agitation

fer·men·ta·tion \ˌfərmən'tāshən, -ˌmen-\ *n* : chemical decomposition of an organic substance in the absence of oxygen

fern \'fərn\ *n* : flowerless seedless green plant

fe·ro·cious \fə'rōshəs\ *adj* : fierce or savage — **fe·ro·cious·ly** *adv* — **fe·ro·cious·ness** *n* — **fe·roc·i·ty** \-'räsətē\ *n*

fer·ret \'ferət\ *n* : white European polecat ~ *vb* : find out by searching

fer·ric \'ferik\ *adj* : relating to or containing iron

fer·rous \'ferəs\ *adj* : relating to or containing iron

fer·rule \'ferəl\ *n* : metal band or ring

fer·ry \'ferē\ *vb* **-ried; -ry·ing** : carry by boat over water ~ *n, pl* **-ries** : boat used in ferrying —**fer·ry·boat** *n*

fer·tile \'fərt²l\ *adj* **1** : producing plentifully **2** : capable of developing or reproducing —**fer·til·i·ty** \(,)fər'tilətē\ *n*

fer·til·ize \'fərt²l,īz\ *vb* **-ized; -iz·ing** : make fertile —**fer·til·iza·tion** \,fərt²lə'zāshən\ *n* —**fer·til·iz·er** *n*

fer·vid \'fərvəd\ *adj* : ardent or zealous —**fer·vid·ly** *adv*

fer·vor \'fərvər\ *n* : passion —**fer·ven·cy** \-vənsē\ *n* —**fer·vent** \-vənt\ *adj* —**fer·vent·ly** *adv*

fes·ter \'festər\ *n* : pus-filled sore ~ *vb* **1** : form pus **2** : become more bitter or malignant

fes·ti·val \'festəvəl\ *n* : time of celebration

fes·tive \-tiv\ *adj* : joyous or happy —**fes·tive·ly** *adv* —**fes·tiv·i·ty** \fes'tivətē\ *n*

fes·toon \fes'tün\ *n* : decorative chain or strip hanging in a curve —**festoon** *vb*

fe·tal \'fēt²l\ *adj* : of, relating to, or being a fetus

fetch \'fech\ *vb* **1** : go or come after and bring or take back **2** : sell for

fetch·ing \'fechiŋ\ *adj* : attractive —**fetch·ing·ly** *adv*

fête \'fāt, 'fet\ *n* : lavish party ~ *vb* **fêt·ed; fêt·ing** : honor or commemorate with a fête

fet·id \'fetəd\ *adj* : having an offensive smell

fe·tish \'fetish, 'fēt-\ *n* **1** : object believed to have magical powers **2** : object of unreasoning devotion or concern

fet·lock \'fet,läk\ *n* : projection on the back of a horse's leg above the hoof

fet·ter \'fetər\ *n* : chain or shackle for the feet —**fetter** *vb*

fet·tle \'fet²l\ *n* : state of fitness

fe·tus \'fētəs\ *n* : vertebrate not yet born or hatched

feud \'fyüd\ *n* : lasting conflict between families or clans —**feud** *vb*

feu·dal \'fyüd²l\ *adj* : of or relating to feudalism

feu·dal·ism \-,izəm\ *n* : medieval political order in which land is granted in return for service —**feu·dal·is·tic** \,fyüd²l'istik\ *adj*

fe·ver \'fēvər\ *n* **1** : abnormal rise in body temperature **2** : state of heightened emotion —**fe·ver·ish** *adj* —**fe·ver·ish·ly** *adv*

few \'fyü\ *pron* : not many ~ *adj* : some but not many —often with *a* ~ *n* : small number —often with *a*

few·er \-ər\ *pron* : smaller number of things

fez \'fez\ *n, pl* **fez·zes** : round flat-crowned hat

fi·an·cé \,fē,än'sā\ *n* : man one is engaged to

fi·an·cée \,fē,än'sā\ *n* : woman one is engaged to

fi·as·co \fē'askō\ *n, pl* **-coes** : ridiculous failure

fi·at \'fēat, -,at, -,ät; 'fīat, -,at\ *n* : decree

fib \'fib\ *n* : trivial lie —**fib** *vb* —**fib·ber** *n*

fi·ber, fi·bre \'fībər\ *n* **1** : threadlike substance or structure (as a muscle cell or fine root) **2** : element that gives texture or substance —**fi·brous** \-brəs\ *adj*

fi·ber·board *n* : construction material made of compressed fibers

fi·ber·glass *n* : glass in fibrous form in various products (as insulation)

fi·bril·la·tion \,fibrə'lāshən, ,fīb-\ *n* : rapid irregular contractions of muscle fibers (as of the heart) —**fib·ril·late** \'fibrə,lāt, 'fīb-\ *vb*

fib·u·la \'fibyələ\ *n, pl* **-lae** \-,lē, -,lī\ *or* **-las** : outer of the two leg bones below the knee —**fib·u·lar** \-lər\ *adj*

fick·le \'fikəl\ *adj* : unpredictably changeable —**fick·le·ness** *n*

fic·tion \'fikshən\ *n* : a made-up story or literature consisting of these —**fic·tion·al** \-sh(ə)nəl\ *adj*

fic·ti·tious \fik'tishəs\ *adj* : made up or pretended

fid·dle \'fid²l\ *n* : violin ~ *vb* **-dled; -dling** **1** : play on the fiddle **2** : move the hands restlessly —**fid·dler** \'fidlər, -²lər\ *n*

fid·dle·sticks *n* : nonsense —used as an interjection

fi·del·i·ty \fə'delətē, fī-\ *n, pl* **-ties 1** : quality or state of being faithful **2** : quality of reproduction

fid·get \'fijət\ *n* **1** *pl* : restlessness **2** : one that fidgets ~ *vb* : move restlessly —**fid·gety** *adj*

fi·du·cia·ry \fə'd(y)üshē,erē, -shərē\ *adj* : held or holding in trust —**fiduciary** *n*

field \'fēld\ *n* 1 : open country 2 : cleared land 3 : land yielding some special product 4 : sphere of activity 5 : area for sports 6 : region or space in which a given effect (as magnetism) exists ~ *vb* : put into the field —**field** *adj* —**field·er** *n*

fiend \'fēnd\ *n* 1 : devil 2 : extremely wicked person —**fiend·ish** *adj* —**fiend·ish·ly** *adv*

fierce \'fiərs\ *adj* **fierc·er; -est** 1 : violently hostile or aggressive 2 : intense 3 : menacing looking —**fierce·ly** *adv* —**fierce·ness** *n*

fi·ery \'fī(ə)rē\ *adj* **fi·er·i·er; -est** 1 : burning 2 : hot or passionate —**fi·eri·ness** \'fī(ə)rēnəs\ *n*

fi·es·ta \fē'estə\ *n* : festival

fife \'fīf\ *n* : small flute

fif·teen \fif'tēn\ *n* : one more than 14 —**fifteen** *adj or pron* —**fif·teenth** \-'tēnth\ *adj or n*

fifth \'fifth\ *n* 1 : one that is number 5 in a countable series 2 : one of 5 equal parts of something —**fifth** *adj or adv*

fif·ty \'fiftē\ *n, pl* **-ties** : 5 times 10 —**fif·ti·eth** \-tēəth\ *adj or n* —**fifty** *adj or pron*

fif·ty-fif·ty *adv or adj* : shared equally

fig \'fig\ *n* : pear-shaped edible fruit

fight \'fīt\ *vb* **fought** \'fȯt\; **fight·ing** 1 : contend against another in battle 2 : box 3 : struggle ~ *n* 1 : hostile encounter 2 : boxing match 3 : verbal disagreement —**fight·er** *n*

fig·ment \'figmənt\ *n* : something imagined or made up

fig·u·ra·tive \'fig(y)ərətiv\ *adj* : metaphorical —**fig·u·ra·tive·ly** *adv*

fig·ure \'figyər\ *n* 1 : symbol representing a number 2 *pl* : arithmetical calculations 3 : price 4 : shape or outline 5 : illustration 6 : pattern or design 7 : prominent person ~ *vb* **-ured; -ur·ing** 1 : be important 2 : calculate —**fig·ured** *adj*

fig·u·rine \,fig(y)ə'rēn\ *n* : small statue

fil·a·ment \'filəmənt\ *n* : fine thread or threadlike part —**fil·a·men·tous** \,filə'mentəs\ *adj*

fil·bert \'filbərt\ *n* : edible nut of a European hazel

filch \'filch\ *vb* : steal furtively

¹file \'fīl\ *n* : tool for smoothing or sharpening ~ *vb* **filed; fil·ing** : rub or smooth with a file

²file *vb* **filed; fil·ing** 1 : arrange in order 2 : enter or record officially ~ *n* : device for keeping papers in order

³file *n* : row of persons or things one behind the other ~ *vb* **filed; fil·ing** : march in file

fil·ial \'fileəl, 'filyəl\ *adj* : relating to a son or daughter

fil·i·bus·ter \'filə,bəstər\ *n* : long speeches to delay a legislative vote —**filibuster** *vb* —**fil·i·bus·ter·er** *n*

fil·i·gree \'filə,grē\ *n* : ornamental designs of fine wire —**fil·i·greed** \-,grēd\ *adj*

fill \'fil\ *vb* 1 : make or become full 2 : stop up 3 : feed 4 : satisfy 5 : occupy fully 6 : spread through ~ *n* 1 : full supply 2 : material for filling —**fill·er** *n* —**fill in** *vb* 1 : provide information to or for 2 : substitute

fil·let \'filət, fil'ā, 'fil(,)ā\ *n* : piece of boneless meat or fish ~ *vb* : cut into fillets

fill·ing *n* : material used to fill something

fil·ly \'filē\ *n, pl* **-lies** : young female horse

film \'film\ *n* 1 : thin skin or membrane 2 : thin coating or layer 3 : strip of material used in taking pictures 4 : movie ~ *vb* : make a movie of —**filmy** *adj*

film·strip *n* : strip of film with photographs for still projection

fil·ter \'filtər\ *n* 1 : device for separating matter from a fluid 2 : device (as on a camera lens) that absorbs light ~ *vb* 1 : pass through a filter 2 : remove by means of a filter —**fil·ter·able** *adj* —**fil·tra·tion** \fil'trāshən\ *n*

filth \'filth\ *n* : repulsive dirt or refuse —**filth·i·ness** *n* —**filthy** \'filthē\ *adj*

fin \'fin\ *n* 1 : thin external process controlling movement in an aquatic animal 2 : fin-shaped part (as on an airplane) 3 : flipper —**finned** \'find\ *adj*

fi·na·gle \fə'nāgəl\ *vb* **-gled; -gling** : get by clever or tricky means —**fi·na·gler** *n*

fi·nal \'fīn²l\ *adj* 1 : not to be changed 2 : ultimate 3 : coming at the end —**final** *n* —**fi·nal·ist** \'fīn²ləst\ *n* —**fi·nal·i·ty** \fī'nalətē, fə-\ *n* —**fi·nal·ize** \-,līz\ *vb* —**fi·nal·ly** *adv*

fi·na·le \fə'nalē, fi'nä-\ *n* : last or climactic part

fi·nance \fə'nans, 'fī,nans\ *n* 1 *pl* : money resources 2 : management of money affairs ~ *vb* **-nanced; -nanc·ing** 1 : raise funds for 2 : give necessary funds to : sell on credit

fi·nan·cial \fə'nanchəl, fī-\ *adj* : relating to finance —**fi·nan·cial·ly** *adv*

fi·nan·cier \,finən'siər, ,fī,nan-\ *n* : person who invests large sums of money

finch \'finch\ *n* : songbird (as a sparrow or linnet)

find \'fīnd\ *vb* **found** \'faund\; **find-ing** 1 : discover or encounter 2 : obtain by effort 3 : experience or perceive 4 : gain or regain the use of 5 : decide on (a verdict) ~ *n* 1 : act or instance of finding 2 : something found —**find-er** *n* —**find-ing** *n* —**find out** *vb* : learn, discover, or verify something

fine \'fīn\ *n* : money paid as a penalty ~ *vb* **fined; fin-ing** : impose a fine on ~ *adj* **fin-er; -est** 1 : free from impurity 2 : small or thin 3 : not coarse 4 : superior in quality or appearance ~ *adv* : finely —**fine-ly** *adv* —**fine-ness** *n*

fin-ery \'fīn(ə)rē\ *n, pl* **-er-ies** : showy clothing and jewels

fi-nesse \fə'nes\ *n* 1 : delicate skill 2 : craftiness —**finesse** *vb*

fin-ger \'fiŋgər\ *n* 1 : one of the 5 divisions at the end of the hand and esp. one other than the thumb 2 : something like a finger 3 : part of a glove for a finger ~ *vb* 1 : touch with the fingers 2 : identify as if by pointing —**fin-gered** *adj* —**fin-ger-nail** *n* —**fin-ger-tip** *n*

fin-ger-ling \-gərliŋ\ *n* : small fish

fin-ger-print *n* 1 : impression of the pattern of marks on the tip of a finger —**fingerprint** *vb*

fin-icky \'finikē\ *adj* : excessively particular in taste or standards

fin-ish \'finish\ *vb* 1 : come or bring to an end 2 : use or dispose of entirely 3 : put a final coat or surface on ~ *n* 1 : end 2 : final treatment given a surface —**fin-ish-er** *n*

fi-nite \'fī,nīt\ *adj* : having definite limits

fink \'fiŋk\ *n* : contemptible person

fiord *var of* FJORD

fir \'fər\ *n* : erect evergreen tree or its wood

fire \'fī(ə)r\ *n* 1 : light or heat and esp. the flame of something burning 2 : destructive burning of something (as a house) 3 : enthusiasm 4 : discharge of firearms ~ *vb* **fired; fir-ing** 1 : kindle 2 : stir up or enliven 3 : dismiss from employment 4 : shoot 5 : bake —**fire-bomb** *n or vb* —**fire-less** *adj* —**fire-proof** *adj or vb* —**fire-wood** *n*

fire-arm *n* : weapon (as a rifle) that works by an explosion of gunpowder

fire-ball *n* 1 : ball of fire 2 : brilliant meteor

fire-boat *n* : ship equipped for fighting fire

fire-box *n* 1 : chamber (as of a furnace) that contains a fire 2 : fire-alarm box

fire-break *n* : cleared land for checking a forest fire

fire-bug *n* : person who deliberately sets destructive fires

fire-crack-er *n* : small firework that makes noise

fire-fly *n* : night-flying beetle that produces a soft light

fire-man \-mən\ *n* 1 : member of a company organized to put out fires 2 : stoker

fire-place *n* : opening made in a chimney to hold an open fire

fire-plug *n* : hydrant

fire-side *n* 1 : place near the fire or hearth 2 : home ~ *adj* : having an informal quality

fire-trap *n* : place apt to catch on fire

fire-work *n* : device that explodes to produce noise or a display of light

¹**firm** \'fərm\ *adj* 1 : securely fixed in place 2 : strong or vigorous 3 : not subject to change 4 : resolute ~ *vb* : make or become firm —**firm-ly** *adv* —**firm-ness** *n*

²**firm** *n* : business enterprise

fir-ma-ment \'fərməmənt\ *n* : sky

first \'fərst\ *adj* 1 : being number one 2 : foremost ~ *adv* 1 : before any other 2 : for the first time ~ *n* 1 : number one 2 : one that is first —**first class** *n* —**first-class** *adj or adv* —**first-ly** *adv* —**first-rate** *adj or adv*

first aid *n* : emergency care

first lieutenant *n* : commissioned officer ranking next below a captain

first sergeant *n* 1 : noncommissioned officer serving as the chief assistant to the commander of a military unit (as a company) 2 : rank in the army below a command sergeant major and in the marine corps below a sergeant major

firth \'fərth\ *n* : estuary

fis-cal \'fiskəl\ *adj* : relating to money

fish \'fish\ *n, pl* **fish** *or* **fish-es** : water animal with fin, gills, and usu. scales ~ *vb* 1 : try to catch fish 2 : grope —**fish-er** *n* —**fish-hook** *n* —**fish-ing** *n*

fish-er-man \-mən\ *n* : one who fishes

fish-ery \'fish(ə)rē\ *n, pl* **-er-ies** : fishing business or a place for this

fishy \'fishē\ *adj* **fish-i-er; -est** 1 : relating to or like fish 2 : questionable

fis-sion \'fishən, 'fizh-\ *n* : splitting of an atomic nucleus —**fis-sion-able** \-(ə)nəbəl\ *adj* —**fis-sion-al** \-ən°l\ *adj*

fis-sure \'fishər\ *n* : crack

fist \'fist\ n : hand doubled up —fist-ed \'fistəd\ adj —fist-ful \-,fûl\ n

fist-i-cuffs \'fisti,kəfs\ n pl : fist fight

1fit \'fit\ n : sudden attack of illness or emotion

2fit adj -tt- 1 : suitable 2 : qualified 3 : sound in body ~ vb -tt- 1 : be suitable to 2 : insert or adjust correctly 3 : make room for 4 : supply or equip 5 : belong ~ n : state of fitting or being fitted —fit-ly adv —fit-ness n —fit-ter n

fit-ful \'fitfəl\ adj : restless —fit-ful-ly adv

fit-ting adj : suitable ~ n : a small part

five \'fiv\ n 1 : one more than 4 2 : 5th in a set or series 3 : something having 5 units —five adj or pron

fix \'fiks\ vb 1 : attach 2 : establish 3 : make right 4 : prepare 5 : improperly influence ~ n 1 : predicament 2 : determination of location —fix-er n

fix-a-tion \fik'sāshən\ n : obsessive attachment —fix-ate \'fik,sāt\ vb

fixed \'fikst\ adj 1 : stationary 2 : settled —fixed-ly \'fiksədlē\ adv —fixed-ness \-nəs\ n

fix-ture \'fikschər\ n : permanent part of something

fizz \'fiz\ vb : make a hissing sound ~ n : effervescence

fiz-zle \'fizəl\ vb -zled; -zling 1 : fizz 2 : fail ~ n : failure

fjord \fē'ôrd\ n : inlet of the sea between cliffs

flab \'flab\ n : flabby flesh

flab-ber-gast \'flabər,gast\ vb : astound

flab-by \'flabē\ adj -bi-er; -est : not firm —flab-bi-ness n

flac-cid \'flaksəd, 'flasəd\ adj : not firm

1flag \'flag\ n : flat stone

2flag n : fabric that is a symbol (as of a country) 2 : something used to signal ~ vb -gg- : signal with a flag —flag-pole n —flag-staff n

3flag vb -gg- : lose strength or spirit

flag-el-late \'flajə,lāt\ vb -lat-ed; -lat-ing : whip —flag-el-la-tion \,flajə'lāshən\ n

flag-on \'flagən\ n : container for liquids

fla-grant \'flāgrənt\ adj : conspicuously bad —fla-grant-ly adv

flag-ship \ n : ship carrying a commander

flag-stone n : flag

flail \'flāl\ n : tool for threshing grain ~ vb : beat with or as if with a flail

flair \'flaər\ n : natural aptitude

flak \'flak\ n, pl flak : antiaircraft fire

flake \'flāk\ n : small flat piece ~ vb

flaked; flak-ing : separate or form into flakes

flam-boy-ant \flam'bóiənt\ adj : showy —flam-boy-ance \-əns\ n —flam-boy-ant-ly adv

flame \'flām\ n 1 : glowing part of a fire 2 : state of combustion 3 : burning passion —flame vb —flam-ing adj

fla-min-go \flə'miŋgō\ n, pl -gos : long-legged long-necked tropical water bird

flam-ma-ble \'flaməbəl\ adj : easily ignited

flange \'flanj\ n : rim

flank \'flaŋk\ n : side of something ~ vb 1 : attack or go around the side of 2 : be at the side of

flan-nel \'flan²l\ n : soft napped fabric

flap \'flap\ n 1 : slap 2 : something flat that hangs loose ~ vb -pp- 1 : move (wings) up and down 2 : swing back and forth noisily

flap-jack \-,jak\ n : pancake

flare \'flaər\ vb flared; flar-ing : become suddenly bright or excited ~ n : blaze of light

flash \'flash\ vb 1 : give off a sudden flame or burst of light 2 : appear or pass suddenly ~ n 1 : sudden burst of light or inspiration 2 : instant ~ adj : coming suddenly

flash-light n : small battery-operated light

flashy \'flashē\ adj flash-i-er; -est : showy —flash-i-ly adv —flash-i-ness n

flask \'flask\ n : flattened bottle

1flat \'flat\ adj -tt- 1 : smooth 2 : broad and thin 3 : definite 4 : uninteresting 5 : deflated 6 : below the true pitch ~ n 1 : level surface of land 2 : flat note in music 3 : deflated tire ~ adv -tt- 1 : exactly 2 : below the true pitch ~ vb -tt- : make flat —flat-ly adv —flat-ness n —flat-ten \-²n\ vb

2flat n 1 : story in a building 2 : apartment

flat-car n : railroad car without sides

flat-fish n : flattened fish with both eyes on the upper side

flat-foot n, pl flat-feet : foot condition in which the arch is flattened —flat-foot-ed adj

flat-ter \'flatər\ vb 1 : praise insincerely 2 : judge or represent too favorably —flat-ter-er n —flat-tery \'flatərē\ n

flat-u-lent \'flachələnt\ adj : full of gas —flat-u-lence \-ləns\ n

flat-ware n : eating utensils

flaunt \'flônt\ vb : display ostentatiously —flaunt n

fla·vor \\'flāvər\ *n* **1** : quality that affects the sense of taste **2** : something that adds flavor ~ *vb* : give flavor to —**fla·vor·ful** *adj* —**fla·vor·ing** \\'flāv(ə)riŋ\ *n* —**fla·vor·some** *adj*

flaw \\'flȯ\ *n* : fault —**flaw·less** *adj* —**flaw·less·ly** *adv*

flax \\'flaks\ *n* : plant from which linen is made

flax·en \\'flaksən\ *adj* : made of or like flax

flay \\'flā\ *vb* **1** : strip off the skin of **2** : criticize harshly

flea \\'flē\ *n* : leaping bloodsucking insect

fleck \\'flek\ *vb or n* : streak or spot

fledg·ling \\'flejliŋ\ *n* : young bird

flee \\'flē\ *vb* **fled** \\'fled\; **flee·ing** : run away

fleece \\'flēs\ *n* : sheep's wool ~ *vb* **fleeced; fleec·ing** **1** : shear **2** : get money from dishonestly —**fleecy** *adj*

¹fleet \\'flēt\ *vb* : pass rapidly ~ *adj* : swift —**fleet·ing** *adj* —**fleet·ness** *n*

²fleet *n* : group of ships

fleet admiral *n* : commissioned officer of the highest rank in the navy

flesh \\'flesh\ *n* : soft parts of an animal's body **2** : soft plant tissue (as fruit pulp) —**fleshed** \\'flesht\ *adj* —**fleshy** *adj*

flesh·ly \\'fleshlē\ *adj* : sensual

flew *past of* FLY

flex \\'fleks\ *vb* : bend

flex·i·ble \\'fleksəbəl\ *adj* **1** : capable of being flexed **2** : adaptable —**flex·i·bil·i·ty** \\,fleksə'bilətē\ *n* —**flex·i·bly** \\-əblē\ *adv*

flick \\'flik\ *n* : light jerky stroke ~ *vb* **1** : strike lightly **2** : flutter

flick·er \\'flikər\ *vb* **1** : waver **2** : burn unsteadily ~ *n* **1** : sudden movement **2** : wavering light

fli·er \\'flī(ə)r\ *n* **1** : aviator **2** : advertising circular

¹flight \\'flīt\ *n* **1** : act or instance of flying **2** : ability to fly **3** : a passing through air or space **4** : series of stairs —**flight·less** *adj*

²flight *n* : act or instance of running away

flighty \\-ē\ *adj* **flight·i·er, -est 1** : capricious **2** : silly

flim·flam \\'flim,flam\ *n* : trickery

flim·sy \\-zē\ *adj* **-si·er; -est 1** : not strong or well made **2** : not believable —**flim·si·ly** *adv* —**flim·si·ness** *n*

flinch \\'flinch\ *vb* : shrink from pain

fling \\'fliŋ\ *vb* **flung** \\'fləŋ\; **fling·ing 1** : move brusquely **2** : throw ~ *n* **1** : act or instance of flinging **2** : attempt **3** : period of self-indulgence

flint \\'flint\ *n* : hard quartz that gives off sparks when struck with steel —**flinty** *adj*

flip \\'flip\ *vb* **-pp- 1** : cause to turn over quickly or many times **2** : move with a quick push ~ *adj* : insolent —**flip** *n*

flip·pant \\'flipənt\ *adj* : not serious enough —**flip·pan·cy** \\-ənsē\ *n*

flip·per \\-ər\ *n* : paddlelike limb (as of a seal) for swimming

flirt \\'flərt\ *vb* **1** : be playfully romantic **2** : trifle ~ *n* : one who flirts —**flir·ta·tion** \\,flər'tāshən\ *n* —**flir·ta·tious** \\-shəs\ *adj*

flit \\'flit\ *vb* **-tt-** : dart

float \\'flōt\ *n* **1** : something that floats **2** : vehicle carrying an exhibit ~ *vb* **1** : rest on or in a fluid without sinking **2** : finance by issuing stock or bonds —**float·er** *n*

flock \\'fläk\ *n* : group of animals (as birds) or people ~ *vb* : gather or move as a group

floe \\'flō\ *n* : mass of floating ice

flog \\'fläg\ *vb* **-gg-** : beat with a rod or whip —**flog·ger** *n*

flood \\'fləd\ *n* **1** : great flow of water over the land **2** : overwhelming volume ~ *vb* : cover or fill esp. with water —**flood·wa·ter** *n*

floor \\'flōr\ *n* **1** : bottom of a room on which one stands **2** : story of a building **3** : lower limit ~ *vb* **1** : furnish with a floor **2** : knock down or overwhelm —**floor·board** *n* —**floor·ing** \\-iŋ\ *n*

floo·zy, floo·zie \\'flüzē\ *n, pl* **-zies** : tawdry woman

flop \\'fläp\ *vb* **-pp- 1** : flap **2** : slump heavily **3** : fail —**flop** *n*

flop·py \\'fläpē\ *adj* **-pi·er; -est** : soft and flexible

flo·ra \\'flōrə\ *n* : plants or plant life of a region

flo·ral \\'flōrəl\ *adj* : relating to flowers

flor·id \\'flōrəd\ *adj* **1** : excessively flowery in style **2** : reddish

flo·rist \\'flōrəst\ *n* : flower dealer

flo·ta·tion \\flō'tāshən\ *n* : process or instance of floating

flo·til·la \\flō'tilə\ *n* : small fleet

flot·sam \\'flätsəm\ *n* : floating wreckage

¹flounce \\'flaúns\ *vb* **flounced; flounc·ing** : move with exaggerated jerky motions —**flounce** *n*

²flounce *n* : fabric border

¹floun·der \\'flaúndər\ *n, pl* **flounder** *or* **flounders** : flatfish

²flounder *vb* **1** : struggle for footing **2** : proceed clumsily

flour \'flaů(ə)r\ n : finely ground meal ~ vb : coat with flour —**floury** adj

flour·ish \'flərish\ vb 1 : thrive 2 : wave threateningly ~ n 1 : embellishment 2 : ostentatious action

flout \'flaůt\ vb : scorn

flow \'flō\ vb 1 : move in a stream 2 : proceed smoothly and readily ~ n : uninterrupted stream

flow·er \'flaů(ə)r\ n 1 : showy plant shoot that bears seeds 2 : state of flourishing ~ vb 1 : produce flowers 2 : flourish —**flow·ered** adj —**flow·er·i·ness** n —**flow·er·less** adj —**flow·er·pot** n —**flow·ery** \-ē\ adj

flown past part of FLY

flu \'flü\ n 1 : influenza 2 : minor virus ailment

flub \'fləb\ vb -bb- : bungle —**flub** n

fluc·tu·ate \'fləkchə,wāt\ vb -at·ed; -at·ing : change rapidly esp. up and down —**fluc·tu·a·tion** \,fləkchə'wāshən\ n

flue \'flü\ n : smoke duct

flu·ent \'flüənt\ adj : speaking with ease —**flu·en·cy** \-ənsē\ n —**flu·ent·ly** adv

fluff \'fləf\ n 1 : something soft and light 2 : blunder ~ vb 1 : make fluffy 2 : make a mistake —**fluffy** \-ē\ adj

flu·id \'flüəd\ adj : flowing ~ n : substance that can flow —**flu·id·i·ty** \flü'idətē\ n

flu·id ounce n : unit of liquid measure equal to ⅟₁₆ pint

fluke \'flük\ n : stroke of luck

flume \'flüm\ n : channel for water

flung past of FLING

flunk \'fləŋk\ vb : fail in school work

flun·ky, **flun·key** \'fləŋkē\ n, pl -kies or -keys : obsequious or insignificant person

flu·o·res·cence \,flů(ə)r'es'ns\ n : emission of light after initial absorption —**flu·o·resce** \-'es\ vb —**flu·o·res·cent** \-'es'nt\ adj

flu·o·ri·date \'flůrə,dāt\ vb -dat·ed; -dat·ing : add a compound of fluorine to —**flu·o·ri·da·tion** \,flůrə'dā-shən\ n

flu·o·ride \'flů(ə)r,īd\ n : compound of fluorine

flu·o·rine \'flů(ə)r,ēn, -ən\ n : toxic gaseous chemical element

flu·o·ro·car·bon \,flů(ə)rō'kärbən\ n : compound containing fluorine and carbon

flu·o·ro·scope \'flůrə,skōp\ n : instrument for internal examination —**flu·o·ro·scop·ic** \,flůrə'skäpik\ adj —**flu·o·ros·co·pist**

\'äskəpəst\ n —**flu·o·ros·co·py** \-pē\

flur·ry \'flərē\ n, pl -ries 1 : light snowfall 2 : bustle 3 : brief burst of activity

¹**flush** \'fləsh\ vb : cause (a bird) to fly from cover

²**flush** n 1 : sudden flow (as of water) 2 : surge of emotion 3 : blush ~ vb 1 : blush 2 : wash out with a rush of liquid ~ adj 1 : filled to overflowing 2 : of a reddish healthy color 3 : smooth or level 4 : abutting —**flush** adv

³**flush** n : cards of the same suit

flus·ter \'fləstər\ vb : upset —**fluster** n

flute \'flüt\ n 1 : pipelike musical instrument 2 : groove —**flut·ed** adj —**flut·ist** \-əst\ n

flut·ter \'flətər\ vb 1 : flap the wings rapidly 2 : move with quick wavering or flapping motions 3 : behave in an agitated manner ~ n 1 : a fluttering 2 : state of confusion —**flut·tery** \-ərē\ adj

flux \'fləks\ n : state of continuous change

¹**fly** \'flī\ vb flew \'flü\; flown \'flōn\; fly·ing 1 : move through the air with wings 2 : float or soar 3 : flee 4 : move or pass swiftly 5 : operate an airplane

²**fly** n, pl flies : garment closure

³**fly** n, pl flies : winged insect

fly-by-night adj : transitory

fly·er var of FLIER

fly·pa·per n : sticky paper for catching flies

fly·speck n 1 : speck of fly dung 2 : something tiny

fly·wheel n : rotating wheel that regulates the speed of machinery

f-number n : number expressing the effectiveness of a camera lens

foal \'fōl\ n : young horse —**foal** vb

foam \'fōm\ n 1 : mass of bubbles on top of a liquid 2 : material of cellular form ~ vb : form foam —**foamy** adj

fob \'fäb\ n : short chain for a pocket watch

fo'·c's'le var of FORECASTLE

fo·cus \'fōkəs\ n, pl -cus·es or -ci \-,sī\ 1 : point at which reflected or refracted rays meet 2 : adjustment (as of eyeglasses) for clear vision 3 : central point ~ vb : bring to a focus —**fo·cal** \-kəl\ adj —**fo·cal·ly** adv

fod·der \'fädər\ n : food for livestock

foe \'fō\ n : enemy

fog \'fog, 'fäg\ n 1 : fine particles of water suspended in the lower atmosphere 2 : mental confusion ~ vb

-gg- : obscure or be obscured with fog —**fog·gy** *adj*

fog-horn *n* : warning horn sounded in a fog

fo-gy \'fōgē\ *n, pl* **-gies** : person with old-fashioned ideas

foi-ble \'fóibəl\ *n* : minor character fault

¹foil \'fóil\ *vb* : defeat ∼ *n* : fencing sword

²foil *n* **1** : thin sheet of metal **2** : one that sets off another by contrast

foist \'fóist\ *vb* : force another to accept

¹fold \'fōld\ *n* **1** : enclosure for sheep **2** : group with a common interest

²fold *vb* **1** : lay one part over another **2** : embrace ∼ *n* : part folded

fold-er \'fōldər\ *n* **1** : one that folds **2** : circular **3** : folded cover or envelope for papers

fol-de-rol \'fäldə,rä̇l\ *n* : nonsense

fo-liage \'fōl(ē)ij\ *n* : plant leaves

fo-lio \'fōlē,ō\ *n, pl* **-li-os** : sheet of paper folded once

folk \'fōk\ *n, pl* **folk** *or* **folks 1** : people in general **2** *folks pl* : one's family ∼ *adj* : relating to the common people

folk-lore *n* : customs and traditions of a people —**folk-lor-ist** *n*

folksy \'fōksē\ *adj* **folks-i-er; -est** : friendly and informal

fol-li-cle \'fälikəl\ *n* : small anatomical cavity or gland

fol-low \'fälō\ *vb* **1** : go or come after **2** : pursue **3** : obey **4** : proceed along **5** : keep one's attention fixed on **6** : result from —**fol-low-er** *n*

fol-low-ing \'fäləwiŋ\ *adj* : next ∼ *n* : group of followers ∼ *prep* : after

fol-ly \'fälē\ *n, pl* **-lies** : foolishness

fo-ment \fō'ment\ *vb* : incite —**fo-men-ta-tion** \,fōmən'tāshən, -,men-\ *n*

fond \'fänd\ *adj* **1** : strongly attracted **2** : affectionate **3** : dear —**fond-ly** \'fän(d)lē\ *adv* —**fond-ness** \-nəs\ *n*

fon-dle \'fänd²l\ *vb* **-dled; -dling** : touch lovingly

fon-due \fän'd(y)ü\ *n* : preparation of melted cheese

font \'fänt\ *n* **1** : baptismal basin **2** : fountain

food \'füd\ *n* : material eaten to sustain life

fool \'fül\ *n* **1** : stupid person **2** : jester ∼ *vb* **1** : waste time **2** : meddle **3** : deceive —**fool-ery** \'fül(ə)rē\ *n* —**fool-ish** \'fülish\ *adj* —**fool-ish-ly** *adv* —**fool-ish-ness** *n* —**fool-proof** *adj*

fool-har-dy \'fül,härdē\ *adj* : rash —**fool-har-di-ness** *n*

foot \'fu̇t\ *n, pl* **feet** \'fēt\ **1** : terminal part of a leg **2** : unit of length equal to ⅓ yard **3** : unit of verse meter **4** : bottom —**foot-age** \-ij\ *n* —**foot-path** *n* —**foot-print** *n* —**foot-race** *n* —**foot-rest** *n* —**foot-wear** *n*

foot-ball *n* : ball game played by 2 teams on a rectangular field

foot-bridge *n* : bridge for pedestrians

foot-ed \'fu̇təd\ *adj* : having feet or such or so many feet

foot-hill *n* : hill at the foot of higher hills

foot-hold *n* : support for the feet

foot-ing *n* **1** : foothold **2** : basis

foot-lights *n pl* : stage lights along the floor

foot-lock-er *n* : small trunk

foot-loose *adj* : having no ties

foot-man \-mən\ *n* : male servant

foot-note *n* : note at the bottom of a page

foot-step *n* **1** : step **2** : distance covered by a step **3** : footprint

foot-stool *n* : stool to support the feet

foot-work *n* : skillful movement of the feet (as in boxing)

fop \'fäp\ *n* : dandy —**fop-pery** \-(ə)rē\ *n* —**fop-pish** *adj*

for \fər, (')fȯr\ *prep* **1** : —used to show preparation or purpose **2** : because of **3** : —used to show a recipient **4** : in support of **5** : so as to support or help care **6** : so as to be equal to **7** : concerning **8** : through the period of ∼ *conj* : because

for-age \'fȯrij\ *n* **1** : food for animals **2** : search for provisions ∼ *vb* **-aged; -ag-ing 1** : hunt food **2** : make a search

for-ay \'fȯr,ā\ *vb* : raid for plunder —**foray** *n*

¹for-bear \fȯr'baər\ *vb* **-bore** \-'bȯr\; **-borne** \-'bȯrn\; **-bear-ing 1** : refrain from **2** : be patient —**for-bear-ance** \-'barəns\ *n*

²forbear *var of* FOREBEAR

for-bid \fər'bid\ *vb* **-bade** \-'bad, -'bād\ *or* **-bad** \-'bad\; **-bid-den** \-'bid²n\; **-bid-ding 1** : prohibit **2** : order not to do something

for-bid-ding *adj* : tending to discourage

force \'fȯrs\ *n* **1** : exceptional strength or energy **2** : military strength **3** : body (as of persons) available for a purpose **4** : violence **5** : influence (as a push or pull) that causes motion ∼ *vb* **forced; forc-ing 1** : compel **2** : gain against resistance **3** : break open —**force-ful** \-fəl\ *adj* —**force-ful-ly** *adv* —**in force 1** : in great numbers **2** : valid

for·ceps \'fȯrsəps\ *n, pl* **forceps** : surgical instrument for grasping objects

forc·ible \'fȯrsəbəl\ *adj* **1** : done by force **2** : showing force —**forc·i·bly** \-blē\ *adv*

ford \'fȯrd\ *n* : place to wade across a stream ~ *vb* : wade across

fore \'fȯr\ *adv* : in or toward the front ~ *adj* : being or coming before in time, place, or order ~ *n* : front

fore-and-aft *adj* : lengthwise

fore·arm \'fȯr-\ *n* : part of the arm between the elbow and the wrist

fore·bear, for·bear \'fȯr,baər, 'fȯr-\ *n* : ancestor

fore·bode \fȯr'bōd, fȯr-\ *vb* : predict —**fore·bod·ing** *n*

fore·cast \'fȯr,kast\ *vb* **-cast** *or* **-casted; -cast·ing** : predict —**forecast** *n* —**fore·cast·er** *n*

fore·cas·tle \'fōksəl\ *n* : forward part of a ship

fore·close \fȯr'klōz\ *vb* : take legal measures to terminate a mortgage —**fore·clo·sure** \-'klōzhər\ *n*

fore·fa·ther \'fȯr-\ *n* : ancestor

fore·fin·ger \'fȯr-\ *n* : finger next to the thumb

fore·foot \'fȯr-\ *n* : front foot of a quadruped

fore·front \'fȯr-\ *n* : foremost position or place

fore·gath·er *var of* FORGATHER

¹fore·go \fȯr'gō\ *vb* **-went; -gone; -go·ing** : precede

²forego *var of* FORGO

fore·go·ing *adj* : preceding

fore·gone *adj* : determined in advance

fore·ground \'fȯr-\ *n* : part of a scene nearest the viewer

fore·hand \'fȯr-\ *n* : a stroke with the palm of the hand turned in the direction of movement —**forehand** *adj*

fore·head \'fȯrəd, 'fȯr,hed\ *n* : part of the face above the eyes

for·eign \'fȯrən\ *adj* **1** : situated outside a place or country and esp. one's own country **2** : belonging to a different place or country **3** : not pertinent **4** : related to or dealing with other nations —**for·eign·er** \-ər\ *n*

fore·know \fȯr'nō\ *vb* **-knew; -known; -know·ing** : know beforehand —**fore·knowl·edge** *n*

fore·leg \'fȯr-\ *n* : front leg

fore·lock \'fȯr-\ *n* : front lock of hair

fore·man \'fȯrmən\ *n* **1** : spokesman of a jury **2** : workman in charge

fore·most \'fȯr-\ *adj* : first in time, place, or order —**foremost** *adv*

fore·noon \'fȯr-\ *n* : morning

fo·ren·sic \fə'rensik\ *adj* : relating to courts or public speaking or debate

fo·ren·sics \-siks\ *n pl* : art or study of speaking or debating

fore·or·dain \,fȯr-\ *vb* : decree beforehand

fore·quar·ter \'fȯr-\ *n* : front half on one side of the body of a quadruped

fore·run·ner \'fȯr-\ *n* : one that goes before

fore·see \fȯr'sē\ *vb* **-saw; -seen; -see·ing** : see or realize beforehand —**fore·see·able** *adj*

fore·shad·ow \fȯr-\ *vb* : hint or suggest beforehand

fore·sight \'fȯr-\ *n* : care or provision for the future —**fore·sight·ed** *adj* —**fore·sight·ed·ness** *n*

for·est \'fȯrəst\ *n* : large thick growth of trees and underbrush —**for·est·ed** \'fȯrəstəd\ *adj* —**for·est·er** \-əstər\ *n* —**for·est·land** \-,land\ *n* —**for·est·ry** \-əstrē\ *n*

fore·stall \fȯr'stȯl, fȯr-\ *vb* : prevent by acting in advance

foreswear *var of* FORSWEAR

fore·taste \'fȯr-\ *n* : advance indication or notion ~ *vb* : anticipate

fore·tell \fȯr'tel\ *vb* **-told; -tell·ing** : predict

fore·thought \'fȯr-\ *n* : foresight

for·ev·er \fȯr'evər, fə-\ *adv* **1** : for a limitless time **2** : always

for·ev·er·more \-,evər'mȯr\ *adv* : forever

fore·warn \fȯr-\ *vb* : warn beforehand

fore·word \'fȯr-\ *n* : preface

for·feit \'fȯrfət\ *n* : something forfeited ~ *vb* : lose or lose the right to by an error or crime —**for·fei·ture** \-fə,chúr\ *n*

for·gath·er, fore·gath·er \fȯr'gathər\ *vb* : assemble

¹forge \'fȯrj\ *n* : smithy ~ *vb* **forged; forg·ing 1** : form (metal) by heating and hammering **2** : imitate falsely esp. to defraud —**forg·er** *n* —**forg·ery** \-(ə)rē\ *n*

²forge *vb* **forged; forg·ing** : move ahead steadily

for·get \fər'get\ *vb* **-got** \-'gät\; **-got·ten** \-'gät²n\ *or* **-got; -get·ting 1** : be unable to think of or recall **2** : fail to think of at the proper time —**for·get·ful** \-fəl\ *adj* —**for·get·ful·ly** *adv*

for·get-me-not *n* : small herb with blue or white flowers

for·give \fər'giv\ *vb* **-gave \-'gāv\; -giv·en \-'givən\; -giv·ing** : pardon —**for·giv·able** *adj* —**for·give·ness** *n*

for·go, fore·go \fȯr'gō, fōr-\ *vb* **-went; -gone; -go·ing** : give up

fork \\'fȯrk\ *n* **1** : implement with prongs for lifting, holding, or digging **2** : forked part **3** : a dividing into branches or a place where something branches ~ *vb* **1** : divide into branches **2** : move with a fork —**forked** \\'fȯrkt, 'fȯrkəd\ *adj*

fork·lift *n* : hoisting machine with a fork-shaped lever

for·lorn \fər'lȯrn\ *adj* **1** : deserted **2** : wretched —**for·lorn·ly** *adv*

form \\'fȯrm\ *n* **1** : shape **2** : set way of doing or saying something **3** : document with blanks to be filled in **4** : behavior or performance with respect to what is expected **5** : mold **6** : variety **7** : one of the ways in which a word is changed to show difference in use ~ *vb* **1** : give form or shape to **2** : train **3** : develop **4** : constitute —**for·ma·tive** \\'fȯrmətiv\ *adj* —**form·less** \-ləs\ *adj*

for·mal \\'fȯrməl\ *adj* : following established custom ~ *n* : formal social event —**for·mal·i·ty** \fȯr'malətē\ *n* —**for·mal·ize** \'fȯrmə,līz\ *vb* —**for·mal·ly** *adv*

form·al·de·hyde \fȯr'maldə,hīd\ *n* : colorless pungent gas used as a preservative and disinfectant

for·mat \\'fȯr,mat\ *n* : general style or arrangement of something —**format** *vb*

for·ma·tion \fȯr'māshən\ *n* **1** : a giving form to something **2** : something formed **3** : arrangement

for·mer \\'fȯrmər\ *adj* : coming before in time —**for·mer·ly** *adv*

for·mi·da·ble \\'fȯrmədəbəl, fȯr'mid-\ *adj* **1** : causing fear or dread **2** : very difficult —**for·mi·da·bly** \-blē\ *adv*

for·mu·la \\'fȯrmyələ\ *n, pl* **-las** *or* **-lae** \-,lē, -,lī\ **1** : set form of words for ceremonial use **2** : recipe **3** : milk mixture for a baby **4** : group of symbols or figures expressing a single rule or idea **5** : set form or method

for·mu·late \-,lāt\ *vb* **-lat·ed; -lat·ing** : state definitely and clearly —**for·mu·la·tion** \,fȯrmyə'lāshən\ *n*

for·ni·ca·tion \,fȯrnə'kāshən\ *n* : illicit sexual intercourse —**for·ni·cate** \\'fȯrnə,kāt\ *vb* —**for·ni·ca·tor** \-,kātər\ *n*

for·sake \fər'sāk\ *vb* **-sook** \-'sůk\; **-sak·en** \-'sākən\; **-sak·ing** : abandon

for·swear, fore·swear \fȯr'swaar, fȯr-, -'swear\ *vb* **-swore; -sworn; -swear·ing 1** : renounce under oath **2** : perjure

for·syth·ia \fər'sithēə\ *n* : shrub grown for its yellow flowers

fort \\'fȯrt\ *n* **1** : fortified place **2** : permanent army post

forte \\'fȯrt, 'fȯr,tā\ *n* : something in which a person excels

forth \\'fȯrth\ *adv* : forward

forth·com·ing *adj* : coming or available soon

forth·right *adj* : direct —**forth·right·ly** *adv* —**forth·right·ness** *n*

forth·with *adv* : immediately

for·ti·fy \\'fȯrtə,fī\ *vb* **-fied; -fy·ing** : make strong —**for·ti·fi·ca·tion** \,fȯrtəfə'kāshən\ *n*

for·ti·tude \\'fȯrtə,t(y)üd\ *n* : ability to endure

fort·night \\'fȯrt,nīt\ *n* : 2 weeks —**fort·night·ly** *adj or adv*

for·tress \\'fȯrtrəs\ *n* : fort

for·tu·itous \fȯr't(y)üətəs\ *adj* : accidental

for·tu·nate \\'fȯrch(ə)nət\ *adj* **1** : coming by good luck **2** : lucky —**for·tu·nate·ly** *adv*

for·tune \\'fȯrchən\ *n* **1** : apparent cause of something that happens to one unexpectedly **2** : good or bad luck **3** : destiny **4** : wealth

for·tune-tell·er \-,telər\ *n* : one who foretells a person's future —**for·tune-tell·ing** \-iŋ\ *n or adj*

for·ty \\'fȯrtē\ *n, pl* **forties** : 4 time 10 —**for·ti·eth** \-ēəth\ *adj or n* —**forty** *adj or pron*

for·ty-nin·er \-'nīnər\ *n* : a person in the gold rush to California in 1849

fo·rum \\'fȯrəm\ *n, pl* **-rums 1** : Roman marketplace **2** : medium for open discussion

for·ward \\'fȯrwərd\ *adj* **1** : being near or at or belonging to the front **2** : brash ~ *adv* : toward what is in front ~ *n* : player near the front of his team ~ *vb* **1** : help onward **2** : send on —**for·ward·er** \-wərdər\ *n* —**for·ward·ness** *n*

for·wards \\'fȯrwərdz\ *adv* : forward

fos·sil \\'fäsəl\ *n* : preserved trace of an ancient plant or animal ~ *adj* : being or originating from a fossil —**fos·sil·ize** *vb*

fos·ter \\'fȯstər\ *adj* : being, having, or relating to substitute parents ~ *vb* : help to grow or develop

fought *past of* FIGHT

foul \\'faůl\ *adj* **1** : offensive **2** : clogged with dirt **3** : abusive **4** : wet and stormy **5** : unfair ~ *n* : a breaking of the rules in a game ~ *adv* : foully ~ *vb* **1** : make or become foul or filthy **2** : tangle —**foul·ly** *adv* —**foul-**

mouthed \-'maüthd, -'maütht\ *adj*
—**foul-ness** *n*

fou-lard \fu̇'lärd\ *n* : lightweight silk

foul-up *n* : error or state of confusion —**foul up** *vb* : bungle

¹**found** \'faünd\ *past of* FIND

²**found** *vb* : establish —**found-er** *n*

³**found** *vb* : melt (metal) and pour into a mold —**found-er** *n* —**found-ry** \'faündrē\ *n*

foun-da-tion \faün'dāshən\ *n* 1 : act of founding 2 : basis for something 3 : endowed institution 4 : supporting structure —**foun-da-tion-al** \-sh(ə)nəl\ *adj*

foun-der \'faündər\ *vb* : sink

found-ling \'faün(d)liŋ\ *n* : abandoned infant that is found

fount \'faünt\ *n* : fountain

foun-tain \'faünt²n\ *n* 1 : spring of water 2 : source 3 : artificial jet of water

four \'fōr\ *n* 1 : one more than 3 2 : 4th in a set or series 3 : something having 4 units —**four** *adj or pron*

four-fold *adj* : quadruple —**four-fold** *adv*

four-score *adj* : 80

four-some \'fōrsəm\ *n* : group of 4

four-teen \fōr'tēn\ *n* : one more than 13 —**fourteen** *adj or pron* —**four-teenth** \-'tēnth\ *adj or n*

fourth \'fōrth\ *n* 1 : one that is 4th 2 : one of 4 equal parts of something —**fourth** *adj or adv*

fowl \'faül\ *n, pl* **fowl** *or* **fowls** 1 : bird 2 : chicken

fox \'fäks\ *n, pl* **fox-es** *or* **fox** 1 : small mammal related to wolves 2 : clever person ~ *vb* : trick —**foxy** \'fäksē\ *adj*

fox-glove *n* : flowering plant that provides digitalis

fox-hole \'fäks,hōl\ *n* : pit for protection against enemy fire

foy-er \'fȯiər, 'fȯi,(y)ā\ *n* : entrance hallway

fra-cas \'frākəs, 'frak-\ *n, pl* **-cas-es** \-əsəz\ : brawl

frac-tion \'frakshən\ *n* 1 : number indicating one or more equal parts of a whole 2 : portion —**frac-tion-al** \-sh(ə)nəl\ *adj* —**frac-tion-al-ly** *adv*

frac-tious \-shəs\ *adj* : hard to control

frac-ture \-chər\ *n* : a breaking of something —**fracture** *vb*

frag-ile \'frajəl, -,īl\ *adj* : easily broken —**fra-gil-i-ty** \frə'jilətē\ *n*

frag-ment \'fragmənt\ *n* : part broken off — *vb* \-,ment\ : break into parts —**frag-men-tary** \'fragmən,terē\ *adj* —**frag-men-ta-tion** \,fragmən'tā-shən, -,men-\ *n*

fra-grant \'frāgrənt\ *adj* : sweet-smelling —**fra-grance** \-grəns\ *n* —**fra-grant-ly** *adv*

frail \'frāl\ *adj* : weak or delicate —**frail-ty** \'frāl(ə)ltē\ *n*

frame \'frām\ *vb* **framed; fram-ing** 1 : plan 2 : formulate 3 : construct or arrange 4 : enclose in a frame 5 : make appear guilty ~ *n* 1 : makeup of the body 2 : supporting or enclosing structure 3 : state or disposition (as of mind) —**frame-work** *n*

franc \'fraŋk\ *n* : monetary unit (as of France)

fran-chise \'fran,chīz\ *n* 1 : special privilege 2 : the right to vote —**fran-chi-see** \,fran,chī'zē, -chə-\ *n*

fran-gi-ble \'franjəbəl\ *adj* : breakable —**fran-gi-bil-i-ty** \,franjə'bilətē\ *n*

¹**frank** \'fraŋk\ *adj* : direct and sincere —**frank-ly** *adv* —**frank-ness** *n*

²**frank** *vb* : mark (mail) with a sign showing it can be mailed free ~ *n* : sign on franked mail

frank-furt-er \'fraŋkfə(r)tər, -,fərt-\, **frank-furt**, **frank-fort** \-fərt\ *n* : cooked sausage

frank-in-cense \'fraŋkən,sens\ *n* : incense resin

fran-tic \'frantik\ *adj* : wildly excited —**fran-ti-cal-ly** \-ik(ə)lē\ *adv* —**fran-tic-ly** \-iklē\ *adv*

fra-ter-nal \frə'tərn²l\ *adj* 1 : brotherly 2 : of a fraternity —**fra-ter-nal-ly** *adv*

fra-ter-ni-ty \frə'tərnətē\ *n, pl* **-ties** : social club of males

frat-er-nize \'fratər,nīz\ *vb* **-nized; niz-ing** 1 : mingle as friends 2 : associate with citizens or troops of a hostile nation —**frat-er-ni-za-tion** \,fratər-nə'zāshən\ *n*

frat-ri-cide \'fratrə,sīd\ *n* : killing of a brother or sister —**frat-ri-cid-al** \,fratrə'sīd³l\ *adj*

fraud \'frȯd\ *n* : trickery —**fraud-u-lent** \'frȯjələnt\ *adj* —**fraud-u-lent-ly** *adv*

fraught \'frȯt\ *adj* : bearing promise or menace

¹**fray** \'frā\ *n* : fight

²**fray** *vb* 1 : wear by rubbing 2 : separate the threads of 3 : irritate

fraz-zle \'frazəl\ *vb* **-zled; -zling** : wear out ~ *n* : exhaustion

freak \'frēk\ *n* 1 : something abnormal or unusual 2 : enthusiast —**freak-ish** *adj* —**freak out** *vb* : experience nightmarish hallucinations from drugs

freck-le \'frekəl\ *n* : brown spot on the skin —**freckle** *vb*

free \'frē\ *adj* **fre-er; fre-est** 1 : having liberty or independence 2 : not taxed 3 : given without charge 4 : volun-

tary **5** : not in use **6** : not fastened ~ *adv* : without charge — *vb* **freed;**
free·ing : set free —**free·born** *adj* —**free·dom** \'frēdəm\ *n* —**free·ly** *adv*

free-boo·ter \-ˌbütər\ *n* : pirate

free-for-all *n* : fight with no rules

free·load *vb* : live off another's generosity —**free·load·er** *n*

free·stand·ing *adj* : standing without support

free·way \'frēˌwā\ *n* : limited-access expressway

free will *n* : independent power to choose —**free·will** *adj*

freeze \'frēz\ *vb* **froze** \'frōz\; **fro·zen** \'frōz²n\; **freez·ing 1** : harden into ice **2** : become chilled **3** : damage by frost **4** : stick fast **5** : become motionless **6** : fix at one stage or level ~ *n* **1** : very cold weather **2** : state of being frozen —**freez·er** *n*

freeze–dry *vb* : preserve by freezing then drying —**freeze–dried** *adj*

freight \'frāt\ *n* **1** : carrying of goods or payment for this **2** : shipped goods ~ *vb* : load or ship goods —**freight·er** *n*

french fry *vb* : fry in deep fat —**french fry** *n*

fre·net·ic \fri'netik\ *adj* : frenzied —**fre·net·i·cal·ly** \-ik(ə)lē\ *adv*

fren·zy \'frenzē\ *n, pl* **-zies** : violent agitation —**fren·zied** \-zēd\ *adj*

fre·quen·cy \'frēkwənsē\ *n, pl* **-cies 1** : frequent or regular occurrence **2** : number of cycles or sound waves per second

fre·quent \'frēkwənt\ *adj* : happening often ~ \frē'kwent, 'frēkwənt\ *vb* : go to habitually —**fre·quent·er** *n* —**fre·quent·ly** *adv*

fres·co \'freskō\ *n, pl* **-coes** *or* **-cos** : painting on fresh plaster

fresh \'fresh\ *adj* **1** : not salt **2** : invigorating **3** : not preserved **4** : not stale **5** : like new **6** : insolent —**fresh·en** \-ən\ *vb* —**fresh·ly** *adv* —**fresh·ness** *n*

fresh·et \-ət\ *n* : overflowing stream

fresh·man \-mən\ *n* : first-year student

fresh·wa·ter \-ˌ\ *n* : water that is not salt

fret \'fret\ *vb* **-tt- 1** : worry or become irritated **2** : fray **3** : agitate ~ *n* **1** : worn spot **2** : irritation —**fret·ful** \'fretfəl\ *adj* —**fret·ful·ly** *adv* —**fret·ful·ness** *n*

fri·a·ble \'frīəbəl\ *adj* : easily pulverized

fri·ar \'frī(ə)r\ *n* : member of a religious order

fri·ary \-ē\ *n, pl* **-ar·ies** : monastery of friars

fric·as·see \'frikəˌsē, ˌfrikə'-\ *n* : meat stewed in a gravy — *vb* **-seed; -see·ing** : stew in gravy

fric·tion \'frikshən\ *n* **1** : a rubbing between 2 surfaces **2** : clash of opinions —**fric·tion·al** *adj*

Fri·day \'frīdē\ *n* : 6th day of the week

friend \'frend\ *n* : person one likes —**friend·less** \'fren(d)ləs\ *adj* —**friend·li·ness** \'fren(d)lēnəs\ *n* —**friend·ly** *adj* —**friend·ship** \'fren(d)ˌship\ *n*

frieze \'frēz\ *n* : ornamental band around a room

frig·ate \'frigət\ *n* : warship larger than a destroyer

fright \'frīt\ *n* : sudden fear —**fright·en** \-²n\ *vb* —**fright·ful** \-fəl\ *adj* —**fright·ful·ly** *adv* —**fright·ful·ness** *n*

frig·id \'frijəd\ *adj* : intensely cold —**fri·gid·i·ty** \frij'idətē\ *n*

frill \'fril\ *n* **1** : ruffle **2** : pleasing but nonessential addition —**frilly** *adj*

fringe \'frinj\ *n* **1** : ornamental border of short hanging threads or strips **2** : border ~ *vb* : furnish with or serve as a fringe

frisk \'frisk\ *vb* **1** : leap about **2** : search (a person) esp. for weapons

frisky \'friskē\ *adj* **frisk·i·er; -est** : frolicsome —**frisk·i·ly** *adv* —**frisk·i·ness** *n*

¹**frit·ter** \'fritər\ *n* : fried batter containing fruit or meat

²**fritter** *vb* : waste little by little

friv·o·lous \'friv(ə)ləs\ *adj* : not important or serious —**fri·vol·i·ty** \friv'älətē\ *n* —**friv·o·lous·ly** *adv*

frizz \'friz\ *vb* : curl tightly —**frizz** *n* —**frizzy** *adj*

fro \'frō\ *adv* : away

frock \'fräk\ *n* **1** : loose outer garment **2** : dress

frog \'frȯg, 'fräg\ *n* **1** : leaping amphibian **2** : hoarseness **3** : ornamental braid fastener **4** : small holder for flowers

frog·man \-ˌman, -mən\ *n* : underwater swimmer

frol·ic \'frälik\ *vb* **-icked; -ick·ing** : romp ~ *n* : fun —**frol·ic·some** \-səm\ *adj*

from \(')frəm, 'främ\ *prep* —used to show a starting point

frond \'fränd\ *n* : fern leaf

front \'frənt\ *n* **1** : face **2** : behavior **3** : main side of a building **4** : forward part **5** : boundary between air masses ~ *vb* **1** : face **2** : serve as a front —**fron·tal** \-²l\ *adj*

front·age \'frəntij\ *n* : length of boundary line on a street

fron·tier \,frən'tiər\ *n* : outer edge of settled territory —**fron·tiers·man** \-'tiərzmən\ *n*

fron·tis·piece \'frəntə,spēs\ *n* : illustration facing a title page

frost \'frȯst\ *n* 1 : freezing temperature 2 : ice crystals on a surface ~ *vb* 1 : cover with frost 2 : put icing on (a cake) —**frosty** *adj*

frost·bite \'frȯs(t),bīt\ *n* : partial freezing of part of the body —**frostbit·ten** \-,bit²n\ *adj*

frost·ing *n* : icing

froth \'frȯth\ *n, pl* **froths** \'frȯths, 'frȯthz\ : bubbles on a liquid —**frothy** *adj*

fro·ward \'frō(w)ərd\ *adj* : willful

frown \'fraún\ *vb or n* : scowl

frow·sy \'fraúzē\ *adj* -**si·er; -est** : untidy

froze *past of* FREEZE

frozen *past part of* FREEZE

fru·gal \'frügəl\ *adj* : thrifty —**fru·gal·i·ty** \frü'galətē\ *n* —**fru·gal·ly** *adv*

fruit \'früt\ *n* 1 : usu. edible and sweet part of a seed plant 2 : result ~ *vb* : bear fruit —**fruit·cake** —**fruit·ed** \-əd\ *adj* —**fruit·ful** *adj* —**fruit·ful·ness** *n* —**fruit·less** *adj* —**fruity** *adj*

fru·ition \frü'ishən\ *n* : completion

frumpy \'frəmpē\ *adj* **frump·i·er; -est** : dowdy

frus·trate \'frəs,trāt\ *vb* -**trat·ed; -trat·ing** 1 : block 2 : cause to fail —**frus·trat·ing·ly** *adv* —**frus·tra·tion** \,frəs'trāshən\ *n*

¹**fry** \'frī\ *vb* **fried; fry·ing** 1 : cook esp. with fat or oil 2 : be cooked by frying ~ *n, pl* **fries** 1 : something fried 2 : social gathering with fried food

²**fry** *n, pl* **fry** : recently hatched fish

fud·dle \'fəd²l\ *vb* -**dled; -dling** : muddle

fud·dy-dud·dy \'fədē,dədē\ *n, pl* -**dies** : one who is old-fashioned or unimaginative

fudge \'fəj\ *vb* **fudged; fudg·ing** : cheat or exaggerate ~ *n* : creamy candy

fu·el \'fyüəl\ *n* : substance burned to produce heat or power ~ *vb* -**eled** *or* -**elled; -el·ing** *or* -**el·ling** : provide with or take in fuel

fu·gi·tive \'fyüjətiv\ *adj* 1 : running away or trying to escape 2 : not lasting —**fugitive** *n*

-**ful** \'fəl\ *adj-suffix* 1 : full of 2 : having the qualities of 3 : -able ~ *n suffix* : quantity that fills

ful·crum \'fulkrəm, 'fəl-\ *n, pl* -**crums** or -**cra** \-krə\ : support on which a lever turns

ful·fill, ful·fil \ful'fil\ *vb* -**filled; -fill·ing** 1 : perform 2 : satisfy —**ful·fill·ment** *n*

¹**full** \'ful\ *adj* 1 : filled 2 : complete 3 : rounded 4 : having an abundance of something ~ *adv* : entirely ~ *n* : utmost degree —**full·ness** \'fulnəs\ *n* —**ful·ly** \-(l)lē\ *adv*

²**full** *vb* : shrink and thicken woolen cloth —**full·er** *n*

full-fledged \'ful'flejd\ *adj* : fully developed

ful·some \'fulsəm\ *adj* : offensive

fum·ble \'fəmbəl\ *vb* -**bled; -bling** : fail to hold something properly —**fumble** *n*

fume \'fyüm\ *n* : irritating gas ~ *vb* **fumed; fum·ing** 1 : give off fumes 2 : show annoyance

fu·mi·gate \'fyümə,gāt\ *vb* -**gat·ed; -gat·ing** : treat with pest-killing fumes —**fu·mi·gant** \'fyümigənt\ *n* —**fu·mi·ga·tion** \,fyümə'gāshən\ *n*

fun \'fən\ *n* 1 : something providing amusement or enjoyment 2 : enjoyment

func·tion \'fəŋkshən\ *n* 1 : special purpose 2 : formal ceremony or social affair ~ *vb* 1 : serve 2 : operate —**func·tion·al** \-sh(ə)nəl\ *adj* —**func·tion·al·ly** *adv* —**func·tion·less** *adj*

func·tion·ary \-shə,nerē\ *n, pl* -**ar·ies** : official

fund \'fənd\ *n* 1 : store 2 : sum of money intended for a special purpose 3 *pl* : available money ~ *vb* : provide funds for

fun·da·men·tal \,fəndə'ment²l\ *adj* 1 : basic 2 : of central importance or necessity —**fundamental** *n* —**fun·da·men·tal·ly** *adv*

fu·ner·al \'fyün(ə)rəl\ *n* : ceremony for a dead person —**funeral** *adj* —**fu·ne·re·al** \fyü'nirēəl\ *adj*

fun·gi·cide \'fənjə,sīd, 'fəŋgə-\ *n* : agent that kills fungi —**fun·gi·cid·al** \,fənjə'sīd²l, ,fəŋgə-\ *adj*

fun·gus \'fəŋgəs\ *n, pl* **fun·gi** \'fən,jī, 'fəŋ,gī\ : lower plant that lacks chlorophyll —**fun·gal** \'fəŋgəl\ *adj* —**fun·gous** \-gəs\ *adj*

funk \'fəŋk\ *n* : state of paralyzed fear

funky \'fəŋkē\ *adj* **funk·i·er; -est** : unconventional and unsophisticated

fun·nel \'fən²l\ *n* 1 : cone-shaped utensil with a tube 2 : ship's smokestack ~ *vb* -**neled; -nel·ing** : move to a central point or into a central channel

fun·nies \\'fənēz\ *n pl* : section of comic strips

fun·ny \\'fənē\ *adj* **-ni·er; -est** 1 : amusing 2 : strange

fur \\'fər\ *n* 1 : hairy coat of a mammal 2 : article of clothing made with fur **—fur** *adj* **—furred** \\'fərd\ *adj* **—fur·ry** \-ē\ *adj*

fur·bish \\'fərbish\ *vb* : make lustrous or new looking

fu·ri·ous \\'fyúrēəs\ *adj* : fierce or angry **—fu·ri·ous·ly** *adv*

fur·long \\'fər,lóṅ\ *n* : a unit of length equal to 220 yards

fur·lough \\'fərlō\ *n* : authorized absence from duty **—furlough** *vb*

fur·nace \\'fərnəs\ *n* : enclosed structure in which heat is produced

fur·nish \\'fərnish\ *vb* 1 : provide with what is needed 2 : make available for use

fur·nish·ings \-iṅs\ *n pl* 1 : articles or accessories of dress 2 : furniture

fur·ni·ture \\'fərnichər\ *n* : movable equipment necessary for a room

fu·ror \\'fyúr,ór\ *n* 1 : anger 2 : sensational craze

fur·ri·er \\'fərēər\ *n* : dealer in furs **—fur·ri·ery** \-ē\ *n*

fur·row \\'fərō\ *n* 1 : trench made by a plow 2 : wrinkle or groove **—furrow** *vb*

fur·ther \\'fərthər\ *adv* 1 : at or to a more advanced point 2 : more **—** *adj* : additional **—** *vb* : promote **—fur·ther·ance** \-(ə)rəns\ *n*

fur·ther·more \\'fərthə(r),mór\ *adv* : in addition

fur·ther·most \-thər,mōst\ *adj* : most distant

fur·thest \\'fərthəst\ *adv or adj* : farthest

fur·tive \\'fərtiv\ *adj* : slyly or secretly

done **—fur·tive·ly** *adv* **—fur·tive·ness** *n*

fu·ry \\'fyúrē\ *n, pl* **-ries** 1 : violent anger 2 : violence

¹fuse \\'fyüz\ *n* 1 : tube lighted to transmit fire to an explosive 2 *usu* **~, fuze** *vb* **fused** *or* **fuzed; fus·ing** *or* **fuz·ing** : equip with a fuse

²fuse *vb* **fused; fus·ing** 1 : melt and run together 2 : unite **—** *n* : electrical safety device **—fus·ible** *adj*

fu·se·lage \\'fyüsə,läzh, -zə-\ *n* : main body of an airplane

fu·sil·lade \\'fyüsə,läd, -,läd, ,fyüsə'-, -zə-\ *n* : volley of fire

fu·sion \\'fyüzhən\ *n* 1 : process of merging by melting 2 : union of atomic nuclei

fuss \\'fəs\ *n* 1 : needless bustle or excitement 2 : unusual amount of attention or interest 3 : objection or protest **~** *vb* 1 : shower flattering attention 2 : pay undue attention to details

fuss·bud·get \-,bəjət\ *n* : one who fusses about trifles

fussy \\'fəsē\ *adj* **fuss·i·er; -est** 1 : irritable 2 : fastidious **—fuss·i·ly** *adv* **—fuss·i·ness** *n*

fu·tile \\'fyütᵊl, 'fyü,tīl\ *adj* : useless or vain **—fu·til·i·ty** \fyü'tilətē\ *n*

fu·ture \\'fyüchər\ *adj* : coming after the present **~** *n* 1 : time yet to come 2 : what will happen **—fu·tur·is·tic** \,fyüchə'ristik\ *adj*

fuze *var of* FUSE

fuzz \\'fəz\ *n* : fine particles or fluff

fuzzy \\'fəzē\ *adj* **fuzz·i·er; -est** 1 : covered with or like fuzz 2 : indistinct **—fuzz·i·ness** *n*

-fy \,fī\ *vb suffix* : make **—-fi·er** \,fī(ə)r\ *n suffix*

G

g \\'jē\ *n, pl* **g's** *or* **gs** \'jēz\ 1 : 7th letter of the alphabet 2 : unit of gravitational force

gab \\'gab\ *vb* **-bb-** : chatter **—gab** *n* **—gab·by** \'gabē\ *adj*

gab·ar·dine \\'gabər,dēn\ *n* : durable twilled fabric

ga·ble \\'gābəl\ *n* : triangular part of the end of a building **—ga·bled** \-bəld\ *adj*

gad \\'gad\ *vb* **-dd-** : roam about **—gad·der** *n*

gad·fly *n* : persistently critical person

gad·get \\'gajət\ *n* : device **—gad·get·ry** \'gajətrē\ *n*

gaff \\'gaf\ *n* : metal hook for lifting fish **—gaff** *vb*

gaffe \\'gaf\ *n* : social blunder

gag \\'gag\ *vb* **-gg-** 1 : prevent from speaking or crying out by stopping up the mouth 2 : retch or cause to retch **~** *n* 1 : something that stops up the mouth 2 : laugh-provoking remark or act

gage *var of* GAUGE

gag·gle \\'gagəl\ *n* : flock of geese

gai·ety \'gāətē\ n, pl **-eties** : gay spirits

gai·ly \'gālē\ adv : in a gay manner

gain \'gān\ n 1 : profit 2 : obtaining of profit or possessions 3 : increase ~ vb 1 : get possession of 2 : win 3 : arrive at 4 : increase or increase in 5 : profit —**gain·er** n —**gain·ful** adj —**gain·ful·ly** adv

gain·say \gān'sā\ vb **-said** \-'sād, -'sed\; **-say·ing**; **-says** \-'sāz, -'sez\ : deny or dispute —**gain·say·er** n

gait \'gāt\ n : manner of walking or running —**gait·ed** adj

gal \'gal\ n : girl

ga·la \'gālə, 'gala, 'gälə\ n : festive celebration —**gala** adj

gal·axy \'galəksē\ n, pl **-ax·ies** : any of the systems that include stars, nebulas, and dust and make up the universe —**ga·lac·tic** \gə'laktik\ adj

gale \'gāl\ n 1 : strong wind 2 : outburst

1gall \'gȯl\ n 1 : bile 2 : insolence

2gall n 1 : sore on the skin caused by chafing 2 : swelling of plant tissue caused by parasites ~ vb 1 : chafe 2 : irritate or vex

gal·lant \gə'lant, -'länt; 'galənt\ n : man very attentive to women ~ \gə'lant; gə'länt, -'länt\ adj 1 : splendid 2 : brave 3 : polite and attentive to women —**gal·lant·ly** adv —**gal·lant·ry** \'galəntrē\ n

gall·blad·der n : pouch attached to the liver in which bile is stored

gal·le·on \'galēən\ n : former ship used for war and commerce esp. by the Spanish

gal·lery \'gal(ə)rē\ n, pl **-ler·ies** 1 : outdoor balcony 2 : long narrow room or passage 3 : room or building for exhibiting art 4 : spectators —**gal·ler·ied** \-rēd\ adj

gal·ley \'galē\ n, pl **-leys** 1 : old ship propelled by oars and sails 2 : kitchen of a ship or airplane

gal·li·um \'galēəm\ n : bluish white metallic chemical element

gal·li·vant \'galə,vant\ vb 1 : be socially active esp. with members of the opposite sex 2 : travel about for pleasure

gal·lon \'galən\ n : unit of liquid measure equal to 4 quarts

gal·lop \-əp\ n : fast 3-beat gait of a horse —**gal·lop** vb —**gal·lop·er** n

gal·lows \-ōz\ n, pl **-lows** or **-lows·es** : upright frame for hanging criminals

gall·stone n : abnormal concretion in the gallbladder or bile passages

ga·lore \gə'lȯr\ adj : in abundance

ga·losh \-'läsh\ n : overshoe —usu. pl.

gal·va·nize \'galvə,nīz\ vb **-nized**; **-niz·ing** 1 : shock into action 2 : coat (iron or steel) with zinc —**gal·va·ni·za·tion** \,galvənə'zāshən\ n —**gal·va·niz·er** n

gam·bit \'gambət\ n 1 : opening tactic in chess 2 : risky stratagem

gam·ble \-bəl\ vb **-bled**; **-bling** 1 : play a game for stakes 2 : bet 3 : take a chance ~ n : risky undertaking —**gam·bler** \-blər\ n

gam·bol \-bəl\ vb **-boled** or **-bolled**; **-bol·ing** or **-bol·ling** : skip about in play —**gambol** n

game \'gām\ n 1 : playing activity 2 : competition according to rules 3 : animals hunted for sport or food ~ vb **gamed**; **gam·ing** : gamble —adj 1 : plucky 2 : lame —**game·ly** adv —**game·ness** n

game·cock n : male fighting cock

game·keep·er n : person in charge of game animals or birds

ga·mete \gə'mēt, 'gam,ēt\ n : matured germ cell —**ga·met·ic** \gə'metik\ adj

ga·mine \ga'mēn\ n : charming tomboy

gam·ut \'gamət\ n : entire range or series

gamy or **gam·ey** \'gāmē\ adj **gam·i·er**; **-est** : having the flavor of game esp. when slightly tainted —**gam·i·ness** n

1gan·der \'gandər\ n : male goose

2gander n : glance

gang \'gaŋ\ n 1 : group of persons working together 2 : group of criminals ~ vb : attack in a gang —with up

gan·gling \'gaŋgliŋ\ adj : lanky

gan·gli·on \'gaŋglēən\ n, pl **-glia** \-glēə\ : mass of nerve cells —**gan·gli·on·ic** \,gaŋglē'änik\ adj

gang·plank n : platform used in boarding or leaving a ship

gan·grene \'gaŋ,grēn, gaŋ'-; 'gan-, gan-\ n : local death of body tissue —**gangrene** vb —**gan·gre·nous** \'gaŋgrənəs\ adj

gang·ster \'gaŋstər\ n : member of criminal gang

gang·way \-,wā\ n : passage in or out

gan·net \'ganət\ n : large fish-eating marine bird

gan·try \'gantrē\ n, pl **-tries** : frame structure supported over or around something

gap \'gap\ n 1 : break in a barrier 2 : mountain pass 3 : empty space

gape \'gāp, 'gap\ vb **gaped**; **gap·ing** 1 : open widely 2 : stare with mouth open —**gape** n

ga·rage \gə'räzh, -'räj\ n : building for housing or repairing automobiles ~ vb **-raged; -rag·ing** : put or keep in a garage

garb \'gärb\ n : clothing ~ vb : dress

gar·bage \'gärbij\ n **1** : food waste **2** : trash

gar·ble \'gärbəl\ vb **-bled; -bling** : distort the sense or sound of

gar·den \'gärd²n\ n **1** : plot for growing fruits, flowers, or vegetables **2** : public recreation area ~ vb : work in a garden —**gar·den·er** \'gärdnər, -²n·ər\ n

gar·de·nia \gär'dēnyə\ n : tree or shrub with fragrant white or yellow flowers or the flower

gar·gan·tuan \gär'ganch(ə)wən\ adj : having tremendous size or volume

gar·gle \'gärgəl\ vb **-gled; -gling** : rinse the throat with liquid —**gargle** n

gar·goyle \'gär,goil\ n : waterspout in the form of a grotesque human or animal

gar·ish \'ga(ə)rish\ adj : offensively bright or gaudy

gar·land \'gärlənd\ n : wreath of leaves or flowers ~ vb : form into or deck with a garland

gar·lic \'gärlik\ n : herb with pungent bulbs used in cooking —**gar·licky** \-likē\ adj

gar·ment \-mənt\ n : article of clothing

gar·ner \'närər\ vb : acquire by effort

gar·net \'närət\ n : deep red mineral

gar·nish \-nish\ vb : add decoration to (as food) —**garnish** n

gar·nish·ee \,gärnə'shē\ vb **-eed; -ee·ing** : take (as a debtor's wages) by legal authority

gar·nish·ment \'gärnishmənt\ n : attachment of property to satisfy a creditor

gar·ret \'garət\ n : attic

gar·ri·son \-rəsən\ n : military post or the troops stationed there —**garrison** vb

gar·ru·lous \'garələs\ adj : talkative —**gar·ru·li·ty** \gə'rülətē\ n —**gar·ru·lous·ly** adv —**gar·ru·lous·ness** n

gar·ter \'gärtər\ n : band to hold up a stocking or sock

gas \'gas\ n, pl **gas·es 1** : fluid (as hydrogen or air) that tends to expand indefinitely **2** : gasoline ~ vb **gassed; gas·sing 1** : treat with gas **2** : fill with gasoline —**gas·eous** \-ēəs, 'gashəs\ adj

gash \'gash\ n : deep long cut —**gash** vb

gas·ket \'gaskət\ n : material to seal a joint against leakage

gas·light n : light of burning illuminating gas

gas·o·line \'gasə,lēn, ,gasə'-\ n : flammable liquid from petroleum

gasp \'gasp\ vb **1** : catch the breath with emotion **2** : breathe laboriously —**gasp** n

gas·tric \'gastrik\ adj : relating to or located near the stomach

gas·tron·o·my \gas'tränəmē\ n : art of good eating —**gas·tro·nom·ic** \,gastrə'nämik\, **gas·tro·nom·i·cal** \-ikəl\ adj

gate \'gāt\ n : an opening for passage in a wall or fence —**gate·keep·er** n —**gate·post** n

gate·way n : way in or out

gath·er \'gathər\ vb **1** : bring or come together **2** : harvest **3** : pick up little by little **4** : deduce —**gath·er·er** n —**gath·er·ing** n

gauche \'gōsh\ adj : crude or tactless

gaudy \'gȯdē\ adj **gaud·i·er; -est** : tastelessly showy —**gaud·i·ly** \'gȯd³lē\ adv —**gaud·i·ness** n

gauge \'gāj\ n : instrument for measuring ~ vb **gauged; gaug·ing** : measure

gaunt \'gȯnt\ adj : thin or emaciated —**gaunt·ness** n

¹gaunt·let \-lət\ n **1** : protective glove **2** : challenge to combat

²gauntlet n : ordeal

gauze \'gȯz\ n : thin often transparent fabric —**gauzy** adj

gave past of GIVE

gav·el \'gavəl\ n : mallet of a presiding officer or auctioneer

gawk \'gȯk\ vb : stare stupidly

gawky \-ē\ adj **gawk·i·er; -est** : clumsy

gay \'gā\ adj **1** : merry **2** : bright and lively **3** : homosexual —**gay** n

gaze \'gāz\ vb **gazed; gaz·ing** : fix the eyes in a steady intent look —**gaze** n —**gaz·er** n

ga·zelle \gə'zel\ n : small swift antelope

ga·zette \-'zet\ n : newspaper

gaz·et·teer \,gazə'tiər\ n : geographical dictionary

gear \'giər\ n **1** : clothing **2** : equipment **3** : toothed wheel that interlocks with another for transmitting motion ~ vb **1** : provide with gears **2** : make ready or adjust —**gear·ing** n

gear·shift n : mechanism by which automobile gears are shifted

geese pl of GOOSE

gei·sha \'gāshə, 'gē-\ n, pl **-sha** or **-shas** : Japanese girl trained to entertain men

gel·a·tin \'jelət²n\ n : sticky substance obtained from animal tissues by boiling —**ge·lat·i·nous** \jə'latnəs, -ᵊnəs\ adj

geld \'geld\ vb : castrate

geld·ing \-iŋ\ n : castrated horse

gem \'jem\ n : cut and polished valuable stone —**gem·stone** n

gen·der \'jendər\ n 1 : sex 2 : division of a class of words (as nouns) that determines agreement of other words

gene \'jēn\ n : complex chemical unit of a chromosome that carries heredity —**gen·ic** \'jēnik\ adj

ge·ne·al·o·gy \jēnē'äläjē, jen-, -'al-\ n, pl -gies : study of family pedigrees —**ge·ne·a·log·i·cal** \-ēə'läjikəl\ adj —**ge·ne·a·log·i·cal·ly** adv —**ge·ne·al·o·gist** \-ē'äləjəst, -'al-\ n

genera pl of GENUS

gen·er·al \'jen(ə)rəl\ adj 1 : relating to the whole 2 : applicable to all of a group 3 : common or widespread ~ n 1 : something that involves or is applicable to the whole 2 : commissioned officer ranking next below a general of the army or a general of the air force 3 : commissioned officer of the highest rank in the marine corps —**gen·er·al·ly** adv —**in general** : for the most part

gen·er·al·i·ty \jenə'ralətē\ n, pl -ties : general statement

gen·er·al·ize \'jen(ə)rə,līz\ vb -ized; -iz·ing : reach a general conclusion esp. on the basis of particular instances —**gen·er·al·iza·tion** \(ə)rələ'zāshən\ n

general of the air force : commissioned officer of the highest rank in the air force

general of the army : commissioned officer of the highest rank in the army

gen·er·ate \'jenə,rāt\ vb -at·ed; -at·ing : create or produce

gen·er·a·tion \jenə'rāshən\ n 1 : living beings constituting a single step in a line of descent 2 : production —**gen·er·a·tive** \'jenə,rātiv, -(ə)rət-\ adj

gen·er·a·tor \'jenə,rātər\ n 1 : one that generates 2 : machine that turns mechanical into electrical energy

ge·ner·ic \jə'nerik\ adj 1 : general 2 : not protected by a trademark 3 : relating to a genus —**generic** n

gen·er·ous \'jen(ə)rəs\ adj 1 : freely giving or sharing —**gen·er·os·i·ty** \jenə'räsətē\ n —**gen·er·ous·ly** adv —**gen·er·ous·ness** n

ge·net·ics \jə'netiks\ n : biology dealing with heredity and variation —**ge·net·ic** \-ik\ adj —**ge·net·i·cal·ly** adv —**ge·net·i·cist** \-'netəsəst\ n

ge·nial \'jēnyəl\ adj : cheerful —**ge·nial·i·ty** \,jēnē'alətē, jēn'yal-\ n —**ge·nial·ly** \'jēnyəlē\ adv

ge·nie \'jēnē\ n : supernatural spirit that often takes human form

gen·i·tal \'jenət⁸l\ adj : concerned with reproduction —**gen·i·tal·ly** \-təlē\ adv

gen·i·ta·lia \jenə'tālyə\ n pl : external genital organs

gen·i·tals \'jenət⁸lz\ n pl : genitalia

ge·nius \'jēnyəs\ n 1 : single strongly marked capacity 2 : extraordinary intellectual power or a person having such power

geno·cide \'jenə,sīd\ n : systematic destruction of a racial or cultural group

genre \'zhänrə, 'zhäⁿrə, 'zhäⁿ(d)rⁱ\ n : category esp. of literary composition

gen·teel \jen'tēl\ adj : polite or refined

gen·tile \'jen,tīl\ n : person who is not Jewish —**gentile** adj

gen·til·i·ty \jen'tilətē\ n, pl -ties 1 : good birth and family 2 : good manners

gen·tle \'jent⁸l\ adj -tler, -tlest 1 : of a family of high social station 2 : not harsh, stern, or violent 3 : soft or delicate ~ vb -tled; -tling : make gentle —**gen·tle·ness** n —**gen·tly** adv

gen·tle·man \-mən\ n : man of good manners —**gen·tle·man·ly** adv

gen·tle·wom·an \-,wùmən\ n : woman of good family or breeding

gen·try \'jentrē\ n, pl -tries : people of good birth or breeding

gen·u·flect \'jenyə,flekt\ vb : bend the knee in worship —**gen·u·flec·tion** \jenyə'flekshən\ n

gen·u·ine \'jenyəwən\ adj : being the same in fact as in appearance —**gen·u·ine·ly** adv —**gen·u·ine·ness** n

ge·nus \'jēnəs\ n, pl **gen·era** \'jenərə\ : category of biological classification

ge·ode \'jē,ōd\ n : stone having a mineral-lined cavity

geo·des·ic \jēə'desik, -'dēs-\ adj : made of a framework of light straight-sided polygons in tension

ge·og·ra·phy \jē'ägrəfē\ n : study of the earth and its climate, products, and inhabitants —**ge·og·ra·pher** \-fər\ n —**geo·graph·ic** \jēə'grafik\, **geo·graph·i·cal** \-ikəl\ adj —**geo·graph·i·cal·ly** adv

ge·ol·o·gy \jē'äləjē\ n : study of the history of the earth and its life esp. as recorded in rocks —**ge·o·log·ic** \jēə'läjik\, **ge·o·log·i·cal** \-ikəl\ adj —**ge·ol·o·gist** \jē'äləjəst\ n ge·om·e·try \jē'ämətrē\ n, pl -tries : mathematics of the relations, properties, and measurements of solids, surfaces, lines, and angles —ge·om·e·ter \-ətər\ n —geo·met·ric \,jēə'metrik\, geo·met·ri·cal \-rikəl\ adj

geo·phys·ics \,jēə'fiziks\ n : physics of the earth —geo·phys·i·cal \-ikəl\ adj —geo·phys·i·cist \-'fizəsəst\ n

geo·ther·mal \,jēo'thərməl\, geo·ther·mic \-mik\ adj : of or relating to the heat of the earth's interior

ge·ra·ni·um \jə'rānēəm\ n : garden plant with clusters of white, pink, or scarlet flowers

ger·bil \'jərbəl\ n : burrowing desert rodent

ge·ri·at·ric \,jerē'atrik\ adj : relating to aging or the aged

ge·ri·at·rics \-triks\ n : medicine dealing with the aged and aging

germ \'jərm\ n 1 : microorganism 2 : source or rudiment

ger·mane \(,)jər'mān\ adj : relevant

ger·ma·ni·um \-'mānēəm\ n : grayish white hard chemical element

ger·mi·cide \'jərmə,sīd\ n : agent that destroys germs —ger·mi·cid·al \,jərmə'sīd⁰l\ adj

ger·mi·nate \'jərmə,nāt\ vb -nat·ed; -nat·ing : begin to develop —ger·mi·na·tion \,jərmə'nāshən\ n

ger·ry·man·der \,jerē'mandər, 'jerē,-, ,gerē'-, 'gerē,-\ vb : divide into election districts so as to give one political party an advantage —gerryman·der n

ger·und \'jerənd\ n : word having the characteristics of both verb and noun

ge·sta·po \gə'stäpō\ n, pl -pos : secret police

ges·ta·tion \je'stāshən\ n : pregnancy or incubation —ges·tate \'jes,tāt\ vb

ges·ture \'jeschər\ n 1 : movement of the body or limbs that expresses something 2 : something said or done for its effect on the attitudes of others —ges·tur·al \-chərəl\ adj —gesture vb

ge·sund·heit \gə'zünt,hīt\ interj —used to wish good health to one who has just sneezed

get \'get\ vb got \'gät\; got or got·ten \'gät⁰n\; get·ting 1 : gain or be in possession of 2 : succeed in coming or going 3 : cause to come or go or to be in a certain condition or position 4 : become 5 : be subjected to 6 : understand 7 : be obliged —get along vb 1 : get by 2 : be on friendly terms —get by vb : meet one's needs

get·away \'getə,wā\ n 1 : escape 2 : a starting or getting under way

gey·ser \'gīzər\ n : spring that intermittently shoots up hot water and steam

ghast·ly \'gastlē\ adj -li·er; -est : horrible or shocking

gher·kin \'gərkən\ n : small pickle

ghet·to \'getō\ n, pl -tos or -toes : part of a city in which members of a minority group live

ghost \'gōst\ n : disembodied soul —ghost·ly adv

ghost·write vb -wrote; -writ·ten : write for and in the name of another —ghost·writ·er n

ghoul \'gül\ n : legendary evil being that feeds on corpses —ghoul·ish adj

GI \(')jē'ī\ n, pl GI's or GIs : member of the U.S. armed forces

gi·ant \'jīənt\ n 1 : huge legendary being 2 : something very large or very powerful —giant adj

gib·ber \'jibər\ vb -bered; -ber·ing : speak rapidly and foolishly

gib·ber·ish \'jib(ə)rish\ n : unintelligible speech or language

gib·bon \'gibən\ n : manlike ape

gibe \'jīb\ vb gibed; gib·ing : jeer at —gibe n

gib·lets \'jibləts\ n pl : edible fowl viscera

gid·dy \'gidē\ adj -di·er; -est 1 : silly 2 : dizzy —gid·di·ness n

gift \'gift\ n 1 : something given 2 : talent —gift·ed adj

gi·gan·tic \jī'gantik\ adj : very big

gig·gle \'gigəl\ vb -gled; -gling : laugh in a silly manner —giggle n —gig·gly \-(ə)lē\ adj

gig·o·lo \'jigə,lō\ n, pl -los : man living on the earnings of a woman

Gi·la monster \,hēlə-\ n : large venomous lizard

gld \'gild\ vb gild·ed \'gildəd\ or gilt \'gilt\; gild·ing : cover with or as if with gold —gild·ing n

gill \'gil\ n : organ of a fish for obtaining oxygen from water

gilt \'gilt\ adj : gold-colored ~ n : gold or goldlike substance on the surface of an object

gim·bal \'gimbəl, 'jim-\ n : device that allows something to incline freely

gim·let \'gimlət\ n : small boring tool

gim·mick \'gimik\ n : new and ingenious scheme, feature, or device —gim·mick·ry n —gim·micky \-ikē\ adj

gimpy \'gimpē\ adj : lame

¹gin \'jin\ n : machine to separate seeds from cotton —gin vb

²**gin** *n* : clear liquor flavored with juniper berries

gin-ger \'jinjər\ *n* : pungent aromatic spice from a tropical plant —**gin-ger-bread** *n*

gin-ger-ly *adj* : very cautious or careful —**gingerly** *adv*

ging-ham \'giŋəm\ *n* : cotton clothing fabric

gin-gi-vi-tis \,jinjə'vītəs\ *n* : inflammation of the gums

gink-go \'giŋ(,)kō\ *n, pl* **-goes** *or* **-gos** : tree of eastern China

gin-seng \'jin,san, -,seŋ, -(,)siŋ\ *n* : aromatic root of a Chinese herb

gi-raffe \jə'raf\ *n* : African mammal with a very long neck

gird \'gərd\ *vb* **gird-ed** \'gərdəd\ *or* **girt** \'gərt\; **gird-ing 1** : encircle or fasten with or as if with a belt **2** : prepare

gird-er \'gərdər\ *n* : horizontal supporting beam

gir-dle \'-ᵊl\ *n* : woman's supporting undergarment ~ *vb* : surround

girl \'gərl\ *n* **1** : female child **2** : sweetheart —**girl-hood** \-,hůd\ *n* —**girl-ish** *adj*

girl friend *n* : frequent or regular female companion of a boy or man

girth \'gərth\ *n* : measure around something

gist \'jist\ *n* : main point of a matter

give \'giv\ *vb* **gave** \'gāv\; **giv-en** \'givən\; **giv-ing 1** : put into the possession or keeping of another **2** : pay **3** : perform **4** : contribute or donate **5** : produce **6** : utter **7** : yield to force, strain, or pressure ~ *n* : capacity or tendency to yield to force or strain —**give in** *vb* : surrender —**give out** *vb* : become used up or exhausted —**give up** *vb* **1** : let out of one's control **2** : cease from trying, doing, or hoping

give-away *n* **1** : unintentional betrayal **2** : something given free

giv-en \'givən\ *adj* **1** : prone or disposed **2** : having been specified

giz-zard \'gizərd\ *n* : muscular usu. horny-lined enlargement following the crop of a bird

gla-cial \'glāshəl\ *adj* : of or relating to glaciers —**gla-cial-ly** *adv*

gla-cier \'glāshər\ *n* : large body of ice moving slowly

glad \'glad\ *adj* **-dd- 1** : experiencing or causing pleasure, joy, or delight **2** : very willing —**glad-den** \-ᵊn\ *vb* —**glad-ly** *adv* —**glad-ness** *n*

glade \'glād\ *n* : grassy open space in a forest

glad-i-a-tor \'gladē,ātər\ *n* : one who fought to the death for the entertainment of ancient Romans —**glad-i-a-to-ri-al** \,gladēə'tōrēəl\ *adj*

glad-i-o-lus \,gladē'ōləs\ *n, pl* **-li** \-(,)lē, -,lī\ : plant related to the irises

glam-our, glam-or \'glamər\ *n* : romantic or exciting attractiveness —**glam-or-ize** \-ə,rīz\ *vb* —**glam-or-ous** \-(ə)rəs\ *adj*

glance \'glans\ *vb* **glanced; glanc-ing 1** : strike and fly off to one side **2** : give a quick look ~ *n* : quick look

gland \'gland\ *n* : group of cells that secretes a substance —**glan-du-lar** \'glanjələr\ *adj*

glans \'glanz\ *n, pl* **glan-des** \'glan,dēz\ : conical vascular body forming the extremity of the penis or clitoris

glare \'glaar\ *vb* **glared; glar-ing 1** : shine with a harsh dazzling light **2** : gaze angrily ~ *n* **1** : harsh dazzling light **2** : angry stare —**glar-ing** \'gla(ə)riŋ\ *adj* —**glar-ing-ly** *adv*

glass \'glas\ *n* **1** : usu. transparent substance made by melting sand and other materials **2** : something made of glass **3** *pl* : lenses used to correct defects of vision —**glass** *adj* —**glass-ful** \-,fůl\ *n* —**glass-ware** \-,waər\ *n* —**glassy** *adj*

glass-blow-ing *n* : art of shaping a mass of molten glass by blowing air into it —**glass-blow-er** *n*

glau-co-ma \glaů'kōmə, glȯ-\ *n* : state of increased pressure within the eyeball

glaze \'glāz\ *vb* **glazed; glaz-ing 1** : furnish with glass **2** : apply glaze to ~ *n* : glassy surface or coating

gla-zier \'glāzhər\ *n* : one who sets glass in window frames

gleam \'glēm\ *n* **1** : transient or partly obscured light **2** : faint trace ~ *vb* : send out gleams

glean \'glēn\ *vb* : collect little by little —**glean-able** *adj* —**glean-er** *n*

glee \'glē\ *n* : joy —**glee-ful** *adj*

glen \'glen\ *n* : valley

glib \'glib\ *adj* **-bb-** : speaking or spoken with ease —**glib-ly** *adv*

glide \'glīd\ *vb* **glid-ed; glid-ing** : move or descend smoothly and effortlessly ~ *n* : smooth motion or descent

glid-er \'glīdər\ *n* : aircraft having no engine

glim-mer \'glimər\ *vb* : shine faintly or unsteadily ~ *n* **1** : faint light **2** : small amount

glimpse \'glimps\ *vb* **glimpsed; glimps-ing** : take a brief look at —**glimpse** *n*

glint \'glint\ *vb* : gleam or sparkle —**glint** *n*

glis·ten \'glis°n\ *vb* : shine or sparkle by reflection —**glisten** *n*

glit·ter \'glitər\ *vb* : shine with brilliant or metallic luster ~ *n* : small glittering ornaments —**glit·tery** *adj*

gloat \'glōt\ *vb* : think of something with pride or self-satisfaction

glob \'gläb\ *n* : large rounded lump

glob·al \'glōbəl\ *adj* : worldwide —**glob·al·ly** *adv*

globe \'glōb\ *n* 1 : sphere 2 : the earth or a model of it

glob·u·lar \'gläbyələr\ *adj* 1 : round 2 : made up of globules

glob·ule \'gläbyül\ *n* : tiny ball

glock·en·spiel \'gläkən,s(h)pēl\ *n* : portable musical instrument consisting of tuned metal bars

gloom \'glüm\ *n* 1 : darkness 2 : sadness —**gloom·i·ly** *adv* —**gloom·i·ness** *n* —**gloomy** *adj*

glop \'gläp\ *n* : messy mass or mixture

glo·ri·fy \'glōrə,fī\ *vb* **-fied; -fy·ing** 1 : make to seem glorious 2 : worship —**glo·ri·fi·ca·tion** \,glōrəfə'kāshən\ *n*

glo·ry \'glōrē\ *n, pl* **-ies** 1 : praise or honor offered in worship 2 : cause for praise or renown 3 : magnificence 4 : heavenly bliss ~ *vb* **-ried; -ry·ing** : rejoice proudly —**glo·ri·ous** \'glō-rēəs\ *adj* —**glo·ri·ous·ly** *adv*

¹**gloss** \'gläs, 'glós\ *n* : luster ~ *vb* : treat rapidly or superficially —**gloss·i·ly** \-əlē\ *adv* —**gloss·i·ness** \-ēnəs\ *n* —**glossy** \-ē\ *adj*

²**gloss** *n* : brief explanation or translation ~ *vb* : translate or explain

glos·sa·ry \'gläs(ə)rē\ *n, pl* **-ries** : dictionary —**glos·sar·i·al** \glä-'sarēəl, glȯ-\ *adj*

glove \'gləv\ *n* : hand covering with sections for each finger

glow \'glō\ *vb* 1 : shine with or as if with intense heat 2 : show exuberance ~ *n* : brightness or warmth of color or feeling

glow·er \'glaü(ə)r\ *vb* : stare angrily —**glower** *n*

glow-worm *n* : insect or insect larva that emits light

glu·cose \'glü,kōs\ *n* : sugar found esp. in blood, plant sap, and fruits

glue \'glü\ *n* : substance used for sticking things together —**glue** *vb* —**glu·ey** \'glüē\ *adj*

glum \'gləm\ *adj* **-mm-** 1 : sullen 2 : dismal

glut \'glət\ *vb* **-tt-** : fill to excess —**glut** *n*

glu·ten \'glüt°n\ *n* : gluey protein substance in flour

glu·ti·nous \'glüt°nəs\ *adj* : sticky

glut·ton \'glət°n\ *n* : one who eats to excess —**glut·ton·ous** \'glət°nəs\ *adj* —**glut·tony** \'glət°nē\ *n*

glyc·er·in, glyc·er·ine \'glis(ə)rən\ *n* : syrupy liquid used as a solvent and moistener

gnarl \'närl\ *n* : hard knob on a tree ~ *vb* : twist or contort —**gnarled** \'närld\ *adj*

gnash \'nash\ *vb* : grind (as teeth) together

gnat \'nat\ *n* : small biting fly

gnaw \'nȯ\ *vb* : bite or chew on —**gnaw·er** \'nȯ(ə)r\ *n*

gnome \'nōm\ *n* : dwarf of folklore —**gnom·ish** *adj*

gnu \'n(y)ü\ *n, pl* **gnu** *or* **gnus** : large African antelope

go \'gō\ *vb* **went** \'went\; **gone** \'gȯn, 'gän\; **go·ing; goes** \'gōz\ 1 : move, proceed, run, or pass 2 : leave 3 : extend or lead 4 : sell or amount —used *with* for 5 : happen 6 —used in present participle to show intent or imminent action 7 : become 8 : fit or harmonize 9 : belong ~ *n, pl* **goes** 1 : act or manner of going 2 : vigor 3 : attempt —**go back on** : betray —**go by the board** : be discarded —**go for** : favor —**go off** : explode —**go one better** : outdo —**go over** 1 : examine 2 : study —**go to town** : be very successful —**on the go** : constantly active

goad \'gōd\ *n* : something that urges —**goad** *vb*

goal \'gōl\ *n* 1 : mark to reach in a race 2 : purpose 3 : object in a game through which a ball is propelled

goal·ie \'gōlē\ *n* : player who defends the goal

goal·keep·er *n* : goalie

goat \'gōt\ *n* : horned ruminant mammal related to the sheep —**goat·skin** *n*

goa·tee \gō'tē\ *n* : small pointed beard

gob \'gäb\ *n* : lump

¹**gob·ble** \'gäbəl\ *vb* **-bled; -bling** : eat greedily

²**gobble** *vb* **-bled; -bling** : make the noise of a turkey (**gobbler**)

gob·ble·dy·gook, gob·ble·de·gook \,gäbəldē'gúk, -'gük\ *n* : nonsense

gob·let \'gäblət\ *n* : large stemmed drinking glass

gob·lin \-lən\ *n* : ugly mischievous sprite

god \'gäd, 'gȯd\ *n* **1** *cap* : supreme being **2** : being with supernatural powers **2** : being with supernatural powers —**god·dess** \-əs\ *n* —**god·like** *adj* —**god·ly** *adj*

god·child *n* : person one sponsors at baptism —**god·daugh·ter** *n* —**god·son** *n*

god·less \-ləs\ *adj* : not believing in God —**god·less·ness** *n*

god·par·ent *n* : sponsor at baptism —**god·fa·ther** *n* —**god·moth·er** *n*

god·send \-,send\ *n* : something needed that comes unexpectedly

goes *pres 3d sing of* GO

go-get·ter \'gō,getər\ *n* : enterprising person —**go–get·ting** \-iŋ\ *adj or n*

gog·gle \'gägəl\ *vb* **-gled; -gling** : stare wide-eyed

gog·gles \-əlz\ *n pl* : protective glasses

go·ings–on \,gōiŋz'ȯn, -'än\ *n pl* : events

goi·ter \'gȯitər\ *n* : abnormally enlarged thyroid gland —**goi·trous** *adj*

gold \'gōld\ *n* : malleable yellow metallic chemical element —**gold·smith** \-,smith\ *n*

gold–brick \-,brik\ *n* : person who shirks duty —**goldbrick** *vb*

gold digger *n* : woman interested only in a man's money

gold·en \'gōldən\ *adj* **1** : made of, containing, or relating to gold **2** : having the color of gold **3** : precious or favorable

gold·en·rod \'gōldən,räd\ *n* : herb having tall stalks with tiny yellow flowers

gold·finch \'gōl(d),finch\ *n* : yellow American finch

gold·fish \-,fish\ *n* : small usu. orange or golden carp

golf \'gälf, 'gȯlf\ *n* : game played by hitting a small ball (**golf ball**) with clubs (**golf clubs**) into holes placed in a field (**golf course**) —**golf** *vb* —**golf·er** *n*

go·nad \'gō,nad\ *n* : sex gland

gon·do·la \'gändələ (*usual for 1*), gän'dō-\ *n* **1** : long narrow boat used on the canals of Venice **2** : car suspended from a cable

gon·do·lier \,gändə'liər\ *n* : gondola boatman

gone \'gȯn\ *adj* **1** : past **2** : involved

gon·er \'gȯnər\ *n* : hopeless case

gong \'gäŋ, 'gȯŋ\ *n* : metallic disk that sounds when struck

gon·or·rhea \,gänə'rēə\ *n* : bacterial inflammatory venereal disease of the genital tract —**gon·or·rhe·al** \-'rēəl\ *adj*

goo \'gü\ *n* : thick or sticky substance —**goo·ey** \-ē\ *adj*

good \'gu̇d\ *adj* **bet·ter** \'betər\; **best** \'best\ **1** : satisfactory **2** : salutary **3** : considerable **4** : desirable **5** : well-behaved, kind, or virtuous ~ *n* **1** : something good **2** : benefit **3** *pl* : personal property **4** *pl* : wares ~ *adv* : well —**good–heart·ed** \-'härtəd\ *adj* —**good·ish** *adj* —**good–look·ing** *adj* —**good–na·tured** *adj* —**good·ness** *n* —**good–tem·pered** \-'tempərd\ *adj* —**for good** : forever

good–bye, good–by \gu̇d'bī, gə(d)\ *n* : parting remark

good–for–noth·ing *n* : idle worthless person

Good Friday *n* : Friday before Easter observed as the anniversary of the crucifixion of Christ

good·ly *adj* **-li·er, -est** : considerable

good·will *n* **1** : good intention **2** : kindly feeling

goody \-ē\ *n, pl* **good·ies** : something that is good esp. to eat

goody–goody *adj* : affectedly or annoyingly sweet or self-righteous —**goody–goody** *n*

goof \'güf\ *vb* **1** : blunder **2** : waste time —usu. with *off* or *around* —**goof** *n* —**goof–off** *n*

goofy \'güfē\ *adj* **goof·i·er, -est** : crazy —**goof·i·ness** *n*

goose \'güs\ *n, pl* **geese** \'gēs\ : large bird with webbed feet

goose·ber·ry \'güs,berē, 'güz-, -b(ə)rē\ *n* : berry of a shrub related to the currant

goose–flesh *n* : roughening of the skin caused usu. by cold or fear

goose pimples *n pl* : gooseflesh

go·pher \'gōfər\ *n* : burrowing rodent

¹gore \'gōr\ *n* : blood

²gore *vb* **gored; gor·ing** : pierce or wound with a horn or tusk

¹gorge \'gȯrj\ *n* : narrow ravine

²gorge *vb* **gorged; gorg·ing** : eat greedily

gor·geous \'gȯrjəs\ *adj* : supremely beautiful

go·ril·la \gə'rilə\ *n* : African manlike ape

gory \'gōrē\ *adj* **gor·i·er, -est** : bloody

gos·hawk \'gäs,hȯk\ *n* : long-tailed hawk with short rounded wings

gos·ling \'gäzliŋ, 'gȯz-\ *n* : young goose

gos·pel \'gäspəl\ *n* **1** : teachings of Christ and the apostles **2** : something accepted as infallible truth —**gospel** *adj*

gos·sa·mer \'gäsəmər, gäz(ə)mər\ n 1 : film of cobweb 2 : light filmy substance

gos·sip \'gäsəp\ n 1 : person who reveals personal information 2 : rumor or report of an intimate nature ~ vb : spread gossip —**gos·sipy** adj

got past of GET

Goth·ic \'gäthik\ adj : relating to a medieval style of architecture

gotten past part of GET

gouge \'gaúj\ n 1 : rounded chisel 2 : cavity or groove scooped out ~ vb gouged; goug·ing 1 : cut or scratch a groove in 2 : overcharge —**goug·er** n

gou·lash \'gü,läsh, -,läsh\ n : beef stew with vegetables and paprika

gourd \'görd, 'gúrd\ n 1 : any of a group of vines including the cucumber, squash, and melon 2 : inedible hard-shelled fruit of a gourd

gour·mand \'gúr,mänd\ n : person who loves good food and drink

gour·met \'gúr,mä, gúr'mä\ n : connoisseur of food and drink

gout \'gaút\ n : disease marked by painful inflammation and swelling of the joints —**gouty** adj

gov·ern \'gəvərn\ vb 1 : control and direct policy in 2 : guide or influence strongly 3 : restrain —**gov·ern·ment** \-ər(n)mənt\ n —**gov·ern·men·tal** \,gəvər(n)'mentᵊl\ adj

gov·ern·ess \'gəvərnəs\ n : female teacher in a private home

gov·er·nor \'gəv(ə)nər, 'gəvərnər\ n 1 : head of a political unit 2 : automatic speed-control device —**gov·er·nor·ship** n

gown \'gaún\ n 1 : loose flowing outer garment 2 : woman's formal evening dress —**gown** vb

grab \'grab\ vb -bb- : take by sudden grasp —**grab** n

grace \'grās\ n 1 : unmerited divine assistance 2 : short prayer before or after a meal 3 : respite 4 : ease of movement or bearing ~ vb graced; grac·ing 1 : honor 2 : adorn —**grace·ful** \-fəl\ adj —**grace·ful·ly** adv —**grace·ful·ness** n —**grace·less** adj

gra·cious \'grāshəs\ adj : marked by kindness and courtesy or charm and taste —**gra·cious·ly** adv —**gra·cious·ness** n

grack·le \'grakəl\ n : American blackbird

gra·da·tion \grā'dāshən, grə-\ n : step, degree, or stage in a series

grade \'grād\ n 1 : stage in a series, order, or ranking 2 : division of school representing one year's work

3 : mark of accomplishment in school 4 : degree of slope ~ vb grad·ed; grad·ing 1 : arrange in grades 2 : make level or evenly sloping 3 : give a grade to —**grad·er** n

grade school n : school including the first 6 or 8 grades

gra·di·ent \'grādēənt\ n : slope

grad·u·al \'graj(əw)əl\ adj : going by steps or degrees —**grad·u·al·ly** adv

grad·u·ate \'graj(ə)wət, -ə,wāt\ n : holder of a diploma ~ adj : of or relating to studies beyond the bachelor's degree ~ \-ə,wāt\ vb -at·ed; -at·ing 1 : grant or receive a diploma 2 : mark with degrees of measurement —**grad·u·a·tion** \,grajə'wāshən\ n

graf·fi·to \grə'fētō, gra-\ n, pl -ti \-(,)ē\ : inscription on a wall

graft \'graft\ vb : join one thing to another so that they grow together ~ n 1 : grafted plant 2 : the getting of money dishonestly or the money so gained —**graft·er** n

grain \'grān\ n 1 : seeds or fruits of cereal grasses 2 : small hard particle 3 : arrangement of fibers in wood —**grained** \'grānd\ adj —**grain·field** n —**grainy** adj

gram, gramme \'gram\ n : metric unit of weight nearly equal to one cubic centimeter of water at its maximum density

gram·mar \'gramər\ n : study of words and their functions and relations in the sentence —**gram·mar·i·an** \grə'merēən, -'mar-\ n —**gram·mat·i·cal** \-'matikəl\ adj —**gram·mat·i·cal·ly** adv

grammar school n : grade school

gra·na·ry \'grān(ə)rē, 'gran-\ n, pl -ries : storehouse for grain

grand \'grand\ adj 1 : large or striking in size or scope 2 : fine and imposing 3 : very good —**grand·ly** \'gran(d)lē\ adv —**grand·ness** \-nəs\ n

grand·child \'gran(d),chīld\ n : child of one's son or daughter —**grand·daugh·ter** n —**grand·son** n

gran·deur \'granjər\ n : quality or state of being grand

gran·dil·o·quence \gran'diləkwəns\ n : pompous speaking —**gran·dil·o·quent** \-kwənt\ adj

gran·di·ose \'grandē,ōs, ,grandē'-\ adj 1 : impressive 2 : affectedly splendid —**gran·di·ose·ly** adv

grand·par·ent \-,parənt\ n : parent of one's father or mother —**grand·fa·ther** \-,fäthər, -,fath-\ n —**grand·mo·ther** \-,məthər\ n

grand·stand \-ˌstand\ *n* : usu. roofed stand for spectators

grange \'grānj\ *n* : farmers association

gran·ite \'granət\ *n* : hard igneous rock —**gra·nit·ic** \grə'nitik\ *adj*

grant \'grant\ *vb* 1 : consent to 2 : give 3 : admit as true ~ *n* 1 : act of granting 2 : something granted —**grant·ee** \grant'ē\ *n* —**grant·er** \grantər\ *n* —**grant·or** \-ər, ˌor\ *n*

gran·u·late \'granyəˌlāt\ *vb* -**lat·ed**; -**lat·ing** : form into grains or crystals —**gran·u·lat·ed** *adj* —**gran·u·la·tion** \ˌgranyə'lāshən\ *n*

gran·ule \'granyül\ *n* : small particle —**gran·u·lar** \-yələr\ *adj* —**gran·u·lar·i·ty** \ˌgranyə'larətē\ *n*

grape \'grāp\ *n* : smooth juicy edible berry of a woody vine (**grape·vine**)

grape·fruit \n : large edible yellow-skinned citrus fruit

graph \'graf\ *n* : diagram that shows relationships between things —**graph** *vb*

graph·ic \'grafik\ *adj* 1 : vividly described 2 : relating to the arts (**graphic arts**) of representation and printing on flat surfaces —**graph·i·cal·ly** \-ik(ə)lē\ *adv* —**graph·ics** \-iks\ *n*

graph·ite \'graf,īt\ *n* : soft carbon used for lead pencils and lubricants

grap·nel \'grapnəl\ *n* : small anchor with several claws

grap·ple \'grapəl\ *vb* -**pled**; -**pling** 1 : seize or hold with or as if with a hooked implement 2 : wrestle

grasp \'grasp\ *vb* 1 : take or seize firmly 2 : understand ~ *n* 1 : one's hold or control 2 : one's reach 3 : comprehension

grass \'gras\ *n* : plant with jointed stem and narrow leaves —**grassy** *adj*

grass·hop·per \-ˌhäpər\ *n* : leaping plant-eating insect

grass·land *n* : land covered with grasses

¹grate \'grāt\ *n* 1 : framework with bars across it 2 : frame of iron bars to hold burning fuel

²grate *vb* **grat·ed**; -**ing** 1 : pulverize by rubbing against something rough 2 : irritate —**grat·er** *n* —**grat·ing·ly** *adv*

grate·ful \'grātfəl\ *adj* : thankful or appreciative —**grate·ful·ly** *adv* —**grate·ful·ness** *n*

grat·i·fy \'gratə,fī\ *vb* -**fied**; -**fy·ing** : give pleasure to —**grat·i·fi·ca·tion** \ˌgratəfə'kāshən\ *n*

grat·ing \'grātiŋ\ *n* : grate

gra·tis \'gratəs, 'grāt-\ *adv or adj* : free

grat·i·tude \'gratə,t(y)üd\ *n* : state of being grateful

gra·tu·itous \grə't(y)üətəs\ *adj* 1 : free 2 : uncalled-for

gra·tu·ity \-ətē\ *n, pl* -**ities** : tip

¹grave \'grāv\ *n* : place of burial —**grave·stone** *n* —**grave·yard** *n*

²grave *adj* **grav·er**; **grav·est** 1 : threatening great harm or danger 2 : solemn —**grave·ly** *adv* —**grave·ness** *n*

grav·el \'gravəl\ *n* : loose rounded fragments of rock —**grav·el·ly** *adj*

grav·i·tate \'gravə,tāt\ *vb* -**tat·ed**; -**tat·ing** : move toward something

grav·i·ta·tion \ˌgravə'tāshən\ *n* : natural force of attraction that tends to draw bodies together —**grav·i·ta·tion·al** \-sh(ə)nəl\ *adj* —**grav·i·ta·tion·al·ly** *adv* —**grav·i·ta·tive** \'gravə,tātiv\ *adj*

grav·i·ty \'gravətē\ *n, pl* -**ties** 1 : serious importance 2 : attraction of bodies toward the center of the earth —**gravity** *adj*

gra·vy \'grāvē\ *n, pl* -**vies** : sauce made from thickened juices of cooked meat

gray \'grā\ *adj* 1 : of the color gray 2 : having gray hair ~ *n* : neutral color between black and white ~ *vb* : make or become gray —**gray·ish** \-ish\ *adj* —**gray·ness** *n*

¹graze \'grāz\ *vb* **grazed**; **graz·ing** : feed on herbage or pasture —**graz·er** *n*

²graze *vb* **grazed**; **graz·ing** : touch lightly in passing

grease \'grēs\ *n* : thick oily material or fat ~ \'grēs, 'grēz\ *vb* **greased**; **greas·ing** : smear or lubricate with grease —**greasy** \'grēsē, -zē\ *adj*

great \'grāt, South also 'gre(ə)t\ *adj* 1 : large in size or number 2 : larger than usual —**great·ly** *adv* —**great·ness** *n*

grebe \'grēb\ *n* : diving bird related to the loon

greed \'grēd\ *n* : selfish desire beyond reason —**greed·i·ly** \-ə^lē\ *adv* —**greed·i·ness** \-ēnəs\ *n* —**greedy** \'grēdē\ *adj*

green \'grēn\ *adj* 1 : of the color green 2 : unripe 3 : inexperienced ~ *vb* : become green ~ *n* 1 : color between blue and yellow 2 *pl* : leafy parts of plants —**green·ish** *adj* —**green·ness** \'grēnnəs\ *n*

green·ery \'grēn(ə)rē\ *n, pl* -**er·ies** : green foliage or plants

green·horn *n* : inexperienced person

green·house *n* : glass structure for the growing of plants

greet \'grēt\ *vb* 1 : address with expressions of kind wishes 2 : react to —**greet·er** *n*

greet·ing \'grētiŋ\ n 1 : friendly address on meeting 2 pl : best wishes

gre·gar·i·ous \gri'garēəs, -'ger-\ adj : social or companionable —**gre·gar·i·ous·ly** adv —**gre·gar·i·ous·ness** n

grem·lin \'gremlən\ n : small mischievous gnome

gre·nade \grə'nād\ n : small missile filled with explosive or chemicals

grew past of GROW

grey var of GRAY

grey·hound \'grā,haůnd\ n : tall slender dog noted for speed

grid \'grid\ n 1 : grate 2 : metal plate for conducting current in a storage battery

grid·dle \'gridᵊl\ n : flat metal surface for cooking

grid·iron \'grid,ī(ə)rn\ n 1 : grate for broiling 2 : football field

grief \'grēf\ n 1 : emotional suffering caused by or as if by bereavement 2 : disaster

griev·ance \'grēvəns\ n : complaint

grieve \'grēv\ vb **grieved; griev·ing** : feel or cause to feel grief or sorrow

griev·ous \'grēvəs\ adj 1 : oppressive 2 : causing grief or sorrow —**griev·ous·ly** adv

grill \'gril\ vb 1 : cook on a grill 2 : question intensely ~ n 1 : griddle 2 : informal restaurant

grille, grill \'gril\ n : grate forming a barrier or screen —**grill·work** n

grim \'grim\ adj **-mm-** 1 : relentless 2 : forbidding in appearance —**grim·ly** adv —**grim·ness** n

gri·mace \'grimas, grim'ās\ n : facial expression of disgust —**grimace** vb

grime \'grīm\ n : embedded or accumulated dirt —**grimy** adj

grin \'grin\ vb **-nn-** : smile so as to show the teeth —**grin** n

grind \'grīnd\ vb **ground** \'graůnd\; **grind·ing** 1 : reduce to powder or wear down or sharpen by friction 2 : operate or produce by turning a crank ~ n : monotonous labor or routine —**grind·er** n —**grind·stone** \'grīn,stōn\ n

grip \'grip\ vb **-pp-** : seize or hold firmly ~ n 1 : grasp 2 : control 3 : device for holding

gripe \'grīp\ vb **griped; grip·ing** 1 : cause pains in the bowels 2 : complain —**gripe** n

grippe \'grip\ n : influenza

gris·ly \'grizlē\ adj **-li·er; -est** : horrible or grusome

grist \'grist\ n : grain to be ground or already ground —**grist·mill** n

gris·tle \'grisəl\ n : cartilage —**gris·tly** \-(ə)lē\ adj

grit \'grit\ n 1 : hard sharp granule 2 : material composed of granules 3 : unyielding courage ~ vb **-tt-** : press with a grating noise —**grit·ty** adj

grits \'grits\ n pl : coarsely ground hulled grain

griz·zled \'grizəld\ adj : streaked with gray

groan \'grōn\ vb 1 : moan 2 : creak under a strain —**groan** n

gro·cer \'grōsər\ n : food dealer —**gro·cery** \'grōs(ə)rē\ n

grog \'gräg\ n : rum diluted with water

grog·gy \-ē\ adj **-gi·er; -est** : dazed and unsteady on the feet —**grog·gi·ly** adv —**grog·gi·ness** n

groin \'gròin\ n : juncture of abdomen and thigh

grom·met \'grämət, 'grəm-\ n : eyelet

groom \'grüm, 'grům\ n 1 : one who cleans and brushes horses 2 : bridegroom ~ vb 1 : clean and care for (as a horse) 2 : make neat, attractive, or acceptable

groove \'grüv\ n 1 : long narrow channel 2 : fixed routine —**groove** vb

grope \'grōp\ vb **groped; grop·ing** : search for by feeling

gros·beak \'grōs,bēk\ n : finch with large conical bill

¹**gross** \'grōs\ adj 1 : glaringly noticeable 2 : bulky 3 : consisting of an overall total exclusive of deductions 4 : vulgar ~ vb : earn as a total —**gross·ly** adv —**gross·ness** n

²**gross** n, pl **gross** : 12 dozen

gro·tesque \grō'tesk\ adj 1 : absurdly distorted or repulsive 2 : ridiculous —**gro·tesque·ly** adv

grot·to \'grätō\ n, pl **-toes** : cave

grouch \'graůch\ n : complaining person —**grouch** vb —**grouchy** adj

¹**ground** \'graůnd\ n 1 : bottom of a body of water 2 pl : sediment 3 : basis for something 4 : surface of the earth 5 : conductor that makes electrical connection with the earth or a framework ~ vb 1 : force or bring down to the ground 2 : instruct in fundamental principles 3 : connect with an electrical ground —**ground·hog** n

²**ground** past of GRIND

ground·hog n : woodchuck

ground·wa·ter n : underground water

ground·work n : foundation

group \'grüp\ n : number of associated

individuals ~ *vb* : gather or collect into groups

grou·per \'grüpər\ *n* : large fish of warm seas

grouse \'graùs\ *n, pl* **grouse** : game bird

grout \'graùt\ *n* : mortar for filling cracks —**grout** *vb*

grove \'grōv\ *n* : small group of trees

grov·el \'grävəl, 'grəv-\ *vb* **-eled** *or* **-elled; -el·ing** *or* **-el·ling** : abase oneself

grow \'grō\ *vb* **grew** \'grü\; **grown** \'grōn\; **grow·ing 1** : come into existence and develop to maturity **2** : be able to grow **3** : advance or increase **4** : become **5** : cultivate —**grow·er** \'grō(ə)r\ *n*

growl \'graùl\ *vb* : utter a deep threatening sound —**growl** *n*

grown-up \'grōn,əp\ *n* : adult —**grown-up** *adj*

growth \'grōth\ *n* **1** : stage in growing **2** : process of growing **3** : result of something growing

grub \'grəb\ *vb* **-bb-** : root out by digging ~ *n* **1** : thick wormlike larva **2** : food

grub·by \'grəbē\ *adj* **-bi·er; -est** : dirty —**grub·bi·ness** *n*

grub·stake *n* : supplies for a prospector

grudge \'grəj\ *vb* **grudged; grudg·ing** : be reluctant to give ~ *n* : feeling of ill will

gru·el \'grüəl\ *n* : thin porridge

gru·el·ing, gru·el·ling \-əliŋ\ *adj* : requiring extreme effort

grue·some \'grüsəm\ *adj* : horribly repulsive

gruff \'grəf\ *adj* : rough in speech or manner —**gruff·ly** *adv*

grum·ble \'grəmbəl\ *vb* **-bled; -bling** : mutter in discontent —**grum·bler** \-b(ə)lər\ *n*

grumpy \-pē\ *adj* **grump·i·er; -est** : cross —**grump·i·ly** *adv* —**grump·i·ness** *n*

grun·ion \'grənyən\ *n* : fish of the California coast

grunt \'grəɪt\ *n* : deep guttural sound —**grunt** *vb*

gua·no \'gwänō\ *n* : excrement of seabirds used as fertilizer

guar·an·tee \,garən'tē\ *n* **1** : assurance of the fulfillment of a condition **2** : something given or held as a security ~ *vb* **-teed; -tee·ing 1** : promise to be responsible for **2** : state with certainty —**guar·an·tor** \,garən'tòr\ *n*

guar·an·ty \'garəntē\ *n, pl* **-ties 1** : promise to answer for another's failure to pay a debt **2** : guarantee **3** : pledge ~ *vb* **-tied; -ty·ing** : guarantee

guard \'gärd\ *n* **1** : defensive position **2** : act of protecting **3** : an individual or group that guards against danger **4** : protective or safety device ~ *vb* **1** : protect or watch over **2** : take precautions —**guard·house** *n* —**guard·room** *n*

guard·ian \'gärdēən\ *n* : one who has responsibility for the care of a person or property —**guard·ian·ship** *n*

gua·va \'gwävə\ *n* : shrubby tree or its mildly acid fruit

gu·ber·na·to·ri·al \,g(y)übə(r)nə'tōrēəl\ *adj* : relating to a governor

guer·ril·la, gue·ril·la \gə'rilə\ *n* : soldier engaged in small-scale harassing tactics

guess \'ges\ *vb* **1** : form an opinion from little evidence **2** : state correctly solely by chance **3** : think or believe —**guess** *n*

guest \'gest\ *n* **1** : person to whom hospitality (as of a house) is extended **2** : patron of a commercial establishment (as a hotel) **3** : person not a regular cast member who appears on a program

guf·faw \(,)gə'fò, 'gəf,ò\ *n* : loud burst of laughter —**guf·faw** \(,)gə'fò\ *vb*

guide \'gīd\ *n* **1** : one that leads or gives direction to another **2** : device on a machine to direct motion ~ *vb* **guid·ed; guid·ing 1** : show the way to **2** : direct —**guid·able** *adj* —**guid·ance** \'gīdⁿns\ *n* —**guide·book** *n*

guild \'gild\ *n* : association

guile \'gīl\ *n* : craftiness —**guile·ful** *adj* —**guile·less** *adj* —**guile·less·ness** *n*

guil·lo·tine \'gilə,tēn; ,gē(y)ə'tēn, 'gē(y)ə-\ *n* : machine for beheading persons —**guillotine** *vb*

guilt \'gilt\ *n* **1** : fact of having committed an offense **2** : feeling of responsibility for offenses —**guilt·i·ly** *adv* —**guilt·i·ness** *n* —**guilty** \'giltē\ *adj*

guin·ea \'ginē\ *n* **1** : old gold coin of United Kingdom **2** : 21 shillings

guinea pig *n* : small So. American rodent

guise \'gīz\ *n* : external appearance

gui·tar \gə'tär, gi-\ *n* : 6-stringed musical instrument played by plucking

gulch \'gəlch\ *n* : ravine

gulf \'gəlf\ *n* **1** : extension of an ocean or a sea into the land **2** : abyss

¹gull \'gəl\ *n* : seabird with webbed feet

²gull *vb* : make a dupe of ~ *n* : dupe —**gull·ible** *adj*

gul·let \'gələt\ *n* : throat

gul·ly \-ē\ *n, pl* **-lies** : trench worn by running water

gulp \'gəlp\ *vb* : swallow hurriedly or greedily —**gulp** *n*

¹gum \'gəm\ *n* : tissue along the jaw at the base of the teeth

²gum *n* **1** : sticky plant substance **2** : gum usu. of sweetened chicle prepared for chewing

gum·bo \'gəmbō\ *n* : thick soup

gum·drop *n* : gumlike candy

gump·tion \'gəmpshən\ *n* : initiative

gun \'gən\ *n* **1** : cannon **2** : portable firearm **3** : discharge of a gun **4** : something like a gun ~ *vb* **-nn-** : hunt with a gun —**gun·fight** *n* —**gun·fight·er** *n* —**gun·fire** *n* —**gun·man** \-mən\ *n* —**gun·pow·der** *n* —**gun·shot** *n* —**gun·smith** *n*

gun·boat *n* : small armed ship

gun·ner \'gənər\ *n* : person who uses a gun

gunnery sergeant *n* : noncommissioned officer in the marine corps ranking next below a first sergeant

gun·ny \'gənē\ *n* : coarse jute material for making sacks (**gunnysacks**)

gun·sling·er \-ˌslinər\ *n* : gunman in the old West

gun·wale, gun·nel \'gənᵊl\ *n* : upper edge of a boat's side

gup·py \'gəpē\ *n, pl* **-pies** : tiny tropical fish

gur·gle \'gərgəl\ *vb* **-gled; -gling** : make a sound like that of a flowing and gently splashing liquid —**gurgle** *n*

gu·ru \'gə̇rü, 'gü(ə)r(ˌ)ü\ *n, pl* **-rus** : personal religious teacher in Hinduism

gush \'gəsh\ *vb* : pour forth violently or enthusiastically —**gush·er** \'gəshər\ *n*

gushy \-ē\ *adj* **gush·i·er; -est** : effusively sentimental

gust \'gəst\ *n* **1** : sudden brief rush of wind **2** : sudden outburst —**gust** *vb* —**gusty** *adj*

gus·ta·to·ry \'gəstəˌtōrē\ *adj* : relating to the sense of taste

gus·to \'gəstō\ *n* : zest

gut \'gət\ *n* **1** *pl* : intestines **2** : digestive canal **3** *pl* : courage ~ *vb* **-tt-** : eviscerate

gut·ter \'gətər\ *n* : channel for carrying off rainwater

gut·tur·al \'gətərəl\ *adj* : sounded in the throat —**guttural** *n*

¹guy \'gī\ *n* : rope, chain, or rod attached to something to steady it —**guy** *vb*

²guy *n* : person

guz·zle \'gəzəl\ *vb* **-zled; -zling** : drink greedily

gym \'jim\ *n* : gymnasium

gym·na·si·um \jim'nāzēəm, -zhəm\ *n, pl* **-si·ums** or **-sia** \-zēə, -zhə\ : place for indoor sports

gym·nas·tics \jim'nastiks\ *n* : physical exercises performed in a gymnasium —**gym·nast** \'jimˌnast\ *n* —**gym·nas·tic** *adj*

gy·ne·col·o·gy \ˌgīnə'käləjē, ˌjin-\ *n* : branch of medicine dealing with the diseases of women —**gy·ne·co·log·ic** \-ikə'läjik\, **gy·ne·co·log·i·cal** \-ikəl\ *adj* —**gy·ne·col·o·gist** \-ə'käləjəst\ *n*

gyp \'jip\ *n* **1** : cheat **2** : trickery —**gyp** *vb*

gyp·sum \'jipsəm\ *n* : calcium-containing mineral

gy·rate \'jīˌrāt\ *vb* **-rat·ed; -rat·ing** : revolve around a center —**gy·ra·tion** \jī'rāshən\ *n*

gy·ro·com·pass \'jīrōˌkəmpəs, -ˌkäm-\ *n* : compass in which the axis of a spinning gyroscope points to the north

gy·ro·scope \-ˌskōp\ *n* : wheel mounted to spin rapidly about an axis that is free to turn in various directions

H

h \'āch\ *n, pl* **h's** or **hs** \'āchəz\ : 8th letter of the alphabet

hab·er·dash·er \'habə(r)ˌdashər\ *n* : men's clothier —**hab·er·dash·ery** \-(ə)rē\ *n*

hab·it \'habət\ *n* **1** : monk's or nun's clothing **2** : usual behavior —**hab·it·form·ing** *adj*

hab·it·able \-əbəl\ *adj* : capable of being lived in

hab·i·tat \'habəˌtat\ *n* : place where a plant or animal naturally occurs

hab·i·ta·tion \ˌhabə'tāshən\ *n* **1** : occupancy **2** : dwelling place

ha·bit·u·al \hə'bichə(wə)l\ *adj* **1** : commonly practiced or observed **2**

: doing, practicing, or acting by habit —**ha·bit·u·al·ly** adv —**ha·bit·u·al·ness** n

ha·bit·u·ate \ha'bicha,wāt\ vb -**at·ed**; -**at·ing** : accustom

ha·ci·en·da \,(h)äsē'endə\ n : ranch house

1hack \'hak\ vb 1 : cut with repeated irregular blows 2 : cough in a short dry manner 3 : manage successfully —**hack** n —**hack·er** n

2hack n 1 : horse or vehicle for hire 2 : saddle horse 3 : writer for hire —**hack** adj —**hack·man** \-mən\ n

hack·le \hakəl\ n 1 : long feather on the neck or lower back of a bird 2 pl : hairs that can be erected 3 pl : temper

hack·ney \-nē\ n, pl -**neys** 1 : horse for riding or driving 2 : carriage for hire

hack·neyed \-nēd\ adj : trite

hack·saw n : saw for metal

had past of HAVE

had·dock \'hadək\ n, pl **haddock** : Atlantic food fish

Ha·des \'hād(,)ēz\ n 1 : mythological abode of the dead 2 : often not cap : hell

haft \'haft\ n : handle of a weapon or tool

hag \'hag\ n 1 : witch 2 : ugly old woman

hag·gard \'hagərd\ adj : worn or emaciated —**hag·gard·ly** adv

hag·gle \'hagəl\ vb -**gled**; -**gling** : argue in bargaining —**hag·gler** n

1hail \'hāl\ n 1 : precipitation in small lumps of ice 2 : something like a rain of hail —vb : rain hail —**hail·stone** n —**hail·storm** n

2hail vb : greet or salute ~ n : expression of greeting or praise —often used as an interjection

hair \'haər\ n : threadlike growth from the skin —**hair·brush** n —**hair·cut** n —**hair·dress·er** n —**haired** adj —**hair·i·ness** n —**hair·less** adj —**hair·pin** n —**hair·style** n —**hair·styl·ing** n —**hair·styl·ist** n —**hairy** adj

hair·breadth \-,bredth\, **hairs·breadth** \'haərz-\ n : tiny distance or margin

hair·do \-,dü\ n, pl -**dos** : style of wearing hair

hair·line n 1 : thin line 2 : outline of the hair on the head

hair·piece n : toupee

hair·rais·ing adj : causing terror or astonishment

hake \'hāk\ n : marine food fish

hal·cy·on \'halsēən\ adj : prosperous or most pleasant

1hale \'hāl\ adj : healthy or robust

2hale vb **haled**; **hal·ing** 1 : haul 2 : compel to go

half \'haf, 'häf\ n, pl **halves** \'havz, 'hävz\ : one of 2 equal parts ~ adj 1 : being a half or nearly a half 2 : partial —**half** adv

half-breed n : offspring of parents of different races —**half-breed** adj

half brother n : brother by one parent only

half-heart·ed \-'härtəd\ adj : without enthusiasm —**half-heart·ed·ly** adv —**half-heart·ed·ness** n

half-life n : time for half of something to undergo a process

half sister n : sister by one parent only

half·way adj : midway between 2 points —**half·way** adv

half-wit \-,wit\ n : foolish person —**half-wit·ted** \-'witəd\ adj

hal·i·but \'haləbət\ n, pl **halibut** : large edible marine flatfish

hal·i·to·sis \,halə'tōsəs\ n : bad breath

hall \'hol\ n 1 : large public or college or university building 2 : lobby 3 : auditorium

hal·le·lu·jah \,halə'lüyə\ interj —used to express praise, joy, or thanks

hall·mark \'hol,märk\ n : distinguishing characteristic

hal·low \'halō\ vb : consecrate —**hallowed** \-ōd, -əwəd\ adj

Hal·low·een \,halə'wēn, ,häl-\ n : evening of October 31 observed esp. by children in merrymaking and masquerading

hal·lu·ci·na·tion \hə,lüs°n'āshən\ n : perception of objects or events that are not real —**hal·lu·ci·nate** \hə'lüs°n,āt\ vb —**hal·lu·ci·na·tive** \-'lüs°n,ātiv\ adj —**hal·lu·ci·na·to·ry** \-°nə,tōrē\ adj

hal·lu·ci·no·gen \hə'lüs°nəjən\ n : substance that induces hallucinations —**hal·lu·ci·no·gen·ic** \-,lüs°nə'jenik\ adj

hall·way n : entrance hall

ha·lo \'hālō\ n, pl -**los** or -**loes** : circle of light appearing to surround a shining body

1halt \'holt\ adj : lame

2halt vb : stop or cause to stop —**halt** n

hal·ter \'holtər\ n 1 : rope or strap for leading or tying an animal 2 : brief blouse held up by straps ~ vb : catch (an animal) with a halter

halt·ing \'holtiŋ\ adj : uncertain —**halt·ing·ly** adv

halve \'hav, 'häv\ vb **halved**; **halv·ing** 1 : divide into halves 2 : reduce to half

halves pl of HALF

ham \'ham\ *n* **1** : thigh **2** : cut esp. of pork from the thigh **3** : showy actor **4** : amateur radio operator ~ *vb* **-mm-** : overlay a part —**ham** *adj*

ham·burg·er \'ham₁bərgər\, **ham·burg** \-₁bərg\ *n* : ground beef or a sandwich made with this

ham·let \'hamlət\ *n* : small village

ham·mer \-ər\ *n* **1** : hand tool for pounding **2** : gun part whose striking explodes the charge ~ *vb* **1** : beat, drive, or shape with a hammer **2** : produce by repeated blows

ham·mer·head *n* **1** : striking part of a hammer **2** : shark with a hammerlike head

ham·mock \'hamək\ *n* : swinging bed hung by cords at each end

¹ham·per \-pər\ *vb* : impede

²hamper *n* : large covered basket

ham·ster \-stər\ *n* : stocky short-tailed rodent

ham·string \-₁striŋ\ *vb* -**strung** \-₁strəŋ\; -**string·ing** \-₁striŋiŋ\ **1** : cripple by cutting the leg tendons **2** : make ineffective or powerless

hand \'hand\ *n* **1** : end of a front limb adapted for grasping **2** : side **3** : promise of marriage **4** : handwriting **5** : assistance or participation **6** : applause **7** : cards held by a player **8** : worker ~ *vb* : lead, assist, give, or pass with the hand —**hand·clasp** *n* —**hand·craft** *vb* —**hand·ful** *n* —**hand·gun** *n* —**hand·less** *adj* —**hand·made** *adj* —**hand·rail** *n* —**hand·saw** *n* —**hand·wo·ven** *adj* —**hand·writ·ing** *n* —**hand·writ·ten** *adj*

hand·bag *n* : woman's purse

hand·ball *n* : game played by striking a ball with the hand

hand·bill *n* : printed advertisement or notice distributed by hand

hand·book *n* : concise reference book

hand·cuffs *n, pl* : locking bracelets that bind the wrists together —**handcuff** *vb*

hand·i·cap \'handi₁kap\ *n* **1** : advantage given or disadvantage imposed to equalize a competition **2** : disadvantage —**handicap** *vb* —**hand·i·cap·per** *n*

hand·i·craft \'handi₁kraft\ *n* **1** : manual skill **2** : article made by hand —**hand·i·craft·er** *n* —**hand·i·crafts·man** \-₁kraftsmən\ *n*

hand·i·work \-₁wərk\ *n* : work done personally

hand·ker·chief \'haŋkərchəf, -₁chēf\ *n, pl* -**chiefs** \-chəfs, -₁chēfs\ : small piece of cloth carried for personal use

han·dle \'hand³l\ *n* : part to be grasped ~ *vb* -**dled**; -**dling 1** : touch, hold, or manage with the hands **2** : deal with **3** : deal or trade in —**han·dle·bar** *n* —**han·dled** \-d³ld\ *adj*

hand·maid·en, hand·maid *n* : female attendant

hand·out *n* : something given out

hand·pick *vb* : select personally

hand·shake *n* : clasping of hands (as in greeting)

hand·some \'hansəm\ *adj* **1** : sizable **2** : generous **3** : nice-looking —**hand·some·ly** *adv* —**hand·some·ness** *n*

hand·spring *n* : somersault on the hands

hand·stand *n* : a balancing upside down on the hands

handy \'handē\ *adj* **hand·i·er**; -**est 1** : conveniently near **2** : easily used **3** : dexterous —**hand·i·ly** *adv* —**hand·i·ness** *n*

handy·man \-₁man\ *n* : one who does odd jobs

hang \'haŋ\ *vb* **hung** \'həŋ\ *or* **hanged** \'haŋd\; **hang·ing 1** : fasten or remain fastened to an elevated point without support from below **2** : put or come to death by suspending with a rope around the neck ~ *n* **1** : way a thing hangs **2** : knack —**hang·er** *n*

han·gar \'haŋər\ *n* : airplane shelter

hang·dog \'haŋ₁dȯg\ *adj* : ashamed or guilty

hang·man \-mən\ *n* : public executioner

hang·nail *n* : loose skin near a fingernail

hang·out *n* : place where one likes to spend time

hang·over *n* : sick feeling following heavy drinking

hank \'haŋk\ *n* : coil or loop

han·ker \'haŋkər\ *vb* : desire strongly —**han·ker·ing** *n*

han·ky-pan·ky \₁haŋkē'paŋkē\ *n* : underhand activity

han·som \'hansəm\ *n* : 2-wheeled covered carriage

Ha·nuk·kah \'känəkə, 'hän-\ *n* : 8-day Jewish holiday commemorating the rededication of the Temple of Jerusalem after its defilement by Antiochus of Syria

hap·haz·ard \hap'hazərd\ *adj* : having no plan or order —**hap·haz·ard·ly** *adv*

hap·less \'hapləs\ *adj* : unfortunate —**hap·less·ly** *adv* —**hap·less·ness** *n*

hap·pen \'hapən\ *vb* **1** : take place **2** : be fortunate to encounter something unexpectedly —often used with infinitive

hap·pen·ing \-(ə)niŋ\ n : occurrence

hap·py \'hapē\ adj -pi·er; -est 1 : fortunate 2 : content, pleased, or joyous —**hap·pi·ly** \'ha₁pəlē\ adv —**hap·pi·ness** n

ha·rangue \hə'raŋ\ n : ranting or scolding speech —harangue vb —**ha·rangu·er** \-'raŋər\ n

ha·rass \hə'ras, 'haras\ vb 1 : worry and impede (an enemy) by repeated raids 2 : annoy continually —**ha·rass·ment** n

har·bin·ger \'härbənjər\ n : one that announces or foreshadows what is coming

har·bor \-bər\ n : protected body of water suitable for anchorage ~ vb 1 : give refuge to 2 : hold as a thought or feeling

hard \'härd\ adj 1 : not easily penetrated 2 : firm or definite 3 : close or searching 4 : severe or unfeeling 5 : strenuous or difficult 6 : physically strong or intense —hard adv —**hard·ness** n

hard·en \'härd³n\ vb : make or become hard or harder —**hard·en·er** n

hard-head·ed \-'hedəd\ adj 1 : stubborn 2 : realistic —**hard-head·ed·ly** adv —**hard-head·ed·ness** n

hard-heart·ed \-'härtəd\ adj : lacking sympathy —**hard-heart·ed·ly** adv —**hard-heart·ed·ness** n

hard·ly \-lē\ adv 1 : only just 2 : certainly not

hard·ship \-₁ship\ n : suffering or privation

hard·tack \-₁tak\ n : hard biscuit

hard·ware n : cutlery or tools made of metal

hard·wood n : wood of a broad-leaved usu. deciduous tree —hardwood adj

har·dy \'härdē\ adj -di·er; -est : able to withstand adverse conditions —**har·di·ly** adv —**har·di·ness** n

hare \'haər\ n, pl hare or hares : long-eared mammal related to the rabbit

hare·lip n : deformity in which the upper lip is vertically split —**hare·lipped** \-'lipt\ adj

ha·rem \'harəm\ n : house or part of a house allotted to women in a Muslim household or the women and servants occupying it

hark \'härk\ vb : listen

har·le·quin \'härlik(w)ən\ n : clown

har·lot \'härlət\ n : prostitute

harm \'härm\ n 1 : physical or mental damage 2 : mischief ~ vb : cause harm —**harm·ful** \-fəl\ adj —**harm·ful·ly** adv —**harm·ful·ness** n —**harm-**

less adj —**harm·less·ly** adv —**harm·less·ness** n

har·mon·ic \här'mänik\ adj 1 : of or relating to musical harmony 2 : pleasing to hear —**har·mon·i·cal·ly** \-ik(ə)lē\ adv

har·mon·i·ca \här'mänikə\ n : small wind instrument with metallic reeds

har·mo·ny \'härmənē\ n, pl -nies 1 : musical combination of sounds 2 : pleasing arrangement of parts 3 : lack of conflict 4 : internal calm —**har·mo·ni·ous** \här'mōnēəs\ adj —**har·mo·ni·ous·ly** adv —**har·mo·ni·ous·ness** n —**har·mo·ni·za·tion** \₁härmənə'zāshən\ n —**har·mo·nize** \'härmə₁nīz\ vb

har·ness \'härnəs\ n : gear of a draft animal ~ vb 1 : put a harness on 2 : put to use

harp \'härp\ n : musical instrument with many strings plucked by the fingers ~ vb 1 : play on a harp 2 : dwell on a subject tiresomely —**harp·er** n —**harp·ist** n

har·poon \här'pün\ n : barbed spear used in hunting whales —harpoon vb —**har·poon·er** n

harp·si·chord \'härpsi₁kórd\ n : keyboard instrument with strings that are plucked

har·py \'härpē\ n, pl -pies : shrewish woman

har·row \'harō\ n : implement used to break up soil ~ vb 1 : cultivate with a harrow 2 : distress

har·ry \'harē\ vb -ried; -ry·ing : torment by or as if by constant attack

harsh \'härsh\ adj 1 : disagreeably rough 2 : severe —**harsh·ly** adv —**harsh·ness** n

hart \'härt\ n : stag

har·um-scar·um \₁harəm'skarəm\ adv : recklessly

har·vest \'härvəst\ n 1 : act or time of gathering in a crop 2 : mature crop —harvest vb —**har·vest·er** n

has pres 3d sing of HAVE

hash \'hash\ vb : chop into small pieces ~ n : chopped meat mixed with potatoes and browned

hash·ish \'hash₁ēsh, -(₁)ish\ n : unadulterated intoxicating resin from female hemp plants

hasp \'hasp\ n : hinged strap fastener esp. for a door

has·sle \'hasəl\ n 1 : quarrel 2 : struggle —hassle vb

has·sock \'hasək\ n : cushion used as a seat or leg rest

haste \'hāst\ n 1 : rapidity of motion 2 : rash action 3 : excessive eagerness

—hast·i·ly \'hāstəlē\ adv —hast·i·ness \-stēnəs\ n

has·ten \'hāsən\ vb : hurry

hat \'hat\ n : covering for the head

¹hatch \'hach\ n : small door or opening —hatch·way n

²hatch vb : emerge from an egg —hatch·ery \-(ə)rē\ n

hatch·et \'hachət\ n : short-handled ax

hate \'hāt\ n : intense hostility and aversion ~ vb hat·ed; hat·ing 1 : express or feel hate 2 : dislike —hate·ful \-fəl\ adj —hate·ful·ly adv —hate·ful·ness n —hat·er n

ha·tred \'hātrəd\ n : hate

hat·ter \'hatər\ n : one that makes or sells hats

haugh·ty \'hòtē\ adj -ti·er; -est : disdainfully proud —haugh·ti·ly adv —haugh·ti·ness n

haul \'hòl\ vb 1 : draw or pull 2 : transport or carry ~ n 1 : amount collected 2 : load or the distance it is transported —haul·age \-ij\ n —haul·er n

haunch \'hònch\ n : hip or hindquarter —usu. pl.

haunt \'hònt\ vb 1 : visit often 2 : visit or inhabit as a ghost ~ n : place habitually frequented —haunt·er n —haunt·ing·ly adv

have \(')hav, (h)əv, v; in sense 2 before "to" usu ¹haf\ vb had \(')had, (h)əd\; hav·ing \'havin\; has \(')haz, (h)əz, in sense 2 before "to" usu ¹has\ 1 : hold in possession, service, or affection 2 : be compelled or forced to 3 —used as an auxiliary with the past participle to form the present perfect, past perfect, or future perfect 4 : obtain or receive 5 : undergo 6 : cause to 7 : bear —have to do with : have in the way of connection or relation with or effect on

ha·ven \'hāvən\ n : place of safety

hav·oc \'havək\ n 1 : wide destruction 2 : great confusion

¹hawk \'hòk\ n : small or mediumsized day-flying bird of prey —hawk·ish adj

²hawk vb : offer for sale by calling out in the street —hawk·er n

haw·ser \'hòzər\ n : large rope

haw·thorn \'hò,thòrn\ n : spiny shrub or tree with pink or white fragrant flowers

hay \'hā\ n : herbage mowed and cured for fodder —hay vb —hay·fork n —hay·loft n —hay·mow \-,maů\ n —hay·stack n

hay·cock \'hā,käk\ n : small pile of hay

hay·rick \-,rik\ n : large outdoor stack of hay

hay·seed \'hā,sēd\ n : bumpkin

hay·wire adj : being out of order

haz·ard \'hazərd\ n 1 : source of danger 2 : chance ~ vb : venture or risk —haz·ard·ous adj

¹haze \'hāz\ n : fine dust, smoke, or light vapor in the air that reduces visibility

²haze vb hazed; haz·ing : harass by abusive and humiliating tricks

ha·zel \'hāzəl\ n : shrub or small tree bearing edible nuts (hazel·nuts)

hazy \'hāzē\ adj haz·i·er; -est 1 : obscured by haze 2 : vague or indefinite —haz·i·ly adv —haz·i·ness n

he \'hē, ē\ pron 1 : that male one 2 : a or the person

head \'hed\ n 1 : front or upper part of the body 2 : mind 3 : upper or higher end 4 : director or leader 5 : place of leadership or honor ~ adj : principal or chief ~ vb 1 : provide with or form a head 2 : put, stand, or be at the head 3 : point or proceed in a certain direction —head·ache n —head·band n —head·dress n —head·ed adj —head·first adv or adj —head·gear n —head·less adj —head·man \-'man, -,man\ n —head·rest n —head·ship n —head·wait·er n

head·ing \-iŋ\ n 1 : direction in which a plane or ship heads 2 : something (as a title) standing at the top or beginning

head·land \'hedlənd, -,land\ n : promontory

head·light n : light on the front of an automobile

head·line n : introductory line of a newspaper story printed in large type

head·long \'hed,lòŋ\ adv 1 : head foremost 2 : in a rash or reckless manner —head·long \-,lòŋ\ adj

head·mas·ter n : male head of a private school

head·mis·tress n : female head of a private school

head-on adj : having the front facing in the direction of initial contact —head-on adv

head·phone n : an earphone held on by a band over the head

head·quar·ters n sing or pl : command or administrative center

head·stone n : stone at the head of a grave

head·strong adj : stubborn or willful

head·wa·ter n : source of a stream —usu. pl.

head·way n : forward motion

heady \'hedē\ adj **head·i·er, -est 1** : intoxicating **2** : shrewd

heal \'hēl\ vb : make or become sound or whole —**heal·er** n

health \'helth\ n : sound physical or mental condition

health·ful \-fəl\ adj : beneficial to health —**health·ful·ly** adv —**health·ful·ness** n

healthy \'helthē\ adj **health·i·er, -est** : enjoying or typical of good health —**health·i·ly** adv —**health·i·ness** n

heap \'hēp\ n : pile ~ vb : throw or lay in a heap

hear \'hiər\ vb **heard** \'hərd\; **hear·ing** \'hi(ə)riŋ\ **1** : perceive by the ear **2** : heed **3** : learn —**hear·er** \'hirər\ n

hear·ing n **1** : process or power of perceiving sound **2** : earshot **3** : session in which witnesses are heard

hear·ken \'härkən\ vb : give attention

hear·say n : rumor

hearse \'hərs\ n : vehicle for carrying the dead to the grave

heart \'härt\ n **1** : hollow muscular organ that keeps up the circulation of the blood **2** : playing card of a suit marked with a red heart **3** : whole personality or the emotional or moral part of it **4** : courage **5** : essential part —**heart·beat** n —**heart·ed** adj

heart·ache n : anguish of mind

heart·break n : crushing grief —**heart·break·ing** adj —**heart·bro·ken** adj

heart·burn n : burning distress behind the lower sternum

heart·en \'härt²ən\ vb : encourage

hearth \'härth\ n **1** : area in front of a fireplace **2** : home —**hearth·stone** n

heart·less \-ləs\ adj : cruel

heart·rend·ing \-,rendiŋ\ adj : causing intense grief or anguish

heart·sick adj : very despondent —**heart·sick·ness** n

heart·strings n pl : deepest emotions

heart·throb n : sweetheart

heart·warm·ing adj : inspiring sympathetic feeling

heart·wood n : central portion of wood

hearty \'härtē\ adj **heart·i·er, -est 1** : vigorously healthy **2** : nourishing —**heart·i·ly** adv —**heart·i·ness** n

heat \'hēt\ vb : make or become warm or hot ~ n **1** : condition of being hot **2** : form of energy that causes a body to rise in temperature **3** : intensity of feeling —**heat·ed·ly** adv —**heat·er** n —**heat·less** adj

heath \'hēth\ n **1** : often evergreen shrubby plant of wet acid soils **2** : tract of wasteland —**heathy** adj

hea·then \'hēthən\ n, pl **-thens** or **-then** : uncivilized or godless person —**heathen** adj

heath·er \'hethər\ n : evergreen heath with lavender flowers —**heath·ery** adj

heat·stroke n : disorder that follows prolonged exposure to excessive heat

heave \'hēv\ vb **heaved** or **hove** \'hōv\; **heav·ing 1** : rise or lift upward **2** : throw **3** : rise and fall ~ n **1** : an effort to lift or raise **2** : throw

heav·en \'hevən\ n **1** pl : sky **2** : abode of the Deity and of the blessed dead **3** : place of supreme happiness —**heav·en·ly** adj —**heav·en·ward** adv or adj

heavy \'hevē\ adj **heavi·er, -est 1** : having great weight **2** : hard to bear **3** : greater than the average —**heav·i·ly** adv —**heav·i·ness** n —**heavy·weight** n

heavy-du·ty adj : able to withstand unusual strain

heavy-set adj : stocky and compact in build

heck·le \'hekəl\ vb **-led; -ling** : harass with gibes —**heck·ler** \-(ə)lər\ n

hec·tic \'hektik\ adj : filled with excitement or confusion —**hec·ti·cal·ly** \-tik(ə)lē\ adv

hedge \'hej\ n **1** : fence or boundary of shrubs or small trees **2** : means of protection ~ vb **hedged; hedg·ing 1** : protect oneself against loss **2** : evade the risk of commitment —**hedg·er** n

hedge·hog n : spiny mammal (as a porcupine)

he·do·nism \'hēd²ⁿ,izəm\ n : way of life devoted to pleasure —**he·do·nist** \-²nəst\ n —**he·do·nis·tic** \,hēd²ⁿistik\ adj

heed \'hēd\ vb : pay attention ~ n : attention —**heed·ful** \-fəl\ adj —**heed·ful·ly** adv —**heed·ful·ness** n —**heed·less** adj —**heed·less·ly** adv —**heed·less·ness** n

¹heel \'hēl\ n **1** : back of the foot **2** : crusty end of a loaf of bread **3** : solid piece forming the back of the sole of a shoe —**heel·less** \'hēlləs\ adj

²heel vb : tilt to one side

heft \'heft\ n : weight ~ vb : judge the weight of by lifting

hefty \'heftē\ adj **heft·i·er, -est** : big and bulky

he·ge·mo·ny \hi'jemənē\ n : preponderant influence esp. of one nation over others

heif·er \'hefər\ n : young cow

height \'hīt, 'hīth\ n **1** : highest part

or point **2** : distance from bottom to top **3** : altitude

height·en \'hīt³n\ vb : increase in amount or degree

hei·nous \'hānəs\ adj : shockingly evil —**hei·nous·ly** adv —**hei·nous·ness** n

heir \'aər\ n : one who inherits or is entitled to inherit property —**heir·ship** n

heir·ess \'arəs\ n : female heir esp. to great wealth

heir·loom \'aər,lüm\ n : something handed on from one generation to another

held past of HOLD

he·li·cal \'helikəl, 'hē-\ adj : spiral

he·li·cop·ter \'helə,käptər, 'hē-\ n : aircraft supported in the air by rotors

he·lio·trope \'hēlyə,trōp\ n : garden herb with small fragrant white or purple flowers

he·li·um \'hēlēəm\ n : very light nonflammable gaseous chemical element

he·lix \'hēliks\ n, pl **-li·ces** \'helə,sēz, 'hē-\ : something spiral

hell \'hel\ n **1** : nether world in which the dead continue to exist **2** : realm of the devil **3** : place or state of torment or destruction —**hell·ish** adj

hell·gram·mite \'helgrə,mīt\ n : aquatic insect larva

hel·lion \'helyən\ n : troublesome person

hel·lo \hə'lō, he-\ n, pl **-los** : expression of greeting

helm \'helm\ n : lever or wheel for steering a ship —**helms·man** \'helmzmən\ n

hel·met \'helmət\ n : protective covering for the head

help \'help\ vb **1** : supply what is needed **2** : be of use **3** : refrain from or prevent ~ n **1** : something that helps or a source of help **2** : one who helps another —**help·er** n —**help·ful** \-fəl\ adj —**help·ful·ly** adv —**help·ful·ness** n —**help·less** adj —**help·less·ly** adv —**help·less·ness** n

help·ing \'helpiŋ\ n : portion of food

help·mate n **1** : helper **2** : wife

help·meet \-,mēt\ n : helpmate

hel·ter-skel·ter \,heltər'skeltər\ adv : in total disorder

hem \'hem\ n : border of an article of cloth doubled back and stitched down ~ vb **-mm- 1** : sew a hem **2** : surround restrictively —**hem·line** n

he·ma·tol·o·gy \,hēmə'täləjē\ n : study of the blood and blood-forming organs —**hem·a·to·log·ic** \-mət³l'äjik\,

hem·a·to·log·i·cal \-ikəl\ adj —**he·ma·tol·o·gist** \-'täləjəst\ n

hemi·sphere \'hemə,sfiər\ n : one of the halves of the earth divided by the equator into northern and southern parts (**northern hemisphere, southern hemisphere**) or by a meridian into eastern and western parts (**eastern hemisphere, western hemisphere**) —**hemi·spher·ic** \,hemə'sfiərik, -'sfer-\, **hemi·spher·i·cal** \-'sfirikəl, -'sfer-\ adj

hem·lock \'hem,läk\ n **1** : poisonous herb related to the carrot **2** : evergreen tree related to the pines

he·mo·glo·bin \'hēmə,glōbən\ n : iron-containing compound found in red blood cells

he·mo·phil·ia \,hēmə'filēə\ n : tendency to severe prolonged bleeding —**he·mo·phil·i·ac** \-ē,ak\ adj or n

hem·or·rhage \'hem(ə)rij\ n : large discharge of blood —**hemorrhage** vb —**hem·or·rhag·ic** \,hemə'rajik\ adj

hem·or·rhoids \'hem(ə),rȯidz\ n pl : swollen mass of dilated veins at or just within the anus

hemp \'hemp\ n : tall Asian herb grown for its tough fiber —**hemp·en** \'hempən\ adj

hen \'hen\ n : female domestic fowl

hence \'hens\ adv **1** : away **2** : therefore **3** : from this source or origin

hence·forth adv : from this point on

hence·for·ward adv : henceforth

hench·man \'henchmən\ n : trusted follower

hen·na \'henə\ n : reddish brown dye obtained from the leaves of a tropical shrub

hen·peck \'hen,pek\ vb : subject (one's husband) to persistent nagging

he·pat·ic \hi'patik\ adj : relating to or resembling the liver

hep·a·ti·tis \,hepə'tītəs\ n, pl **-tit·i·des** \-'titə,dēz\ : inflammation of the liver or a disease of which this is a feature

her \(h)ər, ,hər\ adj : of or relating to her or herself ~ \ər, (')hər\ pron, objective case of SHE

her·ald \'herəld\ n **1** : official crier or messenger **2** : harbinger ~ vb : give notice

her·ald·ry \'herəldrē\ n, pl **-ries** : practice of devising and granting arms —**he·ral·dic** \he'raldik, hə-\ adj

herb \'(h)ərb\ n **1** : seed plant that lacks woody tissue **2** : plant or plant part valued for medicinal or savory qualities —**her·ba·ceous** \,(h)ər'bāshəs\ adj —**herb·age**

\\'(h)ərbij\ *n* —**herb·al** \-bəl\ *n or adj*
—**herb·al·ist** \-bələst\ *n*

her·bi·cide \\'(h)ərbə‚sīd\ *n* : agent that
destroys plants —**her·bi·cid·al**
\‚(h)ərbə'sīd²l\ *adj*

her·biv·o·rous \(‚)hər'bivərəs\ *adj*
: feeding on plants —**her·bi·vore**
\\'(h)ərbə‚vōr\ *n* —**her·biv·o·rous·ly**
adv

her·cu·le·an \‚hərkyə'lēən, ‚hər'kyū-
lēən\ *adj* : of extraordinary power,
size, or difficulty

herd \\'hərd\ *n* : group of animals of
one kind ~ *vb* : assemble or move in
a herd —**herd·er** *n* —**herds·man**
\\'hərdzmən\ *n*

here \\'hiər\ *adv* 1 : in or at this place 2
: now 3 : at or in this point or particular 4 : in the present life or state
~ *n* : this place —**here·abouts**
\\'hirə‚bauts\, **here·about** \-‚baut\
adv

here·af·ter *adv* : in some future time or
state ~ *n* : existence beyond earthly
life

here·by *adv* : by means of this

he·red·i·tary \hə'redə‚terē\ *adj* 1 : genetically passed or passable from
parent to offspring 2 : passing by
inheritance

he·red·i·ty \-ōtē\ *n* : the passing of
characteristics from parent to offspring

here·in *adv* : in this

here·of *adv* : of this

here·on *adv* : on this

her·e·sy \\'herəsē\ *n, pl* **-sies** : opinion
or doctrine contrary to church dog-
ma —**her·e·tic** \-‚tik\ *n* —**he·ret·i·
cal** \hə'retikəl\ *adj*

here·to *adv* : to this document

here·to·fore \\'hirtə‚fōr\ *adv* : up to this
time

here·un·der *adv* : under this

here·un·to *adv* : to this

here·upon *adv* : on this

here·with *adv* 1 : with this 2 : hereby

her·i·tage \\'herətij\ *n* 1 : inheritance 2
: birthright

her·maph·ro·dite \(‚)hər'mafrə‚dīt\ *n*
: animal or plant having both male
and female reproductive organs
—**hermaphrodite** *adj* —**her·maph·ro·
dit·ic** \-‚mafrə'ditik\ *adj*

her·met·ic \hər'metik\ *adj* : sealed airtight —**her·met·i·cal·ly** \-ik(ə)lē\ *adv*

her·mit \\'hərmət\ *n* : one who lives in
solitude

her·nia \\'hərnēə\ *n, pl* **-ni·as** *or* **-ni·ae**
\-nē‚ē, -nē‚ī\ : a protrusion of a
bodily part through the weakened
wall of its enclosure —**her·ni·al** *adj*

—her·ni·ate \-nē‚āt\ *vb* —**her·ni·a·
tion** \‚hərnē'āshən\ *n*

he·ro \\'hērō\ *n, pl* **-roes** : one that is
much admired or shows great cour-
age —**he·ro·ic** \hi'rōik\ *adj* —**he·ro·
i·cal·ly** \-ik(ə)lē\ *adv* —**he·ro·ics**
\-iks\ *n pl* —**he·ro·ism**
\\'herə‚wizəm\ *n*

her·o·in \\'herəwən\ *n* : strongly addictive narcotic

her·o·ine \\'herəwən\ *n* : woman of heroic achievements or qualities

her·on \\'herən\ *n* : long-legged long-
billed wading bird

her·pes \\'hərpēz\ *n* : virus disease
characterized by the formation of
blisters

her·pe·tol·o·gy \‚hərpə'täləjē\ *n*
: study of reptiles and amphibians
—**her·pe·to·log·ic** \-pətᵊl'äjik\, **her·
pe·to·log·i·cal** \-ikəl\ *adj* —**her·pe·
tol·o·gist** \-pə'täləjəst\ *n*

her·ring \\'heriŋ\ *n, pl* **-ring** *or* **-rings**
: narrow-bodied Atlantic food fish

hers \\'hərz\ *pron* : one or the ones belonging to her

her·self \(h)ər'self\ *pron* : she, her
—used reflexively or for emphasis

hertz \\'herts, 'hərts\ *n, pl* **hertz** : unit
of frequency equal to one cycle per
second

hes·i·tant \\'hezətənt\ *adj* : tending to
hesitate —**hes·i·tan·cy** \-tənsē\ *n*
—**hes·i·tant·ly** *adv*

hes·i·tate \\'hezə‚tāt\ *vb* **-tat·ed; -tat·ing**
1 : hold back esp. in doubt 2 : pause
—**hes·i·ta·tion** \‚hezə'tāshən\ *n*

het·er·o·ge·neous \‚het(ə)rə'jēnēəs,
-nyəs\ *adj* : consisting of dissimilar
ingredients or constituents —**het·er·
o·ge·neous·ly** *adv* —**het·er·o·ge·
neous·ness** *n*

het·ero·sex·u·al \‚hetarō'seksh(əw)əl\
adj : oriented toward the opposite
sex —**heterosexual** *n*

hew \\'hyü\ *vb* **hewed; hewed** *or* **hewn**
\\'hyün\; **hew·ing** 1 : cut or shape
with or as if with an ax 2 : conform
strictly —**hew·er** *n*

hex \\'heks\ *vb* : put an evil spell on
—**hex** *n*

hexa·gon \\'heksə‚gän\ *n* : 6-sided
polygon —**hex·ag·o·nal**
\hek'sagənᵊl\ *adj*

hey·day \\'hā‚dā\ *n* : time of flourishing

hi·a·tus \hī'ātəs\ *n* : lapse in continuity

hi·ba·chi \hi'bächē\ *n* : brazier

hi·ber·nate \\'hībər‚nāt\ *vb* **-nat·ed;
-nat·ing** : pass the winter in a torpid
or resting state —**hi·ber·na·tion**
\‚hībər'nāshən\ *n* —**hi·ber·na·tor**
\\'hībər‚nātər\ *n*

hic·cup \'hik(ˌ)əp\ *n* : spasmodic inhalation with sudden closing of the glottis accompanied by a peculiar sound —**hiccup** *vb*

hick \'hik\ *n* : awkward provincial person —**hick** *adj*

hick·o·ry \'hik(ə)rē\ *n, pl* **-ries** : No. American hardwood tree —**hickory** *adj*

¹hide \'hīd\ *vb* **hid** \'hid\; **hid·den** \'hid²n\ *or* **hid**; **hid·ing** : put or remain out of sight

²hide *n* : animal skin

hid·eous \'hidēəs\ *adj* : very ugly —**hid·eous·ly** *adv* —**hid·eous·ness** *n*

hie \'hī\ *vb* **hied**; **hy·ing** *or* **hie·ing** : hurry

hi·er·ar·chy \'hī(ə)ˌrärkē\ *n, pl* **-chies** : persons or things arranged in a graded series —**hi·er·ar·chi·cal** \ˌhīə'rärkikəl\ *adj*

hi·er·o·glyph·ic \ˌhī(ə)rə'glifik\ *n* : character in the picture writing of the ancient Egyptians

high \'hī\ *adj* 1 : having large extension upward 2 : elevated in pitch 3 : exalted in character 4 : of greater degree or amount than average 5 : expensive 6 : excited or stupefied by alcohol or a drug — *adv* : at or to a high place or degree — *n* 1 : elevated point or level 2 : automobile gear giving the highest speed

high·boy *n* : high chest of drawers on legs

high·brow \-ˌbrau̇\ *n* : person of superior learning or culture —**high·brow** *adj*

high-flown *adj* : pretentious

high-hand·ed *adj* : willful and arrogant —**high-hand·ed·ly** *adv* —**high-hand·ed·ness** *n*

high·land \'hīlənd\ *n* : hilly country —**high·land·er** \-ləndər\ *n*

high·light *n* : event or detail of major importance — *vb* 1 : emphasize 2 : be a highlight of

high·ness \-nəs\ *n* 1 : quality or degree of being high 2 —used as a title (as for kings)

high-rise *adj* : having several stories

high school *n* : school usu. comprising the 9th to 12th or 10th to 12th grades

high-spir·it·ed *adj* : lively

high-strung \-'strəŋ\ *adj* : very nervous or sensitive

high·way *n* : public road

high·way·man \-mən\ *n* : one who robs travelers on a road

hi·jack \'hīˌjak\ *vb* : steal esp. by commandeering a vehicle —**hijack** *n* —**hi·jack·er** *n*

hike \'hīk\ *vb* **hiked**; **hik·ing** 1 : raise quickly 2 : take a long walk — *n* 1 : long walk 2 : increase

hi·lar·i·ous \hī'larēəs, hi'lar-\ *adj* : extremely funny —**hi·lar·i·ous·ly** *adv* —**hi·lar·i·ty** \-ətē\ *n*

hill \'hil\ *n* : place where the land rises —**hill·side** *n* —**hill·top** *n* —**hilly** *adj*

hill·bil·ly \'hilˌbilē\ *n, pl* **-lies** : person from a backwoods area

hill·ock \'hilək\ *n* : small hill

hilt \'hilt\ *n* : handle of a sword

him \im, 'him\ *pron*, objective case of HE

him·self \(h)im'self\ *pron* : he, him —used reflexively or for emphasis

¹hind \'hīnd\ *n* : female deer

²hind *adj* : back

hin·der \'hindər\ *vb* : obstruct or hold back

hind·most *adj* : farthest to the rear

hind·quar·ter *n* : back half of a complete side of a carcass

hin·drance \'hindrəns\ *n* : something that hinders

hind·sight *n* : understanding of an event after it has happened

Hin·du·ism \'hindüˌizəm\ *n* : body of religious beliefs and practices native to India —**Hin·du** *n or adj*

hinge \'hinj\ *n* : jointed piece on which one piece (as a door) turns or swings ~ *vb* **hinged**; **hing·ing** 1 : attach by or furnish with hinges 2 : depend

hint \'hint\ *n* 1 : indirect suggestion 2 : clue 3 : very small amount —**hint** *vb*

hin·ter·land \'hintərˌland\ *n* : remote region

hip \'hip\ *n* : part of the body on either side just below the waist —**hip·bone** *n*

hip·pie, hip·py \'hipē\ *n, pl* **-pies** : usu. young person who rejects conventional society —**hip·pie·dom** *n* —**hip·pie·hood** *n*

hip·po·pot·a·mus \ˌhipə'pätəməs\ *n, pl* **-mus·es** *or* **-mi** \-ˌmī\ : large thick-skinned African river animal

hire \'hī(ə)r\ *n* 1 : payment for labor 2 : employment — *vb* **hired**; **hir·ing** : employ for pay

hire·ling \'hī(ə)rliŋ\ *n* : one who serves another only for gain

hir·sute \'hərˌsüt, 'hiər-\ *adj* : hairy

his \(h)iz, ˌhiz\ *adj* : of or belonging to him ~ \'hiz\ *pron* : ones belonging to him

hiss \'his\ *vb* 1 : make a sharp sibilant sound 2 : show dislike by hissing —**hiss** *n*

his·to·ri·an \his'tōrēən\ *n* : writer of history

his·to·ry \'hist(ə)rē\ n, pl **-ries 1** : chronological record of significant events **2** : study of past events —**his·tor·ic** \his'tòrik\, **his·tor·i·cal** \-ikəl\ adj —**his·tor·i·cal·ly** \-k(ə)lē\ adv

hit \'hit\ vb **hit; hit·ting 1** : reach with a blow **2** : come or cause to come in contact **3** : affect detrimentally ~ n **1** : blow **2** : something very successful —**hit·ter** n

hitch \'hich\ vb **1** : move by jerks **2** : catch by a hook **3** : hitchhike ~ n **1** : jerk **2** : sudden halt

hitch·hike \'hich,hīk\ vb : travel by securing free rides from passing vehicles —**hitch·hik·er** n

hith·er \'hithər\ adv : to this place

hith·er·to \-,tü\ adv : up to this time

hive \'hīv\ n **1** : container housing honeybees **2** : colony of bees —**hive** vb

hives \'hīvz\ n sing or pl : allergic disorder

hoard \'hòrd\ n : hidden accumulation —**hoard** vb —**hoard·er** n

hoar·frost \'hòr,fròst\ n : frost

hoarse \'hòrs\ adj **hoars·er; -est 1** : harsh in sound **2** : speaking in a harsh strained voice —**hoarse·ly** adv —**hoarse·ness** n

hoary \'hòrē\ adj **hoar·i·er; -est 1** : gray or white with age —**hoar·i·ness** n

hoax \'hōks\ n : act intended to trick or dupe —**hoax** vb —**hoax·er** n

hob·ble \'häbəl\ vb **-bled; -bling** : limp along ~ n : hobbling movement

hob·by \-ē\ n, pl **-bies** : interest engaged in for relaxation —**hob·by·ist** \-ēəst\ n

hob·gob·lin \'häb,gäblən\ n **1** : mischievous goblin **2** : bogey

hob·nail \-,nāl\ n : short nail for studding shoe soles —**hob·nailed** \-,nāld\ adj

hob·nob \-,näb\ vb **-bb-** : associate socially

ho·bo \'hōbō\ n, pl **-boes** : tramp

¹hock \'häk\ n : joint or region in the hind limb of a quadruped corresponding to the human ankle

²hock n or vb : pawn

hock·ey \'häkē\ n : game played on ice or a field by 2 teams

hod \'häd\ n **1** : carrier for bricks or mortar **2** : scuttle

hodge·podge \'häj,päj\ n : heterogeneous mixture

hoe \'hō\ n : long-handled tool for cultivating or weeding —**hoe** vb

hog \'hog, 'häg\ n **1** : domestic adult swine **2** : glutton ~ vb : take selfishly —**hog·gish** adj

hogs·head \'hògz,hed, 'hägz-\ n : large cask or barrel

hog·wash n : nonsense

hoist \'hòist\ vb : lift ~ n **1** : lift **2** : apparatus for hoisting

¹hold \'hōld\ vb **held; hold·ing 1** : possess **2** : restrain **3** : have a grasp on **4** : remain or keep in a particular situation or position **5** : contain **6** : regard **7** : cause to occur **8** : occupy esp. by appointment or election ~ n **1** : act or manner of holding **2** : restraining or controlling influence —**hold·er** n —**hold forth** : speak at length —**hold to** : adhere to —**hold with** : agree with

²hold n : cargo area of a ship

hold·ing \'hōldiŋ\ n : property owned —usu. pl.

hold·up n **1** : robbery at the point of a gun **2** : delay

hole \'hōl\ n **1** : opening into or through something **2** : hollow place (as a pit) **3** : den —**hole** vb

hol·i·day \'hälə,dā\ n **1** : day of freedom from work **2** : vacation —**holiday** vb

ho·li·ness \'hōlēnəs\ n : quality or state of being holy

hol·ler \'hälər\ vb : cry out —**holler** n

hol·low \-ō\ adj **-low·er** \-əwər\; **-est 1** : sunken **2** : having a cavity within **3** : sounding like a noise made in an empty place **4** : empty of value or meaning ~ vb : make or become hollow ~ n **1** : surface depression **2** : cavity —**hol·low·ness** n

hol·ly \-ē\ n, pl **-lies** : evergreen tree or shrub

hol·ly·hock \-,häk, -,hòk\ n : tall perennial herb grown for its showy flowers

ho·lo·caust \'hälə,kòst, 'hō-, 'hò-\ n : thorough destruction esp. by fire

hol·stein \'hòl,stēn, -,stīn\ n : large black-and-white dairy cow

hol·ster \'hōlstər\ n : case for a pistol

ho·ly \'hōlē\ adj **-li·er; -est 1** : sacred **2** : spiritually pure

hom·age \'(h)ämij\ n : reverent regard

home \'hōm\ n **1** : residence **2** : congenial environment **3** : place of origin or refuge ~ vb **homed; hom·ing 1** : go or return home —**home·bred** adj —**home·com·ing** n —**home·grown** adj —**home·land** \-,land\ n —**home·less** adj —**home·made** \-'mād\ adj

home·ly \-lē\ adj **-li·er; -est** : plain or unattractive —**home·li·ness** n

home·mak·er n : one who manages a household —**home·mak·ing** n

home·sick \ adj : longing for home —**home·sick·ness** n

home·spun \-,spən\ adj : simple

home·stead \-,sted\ n : home and land (as a tract acquired from U.S. public lands) occupied and worked by a family —**home·stead·er** \-ər\ n

home·stretch n 1 : last part of a race-track 2 : final stage

1home·ward \-wərd\, **home·wards** \-wərdz\ adv : toward home

2homeward adj : in the direction of home

home·work n : school lessons to be done outside the classroom

hom·ey \'hōmē\ adj home·er; -est : intimate in nature

ho·mi·cide \'hämə,sīd, 'hō-\ n : the killing of one human being by another —**hom·i·cid·al** \,hämə'sīdəl\ adj

hom·i·ly \'häməlē\ n, pl -lies : sermon —**hom·i·let·ic** \,hämə'letik\ adj

hom·i·ny \'hämənē\ n : type of processed hulled corn

ho·mo·ge·neous \,hōmə'jēnēəs, -nyəs\ adj : of the same or a similar kind —**ho·mo·ge·ne·i·ty** \-jə'nēətē\ n —**ho·mo·ge·neous·ly** adv —**ho·mo·ge·neous·ness** n

ho·mog·e·nize \hō'mäjə,nīz, hə-\ vb -nized; -niz·ing : make the particles in (as milk or paint) of uniform size and even distribution —**ho·mog·e·niz·er** n

ho·mo·graph \'hämə,graf, 'hōmə-\ n : one of 2 or more words (as the noun conduct and the verb conduct) spelled alike but different in origin or meaning or pronunciation

hom·onym \'hämə,nim, 'hōmə-\ n 1 : homophone 2 : homograph 3 : one of 2 or more words (as pool of water and pool the game) spelled and pronounced alike but different in meaning

ho·mo·phone \'hämə,fōn, 'hōmə-\ n : one of 2 or more words (as to, too, and two) pronounced alike but different in origin or meaning or spelling

Ho·mo sa·pi·ens \,hōmō'sapēənz, -'sā-\ n : man or mankind

ho·mo·sex·u·al \,hōmə'seksh(əw)əl\ adj : oriented toward one's own sex —**homosexual** n

hone \'hōn\ n : sharpening stone —**hone** vb —**hon·er** n

hon·est \'änəst\ adj 1 : free from deception 2 : trustworthy 3 : genuine —**hon·est·ly** adv —**hon·es·ty** \-əstē\ n

hon·ey \'hənē\ n, pl -eys : sweet sticky substance made by bees (**hon·ey·bees**) from the nectar of flowers

hon·ey·comb n : mass of 6-sided wax cells built by honeybees or something like it ~ vb : make or become full of holes like a honeycomb

hon·ey·moon n : holiday taken by a newly married couple —**honeymoon** vb

hon·ey·suck·le \-,səkəl\ n : shrub or vine with flowers rich in nectar

honk \'häŋk, 'hȯŋk\ n : cry of a goose or a similar sound —**honk** vb —**honk·er** n

hon·or \'änər\ n 1 : good name 2 : outward respect or symbol of this 3 : privilege 4 : person of superior rank or position —used esp. as a title 5 : something or someone worthy of respect 6 : integrity ~ vb 1 : regard with honor 2 : confer honor on 3 : fulfill the terms of —**hon·or·able** \'än(ə)rəbəl\ adj —**hon·or·ably** \-blē\ adv —**hon·or·ari·ly** \,änə'rerəlē\ adv —**hon·or·ary** \'änə,rerē\ adj

hood \'hüd\ n 1 : part of a garment that covers the head 2 : covering over an automobile engine compartment —**hood·ed** adj

-hood \,hùd\ n suffix 1 : state, condition, or quality 2 : individuals sharing a state or character

hood·lum \'hüdləm, 'hùd-\ n : thug

hood·wink \'hùd,wiŋk\ vb : deceive

hoof \'hùf, 'hüf\ n, pl hooves \'hüvz, 'hùvz\ or hoofs : horny covering of the toes of some mammals (as horses or cattle) —**hoofed** \'hùft, 'hüft\ adj

hook \'hùk\ n : curved or bent device for catching, holding, or pulling ~ vb : seize or make fast with a hook —**hook·er** n

hoo·kah \'hùkə, 'hü-\ n : pipe for smoking so arranged that the smoke passes through water

hook·worm n : parasitic intestinal worm

hoo·li·gan \'hüligən\ n : thug

hoop \'hüp, 'hùp\ n : circular strip, figure, or object

hoot \'hüt\ vb 1 : shout in contempt 2 : make the cry of an owl —**hoot** n —**hoot·er** n

1hop \'häp\ vb -pp- : move by quick springy leaps —**hop** n

2hop n : vine whose ripe dried flowers are used to flavor malt liquors

hope \'hōp\ vb hoped; hop·ing : desire with expectation of fulfillment ~ n 1 : act of hoping 2 : something hoped for —**hope·ful** \-fəl\ adj —**hope·ful·**

ly *adv* —**hope·ful·ness** *n* —**hope·less** *adj* —**hope·less·ly** *adv* —**hope·less·ness** *n*

hop·per \'häpər\ *n* : container that releases its contents through the bottom

horde \'hōrd\ *n* : throng or swarm

hore·hound \'hōr₁haůnd\ *n* : aromatic bitter mint

ho·ri·zon \hə'rīz³n\ *n* : line marking the apparent junction of earth and sky

hor·i·zon·tal \₁hòrə'zänt³l\ *adj* : parallel to the horizon —**hor·i·zon·tal·ly** *adv*

hor·mone \'hòr₁mōn\ *n* : cell product in body fluids that has a specific effect on other cells —**hor·mon·al** \hòr'mōn³l\ *adj*

horn \'hòrn\ *n* **1** : one of the hard bony projections on the head of many hoofed animals **2** : brass wind instrument —**horned** *adj* —**horn·less** *adj* —**horny** *adj*

hor·net \'hòrnət\ *n* : large social wasp

hor·ol·o·gy \hə'räləjē\ *n* : science of measuring time or making clocks —**hor·o·log·i·cal** \₁hòrə'läjikəl\ *adj* —**ho·rol·o·gist** \hə'räləjəst\ *n*

horo·scope \'hòrə₁skōp\ *n* : astrological forecast

hor·ren·dous \hò'rendəs\ *adj* : horrible

hor·ri·ble \'hòrəbəl\ *adj* **1** : having or causing horror **2** : highly disagreeable —**hor·ri·ble·ness** *n* —**hor·ri·bly** \-blē\ *adv*

hor·rid \'hòrəd\ *adj* : horrible —**hor·rid·ly** *adv*

hor·ri·fy \'-ə₁fī\ *vb* -**fied; -fy·ing** : cause to feel horror

hor·ror \-ər\ *n* **1** : intense fear, dread, or dismay **2** : intense repugnance **3** : something horrible

hors d'oeuvre \òr'dərv\ *n, pl* **hors d'oeuvres** \-'dərv(z)\ : appetizer

horse \'hòrs\ *n* : large solid-hoofed domesticated mammal —**horse·back** *n or adv* —**horse·hair** *n* —**horse·hide** *n* —**horse·less** *adj* —**horse·man** \-mən\ *n* —**horse·man·ship** *n* —**horse·wom·an** *n* —**hors·ey, horsy** *adj*

horse·fly *n* : large fly with bloodsucking female

horse·play *n* : rough boisterous play

horse·pow·er *n* : unit of mechanical power

horse·rad·ish *n* : herb with a pungent root used as a condiment

horse·shoe \'hòrs₁shü\ *n* : protective metal plate fitted to the rim of a horse's hoof

hor·ta·to·ry \'hòrtə₁tōrē\ *adj* : giving exhortation

hor·ti·cul·ture \'hòrtə₁kəlchər\ *n* : science of growing fruits, vegetables, and flowers —**hor·ti·cul·tur·al** \₁hòrtə'kəlch(ə)rəl\ *adj* —**hor·ti·cul·tur·ist** \-rəst\ *n*

ho·san·na \hō'zanə, -'zän-\ *interj* —used as a cry of acclamation and adoration

hose \'hōz\ *n* **1** *pl* **hose** : stocking or sock **2** *pl* **hos·es** : flexible tube for conveying fluids ~ *vb* **hosed; hos·ing** : spray, water, or wash with a hose

ho·siery \'hōzh(ə)rē, 'hòz(ə)-\ *n* : stockings or socks

hos·pice \'häspəs\ *n* : lodging (as for travelers) maintained by a religious order

hos·pi·ta·ble \hä'spitəbəl, 'häs(₁)pit-\ *adj* : given to generous and cordial reception of guests —**hos·pi·ta·bly** \-blē\ *adv*

hos·pi·tal \'häs₁pit³l\ *n* : institution where the sick or injured receive medical care —**hos·pi·tal·iza·tion** \₁häs₁pit³lə'zāshən\ *n* —**hos·pi·tal·ize** \'häs₁pit³l₁īz\ *vb*

hos·pi·tal·i·ty \₁häspə'talətē\ *n, pl* -**ties** : hospitable treatment, reception, or disposition

¹host \'hōst\ *n* **1** : army **2** : multitude

²host *n* : one who receives or entertains guests —**host** *vb*

³host *n* : eucharistic bread

hos·tage \'hästij\ *n* : person held to guarantee that promises be kept or demands met

hos·tel \'häst³l\ *n* : lodging for youth —**hos·tel·er** *n*

hos·tel·ry \-rē\ *n, pl* -**ries** : hotel

host·ess \'hōstəs\ *n* : woman who is host

hos·tile \'häst³l, -₁tīl\ *adj* : openly or actively unfriendly or opposed to someone or something —**hostile** *n* —**hos·tile·ly** *adv* —**hos·til·i·ty** \häs'tilətē\ *n*

hot \'hät\ *adj* -**tt-** **1** : having a high temperature **2** : giving a sensation of heat or burning **3** : ardent **4** : pungent —**hot** *adv* —**hot·ly** *adv* —**hot·ness** *n*

hot·bed *n* : environment that favors rapid growth

hot dog *n* : frankfurter

ho·tel \hō'tel\ *n* : building where lodging and personal services are provided

hot·head·ed *adj* : impetuous —**hot·head** *n* —**hot·head·ed·ly** *adv* —**hot·head·ed·ness** *n*

hot·house *n* : glass-enclosed house for raising plants

hound \'haund\ *n* : long-eared hunting dog ~ *vb* : pursue relentlessly

hour \'au̇(ə)r\ *n* 1 : 24th part of a day 2 : time of day —**hour·ly** *adv or adj*

hour·glass *n* : glass vessel for measuring time

house \'haus\ *n, pl* **hous·es** \'hauzəz\ 1 : building to live in 2 : household 3 : legislative body 4 : business firm ~ \'hauz\ *vb* **housed; hous·ing** : provide with or take shelter —**house·boat** \'haus-\ *n* —**house·clean** \'haus-\ *vb* —**house·clean·ing** *n* —**house·ful** \-,fu̇l\ *n* —**house·keep·er** *n* —**house·keep·ing** *n* —**house·maid** *n* —**house·wares** *n pl* —**house·work** *n*

house-bro·ken *adj* : trained to excretory habits acceptable in indoor living

house·fly *n* : two-winged fly common about human habitations

house·hold \-,hōld\ *n* : those who dwell as a family under the same roof ~ *adj* 1 : domestic 2 : common or familiar —**house·hold·er** *n*

house-warm·ing *n* : party to celebrate moving into a house

house·wife \'haus-,wīf\ *n* : married woman in charge of a household —**house·wife·li·ness** *n* —**house·wife·ly** *adj* —**house·wif·ery** \-,wīf(ə)rē\ *n*

hous·ing \'hauziŋ\ *n* 1 : dwellings for people 2 : protective covering

hove *past of* HEAVE

hov·el \'həvəl, 'häv-\ *n* : small wretched house

hov·er \'həvər, 'häv-\ *vb* 1 : remain suspended in the air 2 : move about in the vicinity

how \(')hau̇\ *adv* 1 : in what way or condition 2 : for what reason 3 : to what extent ~ *conj* : in what manner or condition

how·ev·er \hau̇'evər\ *conj* : in whatever manner —*adv* 1 : to whatever degree or in whatever manner 2 : in spite of that

how·itz·er \'hau̇ətsər\ *n* : short cannon

howl \'hau̇l\ *vb* : emit a loud long doleful sound like a dog —**howl** *n* —**howl·er** *n*

hoy·den \'hȯidᵊn\ *n* : girl or woman of saucy or carefree behavior

hub \'həb\ *n* : central part (as of a wheel) —**hub·cap** *n*

hub·bub \'həb,əb\ *n* : uproar

hu·bris \'hyübrəs\ *n* : excessive pride

huck·le·ber·ry \'həkəl,berē\ *n* 1 : shrub related to the blueberry or its berry 2 : blueberry

huck·ster \'həkstər\ *n* : peddler

hud·dle \'hədᵊl\ *vb* **-dled; -dling** 1 : crowd together 2 : confer —**huddle** *n*

hue \'hyü\ *n* : attribute of colors that permits them to be classed as red, yellow, green, blue, or an intermediate color —**hued** \'hyüd\ *adj*

huff \'həf\ *n* : fit of pique —**huffy** *adj*

hug \'həg\ *vb* **-gg-** 1 : press tightly in the arms 2 : stay close to —**hug** *n*

huge \'hyüj\ *adj* **hug·er; hug·est** : very large or extensive —**huge·ly** *adv* —**huge·ness** *n*

hu·la \'hülə\ *n* : Polynesian dance

hulk \'həlk\ *n* 1 : bulky or unwieldy person or thing 2 : old ship unfit for service —**hulk·ing** *adj*

hull \'həl\ *n* 1 : outer covering of a fruit or seed 2 : frame or body of a ship ~ *vb* : remove the hulls of —**hull·er** *n*

hul·la·ba·loo \'hələbə,lü\ *n, pl* **-loos** : uproar

hum \'həm\ *vb* **-mm-** : make a prolonged sound like that of the speech sound \m\ —**hum** *n* —**hum·mer** *n*

hu·man \'(h)yümən\ *adj* 1 : of or relating to the species people belong to 2 : by, for, or like people —**human** *n* —**human·kind** *n* —**hu·man·ly** *adv* —**hu·man·ness** *n*

hu·mane \(h)yü'mān\ *adj* : showing compassion or consideration for others —**hu·mane·ly** *adv* —**hu·mane·ness** *n*

hu·man·ism \'(h)yümə,nizəm\ *n* : doctrine or way of life centered on human interests or values —**hu·man·ist** \-nəst\ *n or adj* —**hu·man·is·tic** \,(h)yümə'nistik\ *adj*

hu·man·i·tar·i·an \(h)yü,manə'terēən\ *n* : person promoting human welfare —**humanitarian** *adj* —**hu·man·i·tar·i·an·ism** *n*

hu·man·i·ty \(h)yü'manətē\ *n, pl* **-ties** 1 : human or humane quality or state 2 : mankind

hu·man·ize \'(h)yümə,nīz\ *vb* **-ized; -izing** : make human or humane —**hu·man·iza·tion** \,(h)yümənə'zāshən\ *n*

hu·man·oid \'(h)yümə,nȯid\ *adj* : having human form —**humanoid** *n*

hum·ble \'(h)əmbəl\ *adj* **-bler; -blest** 1 : not proud or haughty 2 : not pretentious ~ *vb* **-bled; -bling** : make humble —**hum·ble·ness** *n* —**hum·bler** *n* —**hum·bly** \-blē\ *adv*

hum·bug \'həm,bəg\ *n* : nonsense

hum·drum \-,drəm\ *adj* : monotonous

hu·mid \'(h)yüməd\ *adj* : containing or characterized by moisture —**hu·mid·**

i·fi·ca·tion \ˌhyüˌmidəfəˈkāshən\ *n* —**hu·mid·i·fi·er** \-ˈmidəˌfī(ə)r\ *n* —**hu·mid·i·fy** \-ˌfī\ *vb* —**hu·mid·ly** *adv*

hu·mid·i·ty \(h)yüˈmidətē\ *n, pl* **-ties** : atmospheric moisture

hu·mi·dor \ˈ(h)yüməˌdòr\ *n* : humidified storage case

hu·mil·i·ate \(h)yüˈmilēˌāt\ *vb* **-at·ed; -at·ing** : injure the self-respect of —**hu·mil·i·at·ing·ly** *adv* —**hu·mil·i·a·tion** \-ˌmilēˈāshən\ *n*

hu·mil·i·ty \(h)yüˈmilətē\ *n* : humble quality or state

hum·ming·bird \ˈhəmiŋˌbərd\ *n* : tiny American bird

hum·mock \ˈhəmək\ *n* : mound or knoll

hu·mor \ˈ(h)yümər\ *n* **1** : mood **2** : quality of being laughably ludicrous or incongruous **3** : appreciation of what is ludicrous or incongruous **4** : something intended to be funny ~ *vb* : comply with the wishes or mood of —**hu·mor·ist** \-(ə)rəst\ *n* —**hu·mor·less** *adj* —**hu·mor·less·ly** *adv* —**hu·mor·less·ness** *n* —**hu·mor·ous** \ˈ(h)yüm(ə)rəs\ *adj* —**hu·mor·ous·ly** *adv* —**hu·mor·ous·ness** *n*

hump \ˈhəmp\ *n* : rounded protuberance —**humped** *adj*

hump·back *n* : hunchback —**hump·backed** *adj*

hu·mus \ˈ(h)yüməs\ *n* : dark organic part of soil

hunch \ˈhənch\ *vb* : assume or cause to assume a bent or crooked posture ~ *n* : strong intuitive feeling

hunch·back *n* **1** : back with a hump **2** : person with a crooked back —**hunch·backed** *adj*

hun·dred \ˈhəndrəd\ *n, pl* **-dreds** or **-dred** : 10 times 10 —**hundred** *adj* —**hun·dredth** \-drədth\ *adj or n*

hung *past of* HANG

hun·ger \ˈhəŋgər\ *n* **1** : craving or urgent need for food **2** : strong desire —**hunger** *vb* —**hun·gri·ly** \-grəlē\ *adv* —**hun·gry** *adj*

hunk \ˈhəŋk\ *n* : large piece

hun·ker \ˈhəŋkər\ *vb* : squat down

hunt \ˈhənt\ *vb* **1** : pursue for food or sport **2** : try to find ~ *n* : act or instance of hunting —**hunt·er** *n*

hur·dle \ˈhərdəl\ *n* **1** : barrier to leap over **2** : obstacle —**hurdle** *vb* —**hur·dler** *n*

hurl \ˈhərl\ *vb* : throw with violence —**hurl** *n* —**hurl·er** *n*

hur·rah \hüˈrò, -ˈrä\ *interj* —used to express joy or approval

hur·ri·cane \ˈhərəˌkān\ *n* : tropical storm with winds of 74 miles per hour or greater

hur·ry \ˈhərē\ *vb* **-ried; -ry·ing** : go or cause to go with haste ~ *n* : extreme haste —**hur·ried·ly** *adv* —**hur·ried·ness** *n*

hurt \ˈhərt\ *vb* **hurt; hurt·ing** **1** : feel or cause pain **2** : do harm to ~ *n* **1** : bodily injury **2** : harm —**hurt·ful** \-fəl\ *adj*

hur·tle \ˈhərtəl\ *vb* **-tled; -tling** : move with rapid force

hus·band \ˈhəzbənd\ *n* : married man ~ *vb* : manage prudently

hus·band·ry \-bəndrē\ *n* **1** : careful use **2** : agriculture

hush \ˈhəsh\ *vb* : make or become quiet ~ *n* : silence

husk \ˈhəsk\ *n* : outer covering of a seed or fruit ~ *vb* : strip the husk from —**husk·er** *n*

¹hus·ky \ˈhəskē\ *adj* **-ki·er; -est** : hoarse —**hus·ki·ly** *adv* —**hus·ki·ness** *n*

²husky *adj* **-ki·er; -est** : burly —**husk·i·ness** *n*

³husky *n, pl* **-kies** : working dog of the arctic

hus·sy \ˈhəzē, ˈhas-\ *n, pl* **-sies** **1** : brazen woman **2** : mischievous girl

hus·tle \ˈhəsəl\ *vb* **-tled; -tling** **1** : hurry **2** : work energetically —**hustle** *n* —**hus·tler** \ˈhəslər\ *n*

hut \ˈhət\ *n* : small often temporary dwelling

hutch \ˈhəch\ *n* **1** : cupboard with open shelves **2** : pen for an animal

hy·a·cinth \ˈhīəˌ(ˌ)sinth\ *n* : bulbous herb grown for bell-shaped flowers

hy·brid \ˈhībrəd\ *n* : offspring of genetically differing parents —**hybrid** *adj* —**hy·brid·iza·tion** \ˌhībrədəˈzāshən\ *n* —**hy·brid·ize** \ˈhībrədˌīz\ *vb* —**hy·brid·iz·er** *n*

hy·drant \ˈhīdrənt\ *n* : pipe from which water may be drawn to fight fires

hy·drau·lic \hīˈdròlik\ *adj* : operated by liquid forced through a small hole —**hy·drau·lics** \-liks\ *n*

hy·dro·car·bon \ˌhīdrəˈkärbən\ *n* : organic compound of carbon and hydrogen

hy·dro·elec·tric \ˌhīdrōiˈlektrik\ *adj* : producing electricity by waterpower —**hy·dro·elec·tri·cal·ly** \-trik(ə)lē\ *adv* —**hy·dro·elec·tric·i·ty** \-ˌlekˈtrisətē\ *n*

hy·dro·gen \ˈhīdrəjən\ *n* : gaseous colorless odorless flammable chemical element   —hy·drog·e·nous \hī'dräjənəs\ adj

hydrogen bomb n : bomb with violent power from the energy released by the union of atomic nuclei

hy·dro·pho·bia \,hīdrə'fōbēə\ n : rabies

hy·dro·plane \'hīdrə,plān\ n : speedboat whose hull rises out of the water

hy·drous \'hīdrəs\ adj : containing water

hy·e·na \hī'ēnə\ n : nocturnal carnivorous mammal of Asia and Africa

hy·giene \'hī,jēn\ n : conditions or practices conducive to health —hy·gien·ic \,hījē'enik; hī'jen-, -'jēn-\ adj —hy·gien·i·cal·ly \-ik(ə)lē\ adv —hy·gien·ist \hī'jēnəst, -'jen-; 'hī,jēn-\ n

hy·grom·e·ter \hī'grämətər\ n : instrument for measuring atmospheric humidity —hy·grom·e·try \-trē\ n

hying pres part of HIE

hymn \'him\ n : song of praise esp. to God —hymn vb —hym·nal \'himnəl\ n

hyper- prefix 1 : above or beyond 2 : excessively or excessive

hyperacid	hypermasculine
hyperacidity	hypermilitant
hyperactive	hypermoralistic
hyperacute	hypernationalistic
hyperaggressive	
hyperanxious	hyperreactive
hypercautious	hyperrealistic
hyperclean	hyperromantic
hyperconscientious	hypersensitive
	hypersensitiveness
hypercorrect	hypersensitivity
hypercritical	hypersexual
hyperemotional	hypersusceptible
hyperenergetic	hypersuspicious
hyperexcitable	hypertense
hyperfastidious	hypervigilant
hyperintense	

hy·per·bo·le \hī'pərbə(,)lē\ n : extravagant exaggeration

hy·per·ten·sion \'hīpər,tenchən\ n : high blood pressure —hy·per·ten·sive \,hīpər'tensiv\ adj or n

hy·phen \'hīfən\ n : punctuation mark - used to divide or compound words —hyphen vb

hy·phen·ate \'hīfə,nāt\ vb -at·ed; -at·ing : connect or divide with a hyphen —hy·phen·ation \,hīfə'nāshən\ n

hyp·no·sis \hip'nōsəs\ n, pl -no·ses \-,sēz\ : induced state like sleep in which the subject is responsive to suggestions of the inducer (hyp·no·tist \'hipnətəst\) —hyp·no·tism \'hipnə,tizəm\ n —hyp·no·tiz·able \-,tīzəbəl\ adj —hyp·no·tize \-,tīz\ vb

hyp·not·ic \hip'nätik\ adj : relating to hypnosis —hypnotic n —hyp·not·i·cal·ly \-ik(ə)lē\ adv

hy·po·chon·dria \,hīpə'kändrēə\ n : morbid concern for one's health —hy·po·chon·dri·ac \-drē,ak\ adj or n

hy·poc·ri·sy \hip'äkrəsē\ n, pl -sies : a feigning to be what one is not —hyp·o·crite \'hipə,krit\ n —hyp·o·crit·i·cal \,hipə'kritikəl\ adj —hyp·o·crit·i·cal·ly adv

hy·po·der·mic \,hīpə'dərmik\ adj : used for or given by injection beneath the skin ~ n : hypodermic syringe

hy·pot·e·nuse \hī'pät²n,(y)üs, -,(y)üz\ n : side of a right-angled triangle opposite the right angle

hy·poth·e·sis \hī'päthəsəs\ n, pl -e·ses \-,sēz\ : assumption made in order to test its consequences —hy·poth·e·size \-,sīz\ vb —hy·po·thet·i·cal \,hīpə'thetikəl\ adj —hy·po·thet·i·cal·ly adv

hys·ter·ec·to·my \,histə'rektəmē\ n, pl -mies : surgical removal of the uterus —hys·ter·ec·to·mize \-,mīz\ vb

hys·te·ria \his'terēə, -tir-\ n : uncontrollable fear or emotion —hys·ter·ic \-'terik\, hys·ter·i·cal \-ikəl\ adj —hys·ter·i·cal·ly adv

hys·ter·ics \-'teriks\ n pl : uncontrollable laughter or crying

I

i \'ī\ n, pl i's or is \'īz\ : 9th letter of the alphabet

I \(')ī, ə\ pron : the speaker

-ia adj suffix : of, relating to, or characterized by

-ian —see -AN

ibis \'ībəs\ n, pl ibis or ibis·es : wading bird with a down-curved bill

-ible —see -ABLE

-ic \ik\ adj suffix 1 : of, relating to, or being 2 : containing 3 : characteristic of 4 : marked by 5 : caused by

-ical · illegitimately

-i·cal \ikəl\ *adj suffix* : -ic —**i·cal·ly** \ik(ə)lē\ *adv suffix*

ice \'īs\ *n* **1** : frozen water **2** : frozen dessert ∼ *vb* **iced; ic·ing 1** : freeze **2** : chill **3** : cover with icing

ice·berg \'īs,bərg\ *n* : large floating mass of ice

ice·box *n* : refrigerator

ice·break·er *n* : ship equipped to cut through ice

ice cream *n* : sweet frozen food

ice-skate *vb* : skate on ice —**ice skater** *n*

ich·thy·ol·o·gy \,ikthē'äləjē\ *n* : study of fishes —**ich·thy·ol·o·gist** \-jəst\ *n*

ici·cle \'ī,sikəl\ *n* : hanging mass of ice

ic·ing \'īsiŋ\ *n* : sweet usu. creamy coating for baked goods

icon \'ī,kän\ *n* : religious image

icon·o·clast \ī'känə,klast\ *n* : attacker of cherished beliefs or institutions —**icon·o·clasm** \-,klazəm\ *n*

icy \'īsē\ *adj* **ic·i·er; -est 1** : covered or consisting of ice **2** : very cold —**ic·i·ly** *adv* —**ic·i·ness** *n*

id \'id\ *n* : unconscious part of the mind

idea \ī'dēə\ *n* **1** : something imagined in the mind **2** : purpose or plan

ide·al \ī'dēəl\ *adj* **1** : imaginary **2** : perfect ∼ *n* **1** : standard of excellence **2** : model **3** : aim —**ide·al·ly** *adv*

ide·al·ism \ī'dēə,lizəm\ *n* **1** : adherence to ideals **2** : tendency to see things as they should be —**ide·al·ist** \-ləst\ *n* —**ide·al·is·tic** \ī,dēə'listik\ *adj*

ide·al·ize \ī'dē(ə),līz\ *vb* **-ized; -iz·ing** : think of or represent as ideal —**ide·al·iza·tion** \-,dē(ə)lə'zāshən\ *n*

iden·ti·cal \ī'dentikəl\ *adj* **1** : being the same **2** : exactly or essentially alike

iden·ti·fi·ca·tion \ī,dentəfə'kāshən\ *n* **1** : act of identifying **2** : evidence of identity

iden·ti·fy \ī'dentə,fī\ *vb* **-fied; -fy·ing 1** : associate **2** : establish the identity of

iden·ti·ty \ī'dentətē\ *n, pl* **-ties 1** : sameness of essential character **2** : individuality **3** : fact of being what it is supposed

ide·ol·o·gy \,īdē'äləjē, ,id-\ *n, pl* **-gies** : body of beliefs —**ide·o·log·i·cal** \,īdēə'läjikəl, ,id-\ *adj*

id·i·om \'idēəm\ *n* **1** : language peculiar to a person or group **2** : expression with a special meaning —**id·i·om·at·ic** \,idēə'matik\ *adj* —**id·i·om·at·i·cal·ly** \-ik(ə)lē\ *adv*

id·io·syn·cra·sy \,idēə'siŋkrəsē\ *n, pl* **-sies** : personal peculiarity —**id·io·syn·crat·ic** \-ōsin'kratik\ *adj*

id·i·ot \'idēət\ *n* : feebleminded or foolish person —**id·i·o·cy** \-əsē\ *n* —**id·i·ot·ic** \,idē'ätik\ *adj* —**id·i·ot·i·cal·ly** \-ik(ə)lē\ *adv*

idle \'īd⁰l\ *adj* **idler; idlest 1** : worthless **2** : inactive **3** : lazy ∼ *vb* **idled; idling 1** : spend time doing nothing —**idle·ness** *n* —**idler** *n* —**idly** \'īdlē\ *adv*

idol \'īd⁰l\ *n* **1** : image of a god **2** : object of devotion —**idol·ize** \-⁰l,īz\ *vb*

idol·a·ter \ī'dälətər\ *n* : worshiper of idols —**idol·a·trous** \-trəs\ *adj* —**idol·a·try** \-trē\ *n*

-ier —see -ER

if \(,)if, əf\ *conj* **1** : in the event that **2** : whether **3** : even though

-i·fy \ə,fī\ *vb suffix* : -fy

ig·loo \'iglü\ *n, pl* **-loos** : hut made of snow blocks

ig·nite \ig'nīt\ *vb* **-nit·ed; -nit·ing** : set afire or catch fire

ig·ni·tion \ig'nishən\ *n* **1** : a setting on fire **2** : process or means of igniting fuel

ig·no·ble \ig'nōbəl\ *adj* : not honorable —**ig·no·bly** \-blē\ *adv*

ig·no·min·i·ous \,ignə'minēəs\ *adj* **1** : dishonorable **2** : humiliating —**ig·no·min·i·ous·ly** *adv* —**ig·no·min·y** \'ignə,minē, ig'nämənē\ *n*

ig·no·ra·mus \,ignə'rāməs\ *n* : ignorant person

ig·no·rant \'ignərənt\ *adj* **1** : lacking knowledge **2** : stupid **3** : unaware —**ig·no·rance** \-rəns\ *n* —**ig·no·rant·ly** *adv*

ig·nore \ig'nōr\ *vb* **-nored; -nor·ing** : refuse to notice

igua·na \i'gwänə\ *n* : tropical American lizard

ilk \'ilk\ *n* : kind

ill \'il\ *adj* **worse** \'wərs\; **worst** \'wərst\ **1** : sick **2** : bad **3** : inferior **4** : hostile ∼ *adv* **worse; worst 1** : with displeasure **2** : harshly **3** : scarcely **4** : badly ∼ *n* **1** : evil **2** : misfortune **3** : sickness

il·le·gal \il'(l)ēgəl\ *adj* : not lawful —**il·le·gal·i·ty** \,il(l)i'galətē\ *n* —**il·le·gal·ly** \il'(l)ēgəlē\ *adv*

il·leg·i·ble \il'(l)ejəbəl\ *adj* : not legible —**il·leg·i·bil·i·ty** \il,(l)ejə'bilətē\ *n* —**il·leg·i·bly** \il'(l)ejəblē\ *adv*

il·le·git·i·mate \,ili'jitəmət\ *adj* **1** : born of unmarried parents **2** : illegal —**il·le·git·i·ma·cy** \-əməsē\ *n* —**il·le·git·i·mate·ly** *adv* il·lic·it \il¹(l)isət\ adj : not lawful —il·lic·it·ly adv

il·lim·it·able \il¹(l)imətəbəl\ adj : boundless —il·lim·it·ably \-blē\ adv

il·lit·er·ate \il¹(l)it(ə)rət\ adj : unable to read or write —il·lit·er·a·cy \-(ə)rəsē\ n —illiterate n

ill-na·tured \'il¹·nāchərd\ adj : cross —ill·na·tured·ly adv

ill·ness \'ilnəs\ n : sickness

il·log·i·cal \il¹(l)äjikəl\ adj : contrary to logic —il·log·i·cal·ly adv

ill-starred \'il¹stärd\ adj : unlucky

il·lu·mi·nate \il¹ümə₁nāt\ vb -nat·ed; -nat·ing 1 : light up 2 : make clear —il·lu·mi·nat·ing·ly \-₁nātiŋlē\ adv —il·lu·mi·na·tion \-₁ümə¹nāshən\ n

ill-use \-¹¹yüz\ vb : abuse —ill-use \-¹yüs\ n

il·lu·sion \il¹üzhən\ n 1 : mistaken idea 2 : misleading visual image

il·lu·sive \il¹üsiv\ adj : illusory

il·lu·so·ry \il¹üs(ə)rē, -¹üz-\ adj : based on or producing illusion

il·lus·trate \'iləs₁trāt\ vb -trat·ed; -trat·ing 1 : explain by example 2 : provide with pictures or figures —il·lus·tra·tor \-ər\ n

il·lus·tra·tion \₁iləs¹trāshən\ n 1 : example that explains 2 : pictorial explanation

il·lus·tra·tive \il¹əstrativ\ adj : designed to illustrate —il·lus·tra·tive·ly adv

il·lus·tri·ous \il¹·trēəs\ adj : notably or brilliantly outstanding —il·lus·tri·ous·ness n

ill will n : unfriendly feeling

im·age \'imij\ n 1 : likeness 2 : visual counterpart of an object formed by a lens or mirror 3 : mental picture ~ vb -aged; -ag·ing : create a representation of

im·ag·ery \'imij(ə)rē\ n 1 : images 2 : figurative language

imag·i·nary \im¹ajə₁nerē\ adj : existing only in the imagination

imag·i·na·tion \im₁ajə¹nāshən\ n 1 : act or power of forming a mental image 2 : creative ability —imag·i·na·tive \im¹aj(ə)nətiv, -ə₁nātiv\ adj —imag·i·na·tive·ly adv

imag·ine \im¹ajən\ vb -ined; -in·ing : form a mental picture of something not present —imag·in·able \-¹aj(ə)nəbəl\ adj —imag·in·ably \-blē\ adv

im·bal·ance \(¹)im¹baləns\ n : lack of balance

im·be·cile \'imbəsəl, -₁sil\ n : feeble-minded or foolish person —imbecile,

im·be·cil·ic \₁imbə¹silik\ adj —im·be·cil·i·ty \-¹silətē\ n

im·bibe \im¹bīb\ vb -bibed; -bib·ing : drink —im·bib·er n

im·bro·glio \im¹brōlyō\ n, pl -glios : complicated situation

im·brue \im¹brü\ vb -brued; -bru·ing : steep

im·bue \-¹byü\ vb -bued; -bu·ing : fill (as with color or a feeling)

im·i·tate \'imə₁tāt\ vb -tat·ed; -tat·ing 1 : follow as a model 2 : mimic —im·i·ta·tive \-₁tātiv\ adj —im·i·ta·tor \-ər\ n

im·i·ta·tion \₁imə¹tāshən\ n 1 : act of imitating 2 : copy —imitation adj

im·mac·u·late \im¹akyəlat\ adj : without stain or blemish —im·mac·u·late·ly adv

im·ma·te·ri·al \₁imə¹tirēəl\ adj 1 : spiritual 2 : not relevant —im·ma·te·ri·al·i·ty \-₁tirē¹alətē\ n

im·ma·ture \₁imə¹t(y)ur\ adj : not yet mature —im·ma·tu·ri·ty \-ətē\ n

im·mea·sur·able \(¹)im¹ezh(ə)rəbəl\ adj : indefinitely extensive —im·mea·sur·ably \-blē\ adv

im·me·di·a·cy \im¹ēdēəsē\ n, pl -cies : urgency

im·me·di·ate \im¹ēdēət\ adj 1 : direct 2 : being next in line 3 : made or done at once 4 : not distant —im·me·di·ate·ly adv

im·me·mo·ri·al \₁imə¹mōrēəl\ adj : old beyond memory

im·mense \im¹ens\ adj : vast —im·mense·ly adv —im·men·si·ty \-¹ensətē\ n

im·merse \im¹ərs\ vb -mersed; -mers·ing 1 : plunge or dip esp. into liquid 2 : engross —im·mer·sion \-¹ərzhən\ n

im·mi·grant \'imigrənt\ n : one that immigrates

im·mi·grate \'imə₁grāt\ vb -grat·ed; -grat·ing : come into a place and take up residence —im·mi·gra·tion \₁imə¹grāshən\ n

im·mi·nent \'imənənt\ adj : ready to take place —im·mi·nence \-nəns\ n —im·mi·nent·ly adv

im·mo·bile \(¹)im¹ōbəl\ adj : incapable of being moved —im·mo·bil·i·ty \₁imō¹bilətē\ n —im·mo·bi·lize \im¹ōbəlīz\ vb

im·mod·er·ate \(¹)im¹äd(ə)rət\ adj : not moderate —im·mod·er·a·cy \-(ə)rəsē\ n —im·mod·er·ate·ly adv

im·mod·est \(¹)im¹ädəst\ adj : not modest —im·mod·est·ly adv —im·mod·es·ty \-əstē\ n

im·mo·late \\'imə₁lāt\ *vb* **-lat·ed; -lat·ing** : offer in sacrifice —**im·mo·la·tion** \₁imə'lāshən\ *n*

im·mor·al \(')im'ôrəl\ *adj* : not moral —**im·mo·ral·i·ty** \₁imô'ralətē, ₁imə-\ *n* —**im·mor·al·ly** *adv*

im·mor·tal \(')im'ôrtᵊl\ *adj* **1** : not mortal **2** : having lasting fame ~ *n* : one exempt from death or oblivion —**im·mor·tal·i·ty** \₁imôr'talətē\ *n* —**im·mor·tal·ize** \im'ôrtᵊl₁īz\ *vb*

im·mov·able \(')im'üvəbəl\ *adj* **1** : stationary **2** : unyielding —**im·mov·abil·i·ty** \(₁)im₁üvə'bilətē\ *n* —**im·mov·ably** *adv*

im·mune \im'yün\ *adj* : not liable esp. to disease —**im·mu·ni·ty** \im'yünətē\ *n* —**im·mu·ni·za·tion** \₁imyənə'zāshən\ *n* —**im·mu·nize** \'imyə₁nīz\ *vb*

im·mu·nol·o·gy \₁imyə'näləjē\ *n* : science of immunity —**im·mu·no·log·ic** \-yən°l'äjik\, **im·mu·no·log·i·cal** \-ikəl\ *adj* —**im·mu·nol·o·gist** \₁imyə'näləjəst\ *n*

im·mu·ta·ble \(')im'yütəbəl\ *adj* : unchangeable —**im·mu·ta·bil·i·ty** \(₁)im₁yütə'bilətē\ *n* —**im·mu·ta·bly** *adv*

imp \'imp\ *n* **1** : demon **2** : mischievous child

im·pact \im'pakt\ *vb* **1** : press close **2** : have an effect on ~ \'im₁pakt\ *n* **1** : forceful contact **2** : influence

im·pact·ed \im'paktəd\ *adj* : wedged between the jawbone and another tooth

im·pair \im'paər\ *vb* : diminish in quantity or value —**im·pair·ment** *n*

im·pa·la \im'palə\ *n* : large antelope

im·pale \im'pāl\ *vb* **-paled; -pal·ing** : pierce with something pointed —**im·pale·ment** *n*

im·pal·pa·ble \(')im'palpəbəl\ *adj* : incapable of being felt —**im·pal·pa·bly** *adv*

im·pan·el \im'panᵊl\ *vb* : enter in or on a panel

im·part \-'pärt\ *vb* : give from or as if from a store

im·par·tial \(')im'pärshəl\ *adj* : not partial —**im·par·tial·i·ty** \(₁)im₁pärshē'alətē, -₁pärt'shal-\ *n* —**im·par·tial·ly** *adv*

im·pass·able \(')im'pasəbəl\ *adj* : not passable

im·passe \'im₁pas\ *n* : inescapable predicament

im·pas·sioned \im'pashənd\ *adj* : filled with passion

im·pas·sive \(')im'pasiv\ *adj* : showing no feeling or interest —**im·pas·sive·ly** *adv* —**im·pas·siv·i·ty** \₁im₁pas'ivətē\ *n*

im·pa·tiens \im'pāshənz, -shəns\ *n* : annual herb with showy irregular flowers

im·pa·tient \(')im'pāshənt\ *adj* : not patient —**im·pa·tience** \-shəns\ *n* —**im·pa·tient·ly** *adv*

im·peach \im'pēch\ *vb* **1** : charge an official with misconduct **2** : cast doubt on —**im·peach·ment** *n*

im·pec·ca·ble \(')im'pekəbəl\ *adj* : faultless —**im·pec·ca·bly** *adv*

im·pe·cu·nious \₁impi'kyünyəs, -nēəs\ *adj* : broke —**im·pe·cu·nious·ness** *n*

im·pede \im'pēd\ *vb* **-ped·ed; -ped·ing** : interfere with

im·ped·i·ment \-'pedəmənt\ *n* **1** : hindrance **2** : speech defect

im·pel \-'pel\ *vb* **-pelled; -pel·ling** : urge forward

im·pend \-'pend\ *vb* : be about to occur

im·pen·e·tra·ble \(')im'penətrəbəl\ *adj* : incapable of being penetrated or understood —**im·pen·e·tra·bil·i·ty** \(₁)im₁penətrə'bilətē\ *n* —**im·pen·e·tra·bly** *adv*

im·pen·i·tent \im'penətənt\ *adj* : not penitent —**im·pen·i·tence** \-təns\ *n*

im·per·a·tive \im'perətiv\ *adj* **1** : expressing a command **2** : urgent ~ *n* **1** : imperative mood or verb form **2** : unavoidable fact, need, or obligation —**im·per·a·tive·ly** *adv*

im·per·cep·ti·ble \₁impər'septəbəl\ *adj* : not perceptible —**im·per·cep·ti·bly** *adv*

im·per·fect \(')im'pərfikt\ *adj* : not perfect —**im·per·fec·tion** *n* —**im·per·fect·ly** *adv*

im·pe·ri·al \im'pirēəl\ *adj* **1** : relating to an empire or an emperor **2** : royal

im·pe·ri·al·ism \im'pirēə₁lizəm\ *n* : policy of controlling other nations —**im·pe·ri·al·ist** \-ləst\ *n or adj* —**im·pe·ri·al·is·tic** \-₁pirēə'listik\ *adj*

im·per·il \im'perəl\ *vb* **-iled** *or* **-illed; -il·ing** *or* **-il·ling** : endanger

im·pe·ri·ous \im'pirēəs\ *adj* : arrogant or domineering —**im·pe·ri·ous·ly** *adv*

im·per·ish·able \(')im'perishəbəl\ *adj* : not perishable

im·per·ma·nent \-'pərmənənt\ *adj* : not permanent —**im·per·ma·nent·ly** *adv*

im·per·me·able \-'pərmēəbəl\ *adj* : not permeable

im·per·mis·si·ble \₁impər'misəbəl\ *adj* : not permissible

im·per·son·al \(ʹ)imʹpərsnəl, -ᵊnəl\ *adj* : not involving human personality or emotion —**im·per·son·al·ly** \-ē\ *adv*

im·per·son·ate \imʹpərsᵊn‚āt\ *vb* -at·ed; -at·ing : assume the character of —**im·per·son·ation** \-‚pərsᵊnʹāshən\ *n* —**im·per·son·ator** \-ʹpərsᵊn‚ātər\ *n*

im·per·ti·nent \(ʹ)imʹpərtᵊnənt\ *adj* 1 : irrelevant 2 : insolent —**im·per·ti·nence** \-ᵊnəns\ *n* —**im·per·ti·nent·ly** *adv*

im·per·turb·able \‚impərʹtərbəbəl\ *adj* : calm and steady

im·per·vi·ous \(ʹ)imʹpərvēəs\ *adj* : incapable of being penetrated or affected

im·pet·u·ous \imʹpechə)wəs\ *adj* : impulsive —**im·pet·u·os·i·ty** \(‚)im‚pechəʹwäsətē\ *n* —**im·pet·u·ous·ly** *adv*

im·pe·tus \ʹimpətəs\ *n* : driving force

im·pi·ety \(ʹ)imʹpīətē\ *n* : quality or state of being impious

im·pinge \imʹpinj\ *vb* -pinged; -ping·ing : encroach —**im·pinge·ment** \-ʹpinjmənt\ *n*

im·pi·ous \ʹimpēəs, (ʹ)imʹpī-\ *adj* : not pious

imp·ish \ʹimpish\ *adj* : mischievous —**imp·ish·ly** *adv* —**imp·ish·ness** *n*

im·pla·ca·ble \(ʹ)imʹplakəbəl, -ʹplā-\ *adj* : not capable of being appeased or changed —**im·pla·ca·bil·i·ty** \(‚)im‚plakəʹbilətē, -‚plā-\ *n* —**im·pla·ca·bly** \-ʹplakəblē\ *adv*

im·plant \imʹplant\ *vb* 1 : set firmly or deeply 2 : fix in the mind or spirit —**im·plant** \ʹim‚plant\ *n*

im·plau·si·ble \(ʹ)imʹplȯzəbəl\ *adj* : not plausible —**im·plau·si·bil·i·ty** \(‚)im‚plȯzəʹbilətē\ *n*

im·ple·ment \ʹimpləmənt\ *n* : piece of equipment for performing a hand or mechanical operation ~ \-‚ment\ *vb* : put into practice —**im·ple·men·ta·tion** \‚impləmənʹtāshən\ *n*

im·pli·cate \ʹimplə‚kāt\ *vb* -cat·ed; -cat·ing : involve

im·pli·ca·tion \‚impləʹkāshən\ *n* 1 : an implying 2 : something implied

im·plic·it \imʹplisət\ *adj* 1 : understood though only implied 2 : complete and unquestioning —**im·plic·it·ly** *adv*

im·plode \imʹplōd\ *vb* -plod·ed; -plod·ing : burst inward —**im·plo·sion** \-ʹplōzhən\ *n* —**im·plo·sive** \-ʹplō-siv\ *adj*

im·plore \imʹplōr\ *vb* -plored; -plor·ing : entreat

im·ply \-ʹplī\ *vb* -plied; -ply·ing : express indirectly

im·po·lite \‚impəʹlīt\ *adj* : not polite

im·pol·i·tic \(ʹ)imʹpäləʹtik\ *adj* : not politic

im·pon·der·a·ble \(ʹ)imʹpänd(ə)rəbəl\ *adj* : incapable of being precisely evaluated —**imponderable** *n*

im·port \imʹpōrt\ *vb* 1 : mean 2 : bring in from an external source ~ \ʹim‚pōrt\ *n* 1 : meaning 2 : importance 3 : something imported —**im·por·ta·tion** \‚im‚pōrʹtāshən\ *n* —**im·port·er** *n*

im·por·tant \imʹpōrtᵊnt\ *adj* : having great worth, significance, or influence —**im·por·tance** \-ᵊns\ *n* —**im·por·tant·ly** *adv*

im·por·tu·nate \imʹpōrch(ə)nət\ *adj* : troublesomely persistent or urgent

im·por·tune \‚impərʹt(y)ün, imʹpōrchən\ *vb* -tuned; -tun·ing : urge or beg persistently —**im·por·tu·ni·ty** \‚impərʹt(y)ünətē\ *n*

im·pose \imʹpōz\ *vb* -posed; -pos·ing 1 : establish as compulsory 2 : take unwarranted advantage of —**im·po·si·tion** \‚impəʹzishən\ *n*

im·pos·ing \imʹpōzin\ *adj* : impressive —**im·pos·ing·ly** *adv*

im·pos·si·ble \(ʹ)imʹpäsəbəl\ *adj* 1 : incapable of occurring 2 : hopeless —**im·pos·si·bil·i·ty** \(‚)im‚päsəʹbilətē\ *n* —**im·pos·si·bly** \(ʹ)imʹpäsəblē\ *adv*

im·post \ʹim‚pōst\ *n* : tax

im·pos·tor, im·pos·ter \imʹpästər\ *n* : one who assumes an identity or title to deceive —**im·pos·ture** \-ʹpäschər\ *n*

im·po·tent \ʹimpətənt\ *adj* 1 : lacking power 2 : sterile —**im·po·tence** \-pətəns\ *n* —**im·po·ten·cy** \-ᵊnsē\ *n* —**im·po·tent·ly** *adv*

im·pound \imʹpaůnd\ *vb* : seize and hold in legal custody —**im·pound·ment** *n*

im·pov·er·ish \imʹpäv(ə)rish\ *vb* : make poor —**im·pov·er·ish·ment** *n*

im·prac·ti·ca·ble \(ʹ)imʹpraktikəbəl\ *adj* : not practicable

im·prac·ti·cal \-ʹpraktikəl\ *adj* : not practical

im·pre·cise \‚impriʹsīs\ *adj* : not precise —**im·pre·cise·ly** *adv* —**im·pre·cise·ness** *n* —**im·pre·ci·sion** \-ʹsizhən\ *n*

im·preg·na·ble \imʹpregnəbəl\ *adj* : able to resist attack —**im·preg·na·bil·i·ty** \(‚)im‚pregnəʹbilətē\ *n*

im·preg·nate \imʹpreg‚nāt\ *vb* -nat·ed; -nat·ing 1 : make pregnant 2 : saturate with some other substance —**im·preg·na·tion** \‚im‚pregʹnāshən\ *n*

im·pre·sa·rio \ˌimprəˈsärēˌō\ n, pl -ri-os : one who sponsors an entertainment

¹im·press \imˈpres\ vb 1 : apply with or produce by pressure 2 : press, stamp, or print in or upon 3 : produce a vivid impression of 4 : affect (as the mind) forcibly ~ \ˈimˌ-\ n 1 : product of pressure or influence 2 : impression or effect —**im·press·ible** adj

²im·press \imˈpres\ vb : force into naval service —**im·press·ment** n

im·pres·sion \imˈpreshən\ n 1 : mark made by impressing 2 : marked influence or effect 3 : printed copy 4 : vague notion or recollection —**im·pres·sion·able** \-ˈpresh(ə)nəbəl\ adj

im·pres·sive \imˈpresiv\ adj : making a marked impression —**im·pres·sive·ly** adv —**im·pres·sive·ness** n

im·pri·ma·tur \ˌimprəˈmäˌtu̇(ə)r\ n : official approval (as of a publication by a censor)

im·print \imˈprint, ˈimˌ-\ vb : stamp or mark by or as if by pressure ~ \ˈimˌ-\ n : something imprinted or printed

im·pris·on \imˈprizⁿn\ vb : put in prison —**im·pris·on·ment** \imˈprizⁿnmənt\ n

im·prob·a·ble \(ˈ)imˈpräbəbəl\ adj : unlikely to be true or to occur —**im·prob·a·bil·i·ty** \ˌ(ˌ)imˌpräbəˈbilətē\ n —**im·prob·a·bly** adv

im·promp·tu \imˈprämpt(y)ü\ adj : not planned beforehand —**impromptu** adv or n

im·prop·er \(ˈ)imˈpräpər\ adj : not proper —**im·prop·er·ly** adv

im·pro·pri·e·ty \ˌimprəˈprīətē\ n, pl -eties : state or instance of being improper

im·prove \imˈprüv\ vb -proved; -proving 1 : grow or make better 2 : make good use of —**im·prov·able** \-ˈprüvəbəl\ adj —**im·prove·ment** n

im·prov·i·dent \(ˈ)imˈprävədənt\ adj : not providing for the future —**im·prov·i·dence** \-əns\ n

im·pro·vise \ˈimprəˌvīz, ˈimprəˌvīz\ vb -vised; -vis·ing : make, invent, or arrange offhand —**im·pro·vi·sa·tion** \imˌprävəˈzāshən, ˌimprəvə-\ n —**im·pro·vis·er, im·pro·vi·sor** \ˌimprəˈvīzər, ˈimprəˌvī-\ n

im·pru·dent \(ˈ)imˈprüdⁿnt\ adj : not prudent —**im·pru·dence** \-ⁿns\ n

im·pu·dent \ˈimpyədənt\ adj : insolent —**im·pu·dence** \-əns\ n —**im·pu·dent·ly** adv

im·pugn \imˈpyün\ vb : attack as false

im·pulse \ˈimˌpəls\ n 1 : moving force 2 : sudden inclination

im·pul·sion \imˈpəlshən\ n : act of impelling

im·pul·sive \imˈpəlsiv\ adj : acting on impulse —**im·pul·sive·ly** adv —**im·pul·sive·ness** n

im·pu·ni·ty \imˈpyünətē\ n : exemption from punishment or harm

im·pure \(ˈ)imˈpyu̇r\ adj : not pure —**im·pu·ri·ty** \-ˈpyu̇rətē\ n

im·pute \imˈpyüt\ vb -put·ed; -put·ing : credit to or blame on a person or cause —**im·pu·ta·tion** \ˌimpyəˈtāshən\ n

in \(ˈ)in, ən, ᵊn\ prep 1 —used to indicate location, inclusion, situation, or manner 2 : into 3 : during ~ \ˈin\ adv : to or toward the inside ~ \ˈin\ adj : located inside

in- \(ˈ)in, ˌin, ˌin\ prefix 1 : not 2 : lack of

inability	incoherence
inaccessibility	incoherent
inaccessible	incoherently
inaccuracy	incohesive
inaccurate	incombustible
inaction	incommensurate
inactive	incommodious
inactivity	incommunicable
inadequacy	incompatibility
inadequate	incompatible
inadequately	incomplete
inadmissibility	incompletely
inadmissible	incompleteness
inadvisability	incomprehen-
inadvisable	sible
inapparent	inconceivable
inapplicable	inconceivably
inapposite	inconclusive
inappositely	incongruent
inappositeness	inconsecutive
inappreciative	inconsiderate
inapproachable	inconsiderately
inappropriate	inconsiderate-
inappropriately	ness
inappropriate-	inconsistency
ness	inconsistent
inapt	inconsistently
inarguable	inconspicuous
inartistic	inconspicuously
inartistically	inconstancy
inattentive	inconstant
inattentively	inconstantly
inattentiveness	inconsumable
inaudible	incontestable
inaudibly	incontestably
inauspicious	incorporeal
inauthentic	incorporeally
incapability	incorrect
incapable	incorrectly
incautious	incorrectness

incorruptible
inculpable
incurable
incurious
indecency
indecent
indecently
indecipherable
indecisive
indecisively
indecisiveness
indecorous
indecorously
indecorousness
indefensible
indefinable
indefinably
indescribable
indescribably
indestructibility
indestructible
indigestible
indiscernible
indiscreet
indiscretion
indisputable
indisputably
indistinct
indistinctly
indistinctness
indivisibility
indivisible
ineducable
ineffective
ineffectively
ineffectiveness
ineffectual
ineffectually
ineffectualness
inefficiency
inefficient
inefficiently
inelastic
inelasticity
inelegance
inelegant
ineligibility
ineligible
ineradicable
inessential
inexact
inexactly
inexpedient
inexpensive
inexperience
inexperienced
inexpert
inexpertly
inexpertness
inexplicable
inexplicably
inexplicit

inexpressible
inexpressibly
inextinguishable
inextricable
infeasibility
infeasible
infelicitous
infelicity
infertile
infertility
inflexibility
inflexible
inflexibly
infrequent
infrequently
inglorious
ingloriously
ingratitude
inhumane
inhumanely
injudicious
injudiciously
injudiciousness
inoffensive
inoperable
inoperative
insalubrious
insensitive
insensitivity
inseparable
insignificant
insincere
insincerely
insincerity
insolubility
insoluble
instability
insubstantial
insufficiency
insufficient
insufficiently
insupportable
intangibility
intangible
intangibly
intolerable
intolerably
intolerance
intolerant
intractable
intransitive
invariable
invariably
inviable
invisibility
invisible
invisibly
involuntarily
involuntary
invulnerability
invulnerable
invulnerably

in·ad·ver·tent \ˌinəd'vərtᵊnt\ adj : unintentional —**in·ad·ver·tence** \-ᵊns\ n —**in·ad·ver·ten·cy** \-ᵊnsē\ n —**in·ad·ver·tent·ly** adv

in·alien·able \(ˈ)in'ālyənəbəl, -'āliənə-\ adj : incapable of being transferred or given up —**in·alien·abil·i·ty** \(ˌ)in,ālyənə'bilətē, -'āliənə-\ n —**in·alien·ably** adv

inane \in'ān\ adj inan·er; -est : silly or stupid —**inan·i·ty** \in'anətē\ n

in·an·i·mate \(ˈ)in'anəmət\ adj : not animate or animated —**in·an·i·mate·ly** adv —**in·an·i·mate·ness** n

in·a·ni·tion \ˌinə'nishən\ n : weakness from lack of food and water

in·ap·pre·cia·ble \ˌinə'prēshəbəl\ adj : too small to be perceived —**in·ap·pre·cia·bly** adv

in·ar·tic·u·late \ˌinär'tikyələt\ adj : without the power of speech or effective expression —**in·ar·tic·u·late·ly** adv

in·as·much as \ˌinəz,məchəz\ conj : because

in·at·ten·tion \ˌinə'tenchən\ n : failure to pay attention

in·au·gu·ral \in'ȯgyərəl, -g(ə)rəl\ adj : relating to an inauguration ~ n 1 : inaugural speech 2 : inauguration

in·au·gu·rate \in'ȯg(y)ə,rāt\ vb -rat·ed; -rat·ing 1 : install in office 2 : start —**in·au·gu·ra·tion** \-,ȯg(y)ə'rāshən\ n

in·board \'in,bōrd\ adv : inside a boat or ship —**inboard** adj

in·born \'in'bȯrn\ adj : present from birth

in·bred \'in'bred\ adj : inborn

in·breed·ing \'in,brēdin\ n : interbreeding of closely related individuals —**in·breed** \-'brēd\ vb

in·cal·cu·la·ble \(ˈ)in'kalkyələbəl\ adj : too large to be calculated —**in·cal·cu·la·bly** adv

in·can·des·cent \ˌinkən'desᵊnt\ adj 1 : glowing with heat 2 : brilliant —**in·can·des·cence** \-ᵊns\ n

in·can·ta·tion \ˌin,kan'tāshən\ n : use of spoken or sung charms or spells as a magic ritual

in·ca·pac·i·tate \ˌinkə'pasə,tāt\ vb -tat·ed; -tat·ing : disable

in·ca·pac·i·ty \ˌinkə'pasətē\ n, pl -ties : quality or state of being incapable

in·car·cer·ate \in'kärsə,rāt\ vb : imprison —**in·car·cer·a·tion** \(ˌ)in,kärsə'rāshən\ n

in·car·nate \in'kärnət, -,nāt\ adj : having bodily form and substance —**in·car·nate** \-,nāt\ vb —**in·car·na·tion** \-,kär'nāshən\ n

in·cen·di·ary \in'sende͟,erē\ *adj* 1 : pertaining to or used to ignite fire 2 : tending to excite —**incendiary** *n*

in·cense \'in,sens\ *n* : material burned to produce a fragrant odor or its smoke ~ \in'sens\ *vb* -censed; -cens·ing : make very angry

in·cen·tive \in'sentive\ *n* : inducement to do something

in·cep·tion \in'sepshən\ *n* : beginning

in·ces·sant \(')in'sesᵊnt\ *adj* : continuing without interruption —**in·ces·sant·ly** *adv*

in·cest \'in,sest\ *n* : sexual intercourse between close relatives —**in·ces·tu·ous** \in'seschəwəs\ *adj*

inch \'inch\ *n* : unit of length equal to 1/12 foot ~ *vb* : move by small degrees

in·cho·ate \in'kōət, 'inkə,wāt\ *adj* : new and not fully formed or ordered

in·ci·dent \'insədənt\ *n* : occurrence —**in·ci·dence** \-əns\ *n* —**incident** *adj*

in·ci·den·tal \,insə'dentᵊl\ *adj* 1 : subordinate, nonessential, or attendant 2 : met by chance ~ *n* 1 : something incidental 2 *pl* : minor expenses that are not itemized —**in·ci·den·tal·ly** *adv*

in·cin·er·ate \in'sinə,rāt\ *vb* -at·ed; -at·ing : burn to ashes —**in·cin·er·a·tor** \-,rāt-ər\ *n*

in·cip·i·ent \in'sipēənt\ *adj* : beginning to be or appear

in·cise \in'sīz\ *vb* -cised; -cis·ing : carve into

in·ci·sion \in'sizhən\ *n* : surgical wound

in·ci·sive \in'sīsiv\ *adj* : keen and discerning —**in·ci·sive·ly** *adv*

in·ci·sor \in'sīzər\ *n* : tooth for cutting

in·cite \in'sīt\ *vb* -cit·ed; -cit·ing : arouse to action —**in·cite·ment** *n*

in·ci·vil·i·ty \,insə'vilətē\ *n* : rudeness

in·clem·ent \(')in'klemənt\ *adj* : stormy —**in·clem·en·cy** \-mənsē\ *n*

in·cline \in'klīn\ *vb* -clined; -clin·ing 1 : bow 2 : tend toward an opinion 3 : slope ~ *n* : slope —**in·cli·na·tion** \,inklə'nāshən\ *n*

inclose, inclosure *var of* ENCLOSE, ENCLOSURE

in·clude \in'klüd\ *vb* -clud·ed; -clud·ing : take in or comprise —**in·clu·sion** \in'klüzhən\ *n* —**in·clu·sive** \-'klü-siv\ *adj*

in·cog·ni·to \,in,käg'nētō, in'kägnə,tō\ *adv or adj* : with one's identity concealed

in·come \'in,kəm\ *n* : money gained (as from work or investment)

in·com·ing \'in,kəmiŋ\ *adj* : coming in

in·com·mu·ni·ca·do \,inkə,myünə-'kädō\ *adv or adj* : without means of communication

in·com·pa·ra·ble \(')in'kämp(ə)rəbəl\ *adj* : eminent beyond comparison

in·com·pe·tent \(')in'kämpətənt\ *adj* : lacking sufficient knowledge or skill —**in·com·pe·tence** \-pətəns\ *n* —**in·com·pe·ten·cy** \-ənsē\ *n* —**incompetent** *n*

in·con·gru·ous \(')in'käŋgrəwəs\ *adj* : inappropriate or out of place —**in·con·gru·i·ty** \,inkən'grüətē, ,iŋkäŋ-\ *n* —**in·con·gru·ous·ly** *adv*

in·con·se·quen·tial \,in,känsə-'kwenchəl\ *adj* : unimportant —**in·con·se·quence** \(')in'känsə,kwens\ *n* —**in·con·se·quen·tial·ly** *adv*

in·con·sid·er·able \,inkən'sidər(ə)bəl, -'sidrəbəl\ *adj* : trivial

in·con·sol·able \,inkən'sōləbəl\ *adj* : incapable of being consoled —**in·con·sol·ably** *adv*

in·con·ve·nience \inkən'vēnyəns\ *n* 1 : discomfort 2 : something that causes trouble or annoyance ~ *vb* : cause inconvenience to —**in·con·ve·nient** \,inkən'vēnyənt\ *adj* —**in·con·ve·nient·ly** *adv*

in·cor·po·rate \in'kȯrpə,rāt\ *vb* -rat·ed; -rat·ing 1 : blend 2 : form into a legal body —**in·cor·po·rat·ed** *adj* —**in·cor·po·ra·tion** \-,kȯrpə'rāshən\ *n*

in·cor·ri·gi·ble \(')in'kȯrəjəbəl\ *adj* : incapable of being corrected or reformed —**in·cor·ri·gi·bil·i·ty** \(,)in,kȯrəjə'bilətē\ *n* —**in·cor·ri·gi·bly** \(')in'kȯrəjəblē\ *adv*

in·crease \in'krēs, 'in,krēs\ *vb* -creased; -creas·ing : make or become greater ~ \'in,-, in'-\ *n* 1 : enlargement in size 2 : something added —**in·creas·ing·ly** \-'krēsiŋlē\ *adv*

in·cred·i·ble \(')in'kredəbəl\ *adj* : too extraordinary to be believed —**in·cred·i·bil·i·ty** \(,)in,kredə'bilətē\ *n* —**in·cred·i·bly** \(')in'kredəblē\ *adv*

in·cred·u·lous \(')in'krejələs\ *adj* : skeptical —**in·cre·du·li·ty** \,in-kri'd(y)ülətē\ *n* —**in·cred·u·lous·ly** *adv*

in·cre·ment \'iŋkrəmənt, 'in-\ *n* : increase or amount of increase —**in·cre·men·tal** \,iŋkrə'mentᵊl, ,in-\ *adj*

in·crim·i·nate \in'krimə,nāt\ *vb* -nat·ed; -nat·ing : show to be guilty of a crime —**in·crim·i·na·tion** \-,krimə'nāshən\ *n* —**in·crim·i·na·to·ry** \-'krim(ə)nə,tōrē\ *adj* in·cu·bate \'iŋkyə₁bāt, 'in-\ vb -bat·ed; -bat·ing : keep (as eggs) under conditions favorable for development —in·cu·ba·tion \₁iŋkyə'bā-shən, ₁in-\ n —in·cu·ba·tor \'iŋkyə₁bātər, 'in-\ n

in·cul·cate \in'kəl₁kāt, 'in₁kəl-\ -cat·ed; -cat·ing : instill by repeated teaching —in·cul·ca·tion \₁in₁kəl'kāshən\ n

in·cum·bent \in'kəmbənt\ n : holder of an office ∼ adj : obligatory —in·cum·ben·cy \-bənsē\ n

in·cur \in'kər\ vb -rr- : become liable or subject to

in·cur·sion \in'kərzhən\ n : invasion

in·debt·ed \in'detəd\ adj : owing something —in·debt·ed·ness n

in·de·ci·sion \₁indi'sizhən\ n : inability to decide

in·deed \in'dēd\ adv : without question

in·de·fat·i·ga·ble \₁indi'fatigəbəl\ adj : not tiring —in·de·fat·i·ga·bly \-blē\ adv

in·def·i·nite \(')in'def(ə)nət\ adj 1 : not defining or identifying 2 : not precise 3 : having no fixed limit or amount —in·def·i·nite·ly adv

in·del·i·ble \in'deləbəl\ adj : not capable of being removed or erased —in·del·i·bly adv

in·del·i·cate \in'delikət\ adj : improper —in·del·i·ca·cy \in'deləkəsē\ n

in·dem·ni·fy \in'demnə₁fī\ vb -fied; -fy·ing : repay for a loss —in·dem·ni·fi·ca·tion \-₁demnəfə'kāshən\ n

in·dem·ni·ty \in'demnətē\ n, pl -ties : security against loss or damage

¹in·dent \in'dent\ vb : leave a space at the beginning of a paragraph —in·dent n

²indent vb : force inward so as to form a depression or dent

in·den·ta·tion \₁in₁den'tashən\ n 1 : notch, recess, or dent 2 : action of indenting 3 : space at the beginning of a paragraph

in·den·ture \in'denchər\ n : contract binding one person to work for another for a given period —usu. in pl. ∼ vb -tured; -tur·ing : bind by indentures

Independence Day n : July 4 observed as a legal holiday in commemoration of the adoption of the Declaration of Independence in 1776

in·de·pen·dent \₁ində'pendənt\ adj 1 : not governed by another 2 : not requiring or relying on something or somebody else 3 : not easily influenced —in·de·pen·dence \-dəns\ n

—independent n —in·de·pen·dent·ly adv

in·de·ter·mi·nate \₁indi'tərm(ə)nət\ adj : not definitely determined —in·de·ter·mi·na·cy \-(ə)nəsē\ n —in·de·ter·mi·nate·ly adv

in·dex \'in₁deks\ n, pl -dex·es or -di·ces \-də₁sēz\ 1 : alphabetical list of items (as topics in a book) 2 : a number that serves as a measure or indicator of something ∼ vb 1 : provide with an index 2 : serve as an index of

index finger n : forefinger

in·di·cate \'ində₁kāt\ vb -cat·ed; -cat·ing 1 : point out or to 2 : reveal or suggest 3 : state briefly —in·di·ca·tion \₁ində'kāshən\ n —in·di·ca·tor \'ində₁kātər\ n

in·dic·a·tive \in'dikətiv\ adj : serving to indicate

in·dict \in'dīt\ vb : charge with a crime —in·dict·able adj —in·dict·ment n

in·dif·fer·ent \in'difərnt, -'dif(ə)rənt\ adj 1 : having no preference 2 : showing neither interest nor dislike 3 : mediocre —in·dif·fer·ence \-'difərns, -'dif(ə)rəns\ n —in·dif·fer·ent·ly adv

in·dig·e·nous \in'dijənəs\ adj : native to a particular region

in·di·gent \'indijənt\ adj : needy —in·di·gence \-jəns\ n

in·di·ges·tion \₁indī'jeschən, -də-\ n : discomfort from inability to digest food

in·dig·na·tion \₁indig'nāshən\ n : anger aroused by something unjust or unworthy —in·dig·nant \in'dignənt\ adj —in·dig·nant·ly adv

in·dig·ni·ty \in'dignətē\ n, pl -ties 1 : offense against self-respect 2 : humiliating treatment

in·di·go \'indi₁gō\ n, pl -gos or -goes 1 : blue dye 2 : dark blue or violet color

in·di·rect \₁ində'rekt, -dī-\ adj : not straight or straightforward —in·di·rec·tion \-'rekshən\ n —in·di·rect·ly adv —in·di·rect·ness n

in·dis·crim·i·nate \₁indis'krimənət\ adj 1 : not careful or discriminating 2 : haphazard —in·dis·crim·i·nate·ly adv

in·dis·pens·able \₁indis'pensəbəl\ adj : absolutely essential —in·dis·pens·abil·i·ty \-₁pensə'bilətē\ n —in·dis·pensable n —in·dis·pens·ably \-'pensəblē\ adv

in·dis·posed \-'pōzd\ adj : slightly ill —in·dis·po·si·tion \(₁)in₁dispə-'zishən\ n

in·dis·sol·u·ble \,indis'älyəbəl\ *adj* : not capable of being dissolved or broken

in·di·vid·u·al \,ində'vij(əw)əl\ *n* 1 : single member of a category 2 : person —**individual** *adj* —**in·di·vid·u·al·ly** *adv*

in·di·vid·u·al·i·ty \-,vijə'walətē\ *n* : special quality that distinguishes an individual

in·di·vid·u·al·ize \-'vijə(wə),līz\ *vb* -**ized;** -**iz·ing** 1 : make individual 2 : treat individually

in·doc·tri·nate \in'däktrə,nāt\ *vb* -**nat·ed;** -**nat·ing** : instruct in fundamentals (as of a doctrine) —**in·doc·tri·na·tion** \(,)in,däktrə'nāshən\ *n*

in·do·lent \'indələnt\ *adj* : lazy —**in·do·lence** \-ləns\ *n*

in·dom·i·ta·ble \in'dämətəbəl\ *adj* : invincible —**in·dom·i·ta·bly** \-blē\ *adv*

in·door \'in,dōr\ *adj* : relating to the interior of a building

in·doors \in'dōrz\ *adv* : in or into a building

in·du·bi·ta·ble \(')in'd(y)übətəbəl\ *adj* : being beyond question —**in·du·bi·ta·bly** \-blē\ *adv*

in·duce \in'd(y)üs\ *vb* -**duced;** -**duc·ing** 1 : persuade 2 : bring about —**in·duce·ment** *n* —**in·duc·er** *n*

in·duct \in'dəkt\ *vb* 1 : put in office 2 : admit as a member 3 : enroll (as for military service) —**in·duct·ee** \(,)in,dək'tē\ *n*

in·duc·tion \in'dəkshən\ *n* 1 : act or instance of inducting 2 : reasoning from particular instances to a general conclusion

in·duc·tive \in'dəktiv\ *adj* : reasoning by induction

in·dulge \in'dəlj\ *vb* -**dulged;** -**dulg·ing** : yield to the desire of or for —**in·dul·gence** \-'dəljəns\ *n* —**in·dul·gent** \-jənt\ *adj* —**in·dul·gent·ly** *adv*

in·dus·tri·al \in'dəstrēəl\ *adj* : having to do with industry —**in·dus·tri·al·ist** \-ələst\ *n* —**in·dus·tri·al·iza·tion** \-,dəstrēələ'zāshən\ *n* —**in·dus·tri·al·ize** \-'dəstrēə,līz\ *vb* —**in·dus·tri·al·ly** \-ē\ *adv*

in·dus·tri·ous \in'dəstrēəs\ *adj* : diligent or busy —**in·dus·tri·ous·ly** *adv* —**in·dus·tri·ous·ness** *n*

in·dus·try \'in(,)dəstrē\ *n, pl* -**tries** 1 : diligence 2 : manufacturing enterprises or activity

in·e·bri·ate \in'ēbrē,āt\ *vb* -**at·ed;** -**at·ing** : make drunk ~ *n* : one who is drunk —**in·e·bri·a·tion** \-,ēbrē'ā·shən\ *n*

in·ef·fa·ble \(')in'efəbəl\ *adj* : incapable of being expressed in words —**in·ef·fa·bly** \-blē\ *adv*

in·ept \in'ept\ *adj* 1 : inappropriate or foolish 2 : generally incompetent —**in·ep·ti·tude** \in'eptə,t(y)üd\ *n* —**in·ept·ly** *adv* —**in·ept·ness** *n*

in·equal·i·ty \ini'kwälətē\ *n* : quality of being unequal or uneven

in·ert \in'ərt\ *adj* 1 : powerless to move or act 2 : sluggish —**in·ert·ly** *adv* —**in·ert·ness** *n*

in·er·tia \in'ərsh(ē)ə\ *n* : tendency of matter to remain at rest or in motion —**in·er·tial** \-shəl\ *adj*

in·es·cap·able \,inə'skāpəbəl\ *adj* : inevitable —**in·es·cap·ably** \-blē\ *adv*

in·es·ti·ma·ble \(')in'estəməbəl\ *adj* : incapable of being estimated —**in·es·ti·ma·bly** \-blē\ *adv*

in·ev·i·ta·ble \in'evətəbəl\ *adj* : incapable of being avoided or escaped —**in·ev·i·ta·bil·i·ty** \(,)in,evətə'bilətē\ *n* —**in·ev·i·ta·bly** \in'evətəblē\ *adv*

in·ex·cus·able \,inik'skyüzəbəl\ *adj* : being without excuse or justification —**in·ex·cus·ably** \-blē\ *adv*

in·ex·haust·ible \,inig'zóstəbəl\ *adj* : incapable of being used up or tired out —**in·ex·haust·ibly** \-blē\ *adv*

in·ex·o·ra·ble \(')in'eks(ə)rəbəl\ *adj* : unyielding or relentless —**in·ex·o·ra·bly** *adv*

in·fal·li·ble \(')in'faləbəl\ *adj* : incapable of error —**in·fal·li·bil·i·ty** \(,)in,falə'bilətē\ *n* —**in·fal·li·bly** *adv*

in·fa·mous \'infəməs\ *adj* : having the worst kind of reputation —**in·fa·mous·ly** *adv*

in·fa·my \-mē\ *n, pl* -**mies** : evil reputation

in·fan·cy \'infənsē\ *n, pl* -**cies** 1 : early childhood 2 : early period of existence

in·fant \'infənt\ *n* : baby

in·fan·tile \'infən,tīl, -,tᵊl, -,tēl\ *adj* : relating to infants

in·fan·try \'infəntrē\ *n, pl* -**tries** : soldiers that fight on foot

in·fat·u·ate \in'facha,wāt\ *vb* -**at·ed;** -**at·ing** : inspire with foolish love or admiration —**in·fat·u·a·tion** \-,facha'wāshən\ *n*

in·fect \in'fekt\ *vb* : contaminate with disease-producing matter —**in·fec·tion** \-'fekshən\ *n* —**in·fec·tious** \-shəs\ *adj* —**in·fec·tive** \-'fektiv\ *adj*

in·fer \in'fər\ *vb* -**rr-** : deduce —**in·fer·ence** \'inf(ə)rəns\ *n* —**in·fer·en·tial** \,infə'renchəl\ *adj*

in·fe·ri·or \in'firēər\ adj : being lower in position, degree, rank, or merit —**inferior** n —**in·fe·ri·or·i·ty** \(,)in,firē'òrətē\ n

in·fer·nal \in'fərn°l\ adj : of or like hell—often used as a general expression of disapproval —**in·fer·nal·ly** adv

in·fer·no \in'fərnō\ n, pl -nos : place or condition suggesting hell

in·fest \in'fest\ vb : swarm or grow in or over —**in·fes·ta·tion** \,infes'tāshən\ n

in·fi·del \'infəd°l, -fə,del\ n : one who does not believe in a particular religion

in·fi·del·i·ty \,infə'delətē, -fī-\ n, pl -ties : lack of faithfulness

in·field \'in,fēld\ n : baseball field inside the base lines —**in·field·er** n

in·fil·trate \in'fil,trāt, 'in(,)fil-\ vb -trat·ed; -trat·ing : enter or become established in without being noticed —**in·fil·tra·tion** \,in(,)fil'trāshən\ n

in·fi·nite \'infənət\ adj 1 : having no limit or extending indefinitely 2 : vast —**infinite** n —**in·fi·nite·ly** adv —**in·fi·ni·tude** \in'finə,t(y)üd\ n

in·fin·i·tes·i·mal \(,)in,finə'tesəməl\ adj : very minute —**in·fin·i·tes·i·mal·ly** adv

in·fin·i·tive \in'finətiv\ n : verb form in English usu. used with to

in·fin·i·ty \in'finətē\ n, pl -ties 1 : quality or state of being infinite 2 : indefinitely great number or amount

in·firm \in'fərm\ adj : feeble from age —**in·fir·mi·ty** \-'fərmətē\ n

in·fir·ma·ry \in'fərm(ə)rē\ n, pl -ries : place for the care of the sick

in·flame \in'flām\ vb -flamed; -flam·ing 1 : excite to intense action or feeling 2 : affect or become affected with inflammation —**in·flam·ma·to·ry** \-'flamə,tōrē\ adj

in·flam·ma·ble \in'flaməbəl\ adj : flammable

in·flam·ma·tion \,inflə'māshən\ n : response to injury in which an affected area becomes red and painful and congested with blood

in·flate \in'flāt\ vb -flat·ed; -flat·ing 1 : swell or puff up (as with gas) 2 : expand or increase abnormally —**in·flat·able** adj

in·fla·tion \in'flāshən\ n 1 : act of inflating 2 : abnormal increase in the volume of money and credit with a continuing rise in prices —**in·fla·tion·ary** \-shə,nerē\ adj

in·flec·tion \in'flekshən\ n 1 : change in pitch or loudness of the voice 2

: change in form of a word —**in·flect** \-'flekt\ vb —**in·flec·tion·al** \-'flekshənəl\ adj

in·flict \in'flikt\ vb : give by or as if hitting —**in·flic·tion** \-'flikshən\ n

in·flu·ence \'in,flüəns\ n 1 : power or capacity of causing an effect in indirect or intangible ways : one that exerts influence ∼ vb -enced; -enc·ing : affect or alter by influence —**in·flu·en·tial** \,inflü'enchəl\ adj

in·flu·en·za \,inflü'enzə\ n : acute very contagious virus disease

in·flux \'in,fləks\ n : a flowing in

in·form \in'fòrm\ vb : give information or knowledge to —**in·for·mant** \-mənt\ n —**in·form·er** n

in·for·mal \in'fòrməl\ adj 1 : without formality or ceremony 2 : for ordinary or familiar use —**in·for·mal·i·ty** \,infòr'malətē, -fər-\ n —**in·for·mal·ly** adv

in·for·ma·tion \,infər'māshən\ n : knowledge obtained from investigation, study, or instruction —**in·for·ma·tion·al** \-sh(ə)nəl\ adj

in·for·ma·tive \in'fòrmətiv\ adj : giving knowledge

in·frac·tion \in'frakshən\ n : violation

in·fra·red \,infrə'red\ adj : being, relating to, or using invisible heat rays having wavelengths longer than those of red light —**infrared** n

in·fringe \in'frinj\ vb -fringed; -fring·ing : violate another's right or privilege —**in·fringe·ment** n

in·fu·ri·ate \in'fyürē,āt\ vb -at·ed; -at·ing : make furious —**in·fu·ri·at·ing·ly** \-,ātiŋlē\ adv

in·fuse \in'fyüz\ vb -fused; -fus·ing 1 : instill a principle or quality in 2 : steep in liquid without boiling —**in·fu·sion** \-'fyüzhən\ n

¹-ing \iŋ\ vb suffix or adj suffix —used to form the present participle and sometimes an adjective resembling a present participle

²-ing n suffix 1 : action or process 2 : something connected with or resulting from an action or process

in·ge·nious \in'jēnyəs\ adj : very clever —**in·ge·nious·ly** adv —**in·ge·nious·ness** n

in·ge·nue or **in·gé·nue** \'anjə,nü, 'än-; 'aⁿzhə-, 'äⁿ-\ n : naive young woman

in·ge·nu·ity \,injə'n(y)üətē\ n, pl -ities : skill or cleverness in planning or inventing

in·gen·u·ous \in'jenyəwəs\ adj : innocent and candid —**in·gen·u·ous·ly** adv —**in·gen·u·ous·ness** n in-gest \in'jest\ vb : eat —in-ges-tion \-'jeschən\ n

in-gle-nook \'ingəl,núk\ n : corner by the fireplace

in-got \'ingət\ n : block of metal

in-grained \(')in'grānd\ adj : deep-seated

in-grate \'in,grāt\ n : ungrateful person

in-gra-ti-ate \in'grāshē,āt\ vb -at-ed; -at-ing : gain favor for (oneself) —in-gra-ti-at-ing-ly adv

in-gre-di-ent \in'grēdēənt\ n : one of the substances that make up a mixture

in-grown \'in,grōn\ adj : grown in and esp. into the flesh

in-hab-it \in'habət\ vb : live or dwell in —in-hab-it-able adj —in-hab-it-ant \-ətənt\ n

in-hale \in'hāl\ vb -haled; -hal-ing : breathe in —in-hal-ant \-ənt\ n —in-ha-la-tion \,in(h)ə'lāshən\ n —in-hal-er n

in-here \in'hir\ vb -hered; -her-ing : be inherent

in-her-ent \in'hirənt, -'her-\ adj : being an essential part of something —in-her-ent-ly adv

in-her-it \in'herət\ vb : receive from one's ancestors —in-her-i-tance \-ətəns\ n —in-her-i-tor \-ətər\ n

in-hib-it \in'hibət\ vb : hold in check —in-hi-bi-tion \,in(h)ə'bishən\ n

in-hu-man \in'(')in'(h)yümən\ adj : cruel or impersonal —in-hu-man-i-ty \-(h)yü'manətē\ n —in-hu-man-ly adv

in-im-i-cal \in'imikəl\ adj : hostile or harmful —in-im-i-cal-ly adv

in-im-i-ta-ble \(')in'imətəbəl\ adj : not capable of being imitated

in-iq-ui-ty \in'ikwətē\ n, pl -ties : wickedness —in-iq-ui-tous \-wətəs\ adj

ini-tial \in'ishəl\ adj 1 : of or relating to the beginning 2 : first ~ n : 1st letter of a word or name ~ vb -tialed or -tialled; -tial-ing or -tial-ling : put initials on —in-i-tial-ly adv

ini-ti-ate \in'ishē,āt\ vb -at-ed; -at-ing 1 : start 2 : induct into membership —initiate \-ish(ē)ət\ n —in-i-ti-a-tion \-,ishē'āshən\ n —in-i-tia-to-ry \-'ishēə,tōrē\ adj

ini-tia-tive \in'ishətiv\ n 1 : first step 2 : readiness to undertake something on one's own

in-ject \in'jekt\ vb : force or introduce into something —in-jec-tion \-'jekshən\ n

in-junc-tion \in'jəŋkshən\ n : court writ requiring one to do or to refrain from doing a specified act

in-jure \'injər\ vb -jured; -jur-ing : do damage, hurt, or a wrong to

in-ju-ry \'inj(ə)rē\ n, pl -ries 1 : act that injures 2 : hurt, damage, or loss sustained —in-ju-ri-ous \in'júrēəs\ adj

in-jus-tice \(')in'jəstəs\ n : unjust act

ink \'iŋk\ n : usu. liquid and colored material for writing and printing ~ vb : put ink on —ink-well \-,wel\ n —inky adj

in-kling \'iŋkliŋ\ n : hint or idea

in-land \'in,land, -lənd\ n : interior of a country —inland adj or adv

in-law \'in,lò\ n : relative by marriage

in-lay \(')in'lā, 'in,lā\ vb -laid \-'lād\; -lay-ing : set into a surface for decoration ~ \'in,lā\ n 1 : inlaid work 2 : shaped filling cemented into a tooth

in-let \'in,let, -lət\ n : bay or recess in a shore

in-mate \'in,māt\ n : person confined to an asylum or prison

in me-mo-ri-am \,inmə'mōrēəm\ prep : in memory of

in-most \'in,mōst\ adj : deepest within

inn \'in\ n : hotel

in-nards \'inərdz\ n pl : internal parts

in-nate \in'āt\ adj 1 : inborn 2 : inherent —in-nate-ly adv

in-ner \'inər\ adj : being on the inside

in-ner-most \'inər,mōst\ adj : farthest inward

in-ner-sole \,inər'sōl\ n : insole

in-ning \'iniŋ\ n : baseball team's turn at bat

inn-keep-er \'in,kēpər\ n : owner of an inn

in-no-cent \'inəsənt\ adj 1 : free from guilt 2 : harmless 3 : not sophisticated —in-no-cence \-səns\ n —in-no-cent n —in-no-cent-ly adv

in-noc-u-ous \in'äkyəwəs\ adj 1 : harmless 2 : inoffensive

in-no-va-tion \,inə'vāshən\ n : new idea or method —in-no-va-tive \'inə,vātiv\ adj —in-no-va-tor \-,vātər\ n

in-nu-en-do \,inyə'wendō\ n, pl -dos or -does : insinuation

in-nu-mer-a-ble \in'(y)üm(ə)rəbəl\ adj : countless

in-oc-u-late \in'äkyə,lāt\ vb -lat-ed; -lat-ing : treat with something esp. to establish immunity —in-oc-u-la-tion \-,äkyə'lāshən\ n

in-op-por-tune \(,)in,äpər't(y)ün\ adj : happening at the wrong time —in-op-por-tune-ly adv in·or·di·nate \in'ȯrdnət, -ᵊnət\ adj : unusual or excessive —in·or·di·nate·ly adv

in·or·gan·ic \,in,ȯr'ganik\ adj : made of mineral matter

in·pa·tient \'in,pāshənt\ n : patient who stays in a hospital

in·put \'in,pu̇t\ n : something put in —input vb

in·quest \'in,kwest\ n : inquiry esp. before a jury

in·quire \in'kwī(ə)r\ vb -quired; -quiring 1 : ask 2 : investigate —in·quir·er n —in·quir·ing·ly adv —in·qui·ry \'in,kwī(ə)rē, in'kwī(ə)rē; 'inkwərē, 'iṇ-\ n

in·qui·si·tion \,inkwə'zishən, ,iṇ-\ n 1 : official inquiry 2 : severe questioning —in·quis·i·tor \in'kwizətər\ n —in·quis·i·to·ri·al \-,kwizə'tōrēəl\ adj

in·quis·i·tive \in'kwizətiv\ adj : curious —in·quis·i·tive·ly adv —in·quis·i·tive·ness n

in·road \'in,rōd\ n : encroachment

in·rush \'in,rəsh\ n : influx

in·sane \(')in'sān\ adj 1 : not sane 2 : foolish —in·sane·ly adv —in·san·i·ty \in'sanətē\ n

in·sa·tia·ble \(')in'sāshəbəl\ adj : incapable of being satisfied

in·sa·tiate \(')in'sāsh(ē)ət\ adj : insatiable

in·scribe \in'skrīb\ vb 1 : write 2 : engrave 3 : dedicate (a book) to someone —in·scrip·tion \-'skripshən\ n

in·scru·ta·ble \in'skrütəbəl\ adj : mysterious —in·scru·ta·bly adv

in·seam \'in,sēm\ n : inner seam (of a garment)

in·sect \'in,sekt\ n : small usu. winged animal with 6 legs

in·sec·ti·cide \in'sektə,sīd\ n : insect poison —in·sec·ti·cid·al \(,)in,sektə'sīdᵊl\ adj

in·se·cure \,insi'kyu̇r\ adj 1 : uncertain 2 : unsafe 3 : fearful —in·se·cure·ly adv —in·se·cu·ri·ty \-'kyu̇rətē\ n

in·sem·i·nate \in'semə,nāt\ vb -nat·ed; -nat·ing : introduce semen into —in·sem·i·na·tion \-,semə'nāshən\ n

in·sen·si·ble \(')in'sensəbəl\ adj 1 : unconscious 2 : unable to feel 3 : unaware —in·sen·si·bil·i·ty \(,)in,sensə'bilətē\ n —in·sen·si·bly adv

in·sen·tient \(')in'sench(ē)ənt\ adj : lacking feeling —in·sen·tience \-ch(ē)əns\ n

in·sert \in'sərt\ vb : put in —insert \'in,sərt\ n —in·ser·tion \in'sərshən\ n

in·set \'in,set\ vb inset or in·set·ted; in·set·ting : set in —inset n

in·shore \'in'shȯr\ adj 1 : situated near shore 2 : moving toward shore ~ adv : toward shore

in·side \in'sīd, 'in,sīd\ n 1 : inner side 2 pl : innards ~ prep 1 : in or into the inside of 2 : before the end of ~ adv 1 : on the inner side 2 : into the interior —inside adj —in·sid·er \in'sīdər\ n

inside of prep : inside

in·sid·i·ous \in'sidēəs\ adj 1 : treacherous 2 : seductive —in·sid·i·ous·ly adv —in·sid·i·ous·ness n

in·sight \'in,sīt\ n : understanding —in·sight·ful \'in,sītfəl, in'sīt-\ adj

in·sig·nia \in'signēə\, in·sig·ne \-(,)nē\ n, pl -nia or -ni·as : badge of authority or office

in·sin·u·ate \in'sinyə,wāt\ vb -at·ed; -at·ing 1 : imply 2 : bring in artfully —in·sin·u·a·tion \(,)in,sinyə'wāshən\ n

in·sip·id \in'sipəd\ adj 1 : tasteless 2 : not stimulating —in·si·pid·i·ty \,in-sə'pidətē\ n

in·sist \in'sist\ vb : be firmly demanding —in·sis·tence \in'sistəns\ n —in·sis·tent \-tənt\ adj —in·sis·tent·ly adv

insofar as \,insə'färəz\ conj : to the extent that

in·sole \'in,sōl\ n : inside sole of a shoe

in·so·lent \'insələnt\ adj : contemptuously rude —in·so·lence \-ləns\ n

in·sol·vent \(')in'sälvənt\ adj : unable or insufficient to pay debts —in·sol·ven·cy \-vənsē\ n

in·som·nia \in'sämnēə\ n : inability to sleep

in·so·much \,insə'məch\ adv : to such a degree

in·sou·ci·ance \in'süsēəns, aⁿsüsyäⁿs\ n : lighthearted indifference —in·sou·ci·ant \in'süsēənt, aⁿsüsyäⁿ\ adj

in·spect \in'spekt\ vb : view closely and critically —in·spec·tion \-'spekshən\ n —in·spec·tor \-tər\ n

in·spire \in'spī(ə)r\ vb -spired; -spir·ing 1 : inhale 2 : influence by example 3 : bring about 4 : stir to action —in·spi·ra·tion \,inspə'rāshən\ n —in·spi·ra·tion·al \-'rāsh(ə)nəl\ adj —in·spir·er n

in·stall, in·stal \in'stȯl\ vb -stalled; -stall·ing 1 : induct into office 2 : set up for use —in·stal·la·tion \,instə'lāshən\ n

in·stall·ment \in'stȯlmənt\ n : partial payment

in·stance \'instəns\ *n* **1** : request or instigation **2** : example

in·stant \'instənt\ *n* : moment ~ *adj* **1** : immediate **2** : ready to mix —**in·stan·ta·neous** \ˌinstən'tānēəs, adj\ —**in·stan·ta·neous·ly** *adv* —**in·stant·ly** *adv*

in·stead \in'sted\ *adv* : as a substitute or alternative

instead of \in,steda(v), ˌ-stid-\ *prep* : as a substitute for or alternative to

in·step \'in,step\ *n* : part of the foot in front of the ankle

in·sti·gate \'instəˌgāt\ *vb* -**gat·ed**; -**gat·ing** : incite —**in·sti·ga·tion** \ˌinstə'gāshən\ *n* —**in·sti·ga·tor** \'instəˌgātər\ *n*

in·still \in'stil\ *vb* -**stilled**; -**still·ing** : impart gradually

in·stinct \'in,stiŋkt\ *n* **1** : natural talent **2** : natural inherited or subconsciously motivated behavior —**in·stinc·tive** \in'stiŋktiv\ *adj* —**in·stinc·tive·ly** *adv*

in·sti·tute \'instəˌt(y)üt\ *vb* -**tut·ed**; -**tut·ing** **1** : establish **2** : start ~ *n* **1** : organization promoting a cause **2** : school

in·sti·tu·tion \ˌinstə't(y)üshən\ *n* **1** : act of instituting **2** : custom **3** : corporation or society of a public character —**in·sti·tu·tion·al** \-'t(y)üsh(ə)nəl\ *adj* —**in·sti·tu·tion·al·ize** \-ˌīz\ *vb* —**in·sti·tu·tion·al·ly** \-ē\ *adv*

in·struct \in'strəkt\ *vb* : teach —**in·struc·tion** \in'strəkshən\ *n* —**in·struc·tion·al** \-sh(ə)nəl\ *adj* —**in·struc·tive** \in'strəktiv\ *adj* —**in·struc·tor** \in'strəktər\ *n* —**in·struc·tor·ship** *n*

in·stru·ment \'instrəmənt\ *n* **1** : means **2** : implement **3** : something that produces music **4** : legal document **5** : device for controlling or regulating something —**in·stru·men·tal** \ˌinstrə'mentᵊl\ *adj* —**in·stru·men·tal·ist** \-əst, -ˌn-\ *n* —**in·stru·men·tal·i·ty** \ˌinstrəmən'talətē, ˌ-ˌmen-\ *n* —**in·stru·men·ta·tion** \ˌinstrəmən'tāshən, -ˌmen-\ *n*

in·sub·or·di·nate \ˌinsə'bördᵊnət, -ᵊnət\ *adj* : not obeying —**in·sub·or·di·na·tion** \-ˌbördᵊn'āshən\ *n*

in·suf·fer·able \(')in'səf(ə)rəbəl\ *adj* : unbearable —**in·suf·fer·ably** \-blē\ *adv*

in·su·lar \'ins(y)ələr, 'inshələr\ *adj* **1** : relating to an island **2** : isolated **3** : narrow-minded —**in·su·lar·i·ty** \ˌins(y)ə'larətē, ˌinshə'lar-\ *n*

in·su·late \'insəˌlāt\ *vb* -**lat·ed**; -**lat·ing** : protect from heat loss or electricity —**in·su·la·tion** \ˌinsə'lāshən\ *n* —**in·su·la·tor** \'insəˌlātər\ *n*

in·su·lin \'ins(ə)lən\ *n* : hormone used by diabetics

in·sult \in'səlt\ *vb* : treat with contempt ~ \'inˌsəlt\ *n* : insulting act or remark —**in·sult·ing·ly** \-iŋlē\ *adv*

in·su·per·a·ble \(')in'süp(ə)rəbəl\ *adj* : too difficult —**in·su·per·a·bly** \-blē\ *adv*

in·sure \in'shùr\ *vb* -**sured**; -**sur·ing 1** : guarantee against loss **2** : make certain —**in·sur·able** \-əbəl\ *adj* —**in·sur·ance** \-ᵊns\ *n* —**in·sured** \in'shùrd\ *n* —**in·sur·er** *n*

in·sur·gent \in'sərjənt\ *n* : rebel —**in·sur·gence** \-jəns\ *n* —**in·sur·gen·cy** \-jənsē\ *n* —**in·sur·gent** *adj*

in·sur·mount·able \ˌinsər'maùntəbəl\ *adj* : too great to be overcome —**in·sur·mount·ably** \-blē\ *adv*

in·sur·rec·tion \ˌinsə'rekshən\ *n* : revolution —**in·sur·rec·tion·ist** *n*

in·tact \in'takt\ *adj* : undamaged

in·take \'in,tāk\ *n* **1** : opening through which something enters **2** : act of taking in **3** : amount taken in

in·te·ger \'intijər\ *n* : number that is not a fraction and does not include a fraction

in·te·gral \'intigrəl\ *adj* : essential

in·te·grate \'intəˌgrāt\ *vb* -**grat·ed**; -**grat·ing 1** : unite **2** : end segregation of or at —**in·te·gra·tion** \ˌintə'grāshən\ *n*

in·teg·ri·ty \in'tegrətē\ *n* **1** : soundness **2** : adherence to a code of values **3** : completeness

in·tel·lect \'intᵊlˌekt\ *n* : power of knowing or thinking —**in·tel·lec·tu·al** \ˌintᵊl'ekch(əw)əl\ *adj or n* —**in·tel·lec·tu·al·ism** \-chə(wə)ˌlizəm\ *n* —**in·tel·lec·tu·al·ly** *adv*

in·tel·li·gence \in'teləjəns\ *n* **1** : ability to learn and understand **2** : information

in·tel·li·gent \in'teləjənt\ *adj* : having or showing intelligence —**in·tel·li·gent·ly** *adv*

in·tel·li·gi·ble \in'teləjəbəl\ *adj* : understandable —**in·tel·li·gi·bil·i·ty** \-ˌteləjə'bilətē\ *n* —**in·tel·li·gi·bly** *adv*

in·tem·per·ance \(')in'temp(ə)rəns\ *n* : lack of moderation —**in·tem·per·ate** \-p(ə)rət\ *adj* —**in·tem·per·ate·ness** *n*

in·tend \in'tend\ *vb* : have as a purpose

in·tend·ed \-'tendəd\ *n* : engaged person —**intended** *adj*

in-tense \in'tens\ adj 1 : extreme 2 : deeply felt —in-tense-ly adv —in-ten-si-fi-ca-tion \-ˌtensəfə'kāshən\ n —in-ten-si-fy \-'tensəˌfī\ vb —in-ten-si-ty \in'tensətē\ n —in-ten-sive \in'tensiv\ adj —in-ten-sive-ly adv

1in-tent \in'tent\ n : purpose —in-ten-tion \-'tenchən\ n —in-ten-tion-al \-'tench(ə)nəl\ adj —in-ten-tion-al-ly adv

2intent adj : concentrated —in-tent-ly adv —in-tent-ness n

in-ter \in'tər\ vb -rr- : bury

inter- prefix : between or among

interagency
interatomic
interbank
interborough
interbusiness
intercampus
interchurch
intercity
interclass
intercoastal
intercollegiate
intercolonial
intercommunal
intercommunity
intercompany
intercontinental
intercounty
intercultural
interdenomina-
tional
interdepart-
mental
interdivisional
interelectronic
interethnic
interfaculty
interfamily
interfiber
interfraternity
intergalactic
intergang
intergovern-
mental
intergroup
interhemispheric
interindustry
interinstitutional
interisland
interlibrary
intermolecular
intermountain
interoceanic
interoffice
interparticle
interparty
interpersonal
interplanetary
interpopulation
interprovincial
interpupil
interracial
interregional
interreligious
interscholastic
intersectional
interstate
interstellar
intersystem
interterm
interterminal
intertribal
intertroop
intertropical
interuniversity
interurban
intervalley
intervillage
interwar
interzonal
interzone

in-ter-ac-tion \ˌintər'akshən\ n : mutual influence —in-ter-act \-'akt\ vb

in-ter-breed \ˌintər'brēd\ vb -bred \-'bred\; -breed-ing : breed together

in-ter-ca-late \in'tərkəˌlāt\ vb -lat-ed; -lat-ing : insert —in-ter-ca-la-tion \-ˌtərkə'lāshən\ n

in-ter-cede \ˌintər'sēd\ vb -ced-ed; -ced-ing : act to reconcile —in-ter-ces-sion \-'seshən\ n —in-ter-ces-sor

\-'sesər\ n —in-ter-ces-so-ry \-'ses(ə)rē\ adj

in-ter-cept \ˌintər'sept\ vb : interrupt the progress of —intercept \'intərˌsept\ n —in-ter-cep-tion \ˌintər'sepshən\ n —in-ter-cep-tor \-'septər\ n

in-ter-change \ˌintər'chānj\ vb 1 : exchange 2 : change places ~ \'intərˌchānj\ n 1 : exchange 2 : junction of highways —in-ter-change-able \ˌintər'chānjəbəl\ adj

in-ter-course \'intərˌkōrs\ n 1 : relations between persons or nations 2 : copulation

in-ter-de-pen-dent \ˌintərdi'pendənt\ adj : mutually dependent —in-ter-de-pen-dence \-dəns\ n

in-ter-dict \ˌintər'dikt\ vb : prohibit —in-ter-dic-tion \-'dikshən\ n

in-ter-est \'int(ə)rəst, -tərest\ n 1 : right 2 : benefit 3 : charge for borrowed money 4 pl : group financially involved in something 5 : readiness to pay special attention 6 : quality that causes interest ~ vb 1 : concern 2 : get the attention of —in-ter-est-ing adj —in-ter-est-ing-ly adv

in-ter-face \'intərˌfās\ n : common boundary —in-ter-fa-cial \ˌintər'fāshəl\ adj

in-ter-fere \ˌintə(r)'fiər\ vb -fered; -fer-ing 1 : collide or be in opposition 2 : try to run the affairs of others —in-ter-fer-ence \-'firəns\ n

in-ter-im \'intərəm\ n : time between —interim adj

in-te-ri-or \in'tirēər\ adj : being on the inside ~ n 1 : inside 2 : inland area

in-ter-ject \ˌintər'jekt\ vb : stick in between

in-ter-jec-tion \-'jekshən\ n : an exclamatory word —in-ter-jec-tion-al-ly \-sh(ə)nəlē\ adv

in-ter-lace \ˌintər'lās\ vb : cross or cause to cross one over another

in-ter-lard \ˌintər'lärd\ vb : intersperse

in-ter-lin-ear \ˌintər'linēər\ adj : between written or printed lines

in-ter-lock \ˌintər'läk\ vb 1 : interlace 2 : connect for mutual effect —in-ter-lock \'intərˌläk\ n

in-ter-lope \ˌintər'lōp\ vb -loped; -lop-ing 1 : encroach 2 : interfere —in-ter-lop-er n

in-ter-lude \'intərˌlüd\ n : intervening period

in-ter-mar-ry \ˌintər'marē\ vb 1 : marry each other 2 : marry within a group —in-ter-mar-riage \-'marij\ n

in-ter-me-di-ary \ˌintər'mēdēˌerē\ n, pl

-ar·ies : agent between individuals or groups —**intermediary** adj

in·ter·me·di·ate \,intər'mēdēət\ adj : between extremes —**intermediate** n

in·ter·ment \in'tərmənt\ n : burial

in·ter·mi·na·ble \(')in'tərm(ə)nəbəl\ adj : endless —**in·ter·mi·na·bly** adv

in·ter·min·gle \,intər'mingəl\ vb : mingle

in·ter·mis·sion \,intər'mishən\ n : break in a performance

in·ter·mit·tent \-'mit²nt\ adj : coming at intervals —**in·ter·mit·tent·ly** adv

in·ter·mix \,intər'miks\ vb : mix together —**in·ter·mix·ture** \-'mikschər\ n

¹in·tern \'in,tərn, in'tərn\ vb : confine —**in·tern·ee** \,in,tər'nē\ n —**in·tern·ment** n

²in·tern, in·terne \'in,tərn\ n : advanced student (as in medicine) gaining supervised experience — vb : act as an intern —**in·tern·ship** n

in·ter·nal \in'tərn²l\ adj 1 : inward 2 : inside of the body 3 : relating to or existing in the mind —**in·ter·nal·ly** adv

in·ter·na·tion·al \,intər'nash(ə)nəl\ adj : affecting 2 or more nations ~ n : something having international scope —**in·ter·na·tion·al·ism** \-,izəm\ n —**in·ter·na·tion·al·ize** \-,īz\ vb —**in·ter·na·tion·al·ly** adv

in·ter·nist \'in,tərnəst\ n : specialist in nonsurgical medicine

in·ter·play \'intər,plā\ n : interaction

in·ter·po·late \in'tərpə,lāt\ vb -**lat·ed; -lat·ing** : insert —**in·ter·po·la·tion** \-,tərpə'lāshən\ n

in·ter·pose \,intər'pōz\ vb -**posed; -pos·ing** 1 : place between 2 : intrude —**in·ter·po·si·tion** \-pə'zishən\ n

in·ter·pret \in'tərprət\ vb : explain the meaning of —**in·ter·pre·ta·tion** \in,tərprə'tāshən\ n —**in·ter·pre·ta·tive** \-'tərprə,tātiv\ adj —**in·ter·pret·er** n —**in·ter·pre·tive** \-'tərprətiv\ adj

in·ter·re·late \,intə(r)ri'lāt\ vb : have a mutual relationship —**in·ter·re·lat·ed·ness** \-'lātədnəs\ n —**in·ter·re·la·tion** \-'lāshən\ n —**in·ter·re·la·tion·ship** n

in·ter·ro·gate \in'terə,gāt\ vb -**gat·ed; -gat·ing** : question —**in·ter·ro·ga·tion** \-,terə'gāshən\ n —**in·ter·rog·a·tive** \,intə'rägətiv\ adj or n —**in·ter·ro·ga·tor** \-'terə,gātər\ n —**in·ter·rog·a·to·ry** \,intə'räga,tōrē\ adj

in·ter·rupt \,intə'rəpt\ vb : intrude so as to hinder or end continuity —**in·ter·rupt·er** n —**in·ter·rup·tion**

\-'rəpshən\ n —**in·ter·rup·tive** \-'rəptiv\ adv

in·ter·sect \,intər'sekt\ vb 1 : cut across or divide 2 : cross —**in·ter·sec·tion** \-'sekshən\ n

in·ter·sperse \,intər'spərs\ vb -**spersed; -spers·ing** : insert at intervals —**in·ter·sper·sion** \-'spərzhən\ n

in·ter·stice \in'tərstəs\ n, pl -**stic·es** \-stə,sēz, -stəsəz\ : space between —**in·ter·sti·tial** \,intər'stishəl\ adj

in·ter·twine \,intər'twīn\ vb : twist together

in·ter·val \'intərvəl\ n 1 : time between 2 : space between

in·ter·vene \,intər'vēn\ vb -**vened; -ven·ing** 1 : happen between events 2 : intercede —**in·ter·ven·tion** \-'venchən\ n

in·ter·view \'intər,vyü\ n : a meeting to get information —**interview** vb —**in·ter·view·er** n

in·ter·weave \,intər'wēv\ vb -**wove** \-'wōv\, -**wo·ven** \-'wōvən\; -**weav·ing** : weave together —**in·ter·wo·ven** \-'wōvən\ adj

in·tes·tate \in'tes,tāt, -tət\ adj : not leaving a will

in·tes·tine \in'testən\ n : tubular part of the digestive system after the stomach including a long narrow upper part (**small intestine**) followed by a broader shorter lower part (**large intestine**) —**in·tes·ti·nal** \-'ton²l\ adj

in·ti·mate \'intə,māt\ vb -**mat·ed; -mat·ing** : hint ~ \-'intəmət\ adj 1 : very friendly 2 : suggesting privacy 3 : very personal ~ n : close friend —**in·ti·ma·cy** \'intəməsē\ n —**in·ti·mate·ly** adv —**in·ti·ma·tion** \,intə'māshən\ n

in·tim·i·date \in'timə,dāt\ vb -**dat·ed; -dat·ing** : make fearful —**in·tim·i·da·tion** \-,timə'dāshən\ n

in·to \'intə, 'intü\ prep 1 : to the inside of 2 : to the condition of 3 : against

in·to·na·tion \,intə'nāshən\ n : way of singing or speaking

in·tone \in'tōn\ vb -**toned; -ton·ing** : chant

in·tox·i·cate \in'täksə,kāt\ vb -**cat·ed; -cat·ing** : make drunk —**in·tox·i·cant** \-sikənt\ n —**in·tox·i·ca·tion** \-,täksə'kāshən\ n

in·tra·mu·ral \,intrə'myurəl\ adj : within a school

in·tran·si·gent \in'transəjənt\ adj : uncompromising —**in·tran·si·gence** \-jəns\ n —**intransigent** n

in·tra·ve·nous \,intrə'vēnəs\ adj : by way of the veins —**in·tra·ve·nous·ly** adv

in·trep·id \in'trepəd\ *adj* : fearless —**in·tre·pid·i·ty** \ˌintrə'pidətē\ *n*

in·tri·cate \'intrikət\ *adj* : very complex and delicate —**in·tri·ca·cy** \-trikəsē\ *n* —**in·tri·cate·ly** *adv*

in·trigue \in'trēg\ *vb* -**trigued; -trigu·ing 1** : scheme **2** : arouse curiosity of ~ *n* : secret scheme —**in·trigu·ing·ly** \-inˈlē\ *adv*

in·trin·sic \in'trinzik, -sik\ *adj* **1** : essential **2** : actual —**in·trin·si·cal·ly** \-zik(ə)lē, -si-\ *adv*

in·tro·duce \ˌintrə'd(y)üs\ *vb* -**duced; -duc·ing 1** : bring in esp. for the 1st time **2** : cause to be acquainted **3** : bring to notice **4** : put in —**in·tro·duc·tion** \-'dəkshən\ *n* —**in·tro·duc·to·ry** \-'dəkt(ə)rē\ *adj*

in·troit \'in,trȯət, -,trȯit\ *n* : part of the Mass or music for it

in·tro·spec·tion \ˌintrə'spekshən\ *n* : examination of one's own thoughts or feelings —**in·tro·spect** \-'spekt\ *vb* —**in·tro·spec·tive** \-'spektiv\ *adj* —**in·tro·spec·tive·ly** *adv*

in·tro·vert \'intrə,vərt\ *n* : shy or retiring person —**in·tro·ver·sion** \ˌintrə'vərzhən\ *n* —**introvert** —**in·tro·vert·ed** \'intrə,vərtəd\ *adj*

in·trude \in'trüd\ *vb* -**trud·ed; -trud·ing 1** : thrust in **2** : encroach —**in·trud·er** *n* —**in·tru·sion** \-'trüzhən\ *n* —**in·tru·sive** \-'trüsiv\ *adj* —**in·tru·sive·ness** *n*

in·tu·i·tion \ˌint(y)ü'ishən\ *n* : quick and ready insight —**in·tu·it** \in't(y)üət\ *vb* —**in·tu·i·tive** \in't(y)üətiv\ *adj* —**in·tu·i·tive·ly** *adv*

in·un·date \'inən,dāt\ *vb* -**dat·ed; -dat·ing** : flood —**in·un·da·tion** \ˌinən'dāshən\ *n*

in·ure \in'(y)ùr\ *vb* -**ured; -ur·ing** : accustom to accept something undesirable

in·vade \in'vād\ *vb* -**vad·ed; -vad·ing** : enter for conquest —**in·vad·er** *n* —**in·va·sion** \-'vāzhən\ *n*

1in·val·id \in'valəd\ *adj* : not true or legal —**in·va·lid·i·ty** \ˌinvə'lidətē\ *n* —**in·val·id·ly** *adv*

2in·va·lid \'invələd\ *adj* : sickly ~ *n* : one chronically ill —**in·va·lid·ism** \-,izəm\ *n*

in·val·i·date \(')in'valə,dāt\ *vb* : make invalid

in·valu·able \(')in'valyə(wə)bəl\ *adj* : extremely valuable

in·vec·tive \in'vektiv\ *n* : abusive language —**invective** *adj*

in·veigh \in'vā\ *vb* : protest or complain forcefully

in·vei·gle \in'vāgəl, -'vē-\ *vb* -**gled; -gling** : win over or get by flattery

in·vent \in'vent\ *vb* **1** : think up **2** : create for the 1st time —**in·ven·tion** \-'venchən\ *n* —**in·ven·tive** \-iv\ *adj* —**in·ven·tive·ness** *n* —**in·ven·tor** \-'ventər\ *n*

in·ven·to·ry \'invən,tōrē\ *n, pl* -**ries 1** : list of goods **2** : stock —**inventory** *vb*

in·verse \(')in'vərs, 'in,vərs\ *adj* : opposite —**in·verse·ly** *adv*

in·vert \in'vərt\ *vb* **1** : turn upside down or inside out **2** : reverse —**in·ver·sion** \-'vərzhən\ *n*

in·ver·te·brate \(')in'vərtəbrət, -,brāt\ *adj* : lacking a backbone ~ *n* : invertebrate animal

in·vest \in'vest\ *vb* **1** : give power or authority to **2** : endow with a quality **3** : commit money to someone else's use in hope of profit —**in·vest·ment** \-'ves(t)mənt\ *n* —**in·ves·tor** \-'vestər\ *n*

in·ves·ti·gate \in'vestə,gāt\ *vb* -**gat·ed; -gat·ing** : study closely and systematically —**in·ves·ti·ga·tion** \-,vestə'gāshən\ *n* —**in·ves·ti·ga·tor** \-'vestə,gātər\ *n*

in·ves·ti·ture \in'vestə,chùr, -chər\ *n* : act of establishing in office

in·vet·er·ate \in'vet(ə)rət\ *adj* : acting out of habit —**in·vet·er·a·cy** \-(ə)rəsē\ *n*

in·vid·i·ous \in'vidēəs\ *adj* **1** : detestable **2** : injurious —**in·vid·i·ous·ly** *adv*

in·vig·o·rate \in'vigə,rāt\ *vb* -**rat·ed; -rat·ing** : give life and energy to —**in·vig·o·ra·tion** \-,vigə'rāshən\ *n*

in·vin·ci·ble \(')in'vinsəbəl\ *adj* : incapable of being conquered —**in·vin·ci·bil·i·ty** \(,)in,vinsə'bilətē\ *n* —**in·vin·ci·bly** \in'vinsəblē\ *adv*

in·vi·o·la·ble \(')in'vīələbəl\ *adj* : safe from violation or desecration —**in·vi·o·la·bil·i·ty** \(,)in,vīələ'bilətē\ *n*

in·vi·o·late \(')in'vīələt\ *adj* : not violated or profaned

in·vite \in'vīt\ *vb* -**vit·ed; -vit·ing 1** : entice **2** : increase the likelihood of **3** : request the presence or participation of **4** : encourage —**in·vi·ta·tion** \ˌinvə'tāshən\ *n* —**in·vit·ing** \in'vītiŋ\ *adj*

in·vo·ca·tion \ˌinvə'kāshən\ *n* **1** : prayer **2** : incantation

in·voice \'in,vȯis\ *n* : itemized bill for goods shipped ~ *vb* -**voiced; -voic·ing** : bill

in·voke \in'vōk\ *vb* -**voked; -vok·ing 1**

: call on for help **2** : cite as authority
3 : conjure **4** : carry out
in·volve \in'välv\ *vb* -**volved**; -**volv·ing**
1 : draw in as a participant **2** : relate
closely **3** : require as a necessary part
4 : occupy fully —**in·volve·ment** *n*
in·volved \-'välvd\ *adj* : intricate
¹in·ward \'inwərd\ *adj* : inside
²in·ward, in·wards \-wərdz\ *adv*
: toward the inside, center, or inner
being
in·ward·ly *adv* **1** : mentally or spiritually **2** : internally **3** : to oneself
io·dide \'īə,dīd\ *n* : compound of iodine
io·dine \'īə,dīn, - də⁰n\ *n* : nonmetallic
chemical element
io·dize \'īə,dīz\ *vb* -**dized**; -**diz·ing**
: treat with iodine or an iodide
ion \'īən, 'ī,än\ *n* : electrically charged
particle —**ion·ic** \ī'änik\ *adj* —**ion-
iz·able** \'īə,nīzəbəl\ *adj* —**ion·iza-
tion** \,īənə'zāshən\ *n* —**ion·ize**
\'īə,nīz\ *vb* —**ion·iz·er** \'īə,nīzər\ *n*
-ion *suffix* **1** : act or process **2** : state
or condition
ion·o·sphere \ī'änə,sfiər\ *n* : layer of
the atmosphere with charged particles —**ion·o·spher·ic** \ī,änə'sfi(ə)rik,
-'sfer-\ *adj*
io·ta \ī'ōtə\ *n* : small quantity
IOU \,ī,(')ō'yü\ *n* : acknowledgment of
a debt
iras·ci·ble \ir'asəbəl, I'ras-\ *adj*
: marked by hot temper —**iras·ci·bil-
i·ty** \-,asə'bilətē, -,ras-\ *n*
irate \ī'rāt\ *adj* : roused to intense anger —**irate·ly** *adv*
ire \'ī(ə)r\ *n* : anger
ir·i·des·cence \,irə'des⁰ns\ *n* : rain-
bowlike play of colors —**ir·i·des·cent**
\-⁰nt\ *adj*
iris \'īrəs\ *n, pl* **iris·es** *or* **iri·des**
\'īrə,dēz, 'ir-\ **1** : colored part
around the pupil of the eye **2** : plant
with long leaves and large showy
flowers
irk \'ərk\ *vb* : make weary, irritated, or
bored —**irk·some** \-səm\ *adj* —**irk-
some·ly** *adv*
iron \'ī(ə)rn\ *n* **1** : metallic chemical
element **2** : something made of metal
3 : heated device for pressing clothes
~ *vb* : press or smooth out with an
iron —**iron·er** *n* —**iron·ware** *n*
—**iron·work** *n* —**iron·work·er** *n*
—**iron·works** *n pl*
iron·clad \-'klad\ *adj* **1** : sheathed in
iron armor **2** : strict or exacting
iron·ing \'ī(ə)rniŋ\ *n* : clothes to be
ironed

iron·wood \-,wùd\ *n* : tree or shrub
with very hard wood
iro·ny \'īrənē\ *n, pl* -**nies 1** : use of
words to express the opposite of the
literal meaning **2** : incongruity between the actual and expected result
of events —**iron·ic** \ī'ränik\, **iron·i-
cal** \-ikəl\ *adj* —**iron·i·cal·ly**
\-ik(ə)lē\ *adv*
ir·ra·di·ate \ir'ādē,āt\ *vb* -**at·ed**; -**at·ing**
: treat with radiation —**ir·ra·di·a·tion**
\-,ādē'āshən\ *n*
ir·ra·tio·nal \(')ir'ash(ə)nəl\ *adj* **1** : in-
capable of reasoning **2** : not based on
reason —**ir·ra·tio·nal·i·ty** \(,)ir,-
,ashə'nalətē\ *n* —**ir·ra·tio·nal·ly** *adv*
ir·rec·on·cil·able \(,)ir,ekən'sīləbəl\
adj : impossible to reconcile —**ir·rec-
on·cil·abil·i·ty** \-,sīlə'bilətē\ *n*
ir·re·cov·er·able \,iri'kəv(ə)rəbəl\ *adj*
: not capable of being recovered —**ir-
re·cov·er·ably** \-blē\ *adv*
ir·re·deem·able \,iri'dēməbəl\ *adj* : not
redeemable
ir·re·duc·ible \,iri'd(y)üsəbəl\ *adj* : not
reducible —**ir·re·duc·ibly** \-blē\ *adv*
ir·re·fut·able \,iri'fyütəbəl, (')ir'(r)e-
fyət-\ *adj* : impossible to refute
ir·reg·u·lar \(')ir'egyələr\ *adj* : not
regular or normal —**irregular** *n* —**ir-
reg·u·lar·i·ty** \(,)ir,egyə'larətē\ *n*
—**ir·reg·u·lar·ly** *adv*
ir·rel·e·vant \(')ir'eləvənt\ *adj* : not
relevant —**ir·rel·e·vance** \-vəns\ *n*
ir·re·li·gious \,iri'lijəs\ *adj* : not following religious practices
ir·rep·a·ra·ble \(')ir'ep(ə)rəbəl\ *adj*
: impossible to make good, undo, or
remedy
ir·re·place·able \,iri'plāsəbəl\ *adj* : not
replaceable
ir·re·press·ible \,iri'presəbəl\ *adj* : impossible to repress or control
ir·re·proach·able \,iri'prōchəbəl\ *adj*
: blameless
ir·re·sist·ible \,iri'zistəbəl\ *adj* : impossible to successfully resist —**ir·re·sist-
ibly** \-blē\ *adv*
ir·res·o·lute \(')ir'ezəlüt\ *adj* : uncer-
tain —**ir·res·o·lute·ly** *adv* —**ir·res·o-
lu·tion** \-,ezə'lüshən\ *n*
ir·re·spec·tive of \,iri'spektiv-\ *prep*
: without regard to
ir·re·spon·si·ble \,iri'spänsəbəl\ *adj*
: not responsible —**ir·re·spon·si·bil·i-
ty** \-,spänsə'bilətē\ *n* —**ir·re·spon-
si·bly** *adv*
ir·re·triev·able \,iri'trēvəbəl\ *adj* : not
retrievable
ir·rev·er·ence \(')ir'ev(ə)rəns\ *n* **1**
: lack of reverence **2** : irreverent act

or utterance —**ir·rev·er·ent** \-(ə)rənt\ adj

ir·re·vers·ible \ˌiri'vərsəbəl\ adj : incapable of being reversed

ir·re·vo·ca·ble \(')ir'evəkəbəl\ adj : incapable of being revoked —**ir·re·vo·ca·bly** \-blē\ adv

ir·ri·gate \'irə,gāt\ vb -**gat·ed**; -**gat·ing** : supply with water by artificial means —**ir·ri·ga·tion** \ˌirə'gāshən\ n

ir·ri·tate \'irə,tāt\ vb -**tat·ed**; -**tat·ing** 1 : excite to anger 2 : make sore or inflamed —**ir·ri·ta·bil·i·ty** \ˌirə-tə'bilətē\ n —**ir·ri·ta·ble** \'irətəbəl\ adj —**ir·ri·ta·bly** \'irətəblē\ adv —**ir·ri·tant** \'irətənt\ adj or n —**ir·ri·tat·ing·ly** \'irə,tātiŋlē\ adv —**ir·ri·ta·tion** \ˌirə'tā-shən\ n

is pres 3d sing of BE

-**ish** \ish\ adj suffix 1 : characteristic of 2 : somewhat

isin·glass \'īzᵊn,glas, 'īziŋ-\ n 1 : gelatin from the air bladders of fish 2 : mica

Is·lam \is'läm, iz-, -'lam\ n : religious faith of Muslims —**Is·lam·ic** \-ik\ adj

is·land \'īlənd\ n : body of land surrounded by water —**is·land·er** \'īləndər\ n

isle \'īl\ n : small island

is·let \'īlət\ n : small island

-**ism** \ˌizəm\ n suffix 1 : act or practice 2 : characteristic manner 3 : condition 4 : doctrine

iso·late \'īsə,lāt, 'isə-\ vb -**lat·ed**; -**lat·ing** : place or keep by itself —**iso·la·tion** \ˌīsə'lāshən, ˌisə-\ n

iso·met·rics \ˌīsə'metriks\ n sing or pl : exercise against unmoving resistance —**isometric** adj

isos·ce·les \ī'säsə,lēz\ adj : having 2 equal sides

iso·tope \'īsə,tōp\ n : any of 2 or more species of atoms of the same chemical element —**iso·to·pic** \ˌīsə'täpik, -'tō-\ adj —**iso·to·pi·cal·ly** \-ik(ə)lē\ adv

is·sue \'ish(ˌ)ü\ vb -**sued**; -**su·ing** 1 : go, come, or flow out 2 : descend from a

specified ancestor 3 : emanate or result 4 : put forth or distribute officially ~ n 1 : action of issuing 2 : offspring 3 : result 4 : point of controversy 5 : act of giving out or printing 6 : quantity given out or printed —**is·su·ance** \'ishəwəns\ n —**is·su·er** n

-**ist** \əst\ n suffix 1 : one that does 2 : one that plays 3 : one that specializes in 4 : follower of a doctrine

isth·mus \'isməs\ n : narrow strip of land connecting 2 larger portions

it \(')it, ət\ pron 1 : that one —used of a lifeless thing or an abstract entity 2 —used as an anticipatory subject or object ~ n : player who tries to catch others (as in a game of tag)

ital·ic \ə'talik, i-, ī-\ n : style of type with slanting letters —**italic** adj —**ital·i·ci·za·tion** \ə,taləsə'zāshən, i-, ī-\ n —**ital·i·cize** \ə'talə,sīz, i-, ī-\ vb

itch \'ich\ n 1 : uneasy irritating skin sensation 2 : skin disorder 3 : persistent desire —**itch** vb —**itchy** adj

item \'ītəm\ n 1 : particular in a list, account, or series 2 : piece of news —**item·iza·tion** \ˌītəmə'zāshən\ n —**item·ize** \'ītə,mīz\ vb

itin·er·ant \ī'tinərənt, ə-\ adj : traveling from place to place

itin·er·ary \ī'tinə,rerē, ə-\ n, pl -**ar·ies** : route or outline of a journey

its \(ˌ)its, əts\ adj : relating to it

it·self \it'self, ət-\ pron : it—used reflexively or for emphasis

-**ity** \ətē\ n suffix : quality, state, or degree

-**ive** \iv\ adj suffix : that performs or tends toward an action

ivo·ry \'īv(ə)rē\ n, pl -**ries** 1 : hard creamy-white material of elephants' tusks 2 : pale yellow color

ivy \'īvē\ n, pl **ivies** : trailing woody vine with evergreen leaves

-**ize** \ˌīz\ vb suffix 1 : cause to be, become, or resemble 2 : subject to an action 3 : treat or combine with 4 : engage in an activity

J

j \'jā\ n, pl **j's** or **js** \'jāz\ : 10th letter of the alphabet

jab \'jab\ vb -**bb**- : thrust quickly or abruptly ~ n : short straight punch

jab·ber \'jabər\ vb : talk rapidly or unintelligibly —**jabber** n

jack \'jak\ n 1 : mechanical device to

raise a heavy body 2 : small flag 3 : small 6-pointed metal object used in a game (**jacks**) 4 : electrical socket ~ vb 1 : raise with a jack 2 : increase

jack·al \'jakəl, -ˌol\ n : wild dog smaller than a wolf

jack·ass n : male ass

jack·et \'jakət\ *n* : garment for the upper body —**jack·et·ed** *adj*

jack·ham·mer \'jak,hamər\ *n* : pneumatic tool for drilling

jack·knife \'jak,nīf\ *n* : pocketknife

jack-o'-lan·tern \'jakə,lantərn\ · *n* : lantern made of a carved pumpkin

jack·pot \'jak,pät\ *n* : sum of money won

jack·rab·bit \-,rabət\ *n* : large hare of western No. America

jade \'jād\ *n* : usu. green gemstone

jad·ed \'jādəd\ *adj* : dulled or bored by having too much

jag·ged \'jagəd\ *adj* : sharply notched

jag·uar \'jag(yə),wär\ *n* : black-spotted tropical American cat

jai alai \'hī,lī\ *n* : game with a ball propelled by a basket on the hand

jail \'jāl\ *n* : prison ~ *vb* : put in jail —**jail·break** *n* —**jail·er, jail·or** *n*

ja·lopy \jə'läpē\ *n, pl* -**lopies** : dilapidated automobile

jal·ou·sie \'jaləsē\ *n* : door or window with louvers

jam \'jam\ *vb* -**mm-** 1 : press into a close or tight position 2 : cause to become wedged so as to be unworkable ~ *n* 1 : crowded mass that blocks or impedes 2 : difficult situation 3 : thick sweet food made of cooked fruit

jamb \'jam\ *n* : upright framing piece of a door

jam·bo·ree \,jambə'rē\ *n* : large festive gathering

jan·gle \'jaŋgəl\ *vb* -**gled; -gling** : make a harsh ringing sound —**jangle** *n*

jan·i·tor \'janətər\ *n* : person who has the care of a building —**jan·i·to·ri·al** \,janə'tōrēəl\ *adj*

Jan·u·ary \'janyə,werē\ *n* : 1st month of the year having 31 days

¹jar \'jär\ *vb* -**rr-** 1 : have a harsh or disagreeable effect 2 : vibrate or shake ~ *n* 1 : jolt 2 : painful effect

²jar *n* : broad-mouthed container

jar·gon \'järgən, -,gän\ *n* : special vocabulary of a group

jas·mine \'jazmən\ *n* : climbing shrub with fragrant flowers

jas·per \'jaspər\ *n* : red, yellow, or brown opaque quartz

jaun·dice \'jōndəs\ *n* : yellowish discoloration of skin, tissues, and body fluids

jaun·diced \-dəst\ *adj* : exhibiting envy or hostility

jaunt \'jönt\ *n* : short pleasure trip

jaun·ty \'jöntē\ *adj* -**ti·er; -est** : lively in manner or appearance —**jaun·ti·ly** \'jönt³lē\ *adv* —**jaun·ti·ness** *n*

jav·e·lin \'jav(ə)lən\ *n* : light spear

jaw \'jō\ *n* 1 : either of the bony or cartilaginous structures that support the mouth 2 : one of 2 movable parts for holding or crushing ~ *vb* : talk indignantly or at length —**jaw·bone** \-,bōn, -,bōn\ *n* —**jawed** \'jōd\ *adj*

jay \'jā\ *n* : noisy brightly colored bird

jay·bird *n* : jay

jay·walk *vb* : cross a street carelessly —**jay·walk·er** *n*

jazz \'jaz\ *vb* : enliven ~ *n* 1 : kind of American music involving improvisation 2 : empty talk —**jazzy** *adj*

jeal·ous \'jeləs\ *adj* : suspicious of a rival or of one believed to enjoy an advantage —**jeal·ous·ly** *adv* —**jeal·ou·sy** \-əsē\ *n*

jeans \'jēnz\ *n pl* : pants made of durable twilled cotton cloth

jeep \'jēp\ *n* : 4-wheel army vehicle

jeer \'jiər\ *vb* 1 : speak or cry out in derision ?: ridicule ~ *n* : taunt

Je·ho·vah \ji'hōvə\ *n* : God

je·june \ji'jün\ *adj* : dull or childish

jell \'jel\ *vb* 1 : come to the consistency of jelly 2 : take shape

jel·ly \'jelē\ *n, pl* -**lies** : a substance (as food) with a soft somewhat elastic consistency —**jelly** *vb*

jel·ly·fish *n* : sea animal with a saucer-shaped jellylike body

jen·ny \'jenē\ *n, pl* -**nies** : female bird or donkey

jeop·ar·dy \'jepərdē\ *n* : exposure to death, loss, or injury —**jeop·ar·dize** \-ər,dīz\ *vb* —**jeop·ar·dous** \-ərdəs\ *adj*

jerk \'jərk\ *vb* 1 : give a sharp quick push, pull, or twist 2 : move in short abrupt motions ~ *n* 1 : short quick pull or twist 2 : stupid or foolish person —**jerk·i·ly** *adv* —**jerky** *adj*

jer·kin \'jərkən\ *n* : close-fitting sleeveless jacket

jer·ry-built \'jerē,bilt\ *adj* : built cheaply and flimsily

jer·sey \'jərzē\ *n, pl* -**seys** 1 : plain knit fabric 2 : knitted shirt

jest \'jest\ *n* : witty remark —**jest** *vb*

jest·er \'jestər\ *n* : one employed to entertain a court

¹jet \'jet\ *n* : velvet-black coal used for jewelry

²jet *vb* -**tt-** 1 : spout or emit in a stream 2 : travel by jet ~ *n* 1 : forceful rush of fluid through a narrow opening 2 : jet-propelled airplane

jet-propelled *adj* : driven by an engine (**jet engine**) that produces propulsion (**jet propulsion**) by the rearward discharge of a jet of fluid

jet·sam \'jetsəm\ *n* : jettisoned goods

jet·ti·son \'jetəsən\ *vb* **1** : throw (goods) overboard **2** : discard —**jettison** *n*

jet·ty \'jetē\ *n, pl* **-ties** : pier or wharf

Jew \'jü\ *n* : one whose religion is Judaism —**Jew·ish** *adj*

jew·el \'jüəl\ *n* **1** : ornament of precious metal **2** : gem ~ *vb* **-eled** or **-elled; -el·ing** or **-el·ling** : adorn with jewels —**jew·el·er** or **jew·el·ler** \-ər\ *n* —**jew·el·ry** \-rē\ *n*

jib \'jib\ *n* : triangular sail

jibe \'jīb\ *vb* **jibed; jib·ing** : be in agreement

jif·fy \'jifē\ *n, pl* **-fies** : short time

jig \'jig\ *n* : lively dance ~ *vb* **-gg-** : dance a jig

jig·ger \'jigər\ *n* : measure used in mixing drinks

jig·gle \'jigəl\ *vb* **-gled; -gling** : move with quick little jerks —**jiggle** *n*

jig·saw *n* : machine saw with a narrow blade that moves up and down

jilt \'jilt\ *vb* : woman who jilts a man ~ *vb* : drop (one's lover) unfeelingly

jim·my \'jimē\ *n, pl* **-mies** : small crowbar ~ *vb* **-mied; -my·ing** : pry open

jim·son·weed \'jimsən,wēd\ *n* : coarse poisonous weed

jin·gle \'jiŋgəl\ *vb* **-gled; -gling** : make a light tinkling sound ~ *n* **1** : light tinkling sound **2** : short verse or song

jin·go·ism \'jiŋgō,izəm\ *n* : extreme chauvinism or nationalism —**jin·go·ist** \-əst\ *n* —**jin·go·is·tic** \,jiŋgō'istik\ *adj*

jinx \'jiŋks\ *n* : one that brings bad luck —**jinx** *vb*

jit·ney \'jitnē\ *n, pl* **-neys** : small bus

jit·ters \'jitərz\ *n pl* : extreme nervousness —**jit·tery** \-ərē\ *adj*

job \'jäb\ *n* **1** : something that has to be done **2** : regular employment —**job·hold·er** *n* —**job·less** *adj*

job·ber \'jäbər\ *n* : middleman

jock·ey \'jäkē\ *n, pl* **-eys** : one who rides a horse in a race ~ *vb* **-eyed; -ey·ing** : manipulate or maneuver adroitly

jo·cose \jō'kōs\ *adj* : jocular

joc·u·lar \'jäkyələr\ *adj* : marked by jesting —**joc·u·lar·i·ty** \,jäkyə'larətē\ *n*

jo·cund \'jäkənd\ *adj* : full of mirth or gaiety

jodh·purs \'jädpərz\ *n pl* : riding breeches

¹jog \'jäg\ *vb* **-gg- 1** : give a slight shake or push to **2** : run or ride at a slow pace ~ *n* **1** : slight shake **2** : slow pace —**jog·ger** *n*

²jog *n* : brief abrupt change in direction or line

join \'join\ *vb* **1** : come or bring together **2** : become a member of —**join·er** *n*

joint \'joint\ *n* **1** : point of contact between bones **2** : place where 2 parts connect **3** : often disreputable place ~ *adj* : common to 2 or more —**joint·ed** *adj* —**joint·ly** *adv*

joist \'joist\ *n* : beam supporting a floor or ceiling

joke \'jōk\ *n* : something said or done to provoke laughter ~ *vb* **joked; jok·ing** : make jokes —**jok·er** *n* —**jok·ing·ly** \'jōkiŋlē\ *adv*

jol·li·ty \'jälətē\ *n, pl* **-ties** : gaiety or merriment

jol·ly \'jälē\ *adj* **-li·er; -est** : full of high spirits

jolt \'jōlt\ *vb* **1** : move with a sudden jerky motion **2** : give a jolt to ~ *n* **1** : abrupt jerky blow or movement **2** : sudden shock —**jolt·er** *n*

jon·quil \'jänkwəl\ *n* : narcissus with white or yellow flowers

josh \'jäsh\ *vb* : tease or joke

jos·tle \'jäsəl\ *vb* **-tled; -tling** : push or shove

jot \'jät\ *n* : least bit ~ *vb* **-tt-** : write briefly and hurriedly

jounce \'jauns\ *vb* **jounced; jounc·ing** : jolt —**jounce** *n*

jour·nal \'jərn°l\ *n* **1** : brief account of daily events **2** : periodical (as a newspaper)

jour·nal·ism \'jərn°l,izəm\ *n* : business of reporting or printing news —**jour·nal·ist** \-əst\ *n* —**jour·nal·is·tic** \,jərn°l'istik\ *adj*

jour·ney \'jərnē\ *n, pl* **-neys** : a going from one place to another ~ *vb* **-neyed; -ey·ing** : make a journey

jour·ney·man \-mən\ *n* : worker who has learned a trade and works for another person

joust \'jaust\ *n* : combat on horseback between 2 knights with lances —**joust** *vb*

jo·vial \'jōvēəl\ *adj* : marked by good humor —**jo·vi·al·i·ty** \,jōvē'alətē\ *n* —**jo·vi·al·ly** \'jōvēəlē\ *adv*

¹jowl \'jaul\ *n* **1** : lower jaw **2** : cheek

²jowl *n* : loose flesh about the lower jaw or throat

joy \'joi\ *n* **1** : feeling of happiness **2** : source of happiness —**joy** *vb* —**joy·ful** *adj* —**joy·ful·ly** *adv* —**joy·less** *adj*

—**joy·ous** \'jòiəs\ *adj* —**joy·ous·ly**
adv —**joy·ous·ness** *n*

joy·ride *n* : reckless ride for pleasure
—**joy·rid·er** *n* —**joy·rid·ing** *n*

ju·bi·lant \'jübələnt\ *adj* : expressing
great joy —**ju·bi·lant·ly** *adv* —**ju·bi-
la·tion** \,jübə'lāshən\ *n*

ju·bi·lee \'jübə,lē\ *n* **1** : 50th anniversary **2** : season or occasion of celebration

Ju·da·ism \'jüdə,izəm\ *n* : religion developed among the ancient Hebrews
—**Ju·da·ic** \jù'dāik\ *adj*

judge \'jəj\ *vb* **judged; judg·ing 1** : form
an opinion **2** : decide as a judge ~ *n*
1 : public official authorized to decide questions brought before a court
2 : one who gives an authoritative
opinion —**judge·ship** *n*

judg·ment, judge·ment \'jəjmənt\ *n* **1**
: decision or opinion given after
judging **2** : capacity for judging

ju·di·ca·ture \'jüdikə,chùr\ *n* : administration of justice

ju·di·cial \jù'dishəl\ *adj* : relating to
judicature or the judiciary —**ju·di-
cial·ly** *adv*

ju·di·cia·ry \jù'dishē,erē, -'dishərē\ *n*
: system of courts of law or the
judges of them —**judiciary** *adj*

ju·di·cious \jù'dishəs\ *adj* : having or
characterized by sound judgment
—**ju·di·cious·ly** *adv* —**ju·di·cious-
ness** *n*

ju·do \'jüdō\ *n* : form of wrestling
—**judo·ist** *n*

jug \'jəg\ *n* : large deep container with
a narrow mouth and a handle

jug·ger·naut \'jəgər,nòt\ *n* : massive
inexorable force or object

jug·gle \'jəgəl\ *vb* **-gled; -gling 1**
: keep several objects in motion in
the air at the same time **2** : manipulate for an often tricky purpose
—**jug·gler** \'jəglər\ *n*

jug·u·lar \'jəgyələr\ *adj* : in or on the
throat or neck

juice \'jüs\ *n* **1** : extractable fluid contents of cells or tissues **2** : electricity
—**juic·er** *n* —**juic·i·ly** \'jüsəlē\ *adv*
—**juic·i·ness** \-sēnəs\ *n* —**juicy**
\'jüsē\ *adj*

ju·jube \'jü,jüb, 'jüjù,bē\ *n* : gummy
candy

juke·box \'jük,bäks\ *n* : coin-operated
record player

ju·lep \'jüləp\ *n* : mint-flavored bour-
bon drink

Ju·ly \jù'lī\ *n* : 7th month of the year
having 31 days

jum·ble \'jəmbəl\ *vb* **-bled; -bling** : mix
in a disorderly mass —**jumble** *n*

jum·bo \'jəmbō\ *n, pl* **-bos** : very large
version —**jumbo** *adj*

jump \'jəmp\ *vb* **1** : rise into or through
the air esp. by muscular effort **2**
: pass over **3** : give a start **4** : rise or
increase sharply ~ *n* **1** : a jumping
2 : sharp sudden increase **3** : initial
advantage

¹jump·er \'jəmpər\ *n* : one that jumps

²jumper *n* : sleeveless one-piece dress

jumpy \'jəmpē\ *adj* **jump·i·er; -est**
: nervous or jittery

junc·tion \'jəŋkshən\ *n* **1** : a joining **2**
: place or point of meeting

junc·ture \'jəŋkchər\ *n* **1** : joint or connection **2** : critical time or state of
affairs

June \'jün\ *n* : 6th month of the year
having 30 days

jun·gle \'jəŋgəl\ *n* : thick tangled mass
of tropical vegetation

ju·nior \'jünyər\ *n* **1** : person who is
younger or of lower rank than an-
other **2** : student in the next-to-last
year ~ *adj* : younger or lower in
rank

ju·ni·per \'jünəpər\ *n* : evergreen
shrub or tree

¹junk \'jəŋk\ *n* **1** : discarded articles **2**
: shoddy product ~ *vb* : discard or
scrap —**junky** *adj*

²junk *n* : flat-bottomed ship of Chinese
waters

jun·ket \'jəŋkət\ *n* : trip made by an
official at public expense

jun·ta \'hùntə, 'jəntə, 'həntə\ *n*
: group of persons controlling a government

ju·ris·dic·tion \,jùrəs'dikshən\ *n* **1**
: right or authority to interpret and
apply the law **2** : limits within which
authority may be exercised —**ju·ris-
dic·tion·al** \-sh(ə)nəl\ *adj*

ju·ris·pru·dence \-'prüd²ns\ *n* : system of laws **2** : science or philosophy
of law

ju·rist \'jùrəst\ *n* : lawyer or judge

ju·ror \'jùrər\ *n* : member of a jury

ju·ry \'jùrē\ *n, pl* **-ries** : body of persons sworn to give a verdict on a
matter

just \'jəst\ *adj* **1** : reasonable **2** : correct or proper **3** : morally or legally
right **4** : deserved ~ \(,)jəst, (,)jist\
adv **1** : exactly **2** : very recently **3**
: barely **4** : only —**just·ly** *adv* —**just-
ness** *n*

jus·tice \'jəstəs\ *n* **1** : administration
of what is just **2** : judge **3** : administration of law **4** : fairness

jus·ti·fy \'jəstə,fī\ *vb* **-fied; -fy·ing**

: prove to be just, right, or reasonable —**jus·ti·fi·able** *adj* —**jus·ti·fi·ca·tion** \ˌjəstəfə'kāshən\ *n*

jut \'jət\ *vb* **-tt-** : stick out

jute \'jüt\ *n* : strong glossy fiber from a tropical herb

ju·ve·nile \'jüvə,nīl, -vənᵊl\ *adj* : relating to children or young people ~ *n* : young person

jux·ta·pose \'jəkstə,pōz\ *vb* **-posed; -pos·ing** : place side by side —**jux·ta·po·si·tion** \ˌjəkstəpə'zishən\ *n*

K

k \'kā\ *n, pl* **k's** *or* **ks** \'kāz\ : 11th letter of the alphabet

kai·ser \'kīzər\ *n* : German ruler

kale \'kāl\ *n* : curly cabbage

ka·lei·do·scope \kə'līdə,skōp\ *n* : device containing loose bits of colored glass reflecting in many patterns —**ka·lei·do·scop·ic** \-,līdə'skäpik\, **ka·lei·do·scop·i·cal** \-ikəl\ *adj* —**ka·lei·do·scop·i·cal·ly** *adv*

kan·ga·roo \ˌkaŋgə'rü\ *n, pl* **-roos** : large leaping Australian mammal

ka·olin \'kāələn\ *n* : fine white clay

kar·at \'karət\ *n* : unit of gold content

ka·ra·te \kə'rätē\ *n* : art of self-defense by crippling kicks and punches

ka·ty·did \'kātē,did\ *n* : large American grasshopper

kay·ak \'kī,ak\ *n* : Eskimo canoe

ka·zoo \kə'zü\ *n, pl* **-zoos** : toy musical instrument

keel \'kēl\ *n* : central lengthwise strip on the bottom of a ship —**keeled** \'kēld\ *adj*

keen \'kēn\ *adj* 1 : sharp 2 : severe 3 : enthusiastic 4 : mentally alert —**keen·ly** *adv* —**keen·ness** \'kēnnəs\ *n*

keep \'kēp\ *vb* **kept** \'kept\; **keep·ing** 1 : perform 2 : guard 3 : maintain 4 : retain in one's possession 5 : detain 6 : continue in good condition 7 : refrain ~ *n* 1 : fortress 2 : means by which one is kept —**keep·er** *n*

keep·ing \'kēpiŋ\ *n* : conformity

keep·sake \'kēp,sāk\ *n* : souvenir

keg \'keg\ *n* : small cask or barrel

kelp \'kelp\ *n* : coarse brown seaweed

ken \'ken\ *n* : range of sight or understanding

ken·nel \'kenᵊl\ *n* : dog shelter —**ken·nel** *vb*

ker·chief \'kərchəf, -,chēf\ *n* : square of cloth worn as a head covering

ker·nel \'kərnᵊl\ *n* 1 : inner softer part of a seed or nut 2 : whole seed of a cereal 3 : central part

ker·o·sene, ker·o·sine \'kerə,sēn, ˌkerə'-, 'kar-, ˌkar-\ *n* : thin petroleum oil

ketch·up *var of* CATSUP

ket·tle \'ketᵊl\ *n* : vessel for boiling liquids

ket·tle·drum \-,drum\ *n* : brass or copper drum with a top of animal skin

¹key \'kē\ *n* 1 : metal piece to open a lock 2 : explanation 3 : lever pressed by a finger in playing an instrument or operating a machine 4 : leading individual or principle 5 : system of musical tones or pitch ~ *vb* 1 : attune 2 : make nervous ~ *adj* : basic —**key·hole** *n*

²key *n* : low island or reef

key·board *n* : arrangement of keys

key·note \-,nōt\ *n* 1 : 1st note of a scale 2 : central fact, idea, or mood ~ *vb* 1 : set the keynote of 2 : deliver the major speech

key-punch *n* : keyboard machine to punch cards —**keypunch** *vb* —**key-punch·er** *n*

key·stone *n* : wedge-shaped piece at the crown of an arch

kha·ki \'kakē, 'käk-\ *n* : light yellowish brown

khan \'kän, 'kan\ *n* : Mongol leader

kib·butz \kib'üts, -'üts\ *n, pl* **-but·zim** \-,üt'sēm, -,üt-\ : Israeli collective farm or settlement

ki·bitz·er \'kibətsər, kə'bit-\ *n* : one who offers unwanted advice —**kib·itz** \'kibəts\ *vb*

kick \'kik\ *vb* 1 : strike out or hit with the foot 2 : object strongly 3 : recoil ~ *n* 1 : thrust with the foot 2 : recoil of a gun 3 : stimulating effect —**kick·er** *n*

kid \'kid\ *n* 1 : young goat 2 : child ~ *vb* **-dd-** 1 : deceive as a joke 2 : tease —**kid·der** *n* —**kid·ding·ly** *adv* —**kid·dish** \'kidish\ *adj*

kid·nap \'kid,nap\ *vb* **-napped** *or* **-naped** \-,napt\; **-nap·ping** *or* **-nap·ing** : carry a person away by illegal force —**kid·nap·per, kid·nap·er** *n*

kid·ney \'kidnē\ *n, pl* **-neys** : either of a pair of organs that excrete urine

kill \'kil\ *vb* 1 : deprive of life 2 : finish 3 : use up (time) ~ *n* : act of killing —**kill·er** *n*

kiln \'kil(n)\ n : heated enclosure for burning, firing, or drying —**kiln** vb

ki-lo \'kēlō\ n, pl -los 1 : kilogram 2 : kilometer

kilo-cy-cle \'kilə,sīkəl\ n : kilohertz

ki-lo-gram \'kēlə,gram, 'kilə-\ n : 1000 grams

ki-lo-hertz \'kilə,hərts, 'kēlə-, -,herts\ n : 1000 hertz

ki-lo-me-ter \kil'ämətər, 'kilə,mēt-\ n : 1000 meters

ki-lo-volt \ '\ n : 1000 volts

kilo-watt \'kilə,wät\ n : 1000 watts

kilt \'kilt\ n : knee-length pleated skirt

kil-ter \'kiltər\ n : proper condition

ki-mo-no \kə'mōnə\ n, pl -nos : loose robe

kin \'kin\ n 1 : one's relatives 2 : kinsman

kind \'kīnd\ n 1 : essential quality 2 : group with common traits 3 : variety ~ adj 1 : of a sympathetic nature 2 : arising from sympathy —**kind-heart-ed** adj —**kind-ness** n

kin-der-gar-ten \'kindər,gärt³n\ n : class for young children —**kin-der-gart-ner** \-,gärtnər\ n

kin-dle \'kind³l\ vb -dled; -dling 1 : set on fire or start burning 2 : stir up

kin-dling \'kin(d)liŋ, 'kinlən\ n : material for starting a fire

kind-ly \'kīndlē\ adj -li-er; -est : of a sympathetic nature ~ adv 1 : sympathetically 2 : courteously —**kind-li-ness** n

kin-dred \'kindrəd\ n 1 : related individuals 2 : kin ~ adj : of a like nature

kin-folk \'kin,fōk\, **kinfolks** n pl : kin

king \'kiŋ\ n : male sovereign —**king-dom** \-dəm\ n —**king-less** adj —**king-ly** adj —**king-ship** n

king-fish-er \-,fishər\ n : bright-colored crested bird

kink \'kiŋk\ n 1 : short tight twist or curl 2 : cramp —**kinky** adj

kin-ship n : relationship

kins-man \'kinzmən\ n : male relative

kins-wom-an \-,wùmən\ n : female relative

kip-per \'kipər\ n : dried or smoked fish —**kipper** vb

kiss \'kis\ vb : touch with the lips as a mark of affection —**kiss** n

kit \'kit\ n : set of articles (as tools or parts)

kitch-en \'kichən\ n : room with cooking facilities

kite \'kīt\ n 1 : small hawk 2 : covered framework flown at the end of a string

kith \'kith\ n : familiar friends

kit-ten \'kit³n\ n : young cat —**kit-ten-ish** adj

¹**kit-ty** \'kitē\ n, pl -ties : kitten

²**kitty** n, pl -ties : fund or pool (as in a card game)

kit-ty-cor-ner, kit-ty-cor-nered var of CATERCORNER

ki-wi \'kē(,)wē\ n : flightless New Zealand bird

klep-to-ma-nia \,kleptə'mānēə\ n : neurotic impulse to steal —**klep-to-ma-ni-ac** \-nē,ak\ n

knack \'nak\ n 1 : clever way of doing something 2 : natural aptitude

knap-sack \'nap,sak\ n : case for carrying supplies

knave \'nāv\ n : rogue —**knav-ery** \'nāv(ə)rē\ n —**knav-ish** \'nāvish\ adj

knead \'nēd\ vb 1 : work and press with the hands 2 : massage —**knead-er** n

knee \'nē\ n : joint in the middle part of the leg —**kneed** \'nēd\ adj

knee-cap \'nē,kap\ n : bone forming the front of the knee

kneel \'nēl\ vb knelt \'nelt\ or kneeled; kneel-ing : fall or rest on the knees

knell \'nel\ n : stroke of a bell

knew past of KNOW

knick-ers \'nikərz\ n pl : pants gathered at the knee

knick-knack \'nik,nak\ n : small decorative object

knife \'nīf\ n, pl knives \'nīvz\ : sharp blade with a handle ~ vb knifed; knif-ing : stab or cut with a knife

knight \'nīt\ n 1 : mounted warrior of feudal times 2 : man honored by a sovereign ~ vb : make a knight of —**knight-hood** n —**knight-ly** adv

knit \'nit\ vb knit or knit-ted; knit-ting 1 : link firmly or closely 2 : form a fabric by interlacing yarn or thread ~ n : knitted garment —**knit-ter** n

knob \'näb\ n : rounded protuberance or handle —**knobbed** \'näbd\ adj —**knob-by** \'näbē\ adj

knock \'näk\ vb 1 : strike with a sharp blow 2 : collide 3 : find fault with ~ n : sharp blow —**knock out** vb : make unconscious

knock-er n : device hinged to a door to knock with

knoll \'nōl\ n : small round hill

knot \'nät\ n 1 : interlacing (as of string) that forms a lump 2 : base of a woody branch in the stem 3 : group 4 : one nautical mile per hour ~ vb

-tt- : tie in or with a knot **—knot·ty** *adj*

know \\'nō\\ *vb* **knew** \\'n(y)ü\\; **known** \\'nōn\\; **know·ing 1 :** perceive directly or understand **2 :** be familiar with **—know·able** *adj* **—know·er** *n*

know·ing \\'nōin\\ *adj* **:** shrewdly and keenly alert **—know·ing·ly** *adv*

knowl·edge \\'nälij\\ *n* **1 :** understanding gained by experience **2 :** range of information **—knowl·edge·able** *adj*

knuck·le \\'nəkəl\\ *n* **:** rounded knob at a finger joint **—knuck·le·bone** *n*

ko·ala \\kōälə, kə'wäl-\\ *n* **:** furry Australian animal

kohl·ra·bi \\kōl'rabē, -'räb-\\ *n, pl* **-bies :** cabbage that forms no head

Ko·ran \\kə'ran, -'rän\\ *n* **:** book of writings accepted by Muslims as revelations made to Muhammad by Allah

ko·sher \\'kōshər\\ *adj* **:** ritually fit for use according to Jewish law

kow·tow \\kaú'taú, 'kaú,taú\\ *vb* **:** show excessive deference

kryp·ton \\'krip,tän\\ *n* **:** gaseous chemical element

ku·dos \\'k(y)ü,däs, -,dōz\\ *n* **:** fame and renown

kum·quat \\'kəm,kwät\\ *n* **:** small citrus fruit

L

l \\'el\\ *n, pl* **l's** *or* **ls** \\'elz\\ **:** 12th letter of the alphabet

lab \\'lab\\ *n* **:** laboratory

la·bel \\'lābəl\\ *n* **1 :** identification slip **2 :** identifying word or phrase ~ *vb* **-beled** *or* **-belled; -bel·ing** *or* **-bel·ling :** put a label on

la·bi·al \\'lābēəl\\ *adj* **:** of or relating to the lips

la·bor \\'lābər\\ *n* **1 :** physical or mental effort **2 :** physical activities of childbirth **3 :** task **4 :** people who work for wages ~ *vb* **:** work esp. with great effort **—la·bor·er** *n*

lab·o·ra·to·ry \\'lab(ə)rə,tōrē\\ *n, pl* **-ries :** place for experimental testing and analysis

Labor Day *n* **:** 1st Monday in September observed as a legal holiday in recognition of the workingman

la·bo·ri·ous \\lə'bōrēəs\\ *adj* **:** requiring great effort **—la·bo·ri·ous·ly** *adv*

lab·y·rinth \\'labə,rinth\\ *n* **:** maze **—lab·y·rin·thine** \\,labə'rinthən\\ *adj*

lace \\'lās\\ *n* **1 :** cord or string for tying **2 :** fine net usu. figured fabric ~ *vb* **laced; lac·ing 1 :** tie **2 :** adorn with lace **—lacy** \\'lāsē\\ *adj*

lac·er·ate \\'lasə,rāt\\ *vb* **-at·ed; -at·ing :** tear roughly **—lac·er·a·tion** \\,lasə'rāshən\\ *n*

lach·ry·mose \\'lakrə,mōs\\ *adj* **:** tearful

lack \\'lak\\ *vb* **:** be missing or deficient in ~ *n* **:** deficiency

lack·a·dai·si·cal \\,lakə'dāzikəl\\ *adj* **:** lacking spirit **—lack·a·dai·si·cal·ly** \\-k(ə)lē\\ *adv*

lack·ey \\'lakē\\ *n, pl* **-eys 1 :** liveried retainer **2 :** toady

lack·lus·ter \\'lak,ləstər\\ *adj* **:** dull

la·con·ic \\lə'känik\\ *adj* **:** sparing of words **—la·con·i·cal·ly** \\-ik(ə)lē\\ *adv*

lac·quer \\'lakər\\ *n* **:** glossy surface coating **—lacquer** *vb*

la·crosse \\lə'krós\\ *n* **:** ball game played with long-handled rackets

lac·tate \\'lak,tāt\\ *vb* **-tat·ed; -tat·ing :** secrete milk **—lac·ta·tion** \\lak'tā-shən\\ *n*

lac·tic \\'laktik\\ *adj* **:** relating to milk

la·cu·na \\lə'k(y)ünə\\ *n, pl* **-nae** \\-(,)nē\\ *or* **-nas :** blank space or missing part

lad \\'lad\\ *n* **:** boy

lad·der \\'ladər\\ *n* **:** device with steps or rungs for climbing

lad·en \\'lādən\\ *adj* **:** loaded

la·dle \\'lādəl\\ *n* **:** spoon with a deep bowl **—ladle** *vb*

la·dy \\'lādē\\ *n, pl* **-dies 1 :** woman of rank or authority **2 :** woman

la·dy·bird \\'lādē,bərd\\ *n* **:** ladybug

la·dy·bug \\-,bəg\\ *n* **:** brightly colored beetle

lag \\'lag\\ *vb* **-gg- :** fail to keep up ~ *n* **1 :** a falling behind **2 :** interval

la·ger \\'lägər\\ *n* **:** beer

lag·gard \\'lagərd\\ *adj* **:** slow ~ *n* **:** one that lags **—lag·gard·ly** *adv or adj* **—lag·gard·ness** *n*

la·gniappe \\'lan,yap\\ *n* **:** bonus

la·goon \\lə'gün\\ *n* **:** shallow sound, channel, or pond near or connecting with a larger body of water

laid *past of* LAY

lain *past part of* LIE

lair \\'laər\\ *n* **:** den

lais·sez-faire \\,les,ā'faər\\ *n* **:** doctrine opposing government interference in business

la·ity \\'lāətē\\ *n* **:** people who are not clergy

lake \\'lāk\\ *n* **:** inland body of water

la·ma \\'lämə\\ *n* **:** Buddhist monk

lamb \\'lam\ *n* : young sheep or its flesh used as food

lam·baste, lam·bast \lam'bāst, -'bast\ *vb* 1 : beat 2 : censure

lam·bent \\'lambənt\ *adj* : light or bright —**lam·ben·cy** \-bənsē\ *n* —**lam·bent·ly** *adv*

lame \\'lām\ *adj* **lam·er; lam·est** 1 : having a limb disabled 2 : weak ~ *vb* **lamed; lam·ing** : make lame —**lame·ly** *adv* —**lame·ness** *n*

la·mé \la'mā, la-\ *n* : cloth with tinsel threads

lame·brain \\'lām₁brān\ *n* : fool

la·ment \lə'ment\ *vb* 1 : mourn 2 : express sorrow for ~ *n* : mourning —**lam·en·ta·ble** \'lamentəbəl, lə'mentə-\ *adj* —**lam·en·ta·bly** \-blē\ *adv* —**lam·en·ta·tion** \₁lamən'tāshən\ *n*

lam·i·nat·ed \\'lamə₁nātəd\ *adj* : made of thin layers of material —**lam·i·nate** \-₁nāt\ *vb* —**lam·i·nate** \-nət\ *n or adj* —**lam·i·na·tion** \₁lamə'nāshən\ *n*

lamp \\'lamp\ *n* : device for producing light or heat

lam·poon \lam'pün\ *n* : satire —**lampoon** *vb*

lam·prey \\'lamprē\ *n, pl* **-preys** : sucking eellike water animal

lance \\'lans\ *n* : spear ~ *vb* **lanced; lanc·ing** : pierce or open with a lancet

lance corporal *n* : enlisted man in the marine corps ranking above a private first class and below a corporal

lan·cet \\'lansət\ *n* : pointed surgical instrument

land \\'land\ *n* 1 : solid part of the surface of the earth 2 : country ~ *vb* 1 : go ashore 2 : catch or gain 3 : touch the ground or a surface —**land·less** *adj*

land·fill *n* : dump

land·hold·er *n* : owner of land —**land·hold·ing** *adj or n*

land·ing \\'landiŋ\ *n* 1 : action of one that lands 2 : place for loading passengers and cargo 3 : level part of a staircase

land·locked *adj* : enclosed by land

land·lord *n* : owner of property —**land·la·dy** *n*

land·lub·ber \-₁ləbər\ *n* : one with little sea experience

land·mark \\'lan(d)₁märk\ *n* 1 : object that marks a boundary or serves as a guide 2 : event that marks a turning point

land·scape \-₁skāp\ *n* : view of natural scenery ~ *vb* **-scaped; -scap·ing** : beautify a piece of land (as by decorative planting)

land·slide *n* 1 : slipping down of a mass of earth 2 : overwhelming victory

land·ward \\'landwərd\ *adj* : toward the land —**landward** *adv*

lane \\'lān\ *n* : narrow way

lan·guage \\'laŋgwij\ *n* : words and the methods of combining them for communication

lan·guid \\'laŋgwəd\ *adj* 1 : weak 2 : sluggish —**lan·guid·ly** *adv* —**languid·ness** *n*

lan·guish \\'laŋgwish\ *vb* : become languid or discouraged

lan·guor \\'laŋ(g)ər\ *n* : listless indolence —**lan·guor·ous** *adj* —**lan·guor·ous·ly** *adv*

lank \\'laŋk\ *adj* 1 : thin 2 : limp

lanky *adj* **lank·i·er; -est** : tall and thin

lan·o·lin \\'lan²lən\ *n* : fatty wax used in ointments

lan·tern \\'lantərn\ *n* : enclosed portable light

¹lap \\'lap\ *n* 1 : front part of the lower trunk and thighs of a seated person 2 : overlapping part 3 : one complete circuit ~ *vb* **-pp-** : fold over or around

²lap *vb* **-pp-** 1 : scoop up with the tongue 2 : splash gently

lap·dog *n* : small dog

la·pel \lə'pel\ *n* : fold of the front of a coat

lap·i·dary \\'lapə₁derē\ *n* : one who cuts and polishes gems ~ *adj* : relating to gems

lapse \\'laps\ *n* 1 : slight error 2 : termination of a right or privilege 3 : interval ~ *vb* **lapsed; laps·ing** 1 : slip 2 : subside 3 : cease

lar·board \\'lärbərd\ *n* : port side

lar·ce·ny \\'lärsnē, -²nē\ *n, pl* **-nies** : theft —**lar·ce·nous** \\'lärsnos, -²nos\ *adj*

larch \\'lärch\ *n* : conical evergreen

lard \\'lärd\ *n* : pork fat

lar·der \\'lärdər\ *n* : pantry

large \\'lärj\ *adj* **larg·er; larg·est** : greater than average —**large·ly** *adv* —**large·ness** *n*

lar·gess, lar·gesse \lär'zhes, -'jes; 'lär₁jes\ *n* : liberal giving

lar·i·at \\'larēət\ *n* : lasso

¹lark \\'lärk\ *n* : small songbird

²lark *vb or n* : romp

lar·va \\'lärvə\ *n, pl* **-vae** \-(₁)vē\ : wormlike form of an insect —**lar·val** \-vəl\ *adj*

lar·yn·gi·tis \₁larən'jītəs\ *n* : inflammation of the larynx

lar·ynx \'larinks\ *n, pl* **-ryn·ges** \lə'rin,jēz\ *or* **-ynx·es** : upper part of the trachea —**la·ryn·ge·al** \,larən'jēal, lə'rinjēal\ *adj*

las·civ·i·ous \lə'sivēəs\ *adj* : lewd —**las·civ·i·ous·ness** *n*

la·ser \'lāzər\ *n* : device that produces an intense light beam

¹lash \'lash\ *vb* 1 : whip ~ *n* 1 : stroke esp. of a whip 2 : eyelash

²lash *vb* : bind with a rope or cord

lass \'las\ *n* : girl

lass·ie \'lasē\ *n* : girl

las·si·tude \'lasə,t(y)üd\ *n* 1 : fatigue 2 : listlessness

las·so \'lasō, la'sü\ *n, pl* **-sos** *or* **-soes** : rope with a noose for catching livestock —**lasso** *vb*

¹last \'last\ *vb* : continue in existence or operation

²last *adj* 1 : following all the rest 2 : previous —*adv* 1 : at the end 2 : most recently 3 : in conclusion ~ *n* : something that is last —**at last** : finally —**last·ly** *adv*

³last *n* : form on which a shoe is shaped

latch \'lach\ *vb* : catch or get hold ~ *n* : catch that holds a door closed

late \'lāt\ *adj* **later; lat·est** 1 : coming or staying after the proper time 2 : advanced toward the end 3 : recently deceased 4 : recent —**late** *adv* —**late·com·er** \-,kəmər\ *n* —**late·ly** *adv* —**late·ness** *n*

la·tent \'lāt³nt\ *adj* : potential —**la·ten·cy** \-³nsē\ *n*

lat·er·al \'lat(ə)rəl\ *adj* : on or toward the side —**lat·er·al·ly** *adv*

la·tex \'lā,teks\ *n, pl* **-ti·ces** \'lātə,sēz, 'lat-\ *or* **-tex·es** : emulsion of synthetic rubber or plastic

lath \'lath, 'lath\ *n, pl* **laths** *or* **lath** : building material (as a thin strip of wood) used as a base for plaster —**lath·ing** \-iŋ\ *n*

lathe \'lāth\ *n* : machine that rotates material for shaping

lath·er \'lathər\ *n* : foam ~ *vb* : form or spread lather

lat·i·tude \'latə,t(y)üd\ *n* 1 : distance north or south from the earth's equator 2 : freedom of action

la·trine \lə'trēn\ *n* : toilet

lat·ter \'latər\ *adj* 1 : more recent 2 : being the second of 2 —**lat·ter·ly** *adv*

lat·tice \'latəs\ *n* : framework of crossed strips

laud *vb or n* : praise —**laud·able** *adj* —**laud·ably** *adv*

laugh \'laf, 'laf\ *vb* : show mirth, joy, or scorn with a smile and explosive sound —**laugh** *n* —**laugh·able** *adj* —**laugh·ing·ly** \-iŋlē\ *adv*

laugh·ing·stock \'lafiŋ,stäk, 'läf-\ *n* : object of ridicule

laugh·ter \'laftər, 'läf-\ *n* : action or sound of laughing

¹launch \'lönch\ *vb* 1 : hurl or send off 2 : set afloat 3 : start —**launch** *n* —**launch·er** *n*

²launch *n* : small open boat

laun·der \'löndər\ *vb* : wash or iron fabrics —**laun·der·er** *n* —**laun·dress** \-drəs\ *n* —**laun·dry** \-drē\ *n*

lau·re·ate \'lörēət\ *n* : recipient of honors —**lau·re·ate·ship** *n*

lau·rel \'lörəl\ *n* 1 : small evergreen tree 2 : honor

la·va \'lävə, 'lav-\ *n* : volcanic molten rock

lav·a·to·ry \'lavə,tōrē\ *n, pl* **-ries** : bathroom

lav·en·der \'lavəndər\ *n* 1 : aromatic plant used for perfume 2 : pale purple

lav·ish \'lavish\ *adj* : expending or expending profusely ~ *vb* : expend or give freely —**lav·ish·ly** *adv*

law \'lö\ *n* 1 : established rule of conduct 2 : body of such rules 3 : principle of construction or procedure 4 : rule stating uniform behavior under uniform conditions 5 : lawyer's profession —**law·break·er** *n* —**law·giv·er** *n* —**law·less** *adj* —**law·less·ly** *adv* —**law·mak·er** *n* —**law·man** \-mən\ *n* —**law·suit** *n*

law·ful \'lófəl\ *adj* : permitted by law —**law·ful·ly** *adv*

lawn \'lön\ *n* : grass-covered yard

law·yer \'löyər\ *n* : legal practitioner

lax \'laks\ *adj* : not strict or tense —**lax·i·ty** \'laksətē\ *n* —**lax·ly** *adv*

lax·a·tive \'laksətiv\ *n* : drug relieving constipation

¹lay \'lā\ *vb* **laid** \'lād\; **lay·ing** 1 : put on a surface 2 : produce eggs 3 : bet 4 : impose as a duty or burden 5 : place (as stress) on something 6 : put forward ~ *n* : way something lies or is laid

²lay *past of* LIE

³lay *n* : song

⁴lay *adj* : of the laity —**lay·man** \-mən\ *n* —**lay·wom·an** \-,wúmən\ *n*

lay·er \'lāər\ *n* 1 : one that lays 2 : one thickness over or under another

lay·off \'lā,öf\ *n* : temporary dismissal of a worker

lay·out \'lā,aút\ *n* 1 : arrangement 2 : outfit

la·zy \'lāzē\ *adj* **-zi·er; -est** : disliking

activity or exertion —**la·zi·ly** \'lāzǝlē\ adv —**la·zi·ness** n

lea \'lē, 'lā\ n : meadow

leach \'lēch\ vb : remove (a soluble part) with a solvent

¹lead \'lēd\ vb **led** \'led\, **lead·ing 1** : direct or run on a course **2** : direct the activity of **3** : go at the head of **4** : bring or tend to a definite result — n : position in front —**lead·er** n —**lead·er·less** adj —**lead·er·ship** n

²lead \'led\ n **1** : heavy bluish white chemical element **2** : marking substance in a pencil —**lead·en** \'led³n\ adj

leaf \'lēf\ n, pl **leaves** \'lēvz\ **1** : green outgrowth of a plant stem **2** : leaflike thing ~ vb **1** : produce leaves **2** : turn book pages —**leaf·age** \'lēfij\ n —**leafed** \'lēft\ adj —**leaf·less** adj —**leafy** \'lēfē\ adj —**leaved** \'lēfd\ adj

leaf·let \'lēflǝt\ n : pamphlet

¹league \'lēg\ n : unit of distance equal to about 3 miles

²league n : association for a common purpose —**league** vb —**leagu·er** n

leak \'lēk\ vb **1** : enter or escape through a leak **2** : become or make known ~ n : opening that accidentally admits or lets out a substance —**leak·age** \'lēkij\ n —**leaky** adj

¹lean \'lēn\ vb **1** : bend from a vertical position **2** : rely on for support **3** : incline in opinion —**lean** n

²lean adj **1** : lacking in flesh **2** : lacking richness —**lean·ness** \'lēnnǝs\ n

leap \'lēp\ vb **leaped** or **leapt** \'lept, 'lept\; **leap·ing** : jump —**leap** n

leap year n : 366-day year

learn \'lǝrn\ vb **1** : gain understanding or skill by study or experience **2** : memorize **3** : find out —**learn·er** n

learn·ed \-ǝd\ adj : having great learning

learn·ing \-iŋ\ n : knowledge gained by study

lease \'lēs\ n : contract transferring real estate for a term and usu. for rent ~ vb **leased; leas·ing** : grant by or hold under a lease

leash \'lēsh\ n : line to hold an animal —**leash** vb

least \'lēst\ adj **1** : lowest in importance or position **2** : smallest **3** : scantiest ~ n : one that is least ~ adv : in the smallest or lowest degree

leath·er \'lethǝr\ n : dressed animal skin —**leather** adj —**leath·ern** \-ǝrn\ adj —**leath·ery** adj

¹leave \'lēv\ vb **left** \'left\; **leav·ing 1** : bequeath **2** : allow or cause to remain **3** : have as a remainder **4** : go away ~ n **1** : permission **2** : authorized absence **3** : departure

²leave vb **leaved; leav·ing** : leaf

leav·en \'levǝn\ n : substance for producing fermentation ~ vb : raise dough with a leaven

leaves pl of LEAF

lech·ery \'lechǝrē\ n : inordinate indulgence in sex —**lech·er** \'lechǝr\ n —**lech·er·ous** adj —**lech·er·ous·ness** n

lec·ture \'lekchǝr\ n **1** : instructive talk —**lec·ture** vb —**lec·tur·er** n —**lec·ture·ship** n

led past of LEAD

ledge \'lej\ n : shelflike projection

led·ger \'lejǝr\ n : account book

lee \'lē\ n : side sheltered from the wind —**lee** adj

leech \'lēch\ n : segmented freshwater worm

leek \'lēk\ n : onionlike herb

leer \'liǝr\ n : suggestive look —**leer** vb

leery \'li(ǝ)rē\ adj : suspicious or wary

lees \'lēz\ n pl : dregs

lee·ward \'lēwǝrd, 'lüǝrd\ adj : situated away from the wind ~ n : the lee side —**leeward** adv

lee·way \'lē,wā\ n : allowable margin

¹left \'left\ adj : on the same side of the body as the heart ~ n : left hand —**left** adv

²left past of LEAVE

leg \'leg\ n **1** : limb of an animal that supports the body or something like it **2** : clothing to cover the leg ~ vb **-gg-** : walk or run —**legged** \'legǝd\ adj —**leg·less** adj

leg·a·cy \'legǝsē\ n, pl **-cies** : inheritance

le·gal \'lēgǝl\ adj **1** : relating to law or lawyers **2** : lawful —**le·gal·is·tic** \,lēgǝ'listik\ adj —**le·gal·i·ty** \li'galǝtē\ n —**le·gal·ize** \'lēgǝ,līz\ vb —**le·gal·ly** \-gǝlē\ adv

le·gate \'legǝt\ n : official representative

le·ga·tion \li'gāshǝn\ n **1** : diplomatic mission **2** : official residence and office of a diplomat

leg·end \'lejǝnd\ n **1** : story handed down from the past **2** : inscription —**leg·end·ary** \-ǝn,derē\ adj

leg·er·de·main \,lejǝrdǝ'mān\ n : sleight of hand

leg·gings, leg·gins \'leganz, -inz\ n pl : leg coverings

leg·i·ble \'lejǝbǝl\ adj : capable of being read —**leg·i·bil·i·ty** \,lejǝ'bilǝtē\ n —**leg·i·bly** \'lejǝblē\ adv le·gion \'lējən\ n 1 : large military force 2 : multitude 3 : association of former servicemen —le·gion·ary \-,erē\ n —le·gion·naire \,lējən'aər\ n

leg·is·late \'lejə,slāt\ vb -lat·ed; -lat·ing : enact or bring about with laws —leg·is·la·tion \,lejə'slāshən\ n —leg·is·la·tive \'lejə,slātiv\ adj —leg·is·la·tor \-ər\ n

leg·is·la·ture \'lejə,slāchər\ n : organization with authority to make laws

le·git·i·mate \li'jitəmət\ adj 1 : lawfully begotten 2 : genuine 3 : conforming with law or accepted standards —le·git·i·ma·cy \-məsē\ n —le·git·i·mate·ly adv

le·gume \'leg,yüm, li'gyüm\ n : plant bearing pods —le·gu·mi·nous \li'gyümənəs\ adj

lei \'lā(,ē)\ n : necklace of flowers

lei·sure \'lēzhər, 'lezh-, 'lāzh-\ n 1 : free time 2 : comfort 3 : convenience —lei·sure·ly adj

lem·ming \'lemiŋ\ n : short-tailed rodent

lem·on \'lemən\ n : yellow citrus fruit —lem·ony adj

lem·on·ade \,lemə'nād\ n : sweetened lemon beverage

lend \'lend\ vb lent \'lent\; lend·ing 1 : give for temporary use 2 : furnish —lend·er n

length \'leŋth\ n 1 : longest dimension 2 : duration in time 3 : piece to be joined to others —length·en \'leŋthən\ vb —length·wise adv or adj —lengthy adj

le·nient \'lēnēənt, -nyənt\ adj : of mild and tolerant disposition or effect —le·ni·en·cy \'lēnēənsē, -nyənsē,\ n —le·ni·ent·ly adv

len·i·ty \'lenətē\ n : leniency

lens \'lenz\ n 1 : curved piece for forming an image in an optical instrument 2 : transparent body in the eye that focuses light rays

Lent \'lent\ n : 40-day period of penitence and fasting from Ash Wednesday to Easter —Lent·en \'lentˀn\ adj

len·til \'lentˀl\ n : Old World legume

le·o·nine \'lēə,nīn\ adj : like a lion

leop·ard \'lepərd\ n : large tawny black-spotted cat

le·o·tard \'lēə,tärd\ n : close-fitting garment

lep·er \'lepər\ n : person with leprosy

lep·re·chaun \'leprə,kän\ n : mischievous Irish elf

lep·ro·sy \'leprəsē\ n : chronic bacterial disease —lep·rous \-rəs\ adj

les·bi·an \'lezbēən\ n : female homosexual —lesbian adj —les·bi·an·ism \-,izəm\ n

le·sion \'lēzhən\ n : abnormal area in the body due to injury or disease

less \'les\ adj 1 : fewer 2 : of lower rank, degree, or importance 3 : smaller ~ adv : to a lesser degree ~ n, pl less : smaller portion ~ prep : minus —less \ləs\ n -ən\ vb

-less \ləs\ adj suffix 1 : not having 2 : unable to act or be acted on

les·see \le'sē\ n : tenant under a lease

less·er \'lesər\ adj 1 : smaller 2 : inferior

les·son \'lesən\ n 1 : reading or exercise to be studied by a pupil 2 : something learned

les·sor \'les,ör, le'sör\ n : one who transfers property by a lease

lest \'lest\ conj : for fear that

¹let \'let\ n : hindrance or obstacle

²let vb let; let·ting 1 : cause to 2 : rent 3 : permit

-let \lət\ n suffix : small one

le·thal \'lēthəl\ adj : deadly —le·thal·ly adv

leth·ar·gy \'lethərjē\ n : state of being lazy or indifferent —le·thar·gic \li'thärjik\ adj

let·ter \'letər\ n 1 : unit of an alphabet 2 : written or printed communication 3 pl : literature or learning 4 : literal meaning ~ vb : mark with letters —let·ter·er n

let·tuce \'letəs\ n : garden plant with crisp leaves

leu·ke·mia \lü'kēmēə\ n : cancerous blood disease —leu·ke·mic \-mik\ adj or n

lev·ee \'levē\ n : embankment to prevent flooding

lev·el \'levəl\ n 1 : device for establishing a flat surface 2 : horizontal surface 3 : position in a scale ~ vb -eled or -elled; -el·ing or -el·ling 1 : make flat or level 2 : aim 3 : raze ~ adj 1 : having a smooth surface 2 : of the same height or rank —lev·el·er n —lev·el·ly adv —lev·el·ness n

le·ver \'levər, 'lē-\ n : bar for prying or dislodging something —le·ver·age \'lev(ə)rij, 'lēv-\ n

le·vi·a·than \li'vīəthən\ n 1 : large sea animal 2 : enormous thing

lev·i·ty \'levətē\ n : unseemly frivolity

levy \'levē\ n, pl lev·ies : imposition or collection of a tax ~ vb lev·ied; levy·ing 1 : impose or collect legally 2 : enlist for military service 3 : wage

lewd \'lüd\ adj 1 : sexually unchaste 2

: salacious —**lewd·ly** adv —**lewd·ness** n

lex·i·cog·ra·phy \\leksə'kägrəfē\ n : dictionary making —**lex·i·cog·ra·pher** \-fər\ n —**lex·i·co·graph·i·cal** \-kō'grafikəl\ or **lex·i·co·graph·ic** \-ik\ adj

lex·i·con \'leksə,kän\ n, pl **-i·ca** \-sikə\ or **-icons** : dictionary

li·a·ble \'līəbəl\ adj 1 : legally obligated 2 : probable 3 : susceptible —**li·a·bil·i·ty** \,līə'bilətē\ n

li·ai·son \'lēə,zän, lē'ā-\ n 1 : close bond 2 : communication between groups

li·ar \'līər\ n : one who lies

li·bel \'lībəl\ n : action, crime, or an instance of injuring a person's reputation esp. by something written ~ vb **-beled** or **-belled; -bel·ing** or **-bel·ling** : make or publish a libel —**li·bel·er** n —**li·bel·ist** n —**li·bel·ous, li·bel·lous** \-bələs\ adj

lib·er·al \'lib(ə)rəl\ adj : not stingy, narrow, or conservative —**liberal** n —**lib·er·al·ism** \-,izəm\ n —**lib·er·al·i·ty** \,libə'ralətē\ n —**lib·er·al·ize** \'lib(ə)rə,līz\ vb —**lib·er·al·ly** \-rəlē\ adv

lib·er·ate \'libə,rāt\ vb **-at·ed; -at·ing** : set free —**lib·er·a·tion** \,libə'rāshən\ n —**lib·er·a·tor** \'libə,rātər\ n

lib·er·tine \'libər,tēn\ n : one who leads a dissolute life

lib·er·ty \'libərtē\ n, pl **-ties** 1 : quality or state of being free 2 : action going beyond normal limits

li·bi·do \lə'bēdō, -'bīd\ n, pl **-dos** : sexual drive —**li·bid·i·nal** \lə'bid⁰nəl\ adj —**li·bid·i·nous** \-əs\ adj

li·brary \'lī,brerē\ n, pl **-brar·ies** 1 : place where books are kept for use 2 : collection of books —**li·brar·i·an** \lī'brerēən\ n

li·bret·to \lə'bretō\ n, pl **-tos** or **-ti** \-ē\ : text of an opera —**li·bret·tist** \-əst\ n

lice pl of LOUSE

li·cense, li·cence \'līs⁰ns\ n 1 : legal permission to engage in some activity 2 : document or tag evidencing a license granted 3 : irresponsible use of freedom —**license** vb —**li·cens·ee** \,līs⁰n'sē\ n

li·cen·tious \lī'senchəs\ adj : disregarding sexual restraints —**li·cen·tious·ly** adv —**li·cen·tious·ness** n

li·chen \'līkən\ n : complex lower plant made up of an alga and a fungus —**li·chen·ous** adj

lic·it \'lisət\ adj : lawful

lick \'lik\ vb 1 : draw the tongue over 2 : beat ~ n 1 : stroke of the tongue 2 : small amount

lic·o·rice \'lik(ə)rish, -rəs\ n : dried root of a European leguminous plant or candy flavored with an extract from it

lid \'lid\ n 1 : movable cover 2 : eyelid

¹lie \'lī\ vb **lay** \'lā\; **lain** \'lān\; **ly·ing** \'līiŋ\ 1 : be in, rest in, or assume a horizontal position 2 : occupy a certain relative position ~ n : position in which something lies

²lie vb **lied; ly·ing** \'līiŋ\ : tell a lie ~ n : untrue statement

liege \'lēj\ n : feudal superior or vassal

lien \'lēn, 'lēən\ n : legal claim on the property of another

lieu·ten·ant \lü'tenənt\ n 1 : representative 2 : first lieutenant or second lieutenant 3 : commissioned officer in the navy ranking next below a lieutenant commander —**lieu·ten·an·cy** \-ənsē\ n

lieutenant colonel n : commissioned officer (as in the army) ranking next below a colonel

lieutenant commander n : commissioned officer in the navy ranking next below a commander

lieutenant general n : commissioned officer (as in the army) ranking next below a general

lieutenant junior grade n, pl **lieutenants junior grade** : commissioned officer in the navy ranking next below a lieutenant

life \'līf\ n, pl **lives** \'līvz\ 1 : quality that distinguishes a vital and functional being from a dead body or inanimate matter 2 : physical and mental experiences of an individual 3 : biography 4 : period of existence 5 : way of living 6 : liveliness —**life·less** adj —**life·like** adj

life·blood n : basic source of strength and vitality

life·boat n : boat for use in saving lives at sea

life·guard n : one employed to safeguard bathers

life·long adj : continuing through life

life·sav·ing n : art or practice of saving lives —**life·sav·er** \-,sāvər\ n

life·time n : duration of an individual's existence

lift \'lift\ vb 1 : move upward or cause to move upward 2 : put an end to —**lift** n

lift-off \'lif,tȯf\ n : vertical takeoff by a rocket

184

lig·a·ment \'ligəmənt\ *n* : band of tough tissue that holds bones together

lig·a·ture \'ligə,chùr, -chər\ *n* : something that binds or ties

¹light \'līt\ *n* **1** : radiation that makes vision possible **2** : daylight **3** : source of light **4** : public knowledge **5** : aspect **6** : celebrity **7** : flame for lighting — *adj* **1** : bright **2** : weak in color — *vb* **light·ed** *or* **lit; light·ing 1** : make or become light **2** : cause to burn —**light·er** *n* —**light·ness** *n* —**light·proof** *adj*

²light *adj* : not heavy, serious, or abundant —**light** *adv* —**light·ly** *adv* —**light·ness** *n*

³light *vb* **light·ed** *or* **lit** \'līt\; **light·ing 1** : settle or dismount

light·en \'līt⁀n\ *vb* **1** : make light or bright **2** : give out flashes of lightning

light·en *vb* **1** : relieve of a burden **2** : become lighter

light·heart·ed \-'härtəd\ *adj* : GAY —**light·heart·ed·ly** *adv* —**light·heart·ed·ness** *n*

light·house *n* : structure with a powerful light for guiding sailors

light·ning \'lītniŋ\ *n* : flashing discharge of atmospheric electricity

light-year \'līt,yiər\ *n* : distance traveled by light in one year equal to about 5.878 trillion miles

lig·nite \'lig,nīt\ *n* : brownish black soft coal

¹like \'līk\ *vb* **liked; lik·ing 1** : enjoy **2** : desire — *n* : preference —**lik·able, like·able** \'līkəbəl\ *adj*

²like *adj* : similar — *prep* **1** : similar or similarly to **2** : typical of **3** : such as — *n* : counterpart — *conj* : as or as if —**like·ness** *n* —**like·wise** *adv*

-like \,līk\ *adj comb form* : resembling, suggesting, or characteristic of

like·li·hood \'līklē,hùd\ *n* : probability

like·ly \'līklē\ *adj* **-li·er; -est 1** : probable **2** : believable — *adv* **1** : in all probability

lik·en \'līkən\ *vb* : compare

lik·ing \'līkiŋ\ *n* : favorable regard

li·lac \'līlak, -lak, -läk\ *n* : shrub with clusters of fragrant pink, purple, or white flowers

lilt \'lilt\ *n* : rhythmical swing or flow

lily \'lilē\ *n, pl* **lil·ies** : tall bulbous herb with funnel-shaped flowers

lima bean \,līmə-\ *n* : flat edible seed of a bean grown for its flat edible seed or the seed

limb \'lim\ *n* **1** : projecting appendage used in moving or grasping **2** : tree branch —**limb·less** *adj*

lim·ber \'limbər\ *adj* : supple or agile — *vb* : make or become limber

lim·bo \'limbō\ *n, pl* **-bos** : place or state of confinement or oblivion

¹lime \'līm\ *n* : caustic white oxide of calcium

²lime *n* : small green lemonlike citrus fruit —**lime·ade** \-,ād\ *n*

lime·light *n* : center of public attention

lim·er·ick \'lim(ə)rik\ *n* : light poem of 5 lines

lime·stone *n* : rock that yields lime when burned

lim·it \'limət\ *n* **1** : boundary **2** : something that restrains or confines — *vb* **1** : set limits on —**lim·i·ta·tion** \,limə'tāshən\ *n* —**lim·it·less** *adj*

lim·ou·sine \'limə,zēn, ,limə'-\ *n* : large luxurious sedan

limp \'limp\ *vb* : walk lamely — *n* : limping movement or gait — *adj* : lacking firmness and body —**limp·ly** *adv* —**limp·ness** *n*

lim·pid \'limpəd\ *adj* : clear or transparent

lin·den \'lindən\ *n* : tree with large heart-shaped leaves

¹line \'līn\ *vb* **lined; lin·ing** : cover the inner surface of —**lin·ing** *n*

²line *n* **1** : cord, rope, or wire **2** : row or something like a row **3** : note **4** : course of action or thought **5** : state of agreement **6** : occupation **7** : limit **8** : transportation system **9** : long narrow mark — *vb* **lined; lin·ing 1** : mark with a line **2** : place in a line **3** : form a line

lin·eage \'linēij\ *n* : descent from a common ancestor

lin·eal \'linēəl\ *adj* **1** : linear **2** : in a direct line of ancestry

lin·ea·ments \'linēəmənts\ *n pl* : features or contours esp. of a face

lin·ear \'linēər\ *adj* **1** : straight **2** : long and narrow

lin·en \'linən\ *n* **1** : cloth or thread made of flax **2** : household articles made of cloth

lin·er \'līnər\ *n* **1** : one that lines **2** : ship or airplane belonging to a line

line·up \'līn,əp\ *n* **1** : line of persons for inspection or identification **2** : list of players in a game

-ling \liŋ\ *n suffix* **1** : one connected with or having the quality of **2** : young, small, or inferior one

lin·ger \'liŋgər\ *vb* : be slow to leave or act

lin·ge·rie \,länjə'rā, ,lan͡zhə-, -'rē\ *n* : women's underwear

lin·go \'liŋgō\ *n, pl* **-goes** : usu. strange language

lin·guist \'liŋgwəst\ *n* 1 : person skilled in speech or la*n*guages 2 : student of language —**lin·guis·tic** \liŋ'gwistik\ *adj* —**lin·guis·tics** *n pl*

lin·i·ment \'linəmənt\ *n* : liquid medication rubbed on the skin

link \'liŋk\ *n* 1 : connecting structure (as a ring of a chain) 2 : bond —**link** *vb* —**link·age** \-ij\ *n* —**link·er** *n*

li·no·leum \lə'nōlēəm\ *n* : floor covering with hard surface

lin·seed \'lin₁sēd\ *n* : seeds of flax yielding an oil (linseed oil)

lint \'lint\ *n* : fine fluff or loose short fibers from fabric

lin·tel \'lint²l\ *n* : horizontal piece over a door or window

li·on \'līən\ *n* : large cat of Africa and Asia —**li·on·ess** \'līənəs\ *n*

li·on·ize \'līə₁nīz\ *vb* **-ized; -iz·ing** : treat as very important —**li·on·iza·tion** \₁līənə'zāshən\ *n*

lip \'lip\ *n* 1 : either of the 2 fleshy folds surrounding the mouth 2 : edge of something hollow —**lipped** \'lipt\ *adj* —**lip-read·ing** *n*

lip·stick \'lip₁stik\ *n* : stick of cosmetic to color lips

liq·ue·fy \'likwə₁fī\ *vb* **-fied; -fy·ing** : reduce to liquid —**liq·ue·fac·tion** \₁likwə'fakshən\ *n* —**liq·ue·fi·able** \-'fīəbəl\ *adj* —**liq·ue·fi·er** \'likwə₁fīər\ *n*

li·queur \li'kər\ *n* : sweet or aromatic alcoholic liquor

liq·uid \'likwəd\ *adj* 1 : flowing freely like water 2 : neither solid nor gaseous 3 : of or convertible to cash —**liquid** *n* —**li·quid·i·ty** \lik'widətē\ *n*

liq·ui·date \'likwə₁dāt\ *vb* **-dat·ed; -dat·ing** 1 : pay off 2 : dispose of —**liq·ui·da·tion** \₁likwə'dāshən\ *n*

li·quor \'likər\ *n* : liquid substance and esp. a distilled alcoholic beverage

lisp \'lisp\ *vb* : pronounce *s* and *z* imperfectly —**lisp** *n*

lis·some \'lisəm\ *adj* : supple or agile

¹list \'list\ *n* 1 : series of names or items — *vb* 1 : make a list of 2 : put on a list

²list *vb* : tilt or lean over ~ *n* : slant

lis·ten \'lis²n\ *vb* 1 : pay attention in order to hear 2 : heed —**lis·ten·er** \'lisnər, -²nər\ *n*

list·less \'listləs\ *adj* : having no desire to act —**list·less·ly** *adv* —**list·less·ness** *n*

lit \'lit\ *past of* LIGHT

lit·a·ny \'lit²nē\ *n, pl* **-nies** : prayer said as a series of responses to a leader

li·ter \'lētər\ *n* : unit of liquid measure equal to about 1.06 quarts

lit·er·al \'lit(ə)rəl\ *adj* : being exactly as stated —**lit·er·al·ly** *adv*

lit·er·ary \'litə₁rerē\ *adj* : relating to literature

lit·er·ate \'lit(ə)rət\ *adj* : able to read and write —**lit·er·a·cy** \'lit(ə)rəsē\ *n*

lit·er·a·ture \'lit(ə)rə₁chùr, -chər\ *n* : writings of enduring interest

lithe \'līth, 'līth\ *adj* 1 : supple 2 : graceful —**lithe·some** \-səm\ *adj*

lith·o·graph \'lithə₁graf\ *n* : print from drawing on stone —**li·thog·ra·pher** \lith'ägrəfər, 'lithə₁grafər\ *n* —**lith·o·graph·ic** \₁lithə'grafik\ *adj* —**li·thog·ra·phy** \lith'ägrəfē\ *n*

lit·i·gate \'litə₁gāt\ *vb* **-gat·ed; -gat·ing** : carry on a lawsuit —**lit·i·gant** \'litigənt\ *n* —**lit·i·ga·tion** \₁litə'gāshən\ *n* —**li·ti·gious** \lə'tijəs, li-\ *adj* —**li·ti·gious·ness** *n*

lit·mus \'litməs\ *n* : coloring matter that turns red in acid solutions and blue in alkaline

lit·ter \'litər\ *n* 1 : animal offspring of one birth 2 : stretcher 3 : rubbish ~ *vb* 1 : give birth to young 2 : strew with litter

lit·tle \'lit²l\ *adj* **lit·tler** \litlər, -²lər\ *or* **less** \'les\ *or* **less·er** \'lesər\; **lit·tlest** \'litləst, -²ləst\ *or* **least** \'lēst\ 1 : not big 2 : not much 3 : not important — *adv* **less** \'les\; **least** \'lēst\ 1 : slightly 2 : not often ~ *n* : small amount —**lit·tle·ness** *n*

lit·ur·gy \'litərjē\ *n, pl* **-gies** : rite of worship —**li·tur·gi·cal** \lə'tərjikəl\ *adj* —**li·tur·gi·cal·ly** \-k(ə)lē\ *adv* —**lit·ur·gist** \'litərjəst\ *n*

liv·able \'livəbəl\ *adj* : suitable for living in or with —**liv·a·bil·i·ty** \₁livə'bilətē\ *n*

¹live \'liv\ *vb* **lived; liv·ing** 1 : be alive 2 : conduct one's life 3 : subsist 4 : reside

²live \'līv\ *adj* 1 : having life 2 : burning 3 : connected to electric power 4 : not exploded 5 : of continuing interest 6 : involving the actual presence of real people

live·li·hood \'līvlē₁hùd\ *n* : means of subsistence

live·long \'liv'lòŋ\ *adj* : whole

live·ly \'līvlē\ *adj* **-li·er; -est** : full of life and vigor —**live·li·ness** *n*

liv·en \'līvən\ *vb* : enliven

liv·er \'livər\ *n* : organ that secretes bile —**liv·ered** \'livərd\ *adj*

liv·ery \'liv(ə)rē\ *n, pl* **-er·ies** 1 : uniform for household servants 2 : care of horses for pay —**liv·er·ied** \-rēd\ *adj* —**liv·ery·man** \-mən\ *n*

lives *pl of* LIFE

live·stock \'līv,stäk\ *n* : farm animals

liv·id \'livəd\ *adj* 1 : discolored by bruising 2 : pale 3 : enraged

liv·ing \'liviŋ\ *adj* : having life ~ *n* : livelihood

liz·ard \'lizərd\ *n* : scaly reptile

lla·ma \'lämə\ *n* : So. American mammal related to the camel

lo \'lō\ *interj* —used to call attention

load \'lōd\ *n* 1 : cargo 2 : supported weight 3 : burden ~ *vb* 1 : put a load on 2 : burden 3 : put ammunition in

¹loaf \'lōf\ *n, pl* **loaves** \'lōvz\ : mass of bread

²loaf *vb* : waste time —**loaf·er** *n*

loam \'lōm, 'lüm\ *n* : soil —**loamy** *adj*

loan \'lōn\ *n* 1 : money borrowed at interest 2 : something lent temporarily 3 : permission to use ~ *vb* : lend

loath \'lōth, 'lōth\ *adj* : very reluctant

loathe \'lōth\ *vb* **loathed; loath·ing** : hate

loath·ing \'lōthiŋ\ *n* : extreme disgust

loath·some \'lōthsəm, 'lōth-\ *adj* : repulsive

lob \'läb\ *vb* **-bb-** : throw or hit in a high arc —**lob** *n*

lob·by \'läbē\ *n, pl* **-bies** 1 : public waiting room at the entrance of a building 2 : persons lobbying ~ *vb* **-bied; -by·ing** : try to influence legislators —**lob·by·ist** *n*

lobe \'lōb\ *n* : rounded part —**lo·bar** \'lōbər\ *adj* —**lobed** \'lōbd\ *adj*

lo·bot·o·my \lō'bätəmē\ *n, pl* **-mies** : severance of nerve fibers in the brain

lob·ster \'läbstər\ *n* : marine crustacean with 2 large pincerlike claws

lo·cal \'lōkəl\ *adj* : confined to or serving a limited area —**local** *n* —**lo·cal·ly** *adv*

lo·cale \lō'kal\ *n* : setting for an event

lo·cal·i·ty \lō'kalətē\ *n, pl* **-ties** : particular place

lo·cal·ize \'lōkə,līz\ *vb* **-ized; -iz·ing** : confine to a definite place —**lo·cal·iza·tion** \,lōkələ'zāshən\ *n*

lo·cate \'lō,kāt, lō'kāt\ *vb* **-cat·ed; -cat·ing** 1 : settle 2 : find a site for 3 : discover the place of —**lo·ca·tion** \lō'kāshən\ *n*

¹lock \'läk\ *n* : tuft or strand of hair

²lock *n* 1 : fastener using a bolt 2 : enclosure in a canal to raise or lower boats ~ *vb* 1 : make fast with a lock 2 : confine 3 : interlock

lock·er \'läkər\ *n* : storage compartment

lock·et \'läkət\ *n* : small case worn on a necklace

lock·jaw *n* : tetanus

lock·out *n* : closing of a plant by an employer during a labor dispute

lock·smith \-,smith\ *n* : one who makes or repairs locks

lo·co·mo·tion \,lōkə'mōshən\ *n* : power of moving —**lo·co·mo·tive** \-'mōtiv\ *adj*

lo·co·mo·tive \-'mōtiv\ *n* : vehicle that moves railroad cars

lo·co·weed \'lōkō,wēd\ *n* : western plant poisonous to livestock

lo·cust \'lōkəst\ *n* 1 : migratory grasshopper 2 : cicada 3 : tree with hard wood

lo·cu·tion \lō'kyüshən\ *n* : way of saying something

lode \'lōd\ *n* : ore deposit

lode·stone *n* : magnetic rock

lodge \'läj\ *vb* **lodged; lodg·ing** 1 : provide quarters for 2 : come to rest 3 : file ~ *n* 1 : special house (as for hunters) 2 : animal's den 3 : branch of a fraternal organization —**lodg·er** \'läjər\ *n* —**lodg·ing** *n* —**lodg·ment, lodge·ment** \-mənt\ *n*

loft \'lȯft\ *n* 1 : attic 2 : upper floor (as of a warehouse)

lofty \'lȯftē\ *adj* **loft·i·er; -est** : tall or high —**loft·i·ly** *adv* —**loft·i·ness** *n*

¹log \'lȯg, 'läg\ *n* 1 : unshaped timber 2 : daily record of a ship's or plane's progress ~ *vb* **-gg-** 1 : cut trees for lumber 2 : enter in a log

²log *n* : logarithm

log·a·rithm \'lȯgə,rithəm, 'läg-\ *n* : exponent to which a base number is raised to produce a given number —**log·a·rith·mic** \,lȯgə'rithmik, ,läg-\ *adj*

loge \'lōzh\ *n* : box in a theater

log·ger \-ər\ *n* : one engaged in logging

log·ger·head \'lȯgər,hed, 'läg-\ *n* : large Atlantic sea turtle —**at loggerheads** : in disagreement

log·ic \'läjik\ *n* 1 : science of reasoning 2 : sound reasoning —**log·i·cal** \-ikəl\ *adj* —**log·i·cal·ly** *adv* —**lo·gi·cian** \lō'jishən\ *n*

lo·gis·tics \lō'jistiks\ *n sing or pl* : procurement and movement of people and supplies —**lo·gis·tic** *adj*

logo \'lōgō, 'lȯg-, 'läg-\ *n, pl* **log·os** \-ōz\ : advertising symbol

loin \'lȯin\ *n* 1 : part of the body on each side of the spine between the hip and lower ribs 2 *pl* : abdominal regions

loi·ter \'lȯitər\ *vb* : remain around a place idly —**loi·ter·er** *n*

loll \\'läl\\ vb : lounge

lol·li·pop, lol·ly·pop \\'läli,päp\\ n : hard candy on a stick

lone \\'lōn\\ adj 1 : alone or isolated 2 : only —**lone·li·ness** n —**lone·ly** adj —**lon·er** \\'lōnər\\ n

lone·some \\-səm\\ adj : sad from lack of company —**lone·some·ly** adv —**lone·some·ness** n

long \\'lȯŋ\\ adj **lon·ger** \\'lȯŋgər\\; **lon·gest** \\'lȯŋgəst\\ 1 : extending far or for a considerable time 2 : having a specified length 3 : tedious 4 : well supplied—used with on ~ adv : for a long time ~ n : long period ~ vb : feel a strong desire —**long·ing** \\'lȯŋiŋ\\ n —**long·ing·ly** adv

lon·gev·i·ty \\län'jevətē\\ n : long life

long·hand n : handwriting

long·horn n : cattle with long horns

lon·gi·tude \\'länjə,t(y)üd\\ n : angular distance east or west from a meridian

lon·gi·tu·di·nal \\,länjə't(y)üdənəl, -'nəl\\ adj : lengthwise —**lon·gi·tu·di·nal·ly** adv

long·shore·man \\'lȯŋ'shōrmən\\ n : one who loads and unloads ships

look \\'lük\\ vb 1 : see 2 : seem 3 : direct one's attention 4 : face ~ n 1 : movement of the eyes to see something 2 : appearance of the face 3 : aspect —**look after** : take care of —**look for** 1 : expect 2 : search for

look·out n 1 : one who watches 2 : careful watch

¹loom \\'lüm\\ n : frame or machine for weaving

²loom vb : appear large and indistinct or impressive

loon \\'lün\\ n : black-and-white diving bird

loo·ny, loo·ney \\'lünē\\ adj -**ni·er; -est** : crazy

loop \\'lüp\\ n 1 : doubling of a line that leaves an opening 2 : something like a loop —**loop** vb

loop·hole \\'lüp,hōl\\ n : means of evading

loose \\'lüs\\ adj **loos·er; -est** 1 : not fixed tight 2 : not restrained 3 : not dense 4 : slack 5 : not exact ~ vb **loosed; loos·ing** 1 : release 2 : untie or relax —**loose** adv —**loose·ly** adv —**loos·en** \\'lüsən\\ vb —**loose·ness** n

loot \\'lüt\\ n or vb : plunder —**loot·er** n

lop \\'läp\\ vb -**pp-** : cut off

lope \\'lōp\\ n : bounding gait —**lope** vb

lop·sid·ed \\'läp'sīdəd\\ adj : leaning to one side 2 : not symmetrical —**lop·sid·ed·ly** adv —**lop·sid·ed·ness** n

lo·qua·cious \\lō'kwāshəs\\ adj : very talkative —**lo·quac·i·ty** \\-'kwasətē\\ n

lord \\'lȯrd\\ n 1 : one with authority over others 2 : British nobleman

lord·ly \\-lē\\ adj **-li·er; -est** : haughty

lord·ship \\-,ship\\ n : rank of a lord

Lord's Supper n : Communion

lore \\'lōr\\ n : traditional knowledge

lose \\'lüz\\ vb **lost** \\'lȯst\\; **los·ing** \\'lüziŋ\\ 1 : have pass from one's possession 2 : be deprived of 3 : waste 4 : be defeated in 5 : fail to keep to or hold —**los·er** n

loss \\'lȯs\\ n 1 : something lost 2 pl : killed, wounded, or captured soldiers 3 : failure to win

lost \\'lȯst\\ adj 1 : not used, won, or claimed 2 : unable to find the way

lot \\'lät\\ n 1 : object used in deciding something by chance 2 : share 3 : fate 4 : plot of land 5 : much

loth \\'lōth, 'lōth\\ var of LOATH

lo·tion \\'lōshən\\ n : liquid to rub on the skin

lot·tery \\'lätərē\\ n, pl -**ter·ies** : drawing of lots with prizes going to winners

lo·tus \\'lōtəs\\ n 1 : legendary fruit that causes forgetfulness 2 : water lily

loud \\'laüd\\ adj 1 : high in volume of sound 2 : noisy 3 : obtrusive in color or pattern —**loud** adv —**loud·ly** adv —**loud·ness** n

loud·speak·er n : device that amplifies sound

lounge \\'laünj\\ vb **lounged; loung·ing** : act or move lazily ~ n : room with comfortable furniture

lour \\'laü(ə)r\\ var of LOWER

louse \\'laüs\\ n, pl **lice** \\'līs\\ : parasitic insect

lousy \\'laüzē\\ adj **lous·i·er; -est** 1 : infested with lice 2 : not good —**lous·i·ly** adv —**lous·i·ness** n

lout \\'laüt\\ n : stupid awkward person —**lout·ish** adj —**lout·ish·ly** adv

lou·ver, lou·vre \\'lüvər\\ n 1 : opening having parallel slanted slats for ventilation or such a slat

love \\'ləv\\ n 1 : strong affection 2 : warm attachment 3 : beloved person ~ vb **loved; lov·ing** 1 : feel affection for 2 : enjoy greatly —**lov·able** \\-əbəl\\ adj —**love·less** adj —**lov·er** n —**lov·ing·ly** adv

love·lorn \\-,lȯrn\\ adj : deprived of love or of a lover

love·ly \\'ləvlē\\ adj **-li·er; -est** : beautiful —**love·li·ness** n

¹low \\'lō\\ vb or n : moo

²low adj **low·er; low·est** 1 : not high or tall 2 : below the normal level 3 : not loud 4 : humble 5 : sad 6 : less than usual **7** : falling short of a standard **8** : unfavorable ~ *n* **1** : something low **2** : automobile gear giving the slowest speed —**low** *adj* —**low-ness** *n*

low-brow \'lō,braủ\ *n* : person without intellectual interests or culture

1low-er \'laủ(ə)r\ *vb* **1** : scowl **2** : become dark and threatening

2low-er \'lō(ə)r\ *adj* : relatively low (as in rank)

3low-er \'lō(ə)r\ *vb* **1** : drop **2** : let descend **3** : reduce in value

low-land \'lōlənd, -,land\ *n* : low flat country

low-ly \'lōlē\ *adj* **-li-er; -est** : humble —**low-li-ness** *n*

loy-al \'lȯi(ə)l\ *adj* : faithful to a country, cause, or friend —**loy-al-ist** *n* —**loy-al-ly** *adv* —**loy-al-ty** \'lȯi(ə)ltē\ *n*

loz-enge \'läz²nj\ *n* : small medicated candy

LSD \,el,es'dē\ *n* : hallucinogenic drug

lu-bri-cant \'lübrikənt\ *n* : material to reduce friction

lu-bri-cate \-,kāt\ *vb* **-cat-ed; -cat-ing** : apply a lubricant to —**lu-bri-ca-tion** \,lübrə'kāshən\ *n* —**lu-bri-ca-tor** \'lübrə,kātər\ *n*

lu-cid \'lüsəd\ *adj* **1** : clear-minded **2** : easily understood —**lu-cid-i-ty** \lü'sidətē\ *n* —**lu-cid-ly** *adv* —**lu-cid-ness** *n*

luck \'lək\ *n* **1** : chance **2** : good fortune —**luck-i-ly** *adv* —**luck-i-ness** *n* —**luck-less** *adj* —**lucky** *adj*

lu-cra-tive \'lükrətiv\ *adj* : profitable —**lu-cra-tive-ly** *adv* —**lu-cra-tive-ness** *n*

lu-di-crous \'lüdəkrəs\ *adj* : comically ridiculous —**lu-di-crous-ly** *adv* —**lu-di-crous-ness** *n*

lug \'ləg\ *vb* **-gg-** : drag or carry laboriously

lug-gage \'ləgij\ *n* : baggage

lu-gu-bri-ous \lủ'gübrēəs\ *adj* : mournful —**lu-gu-bri-ous-ly** *adv* —**lu-gu-bri-ous-ness** *n*

luke-warm \'lük'wȯrm\ *adj* **1** : moderately warm **2** : not enthusiastic

lull \'ləl\ *vb* : make or become quiet or relaxed ~ *n* **1** : temporary calm

lul-la-by \'lələ,bī\ *n*, *pl* **-bies** : song to lull children to sleep

lum-ba-go \,ləm'bāgō\ *n* : rheumatic back pain

lum-ber \'ləmbər\ *n* : timber dressed for use ~ *vb* : cut logs —**lum-ber-man** *n* —**lum-ber-yard** *n*

lum-ber-jack \-,jak\ *n* : logger

lu-mi-nary \'lümə,nerē\ *n*, *pl* **-nar-ies** : very famous person

lu-mi-nes-cence \,lümə'nes²ns\ *n* : low-temperature emission of light —**lu-mi-nes-cent** \-²nt\ *adj*

lu-mi-nous \'lümənəs\ *adj* : emitting light —**lu-mi-nance** \-nəns\ *n* —**lu-mi-nos-i-ty** \,lümə'näsətē\ *n* —**lu-mi-nous-ly** *adv*

lump \'ləmp\ *n* **1** : mass of irregular shape **2** : abnormal swelling ~ *vb* : heap together —**lump-ish** *adj* —**lumpy** *adj*

lu-na-cy \'lünəsē\ *n*, *pl* **-cies** : insanity

lu-nar \'lünər\ *adj* : of the moon

lu-na-tic \'lünə,tik\ *adj* : insane —**lunatic** *n*

lunch \'lənch\ *n* : noon meal ~ *vb* : eat lunch

lun-cheon \'lənchən\ *n* : usu. formal lunch

lung \'ləŋ\ *n* : breathing organ in the chest —**lunged** \'ləŋd\ *adj*

lunge \'lənj\ *n* **1** : sudden thrust **2** : sudden move forward —**lunge** *vb*

lurch \'lərch\ *n* : sudden swaying —**lurch** *vb*

lure \'lủr\ *n* **1** : something that attracts **2** : artificial fish bait ~ *vb* **lured; lur-ing** : attract

lu-rid \'lủrəd\ *adj* **1** : gruesome **2** : sensational —**lu-rid-ly** *adv*

lurk \'lərk\ *vb* : lie in wait

lus-cious \'ləshəs\ *adj* **1** : pleasingly sweet in taste or smell **2** : sensually appealing —**lus-cious-ly** *adv* —**lus-cious-ness** *n*

lush \'ləsh\ *adj* : covered with abundant growth

lust \'ləst\ *n* **1** : intense sexual desire **2** : intense longing —**lust** *vb* —**lust-ful** *adj*

luster, lustre \'ləstər\ *n* **1** : brightness from reflected light **2** : magnificence —**lus-ter-less** *adj* —**lus-trous** \-trəs\ *adj*

lusty \'ləstē\ *adj* **lust-i-er; -est** : full of vitality —**lust-i-ly** *adv* —**lust-i-ness** *n*

lute \'lüt\ *n* : pear-shaped stringed instrument —**lute-nist, lu-ta-nist** \'lüt²nəst\ *n*

lux-u-ri-ant \,ləg'zhùrēənt, ,lək'shủr-\ *adj* **1** : growing plentifully **2** : rich and varied —**lux-u-ri-ance** \-ēəns\ *n* —**lux-u-ri-ant-ly** *adv*

lux-u-ri-ate \-ē,āt\ *vb* **-at-ed; -at-ing** : revel

lux-u-ry \'ləksh(ə)rē, 'ləgzh-\ *n*, *pl* **-ries** **1** : great comfort **2** : something desirable but costly **3** : something adding to pleasure or comfort —**lux-u-ri-ous**

\ˌlag'zhu̇rēəs, ˌlək'shu̇r-\ *adj* —**lux-u·ri·ous·ly** *adv*

-ly \lē, *after* i *usu* ē; *(corresponding adjectives may end in* əl, *as* "double"); *-ically* is ik(ə)lē\ *adv suffix* **1** : in a specified way **2** : from a specified point of view

ly·ce·um \lī'sēəm, 'līsē-\ *n* : hall for public lectures

lye \'līl\ *n* : corrosive alkaline substance

lying *pres part of* LIE

lymph \'limf\ *n* : bodily liquid consisting chiefly of blood plasma and white blood cells —**lym·phat·ic** \lim'fatik\ *adj*

lynch \'linch\ *vb* : to put to death by mob action —**lynch·er** *n*

lynx \'links\ *n, pl* **lynx** *or* **lynx·es** : wildcat

lyre \'lī(ə)r\ *n* : ancient Greek stringed instrument

lyr·ic \'lirik\ *adj* **1** : suitable for singing **2** : expressing direct personal emotion ~ *n* **1** : lyric poem **2** *pl* : words of a song —**lyr·i·cal** \-ikəl\ *adj*

M

m \'em\ *n, pl* **m's** *or* **ms** \'emz\ : 13th letter of the alphabet

ma'am \'mam, *after* "yes" *often* əm\ *n* : madam

ma·ca·bre \mə'käb(rə), -'käbər, -'käbrə\ *adj* : gruesome

mac·ad·am \mə'kadəm\ *n* : pavement of cemented broken stone —**mac·ad·am·ize** \-ˌīz\ *vb*

mac·a·ro·ni \ˌmakə'rōnē\ *n* : tubes of dried wheat paste used as food

mac·a·roon \ˌmakə'rün\ *n* : cookie of ground almonds or coconut

ma·caw \mə'kȯ\ *n* : large long-tailed parrot

¹mace \'mās\ *n* **1** : heavy spiked club **2** : ornamental staff as a symbol of authority

²mace *n* : spice from the fibrous coating of the nutmeg

ma·chete \mə'shetē\ *n* : large heavy knife

mach·i·na·tion \ˌmakə'nāshən, ˌmashə-\ *n* : plot or scheme —**mach·i·nate** \'makəˌnāt, 'mash-\ *vb*

ma·chine \mə'shēn\ *n* : combination of mechanical or electrical parts ~ *vb* -**chined; -chin·ing** : modify by machine-operated tools —**ma·chin·able** *adj* —**ma·chin·ery** \-(ə)rē\ *n* —**ma·chin·ist** *n*

mack·er·el \'mak(ə)rəl\ *n, pl* **-el** *or* **-els** : No. Atlantic food fish

mack·i·naw \'makəˌnȯ\ *n* : short heavy plaid coat

mac·ra·me \ˌmakrə'mā\ *n* : coarse lace or fringe made by knotting

mac·ro \'mak(ˌ)rō\ *adj* : very large

mac·ro·cosm \'makrəˌkäzəm\ *n* : universe

mad \'mad\ *adj* **-dd-** **1** : insane or rabid **2** : rash and foolish **3** : angry **4** : carried away by enthusiasm —**mad·den** \'madᵊn\ *vb* —**mad·den·ing·ly** \'madninlē, -ᵊninl-\ *adv* —**mad·ly** *adv* —**mad·ness** *n*

mad·am \'madəm\ *n, pl* **mes·dames** \mā'däm\ —used in polite address to a woman

ma·dame \mə'dam, *before a surname also* ˌmadəm\ *n, pl* **mes·dames** \mā'däm\ —used as a title for a woman not of English-speaking nationality

mad·cap \'madˌkap\ *adj* : wild or zany —**madcap** *n*

made *past of* MAKE

Ma·dei·ra \mə'dirə\ *n* : amber-colored dessert wine

ma·de·moi·selle \ˌmad(ə)m(w)ə'zel, mam'zel\ *n, pl* **ma·de·moi·selles** \-'zelz\ *or* **mes·de·moi·selles** \ˌmād(ə)m(w)ə'zel\ : an unmarried girl or woman —used as a title for a woman esp. of French nationality

mad·house *n* **1** : insane asylum **2** : place of great uproar or confusion

mad·man \-ˌman, -mən\ *n* : lunatic —**mad·wom·an** *n*

mad·ri·gal \'madrigəl\ *n* : elaborate song for several voice parts

mael·strom \'mālstrəm\ *n* : whirlpool

mae·stro \'mīstrō\ *n, pl* **-stros** *or* **-stri** \-ˌstrē\ : eminent composer or conductor

Ma·fia \'mäfēə\ *n* : secret criminal organization

ma·fi·o·so \ˌmäfē'ō(ˌ)sō\ *n, pl* **-si** \-(ˌ)sē\ : member of the Mafia

mag·a·zine \ˌmagə,zēn\ *n* **1** : storehouse **2** : publication issued at regular intervals **3** : cartridge container in a gun

ma·gen·ta \mə'jentə\ *n* : deep purplish red

mag·got \'magət\ *n* : wormlike fly larva —**mag·goty** *adj*

mag·ic \'majik\ *n* **1** : art of using supernatural powers **2** : extraordinary power or influence **3** : sleight of hand —**magic, magical** \-ikəl\ *adj* —**mag·i·cal·ly** \-ik(ə)lē\ *adv* —**ma·gi·cian** \mə'jishən\ *n*

mag·is·te·ri·al \,majə'stirēəl\ *adj* **1** : authoritative **2** : relating to a magistrate

mag·is·trate \'majə,strāt\ *n* : judge —**mag·is·tra·cy** \-strəsē\ *n*

mag·ma \'magmə\ *n* : molten rock —**mag·mat·ic** \mag'matik\ *adj*

mag·nan·i·mous \mag'nanəməs\ *adj* : noble or generous —**mag·na·nim·i·ty** \,magnə'nimətē\ *n* —**mag·nan·i·mous·ly** *adv* —**mag·nan·i·mous·ness** *n*

mag·ne·sia \mag'nēshə, -zhə\ *n* : oxide of magnesium used as a laxative

mag·ne·sium \mag'nēzēəm, -zhəm\ *n* : silver-white metallic chemical element

mag·net \'magnət\ *n* **1** : body that attracts iron **2** : something that attracts —**mag·net·ic** \mag'netik\ *adj* —**mag·net·i·cal·ly** \-ik(ə)lē\ *adv* —**mag·ne·tism** \'magnə,tizəm\ *n*

mag·ne·tite \'magnə,tīt\ *n* : black iron ore

mag·ne·tize \'magnə,tīz\ *vb* **-tized; -tiz·ing 1** : attract like a magnet **2** : give magnetic properties to —**mag·ne·tiz·able** *adj* —**mag·ne·ti·za·tion** \,magnətə'zāshən\ *n* —**mag·ne·tiz·er** *n*

mag·nif·i·cent \mag'nifəsənt\ *adj* : splendid —**mag·nif·i·cence** \-səns\ *n* —**mag·nif·i·cent·ly** *adv*

mag·ni·fy \'magnə,fī\ *vb* **-fied; -fy·ing 1** : intensify **2** : enlarge —**mag·ni·fi·ca·tion** \,magnəfə'kāshən\ *n* —**mag·ni·fi·er** \'magnə,fī(ə)r\ *n*

mag·ni·tude \'magnə,t(y)üd\ *n* **1** : greatness of size or extent **2** : quantity

mag·no·lia \mag'nōlyə\ *n* : shrub with large fragrant flowers

mag·pie \'mag,pī\ *n* : long-tailed black-and-white bird

ma·hog·a·ny \mə'häg(ə)nē\ *n, pl* **-nies** : tropical evergreen tree or its reddish brown wood

maid \'mād\ *n* **1** : unmarried young woman **2** : female servant

maid·en \'mād²n\ *n* : unmarried young woman ~ *adj* **1** : unmarried **2** : first —**maid·en·hood** \-,hùd\ *n* —**maid·en·ly** *adj*

maid·en·hair \-,haər\ *n* : fern with delicate feathery fronds

¹mail \'māl\ *n* **1** : something sent or carried in the postal system **2** : postal system ~ *vb* : send by mail —**mail·box** *n* —**mail·man** \-,man, -mən\ *n*

²mail *n* : armor of metal links or plates

maim \'mām\ *vb* : seriously wound or disfigure

main \'mān\ *n* **1** : force **2** : ocean **3** : principal pipe, duct, or circuit of a utility system ~ *adj* : chief —**main·ly** *adv*

main·land \'mān,land, -lənd\ *n* : part of a country on a continent

main·stay *n* : chief support

main·stream *n* : prevailing current or direction of activity or influence —**mainstream** *adj*

main·tain \mān'tān\ *vb* **1** : keep in an existing state (as of repair) **2** : sustain **3** : declare —**main·tain·abil·i·ty** \-,tānə'bilətē\ *n* —**main·tain·able** \-'tānəbəl\ *adj* —**main·te·nance** \'māntnəns, -²nəns\ *n*

mai·tre d'hô·tel \,mātrədō'tel, ,me-\ *n* : head of a dining room staff

maize \'māz\ *n* : corn

maj·es·ty \'majəstē\ *n, pl* **-ties 1** : sovereign power or dignity —used as a title **2** : grandeur or splendor —**ma·jes·tic** \mə'jestik\, **ma·jes·ti·cal** \-tikəl\ *adj* —**ma·jes·ti·cal·ly** \-tik(ə)lē\ *adv*

ma·jor \'mājər\ *adj* **1** : larger or greater **2** : noteworthy or conspicuous ~ *n* **1** : commissioned officer (as in the army) ranking next below a lieutenant colonel **2** : main field of study ~ *vb* **-jored; -jor·ing** : pursue an academic major

ma·jor·do·mo \,mājər'dōmō\ *n, pl* **-mos** : head steward

major general *n* : commissioned officer (as in the army) ranking next below a lieutenant general

ma·jor·i·ty \mə'jorətē\ *n, pl* **-ties 1** : age of full civil rights **2** : quantity more than half

make \'māk\ *vb* **made** \'mād\; **mak·ing 1** : cause to exist, occur, or appear **2** : fashion or manufacture **3** : formulate in the mind **4** : constitute **5** : prepare **6** : cause to be or become **7** : carry out or perform **8** : compel **9** : gain **10** : have an effect —used *with for* ~ *n* : brand —**mak·er** *n* —**make do** *vb* : get along with what is available —**make good** *vb* **1** : repay **2** : succeed —**make out** *vb* **1** : draw up or write **2** : discern or understand **3** : fare —**make up** *vb* **1** : invent **2** : become reconciled **3** : compensate for

make-be-lieve n : a pretending to believe ~ adj : imagined or pretended

make-shift n : temporary substitute —**makeshift** adj

make-up \-,əp\ n **1** : way in which something is constituted **2** : cosmetics

mal-ad-just-ed \,malə'jəstəd\ adj : poorly adjusted (as to one's environment) —**mal-ad-just-ment** \-'jəs(t)mənt\ n

mal-adroit \,malə'dròit\ adj : clumsy or inept

mal-a-dy \'malədē\ n, pl -dies : disease or disorder

mal-aise \mə'lāz, ma-\ n : sense of being unwell

mal-a-mute \'malə,myüt\ n : powerful heavy-coated dog

mal-a-prop-ism \'malə,präp,izəm\ n : humorous misuse of a word

ma-lar-ia \mə'lerēə\ n : disease transmitted by a mosquito —**ma-lar-i-al** \-əl\ adj

ma-lar-key \mə'lärkē\ n : foolishness

mal-con-tent \,malkən'tent\ adj : dissatisfied with the state of affairs —**malcontent** n

male \'māl\ adj **1** : relating to the sex that performs a fertilizing function **2** : masculine ~ n : male individual —**male-ness** n

male-dic-tion \,malə'dikshən\ n : curse

male-fac-tor \'malə,faktər\ n : one who commits an offense esp. against the law

ma-lef-i-cent \mə'lefəsənt\ adj : harmful —**ma-lef-i-cence** \-səns\ n

ma-lev-o-lent \mə'levələnt\ adj : malicious or spiteful —**ma-lev-o-lence** \-ləns\ n

mal-fea-sance \mal'fēz³ns\ n : misconduct by a public official

mal-for-ma-tion \,malfòr'māshən\ n : distortion or faulty formation —**mal-formed** \mal'fòrmd\ adj

mal-func-tion \mal'fəŋkshən\ vb : fail to operate properly —**malfunction** n

mal-ice \'maləs\ n : ill will —**ma-li-cious** \mə'lishəs\ adj —**ma-li-cious-ly** adv

ma-lign \mə'līn\ adj **1** : wicked **2** : malignant ~ vb : speak evil of

ma-lig-nant \mə'lignənt\ adj **1** : harmful **2** : likely to cause death —**ma-lig-nan-cy** \-nənsē\ n —**ma-lig-nant-ly** adv —**ma-lig-ni-ty** \-nətē\ n

ma-lin-ger \mə'liŋgər\ vb : pretend illness to avoid duty —**ma-lin-ger-er** n

mall \'mòl\ n **1** : shaded promenade **2** : concourse providing access to rows of shops

mal-lard \'malərd\ n, pl **-lard** or **-lards** : common wild duck

mal-lea-ble \'malēəbəl\ adj : easily shaped —**mal-le-a-bil-i-ty** \,malēə'bilətē\ n

mal-let \'malət\ n : hammerlike tool

mal-nour-ished \mal'nərisht\ adj : poorly nourished

mal-nu-tri-tion \,maln(y)ü'trishən\ n : inadequate nutrition

mal-odor-ous \mal'ōdərəs\ adj : foul-smelling —**mal-odor-ous-ly** adv —**mal-odor-ous-ness** n

mal-prac-tice \-'praktəs\ n : failure of professional duty

malt \'mòlt\ n : sprouted grain used in brewing

mal-treat \mal'trēt\ vb : treat badly —**mal-treat-ment** n

ma-ma, mam-ma \'mämə\ n : mother

mam-mal \'maməl\ n : vertebrate animal that nourishes its young with milk —**mam-ma-li-an** \mə'mālēən, ma-\ adj or n

mam-ma-ry \'mamərē\ adj : relating to the milk-secreting glands

mam-moth \'maməth\ n : large hairy extinct elephant ~ adj : enormous

man \'man\ n, pl **men** \'men\ **1** : human being **2** : adult male **3** : mankind —vb -nn- **1** : station people to work on or at **2** : physically operate —**man-hood** n —**man-hunt** n —**man-like** adj —**man-li-ness** n —**man-ly** adj or adv —**man-made** adj —**man-nish** adj —**man-nish-ly** adv —**man-nish-ness** n —**man-size, man-sized** adj

man-a-cle \'manikəl\ n : shackle for the hands —**manacle** vb

man-age \'manij\ vb -aged; -ag-ing **1** : control **2** : direct or carry on business or affairs **3** : cope —**man-age-abil-i-ty** \,manijə'bilətē\ n —**man-age-able** \'manijəbəl\ adj —**man-age-able-ness** n —**man-age-ably** \-blē\ adv —**man-age-ment** \'manijmənt\ n —**man-age-men-tal** \,manij'ment³l\ adj —**man-ag-er** \'manijər\ n —**man-a-ge-ri-al** \,manə'jirēəl\ adj

man-da-rin \'mandərən\ n : Chinese imperial official

man-date \'man,dāt\ n : authoritative command

man-da-to-ry \'mandə,tōrē\ adj : obligatory

man-di-ble \'mandəbəl\ n : lower jaw —**man-dib-u-lar** \man'dibyələr\ adj

man-do-lin \,mandə'lin, 'mand³lən\ n : stringed musical instrument

man-drake \'man,drāk\ n : herb with a large forked root

mane \'mān\ *n* : animal's neck hair —**maned** \'mānd\ *adj*

ma·neu·ver \mə'n(y)üvər\ *n* **1** : planned movement of troops or ships **2** : military training exercise **3** : procedure involving expert physical movement **4** : skillful often evasive action or management —**maneuver** *vb* —**ma·neu·ver·abil·i·ty** \-ˌn(y)üvərə'bilətē\ *n*

man·ful \'manfəl\ *adj* : courageous —**man·ful·ly** *adv*

man·ga·nese \'maŋgəˌnēz, -ˌnēs\ *n* : gray metallic chemical element —**man·ga·ne·sian** \ˌmaŋgə'nēzhən, -shən\ *adj*

mange \'mānj\ *n* : skin disease of domestic animals —**mangy** \'mānjē\ *adj*

man·ger \'mānjər\ *n* : feeding trough for livestock

man·gle \'maŋgəl\ *vb* **-gled; -gling 1** : mutilate **2** : bungle —**man·gler** \-g(ə)lər\ *n*

man·go \'maŋgō\ *n, pl* **-goes** *or* **-gos** : yellowish red tropical fruit

man·grove \'manˌgrōv, 'maŋ-\ *n* : tropical tree growing in salt water

man·han·dle *vb* : handle roughly

man·hole *n* : entry to a sewer

ma·nia \'mānēə, -nyə\ *n* **1** : insanity **2** : excessive enthusiasm —**ma·ni·ac** \-nēˌak\ *n* —**ma·ni·a·cal** \mə'nīəkəl\ *adj* —**man·ic** \'manik\ *adj or n*

man·i·cure \'manəˌkyùər\ *n* : treatment for the fingernails ~ *vb* **-cured; -cur·ing 1** : do manicure work on **2** : trim precisely —**man·i·cur·ist** \-ˌkyùrəst\ *n*

1man·i·fest \'manəˌfest\ *adj* : clear to the senses or to the mind ~ *vb* : make evident —**man·i·fes·ta·tion** \ˌmanəfə'stāshən\ *n* —**man·i·fest·ly** *adv*

2manifest *n* : invoice of cargo or list of passengers

man·i·fes·to \ˌmanə'festō\ *n, pl* **-tos** *or* **-toes** : public declaration of policy or views

man·i·fold \'manəˌfōld\ *adj* : marked by diversity or variety ~ *n* : pipe fitting with several outlets for connections

ma·nila paper \mə'nilə-\ *n* : durable brownish paper

ma·nip·u·late \mə'nipyəˌlāt\ *vb* **-lat·ed; -lat·ing 1** : treat or operate manually or mechanically **2** : influence esp. by cunning —**ma·nip·u·la·tion** \mə,nip-yə'lāshən\ *n* —**ma·nip·u·la·tor** \-'nipyəˌlātiv\ *adj* —**ma·nip·u·la·tor** \-ˌlātər\ *n*

man·kind \'man'kīnd\ *n* : human race

man·na \'manə\ *n* : something valuable that comes unexpectedly

manned \'mand\ *adj* : carrying or performed by a man

man·ne·quin \'manikən\ *n* : dummy used to display clothes

man·ner \'manər\ *n* **1** : kind **2** : usual way of acting **3** : artistic method **4** *pl* : social conduct

man·nered \-ərd\ *adj* **1** : having manners of a specified kind **2** : artificial

man·ner·ism \'manəˌrizəm\ *n* : individual peculiarity of action

man·ner·ly \-lē\ *adj* : polite —**man·ner·li·ness** *n*

man-of-war \ˌmanə(v)'wòr\ *n, pl* **men-of-war** \ˌmen-\ : warship

man·or \'manər\ *n* : country estate —**ma·no·ri·al** \mə'nōrēəl\ *adj* —**ma·no·ri·al·ism** \-ēəˌlizəm\ *n*

man·pow·er *n* : supply of people available for service

man·sard \'manˌsärd\ *n* : roof with two slopes on all sides and the lower slope the steeper

manse \'mans\ *n* : parsonage

man·ser·vant *n, pl* **men·ser·vants** : a male servant

man·sion \'manchən\ *n* : very big house

man·slaugh·ter *n* : unintentional killing of a person

man·tel \'mantᵊl\ *n* : shelf above a fireplace

man·tis \'mantəs\ *n, pl* **-tis·es** *or* **-tes** \'manˌtēz\ : large insect with stout forelegs

man·tle \'mantᵊl\ *n* **1** : sleeveless cloak **2** : something that covers, enfolds, or envelopes ~ *vb* **-tled; -tling** : cover

man·tra \'mantrə\ *n* : mystical chant

man·u·al \'manyə(wə)l\ *adj* : involving the hands or physical force ~ *n* : handbook —**man·u·al·ly** *adv*

man·u·fac·ture \ˌmanyə'fakchər\ *n* : process of making wares by hand or by machinery ~ *vb* **-tured; -tur·ing** : make from raw materials —**man·u·fac·tur·er** *n*

ma·nure \mə'nùr\ *n* : animal excrement used as fertilizer —**ma·nu·ri·al** *adj*

man·u·script \'manyəˌskript\ *n* : something written or typed

many \'menē\ *adj* **more** \'mòr\; **most** \'mōst\ : consisting of a large number —**many** *n or pron*

map \'map\ *n* : representation of a geographical area ~ *vb* **-pp- 1** : make a **map of 2** : plan in detail —**map·pa·ble** \-əbəl\ *adj* —**map·per** *n*

ma·ple \'māpəl\ *n* : tree with hard light-colored wood

mar \'mär\ *vb* -**rr-** : damage

ma·ra·schi·no \ˌmarə'skēnō, -'shē-\ *n, pl* -**nos** : preserved cherry

mar·a·thon \'marəˌthän\ *n* 1 : long-distance race 2 : test of endurance

ma·raud \mə'rȯd\ *vb* : plunder —**ma·raud·er** *n*

mar·ble \'märbəl\ *n* 1 : crystallized limestone 2 : small glass ball used in a children's game (**marbles**)

mar·bling \-b(ə)liŋ\ *n* : intermixture of fat and lean in meat

march \'märch\ *vb* : move with regular steps or in a purposeful manner ~ *n* 1 : distance covered in a march 2 : measured stride 3 : forward movement 4 : music for marching —**march·er** *n*

March *n* : 3d month of the year having 31 days

mar·chio·ness \'märshənəs\ *n* 1 : wife or widow of a marquess 2 : woman holding the rank of a marquess

Mar·di Gras \'märdēˌgrä\ *n* : Tuesday before the beginning of Lent often observed with parades and merry-making

mare \'maar\ *n* : female horse

mar·ga·rine \'märj(ə)rən, -əˌrēn\ *n* : butter substitute made usu. from vegetable oils

mar·gin \'märjən\ *n* 1 : edge 2 : spare amount, measure, or degree —**mar·gin·al** \-ᵊl\ *adj* —**mar·gin·al·ly** *adv*

mari·gold \'marəˌgōld, 'mer-\ *n* : garden plant with showy flower heads

mari·jua·na, mari·hua·na \ˌmarə'(h)wänə\ *n* : intoxicating drug obtained from the hemp plant

ma·ri·na \mə'rēnə\ *n* : place for mooring boats

mar·i·nate \'marəˌnāt\ *vb* -**nat·ed; -nat·ing** : soak in a savory sauce

ma·rine \mə'rēn\ *adj* 1 : relating to the sea 2 : relating to marines ~ *n* : infantry soldier associated with a navy

mar·i·ner \'marənər\ *n* : sailor

mar·i·o·nette \ˌmarēə'net, ˌmer-\ *n* : puppet

mar·i·tal \'marətᵊl\ *adj* : relating to marriage

mar·i·time \'marəˌtīm\ *adj* : relating to the sea or commerce on the sea

mar·jo·ram \'märj(ə)rəm\ *n* : aromatic mint used as a seasoning

¹**mark** \'märk\ *n* 1 : something aimed at 2 : something (as a line) designed to record position 3 : visible sign 4 : written symbol 5 : grade 6 : lasting impression 7 : blemish ~ *vb* 1 : designate or set apart by a mark or make a mark on 2 : characterize 3 : remark —**mark·er** *n*

²**mark** *n* : monetary unit of East Germany

marked \'märkt\ *adj* : noticeable —**mark·ed·ly** \'märkədlē\ *adv*

mar·ket \'märkət\ *n* 1 : buying and selling of goods or the place this happens 2 : demand for commodities 3 : store ~ *vb* : sell —**mar·ket·able** *adj*

mar·ket·place *n* 1 : market 2 : world of trade or economic activity

marks·man \'märksmən\ *n* : good shooter —**marks·man·ship** *n*

mar·lin \'märlən\ *n* : large oceanic fish

mar·ma·lade \'märməˌlād\ *n* : jam with pieces of fruit and rind

mar·mo·set \'märməˌset\ *n* : small bushy-tailed monkey

mar·mot \'märmət\ *n* : burrowing rodent

¹**ma·roon** \mə'rün\ *vb* : isolate without hope of escape

²**maroon** *n* : dark red

mar·quee \mär'kē\ *n* : canopy over an entrance

mar·quess \'märkwəs\ *n* : British noble ranking next below a duke

mar·quis \'märkwəs, mär'kē\ *n* : marquess

mar·quise \mär'kēz\ *n, pl* **mar·quises** \-'kēz(əz)\ : marchioness

mar·riage \'marij\ *n* 1 : state of being married 2 : wedding ceremony —**mar·riage·able** *adj*

mar·row \'marō\ *n* : soft tissue in the cavity of bone

mar·ry \'marē\ *vb* -**ried; -ry·ing** 1 : join as husband and wife 2 : take or give in marriage —**mar·ried** *adj or n*

marsh \'märsh\ *n* : soft wet land —**marshy** *adj*

mar·shal \'märshəl\ *n* 1 : leader of ceremony 2 : usu. high military or administrative officer ~ *vb* -**shaled** or -**shalled; -shal·ing** or -**shal·ling** 1 : arrange in order, rank, or position 2 : lead with ceremony

marsh·mal·low \'märsh,melō, -,mal\ *n* : spongy candy

mar·su·pi·al \mär'süpēəl\ *n* : Australian mammal that nourishes young in an abdominal pouch —**marsupial** *adj*

mart \'märt\ *n* : market

mar·ten \'märtᵊn\ *n, pl* -**ten** or -**tens** : weasellike mammal

mar·tial \'märshəl\ *adj* : relating to war or an army 2 : warlike

mar·tin \'märt°n\ n : small swallow

mar·ti·net \ˌmärt°n'et\ n : strict disciplinarian

mar·tyr \'märtər\ n : one who dies or makes a great sacrifice for a cause ~ vb : make a martyr of —**mar·tyr·dom** \-dəm\ n

mar·vel \'märvəl\ vb -**veled** or -**velled**; -**vel·ing** or -**vel·ling** : feel surprise or wonder ~ n : something amazing —**mar·vel·ous**, **mar·vel·lous** \'märv(ə)ləs\ adj —**mar·vel·ous·ly** adv —**mar·vel·ous·ness** n

Marx·ism \'märkˌsizəm\ n : political and social principles of Karl Marx —**Marx·ist** \-səst\ n or adj

mas·cara \mas'karə\ n : eye cosmetic

mas·cot \'masˌkät, -kət\ n : one believed to bring good luck

mas·cu·line \'maskyələn\ adj : relating to the male sex —**mas·cu·lin·i·ty** \ˌmaskyə'linətē\ n

mash \'mash\ n 1 : crushed steeped grain for fermenting 2 : soft pulpy mass ~ vb 1 : reduce to a pulpy mass 2 : smash —**mash·er** n

mask \'mask\ n : disguise for the face ~ vb 1 : disguise 2 : cover to protect —**mask·er** n

mas·och·ism \'masəˌkizəm, 'maz-\ n : pleasure in being abused —**mas·och·ist** \-kəst\ n —**mas·och·is·tic** \ˌmasə'kistik, ˌmaz-\ adj

ma·son \'mās°n\ n : workman who builds with stone or brick —**ma·son·ry** \-rē\ n

mas·quer·ade \ˌmaskə'rād\ n 1 : costume party 2 : disguise ~ vb -**ad·ed**; -**ad·ing** 1 : disguise oneself 2 : take part in a costume party —**mas·quer·ad·er** n

mass \'mas\ n 1 : large amount of matter or number of things 2 : expanse or magnitude 3 : great body of people —usu. pl. ~ vb : form into a mass —**mass·less** \-ləs\ adj —**mass·less·ness** n —**massy** adj

Mass \'mas\ n : worship service of the Roman Catholic Church

mas·sa·cre \'masikər\ n : wholesale slaughter —**massacre** vb

mas·sage \mə'säzh, -'säj\ n : a rubbing of the body —**massage** vb

mas·seur \ma'sər\ n : man who massages

mas·seuse \-'sə(r)z, -'süz\ n : woman who massages

mas·sive \'masiv\ adj 1 : being a large mass 2 : large in scope —**mas·sive·ly** adv —**mas·sive·ness** n

mast \'mast\ n : tall pole supporting sails —**mast·ed** adj

mas·ter \'mastər\ n 1 : male teacher 2 : holder of an academic degree between a bachelor's and a doctor's 3 : one highly skilled 4 : one in authority ~ vb 1 : subdue 2 : become proficient in —**mas·ter·ful** \-fəl\ adj —**mas·ter·ful·ly** adv —**mas·ter·ly** adj —**mas·ter·ship** \-ˌship\ n —**mas·tery** \'mast(ə)rē\ n

master chief petty officer n : petty officer of the highest rank in the navy

master gunnery sergeant n : noncommissioned officer in the marine corps ranking above a master sergeant

mas·ter·piece \'mastərˌpēs\ n : great piece of work

master sergeant n 1 : noncommissioned officer in the army ranking next below a sergeant major 2 : noncommissioned officer in the air force ranking next below a senior master sergeant 3 : noncommissioned officer in the marine corps ranking next below a master gunnery sergeant

mas·ter·work n : masterpiece

mas·tic \'mastik\ n : pasty glue

mas·ti·cate \'mastəˌkāt\ vb -**cat·ed**; -**cat·ing** : chew —**mas·ti·ca·tion** \ˌmastə'kāshən\ n

mas·tiff \'mastəf\ n : large dog

mas·to·don \'mastəˌdän\ n : extinct elephantlike animal

mas·toid \'masˌtȯid\ n : bone behind the ear —**mastoid** adj

mas·tur·ba·tion \ˌmastər'bāshən\ n : stimulation of sex organs by hand —**mas·tur·bate** \'mastərˌbāt\ vb

¹**mat** \'mat\ n 1 : coarse woven or plaited fabric 2 : mass of tangled strands 3 : thick pad ~ vb -**tt**- : form into a mat

²**mat, matt, matte** \'mat\ adj : not shiny ~ n 1 : border around a picture 2 : dull finish

mat·a·dor \'matəˌdȯr\ n : bullfighter

¹**match** \'mach\ n 1 : one equal to another 2 : 2 things that go well together 3 : game 4 : marriage ~ vb 1 : set in competition 2 : marry 3 : be or provide the equal of 4 : fit or go together —**match·less** adj —**match·mak·er** n

²**match** n : piece of wood or paper material with a combustible tip

mate \'māt\ n 1 : companion 2 : subordinate officer on a ship 3 : one of a pair ~ vb **mat·ed**; **mat·ing** 1 : fit together 2 : come together as a pair

ma·te·ri·al \mə'tirēəl\ adj 1 : natural 2 : relating to matter 3 : important 4 : of a physical or worldly nature ~ n

: stuff something is made of —**ma·te·ri·al·ly** adv

ma·te·ri·al·ism \mə'tirēə,lizəm\ n 1 : theory that matter is the only reality 2 : preoccupation with material and not spiritual things —**ma·te·ri·al·ist** \-ləst\ n or adj —**ma·te·ri·al·is·tic** \-,tirēə'listik\ adj

ma·te·ri·al·ize \mə'tirēə,līz\ vb -ized; -iz·ing : take or cause to take bodily form —**ma·te·ri·al·i·za·tion** \mə-,tirēələ'zāshən\ n

ma·té·ri·el \mə,tir'el\ n : military supplies

ma·ter·nal \mə'tərnᵊl\ adj : motherly —**ma·ter·nal·ly** adv

ma·ter·ni·ty \mə'tərnətē\ n, pl -ties 1 : state of being a mother 2 : hospital's childbirth facility —**maternity** adj

math \'math\ n : mathematics

math·e·mat·ics \,mathə'matiks\ n pl : science of numbers and of space configurations —**math·e·mat·i·cal** \-ikəl\ adj —**math·e·mat·i·cal·ly** adv —**math·e·ma·ti·cian** \,mathə-mə'tishən\ n

mat·i·née \,matᵊn'ā\ n : afternoon performance

mat·ins \'matᵊnz\ n : morning prayers

ma·tri·arch \'mātrē,ärk\ n : woman who rules a family —**ma·tri·ar·chal** \,mātrē'ärkəl\ adj —**ma·tri·ar·chy** \'mātrē,ärkē\ n

ma·tri·cide \'matrə,sīd, 'mā-\ n : murder of one's mother —**ma·tri·cid·al** \,matrə'sīdᵊl, ,mā-\ adj

ma·tric·u·late \mə'trikyə,lāt\ vb -lat·ed; -lat·ing : enroll in school —**ma·tric·u·la·tion** \-,trikyə'lāshən\ n

mat·ri·mo·ny \'matrə,mōnē\ n : marriage —**mat·ri·mo·ni·al** \,matrə'mō-nēəl\ adj —**mat·ri·mo·ni·al·ly** adv

ma·trix \'mātriks\ n, pl -tri·ces \'mā-trə,sēz, 'ma-\ or -trix·es \'mā-triksəz\ 1 : something within which something else originates or develops 2 : mold

ma·tron \'mātrən\ n 1 : dignified mature woman 2 : woman supervisor —**ma·tron·ly** adj

matt, matte var of MAT

mat·ter \'matər\ n 1 : subject of interest 2 pl : circumstances 3 : trouble 4 : physical substance ~ vb : be important

mat·tock \'matək\ n : a digging tool

mat·tress \'matrəs\ n : pad to sleep on

ma·ture \mə't(y)u̇r\ adj -tur·er; -est 1 : carefully considered 2 : fully grown or developed 3 : due for payment ~ vb -tured; -tur·ing : become mature

mat·u·ra·tion \,machə'rāshən\ n —**mat·u·ra·tion·al** \-sh(ə)nəl\ adj —**ma·tu·ra·tive** \mə't(y)u̇rətiv\ adj —**ma·tu·ri·ty** \-ətē\ n

maud·lin \'mȯdlən\ adj : stupidly sentimental

maul \'mȯl\ n : heavy wooden hammer ~ vb 1 : beat 2 : handle roughly

mau·so·le·um \,mȯsə'lēəm, ,mȯzə-\ n, pl -leums or -lea \-'lēə\ : large above-ground tomb

mauve \'mōv, 'mȯv\ n : lilac color

ma·ven, ma·vin, may·vin \'māvən\ n : expert

mav·er·ick \'mav(ə)rik\ n 1 : unbranded range animal 2 : nonconformist

maw \'mȯ\ n 1 : stomach 2 : throat, esophagus, or jaws

mawk·ish \'mȯkish\ adj : sickly sentimental —**mawk·ish·ly** adv —**mawk·ish·ness** n

max·im \'maksəm\ n : proverb

max·i·mum \'maks(ə)məm\ n, pl -ma \-səmə\ or -mums \-s(ə)məmz\ 1 : greatest quantity 2 : upper limit 3 : largest number —**maximum** adj —**max·i·mize** \-sə,mīz\ vb

may \(')mā\ verbal auxiliary, past **might** \(')mīt\; pres sing & pl **may** 1 : have permission 2 : be likely to 3 —used to express desire, purpose, or contingency

May \'mā\ n : 5th month of the year having 31 days

may·ap·ple n : woodland herb having edible fruit

may·be \'mābē, 'mebē\ adv : perhaps

may·flow·er n : spring-blooming herb

may·fly n : fly with an aquatic larva

may·hem \'mā,hem, 'māəm\ n : crippling or mutilation of a person

may·on·naise \'māə,nāz\ n : thick salad dressing

may·or \'māər\ n : chief city official —**may·or·al** \-əl\ adj —**may·or·al·ty** \-əltē\ n —**may·or·ess** \'māərəs\ n

maze \'māz\ n : confusing network of passages —**mazy** adj

ma·zur·ka \mə'zərkə\ n : Polish dance

me \(')mē\ pron, objective case of I

mead \'mēd\ n : alcoholic beverage brewed from honey

mead·ow \'medō\ n : low-lying usu. level grassland —**mead·ow·land** \-,land\ n —**mead·owy** \'medəwē\ adj

mead·ow·lark n : songbird with a yellow breast

mea·ger, mea·gre \'mēgər\ adj 1 : thin 2 : scanty —**mea·ger·ly** adv —**mea·ger·ness** n

¹meal \'mēl\ *n* **1** : food to be eaten at one time **2** : act of eating —**meal-time** *n*

²meal *n* : ground grain —**mealy** *adj*

¹mean \'mēn\ *adj* **1** : humble **2** : worthy of or showing little regard **3** : stingy **4** : malicious —**mean-ly** *adv* —**mean-ness** *n*

²mean \'mēn\ *vb* **meant** \'ment\; **mean-ing** \'mēniŋ\ **1** : intend **2** : serve to convey, show, or indicate **3** : be important

³mean *n* **1** : middle point **2** *pl* : something that helps gain an end **3** *pl* : material resources **4** : sum of several quantities divided by the number of quantities ~ *adj* : being a mean

me-an-der \mē'andər\ *vb* **-dered; -der-ing** \-d(ə)riŋ\ **1** : follow a winding course **2** : wander aimlessly —**mean-der** *n*

mean-ing \'mēniŋ\ *n* : idea conveyed or intended to be conveyed —**mean-ing-ful** \-fəl\ *adj* —**mean-ing-ful-ly** *adv* —**mean-ing-less** *adj*

mean-time \'mēn,tīm\ *n* : intervening time —**meantime** *adv*

mean-while \-,hwīl\ *n* : meantime —**meanwhile** *adv*

mea-sles \'mēzəlz\ *n pl* : disease that is marked by red spots on the skin

mea-sly \'mēz(ə)lē\ *adj* **-sli-er; -est** : contemptibly small in amount

mea-sure \'mezhər, 'māzh-\ *n* **1** : moderate amount **2** : dimensions or amount **3** : something to show amount **4** : unit or system of measurement **5** : act of measuring **6** : means to an end ~ *vb* **-sured; -sur-ing 1** : regulate by a standard **2** : find out or mark off size or amount of **3** : have a specified measurement —**mea-sur-able** \'mezh(ə)rəbəl, 'māzh-\ *adj* —**mea-sur-ably** \-blē\ *adv* —**mea-sure-less** *adj* —**mea-sure-ment** *n* —**mea-sur-er** *n*

meat \'mēt\ *n* **1** : food **2** : animal flesh used as food —**meat-ball** *n* —**meaty** *adj*

me-chan-ic \mi'kanik\ *adj* **1** : manual **2** : like a machine ~ *n* : worker who repairs machines

me-chan-i-cal \mi'kanikəl\ *adj* **1** : relating to machines or mechanics **2** : involuntary —**me-chan-i-cal-ly** *adv*

me-chan-ics \-iks\ *n sing or pl* **1** : branch of physics dealing with energy and forces in relation to bodies **2** : mechanical details

mech-a-nism \'mekə,nizəm\ *n* **1** : piece of machinery **2** : technique for gaining a result **3** : basic processes producing a phenomenon —**mech-a-nis-tic** \,mekə'nistik\ *adj* —**mech-a-nis-ti-cal-ly** \-ti-k(ə)lē\ *adv* —**mech-a-ni-za-tion** \,mekənə'zāshən\ *n* —**mech-a-nize** \'mekə,nīz\ *vb* —**mech-a-niz-er** *n*

med-al \'medᵊl\ *n* **1** : religious pin or pendant **2** : coinlike commemorative metal piece

me-dal-lion \mə'dalyən\ *n* : large medal

med-dle \'medᵊl\ *vb* **-dled; -dling** : interfere —**med-dler** \'medlər, -ᵊlər\ *n* —**med-dle-some** \'medᵊlsəm\ *adj*

me-dia \'mēdēə\ *n pl* : communications organizations

me-di-an \'mēdēən\ *n* : middle value in a range —**median** *adj*

me-di-ate \'mēdē,āt\ *vb* **-at-ed; -at-ing** : help settle a dispute —**me-di-a-tion** \,mēdē'āshən\ *n* —**me-di-a-tor** \'mēdē,ātər\ *n*

med-ic \'medik\ *n* : medical worker esp. in the military

med-i-ca-ble \'medikəbəl\ *adj* : curable —**med-i-ca-bly** \-blē\ *adv*

med-ic-aid \'medi,kād\ *n* : government program of medical aid for the poor

med-i-cal \'medikəl\ *adj* : relating to medicine —**med-i-cal-ly** \-k(ə)lē\ *adv*

medi-care \'medi,keər\ *n* : government program of medical care for the aged

med-i-cate \'medə,kāt\ *vb* **-cat-ed; -cat-ing** : treat with medicine —**med-i-ca-tion** \,medə'kāshən\ *n*

med-i-cine \'medəsən\ *n* **1** : preparation used to treat disease **2** : science dealing with the cure of disease —**me-dic-i-nal** \mə'disnəl, -ᵊnəl\ *adj* —**me-dic-i-nal-ly** *adv*

me-di-eval, me-di-ae-val \,mēd(ē)'ēval, ,med-, ,mid-\ *adj* : of or relating to the Middle Ages —**me-di-e-val-ism** \-,izəm\ *n* —**me-di-e-val-ist** \-əst\ *n*

me-di-o-cre \,mēdē'ōkər\ *adj* : not very good —**me-di-oc-ri-ty** \-'äkrətē\ *n*

med-i-tate \'medə,tāt\ *vb* **-tat-ed; -tat-ing** : contemplate —**med-i-ta-tion** \,medə'tāshən\ *n* —**med-i-ta-tive** \'medə,tātiv\ *adj* —**med-i-ta-tive-ly** *adv*

me-di-um \'mēdēəm\ *n, pl* **-diums** or **-dia** \-ēə\ **1** : middle position or degree **2** : means of effecting or conveying something **3** : surrounding substance **4** : means of communication **5** : mode of artistic expression —**medium** *adj*

med-ley \'medlē\ *n, pl* **-leys** : series of songs performed as one meek \'mēk\ *adj* 1 : mild-mannered 2 : weak —**meek·ly** *adv* —**meek·ness** *n*

meer·schaum \'miərshəm, -,shòm\ *n* : claylike tobacco pipe

¹meet \'mēt\ *vb* met \'met\; **meet·ing** 1 : run into 2 : join 3 : oppose 4 : assemble 5 : satisfy 6 : be introduced to ~ *n* : sports team competition

²meet *adj* : proper

meet·ing \'mētin\ *n* : a getting together —**meet·ing·house** *n*

mega·cy·cle \'megə,sīkəl\ *n* : megahertz

mega·hertz \-,hərts, -,heərts\ *n* : one million hertz

mega·phone \'megə,fōn\ *n* : coneshaped device to intensify or direct the voice

mel·an·choly \'melən,kälē\ *n* : depression —**mel·an·chol·ic** \,melən'kälik\ *adj* —**melancholy** *adj*

mel·a·no·ma \,melə'nōmə\ *n, pl* -mas *also* -ma·ta \-mətə\ : usu. malignant tumor

me·lee \'mā,lā, mā'lā\ *n* : brawl

me·lio·rate \'mēlyə,rāt, 'mēlēə-\ *vb* -rat·ed; -rat·ing : improve —**me·lio·ra·tion** \,mēlyə'rāshən, ,mēlēə-\ *n* —**me·lio·ra·tive** \'mēlyə,rātiv, 'mēlēə-\ *adj*

mel·lif·lu·ous \me'lifləwəs, mə-\ *adj* : sweetly flowing —**mel·lif·lu·ous·ly** *adv* —**mel·lif·lu·ous·ness** *n*

mel·low \'melō\ *adj* : grown gentle or mild 2 : rich and full —**mellow** *vb* —**mel·low·ness** *n*

melo·dra·ma \'melə,drämə, -,dram-\ *n* : overly theatrical play —**melo·dra·mat·ic** \,melədrə'matik\ *adj* —**melo·dra·ma·tist** \-,melə'dramətəst, -'dräm-\ *n*

mel·o·dy \'melədē\ *n, pl* -dies 1 : agreeable sound 2 : succession of musical notes —**me·lod·ic** \mə'lädik\ *adj* —**me·lod·i·cal·ly** \-ik(ə)lē\ *adv* —**me·lo·di·ous** \mə'lōdēəs\ *adj* —**me·lo·di·ous·ly** *adv* —**me·lo·di·ous·ness** *n*

mel·on \'melən\ *n* : gourdlike fruit

melt \'melt\ *vb* 1 : change from solid to liquid usu. by heat 2 : dissolve or disappear gradually 3 : move or be moved emotionally

mem·ber \'membər\ *n* 1 : part of a person, animal, or plant 2 : one of a group 3 : part of a whole —**mem·ber·ship** \-,ship\ *n*

mem·brane \'mem,brān\ *n* : thin layer esp. of animal or plant tissue —**mem·bra·nous** \-brənəs\ *adj*

me·men·to \mi'mentō\ *n, pl* -tos *or* -toes : souvenir

memo \'memō\ *n, pl* mem·os : memorandum

mem·oirs \'mem,wärz\ *n pl* : autobiography

mem·o·ra·bil·ia \,memərə'bilēə, -'bilyə\ *n pl* 1 : memorable things 2 : mementos

mem·o·ra·ble \'mem(ə)rəbəl\ *adj* : worth remembering —**mem·o·ra·bil·i·ty** \,memərə'bilətē\ *n* —**mem·o·ra·ble·ness** \'mem(ə)rəbəlnəs\ *n* —**mem·o·ra·bly** \-blē\ *adv*

mem·o·ran·dum \,memə'randəm\ *n, pl* -dums *or* -da \-də\ : informal note

me·mo·ri·al \mə'mōrēəl\ *n* : something (as a monument) meant to keep remembrance alive —**memorial** *adj* —**me·mo·ri·al·ize** *vb*

Memorial Day *n* : last Monday in May or formerly May 30 observed as a legal holiday in commemoration of dead servicemen

mem·o·ry \'mem(ə)rē\ *n, pl* -ries 1 : power of remembering 2 : something remembered 3 : commemoration 4 : time within which past events are remembered —**mem·o·ri·za·tion** \,mem(ə)rə'zāshən\ *n* —**mem·o·rize** \'memə,rīz\ *vb* —**mem·o·riz·er** *n*

men *pl of* MAN

men·ace \'menəs\ *n* : threat of danger ~ *vb* -aced; -ac·ing 1 : threaten 2 : endanger —**men·ac·ing·ly** *adv*

me·nag·er·ie \mə'naj(ə)rē\ *n* : collection of wild animals

mend \'mend\ *vb* 1 : improve 2 : repair 3 : heal —**mend** *n* —**mend·er** *n*

men·da·cious \men'dāshəs\ *adj* : dishonest —**men·da·cious·ly** *adv* —**men·dac·i·ty** \-'dasətē\ *n*

men·di·cant \'mendikənt\ *n* : beggar —**men·di·can·cy** \-kənsē\ *n* —**mendicant** *adj*

men·ha·den \men'hād³n, mən-\ *n, pl* -den : fish related to the herring

me·nial \'mēnēəl, -nyəl\ *adj* 1 : relating to servants 2 : humble ~ *n* : domestic servant —**me·ni·al·ly** *adv*

men·in·gi·tis \,menən'jītəs\ *n, pl* -git·i·des \-'jitə,dēz\ : disease of the brain and spinal cord

meno·pause \'menə,pòz\ *n* : time when menstruation ends —**meno·paus·al** \,menə'pòzəl\ *adj*

men·stru·a·tion \,menstrə'wāshən, men'strā-\ *n* : monthly discharge of blood from the uterus —**men·stru·al** \'menstrə(wə)l\ *adj* —**men·stru·ate** \'menstrə,wāt, -,strāt\ *vb*

-ment \mənt\ *n suffix* **1** : result or means of an action **2** : action or process **3** : place of an action **4** : state or condition

men·tal \'ment³l\ *adj* : relating to the mind or its disorders —**men·tal·i·ty** \men'talətē\ *n* —**men·tal·ly** *adv*

men·thol \'men,thòl, -,thōl\ *n* : soothing substance from oil of peppermint —**men·tho·lat·ed** \-tha,lātəd\ *adj*

men·tion \'menchən\ *vb* : refer to —**mention** *n*

men·tor \'men,tòr, 'mentər\ *n* : instructor

menu \'menyü, 'mān-\ *n* : restaurant's list of food

me·ow \mē'aù\ *n* : characteristic cry of a cat —**meow** *vb*

mer·can·tile \'mərkən,tēl, -,tīl\ *adj* : relating to merchants or trade

mer·ce·nary \'mərs³n,erē\ *n, pl* **-nar·ies** : hired soldier ~ *adj* : serving only for money —**mer·ce·nari·ly** \,mərs³n'erəlē\ *adv* —**mer·ce·nari·ness** \'mərs³nerēnəs\ *n*

mer·cer \'mərsər\ *n* : textile dealer

mer·chan·dise \'mərchən,dīz, -,dīs\ *n* : goods bought and sold ~ *vb* -**dised;** **-dis·ing** : buy and sell —**mer·chan·dis·er** *n*

mer·chant \'mərchənt\ *n* : one who buys and sells

merchant marine *n* : commercial ships

mer·cu·ri·al \,mər'kyùrēəl\ *adj* : unpredictable —**mer·cu·ri·al·ly** *adv* —**mer·cu·ri·al·ness** *n*

mer·cu·ry \'mərkyərē\ *n* : liquid metallic chemical element —**mer·cu·ric** \,mər'kyùrik\ *adj* —**mer·cu·rous** \,mər'kyùrəs, 'mərkyərəs\ *adj*

mer·cy \'mərsē\ *n, pl* **-cies** **1** : show of pity or leniency **2** : divine blessing —**mer·ci·ful** \-sifəl\ *adj* —**mer·ci·ful·ly** *adv* —**mer·ci·less** \-siləs\ *adj* —**mer·ci·less·ly** *adv* —**mercy** *adj*

mere \'mir\ *adj* **mer·est** : simple —**mere·ly** *adv*

merge \'mərj\ *vb* **merged; merg·ing** **1** : unite **2** : blend —**merg·er** \'mərjər\ *n*

me·rid·i·an \mə'ridēən\ *n* : imaginary circle on the earth's surface passing through the poles —**meridian** *adj*

me·ringue \mə'raŋ\ *n* : dessert topping of baked beaten egg whites

me·ri·no \mə'rēnō\ *n, pl* **-nos** **1** : kind of sheep **2** : fine soft woolen yarn

mer·it \'merət\ *n* **1** : praiseworthy quality **2** *pl* : rights and wrongs of a legal case ~ *vb* : deserve —**mer·i·to·ri·ous** \,merə'tōrēəs\ *adj* —**mer·i·to·ri·ous·ly** *adv* —**mer·i·to·ri·ous·ness** *n*

mer·maid \'mər,mād\ *n* : legendary female sea creature

mer·ry \'merē\ *adj* **-ri·er; -est** : full of high spirits —**mer·ri·ly** *adv* —**mer·ri·ment** \'merimənt\ *n* —**mer·ry·mak·er** \'merē,mākər\ *n* —**mer·ry·mak·ing** \'merē,mākiŋ\ *n*

merry-go-round *n* : revolving amusement ride

me·sa \'māsə\ *n* : steep flat-topped hill

mesdames *pl of* MADAM *or of* MADAME *or of* MRS.

mesdemoiselles *pl of* MADEMOISELLE

mesh \'mesh\ *n* **1** : one of the openings in a net **2** : net fabric **3** : working contact ~ *vb* : fit together properly —**meshed** \'mesht\ *adj*

mes·mer·ize \'mezmə,rīz\ *vb* -**ized; -ing** : hypnotize —**mes·mer·ic** \mez'merik\ *adj* —**mes·mer·ism** \'mezmə,rizəm\ *n*

mess \'mes\ *n* **1** : meal eaten by a group **2** : confused, dirty, or offensive state **3** : state of disorder or distress ~ *vb* **1** : make dirty or untidy **2** : putter **3** : interfere

mes·sage \'mesij\ *n* : news, information, or a command sent by one person to another

mes·sen·ger \'mes³njər\ *n* : one who carries a message or does an errand

Mes·si·ah \mə'sīə\ *n* **1** : expected deliverer of the Jews **2** : Jesus Christ **3** *not cap* : great leader

messieurs *pl of* MONSIEUR

Messrs. *pl of* MR.

mes·ti·zo \me'stēzō\ *n, pl* **-zos** : person of mixed blood

met *past of* MEET

me·tab·o·lism \mə'tabə,lizəm\ *n* : sum of the processes of life support and esp. the processes by which a substance is assimilated or eliminated by the body —**met·a·bol·ic** \,metə'bälik\ *adj* —**me·tab·o·lize** \mə'tabə,līz\ *vb*

met·al \'met³l\ *n* : lustrous, fusible, ductile substance —**me·tal·lic** \mə'talik\ *adj* —**met·al·ware** *n* —**met·al·work** *n* —**met·al·work·er** *n* —**met·al·work·ing** *n*

met·al·lur·gy \'met³l,ərjē\ *n* : science of metals —**met·al·lur·gi·cal** \,met³l'ərjikəl\ *adj* —**met·al·lur·gi·cal·ly** *adv* —**met·al·lur·gist** \'met³l,ərjist\ *n*

meta·mor·pho·sis \,metə'mòrfəsəs\ *n, pl* **-pho·ses** \-,sēz\ : sudden and drastic change (as of form) —**meta·mor·phose** \-,fōz, -,fōs\ *vb*

met·a·phor \'metə,fòr, -fər\ *n* : use of a word denoting one kind of object or idea in place of another to suggest a likeness between them —**met·a·phor·i·cal** \ˌmetəˈfôrikəl\ adj

meta·phys·ics \ˌmetəˈfiziks\ n : study of the causes and nature of things —**meta·phys·i·cal** \-ˈfizəkəl\ adj —**meta·phy·si·cian** \-fəˈzishən\ n

mete \ˈmēt\ vb met·ed; met·ing : allot

me·te·or \ˈmētēər, -ē̇ˌȯr\ n : small piece of matter in the solar system

me·te·or·ic \ˌmētēˈȯrik\ adj 1 : relating to a meteor 2 : sudden and brilliant —**me·te·or·i·cal·ly** \-ik(ə)lē\ adv

me·te·or·ite \ˈmētēəˌrīt\ n : meteor that reaches the earth —**me·te·or·it·ic** \ˌmētēəˈritik\ adj

me·te·o·rol·o·gy \ˌmētēəˈräləjē\ n : science of weather —**me·te·o·ro·log·i·cal** \-ē̇ˌȯrəˈläjikəl\ adj —**me·te·o·rol·o·gist** \-ēəˈräləjəst\ n

¹me·ter \ˈmētər\ n : rhythm in verse or music

²me·ter \ˈmētər\ n : unit of length equal to 39.37 inches

³me·ter \ˈmētər\ n : measuring instrument

meth·a·done \ˈmethəˌdōn\, **meth·a·don** \-ˌdän\ n : synthetic addictive narcotic

meth·ane \ˈmethˌān\ n : colorless odorless flammable gas

meth·a·nol \ˈmethəˌnȯl, -ˌnōl\ n : volatile flammable poisonous liquid

meth·od \ˈmethəd\ n 1 : procedure for achieving an end 2 : orderly arrangement or plan —**me·thod·i·cal** \məˈthädikəl\ adj —**me·thod·i·cal·ly** \-k(ə)lē\ adv —**me·thod·i·cal·ness** n

me·tic·u·lous \məˈtikyələs\ adj : extremely careful in attending to details —**me·tic·u·lous·ly** adv —**me·tic·u·lous·ness** n

met·ric \ˈmetrik\, **met·ri·cal** \-trikəl\ adj : relating to meter or the metric system —**met·ri·cal·ly** adv

met·ri·ca·tion \ˌmetriˈkāshən\ n : conversion into or expression in the metric system

metric system n : system of weights and measures using the meter and kilogram

met·ro·nome \ˈmetrəˌnōm\ n : instrument that produces regular repeated ticks

me·trop·o·lis \məˈträp(ə)ləs\ n : major city —**met·ro·pol·i·tan** \ˌmetrəˈpälətən\ adj

met·tle \ˈmetᵊl\ n : spirit or courage —**met·tle·some** \-səm\ adj

mez·za·nine \ˈmezᵊnˌēn, ˌmezᵊnˈēn\ n 1 : shopping level between 2 main floors 2 : lowest balcony

mez·zo-so·pra·no \ˌmetsōsəˈpranō, ˌme(d)zō-\ n : voice between soprano and contralto

mi·as·ma \mīˈazmə\ n : noxious vapor —**mi·as·mic** \-mik\ adj

mi·ca \ˈmīkə\ n : mineral separable into thin transparent sheets

mice pl of MOUSE

mi·cro \ˈmīkrō\ adj : very small

mi·crobe \ˈmīˌkrōb\ n : disease-causing microorganism —**mi·cro·bi·al** \mīˈkrōbēəl\ adj

mi·cro·bi·ol·o·gy \ˌmīkrōbīˈäləjē\ n : biology dealing with microscopic life —**mi·cro·bi·o·log·i·cal** \-ˌbīəˈläjikəl\ adj —**mi·cro·bi·ol·o·gist** \ˌmīkrōbīˈäləjəst\ n

mi·cro·cosm \ˈmīkrəˌkäzəm\ n 1 : miniature universe 2 : human nature as an epitome of the world

mi·cro·film \-ˌfilm\ n : small film recording printed matter —**microfilm** vb

mi·crom·e·ter \mīˈkrämətər\ n : instrument for measuring minute distances

mi·cro·min·ia·ture \ˌmīkrōˈminēə,chu̇r, -ˈminiˌchu̇r, -chər\ adj : suitable for use with parts reduced to a very small size —**mi·cro·min·ia·tur·iza·tion** \-ˌminēəˌchu̇rəˈzāshən, -ˌminiˌchu̇r-, -chər-\ n —**mi·cro·min·ia·tur·ized** \-ˈminēəchəˌrīzd, -ˈminichə-\ adj

mi·cron \ˈmīˌkrän\ n : 1/1000 millimeter

mi·cro·or·gan·ism \ˌmīkrōˈȯrgəˌnizəm\ n : tiny being

mi·cro·phone \ˈmīkrəˌfōn\ n : instrument for transmitting or recording sound by changing sound waves into variations of an electric current

mi·cro·scope \-ˌskōp\ n : optical device for magnifying tiny objects —**mi·cro·scop·ic** \ˌmīkrəˈskäpik\ adj, **mi·cro·scop·i·cal** \-ikəl\ adj —**mi·cro·scop·i·cal·ly** adv —**mi·cros·co·py** \mīˈkräskəpē\ n

mi·cro·wave \ˈmīkrəˌwāv\ n : short radio wave

mid \ˈmid\ adj : middle —**mid·point** n —**mid·stream** n —**mid·sum·mer** n —**mid·town** n or adj —**mid·week** n —**mid·win·ter** n —**mid·year** n

mid-air n : a point well above the ground

mid·day n : noon

mid·dle \ˈmidᵊl\ adj 1 : equally distant from the extremes 2 : being at neither extreme ~ n : middle part or point

Middle Ages n pl : period from about A.D. 500 to about 1500

mid·dle·man \-₁man\ n : dealer or agent between the producer and consumer

mid·dling \'midlin, -lən\ adj 1 : of middle or medium size, degree, or quality 2 : mediocre

midge \'mij\ n : very tiny fly

midg·et \'mijət\ n : very small person or thing

mid·land \'midlənd, -₁land\ n : interior of a country

mid·most adj : being nearest the middle —**midmost** adv

mid·night n : 12 o'clock at night

mid·riff \'mid₁rif\ n : mid-region of the torso

mid·ship·man \'mid₁shipmən, (')mid'ship-\ n : student naval officer

midst \'midst\ n : position close to or surrounded by others —**midst** prep

mid·way \'mid₁wā\ n : concessions and amusements at a carnival ~ adv : in the middle

mid·wife \'mid₁wīf\ n : woman who aids at childbirth —**mid·wife·ry** \-₁wīf(ə)rē\ n

mien \'mēn\ n : appearance

miff \'mif\ vb : upset or peeve

¹might \(')mīt\ past of MAY —used to express permission or possibility or as a polite alternative to may

²might \'mīt\ n : power or resources

mighty \'mītē\ adj might·i·er; -est 1 : very strong 2 : great —**might·i·ly** adv —**might·i·ness** n —**mighty** adv

mi·graine \'mī₁grān\ n : severe headache and often nausea

mi·grant \'mīgrənt\ n : one who moves frequently to find work

mi·grate \'mī₁grāt\ vb -grat·ed; -grat·ing 1 : move from one place to another 2 : pass periodically from one region or climate to another —**mi·gra·tion** \mī'grāshən\ n —**mi·gra·tion·al** \-sh(ə)nəl\ adj —**mi·gra·to·ry** \'mīgrə₁tōrē\ adj

mild \'mīld\ adj 1 : gentle in nature or behavior 2 : moderate in action or effect —**mild·ly** adv —**mild·ness** n

mil·dew \'mil₁d(y)ü\ n : whitish fungal growth —**mildew** vb

mile \'mīl\ n : unit of length equal to 5280 feet

mile·age \'mīlij\ n 1 : allowance per mile for traveling expenses 2 : amount or rate of use expressed in miles

mile·stone n : significant point in development

mi·lieu \mēl'yə(r), -'yü\ n, pl -lieus or -lieux \-'yə(r)(z), -'yüz\ : surroundings or setting

mil·i·tant \'milətənt\ adj : aggressively active or hostile —**mil·i·tan·cy** \-tənsē\ n —**militant** n —**mil·i·tant·ly** adv

mil·i·ta·rism \'milətə₁rizəm\ n : dominance of military ideals or of a policy of aggressive readiness for war —**mil·i·ta·rist** \-₁rəst\ n —**mil·i·ta·ris·tic** \₁milətə'ristik\ adj

mil·i·tary \'milə₁terē\ adj 1 : relating to soldiers, arms, or war 2 : relating to or performed by armed forces ~ n : armed forces or the people in them —**mil·i·tar·i·ly** \₁milə'terəlē\ adv

mil·i·tate \'-₁tāt\ vb -tat·ed; -tat·ing : have an effect

mi·li·tia \mə'lishə\ n : civilian soldiers —**mi·li·tia·man** \-mən\ n

milk \'milk\ n : nutritive fluid secreted by female mammals for feeding their young ~ vb : draw off the milk of —**milk·er** n —**milk·i·ness** \-ēnəs\ n —**milky** adj

milk·man \-₁man, -mən\ n : man who sells or delivers milk

milk·weed n : herb with milky juice

¹mill \'mil\ n 1 : building in which grain is ground into flour 2 : manufacturing plant 3 : machine used esp. for forming or processing ~ vb 1 : subject to a process in a mill 2 : move in a circle —**mill·er** n

²mill n : 1/10 cent

mil·len·ni·um \mə'lenēəm\ n, pl -nia \-ēə\ or -niums : a period of 1000 years

mil·let \'milət\ n : cereal and forage grass with small seeds

mil·li·gram \'milə₁gram\ n : 1/1000 gram

mil·li·li·ter \-₁lētər\ n : 1/1000 liter

mil·li·me·ter \-₁mētər\ n : 1/1000 meter

mil·li·ner \'milənər\ n : person who makes or sells women's hats —**mil·li·nery** \'milə₁nerē\ n

mil·lion \'milyən\ n, pl millions or million : 1000 thousands —**million** adj —**mil·lionth** \-yənth\ adj or n

mil·lion·aire \₁milyə'naər, 'milyə₁naər\ n : person worth a million or more (as of dollars)

mil·li·pede \'milə₁pēd\ n : long-bodied arthropod with 2 pairs of legs on most segments

mill·stone n : either of 2 round flat stones used for grinding grain

mime \'mīm, 'mēm\ n 1 : mimic 2 : art of telling a story by body movements —**mime** vb

mim-eo-graph \'mimē-ə,graf\ *n* : machine for making many stencil copies —**mimeograph** *vb*

mim-ic \'mimik\ *n* : one that mimics ~ *vb* **-icked; -ick-ing** 1 : imitate closely 2 : ridicule by imitation —**mim-ic-ry** \'mimikrē\ *n*

min-a-ret \,minə'ret\ *n* : tower attached to a mosque

mince \'mins\ *vb* **minced; minc-ing** 1 : cut into small pieces 2 : choose (one's words) carefully 3 : walk in a prim affected manner —**minc-ing** *adj*

mind \'mīnd\ *n* 1 : memory 2 : the part of an individual that feels, perceives, and esp. reasons 3 : intention 4 : normal mental condition 5 : opinion 6 : intellectual ability ~ *vb* 1 : attend to 2 : obey 3 : be concerned about 4 : be careful —**mind-ed** *adj* —**mind-less** \-ləs\ *adj* —**mind-less-ly** *adv* —**mind-less-ness** *n*

mind-ful \-fəl\ *adj* : aware or attentive —**mind-ful-ly** *adv* —**mind-ful-ness** *n*

¹mine \'mīn\ *pron* : one or the ones belonging to me

²mine \'mīn\ *n* 1 : excavation from which mineral substances are taken 2 : encased explosive for destroying enemy vehicles or vessels ~ *vb* **mined; min-ing** 1 : get ore from 2 : place military mines in —**min-er** *n*

min-er-al \'min(ə)rəl\ *n* 1 : crystalline substance not of animal or vegetable origin 2 : useful natural substance (as coal) obtained from the ground —**mineral** *adj* —**min-er-al-ize** \-,īz\ *vb*

min-er-al-o-gy \,minə'rälǝjē, -'ral-\ *n* : science dealing with minerals —**min-er-al-og-i-cal** \,min(ə)rə'läjikəl\ *adj* —**min-er-al-o-gist** \,minə'rälǝjəst, -'ral-\ *n*

min-gle \'mingəl\ *vb* **-gled; -gling** : bring together or mix

mini- *comb form* : miniature or of small dimensions

minibook	minicourse
miniboom	minicrisis
minibrain	minidrama
minibudget	minidress
minibus	minifair
minicab	minifarm
minicalculator	minifestival
minicamera	minifeud
minicar	miniflaw
niniclock	minigarden
minicoat	minigrant
minicomponent	minigroup
minicomputer	miniguide
miniconvention	minihospital

minileague	minischool
minilecture	minisearch
minimarket	minisedan
minimiracle	miniseries
minimuseum	miniski
minination	miniskirt
mininetwork	minislump
mininovel	minisociety
mini-opera	ministate
minipanic	ministrike
minipark	minisub
miniplan	minisubmarine
minipool	minisurvey
miniprice	minisystem
miniproblem	miniterritory
minipump	minitheater
minirebellion	minitrain
minirecession	minivacation
miniriot	minivan
minirobot	miniversion
minirose	miniwar
miniscandal	minizoo

min-ia-ture \'minē-ə,chúr, 'mini,chúr, -chər\ *n* : tiny copy or very small version —**miniature** *adj* —**min-ia-tur-ist** \-,chúrəst, -chərəst\ *n* —**min-ia-tur-ize** \-ē-əchə,rīz, -ichə-\ *vb*

min-i-mal \'minəməl\ *adj* : relating to or being a minimum —**min-i-mal-ly** *adv*

min-i-mize \'minə,mīz\ *vb* **-mized; -miz-ing** 1 : reduce to a minimum 2 : estimate at a minimum

min-i-mum \'minəməm\ *n*, *pl* **-ma** \-mə\ *or* **-mums** : lowest quantity or amount —**minimum** *adj*

min-ion \'minyən\ *n* 1 : servile dependent 2 : subordinate official

min-is-ter \'minəstər\ *n* 1 : Protestant clergyman 2 : high officer of state 3 : diplomatic representative ~ *vb* : give aid or service —**min-is-te-ri-al** \,minə'stirēəl\ *adj* —**min-is-tra-tion** *n*

min-is-try \'minəstrē\ *n*, *pl* **-tries** 1 : office or duties of a minister 2 : body of ministers 3 : government department headed by a minister

mink \'miŋk\ *n*, *pl* **mink** *or* **minks** : weasellike mammal or its soft brown fur

min-now \'minō\ *n*, *pl* **-nows** : small freshwater fish

mi-nor \'mīnər\ *adj* : less in size, importance, or value ~ *n* 1 : person not yet of legal age 2 : secondary field of academic specialization

mi-nor-i-ty \mə'nórətē, mī-\ *n*, *pl* **-ties** 1 : time or state of being a minor 2 : smaller number (as of votes) 3

: part of a population differing from others (as in race or religion)

min·strel \'minstrəl\ n 1 : medieval singer of verses 2 : performer in a program usu. of Negro songs and jokes —**min·strel·sy** \-sē\ n

¹mint \'mint\ n 1 : place where coins are made 2 : vast sum —**mint** vb —**mint·age** \-ij\ n —**mint·er** n

²mint n : herb with fragrant foliage —**minty** adj

min·u·et \,minyə'wet\ n : slow graceful dance

mi·nus \'mīnəs\ prep 1 : diminished by 2 : lacking ~ n : negative quantity or quality

mi·nus·cule \'minəs,kyül, min'əs-\ or **min·is·cule** \'minəs-\ adj : very small

¹min·ute \'minət\ n 1 : 60th part of an hour or of a degree 2 : short time 3 pl : official record of a meeting

²mi·nute \mī'n(y)üt, mə-\ adj -**nut·er; -est** 1 : very small 2 : marked by close attention to details —**mi·nute·ly** adv —**mi·nute·ness** n

mir·a·cle \'mirikəl\ n 1 : event that cannot be explained by known laws of nature 2 : marvel —**mi·rac·u·lous** \mə'rakyələs\ adj —**mi·rac·u·lous·ly** adv

mi·rage \mə'räzh\ n : reflection visible at sea or in deserts of some distant object

mire \'mī(ə)r\ n : heavy deep mud ~ vb **mired; mir·ing** : stick or sink in mire —**miry** adj

mir·ror \'mirər\ n : smooth substance (as of glass) that reflects images ~ vb : reflect in or as if in a mirror

mirth \'mərth\ n : gladness and laughter —**mirth·ful** \-fəl\ adj —**mirth·ful·ly** adv —**mirth·ful·ness** n —**mirth·less** adj

mis·an·thrope \'mis²n,thrōp\ n : one who hates mankind —**mis·an·throp·ic** \,mis²n'thräpik\ adj —**mis·an·thro·py** \mis'anthrəpē\ n

mis·ap·pre·hend \,mis-\ vb : misunderstand —**mis·ap·pre·hen·sion** n

mis·ap·pro·pri·ate \,mis-\ vb : take dishonestly for one's own use —**mis·ap·pro·pri·a·tion** n

mis·be·have \,mis-\ vb : behave improperly —**mis·be·hav·er** n —**mis·be·hav·ior** n

mis·cal·cu·late \mis-\ vb : calculate wrongly —**mis·cal·cu·la·tion** \,mis-\ n

mis·car·ry \mis-\ vb 1 : give birth prematurely before the fetus can survive 2 : go wrong or be unsuccessful —**mis·car·riage** n

mis·ce·ge·na·tion \mis,ejə'nāshən, ,misjə2'nā-\ n : marriage between members of different races

mis·cel·la·neous \,misə'lānēəs\ adj 1 : consisting of many things of different kinds —**mis·cel·la·neous·ly** adv —**mis·cel·la·neous·ness** n

mis·cel·la·ny \'misə,lānē\ n, pl -**nies** : collection of various things

mis·chance \mis-\ n : bad luck

mis·chief \'mischəf\ n : conduct esp. of a child that annoys or causes minor damage

mis·chie·vous \'mischəvəs\ adj 1 : causing annoyance or minor injury 2 : irresponsibly playful —**mis·chie·vous·ly** adv —**mis·chie·vous·ness** n

mis·con·ceive \,mis-\ vb : interpret incorrectly —**mis·con·cep·tion** n

mis·con·duct \mis-\ n 1 : mismanagement 2 : bad behavior

mis·con·strue \,mis-\ vb : misinterpret —**mis·con·struc·tion** n

mis·cre·ant \'miskrēənt\ n : one who behaves criminally or viciously —**miscreant** adj

mis·deed \mis-\ n : wrong deed

mis·de·mean·or \,misdi'mēnər\ n : crime less serious than a felony

mi·ser \'mīzər\ n : person who hoards money —**mi·ser·li·ness** \-lēnəs\ n —**mi·ser·ly** adj

mis·er·a·ble \'mizərbəl, 'miz(ə)rəbəl\ adj 1 : wretchedly deficient 2 : causing extreme discomfort —**mis·er·a·ble·ness** n —**mis·er·a·bly** \-blē\ adv

mis·ery \'miz(ə)rē\ n, pl -**er·ies** : suffering and want caused by distress or poverty

mis·fire \mis-\ vb 1 : fail to fire 2 : miss an intended effect —**misfire** n

mis·fit \'mis,fit, mis'fit\ n : person poorly adjusted to his environment

mis·for·tune \mis-\ n 1 : bad luck 2 : unfortunate condition or event

mis·giv·ing \mis-\ n : doubt or concern

mis·guid·ed \mis-\ adj : mistaken, uninformed, or deceived

mis·hap \'mis,hap\ n : accident

mis·in·form \,mis²n'fôrm\ vb : give false information to —**mis·in·for·ma·tion** \,mis-\ n

mis·in·ter·pret \,mis²n'tərprət\ vb : understand or explain wrongly —**mis·in·ter·pre·ta·tion** \,tərprə'tāshən\ n

mis·judge \mis-\ vb : judge incorrectly or unjustly —**mis·judg·ment** n

mis·lay \mis-\ vb -**laid; -lay·ing** : misplace

mis·lead \mis-\ *vb* **-led; -lead·ing** : lead in a wrong direction or into error —**mis·lead·ing·ly** *adv*

mis·man·age \mis-\ *vb* : manage badly —**mis·man·age·ment** *n*

mis·no·mer \mis-'nōmər\ *n* : wrong name

mi·sog·y·nist \mə'säjənəst\ *n* : one who hates or distrusts women —**mi·sog·y·ny** \-nē\ *n*

mis·place \mis-\ *vb* : put in an unremembered place or in the wrong place

mis·print \'mis,print, mis'-\ *n* : error in something printed

mis·pro·nounce \,mis-\ *vb* : pronounce incorrectly —**mis·pro·nun·ci·a·tion** *n*

mis·quote \mis-\ *vb* : quote incorrectly —**mis·quo·ta·tion** \,mis-\ *n*

mis·read \mis-\ *vb* **-read; -read·ing** : read or interpret incorrectly

mis·rep·re·sent \,mis-\ *vb* : represent falsely or unfairly —**mis·rep·re·sen·ta·tion** *n*

mis·rule \mis-\ *vb* : govern badly ~ *n* **1** : bad or corrupt government **2** : disorder

¹miss \'mis\ *vb* **1** : fail to hit, reach, or contact **2** : notice the absence of **3** : fail to obtain **4** : avoid **5** : omit —**miss** *n*

²miss *n* : young unmarried woman or girl —often used as a title

mis·sal \'misəl\ *n* : book containing what is said at mass during the year

mis·shap·en \mis(h)'shāpən\ *adj* : distorted

mis·sile \'misəl\ *n* **1** : object (as a stone or weapon) propelled **2** : self-propelled rocket weapon

miss·ing \'misiŋ\ *adj* : absent or lost

mis·sion \'mishən\ *n* **1** : ministry sent by a church to spread its teaching **2** : group of diplomats sent to a foreign country **3** : task

mis·sion·ary \'misha,nerē\ *adj* : relating to religious missions ~ *n, pl* **-ar·ies** : person sent to spread religious faith

mis·sive \'misiv\ *n* : letter

mis·spell \mis-\ *vb* : spell incorrectly —**mis·spell·ing** *n*

mis·state \mis-\ *vb* : state incorrectly —**mis·state·ment** *n*

mis·step \mis-\ *n* **1** : wrong step **2** : mistake

mist \'mist\ *n* : particles of water falling as fine rain

mis·take \mə'stāk\ *n* **1** : misunderstanding or wrong belief **2** : wrong action or statement —**mistake** *vb*

mis·tak·en \-'stākən\ *adj* : having a wrong opinion or incorrect information —**mis·tak·en·ly** *adv*

mis·ter \'mistər\ *n* : sir —used without a name in addressing a man

mis·tle·toe \'misəl,tō\ *n* : parasitic green plant

mis·treat \mis'trēt\ *vb* : treat badly —**mis·treat·ment** *n*

mis·tress \'mistrəs\ *n* **1** : woman in control **2** : woman with whom a man lives unmarried

mis·tri·al \mis'trī(ə)l\ *n* : trial that has no legal effect

mis·trust \-'trəst\ *n* : lack of confidence ~ *vb* : have no confidence in —**mis·trust·ful** \-fəl\ *adj* —**mis·trust·ful·ly** *adv* —**mis·trust·ful·ness** *n*

misty \'mistē\ *adj* **mist·i·er; -est** : obscured by mist —**mist·i·ly** *adv* —**mist·i·ness** *n*

mis·un·der·stand \,mis,əndər'stand\ *vb* **1** : fail to understand **2** : interpret incorrectly

mis·un·der·stand·ing \-'standiŋ\ *n* **1** : wrong interpretation **2** : disagreement

mis·use \mish'ūz, mis(h)'yüz\ *vb* **1** : use incorrectly **2** : mistreat —**mis·use** \-'üz, -'yüs\ *n*

mite \'mīt\ *n* **1** : tiny spiderlike animal **2** : small amount

mi·ter, mi·tre \'mītər\ *n* **1** : bishop's headdress **2** : angular joint in wood ~ *vb* **-tered** *or* **-tred; -ter·ing** *or* **-tring** \'mītəriŋ\ : bevel the ends of for a miter joint

mit·i·gate \'mitə,gāt\ *vb* **-gat·ed; -gat·ing** : make less severe —**mit·i·ga·tion** \,mitə'gāshən\ *n* —**mit·i·ga·tive** \'mitə,gātiv\ *adj* —**mit·i·ga·tor** \-,gātər\ *n* —**mit·i·ga·to·ry** \-gə,tōrē\ *adj*

mi·to·sis \mī'tōsəs\ *n, pl* **-to·ses** \-,sēz\ : process of forming 2 cell nuclei from one —**mi·tot·ic** \-'tätik\ *adj*

mitt \'mit\ *n* : mittenlike baseball glove

mit·ten \'mitᵊn\ *n* : hand covering without finger sections

mix \'miks\ *vb* : combine or join into one mass *or* group ~ *n* : commercially prepared food mixture —**mix·able** *adj* —**mix·er** *n* —**mix up** *vb* : confuse

mix·ture \'miks·chər\ *n* : act or product of mixing

mix-up *n* : instance of confusion

mne·mon·ic \ni'mänik\ *adj* : assisting memory

moan \'mōn\ n : low prolonged sound of pain or grief —**moan** vb

moat \'mōt\ n : deep wide trench around a castle

mob \'mäb\ n 1 : large disorderly crowd 2 : criminal gang ~ vb -**bb**- : crowd around and attack or annoy

mo·bile \'mōbəl, -ˌbēl, -ˌbīl\ adj : capable of moving or being moved ~ \'mō-ˌbēl\ n : suspended art construction with freely moving parts —**mo·bil·i·ty** \mō'bilətē\ n

mo·bi·lize \'mōbəˌlīz\ vb -**lized; -liz·ing** : assemble and make ready for war duty —**mo·bi·li·za·tion** \ˌmōbə-lə'zāshən\ n —**mo·bi·liz·er** \'mōbə,līzər\ n

moc·ca·sin \'mäkəsən\ n 1 : heelless shoe 2 : venomous U.S. snake

mock \'mäk, 'mȯk\ vb 1 : ridicule 2 : mimic in derision ~ adj 1 : simulated 2 : phony —**mock·er** n —**mock·ery** \-(ə)rē\ n —**mock·ing·ly** adv

mock·ing·bird \'mäkiŋˌbərd, 'mȯk-\ n : songbird that mimics other birds

mode \'mōd\ n 1 : particular form or variety 2 : style —**mod·al** \-ᵊl\ adj —**mod·ish** \'mōdish\ adj

mod·el \'mädᵊl\ n 1 : structural design 2 : miniature representation 3 : something worthy of copying 4 : one who poses for an artist or displays clothes 5 : type or design ~ vb -**eled** or -**elled; -el·ing** or -**el·ling** 1 : shape 2 : work as a model ~ adj 1 : serving as a pattern 2 : being a miniature representation of

mod·er·ate \'mäd(ə)rət\ adj : avoiding extremes — \'mädəˌrāt\ vb -**at·ed; -at·ing** 1 : lessen the intensity of 2 : act as a moderator —**moderate** n —**mod·er·ate·ly** adv —**mod·er·ate·ness** n —**mod·er·a·tion** \ˌmädə'rā-shən\ n

mod·er·a·tor \'mädəˌrātər\ n : one who presides

mod·ern \'mädərn\ adj : relating to or characteristic of the present —**modern** n —**mo·der·ni·ty** \mä'dərnətē\ n —**mod·ern·iza·tion** \ˌmädərnə'zā-shən\ n —**mod·ern·ize** \'mädər,nīz\ vb —**mod·ern·iz·er** \'mädər,nīzər\ n —**mod·ern·ly** adv —**mod·ern·ness** n

mod·est \'mädəst\ adj 1 : having a moderate estimate of oneself 2 : reserved or decent in thoughts or actions 3 : limited in size, amount, or aim —**mod·est·ly** adv —**mod·es·ty** \-əstē\ n

mod·i·cum \'mädikəm\ n : small amount

mod·i·fy \'mädəˌfī\ vb -**fied; -fy·ing** 1 : limit the meaning of 2 : change —**mod·i·fi·ca·tion** \ˌmädəfə'kāshən\ n —**mod·i·fi·er** \'mädəˌfī(ə)r\ n

mod·u·lar \'mäjələr\ adj : built with standardized units —**mod·u·lar·ized** \-lə,rīzd\ adj

mod·u·late \'mäjə,lāt\ vb -**lat·ed; -lat·ing** 1 : keep in proper measure or proportion 2 : vary a radio wave —**mod·u·la·tion** \ˌmäjə'lāshən\ n —**mod·u·la·tor** \'mäjə,lātər\ n —**mod·u·la·to·ry** \-lə,tōrē\ adj

mod·ule \'mäjül\ n : standardized unit

mo·gul \'mōgəl, mō'gəl\ n : important person

mo·hair \'mō,haər\ n : fabric made from the hair of the Angora goat

moist \'mȯist\ adj : slightly or moderately wet —**moist·en** \'mȯis²n\ vb —**moist·en·er** \'mȯisnər, -ᵊnər\ n —**moist·ly** adv —**moist·ness** n

mois·ture \'mȯischər\ n : small amount of liquid that causes dampness

mo·lar \'mōlər\ n : grinding tooth —**molar** adj

mo·las·ses \mə'lasəz\ n : thick brown syrup from raw sugar

¹mold \'mōld\ n : crumbly organic soil

²mold n : frame or cavity for forming ~ vb : shape in or as if in a mold —**mold·er** n

³mold n : surface growth of fungus ~ vb : become moldy —**mold·i·ness** \'mōldēnəs\ n —**moldy** adj

mold·er \'mōldər\ vb : crumble

mold·ing \'mōldiŋ\ n : decorative surface, plane, or strip

¹mole \'mōl\ n : spot on the skin

²mole n : small burrowing mammal —**mole·hill** n

mol·e·cule \'mäliˌkyül\ n : small particle of matter —**mo·lec·u·lar** \mə'lek-yələr\ adj

mole·skin \-ˌskin\ n : heavy cotton fabric

mo·lest \mə'lest\ vb : annoy esp. by improper or rough handling —**mo·les·ta·tion** \ˌmōl,es'tāshən\ n —**mo·lest·er** n

mol·li·fy \'mälə,fī\ vb -**fied; -fy·ing** : soothe in temper —**mol·li·fi·ca·tion** \ˌmäləfə'kāshən\ n

mol·lusk, mol·lusc \'mäləsk\ n : shelled aquatic invertebrate —**mol·lus·can** \mə'ləskən\ adj

mol·ly·cod·dle \'mälē,kädᵊl\ vb -**dled; -dling** : pamper

molt \'mōlt\ vb : shed hair, feathers, outer skin, or horns periodically —**molt** n —**molt·er** n

mol·ten \'mōlt°n\ *adj* : fused or liquefied by heat

mom \'mäm, 'məm\ *n* : mother

mo·ment \'mōmənt\ *n* 1 : tiny portion of time 2 : time of excellence 3 : importance

mo·men·tar·i·ly \,mōmən'terəlē\ *adv* 1 : for a moment 2 : at any moment

mo·men·tary \'mōmən,terē\ *adj* : continuing only a moment —**mo·men·tar·i·ness** *n*

mo·men·tous \mō'mentəs\ *adj* : very important —**mo·men·tous·ly** *adv* —**mo·men·tous·ness** *n*

mo·men·tum \-əm\ *n, pl* **-ta** \-ə\ *or* **-tums** : force of a moving body

mon·arch \'mänərk, -,ärk\ *n* 1 : ruler 2 : large orange and black migratory butterfly —**mo·nar·chi·cal** \mə'närkikəl\, **mo·nar·chic** \-'närkik\ *adj*

mon·ar·chy \'mänərkē\ *n, pl* **-chies** : realm of a monarch

mon·as·tery \'mänə,sterē\ *n, pl* **-ter·ies** : house for monks —**mon·as·te·ri·al** \,mänə'stirēəl\ *adj*

mo·nas·tic \mə'nastik\ *adj* : relating to monasteries, monks, or nuns —**monastic** *n* —**mo·nas·ti·cal·ly** \-tik(ə)lē\ *adv* —**mo·nas·ti·cism** \-tə,sizəm\ *n*

Mon·day \'məndē\ *n* : 2d day of the week

mon·e·tary \'mänə,terē, 'mən-\ *adj* : relating to money

mon·ey \'mənē\ *n, pl* **-eys** *or* **-ies** \'mənēz\ 1 : something (as coins or paper currency) used in buying 2 : wealth —**mon·eyed** \-ēd\ *adj* —**mon·ey·lend·er** *n*

mon·ger \'məŋgər, 'mäŋ-\ *n* : dealer

mon·gol·ism \'mäŋgə,lizəm\ *n* : congenital idiocy —**Mon·gol·oid** \-gə,lóid\ *adj or n*

mon·goose \'män,güs, 'mäŋ-\ *n, pl* **-goos·es** : small agile mammal of India

mon·grel \'məŋgrəl, 'mäŋ-\ *n* : offspring of mixed breed

mon·i·tor \'mänətər\ *n* 1 : student assistant 2 : television screen ~ *vb* : watch or observe esp. for quality

monk \'məŋk\ *n* : member of a religious order living in a monastery —**monk·ish** *adj* —**monk·ish·ly** *adv* —**monk·ish·ness** *n*

mon·key \'məŋkē\ *n, pl* **-keys** : small long-tailed arboreal primate ~ *vb* 1 : fool 2 : tamper

mon·key·shines \-,shīnz\ *n pl* : pranks

monks·hood \'məŋks,húd\ *n* : poisonous herb with showy flowers

mon·o·cle \'mänikəl\ *n* : eyeglass for one eye

mo·nog·a·my \mə'nägəmē\ *n* : marriage with one person at a time —**mo·nog·a·mic** \,mänə'gamik\ *adj* —**mo·nog·a·mist** \mə'nägəməst\ *n* —**mo·nog·a·mous** \-məs\ *adj*

mono·gram \'mänə,gram\ *n* : sign of identity made of initials —**monogram** *vb*

mono·graph \-,graf\ *n* : learned treatise

mono·lin·gual \,mänə'liŋgwəl\ *adj* : using only one language

mono·lith \'mänə°l,ith\ *n* 1 : single great stone 2 : single uniform massive whole —**mono·lith·ic** \,mänə°l'ithik\ *adj*

mono·logue \'mänə°l,óg\ *n* : long speech —**mono·log·ist** \-,ógəst\, **mo·no·lo·gist** \mə'näləjəst, 'mänə°l,ógəst\ *n*

mono·nu·cle·o·sis \,mänō,n(y)üklē'ōsəs\ *n* : acute infectious disease

mo·nop·o·ly \mə'näp(ə)lē\ *n, pl* **-lies** 1 : exclusive ownership or control of a commodity 2 : one controlling a monopoly —**mo·nop·o·list** \-ləst\ *n* —**mo·nop·o·lis·tic** \mə,näpə'listik\ *adj* —**mo·nop·o·li·za·tion** \-lə'zāshən\ *n* —**mo·nop·o·lize** \mə'näpə,līz\ *vb*

mono·rail \'mänə,rāl\ *n* : single rail for a wheeled vehicle or a vehicle or system using it

mono·syl·la·ble \-,silabəl\ *n* : word of one syllable —**mono·syl·lab·ic** \-sə'labik\ *adj*

mono·the·ism \'mänə(,)thē,izəm\ *n* : doctrine or belief that there is only one deity —**mono·the·ist** \-,thēəst\ *n* —**mono·the·is·tic** \-,thēəst\ *adj*

mono·tone \'mänə,tōn\ *n* : succession of words in one unvarying tone

mo·not·o·nous \mə'nät°nəs\ *adj* 1 : sounded in one unvarying tone 2 : tediously uniform —**mo·not·o·nous·ly** *adv* —**mo·not·o·nous·ness** *n* —**mo·not·o·ny** \-°nē\ *n*

mon·ox·ide \mə'näk,sīd\ *n* : oxide containing one atom of oxygen in the molecule

mon·sieur \məs(h)(')yə(r), mə'si(ə)r\ *n, pl* **mes·sieurs** \məs(h)(')yə(r)(z), mäs-; mə'si(ə)r(z)\ : man of high rank or station —used as a title for a man esp. of French nationality

mon·si·gnor \män'sēnyər\ *n, pl* **monsignors** *or* **mon·si·gno·ri** \,mänsēn'yōrē\ : Roman Catholic prelate —used as a title

mon·soon \män'sün\ *n* : periodic rainy season —**mon·soon·al** \-°l\ *adj*

mon·ster \'mänstər\ *n* 1 : abnormal or terrifying animal 2 : ugly, wicked, or cruel person —**mon·stros·i·ty**

\mänˈsträsətē\ n —mon·strous \ˈmänstrəs\ adj —mon·strous·ly adv

mon·tage \mänˈtäzh\ n : composite photo

month \ˈmənth\ n : 12th part of a year —month·ly adv or adj or n

mon·u·ment \ˈmänyəmənt\ n : structure erected in remembrance —mon·u·men·tal \ˌmänyəˈmentᵊl\ adj —mon·u·men·tal·ly adv

moo \ˈmü\ vb : make the noise of a cow —moo n

mood \ˈmüd\ n : state of mind or emotion

moody \ˈmüdē\ adj mood·i·er; -est 1 : sad 2 : subject to changing moods and esp. to bad moods —mood·i·ly \ˈmüdᵊlē\ adv —mood·i·ness \-ēnəs\ n

moon \ˈmün\ n : earth's satellite —moon·beam n —moon·light n —moon·lit adj

moon·light \-ˌlīt\ vb -ed; -ing : hold a 2d job —moon·light·er n

moon·shine n 1 : moonlight 2 : illegally distilled liquor

¹moor \ˈmu̇r\ n : open usu. swampy wasteland —moor·land \-lənd, -ˌland\ n

²moor vb : fasten with line or cable

moor·ing \-iŋ\ n : place where boat can be moored

moose \ˈmüs\ n, pl moose : large heavy-antlered deer

moot \ˈmüt\ adj : open to question

mop \ˈmäp\ n : floor-cleaning implement ~ vb -pp- : use a mop on

mope \ˈmōp\ vb moped; mop·ing : be sad or listless

mo·ped \ˈmōˌped\ n : low-powered motorbike

mo·raine \məˈrān\ n : glacial deposit of earth and stones

mor·al \ˈmȯrəl\ adj 1 : relating to principles of right and wrong 2 : conforming to a standard of right behavior 3 : relating to or acting on the mind, character, or will ~ n 1 : point of a story 2 pl : moral practices or teachings —mor·al·ist \ˈmȯrələst\ n —mor·al·is·tic \ˌmȯrəˈlistik\ adj —mor·al·i·ty \məˈralətē\ n —mor·al·ize \ˈmȯrəˌlīz\ vb —mor·al·ly adv

mo·rale \məˈral\ n : emotional attitude

mo·rass \məˈras\ n : swamp

mor·a·to·ri·um \ˌmȯrəˈtōrēəm\ n, pl -ri·ums or -ria \-ēə\ : suspension of activity

mo·ray \məˈrā, ˈmȯrˌā\ n : savage eel

mor·bid \ˈmȯrbəd\ adj 1 : relating to disease 2 : gruesome —mor·bid·i·ty

\mȯrˈbidətē\ n —mor·bid·ly adv —mor·bid·ness n

mor·dant \ˈmȯrdᵊnt\ adj : incisive —mor·dant·ly adv

more \ˈmȯr\ adj 1 : greater 2 : additional ~ adv 1 : in addition 2 : to a greater degree ~ n 1 : greater quantity 2 : additional amount ~ pron : additional ones

mo·rel \məˈrel\ n : pitted edible mushroom

more·over \mȯrˈōvər\ adv : in addition

mo·res \ˈmȯrˌāz, -(ˌ)ēz\ n, pl : customs

morgue \ˈmȯrg\ n : mortuary for persons found dead

mor·i·bund \ˈmȯrə(ˌ)bənd\ adj : dying —mor·i·bun·di·ty \ˌmȯrəˈbəndətē\ n

morn \ˈmȯrn\ n : morning

morn·ing \ˈmȯrniŋ\ n : time from sunrise to noon

mo·ron \ˈmȯrˌän\ n : mentally deficient person —mo·ron·ic \məˈränik\ adj —mo·ron·i·cal·ly \-ik(ə)lē\ adv

mo·rose \məˈrōs\ adj : sullen —mo·rose·ly adv —mo·rose·ness n

mor·phine \ˈmȯrˌfēn\ n : addictive painkilling drug

mor·row \ˈmärō\ n : next day

Morse code \ˈmȯrs-\ n : code of dots and dashes or long and short sounds used for transmitting messages

mor·sel \ˈmȯrsəl\ n : small piece or quantity

mor·tal \ˈmȯrtᵊl\ adj 1 : causing or subject to death 2 : extreme —mortal n —mor·tal·i·ty \mȯrˈtalətē\ n —mor·tal·ly \ˈmȯrtᵊlē\ adv

mor·tar \ˈmȯrtər\ n 1 : strong bowl 2 : short-barreled cannon 3 : masonry material that hardens —mortar vb

mort·gage \ˈmȯrgij\ n : transfer of property rights as security for a loan —mortgage vb —mort·gag·ee \ˌmȯrgiˈjē\ n —mort·ga·gor \ˌmȯrgiˈjȯr\ n

mor·ti·fy \ˈmȯrtəˌfī\ vb -fied; -fy·ing 1 : subdue by abstinence or self-inflicted pain 2 : humiliate —mor·ti·fi·ca·tion \ˌmȯrtəfəˈkāshən\ n

mor·tu·ary \ˈmȯrchəˌwerē\ n, pl -ar·ies : place in which dead bodies are kept until burial

mo·sa·ic \mōˈzāik\ n : inlaid stone decoration

Mos·lem \ˈmäzləm\ var of MUSLIM

mosque \ˈmäsk\ n : building where Muslims worship

mos·qui·to \məˈskētō\ n, pl -toes : biting insect

moss \ˈmȯs\ n : green seedless plant —mossy adj

most \ˈmōst\ adj 1 : majority of 2 : greatest ~ adv : to the greatest or a very great degree ~ *n* : greatest amount ~ *pron* : greatest number or part

-most \ˌmōst\ *adj suffix* : most : most toward

most·ly \ˈmōstlē\ *adv* : mainly

mote \ˈmōt\ *n* : small particle

mo·tel \mōˈtel\ *n* : hotel with outdoor parking area

moth \ˈmoth\ *n* : small pale insect related to the butterflies

moth·er \ˈməthər\ *n* **1** : female parent **2** : source ~ *vb* **1** : give birth to **2** : cherish or protect —**moth·er·hood** \-ˌhůd\ *n* —**moth·er·land** \-ˌland\ *n* —**moth·er·less** *adj* —**moth·er·ly** *adj*

moth·er-in-law \ˈməth(ə)rən-ˌlò, ˈməthərn-ˌlò\ *n, pl* **mothers-in-law** : spouse's mother

mo·tif \mōˈtēf\ *n* : dominant theme

mo·tion \ˈmōshən\ *n* **1** : proposal for action **2** : act or instance of moving ~ *vb* : direct by a motion —**mo·tion·less** *adj* —**mo·tion·less·ly** *adv* —**mo·tion·less·ness** *n*

motion picture *n* : movie

mo·ti·vate \ˈmōtəˌvāt\ *vb* **-vat·ed; -vat·ing** : provide with a motive —**mo·ti·va·tion** \ˌmōtəˈvāshən\ *n*

mo·tive \ˈmōtiv\ *n* : cause of a person's action ~ *adj* **1** : moving to action **2** : relating to motion —**mo·tive·less** *adj*

mot·ley \ˈmätlē\ *adj* : of diverse colors or elements

mo·tor \ˈmōtər\ *n* : unit that supplies power or motion ~ *vb* : travel by automobile —**mo·tor·ist** \-əst\ *n* —**mo·tor·ize** \ˈmōtəˌrīz\ *vb*

mo·tor·bike *n* : lightweight motorcycle

mo·tor·boat *n* : engine-driven boat

mo·tor·car *n* : automobile

mo·tor·cy·cle *n* : 2-wheeled automotive vehicle —**mo·tor·cy·clist** *n*

mo·tor·truck *n* : automotive truck

mot·tle \ˈmätᵊl\ *vb* **-tled; -tling** : mark with spots of different color

mot·to \ˈmätō\ *n, pl* **-toes** : brief guiding rule

mould \ˈmōld\ *var of* MOLD

mound \ˈmaůnd\ *n* : pile (as of earth)

¹mount \ˈmaůnt\ *n* : mountain

²mount *vb* **1** : increase in amount **2** : get up on **3** : put in position ~ *n* **1** : frame or support **2** : horse to ride —**mount·able** *adj* —**mount·er** *n*

moun·tain \ˈmaůntᵊn\ *n* : elevated land higher than a hill —**moun·tain·ous** \ˈmaůntᵊnəs, -ᵊnəs\ *adj* —**moun·tain·top** *n*

moun·tain·eer \ˌmaůntᵊnˈiər\ *n* : mountain resident or climber —**mountaineer** *vb*

moun·te·bank \ˈmaůntiˌbaŋk\ *n* : impostor

mourn \ˈmōrn\ *vb* : feel or express grief —**mourn·er** *n* —**mourn·ful** \-fəl\ *adj* —**mourn·ful·ly** *adv* —**mourn·ful·ness** *n* —**mourn·ing** *n*

mouse \ˈmaůs\ *n, pl* **mice** \ˈmīs\ : small rodent —**mouse·trap** *n or vb*

mous·tache \ˈməsˌtash, (ˌ)məsˈtash\ *var of* MUSTACHE

mouth \ˈmaůth\ *n* : opening through which an animal takes in food ~ \ˈmaůth\ *vb* : speak —**mouthed** \ˈmaůthd, ˈmaůtht\ *adj* —**mouth·ful** \-ˌfůl\ *n*

mouth·piece *n* **1** : part (as of a musical instrument) held in or to the mouth **2** : spokesman

mou·ton \ˈmüˌtän\ *n* : processed sheepskin

move \ˈmüv\ *vb* **moved; mov·ing 1** : go or cause to go to another point **2** : change residence **3** : change or cause to change position **4** : take or cause to take action **5** : make a formal request **6** : stir the emotions ~ *n* **1** : act or instance of moving —**mov·able, move·able** \-əbəl\ *adj* —**move·ment** *n* —**mov·er** *n*

mov·ie \ˈmüvē\ *n* : projected picture in which persons and objects seem to move

¹mow \ˈmaů\ *n* : part of a barn where hay or straw is stored

²mow \ˈmō\ *vb* **mowed; mowed** or **mown** \ˈmōn\; **mow·ing** : cut with a machine —**mow·er** *n*

Mr. \ˈmistər\ *n, pl* **Messrs.** \ˈmesərz\ : conventional title for a man

Mrs. \ˈmisəz, -əs, *esp South* ˌmizəz, -əs, or (ˌ)miz, *or before first names* (ˌ)mis\ *n, pl* **Mes·dames** \mā'däm, -ˈdam\ : conventional title for a married woman

Ms. \(ˈ)miz\ *n* : conventional title for a woman

much \ˈməch\ *adj* **more** \ˈmōr\; **most** \ˈmōst\ : great in quantity, extent, or degree ~ *adv* **more; most** : to a great degree or extent ~ *n* : great quantity, extent, or degree

mu·ci·lage \ˈmyüs(ə)lij\ *n* : weak glue —**mu·ci·lag·i·nous** \ˌmyüsəˈlajənəs\ *adj*

muck \ˈmək\ *n* : manure, dirt, or mud —**mucky** *adj*

mu·cus \ˈmyükəs\ *n* : slippery protective secretion of membranes (**mucous membranes**) lining body cavities —**mu·cous** \-kəs\ *adj* mud \'məd\ *n* : soft wet earth —**mud-di-ly** \'məd²l`ē\ *adv* —**mud-di-ness** \-ēnəs\ *n* —**mud-dy** *adj or vb*

mud-dle \'məd²l\ *vb* -dled; -dling 1 : make, be, or act confused 2 : make a mess of —**muddle** *n* —**mud-dle-head-ed** \ˌməd²l'hedəd\ *adj*

mu-ez-zin \mü'ez²n\ *n* : Muslim who calls the hour of daily prayer

¹muff \'məf\ *n* : tubular hand covering

²muff *vb* : bungle —**muff** *n*

muf-fin \'məfən\ *n* : soft biscuit baked in a cup-shaped container

muf-fle \'məfəl\ *vb* -fled; -fling 1 : wrap up 2 : dull the sound of —**muf-fler** \'məflər\ *n*

muf-ti \'məftē\ *n* : civilian clothes

¹mug \'məg\ *n* : drinking cup ∼ *vb* -gg- : make faces

²mug *vb* -gg- : assault with intent to rob —**mug-ger** *n*

mug-gy \'məgē\ *adj* -gi-er; -est : hot and humid —**mug-gi-ness** *n*

Mu-ham-mad-an \mō'hamədən, -'häm-; mü-\ *n* : Muslim —**Mu-ham-mad-an-ism** \-ˌizəm\ *n*

mu-lat-to \m(y)ü'lätō, -lät-\ *n, pl* -toes *or* tos : 1st-generation offspring of a Negro and a white

mul-ber-ry \'məlˌberē\ *n* : tree with small edible fruit

mulch \'məlch\ *n* : protective ground covering —**mulch** *vb*

mulct \'məlkt\ *n or vb* : fine

¹mule \'myül\ *n* : offspring of a male ass and a female horse 2 : stubborn person —**mul-ish** \'myülish\ *adj* —**mul-ish-ly** *adv* —**mu-lish-ness** *n*

²mule *n* : backless shoe

mull \'məl\ *vb* : ponder

mul-let \'məlat\ *n, pl* -let *or* lets : marine food fish

multi- *comb form* 1 : many or multiple 2 : many times over

multiarmed	multidivisional
multibarreled	multidwelling
multibillion	multifaceted
multibranched	multifamily
multibuilding	multifilament
multicenter	multifunction
multichambered	multifunctional
multichannel	multigrade
multicolored	multiheaded
multicounty	multihospital
multicultural	multihued
multidenomina-	multilane
tional	multilevel
multidimensional	multimedia
multidirectional	multimember
multidisciplinary	multimillion
multidiscipline	multimillionaire

multipart	multispeed
multipartite	multistage
multiparty	multistep
multiplant	multistory
multipolar	multisyllabic
multiproblem	multitalented
multiproduct	multitrack
multipurpose	multiunion
multiracial	multiunit
multiroomed	multiuse
multisense	multiwarhead
multiservice	multiyear
multisided	

mul-ti-far-i-ous \ˌməltə'farēəs\ *adj* : diverse —**mul-ti-far-i-ous-ly** *adv*

mul-ti-lat-er-al \ˌməlti'latərəl, -ˌtī-, -'latrəl\ *adj* : having many sides or participants

mul-ti-lin-gual \-'lingwəl\ *adj* : involving several languages —**mul-ti-lin-gual-ism** \-gwəˌlizəm\ *n*

mul-ti-ple \'məltəpəl\ *adj* 1 : several or many 2 : complex ∼ *n* : product of one number by another

multiple sclerosis *n* : brain or spinal disease affecting muscle control

mul-ti-pli-ca-tion \ˌməltəplə'kāshən\ *n* 1 : increase 2 : short method of repeated addition

mul-ti-plic-i-ty \ˌməltə'plisətē\ *n, pl* -ties : great number or variety

mul-ti-ply \'məltəˌplī\ *vb* -plied; -ply-ing 1 : increase in number 2 : perform multiplication —**mul-ti-pli-er** \-ˌplī(ə)r\ *n*

mul-ti-tude \'məltəˌt(y)üd\ *n* : great number —**mul-ti-tu-di-nous** \ˌməltə't(y)üdnəs, -²nəs\ *adj*

¹mum \'məm\ *adj* : silent

²mum *n* : chrysanthemum

mum-ble \'məmbəl\ *vb* -bled; -bling : speak indistinctly —**mumble** *n* —**mum-bler** *n*

mum-mer \'məmər\ *n* 1 : actor esp. in a pantomime 2 : diguised merry-maker —**mum-mery** *n*

mum-my \'məmē\ *n, pl* -mies : embalmed body —**mum-mi-fi-ca-tion** \ˌməmifə'kāshən\ *n* —**mum-mi-fy** \-miˌfī\ *vb*

mumps \'məmps\ *n sing or pl* : virus disease with swelling esp. of the salivary glands

munch \'mənch\ *vb* : chew

mun-dane \ˌmən'dān, 'mən,-\ *adj* 1 : relating to the world 2 : lacking concern for the ideal or spiritual —**mun-dane-ly** *adv*

mu-nic-i-pal \myü'nisəpəl\ *adj* : of or relating to a town or city —**mu-nic-i-**

pal·i·ty \,myu̇,nisə'palətē\ n —**mu·nic·i·pal·ly** adv

mu·nif·i·cent \myu̇'nifəsənt\ adj : generous —**mu·nif·i·cence** \-səns\ n

mu·ni·tions \myu̇'nishənz\ n pl : armaments

mu·ral \'myu̇rəl\ adj : relating to a wall ~ n : wall painting —**mu·ra·list** n

mur·der \'mərdər\ n : unlawful killing of a person ~ vb : commit a murder —**mur·der·er** n —**mur·der·ess** \-əs\ n —**mur·der·ous** \-əs\ adj —**mur·der·ous·ly** adv

murk \'mərk\ n : darkness —**murk·i·ly** \'mərkəlē\ adv —**murk·i·ness** \-kēnəs\ n —**murky** adj

mur·mur \'mərmər\ n 1 : muttered complaint 2 : low indistinct sound —**murmur** vb —**mur·mur·er** n —**mur·mur·ous** adj

mus·ca·tel \,məskə'tel\ n : sweet wine

mus·cle \'məsəl\ n 1 : body tissue capable of contracting 2 : strength ~ vb -**cled; -cling** : force one's way —**mus·cled** adj —**mus·cu·lar** \'məskyələr\ adj —**mus·cu·lar·i·ty** \,məskyə'larətē\ n

muscular dystrophy n : disease marked by progressive wasting of muscles

mus·cu·la·ture \'məskyələ,chu̇r\ n : bodily muscles

¹**muse** \'myüz\ vb **mused; mus·ing** : ponder —**mus·ing·ly** adv

²**muse** n : source of inspiration

mu·se·um \myu̇'zēəm\ n : institution displaying objects of interest

mush \'məsh\ n 1 : corn meal boiled in water or something of similar consistency 2 : sentimental nonsense —**mushy** adj

mush·room \'məsh,rüm, -,rúm\ n : caplike organ of a fungus ~ vb : grow rapidly

mu·sic \'myüzik\ n : vocal or instrumental sounds —**mu·si·cal** \-zikəl\ adj or n —**mu·si·cal·ly** adv

mu·si·cian \myu̇'zishən\ n : composer or performer of music —**mu·si·cian·ly** adj —**mu·si·cian·ship** n

musk \'məsk\ n : strong-smelling substance from an Asiatic deer used in perfume —**musk·i·ness** \'məskēnəs\ n —**musky** adj

mus·kel·lunge \'məskə,lənj\ n, pl -**lunge** : large No. American pike

mus·ket \'məskət\ n : shoulder firearm —**mus·ke·teer** \,məskə'tiər\ n

musk·mel·on \'məsk,melən\ n : small edible melon

musk-ox \'məsk,äks\ n : shaggy-coated wild ox of the arctic

musk·rat \'məs,krat\ n, pl -**rat** or -**rats** : No. American water rodent

Mus·lim \'məzləm\ n : adherent of the religion founded by Muhammad

mus·lin \'mazlən\ n : cotton fabric

muss \'məs\ n : untidy state ~ vb : disarrange —**muss·i·ly** \'məsəlē\ adv —**muss·i·ness** \-ēnəs\ n —**mussy** adj

mus·sel \'məsəl\ n : edible mollusk

must \'(')məst\ vb —used as an auxiliary esp. to express a command, obligation, or necessity ~ \'məst\ n : something necessary

mus·tache \'məs,tash, (,)məs'-\ n : hair of the human upper lip

mus·tang \'məs,taŋ\ n : wild horse of Western America

mus·tard \'məstərd\ n : pungent yellow seasoning

mus·ter \'məstər\ vb 1 : assemble 2 : rouse ~ n : assembled group

musty \'məstē\ adj **mus·ti·er; -est** : stale —**must·i·ly** adv —**must·i·ness** n

mu·ta·ble \'myütəbəl\ adj : changeable —**mu·ta·bil·i·ty** \,myütə'bilətē\ n

mu·tant \'myüt°nt\ adj : relating to or produced by mutation —**mutant** n

mu·tate \'myü,tāt\ vb -**tat·ed; -tat·ing** : undergo mutation —**mu·ta·tive** \'myü,tātiv, 'myütət-\ adj

mu·ta·tion \myu̇'tāshən\ n : change in a hereditary character —**mu·ta·tion·al** adj

mute \'myüt\ adj **mut·er; mut·est** 1 : unable to speak 2 : silent ~ n 1 : one who is speechless 2 : muffling device ~ vb **mut·ed; mut·ing** : muffle —**mute·ly** adv —**mute·ness** n

mu·ti·late \'myüt°l,āt\ vb -**lat·ed; -lat·ing** : damage seriously (as by cutting off or altering an essential part) —**mu·ti·la·tion** \,myüt°l'āshən\ n —**mu·ti·la·tor** \'myüt°l,ātər\ n

mu·ti·ny \'myüt°nē\ n, pl -**nies** : rebellion —**mu·ti·neer** \,myüt°n'iər\ n —**mu·ti·nous** \'myüt°nəs\ adj —**mu·ti·nous·ly** adv

mutt \'mət\ n : mongrel

mut·ter \'mətər\ vb 1 : speak indistinctly or softly 2 : grumble —**mutter** n

mut·ton \'mət°n\ n : flesh of a mature sheep —**mut·tony** adj

mu·tu·al \'myüchə(wə)l\ adj 1 : given or felt by one another in equal amount 2 : common —**mu·tu·al·ly** adv

muz·zle \'məzəl\ n 1 : nose and jaws of

an animal **2** : muzzle covering to immobilize an animal's jaws **3** : discharge end of a gun ~ *vb* **-zled; -zling** : restrain with or as if with a muzzle

my \\(')mī, mə\ *adj* **1** : relating to me or myself **2** —used interjectionally esp. to express surprise

my·na, my·nah \'mīnə\ *n* : Asian starling

my·o·pia \mī'ōpēə\ *n* : nearsightedness —**my·o·pic** \-'ōpik, -'äpik\ *adj* —**my·o·pi·cal·ly** \-(ə)lē\ *adv*

myr·i·ad \'mirēəd\ *n* : indefinitely large number —**myriad** *adj*

myrrh \'mər\ *n* : aromatic plant gum

myr·tle \'mərtᵊl\ *n* : shiny evergreen

my·self \mī'self, mə-\ *pron* : I, me —used reflexively or for emphasis

mys·tery \'mist(ə)rē\ *n, pl* **-ter·ies 1** : religious truth **2** : something not understood **3** : puzzling or secret quality or state —**mys·te·ri·ous**

\mis'tirēəs\ *adj* —**mys·te·ri·ous·ly** *adv* —**mys·te·ri·ous·ness** *n*

mys·tic \'mistik\ *adj* : mystical or mysterious ~ *n* : one who has mystical experiences —**mys·ti·cism** \-tə,sizəm\ *n*

mys·ti·cal \'mistikəl\ *adj* **1** : spiritual **2** : relating to direct communion with God

mys·ti·fy \'mistə,fī\ *vb* **-fied; -fy·ing** : perplex —**mys·ti·fi·ca·tion** \,mistəfə'kāshən\ *n*

mys·tique \mis'tēk\ *n* : beliefs and attitudes associated with something

myth \'mith\ *n* **1** : legendary narrative explaining a belief or phenomenon **2** : imaginary person or thing —**myth·i·cal** \-ikəl\ *adj*

my·thol·o·gy \mith'äləjē\ *n, pl* **-gies** : body of myths —**myth·o·log·i·cal** \,mithə'läjikəl\ *adj* —**my·thol·o·gist** \mith'äləjəst\ *n*

N

n \'en\ *n, pl* **n's** *or* **ns** \'enz\ : 14th letter of the alphabet

nab \'nab\ *vb* **-bb-** : seize or arrest

na·dir \'nā,diər, 'nādər\ *n* : lowest point

¹nag \'nag\ *n* : old or decrepit horse

²nag *vb* **-gg-** **1** : scold or urge continually **2** : be persistently annoying ~ *n* : one who nags habitually

na·iad \'nāəd, 'nī-, -,ad\ *n, pl* **-iads** *or* **-ia·des** \-ə,dēz\ : mythological water nymph

nail \'nāl\ *n* **1** : horny sheath at the end of each finger and toe **2** : pointed metal fastener ~ *vb* : fasten with a nail —**nail·er** *n*

na·ive, na·ïve \nä'ēv\ *adj* **-iv·er; -est 1** : innocent and unsophisticated **2** : easily deceived —**na·ive·ly** *adv* —**na·ive·ness** *n*

na·ive·té, na·ïve·té \,nä,ēv(ə)'tā, nä'ēvə,-\ *n* : quality or state of being naive

na·ked \'nākəd, 'nekəd\ *adj* **1** : having no clothes on **2** : uncovered **3** : plain or obvious **4** : unaided —**na·ked·ly** *adv* —**na·ked·ness** *n*

nam·by-pam·by \,nambē'pambē\ *adj* : weak or indecisive

name \'nām\ *n* **1** : word by which a person or thing is known **2** : disparaging word for someone **3** : distinguished reputation ~ *vb* **named; nam·ing 1** : give a name to **2** : mention or identify by name **3** : nomi-

nate or appoint ~ *adj* **1** : relating to a name **2** : prominent —**name·able** *adj* —**name·less** *adj* —**name·less·ly** *adv*

name·ly \'nāmlē\ *adv* : that is to say

name·sake \-,sāk\ *n* : one named after another

¹nap \'nap\ *vb* **-pp-** **1** : sleep briefly **2** : be off guard ~ *n* : short sleep

²nap *n* : soft downy surface —**nap·less** *adj* —**napped** \'napt\ *adj*

na·palm \'nā,pä(l)m\ *n* : gasoline in the form of a jelly

nape \'nāp, 'nap\ *n* : back of the neck

naph·tha \'nafthə, 'nap-\ *n* : flammable solvent

nap·kin \'napkən\ *n* : small cloth for use at the table

nar·cis·sism \'närsə,sizəm\ *n* : self-love —**nar·cis·sist** \-səst\ *n or adj*

nar·cis·sus \när'sisəs\ *n, pl* **-cis·sus** *or* **-cis·sus·es** *or* **-cis·si** \-'sis,ī, -,ē\ : plant with flowers usu. borne separately

nar·cot·ic \när'kätik\ *n* : painkilling addictive drug —**narcotic** *adj*

nar·rate \'nar,āt\ *vb* **nar·rat·ed; nar·rat·ing** : tell (a story) —**nar·ra·tion** \na'rāshən\ *n* —**nar·ra·tive** \'närətiv\ *n or adj* —**nar·ra·tor** \'nar,ātər\ *n*

nar·row \'narō\ *adj* **1** : of less than standard width **2** : limited **3** : not liberal **4** : barely successful ~ *vb*

: make narrow —**nar·row·ly** *adv*
—**nar·row·ness** *n*

nar·row-mind·ed \\narō'mīndəd\ *adj*
: shallow, provincial, or bigoted

nar·rows \'narōz\ *n pl* : narrow passage

nar·whal \'när,hwäl, 'närwəl\ *n* : sea
mammal with a tusk

nasal \'nāzəl\ *adj* : relating to or uttered through the nose —**na·sal·ly**
adv

nas·tur·tium \nə'stərshəm, na-\
: herb with showy flowers

nas·ty \'nastē\ *adj* **nas·ti·er; -est 1**
: filthy **2** : indecent **3** : malicious or
spiteful —**nas·ti·ly** \'nastəlē\ *adv*
—**nas·ti·ness** \-tēnəs\ *n*

na·tal \'nāt³l\ *adj* : relating to birth

na·tion \'nāshən\ *n* **1** : people of similar characteristics **2** : community
with its own territory and government —**na·tion·al** \'nash(ə)nəl\ *adj
or n* —**na·tion·al·ly** *adv* —**na·tion·hood** *n*

na·tion·al·ism \'nash(ə)nəl,izəm\ *n*
: devotion to national interests,
unity, and independence —**na·tion·al·ist** \-əst\ *n or adj* —**na·tion·al·is·tic** \,nash(ə)nəl'istik\ *adj*

na·tion·al·i·ty \,nash(ə)'nalətē\ *n, pl*
-ties 1 : national character **2** : membership in a nation **3** : political independence **4** : ethnic group

na·tion·al·ize \'nash(ə)nəl,īz\ *vb* **-ized;
-iz·ing 1** : make national **2** : place
under government control —**na·tion·al·iza·tion** \,nash(ə)nələ'zāshən\ *n*

na·tive \'nātiv\ *adj* **1** : belonging to a
person at or by way of birth **2** : born
or produced in a particular place ~
n : one who belongs to a country by
birth

Na·tiv·i·ty \nə'tivətē, nā-\ *n, pl* **-ties 1**
: birth of Christ **2** : Christmas **3** *not
cap* : birth

nat·ty \'natē\ *adj* **-ti·er; -est** : smartly
dressed —**nat·ti·ly** \'nat³lē\ *adv*
—**nat·ti·ness** \-ēnəs\ *n*

nat·u·ral \'nach(ə)rəl\ *adj* **1** : relating
to or determined by nature **2** : not
artificial **3** : simple and sincere **4**
: lifelike —**nat·u·ral·ness** *n*

nat·u·ral·ism \'nach(ə)rə,lizəm\ *n*
: realism in art and literature —**nat·u·ral·is·tic** \,nach(ə)rə'listik\ *adj*

nat·u·ral·ist \-ləst\ *n* **1** : one who practices naturalism **2** : student of animals or plants

nat·u·ral·ize \-,īz\ *vb* **-ized; -iz·ing 1**
: become or cause to become established **2** : confer citizenship on

—**nat·u·ral·iza·tion** \,nach(ə)-
rələ'zāshən\ *n*

nat·u·ral·ly \'nach(ə)rəlē, 'nachərlē\
adv **1** : in a natural way **2** : as might
be expected

na·ture \'nāchər\ *n* **1** : basic quality of
something **2** : kind **3** : disposition **4**
: physical universe **5** : natural environment —**natured** *adj*

naught \'nȯt, 'nät\ *n* **1** : nothing **2**
: zero

naugh·ty \'nȯtē, 'nät-\ *adj* **-ti·er; -est 1**
: disobedient or misbehaving **2** : improper —**naught·i·ly** \'nȯt³lē, 'nät-\
adv —**naught·i·ness** \-ēnəs\ *n*

nau·sea \'nȯzēə, -shə\ *n* **1** : sickness of
the stomach with a desire to vomit **2**
: extreme disgust —**nau·seous** \-shəs,
-zēəs\ *adj*

nau·se·ate \'nȯzē(h)āt, -sē-, -s(h)ē-\ *vb* **-at·ed; -at·ing** : affect or become affected
with nausea —**nau·se·at·ing·ly**
\-,ātiŋlē\ *adv*

nau·ti·cal \'nȯtikəl\ *adj* : relating to
ships and sailing —**nau·ti·cal·ly**
\-k(ə)lē\ *adv*

nau·ti·lus \'nȯt³ləs\ *n, pl* **-lus·es** *or* **-li**
\-³l,ī, -,ē\ : sea mollusk

na·val \'nāvəl\ *adj* : relating to a navy

nave \'nāv\ *n* : central part of a church

na·vel \'nāvəl\ *n* : depression in the
abdomen

nav·i·ga·ble \'navigəbəl\ *adj* : capable
of being navigated —**nav·i·ga·bil·i·ty**
\,navigə'bilətē\ *n* —**nav·i·ga·bly**
\'navigəblē\ *adv*

nav·i·gate \'navə,gāt\ *vb* **-gat·ed; -gat·ing 1** : sail on or through **2** : direct
the course of —**nav·i·ga·tion**
\,navə'gāshən\ *n* —**nav·i·ga·tor**
\'navəgātər\ *n*

na·vy \'nāvē\ *n, pl* **-vies 1** : fleet **2** : nation's organization for sea warfare

nay \'nā\ *adv* : no—used in oral voting
~ *n* : negative vote

Na·zi \'nätsē, 'nat-\ *n* : member of a
German fascist party from 1933 to
1945 —**Nazi** *adj* —**Na·zism**
\'nät,sizəm, 'nat-\, **Na·zi·ism**
\-sē,izəm\ *n*

near \'niər\ *adv* : at or close to ~ *prep*
: close to ~ *adj* **1** : not far away **2**
: very much like ~ *vb* : approach
—**near·ness** *n*

near·by \niər'bī, -,bī\ *adv or adj* : near

near·sight·ed \'niər'sītəd\ *adj* : seeing
well at short distances only —**near·sight·ed·ly** *adv* —**near·sight·ed·ness** *n*

neat \'nēt\ *adj* **1** : not diluted **2** : tastefully simple **3** : orderly and clean
—**neat** *adv* —**neat·ly** *adv* —**neat·ness**
n

neb·u·la \\'nebyələ\ *n, pl* **-las** *or* **-lae** \-,lē, -,lī\ : vast mass of interstellar gas —**neb·u·lar** \-lər\ *adj*

neb·u·lous \-ləs\ *adj* : indistinct

nec·es·sary \\'nesə,serē\ *n, pl* **-saries** : indispensable item ~ *adj* **1** : inevitable **2** : compulsory **3** : positively needed —**nec·es·sar·i·ly** \,nesə'serəlē\ *adv*

ne·ces·si·tate \ni'sesə,tāt\ *vb* **-tat·ed; -tat·ing** : make necessary

ne·ces·si·ty \ni'sesətē\ *n, pl* **-ties 1** : very great need **2** : something that is necessary **3** : poverty **4** : circumstances that force a course of action or that cannot be changed

neck \\'nek\ *n* **1** : body part connecting the head and trunk **2** : part of a garment at the neck **3** : narrow part ~ *vb* : kiss and caress —**necked** \\'nekt\ *adj*

neck·er·chief \\'nekərchəf, -,chēf\ *n, pl* **-chiefs** \-chəfs, -,chēfs\ : cloth worn tied about the neck

neck·lace \\'nekləs\ *n* : ornamental chain for the neck

neck·tie *n* : ornamental cloth tied under a collar

ne·crol·o·gy \nə'kräləjē\ *n, pl* **-gies** : obituary list

nec·ro·man·cy \\'nekrə,mansē\ *n* : art of conjuring —**nec·ro·man·cer** \-sər\ *n*

ne·cro·sis \nə'krōsəs, ne-\ *n, pl* **-cro·ses** \-,sēz\ : death of body tissue —**ne·crot·ic** \-'krätik\ *adj*

nec·tar \\'nektər\ *n* : sweet plant secretion

nec·tar·ine \,nektə'rēn\ *n* : smooth-skinned peach

née, nee \\'nā\ *adj*—used to identify a married woman by maiden name

need \\'nēd\ *n* **1** : obligation **2** : lack of something or what is lacking **3** : poverty ~ *vb* **1** : be in want **2** : have cause for **3** : be under obligation —**need·ful** \-fəl\ *adj* —**need·less** *adj* —**need·less·ly** *adv* —**needy** *adj*

nee·dle \\'nēd³l\ *n* **1** : pointed sewing implement or something like it **2** : movable bar in a compass **3** : hollow instrument for injecting or withdrawing material ~ *vb* **-dled; -dling** : incite to action by repeated gibes —**nee·dle·work** \-,wərk\ *n*

nee·dle·point \\'nēd³l,pȯint\ *n* **1** : lace work **2** : embroidery on canvas —**needlepoint** *adj*

ne·far·i·ous \ni'farēəs\ *adj* : very wicked —**ne·far·i·ous·ly** *adv*

ne·gate \ni'gāt\ *vb* **-gat·ed; -gat·ing** : deny **2** : nullify —**ne·ga·tion** \-'gāshən\ *n*

neg·a·tive \\'negtiv\ *adj* **1** : marked by denial or refusal **2** : showing a lack of something suspected or desirable **3** : less than zero **4** : having more electrons than protons **5** : having light and shadow images reversed ~ *n* **1** : negative word or vote **2** : negative photographic image —**neg·a·tive·ly** *adv*

ne·glect \ni'glekt\ *vb* **1** : disregard **2** : leave unattended to ~ *n* **1** : act of neglecting **2** : condition of being neglected —**ne·glect·ful** *adj*

neg·li·gee \,negli'zhā\ *n* : woman's loose robe

neg·li·gent \\'neglijənt\ *adj* : marked by neglect —**neg·li·gence** \-jəns\ *n* —**neg·li·gent·ly** *adv*

neg·li·gi·ble \\'neglijəbəl\ *adj* : insignificant

ne·go·ti·ate \ni'gōshē,āt\ *vb* **-at·ed; -at·ing 1** : confer with another to settle a matter **2** : obtain cash for **3** : get through successfully —**ne·go·tia·ble** \-sh(ē)əbəl\ *adj* —**ne·go·ti·a·tion** \-,gōsh(ē)'āshən\ *n* —**ne·go·ti·a·tor** \-'gōshē,ātər\ *n*

Ne·gro \\'nēgrō\ *n, pl* **-groes** : member of the black race —**Negro** *adj* —**Ne·groid** \\'nē,grȯid\ *n or adj, often not cap*

neigh \\'nā\ *n* : cry of a horse —**neigh** *vb*

neigh·bor \\'nābər\ *n* **1** : one living nearby **2** : fellowman ~ *vb* : be near or next to —**neigh·bor·hood** \-,húd\ *n* —**neigh·bor·li·ness** *n* —**neigh·bor·ly** *adv*

nei·ther \\'nēthər, 'nī-\ *pron or adj* : not the one or the other ~ *conj* **1** : not either **2** : nor

nem·e·sis \\'neməsəs\ *n, pl* **-e·ses** \-ə,sēz\ **1** : old and usu. frustrating rival **2** : retaliation

ne·ol·o·gism \nē'älə,jizəm\ *n* : new word

ne·on \\'nē,än\ *n* : gaseous colorless chemical element —**neon** *adj*

neo·phyte \\'nēə,fīt\ *n* : beginner

neph·ew \\'nefyü, chiefly Brit 'nev-\ *n* : a son of one's brother, sister, brother-in-law, or sister-in-law

ne·po·tism \\'nepə,tizəm\ *n* : favoritism shown in hiring a relative

nerve \\'nərv\ *n* **1** : strand of body tissue that connects the brain with other parts of the body **2** : self-control **3** : daring **4** *pl* : nervousness —**nerved** \\'nərvd\ *adj* —**nerve·less** *adj*

ner·vous \'nərvəs\ *adj* **1** : relating to or made up of nerves **2** : easily excited **3** : fearful —**ner·vous·ly** *adv* —**nervous·ness** *n*

nervy \'nərvē\ *adj* **nerv·i·er; -est** : insolent or presumptuous

-ness \nəs\ *n suffix* : condition or quality

nest \'nest\ *n* **1** : shelter prepared by a bird for its eggs **2** : place where eggs (as of insects or fish) are laid and hatched **3** : snug retreat **4** : set of objects fitting one inside or under another — *vb* : build or occupy a nest

nes·tle \'nesəl\ *vb* **-tled; -tling** : settle snugly (as in a nest)

¹net \'net\ *n* : fabric with spaces between strands or something made of this — *vb* **-tt-** : cover with or catch in a net

²net *adj* : remaining after deductions — *vb* **-tt-** : have as profit

neth·er \'nethər\ *adj* : situated below

net·tle \'net³l\ *n* : coarse herb with stinging hairs — *vb* **-tled; -tling** : provoke or vex —**net·tle·some** *adj*

net·work *n* : system of crossing or connected elements

neu·ral \'n(y)ùrəl\ *adj* : relating to a nerve

neu·ral·gia \n(y)ù'raljə\ *n* : pain along a nerve —**neu·ral·gic** \-jik\ *adj*

neu·ri·tis \n(y)ù'rītəs\ *n, pl* **-rit·i·des** \-'rītə,dēz\ *or* **-ri·tis·es** : inflammation of a nerve —**neu·rit·ic** \-'ritik\ *adj or n*

neu·rol·o·gy \n(y)ù'räləjē\ *n* : study of the nervous system —**neu·ro·log·i·cal** \,n(y)ùrə'läjikəl\, —**neu·ro·log·ic** \-ik\ *adj* —**neu·ro·log·i·cal·ly** *adv* —**neu·rol·o·gist** \n(y)ù'räləjəst\ *n*

neu·ro·sis \n(y)ù'rōsəs\ *n, pl* **-ro·ses** \-,sēz\ : nervous disorder

neu·rot·ic \n(y)ù'rätik\ *adj* : relating to neurosis ~ *n* : unstable person —**neu·rot·i·cal·ly** \-ik(ə)lē\ *adv*

neu·ter \'n(y)ütər\ *adj* : neither masculine nor feminine

neu·tral \'n(y)ütrəl\ *adj* **1** : not favoring either side **2** : being neither one thing nor the other **3** : not decided in color **4** : not electrically charged ~ *n* **1** : one that is neutral **2** : position of gears that are not engaged —**neu·tral·iza·tion** \,n(y)ütrələ'zāshən\ *n* —**neu·tral·ize** \'n(y)ütrə,līz\ *vb*

neu·tral·i·ty \n(y)ù'tralətē\ *n* : state of being neutral

neu·tron \'n(y)ü,trän\ *n* : uncharged atomic particle

nev·er \'nevər\ *adv* **1** : not ever **2** : in no degree, way, or condition

nev·er·more *adv* : never again

nev·er·the·less *adv* : in spite of that

new \'n(y)ü\ *adj* **1** : not old or familiar **2** : different from the former **3** : recently discovered or learned **4** : not accustomed **5** : refreshed or regenerated **6** : being such for the first time — *adv* : newly —**new·ish** *adj* —**new·ness** *n*

new·born *adj* **1** : recently born **2** : born anew ~ *n, pl* **-born** *or* **-borns** : newborn individual

new·ly \'n(y)ülē\ *adv* : recently

news \'n(y)üz\ *n* : report of recent events —**news·let·ter** *n* —**news·maga·zine** *n* —**news·man** \-,man, -,mən\ *n* —**news·pa·per** *n* —**news·pa·per·man** \-,man\ *n* —**news·stand** *n* —**news·wor·thy** *adj*

news·cast \-,kast\ *n* : broadcast of news —**news·cast·er** \-,kastər\ *n*

news·print *n* : cheap paper made from wood pulp

newsy \'n(y)üzē\ *adj* **news·i·er; -est** : filled with news

newt \'n(y)üt\ *n* : small salamander

New Year *n* : New Year's Day

New Year's Day *n* : January 1 observed as a legal holiday

next \'nekst\ *adj* : immediately preceding or following — *adv* **1** : in the time or place nearest **2** : at the first time yet to come — *prep* : nearest to

nex·us \'neksəs\ *n, pl* **-us·es** \-səsəz\ *or* **-us** \-səs, -,süs\ : connection or bond

nib \'nib\ *n* : pen point

nib·ble \'nibəl\ *vb* **-bled; -bling** : bite gently or bit by bit — *n* : small bite

nice \'nīs\ *adj* **nic·er; nic·est** **1** : fastidious **2** : very precise or delicate **3** : pleasing **4** : respectable —**nice·ly** *adv* —**nice·ness** *n*

nice·ty \'nīsətē\ *n, pl* **-ties** **1** : dainty or elegant thing **2** : fine detail **3** : exactness

niche \'nich\ *n* **1** : recess in a wall **2** : fitting place, work, or use

nick \'nik\ *n* **1** : small broken area or chip **2** : critical moment ~ *vb* : make a nick in

nick·el \'nikəl\ *n* **1** : hard silver-white metallic chemical element used in alloys **2** : U.S. 5-cent piece ~ *vb* **-eled** *or* **-elled; -el·ing** *or* **-el·ling** : plate with nickel

nick·name \'nik,nām\ *n* : informal substitute name —**nickname** *vb*

nic·o·tine \'nikə,tēn\ *n* : poisonous substance in tobacco

niece \'nēs\ *n* : a daughter of one's brother, sister, brother-in-law, or sister-in-law

nig·gard·ly \'nigərdlē\ *adj* : stingy —**nig·gard** *n* —**nig·gard·li·ness** *n*

nig·gling \'nig(ə)liŋ\ *adj* : petty and annoying

nigh \'nī\ *adv or adj or prep* : near

night \'nīt\ *n* **1** : period between dusk and dawn **2** : the coming of night —**night** *adj* —**night·ly** *adj or adv* —**night-time** *n*

night-clothes *n pl* : garments worn in bed

night-club \-,kləb\ *n* : place for drinking and entertainment open at night

night crawler *n* : earthworm

night-fall *n* : the coming of night

night-gown *n* : gown worn for sleeping

night-in-gale \'nītᵊn,gāl, -iŋ-\ *n* : Old World thrush that sings at night

night-mare \'nīt,mar\ *n* : frightening dream —**nightmare** *adj* —**night-mar-ish** \-,marish\ *adj*

night-shade \'nīt,shād\ *n* : group of plants with berries of which some forms are used as food while others are poisonous

nil \'nil\ *n* : nothing

nim·ble \'nimbəl\ *adj* **-bler; -blest 1** : agile **2** : clever —**nim·ble·ness** *n* —**nim·bly** \-blē\ *adv*

nine \'nīn\ *n* **1** : one more than 8 **2** : 9th in a set or series —**nine** *adj or pron* —**ninth** \'nīnth\ *adj or adv or n*

nine-pins *n* : bowling game using 9 pins

nine·teen \'nīn'tēn\ *n* : one more than 18 —**nineteen** *adj or pron* —**nine·teenth** \-'tēnth\ *adj or n*

nine·ty \'nīntē\ *n, pl* **-ties** : 9 times 10 —**nine·ti·eth** \-ēəth\ *adj or n* —**ninety** *adj or pron*

nin·ny \'ninē\ *n, pl* **ninnies** : fool

¹nip \'nip\ *vb* **-pp- 1** : catch hold of and squeeze tightly **2** : pinch or bite off **3** : destroy the growth or fulfillment of ~ *n* **1** : biting cold **2** : tang **3** : pinch or bite

²nip *n* : small quantity of liquor ~ *vb* **-pp-** : take liquor in nips

nip·per \'nipər\ *n* **1** : one that nips **2** *pl* : pincers **3** : large claw of a crustacean **4** : small boy

nip·ple \'nipəl\ *n* : tip of the breast or something resembling it

nip·py \'nipē\ *adj* **-pi·er; -est 1** : pungent **2** : chilly

nir·va·na \nir'vänə\ *n* : state of blissful oblivion

nit \'nit\ *n* : parasitic insect egg

ni·ter \'nītər\ *n* : nitrate of potassium or sodium used in gunpowder or fertilizer or in curing meat

ni·trate \'nī,trāt, -trət\ *n* : chemical salt used esp. in curing meat

ni·tric \'nītrik\ *adj* : relating to nitrogen

ni·trite \-,trīt\ *n* : chemical salt used in curing meat

ni·tro \-trō\ *n, pl* **-tros** : nitroglycerin

ni·tro·gen \'nītrəjən\ *n* : tasteless odorless gaseous chemical element —**ni·trog·e·nous** \nī'träjənəs\ *adj* —**ni·trous** \'nītrəs\ *adj*

ni·tro·glyc·er·in, ni·tro·glyc·er·ine \,nītrə'glis(ə)rən\ *n* : heavy oily explosive liquid

nit·wit \'nit,wit\ *n* : stupid person

no \(')nō\ *adv* **1** —used to express the negative **2** : in no respect or degree **3** : not so **4** —used as an interjection of surprise or doubt ~ *adj* **1** : not any **2** : not a ~ *n, pl* **noes** *or* **nos** \'nōz\ **1** : refusal **2** : negative vote

no·bil·i·ty \nō'bilətē\ *n* **1** : quality or state of being noble **2** : noble rank **3** : class of people of noble rank

no·ble \'nōbəl\ *adj* **-bler; -blest 1** : illustrious **2** : aristocratic **3** : stately **4** : of outstanding character ~ *n* : nobleman —**no·ble·ness** *n* —**no·bly** \-blē\ *adv*

no·ble·man \-mən\ *n* : member of the nobility

no·body \'nō,bädē, -bədē\ *pron* : no person ~ *n, pl* **-bod·ies** : person of no influence or social standing

noc·tur·nal \näk'tərnᵊl\ *adj* : relating to, occurring at, or active at night

noc·turne \'näk,tərn\ *n* : dreamy pensive instrumental composition

nod \'näd\ *vb* **-dd- 1** : bend the head downward or forward (as in bowing or going to sleep or as a sign of assent) **2** : move up and down **3** : show by a nod of the head —**nod** *n*

node \'nōd\ *n* : stem part from which a leaf arises —**nod·al** \-ᵊl\ *adj*

nod·ule \'näjül\ *n* : small lump or swelling —**nod·u·lar** \'näjələr\ *adj*

no·el \nō'el\ *n* **1** : Christmas carol **2** *cap* : Christmas season

noes *pl of* NO

nog·gin \'nägən\ *n* **1** : small mug **2** : person's head

no·how \'nō,haù\ *adv* : in no manner

noise \'nòiz\ *n* : loud or unpleasant sound ~ *vb* **noised; nois·ing** : spread by rumor —**noise·mak·er** *n* —**nois·i·ly** \'nòizəlē\ *adv* —**nois·i·ness** \-zēnəs\ *n* —**noisy** \'nòizē\ *adj*

noi·some \'nòisəm\ *adj* : harmful or offensive

no·mad \'nō,mad\ *n* : one who has no permanent home —**nomad** *adj* —**no·mad·ic** \nō'madik\ *adj*

no·men·cla·ture \'nōmən,klāchər\ *n* : system of names

nom·i·nal \'nämən^əl\ *adj* **1** : being something in name only **2** : very small or negligible —**nom·i·nal·ly** *adv*

nom·i·nate \'nämə‚nāt\ *vb* **-nat·ed; -nat·ing** : propose or choose as a candidate —**nom·i·na·tion** \‚nämə'nā- shən\ *n*

nom·i·na·tive \'näm(ə)nətiv\ *adj* : relating to or being a grammatical case marking typically the subject of a verb —**nominative** *n*

nom·i·nee \‚nämə'nē\ *n* : person nominated

non- \(')nän‚ ‚nän\ *prefix* : not, reverse of, or absence of

nonabrasive	noncontroversial
nonabsorbent	noncorrosive
nonacademic	noncriminal
nonaccredited	noncritical
nonacid	noncumulative
nonaddictive	noncurrent
nonadherence	nondeductible
nonadhesive	nondefense
nonadjacent	nondeferrable
nonadjustable	nondegradable
nonaffiliated	nondelivery
nonaggression	nondemocratic
nonalcoholic	nondenomina-
nonaligned	tional
nonappearance	nondestructive
nonautomatic	nondiscrimi-
nonbeliever	nation
nonbinding	nondiscrimi-
nonbreakable	natory
noncancerous	noneducational
noncandidate	nonelastic
noncarbonated	nonelected
non-Catholic	nonelective
nonchargeable	nonelectric
non-Christian	nonelectronic
nonchurchgoer	nonemotional
noncitizen	nonenforceable
nonclassical	nonenforcement
nonclassified	nonessential
noncombat	nonexchangeable
noncombatant	nonexistence
noncombustible	nonexistent
noncommercial	nonexplosive
noncommuni-	nonfat
cable	nonfatal
non-Communist	nonfattening
noncompliance	nonfictional
nonconclusive	nonflammable
nonconflicting	nonflowering
nonconforming	nonfunctional
nonconsecutive	nongovernmental
nonconstructive	nongraded
nonconsumable	nonhazardous
noncontagious	nonhereditary
noncontributing	nonindustrial
noncontrollable	nonindustrialized

noninfectious	nonrefundable
noninflationary	nonregistered
nonintegrated	nonreligious
nonintellectual	nonrenewable
noninterference	nonrepresent-
nonintoxicating	ative
noninvolvement	nonresident
non-Jewish	nonresponsive
nonlegal	nonrestricted
nonlethal	nonreusable
nonliterary	nonreversible
nonliving	nonscientific
nonmagnetic	nonscientist
nonmalignant	nonsegregated
nonmedical	non-self-gov-
nonmember	erning
nonmetal	nonsexist
nonmetallic	nonsexual
nonmilitary	nonsignificant
nonmusical	nonskier
nonnarcotic	nonsmoker
nonnative	nonsmoking
nonnegotiable	nonspeaking
nonobjective	nonspecialist
nonobservance	nonspecific
nonorthodox	nonstaining
nonparallel	nonstandard
nonparticipant	nonstrategic
nonparticipating	nonstriker
nonpaying	nonstriking
nonpayment	nonstudent
nonperformance	nonsubscriber
nonperishable	nonsugar
nonpermanent	nonsurgical
nonphysical	nonswimmer
nonpoisonous	nontaxable
nonpolitical	nonteaching
nonpolluting	nontechnical
nonporous	nontoxic
nonpregnant	nontraditional
nonproductive	nontransferable
nonprofessional	nontropical
nonprofit	nontypical
nonracial	nonunion
nonradioactive	nonuser
nonrated	nonvenomous
nonrealistic	nonverbal
nonrecoverable	nonvoter
nonrecurring	nonwhite
nonrefillable	nonworker

non·age \'nänij‚ 'nōnij\ *n* : period of youth and esp. legal minority

nonce \'näns\ *n* : present occasion ~ *adj* : occurring, used, or made only once

non·cha·lant \‚nänshə'länt\ *adj* : showing indifference —**non·cha·lance** \-'läns\ *n* —**non·cha·lant·ly** *adv*

non·com·mis·sioned officer \‚nän- kə‚mishənd-\ *n* : subordinate officer in the armed forces appointed from enlisted personnel

non·com·mit·tal \,nänkə'mit°l\ *adj* : indicating neither consent nor dissent

non·con·duc·tor \,nän-\ *n* : substance that is a very poor conductor

non·con·form·ist \,nän-\ *n* : one who does not conform to an established belief or mode of behavior —**non·con·for·mi·ty** *n*

non·de·script \,nändi'skript\ *adj* : not easily described

none \'nən\ *pron* : not any ~ *adv* : not at all

non·en·ti·ty \nä'nentətē\ *n* : one of no consequence

none·the·less \,nənthə'les\ *adv* : nevertheless

non·pa·reil \,nänpə'rel\ *adj* : having no equal ~ *n* 1 : one who has no equal 2 : chocolate candy disk

non·par·ti·san \,nän-\ *adj* : not influenced by political party bias

non·per·son \'nän-\ *n* : person without ordinary rights or respect

non·plus \nän'pləs\ *vb* -ss- : perplex

non·pro·lif·er·a·tion \,nän-\ *adj* : aimed at ending increased use of nuclear arms

non·sched·uled \'nän-\ *adj* : licensed to carry by air without a regular operating schedule

non·sense \'nän,sens, -səns\ *n* : foolish or meaningless words or actions —**non·sen·si·cal** \nän'sensikəl\ *adj* —**non·sen·si·cal·ly** \-k(ə)lē\ *adv*

non·sup·port \,nän-\ *n* : failure in a legal obligation to provide for someone's needs

non·vi·o·lence \'nän-\ *n* : avoidance of violence esp. in political demonstrations —**non·vi·o·lent** *adj*

noo·dle \'nüd°l\ *n* : ribbon-shaped dried food paste

nook \'nük\ *n* 1 : inside corner 2 : private place

noon \'nün\ *n* : middle of the day —**noon** *adj*

noon·day \-,dā\ *n* : noon

no one *pron* : no person

noon·time *n* : noon

noose \'nüs\ *n* : rope loop that slips down tight

nor \nər, 'nȯr\ *conj* —used esp. after *neither* 1') to introduce and negate the 2d member of a series

norm \'nȯrm\ *n* : standard usu. derived from an average

nor·mal \'nȯrməl\ *adj* : average, regular, or standard —**nor·mal·cy** \-sē\ *n* —**nor·mal·i·ty** \nȯr'malətē\ *n*

mal·iza·tion \,nȯrmələ'zāshən\ *n* —**nor·mal·ize** \'nȯrmə,līz\ *vb* —**nor·mal·ly** *adv*

north \'nȯrth\ *adv* : to or toward the north ~ *adj* : situated toward, at, or coming from the north ~ *n* 1 : direction to the left of one facing east 2 *cap* : regions to the north —**north·er·ly** \'nȯrthərlē\ *adv or adj* —**north·ern** \-ərn\ *adj* —**North·ern·er** *n* —**north·ern·most** \-,mōst\ *adj* —**north·ward** \-wərd\ *adv or adj* —**north·wards** \-wərdz\ *adv*

north·east \nȯrth'ēst\ *n* 1 : direction between north and east 2 *cap* : regions to the northeast —**northeast** *adj or adv* —**north·east·er·ly** \-ərlē\ *adv or adj* —**north·east·ern** \-ərn\ *adj*

northern lights *n pl* : aurora borealis

north pole *n* : northernmost point of the earth

north·west \-'west\ *n* 1 : direction between north and west 2 *cap* : regions to the northwest —**northwest** *adj or adv* —**north·west·er·ly** \-ərlē\ *adv or adj* —**north·west·ern** \-ərn\ *adj*

nose \'nōz\ *n* 1 : part of the face containing the nostrils 2 : sense of smell 3 : front part ~ *vb* nosed; nos·ing 1 : detect by smell 2 : push aside with the nose 3 : defeat narrowly 4 : pry 5 : inch ahead —**nose·bleed** *n* —**nosed** \'nōzd\ *adj*

nose·gay \-,gā\ *n* : small bunch of flowers

nosh \'näsh\ *vb* : eat a snack —**nosh** *n*

nos·tal·gia \nä'staljə, nə-\ *n* : wistful yearning for something past —**nos·tal·gic** \-jik\ *adj*

nos·tril \'nästrəl\ *n* : opening of the nose

nos·trum \-trəm\ *n* : questionable medicine

nosy, nos·ey \'nōzē\ *adj* nos·i·er; -est : tending to pry

not \(')nät\ *adv* —used to make a statement negative

no·ta·ble \'nōtəbəl\ *adj* 1 : noteworthy 2 : distinguished ~ *n* : notable person —**no·ta·bil·i·ty** \,nōtə'bilətē\ *n* —**no·ta·bly** \-blē\ *adv*

no·ta·rize \'nōtə,rīz\ *vb* -rized; -riz·ing : attest as a notary public

no·ta·ry public \,nōtərē\ *n, pl* -aries public *or* -ry publics : public official who attests writings to make them legally authentic

no·ta·tion \nō'tāshən\ *n* 1 : note 2 : act, process, or method of marking things down

notch \'näch\ *n* : V-shaped hollow —**notch** *vb*

note \\'nōt\\ *vb* **not·ed; not·ing** **1** : notice **2** : write down ~ *n* **1** : musical tone **2** : written comment or record **3** : notice or heed —**note-book** *n*

not·ed \\'nōtəd\\ *adj* : famous

note-wor·thy \\-,wərthē\\ *adj* : worthy of special mention

noth·ing \\'nəthiŋ\\ *pron* **1** : no thing **2** : no part **3** : one of no value or importance ~ *adv* : not at all ~ *n* **1** : something that does not exist **2** : zero **3** : one of little or no importance —**noth·ing·ness** *n*

no·tice \\'nōtəs\\ *n* **1** : warning or announcement **2** : attention ~ *vb* **-ticed; -tic·ing** : take notice of —**no-tice·able** *adj* —**no·tice·ably** *adv*

no·ti·fy \\'nōtə,fī\\ *vb* **-fied; -fy·ing** : give notice of or to —**no·ti·fi·ca·tion** \\,nōtəfə'kāshən\\ *n*

no·tion \\'nōshən\\ *n* **1** : idea or opinion **2** : whim **3** *pl* : small sewing or personal articles

no·to·ri·ous \\nō'tōrēəs\\ *adj* : widely and unfavorably known —**no·to·ri·ety** \\,nōtə'rīətē\\ *n* —**no·to·ri·ous·ly** *adv*

not·with·stand·ing \\,nätwith'standiŋ, -with-\\ *prep* : in spite of ~ *adv* : nevertheless ~ *conj* : although

nou·gat \\'nügat\\ *n* : nuts or fruit pieces in a sugar paste

nought \\'nót, 'nät\\ *var of* NAUGHT

noun \\'naún\\ *n* : word that is the name of a person, place, or thing

nour·ish \\'nərish\\ *vb* : promote the growth of —**nour·ish·ing** *adj* —**nour·ish·ment** *n*

no·va \\'nōvə\\ *n, pl* **-vas** *or* **-vae** \\-(,)vē, -,vī\\ : star that suddenly brightens and then fades

nov·el \\'nävəl\\ *adj* : new or strange ~ *n* : long invented prose story —**nov·el·ist** \\-(ə)ləst\\ *n*

nov·el·ty \\'nävəltē\\ *n, pl* **-ties 1** : something new or unusual **2** : newness **3** : small manufactured article—usu. *pl.*

No·vem·ber \\nō'vembər\\ *n* : 11th month of the year having 30 days

nov·ice \\'nävəs\\ *n* **1** : one preparing to take vows in a religious order **2** : one who is inexperienced or untrained

no·vi·tiate \\nō'vishət, nə-\\ *n* : period or state of being a novice

now \\(')naú\\ *adv* **1** : at the present time or moment **2** : forthwith **3** : under these circumstances ~ *conj* : in view of the fact — ~ \\'naú\\ *n* : present time

now·a·days \\'naú(ə),dāz\\ *adv* : now

no·where \\-,hwear\\ *adv* : not anywhere —**no·where** *n*

nox·ious \\'näkshəs\\ *adj* : harmful

noz·zle \\'näzəl\\ *n* : device to direct or control flow of fluid

nu·ance \\'nü,äns, n(y)ü'äns\\ *n* : subtle distinction or variation

nub \\'nəb\\ *n* **1** : knob or lump **2** : gist —**nub·by** *adj*

nu·bile \\'n(y)übəl, -,bīl\\ *adj* : of marriageable condition or age

nu·cle·ar \\'n(y)üklēər\\ *adj* : relating to the atomic nucleus or atomic energy

nu·cle·us \\'n(y)üklēəs\\ *n, pl* **-clei** \\-klē,ī\\ : central mass or part (as of a cell or an atom)

nude \\'n(y)üd\\ *adj* **nud·er; nud·est** : naked ~ *n* : nude human figure —**nu·di·ty** \\'n(y)üdətē\\ *n*

nudge \\'nəj\\ *vb* **nudged; nudg·ing** : touch or push gently —**nudge** *n*

nud·ism \\'n(y)üd,izəm\\ *n* : practice of going nude —**nud·ist** \\'n(y)üdəst\\ *n*

nug·get \\'nəgət\\ *n* : lump of gold

nui·sance \\'n(y)üsəns\\ *n* : something annoying

null \\'nəl\\ *adj* : having no legal or binding force —**nul·li·ty** \\'nələtē\\ *n*

nul·li·fy \\'nələ,fī\\ *vb* **-fied; -fy·ing** : make null or valueless —**nul·li·fi·ca·tion** \\,nələfə'kāshən\\ *n*

numb \\'nəm\\ *adj* : lacking feeling —**numb** *vb* —**numb·ly** *adv* —**numb·ness** *n*

num·ber \\'nəmbər\\ *n* **1** : total of individuals taken together **2** : group not specif. enumerated **3** : unit of a mathematical system **4** : numeral **5** : one in a sequence ~ *vb* **1** : count **2** : assign a number to **3** : comprise in number —**num·ber·less** *adj*

nu·mer·al \\'n(y)üm(ə)rəl\\ *n* : word or symbol representing a number

nu·mer·a·tor \\'n(y)üma,rātər\\ *n* : part of a fraction above the line

nu·mer·ic \\n(y)ü'merik\\ *adj* : numerical

nu·mer·i·cal \\n(y)ü'merikəl\\ *adj* **1** : of or relating to numbers **2** : denoting a number or expressed in numbers —**nu·mer·i·cal·ly** \\-k(ə)lē\\ *adv*

nu·mer·ol·o·gy \\,n(y)ümə'räləjē\\ *n* : occult study of numbers —**nu·mer·ol·o·gist** \\-jəst\\ *n*

nu·mer·ous \\'n(y)üm(ə)rəs\\ *adj* : consisting of a great number

nu·mis·mat·ics \\,n(y)üməz'matiks\\ *n* : study or collection of monetary objects —**nu·mis·mat·ic** \\-ik\\ *adj* —**nu·mis·ma·tist** \\n(y)ü'mizmətəst\\ *n*

num·skull \\'nəm,skəl\\ *n* : stupid person

nun \\'nən\\ *n* : woman belonging to a religious community —**nun·nery** \\-(ə)rē\\ *n*

nup·tial \'nəpshəl\ *adj* : relating to marriage or a wedding ~ *n* : marriage or wedding—usu. pl.

nurse \'nərs\ *n* 1 : one hired to care for children 2 : person trained to care for sick people ~ *vb* **nursed; nurs·ing** 1 : suckle 2 : care for

nurs·ery \'nərs(ə)rē\ *n, pl* **-er·ies** 1 : place where children are cared for 2 : place where young plants are grown

nursing home *n* : private establishment where care is provided for persons who are unable to care for themselves

nur·ture \'nərchər\ *n* 1 : training or upbringing 2 : food or nourishment ~ *vb* **-tured; -tur·ing** 1 : care for or feed 2 : educate

nut \'nət\ *n* 1 : dry hard-shelled fruit or seed with a firm inner kernel 2 : metal block with a screw hole through it 3 : foolish, eccentric, or crazy person 4 : enthusiast —**nut·crack·er** *n* —**nut·shell** *n* —**nut·ty** *adj*

nut·hatch \'nət,hach\ *n* : small bird

nut·meg \'nət,meg, -,mãg\ *n* : nutlike aromatic seed of a tropical tree

nu·tri·ent \'n(y)ütrēənt\ *n* : something giving nourishment —**nutrient** *adj*

nu·tri·ment \-trəmənt\ *n* : nutrient

nu·tri·tion \n(y)ü'trishən\ *n* : act or process of nourishing esp. with food —**nu·tri·tion·al** \-'trish(ə)nəl\ *adj* —**nu·tri·tious** \-'trishəs\ *adj* —**nu·tri·tive** \'n(y)ütrətiv\ *adj*

nuts \'nəts\ *adj* 1 : enthusiastic 2 : crazy

nuz·zle \'nəzəl\ *vb* **-zled; -zling** 1 : touch with or as if with the nose 2 : snuggle

ny·lon \'nī,län\ *n* 1 : tough synthetic material used esp. in textiles 2 *pl* : stockings made of nylon

nymph \'nimf\ *n* 1 : lesser goddess in ancient mythology 2 : immature insect

nym·pho·ma·nia \,nimfə'mānēə, -nyə\ *n* : excessive sexual desire by a female —**nym·pho·ma·ni·ac** \-nē,ak\ *n or adj*

O

o \'ō\ *n, pl* **o's** *or* **os** \'ōz\ : 15th letter of the alphabet

O *var of* OH

oaf \'ōf\ *n* : stupid or awkward person —**oaf·ish** \'ōfish\ *adj*

oak \'ōk\ *n, pl* **oaks** *or* **oak** : tree bearing a thin-shelled nut or its wood —**oak·en** \'ōkən\ *adj*

oa·kum \'ōkəm\ *n* : loosely twisted tarred hemp or jute fiber for caulking ships

oar \'ōr\ *n* : implement used to propel a boat

oar·lock \-,läk\ *n* : device for holding an oar

oa·sis \ō'āsəs\ *n, pl* **oa·ses** \-,sēz\ : fertile area in a desert

oat \'ōt\ *n* : cereal grass or its edible seed —**oat·cake** *n* —**oat·en** \-ᵊn\ *adj* —**oat·meal** *n*

oath \'ōth\ *n, pl* **oaths** \'ōthz, 'ōths\ 1 : solemn appeal to God as a pledge of sincerity 2 : profane utterance

ob·du·rate \'äbd(y)ərət\ *adj* : stubbornly resistant —**ob·du·ra·cy** \-rəsē\ *n*

obe·di·ent \ō'bēdēənt\ *adj* : willing to obey —**obe·di·ence** \-əns\ *n* —**obe·di·ent·ly** *adv*

obei·sance \ō'bāsəns, -'bēs-\ *n* : bow of respect or submission

ob·e·lisk \'äbə,lisk\ *n* : 4-sided tapering pillar

obese \ō'bēs\ *adj* : extremely fat —**obe·si·ty** \-'bēsətē\ *n*

obey \ō'bā\ *vb* **obeyed; obey·ing** 1 : follow the commands or guidance of 2 : behave in accordance with

ob·fus·cate \'äbfə,skāt\ *vb* **-cat·ed; -cat·ing** : confuse —**ob·fus·ca·tion** \,äbfəs'kāshən\ *n*

obit·u·ary \ō'bichə,werē\ *n, pl* **-ar·ies** : death notice

¹ob·ject \'äbjikt\ *n* 1 : something that may be seen or felt 2 : purpose 3 : noun or equivalent toward which the action of a verb is directed or which follows a preposition

²ob·ject \əb'jekt\ *vb* : offer opposition or disapproval —**ob·jec·tion** \-'jekshən\ *n* —**ob·jec·tion·able** \-sh(ə)nəbəl\ *adj* —**ob·jec·tor** \-'jektər\ *n*

ob·jec·tive \əb'jektiv\ *adj* 1 : relating to an object or end 2 : existing outside an individual's thoughts or feelings 3 : treating facts without distortion 4 : relating to or being a grammatical case marking objects ~ *n* : aim or end of action —**ob·jec·tive·ly** *adv* —**ob·jec·tive·ness** *n* —**ob·jec·tiv·i·ty** \,äb,jek'tivətē\ *n*

ob·li·gate \'äblə₁gāt\ *vb* **-gat·ed; -gat·ing** : bind legally or morally —**ob·li·ga·tion** \₁äblə'gāshən\ *n* —**ob·li·ga·to·ry** \ə'bligə₁tōrē, 'äbligə-\ *adj*

oblige \ə'blīj\ *vb* **obliged; oblig·ing** 1 : compel 2 : do a favor for —**oblig·ing** *adj* —**oblig·ing·ly** *adv*

oblique \ō'blēk, -'blīk\ *adj* 1 : lying at a slanting angle 2 : indirect —**oblique·ly** *adv* —**oblique·ness** *n* —**obliq·ui·ty** \-'blikwətē\ *n*

oblit·er·ate \ə'blitə₁rāt\ *vb* **-at·ed; -at·ing** : completely remove or destroy —**oblit·er·a·tion** \-₁blitə'rāshən\ *n*

obliv·i·on \ə'blivēən\ *n* 1 : state of having lost conscious awareness 2 : state of being unknown or forgotten

obliv·i·ous \-ēəs\ *adj* : not aware or mindful—with *to* or *of* —**obliv·i·ous·ly** *adv* —**obliv·i·ous·ness** *n*

ob·long \'äb₁lȯṅ\ *adj* : longer in one direction than in the other with opposite sides parallel —**oblong** *n*

ob·lo·quy \'äbləkwē\ *n, pl* **-quies** 1 : strongly condemning utterance 2 : bad repute

ob·nox·ious \äb'näkshəs, əb-\ *adj* : repugnant —**ob·nox·ious·ly** *adv* —**ob·nox·ious·ness** *n*

oboe \'ōbō\ *n* : slender woodwind instrument with a reed mouthpiece —**obo·ist** \'ō₁bōəst\ *n*

ob·scene \äb'sēn, əb-\ *adj* : repugnantly indecent —**ob·scene·ly** *adv* —**ob·scen·i·ty** \-'senətē\ *n*

ob·scure \äb'skyür, əb-\ *adj* 1 : dim or hazy 2 : not well known 3 : vague ~ *vb* : make indistinct or unclear —**ob·scure·ly** *adv* —**ob·scu·ri·ty** \-'skyürətē\ *n*

ob·se·quies \'äbsəkwēz\ *n pl* : funeral or burial rite

ob·se·qui·ous \əb'sēkwēəs\ *adj* : excessively attentive or flattering —**ob·se·qui·ous·ly** *adv* —**ob·se·qui·ous·ness** *n*

ob·ser·va·to·ry \əb'zərvə₁tōrē\ *n, pl* **-ries** : place for observing astronomical phenomena

ob·serve \əb'zərv\ *vb* **-served; -serv·ing** 1 : conform to 2 : celebrate 3 : see, watch, or notice 4 : remark —**ob·serv·able** *adj* —**ob·ser·vance** \-'zərvəns\ *n* —**ob·ser·vant** \-vənt\ *adj* —**ob·ser·va·tion** \₁äbsər'vāshən, -zər-\ *n*

ob·sess \əb'ses\ *vb* : preoccupy intensely or abnormally —**ob·ses·sion** \äb'seshən, əb-\ *n* —**ob·ses·sive** \-'sesiv\ *adj* —**ob·ses·sive·ly** *adv*

ob·so·les·cent \₁äbsə'les³nt\ *adj* : going out of use —**ob·so·les·cence** \-³ns\ *n*

ob·so·lete \₁äbsə'lēt, 'äbsə₁-\ *adj* : no longer in use

ob·sta·cle \'äbstikəl\ *n* : something that stands in the way or opposes

ob·stet·rics \əb'stetriks\ *n sing or pl* : branch of medicine that deals with childbirth —**ob·stet·ri·cal** \-rikəl\ *adj* —**ob·ste·tri·cian** \₁äbstə'trishən\ *n*

ob·sti·nate \'äbstənət\ *adj* : stubborn —**ob·sti·na·cy** \-nəsē\ *n* —**ob·sti·nate·ly** *adv*

ob·strep·er·ous \äb'strep(ə)rəs\ *adj* : uncontrollably noisy or defiant —**ob·strep·er·ous·ness** *n*

ob·struct \əb'strəkt\ *vb* : block or impede —**ob·struc·tion** \-'strəkshən\ *n* —**ob·struc·tive** \-'strəktiv\ *adj* —**ob·struc·tor** \-tər\ *n*

ob·tain \əb'tān\ *vb* 1 : gain by effort 2 : be generally recognized —**ob·tain·able** *adj*

ob·trude \äb'trüd\ *vb* **-trud·ed; -trud·ing** 1 : thrust out 2 : intrude —**ob·tru·sion** \-'trüzhən\ *n* —**ob·tru·sive** \-'trüsiv\ *adj* —**ob·tru·sive·ly** *adv* —**ob·tru·sive·ness** *n*

ob·tuse \äb't(y)üs, əb-\ *adj* 1 : slow-witted 2 : exceeding 90 but less than 180 degrees —**ob·tuse·ly** *adv* —**ob·tuse·ness** *n*

ob·verse \'äb₁vərs, äb'-\ *n* : principal side (as of a coin)

ob·vi·ate \'äbvē₁āt\ *vb* **-at·ed; -at·ing** : make unnecessary —**ob·vi·a·tion** \₁äbvē'āshən\ *n*

ob·vi·ous \'äbvēəs\ *adj* : plain or unmistakable —**ob·vi·ous·ly** *adv* —**ob·vi·ous·ness** *n*

oc·ca·sion \ə'kāzhən\ *n* 1 : favorable opportunity 2 : cause 3 : time of an event 4 : special event ~ *vb* : cause —**oc·ca·sion·al** \-'kāzh(ə)nəl\ *adj* —**oc·ca·sion·al·ly** *adv*

oc·ci·den·tal \₁äksə'dent³l\ *adj* : western —**Occidental** *n*

oc·cult \ə'kəlt, 'äk₁əlt\ *adj* : secret or mysterious

oc·cu·pan·cy \'äkyəpənsē\ *n, pl* **-cies** : an occupying

oc·cu·pant \-pənt\ *n* : one who occupies

oc·cu·pa·tion \₁äkyə'pāshən\ *n* 1 : vocation 2 : action or state of occupying —**oc·cu·pa·tion·al** \-sh(ə)nəl\ *adj* —**oc·cu·pa·tion·al·ly** *adv*

oc·cu·py \'äkyə₁pī\ *vb* **-pied; -py·ing** 1 : engage the attention of 2 : fill up 3 : sit or lie in 4 : reside in —**oc·cu·pi·er** \-₁pī(ə)r\ *n*

oc·cur \ə'kər\ *vb* **-rr-** 1 : be found or

met with **2** : take place **3** : come to mind

oc·cur·rence \ə'kərəns\ *n* : something that takes place

ocean \'ōshən\ *n* **1** : whole body of salt water **2** : large body of water —**ocean-front** *n* —**ocean-go·ing** *adj* —**oce-an·ic** \ˌōshē'anik\ *adj*

ocean-og·ra·phy \ˌōshə'nägrəfē\ *n* : science dealing with the ocean —**ocean-og·ra·pher** \-fər\ *n* —**ocean-o·graph·ic** \-nə'grafik\ *adj*

oce·lot \'äsə,lät, 'ōsə-\ *n* : medium-sized American wildcat

ocher, ochre \'ōkər\ *n* : red or yellow pigment

o'·clock \ə'kläk\ *adv* : according to the clock

oc·ta·gon \'äktə,gän\ *n* : 8-sided polygon —**oc·tag·o·nal** \äk'tagənəl\ *adj*

oc·tave \'äktiv\ *n* : musical interval of 8 steps or the notes within this interval

Oc·to·ber \äk'tōbər\ *n* : 10th month of the year having 31 days

oc·to·pus \'äktəpəs\ *n, pl* **-pus·es** *or* **-pi** \-ˌpī\ : sea mollusk with 8 arms

oc·u·lar \'äkyələr\ *adj* : relating to the eye

oc·u·list \'äkyələst\ *n* **1** : ophthalmologist **2** : optometrist

odd \'äd\ *adj* **1** : being only one of a pair or set **2** : not divisible by two without a remainder **3** : additional to what is usual or to the number mentioned **4** : queer —**odd·ly** *adv* —**odd·ness** *n*

odd·i·ty \'ädətē\ *n, pl* **-ties** : something odd

odds \'ädz\ *n pl* **1** : difference by which one thing is favored **2** : equalizing allowance **3** : disagreement

ode \'ōd\ *n* : solemn lyric poem

odi·ous \'ōdēəs\ *adj* : hated —**odi·ous·ly** *adv* —**odi·ous·ness** *n*

odi·um \'ōdēəm\ *n* **1** : merited loathing **2** : disgrace

odor \'ōdər\ *n* : quality that affects the sense of smell —**odor·less** *adj* —**odor·ous** *adj*

od·ys·sey \'ädəsē\ *n, pl* **-seys** : long wandering

o'er \'ō(ə)r\ *adv or prep* : OVER

of \(')əv, ˈəv\ *prep* **1** : from **2** : distinguished by **3** : because of **4** : made or written by **5** : made with, being, or containing **6** : belonging to or connected with **7** : about **8** : that is **9** : concerning **10** : before

off \'òf\ *adv* **1** : from a place **2** : unattached or removed **3** : to a state of being no longer in use **4** : away from

work **5** : at a distance in time or space ~ \(')òf\ *prep* **1** : away from esp. the surface or top of **2** : at the expense of **3** : not engaged in or abstaining from **4** : below the usual level of ~ \(')òf\ *adj* **1** : not operating, up to standard, or correct **2** : remote **3** : provided for

of·fal \'òfəl\ *n* **1** : waste **2** : viscera and trimmings of a butchered animal

of·fend \ə'fend\ *vb* **1** : sin or act in violation **2** : hurt, annoy, or insult —**of·fend·er** *n*

of·fense, of·fence \ə'fens, 'äf,ens\ *n* : attack, misdeed, or insult

of·fen·sive \ə'fensiv, 'äf,en-\ *adj* : causing offense ~ *n* : attack —**of·fen·sive·ly** *adv* —**of·fen·sive·ness** *n*

of·fer \'òfər\ *vb* **1** : present for acceptance **2** : propose **3** : put up (an effort) ~ *n* **1** : proposal **2** : bid —**of·fer·ing** *n*

of·fer·to·ry \'òfə(r)ˌtōrē\ *n, pl* **-ries** : presentation of offerings or its musical accompaniment

off·hand *adv or adj* : without previous thought or preparation

of·fice \'òfəs\ *n* **1** : position of authority (as in government) **2** : rite **3** : place where a business is transacted —**of·fice·hold·er** *n*

of·fi·cer \'òfəsər\ *n* **1** : one charged with law enforcement **2** : one who holds an office of trust or authority **3** : one who holds a commission in the armed forces

of·fi·cial \ə'fishəl\ *n* : one in office ~ *adj* : authorized or authoritative —**of·fi·cial·dom** \-dəm\ *n* —**of·fi·cial·ly** *adv*

of·fi·ci·ate \ə'fishē,āt\ *vb* **-at·ed; -at·ing** : perform a ceremony or function

of·fi·cious \ə'fishəs\ *adj* : volunteering one's services unnecessarily —**of·fi·cious·ly** *adv* —**of·fi·cious·ness** *n*

off·ing \'òfiŋ\ *n* : future

off·set \'òf,set\ *vb* **-set; -set·ting** : provide an opposite or equaling effect to

off·shoot \'òf,shüt\ *n* : outgrowth

off·shore *adv* : at a distance from the shore ~ *adj* : moving away from or situated off the shore

off·spring \'òf,spriŋ\ *n, pl* **offspring** : one coming into being through animal or plant reproduction

of·ten \'òf(t)ən\ *adv* : many times —**of·ten·times** *adv*

ogle \'ōgəl\ *vb* **ogled; ogling** : stare at lustily —**ogle** *n* —**ogler** \-(ə)lər\ *n*

ogre \'ōgər\ *n* **1** : monster **2** : dreaded person —**ogress** \'ōg(ə)rəs\ *n*

oh \'(')ō\ *interj* **1**—used to express an emotion **2**—used in direct address

ohm \'ōm\ *n* : unit of electrical resistance —**ohm·ic** \'ō-mik\ *adj* —**ohm-me·ter** \'ō(m)₁mētər\ *n*

oil \'ȯil\ *n* **1** : greasy liquid substance **2** : petroleum ~ *vb* : treat, furnish, or lubricate with oil —**oil·er** *n* —**oil·i-ness** \'ȯilēnəs\ *n* —**oily** \'ȯilē\ *adj*

oil·cloth *n* : cloth treated with oil or paint and used for coverings

oil·skin *n* : oiled waterproof cloth

oink \'ȯiŋk\ *n* : natural noise of a hog —**oink** *vb*

oint·ment \'ȯintmənt\ *n* : oily medicinal preparation

OK *or* **okay** \ō'kā\ *adv or adj* : all right ~ *vb* **OK'd** *or* **okayed; OK'·ing** *or* **okay·ing** : approve ~ *n* : approval

okra \'ōkrə, *South also* -krē\ *n* : leafy vegetable with edible green pods

old \'ōld\ *adj* **1** : of long standing **2** : of a specified age **3** : relating to a past era **4** : having existed a long time —**old·ish** \'ōldish\ *adj*

old·en \'ōldən\ *adj* : of or relating to a bygone era

old-fash·ioned \'ōld(')fashənd\ *adj* **1** : out-of-date **2** : conservative

old maid *n* : spinster

old-tim·er \ōl(d)'tīmər\ *n* **1** : veteran **2** : one who is old

ole·an·der \'ōlē₁andər\ *n* : poisonous evergreen shrub

oleo·mar·ga·rine \₁ōlēō'märj(ə)rən, -'märjə₁rēn\ *n* : margarine

ol·fac·to·ry \äl'fakt(ə)rē, ōl-\ *adj* : relating to the sense of smell

oli·gar·chy \'älə₁gärkē, 'ōlə-\ *n, pl -chies* **1** : government by a few people **2** : those holding power in an oligarchy —**oli·garch** \-₁gärk\ *n* —**oli·gar·chic** \₁älə'gärkik, ₁ōlə-\ *or* **oli·gar·chi·cal** \-kikəl\ *adj*

ol·ive \'äliv, -əv\ *n* **1** : evergreen tree bearing small edible fruit *or* the fruit **2** : dull yellow to yellowish green color

om·buds·man \'äm₁budzmən, äm'budz-\ *n, pl -men* \-mən\ : complaint investigator

om·elet, om·elette \'äm(ə)lət\ *n* : beaten eggs lightly fried and folded

omen \'ōmən\ *n* : sign or warning for the future

om·i·nous \'ämənəs\ *adj* : threatening —**om·i·nous·ly** *adv* —**om·i·nous·ness** *n*

omit \ō'mit\ *vb* **-tt-** **1** : leave out **2** : fail to perform —**omis·sion** \-'mishən\ *n*

om·nip·o·tent \äm'nipətənt\ *adj* : al-mighty —**om·nip·o·tence** \-əns\ *n* —**om·nip·o·tent·ly** *adv*

om·ni·pres·ent \₁ämni'prez³nt\ *adj* : ever-present —**om·ni·pres·ence** \-³ns\ *n*

om·ni·scient \äm'nishənt\ *adj* : all-knowing —**om·ni·science** \-əns\ *n* —**om·ni·scient·ly** *adv*

om·niv·o·rous \äm'niv(ə)rəs\ *adj* **1** : eating both meat and vegetables **2** : avid —**om·niv·o·rous·ly** *adv* —**om·niv·o·rous·ness** *n*

on \'ȯn, (')än\ *prep* **1** : in or to a position over and in contact with **2** : at or to **3** : about **4** : from **5** : with regard to **6** : in a state or process **7** : during the time of ~ \'ȯn, 'än\ *adv* **1** : in or into contact with **2** : forward **3** : into operation

once \'wəns\ *adv* **1** : one time only **2** : at any one time **3** : formerly ~ *n* : one time ~ *conj* : as soon as —**at once 1** : simultaneously **2** : immediately **3** : both

once-over *n* : swift examination

on·com·ing *adj* : approaching

one \'wən\ *adj* **1** : being a single thing **2** : being one in particular **3** : united ~ *pron* **1** : a single member **2** : a person in general ~ *n* **1** : 1st in a series **2** : single person or thing —**one·ness** *n*

oner·ous \'änərəs, 'ōnə-\ *adj* : oppressive

one·self \(₁)wən'self\ *pron* : one's own self—usu. used reflexively or for emphasis

one-sid·ed \-'sīdəd\ *adj* **1** : unequal **2** : partial

one·time *adj* : former

one-way *adj* : made for or use in only one direction

on·go·ing *adj* : continuing

on·ion \'ənyən\ *n* : plant grown for its pungent edible bulb

on·ly \'ōnlē\ *adj* : alone in its class ~ *adv* **1** : nothing more than **2** : without respect to anyone or anything else ~ *conj* : but

on·set *n* : start

on·shore *adj* **1** : moving toward shore **2** : lying on or near the shore —**on·shore** *adv*

on·slaught \'än₁slȯt, 'ȯn-\ *n* : attack

on·to \₁ȯntə, ₁än-; 'ȯntü, 'än-\ *prep* : to a position or point on

onus \'ōnəs\ *n* : burden (as of obligation or blame)

on·ward \'ȯnwərd, 'än-\ *adv or adj* : forward

on·yx \'äniks\ *n* : quartz used as a gem

¹ooze \ˈüz\ *n* : soft mud —**ooz·y** \ˈüzē\ *adj*

²ooze *vb* **oozed; ooz·ing** : flow or leak out slowly

opac·i·ty \ō'pasətē\ *n* : quality or state of being opaque or an opaque spot

opal \ˈōpəl\ *n* : gem with delicate colors

opaque \ō'pāk\ *adj* **1** : impervious to light **2** : not easily understood **3** : dull-witted —**opaque·ly** *adv* —**opaque·ness** *n*

open \ˈōpən\ *adj* **1** : not shut or shut up **2** : not secret or hidden **3** : frank or generous **4** : extended **5** : free from controls **6** : not decided ~ *vb* **1** : make or become open **2** : make or become functional **3** : start ~ *n* : outdoors —**open·er** \ˈōp(ə)nər\ —**open·ly** *adv* —**open·ness** *n*

open-hand·ed \-'handəd\ *adj* : generous

open·ing \ˈōp(ə)niŋ\ *n* **1** : act or instance of causing to be open **2** : something that is open **3** : opportunity

opera \ˈäp(ə)rə\ *n* : drama set to music —**op·er·at·ic** \ˌäpə'ratik\ *adj*

op·er·a·ble \ˈäp(ə)rabəl\ *adj* **1** : usable or in working condition **2** : suitable for surgical treatment

op·er·ate \ˈäpə,rāt\ *vb* **-at·ed; -at·ing** **1** : perform work **2** : perform an operation **3** : manage —**op·er·a·tor** \-ˌrātər\ *n*

op·er·a·tion \ˌäpə'rāshən\ *n* **1** : act or process of operating **2** : surgical work on a living body **3** : military action or mission —**op·er·a·tion·al** \-sh(ə)nəl\ *adj*

op·er·a·tive \ˈäp(ə)rətiv, ˈäpə,rāt-\ *adj* : working or having an effect

op·er·et·ta \ˌäpə'retə\ *n* : light opera

oph·thal·mol·o·gy \ˌäf,thal'mäləjē, ˌäp-\ *n* : branch of medicine dealing with the eye —**oph·thal·mol·o·gist** \-jəst\ *n*

opi·ate \ˈōpēət, -pē,āt\ *n* : preparation or derivative of opium

opin·ion \ə'pinyən\ *n* **1** : belief **2** : judgment **3** : formal statement by an expert

opin·ion·at·ed \-yə,nātəd\ *adj* : stubborn in one's opinions

opi·um \ˈōpēəm\ *n* : addictive narcotic drug that is the dried juice of a poppy

opos·sum \ə'päsəm\ *n* : common tree-dwelling mammal

op·po·nent \ə'pōnənt\ *n* : one that opposes

op·por·tune \ˌäpər't(y)ün\ *adj* **1** : suitable **2** : occurring at a suitable time —**op·por·tune·ly** *adv*

op·por·tun·ism \-'t(y)ü,nizəm\ *n* : a taking advantage of opportunities —**op·por·tun·ist** \-nəst\ *n* —**op·por·tu·nis·tic** \-t(y)ü'nistik\ *adj*

op·por·tu·ni·ty \-'t(y)ünətē\ *n, pl* **-ties** : favorable time

op·pose \ə'pōz\ *vb* **-posed; -pos·ing** **1** : place opposite or against something **2** : resist —**op·po·si·tion** \ˌäpə'zishən\ *n*

op·po·site \ˈäpəzət\ *n* : one that is opposed ~ *adj* **1** : set facing something that is at the other side or end **2** : opposed or contrary ~ *adv* : on opposite sides ~ *prep* : across from —**op·po·site·ly** *adv* —**op·po·site·ness** *n*

op·press \ə'pres\ *vb* **1** : persecute **2** : weigh down —**op·pres·sion** \-'preshən\ *n* —**op·pres·sive** \-'presiv\ *adj* —**op·pres·sive·ly** *adv* —**op·pres·sor** \-'presər\ *n*

op·pro·bri·ous \ə'prōbrēəs\ *adj* : expressing or deserving opprobrium —**op·pro·bri·ous·ly** *adv*

op·pro·bri·um \-brēəm\ *n* **1** : something that brings disgrace **2** : infamy

opt \ˈäpt\ *vb* : choose

op·tic \ˈäptik\ *adj* : relating to vision or the eye

op·ti·cal \ˈäptikəl\ *adj* : relating to optics, vision, or the eye

op·ti·cian \äp'tishən\ *n* : maker of or dealer in eyeglasses

op·tics \ˈäptiks\ *n pl* : science of light and vision

op·ti·mal \ˈäptəməl\ *adj* : most favorable —**op·ti·mal·ly** *adv*

op·ti·mism \ˈäptə,mizəm\ *n* : tendency to hope for the best —**op·ti·mist** \-məst\ *n* —**op·ti·mis·tic** \ˌäptə'mistik\ *adj* —**op·ti·mis·ti·cal·ly** \-tik(ə)lē\ *adv*

op·ti·mum \ˈäptəməm\ *n, pl* **-ma** \-mə\ : amount or degree of something most favorable to an end

op·tion \ˈäpshən\ *n* **1** : ability to choose **2** : right to buy or sell a stock **3** : alternative —**op·tion·al** \-sh(ə)nəl\ *adj*

op·tom·e·try \äp'tämətrē\ *n* : profession of examining the eyes —**op·tom·e·trist** \-trəst\ *n*

op·u·lent \ˈäpyələnt\ *adj* : lavish —**op·u·lence** \-ləns\ *n*

opus \ˈōpəs\ *n, pl* **opera** \ˈōpərə, ˈäpə-\ : work esp. of music

or \ər,(ˌ)ȯr\ *conj*—used to indicate an alternative

-or \ər\ *n suffix* : one that performs an action

or·a·cle \'ȯrəkəl\ *n* **1** : one held to give divinely inspired answers or revelations **2** : wise person or an utterance of such a person —**orac·u·lar** \ȯ'rakyələr\ *adj*

oral \'ȯrəl, 'ȯr-\ *adj* **1** : spoken **2** : relating to the mouth —**oral·ly** *adv*

or·ange \'ȯrinj\ *n* **1** : reddish yellow citrus fruit **2** : color between red and yellow —**or·ange·ade** \ȯrinj'ād\ *n*

orang·utan, orang·ou·tan \ə'raŋə,taŋ, -,taŋ\ *n* : reddish brown ape

ora·tion \ə'rāshən\ *n* : elaborate formal speech

or·a·tor \'ȯrətər\ *n* : one who delivers an oration

or·a·to·rio \ȯrə'tōrē,ō\ *n, pl* **-ri·os** : major choral work

or·a·to·ry \'ȯrə,tōrē\ *n* : art of public speaking —**or·a·tor·i·cal** \ȯrə'tȯr·ikəl\ *adj*

orb \'ȯrb\ *n* **1** : sphere **2** : celestial body —**or·bic·u·lar** \ȯr'bikyələr\ *adj*

or·bit \'ȯrbət\ *n* : path made by one body revolving around another ~ *vb* : revolve around —**or·bit·al** \-ᵊl\ *adj* —**or·bit·er** *n*

or·chard \'ȯrchərd\ *n* : place where fruit or nut trees are grown —**or·chard·ist** \-əst\ *n*

or·ches·tra \'ȯrkəstrə\ *n* **1** : group of musicians **2** : front seats of a theater's main floor —**or·ches·tral** \ȯr'kestrəl\ *adj*

or·ches·trate \'ȯrkə,strāt\ *vb* **-trat·ed; -trat·ing** : compose or arrange for an orchestra —**or·ches·tra·tion** \ȯrkə'strāshən\ *n*

or·chid \'ȯrkəd\ *n* : plant with showy 3-petal flowers or its flower

or·dain \ȯr'dān\ *vb* **1** : admit to the clergy **2** : decree

or·deal \ȯr'dē(ə)l, 'ȯr,dē(ə)l\ *n* : severely trying experience

or·der \'ȯrdər\ *n* **1** : rank, class, or special group **2** : arrangement **3** : rule of law **4** : authoritative regulation or instruction **5** : working condition **6** : special request for a purchase or what is purchased ~ *vb* **1** : arrange **2** : give an order to **3** : place an order for

or·der·ly \-lē\ *adj* **1** : being in order or tidy **2** : well behaved ~ *n, pl* **-lies 1** : officer's attendant **2** : hospital attendant —**or·der·li·ness** *n*

or·di·nal \'ȯrdᵊnəl, -ᵊnᵊl\ *n* : number indicating order in a series

or·di·nance \-nəns, -ᵊnəns\ *n* : municipal law

or·di·nary \'ȯrdᵊn,erē\ *adj* : of common occurrence, quality, or ability —**or·di·nar·i·ly** \ȯrdᵊn'erəlē\ *adv*

or·di·na·tion \ȯrdᵊn'āshən\ *n* : act of ordaining

ord·nance \'ȯrdnəns\ *n* : military supplies

ore \'ȯr\ *n* : mineral containing a valuable constituent

or·gan \'ȯrgən\ *n* **1** : air-powered or electronic keyboard instrument **2** : animal or plant structure with special function **3** : periodical

or·gan·ic \ȯr'ganik\ *adj* **1** : relating to a bodily organ **2** : relating to living things **3** : relating to or containing carbon or its compounds —**or·gan·i·cal·ly** \-ik(ə)lē\ *adv*

or·gan·ism \'ȯrgə,nizəm\ *n* : living person, animal, or plant

or·gan·ist \'ȯrgənəst\ *n* : organ player

or·ga·nize \'ȯrgə,nīz\ *vb* **-nized; -niz·ing** : form parts into a functioning whole —**or·ga·ni·za·tion** \ȯrg(ə)nə'zāshən\ *n* —**or·ga·niz·er** *n*

or·gasm \'ȯr,gazəm\ *n* : climax of sexual excitement

or·gy \'ȯrjē\ *n, pl* **-gies** : unrestrained indulgence

ori·ent \'ȯrē,ent\ *vb* **1** : set in a definite position **2** : acquaint with a situation —**ori·en·ta·tion** \ȯrēən'tāshən\ *n*

ori·en·tal \ȯrē'entᵊl\ *adj* : Eastern —**Oriental** *n*

or·i·fice \'ȯrəfəs\ *n* : opening

or·i·gin \'ȯrəjən\ *n* **1** : ancestry **2** : rise, beginning, or derivation from a source —**orig·i·nate** \ə'rijə,nāt\ *vb* —**orig·i·na·tor** \-ər\ *n*

orig·i·nal \ə'rij(ə)nəl\ *n* : something from which a copy is made ~ *adj* **1** : first **2** : not copied from something else **3** : inventive —**orig·i·nal·i·ty** \-'nal-\ *n* —**orig·i·nal·ly** *adv*

ori·ole \'ȯrē,ōl\ *n* : American songbird

or·na·ment \'ȯrnəmənt\ *n* : something that adorns ~ *vb* : provide with ornament —**or·na·men·tal** \ȯrnə'mentᵊl\ *adj* —**or·na·men·ta·tion** \-mən'tāshən\ *n*

or·nate \ȯr'nāt\ *adj* : elaborately decorated —**or·nate·ly** *adv* —**or·nate·ness** *n*

or·nery \'ȯrn(ə)rē, 'än-\ *adj* : irritable

or·ni·thol·o·gy \ȯrnə'thäləjē\ *n, pl* **-gies** : study of birds —**or·ni·tho·log·i·cal** \-thə'läjikəl\ *adj* —**or·ni·thol·o·gist** \-'thäləjəst\ *n*

or·phan \'ȯrfən\ *n* : child whose parents are dead —**orphan** *vb* —**or·phan·age** \-(ə)nij\ *n* or·tho·don·tics \ˌȯrthəˈdäntiks\ n : dentistry dealing with straightening teeth —or·tho·don·tist \-ˈdäntəst\ n

or·tho·dox \ˈȯrthəˌdäks\ adj 1 : conforming to established doctrine 2 cap : of or relating to a Christian church originating in the Eastern Roman Empire —or·tho·doxy \-ˌdäksē\ n

or·thog·ra·phy \ȯrˈthägrəfē\ n : spelling —or·tho·graph·ic \ˌȯrthəˈgrafik\ adj

or·tho·pe·dics \ˌȯrthəˈpēdiks\ n sing or pl : correction or prevention of skeletal deformities —or·tho·pe·dic \-ik\ adj —or·tho·pe·dist \-ˈpēdəst\ n

-o·ry \ōrē, ȯrē, (ə)rē\ adj suffix 1 : of, relating to, or characterized by 2 : serving for, producing, or maintaining

os·cil·late \ˈäsəˌlāt\ vb -lat·ed; -lat·ing : swing back and forth —os·cil·la·tion \ˌäsəˈlāshən\ n

os·mo·sis \äzˈmōsəs, äs-\ n : diffusion esp. of water through a membrane —os·mot·ic \-ˈmätik\ adj

os·prey \ˈäsprē, -ˌprā\ n, pl -preys : large hawk

os·ten·si·ble \äˈstensəbəl\ adj : seeming —os·ten·si·bly \-blē\ adv

os·ten·ta·tion \ˌästənˈtāshən\ n : pretentious display —os·ten·ta·tious \-shəs\ adj —os·ten·ta·tious·ly adv

os·te·op·a·thy \ˌästēˈäpəthē\ n : system of healing that emphasizes manipulation (as of joints) —os·te·o·path \ˈästēəˌpath\ n —os·teo·path·ic \ˌästēəˈpathik\ adj

os·tra·cize \ˈästrəˌsīz\ vb -cize; -ciz·ing : exclude by common consent —os·tra·cism \-ˌsizəm\ n

os·trich \ˈästrich, ˈȯs-\ n : very large flightless bird

oth·er \ˈəthər\ adj 1 : being the one left 2 : alternate 3 : additional ~ pron 1 : remaining one 2 : different one

oth·er·wise \ˈəthərˌwīz\ adv 1 : in a different way 2 : in different circumstances 3 : in other respects —otherwise adj

ot·ter \ˈätər\ n : mammal with webbed feet

ot·to·man \ˈätəmən\ n : upholstered footstool

ought \ˈȯt\ verbal auxiliary —used to express obligation, advisability, or expectation

ounce \ˈaůns\ n 1 : unit of weight equal to about 28.3 grams 2 : unit of capacity equal to about 29.6 milliliters

our \ȧr, (ˈ)aů(ə)r\ adj : of or relating to us

ours \ˈaů(ə)rz, ärz\ pron : one belonging to us

our·selves \ȧrˈselvz, aů(ə)r-\ pron : we, us—used reflexively or for emphasis

-ous \əs\ adj suffix : having or having the qualities of

oust \ˈaůst\ vb : expel or eject

oust·er \ˈaůstər\ n : expulsion

out \ˈaůt\ adv 1 : away from the inside or center 2 : beyond control 3 : to extinction, exhaustion, or completion 4 : in or into the open ~ vb : become known ~ adj 1 : situated outside 2 : absent ~ prep 1 : out through 2 : outward on or along —out·bound adj —out·build·ing n

out·board \ˈaůtˌbōrd\ adv : outside a boat or ship —outboard adj

out·break \ˈaůtˌbrāk\ n : sudden occurrence

out·burst \ˈaůtˌbərst\ n : violent expression of feeling

out·cast \-ˌkast\ n : person cast out by society

out·come \-ˌkəm\ n : result

out·crop \-ˌkräp\ n : part of a rock stratum that appears above the ground —outcrop vb

out·cry \-ˌkrī\ n : loud cry

out·dat·ed \aůtˈdātəd\ adj : out-of-date

out·dis·tance vb : go far ahead of

out·do \aůtˈdü\ vb -did \-ˈdid\; -done \-ˈdən\; -do·ing \-ˈdüiŋ\; -does \-ˈdəz\ : do better than

out·doors \aůtˈdōrz\ adv : in or into the open air ~ n : open air —out·door adj

out·er \ˈaůtər\ adj : external 2 : farther out —out·er·most adj

out·field \ˈaůtˌfēld\ n : baseball field beyond the infield —out·field·er \-ˌfēldзr\ n

out·fit \ˈaůtˌfit\ n 1 : equipment for a special purpose 2 : group ~ vb -tt- : equip —out·fit·ter n

out·go \ˈaůtˌgō\ n, pl outgoes : expenditure

out·go·ing \ˈaůtˌgōiŋ\ adj 1 : retiring from a position 2 : friendly

out·grow \aůtˈgrō\ vb -grew \-ˈgrü\; -grown \-ˈgrōn\; -grow·ing 1 : grow faster than 2 : grow too large for

out·growth \ˈaůtˌgrōth\ n 1 : product of growing out 2 : consequence

out·ing \ˈaůtiŋ\ n : excursion

out·land·ish \aůtˈlandish\ adj : very strange —out·land·ish·ly adv

out·last vb : last longer than

out·law \ˈaůtˌlȯ\ n : lawless person ~ vb : make illegal —out·law·ry \-ˌlȯ)rē\ n

out·lay \'autˌlā\ *n* : expenditure

out·let \'autˌlet, -lət\ *n* **1** : exit **2** : means of release **3** : market for goods **4** : electrical device that gives access to wiring

out·line \'autˌlīn\ *n* **1** : line marking the outer limits **2** : summary ~ *vb* **1** : draw the outline of **2** : indicate the chief parts of

out·live \aut'liv\ *vb* : live longer than

out·look \'autˌluk\ *n* **1** : viewpoint **2** : prospect for the future

out·ly·ing \'autˌlīiŋ\ *adj* : far from a central point

out·mod·ed \aut'mōdəd\ *adj* : out-of-date

out·num·ber \-'nəmbər\ *vb* : exceed in number

out of *prep* **1** : out from within **2** : beyond the limits of **3** : among **4**—used to indicate absence or loss **5** : because of **6** : from or with

out-of-date *adj* : no longer in fashion or in use

out·pa·tient *n* : person treated at a hospital who does not stay

out·post *n* : remote military post

out·put *n* : amount produced ~ *vb* **-put·ted** *or* **-put; -put·ting** : produce

out·rage \'autˌrāj\ *n* **1** : violent or shameful act **2** : injury or insult ~ *vb* **-raged; -rag·ing 1** : subject to violent injury **2** : make very angry —**out·ra·geous** \aut'rājəs\ *adj* —**out·ra·geous·ly** *adv*

out·right *adv* **1** : completely **2** : instantly ~ *adj* **1** : complete **2** : given without reservation

out·set *n* : beginning

out·side \aut'sīd, 'aut-\ *n* **1** : place beyond a boundary **2** : exterior **3** : utmost limit ~ *adj* **1** : outer **2** : coming from without **3** : remote ~ *adv* : on or to the outside ~ *prep* **1** : on or to the outside of **2** : beyond the limits of

outside of *prep* **1** : outside **2** : besides

out·sid·er \-'sīdər\ *n* : one who does not belong to a group

out·skirts *n pl* : outlying parts (as of a city)

out·smart \aut-\ *vb* : outwit

out·spo·ken *adj* : direct and open in speech —**out·spo·ken·ness** *n*

out·stand·ing *adj* **1** : unpaid **2** : very good —**out·stand·ing·ly** *adv*

out·strip \aut'strip\ *vb* **1** : go faster than **2** : surpass

¹out·ward \'autwərd\ *adj* **1** : being toward the outside **2** : showing outwardly

²outward, out·wards \-wərdz\ *adv* : toward the outside —**out·ward·ly** *adv*

out·wit \aut'wit\ *vb* : get the better of by superior cleverness

ova *pl of* OVUM

oval \'ōvəl\ *adj* : egg-shaped —**oval** *n*

ova·ry \'ōv(ə)rē\ *n, pl* **-ries 1** : egg-producing organ **2** : seed-producing part of a flower —**ovar·i·an** \ō'varēən, -'ver-\ *adj*

ova·tion \ō'vāshən\ *n* : enthusiastic applause

ov·en \'əvən\ *n* : chamber (as in a stove) for baking

over \'ōvər\ *adv* **1** : across **2** : upside down **3** : in excess or addition **4** : above **5** : at an end **6** : again ~ *prep* **1** : above in position or authority **2** : more than **3** : along, through, or across **4** : because of ~ *adj* **1** : upper **2** : remaining **3** : ended

over- *prefix* **1** : so as to exceed or surpass **2** : excessive or excessively

overabundance	overconfidence
overabundant	overconfident
overacceptance	overconscien-
overachiever	tious
overactive	overconsume
overaggressive	overconsumption
overambitious	overcontrol
overamplify	overcook
overanalyze	overcorrect
overanxiety	overcritical
overanxious	overcrowd
overapologetic	overdecorate
overarousal	overdepend
overarouse	overdependent
overassertive	overdevelop
overbake	overdose
overbid	overdramatic
overbill	overdramatize
overbold	overdress
overborrow	overdrink
overbright	overdue
overbroad	overeager
overbuild	overeat
overburden	overeducate
overbusy	overelaborate
overbuy	overemotional
overcapacity	overemphasis
overcapitalize	overemphasize
overcareful	overenergetic
overcautious	overenthusiastic
overcharge	overestimate
overcivilized	overexaggerate
overclean	overexaggeration
overcommit	overexcite
overcompensate	overexcitement
overcomplicate	overexercise
overconcern	overexert

overexertion
overexhaust
overexpand
overexpansion
overexplain
overexploit
overexpose
overextend
overextension
overexuberant
overfamiliar
overfatigue
overfeed
overfertilize
overfill
overfond
overgenerous
overglamorize
overgraze
overharvest
overhasty
overheat
overidealize
overimaginative
overimbibe
overimpressed
overindebted
overindulge
overindulgence
overindulgent
overinflate
overinfluence
overinsistent
overintense
overintensity
overinvest
overinvolve
overladen
overlarge
overlend
overliberal
overload
overlong
overloud
overmedicate
overmodest
overmuch
overobvious
overoptimistic
overorganize
overpack
overparticular
overpatriotic
overpay
overpayment
overpermissive
overplay

overpopulated
overpossessive
overpraise
overprescribe
overpressure
overprice
overprivileged
overproduce
overproduction
overpromise
overprotect
overprotective
overpublicize
overqualified
overrate
overreact
overreaction
overrefine
overregulate
overregulation
overreliance
overrepresent
overrespond
overripe
oversaturate
oversell
oversensitive
overserious
oversexed
oversimple
oversimplify
oversolicitous
overspecialize
overspend
overstaff
overstimulate
overstock
overstrain
overstress
overstrict
oversubtle
oversupply
oversuspicious
oversweeten
overtax
overtighten
overtip
overtired
overtrain
overtreat
overuse
overutilize
overvalue
overweight
overwork
overzealous

over·all \ˌōvər'ȯl\ adj : including everything

over·alls \'ōvər͵ȯlz\ n pl : work garment

over·awe vb : restrain by awe

over·bear·ing \-¹ba(ə)riŋ\ adj : arrogant

over·blown \-¹blōn\ adj : pretentious

over·board adv : over the side into the water

over·cast adj : clouded over ~ n : cloud covering

over·coat n : outer coat

over·come vb **-came** \-¹kām\; **-come; -com·ing** 1 : defeat 2 : make helpless or exhausted

over·do vb **-did; -done; -do·ing; -does** : do too much

over·draft n : overdrawn sum

over·draw vb **-drew; -drawn; -draw·ing** : write checks for more than one's bank balance

over·flow \ˌōvər'flō\ vb 1 : flood 2 : flow over —**over·flow** \'ōvər͵flō\ n

over·grow vb **-grew; -grown; -grow·ing** : grow over

over·hand adj : made with the hand brought down from above —**over·hand** adv

over·hang vb **-hung; -hang·ing** : jut out over ~ n : something that overhangs

over·haul vb 1 : repair 2 : overtake

over·head \ˌōvər'hed\ adv : aloft ~ \'ōvər͵-\ adj : situated above ~ \'ōvər͵-\ n : general business expenses

over·hear vb **-heard; -hear·ing** : hear without the speaker's knowledge

over·joy vb : fill with joy

over·land \-͵land, -lənd\ adv or adj : by, on, or across land

over·lap vb : lap over

over·lay \ˌōvər'lā\ vb **-laid; -lay·ing** : lay over or across —**over·lay** \'ōvər͵lā\ n

over·look \ˌōvər'lůk\ vb 1 : look down on 2 : fail to see 3 : ignore 4 : pardon 5 : supervise ~ \'ōvər͵-\ n : observation point

over·ly \'ōvərlē\ adv : excessively

over·night adv : through the night —**overnight** adj

over·pass n : bridge over a road

over·pow·er vb 1 : conquer 2 : overwhelm

over·reach \ˌōvər(r)'rēch\ vb : try or seek too much

over·ride vb **-rode; -rid·den; -rid·ing** : neutralize action of

over·rule vb : rule against or set aside

over·run vb **-ran; -run·ning** 1 : swarm or

¹**over·age** \ˌōvər'āj\ adj : too old

²**over·age** \'ōv(ə)rij\ n : surplus

flow over 2 : go beyond ~ *n* : an exceeding of estimated costs

over-seas *adv or adj* : beyond or across the sea

over-see \ˌōvər'sē\ *vb* -saw; -seen; -see-ing : supervise —**over-seer** \'ōvərˌsiər\ *n*

over-shad-ow *vb* : exceed in importance

over-shoe *n* : protective outer shoe

over-shoot *vb* -shot; -shoot-ing : shoot or pass beyond

over-sight *n* : inadvertent omission or error

over-sleep *vb* -slept; -sleep-ing : sleep longer than intended

over-spread *vb* -spread; -spread-ing : spread over or above

over-state *vb* : exaggerate —**over-state-ment** *n*

over-stay *vb* : stay too long

over-step *vb* : exceed

overt \ō'vərt, 'ōˌvərt\ *adj* : not secret

over-take *vb* -took; -tak-en; -tak-ing : catch up with

over-throw \ˌōvər'thrō\ *vb* -threw; -thrown; -throw-ing 1 : upset 2 : bring to defeat —**over-throw** \'ōvərˌ-\ *n*

over-time *n* : extra working time —**overtime** *adv*

over-tone *n* 1 : higher tone in a complex musical tone 2 : suggestion

over-ture \'ōvərˌchùr, -chər\ *n* 1 : opening offer 2 : musical introduction

over-turn *vb* 1 : turn over 2 : overthrow

over-view *n* : brief survey

over-ween-ing \ˌōvər'wēniŋ\ *adj* 1 : arrogant 2 : excessive

over-whelm \ˌōvər'hwelm\ *vb* : overcome completely —**over-whelm-ing-ly** \-'hwelmiŋlē\ *adv*

over-wrought \ˌōvər(r)'ròt\ *adj* : extremely excited

ovoid \'ōˌvòid\, **ovoi-dal** \ō'vòidᵊl\ *adj* : egg-shaped

ovu-late \'ävyəˌlāt, 'ōv-\ *vb* -lat-ed; -lat-ing : produce eggs —**ovu-la-tion** \ˌävyə'lāshən, ˌōv-\ *n*

ovum \'ōvəm\ *n, pl* **ova** \-və\ : female germ cell

owe \'ō\ *vb* **owed; ow-ing 1** : have an obligation to pay **2** : be indebted to or for

owing to *prep* : because of

owl \'aùl\ *n* : nocturnal bird of prey —**owl-ish** *adj* —**owl-ish-ly** *adv*

own \'ōn\ *adj* : belonging to oneself ~ *vb* **1** : have as property **2** : acknowledge — *pron* : one or ones belonging to oneself —**own-er** *n* —**own-er-ship** *n*

ox \'äks\ *n, pl* **ox-en** \'äksən\ : bovine mammal and esp. a castrated bull

ox-ide \'äkˌsīd\ *n* : compound of oxygen

ox-i-dize \'äksəˌdīz\ *vb* -dized; -diz-ing : combine with oxygen —**ox-i-da-tion** \ˌäksə'dāshən\ *n* —**ox-i-diz-able** \ˌäksə'dīzəbəl\ *adj* —**ox-i-diz-er** *n*

ox-y-gen \'äksijən\ *n* : gaseous chemical element —**ox-y-gen-ic** \ˌäksi'jenik\ *adj*

oys-ter \'óistər\ *n* : bivalve mollusk —**oys-ter-ing** \'óist(ə)riŋ\ *n* —**oys-ter-man** \-mən\ *n*

ozone \'ōˌzōn\ *n* : faintly blue form of oxygen

P

p \'pē\ *n, pl* **p's** *or* **ps** \'pēz\ : 16th letter of the alphabet

pace \'pās\ *n* **1** : walking step **2** : rate of progress ~ *vb* **paced; pac-ing 1** : go at a pace **2** : cover with slow steps **3** : set the pace of

pace-mak-er *n* : electrical device to regulate heartbeat

pachy-derm \'pakiˌdərm\ *n* : elephant

pa-cif-ic \pə'sifik\ *adj* : calm or peaceful

pac-i-fism \'pasəˌfizəm\ *n* : opposition to war or violence —**pac-i-fist** \-fəst\ *n or adj* —**pac-i-fis-tic** \ˌpasə'fistik\ *adj*

pac-i-fy \'pasəˌfī\ *vb* -fied; -fy-ing : make calm —**pac-i-fi-ca-tion** \ˌpasəfə'kāshən\ *n* —**pac-i-fi-er** \'pasəˌfī(ə)r\ *n*

pack \'pak\ *n* **1** : compact bundle **2** : group of animals ~ *vb* **1** : put into a container **2** : fill tightly or completely **3** : send without ceremony —**pack-er** *n*

pack-age \'pakij\ *n* : items bundled together ~ *vb* -aged; -ag-ing : enclose in a package

pack-et \'pakət\ *n* : small package

pact \'pakt\ *n* : agreement

pad \'pad\ *n* **1** : cushioning part or thing **2** : floating leaf of a water plant **3** : tablet of paper ~ *vb* -dd- **1** : furnish with a pad **2** : expand with needless matter —**pad-ding** *n*

pad·dle \'pad³l\ *n* : implement with a flat blade ~ *vb* **-dled; -dling** : move, beat, or stir with a paddle

pad·dock \'padək\ *n* : enclosed area for racehorses

pad·dy \'padē\ *n, pl* **-dies** : wet land where rice is grown

pad·lock *n* : lock with a U-shaped catch **—padlock** *vb*

pa·dre \'pädrā\ *n* : priest

pae·an \'pēən\ *n* : song of praise

pa·gan \'pāgən\ *n or adj* :. heathen **—pa·gan·ism** \-,izəm\ *n*

¹page \'pāj\ *n* : messenger ~ *vb* **paged; pag·ing** : summon by repeated calls

²page *n* : single leaf (as of a book) or one side of the leaf

pag·eant \'pajənt\ *n* : elaborate spectacle or procession **—pag·eant·ry** \-əntrē\ *n*

pa·go·da \pə'gōdə\ *n* : tower with roofs curving upward

paid *past of* PAY

pail \'pāl\ *n* : cylindrical container with a handle **—pail·ful** \-,fûl\ *n*

pain \'pān\ *n* **1** : punishment or penalty **2** : suffering of body or mind **3** *pl* : great care ~ *vb* : cause or experience pain **—pain·ful** \-fəl\ *adj* **—pain·ful·ly** *adv* **—pain·kill·er** *n* **—pain·kill·ing** *adj* **—pain·less** *adj* **—pain·less·ly** *adv*

pains·tak·ing \'pān,stākiŋ\ *adj* : taking pains **—painstaking** *n* **—pains·tak·ing·ly** *adv*

paint \'pānt\ *vb* **1** : apply color or paint to **2** : portray esp. in color ~ *n* : mixture of pigment and liquid **—paint·brush** *n* **—paint·er** *n* **—paint·ing** *n*

pair \'paər\ *n* : a set of two ~ *vb* : put or go together as a pair

pa·ja·mas \pə'jäməz, -'jam-\ *n pl* : loose suit for sleeping

pal \'pal\ *n* : close friend

pal·ace \'paləs\ *n* **1** : residence of a sovereign **2** : mansion **—pa·la·tial** \pə'lāshəl\ *adj*

pal·a·din \'palədən\ *n* : knight

pal·at·able \'palətəbəl\ *adj* : agreeable to the taste

pal·ate \'palət\ *n* **1** : roof of the mouth **2** : taste **—pal·a·tal** \-ət³l\ *adj*

pa·la·ver \pə'lavər, -'läv-\ *n* : talk **—palaver** *vb*

¹pale \'pāl\ *adj* **pal·er; pal·est** : lacking in color or brightness **2** : light in color or shade ~ *vb* **paled; pal·ing** : make or become pale **—pale·ness** *n*

²pale *n* **1** : fence stake **2** : enclosed place

pal·ette \'palət\ *n* : board on which paints are laid and mixed

pal·frey \'pólfrē\ *n, pl* **-freys** : saddle horse

pal·i·sade \,palə'sād\ *n* **1** : high fence **2** : line of cliffs

¹pall \'pól\ *n* : cloth draped over a coffin

²pall *vb* : lose in interest or attraction

pall·bear·er *n* : one who attends the coffin at a funeral

¹pal·let \'palət\ *n* : makeshift bed

²pallet *n* : portable storage platform

pal·li·ate \'palē,āt\ *vb* **-at·ed; -at·ing 1** : ease without curing **2** : cover or conceal by excusing **—pal·li·a·tion** \,palē'āshən\ *n* **—pal·li·a·tive** \'palē,ātiv\ *adj or n*

pal·lid \'paləd\ *adj* : pale

pal·lor \'palər\ *n* : paleness

¹palm \'päm, 'pälm\ *n* **1** : tall tropical tree crowned with large leaves **2** : symbol of victory

²palm *n* : underside of the hand ~ *vb* **1** : conceal in the hand **2** : impose by fraud

palm·ist·ry \'päməstrē, 'pälmə-\ *n* : reading a person's character or future in his palms **—palm·ist** \'päməst, 'pälməst\ *n*

palmy \'pämē, 'pälmē\ *adj* **palm·i·er; -est** : flourishing

pal·o·mi·no \,palə'mēnō\ *n, pl* **-nos** : light-colored horse

pal·pa·ble \'palpəbəl\ *adj* **1** : capable of being touched **2** : obvious **—pal·pa·bly** \-blē\ *adv*

pal·pi·tate \'palpə,tāt\ *vb* **-tat·ed; -tat·ing** : pulsate **—pal·pi·ta·tion** \,palpə'tāshən\ *n*

pal·sy \'pólzē\ *n, pl* **-sies 1** : paralysis **2** : condition marked by tremor **—pal·sied** \-zēd\ *adj*

pal·try \'póltrē\ *adj* **-tri·er; -est** : trivial

pam·pa \'pampə\ *n, pl* **-pas** \-pəz, -pəs\ : grassy So. American plain

pam·per \'pampər\ *vb* : spoil or indulge

pam·phlet \'pamflət\ *n* : unbound publication **—pam·phle·teer** \,pamflə'tiər\ *n*

pan \'pan\ *n* : broad, shallow, and open container ~ *vb* **1** : wash gravel in a pan to search for gold **2** : criticize severely

pan·a·cea \,panə'sēə\ *n* : universal remedy

pan·cake *n* : fried flat cake

pan·cre·as \'paŋkrēəs, 'pan-\ *n* : gland that produces insulin **—pan·cre·at·ic** \,paŋkrē'atik, ,pan-\ *adj*

pan·da \'pandə\ *n* : black-and-white bearlike animal

pan·de·mo·ni·um \ˌpandə'mōnēəm\ *n* : wild uproar

pan·der \'pandər\ *n* 1 : pimp 2 : one who caters to others' desires or weaknesses ~ *vb* : act as a pander

pane \'pān\ *n* : sheet of glass

pan·e·gyr·ic \ˌpanə'jirik\ *n* : eulogistic oration —**pan·e·gyr·ist** \-'jirəst\ *n*

pan·el \'pan³l\ *n* 1 : list of persons (as jurors) 2 : discussion group 3 : flat piece of construction material 4 : board with instruments or controls ~ *vb* -**eled** *or* -**elled**; -**el·ing** *or* -**el·ling** : decorate with panels —**pan·el·ing** *n* —**pan·el·ist** \-əst\ *n*

pang \'paŋ\ *n* : sudden sharp pain

pan·han·dle \'pan,hand³l\ *vb* -**dled**; -**dling** : ask for money on the street —**pan·han·dler** \-dlər, -d³lər\ *n*

pan·ic \'panik\ *n* : sudden overpowering fright ~ *vb* -**icked**; -**ick·ing** : affect or be affected with panic —**pan·icky** \-ikē\ *adj*

pan·o·ply \'panəplē\ *n, pl* -**plies** 1 : full suit of armor 2 : impressive array

pan·ora·ma \ˌpanə'ramə, -'rämə\ *n* : view in every direction —**pan·oram·ic** \-'ramik\ *adj*

pan·sy \'panzē\ *n, pl* -**sies** : low-growing garden herb with showy flowers

pant \'pant\ *vb* 1 : breathe with great effort 2 : yearn ~ *n* : panting sound

pan·ta·loons \ˌpant³l'ünz\ *n pl* : pants

pan·ther \'panthər\ *n* : large wild cat

pant·ies \'pantēz\ *n pl* : undergarment with closed crotch and short legs

pan·to·mime \'pantə,mīm\ *n* 1 : play without words 2 : expression by bodily or facial movements ~ *vb* : represent by pantomime

pan·try \'pantrē\ *n, pl* -**tries** : storage room for food and dishes

pants \'pants\ *n pl* 1 : 2-legged outer garment 2 : panties

pap \'pap\ *n* : soft food

pa·pa·cy \'pāpəsē\ *n, pl* -**cies** : office of pope

pa·pal \'pāpəl\ *adj* : relating to the pope

pa·pa·ya \pə'pīə\ *n* : tropical tree with large edible fruit

pa·per \'pāpər\ *n* 1 : pliable substance used to write or print on, to wrap things in, or to cover walls 2 : printed or written document 3 : newspaper —**paper** *adj or vb* —**pa·per·hang·er** *n* —**pa·per·hang·ing** *n* —**pa·per·weight** *n* —**pa·pery** \'pāp(ə)rē\ *adj*

pa·per·board *n* : cardboard

pa·pier-mâ·ché \ˌpāpərmə'shā, ˌpap,yām>-, -ma-\ *n* : molding material of waste paper

pa·poose \pa'püs, pə-\ *n* : young child of American Indian parents

pa·pri·ka \pə'prēkə, pa-\ *n* : mild red spice

pa·py·rus \pə'pīrəs\ *n, pl* -**rus·es** *or* -**ri** \-(,)rē, -,rī\ 1 : tall grasslike plant 2 : paper from papyrus

par \'pär\ *n* 1 : stated value 2 : common level 3 : accepted standard or normal condition —**par** *adj*

par·a·ble \'parəbəl\ *n* : simple story illustrating a moral truth

para·chute \'parə,shüt\ *n* : large umbrella-shaped device for making a descent from an airplane —**parachute** *vb* —**pa·ra·chut·ist** \-,shütəst\ *n*

pa·rade \pə'rād\ *n* 1 : pompous display 2 : ceremonial formation and march ~ *vb* -**rad·ed**; -**rad·ing** 1 : march in a parade 2 : show off

par·a·digm \'parə,dīm, -,dim\ *n* : model

par·a·dise \'parə,dīs, -,dīz\ *n* : place of bliss

par·a·dox \'parə,däks\ *n* : statement that seems contrary to common sense yet is perhaps true —**par·a·dox·i·cal** \ˌparə'däksikəl\ *adj* —**par·a·dox·i·cal·ly** *adv*

par·af·fin \'parəfən\ *n* : white waxy substance used esp. for making candles and sealing bottles —**paraffin** *vb* —**par·af·fin·ic** \ˌparə'finik\ *adj*

par·a·gon \'parə,gän, -gən\ *n* : model of perfection

para·graph \'parə,graf\ *n* : unified division of a piece of writing ~ *vb* : divide into paragraphs

par·a·keet \'parə,kēt\ *n* : small slender parrot

par·al·lel \'parə,lel\ *adj* 1 : lying or moving in the same direction but always the same distance apart 2 : similar ~ *n* 1 : parallel line, curve, or surface 2 : line of latitude 3 : similarity ~ *vb* 1 : compare 2 : correspond to —**par·al·lel·ism** \-,izəm\ *n*

par·al·lel·o·gram \ˌparə'lelə,gram\ *n* : 4-sided polygon with opposite sides equal and parallel

pa·ral·y·sis \pə'raləsəs\ *n, pl* -**y·ses** \-,sēz\ : loss of function and esp. of voluntary motion —**par·a·lyt·ic** \ˌparə'litik\ *adj or n*

par·a·lyze \'parə,līz\ *vb* -**lyzed**; -**lyz·ing** : affect with paralysis —**par·a·lyz·ing·ly** *adv*

pa·ram·e·ter \pə'ramətər\ n : characteristic element —**para·met·ric** \,parə'metrik\ adj

par·a·mount \'parə,maunt\ adj : superior to all others

par·amour \'parə,mur\ n : illicit lover

para·noia \,parə'nóiə\ n : mental disorder marked by irrational suspicion —**para·noid** \'parə,nóid\ adj or n

par·a·pet \'parəpət, -,pet\ n : protecting rampart in a fort

par·a·pher·na·lia \,parəfə(r)'nālyə\ n sing or pl : equipment

para·phrase \'parə,frāz\ n : restatement of a text giving the meaning in different words —**paraphrase** vb

para·ple·gia \,parə'plē(ē)ə\ n : paralysis of the lower trunk and legs —**para·ple·gic** \-jik\ adj or n

par·a·site \'parə,sīt\ n : organism living on another —**par·a·sit·ic** \,parə'sitik\ adj —**par·a·sit·ism** \'parəsə,tizəm, -,sīt,iz-\ n

par·a·sol \'parə,sól\ n : umbrella used to keep off the sun

para·troops \-,trüps\ n pl : troops trained to parachute from an airplane —**para·troop·er** \-,trüpər\ n

par·boil \'pär,bóil\ vb : boil briefly

par·cel \'pärsəl\ n 1 : lot 2 : package ~ vb -celed or -celled; -cel·ing or -cel·ling : divide into portions

parch \'pärch\ vb : toast or shrivel with dry heat

parch·ment \'pärchmənt\ n : animal skin prepared to write on

par·don \'pärdən\ n : excuse of an offense ~ vb : free from penalty —**par·don·able** \'pärdnəbəl, -ənəbəl\ adj —**par·don·er** \-nər, -ənər\ n

pare \'paər\ vb pared; par·ing 1 : trim off an outside part 2 : reduce as if by paring —**par·er** n

par·e·gor·ic \,parə'górik\ n : tincture of opium and camphor

par·ent \'parənt\ n : one that begets offspring —**par·ent·age** \-ij\ n —**pa·ren·tal** \pə'rentəl\ adj —**par·ent·hood** n

pa·ren·the·sis \pə'renthəsəs\ n, pl -the·ses \-,sēz\ 1 : word or phrase inserted in a passage 2 : one of a pair of punctuation marks ( ) —**par·en·thet·ic** \,parən'thetik\, **par·en·thet·i·cal** \-ikəl\ adj —**par·en·thet·i·cal·ly** \-k(ə)lē\ adv

par·fait \pär'fā\ n : layered cold dessert

pa·ri·ah \pə'rīə\ n : outcast

par·ish \'parish\ n : local church community

pa·rish·io·ner \pə'rish(ə)nər\ n : member of a parish

par·i·ty \'parətē\ n, pl -ties : equality

park \'pärk\ n 1 : land reserved for recreation or beauty ~ vb : leave a vehicle standing

par·ka \'pärkə\ n : usu. hooded heavy jacket

park·way \'pärk,wā\ n : broad thoroughfare

par·lance \'pärləns\ n : manner of speaking

par·lay \'pär,lā\ n : the risking of a stake plus its winnings —**parlay** vb

par·ley \'pärlē\ n, pl -leys : conference about a dispute —**parley** vb

par·lia·ment \'pärləmənt\ n : legislative assembly —**par·lia·men·tar·i·an** n —**par·lia·men·ta·ry** \,pärlə'ment(ə)rē\ adj

par·lor \'pärlər\ n 1 : reception room 2 : place of business

pa·ro·chi·al \pə'rōkēəl\ adj 1 : relating to a church parish 2 : provincial —**pa·ro·chi·al·ism** \-ə,lizəm\ n

par·o·dy \'parədē\ n, pl -dies : humorous or satirical imitation —**parody** vb

pa·role \pə'rōl\ n : conditional release of a prisoner —**parole** vb —**pa·rol·ee** \-,rō'lē, -'rō,lē\ n

par·ox·ysm \'parək,sizəm, pə'räk-\ n : spasm —**par·ox·ys·mal** \,parək-'sizməl, pə,räk-\ adj

par·que·try \'pärkətrē\ n, pl -tries : inlaid woodwork

par·ra·keet var of PARAKEET

par·rot \'parət\ n : bright-colored tropical bird

par·ry \'parē\ vb -ried; -ry·ing 1 : ward off a blow 2 : evade adroitly —**parry** n

parse \'pärs, 'pärz\ vb parsed; pars·ing : analyze grammatically

par·si·mo·ny \'pärsə,mōnē\ n : extreme frugality —**par·si·mo·ni·ous** \,pärsə'mōnēəs\ adj —**par·si·mo·ni·ous·ly** adv

pars·ley \'pärslē\ n : garden plant used as a seasoning

pars·nip \'pärsnəp\ n : carrotlike vegetable

par·son \'pärsən\ n : minister

par·son·age \'pärsnij, -ənij\ n : parson's house

part \'pärt\ n 1 : one of the units into which a larger whole is divided 2 : function or role ~ vb 1 : take leave 2 : separate 3 : go away 4 : give up

par·take \pär'tāk, pər-\ vb -took; -tak·en; -tak·ing : have or take a share —**par·tak·er** n

par·tial \'pärshəl\ *adj* 1 : favoring one over another 2 : affecting a part only —**par·tial·i·ty** \ˌpärsh(ē)'alətē\ *n* —**par·tial·ly** \'pärsh(ə)lē\ *adv*

par·tic·i·pate \pər'tisəˌpāt, pär-\ *vb* -**pat·ed; -pat·ing** : take part in something —**par·tic·i·pant** \-pənt\ *adj or n* —**par·tic·i·pa·tion** \-ˌtisə'pāshən\ *n* —**par·tic·i·pa·to·ry** \-'tisəpəˌtōrē\ *adj*

par·ti·ci·ple \'pärtəˌsipəl\ *n* : verb form with functions of both verb and adjective —**par·ti·cip·i·al** \ˌpärtə'sipēəl\ *adj*

par·ti·cle \'pärtikəl\ *n* : small bit

par·tic·u·lar \pə(r)'tikyələr\ *adj* 1 : relating to a specific person or thing 2 : individual 3 : hard to please ∼ *n* : detail —**par·tic·u·lar·ly** *adv*

par·ti·san, par·ti·zan \'pärtəzən, -sən\ *n* 1 : adherent 2 : guerrilla —**partisan** *adj* —**par·ti·san·ship** *n*

par·tite \'pärˌtīt\ *adj* : divided into parts

par·ti·tion \pər'tishən, pär-\ *n* 1 : distribution 2 : something that divides —**partition** *vb*

part·ly \'pärtlē\ *adv* : in some degree

part·ner \'pärtnər\ *n* 1 : associate 2 : companion 3 : business associate —**part·ner·ship** *n*

part of speech : class of words distinguished esp. according to function

par·tridge \'pärtrij\ *n, pl* -**tridge** *or* -**tridg·es** : stout-bodied game bird

par·tu·ri·tion \ˌpärt(y)ə'rishən, ˌpärchə-, ˌpärtyü-\ *n* : childbirth

par·ty \'pärtē\ *n, pl* -**ties** 1 : political organization 2 : participant 3 : company of persons esp. with a purpose 4 : social gathering

par·ve·nu \'pärvəˌn(y)ü\ *n* : social upstart

pass \'pas\ *vb* 1 : move past, over, or through 2 : go away or die 3 : allow to elapse 4 : go unchallenged 5 : transfer or undergo transfer 6 : render a judgment 7 : occur 8 : enact 9 : undergo testing successfully 10 : be regarded 11 : decline ∼ *n* 1 : low place in a mountain range 2 : act of passing 3 : accomplishment 4 : permission to leave, enter, or move about —**pass·able** *adj* —**pass·er** *n* —**pass·er·by** *n*

pas·sage \'pasij\ *n* 1 : process of passing 2 : means of passing 3 : voyage 4 : right to pass 5 : literary selection —**pas·sage·way** *n*

pass·book *n* : bankbook

pas·sé \pa'sā\ *adj* : out-of-date

pas·sen·ger \'pas°njər\ *n* : traveler in a conveyance

pass·ing \'pasiŋ\ *n* : death

pas·sion \'pashən\ *n* 1 : strong feeling esp. of anger, love, or desire 2 : object of affection or enthusiasm —**pas·sion·ate** \'pash(ə)nət\ *adj* —**pas·sion·ate·ly** *adv* —**pas·sion·less** *adj*

pas·sive \'pasiv\ *adj* 1 : not active but acted upon 2 : submissive —**passive** *n* —**pas·sive·ly** *adv* —**pas·siv·i·ty** \pa'sivətē\ *n*

Pass·over \'pasˌōvər\ *n* : Jewish holiday celebrated in March or April in commemoration of the Hebrews' liberation from slavery in Egypt

pass·port \'pasˌpōrt\ *n* : government document needed for travel abroad

pass·word *n* : word or phrase spoken to pass a guard

past \'past\ *adj* 1 : ago 2 : just gone by 3 : having existed before the present 4 : expressing past time ∼ *prep or adv* : beyond ∼ *n* 1 : time gone by 2 : verb tense expressing past time 3 : past life

pas·ta \'pästə\ *n* : fresh or dried shaped dough

paste \'pāst\ *n* 1 : smooth ground food 2 : moist adhesive ∼ *vb* **past·ed; past·ing** : attach with paste —**pasty** *adj*

paste·board *n* : cardboard

pas·tel \pas'tel\ *n* : light color —**pastel** *adj*

pas·teur·ize \'paschəˌrīz, 'pastə-\ *vb* -**ized; -iz·ing** : heat (as milk) so as to kill germs —**pas·teur·i·za·tion** \ˌpaschərə'zāshən, ˌpastə-\ *n* —**pas·teur·iz·er** *n*

pas·time \'pasˌtīm\ *n* : amusement

pas·tor \'pastər\ *n* : clergyman serving a church or parish —**pas·tor·ate** \-t(ə)rət\ *n*

pas·to·ral \'past(ə)rəl\ *adj* 1 : relating to rural life 2 : of or relating to spiritual guidance or a pastor ∼ *n* : literary work dealing with rural life

pas·try \'pāstrē\ *n, pl* -**tries** : sweet baked goods

pas·ture \'paschər\ *n* : land used for grazing ∼ *vb* -**tured; -tur·ing** : graze

pat \'pat\ *n* 1 : light tap 2 : small mass ∼ *vb* -**tt-** : tap gently ∼ *adj or adv* 1 : apt or glib 2 : unyielding

patch \'pach\ *n* 1 : piece used for mending 2 : small area distinct from surrounding area ∼ *vb* 1 : mend with a patch 2 : make of fragments 3 : repair hastily

patch·work *n* : something made of pieces of different materials, shapes, or colors

pate \'pāt\ n : crown of the head

pa·tel·la \pə'telə\ n, pl -lae \-'tel(₁)ē, -₁lī\ or -las : kneecap

¹pa·tent adj 1 \'pat²nt, 'pāt-\ : obvious 2 \'pat-\ : protected by a patent

²pat·ent \'pat-\ n : document conferring or securing a right ~ vb : secure by patent —**pat·en·tee** \₁pat²n'tē\ n

pa·ter·nal \pə'tərn³l\ adj 1 : fatherly 2 : related through or inherited from a father —**pa·ter·nal·ly** adv

pa·ter·ni·ty \pə'tərnətē\ n : fatherhood

path \'path, 'päth\ n 1 : trodden way 2 : route or course —**path·find·er** n —**path·way** n —**path·less** adj

pa·thet·ic \pə'thetik\ adj : pitiful —**pa·thet·i·cal·ly** \-ik(ə)lē\ adv

pa·thol·o·gy \pa'thäləjē\ n, pl -gies 1 : study of disease 2 : physical abnormality —**path·o·log·i·cal** \₁pathə'läjikəl\ adj —**pa·thol·o·gist** \pə'thäləjəst\ n

pa·thos \'pā₁thäs\ n : element evoking pity

pa·tience \'pāshəns\ n : habit or fact of being patient

pa·tient \'pāshənt\ adj : bearing pain or trials without complaint ~ n : person under medical care —**pa·tient·ly** adv

pa·ti·na \'patənə, pə'tēnə\ n, pl -nas \-nəz\ or -nae \'patə,nē, -,nī\ : green film formed on copper and bronze

pa·tio \'patē,ō, 'pät-\ n, pl -ti·os 1 : courtyard 2 : paved recreation area near a house

pa·tri·arch \'pātrē,ärk\ n 1 : man revered as father or founder 2 : venerable old man —**pa·tri·ar·chal** \₁pātrē'ärkəl\ adj —**pa·tri·ar·chy** \-,ärkē\ n

pa·tri·cian \pə'trishən\ n : person of high birth —**patrician** adj

pat·ri·cide \'patrə,sīd\ n : murder of one's father

pat·ri·mo·ny \'patrə,mōnē\ n : something inherited —**pat·ri·mo·ni·al** \₁patrə'mōnēəl\ adj

pa·tri·ot \'pātrēət, -,ät\ n : one who loves his country —**pa·tri·ot·ic** \₁pātrē'ätik\ adj —**pa·tri·ot·i·cal·ly** \-ik(ə)lē\ adv —**pa·tri·o·tism** \'pātrēə,tizəm\ n

pa·trol \pə'trōl\ n : a going around for observation or security 2 : group on patrol ~ vb -ll- : carry out a patrol

pa·trol·man \-mən\ n : police officer

pa·tron \'pātrən\ n 1 : special protector 2 : wealthy supporter 3 : customer

pa·tron·age \'patrənij, 'pā-\ n 1 : support or influence of a patron 2 : trade of customers 3 : control of government appointments

pa·tron·ize \'pātrə,nīz, 'pa-\ vb -ized; -iz·ing 1 : be a customer of 2 : treat with condescension

¹pat·ter \'patər\ vb : talk glibly or mechanically ~ n : rapid talk

²patter vb : pat or tap rapidly ~ n : quick succession of pats or taps

pat·tern \'patərn\ n 1 : model for imitation or for making things 2 : artistic design 3 : noticeable formation or set of characteristics ~ vb : form according to a pattern

pat·ty \'patē\ n, pl -ties : small flat cake

pau·ci·ty \'pósətē\ n : shortage

paunch \'pónch\ n : large belly —**paunchy** adj

pau·per \'pópər\ n : person without means of support —**pau·per·ism** \-pə,rizəm\ n —**pau·per·ize** \-pə,rīz\ vb

pause \'póz\ n : temporary stop ~ vb paused; paus·ing : stop briefly

pave \'pāv\ vb paved; pav·ing : cover to smooth or firm the surface —**pave·ment** \-mənt\ n —**pav·ing** n

pa·vil·ion \pə'vilyən\ n 1 : large tent 2 : light structure used for entertainment

paw \'pó\ n : foot of a 4-legged clawed animal ~ vb 1 : handle clumsily or rudely 2 : touch or strike with a paw, hoof, or foot

pawn \'pón\ n 1 : goods deposited as security for a loan 2 : state of being pledged ~ vb : deposit as a pledge —**pawn·bro·ker** n —**pawn·shop** n

pay \'pā\ vb paid \'pād\; pay·ing 1 : make due return for goods or services 2 : discharge indebtedness for 3 : requite 4 : give or make freely or as fitting 5 : be profitable ~ n 1 : state of being paid 2 : something paid —**pay·able** adj —**pay·check** n —**pay·ee** \pā'ē\ n —**pay·er** n —**pay·ment** n

pea \'pē\ n : round edible seed of a leguminous vine

peace \'pēs\ n : state of calm and quiet 2 : absence of war or strife —**peace·able** \-əbəl\ adj —**peace·ably** \-blē\ adv —**peace·ful** \-fəl\ adj —**peace·ful·ly** adv —**peace·keep·er** n —**peace·keep·ing** n —**peace·mak·er** n —**peace·time** n

peach \'pēch\ n : sweet juicy fruit of a flowering tree

pea·cock \'pē,käk\ n : brilliantly colored male pheasant

peak \'pēk\ *n* **1** : pointed or projecting part **2** : top of a hill **3** : highest level ~ *vb* : reach a maximum —**peak** *adj*

peak·ed \'pēkəd\ *adj* : sickly

peal \'pēl\ *n* : loud sound (as of ringing bells) ~ *vb* : give out peals

pea·nut \'pē(ˌ)nət\ *n* : annual herb that bears underground pods or the pod or the edible seed inside

pear \'paər\ *n* : fleshy fruit of a tree related to the apple

pearl \'pərl\ *n* : gem formed within an oyster —**pearly** \'pərlē\ *adj*

peas·ant \'pez⁰nt\ *n* : tiller of the soil —**peas·ant·ry** \-rē\ *n*

peat \'pēt\ *n* : decayed organic deposit often dried for fuel —**peaty** *adj*

peb·ble \'pebəl\ *n* : small stone —**peb·bly** *adj*

pe·can \pi'kän, -'kan\ *n* : hickory tree bearing a smooth-shelled nut or the nut

pec·ca·dil·lo \ˌpekə'dilō\ *n, pl* -**loes** *or* -**los** : slight offense

¹peck \'pek\ *n* : unit of dry measure equal to 8 quarts

²peck *vb* : strike or pick up with the bill ~ *n* : quick sharp stroke

pec·tin \'pektən\ *n* : water-soluble plant substance that causes fruit jellies to set —**pec·tic** \-tik\ *adj*

pec·to·ral \'pekt(ə)rəl\ *adj* : relating to the breast or chest

pec·u·late \'pekyəˌlāt\ *vb* -**lat·ed**; -**lat·ing** : embezzle —**pec·u·la·tion** \ˌpekyə'lāshən\ *n*

pe·cu·liar \pi'kyülyər\ *adj* **1** : characteristic of only one **2** : strange —**pe·cu·liar·i·ty** \-ˌkyül'yarətē, -ē'ar-\ *n* —**pe·cu·liar·ly** *adv*

pe·cu·ni·ary \pi'kyünēˌerē\ *adj* : relating to money

ped·a·go·gy \'pedəˌgōjē, -ˌgäj-\ *n* : art or profession of teaching —**ped·a·gog·ic** \ˌpedə'gäjik, -'gōj-\, **ped·a·gog·i·cal** \-ikəl\ *adj* —**ped·a·gogue** \'pedəˌgäg\ *n*

ped·al \'ped⁰l\ *n* : lever worked by the foot ~ *adj* : relating to the foot ~ *vb* : use a pedal

ped·ant \'ped⁰nt\ *n* : learned bore —**pe·dan·tic** \pi'dantik\ *adj* —**ped·ant·ry** \'ped⁰ntrē\ *n*

ped·dle \'ped⁰l\ *vb* -**dled**; -**dling** : offer for sale —**ped·dler, ped·lar** \'pedlər\ *n*

ped·es·tal \'pedəst⁰l\ *n* : support or foot of something upright

pe·des·tri·an \pə'destrēən\ *adj* **1** : ordinary **2** : walking ~ *n* : person who walks

pe·di·at·rics \ˌpēdē'atriks\ *n* : branch of medicine dealing with children —**pe·di·at·ric** \-trik\ *adj* —**pe·di·a·tri·cian** \ˌpēdēə'trishən\ *n*

ped·i·gree \'pedəˌgrē\ *n* : line of ancestors or a record of them

ped·i·ment \'pedəmənt\ *n* : triangular gablelike decoration on a building

peek \'pēk\ *vb* **1** : look furtively **2** : glance —**peek** *n*

peel \'pēl\ *vb* **1** : strip the skin or rind from **2** : lose the outer layer ~ *n* : skin or rind —**peel·ing** *n*

¹peep \'pēp\ *vb or n* : cheep

²peep *vb* **1** : look slyly **2** : begin to emerge ~ *n* : brief look —**peep·er** *n* —**peep·hole** *n*

peer \'piər\ *n* **1** : one's equal **2** : nobleman —**peer·age** \-ij\ *n*

²peer *vb* : look intently or curiously

peer·less \-ləs\ *adj* : having no equal

peeve \'pēv\ *vb* **peeved**; **peev·ing** : make resentful ~ *n* : complaint —**peev·ish** \-ish\ *adj* —**peev·ish·ly** *adv* —**peev·ish·ness** *n*

peg \'peg\ *n* : small pinlike piece ~ *vb* -**gg**- **1** : put a peg into **2** : fix or mark with or as if with pegs

pei·gnoir \pān'wär, pen-\ *n* : negligee

pelf \'pelf\ *n* : money

pel·i·can \'pelikən\ *n* : large-billed seabird

pel·la·gra \pə'lagrə, -'läg-\ *n* : protein-deficiency disease

pel·let \'pelət\ *n* : little ball —**pel·let·al** \-⁰l\ *adj* —**pel·let·ize** \-ˌīz\ *vb*

pell-mell \'pel'mel\ *adv* : in confusion or haste

pel·lu·cid \pə'lüsəd\ *adj* : very clear

¹pelt \'pelt\ *n* : skin of a fur-bearing animal

²pelt *vb* : strike with blows or missiles

pel·vis \'pelvəs\ *n, pl* -**vis·es** \-vəsəz\ *or* -**ves** \-ˌvēz\ : cavity formed by the hip bones —**pel·vic** \-vik\ *adj*

pem·mi·can \'pemikən\ *n* : dried meat

¹pen \'pen\ *n* : enclosure for animals ~ *vb* -**nn**- : shut in a pen

²pen *n* : tool for writing with ink ~ *vb* -**nn**- : write

pe·nal \'pēn⁰l\ *adj* : relating to punishment

pe·nal·ize \'pēn⁰lˌīz, 'pen-\ *vb* -**ized**; -**iz·ing** : put a penalty on

pen·al·ty \'pen⁰ltē\ *n, pl* -**ties 1** : punishment for crime **2** : disadvantage, loss, or hardship due to an action

pen·ance \'penəns\ *n* : act performed to show repentance

pence \'pens\ *pl of* PENNY

pen·chant \'penchənt\ *n* : strong inclination

pen·cil \'pensəl\ *n* : writing or drawing tool with a solid marking substance as its core ~ *vb* -ciled *or* -cilled; -cil·ing *or* cil·ling : draw or write with a pencil

pen·dant \'pendənt\ *n* : hanging ornament

pen·dent, pen·dant \'pendənt\ *adj* : hanging

pend·ing \'pendiŋ\ *prep* : while awaiting ~ *adj* : not yet decided

pen·du·lous \'penjələs, -də-\ *adj* : hanging loosely

pen·du·lum \-ləm\ *n* : weight that swings from a fixed point

pen·e·trate \'penə,trāt\ *vb* -trat·ed; -trat·ing 1 : enter into 2 : permeate 3 : see into —**pen·e·tra·ble** \-trəbəl\ *adj* —**pen·e·tra·tion** \,penə'trāshən\ *n* —**pen·e·tra·tive** \'penə,trātiv\ *adj*

pen·guin \'peŋgwən, 'pen-\ *n* : short-legged flightless seabird

pen·i·cil·lin \,penə'silən\ *n* : anitbiotic produced by a mold

pen·in·su·la \pə'ninsələ, -'ninchə-\ *n* : land extending out into the water —**pen·in·su·lar** \-lər\ *adj*

pe·nis \'pēnəs\ *n, pl* -nes \-,nēz\ *or* -nis·es : male organ of copulation

pen·i·tent \'penətənt\ *adj* : feeling sorrow for sins or offenses ~ *n* : penitent person —**pen·i·tence** \-təns\ *n* —**pen·i·ten·tial** \,penə'tenchəl\ *adj*

pen·i·ten·tia·ry \,penə'tench(ə)rē\ *n, pl* -ries : state or federal prison

pen·man·ship \'penmən,ship\ *n* : art or practice of writing

pen·nant \'penənt\ *n* : nautical or championship flag

pen·ny \'penē\ *n, pl* -nies \-ēz\ *or* pence \'pens\ 1 : monetary unit equal to 1/100 pound 2 *pl* -nies : cent —**pen·ni·less** \'penilэs\ *adj*

pen·sion \'penchən\ *n* : retirement income ~ *vb* : pay a pension to —**pen·sion·er** *n*

pen·sive \'pensiv\ *adj* : thoughtful —**pen·sive·ly** *adv*

pent \'pent\ *adj* : confined

pent·a·gon \'pentə,gän\ *n* : 5-sided polygon —**pen·tag·o·nal** \pen'tagən⁹l\ *adj*

pen·tam·e·ter \pen'tamətər\ *n* : line of 5 metrical feet

pent·house \'pent,haùs\ *n* : rooftop apartment

pe·nu·ri·ous \pə'n(y)ùrēəs\ *adj* 1 : marked by penury 2 : stingy

pen·u·ry \'penyərē\ *n* : poverty

pe·on \'pē,än, -ən\ *n, pl* -ons *or* -ones \pā'ōnēz\ : landless laborer in Spanish America —**pe·on·age** \-ənij\ *n*

pe·o·ny \'pēənē\ *n, pl* -nies : garden plant having large flowers

peo·ple \'pēpəl\ *n, pl* **people** 1 *pl* : human beings in general 2 *pl* : human beings in a certain group (as a family) or community 3 *pl* **peoples** : tribe, nation, or race ~ *vb* -pled; -pling : constitute the population of

pep \'pep\ *n* : brisk energy ~ *vb* pepped; **pep·ping** : put pep into —**pep·py** *adj*

pep·per \'pepər\ *n* 1 : pungent seasoning from the berry (**peppercorn**) of a shrub 2 : vegetable grown for its hot or sweet fruit ~ *vb* : season with pepper —**pep·pery** \-(ə)rē\ *adj*

pep·per·mint \-,mint, -mənt\ *n* : pungent aromatic mint

pep·tic \'peptik\ *adj* : relating to digestion or the effect of digestive juices

per \(,)pər\, *prep* 1 : by means of 2 : for each 3 : according to

per·am·bu·late \pə'rambyə,lāt\ *vb* -lat·ed; -lat·ing : travel over esp. on foot —**per·am·bu·la·tion** \-,rambyə'lāshən\ *n*

per·cale \(,)pər'kāl, 'pər-,; (,)pər'kal\ *n* : fine woven cotton cloth

per·ceive \pər'sēv\ *vb* -ceived; -ceiv·ing 1 : realize 2 : become aware of through the senses —**per·ceiv·able** *adj*

per·cent \pər'sent\ *adv* : in each hundred ~ *n, pl* -cent *or* -cents 1 : one part in a hundred 2 : percentage

per·cent·age \pər'sentij\ *n* : part of a whole expressed in hundredths

per·cep·ti·ble \pər'septəbəl\ *adj* : capable of being perceived —**per·cep·ti·bly** \-blē\ *adv*

per·cep·tion \pər'sepshən\ *n* 1 : act or result of perceiving 2 : ability to perceive

per·cep·tive \pər'septiv\ *adj* : showing perception —**per·cep·tive·ly** *adv*

¹perch \'pərch\ *n* : roost for birds ~ *vb* : roost

²perch *n, pl* **perch** *or* **perch·es** : freshwater spiny-finned food fish

per·co·late \'pərkə,lāt\ *vb* -lat·ed; -lat·ing : trickle or cause to trickle down through a substance —**per·co·la·tor** \-,lātər\ *n*

per·cus·sion \pər'kəshən\ *n* 1 : sharp blow 2 : musical instrument sounded by striking

per·emp·to·ry \pə'rempt(ə)rē\ *adj* 1 : imperative 2 : domineering —**pe·remp·to·ri·ly** \-t(ə)rəlē\ *adv*

pe·ren·ni·al \pə'renēəl\ *adj* 1 : present at all seasons of the year 2 : continuing to live from year to year 3 : recurring regularly ~ n : plant that lives for a number of years —per·en·ni·al·ly adv

per·fect \'pərfikt\ adj 1 : being without fault or defect 2 : exact 3 : complete ~ vb : make perfect —per·fect·ibil·i·ty \pər,fektə'bilətē, ,pərfik-\ n —per·fect·ible \pər'fektəbəl, 'perfik-\ adj —per·fect·ly adv —per·fect·ness n

per·fec·tion \pər'fekshən\ n 1 : quality or state of being perfect 2 : highest degree of excellence —per·fec·tion·ist \-sh(ə)nəst\ n

per·fi·dy \'pərfədē\ n : treachery —per·fid·i·ous \pər'fidēəs\ adj —per·fid·i·ous·ly adv

per·fo·rate \'pərfə,rāt\ vb -rat·ed; -rat·ing : make a hole in —per·fo·ra·tion \,pərfə'rāshən\ n

per·force \pər'fōrs\ adv : of necessity

per·form \pə(r)'fόrm\ vb 1 : adhere to the terms of 2 : carry out 3 : give a performance —per·form·er n

per·for·mance \pər'fόr,məns\ n 1 : act or process of performing 2 : public presentation

per·fume \'pər,fyüm, pər'-\ n 1 : pleasant odor 2 : preparation used for scenting ~ \pər'-, 'pər,-\ vb -fumed; -fum·ing : add a pleasing smell to

per·func·to·ry \pər'fəŋkt(ə)rē\ adj : done merely as a duty —per·func·to·ri·ly \-t(ə)rəlē\ adv

per·haps \pər'(h)aps, 'praps\ adv : possibly but not certainly

per·il \'perəl\ n : danger —per·il·ous adj —per·il·ous·ly adv

per·im·e·ter \pə'rimətər\ n : outer boundary of a body or figure

pe·ri·od \'pirēəd\ n 1 : punctuation mark . used esp. to mark the end of a declarative sentence or an abbreviation 2 : division of time 3 : stage or division in a process or development

pe·ri·od·ic \,pirē'ädik\ adj : occurring at regular intervals —pe·ri·od·i·cal·ly \-ik(ə)lē\ adv

pe·ri·od·i·cal \,pirē'ädikəl\ n : newspaper or magazine

pe·riph·ery \pə'rif(ə)rē\ n, pl -er·ies : outer boundary —pe·riph·er·al \-(ə)rəl\ adj

peri·scope \'perə,skōp\ n : optical instrument for viewing from a submarine

per·ish \'perish\ vb : die or spoil —per·ish·able \-əbəl\ adj or n

per·ju·ry \'pərj(ə)rē\ n : voluntary violation of an oath to tell the truth —per·jure \'pərjər\ vb —per·jur·er n

¹perk \'pərk\ vb 1 : thrust (as the head) up jauntily 2 : make trim or brisk 3 : gain vigor or spirit —perky adj

²perk vb : percolate

¹per·ma·nent \'pərmənənt\ adj : lasting —per·ma·nence \-nəns\ n —per·ma·nen·cy \-nənsē\ n —per·ma·nent·ly adv

²permanent n : long-lasting hair wave or straightening

per·me·able \'pərmēəbəl\ adj : permitting liquids or gases to seep through —per·me·a·bil·i·ty \,pərmēə'bilətē\ n

per·me·ate \'pərmē,āt\ vb -at·ed; -at·ing 1 : seep through 2 : pervade —per·me·ation \,pərmē'āshən\ n

per·mis·si·ble \pər'misəbəl\ adj : that may be permitted

per·mis·sion \pər'mishən\ n : formal consent

per·mis·sive \pər'misiv\ adj : granting freedom esp. to excess —per·mis·sive·ness n

per·mit \pər'mit\ vb -mit·ted; -mit·ting 1 : give approval for 2 : make possible ~ \'pər,-, pər'-\ n : license

per·ni·cious \pər'nishəs\ adj : harmful —per·ni·cious·ly adv

per·ox·ide \pə'räk,sīd\ n : compound (as hydrogen peroxide) in which oxygen is joined to oxygen

per·pen·dic·u·lar \,pərpən'dikyələr\ adj 1 : vertical 2 : meeting another line at a right angle —perpendicular n —per·pen·dic·u·lar·i·ty \-,dikyə'larətē\ n —per·pen·dic·u·lar·ly adv

per·pe·trate \'pərpə,trāt\ vb -trat·ed; -trat·ing : be guilty of doing —per·pe·tra·tion \,pərpə'trāshən\ n —per·pe·tra·tor \'pərpə,trātər\ n

per·pet·u·al \pər'pech(əw)əl\ adj 1 : continuing forever 2 : occurring continually —per·pet·u·al·ly adv —per·pe·tu·ity \,pərpə't(y)üətē\ n

per·pet·u·ate \pər'pechə,wāt\ vb -at·ed; -at·ing : make perpetual —per·pet·u·a·tion \-,pechə'wāshən\ n

per·plex \pər'pleks\ vb : confuse —per·plex·i·ty \-ətē\ n

per·qui·site \'pərkwəzət\ n : privilege or profit beyond regular pay

per·se·cute \'pərsi,kyüt\ vb -cut·ed; -cut·ing : harass in such a way as to injure or afflict —per·se·cu·tion \,pərsi'kyüshən\ n —per·se·cu·tor \'pərsi,kyütər\ n

per·se·vere \,pərsə'viər\ vb -vered; -ver·ing : persist —per·se·ver·ance \-'virəns\ n

per·sist \pər'sist, -'zist\ *vb* 1 : go on resolutely in spite of difficulties 2 : continue to exist —**per·sis·tence** \-'sistəns, -'zis-\ *n* —**per·sis·ten·cy** \-tənsē\ *n* —**per·sis·tent** \-tənt\ *adj* —**per·sis·tent·ly** *adv*

per·son \'pərsᵊn\ *n* 1 : human being 2 : human being's body or individuality 3 : reference to the speaker, one spoken to, or one spoken of

per·son·able \'pərsnəbəl, -ᵊnəbəl\ *adj* : having a pleasing personality

per·son·age \'pərsnij, -ᵊnij\ *n* : person of rank or distinction

per·son·al \'pərsnəl, -ᵊnəl\ *adj* 1 : relating to or affecting a particular person 2 : done in person 3 : affecting an individual's body 4 : indicating grammatical person —**per·son·al·ly** *adv*

per·son·al·i·ty \,pərsᵊn'alətē\ *n, pl* **-ties** 1 : offensive personal remark 2 : manner and disposition of an individual 3 : distinctive person

per·son·al·ize \'pərsnə,līz, -ᵊnə,līz\ *vb* **-ized; -iz·ing** : mark as belonging to a particular person

per·son·i·fy \pər'sänə,fī\ *vb* **-fied; -fy·ing** 1 : represent as a human being 2 : be the embodiment of —**per·son·i·fi·ca·tion** \-,sänəfə'kāshən\ *n*

per·son·nel \,pərsᵊn'el\ *n* : body of persons employed in an organization

per·spec·tive \pər'spektiv\ *n* 1 : apparent depth and distance in painting 2 : view of things in their true relationship or importance

per·spi·cac·i·ty \,pərspə'kasətē\ *n* : acuteness of understanding or judgment —**per·spi·ca·cious** \-'kāshəs\ *adj*

per·spire \pər'spīr\ *vb* **-spired; -spir·ing** : sweat —**per·spi·ra·tion** \,pərspə-'rāshən\ *n*

per·suade \pər'swād\ *vb* **-suad·ed; -suad·ing** : cause to do or believe by argument or entreaty —**per·sua·sive** \-'swāsiv, -ziv\ *adj* —**per·sua·sive·ly** *adv* —**per·sua·sive·ness** *n*

per·sua·sion \pər'swāzhən\ *n* : act or process of persuading

pert \'pərt\ *adj* : flippant or irreverent

per·tain \pər'tān\ *vb* 1 : belong 2 : relate

per·ti·na·cious \,pərtᵊn'āshəs\ *adj* : obstinately persistent —**per·ti·nac·i·ty** \-'asətē\ *n*

per·ti·nent \'pərtᵊnənt\ *adj* : relevant —**per·ti·nence** \-əns\ *n*

per·turb \pər'tərb\ *vb* : make uneasy —**per·tur·ba·tion** \,pərtər'bāshən\ *n*

pe·ruse \pə'rüz\ *vb* **-rused; -rus·ing** : read attentively —**pe·rus·al** \-'rüzəl\ *n*

per·vade \pər'vād\ *vb* **-vad·ed; -vad·ing** : spread through every part of —**per·va·sive** \-'vāsiv, -ziv\ *adj*

per·verse \pər'vərs\ *adj* 1 : corrupt 2 : unreasonably contrary —**per·verse·ly** *adv* —**per·verse·ness** *n* —**per·ver·sion** \pər'vərzhən\ *n* —**per·ver·si·ty** \-'vərsətē\ *n*

per·vert \pər'vərt\ *vb* : corrupt or distort ~ \'pər,-\ *n* : one that is perverted

pe·so \'pāsō\ *n, pl* **-sos** : monetary unit (as of Mexico)

pes·si·mism \'pesə,mizəm\ *n* : inclination to expect the worst —**pes·si·mist** \-məst\ *n* —**pes·si·mis·tic** \,pesə-'mistik\ *adj*

pest \'pest\ *n* 1 : nuisance 2 : plant or animal detrimental to man —**pes·ti·cide** \'pestə,sīd\ *n*

pes·ter \'pestər\ *vb* **-tered; -ter·ing** : harass persistently with petty matters

pes·ti·lence \'pestələns\ *n* : plague —**pes·ti·lent** \-lənt\ *adj*

pes·tle \'pesəl, 'pestᵊl\ *n* : implement for grinding substances in a mortar

pet \'pet\ *n* 1 : domesticated animal kept for pleasure rather than utility 2 : favorite ~ *vb* : stroke gently or lovingly

pet·al \'petᵊl\ *n* : modified leaf of a flower head

pe·tite \pə'tēt\ *adj* : having a small trim figure

pe·ti·tion \pə'tishən\ *n* : formal written request ~ *vb* : make a petition —**pe·ti·tion·er** *n*

pe·trel \'petrəl\ *n* : small seabird

pet·ri·fy \'petrə,fī\ *vb* **-fied; -fy·ing** 1 : change into stony material 2 : make rigid or inactive (as from fear) —**pet·ri·fac·tion** \,petrə'fakshən\ *n*

pe·tro·leum \pə'trōlēəm\ *n* : raw oil obtained from the ground

pet·ti·coat \'petē,kōt\ *n* : skirt worn under a dress

pet·ty \'petē\ *adj* **-ti·er; -est** 1 : being small or minor and of no importance 2 : narrow-minded or unsympathetic —**pet·ti·ly** \'petᵊlē\ *adv* —**pet·ti·ness** *n*

petty officer *n* : subordinate officer in the navy or coast guard appointed from among the enlisted men

petty officer first class *n* : petty officer ranking below a chief petty officer

petty officer second class *n* : petty officer ranking below a petty officer first class

petty officer third class *n* : petty officer ranking below a petty officer second class

pet·u·lant \'pechələnt\ *adj* : irritable —**pet·u·lance** \-ləns\ *n* —**pet·u·lant·ly** *adv*

pe·tu·nia \pi¹t(y)ünyə\ *n* : garden plant with bright flowers

pew \'pyü\ *n* : bench with a back used in a church

pew·ter \'pyütər\ *n* : alloy of tin used for kitchen or table utensils

pH \¹)pē¹āch\ *n* : number expressing relative acidity and alkalinity

pha·lanx \'fā,lanks\ *n, pl* **-lanx·es** or **-lan·ges** \'fə¹lan,jēz\ **1** : body (as of troops) in compact formation **2** *pl* **phalanges** : digital bone of the hand or foot

phal·lus \'faləs\ *n, pl* **-li** \'fal,ī\ or **-lus·es** : penis —**phal·lic** *adj*

phantasy *var of* FANTASY

phan·tom \'fantəm\ *n* : something that only appears to be real —**phantom** *adj*

pha·raoh \'fe(ə)rō, 'fārō\ *n* : ruler of ancient Egypt

phar·i·see \'fara,sē\ *n* : a self-righteous or hypocritical person —**phar·i·sa·ic** \,farə¹sāik\ *adj*

phar·ma·ceu·ti·cal \,färmə¹sütikəl\ *adj* **1** : relating to pharmacy or pharmacists **2** : medicinal —**pharmaceutical** *n*

phar·ma·col·o·gy \,färmə¹käləjē\ *n* : science of drugs esp. as related to medicinal uses —**phar·ma·co·log·ic** \-kə¹läjik\, **phar·ma·co·log·i·cal** \-ikəl\ *adj* —**phar·ma·col·o·gist** \-¹kāləʒəst\ *n*

phar·ma·cy \'färməsē\ *n, pl* **-cies 1** : art or practice of preparing and dispensing drugs **2** : drugstore —**phar·ma·cist** \-səst\ *n*

phar·ynx \'farinks\ *n, pl* **pha·ryn·ges** \fə¹rin,jēz\ : space behind the mouth into which the nostrils, esophagus, and windpipe open —**pha·ryn·ge·al** \fə¹rinj(ē)əl, ,farən¹jēəl\ *adj*

phase \'fāz\ *n* **1** : particular appearance or stage in a recurring series of changes **2** : stage in a process

pheas·ant \'fez²nt\ *n, pl* **-ant** or **-ants** : long-tailed brilliantly colored game bird

phe·nom·e·non \fi¹nämə,nän, -nən\ *n, pl* **-na** \-nə\ or **-nons 1** : observable fact or event **2** *pl* **-nons** : prodigy —**phe·nom·e·nal** \-¹nämən²l\ *adj*

phi·lan·der \fə¹landər\ *vb* : make love without serious intent —**phi·lan·der·er** *n*

phi·lan·thro·py \fə¹lanthrəpē\ *n, pl* **-pies** : charitable act or gift or an organization that distributes such gifts —**phil·an·throp·ic** \,filən¹thräpik\ *adj* —**phi·lan·thro·pist** \fə¹lanthrəpəst\ *n*

phi·lat·e·ly \fə¹lat²lē\ *n* : collection and study of postage stamps —**phi·lat·e·list** \-²ləst\ *n*

phil·har·mon·ic \,filər¹mänik, ,fil(h)är-\ *adj* : relating to a symphony orchestra

phi·lis·tine \'filə,stēn; fə¹listən\ *n* : one who is smugly indifferent to ideas or art —**philistine** *adj*

philo·den·dron \,filə¹dendrən\ *n, pl* **-drons** or **-dra** \-drə\ : plant grown for its showy leaves

phi·los·o·pher \fə¹läsəfər\ *n* **1** : reflective thinker **2** : student of or specialist in philosophy

phi·los·o·phy \fə¹läsəfē\ *n, pl* **-phies 1** : critical study of fundamental beliefs **2** : sciences and liberal arts exclusive of medicine, law, and theology **3** : system of ideas **4** : sum of personal convictions **5** : calmness —**philo·soph·ic** \,filə¹säfik\, **phil·o·soph·i·cal** \-ikəl\ *adj* —**phil·o·soph·i·cal·ly** \-k(ə)lē\ *adv* —**phi·los·o·phize** \fə¹läsə,fīz\ *vb*

phle·bi·tis \fli¹bītəs\ *n* : inflammation of a vein

phlegm \'flem\ *n* : thick mucus in the nose and throat

phleg·mat·ic \fleg¹matik\ *adj* : slow and stolid

phlox \'fläks\ *n, pl* **phlox** or **phlox·es** : herb grown for its flower clusters

pho·bia \'fōbēə\ *n* : irrational persistent fear

phoe·nix \'fēniks\ *n* : legendary bird held to burn itself to death and rise fresh and young from its ashes

phone \'fōn\ *n* : telephone ~ *vb* **phoned; phon·ing** : call on a telephone

pho·neme \'fō,nēm\ *n* : smallest distinguishable unit of speech —**pho·ne·mic** \fō¹nēmik\ *adj*

pho·net·ics \fə¹netiks\ *n* : study of speech sounds —**pho·net·ic** \-ik\ *adj* —**pho·ne·ti·cian** \,fōnə¹tishən\ *n*

pho·no·graph \'fōnə,graf\ *n* : instrument that reproduces sound from a grooved disc —**pho·no·graph·ic** \,fōnə¹grafik\ *adj* —**pho·no·graph·i·cal·ly** \-ik(ə)lē\ *adv*

pho·ny or **pho·ney** \'fōnē\ adj **-ni·er; -est** : not sincere or genuine —**phony** n

phos·phate \'fäs₁fāt\ n : chemical salt used in fertilizers —**phos·phat·ic** \fäs'fatik\ adj

phos·phor \'fäsfər\ n : phosphorescent substance

phos·pho·res·cence \₁fäsfə'res²ns\ n : luminescence without heat —**phos·pho·res·cent** \-²nt\ adj —**phos·pho·res·cent·ly** adv

phos·pho·rus \'fäsf(ə)rəs\ n : poisonous waxy chemical element —**phos·phor·ic** \fäs'fōrik, -'fär-\ adj —**phos·pho·rous** \'fäsf(ə)rəs; fäs'fōrəs, -'fôr-\ adj

pho·to \'fōtō\ n, pl **-tos** : photograph —**photo** vb or adj

pho·to·elec·tric \₁fōtōi'lektrik\ adj : relating to an electrical effect due to the interaction of light with matter —**pho·to·elec·tri·cal·ly** \-'trik(ə)lē\ adv

pho·to·gen·ic \₁fōtə'jenik\ adj : suitable for being photographed

pho·to·graph \'fōtə₁graf\ n : picture taken by photography —**photograph** vb —**pho·tog·ra·pher** \fə'tägrəfər\ n

pho·tog·ra·phy \fə'tägrəfē\ n : process of using light to produce images on a sensitized surface —**pho·to·graph·ic** \₁fōtə'grafik\ adj —**pho·to·graph·i·cal·ly** \-ik(ə)lē\ adv

pho·to·syn·the·sis \₁fōtō'sinthəsəs\ n : formation of carbohydrates by chlorophyll-containing plants exposed to sunlight —**pho·to·syn·the·size** \-₁sīz\ vb —**pho·to·syn·thet·ic** \-'sin'thetik\ adj

phrase \'frāz\ n : brief expression 2 : group of related words that express a thought ~ vb **phrased; phras·ing** : express in a particular manner

phrase·ol·o·gy \₁frāzē'äləjē\ n, pl **-gies** : manner of phrasing

phy·lum \'fīləm\ n, pl **-la** \-lə\ : major division of the plant or animal kingdom

phys·ic \'fizik\ n : medicine that purges

phys·i·cal \'fizikəl\ adj **1** : relating to nature **2** : material as opposed to mental or spiritual **3** : relating to the body —**phys·i·cal·ly** \-k(ə)lē\ adv

phy·si·cian \fə'zishən\ n : doctor of medicine

phys·i·cist \'fizəsəst\ n : specialist in physics

phys·ics \'fiziks\ n : science that deals with matter and motion

phys·i·og·no·my \₁fizē'ä(g)nəmē\ n, pl -mies : facial appearance esp. as a reflection of inner character

phys·i·ol·o·gy \₁fizē'äləjē\ n **1** : science dealing with the functioning of living matter and beings **2** : functional processes in an organism —**phys·i·o·log·i·cal** \-ēə'läjikəl\, **phys·i·o·log·ic** \-ik\ adj —**phys·i·ol·o·gist** \-ē'äləjəst\ n

phy·sique \fə'zēk\ n : build of a person's body

pi \'pī\ n, pl **pis** \'pīz\ : symbol π denoting the ratio of the circumference of a circle to its diameter or the ratio itself

pi·a·nist \pē'anəst, 'pēanəst\ n : one who plays the piano

pi·ano \pē'anō\ n, pl **-anos** : musical instrument with strings sounded by hammers operated from a keyboard

pi·az·za \pē'azə, -'atsə\ n, pl **-zas** or **-ze** \-'at(₁)sā, -'ät-\ : open square in a town

pic·a·yune \₁pikē'(y)ün\ adj : trivial or petty

pic·co·lo \'pikə₁lō\ n, pl **-los** : small shrill flute

¹pick \'pik\ vb **1** : break up with a pointed instrument **2** : remove bit by bit **3** : gather by plucking **4** : select **5** : rob **6** : provoke **7** : unlock with a wire **8** : eat sparingly ~ n **1** : act of choosing **2** : choicest one —**pick·er** n —**pick up** vb **1** : improve **2** : put in order

²pick n : pointed digging tool

pick·ax n : pick

pick·er·el \'pik(ə)rəl\ n, pl **-el** or **-els** : small pike

¹pick·et \'pikət\ n **1** : pointed stake (as for a fence) **2** : worker demonstrating on strike ~ vb : demonstrate as a picket

pick·le \'pikəl\ n : brine or vinegar solution for preserving foods or a food preserved in a pickle —**pickle** vb

pick·pock·et n : one who steals from pockets

pick-up \'pik₁əp\ n **1** : revival or acceleration **2** : light truck with an open body

pic·nic \'pik₁nik\ n : outing with food usu. eaten in the open ~ vb **-nicked; -nick·ing** : go on a picnic

pic·to·ri·al \pik'tōrēəl\ adj : relating to pictures

pic·ture \'pikchər\ n **1** : representation by painting, drawing, or photography **2** : vivid description **3** : image or copy **4** : movie ~ vb **-tured; -tur·ing** : form a mental image of

pic·tur·esque \,pikchə'resk\ *adj* : attractive or charming enough to be suitable for a picture —**pic·tur·esque·ness** *n*

pie \'pī\ *n* : pastry crust and a filling

pie·bald \'pī,bȯld\ *adj* : blotched with white and black

piece \'pēs\ *n* **1** : part of a whole **2** : one of a group or set ~ *vb* **pieced; piec·ing** : join into a whole

piece·meal \-,mēl\ *adv or adj* : gradually

pied \'pīd\ *adj* : colored in blotches

pier \'piər\ *n* **1** : support for a bridge span **2** : deck or wharf built out over water **3** : pillar

pierce \'piərs\ *vb* **pierced; pierc·ing** **1** : enter or thrust into or through **2** : penetrate **3** : see through

pi·ety \'pīətē\ *n, pl* **-eties** : devotion to religion

pig \'pig\ *n* **1** : young swine **2** : dirty or greedy individual **3** : a casting (as of iron) run directly from a furnace into a mold —**pig·let** \-lət\ *n* —**pig·pen** *n* —**pig·sty** *n*

pi·geon \'pijən\ *n* : stout-bodied short-legged bird

pi·geon·hole *n* : small open compartment for letters or documents ~ *vb* **1** : place in a pigeonhole **2** : classify

pig·gish \'pigish\ *adj* : greedy

pig·gy·back \'pigē,bak\ *adv or adj* : up on the back and shoulders

pig·head·ed \-'hedəd\ *adj* : stubborn

pig·ment \'pigmənt\ *n* : coloring matter —**pig·men·ta·tion** *n*

pigmy *var of* PYGMY

pig·tail *n* : tight braid of hair

¹pike \'pīk\ *n, pl* **pike** *or* **pikes** : large freshwater fish

²pike *n* : former weapon consisting of a long wooden staff with a steel point —**pike·staff** *n*

³pike *n* : turnpike

pi·las·ter \'pī,lastər, pə'las-\ *n* : slightly projecting upright column

¹pile \'pīl\ *n* : supporting pillar driven into the ground

²pile *n* : quantity of things thrown on one another ~ *vb* **piled; pil·ing** : heap up or accumulate

³pile *n* : surface of fine hairs or threads —**piled** *adj*

piles \'pīls\ *n pl* : hemorrhoids

pil·fer \'pilfər\ *vb* : steal in small quantities at a time

pil·grim \'pilgrəm\ *n* **1** : one who travels to a shrine or holy place in devotion **2** *cap* : one of the founding settlers in America in 1620

pil·grim·age \-grəmij\ *n* : pilgrim's journey

pill \'pil\ *n* : small rounded mass of medicine —**pill·box** *n*

pil·lage \'pilij\ *vb* **-laged; -lag·ing** : take booty —**pillage** *n*

pil·lar \'pilər\ *n* : upright usu. supporting column or shaft —**pil·lared** *adj*

pil·lo·ry \'pil(ə)rē\ *n, pl* **-ries** : wooden frame for public punishment with holes for the head and hands ~ *vb* **-ried; -ry·ing** **1** : set in a pillory **2** : expose to public scorn

pil·low \'pilō\ *n* : soft cushion for the head —**pil·low·case** *n*

pi·lot \'pīlət\ *n* **1** : helmsman **2** : person licensed to take ships into and out of a port **3** : guide **4** : one that flies an aircraft or spacecraft ~ *vb* : act as pilot of —**pi·lot·age** \-ij\ *n* —**pi·lot·less** *adj*

pi·men·to \pə'mentō\ *n, pl* **-tos** *or* **-to 1** : pimiento **2** : allspice

pi·mien·to \pə'm(y)entō\ *n, pl* **-tos** : mild red sweet pepper fruit

pimp \'pimp\ *n* : man who solicits clients for a prostitute —**pimp** *vb*

pim·ple \'pimpəl\ *n* : small inflamed swelling on the skin —**pim·ply** \-p(ə)lē\ *adj*

pin \'pin\ *n* **1** : fastener made of a small pointed piece of wire **2** : ornament or emblem fastened to clothing with a pin **3** : wooden object used as a target in bowling ~ *vb* **-nn- 1** : fasten with a pin **2** : hold fast or immobile —**pin·hole** *n*

pin·afore \'pinə,fōr\ *n* : sleeveless dress or apron fastened at the back

pin·cer \'pinsər\ *n* **1** *pl* : gripping tool with 2 jaws **2** : pincerlike claw

pinch \'pinch\ *vb* **1** : squeeze between the finger and thumb or between the jaws of a tool **2** : compress painfully ~ *n* **1** : critical point **2** : painful effect **3** : act of pinching **4** : very small quantity

pin·cush·ion *n* : cushion for storing pins

¹pine \'pīn\ *vb* **pined; pin·ing** **1** : lose health through distress **2** : yearn for intensely

²pine *n* : evergreen cone-bearing tree or its wood

pine·ap·ple *n* : tropical plant bearing an edible juicy fruit

pin·feath·er *n* : new feather just coming through the skin

¹pin·ion \'pinyən\ *vb* : restrain by binding the arms

²pinion *n* : small gear

pink \'piŋk\ *n* **1** : plant with narrow leaves and showy flowers **2** : light red

3 : highest degree —**pink** adj —**pink·ish** adj

pink·eye n : contagious eye inflammation

pin·na·cle \'pinikəl\ n : highest point

pi·noch·le \'pē,nəkəl\ n : card game played with a 48-card deck

pin·point vb : locate, hit, or aim with great precision

pint \'pīnt\ n : 1/2 quart

pin·to \'pin,tō\ n, pl **pintos** : spotted horse

pin·worm n : small parasitic intestinal worm

pi·o·neer \ˌpīə'niər\ n 1 : one that originates or helps open up a new line of thought or activity 2 : early settler ~ vb : act as a pioneer

pi·ous \'pīəs\ adj 1 : conscientious in religious practices 2 : affectedly religious —**pi·ous·ly** adv

pipe \'pīp\ n 1 : tube that produces music when air is forced through 2 : bagpipe 3 : long tube for conducting a fluid 4 : smoking tool ~ vb **piped; pip·ing 1** : play on a pipe 2 : speak in a high voice 3 : convey by pipes —**pip·er** n

pipe·line n 1 : line of pipe 2 : channel for information

pip·ing \'pīpiŋ\ n 1 : music of pipes 2 : narrow fold of material used to decorate edges or seams

pi·quant \'pēkənt\ adj 1 : tangy 2 : provocative or charming —**pi·quan·cy** \-kənsē\ n

pique \'pēk\ n : resentment ~ vb **piqued; piqu·ing 1** : offend 2 : arouse

pi·qué, pi·que \pi'kā\ n : durable ribbed clothing fabric

pi·ra·cy \'pīrəsē\ n, pl **-cies 1** : robbery on the seas 2 : unauthorized use of another's production or invention

pi·ra·nha \pə'ranyə, -'ränyə\ n : small voracious So. American fish

pi·rate \'pīrət\ n : one who commits piracy —**pirate** vb —**pi·rat·i·cal** \pə'ratikəl, pī-\ adj

pir·ou·ette \ˌpirü'wet\ n : full turn on the toe or ball of one foot in ballet —**pirouette** vb

pis pl of PI

pis·ta·chio \pə'stashēˌō, -'stäsh-\ n, pl **-chios** : small tree bearing a greenish edible seed or its seed

pis·til \'pistᵊl\ n : female reproductive organ in a flower —**pis·til·late** \'pistə,lāt\ adj

pis·tol \'pistᵊl\ n : firearm held with one hand

pis·ton \'pistən\ n : sliding piece that

receives and transmits motion usu. inside a cylinder

¹**pit** \'pit\ n 1 : hole or shaft in the ground 2 : sunken or enclosed place for a special purpose 3 : hell 4 : hollow or indentation ~ vb **-tt- 1** : form pits in 2 : become marred with pits

²**pit** n : stony seed of some fruits ~ vb **-tt-** : remove the pit from

¹**pitch** \'pich\ n : resin from conifers

²**pitch** vb 1 : erect and fix firmly in place 2 : throw 3 : set at a particular level 4 : fall headlong ~ n 1 : action or manner of pitching 2 : degree of slope 3 : relative highness of a tone —**pitched** adj

pitch·blende \'pich,blend\ n : mineral source of uranium

¹**pitch·er** \'pichər\ n : container for liquids

²**pitcher** n : one that pitches

pitch·fork n : long-handled fork for pitching hay

pit·e·ous \'pitēəs\ adj : arousing pity —**pit·e·ous·ly** adv

pit·fall \'pit,fól\ n : hidden danger

pith \'pith\ n 1 : spongy plant tissue 2 : essential or meaningful part —**pithy** adj

piti·able \'pitēəbəl\ adj : pitiful

piti·ful \'pitifəl\ adj 1 : arousing or deserving pity 2 : contemptible —**piti·ful·ly** \-f(ə)lē\ adv

pit·tance \'pitᵊns\ n : small portion or amount

pi·tu·itary \pə't(y)üəˌterē\ adj : relating to or being a small gland attached to the brain

pity \'pitē\ n, pl **pit·ies 1** : sympathetic sorrow 2 : something to be regretted ~ vb **pit·ied; pity·ing** : feel pity for —**piti·less** adj —**piti·less·ly** adv

piv·ot \'pivət\ n : fixed pin on which something turns ~ vb : turn on or as if on a pivot —**pivot** adj —**piv·ot·al** adj

pix·ie, pixy \'piksē\ n, pl **pix·ies** : mischievous sprite

piz·za \'pētsə\ n : thin pie of bread dough spread with a spiced mixture (as of tomatoes, cheese, and meat)

piz·ze·ria \ˌpētsə'rēə\ n : pizza restaurant

plac·ard \'plakərd, -ˌärd\ n : poster ~ vb : display placards on or on

pla·cate \'plā,kāt, 'plak,āt\ vb **-cat·ed; -cat·ing** : appease —**plac·a·ble** \'plakəbəl, 'plāka-\ adj

place \'plās\ n 1 : space or room 2 : indefinite area 3 : a particular building, locality, area, or part 4

: relative position in a scale or sequence 5 : seat 6 : job ~ *vb* placed; plac·ing 1 : put in a place 2 : identify —place·ment *n*

pla·cen·ta \plə'sentə\ *n, pl* -tas *or* -tae \-(,)ē\ : structure by which a mammal is nourished before birth —pla·cen·tal \-'sent²l\ *adj*

plac·id \'plasəd\ *adj* : undisturbed or peaceful —pla·cid·i·ty \pla'sidətē\ *n* —plac·id·ly *adv*

pla·gia·rize \'plājə,rīz\ *vb* -rized; -riz·ing : use (words or ideas) of another as if your own —pla·gia·rism \-,rizəm\ *n* —pla·gia·rist \-rəst\ *n*

plague \'plāg\ *n* 1 : disastrous evil 2 : destructive contagious bacterial disease ~ *vb* plagued; plagu·ing 1 : afflict with disease or disaster 2 : harass

plaid \'plad\ *n* : woolen fabric with a pattern of crossing stripes or the pattern itself —plaid *adj*

¹plain \'plān\ *n* : expanse of relatively level treeless country

²plain *adj* 1 : lacking ornament 2 : not concealed or disguised 3 : easily understood 4 : frank 5 : not fancy or pretty —plain·ly *adv* —plain·ness \'plānnəs\ *n*

plaint \'plānt\ *n* : complaint

plain·tiff \'plāntəf\ *n* : complaining party in a lawsuit

plain·tive \'plāntiv\ *adj* : expressive of suffering or woe —plain·tive·ly *adv*

plait \'plāt, 'plat\ *n* 1 : pleat 2 : braid of hair or straw —plait *vb*

plan \'plan\ *n* 1 : drawing or diagram 2 : method for accomplishing something ~ *vb* -nn- 1 : form a plan of 2 : intend —plan·less *adj* —plan·ner *n*

¹plane \'plān\ *vb* planed; plan·ing : smooth or level off with a plane ~ *n* : smoothing or shaping tool —plan·er *n*

²plane *n* 1 : level surface 2 : level of existence, consciousness, or development 3 : airplane ~ *adj* 1 : flat 2 : dealing with flat surfaces or figures

plan·et \'planət\ *n* : celestial body that revolves around the sun —plan·e·tary \-ə,terē\ *adj*

plan·e·tar·i·um \,planə'terēəm\ *n, pl* -iums *or* -ia \-ēə\ : building or room housing a device to project images of celestial bodies

plank \'plaŋk\ *n* 1 : heavy thick board 2 : article in the platform of a political party —plank·ing *n*

plank·ton \'plaŋktən\ *n* : tiny aquatic animal and plant life —plank·ton·ic \plaŋk'tänik\ *adj*

plant \'plant\ *vb* 1 : set in the ground to grow 2 : place firmly or forcibly ~ *n* 1 : living thing without sense organs that cannot move about 2 : land, buildings, and machinery used esp. in manufacture

¹plan·tain \'plant²n\ *n* : short-stemmed herb with tiny greenish flowers

²plantain *n* : banana plant with starchy greenish fruit

plan·ta·tion \plan'tāshən\ *n* : agricultural estate worked by resident laborers

plant·er \'plantər\ *n* 1 : plantation owner 2 : plant container

plaque \'plak\ *n* : commemorative tablet

plas·ma \'plazmə\ *n* : watery part of blood —plas·mat·ic \plaz'matik\ *adj*

plas·ter \'plastər\ *n* 1 : medicated dressing 2 : hardening paste for coating walls and ceilings ~ *vb* : cover with plaster —plas·ter·er *n* —plas·tery *adj*

plas·tic \'plastik\ *adj* : capable of being molded ~ *n* : material that can be formed into rigid objects, films, or filaments —plas·tic·i·ty \plas'tisətē\ *n*

plate \'plāt\ *n* 1 : flat thin piece 2 : plated metalware 3 : shallow usu. circular dish 4 : denture or the part of it that fits to the mouth 5 : something printed from an engraving ~ *vb* plat·ed; plat·ing : overlay with metal —plat·ing *n*

pla·teau \pla'tō\ *n, pl* -teaus *or* -teaux \-'tōz\ : large level area raised above adjacent land

plat·form \'plat,fòrm\ *n* 1 : raised flooring or stage 2 : declaration of principles for a political party

plat·i·num \'platnəm, -³nəm\ *n* : heavy silver-white metallic chemical element

plat·i·tude \'platə,t(y)üd\ *n* : trite remark —plat·i·tu·di·nous \,platə't(y)üdnəs, -³nəs\ *adj*

pla·toon \plə'tün\ *n* : small military unit

platoon sergeant *n* : noncommissioned officer in the army ranking below a first sergeant

plat·ter \'platər\ *n* : large serving plate

platy·pus \'platipəs\ *n* : small aquatic egg-laying mammal

plau·dit \'plòdət\ *n* : act of applause

plau·si·ble \'plòzəbəl\ *adj* : reasonable or believeable —plau·si·bil·i·ty \,plòzə'bilətē\ *n* —plau·si·bly \-blē\ *adv*

play \'plā\ *n* **1** : action in a game **2** : recreational activity **3** : stage representation of a drama **4** : light or fitful movement **5** : free movement ~ *vb* **1** : engage in recreation **2** : move or toy with aimlessly **3** : perform music **4** : act in a drama —**play·act·ing** *n* —**play·er** *n* —**play·ful** \-fəl\ *adj* —**play·ful·ly** *adv* —**play·ful·ness** *n* —**play·go·er** *n* —**play·let** \-lət\ *n* —**play·pen** *n* —**play·suit** *n*

play·ground *n* : place for children to play

play·house *n* **1** : theater **2** : small house for children to play in

playing card *n* : one of a set of 24 to 78 cards marked to show its rank and suit and used to play a game of cards

play·mate *n* : companion in play

play·off *n* : contest or series of contests to determine a champion

play·thing *n* : toy

play·wright \-₁rīt\ *n* : writer of plays

pla·za \'plazə, 'pläz-\ *n* : public square

plea \'plē\ *n* **1** : defendant's answer to charges **2** : urgent request

plead \'plēd\ *vb* **plead·ed** \'plēdəd\ *or* **pled** \'pled\; **plead·ing 1** : argue for or against in court **2** : answer to a charge or indictment **3** : appeal earnestly —**plead·er** *n*

pleas·ant \'plez²nt\ *adj* **1** : giving pleasure **2** : marked by pleasing behavior or appearance —**pleas·ant·ly** *adv* —**pleas·ant·ness** *n*

pleas·ant·ries \-²ntrēz\ *n pl* : pleasant and casual conversation

please \'plēz\ *vb* **pleased; pleas·ing 1** : give pleasure or satisfaction to **2** : desire or intend **3** : be willing to

pleas·ing \'plēziŋ\ *adj* : giving pleasure —**pleas·ing·ly** *adv*

plea·sur·able \'plezh(ə)rəbəl\ *adj* : pleasant —**plea·sur·ably** \-blē\ *adv*

plea·sure \'plezhər\ *n* **1** : desire or inclination **2** : enjoyment **3** : source of delight

pleat \'plēt\ *vb* : arrange in pleats ~ *n* : fold in cloth

ple·be·ian \pli'bēən\ *n* : one of the common people ~ *adj* : ordinary

pleb·i·scite \'plebə₁sīt, -sət\ *n* : vote of the people (as of a country) on a proposal submitted to them

pledge \'plej\ *n* **1** : something given as security **2** : promise or vow ~ *vb* **pledged; pledg·ing 1** : offer as or bind by a pledge **2** : promise

ple·na·ry \'plēnərē, 'plen-\ *adj* : full

pleni·po·ten·tia·ry \₁plenəpə-'tench(ə)rē, -¹'tenchē₁erē\ *n* : diplomatic agent having full authority —**plenipotentiary** *adj*

plen·i·tude \'plenə₁t(y)üd\ *n* **1** : completeness **2** : abundance

plen·te·ous \'plentēəs\ *adj* : existing in plenty

plen·ti·ful \'plentifəl\ *adj* : abundant —**plen·ti·ful·ly** *adv*

plen·ty \'plentē\ *n* : more than adequate number or amount

pleth·o·ra \'plethərə\ *n* : excess

pleu·ri·sy \'plurəsē\ *n* : inflammation of the chest membrane

pli·able \'plīabəl\ *adj* : flexible

pli·ant \'plīənt\ *adj* : flexible —**pli·an·cy** \-ənsē\ *n*

pli·ers \'plī(ə)rz\ *n pl* : pinching or gripping tool

¹plight \'plīt\ *vb* : pledge

²plight *n* : bad state

plod \'pläd\ *vb* -**dd**- **1** : walk heavily or slowly **2** : work laboriously and monotonously —**plod·der** *n* —**plod·ding·ly** \-iŋlē\ *adv*

plot \'plät\ *n* **1** : small area of ground **2** : ground plan **3** : main story development (as of a book or movie) **4** : secret plan for doing something ~ *vb* -**tt**- **1** : make a plot or plan of **2** : plan or contrive —**plot·ter** *n*

plo·ver \'pləvər, 'plōvər\ *n, pl* -**ver** *or* -**vers** : shorebird related to the sandpiper

plow, plough \'plaù\ *n* **1** : tool used to turn soil **2** : plowlike device ~ *vb* **1** : break up with a plow **2** : cleave or move through like a plow —**plow·able** *adj* —**plow·er** *n* —**plow·man** \-mən, -₁man\ *n*

plow·share \-₁she(ə)r\ *n* : plow part that cuts the earth

ploy \'plòi\ *n* : clever plan or maneuver

pluck \'plək\ *vb* **1** : pull off or out **2** : tug or twitch ~ *n* **1** : act or instance of plucking **2** : spirit or courage

plucky \'pləkē\ *adj* **pluck·i·er; -est** : courageous or spirited

plug \'pləg\ *n* **1** : something for sealing an opening **2** : electrical connector at the end of a cord **3** : piece of favorable publicity ~ *vb* -**gg**- **1** : stop or make tight or secure by inserting a plug **2** : publicize

plum \'pləm\ *n* **1** : smooth-skinned juicy fruit **2** : fine reward

plum·age \'plümij\ *n* : feathers of a bird

plumb \'pləm\ *n* : weight on the end of a line to show vertical direction ~ *adv* **1** : vertically **2** : completely ~ *vb*

: sound or test with a plumb ~ *adj* : vertical

plumb·er \'pləmər\ *n* : one who repairs usu. water pipes and fixtures

plumb·ing \'pləmiŋ\ *n* : system of water pipes in a building

plume \'plüm\ *n* : large, conspicuous, or showy feather ~ *vb* **plumed; plum·ing 1** : provide or deck with feathers **2** : indulge in pride —**plumed** \'plümd\ *adj* —**plumy** \'plümē\ *adj*

plum·met \'pləmət\ *vb* : drop straight down

¹plump \'pləmp\ *vb* : drop suddenly or heavily ~ *adv* **1** : suddenly and heavily **2** : directly

²plump *adj* : having a full rounded form —**plump·ness** *n*

plun·der \'pləndər\ *vb* : rob or take goods by force (as in war) ~ *n* : something taken in plundering —**plun·der·er** *n*

plunge \'plənj\ *vb* **plunged; plung·ing 1** : thrust or dive into something **2** : begin an action suddenly **3** : dive or throw oneself forward or down ~ *n* : act or instance of plunging —**plung·er** *n*

plu·ral \'plürəl\ *adj* : relating to a word form denoting more than one —**plu·ral** *n*

plu·ral·i·ty \plü'ralətē\ *n, pl* **-ties** : greatest number of votes cast when not a majority

plu·ral·ize \'plürə,līz\ *vb* **-ized; -iz·ing** : make plural —**plu·ral·iza·tion** \,plürələ'zāshən\ *n*

plus \'pləs\ *prep* : with the addition of ~ *n* **1** : sign + (**plus sign**) in mathematics to require addition **2** : added or positive quantity **3** : advantage ~ *adj* : being more or in addition

plush \'pləsh\ *n* : fabric with a long pile ~ *adj* : luxurious —**plush·ly** *adv* —**plushy** *adj*

plu·toc·ra·cy \plü'täkrəsē\ *n* **1** : government by the wealthy **2** : a controlling class of rich men —**plu·to·crat** \'plütə,krat\ *n* —**plu·to·crat·ic** \,plütə'kratik\ *adj*

plu·to·ni·um \plü'tōnēəm\ *n* : radioactive chemical element

¹ply \'plī\ *n, pl* **plies** : fold, thickness, or strand of which something is made

²ply *vb* **plied; ply·ing 1** : use or work at **2** : keep supplying something to **3** : travel over regularly

ply·wood \-\ *n* : sheets of wood glued and pressed together

pneu·mat·ic \n(y)ü'matik\ *adj* **1** : moved by air pressure **2** : filled with

compressed air —**pneu·mat·i·cal·ly** \-ik(ə)lē\ *adv*

pneu·mo·nia \n(y)ü'mōnyə\ *n* : inflammatory lung disease

¹poach \'pōch\ *vb* : cook in simmering liquid

²poach *vb* : hunt or fish illegally —**poach·er** *n*

pock \'päk\ *n* : small swelling on the skin or its scar —**pock·mark** *n* —**pock-marked** *adj*

pock·et \'päkət\ *n* **1** : small open bag sewn into a garment **2** : container or receptacle **3** : isolated area or group ~ *vb* : put in a pocket —**pock·et·ful** \-,fül\ *n*

pock·et·book *n* **1** : purse **2** : financial resources

pock·et·knife *n* : knife with a folding blade for the pocket

pod \'päd\ *n* **1** : dry fruit that splits open when ripe **2** : detachable spacecraft compartment

po·di·a·try \pə'dīətrē, pō-\ *n* : branch of medicine dealing with the foot —**po·di·a·trist** \pə'dīətrəst, pō-\ *n*

po·di·um \'pōdēəm\ *n, pl* **-di·ums** or **-dia** \-ēə\ : dais

po·em \'pōəm\ *n* : composition in verse

po·et \'pōət\ *n* : writer of poetry

po·et·ry \'pōətrē\ *n* **1** : metrical writing **2** : poems —**po·et·ic** \pō'etik\, **po·et·i·cal** \-ikəl\ *adj*

po·grom \pə'gräm, 'pōgrəm, 'pägrəm\ *n* : organized massacre

poi·gnant \'pòinyənt\ *adj* **1** : emotionally painful **2** : deeply moving —**poi·gnan·cy** \-nyənsē\ *n*

poin·set·tia \pòin'setēə, -'setə\ *n* : showy tropical American plant

point \'pòint\ *n* **1** : individual often essential detail **2** : purpose **3** : particular place, time, or stage **4** : sharp end **5** : projecting piece of land **6** : dot or period **7** : division of the compass **8** : unit of counting ~ *vb* **1** : sharpen **2** : indicate direction by extending a finger **3** : direct attention to **4** : aim —**point·less** *adj*

point-blank *adj* **1** : so close to a target that a missile fired goes straight to it **2** : direct —**point-blank** *adv*

point·er \'pòintər\ *n* **1** : one that points out **2** : large short-haired hunting dog **3** : hint or tip

poise \'pòiz\ *vb* **poised; pois·ing** : balance ~ *n* : self-possessed calmness

poi·son \'pòiz²n\ *n* : chemical that can injure or kill ~ *vb* **1** : injure or kill with poison **2** : apply poison to **3** : affect destructively —**poi·son·er**

\-nər, -ᵊnər\ *n* —**poi·son·ous** \'póiznəs, -ᵊnəs\ *adj*

poke \'pōk\ *vb* **poked; pok·ing 1** : prod **2** : dawdle ~ *n* : quick thrust

¹pok·er \'pōkər\ *n* : rod for stirring a fire

²po·ker *n* : card game

po·lar \'pōlər\ *adj* : relating to a geographical or magnetic pole

po·lar·ize \'pōlə,rīz\ *vb* **-ized; -iz·ing** : cause to have magnetic poles —**po·lar·iza·tion** \,pōlərə'zāshən\ *n*

¹pole \'pōl\ *n* : long slender piece of wood or metal

²pole *n* **1** : either end of the earth's axis **2** : battery terminal **3** : either end of a magnet

pole·cat \'pōl,kat\ *n, pl* **polecats** or **polecat 1** : European carnivorous mammal **2** : skunk

po·lem·ics \pə'lemiks\ *n sing* or *pl* : practice of disputation —**polemic, po·lem·i·cal** \-ikəl\ *adj* —**po·lem·i·cist** \-səst\ *n*

po·lice \pə'lēs\ *n, pl* **-lice 1** : department of government that keeps public order and enforces the laws **2** : members of the police ~ *vb* **-liced; -lic·ing** : regulate and keep in order —**po·lice·man** \-mən\ *n* —**po·lice·wom·an** *n*

¹pol·i·cy \'pāləsē\ *n, pl* **-cies** : course of action selected to guide decisions

²policy *n, pl* **-cies** : insurance contract —**pol·i·cy·hold·er** *n*

po·lio \'pōlē,ō\ *n* : poliomyelitis —**polio** *adj*

po·lio·my·eli·tis \-,mīə'lītəs\ *n* : acute virus disease marked by fever, paralysis, and atrophy of skeletal muscles

pol·ish \'pālish\ *vb* **1** : make smooth and glossy **2** : develop or refine ~ *n* **1** : shiny surface **2** : refinement

po·lite \pə'līt\ *adj* **-lit·er; -est** : marked by correct social conduct —**po·lite·ly** *adv* —**po·lite·ness** *n*

pol·i·tic \'pālə,tik\ *adj* : shrewdly tactful

pol·i·tics \'pālə,tiks\ *n sing* or *pl* : practice of government and managing of public affairs —**po·lit·i·cal** \pə'litikəl\ *adj* —**pol·i·ti·cian** \,pālə'tishən\ *n*

pol·ka \'pōlkə\ *n* : lively couple dance —**polka** *vb*

poll \'pōl\ *n* **1** : head **2** : place where votes are cast —usu. pl. **3** : a sampling of opinion ~ *vb* **1** : cut off **2** : receive or record votes **3** : question in a poll —**poll·ster** \-stər\ *n*

pol·len \'pālən\ *n* : spores of a seed plant

pol·li·na·tion \,pālə'nāshən\ *n* : the carrying of pollen to fertilize the seed —**pol·li·nate** \'pālə,nāt\ *vb* —**pol·li·na·tor** \-ər\ *n*

pol·li·wog, pol·ly·wog \'pālē,wäg\ *n* : tadpole

pol·lute \pə'lüt\ *vb* **-lut·ed; -lut·ing** : make impure esp. by contaminating with man-made waste —**pol·lut·ant** \-'lüt⁹nt\ *n* —**pol·lut·er** *n* —**pol·lu·tion** \-'lüshən\ *n*

po·lo \'pōlō\ *n* : game played by 2 teams on horseback using long-handled mallets to drive a wooden ball

pol·troon \pal'trün\ *n* : coward

poly·es·ter \'pälē,estər\ *n* : synthetic fiber

po·lyg·a·my \pə'ligəmē\ *n* : marriage to several spouses at the same time —**po·lyg·a·mist** \-məst\ *n* —**po·lyg·a·mous** \-məs\ *adj*

poly·gon \'päli,gän\ *n* : closed plane figure with straight sides —**po·lyg·o·nal** \pə'ligən⁹l\ *adj*

poly·syl·la·ble \'päli,siləbəl\ *n* : a word of more than 3 syllables —**poly·syl·lab·ic** \,pälisə'labik\ *adj*

poly·tech·nic \,päli'teknik\ *adj* : relating to many arts or sciences

poly·the·ism \'pälithē,izəm\ *n* : worship of many gods —**poly·the·ist** \-,thēəst\ *adj* or *n*

po·made \pō'mād, -'mäd\ *n* : perfumed hair ointment

pome·gran·ate \'päm(ə),granət\ *n* : tropical reddish fruit with many seeds

pom·mel \'pəmal, 'päm-\ *n* **1** : knob on the hilt of a sword **2** : knob at the front of a saddle ~ \'pəmal\ *vb* **-meled** or **-melled; -mel·ing** or **-mel·ling** : pummel

pomp \'pämp\ *n* **1** : brilliant display **2** : ostentation

pomp·ous \'pämpəs\ *adj* : pretentiously dignified —**pom·pos·i·ty** \päm'päsətē\ *n* —**pomp·ous·ly** *adv*

pon·cho \'pänchō\ *n, pl* **-chos** : blanketlike cloak

pond \'pänd\ *n* : small body of water

pon·der \'pändər\ *vb* : weigh in the mind

pon·der·ous \'pänd(ə)rəs\ *adj* **1** : very heavy **2** : clumsy **3** : oppressively dull

pon·tiff \'päntəf\ *n* **1** : bishop **2** : pope —**pon·tif·i·cal** \pän'tifikəl\ *adj*

pon·tif·i·cate \pän'tifə,kāt\ *vb* **-cat·ed; -cat·ing** : talk pompously

pon·toon \pän'tün\ n : flat-bottomed boat or float

po·ny \'pōnē\ n, pl **-nies** : small horse

poo·dle \'püd³l\ n : dog with a curly coat

¹pool \'pül\ n 1 : small body of water 2 : puddle

²pool n 1 : game of pocket billiards 2 : amount contributed by participants in a joint venture ~ vb : contribute to a common fund

poop \'püp\ n : enclosed super-structure at the stern of a ship

poor \'pur\ adj 1 : lacking material possessions 2 : less than adequate —**poor·ly** adv

pop \'päp\ vb **-pp-** 1 : move suddenly 2 : burst with or make a sharp sound 3 : protrude ~ n 1 : sharp explosive sound 2 : flavored soft drink

pop·corn \'päp,korn\ n : corn whose kernels burst open into a white mass when heated

pope \'pōp\ n, often cap : head of the Roman Catholic Church

pop·lar \'päplər\ n : slender quick-growing tree

pop·lin \'päplən\ n : strong plain-woven fabric with crosswise ribs

pop·over \'päp,ōvər\ n : egg-rich biscuit that expands into a hollow shell as it bakes

pop·py \'päpē\ n, pl **-pies** : herb with showy flowers

pop·u·lace \'päpyələs\ n 1 : common people 2 : population

pop·u·lar \'päpyələr\ adj 1 : relating to the general public 2 : widely accepted 3 : commonly liked —**pop·u·lar·i·ty** \,päpyə'larətē\ n —**pop·u·lar·ize** \'päpyələ,rīz\ vb —**pop·u·lar·ly** \-lərlē\ adv

pop·u·late \'päpyə,lāt\ vb **-lat·ed; -lat·ing** : inhabit or occupy

pop·u·la·tion \,päpyə'lāshən\ n : people or number of people in a country or area

pop·u·list \'päpyələst\ n : advocate of the rights of the common people —**pop·u·lism** \-,lizəm\ n

pop·u·lous \'päpyələs\ adj : densely populated —**pop·u·lous·ness** n

por·ce·lain \'pors(ə)lən\ n : fine-grained ceramic ware

porch \'pōrch\ n : covered entrance

por·cine \'por,sīn\ adj : relating to or suggesting swine

por·cu·pine \'porkyə,pīn\ n : mammal with sharp quills

¹pore \'por\ vb **pored; por·ing** : read attentively

²pore n : tiny hole —**pored** adj

pork \'pork\ n : pig meat

por·nog·ra·phy \por'nägrəfē\ n : depiction of erotic behavior meant chiefly to cause sexual excitement —**por·no·graph·ic** \,pornə'grafik\ adj

po·rous \'porəs\ adj : permeable to fluids —**po·ros·i·ty** \pə'räsətē\ n

por·poise \'porpəs\ n 1 : small whale with a blunt snout 2 : dolphin

por·ridge \'porij\ n : soft boiled cereal

por·rin·ger \'porənjər\ n : low one-handled metal bowl or cup for children

¹port \'port\ n 1 : harbor 2 : city with a harbor

²port n : inlet or outlet (as in an engine) for a fluid 2 : porthole

³port n : left side of a ship or airplane looking forward —**port** adj

⁴port n : sweet wine

por·ta·ble \'portəbəl\ adj : capable of being carried —**portable** n

por·tage \'portij, por'täzh\ n : carrying of boats overland between navigable bodies of water or the route where this is done —**portage** vb

por·tal \'port³l\ n : entrance

por·tend \por'tend\ vb : give a warning of beforehand

por·tent \'por,tent\ n : something that foreshadows a coming event —**por·ten·tous** \por'tentəs\ adj

por·ter \'portər\ n : baggage carrier

por·ter·house \-,haus\ n : choice cut of steak

port·fo·lio \port'fōlē,ō\ n, pl **-lios** 1 : portable case for papers 2 : investor's securities

port·hole \'port,hōl\ n : opening in the side of a ship or aircraft

por·ti·co \'porti,kō\ n, pl **-coes** or **-cos** : colonnade forming a porch

por·tion \'porshən\ n : part or share of a whole ~ vb : divide into or allot portions

port·ly \'portlē\ adj **-li·er; -est** : somewhat stout

por·trait \'portrət, -,trāt\ n : picture of a person —**por·trait·ist** \-əst\ n —**por·trai·ture** \'portrə,chùr\ n

por·tray \por'trā\ vb 1 : make a picture of 2 : describe in words 3 : play the role of —**por·tray·al** n

pose \'pōz\ vb **posed; pos·ing** 1 : assume a posture or attitude 2 : propose 3 : pretend to be what one is not ~ n 1 : sustained posture 2 : pretense —**pos·er** n

posh \'päsh\ adj : elegant

po·si·tion \pə'zishən\ n 1 : stand taken on a question 2 : place or location 3 : status 4 : job —**position** vb

pos·i·tive \'päzətiv\ *adj* **1** : definite **2** : confident **3** : relating to or being an adjective or adverb form that denotes no increase **4** : greater than zero **5** : having a deficiency of electrons **6** : affirmative —**pos·i·tive·ly** *adv* —**pos·i·tive·ness** *n*

pos·se \'päsē\ *n* : emergency assistants of a sheriff

pos·sess \pə'zes\ *vb* **1** : have as property or as a quality **2** : control —**pos·ses·sion** \-'zeshən\ *n* —**pos·ses·sor** \-'zesər\ *n*

pos·ses·sive \pə'zesiv\ *adj* **1** : relating to a grammatical case denoting ownership **2** : jealous —**possessive** *n* —**pos·ses·sive·ness** *n*

pos·si·ble \'päsəbəl\ *adj* : that can be done **2** : potential —**pos·si·bil·i·ty** \ˌpäsə'bilətē\ *n* —**pos·si·bly** *adv*

pos·sum \'päsəm\ *n* : opossum

¹post \'pōst\ *n* : upright stake serving to support or mark ~ *vb* : put up or announce by a notice

²post *vb* **1** : mail **2** : inform

³post *n* **1** : sentry's station **2** : assigned task **3** : army camp ~ *vb* : station

post- *prefix* : after or subsequent to

postadolescence	postinoculation
postadolescent	postmarital
postattack	postmenopausal
postbaccalau-	postnatal
reate	postnuptial
postbiblical	postproduction
postcollege	postpubertal
postcolonial	postpuberty
postelection	postradiation
postexercise	postrecession
postfertilization	postretirement
postflight	postrevolutionary
postgame	postseason
postgraduate	postsecondary
postgraduation	postsurgical
postharvest	posttreatment
posthospital	posttrial
postimperial	postvaccination
postinaugural	postwar
postindustrial	

post·age \'pōstij\ *n* : fee for mail

post·al \'pōstᵊl\ *adj* : relating to the mail

post·card *n* : card for mailing a message

post·er \'pōstər\ *n* : large usu. printed notice

pos·te·ri·or \pō'stirēər, pä-\ *adj* : later **2** : situated behind ~ *n* : buttocks

pos·ter·i·ty \pä'sterətē\ *n* : succeeding generations

post·haste \'pōst'hāst\ *adv* : speedily

post·hu·mous \'päschəməs\ *adj* : occurring after one's death

post·man \'pōs(t)mən, -ˌman\ *n* : mailman

post·mark *n* : official mark on mail —**postmark** *vb*

post·mas·ter *n* : chief of a post office

post me·ri·di·em \'pōs(t)mə'ridēəm, -ˌem\ *adj* : being after noon

post·mor·tem \(')pōs(t)'mōrtəm\ *adj* : occurring or done after death ~ *n* : medical examination of a corpse

post office *n* : agency or building for mail service

post·op·er·a·tive \(')pōst'äp(ə)rətiv, -'äpəˌrāt-\ *adj* : following surgery

post·paid *adv* : with postage paid by the sender

post·par·tum \(')pōst'pärtəm\ *adj* : following childbirth —**postpartum** *adv*

post·pone \-'pōn\ *vb* **-poned; -pon·ing** : hold back to a later time —**post·pone·ment** *n*

post·script \'pō(s),skript\ *n* : added note

pos·tu·lant \'päschələnt\ *n* : candidate for a religious order

pos·tu·late \'päschəˌlāt\ *vb* **-lat·ed; -lat·ing** : assume as true ~ *n* : assumption

pos·ture \'päschər\ *n* : bearing of the body ~ *vb* **-tured; -tur·ing** : strike a pose

po·sy \'pōzē\ *n, pl* **-sies** : flower or bunch of flowers

pot \'pät\ *n* **1** : rounded container **2** : marijuana ~ *vb* **-tt-** : place in a pot —**pot·ful** *n*

po·ta·ble \'pōtəbəl\ *adj* : drinkable

pot·ash \'pätˌash\ *n* : white chemical salt

po·tas·si·um \pə'tasēəm\ *n* : silver-white metallic chemical element

po·ta·to \pə'tātō\ *n, pl* **-toes** : edible plant tuber

pot·bel·ly *n* : paunch —**pot·bel·lied** *adj*

po·tent \'pōtᵊnt\ *adj* : powerful or effective —**po·ten·cy** \-ᵊnsē\ *n*

po·ten·tate \'pōtᵊnˌtāt\ *n* : powerful ruler

po·ten·tial \pə'tenchəl\ *adj* : capable of becoming actual ~ *n* **1** : something that can become actual **2** : degree of electrification with reference to a standard —**po·ten·ti·al·i·ty** \pəˌtenchē'alətē\ *n* —**po·ten·tial·ly** *adv*

poth·er \'päthər\ *n* : fuss

po·tion \'pōshən\ *n* : liquid medicine or poison

pot·luck *n* : whatever food is available

pot·pour·ri \ˌpōpu̇'rē\ n : miscellaneous collection

pot-shot n 1 : casual or easy shot 2 : random critical remark

pot·ter \'pätər\ n : pottery maker

pot·tery \'pätərē\ n, pl **-ter·ies** : objects (as dishes) made from clay

pouch \'pau̇ch\ n 1 : small bag 2 : bodily sac

poul·tice \'pōltəs\ n : warm medicated dressing —**poultice** vb

poul·try \'pōltrē\ n : domesticated fowl

pounce \'pau̇ns\ vb **pounced; pounc·ing** : spring or swoop upon and seize

1pound \'pau̇nd\ n 1 : unit of weight equal to 16 ounces 2 : monetary unit (as of the United Kingdom) —**pound·age** \-ij\ n

2pound vb 1 : crush by beating 2 : strike heavily 3 : throb

3pound n : shelter for stray animals

pour \'pōr\ vb 1 : flow or supply copiously 2 : rain hard

pout \'pau̇t\ vb : look sullen —**pout** n

pov·er·ty \'pävərtē\ n 1 : lack of money or possessions 2 : poor quality

pow·der \'pau̇dər\ n : dry material of fine particles ~ vb 1 : sprinkle or cover with powder 2 : reduce to powder —**pow·dery** adj

pow·er \'pau̇(ə)r\ n 1 : position of authority 2 : ability to act 3 : one that has power 4 : physical might 5 : force or energy used to do work ~ vb : supply with power —**pow·er·ful** \-fəl\ adj —**pow·er·ful·ly** adv —**pow·er·less** adj

pow-wow \'pau̇ˌwau̇\ n : conference

pox \'päks\ n, pl **pox** or **pox·es** : disease marked by skin rash

prac·ti·ca·ble \'praktikəbəl\ adj : feasible —**prac·ti·ca·bil·i·ty** \ˌpraktikə'bilətē\ n

prac·ti·cal \'praktikəl\ adj 1 : relating to practice 2 : virtual 3 : capable of being put to use 4 : inclined to action as opposed to speculation —**prac·ti·cal·i·ty** \ˌprakti'kalətē\ n —**prac·ti·cal·ly** \'praktik(ə)lē\ adv

prac·tice, prac·tise \'praktəs\ vb **-ticed** or **-tised; -tic·ing** or **-tis·ing** 1 : perform repeatedly to become proficient 2 : do or perform customarily 3 : be professionally engaged in ~ n 1 : actual performance 2 : habit 3 : exercise for proficiency 4 : exercise of a profession

prac·ti·tio·ner \prak'tish(ə)nər\ n : one who practices a profession

prag·ma·tism \'pragmə,tizəm\ n

: practical approach to problems —**prag·mat·ic** \prag'matik\ adj

prai·rie \'pre(ə)rē\ n : broad grassy rolling tract of land

praise \'prāz\ vb **praised; prais·ing** 1 : express approval of 2 : glorify —**praise** n —**praise·wor·thy** adj

prance \'prans\ vb **pranced; pranc·ing** 1 : spring from the hind legs 2 : swagger —**prance** n —**pranc·er** n

prank \'praŋk\ n : playful or mischievous act —**prank·ster** \-stər\ n

prate \'prāt\ vb **prat·ed; prat·ing** : talk long and foolishly

prat·fall \'prat,-\ n : fall on the buttocks

prat·tle \'prat³l\ vb **-tled; -tling** : babble —**prattle** n

prawn \'prȯn\ n : shrimplike crustacean

pray \'prā\ vb 1 : entreat 2 : ask earnestly for something 3 : address a divinity

prayer \'praər\ n 1 : earnest request 2 : an addressing of a divinity 3 : words used in praying

praying mantis n : mantis

pre- prefix : before, prior to, or in advance

preadapt	precolonial
preaddress	precombustion
preadmission	precompute
preadolescence	preconceive
preadolescent	preconception
preadult	preconcerted
prealert	precondition
prealign	preconference
preallocate	preconstruct
preanesthetic	preconvention
prearraignment	precook
prearrange	precool
prearrangement	precut
preassemble	predawn
preassign	predefine
preaudit	predelinquent
preauthorize	predeparture
prebattle	predesignate
prebiblical	predesignation
prebirth	predetermine
prebreakfast	predischarge
prebuilt	predrill
precalculate	predug
precalculus	preedit
precampaign	preelection
precancel	preelectric
precancellation	preelectronic
precivilization	preemployment
preclean	preestablish
preclear	preexist
preclearance	preexistence
precollege	preexistent

prefight
prefilter
preform
pregame
preheat
preimmunization
preimmunize
preinaugural
preindustrial
preinoculate
preinoculation
preinterview
prejudge
prekindergarten
prelaunch
prelife
preload
premarital
premenopausal
premenstrual
premix
premodern
premodify
premoisten
premold
prenatal
prenotification
prenotify
prenuptial
preopening
preoperational
preordain
prepack
prepackage
prepay
preplan
preprocess
preproduction

preprofessional
preprogram
prepubertal
prepublication
prepunch
prepurchase
prerecord
preregister
preregistration
prerehearsal
prerelease
pre-Renaissance
preretirement
prerevolutionary
prerinse
preseason
preselect
preset
preshrink
presoak
presort
prestamp
presterilize
prestrike
presurgical
presweeten
pretape
preteen
pretelevision
pretournament
pretreat
pretreatment
pretrial
pretrip
prewar
prewash
prewrap

preach \\'prēch\\ vb 1 : deliver a sermon 2 : advocate earnestly —**preach·er** n —**preach·ment** n

pre·am·ble \\'prē,ambəl\\ n : introduction

pre·car·i·ous \\pri'karēəs\\ adj : dangerously insecure —**pre·car·i·ous·ly** adv —**pre·car·i·ous·ness** n

pre·cau·tion \\pri'kóshən\\ n : care taken beforehand —**pre·cau·tion·ary** \\-shə,nerē\\ adj

pre·cede \\pri'sēd\\ vb -**ced·ed**; -**ced·ing** : be, go, or come ahead of —**prec·e·dence** \\'presədəns, pri'sēd²ns\\ n

prec·e·dent \\'presədənt\\ n : something said or done earlier that serves as an example

pre·ced·ing \\pri'sēdiŋ\\ adj : that precedes

pre·cept \\'prē,sept\\ n : rule of action or conduct

pre·cep·tor \\pri'septər, 'prē,sep-\\ n : tutor

pre·cinct \\'prē,siŋkt\\ n 1 : district of a city 2 pl : vicinity

pre·cious \\'preshəs\\ adj 1 : of great value 2 : greatly cherished 3 : affected

prec·i·pice \\'presəpəs\\ n : steep cliff

pre·cip·i·tate \\pri'sipə,tāt\\ vb -**tat·ed**; -**tat·ing** 1 : cause to happen quickly or abruptly 2 : cause to separate out of a liquid ~ n : solid matter precipitated from a liquid ~ \\-'sipətət, -ə,tāt\\ adj : unduly hasty —**pre·cip·i·tate·ly** adv —**pre·cip·i·tate·ness** n —**pre·cip·i·tous** \\pri'sipətəs\\ adj —**pre·cip·i·tous·ly** adv

pre·cip·i·ta·tion \\pri,sipə'tāshən\\ n 1 : rash haste 2 : rain, snow, or hail

pré·cis \\prā'sē\\ n, pl **pré·cis** \\-'sēz\\ : concise summary of essential points

pre·cise \\pri'sīs\\ adj 1 : definite 2 : highly accurate —**pre·cise·ly** adv —**pre·cise·ness** n

pre·ci·sion \\pri'sizhən\\ n : quality or state of being precise

pre·clude \\pri'klüd\\ vb -**clud·ed**; -**clud·ing** : make impossible

pre·co·cious \\pri'kōshəs\\ adj : exceptionally advanced —**pre·co·cious·ly** adv —**pre·coc·i·ty** \\pri'käsətē\\ n

pre·cur·sor \\pri'kərsər\\ n : harbinger

pred·a·to·ry \\'predə,tōrē\\ adj : preying upon others —**pred·a·tor** \\'predətər\\ n

pre·de·ces·sor \\'predə,sesər, 'prēd-\\ n : one who has previously held a position

pre·des·tine \\prē'destən\\ vb : settle beforehand

pre·dic·a·ment \\pri'dikəmənt\\ n : difficult situation

pred·i·cate \\'predikət\\ n : part of a sentence that states something about the subject ~ \\'predə,kāt\\ vb -**cat·ed**; -**cat·ing** 1 : affirm 2 : establish —**pred·i·ca·tion** \\,predə'kāshən\\ n

pre·dict \\pri'dikt\\ vb : declare in advance —**pre·dict·able** \\-'diktəbəl\\ adj —**pre·dict·ably** \\-blē\\ adv —**pre·dic·tion** \\-'dikshən\\ n

pre·di·lec·tion \\,predəl'ekshən, ,prēd-\\ n : favorable inclination

pre·dis·pose \\,prēdis'pōz\\ vb : cause to be favorable to something beforehand —**pre·dis·po·si·tion** \\,prē,dispə'zishən\\ n

pre·dom·i·nate \\pri'dämə,nāt\\ vb : be superior —**pre·dom·i·nance** \\-nəns\\ n —**pre·dom·i·nant** \\-nənt\\ adj —**pre·dom·i·nant·ly** adv

pre·em·i·nent \\prē'emənənt\\ adj : having highest rank —**pre·em·i·nence** \\-nəns\\ n —**pre·em·i·nent·ly** adv

pre·empt \prē'empt\ vb 1 : seize for oneself 2 : take the place of —**pre·emp·tion** \-'empshən\ n

preen \'prēn\ vb : dress or smooth up (as feathers)

pre·fab·ri·cat·ed \'prē'fabrə,kātəd\ adj : manufactured for rapid assembly elsewhere —**pre·fab·ri·ca·tion** \,prē,fabri'kāshən\ n

pref·ace \'prefəs\ n : introductory comments ~ vb -aced; -ac·ing : introduce with a preface —**pref·a·to·ry** \'prefə,tōrē\ adj

pre·fect \'prē,fekt\ n : chief officer or judge —**pre·fec·ture** \-,fekchər\ n

pre·fer \pri'fər\ vb -rr- 1 : like better 2 : bring (as a charge) against a person —**pref·er·a·ble** \'pref(ə)rəbəl\ adj —**pref·er·a·bly** adv —**pref·er·ence** \-(ə)rəns\ n —**pref·er·en·tial** \,prefə'renchəl\ adj

pre·fer·ment \pri'fərmənt\ n : promotion

pre·fig·ure \prē'figyər\ vb : foreshadow

¹pre·fix \'prē,fiks, prē'fiks\ vb : place before

²pre·fix \'prē,fiks\ n : affix at the beginning of a word

preg·nant \'pregnənt\ adj 1 : containing unborn young 2 : meaningful —**preg·nan·cy** \-nənsē\ n

pre·hen·sile \prē'hensəl, -,sīl\ adj : adapted for grasping

pre·his·tor·ic \,prē(h)is'tòrik\, **pre·his·tor·i·cal** \-ikəl\ adj : relating to the period before written history

prej·u·dice \'prejədəs\ n 1 : damage esp. to one's rights 2 : unreasonable attitude for or against something ~ vb -diced; -dic·ing 1 : damage 2 : cause to have prejudice —**prej·u·di·cial** \,prejə'dishəl\ adj

prel·ate \'prelət\ n : clergyman of high rank —**prel·a·cy** \-əsē\ n

pre·lim·i·nary \pri'limə,nerē\ n, pl -nar·ies : something that precedes or introduces —**preliminary** adj

pre·lude \'prel,(y)üd, 'prā,lüd\ n : introductory performance, event, or musical piece

pre·ma·ture \,prēmə't(y)ùar, -'chù(ə)r\ adj : coming before the usual or proper time —**pre·ma·ture·ly** adv

pre·med·i·tate \pri'medə,tāt\ vb : plan beforehand —**pre·med·i·ta·tion** \-,medə'tāshən\ n

pre·mier \pri'm(y)iər, 'prēmēər\ adj : first in rank or importance ~ n : prime minister —**pre·mier·ship** n

pre·miere \pri'myeər, -'miər\ n : 1st performance ~ vb -miered; -mier·ing : give a 1st performance of

prem·ise \'preməs\ n 1 : statement made or implied as a basis of argument 2 pl : piece of land with the structures on it

pre·mi·um \'prēmēəm\ n 1 : bonus 2 : sum over the stated value 3 : sum paid for insurance 4 : high value

pre·mo·ni·tion \,prēmə'nishən, ,premə-\ n : feeling that something is about to happen —**pre·mon·i·to·ry** \pri'mänə,tōrē\ adj

pre·oc·cu·pied \prē'äkyə,pīd\ adj : lost in thought

pre·oc·cu·py \-,pī\ vb : occupy the attention of —**pre·oc·cu·pa·tion** \prē,äkyə'pāshən\ n

pre·pare \pri'paər\ vb -pared; -par·ing 1 : make or get ready 2 : put together or compound —**prep·a·ra·tion** \,prepə'rāshən\ n —**pre·par·a·to·ry** \pri'parə,tōrē\ adj —**pre·pared·ness** \-'parədnəs\ n

pre·pon·der·ate \pri'pändə,rāt\ vb -at·ed; -at·ing : exceed in weight, power, importance, or numbers —**pre·pon·der·ance** \-d(ə)rəns\ n —**pre·pon·der·ant** \-d(ə)rənt\ adj —**pre·pon·der·ant·ly** adv

prep·o·si·tion \,prepə'zishən\ n : word that combines with a noun or pronoun to form a phrase —**prep·o·si·tion·al** \-'zish(ə)nəl\ adj

pre·pos·sess·ing \,prēpə'zesiŋ\ adj : tending to create a favorable impression

pre·pos·ter·ous \pri'päst(ə)rəs\ adj : absurd

pre·req·ui·site \prē'rekwəzət\ n : something required beforehand —**prerequisite** adj

pre·rog·a·tive \pri'rägətiv\ n : special right or power

pre·sage \'presij, pri'sāj\ vb -saged; -sag·ing 1 : give a warning of 2 : predict —**pres·age** \'presij\ n

pres·by·ter \'prezbətər\ n : priest or minister

pre·science \'prēsh(ē)əns, 'presh-\ n : foreknowledge of events —**pre·scient** \-(ē)ənt\ adj

pre·scribe \pri'skrīb\ vb -scribed; -scrib·ing 1 : lay down as a guide 2 : direct the use of as a remedy

pre·scrip·tion \pri'skripshən\ n : written direction for the preparation and use of a medicine or the medicine prescribed

pres·ence \'prez³ns\ n 1 : fact or condition of being present 2 : appearance or bearing

¹pres·ent \'prez³nt\ n : something

given or received without compensation

²pre·sent \pri'zent\ vb 1 : introduce 2 : bring before the public 3 : make a gift to or of 4 : bring before a court for inquiry —pre·sent·able adj —pre·sen·ta·tion \ˌprē,zenˈtāshən, ˌprezᵊn-\ n —pre·sent·ment \priˈzentmənt\ n

³pres·ent \'prezᵊnt\ adj : now existing, in progress, or attending ~ n : present time

pre·sen·ti·ment \priˈzentəmənt\ n : premonition

pres·ent·ly \'prezᵊntlē\ adv 1 : soon 2 : now

present participle n : participle that typically expresses present action

pre·serve \priˈzərv\ vb -served; -serv·ing 1 : keep safe from danger or spoilage 2 : maintain ~ n 1 : preserved fruit —often in pl. 2 : area for protection of natural resources —pres·er·va·tion \ˌprezərˈvāshən\ n —pre·ser·va·tive \priˈzərvətiv\ adj or n —pre·serv·er \-'zərvər\ n

pre·side \priˈzīd\ vb -sid·ed; -sid·ing 1 : act as chairman 2 : exercise control

pres·i·dent \'prezədənt\ n 1 : one chosen to preside 2 : chief official (as of a company or nation) —pres·i·den·cy \-ənsē\ n —pres·i·den·tial \ˌprezəˈdenchəl\ adj

press \'pres\ n 1 : crowded condition 2 : machine or device for exerting pressure and esp. for printing 3 : pressure 4 : printing or publishing establishment 5 : news media and esp. newspapers ~ vb 1 : lie against and exert pressure on 2 : smooth with an iron or squeeze with something heavy 3 : urge 4 : crowd 5 : force one's way —press·er n

press·ing adj : urgent

pres·sure \'preshər\ n 1 : burden of distress or urgent business 2 : direct application of force —pressure vb —pres·sur·iza·tion \ˌpresh(ə)rəˈzāshən\ n —pres·sur·ize \-ˌīz\ vb

pres·ti·dig·i·ta·tion \ˌprestə,dijəˈtāshən\ n : sleight of hand

pres·tige \presˈtēzh, -ˈtēj\ n : estimation in the eyes of people —pres·ti·gious \-ˈtijəs\ adj

pres·to \'prestō\ adv or adj : quickly

pre·sume \priˈzüm\ vb -sumed; -sum·ing 1 : assume authority without right to do so 2 : take for granted —pre·sum·able \-ˈzüməbəl\ adj —pre·sum·ably \-blē\ adv

pre·sump·tion \priˈzəmpshən\ n 1 : presumptuous attitude or conduct 2 : belief supported by probability —pre·sump·tive \-tiv\ adj

pre·sump·tu·ous \priˈzəmpcho(wə)s\ adj : too bold or forward

pre·sup·pose \ˌprēsəˈpōz\ vb : take for granted —pre·sup·po·si·tion \(ˌ)prē,səpəˈzishən\ n

pre·tend \priˈtend\ vb 1 : act as if something is real or true when it is not 2 : act in a way that is false 3 : lay claim —pre·tend·er n

pre·tense, pre·tence \'prē,tens, priˈtens\ n 1 : insincere effort 2 : deception —pre·ten·sion \priˈtenchən\ n

pre·ten·tious \priˈtenchəs\ adj : overly showy or self-important —pre·ten·tious·ly adv —pre·ten·tious·ness n

pre·ter·nat·u·ral \ˌprētərˈnach(ə)rəl\ adj 1 : exceeding what is natural 2 : inexplicable by ordinary means —pre·ter·nat·u·ral·ly adv

pre·text \'prē,tekst\ n : falsely stated purpose

pret·ty \'pritē, 'pùrt\ adj -ti·er; -est : pleasing by delicacy or attractiveness ~ \'pritē, pərt-, ˌprit-\ adv : in some degree ~ \'pritē, 'pùrtē\ vb -tied; -ty·ing : make pretty —pret·ti·ly \'pritᵊlē\ adv —pret·ti·ness n

pret·zel \'pretsəl\ n : twisted cracker that is glazed and salted

pre·vail \priˈvāl\ vb 1 : triumph 2 : urge successfully 3 : be frequent, widespread, or dominant —pre·vail·ing·ly \-inlē\ adv

prev·a·lent \'prevələnt\ adj : widespread —prev·a·lence \-ləns\ n

pre·var·i·cate \priˈvarəˌkāt\ vb -cat·ed; -cat·ing : deviate from the truth —pre·var·i·ca·tion \-ˌvarəˈkāshən\ n —pre·var·i·ca·tor \-ˈvarəˌkātər\ n

pre·vent \priˈvent\ vb : keep from happening or acting —pre·vent·able adj —pre·ven·tion \-ˈvenchən\ n —pre·ven·tive \-ˈventiv\ n, pre·ven·ta·tive \-ˈventətiv\ adj or n

pre·view \'prē,vyü\ vb : view or show beforehand —preview n

pre·vi·ous \'prēvēəs\ adj : having gone, happened, or existed before —pre·vi·ous·ly adv

prey \'prā\ n, pl preys 1 : animal taken for food by another 2 : victim ~ vb 1 : seize and devour animals as prey 2 : have a harmful effect on

price \'prīs\ n : cost ~ vb priced; pric·ing : set a price on

price·less \-ləs\ adj : too precious to have a price

prick \'prik\ n 1 : tear or small wound

made by a point **2** : something sharp or pointed ~ *vb* : pierce slightly with a sharp point —**prick·er** *n*

prick·le \'prikəl\ *n* **1** : small sharp spine or thorn **2** : slight stinging pain ~ *vb* **-led; -ling** : tingle —**prick·ly** \'priklē\ *adj*

pride \'prīd\ *n* : quality or state of being proud ~ *vb* **prid·ed; prid·ing** : indulge in pride —**pride·ful** *adj*

priest \'prēst\ *n* : person having authority to perform the sacred rites of a religion —**priest·ess** \-əs\ *n* —**priest·hood** *n* —**priest·li·ness** \-lēnəs\ *n* —**priest·ly** *adj*

prig \'prig\ *n* : one who irritates by rigid or pointed observance of proprieties —**prig·gish** \-ish\ *adj* —**prig·gish·ly** *adv*

prim \'prim\ *adj* **-mm-** : stiffly formal and proper —**prim·ly** *adv* —**prim·ness** *n*

pri·mal \'prīmal\ *adj* : original or primitive

pri·ma·ry \'prī,merē, 'prīm(ə)rē\ *adj* : first in order of time, rank, or importance ~ *n, pl* **-ries** : preliminary election —**pri·mar·i·ly** \prī'merəlē\ *adv*

primary school *n* : elementary school

pri·mate *n* **1** \'prī,māt, -mət\ : highest-ranking bishop **2** \-,māt\ : mammal of the group that includes man and monkeys

prime \'prīm\ *n* : earliest or best part or period ~ *adj* : standing first (as in significance or quality) ~ *vb* **primed; prim·ing 1** : fill or load **2** : lay a preparatory coating on

prime minister *n* : chief executive of a parliamentary government

¹**prim·er** \'primər\ *n* : small introductory book

²**prim·er** \'prīmər\ *n* **1** : device for igniting an explosive **2** : material for priming a surface

pri·me·val \prī'mēvəl\ *adj* : relating to the earliest ages

prim·i·tive \'primətiv\ *adj* : relating to or characteristic of an early stage of development ~ *n* : one that is primitive —**prim·i·tive·ly** *adv* —**prim·i·tive·ness** *n* —**prim·i·tiv·i·ty** \,primə'tivətē\ *n*

pri·mor·di·al \prī'mòrdēəl\ *adj* : primeval

primp \'primp\ *vb* : dress or groom in a finicky manner

prim·rose \'prim,rōz\ *n* : low herb with clusters of showy flowers

prince \'prins\ *n* **1** : ruler **2** : son of a king or queen —**prince·ly** *adj*

prin·cess \'prinsəs, -,ses\ *n* **1** : daughter of a king or queen **2** : wife of a prince

prin·ci·pal \'prinsəpəl\ *adj* : most important ~ *n* **1** : leading person **2** : head of a school **3** : sum lent at interest —**prin·ci·pal·ly** *adv*

prin·ci·pal·i·ty \,prinsə'palətē\ *n, pl* **-ties** : territory of a prince

prin·ci·ple \'prinsəpəl\ *n* **1** : general or fundamental law **2** : rule or code of conduct or devotion to such a code

print \'print\ *n* **1** : mark made by pressure **2** : printed state or form **3** : printed matter **4** : copy made by printing **5** : cloth with a figure stamped on it ~ *vb* **1** : produce impressions of (as from type) **2** : write in letters like those of printer's type —**print·able** *adj* —**print·er** *n*

print·ing \'printiŋ\ *n* : art or business of a printer

print·out \'print,aút\ *n* : printed record produced by a computer —**print out** \(')print'aút\ *vb*

¹**pri·or** \'prī(ə)r\ *n* : head of a religious house —**pri·or·ess** \'prīərəs\ *n* —**pri·o·ry** \'prī(ə)rē\ *n*

²**pri·or** *adj* : coming before in time, order, or importance —**pri·or·i·ty** \prī'òrətē\ *n*

prism \'prizəm\ *n* : transparent 3-sided object that separates light into colors —**pris·mat·ic** \priz'matik\ *adj*

pris·on \'priz²n\ *n* : place where criminals are confined

pris·on·er \'priznər, -²nər\ *n* : person on trial or in prison

pris·sy \'prisē\ *adj* **-si·er; -est** : prim —**pris·si·ness** *n*

pris·tine \'pris,tēn\ *adj* : pure

pri·va·cy \'prīvəsē\ *n, pl* **-cies** : quality or state of being apart from others

pri·vate \'prīvət\ *adj* **1** : belonging to a particular individual or group **2** : carried on independently **3** : withdrawn from company or observation ~ *n* : enlisted man of the lowest rank in the marine corps or one of the two lowest ranks in the army —**pri·vate·ly** *adv*

pri·va·teer \,prīvə'tiər\ *n* : private ship armed to attack enemy ships and commerce

private first class *n* : enlisted man ranking next below a corporal in the army and next below a lance corporal in the marine corps

pri·va·tion \prī'vāshən\ *n* : lack of what is needed for existence

priv·i·lege \'priv(ə)lij\ *n* : right granted

as an advantage or favor —**priv·i·leged** *adj*

privy \'privē\ *adj* : private or secret ~ *n* : outdoor toilet —**priv·i·ly** \'privəlē\ *adv*

¹prize \'prīz\ *n* **1** : something offered or striven for in competition or in contests of chance **2** : something very desirable —**prize** *adj* —**prize-win·ner** *n*

²prize *vb* **prized; priz·ing** : value highly

³prize \'prīz\ *vb* **prized; priz·ing** : pry

prize-fight *n* : professional boxing match —**prize-fight·er** *n* —**prize-fight·ing** *n*

¹pro \'prō\ *n* : favorable argument or person ~ *adv* : in favor

²pro *n or adj* : professional

prob·a·ble \'präbəbəl\ *adj* : seeming true or real or to have a good chance of happening —**prob·a·bil·i·ty** \ˌpräbə'bilətē\ *n* —**prob·a·bly** \'präbəblē, 'präblē\ *adv*

pro·bate \'prō,bāt\ *n* : judicial determination of the validity of a will ~ *vb* **-bat·ed; -bat·ing** : establish by probate

pro·ba·tion \prō'bāshən\ *n* **1** : period of testing and trial **2** : freedom of a convict during good behavior under supervision —**pro·ba·tion·ary** \-shə,nerē\ *adj* —**pro·ba·tion·er** *n*

probe \'prōb\ *n* **1** : slender instrument for examining a cavity **2** : investigation ~ *vb* **probed; prob·ing 1** : examine with a probe **2** : investigate

pro·bi·ty \'prōbətē\ *n* : honest behavior

prob·lem \'präbləm\ *n* **1** : question to be solved **2** : source of perplexity or vexation —**problem** *adj* —**prob·lem·at·ic** \ˌpräblə'matik\ *adj* —**prob·lem·at·i·cal** \-ikəl\ *adj*

pro·bos·cis \prə'bäsəs, -kəs\ *n, pl* **-cis·es** *also* **-ci·des** \-ə,dēz\ : long flexible snout

pro·ce·dure \prə'sējər\ *n* **1** : way of doing something **2** : series of steps in regular order —**pro·ce·dur·al** \-'sējə(ə)rəl\ *adj*

pro·ceed \prō'sēd\ *vb* **1** : come forth **2** : go on in an orderly way **3** : begin and carry on an action **4** : advance

pro·ceed·ing *n* **1** : procedure **2** *pl* : something said or done or its official record

pro·ceeds \'prō,sēdz\ *n pl* : total money taken in

pro·cess \'präs,es, 'prōs-\ *n, pl* **-cess·es** \-,esəz, -əsəz, -ə,sēz\ **1** : natural phenomenon marked by gradual changes **2** : series of actions or operations directed toward a result **3**

: summons **4** : projecting part ~ *vb* : subject to a process —**pro·ces·sor** \-ər\ *n*

pro·ces·sion \prə'seshən\ *n* : group moving along in an orderly way

pro·ces·sion·al \-'sesh(ə)nəl\ *n* : music for a procession

pro·claim \prō'klām\ *vb* : announce publicly or with conviction —**proc·la·ma·tion** \ˌpräklə'māshən\ *n*

pro·cliv·i·ty \prō'klivətē\ *n, pl* **-ties** : inclination

pro·cras·ti·nate \prə'krastə,nāt\ *vb* **-nat·ed; -nat·ing** : put something off until later —**pro·cras·ti·na·tion** \-,krastə'nāshən\ *n* —**pro·cras·ti·na·tor** \-'krastə,nātər\ *n*

pro·cre·ate \'prōkrē,āt\ *vb* **-at·ed; -at·ing** : produce offspring —**pro·cre·ation** \ˌprōkrē'āshən\ *n* —**pro·cre·ative** \'prōkrē,ātiv\ *adj* —**pro·cre·ator** \-,ātər\ *n*

proc·tor \'präktər\ *n* : supervisor of students (as at an examination) —**proctor** *vb* —**proc·to·ri·al** \präk'tōrēəl\ *adj*

pro·cure \prə'kyủər\ *vb* **-cured; -cur·ing** : get possession of —**pro·cur·able** \-'kyủrəbəl\ *adj* —**pro·cure·ment** *n* —**pro·cur·er** *n*

prod \'präd\ *vb* **-dd-** : push with or as if with a pointed instrument —**prod** *n*

prod·i·gal \'prädigəl\ *adj* : recklessly extravagant or wasteful —**prodigal** *n* —**prod·i·gal·i·ty** \ˌprädə'galətē\ *n*

pro·di·gious \prə'dijəs\ *adj* : extraordinary in size or degree —**pro·di·gious·ly** *adv*

prod·i·gy \'prädəjē\ *n, pl* **-gies** : extraordinary person or thing

pro·duce \prə'd(y)üs\ *vb* **-duced; -duc·ing 1** : present to view **2** : give birth to **3** : bring into existence ~ \'präd(,)üs, 'prōd- *also* -(,)yüs\ *n* **1** : product **2** : agricultural products for sale —**pro·duc·er** \prə'd(y)üsər\ *n*

prod·uct \'präd(,)əkt\ *n* **1** : number resulting from multiplication **2** : something produced

pro·duc·tion \prə'dəkshən\ *n* : act, process, or result of producing —**pro·duc·tive** \-'dəktiv\ *adj* —**pro·duc·tive·ness** *n* —**pro·duc·tiv·i·ty** \(,)prō,dək'tivətē, ,präd(,)ək-\ *n*

pro·fane \prō'fān\ *vb* **-faned; -fan·ing** : treat with irreverence ~ *adj* **1** : not concerned with religion **2** : serving to debase what is holy —**pro·fane·ly** *adv* —**pro·fane·ness** \-'fānnəs\ *n* —**pro·fan·i·ty** \prō'fanətē\ *n*

pro·fess \prə'fes\ *vb* 1 : declare openly 2 : confess one's faith in —**pro·fess·ed·ly** \-ədlē\ *adv*

pro·fes·sion \prə'feshən\ *n* 1 : open declaration of belief 2 : occupation requiring specialized knowledge and academic training

pro·fes·sion·al \prə'fesh(ə)nəl\ *adj* 1 : of, relating to, or engaged in a profession 2 : playing sport for pay —**professional** *n* —**pro·fes·sion·al·ism** *n* —**pro·fes·sion·al·ize** *vb* —**pro·fes·sion·al·ly** *adv*

pro·fes·sor \prə'fesər\ *n* : university or college teacher —**pro·fes·so·ri·al** \₁prōfə'sōrēəl, ₁präfə-\ *adj* —**pro·fes·sor·ship** *n*

prof·fer \'präfər\ *vb* -fered; -fer·ing : offer —**proffer** *n*

pro·fi·cient \prə'fishənt\ *adj* : very good at something —**pro·fi·cien·cy** \-ənsē\ *n* —**proficient** *n* —**pro·fi·cient·ly** *adv*

pro·file \'prō₁fīl\ *n* : picture in outline —**profile** *vb*

prof·it \'präfət\ *n* 1 : valuable return 2 : excess of the selling price of goods over cost ~ *vb* : gain a profit —**prof·it·able** \'präfətəbəl, 'präftə-\ *adj* —**prof·it·ably** *adv* —**prof·it·less** *adj*

prof·i·teer \₁präfə'tir\ *n* : one who makes an unreasonable profit —**profiteer** *vb*

prof·li·gate \'präfligət, -lə₁gāt\ *adj* 1 : shamelessly immoral 2 : wildly extravagant —**prof·li·ga·cy** \-gəsē\ *n* —**profligate** *n* —**prof·li·gate·ly** *adv*

pro·found \prə'faùnd\ *adj* 1 : marked by intellectual depth or insight 2 : deeply felt —**pro·found·ly** *adv* —**pro·fun·di·ty** \-'fəndətē\ *n*

pro·fuse \prə'fyüs\ *adj* : pouring forth liberally —**pro·fuse·ly** *adv* —**pro·fu·sion** \-'fyüzhən\ *n*

pro·gen·i·tor \prō'jenətər\ *n* : direct ancestor

prog·e·ny \'präjənē\ *n, pl* -nies : offspring

prog·no·sis \präg'nōsəs\ *n, pl* -no·ses \-₁sēz\ : forecast esp. of the course of a disease

prog·nos·ti·cate \präg'nästə₁kāt\ *vb* -cat·ed; -cat·ing : predict from signs or symptoms —**prog·nos·ti·ca·tion** \-₁nästə'kāshən\ *n* —**prog·nos·ti·ca·tor** \-'nästə₁kātər\ *n*

pro·gram, pro·gramme \'prō₁gram, -grəm\ *n* 1 : outline of the order to be pursued or the subjects included (as in a performance) 2 : plan of procedure 3 : coded instructions for a computer ~ *vb* -**grammed** *or*

-**gramed**; -**gram·ming** *or* -**gram·ing** 1 : enter in a program 2 : provide a computer with a program —**pro·gram·ma·bil·i·ty** \(₁)prō₁gramə'bilətē\ *n* —**pro·gram·ma·ble** \'prō₁graməbəl\ *adj* —**pro·gram·mer** \'prō₁gramər, -grəmər\ *n*

prog·ress \'prägrəs, -₁res\ *n* : movement forward or to a better condition ~ \prə'gres\ *vb* 1 : move forward 2 : improve —**pro·gres·sive** \-'gresiv\ *adj* —**pro·gres·sive·ly** *adv*

pro·gres·sion \prə'greshən\ *n* 1 : act of progressing 2 : continuous connected series

pro·hib·it \prō'hibət\ *vb* : prevent by authority

pro·hi·bi·tion \₁prōə'bishən\ *n* 1 : act of prohibiting 2 : legal restriction on sale or manufacture of alcoholic beverages —**pro·hi·bi·tion·ist** \-'bish(ə)nəst\ *n* —**pro·hib·i·tive** \prō'hibətiv\ *adj* —**pro·hib·i·tive·ly** *adv* —**pro·hib·i·to·ry** \-'hibə₁tōrē\ *adj*

pro·ject \'präj₁ekt, -ikt\ *n* : planned undertaking ~ \prə'jekt\ *vb* 1 : design or plan 2 : protrude 3 : throw forward —**pro·jec·tion** \-'jekshən\ *n*

pro·jec·tile \prə'jekt[ə]l\ *n* : missile hurled by external force

pro·jec·tor \-'jektər\ *n* : device for projecting pictures on a screen

pro·le·tar·i·an \₁prōlə'terēən\ *n* : member of the proletariat —**proletarian** *adj*

pro·le·tar·i·at \-ēət\ *n* : laboring class

pro·lif·er·ate \prə'lifə₁rāt\ *vb* -at·ed; -at·ing : grow or increase in number rapidly —**pro·lif·er·a·tion** \-₁lifə'rāshən\ *n*

pro·lif·ic \prə'lifik\ *adj* : producing abundantly —**pro·lif·i·cal·ly** \-ik(ə)lē\ *adv*

pro·logue \'prō₁lòg, -₁läg\ *n* : preface

pro·long \prə'lòŋ\ *vb* : lengthen in time or extent —**pro·lon·ga·tion** \₁prō₁lòŋ'gāshən\ *n*

prom \'präm\ *n* : formal school dance

prom·e·nade \₁prämə'nād, -'näd\ *n* 1 : leisurely walk 2 : place for strolling —**promenade** *vb*

prom·i·nence \'präm(ə)nəns\ *n* 1 : quality, state, or fact of being readily noticeable or distinguished 2 : something that stands out —**prom·i·nent** \-nənt\ *adj* —**prom·i·nent·ly** *adv*

pro·mis·cu·ous \prə'miskyəwəs\ *adj* : not restricted to one sexual partner —**prom·is·cu·i·ty** \₁prämis'kyütē,

ˌprōˌmis-\ n —pro·mis·cu·ous·ly adv —pro·mis·cu·ous·ness n

prom·ise \'präməs\ n 1 : statement that one will do or not do something 2 : basis for expectation —promise vb —prom·is·so·ry \-ˌsōrē\ adj

prom·is·ing \'präməsiŋ\ adj : likely to succeed —prom·is·ing·ly adv

prom·on·to·ry \'prämənˌtōrē\ n, pl -ries : point of land jutting into the sea

pro·mote \prə'mōt\ vb -mot·ed; -mot·ing 1 : advance in rank 2 : contribute to the growth, development, or prosperity of —pro·mot·er n —pro·mo·tion \-'mōshən\ n —pro·mo·tion·al \-'mōsh(ə)nəl\ adj

¹prompt \'prämpt\ vb 1 : incite 2 : give a cue to (an actor or singer) —prompt·er n

²prompt adj : ready and quick —prompt·ly adv —prompt·ness n

prone \'prōn\ adj 1 : having a tendency 2 : lying face downward —prone·ness \'prōnnəs\ n

prong \'prȯŋ\ n : sharp point of a fork —pronged \'prȯŋd\ adj

pro·noun \'prō̩naùn\ n : word used as a substitute for a noun

pro·nounce \prə'naùns\ vb -nounced; -nounc·ing 1 : utter officially or as an opinion 2 : say or speak esp. correctly —pro·nounce·able adj —pro·nounce·ment n —pro·nun·ci·a·tion \-ˌnənsēˈāshən\ n

pro·nounced \-'naùnst\ adj : strongly marked

¹proof \'prüf\ n 1 : evidence of a truth or fact 2 : trial impression or print

²proof adj : designed for or successful in resisting or repelling

proof·read vb : read and mark corrections in (printer's proof) —proof·read·er n

prop \'präp\ vb -pp- 1 : support 2 : sustain —prop n

pro·pa·gan·da \ˌpräpə'gandə, ˌprōpə-\ n : the spreading of ideas or information to further or damage a cause —prop·a·gan·dist \-dəst\ n —pro·pa·gan·dize \-ˌdīz\ vb

prop·a·gate \'präpəˌgāt\ vb -gat·ed; -gat·ing 1 : reproduce biologically 2 : cause to spread —prop·a·ga·tion \ˌpräpə'gāshən\ n

pro·pane \'prō̩pān\ n : heavy flammable gaseous fuel

pro·pel \prə'pel\ vb -ll- : drive forward —pro·pel·lant, pro·pel·lent n or adj

pro·pel·ler \prə'pelər\ n : hub with revolving blades that drives a craft

pro·pen·si·ty \prə'pensətē\ n, pl -ties : particular interest or inclination

prop·er \'präpər\ adj 1 : suitable or right 2 : limited to a specified thing 3 : correct 4 : strictly adhering to standards of social manners, dignity, or good taste —prop·er·ly adv

prop·er·ty \'präpərtē\ n, pl -ties 1 : quality peculiar to an individual 2 : something owned 3 : piece of real estate 4 : ownership

proph·e·cy \'präfəsē\ n, pl -cies : prediction

proph·e·sy \-ˌsī\ vb -sied; -sy·ing : predict —proph·e·si·er \-ˌsī(ə)r\ n

proph·et \'präfət\ n : one who utters revelations or predicts events —proph·et·ess \-əs\ n —pro·phet·ic \prə'fetik\, pro·phet·i·cal \-ikəl\ adj —pro·phet·i·cal·ly \-ik(ə)lē\ adv

pro·pin·qui·ty \prə'piŋkwətē\ n : nearness

pro·pi·ti·ate \prō'pishēˌāt\ vb -at·ed; -at·ing : gain or regain the favor of —pro·pi·ti·a·tion \-ˌpish(ē)'āshən\ n —pro·pi·ti·a·to·ry \-'pish(ē)ə,tōrē\ adj

pro·pi·tious \prə'pishəs\ adj : favorable

pro·po·nent \prə'pōnənt\ n : one who argues in favor of something

pro·por·tion \prə'pōrshən\ n 1 : relation of one part to another or to the whole with respect to magnitude, quantity, or degree 2 : symmetry 3 : share ~ vb : adjust in size in relation to others —pro·por·tion·al \-sh(ə)nəl\ adj —pro·por·tion·al·ly adv —pro·por·tion·ate \-sh(ə)nət\ adj —pro·por·tion·ate·ly adv

pro·pose \prə'pōz\ vb -posed; -pos·ing 1 : plan or intend 2 : make an offer of marriage 3 : present for consideration —pro·pos·al \-'pōzəl\ n —pro·pos·er n

prop·o·si·tion \ˌpräpə'zishən\ n : something proposed ~ vb : suggest sexual intercourse to

pro·pound \prə'paúnd\ vb : set forth for consideration

pro·pri·e·tor \prə'prīətər\ n : owner —pro·pri·e·tary \prə'prīəˌterē\ adj —pro·pri·e·tor·ship n —pro·pri·e·tress \-'prīətrəs\ n

pro·pri·e·ty \prə'prīətē\ n, pl -eties : standard of acceptability in social conduct

pro·pul·sion \prə'pəlshən\ n 1 : action of propelling 2 : driving power —pro·pul·sive \-siv\ adj

pro·sa·ic \prō'zāik\ adj : dull

pro·scribe \prō'skrīb\ vb -scribed; -scrib·ing : prohibit —**pro·scrip·tion** \-'skripshən\ n

prose \'prōz\ n : ordinary language

pros·e·cute \'präsi‚kyüt\ vb -cut·ed; -cut·ing 1 : follow to the end 2 : seek legal punishment of —**pros·e·cu·tion** \‚präsi'kyüshən\ n —**pros·e·cu·tor** \'präsi‚kyütər\ n

pros·e·lyte \'präsə‚līt\ n : new convert —**pros·e·ly·tize** \'präs(ə)lə‚tīz\ vb

pros·pect \'präs‚pekt\ n 1 : extensive view 2 : something awaited 3 : potential buyer ~ vb : look for mineral deposits —**pro·spec·tive** \prə'spektiv, 'präs‚pek-\ adj —**pro·spec·tive·ly** adv —**pros·pec·tor** \-‚pektər, -'pek-\ n

pro·spec·tus \prə'spektəs\ n : introductory description of an enterprise

pros·per \'präspər\ vb : thrive or succeed —**pros·per·ous** \-p(ə)rəs\ adj

pros·per·i·ty \präs'perətē\ n : economic well-being

pros·tate \'präs‚tāt\ n : glandular body about the base of the male urethra —**prostate** adj

pros·the·sis \präs'thēsəs, 'prästhə-\ n, pl -**the·ses** \-‚sēz\ : artificial replacement for a body part —**pros·thet·ic** \präs'thetik\ adj

pros·ti·tute \'prästə‚t(y)üt\ vb -tut·ed; -tut·ing : put to corrupt or unworthy purposes ~ n : one who engages in sexual intercourse for pay —**pros·ti·tu·tion** \‚prästə't(y)üshən\ n

pros·trate \'präs‚trāt\ adj : stretched out with face on the ground ~ vb -trat·ed; -trat·ing 1 : fall or throw (oneself) into a prostrate position 2 : reduce to helplessness —**pros·tra·tion** \präs'trāshən\ n

pro·tect \prə'tekt\ vb : shield from injury —**pro·tec·tor** \-tər\ n

pro·tec·tion \prə'tekshən\ n 1 : act of protecting 2 : one that protects —**pro·tec·tive** \-'tektiv\ adj

pro·tec·tor·ate \-t(ə)rət\ n : state dependent upon the authority of another state

pro·té·gé \'prōtə‚zhā\ n : one under the care and protection of an influential person —**pro·té·gée** \-‚zhā\ n

pro·tein \'prō‚tēn, 'prōtēən\ n : complex combination of amino acids present in living matter

pro·test \'prō‚test\ n 1 : organized public demonstration of disapproval 2 : strong objection ~ \prə'test\ vb 1 : assert positively 2 : object strongly —**prot·es·ta·tion**

\‚prätəs'tāshən\ n —**pro·test·er, pro·tes·tor** \-ər\ n

Prot·es·tant \'prätəstənt\ n : Christian not of a Catholic or Orthodox church —**Prot·es·tant·ism** \'prätəstənt‚izəm\ n

pro·to·col \'prōtə‚kȯl\ n : diplomatic etiquette

pro·ton \'prō‚tän\ n : positively charged particle

pro·to·plasm \'prōtə‚plazəm\ n : complex colloidal living substance of plant and animal cells —**pro·to·plas·mic** \‚prōtə'plazmik\ adj

pro·to·type \'prōtə‚tīp\ n : original model

pro·to·zo·an \‚prōtə'zōən\ n : single-celled lower invertebrate animal

pro·tract \prō'trakt\ vb : prolong

pro·trac·tor \-'traktər\ n : instrument for constructing and measuring angles

pro·trude \prō'trüd\ vb -trud·ed; -trud·ing : stick out or cause to stick out —**pro·tru·sion** \-'trüzhən\ n —**pro·tru·sive** \-'trüsiv\ adj

pro·tu·ber·ance \prō't(y)üb(ə)rəns\ n : something that protrudes —**pro·tu·ber·ant** adj

proud \'praud\ adj 1 : having or showing excessive self-esteem 2 : highly pleased 3 : having proper self-respect 4 : glorious —**proud·ly** adv

prove \'prüv\ vb proved; proved or prov·en \'prüvən\; prov·ing 1 : test by experiment or by a standard 2 : establish the truth of by argument or evidence 3 : turn out esp. after trial or test —**prov·able** \'prüvəbəl\ adj

prov·en·der \'prävəndər\ n : dry food for domestic animals

prov·erb \'präv‚ərb\ n : short meaningful popular saying —**pro·ver·bi·al** \prə'vərbēəl\ adj

pro·vide \prə'vīd\ vb -vid·ed; -vid·ing 1 : take measures beforehand 2 : make a stipulation 3 : supply what is needed —**pro·vid·er** n

pro·vid·ed conj : if

prov·i·dence \'prävədəns\ n 1 often cap : divine guidance 2 cap : God 3 : quality of being provident

prov·i·dent \-ədənt\ adj 1 : making provision for the future 2 : thrifty —**prov·i·dent·ly** adv

prov·i·den·tial \‚prävə'denchəl\ adj 1 : relating to Providence 2 : opportune

prov·ince \'prävəns\ n 1 : administrative district 2 pl : all of a country outside the metropolis 3 : sphere

pro·vin·cial \prə'vinchəl\ *adj* 1 : relating to a province 2 : not cosmopolitan —**pro·vin·cial·ism** \-,izəm\ *n*

pro·vi·sion \prə'vizhən\ *n* 1 : act of providing 2 : stock of food —usu. in pl. 3 : stipulation ~ *vb* : supply with provisions

pro·vi·sion·al \-'vizh(ə)nəl\ *adj* : provided for a temporary need

pro·vi·so \prə'vīzō\ *n, pl* -sos *or* -soes : article or clause that introduces a condition

pro·voke \prə'vōk\ *vb* -voked; -vok·ing 1 : incite to anger 2 : stir up on purpose —**prov·o·ca·tion** \,prävə'kāshən\ *n* —**pro·voc·a·tive** \prə'väkətiv\ *adj*

prow \'prau̇\ *n* : bow of a ship

prow·ess \'prau̇əs\ *n* 1 : valor 2 : extraordinary ability

prowl \'prau̇l\ *vb* : roam about stealthily —**prowl** *n* —**prowl·er** *n*

prox·i·mate \'präksəmət\ *adj* : very near

prox·im·i·ty \präk'simətē\ *n* : nearness

proxy \'präksē\ *n, pl* **prox·ies** : authority to act for another —**proxy** *adj*

prude \'prüd\ *n* : one who shows extreme modesty —**prud·ery** \'prüdərē\ *n* —**prud·ish** \'prüdish\ *adj*

pru·dent \'prüd⁰nt\ *adj* 1 : shrewd 2 : cautious 3 : thrifty —**pru·dence** \-⁰ns\ *n* —**pru·den·tial** \prü'denchəl\ *adj* —**pru·dent·ly** *adv*

¹prune \'prün\ *n* : dried plum

²prune *vb* **pruned; prun·ing** : cut off unwanted parts

pru·ri·ent \'prürēənt\ *adj* : lewd —**pru·ri·ence** \-ēəns\ *n*

¹pry \'prī\ *vb* **pried; pry·ing** : look closely or inquisitively

²pry *vb* **pried; pry·ing** : raise, move, or pull apart with a lever

psalm \'säm, 'sälm\ *n* : sacred song or poem —**psalm·ist** *n*

pseud·onym \'süd⁰n,im\ *n* : fictitious name —**pseud·on·y·mous** \sü'dänəməs\ *adj*

pso·ri·a·sis \sə'rīəsəs\ *n* : chronic skin disease

psy·che \'sīkē\ *n* : soul or mind

psy·chi·a·try \sə'kīətrē, sī-\ *n* : branch of medicine dealing with mental disorders —**psy·chi·at·ric** \,sīkē'atrik\ *adj* —**psy·chi·a·trist** \sə'kīətrəst, sī-\ *n*

psy·chic \'sīkik\ *adj* 1 : relating to the psyche 2 : sensitive to supernatural forces ~ *n* : person sensitive to supernatural forces —**psy·chi·cal·ly** \-k(ə)lē\ *adv*

psy·cho·anal·y·sis \,sīkōə'naləsəs\ *n* : study of the normally hidden content of the mind esp. to resolve conflicts —**psy·cho·an·a·lyst** \-'an⁰l,ast\ *n* —**psy·cho·an·al·yt·ic** \-,an⁰l'itik\ *adj* —**psy·cho·an·a·lyze** \-'an⁰l,īz\ *vb*

psy·chol·o·gy \sī'käləjē\ *n, pl* -gies 1 : science of mind and behavior 2 : mental and behavioral aspect (as of an individual) —**psy·cho·log·i·cal** \,sīkə'läjikəl\ *adj* —**psy·cho·log·i·cal·ly** \-ik(ə)lē\ *adv* —**psy·chol·o·gist** \sī'käləjəst\ *n*

psy·cho·path \'sīkə,path\ *n* : mentally ill or unstable person —**psy·cho·path·ic** \,sīkə'pathik\ *adj*

psy·cho·sis \sī'kōsəs\ *n, pl* -cho·ses \-,sēz\ : mental derangement (as paranoia) —**psy·chot·ic** \-'kätik\ *adj or n*

psy·cho·so·mat·ic \,sīkəsə'matik\ *adj* : caused by the interaction of mind and body

psy·cho·ther·a·py \,sīkō'therəpē\ *n* : treatment of mental disorder by psychological means —**psy·cho·ther·a·pist** \-pəst\ *n*

pto·maine \'tō,mān\ *n* : bacterial decay product

pu·ber·ty \'pyübərtē\ *n* : time of sexual maturity —**pu·ber·tal** \-bərt⁰l\ *adj*

pu·bic \'pyübik\ *adj* : relating to the lower abdominal region

pub·lic \'pəblik\ *adj* 1 : relating to the people as a whole 2 : civic 3 : not private 4 : open to all 5 : well-known ~ *n* : people as a whole —**pub·lic·ly** *adv*

pub·li·ca·tion \,pəblə'kāshən\ *n* 1 : process of publishing 2 : published work

pub·lic·i·ty \(,)pə'blisətē\ *n* 1 : news information given out to gain public attention 2 : public attention

pub·li·cize \'pəblə,sīz\ *vb* -cized; -ciz·ing : give publicity to —**pub·li·cist** \-səst\ *n*

pub·lish \'pəblish\ *vb* 1 : announce publicly 2 : reproduce for sale esp. by printing —**pub·lish·er** *n*

puck·er \'pəkər\ *vb* : pull together into folds or wrinkles ~ *n* : wrinkle

pud·ding \'pu̇diŋ\ *n* : creamy dessert

pud·dle \'pəd⁰l\ *n* : very small pool of water

pudgy \'pəjē\ *adj* **pudg·i·er; -est** : short and plump

pu·er·ile \'pyu̇ərəl\ *adj* : childish —**pu·er·il·i·ty** \,pyu̇ə'rilətē\ *n*

puff \'pəf\ *vb* 1 : blow in short gusts 2 : pant 3 : enlarge ~ *n* 1 : short discharge (as of air) **2** : slight swelling **3** : something light and fluffy —**puffy** *adj*

pug \'pəg\ *n* : small stocky dog

pu·gil·ism \'pyüjə,lizəm\ *n* : boxing —**pu·gil·ist** \-ləst\ *n* —**pu·gi·lis·tic** \,pyüjə'listik\ *adj*

pug·na·cious \,pəg'nāshəs\ *adj* : prone to fighting —**pug·nac·i·ty** \-'nasət\ *n*

puke \'pyük\ *vb* **puked; puk·ing** : vomit —**puke** *n*

pul·chri·tude \'pəlkrə,t(y)üd\ *n* : beauty —**pul·chri·tu·di·nous** \,pəlkrə't(y)üdnəs, -ᵊnəs\ *adj*

pull \'pul\ *vb* **1** : exert force so as to draw (something) toward or out **2** : move **3** : stretch or tear ~ *n* **1** : act of pulling **2** : influence **3** : device for pulling something —**pull·er** *n*

pul·let \'pulət\ *n* : young hen

pul·ley \'pulē\ *n, pl* **-leys** : wheel with a grooved rim

Pull·man \'pulmən\ *n* : railroad car with berths

pull·over \,pul,ōvər\ *adj* : put on by being pulled over the head —**pull·over** \'pul,ōvər\ *n*

pul·mo·nary \'pulmə,nerē, 'pəl-\ *adj* : relating to the lungs

pulp \'pəlp\ *n* **1** : soft part of a fruit or vegetable **2** : soft moist mass (as of mashed wood) —**pulpy** *adj*

pul·pit \'pul,pit\ *n* : raised desk used in preaching

pul·sate \'pəl,sāt\ *vb* **-sat·ed; -sat·ing** : expand and contract rhythmically —**pul·sa·tion** \,pəl'sāshən\ *n*

pulse \'pəls\ *n* : arterial throbbing caused by heart contractions —**pulse** *vb*

pul·ver·ize \'pəlvə,rīz\ *vb* **-ized; -iz·ing** : beat or grind into a powder

pu·ma \'p(y)ümə\ *n* : cougar

pum·ice \'pəməs\ *n* : light porous volcanic glass used in polishing

pum·mel \'pəməl\ *vb* **-meled** *or* **-melled; -mel·ing** *or* **-mel·ling** \-(ə)liŋ\ : beat

¹pump \'pəmp\ *n* : device for moving or compressing fluids ~ *vb* **1** : raise (as water) with a pump **2** : fill by means of a pump —with *up* **3** : move like a pump —**pump·er** *n*

²pump *n* : woman's low shoe

pum·per·nick·el \'pəmpər,nikəl\ *n* : dark rye bread

pump·kin \'pəŋkən, 'pəm(p)kən\ *n* : large yellow fruit of a vine related to the gourd

pun \'pən\ *n* : humorous use of a word in a way that suggests two interpretations —**pun** *vb*

¹punch \'pənch\ *vb* **1** : strike with the fist **2** : perforate with a punch ~ *n* : quick blow with the fist —**punch·er** *n*

²punch *n* : tool for piercing or stamping

³punch *n* : mixed beverage often including fruit juice

punc·til·i·ous \,(,)pəŋk'tiLēəs\ *adj* : marked by precise accordance with conventions

punc·tu·al \'pəŋkchə(wə)l\ *adj* : prompt —**punc·tu·al·i·ty** \,pəŋkchə'walətē\ *n* —**punc·tu·al·ly** *adv*

punc·tu·ate \'pəŋkchə,wāt\ *vb* **-at·ed; -at·ing** : mark with punctuation

punc·tu·a·tion \,pəŋkchə'wāshən\ *n* : standardized marks inserted in written matter to clarify the meaning or their use

punc·ture \'pəŋkchər\ *n* : act or result of puncturing ~ *vb* **-tured; -tur·ing** : make a hole in

pun·dit \'pəndət\ *n* **1** : learned man **2** : expert

pun·gent \'pənjənt\ *adj* : having a sharp or stinging odor or taste —**pun·gen·cy** \-jənsē\ *n* —**pun·gent·ly** *adv*

pun·ish \'pənish\ *vb* : impose a penalty on or for —**pun·ish·able** *adj* —**pun·ish·ment** *n*

pu·ni·tive \'pyünətiv\ *adj* : inflicting punishment

pun·kin *var of* PUMPKIN

¹punt \'pənt\ *n* : long narrow flat-bottomed boat ~ *vb* : propel (a boat) by pushing with a pole

²punt *vb* : kick a ball dropped from the hands ~ *n* : act of punting a ball

pu·ny \'pyünē\ *adj* **-ni·er; -est** : slight in power or size

pup \'pəp\ *n* : young dog

pu·pa \'pyüpə\ *n, pl* **-pae** \-(,)pē, -,pī\ *or* **-pas** : insect (as a moth) when it is in a case or cocoon —**pu·pal** \-pəl\ *adj*

¹pu·pil \'pyüpəl\ *n* : young person in school

²pupil *n* : dark central opening of the iris of the eye

pup·pet \'pəpət\ *n* : small doll moved by hand or by strings —**pup·pe·teer** \,pəpə'tiər\ *n*

pup·py \'pəpē\ *n, pl* **-pies** : young dog

pur·chase \'pərchəs\ *vb* **-chased; -chas·ing** : obtain in exchange for money ~ *n* **1** : act of purchasing **2** : something purchased **3** : secure grasp —**pur·chas·er** *n*

pure \'pyur\ *adj* **pur·er; pur·est** : free

of foreign matter, contamination, or corruption

pu·ree \pyü'rā, -'rē\ *n* : thick liquid mass of food

pur·ga·to·ry \'pərgə,tōrē\ *n, pl* **-ries** : intermediate state after death for purification by expiating sins —**pur·ga·tor·i·al** \,pərgə'tōrēəl\ *adj*

purge \'pərj\ *vb* **purged; purg·ing 1** : purify esp. from sin **2** : have or cause free evacuation from the bowels **3** : rid (as a political party) by a purge ~ *n* **1** : act or result of purging **2** : something that purges —**pur·ga·tive** \'pərgətiv\ *adj or n*

pu·ri·fy \'pyùrə,fī\ *vb* **-fied; -fy·ing** : make or become pure —**pu·ri·fi·ca·tion** \,pyùrəfə'kāshən\ *n* —**pu·ri·fi·er** \-'fī(ə)r\ *n*

Pu·rim \'pùr(,)im\ *n* : a Jewish holiday celebrated in February or March in commemoration of the deliverance of the Jews from the massacre plotted by Haman

pu·ri·tan \'pyùrətⁿn\ *n* : one who practices or preaches a very strict moral code —**pu·ri·tan·i·cal** \,pyùrə'tanikəl\ *adj*

pu·ri·ty \'pyùrətē\ *n* : quality or state of being pure

purl \'pərl\ *n* : stitch in knitting ~ *vb* : knit in purl stitch

pur·loin \(,)pər'lòin, 'pər,lòin\ *vb* : steal

pur·ple \'pərpəl\ *n* : bluish red color —**pur·plish** \'pərp(ə)lish\ *adj*

pur·port \(,)pər'pōrt\ *vb* : convey outwardly as the meaning ~ \'pər,pōrt\ *n* : meaning —**pur·port·ed·ly** \-'ōdlē\ *adv*

pur·pose \'pərpəs\ *n* **1** : something (as a result) aimed at **2** : resolution ~ *vb* **-posed; -pos·ing** : intend —**pur·pose·ful** \-fəl\ *adj* —**pur·pose·ful·ly** *adv* —**pur·pose·less** *adj* —**pur·pose·ly** *adv*

purr \'pər\ *n* : low murmur typical of a contented cat —**purr** *vb*

¹purse \'pərs\ *n* **1** : bag or pouch for money and small objects **2** : financial resource **3** : prize money

²purse *vb* **pursed; purs·ing** : pucker

pur·su·ance \pər'süəns\ *n* : act of carrying into effect

pursuant to \-'süənt-\ *prep* : according to

pur·sue \pər'sü\ *vb* **-sued; -su·ing 1** : follow in order to overtake **2** : seek to accomplish **3** : engage in —**pur·su·er** *n*

pur·suit \pər'süt\ *n* **1** : act of pursuing **2** : occupation

pur·vey \(,)pər'vā\ *vb* **-veyed; -vey·ing** : supply (as provisions) usu. as a business —**pur·vey·ance** \-əns\ *n* —**pur·vey·or** \-ər\ *n*

pus \'pəs\ *n* : thick yellowish fluid (as in a boil)

push \'pùsh\ *vb* **1** : press against to move forward **2** : urge on or provoke ~ *n* **1** : vigorous effort **2** : act of pushing —**push·cart** *n*

pushy \'pùshē\ *adj* **push·i·er; -est** : objectionably aggressive

pu·sil·lan·i·mous \,pyüsə'lanəməs\ *adj* : cowardly

pussy \'pùsē\ *n, pl* **puss·ies** : cat

pus·tule \'pəschül\ *n* : pus-filled pimple

put \'pùt\ *vb* **put; put·ting 1** : bring to a specified position or condition **2** : subject to pain, suffering, or death **3** : impose or cause to exist **4** : express **5** : cause to be used or employed —**put out** *vb* : bother or inconvenience —**put up with** : endure

pu·tre·fy \'pyütrə,fī\ *vb* **-fied; -fy·ing** : make or become putrid —**pu·tre·fac·tion** \,pyütrə'fakshən\ *n* —**pu·tre·fac·tive** \-'fak,tiv\ *adj*

pu·trid \'pyütrəd\ *adj* : rotten —**pu·trid·i·ty** \pyü'tridətē\ *n*

put·ter \'pətər\ *vb* : occupy oneself with casual or unimportant work

put·ty \'pətē\ *n, pl* **-ties** : doughlike cement —**putty** *vb*

puz·zle \'pəzəl\ *vb* **-zled; -zling 1** : confuse **2** : attempt to solve —with *out* or *over* ~ *n* : something that confuses or tests ingenuity —**puz·zle·ment** \-mənt\ *n* —**puz·zler** \-(ə)lər\ *n*

pyg·my \'pigmē\ *n, pl* **-mies** : dwarf —**pygmy** *adj*

py·lon \'pī,län, -lən\ *n* : tower or tall post

pyr·a·mid \'pirə,mid\ *n* : structure with a square base and 4 triangular sides meeting at a point —**py·ra·mi·dal** \pə'ramədⁿl, ,pirə'mid-\ *adj*

pyre \'pī(ə)r\ *n* : material heaped for a funeral fire

py·ro·ma·nia \,pīrō'mānēə\ *n* : irresistible impulse to start fires —**py·ro·ma·ni·ac** \-nē,ak\ *n*

py·ro·tech·nics \,pīrō'tekniks\ *n pl* : spectacular display (as of fireworks) —**py·ro·tech·nic** \-nik\ *adj*

py·thon \'pī,thän, -thən\ *n* : very large constricting snake

Q

q \'kyü\ *n, pl* **q's** *or* **qs** \'kyüz\ : 17th letter of the alphabet

¹quack \'kwak\ *vb* : make a cry like that of a duck —**quack** *n*

²quack *n* : one who pretends to have medical or healing skill —**quack** *adj* —**quack·ery** \-ərē\ *n* —**quack·ish** *adj*

quad·ran·gle \'kwäd,raŋgəl\ *n* : flat geometrical figure having 4 angles and 4 sides —**quad·ran·gu·lar** \kwä'draŋgyələr\ *adj*

quad·rant \'kwädrənt\ *n* : 1/4 of a circle

quad·ri·lat·er·al \,kwädrə'lat(ə)rəl\ *adj* : having 4 sides ~ *n* : 4-sided polygon

qua·drille \kwä'dril, k(w)ə-\ *n* : square dance of 5 or 6 figures in various rhythms

quad·ru·ped \'kwädrə,ped\ *n* : animal having 4 feet —**qua·dru·pe·dal** \kwä'drüpəd³l, ,kwädrə'ped-\ *adj*

qua·dru·ple \kwä'drüpəl, -'drəp-; 'kwädrəp-\ *vb* **-pled; -pling** \-(ə)liŋ\ : multiply by 4 ~ *adj* : being 4 times as great as many

qua·dru·plet \kwä'drəplət, -'drüp-; 'kwädrəp-\ *n* : one of 4 offspring born at one birth

quaff \'kwäf, 'kwaf\ *vb* : drink deeply or repeatedly —**quaff** *n*

quag·mire \'kwag,mī(ə)r, 'kwäg-\ *n* : soft land or bog

qua·hog \'kō,hȯg, 'kwȯ-, 'kwö-, -,häg\ *n* : thick-shelled clam

¹quail \'kwāl\ *n, pl* **quail** *or* **quails** : short-winged stout-bodied game bird

²quail *vb* : lose courage or cower in fear

quaint \'kwānt\ *adj* : pleasingly old-fashioned or odd —**quaint·ly** *adv* —**quaint·ness** *n*

quake \'kwāk\ *vb* **quaked; quak·ing** : shake or tremble ~ *n* : earthquake

qual·i·fi·ca·tion \,kwäləfə'kāshən\ *n* **1** : limitation or stipulation **2** : special skill or experience for a job

qual·i·fy \'kwälə,fī\ *vb* **-fied; -fy·ing 1** : modify or limit **2** : fit by skill or training for some purpose **3** : become eligible —**qual·i·fied** *adj* —**qual·i·fi·er** \-,fī(ə)r\ *n*

qual·i·ty \'kwälətē\ *n, pl* **-ties 1** : peculiar and essential character, nature, or feature **2** : excellence or distinction

qualm \'kwäm, 'kwälm, 'kwȯm\ *n* : scruple

quan·da·ry \'kwänd(ə)rē\ *n, pl* **-ries** : state of perplexity or doubt

quan·ti·ty \'kwäntətē\ *n, pl* **-ties 1** : something that can be measured or numbered **2** : considerable amount

quar·an·tine \'kwȯrən,tēn\ *n* **1** : restraint on the movements of persons or goods to prevent the spread of pests or disease **2** : place or period of quarantine —**quarantine** *vb*

quar·rel \'kwȯr(ə)l\ *n* : basis of conflict —**quarrel** *vb* —**quar·rel·some** \-səm\ *adj*

¹quar·ry \'kwȯrē\ *n, pl* **quarries** : prey

²quarry *n, pl* **-ries** : excavation for obtaining stone —**quarry** *vb*

quart \'kwȯrt\ *n* : unit of liquid measure equal to .95 liter or of dry measure equal to 1.10 liters

quar·ter \'kwȯrtər\ *n* **1** : 1/4 part **2** : 1/4 of a dollar **3** : city district **4** *pl* : place to live esp. for a time **5** : mercy ~ *vb* : divide into 4 equal parts

quar·ter·ly \'kwȯrtərlē\ *adv or adj* : at 3-month intervals ~ *n, pl* **-lies** : periodical published 4 times a year

quar·ter·mas·ter \-,mastər\ *n* **1** : ship's helmsman **2** : army supply officer

quar·tet \kwȯr'tet\ *n* **1** : music for 4 performers **2** : group of 4

quar·to \'kwȯrtō\ *n, pl* **-tos** : book printed on pages cut 4 from a sheet

quartz \'kwȯrts\ *n* : transparent crystalline mineral

quash \'kwäsh, 'kwȯsh\ *vb* **1** : set aside by judicial action **2** : suppress summarily and completely

qua·si \'kwā,zī, -sī; 'kwäzē, 'kwäs-; 'kwäzē\ *adj* : similar or nearly identical

qua·train \'kwä,trān\ *n* : unit of 4 lines of verse

qua·ver \'kwāvər\ *vb* : tremble or trill —**quaver** *n*

quay \'kē, 'k(w)ā\ *n* : wharf

quea·sy \'kwēzē\ *adj* **-si·er; -est** : nauseated —**quea·si·ly** \-zəlē\ *adv* —**quea·si·ness** \-zēnəs\ *n*

queen \'kwēn\ *n* **1** : wife or widow of a king **2** : female monarch **3** : woman of rank, power, or attractiveness **4** : fertile female of a social insect —**queen·ly** *adj*

queer \'kwiər\ *adj* : differing from the

usual or normal —**queer·ly** adv
—**queer·ness** n

quell \'kwel\ vb : put down

quench \'kwench\ vb 1 : put out 2 : satisfy (a thirst) —**quench·able** adj —**quench·less** adj

quer·u·lous \'kwer(y)ələs\ adj : fretful or whining —**quer·u·lous·ly** adv —**quer·u·lous·ness** n

que·ry \'kwi(ə)rē, 'kwe(ə)r-\ n, pl -**ries** : question —**query** vb

quest \'kwest\ n or vb : search

ques·tion \'kweschən\ n 1 : something asked 2 : subject for discussion 3 : dispute ~ vb 1 : ask questions 2 : doubt or dispute 3 : subject to analysis —**ques·tion·er** n

ques·tion·able \'kweschənəbəl\ adj 1 : not certain 2 : of doubtful truth or morality

question mark n : a punctuation mark ? used esp. at the end of a sentence to indicate a direct question

ques·tion·naire \,kweschə'na(ə)r\ n : set of questions

queue \'kyü\ n 1 : braid of hair 2 : line of persons or vehicles ~ vb queued; **queu·ing** or **queue·ing** : line up

quib·ble \'kwibəl\ n : minor objection —**quibble** vb

quick \'kwik\ adj 1 : rapid 2 : alert or perceptive ~ n 1 : sensitive area (as under a fingernail) —**quick** adv —**quick·ly** adv —**quick·ness** n

quick·en \'kwikən\ vb 1 : come to life 2 : hurry

quick·sand n : deep mass of sand and water

quick·sil·ver n : mercury

qui·es·cent \kwī'es⁵nt\ adj : being at rest —**qui·es·cence** \-⁵ns\ n

qui·et \'kwīət\ adj 1 : marked by little motion or activity 2 : gentle 3 : free from noise 4 : not showy 5 : secluded ~ vb : pacify —**quiet** adv or n —**qui·et·ly** adv —**qui·et·ness** n

qui·etude \'kwīə,t(y)üd\ n : quietness or repose

quill \'kwil\ n 1 : a large stiff feather 2 : porcupine's spine

quilt \'kwilt\ n : padded bedspread ~ vb : stitch or sew in layers with padding in between

quince \'kwins\ n : hard yellow apple-like fruit

qui·nine \'kwī,nīn\ n : bitter drug used against malaria

quin·tes·sence \kwin'tes⁵ns\ n 1 : purest essence of something 2 : most typical example —**quint·es·sen·tial** \,kwintə'senchəl\ adj

quin·tet \kwin'tet\ n 1 : music for 5 performers 2 : group of 5

quin·tu·ple \kwin't(y)üpəl, -'təp-; 'kwintəp-\ adj 1 : having 5 units or members 2 : being 5 times as great or as many —**quintuple** n or vb

quin·tu·plet \kwin'təplət, -'t(y)üp-; 'kwintəp-\ n : one of 5 offspring at one birth

quip \'kwip\ vb -**pp**- : make a clever remark —**quip** n

quire \'kwī(ə)r\ n : 24 or 25 sheets of paper of the same size and quality

quirk \'kwərk\ n : peculiarity of action or behavior —**quirky** adj

quit \'kwit\ vb quit; **quit·ting** 1 : stop 2 : leave —**quit·ter** n

quite \'kwīt\ adv 1 : completely 2 : to a considerable extent

quits \'kwits\ adj : even or equal with another (as by repaying a debt)

¹**quiv·er** \'kwivər\ n : case for arrows

²**quiver** vb : shake or tremble —**quiver** n

quix·ot·ic \kwik'sätik\ adj : idealistic to an impractical degree

quiz \'kwiz\ n, pl **quiz·zes** : short test ~ vb -**zz**- : question closely

quiz·zi·cal \'kwizikəl\ adj 1 : teasing 2 : curious

quoit \'kwät, 'kwȯit, 'k(w)ȯit\ n : ring thrown at a peg in a game (**quoits**)

quon·dam \'kwändəm, -,dam\ adj : former

quo·rum \'kwȯrəm\ n : required number of members present

quo·ta \'kwōtə\ n : proportional part or share

quotation mark n : one of a pair of punctuation marks " " or ' ' used esp. to indicate the beginning and the end of a quotation

quote \'kwōt\ vb quot·ed; **quot·ing** 1 : speak or write another's words 2 : state (a price) —**quot·able** adj —**quo·ta·tion** \kwō'tāshən\ n —**quote** n

quo·tient \'kwōshənt\ n : number resulting from division

R

r \\'är\\ *n, pl* **r's** *or* **rs** \\'ärz\\ : 18th letter of the alphabet

rab·bet \\'rabət\\ *n* : groove in a board

rab·bi \\'rab,ī\\ *n* : Jewish religious leader —**rab·bin·ic** \\rə'binik\\, **rab·bin·i·cal** \\-ikəl\\ *adj*

rab·bin·ate \\'rabənət, -,nāt\\ *n* : office of a rabbi

rab·bit \\'rabət\\ *n, pl* **-bit** *or* **-bits** : long-eared burrowing mammal

rab·ble \\'rabəl\\ *n* : mob

ra·bid \\'rabəd\\ *adj* 1 : violent 2 : fanatical 3 : affected with rabies —**ra·bid·ly** *adv*

ra·bies \\'rābēz\\ *n, pl* **rabies** : acute deadly virus disease

rac·coon \\ra'kün\\ *n, pl* **-coon** *or* **-coons** : tree-dwelling mammal with a bushy ringed tail

¹race \\'rās\\ *n* 1 : strong current of water 2 : contest of speed 3 : election campaign ~ *vb* **raced; rac·ing** 1 : run in a race 2 : rush —**race·course** *n* —**rac·er** *n* —**race·track** *n*

²race *n* 1 : family, tribe, people, or nation of the same stock 2 : division of mankind based on hereditary traits —**ra·cial** \\'rāshəl\\ *adj* —**ra·cial·ly** *adv*

race·horse *n* : horse used for racing

rac·ism \\'rās,izəm\\ *n* : discrimination based on the belief that some races are by nature superior —**rac·ist** \\-əst\\ *n*

rack \\'rak\\ *n* 1 : framework for display or storage 2 : instrument that stretches the body for torture ~ *vb* : torture with or as if with a rack

¹rack·et \\'rakət\\ *n* : bat with a tight netting across an open frame

²racket *n* 1 : confused noise 2 : fraudulent scheme —**rack·e·teer** \\,rakə'tiər\\ *n* —**rack·e·teer·ing** *n*

ra·con·teur \\,rak,än'tər\\ *n* : storyteller

racy \\'rāsē\\ *adj* **rac·i·er; -est** : risqué —**rac·i·ly** *adv* —**rac·i·ness** *n*

ra·dar \\'rā,där\\ *n* : radio device for determining distance, shape, or position of distant objects

ra·di·al \\'rādēəl\\ *adj* : having parts arranged like rays coming from a common center —**ra·di·al·ly** *adv*

ra·di·ant \\'rādēənt\\ *adj* 1 : glowing 2 : beaming with happiness 3 : transmitted by radiation —**ra·di·ance** \\-əns\\ *n* —**ra·di·an·cy** \\-ənsē\\ *n* —**ra·di·ant·ly** *adv*

ra·di·ate \\'rādē,āt\\ *vb* **-at·ed; -at·ing** 1 : issue rays or in rays 2 : spread from a center —**ra·di·a·tion** \\,rādē'āshən\\ *n*

ra·di·a·tor \\'rādē,ātər\\ *n* : cooling or heating device

rad·i·cal \\'radikəl\\ *adj* 1 : fundamental 2 : extreme ~ *n* 1 : person favoring extreme changes 2 : group of atoms replaceable by one atom —**rad·i·cal·ism** \\-,izəm\\ *n* —**rad·i·cal·ly** *adv*

radii *pl of* RADIUS

ra·dio \\'rādē,ō\\ *n, pl* **-di·os** 1 : transmission or reception of sound by means of electric waves 2 : radio receiving set ~ *vb* : send a message to by radio —**radio** *adj*

ra·dio·ac·tiv·i·ty \\,rādēō,ak'tivətē\\ *n* : property of an element that emits energy through nuclear disintegration —**ra·dio·ac·tive** \\-'aktiv\\ *adj*

ra·di·ol·o·gy \\,rādē'äləjē\\ *n* : medical use of radiation —**ra·di·ol·o·gist** \\-jəst\\ *n*

rad·ish \\'radish\\ *n* : pungent fleshy root usu. eaten raw

ra·di·um \\'rādēəm\\ *n* : metallic radioactive chemical element

ra·di·us \\'rādēəs\\ *n, pl* **-dii** \\-ē,ī\\ 1 : line from the center of a circle or sphere to the circumference or surface 2 : area defined by a radius

raff·ish \\'rafish\\ *adj* : flashily vulgar —**raff·ish·ly** *adv* —**raff·ish·ness** *n*

raf·fle \\'rafəl\\ *n* : lottery among people who have bought tickets ~ *vb* **-fled; -fling** : offer in a raffle

¹raft \\'raft\\ *n* 1 : flat floating platform ~ *vb* : travel or transport by raft

²raft *n* : large amount or number

raf·ter \\'raftər\\ *n* : usu. sloping timber of a roof

¹rag \\'rag\\ *n* : waste piece of cloth

²rag *n* : composition in ragtime

rag·a·muf·fin \\'ragə,məfən\\ *n* : ragged dirty person

rage \\'rāj\\ *n* 1 : violent anger 2 : vogue ~ *vb* **raged; rag·ing** 1 : be extremely angry or violent 2 : be out of control

rag·ged \\'ragəd\\ *adj* : torn —**rag·ged·ly** *adv* —**rag·ged·ness** *n*

ra·gout \\ra'gü\\ *n* : meat stew

rag·time *n* : syncopated rhythm

rag·weed \'rag-̧wēd\ n : coarse weedy herb with allergenic pollen

raid \'rād\ n : sudden usu. surprise attack —**raid** vb —**raid·er** n

¹**rail** \'rāl\ n 1 : bar serving as a guard or barrier 2 : bar forming a track for wheeled vehicles 3 : railroad

²**rail** vb : scold someone vehemently —**rail·er** n

rail·ing \'rā-liŋ\ n : rail or a barrier of rails

rail·lery \'rā-lə-rē\ n, pl **-ler·ies** : good-natured ridicule

rail·road \'rāl-̧rōd\ n : road for a train laid with iron rails and wooden ties ~ vb : force something hastily —**rail·road·er** n —**rail·road·ing** n

rail·way \-̧wā\ n : railroad

rai·ment \'rā-mənt\ n : clothing

rain \'rān\ n 1 : water falling in drops from the clouds 2 : shower of objects ~ vb : fall as or like rain —**rain·coat** n —**rain·drop** n —**rain·fall** n —**rain·mak·er** n —**rain·mak·ing** n —**rain·storm** n —**rain·water** n —**rainy** adj

rain·bow \-̧bō\ n : arc of colors formed by the sun shining through moisture

raise \'rāz\ vb **raised; rais·ing** 1 : lift 2 : arouse 3 : erect 4 : collect 5 : breed, grow, or bring up 6 : increase 7 : make light ~ n : increase esp. in pay —**rais·er** n

rai·sin \'rāz-ᵊn\ n : dried grape

ra·ja, ra·jah \'rä-jə\ n : Indian prince

¹**rake** \'rāk\ n : tool for smoothing or sweeping ~ vb **raked; rak·ing** 1 : gather, loosen, or smooth with or as if with a rake 2 : sweep with gunfire

²**rake** n : dissolute man —**rak·ish** \'rā-kish\ adj

rakish \'rā-kish\ adj : smart or jaunty —**rak·ish·ly** adv —**rak·ish·ness** n

ral·ly \'ra-lē\ vb **-lied; -ly·ing** 1 : bring or come together 2 : revive or recover ~ n, pl **-lies** 1 : act of rallying 2 : mass meeting

ram \'ram\ n 1 : male sheep 2 : beam used in battering down walls or doors ~ vb **-mm-** 1 : force or drive in or through 2 : strike against violently

ram·ble \'ram-bəl\ vb **-bled; -bling** : wander —**ramble** n —**ram·bler** \-blər\ n

ram·bunc·tious \ram-'bəŋk-shəs\ adj : unruly

ram·i·fi·ca·tion \̧ra-mə-fə-'kā-shən\ n : consequence

ram·i·fy \'ra-mə-̧fī\ vb **-fied; -fy·ing** : branch out

ramp \'ramp\ n : sloping passage or connecting roadway

ram·page \'ram-̧pāj, (̧)ram-'pāj\ vb **-paged; -pag·ing** : rush about wildly ~ \'ram-̧-\ n : violent or riotous action or behavior

ram·pant \'ram-pənt\ adj : widespread —**ram·pant·ly** adv

ram·part \'ram-̧pärt\ n : embankment of a fortification

ram·rod n : rod used to load or clean a gun

ram·shack·le \'ram-̧sha-kəl\ adj : shaky

ran past of RUN

ranch \'ranch\ n 1 : establishment for the raising of cattle, sheep, or horses 2 : specialized farm ~ vb : operate a ranch —**ranch·er** n —**ranch·land** \-̧land\ n

ran·cid \'ran-səd\ adj : smelling or tasting as if spoiled —**ran·cid·i·ty** \ran-'si-də-tē\ n —**ran·cid·ness** n

ran·cor \'raŋ-kər\ n : deep hatred —**ran·cor·ous** adj

ran·dom \'ran-dəm\ adj : occurring by chance —**ran·dom·ly** adv —**ran·dom·ness** n —**at random** : without definite aim or method

ran·dom·ize \'ran-də-̧mīz\ vb **-ized; -iz·ing** : distribute or treat in a random way —**ran·dom·iza·tion** \̧ran-də-mə-'zā-shən\ n

rang past of RING

range \'rānj\ n 1 : series of things in a row 2 : open land for grazing 3 : cooking stove 4 : variation within limits 5 : place for target practice 6 : extent ~ vb **ranged; rang·ing** 1 : set in a row or in order 2 : roam at large, freely, or over 3 : vary within limits —**range·land** \-̧land\ n

rang·er \'rān-jər\ n : lawman or soldier who patrols a large area

rangy \'rān-jē\ adj **rang·i·er; -est** : being slender with long limbs —**rang·i·ness** n

¹**rank** \'raŋk\ adj 1 : vigorous in growth 2 : unpleasantly strong-smelling —**rank·ly** adv —**rank·ness** n

²**rank** n 1 : line of soldiers 2 : orderly arrangement 3 : grade of official standing 4 : position within a group ~ vb 1 : arrange in formation or according to class 2 : take or give a relative position

rank and file n : general membership

ran·kle \'raŋ-kəl\ vb **-kled; -kling** 1 : become inflamed 2 : cause anger, irritation, or bitterness

ran·sack \'ran-̧sak\ vb : search through and rob

ran·som \'ran-səm\ n : something demanded for the freedom of a captive

~ *vb* : gain the freedom of by paying a price —**ran·som·er** *n*

rant \\'rant\\ *vb* : talk or scold violently —**rant·er** *n* —**rant·ing·ly** *adv*

¹rap \\'rap\\ *n* : sharp blow or rebuke ~ *vb* **-pp-** : strike or criticize sharply

²rap *vb* **-pp-** : talk freely

ra·pa·cious \\rə'pāshəs\\ *adj* **1** : excessively greedy **2** : ravenous —**ra·pa·cious·ly** *adv* —**ra·pa·cious·ness** *n* —**ra·pac·i·ty** \\-'pasətē\\ *n*

¹rape \\'rāp\\ *n* : herb grown as a forage crop and for its seeds (**rape·seed**)

²rape *vb* **raped; rap·ing** : force to have sexual intercourse —**rape** *n* —**rap·er** *n* —**rap·ist** \\'rāpəst\\ *n*

rap·id \\'rapəd\\ *adj* : very fast —**ra·pid·i·ty** \\rə'pidətē\\ *n* —**rap·id·ly** *adv*

rap·ids \\-ədz\\ *n pl* : place in a stream where the current is swift

ra·pi·er \\'rāpēər\\ *n* : narrow 2-edged sword

rap·ine \\'rapən, -ˌīn\\ *n* : plunder

rap·port \\ra'pōr\\ *n* : harmonious relationship

rapt \\'rapt\\ *adj* : engrossed —**rapt·ly** *adv* —**rapt·ness** *n*

rap·ture \\'rapchər\\ *n* : spiritual or emotional ecstasy —**rap·tur·ous** \\-chərəs\\ *adj*

¹rare \\'ra(ə)r\\ *adj* **rar·er; rar·est** : having a portion relatively uncooked

²rare *adj* **rar·er; rar·est** **1** : not dense **2** : unusually fine **3** : seldom met with —**rare·ly** *adv* —**rare·ness** *n* —**rar·i·ty** \\'rarətē\\ *n*

rar·efy \\'rarə,fī\\ *vb* **-efied; -efy·ing** : make or become rare, thin, or less dense —**rar·efac·tion** \\ˌrarə'fakshən\\ *n*

rar·ing \\'ra(ə)rən, -iŋ\\ *adj* : full of enthusiasm

ras·cal \\'raskəl\\ *n* : mean, dishonest, or mischievous person —**ras·cal·i·ty** \\ras-'kal-ət-ē\\ *n* —**ras·cal·ly** \\raskəlē\\ *adj*

¹rash \\'rash\\ *adj* : too hasty in decision or action —**rash·ly** *adv* —**rash·ness** *n*

²rash *n* : a breaking out of the skin with red spots

rasp \\'rasp\\ *vb* **1** : rub with or as if with a rough file **2** : to speak in a grating tone ~ *n* : coarse file

rasp·ber·ry \\'raz,berē, -b(ə)rē\\ *n* : edible red or black berry

rat \\'rat\\ *n* : destructive rodent larger than the mouse

ratch·et \\'rachət\\ *n* : notched device for allowing motion in one direction

rate \\'rāt\\ *n* **1** : quantity, amount, or degree measured in relation to some other quantity **2** : rank ~ *vb* **rat·ed;**

rat·ing **1** : estimate or determine the rank or quality of **2** : deserve —**rat·er** *n*

rath·er \\'rathər, 'rəth-, 'räth-\\ *adv* **1** : preferably **2** : on the other hand **3** : more properly **4** : somewhat

rat·i·fy \\'ratə,fī\\ *vb* **-fied; -fy·ing** : approve and accept formally —**rat·i·fi·ca·tion** \\ˌratəfə'kāshən\\ *n*

rat·ing \\'rātiŋ\\ *n* : classification according to grade

ra·tio \\'rāsh(ē)ō\\ *n, pl* **-tios** : relation in number, quantity, or degree between things

ra·tion \\'rashən, 'räshən\\ *n* : share or allotment (as of food) ~ *vb* : use or allot sparingly

ra·tio·nal \\'rash(ə)nəl\\ *adj* **1** : having reason or sanity **2** : relating to reason —**ra·tio·nal·ly** *adv*

ra·tio·nale \\ˌrashə'nal\\ *n* **1** : explanation of principles of belief or practice **2** : underlying reason

ra·tio·nal·ize \\-ˌīz\\ *vb* **-ized; -iz·ing** **1** : justify (as one's behavior or weaknesses) esp. to oneself —**ra·tio·nal·iza·tion** \\ˌrash(ə)nələ'zāshən\\ *n*

rat·tan \\ra'tan, rə-\\ *n* : palm with long stems used esp. for canes and wickerwork

rat·tle \\'ratᵊl\\ *vb* **-tled; -tling** **1** : make a series of clattering sounds **2** : say briskly **3** : confuse or upset ~ *n* **1** : series of clattering sounds **2** : toy that rattles

rat·tler \\'ratlər\\ *n* : rattlesnake

rat·tle·snake *n* : American venomous snake with a rattle at the end of the tail

rau·cous \\'rókəs\\ *adj* : harsh or boisterous —**rau·cous·ly** *adv* —**rau·cous·ness** *n*

rav·age \\'ravij\\ *n* : destructive effect ~ *vb* **-aged; -ag·ing** : lay waste —**rav·ag·er** *n*

rave \\'rāv\\ *vb* **raved; rav·ing** **1** : talk wildly in or as if in delirium **2** : talk with extreme enthusiasm ~ *n* **1** : act of raving **2** : enthusiastic praise

rav·el \\'ravəl\\ *vb* **-eled** or **-elled; -el·ing** or **-el·ling** **1** : unravel **2** : tangle ~ *n* **1** : something tangled **2** : loose thread

ra·ven \\'rāvən\\ *n* : large black bird ~ *adj* : black and shiny

rav·en·ous \\'rav(ə)nəs\\ *adj* : very hungry —**rav·en·ous·ly** *adv* —**rav·en·ous·ness** *n*

ra·vine \\rə'vēn\\ *n* : narrow steep-sided valley

rav·ish \\'ravish\\ *vb* **1** : seize and take away by violence **2** : overcome with

joy or delight **3** : rape —**rav·ish·er** *n*
—**rav·ish·ment** *n*

raw \'rȯ\ *adj* **raw·er** \'rȯ(ə)r\; **raw·est**
\'rȯəst\ **1** : not cooked **2** : not processed **3** : not trained **4** : having the
skin rubbed off **5** : cold and damp **6**
: vulgar —**raw·ness** *n*

raw·hide \'rȯ,hīd\ *n* : untanned skin of
cattle

ray \'rā\ *n* **1** : thin beam of radiant
energy (as light) **2** : tiny bit

ray·on \'rā,än\ *n* : fabric made from
cellulose fiber

raze \'rāz\ *vb* **razed; raz·ing** : destroy
or tear down

ra·zor \'rāzər\ *n* : sharp cutting instrument used to shave off hair

re- \rē, ,rē, 'rē\ *prefix* **1** : again or
anew **2** : back or backward

reaccelerate	reassociate
reaccept	reattach
reacclimatize	reattain
reaccredit	reawaken
reaccumulate	rebalance
reachieve	rebaptize
reacquaint	rebid
reacquire	rebind
reactivate	reborn
reactivation	rebroadcast
readapt	rebuild
readdict	rebury
readdress	recalculate
readjust	recapture
readjustable	recast
readjustment	recertification
readmit	recertify
readopt	rechannel
reaffirm	recharge
realign	recheck
realignment	rechristen
reallocate	recirculate
reanalysis	recirculation
reanalyze	reclassification
reanesthetize	reclassify
reappear	recolonize
reappearance	recombine
reapply	recompute
reappoint	reconceive
reapportion	reconnect
reappraisal	reconquer
reappraise	reconquest
reapprove	reconsider
reargue	reconsideration
rearrange	reconsolidate
rearrest	reconstruct
reassemble	recontaminate
reassert	reconvene
reassess	reconvict
reassessment	recopy
reassign	recross
reassignment	redeal

redecorate	reinstall
rededicate	reinstitute
rededication	reintegrate
redefine	reintegration
redeposit	reinter
redesign	reintroduce
redesignate	reinvent
redevelop	reinvestigate
rediscover	reinvestigation
rediscovery	reinvigorate
redissolve	rejudge
redistribute	rekindle
redraft	reknit
redraw	relabel
reemerge	relandscape
reemergence	relaunch
reemphasize	relearn
reenergize	relight
reengage	reline
reenlist	reload
reenlistment	remarriage
reenroll	remarry
reenter	remelt
reequip	remobilize
reestablish	remoisten
reestablishment	remold
reestimate	remotivate
reevaluate	rename
reevaluation	renegotiate
reexamination	reoccupy
reexamine	reoccur
refilm	reoccurrence
refinance	reoperate
refire	reorchestrate
refloat	reorganization
reflood	reorganize
refocus	reorient
refold	repack
reformulate	repaint
refreeze	repave
regrow	rephotograph
regrowth	replan
rehear	replaster
reheat	replay
rehire	replot
rehospitalization	repolish
rehospitalize	repopulate
reidentify	repressurize
reignite	reprice
reimplant	reprint
reimpose	reprocess
reincorporate	reprogram
reindict	repropose
reinfection	reread
reinfest	rerecord
reinflate	reregister
reinject	reroof
reinjection	reroute
reinoculate	resalable
reinsert	resale
reinsertion	reschedule
reinspect	reseal

resegregate retarget
resell reteach
resentence retell
reset retest
resettle rethink
resew retighten
reshoot retitle
reshow retrain
resod retranslate
resolidify retransmit
restage retransplant
restart retrap
restate retry
restatement retune
restimulate retype
restock reupholster
restructure reutilize
restudy revaccinate
restyle revaccination
resubmit revisit
resupply rewash
resurface rewax
resurvey reweave
resuspend rewind
resynthesis rewire
resynthesize rewrap

reach \'rēch\ vb 1 : stretch out 2 : touch or try to touch or grasp 3 : extend to or arrive at 4 : communicate with ~ n 1 : act of reaching 2 : distance or extent of reaching —reach·able adj —reach·er n

re·act \rē'akt\ vb 1 : act in response to some influence or stimulus 2 : undergo chemical reaction —re·active \-'aktiv\ adj

re·ac·tion \rē'akshən\ n 1 : action or emotion caused by and directly related or counter to another action 2 : chemical change

re·ac·tion·ary \-shə,nerē\ adj : relating to or favoring return to an earlier political order or policy ~ n, pl -ar·ies : reactionary person

re·ac·tor \rē'aktər\ n 1 : one that reacts 2 : apparatus for the controlled release of atomic energy

read \'rēd\ vb read \'red\; read·ing \'rēdiŋ\ 1 : understand written language 2 : utter aloud printed words 3 : interpret 4 : study 5 : indicate ~ adj \'red\ : informed by reading —read·a·bil·i·ty \,rēdə'bilətē\ n —read·able adj —read·ably adv —read·er n —read·er·ship n

read·ing \'rēdiŋ\ n 1 : something read or for reading 2 : particular version, interpretation, or performance 3 : indication of data made by an instrument

ready \'redē\ adj readi·er; -est 1 : prepared or available for use or action 2 : willing to do something ~ vb read·ied; ready·ing : make ready ~ n : state of being ready —read·i·ly adv —read·i·ness n

re·al \'rē(ə)l\ adj 1 : actually existing 2 : genuine ~ adv : very —re·al·ness n —for real 1 : in earnest 2 : genuine

real estate n : property in houses and land

re·al·ism \'rēə,lizəm\ n 1 : disposition to deal with facts practically 2 : faithful portrayal of reality —re·al·ist \-list\ adj or n —re·al·is·tic \,rēə'listik\ adj —re·al·is·ti·cally \-tik(ə)lē\ adv

re·al·i·ty \rē'alətē\ n, pl -ties 1 : quality or state of being real 2 : something real

re·al·ize \'rēə,līz\ vb -ized; -iz·ing 1 : make actual 2 : obtain 3 : be aware of —re·al·iz·able adj —re·al·i·za·tion \,rēələ'zāshən\ n

re·al·ly \'rē(ə)lē\ adv : in truth

realm \'relm\ n 1 : kingdom 2 : sphere

¹ream \'rēm\ n : quantity of paper that is 480, 500, or 516 sheets

²ream vb : enlarge or clean (a hole) with a specially shaped tool (reamer)

reap \'rēp\ vb : cut or clear (as a crop) with a scythe or machine —reap·er n

¹rear \'riər\ vb 1 : raise upright 2 : breed or bring up 3 : rise on the hind legs

²rear n 1 : back 2 : position at the back of something ~ adj : being at the back —rear·ward \-wərd\ adj or adv

rear admiral n : commissioned officer in the navy or coast guard ranking next below a vice admiral

rea·son \'rēz°n\ n 1 : explanation or justification 2 : motive for action or belief 3 : power or process of thinking ~ vb 1 : use the faculty of reason 2 : try to persuade another —rea·son·er n —rea·son·ing \'rēz-,niŋ, -°niŋ\ n

rea·son·able \'rēznəbəl, -°nəbəl\ adj 1 : being within the bounds of reason 2 : inexpensive —rea·son·able·ness n —rea·son·ably \-blē\ adv

re·as·sure \,rēə'shùr\ vb : restore one's confidence —re·as·sur·ance \-'shùrəns\ n —re·as·sur·ing·ly adv

re·bate \'rē,bāt\ n : return of part of a payment —rebate vb

¹reb·el \'rebəl\ n : one that resists authority —rebel \'rebəl\ adj

²re·bel \ri'bel\ vb -belled; -bel·ling 1 : resist authority 2 : feel or exhibit anger

re·bel·lion \ri'belyən\ n : resistance to authority and esp. to one's government

re·bel·lious \-yəs\ adj 1 : engaged in rebellion 2 : inclined to resist authority —re·bel·lious·ly adv —re·bel·lious·ness n

re·birth \'rē'bərth\ n 1 : new or second birth 2 : revival

re·bound \'rē'baùnd, ri-\ vb 1 : spring back on striking something 2 : recover from a reverse ~ \'rē,-\ n 1 : action of rebounding 2 : immediate reaction to a reverse

re·buff \ri'bəf\ vb : refuse or repulse rudely —rebuff n

re·buke \-'byük\ vb -buked; -buk·ing : reprimand sharply —rebuke n

re·bus \'rēbəs\ n : riddle representing syllables or words with pictures

re·but \ri'bət\ vb -but·ted; -but·ting : refute —re·but·ter n

re·but·tal \-ᵊl\ n : opposing argument

re·cal·ci·trant \ri'kalsətrənt\ adj 1 : stubbornly resisting authority 2 : resistant to handling or treatment —re·cal·ci·trance \-trəns\ n

re·call \ri'kȯl\ vb 1 : call back 2 : remember 3 : revoke ~ \ri'-, 'rē,-\ n 1 : a summons to return 2 : remembrance 3 : act of revoking

re·cant \ri'kant\ vb : take back (something said) publicly

re·ca·pit·u·late \,rēkə'pichə,lāt\ vb -lat·ed; -lat·ing : summarize —re·ca·pit·u·la·tion \-,pichə'lāshən\ n

re·cede \ri'sēd\ vb -ced·ed; -ced·ing 1 : move back or away 2 : slant backward

re·ceipt \-'sēt\ n 1 : act of receiving 2 : something (as payment) received —usu. in pl. 3 : writing acknowledging something received

re·ceive \ri'sēv\ vb -ceived; -ceiv·ing 1 : take in or accept 2 : greet or entertain (visitors) 3 : pick up radio waves and convert into sounds or pictures —re·ceiv·able adj

re·ceiv·er \ri'sēvər\ n 1 : one that receives 2 : one having charge of property or money involved in a lawsuit 3 : apparatus for receiving radio waves —re·ceiv·er·ship n

re·cent \'rēsᵊnt\ adj 1 : lately made or used 2 : of the present time or time just past —re·cent·ly adv —re·cent·ness n

re·cep·ta·cle \ri'septikəl\ n : container

re·cep·tion \ri'sepshən\ n 1 : act of receiving 2 : social gathering at which guests are formally welcomed

re·cep·tion·ist \-sh(ə)nəst\ n : one who greets callers

re·cep·tive \ri'septiv\ adj : open and responsive to ideas, impressions, or suggestions —re·cep·tive·ly adv —re·cep·tive·ness n —re·cep·tiv·i·ty \,rē,sep'tivətē\ n

re·cess \'rē,ses, ri'ses\ n 1 : indentation in a line or surface 2 : suspension of a session for rest ~ vb 1 : make a recess in or put into a recess 2 : interrupt a session to take a recess

re·ces·sion \ri'seshən\ n 1 : departing procession 2 : period of reduced economic activity

rec·i·pe \'resə,pē\ n : instructions for making something

re·cip·i·ent \ri'sipēənt\ n : one that receives

re·cip·ro·cal \ri'siprəkəl\ adj 1 : affecting each in the same way 2 : so related that one is equivalent to the other —re·cip·ro·cal·ly \-k(ə)lē\ adv —rec·i·proc·i·ty \,resə'präsətē\ n

re·cip·ro·cate \-,kāt\ vb -cat·ed; -cat·ing : make a return for something done or given —re·cip·ro·ca·tion \-,siprə'kāshən\ n

re·cit·al \ri'sītᵊl\ n 1 : public reading or recitation 2 : music or dance concert or exhibition by pupils —re·cit·al·ist \-ᵊl·əst\ n

rec·i·ta·tion \,resə'tāshən\ n : a reciting or recital

re·cite \ri'sīt\ vb -cit·ed; -cit·ing 1 : repeat verbatim 2 : recount —re·cit·er n

reck·less \'rekləs\ adj : lacking caution —reck·less·ly adv —reck·less·ness n

reck·on \'rekən\ vb 1 : count or calculate 2 : consider —reck·on·er n

reck·on·ing n 1 : act or instance of reckoning 2 : calculation of a ship's position 3 : settling of accounts

re·claim \ri'klām\ vb : obtain from a waste product or by-product —rec·claim·able adj —rec·la·ma·tion \,reklə'māshən\ n

re·cline \ri'klīn\ vb -clined; -clin·ing : lean backward or lie down

re·cluse \'rek,lüs, ri'klüs\ n : one who lives in seclusion

rec·og·ni·tion \,rekig'nishən, -əg-\ n : act of recognizing or state of being recognized

re·cog·ni·zance \ri'kä(g)nəzəns\ n : promise recorded before a court

rec·og·nize \'rekig,nīz, -əg-\ vb -nized; -niz·ing 1 : identify as previously known 2 : take notice of 3 : acknowledge esp. with appreciation —rec·og-

niz·able \'rekəg͵nīzəbəl, -ig-\ *adj*
—**rec·og·niz·ably** \-blē\ *adv*

re·coil \ri'kȯil\ *vb* : draw or spring
back — \'rē͵-, ri'-\ *n* : action of re-
coiling

rec·ol·lect \͵rekə'lekt\ *vb* : remember

rec·ol·lec·tion \͵rekə'lekshən\ *n* 1 : act
or power of recollecting 2 : something recollected

rec·om·mend \͵rekə'mend\ *vb* 1 : present as deserving of acceptance or
trial 2 : advise —**rec·om·mend·able**
\-'mendəbəl\ *adj* **rec·om·men·da·to-**
ry \-də͵tōrē, -͵tȯr-\ *adj* —**rec·om-**
mend·er *n*

rec·om·men·da·tion \͵rekəmən-
'dāshən\ *n* 1 : act of recommending
2 : statement or letter recommending
someone

rec·om·pense \'rekəm͵pens\ *vb*
-pensed; -pens·ing : give compensation to ~ *n* : compensation

rec·on·cile \'rekən͵sīl\ *vb* **-ciled; -cil-**
ing 1 : cause to be friendly again 2
: adjust or settle 3 : bring to acceptance —**rec·on·cil·able** *adj* —**rec·on-**
cile·ment *n* —**rec·on·cil·er** *n* —**rec-**
on·cil·i·a·tion \͵rekən͵silē'āshən\ *n*

re·con·nais·sance \ri'känəzəns, -səns\
n : exploratory survey of enemy territory

re·con·noi·ter \͵rēkə'nȯitər, ͵rekə-\ *vb*
: make a reconnaissance

re·con·dite \'rekən͵dīt\ *adj* 1 : hard to
understand 2 : little known

re·cord \ri'kȯrd\ *vb* 1 : set down in
writing 2 : register permanently 3
: indicate 4 : preserve (as sound or
images) for later reproduction ~
\'rekərd\ *n* 1 : something recorded 2
: best performance

re·cord·er \ri'kȯrdər\ *n* 1 : one who
records transactions officially 2
: wind instrument with finger holes 3
: recording device

1re·count \ri'kaúnt\ *vb* : relate in detail

2re·count \'rē-, -'\ *vb* : count again —**re-**
count \'rē͵-, (-')rē'-\ *n*

re·coup \ri'küp\ *vb* : make up for (an
expense or loss)

re·course \'rē͵kōrs, ri'-\ *n* : source of
aid or a turning to such a source

re·cov·er \ri'kəvər\ *vb* 1 : regain position, poise, or health 2 : recoup —**re-**
cov·er·able *adj* —**re·cov·ery**
\-'kəv(ə)rē\ *n*

re·cre·ation \͵rekrē'āshən\ *n* : a refreshing of strength or spirits as a
change from work or study —**rec·re-**
ation·al \-'sh(ə)nəl\ *adj* —**rec·re·ative**
\'rekrē͵ātiv\ *adj*

re·crim·i·na·tion \ri͵krimə'nāshən\ *n*
: accusation —**re·crim·i·nate** *vb* —**re-**
crim·i·na·to·ry \-'krim(ə)nə͵tōrē\
adj

re·cruit \ri'krüt\ *n* : newly enlisted
member ~ *vb* : enlist the membership or services of —**re·cruit·er** *n*
—**re·cruit·ment** *n*

rect·an·gle \'rek͵tangəl\ *n* : 4-sided figure with 4 right angles —**rect·an·gu-**
lar \rek'tangyələr\ *adj*

rec·ti·fy \'rektə͵fī\ *vb* **-fied; -fy·ing**
: make or set right —**rec·ti·fi·ca·tion**
\͵rektəfə'kāshən\ *n* —**rec·ti·fi·er**
\'rektə͵fī(ə)r\ *n*

rec·ti·tude \'rektə͵t(y)üd\ *n* : moral integrity

rec·tor \'rektər\ *n* : clergyman in
charge of a parish —**rec·tor·ate**
\-t(ə)rət\ *n* —**rec·to·ri·al**
\rek'tōrēəl\ *adj*

rec·to·ry \'rekt(ə)rē\ *n, pl* **-ries** : rec-
tor's residence

rec·tum \'rektəm\ *n, pl* **-tums** *or* **-ta**
\-tə\ : last part of the intestine joining colon and anus —**rec·tal** \-t²l\
adj

re·cum·bent \ri'kəmbənt\ *adj* : lying
down

re·cu·per·ate \ri'k(y)üpə͵rāt\ *vb* **-at·ed;**
-at·ing : recover (as from illness)
—**re·cu·per·a·tion** \-͵k(y)üpə-
'rāshən\ *n* —**re·cu·per·a·tive**
\-'k(y)üpə͵rātiv\ *adj*

re·cur \ri'kər\ *vb* **-rr-** 1 : return in
thought or talk 2 : happen or occur
again —**re·cur·rence** \-'kərəns\ *n*
—**re·cur·rent** \-ənt\ *adj*

red \'red\ *n* 1 : color of blood or of the
ruby 2 *cap* : communist —**red** *adj*
—**red·dish** *adj* —**red·ness** *n*

red·den \'red²n\ *vb* : make or become
red or reddish

re·deem \ri'dēm\ *vb* 1 : regain, free, or
rescue by paying a price 2 : atone for
3 : free from sin 4 : convert into
something of value —**re·deem·able**
adj —**re·deem·er** *n*

re·demp·tion \-'dempshən\ *n* : act of
redeeming —**re·demp·tive** \-tiv\ *adj*
—**re·demp·to·ry** \-t(ə)rē\ *adj*

red·head \-͵hed\ *n* : one having red
hair —**red·head·ed** \-'hedəd\ *adj*

red·o·lent \'red²lənt\ *adj* 1 : having a
fragrance 2 : suggestive —**red·o-**
lence \-əns\ *n* —**red·o·lent·ly** *adv*

re·doubt \ri'daút\ *n* : small fortification

re·doubt·able \-əbəl\ *adj* : arousing
dread

re·dound \ri'daúnd\ *vb* : have an effect

re-dress \ri'dres\ *vb* : set right ~ *n* 1 : relief or remedy 2 : compensation

red tape *n* : complex obstructive official routine

re-duce \ri'd(y)üs\ *vb* **-duced; -duc-ing** 1 : lessen 2 : put in a lower rank 3 : lose weight —**re-duc-er** *n* —**re-duc-ible** \-'d(y)üsabal\ *adj*

re-duc-tion \ri'dakshan\ *n* 1 : act of reducing 2 : amount lost in reducing 3 : something made by reducing

re-dun-dant \ri'dandant\ *adj* : using more words than necessary —**re-dun-dan-cy** \-dansē\ *n* —**re-dun-dant-ly** *adv*

red-wood *n* : tall coniferous timber tree

reed \'rēd\ *n* 1 : tall slender grass of wet areas 2 : elastic strip that vibrates to produce tones in certain wind instruments —**reedy** *adj*

reef \'rēf\ *n* : ridge of rocks or sand at or near the surface of the water —**reefy** *adj*

reek \'rēk\ *n* : strong or disagreeable fume or odor ~ *vb* : give off a reek —**reeky** *adj*

¹reel \'rēl\ *n* : revolvable device on which something flexible may be wound or quantity of something wound on it ~ *vb* 1 : wind on a reel 2 : pull in by reeling —**reel-able** *adj* —**reel-er** *n*

²reel *vb* 1 : whirl or waver as from a blow 2 : walk or move unsteadily ~ *n* : reeling motion

³reel *n* : lively dance

re-fer \ri'far\ *vb* **-rr-** 1 : direct or send to some person or place 2 : submit for consideration or action 3 : have connection 4 : mention or allude to something —**re-fer-able** \'ref(a)rabal, ri'fara-\ *adj* —**re-fer-ral** \ri'faral\ *n*

ref-er-ee \,refa'rē\ *n* 1 : one to whom an issue is referred for settlement 2 : sports official ~ *vb* **-eed; -ee-ing** : act as referee

ref-er-ence \'refarns, 'ref(a)rans\ *n* 1 : act of referring 2 : a bearing on a matter 3 : consultation for information 4 : person who can speak for one's character or ability or a recommendation given by such a person

ref-er-en-dum \,refa'rendam\ *n, pl* **-da** \-da\ *or* **-dums** : a seeking of voters' approval for a legislative proposal

re-fill \'rē-\ *vb* : fill again —**re-fill** \'rē-\ *n* —**re-fill-able** *adj*

re-fine \ri'fīn\ *vb* **-fined; -fin-ing** 1 : free from impurities or waste matter 2 : improve or perfect 3 : free or become free of what is coarse or un-

couth —**re-fine-ment** \-mant\ *n* —**re-fin-er** *n*

re-fin-ery \ri'fīn(a)rē\ *n, pl* **-er-ies** : place for refining (as oil or sugar)

re-flect \ri'flekt\ *vb* 1 : bend or cast back (as light or heat) 2 : bring as a result 3 : cast reproach or blame 4 : ponder —**re-flec-tion** \-'flekshan\ *n* —**re-flec-tive** \-tiv\ *adj* —**re-flec-tor** \-tar\ *n*

re-flex \'rē,fleks\ *n* : automatic response to a stimulus ~ *adj* 1 : bent back 2 : relating to a reflex —**re-flex-ly** *adv*

re-flex-ive \ri'fleksiv\ *adj* : of or relating to an action directed back upon the doer or the grammatical subject —**reflexive** *n* —**re-flex-ive-ly** *adv* —**re-flex-ive-ness** *n*

re-form \ri'fȯrm\ *vb* : make or become better esp. by correcting bad habits —**reform** *n* —**re-form-able** *adj* —**re-for-ma-tive** \-'fȯrmativ\ *adj* —**re-form-er** *n*

re-for-ma-to-ry \ri'fȯrma,tȯrē\ *n, pl* **-ries** : penal institution for reforming young offenders

re-fract \ri'frakt\ *vb* : subject to refraction

re-frac-tion \-'frakshan\ *n* : the bending of a ray (as of light) when it passes from one medium into another —**re-frac-tive** \-tiv\ *adj*

re-frac-to-ry \ri'frakt(a)rē\ *adj* : obstinate or unmanageable

re-frain \ri'frān\ *vb* : hold oneself back ~ *n* : verse recurring regularly in a song —**re-frain-ment** *n*

re-fresh \ri'fresh\ *vb* 1 : make or become fresh or fresher 2 : supply or take refreshment —**re-fresh-er** *n* —**re-fresh-ing-ly** *adv*

re-fresh-ment \-mant\ *n* 1 : act of refreshing 2 *pl* : light meal

re-frig-er-ate \ri'frija,rāt\ *vb* **-at-ed; -at-ing** : chill or freeze (food) for preservation —**re-frig-er-ant** \-(a)rant\ *adj or n* —**re-frig-er-a-tion** \-,frija'rāshan\ *n* —**re-frig-er-a-tor** \-'frija,rātar\ *n*

ref-uge \'ref,yüj\ *n* 1 : protection from danger 2 : place that provides protection

ref-u-gee \,refyù'jē\ *n* : one who flees for safety

re-fund \ri'fand, 'rē,fand\ *vb* : give or put back (money) ~ \'rē-\ *n* 1 : act of refunding 2 : sum refunded —**re-fund-able** *adj*

re-fur-bish \ri'farbish\ *vb* : renovate

¹re-fuse \ri'fyüz\ *vb* **-fused; -fus-ing**

: decline to accept, do, or give —**re·fus·al** \-'fyüzəl\ *n*

²**re·fuse** \'ref,yüs, -,yüz\ *n* : worthless matter

re·fute \ri'fyüt\ *vb* -**fut·ed; -fut·ing** : prove to be false —**ref·u·ta·tion** \,refyü'tāshən\ *n* —**re·fut·er** \ri'fyütər\ *n*

re·gain \ri'gān\ *vb* : get again

re·gal \'rēgəl\ *adj* 1 : befitting a king 2 : stately —**re·gal·ly** *adv*

re·gale \ri'gāl\ *vb* -**galed; -gal·ing** 1 : entertain richly or agreeably 2 : delight —**re·gale·ment** *n*

re·ga·lia \ri'gālyə\ *n pl* 1 : symbols of royalty 2 : insignia of an office or order 3 : finery

re·gard \ri'gärd\ *n* 1 : consideration 2 : feeling of approval and liking 3 *pl* : friendly greetings 4 : relation ~ *vb* 1 : pay attention to 2 : show respect 3 : have an opinion of 4 : look at 5 : relate to —**re·gard·ful** *adj* —**re·gard·less** *adj*

re·gard·ing *prep* : concerning

regardless of \ri'gärdləs-\ *prep* : in spite of

re·gen·er·ate \ri'jen(ə)rət\ *adj* 1 : formed or created again 2 : spiritually reborn ~ *vb* 1 : reform completely 2 : get new life —**re·gen·er·a·tion** \-,jenə'rāshən\ *n* —**re·gen·er·a·tive** \-'jenə,rātiv\ *adj* —**re·gen·er·a·tor** \-,rātər\ *n*

re·gent \'rējənt\ *n* 1 : person who rules during the childhood, absence, or incapacity of the sovereign 2 : member of a governing board —**re·gen·cy** \-jənsē\ *n*

re·gime \rā'zhēm, ri-\ *n* : government in power

reg·i·men \'rejəmən\ *n* : systematic course of treatment

reg·i·ment \'rejəmənt\ *n* : military unit ~ \-,ment\ *vb* : organize rigidly for control —**reg·i·men·tal** \,rejə'ment³l\ *adj* —**reg·i·men·ta·tion** \-mən'tāshən\ *n*

re·gion \'rējən\ *n* : indefinitely defined area —**re·gion·al** \'rej(ə)nəl\ *adj* —**re·gion·al·ly** *adv*

reg·is·ter \'rejəstər\ *n* 1 : record of items or details or a book for keeping such a record 2 : device to regulate ventilation 3 : counting or recording device 4 : range of a voice or instrument ~ *vb* 1 : enter in a register 2 : record automatically 3 : get special care for mail by paying more postage

reg·is·trar \-,strär\ *n* : official keeper of records

reg·is·tra·tion \,rejə'strāshən\ *n* 1 : act of registering 2 : entry in a register

re·gress \ri'gres\ *vb* : go or cause to go back or to a lower level —**re·gres·sion** \-'greshən\ *n* —**re·gres·sive** *adj* —**re·gres·sor** \-'gresər\ *n*

re·gret \ri'gret\ *vb* -**tt**- 1 : mourn the loss or death of 2 : be keenly sorry for ~ *n* 1 : sorrow or the expression of sorrow 2 *pl* : message declining an invitation —**re·gret·ful** \-fəl\ *adj* —**re·gret·ful·ly** *adv* —**re·gret·ta·ble** \-əbəl\ *adj* —**re·gret·ta·bly** \-blē\ *adv* —**re·gret·ter** *n*

reg·u·lar \'regyələr\ *adj* 1 : conforming to what is usual, normal, or average 2 : steady, uniform, or unvarying —**regular** *n* —**reg·u·lar·i·ty** \,regyə'larətē\ *n* —**reg·u·lar·ize** \'regyələ,rīz\ *vb* —**reg·u·lar·ly** *adv*

reg·u·late \'regyə,lāt\ *vb* -**lat·ed; -lat·ing** 1 : govern according to rule 2 : adjust to a standard —**reg·u·la·tive** \-,lātiv\ *adj* —**reg·u·la·tor** \-,lātər\ *n* —**reg·u·la·to·ry** \-lə,tōrē\ *adj*

reg·u·la·tion \,regyə'lāshən\ *n* 1 : act of regulating 2 : rule dealing with details of procedure

re·gur·gi·tate \rē'gərjə,tāt\ *vb* -**tat·ed; -tat·ing** : vomit —**re·gur·gi·ta·tion** \-,gərjə'tāshən\ *n*

re·ha·bil·i·tate \,rē(h)ə'bilə,tāt\ *vb* -**tat·ed; -tat·ing** 1 : reinstate 2 : make good or usable again —**re·ha·bil·i·ta·tion** \-,bilə'tāshən\ *n* —**re·ha·bil·i·ta·tive** \-,tātiv\ *adj*

re·hears·al \ri'hərsəl\ *n* : practice session or performance

re·hearse \-'hərs\ *vb* -**hearsed; -hears·ing** 1 : repeat or recount 2 : engage in a rehearsal of —**re·hears·er** *n*

reign \'rān\ *n* : sovereign's authority or rule ~ *vb* : rule as a sovereign

re·im·burse \,rēəm'bərs\ *vb* -**bursed; -burs·ing** : repay —**re·im·burs·able** *adj* —**re·im·burse·ment** *n*

rein \'rān\ *n* 1 : line of a bridle to control an animal 2 : restraining influence ~ *vb* : direct by reins

re·in·car·na·tion \,rē,in,kär'nāshən\ *n* : rebirth of the soul —**re·in·car·nate** \,rēin'kär,nāt\ *vb*

rein·deer \'rān,diər\ *n* : large deer of northern regions

re·in·force \,rēən'fōrs\ *vb* : strengthen or support —**re·in·force·ment** *n* —**re·in·forc·er** *n*

re·in·state \,rēən'stāt\ *vb* : restore to a former position —**re·in·state·ment** *n*

re·it·er·ate \rē'itə,rāt\ *vb* : say again —**re·it·er·a·tion** \-,itə'rāshən\ *n*

re·ject \ri'jekt\ vb 1 : refuse to acknowledge or grant 2 : refuse to accept or keep ~ \'rē-\ n : rejected person or thing —**re·jec·tion** \-'jekshən\ n

re·joice \ri'jóis\ vb -joiced; -joic·ing : feel joy —**re·joic·er** n —**re·joic·ing** n

re·join vb 1 \'rē'jóin\ : join again 2 : \ri'-\ : say in answer

re·join·der \ri'jóindər\ n : answer

re·ju·ve·nate \ri'jüvə₁nāt\ vb -nat·ed; -nat·ing : make young again —**re·ju·ve·na·tion** \-₁jüvə'nāshən\ n

re·lapse \ri'laps, 'rē₁laps\ n : recurrence of illness after a period of improvement ~ \ri'-\ vb : suffer a relapse

re·late \ri'lāt\ vb -lat·ed; -lat·ing 1 : give a report of 2 : show a connection between 3 : have a relationship —**re·lat·able** adj —**re·lat·er** n

re·la·tion \-'lāshən\ n 1 : account 2 : connection 3 : relationship 4 : reference 5 pl : dealings

re·la·tion·ship \-₁ship\ n : the state of being related or interrelated

rel·a·tive \'relətiv\ n : person connected with another by blood or marriage ~ adj : considered in comparison with something else —**rel·a·tive·ly** adv —**rel·a·tive·ness** n

re·lax \ri'laks\ vb 1 : make or become less tense or rigid 2 : make less severe 3 : seek rest or recreation —**re·lax·er** n

re·lax·ation \₁rē₁lak'sāshən\ n 1 : lessening of tension 2 : recreation

re·lay \'rē₁lā\ n : fresh supply (as of horses or people) arranged to relieve others ~ \'rē₁-, ri'lā\ vb -layed; -lay·ing : pass along in stages

re·lease \ri'lēs\ vb -leased; -leas·ing 1 : free from confinement or oppression 2 : relinquish 3 : permit publication or performance ~ n 1 : relief from trouble 2 : discharge from an obligation 3 : act of releasing or what is released

rel·e·gate \'relə₁gāt\ vb -gat·ed; -gat·ing 1 : remove to some less prominent position 2 : assign to a particular class or sphere —**rel·e·ga·tion** \₁relə'gāshən\ n

re·lent \ri'lent\ vb : become less severe

re·lent·less \-ləs\ adj : mercilessly severe or persistent —**re·lent·less·ly** adv —**re·lent·less·ness** n

rel·e·vance \'reləvəns\ n : relation to the matter at hand —**rel·e·vant** \-vənt\ adj —**rel·e·vant·ly** adv

re·li·able \ri'līəbəl\ adj : fit to be trusted —**re·li·a·bil·i·ty** \-₁līə'bilətē\ n —**re·li·able·ness** n —**re·li·ably** \-'līəblē\ adv

re·li·ance \ri'līəns\ n : act or result of relying —**re·li·ant** \-ənt\ adj

rel·ic \'relik\ n 1 : object venerated because of its association with a saint or martyr 2 : remaining trace

re·lief \ri'lēf\ n 1 : lightening of something oppressive 2 : aid in the form of money or necessities (as for the elderly)

re·lieve \ri'lēv\ vb -lieved; -liev·ing 1 : free from a burden or distress 2 : release from a post or duty 3 : break the monotony of —**re·liev·er** n

re·li·gion \ri'lijən\ n 1 : service and worship of God 2 : organized system of faith and worship —**re·li·gion·ist** n

re·li·gious \-'lijəs\ adj 1 : relating or devoted to the divine 2 : relating to religious beliefs or observances —**re·li·gious·ly** adv

re·lin·quish \-'linkwish, -'lin-\ vb 1 : renounce 2 : let go of —**re·lin·quish·ment** n

rel·ish \'relish\ n 1 : keen enjoyment 2 : highly seasoned sauce (as of pickles) ~ vb : enjoy —**rel·ish·able** adj

re·live \(')rē'liv\ vb : live over again (as in the imagination)

re·lo·cate \(')rē'lō₁kāt, ₁rēlō'kāt\ vb : move to a new location —**re·lo·ca·tion** \₁rēlō'kāshən\ n

re·luc·tance \ri'ləktəns\ n : state of being reluctant

re·luc·tant \-tənt\ adj : holding back (as from acting) —**re·luc·tant·ly** adv

re·ly \ri'lī\ vb -lied; -ly·ing : place faith or confidence—often with on

re·main \ri'mān\ vb 1 : be left after others have been removed 2 : be something yet to be done 3 : stay behind 4 : continue unchanged

re·main·der \-'māndər\ n : that which is left over

re·mains \-'mānz\ n pl 1 : remaining part or trace 2 : dead body

re·mark \ri'märk\ vb : express as an observation ~ n : passing comment

re·mark·able \-'märkəbəl\ adj : extraordinary —**re·mark·able·ness** n —**re·mark·ably** \-blē\ adv

re·me·di·al \ri'mēdēəl\ adj : intended to remedy or improve —**re·me·di·al·ly** adv

rem·e·dy \'remədē\ n, pl -dies 1 : medicine that cures 2 : something that corrects an evil or compensates for a loss ~ *vb* **-died; -dy·ing** : provide or serve as a remedy for

re·mem·ber \ri'membər\ *vb* 1 : recall to mind 2 : keep from forgetting 3 : convey greetings from

re·mem·brance \-brəns\ *n* 1 : act of remembering 2 : something that serves to bring to mind

re·mind \ri'mīnd\ *vb* : cause to remember —**re·mind·er** *n*

rem·i·nisce \,remə'nis\ *vb* **-nisced; -nisc·ing** : indulge in reminiscence

rem·i·nis·cence \-'nis²ns\ *n* 1 : recalling of a past experience 2 : account of a memorable experience

rem·i·nis·cent \-²nt\ *adj* 1 : relating to reminiscence 2 : serving to remind —**rem·i·nis·cent·ly** *adv*

re·miss \ri'mis\ *adj* : negligent or careless in performance of duty —**re·miss·ly** *adv* —**re·miss·ness** *n*

re·mis·sion \ri'mishən\ *n* 1 : act of forgiving 2 : a period of relief from or easing of symptoms of a disease

re·mit \ri'mit\ *vb* **-tt-** 1 : pardon 2 : send money in payment

re·mit·tance \ri'mit²ns\ *n* : sum of money remitted

rem·nant \'remnənt\ *n* : small part or trace remaining

re·mod·el \'rē'mäd²l\ *vb* : alter the structure of

re·mon·strance \ri'mänstrəns\ *n* : act or instance of remonstrating

re·mon·strate \ri'män,strāt\ *vb* **-strat·ed; -strat·ing** : speak in protest, reproof, or opposition —**re·mon·stra·tion** \,ri,män'strāshən,,reman-\

re·morse \ri'mórs\ *n* : distress arising from a sense of guilt —**re·morse·ful** *adj* —**re·morse·less** *adj*

re·mote \ri'mōt\ *adj* **-mot·er; -est** 1 : far off in place or time 2 : hard to reach or find 3 : slight 4 : distant in manner —**re·mote·ly** *adv* —**re·mote·ness** *n*

re·move \ri'müv\ *vb* **-moved; -mov·ing** 1 : move by lifting or taking off or away 2 : get rid of —**re·mov·able** *adj* —**re·mov·al** \-vəl\ *n* —**re·mov·er** *n*

re·mu·ner·ate \ri'myünə,rāt\ *vb* **-at·ed; -at·ing** : pay —**re·mu·ner·a·tion** —**re·mu·ner·a·tor** \-,rātər\ *n* —**re·mu·ner·a·to·ry** \-rə,tōrē\ *adj*

re·mu·ner·a·tive \ri'myünərətiv,,-rāt-\ *adj* : gainful —**re·mu·ner·a·tive·ly** *adv* —**re·mu·ner·a·tive·ness** *n*

re·nais·sance \,renə'säns, -'zäns\ *n* : rebirth or revival

re·nal \'rēn²l\ *adj* : relating to the kidneys

rend \'rend\ *vb* **rent** \'rent\; **rend·ing** : tear apart forcibly

ren·der \'rendər\ *vb* 1 : extract by heating 2 : hand over or give up 3 : do (a service) for another 4 : cause to be or become

ren·dez·vous \'rändi,vü, -dā-\ *n, pl* **ren·dez·vous** \-,vüz\ 1 : place appointed for a meeting 2 : meeting at an appointed place ~ *vb* **-voused; -vous·ing** : meet at a rendezvous

ren·di·tion \ren'dishən\ *n* : version

ren·e·gade \'reni,gād\ *n* : one who deserts one faith or cause for another

re·nege \ri'nig, -'neg, -'nēg, -'nāg\ *vb* **-neged; -neg·ing** : go back on a promise —**re·neg·er** *n*

re·new \ri'n(y)ü\ *vb* 1 : make or become new, fresh, or strong again 2 : begin again 3 : grant or obtain an extension of —**re·new·able** *adj* —**re·new·al** *n* —**re·new·er** *n*

re·nounce \ri'naúns\ *vb* **-nounced; -nounc·ing** : give up, refuse, or resign —**re·nounce·ment** *n*

ren·o·vate \'renə,vāt\ *vb* **-vat·ed; -vat·ing** : make like new again —**ren·o·va·tion** \,renə'vāshən\ *n* —**ren·o·va·tor** \'renə,vātər\ *n*

re·nown \ri'naún\ *n* : state of being widely known and honored —**re·nowned** \-'naúnd\ *adj*

¹**rent** \'rent\ *n* : money paid or due for the use of another's property ~ *vb* : hold or give possession and use of for rent —**rent·al** *n or adj* —**rent·er** *n*

²**rent** *n* : a tear in cloth

re·nun·ci·a·tion \ri,nənsē'āshən\ *n* : act of renouncing

¹**re·pair** \ri'paər\ *vb* : go

²**repair** *vb* : restore to good condition ~ *n* 1 : act or instance of repairing 2 : condition —**re·pair·er** *n* —**re·pair·man** \-,man\ *n*

rep·a·ra·tion \,repə'rāshən\ *n* : money paid for redress—usu. pl.

rep·ar·tee \,repər'tē\ *n* : clever replies

re·past \ri'past, 'rē,past\ *n* : meal

re·pa·tri·ate \rē'pātrē,āt\ *vb* **-at·ed; -at·ing** : send back to one's own country —**re·pa·tri·ate** \-trēət, -trē,āt\ *n* —**re·pa·tri·a·tion** \-,pātrē'āshən\ *n*

re·pay \rē'pā\ *vb* **-paid; -pay·ing** : pay back —**re·pay·able** *adj* —**re·pay·ment** *n*

re·peal \ri'pēl\ *vb* : annul by legislative action —**repeal** *n* —**re·peal·er** *n*

re·peat \ri'pēt\ *vb* : say or do again ~ *n* 1 : act of repeating 2 : something repeated —**re·peat·able** *adj* —**re·peat·ed·ly** *adv* —**re·peat·er** *n*

re·pel \ri'pel\ *vb* -**pelled**; -**pel·ling** 1 : drive away 2 : disgust —**re·pel·lent** \-'pelənt\ *adj or n*

re·pent \ri'pent\ *vb* 1 : turn from sin 2 : regret —**re·pen·tance** \ri'pent³ns\ *n* —**re·pen·tant** \-³nt\ *adj*

re·per·cus·sion \ˌrēpər'kəshən, ˌrepər-\ *n* : effect of something done or said

rep·er·toire \'repə(r)ˌtwär\ *n* : pieces or parts a company or performer can present

rep·er·to·ry \'repə(r)ˌtōrē\ *n, pl* -**ries** 1 : repertoire 2 : theater with a resident company doing several plays

rep·e·ti·tion \ˌrepə'tishən\ *n* : act or instance of repeating

rep·e·ti·tious \-'tishəs\ *adj* : tediously repeating —**rep·e·ti·tious·ly** *adv* —**rep·e·ti·tious·ness** *n*

re·pet·i·tive \ri'petətiv\ *adj* : repetitious —**re·pet·i·tive·ly** *adv* —**re·pet·i·tive·ness** *n*

re·pine \ri'pīn\ *vb* re·**pined**; re·**pin·ing** 1 : feel or express discontent

re·place \ri'plās\ *vb* 1 : restore to a former position 2 : take the place of 3 : put something new in the place of —**re·place·able** *adj* —**re·place·ment** *n* —**re·plac·er** *n*

re·plen·ish \ri'plenish\ *vb* : stock or supply anew —**re·plen·ish·ment** *n*

re·plete \ri'plēt\ *adj* : full —**re·plete·ness** *n* —**re·ple·tion** \-'plēshən\ *n*

rep·li·ca \'replikə\ *n* : copy

rep·li·cate \'replə.kāt\ *vb* -**cat·ed**; -**cat·ing** : duplicate or repeat —**rep·li·cate** \-likət\ *n*

re·ply \ri'plī\ *vb* -**plied**; -**ply·ing** : say or do in answer ~ *n, pl* -**plies** : answer

re·port \ri'pōrt\ *n* 1 : rumor 2 : statement of information (as events or causes) 3 : explosive noise ~ *vb* 1 : give an account of 2 : present an account of (an event) as news 3 : present oneself 4 : make known to authorities —**re·port·age** \ri'pōrtij, ˌrepər'täzh, ˌrepˌor'-\ *n* —**re·port·ed·ly** *adv* —**re·port·er** *n* —**re·por·to·ri·al** \ˌrepə(r)'tōrēəl\ *adj*

re·pose \ri'pōz\ *vb* -**posed**; -**pos·ing** : lay or lie at rest ~ *n* 1 : state of resting 2 : calm or peace —**re·pose·ful** *adj*

re·pos·i·to·ry \ri'päzəˌtōrē\ *n, pl* -**ries** : place where something is stored

re·pos·sess \ˌrēpə'zes\ *vb* : regain possession and legal ownership of —**re·pos·ses·sion** \-'zeshən\ *n*

rep·re·hend \ˌrepri'hend\ *vb* : express disapproval of —**rep·re·hen·si·ble**

\-'hensəbəl\ *adj* —**rep·re·hen·si·bly** *adv* —**rep·re·hen·sion** \-'henchən\ *n*

rep·re·sent \ˌrepri'zent\ *vb* 1 : serve as a sign or symbol of 2 : act or speak for 3 : describe as having a specified quality or character —**rep·re·sen·ta·tion** \ˌrepriˌzen'tāshən\ *n*

rep·re·sen·ta·tive \ˌrepri'zentətiv\ *adj* 1 : standing or acting for another 2 : carried on by elected representatives ~ *n* 1 : typical example 2 : one that represents another 3 : member of usu. the lower house of a legislature —**rep·re·sen·ta·tive·ly** *adv* —**rep·re·sen·ta·tive·ness** *n*

re·press \ri'pres\ *vb* : restrain or suppress —**re·pres·sion** \-'preshən\ *n* —**re·pres·sive** \-'presiv\ *adj*

re·prieve \ri'prēv\ *vb* -**prieved**; -**priev·ing** : delay the punishment or execution of —**reprieve** *n*

rep·ri·mand \'reprəˌmand\ *n* : formal reproof —**reprimand** *vb*

re·pris·al \ri'prīzəl\ *n* : act in retaliation

re·prise \ri'prēz\ *n* : musical repetition

re·proach \ri'prōch\ *n* 1 : disgrace 2 : rebuke ~ *vb* : express disapproval to —**re·proach·ful** *adj* —**re·proach·ful·ly** *adv* —**re·proach·ful·ness** *n*

rep·ro·bate \'reprəˌbāt\ *n* : scoundrel —**reprobate** *adj*

rep·ro·ba·tion \ˌreprə'bāshən\ *n* : strong disapproval

re·pro·duce \ˌrēprə'd(y)üs\ *vb* 1 : produce again or anew 2 : bear offspring —**re·pro·duc·ible** \-'d(y)üsəbəl\ *adj* —**re·pro·duc·tion** \-'dəkshən\ *n* —**re·pro·duc·tive** \-'dəktiv\ *adj*

re·proof \ri'prüf\ *n* : blame or censure for a fault

re·prove \ri'prüv\ *vb* -**proved**; -**prov·ing** : express disapproval to or of —**re·prov·er** *n*

rep·tile \'rept³l, -ˌtīl\ *n* : air-breathing scaly vertebrate —**rep·til·i·an** \rep'tilēən\ *adj or n*

re·pub·lic \ri'pəblik\ *n* : country with representative government

re·pub·li·can \-likən\ *adj* 1 : relating to or resembling a republic 2 : supporting a republic —**republican** *n* —**re·pub·li·can·ism** *n*

re·pu·di·ate \ri'pyüdēˌāt\ *vb* -**at·ed**; -**at·ing** : refuse to have anything to do with —**re·pu·di·a·tion** \-ˌpyüdē'āshən\ *n* —**re·pu·di·a·tor** \-'pyüdēˌātər\ *n*

re·pug·nant \ri'pəgnənt\ *adj* : contrary to one's tastes or principles —**re·pug·nance** \-nəns\ *n* —**re·pug·nant·ly** *adv*

re·pulse \ri'pəls\ vb -pulsed; -puls·ing 1 : drive or beat back 2 : rebuff 3 : be repugnant to —repulse n —re·pul·sion \-'pəlshən\ n

re·pul·sive \-siv\ adj : arousing aversion or disgust —re·pul·sive·ly adv —re·pul·sive·ness n

rep·u·ta·ble \'repyətəbəl\ adj : having a good reputation —rep·u·ta·bly \-blē\ adv

rep·u·ta·tion \,repyə'tāshən\ n : one's character or public esteem

re·pute \ri'pyüt\ vb -put·ed; -put·ing : think of as being ~ n : reputation —re·put·ed adj —re·put·ed·ly adv

re·quest \ri'kwest\ n : act or instance of asking for something or a thing asked for ~ vb 1 : make a request of 2 : ask for —re·quest·er n

re·qui·em \'rekwēəm, 'rāk-\ n : Mass for a dead person or a musical setting for this

re·quire \ri'kwī(ə)r\ vb -quired; -quir·ing 1 : insist on 2 : call for as essential —re·quire·ment n

req·ui·site \'rekwəzət\ adj : necessary —requisite n

req·ui·si·tion \,rekwə'zishən\ n : formal application or demand —requisition vb

re·quite \ri'kwīt\ vb -quit·ed; -quit·ing : make return for or to —re·quit·al \-'kwīt⁹l\ n

re·scind \ri'sind\ vb : repeal or cancel —re·scis·sion \-'sizhən\ n

res·cue \'reskyü\ vb -cued; -cu·ing : set free from danger or confinement —rescue n —res·cu·er n

re·search \ri'sərch, 'rē,sərch\ n : careful or diligent search esp. for new knowledge —research vb —re·search·er n

re·sem·ble \ri'zembəl\ vb -sem·bled; -sem·bling : be like or similar to —re·sem·blance \-'zembləns\ n

re·sent \ri'zent\ vb : feel or show annoyance at —re·sent·ful adj —re·sent·ful·ly adv —re·sent·ment n

res·er·va·tion \,rezər'vāshən\ n 1 : act of reserving or something reserved 2 : limiting condition

re·serve \ri'zərv\ vb -served; -serv·ing 1 : store for future use 2 : set aside for special use ~ n 1 : something reserved 2 : restraint in words or bearing 3 : military forces withheld from action or not part of the regular services —re·served adj

res·er·voir \'rezə(r)v,wär, -ə(r),vȯi\ n : place where something (as water) is kept in store

re·side \ri'zīd\ vb -sid·ed; -sid·ing 1 : make one's home 2 : be present

res·i·dence \'rezədəns\ n 1 : act or fact of residing in a place 2 : place where one lives —res·i·dent \-ənt\ adj or n —res·i·den·tial \,rezə'denchəl\ adj

res·i·due \'rezə,d(y)ü\ n : part remaining —re·sid·u·al \ri'zij(əw)əl\ adj

re·sign \ri'zīn\ vb 1 : give up deliberately 2 : give (oneself) over without resistance —res·ig·na·tion \,rezig'nāshən\ n

re·signed \ri'zīnd\ adj : submissive —re·sign·ed·ly \-'zīnədlē\ adv

re·sil·ience \ri'zilyəns\ n : ability to recover or adjust easily

re·sil·ien·cy \-yənsē\ n : resilience

re·sil·ient \-yənt\ adj : elastic

res·in \'rez⁹n\ n : substance from the gum or sap of trees —res·in·ous adj

re·sist \ri'zist\ vb 1 : withstand the force or effect of 2 : fight against —re·sist·i·ble \-'zistəbəl\ adj —re·sist·less adj

re·sis·tance \ri'zistəns\ n 1 : act of resisting 2 : opposition to electric current

re·sis·tant \-tənt\ adj : giving resistance

res·o·lute \'rezə,lüt\ adj : having a fixed purpose —res·o·lute·ly adv —res·o·lute·ness n

res·o·lu·tion \,rezə'lüshən\ n 1 : process of resolving 2 : firmness of purpose 3 : statement of the opinion, will, or intent of a body

re·solve \ri'zälv\ vb -solved; -solv·ing 1 : find an answer to 2 : make a formal resolution ~ n 1 : something resolved 2 : steadfast purpose —re·solv·able adj

res·o·nant \'rez⁹nənt\ adj 1 : continuing to sound 2 : relating to intensification or prolongation of sound (as by a vibrating body) —res·o·nance \-əns\ n —res·o·nant·ly adv

re·sort \ri'zȯrt\ n 1 : source of help 2 : place to go for vacation ~ vb 1 : go often or habitually 2 : have recourse

re·sound \ri'zaùnd\ vb : become filled with sound

re·sound·ing \-iŋ\ adj : impressive —re·sound·ing·ly adv

re·source \'rē,sȯrs, ri'sȯrs\ n 1 : new or reserve source 2 pl : available funds 3 : ability to handle situations —re·source·ful adj —re·source·ful·ness n

re·spect \ri'spekt\ n 1 : relation to something 2 : high or special regard 3 : detail ~ vb : consider deserving of high regard —re·spect·er n —re-

spect·ful \adj\ —re·spect·ful·ly \adv\
—re·spect·ful·ness n

re·spect·able \ri'spektəbəl\ adj 1 : worthy of respect 2 : fair in size, quantity, or quality —re·spect·abil·i·ty
\-,spektə'bilətē\ n —re·spect·ably
\-'spektəblē\ adv

re·spec·tive \-tiv\ adj : individual and
specific

re·spec·tive·ly \-lē\ adv 1 : as relating
to each 2 : each in the order given

res·pi·ra·tion \,respə'rāshən\ n 1 : act
or process of breathing 2 : energy-
yielding oxidation in living matter
—re·spi·ra·to·ry \'resp(ə)rə,tōrē,
ri'spīrə-\ adj —re·spire \ri'spī(ə)r\
vb

res·pi·ra·tor \'respə,rātər\ n : device
for artificial respiration

re·spite \'respət\ n : temporary delay
or rest

re·splen·dent \ri'splendənt\ adj : shining brilliantly —re·splen·dence
\-dəns\ n —re·splen·dent·ly adv

re·spond \ri'spänd\ vb 1 : answer 2
: react —re·spon·dent \-'spändənt\ n
or adj —re·spond·er n

re·sponse \ri'späns\ n 1 : act of re-
sponding 2 : answer

re·spon·si·ble \ri'spänsəbəl\ adj 1 : an-
swerable for acts or decisions 2 : able
to fulfill obligations 3 : having important duties —re·spon·si·bil·i·ty
\ri,spänsə'bilətē\ n —re·spon·si·ble-
ness n —re·spon·si·bly \-blē\ adv

re·spon·sive \-siv\ adj : quick to respond —re·spon·sive·ly adv —re·
spon·sive·ness n

¹rest \'rest\ n 1 : sleep 2 : freedom
from work or activity 3 : state of
inactivity 4 : something used as a
support ~ vb 1 : get rest 2 : cease
action or motion 3 : give rest to 4
: sit or lie fixed or supported 5 : depend —rest·ful adj —rest·ful·ly adv

²rest n : remainder

res·tau·rant \'rest(ə)rənt, -tə,ränt\ n
: public eating place

res·ti·tu·tion \,restə't(y)üshən\ n : act
or fact of restoring something or repaying someone

res·tive \'restiv\ adj : uneasy or fidgety
—res·tive·ly adv —res·tive·ness n

rest·less \'restləs\ adj 1 : lacking or
giving no rest 2 : never resting or
ceasing 3 : lacking in repose —rest-
less·ly adv —rest·less·ness n

re·store \ri'stōr\ vb -stored; -stor·ing 1
: give back 2 : put back into use or
into a former state —re·stor·able adj
—res·to·ra·tion \,restə'rāshən\ n

re·stor·a·tive \ri'stōrətiv\ n or adj
—re·stor·er n

re·strain \ri'strān\ vb : limit or keep
under control —re·strain·able adj
—re·strained \-'strānd\ adj —re·
strain·ed·ly \-'strānədlē\ adv —re·
strain·er n

re·straint \-'strānt\ n 1 : act of restraining 2 : restraining force 3 : control over feelings

re·strict \ri'strikt\ vb 1 : confine within
bounds 2 : limit use of —re·stric·tion
\-'strikshən\ n —re·stric·tive adj
—re·stric·tive·ly adv

re·sult \ri'zəlt\ vb 1 : come about because of something else 2 : end ~ n
1 : thing that results 2 : something
obtained by calculation or investigation —re·sul·tant \-'zəltənt\ adj or n

re·sume \ri'züm\ vb -sumed; -sum·ing
: return to or take up again after interruption —re·sump·tion
\-'zəmpshən\ n

ré·su·mé \'rezə,mā, ,rezə'-\ n : summary of one's career and qualifications

re·sur·gence \ri'sərjəns\ n : a rising
again —re·sur·gent \-jənt\ adj

res·ur·rect \,rezə'rekt\ vb 1 : raise
from the dead 2 : bring to attention
or use again —res·ur·rec·tion
\-'rekshən\ n

re·sus·ci·tate \ri'səsə,tāt\ vb -tat·ed;
-tat·ing : revive from a deathlike condition —re·sus·ci·ta·tion
\ri,səsə'tāshən, ,rē-\ n —re·sus·ci·
ta·tor \-,tātər\ n

re·tail \'rē,tāl\ vb : sell in small quantities directly to the consumer ~ n
: business of selling to consumers
—retail adj or adv —re·tail·er n

re·tain \ri'tān\ vb 1 : keep or hold onto
2 : engage the services of

re·tain·er n 1 : household servant 2
: retaining fee

re·tal·i·ate \ri'talē,āt\ vb -at·ed; -at·ing
: get revenge —re·tal·i·a·tion
\-,talē'āshən\ n —re·tal·i·a·to·ry
\-'talyə,tōrē\ adj

re·tard \ri'tärd\ vb : hold back —re·
tar·da·tion \,rē,tär'dāshən, ri-\ n
—re·tard·er n

re·tard·ed \ri'tärdəd\ adj : slow or limited in intellectual development

retch \'rech, 'rēch\ vb : try to vomit

re·ten·tion \ri'tenchən\ n 1 : state of
being retained 2 : ability to retain
—re·ten·tive \-'tentiv\ adj

ret·i·cent \'retəsənt\ adj : inclined to
be silent or secretive —ret·i·cence
\-səns\ n —ret·i·cent·ly adv

ret·i·na \\'ret³nə\ *n, pl* **-nas** *or* **-nae** \\-³n,ē\ : sensory membrane lining the eye —**ret·i·nal** \\'ret³nəl\ *adj*

ret·i·nue \\'ret³n,(y)ü\ *n* : attendants or followers of a distinguished person

re·tire \\ri'tī(ə)r\ *vb* **-tired; -tir·ing 1** : withdraw for privacy **2** : end a career **3** : go to bed —**re·tir·ee** \\ri,tī'rē\ *n* —**re·tire·ment** *n*

re·tir·ing \\ri'tī(ə)riŋ\ *adj* : shy or reserved

¹re·tort \\ri'tort\ *vb* : say in reply ~ *n* : quick, witty, or cutting answer

²re·tort \\ri'tort, 'rē,tort\ *n* : vessel in which substances are distilled or broken up by heat

re·trace \\(')rē'trās\ *vb* **1** : trace again **2** : go over again in reverse

re·tract \\ri'trakt\ *vb* **1** : to draw back or in **2** : withdraw a charge or promise —**re·tract·able** *adj* —**re·trac·tion** \\-'trakshən\ *n*

re·treat \\ri'trēt\ *n* **1** : act of withdrawing **2** : place of privacy or safety or meditation and study ~ *vb* : make a retreat

re·trench \\ri'trench\ *vb* : cut down (as expenses) —**re·trench·ment** *n*

ret·ri·bu·tion \\,retrə'byüshən\ *n* : retaliation —**re·trib·u·tive** \\ri'tribyətiv\ *adj* —**re·trib·u·to·ry** \\-yə,tōrē\ *adj*

re·trieve \\ri'trēv\ *vb* **-trieved; -triev·ing 1** : search for and bring in game **2** : recover —**re·triev·able** *adj* —**re·triev·al** \\-'trēvəl\ *n*

re·triev·er \\ri'trēvər\ *n* : dog for retrieving game

ret·ro·ac·tive \\,retrō'aktiv\ *adj* : made effective as of a prior date —**ret·ro·ac·tive·ly** *adv*

ret·ro·grade \\'retrə,grād\ *adj* **1** : moving backward **2** : becoming worse

ret·ro·gress \\,retrə'gres\ *vb* : move backward —**ret·ro·gres·sion** \\-'greshən\ *n*

ret·ro·spect \\'retrə,spekt\ *n* : review of past events —**ret·ro·spec·tion** \\,retrə'spekshən\ *n* —**ret·ro·spec·tive** \\-'spektiv\ *adj* —**ret·ro·spec·tive·ly** *adv*

re·turn \\ri'tərn\ *vb* **1** : go or come back **2** : pass, give, or send back to an earlier possessor **3** : answer **4** : bring in as a profit **5** : give or do in return ~ *n* **1** : act of returning or something returned **2** *pl* : report of balloting results **3** : statement of taxable income ~ *adj* : profit —**return** *adj* —**turn·able** *adj* —**re·turn·er** *n*

re·union \\rē'yünyən\ *n* **1** : act of re-

uniting **2** : meeting of persons who have been separated

re·vamp \\(')rē'vamp\ *vb* : give a new form to old materials

re·veal \\ri'vēl\ *vb* **1** : make known **2** : show plainly

re·veil·le \\'revəlē\ *n* : military signal sounded about sunrise

rev·el \\'revəl\ *vb* **-eled** *or* **-elled; -el·ing** *or* **-el·ling 1** : take part in a revel **2** : take great delight ~ *n* : wild party or celebration —**rev·el·er, rev·el·ler** \\-ər\ *n* —**rev·el·ry** \\-rē\ *n*

rev·e·la·tion \\,revə'lāshən\ *n* **1** : act of revealing **2** : something enlightening or astonishing

re·venge \\ri'venj\ *vb* **-venged; -veng·ing** : inflict harm or injury in return for a wrong ~ *n* **1** : act of revenging **2** : desire to return evil —**re·venge·ful** *adj* —**re·veng·er** *n*

rev·e·nue \\'revə,n(y)ü\ *n* : money collected by a government

re·ver·ber·ate \\ri'vərbə,rāt\ *vb* **-at·ed; -at·ing** : resound in a series of echoes —**re·ver·ber·a·tion** \\-,vərbə'rāshən\ *n*

re·vere \\ri'viər\ *vb* **-vered; -ver·ing** : show honor and devotion to —**rev·er·ence** \\'rev(ə)rəns\ *n* —**rev·er·ent** \\-rənt\ *adj* —**rev·er·ent·ly** *adv*

rev·er·end \\'rev(ə)rənd\ *adj* : worthy of reverence ~ *n* : clergyman

rev·er·ie, rev·ery \\'rev(ə)rē\ *n, pl* **-er·ies** : daydream

re·verse \\ri'vərs\ *adj* **1** : opposite to a previous or normal condition **2** : acting in an opposite way ~ *vb* **-versed; -vers·ing 1** : turn upside down or completely around **2** : change to the contrary or in the opposite direction ~ *n* **1** : something contrary **2** : change for the worse **3** : back of something —**re·ver·sal** \\-səl\ *n* —**re·verse·ly** *adv* —**re·vers·ible** \\-'vərsəbəl\ *adj*

re·vert \\ri'vərt\ *vb* : return to an original type or condition —**re·ver·sion** \\-'vərzhən\ *n*

re·view \\ri'vyü\ *n* **1** : formal inspection **2** : general survey **3** : critical evaluation **4** : second or repeated study or examination ~ *vb* **1** : examine or study again **2** : reexamine judicially **3** : view in retrospect **4** : write a critical examination of **5** : inspect —**re·view·er** *n*

re·vile \\ri'vīl\ *vb* **-viled; -vil·ing** : abuse verbally —**re·vile·ment** *n* —**re·vil·er** *n*

re·vise \\-'vīz\ *vb* **-vised; -vis·ing 1** : look over something written to correct or improve **2** : make a new version of —**re·vis·able** adj —**revise** n —**re·vis·er**, **re·vi·sor** \-'vīzər\ n —**re·vi·sion** \-'vizhən\ n

re·viv·al \-'vīvəl\ n **1** : act of reviving or state of being revived **2** : evangelistic meeting

re·vive \-'vīv\ vb -**vived**; -**viv·ing 1** : return to consciousness or life **2** : bring back into use —**re·viv·er** n

re·vo·ca·tion \revə'kāshən\ n : act or instance of revoking

re·voke \ri'vōk\ vb -**voked**; -**vok·ing** : annul by recalling —**re·vok·er** n

re·volt \-'vōlt\ vb **1** : throw off allegiance **2** : cause or experience disgust or shock ~ n : rebellion or revolution —**re·volt·er** n

rev·o·lu·tion \revə'lüshən\ n **1** : rotation **2** : progress in an orbit **3** : cycle **4** : overthrow of a ruler or government —**rev·o·lu·tion·ary** \-shə,nərē\ adj or n

rev·o·lu·tion·ize \-shə,nīz\ vb -**ized**; -**iz·ing** : change radically —**rev·o·lu·tion·iz·er** n

re·volve \ri'välv\ vb -**volved**; -**volv·ing 1** : ponder **2** : move in an orbit **3** : rotate —**re·volv·able** adj

re·volv·er \ri'välvər\ n : pistol with a revolving cylinder

re·vue \ri'vyü\ n : theatrical production of brief numbers

re·vul·sion \ri'vəlshən\ n : complete dislike or repugnance

re·ward \ri'wòrd\ vb : give a reward to or for ~ n : something offered for service or achievement

rhap·so·dy \'rapsədē\ n, pl -**dies 1** : extravagantly rapturous discourse **2** : flowing free-form musical composition —**rhap·sod·ic** \rap'sädik\ adj —**rhap·sod·i·cal·ly** \-ik(ə)lē\ adv —**rhap·so·dize** \'rapsə,dīz\ vb

rhet·o·ric \'retərik\ n : art of speaking or writing effectively —**rhe·tor·i·cal** \ri'tòrikəl\ adj —**rhet·o·ri·cian** \,retə'rishən\ n

rheu·ma·tism \'rümə,tizəm, 'rüm-\ n : disorder marked by inflammation or pain in muscles or joints —**rheu·mat·ic** \rü'matik\ adj

rhine·stone \'rīn,stōn\ n : a colorless imitation gem

rhi·no \'rīnō\ n, pl -**no** or -**nos** : rhinoceros

rhi·noc·er·os \rī'näs(ə)rəs\ n, pl -**noc·er·os·es** or -**noc·er·os** or -**noc·eri** \-'näsə,rī\ : large thick-skinned mammal with 1 or 2 horns on the snout

rho·do·den·dron \,rōdə'dendrən\ n : flowering evergreen shrub

rhom·bus \'rämbəs\ n, pl -**bus·es** or -**bi** \-,bī\ : parallelogram with equal sides and usu. oblique angles

rhu·barb \'rü,bärb\ n : garden plant with edible stalks

rhyme \'rīm\ n **1** : correspondence in terminal sounds **2** : verse that rhymes ~ vb **rhymed**; **rhym·ing** : make or have rhymes

rhythm \'riT͟həm\ n : regular succession of sounds or motions —**rhyth·mic** \'riT͟hmik\, **rhyth·mi·cal** \-mikəl\ —**rhyth·mi·cal·ly** adv

rhythm and blues n : popular music based on blues and black folk music

rib \'rib\ n **1** : curved bone joined to the spine **2** : riblike thing ~ vb -**bb**- **1** : furnish or mark with ribs **2** : tease —**rib·ber** n

rib·ald \'ribəld\ adj : coarse or vulgar —**rib·ald·ry** \-əldrē\ n

rib·bon \'ribən\ n **1** : narrow strip of fabric used esp. for decoration **2** : strip of inked cloth (as in a typewriter)

ri·bo·fla·vin \,rībə'flāvən, 'rībə,-\ n : growth-promoting vitamin

rice \'rīs\ n, pl **rice** : edible seeds of an annual cereal grass

rich \'rich\ adj **1** : having a lot of money or possessions **2** : valuable **3** : containing much sugar, fat, or seasoning **4** : abundant **5** : deep and pleasing in color or tone **6** : fertile —**rich·ly** adv —**rich·ness** n

rich·es \'richəz\ n pl : wealth

rick·ets \'rikəts\ n : childhood bone disease

rick·ety \'rikətē\ adj : shaky

rick·sha, **rick·shaw** \'rik,shò\ n : small covered 2-wheeled vehicle pulled by one man

ric·o·chet \'rikə,shā, Brit also \-,shet\ vb -**cheted** \-,shād\ or -**chet·ted** \-,shet-əd\; -**chet·ing** \-,shāiŋ\ or -**chet·ting** \-,shetiŋ\ : skip with or as if while glancing rebounds —**ricochet** n

rid \'rid\ vb **rid**; **rid·ding** : make free of something unwanted —**rid·dance** \'rid⁰ns\ n

rid·den \'rid⁰n\ adj : overburdened with

¹**rid·dle** \'rid⁰l\ n : puzzling question ~ vb -**dled**; -**dling** : speak in riddles

²**rid·dle** vb -**dled**; -**dling** : fill full of holes

ride \'rīd\ vb **rode** \'rōd\; **rid·den** \'rid⁰n\; **rid·ing** \'rīdiŋ\ **1** : be carried along by an animal or vehicle **2** : sit on and cause to move **3** : travel over a surface 4 : tease or nag ~ n 1 : trip on an animal or in a vehicle 2 : mechanical device ridden for amusement

rid·er \'rīd-\ n 1 : one that rides 2 : attached clause or document —**rid·er·less** adj

ridge \'rij\ n 1 : range of hills 2 : raised line or strip 3 : point of intersection of 2 sloping surfaces —**ridgy** adj

rid·i·cule \'rida,kyül\ vb -culed; -cul·ing : laugh at or make fun of —**ridi·cule** n

ri·dic·u·lous \rə'dikyələs\ adj : arousing ridicule —**ri·dic·u·lous·ly** adv —**ri·dic·u·lous·ness** n

rife \'rīf\ adj : abounding —**rife** adv —**rife·ness** n

riff·raff \'rif,raf\ n : mob

¹**ri·fle** \'rī-\ vb -fled; -fling : ransack esp. in order to steal —**ri·fler** \-f(ə)lər\ n

²**rifle** n : long shoulder weapon with spiral grooves in the bore —**ri·fle·man** \-mən\ n —**ri·fling** n

rift \'rift\ n : separation —**rift** vb

¹**rig** \'rig\ vb -gg- 1 : fit out with rigging 2 : set up esp. as a makeshift ~ n 1 : distinctive shape, number, and arrangement of sails and masts of a ship 2 : equipment 3 : carriage with its horses

²**rig** vb -gg- : manipulate esp. by deceptive or dishonest means

rig·ging \'rigin, -ən\ n : lines that hold and move masts, sails, and spars of a ship

right \'rīt\ adj 1 : meeting a standard of conduct 2 : correct 3 : genuine 4 : normal 5 : opposite of left ~ n 1 : something that is correct, just, proper, or honorable 2 : something to which one has a just claim 3 : something that is on the right side ~ adv 1 : according to what is right 2 : immediately 3 : completely 4 : on or to the right ~ vb 1 : restore to a proper state 2 : bring or become upright again —**right·er** n —**right·ness** n —**right·ward** \-wərd\ adj

right angle n : angle bounded by 2 lines perpendicular to each other —**right-an·gled** \'rīt'aŋgəld\ adj

righ·teous \'rīchəs\ adj : acting or being in accordance with what is just or moral —**righ·teous·ly** adv —**righ·teous·ness** n

right·ful \'rītfəl\ adj : lawful —**right·ful·ly** \-ē\ adv —**right·ful·ness** n

right·ly \'rītlē\ adv 1 : justly 2 : properly 3 : correctly

rig·id \'rijəd\ adj : lacking flexibility

—**ri·gid·i·ty** \rə'jidətē\ n —**rig·id·ly** adv

rig·ma·role \'rig(ə)mə,rōl\ n : meaningless talk or procedure

rig·or \'rigər\ n : severity —**rig·or·ous** adj —**rig·or·ous·ly** adv

rig·or mor·tis \,rigər'mōrtəs\ n : temporary stiffness of muscles occurring after death

rile \'rīl\ vb riled; ril·ing : anger

rill \'ril\ n : small brook

rim \'rim\ n : edge esp. of something curved ~ vb -mm- 1 : furnish with a rim 2 : run around the rim of

¹**rime** \'rīm\ n : frostlike ice formed on exposed objects —**rimy** \'rīmē\ adj

²**rime** var of RHYME

rind \'rīnd\ n : usu. hard or tough outer layer

¹**ring** \'riŋ\ n 1 : circular band used as an ornament or for holding or fastening 2 : something circular 3 : place for contest or display 4 : group with a selfish or dishonest aim ~ vb : surround —**ringed** adj —**ring-like** adj

²**ring** vb rang \'raŋ\; rung \'rəŋ\; ring·ing 1 : sound resonantly when struck 2 : cause to make a metallic sound by striking ~ n 1 : resonant sound or tone 2 : act or instance of ringing

ring·er \'riŋər\ n 1 : one that sounds by ringing 2 : illegal substitute

ring·lead·er \'riŋ,lēdər\ n : leader esp. of troublemakers

ring·let n : long curl

ring·worm n : a contagious fungous skin disease

rink \'riŋk\ n : enclosed place for skating

rinse \'rins\ vb rinsed; rins·ing 1 : cleanse usu. with water only 2 : treat (hair) with a rinse ~ n : liquid used for rinsing —**rins·er** n

ri·ot \'rīət\ n 1 : violent public disorder 2 : random or disorderly profusion —**riot** vb —**ri·ot·er** n —**ri·ot·ous** adj

rip \'rip\ vb -pp- : cut or tear open ~ n : rent made by ripping —**rip·per** n

ripe \'rīp\ adj rip·er; rip·est : fully grown, developed, or prepared —**ripe·ly** adv —**rip·en** \'rīpən\ vb —**ripe·ness** n

rip-off n : theft —**rip off** vb

rip·ple \'ripəl\ vb -pled; -pling 1 : become lightly ruffled on the surface 2 : sound like rippling water —**ripple** n

rise \'rīz\ vb rose \'rōz\; ris·en \'riz²n\; ris·ing \'rīziŋ\ 1 : get up from sitting, kneeling, or lying 2 : rebel 3 : appear above the horizon 4 : ascend 5 : gain a higher position or rank 6 : increase ~ n 1 : act of rising 2 : origin 3 : elevation 4 : increase 5 : upward slope 6 : area of high ground —**ris-er** \'rīzər\ n

ris-i-ble \'rizəbəl\ adj 1 : able or inclined to laugh 2 : arousing laughter —**ris-i-bil-i-ty** \ˌrizə'bilətē\ n

risk \'risk\ n : exposure to loss or injury —**risk** vb —**risk-i-ness** n —**risky** adj

ris-qué \ris'kā\ adj : nearly indecent

rite \'rīt\ n 1 : set form of conducting a ceremony 2 : liturgy of a church 3 : ceremonial action

rit-u-al \'rich(əw)əl\ n : rite —**ritual** adj —**rit-u-al-ism** \-ˌizəm\ n —**rit-u-al-is-tic** \ˌrich(əw)əl'istik\ adj —**rit-u-al-is-ti-cal-ly** \-tik(ə)lē\ adv —**rit-u-al-ly** \'rich(əw)əlē\ adv

ri-val \'rīvəl\ n 1 : competitor 2 : peer ~ vb -valed or -valled; -val-ing or -val-ling 1 : be in competition with 2 : equal —**rival** adj —**ri-val-ry** \-rē\ n

riv-er \'rivər\ n : natural stream larger than a brook —**riv-er-bank** n —**riv-er-bed** n —**riv-er-boat** n —**riv-er-side** n

riv-et \'rivət\ n : headed metal bolt ~ vb : fasten with a rivet —**riv-et-er** n

riv-u-let \'riv(y)ələt\ n : small stream

roach \'rōch\ n : cockroach

road \'rōd\ n : open way for vehicles, persons, and animals —**road-bed** n —**road-way** n

road-block n : obstruction on a road

road-run-ner n : large fast-running bird

road-side n : strip of land along a road —**roadside** adj

roam \'rōm\ vb : wander

roan \'rōn\ adj : having a dark coat with white hairs interspersed ~ n : animal with a roan coat or its color

roar \'rōr\ vb : utter a full loud prolonged sound —**roar** n —**roar-er** n

roast \'rōst\ vb 1 : cook by dry heat 2 : criticize severely ~ n : piece of meat suitable for roasting —**roast** adj —**roast-er** n

rob \'räb\ vb -bb- 1 : steal from 2 : commit robbery —**rob-ber** n

rob-bery \'räb(ə)rē\ n, pl -ber-ies : theft of something from a person by use of violence or threat

robe \'rōb\ n 1 : long flowing outer garment 2 : covering for the lower body ~ vb robed; rob-ing 1 : clothe with or as if with a robe

rob-in \'räbən\ n : No. American thrush with a reddish breast

ro-bot \'rō,bät, -bət\ n 1 : machine that looks and acts like a human being 2 : efficient but insensitive person

ro-bust \rō'bəst, 'rō(ˌ)bəst\ adj : strong and vigorously healthy —**ro-bust-ly** adv —**ro-bust-ness** n

¹rock \'räk\ vb : sway or cause to sway back and forth ~ n 1 : rocking movement 2 : popular music marked by repetition and a strong beat

²rock n : mass of hard mineral material —**rock** adj —**rocky** adj

rock-er n 1 : curved piece on which a chair or cradle rocks

rock-et \'räkət\ n 1 : self-propelled firework or missile 2 : jet engine ~ vb : rise abruptly and rapidly —**rock-et-ry** \-ətrē\ n

rod \'räd\ n 1 : straight slender stick 2 : unit of length equal to 5½ yards

rode past of RIDE

ro-dent \'rōd²nt\ n : small gnawing mammal

ro-deo \'rōdēˌō, rə'dā̇ō\ n, pl -de-os : contest of cowboy skills

roe \'rō\ n : fish eggs

rogue \'rōg\ n : dishonest or mischievous person —**ro-guery** \'rōgərē\ n —**ro-guish** \'rōgish\ adj —**ro-guish-ly** adv —**ro-guish-ness** n

roil \'rȯil, for 2 also 'rīl\ vb 1 : make cloudy or muddy by stirring up 2 : make angry

role \'rōl\ n 1 : part to play 2 : function

roll \'rōl\ n 1 : official record or list of names 2 : something rolled up or rounded 3 : bread baked in a small rounded mass 4 : sound of rapid drum strokes 5 : heavy reverberating sound 6 : rolling movement ~ vb 1 : move by turning over and over 2 : move on wheels 3 : flow in a continuous stream 4 : swing from side to side 5 : shape or become shaped in rounded form 6 : press with a roller

roll-er n 1 : revolving cylinder 2 : rod on which something is rolled up

roller skate n : a skate with wheels instead of a runner —**roller-skate** vb —**roller skater** n

rol-lick-ing \'rälikiŋ\ adj : gay or boisterous

Ro-man Catholic \ˌrōmən-\ n : member of a Christian church led by a pope —**Roman Catholic** adj —**Roman Catholicism** n

ro-mance \rō'mans, 'rōˌmans\ n 1 : medieval tale of knightly adventure 2 : love story 3 : love affair ~ vb -manced; -manc-ing 1 : have romantic fancies 2 : have a love affair with —**ro-manc-er** n

ro·man·tic \rō'mantik\ *adj* **1** : visionary or imaginative **2** : appealing to one's emotions —**ro·man·ti·cal·ly** \-ik(ə)lē\ *adv*

romp \'rämp\ *vb* : play actively and noisily —**romp** *n*

roof \'rüf, 'rùf\ *n, pl* **roofs** \'rüfs, 'rùfs; 'rüvz, 'rùvz\ : upper covering part of a building ~ *vb* : cover with a roof —**roofed** \'rüft, 'rùft\ *adj* —**roof·ing** *n* —**roof·less** *adj* —**roof·top** *n*

¹rook \'rùk\ *n* : crowlike bird

²rook *vb* : cheat

rook·ie \'rùkē\ *n* : novice

room \'rüm, 'rùm\ *n* **1** : sufficient space **2** : partitioned part of a building ~ *vb* : occupy lodgings —**room·er** *n* —**room·ful** *n* —**roomy** *adj*

room·mate *n* : one sharing the same lodgings

roost \'rüst\ *n* : support on which birds perch ~ *vb* : settle on a roost

roost·er \'rüstər, 'rùs-\ *n* : adult male domestic fowl

¹root \'rüt, 'rùt\ *n* **1** : leafless underground part of a seed plant **2** : rootlike thing or part **3** : source **4** : essential core ~ *vb* : form, fix, or become fixed by roots —**root·less** *adj* —**root·let** \-lət\ *n* —**root·like** *adj*

²root *vb* : turn up with the snout

³root \'rüt, 'rùt\ *vb* : applaud or encourage noisily —**root·er** *n*

rope \'rōp\ *n* : strong cord of strands of fiber ~ *vb* **roped; rop·ing 1** : tie with a rope **2** : lasso

ro·sa·ry \'rōzərē\ *n, pl* **-ries 1** : string of beads used in praying **2** : Roman Catholic devotion

¹rose *past of* RISE

²rose \'rōz\ *n* **1** : prickly shrub with bright flowers **2** : purplish red —**rose** *adj* —**rose·bud** *n* —**rose·bush** *n*

rose·mary \'rōz₁merē\ *n, pl* **-mar·ies** : fragrant shrubby mint

ro·sette \rō'zet\ *n* : rose-shaped ornament

Rosh Ha·sha·nah \₁rōsh(h)ə'shōnə\ *n* : Jewish New Year observed as a religious holiday in September or October

ros·in \'räz²n\ *n* : brittle resin

ros·ter \'rästər\ *n* : list of names

ros·trum \'rästrəm\ *n, pl* **-trums** *or* **-tra** \-trə\ : speaker's platform

rosy \'rōzē\ *adj* **ros·i·er; -est 1** : of the color rose **2** : hopeful —**ros·i·ly** *adv* —**ros·i·ness** *n*

rot \'rät\ *vb* **-tt-** : undergo decomposition ~ *n* **1** : decay **2** : disease in which tissue breaks down

ro·ta·ry \'rōtərē\ *adj* **1** : turning on an axis **2** : having a rotating part

ro·tate \'rō₁tāt\ *vb* **-tat·ed; -tat·ing 1** : turn about an axis or a center **2** : alternate in a series —**ro·ta·tion** \rō'tāshən\ *n* —**ro·ta·tor** \'rō₁tātər\ *n*

rote \'rōt\ *n* : repetition from memory

ro·tor \'rōtər\ *n* **1** : part that rotates **2** : system of rotating horizontal blades for supporting a helicopter

rot·ten \'rät²n\ *adj* **1** : having rotted **2** : corrupt **3** : extremely unpleasant or inferior —**rot·ten·ness** \-²n(n)əs\ *n*

ro·tund \rō'tənd\ *adj* : rounded —**ro·tun·di·ty** \-'təndətē\ *n*

ro·tun·da \rō'təndə\ *n* : building or room with a dome

roué \rù'ā\ *n* : man given to debauched living

rouge \'rüzh, 'rüj\ *n* : cosmetic for the cheeks —**rouge** *vb*

rough \'rəf\ *adj* **1** : not smooth **2** : not calm **3** : harsh, violent, or rugged **4** : crudely or hastily done ~ *n* : rough state or something in that state ~ *vb* **1** : roughen **2** : manhandle **3** : make roughly —**rough·ly** *adv* —**rough·ness** *n*

rough·age \'rəfij\ *n* : coarse bulky food

rough·en \'rəfən\ *vb* : make or become rough

rough·neck \'rəf₁nek\ *n* : rowdy

rou·lette \rü'let\ *n* : gambling game using a whirling numbered wheel

¹round \'raùnd\ *adj* **1** : having every part the same distance from the center **2** : cylindrical **3** : complete **4** : approximate **5** : blunt **6** : moving in or forming a circle ~ *n* **1** : round thing **2** : curved part **3** : series of recurring actions or events **4** : period of time or a unit of action **5** : fired shot **6** : cut of beef ~ *vb* **1** : make or become round **2** : go around **3** : finish **4** : express as an approximation —**round·ish** *adj* —**round·ly** *adv* —**round·ness** *n*

²round *prep or adv* : around

round·about *adj* : indirect

round·up \'raùnd₁əp\ *n* **1** : gathering together of range cattle **2** : summary —**round·up** *vb*

rouse \'raùz\ *vb* **roused; rous·ing 1** : wake from sleep **2** : excite to activity

rout \'raùt\ *n* **1** : state of wild confusion **2** : disastrous defeat ~ *vb* : defeat decisively

route \'rüt, 'raùt\ *n* : line of travel ~ *vb* **rout·ed; rout·ing** : send by a selected route

rou·tine \rü'tēn\ n : procedure or course of action regularly followed —**routine** adj —**rou·tine·ly** adv

rove \'rōv\ vb **roved; rov·ing** : wander without definite direction —**rov·er** n

¹row \'rō\ vb **1** : propel a boat with oars **2** : travel or convey in a rowboat ~ n : act of rowing —**row·boat** n —**row·er** \'rō(ə)r\ n

²row n : number of objects in a line

³row \'rau\ n : noisy quarrel —**row** vb

row·dy \'raudē\ adj **-di·er; -est** : coarse or boisterous in behavior —**row·di·ness** n —**rowdy** n —**row·dy·ism** n

roy·al \'rȯiəl\ adj : relating to or befitting a king —**roy·al·ly** adv

roy·al·ty \'rȯiəltē\ n, pl **-ties 1** : state of being royal **2** : royal person **3** : payment for use of property

rub \'rəb\ vb **-bb- 1** : use pressure and friction on a body **2** : scour, polish, erase, or smear by pressure and friction **3** : chafe with friction ~ n **1** : act of rubbing **2** : difficulty

rub·ber \'rəbər\ n **1** : one that rubs **2** : waterproof elastic substance or something made of it —**rubber** adj —**rub·ber·ize** \-ˌīz\ vb —**rub·bery** adj

rub·bish \'rəbish\ n : waste or trash

rub·ble \'rəbəl\ n : broken stones or bricks

ru·ble \'rübəl\ n : monetary unit of the U.S.S.R.

ru·by \'rübē\ n, pl **-bies** : precious red stone

rud·der \'rədər\ n : steering device at the rear of a boat or aircraft

rud·dy \'rədē\ adj **-di·er; -est** : reddish —**rud·di·ness** n

rude \'rüd\ adj **rud·er; rud·est 1** : roughly made **2** : impolite —**rude·ly** adv —**rude·ness** n

ru·di·ment \'rüdəmənt\ n **1** : something not fully developed **2** : elementary principle —**ru·di·men·ta·ry** \ˌrüdə'mentə)rē\ adj

rue \'rü\ vb **rued; ru·ing** : feel regret for ~ n : regret —**rue·ful** \-fəl\ adj —**rue·ful·ly** adv —**rue·ful·ness** n

ruf·fi·an \'rəfēən\ n : brutal person

ruf·fle \'rəfəl\ vb **-fled; -fling 1** : draw into or provide with pleats **2** : roughen the surface of **3** : irritate ~ n : strip of fabric pleated on one edge

rug \'rəg\ n : piece of heavy fabric used as a floor covering

rug·ged \'rəgəd\ adj **1** : having a rough uneven surface **2** : severe **3** : strong —**rug·ged·ly** adv —**rug·ged·ness** n

ru·in \'rüən\ n **1** : complete collapse or destruction **2** : remains of something destroyed—usu. in pl. **3** : cause of destruction ~ vb **1** : destroy **2** : damage beyond repair **3** : bankrupt

ru·in·ous \'rüənəs\ adj : causing ruin —**ru·in·ous·ly** adv

rule \'rül\ n **1** : guide or principle for governing action **2** : usual way of doing something **3** : government **4** : straight strip (as of wood or metal) marked off in units for measuring ~ vb **ruled; rul·ing 1** : govern **2** : give as a decision —**rul·er** n

rum \'rəm\ n : liquor distilled from a fermented sugarcane product

rum·ble \'rəmbəl\ vb **-bled; -bling** : make a low heavy rolling sound —**rum·ble** n

ru·mi·nant \'rümənənt\ n : hoofed mammal (as a cow or deer) that chews the cud —**ruminant** adj

rum·mage \'rəmij\ vb **-maged; -mag·ing** : poke around looking for something —**rum·mag·er** n

rum·my \'rəmē\ n : card game

ru·mor \'rümər\ n **1** : common talk **2** : widespread statement not authenticated —**rumor** vb

rump \'rəmp\ n : rear part of an animal

rum·ple \'rəmpəl\ vb **-pled; -pling** : tousle or wrinkle —**rumple** n

rum·pus \'rəmpəs\ n : disturbance

run \'rən\ vb **ran** \'ran\; **run; run·ning 1** : go rapidly or hurriedly **2** : enter a race or election **3** : operate **4** : continue in force **5** : flow rapidly **6** : take a certain direction **7** : manage **8** : incur ~ n **1** : act of running **2** : brook **3** : continuous series **4** : usual kind **5** : freedom of movement **6** : lengthwise ravel

run·around n : evasive or delaying action

run·away \'rənəˌwā\ n : fugitive ~ adj **1** : fugitive **2** : out of control

run-down adj : being in poor condition

¹rung past part of RING

²rung \'rəŋ\ n : a round of a chair or ladder

run·ner \'rənər\ n **1** : one that runs **2** : lengthwise supporting part of a sled, skate, or drawer

run·ner-up n, pl **run·ners-up** : competitor who finishes next to the winner

run·ning \'rəniŋ\ adj **1** : flowing **2** : continuous

runt \'rənt\ n : small person or animal —**runty** adj

run·way \'rənˌwā\ n : strip on which aircraft land and take off

ru·pee \rü'pē, 'rü,-\ n : monetary unit (as of India)

rup·ture \'rəpchər\ *n* 1 : breaking or tearing apart 2 : hernia ~ *vb* **-tured; -tur·ing** : cause or undergo rupture

ru·ral \'rúrəl\ *adj* : relating to the country or agriculture

ruse \'rüs, 'rüz\ *n* : trick

¹rush \'rəsh\ *n* : grasslike marsh plant

²rush *vb* 1 : move forward or act with too great haste 2 : perform in a short time ~ *n* : violent forward motion ~ *adj* : requiring speed **—rush·er** *n*

rus·set \'rəsət\ *n* 1 : reddish brown color 2 : winter apple **—russet** *adj*

rust \'rəst\ *n* 1 : reddish coating on exposed metal (as iron) 2 : reddish orange color **—rust** *vb* **—rusty** *adj*

rus·tic \'rəstik\ *adj* 1 : rural 2 : boorish 3 : simple ~ *n* : rustic person **—rus·ti·cal·ly** \-k(ə)lē\ *adv* **—rus·tic·i·ty** \,rəs'tisətē\ *n*

rus·tle \'rəsəl\ *vb* **-tled; -tling** 1 : make or cause a rustle 2 : forage food 3 : steal cattle from the range ~ *n* : succession of small sounds **—rus·tler** \-(ə)lər\ *n*

rut \'rət\ *n* 1 : track worn by wheels or feet 2 : set routine **—rut·ted** *adj*

ruth·less \'rüthləs\ *adj* : having no pity **—ruth·less·ly** *adv* **—ruth·less·ness** *n*

-ry \rē\ *n suffix* : -ery

rye \'rī\ *n* : cereal grass grown for grain

S

s \'es\ *n, pl* **s's** *or* **ss** \'esəz\ : 19th letter of the alphabet

¹-s \s *after sounds* f, k, k̲, p, t, th; əz *after sounds* ch, j, s, sh, z, zh; z *after other sounds*\ —used to form the plural of most nouns

²-s *vb suffix* —used to form the 3d person singular present of most verbs

Sab·bath \'sabəth\ *n* 1 : Saturday observed as a day of worship by Jews and some Christians 2 : Sunday observed as a day of worship by Christians

sa·ber, sa·bre \'sābər\ *n* : cavalry sword

sa·ble \'sābəl\ *n* 1 : black 2 : dark brown mammal or its fur

sab·o·tage \'sabə,täzh\ *n* : deliberate destruction or hampering ~ *vb* **-taged; -tag·ing** : wreck through sabotage

sab·o·teur \,sabə'tər\ *n* : person who commits sabotage

sac \'sak\ *n* : baglike part

sac·cha·rin \'sak(ə)rən\ *n* : very sweet white substance

sac·cha·rine \-(ə)rən\ *adj* : nauseatingly sweet

sa·chet \sa'shā\ *n* : small bag with perfumed powder (**sachet powder**)

¹sack \'sak\ *n* : bag

²sack *vb* : plunder a captured place

sack·cloth *n* : rough garment worn as a sign of penitence

sac·ra·ment \'sakrəmənt\ *n* : formal religious act or rite **—sac·ra·men·tal** \,sakrə'mentᵊl\ *adj*

sa·cred \'sākrəd\ *adj* 1 : set apart for or worthy of worship 2 : worthy of

reverence 3 : relating to religion **—sa·cred·ly** *adv* **—sa·cred·ness** *n*

sac·ri·fice \'sakrə,fīs\ *n* 1 : the offering of something precious to a deity or the thing offered 2 : loss or deprivation ~ *vb* **-ficed; -fic·ing** : offer or give up as a sacrifice **—sac·ri·fi·cial** \,sakrə'fishəl\ *adj* **—sac·ri·fi·cial·ly** *adv*

sac·ri·lege \'sakrəlij\ *n* : violation of something sacred **—sac·ri·le·gious** \,sakrə'lijəs, -'lējəs\ *adj* **—sac·ri·le·gious·ly** *adv*

sac·ro·sanct \'sakrō,saŋkt\ *adj* : sacred

sad \'sad\ *adj* **-dd-** 1 : affected with grief or sorrow 2 : causing sorrow **—sad·den** \'sadᵊn\ *vb* **—sad·ly** *adv* **—sad·ness** *n*

sad·dle \'sadᵊl\ *n* : seat for riding on horseback ~ *vb* **-dled; -dling** : put a saddle on

sa·dism \'sā,dizəm, 'sad,iz-\ *n* : delight in cruelty **—sa·dist** \'sādəst, 'sad-\ *n* **—sa·dis·tic** \sə'distik\ *adj* **—sa·dis·ti·cal·ly** \-tik(ə)lē\ *adv*

sa·fa·ri \sə'färē, -'far-\ *n* : hunting expedition in Africa

safe \'sāf\ *adj* **saf·er; saf·est** 1 : freed or secure from danger 2 : providing safety ~ *n* : container to keep valuables safe **—safe·keep·ing** *n* **—safe·ly** *adv*

safe·guard *n* : measure or device for preventing accidents **—safeguard** *vb*

safe·ty \'sāftē\ *n, pl* **-ties** 1 : freedom from danger 2 : protective device

saf·flow·er \'saf,laü(ə)r\ *n* : herb with seeds rich in edible oil

saf·fron \'safrən\ *n* : orange powder from a crocus flower used in cooking

sag \'sag\ *vb* **-gg-** : droop, sink, or settle —**sag** *n*

sa·ga \'sägə\ *n* : story of heroic deeds

sa·ga·cious \sə'gāshəs\ *adj* : shrewd —**sa·gac·i·ty** \-'gasətē\ *n*

¹sage \'sāj\ *adj* : wise or prudent ~ *n* : wise man —**sage·ly** *adv*

²sage *n* : shrublike mint

sage·brush *n* : low shrub of the western U.S.

said *past of* SAY

sail \'sāl\ *n* **1** : a fabric used to catch the wind and push a ship **2** : trip on a sailboat ~ *vb* **1** : travel on a ship **2** : glide through the air —**sail·boat** *n* —**sail·or** \'sālər\ *n*

sail·fish *n* : large fish with a very large dorsal fin

saint \'sānt, *before a name* (₁)sānt *or* sənt\ *n* : holy or godly person —**saint·ed** \-əd\ *adj* —**saint·hood** \-,hŭd\ *n* —**saint·li·ness** *n* —**saint·ly** *adj*

¹sake \'sāk\ *n* **1** : purpose or reason **2** : one's good or benefit

²sa·ke, sa·ki \'säkē\ *n* : Japanese rice wine

sa·la·cious \sə'lāshəs\ *adj* : sexually suggestive

sal·ad \'saləd\ *n* : dish usu. of raw lettuce, vegetables, or fruit

sal·a·man·der \'salə,mandər\ *n* : lizardlike amphibian

sa·la·mi \sə'lämē\ *n* : highly seasoned dried sausage

sal·a·ry \'sal(ə)rē\ *n*, *pl* **-ries** : regular payment for services

sale \'sāl\ *n* **1** : transfer of ownership of property for money **2** : selling at bargain prices —**sal·able, sale·able** \'sāləbəl\ *adj* —**sales·man** \-mən\ *n* —**sales·woman** *n*

sa·lient \'sālyənt\ *adj* : standing out conspicuously

sa·line \'sā,lēn, -,līn\ *adj* : containing salt —**sa·lin·i·ty** \sā'linətē, sə-\ *n*

sa·li·va \sə'līvə\ *n* : liquid secreted into the mouth —**sal·i·vary** \'salə,verē\ *adj* —**sal·i·vate** \-,vāt\ *vb* —**sal·i·va·tion** \,salə'vāshən\ *n*

sal·low \'salō\ *adj* : of a yellowish sickly color

sal·ly \'salē\ *n*, *pl* **-lies 1** : rushing attack against troops **2** : witty remark —**sally** *vb*

salm·on \'samən\ *n*, *pl* **salmon** : soft-finned food fish

sa·loon \sə'lün\ *n* **1** : large room or ballroom on a passenger ship **2** : barroom

: elegant room or shop

salt \'sōlt\ *n* **1** : white crystalline substance that consists of sodium and chlorine **2** : compound formed usu. from acid and metal —**salt** *vb* or *adj* —**salt·i·ness** *n* —**salty** *adj*

salt·wa·ter *adj* : relating to or living in salt water

sa·lu·bri·ous \sə'lübrēəs\ *adj* : good for health

sal·u·tary \'salyə,terē\ *adj* : health-giving or beneficial

sal·u·ta·tion \,salyə'tāshən\ *n* : greeting

sa·lute \sə'lüt\ *vb* **-lut·ed; -lut·ing** : honor by ceremony or formal movement —**salute** *n*

sal·vage \'salvij\ *n* : something saved from destruction ~ *vb* **-vaged; -vag·ing** : rescue or save

sal·va·tion \sal'vāshən\ *n* : saving of a person from sin or danger

salve \'sav, 'sàv\ *n* : medicinal ointment ~ *vb* **salved; salv·ing** : soothe

sal·ver \'salvər\ *n* : small tray

sal·vo \'salvō\ *n*, *pl* **-vos** *or* **-voes** : simultaneous discharge of guns

same \'sām\ *adj* : being the one referred to ~ *pron* : the same one or ones ~ *adv* : in the same manner —**same·ness** *n*

sam·ple \'sampəl\ *n* : piece or item that shows the quality of the whole ~ *vb* **-pled; -pling** : judge by a sample

sam·pler \'samplər\ *n* : piece of needlework testing skill in embroidering

san·a·to·ri·um \,sanə'tōrēəm\ *n*, *pl* **-riums** *or* **-ria** \-ēə\ : hospital for the chronically ill

sanc·ti·fy \'saŋktə,fī\ *vb* **-fied; -fy·ing** : make holy —**sanc·ti·fi·ca·tion** \,saŋktəfə'kāshən\ *n*

sanc·ti·mo·nious \,saŋktə'mōnēəs\ *adj* : hypocritically pious

sanc·tion \'saŋkshən\ *n* **1** : authoritative approval **2** : coercive measure —usu. *pl* ~ *vb* : approve

sanc·ti·ty \'saŋktətē\ *n*, *pl* **-ties** : quality or state of being holy or sacred

sanc·tu·ary \'saŋktchə,werē\ *n*, *pl* **-ar·ies 1** : consecrated place **2** : place of refuge

sand \'sand\ *n* : loose granular particles of rock ~ *vb* : smooth with an abrasive —**sand·bank** *n* —**sand·er** *n* —**sand·storm** *n* —**sandy** *adj*

san·dal \'sand²l\ *n* : shoe consisting of a sole strapped to the foot

sand·pa·per *n* : abrasive paper —**sand·paper** *vb*

sand·pip·er \-,pīpər\ *n* : long-billed shorebird

sand·stone n : rock made of naturally cemented sand

sand·wich \'san(d̩)wich\ n : 2 or more slices of bread with a filling between them ~ vb : squeeze or crowd in

sane \'sān\ adj **san·er; san·est 1** : mentally healthy **2** : sensible —**sane·ly** adv

sang past of SING

san·gui·nary \'saŋgwə,nerē\ adj : bloody

san·guine \'saŋgwən\ adj **1** : reddish **2** : cheerful

san·i·tar·i·um \,sanə'terēəm\ n, pl -iums or -ia \-ēə\ : sanatorium

san·i·tary \'sanə,terē\ adj **1** : relating to health **2** : free from filth or infective matter

san·i·ta·tion \,sanə'tāshən\ n : protection of health by maintenance of sanitary conditions

san·i·ty \'sanətē\ n : soundness of mind

sank past of SINK

¹**sap** \'sap\ n **1** : vital fluid **2** : watery fluid that circulates through a vascular plant —**sap·less** adj —**sap·py** adj

²**sap** vb **-pp- 1** : undermine **2** : weaken or exhaust gradually

sa·pi·ent \'sāpēənt, 'sapē-\ adj : wise —**sa·pi·ence** \-əns\ n

sap·ling \'sapliŋ\ n : young tree

sap·phire \'saf,ī(ə)r\ n : hard transparent blue precious stone

sap·suck·er \'sap,səkər\ n : small American woodpecker

sar·casm \'sär,kazəm\ n **1** : cutting remark **2** : ironical criticism or reproach —**sar·cas·tic** \sär'kastik\ adj —**sar·cas·ti·cal·ly** \-tik(ə)lē\ adv

sar·coph·a·gus \sär'käfəgəs\ n, pl -gi \-,gī, -,jī\ : large stone coffin

sar·dine \sär'dēn\ n : small fish preserved esp. in oil for use as food

sar·don·ic \sär'dänik\ adj : bitterly disdainful —**sar·don·i·cal·ly** \-ik(ə)lē\ adv

sa·rong \sə'röŋ, -'räŋ\ n : loose skirt worn esp. by people of the Pacific islands

sar·sa·pa·ril·la \,sas(ə)pə'rilə, ,särs-\ n : root of a tropical American plant used esp. for flavoring

sar·to·ri·al \sär'tōrēəl\ adj : relating to a tailor or men's clothes

¹**sash** \'sash\ n : broad band worn around the waist or over the shoulder

²**sash** n, pl **sash 1** : frame for a pane of glass in a door or window **2** : movable part of a window

sas·sa·fras \'sasə,fras\ n : No. Ameri-

can tree or its dried bark used in medicine and as flavoring

sassy \'sasē\ adj **sass·i·er; -est** : saucy

sat past of SIT

Sa·tan \'sāt³n\ n : devil

satch·el \'sachəl\ n : small bag

sate \'sāt\ vb **sat·ed; sat·ing** : satisfy to the full

sat·el·lite \'sat³l,īt\ n **1** : one that is dependent **2** : body that revolves around a larger celestial body

sa·ti·ate \'sāshē,āt\ vb **-at·ed; -at·ing 1** : satisfy fully **2** : surfeit —**sa·ti·ety** \sə'tīətē\ n

sat·in \'sat³n\ n : glossy fabric

sat·ire \'sa,tī(ə)r\ n : literary ridicule done with humor —**sa·tir·ic** \sə'tirik\, **sa·tir·i·cal** \-ikəl\ adj —**sa·tir·i·cal·ly** adv —**sat·i·rist** \'satərəst\ n —**sat·i·rize** \-ə,rīz\ vb

sat·is·fac·tion \,satəs'fakshən\ n : state of being satisfied —**sat·is·fac·to·ri·ly** \-'fakt(ə)ralē\adv —**sat·is·fac·to·ry** \-'fakt(ə)rē\ adj

sat·is·fy \'satəs,fī\ vb **-fied; -fy·ing 1** : make happy **2** : pay what is due to or on —**sat·is·fy·ing·ly** adv

sat·u·rate \'sachə,rāt\ vb **-rat·ed; -rat·ing** : soak or charge thoroughly —**sat·u·ra·tion** \,sachə'rāshən\ n

Sat·ur·day \'satərdē\ n : 7th day of the week

sat·ur·nine \'satər,nīn\ adj : sardonic or sullen

sa·tyr \'sātər, 'sat-\ n : partly horselike or goatlike deity of Greek mythology

sauce \'sös\ n : dressing for salads or meats —**sauce·pan** n

sau·cer \'sösər\ n : small shallow dish under a cup

saucy \'sasē, 'sösē\ adj **sauc·i·er; -est** : insolent —**sauc·i·ly** adv —**sauc·i·ness** n

sau·er·kraut \'saú(ə)r,kraút\ n : finely cut and fermented cabbage

sau·na \'saúnə\ n : steam or dry heat bath or a room or cabinet used for such a bath

saun·ter \'söntər, 'sänt-\ vb : stroll

sau·sage \'sösij\ n : minced and highly seasoned meat

sau·té \sö'tā, sō-\ vb **-téed or -téd; -té·ing** : fry in a little fat —**sauté** n

sav·age \'savij\ adj **1** : wild **2** : cruel ~ n : person belonging to a primitive society —**sav·age·ly** adv —**sav·age·ness** n —**sav·age·ry** \-əjrē\ n

¹**save** \'sāv\ vb **saved; sav·ing 1** : rescue from danger **2** : guard from destruction **3** : redeem from sin **4** : put aside as a reserve —**sav·er** n

²**save** \(,)sāv\ prep : except

sav·ior, sav·iour \'sāvyər\ *n* **1** : one who saves **2** *cap* : Jesus Christ

sa·vor \'sāvər\ *n* : special flavor ~ *vb* : taste with pleasure —**sa·vory** *adj*

¹saw *past of* SEE

²saw \'sȯ\ *n* **1** : cutting tool with teeth ~ *vb* **sawed; sawed** *or* **sawn; saw·ing** : cut with a saw —**saw·dust** \-₁dəst\ *n* —**saw·mill** *n* —**saw·yer** \-yər\ *n*

saw-horse *n* : support for wood being sawed

sax·o·phone \'saksə₁fōn\ *n* : wind instrument with a reed mouthpiece and usu. a bent metal body

say \'sā\ *vb* **said** \'sed\; **say·ing** \'sāiŋ\; **says** \'sez\ **1** : express in words **2** : state positively ~ *n*, *pl* **says** **1** : expression of opinion **2** : power of decision

say·ing \'sāiŋ\ *n* : commonly repeated statement

scab \'skab\ *n* **1** : protective crust over a sore or wound **2** : worker taking a striker's job ~ *vb* **-bb- 1** : become covered with a scab **2** : work as a scab —**scab·by** *adj*

scab·bard \'skabərd\ *n* : sheath for the blade of a weapon

scaf·fold \'skafəld, -₁ōld\ *n* **1** : raised platform for workmen **2** : platform on which a criminal is executed

scald \'skȯld\ *vb* **1** : burn with hot liquid or steam **2** : heat to the boiling point

¹scale \'skāl\ *n* : weighing device ~ *vb* **scaled; scal·ing** : weigh

²scale *n* **1** : thin plate esp. on the body of a fish or reptile **2** : thin coating or layer ~ *vb* **scaled; scal·ing** : strip of scales —**scaled** \'skāld\ *adj* —**scale·less** *adj* —**scaly** *adj*

³scale *n* **1** : graduated series **2** : size of a sample (as a model) in proportion to the size of the actual thing **3** : standard of estimation or judgment **4** : series of musical tones ~ *vb* **scaled; scal·ing 1** : go up by a ladder **2** : arrange in a graded series

scal·lion \'skalyən\ *n* : bulbless onion

scal·lop \'skäləp, 'skal-\ *n* **1** : marine mollusk **2** : rounded projection on a border

scalp \'skalp\ *n* : skin and flesh of the head ~ *vb* **1** : tear the scalp from **2** : sell again at a greatly increased price —**scalp·er** *n*

scal·pel \'skalpəl\ *n* : surgical knife

scamp \'skamp\ *n* : rascal

scam·per \'skampər\ *vb* : run nimbly —**scamper** *n*

scan \'skan\ *vb* **-nn- 1** : read (verses) so

as to show meter **2** : examine closely or hastily —**scan** *n* —**scan·ner** *n*

scan·dal \'skand²l\ *n* **1** : disgraceful situation **2** : malicious gossip —**scan·dal·ize** *vb* —**scan·dal·ous** *adj*

scant \'skant\ *adj* : barely sufficient ~ *vb* : stint —**scant·i·ly** *adv* —**scanty** *adj*

scape·goat \'skāp₁gōt\ *n* : one that bears the blame for others

scap·u·la \'skapyələ\ *n*, *pl* **-lae** \-₁lē\ *or* **-las** : shoulder blade

scar \'skär\ *n* : mark where a wound has healed —**scar** *vb*

scar·ab \'skarəb\ *n* : large dark beetle or an ornament representing one

scarce \'skers\ *adj* **scarc·er; scarc·est** **1** : not plentiful **2** : rare —**scar·ci·ty** \'skersətē\ *n*

scarce·ly \'skerslē\ *adv* **1** : barely **2** : almost not

scare \'sker\ *vb* **scared; scar·ing** : frighten ~ *n* : fright —**scary** *adj*

scare·crow \'skeər₁krō\ *n* : figure for scaring birds from crops

scarf \'skärf\ *n*, *pl* **scarves** \'skärvz\ *or* **scarfs** : cloth worn about the shoulders or the neck

scar·let \'skärlət\ *n* : bright red —**scarlet** *adj*

scarlet fever *n* : acute contagious disease marked by fever, sore throat, and red rash

scath·ing \'skāthiŋ\ *adj* : bitterly severe

scat·ter \'skatər\ *vb* **1** : spread about irregularly **2** : disperse

scav·en·ger \'skavənjər\ *n* **1** : person that collects refuse or waste **2** : animal that feeds on decayed matter —**scav·enge** \'skavənj\ *vb*

sce·nar·io \sə¹narē₁ō\ *n*, *pl* **-i·os** : plot of a movie

scene \'sēn\ *n* **1** : single situation in a play or movie **2** : stage setting **3** : view **4** : display of emotion —**sce·nic** \'sēnik\ *adj*

scen·ery \'sēn(ə)rē\ *n*, *pl* **-er·ies 1** : painted setting for a stage **2** : picturesque view

scent \'sent\ *vb* **1** : smell **2** : fill with odor ~ *n* **1** : odor **2** : sense of smell **3** : perfume

scep·ter \'septər\ *n* : staff signifying authority

scep·tic \'skeptik\ *var of* SKEPTIC

sched·ule \'skejül, *esp Brit* 'shedyül\ *n* : list showing sequence of events ~ *vb* **-uled; -ul·ing** : make a schedule of

scheme \'skēm\ *n* **1** : crafty plot **2** : systematic design ~ *vb* **schemed;**

schem·ing : form a plot —**sche·mat·ic** \ski'matik\ adj —**schem·er** n

schism \'sizəm, 'skiz-\ n : split —**schis·mat·ic** \siz'matik, skiz-\ n or adj

schizo·phre·nia \ˌskitsə'frēnēə\ n : severe mental disorder —**schiz·oid** \'skit,sȯid\ adj or n —**schizo·phren·ic** \ˌskitsə'frenik\ adj or n

schol·ar \'skälər\ n : student or learned person —**schol·ar·ly** adj

schol·ar·ship \-ˌship\ n 1 : qualities or learning of a scholar 2 : money given to a student to pay for education

scho·las·tic \skə'lastik\ adj : relating to schools, scholars, or scholarship

¹**school** \'skül\ n 1 : institution for learning 2 : pupils in a school 3 : group with shared beliefs ~ vb : teach —**school·boy** n —**school·girl** n —**school·house** n —**school·mate** n —**school·room** n —**school·teacher** n

²**school** n : large number of fish swimming together

schoo·ner \'skünər\ n : sailing ship

sci·ence \'sīəns\ n : branch of systematic study esp. of the physical world —**sci·en·tif·ic** \ˌsīən'tifik\ adj —**sci·en·tif·i·cal·ly** \-ik)lē\ adv —**sci·en·tist** \'sīəntəst\ n

scin·til·late \'sint²lˌāt\ vb -**lat·ed**; -**lat·ing** : flash —**scin·til·la·tion** \ˌsint²l'āshən\ n

sci·on \'sīən\ n 1 : shoot of a plant 2 : descendant

scis·sors \'sizərz\ n pl : small shears

scle·ro·sis \sklə'rōsəs\ n : hardening of an artery —**scle·rot·ic** \-'rätik\ adj

scoff \'skäf\ vb : mock —**scoff·er** n

scold \'skōld\ n : person who scolds ~ vb : criticize severely

scoop \'sküp\ n : shovellike utensil ~ vb 1 : take out with a scoop 2 : dig out

scoot \'scüt\ vb : go suddenly and swiftly

scoot·er \'scütər\ n : child's foot-propelled vehicle

¹**scope** \'skōp\ n 1 : extent 2 : room for development

²**scope** n : viewing device (as a microscope)

scorch \'skȯrch\ vb : burn the surface of

score \'skȯr\ n, pl **scores** or pl **score** 1 : twenty 2 : cut 3 : record of points made (as in a game) 4 : debt 5 : music of a composition ~ vb **scored**; **scor·ing** 1 : record 2 : mark with lines 3 : gain in a game 4 : assign a grade to 5 : compose a score for —**score·less** adj —**scor·er** n

scorn \'skȯrn\ n : emotion involving both anger and disgust ~ vb : hold in contempt —**scorn·er** n —**scorn·ful** \-fəl\ adj —**scorn·ful·ly** adv

scor·pi·on \'skȯrpēən\ n : poisonous spider-like animal

scoun·drel \'skaündrəl\ n : mean worthless person

¹**scour** \'skaü(ə)r\ vb : examine thoroughly

²**scour** vb : rub (as with a gritty substance) in order to clean

scourge \'skərj\ n 1 : whip 2 : punishment —vb **scourged**; **scourg·ing** 1 : lash 2 : punish severely

scout \'skaüt\ vb : inspect or observe to get information ~ n : person sent out to get information

scow \'skaü\ n : large flat-bottomed boat with square ends

scowl \'skaül\ vb : make a face in expression of displeasure —**scowl** n

scrag·gly \'skraglē\ adj : irregular or unkempt

scram \'skram\ vb -**mm**- : go away at once

scram·ble \'skrambəl\ vb -**bled**; -**bling** 1 : clamber clumsily around 2 : struggle for possession of something 3 : mix together 4 : stir during frying —**scramble** n

¹**scrap** \'skrap\ n 1 : fragment 2 : discarded material ~ vb -**pp**- : get rid of as useless

²**scrap** vb -**pp**- : fight —**scrap** n —**scrap·per** n

scrap·book n : blank book in which mementos are kept

scrape \'skrāp\ vb **scraped**; **scrap·ing** 1 : remove by drawing a knife over 2 : clean or smooth by rubbing 3 : get (money) together 4 : get along with difficulty ~ n 1 : act of scraping 2 : predicament —**scrap·er** n

scratch \'skrach\ vb 1 : scrape or dig with or as if with claws or nails 2 : cause to move gratingly ~ n : mark or sound made in scratching —**scratchy** adj

scrawl \'skrȯl\ vb : write hastily and carelessly —**scrawl** n

scraw·ny \'skrȯnē\ adj -**ni·er**; -**est** : very thin

scream \'skrēm\ vb : cry out loudly and shrilly ~ n : loud shrill cry

screech \'skrēch\ vb or n : shriek

screen \'skrēn\ n 1 : device or partition used to protect or decorate 2 : surface on which pictures appear (as in movies) ~ vb 1 : shield with a screen 2 : separate with or as if with a screen

screw \'skrü\ n 1 : grooved fastening

device 2 : propeller ~ vb 1 : fasten by means of a screw 2 : move spirally

screw-driv-er \'skrü,drīvər\ n : tool for turning screws

scrib-ble \'skribəl\ vb **-bled; -bling** : write hastily or carelessly —**scribble** n —**scrib-bler** \-(ə)lər\ n

scribe \'skrīb\ n : one who writes or copies writing

scrimp \'skrimp\ vb : economize greatly

scrip \'skrip\ n 1 : paper money for less than a dollar 2 : certificate entitling one to something (as stock)

script \'skript\ n : text (as of a play)

scrip-ture \'skripchər\ n : sacred writings of a religion —**scrip-tur-al** \'skripchərəl\ adj

scroll \'skrōl\ n 1 : roll of paper for writing a document 2 : spiral or coiled design

scro-tum \'skrōtəm\ n, pl **-ta** \-ə\ or **-tums** : pouch containing the testes

scrounge \'skraünj\ vb **scrounged; scroung-ing** : collect by or as if by foraging

¹**scrub** \'skrəb\ n : stunted tree or shrub or a growth of these —**scrub** adj —**scrub-by** adj

²**scrub** vb **-bb-** 1 : rub in washing 2 : wash by rubbing —**scrub** n

scruff \'skrəf\ n : loose skin of the back of the neck

scru-ple \'skrüpəl\ n : reluctance due to ethical considerations —**scruple** vb —**scru-pu-lous** \-pyələs\ adj —**scru-pu-lous-ly** adv

scru-ti-ny \'skrüt²nē\ n, pl **-nies** : careful inspection —**scru-ti-nize** \-ⁿn,īz\ vb

scud \'skəd\ vb **-dd-** : move speedily

scuff \'skəf\ vb : scratch, scrape, or wear away —**scuff** n

scuf-fle \'skəfəl\ vb **-fled; -fling** 1 : struggle at close quarters 2 : shuffle one's feet —**scuffle** n

scull \'skəl\ n 1 : oar for sculling 2 : racing shell propelled with sculls ~ vb : propel a boat by an oar over the stern

scul-lery \'skəl(ə)rē\ n, pl **-ler-ies** : small room near the kitchen for cleaning

sculp-ture \'skəlpchər\ n : work of art carved or molded ~ vb **-tured; -tur-ing** : form as sculpture —**sculp-tor** \-tər\ n —**sculp-tur-al** \-chərəl\ adj

scum \'skəm\ n : filthy film on a liquid

scurf \'skərf\ n : thin dry scales of skin

scur-ri-lous \'skərələs\ adj : coarsely jesting

scur-ry \'skərē\ vb **-ried; -ry-ing** : scamper

scur-vy \'skərvē\ n : vitamin-deficiency disease

¹**scut-tle** \'skət³l\ n : pail for coal

²**scuttle** vb **-tled; -tling** : cut a hole in a ship to sink it

³**scuttle** vb **-tled; -tling** : scamper

scythe \'sīth\ n : mowing tool —**scythe** vb

sea \'sē\ n 1 : large body of salt water 2 : ocean 3 : rough water —**sea** adj —**sea-coast** n —**sea-food** n —**sea level** n —**sea-port** n —**sea-shore** n —**sea-water** n

sea-bird n : bird frequenting the open ocean

sea-board n : country's seacoast

sea-far-er \-,farər\ n : seaman —**sea-far-ing** \-,farin\ adj or n

sea horse n : small fish with a horselike head

¹**seal** \'sēl\ n : large sea mammal of cold regions —**seal-skin** n

²**seal** n 1 : device for stamping a design 2 : something that closes ~ vb 1 : affix a seal to 2 : close up securely 3 : determine finally —**seal-ant** \-ənt\ n —**seal-er** n

sea lion n : large Pacific seal with external ears

seam \'sēm\ n 1 : line of junction of 2 edges 2 : layer of a mineral ~ vb : join by sewing —**seam-less** adj

sea-man \'sēmən\ n 1 : one who helps to handle a ship 2 : enlisted man in the navy ranking next below a petty officer third class —**sea-man-ship** n

seaman apprentice n : enlisted man in the navy ranking next below a seaman

seaman recruit n : enlisted man of the lowest rank in the navy

seam-stress \'sēmstrəs\ n : woman who sews

seamy \'sēmē\ adj **seam-i-er; -est** : unpleasant or sordid

sé-ance \'sā,äns\ n : meeting for communicating with spirits

sea-plane n : airplane that can take off from and land on the water

sear \'sir\ vb : scorch

search \'sərch\ vb 1 : look through 2 : seek —**search** n —**search-er** n —**search-light** n

sea-sick adj : nauseated by the motion of a ship —**sea-sick-ness** n

¹**sea-son** \'sēz³n\ n 1 : division of the year 2 : customary time for something —**sea-son-al** \'sēznəl, -³n³l\ adj —**sea-son-al-ly** adv

²**season** vb **-soned; -soning** 1 : add spice to (food) 2

: make strong or fit for use —**sea-son-ing** \-niŋ, ͦniŋ\ n

sea-son-able \'sēznəbəl\ adj : occurring at a suitable time —**sea-son-ably** \-blē\ adv

seat \'sēt\ n 1 : place to sit 2 : chair, bench, or stool for sitting on 3 : place that serves as a capital or center ~ vb 1 : place in or on a seat 2 : provide seats for

sea-weed n : marine alga

sea-wor-thy adj : strong enough to hold up to a sea voyage

se-cede \si'sēd\ vb -ced·ed; -ced·ing : withdraw from a body (as a nation)

se-clude \si'klüd\ vb -clud·ed; -clud·ing : shut off alone —**se-clu-sion** \si'klüzhən\ n

¹**sec-ond** \'sekənd\ adj : next after the 1st ~ n 1 : one that is second 2 : one who assists (as in a duel) —**second, sec-ond-ly** adv

²**second** n 1 : 60th part of a minute of time or of a degree 2 : moment

sec-ond-ary \'sekən‚derē\ adj 1 : second in rank or importance 2 : coming after the primary or elementary

sec-ond-hand adj 1 : not original 2 : used before

second lieutenant n : commissioned officer ranking next below a first lieutenant

se-cret \'sēkrət\ adj 1 : hidden 2 : kept from general knowledge —**se-cre-cy** \-krəsē\ n —**secret** n —**se-cre-tive** \'sēkrətiv, si'krēt-\ adj —**se-cret-ly** adv

sec-re-tar-i-at \‚sekrə'terēət\ n 1 : body of secretaries in an office 2 : administrative department

sec-re-tary \'sekrə‚terē\ n, pl -tar-ies 1 : one hired to handle correspondence and other tasks for a superior 2 : official in charge of correspondence or records 3 : head of a government department —**sec-re-tar-i-al** \‚sekrə'terēəl\ adj

¹**se-crete** \si'krēt\ vb -cret-ed; -cret-ing : produce as a secretion

²**se-crete** \si'krēt, 'sēkrət\ vb -cret-ed; -cret-ing : hide

se-cre-tion \si'krēshən\ n 1 : act or process of secreting 2 : product of glandular activity

sect \'sekt\ n : religious group

sec-tar-i-an \sek'terēən\ adj 1 : relating to a sect 2 : limited in character or scope ~ n : member of a sect

sec-tion \'sekshən\ n : distinct part —**sec-tion-al** \-sh(ə)nəl\ adj

sec-tor \'sektər\ n 1 : part of a circle between 2 radii 2 : distinctive part

sec-u-lar \'sekyələr\ adj 1 : not sacred 2 : not monastic

se-cure \si'kyür\ adj -cur-er; -est : free from danger or loss ~ vb 1 : fasten safely 2 : get —**se-cure-ly** adv

se-cu-ri-ty \si'kyürətē\ n, pl -ties 1 : safety 2 : something given to guarantee payment 3 pl : bond or stock certificates

se-dan \si'dan\ n 1 : chair carried by 2 men 2 : enclosed automobile

se-date \si'dāt\ adj : quiet and dignified —**se-date-ly** adv

sed-a-tive \'sedətiv\ adj : serving to relieve tension ~ n : sedative drug —**se-da-tion** \si'dāshən\ n

sed-en-tary \'sedən‚terē\ adj : characterized by much sitting

sedge \'sej\ n : grasslike marsh plant

sed-i-ment \'sedəmənt\ n : material that settles to the bottom of a liquid or is deposited by water or a glacier —**sed-i-men-ta-ry** \‚sedə'ment(ə)rē\ adj —**sed-i-men-ta-tion** \-‚mən'tāshən, -‚men-\ n

se-di-tion \si'dishən\ n : revolution against a government —**se-di-tious** \-əs\ adj

se-duce \si'd(y)üs\ vb -duced; -duc-ing 1 : lead astray 2 : entice to unlawful sexual intercourse —**se-duc-er** n —**se-duc-tion** \-'dəkshən\ n —**se-duc-tive** \-tiv\ adj

sed-u-lous \'sejələs\ adj : diligent

¹**see** \'sē\ vb saw \'sô\; seen \'sēn\; see·ing 1 : perceive by the eye 2 : notice or heed 3 : understand 4 : make sure 5 : meet with or escort

²**see** n : jurisdiction of a bishop

seed \'sēd\ n, pl seed or seeds 1 : part by which a plant is propagated 2 : source ~ vb 1 : sow 2 : remove seeds from —**seed-less** adj

seed-ling \-liŋ\ n : plant grown from seed

seedy \-ē\ adj seed·i·er; -est 1 : full of seeds 2 : inferior

seek \'sēk\ vb sought \'sôt\; seek·ing 1 : search for 2 : try to reach or obtain —**seek-er** n

seem \'sēm\ vb : give the impression of being —**seem-ing-ly** adv

seem-ly \-lē\ adj seem·li·er; -est : proper

seep \'sēp\ vb : leak through fine pores or cracks —**seep-age** \'sēpij\ n

seer \'sir\ n : one who foresees or predicts events

seer-suck-er \'sir‚səkər\ n : light puckered fabric

see-saw \'sē‚sô\ n : board balanced in the middle —**seesaw** vb seethe \'sēth\ vb seethed; seeth·ing : become violently agitated

seg·ment \'segmənt\ n : division of a thing —seg·ment·ed \-,mentəd\ adj

seg·re·gate \'segri,gāt\ vb -gat·ed; -gat·ing : cut off from others —seg·re·ga·tion \,segri'gāshən\ n

seine \'sān\ n : large weighted fishing net ~ vb : fish with a seine

seis·mic \'sīzmik, 'sīs-\ adj : relating to an earthquake

seis·mo·graph \-mə,graf\ n : apparatus for measuring earthquakes

seize \'sēz\ vb seized; seiz·ing : take by force —sei·zure \'sēzhər\ n

sel·dom \'seldəm\ adv : not often

se·lect \sə'lekt\ adj 1 : favored 2 : discriminating ~ vb : take by preference —se·lec·tive \-'lektiv\ adj

se·lec·tion \sə'lekshən\ n : act of selecting or thing selected

se·lect·man \si'lek(t),man, -mən\ n : New England town official

self \'self\ n, pl selves \'selvz\ : essential person distinct from others

self- comb form 1 : oneself or itself 2 : of oneself or itself 3 : by oneself or automatic 4 : to, for, or toward oneself

self-addressed	self-determina-
self-adminis-	tion
tered	self-determined
self-analysis	self-discipline
self-appointed	self-doubt
self-assertive	self-educated
self-assurance	self-employed
self-assured	self-employment
self-awareness	self-esteem
self-cleaning	self-evident
self-closing	self-explanatory
self-complacent	self-expression
self-conceit	self-fulfilling
self-confessed	self-fulfillment
self-confidence	self-governing
self-confident	self-government
self-contained	self-help
self-contempt	self-image
self-contradic-	self-importance
tion	self-important
self-contradic-	self-imposed
tory	self-improve-
self-control	ment
self-created	self-indulgence
self-criticism	self-inflicted
self-defeating	self-interest
self-defense	self-love
self-denial	self-operating
self-denying	self-pity
self-destruction	self-portrait
self-destructive	

self-possessed	self-sacrifice
self-possession	self-satisfaction
self-preservation	self-satisfied
self-proclaimed	self-service
self-propelled	self-serving
self-propelling	self-starting
self-protection	self-styled
self-reliance	self-sufficiency
self-reliant	self-sufficient
self-respect	self-supporting
self-respecting	self-winding
self-restraint	

self-cen·tered adj : concerned only with one's own self

self-con·scious adj : ill at ease —self-con·scious·ly adv —self-con·scious·ness n

self·ish \'selfish\ adj : taking care of oneself without regard for others —self·ish·ly adv —self·ish·ness n

self·less \'selfləs\ adj : having no concern for self —self·less·ness n

self-made adj : rising by one's own efforts

self-right·eous adj : strongly convinced of one's own righteousness

self·same \'self,sām\ adj : precisely the same

sell \'sel\ vb sold \'sōld\; sell·ing 1 : transfer (property) esp. for money 2 : deal in as a business 3 : be sold —sell·er n

selves pl of SELF

se·man·tic \si'mantik\ adj : relating to meaning —se·man·tics \-iks\ n sing or pl

sema·phore \'semə,fōr\ n 1 : visual signaling apparatus 2 : signaling by flags

sem·blance \'sembləns\ n : appearance

se·men \'sēmən\ n : male reproductive fluid

se·mes·ter \sə'mestər\ n : half a school year

semi- \,semi, 'sem-, -,ī\ prefix 1 : half 2 : partial

semi·co·lon \'semi,kōlən\ n : punctuation mark ;

semi·con·duc·tor \,semi-, -,ī-\ n : electronic device used to regulate flow of electricity —semi·con·duct·ing adj

semi·fi·nal \,semi-\ adj : being next to the final —semifinal \'semi-\ n

semi·for·mal \,semi-\ adj : being or suitable for an occasion of moderate formality

sem·i·nal \'semənᵊl\ adj 1 : relating to seed or semen 2 : causing or influencing later development

sem·i·nar \'semə,när\ n : conference or conference-like study

sem·i·nary \'semə,nerē\ n, pl -nar·ies

: school and esp. a theological school —**sem·i·nar·i·an** \\,semə'nerēən\ *n*

sen·ate \'senət\ *n* : upper branch of a legislature —**sen·a·tor** \-ər\ *n* —**sen·a·to·ri·al** \\,senə'tōrēəl\ *adj*

send \'send\ *vb* **sent** \'sent\; **send·ing** **1** : cause to go **2** : propel —**send·er** *n*

se·nile \'sēn,īl, 'sen-\ *adj* : mentally deficient through old age —**se·nil·i·ty** \si'nilətē\ *n*

se·nior \'sēnyər\ *adj* : older or higher ranking —**senior** *n* —**se·nior·i·ty** \\,sēn'yórətē\ *n*

senior chief petty officer *n* : petty officer in the navy ranking next below a master chief petty officer

senior master sergeant *n* : noncommissioned officer in the air force ranking next below a chief master sergeant

sen·sa·tion \sen'sāshən\ *n* **1** : bodily feeling **2** : condition of excitement or the cause of it —**sen·sa·tion·al** \-sh(ə)nəl\ *adj*

sense \'sens\ *n* **1** : meaning **2** : faculty of perceiving something physical **3** : sound mental capacity ~ *vb* **sensed**; **sens·ing** : perceive by the senses —**sense·less** *adj* —**sense·less·ly** *adv*

sen·si·bil·i·ty \\,sensə'bilətē\ *n, pl* **-ties** : delicacy of feeling

sen·si·ble \'sensəbəl\ *adj* **1** : capable of sensing or being sensed **2** : aware or conscious **3** : intelligent —**sen·si·bly** \-blē\ *adv*

sen·si·tive \'sensətiv\ *adj* **1** : subject to excitation by or responsive to stimuli **2** : having power of feeling **3** : easily affected —**sen·si·tive·ness** *n* —**sen·si·tiv·i·ty** \\,sensə'tivətē\ *n*

sen·si·tize \'sensə,tīz\ *vb* **-tized**; **-tiz·ing** : make or become sensitive

sen·so·ry \'sens(ə)rē\ *adj* : relating to sensation or the senses

sen·su·al \'sench(ə)wəl, 'senshə\ *adj* **1** : pleasing the senses **2** : devoted to the pleasures of the senses —**sen·su·al·ist** *n* —**sen·su·al·i·ty** \\,sencha-'walətē\ *n* —**sen·su·al·ly** *adv*

sen·su·ous \'sench(ə)wəs\ *adj* : having strong appeal to the senses —**sen·su·ous·ly** *adv* —**sen·su·ous·ness** *n*

sent *past of* SEND

sen·tence \'sent²ns, -²nz\ *n* **1** : judgment of a court **2** : grammatically self-contained speech unit ~ *vb* **-tenced**; **-tenc·ing** : impose a sentence on

sen·ten·tious \sen'tenchəs\ *adj* : using pompous language

sen·tient \'sench(ē)ənt\ *adj* : capabable of feeling

sen·ti·ment \'sentəmənt\ *n* **1** : belief **2** : feeling

sen·ti·men·tal \\,sentə'ment²l\ *adj* : influenced by tender feelings —**sen·ti·men·tal·ism** *n* —**sen·ti·men·tal·ist** *n* —**sen·ti·men·tal·i·ty** \-,men'talətē, -mən-\ *n* —**sen·ti·men·tal·ize** \-'ment²l,īz\ *vb* —**sen·ti·men·tal·ly** *adv*

sen·ti·nel \'sentnəl, -²nəl\ *n* : sentry

sen·try \'sentrē\ *n, pl* **-tries** : one who stands guard

se·pal \'sēpəl, 'sep-\ *n* : one of the modified leaves comprising a flower calyx

sep·a·rate \'sepə,rāt\ *vb* **-rat·ed**; **-rat·ing 1** : set or keep apart **2** : become divided or detached ~ \'sep(ə)rət\ *adj* **1** : not connected or shared **2** : distinct from each other —**sep·a·ra·ble** \'sep(ə)rəbəl\ *adj* —**sep·a·rate·ly** \'sep(ə)rətlē\ *adv* —**sep·a·ra·tion** \\,sepə'rāshən\ *n* —**sep·a·ra·tor** \'sepə,rātər\ *n*

se·pia \'sēpēə\ *n* : brownish gray

Sep·tem·ber \sep'tembər\ *n* : 9th month of the year having 30 days

sep·tic \'septik\ *adj* : relating to or using the action of bacteria

sep·ul·cher, sep·ul·chre \'sepəlkər\ *n* : burial vault —**se·pul·chral** \sə'pəlkrəl\ *adj*

se·quel \'sēkwəl\ *n* **1** : consequence or result **2** : continuation of a story

se·quence \'sēkwəns\ *n* : continuous or connected series —**se·quen·tial** \si'kwenchəl\ *adj*

se·ques·ter \si'kwestər\ *vb* : segregate

se·quin \'sēkwən\ *n* : spangle

se·quoia \si'kwóiə\ *n* : huge California coniferous tree

sera *pl of* SERUM

ser·aph \'serəf\ *n, pl* **-a·phim** \-ə,fim\ *or* **-aphs** : angel —**se·raph·ic** \sə'rafik\ *adj*

sere \'siər\ *adj* : dried up or withered

ser·e·nade \\,serə'nād\ *n* : music sung esp. to a lady —**serenade** *vb*

ser·en·dip·i·ty \\,serən'dipətē\ *n* : good luck in finding things not sought for —**ser·en·dip·i·tous** \-əs\ *adj*

se·rene \sə'rēn\ *adj* : tranquil —**se·rene·ly** *adv* —**se·ren·i·ty** \sə'renətē\ *n*

serf \'sərf\ *n* : peasant obligated to work the land —**serf·dom** \-dəm\ *n*

serge \'sərj\ *n* : twilled woolen cloth

ser·geant \'särjənt\ *n* : noncommissioned officer (as in the army) ranking next below a staff sergeant

sergeant first class *n* : noncommissioned officer in the army ranking next below a master sergeant

ser·geant major n, pl **sergeants major** or **sergeant majors 1** : noncommissioned officer serving as chief administrative assistant in a headquarters **2** : noncommissioned officer in the marine corps ranking above a first sergeant

se·ri·al \'sirēəl\ adj **1** : story told a little bit at a time —**serial** adj —**se·ri·al·ly** adv

se·ries \'si(ə)rēz\ n, pl **series** : number of things in order

se·ri·ous \'sirēəs\ adj **1** : subdued in appearance or manner **2** : sincere **3** : of great importance —**se·ri·ous·ly** adv —**se·ri·ous·ness** n

ser·mon \'sərmən\ n : lecture on religion or behavior

ser·pent \'sərpənt\ n : snake —**ser·pen·tine** \-pən‚tēn, -‚tīn\ adj

ser·rated \'ser‚ātəd\ adj : saw-toothed

se·rum \'sirəm\ n, pl **-rums** or **-ra** \-ə\ : watery part of blood —**se·rous** \-əs\ adj

ser·vant \'sərvənt\ n : person employed for domestic work

serve \'sərv\ vb **served; serv·ing 1** : work through or perform a term of service **2** : be of use **3** : prove adequate **4** : hand out (food or drink) **5** : be of service to —**serv·er** n

ser·vice \'sərvəs\ n **1** : act or means of serving **2** : required duty **3** : meeting for worship **4** : branch of public employment or the persons in it **5** : set of dishes or silverware **6** : benefit ∼ vb -**viced; -vic·ing** : do repair work on —**ser·vice·able** adj —**ser·vice·man** \-‚man, -mən\ n

ser·vile \'sərvəl, -‚vīl\ adj : behaving like a slave —**ser·vil·i·ty** \sər'vilətē\ n

ser·vi·tude \'sərvə‚t(y)üd\ n : slavery

ses·a·me \'sesəmē\ n : East Indian annual herb or its seeds

ses·sion \'seshən\ n : meeting

set \'set\ vb **set; set·ting 1** : cause to sit **2** : place **3** : settle, arrange, or adjust **4** : cause to be or do **5** : become fixed or solid **6** : sit on eggs to hatch them **7** : sink below the horizon ∼ adj : settled ∼ n **1** : group classed together **2** : setting for the scene of a play or film **3** : electronic apparatus **4** : collection of mathematical elements —**set forth** : begin a trip —**set off** : set forth —**set out** : begin a trip or undertaking —**set up** vb **1** : assemble or erect **2** : cause

set·back n : reverse

set·tee \se'tē\ n : bench or sofa

set·ter \'setər\ n : large long-coated hunting dog

set·ting \'setiŋ\ n : background or surroundings

set·tle \'set³l\ vb -**tled; -tling 1** : come to rest **2** : sink gradually **3** : become established in a place or a home **4** : adjust or arrange **5** : calm **6** : dispose of (as by paying) **7** : decide or agree on —**set·tle·ment** \-mənt\ n —**set·tler** \'setlər, -³lər\ n

sev·en \'sevən\ n : one more than 6 —**seven** adj or pron —**sev·enth** \-ənth\ adj or adv or n

sev·en·teen \‚sevən'tēn\ n : one more than 16 —**seventeen** adj or pron —**sev·en·teenth** \-'tēnth\ adj or n

sev·en·ty \'sevəntē\ n, pl **-ties** : 7 times 10 —**sev·en·ti·eth** \-tēəth\ adj or n —**seventy** adj or pron

sev·er \'sevər\ vb -**ered; -er·ing** : cut off or apart —**sev·er·ance** \-(ə)rəns\ n

sev·er·al \'sev(ə)rəl\ adj **1** : distinct **2** : consisting of an indefinite but not large number —**sev·er·al·ly** \-ē\ adv

se·vere \sə'viər\ adj -**ver·er; -est 1** : allowing no evasion or compromise **2** : restrained or unadorned **3** : painful or distressing **4** : hard to endure —**se·vere·ly** adv —**se·ver·i·ty** \-'verətē\ n

sew \'sō\ vb **sewed; sewn** \'sōn\ or **sewed; sew·ing** : fasten by stitches made with thread and needle —**sew·ing** n

sew·age \'süij\ n : liquid household waste

[1]**sew·er** \'sō(ə)r\ n : one that sews

[2]**sew·er** \'süər\ n : pipe or channel to carry off waste matter

sex \'seks\ n **1** : either of 2 divisions of organisms distinguished respectively as male and female or the qualities which differentiate them **2** : copulation —**sexed** \'sekst\ adj —**sex·less** adj —**sex·u·al** \'seksh(əw)əl\ adj —**sex·u·al·i·ty** \‚seksha'walətē\ n —**sex·u·al·ly** adv —**sexy** adj

sex·ism \'sek‚sizəm\ n : discrimination based on sex and esp. against women —**sex·ist** \'seksəst\ adj or n

sex·tant \'sekstənt\ n : instrument for navigation

sex·tet \sek'stet\ n **1** : music for 6 performers **2** : group of 6

sex·ton \'sekstən\ n : church caretaker

shab·by \'shabē\ adj -**bi·er; -est 1** : worn and faded **2** : dressed in worn clothes **3** : not generous or fair —**shab·bi·ly** adv —**shab·bi·ness** n

shack \'shak\ n : hut

shack·le \'shakəl\ *n* : metal device to bind legs or arms ~ *vb* -**led**; -**ling** : fasten with shackles

shad \'shad\ *n* : Atlantic food fish

shade \'shād\ *n* **1** : space sheltered from the light esp. of the sun **2** : gradation of color **3** : small difference **4** : something that shades ~ *vb* **shad·ed**; **shad·ing** : shelter from light and heat —**shady** *adj*

shad·ow \'shadō\ *n* **1** : shade cast upon a surface by something blocking light **2** : trace **3** : gloomy influence ~ *vb* **1** : cast a shadow **2** : follow closely —**shad·owy** *adj*

shaft \'shaft\ *n* **1** : long slender cylindrical part **2** : deep vertical opening (as of a mine)

shag \'shag\ *n* : shaggy tangled mat

shag·gy \'shagē\ *adj* -**gi·er**; -**est** **1** : covered with long hair or wool **2** : not neat and combed

shah \'shä, 'shȯ\ *n* : monarch in Iran

shake \'shāk\ *vb* **shook** \'shu̇k\; **shak·en** \'shākən\; **shak·ing 1** : move or cause to move quickly back and forth **2** : distress **3** : clasp (hands) as friendly gesture —**shake** *n* —**shak·er** \-ər\ *n*

shake-up *n* : reorganization

shaky \'shākē\ *adj* **shak·i·er**; -**est** : not sound, stable, or reliable —**shak·i·ly** *adv* —**shak·i·ness** *n*

shale \'shāl\ *n* : stratified rock

shall \shəl, (ˌ)shal\ *vb, past* **should** \shəd, (ˌ)shu̇d\; *pres sing & pl* **shall** —used as an auxiliary to express a command, futurity, or determination

shal·low \'shalō\ *adj* **1** : not deep **2** : not intellectually profound

shal·lows \-ōz\ *n pl* : area of shallow water

sham \'sham\ *adj or n or vb* : fake

sham·ble \'shambəl\ *vb* -**bled**; -**bling** : shuffle along —**sham·ble** *n*

sham·bles \'shambəlz\ *n* : state of disorder

shame \'shām\ *n* **1** : distress over guilt or disgrace **2** : cause of shame or regret ~ *vb* **shamed**; **sham·ing 1** : make ashamed **2** : disgrace —**shame·ful** \-fəl\ *adj* —**shame·ful·ly** \-ē\ *adv* —**shame·less** *adj* —**shame·less·ly** *adv*

shame-faced \'shām'fāst\ *adj* : ashamed

sham·poo \sham'pü\ *vb* : wash one's hair ~ *n, pl* -**poos** : act of preparation used in shampooing

sham·rock \'sham,räk\ *n* : plant with 3-lobed leaves

shank \'shaŋk\ *n* : part of the leg between the knee and ankle

shan·ty \'shantē\ *n, pl* -**ties** : hut

shape \'shāp\ *vb* **shaped**; **shap·ing** : form esp. in a particular structure or appearance ~ *n* **1** : distinctive appearance or arrangement of parts **2** : condition —**shape·less** \-ləs\ *adj*

shard \'shärd\ *n* : broken piece

share \'sher\ *n* **1** : portion belonging to one **2** : interest in a company's stock ~ *vb* **shared**; **shar·ing** : divide or use with others —**share·hol·der** *n* —**shar·er** *n*

share·crop·per \-,kräpər\ *n* : farmer who works another's land in return for a share of the crop —**share·crop** *vb*

shark \'shärk\ *n* : voracious sea fish

sharp \'shärp\ *adj* **1** : having a good point or cutting edge **2** : alert, clever, or sarcastic **3** : vigorous or fierce **4** : having prominent angles or a sudden change in direction **5** : distinct **6** : higher than the true pitch ~ *adj* : exactly ~ *n* : sharp note —**sharp·ly** *adv* —**sharp·ness** *n*

sharp·en \'shärpən\ *vb* : make sharp —**sharp·en·er** \'shärp(ə)nər\ *n*

sharp·shoot·er *n* : expert marksman —**sharp·shoot·ing** *n*

shat·ter \'shat·ər\ *vb* : smash or burst into fragments

shave \'shāv\ *vb* **shaved** *or* **shav·en** \'shāvən\; **shav·ing 1** : cut off with a razor **2** : make bare by cutting the hair from **3** : slice very thin ~ *n* : act of instance of shaving —**shav·er** *n*

shawl \'shȯl\ *n* : loose covering for the head or shoulders

she \(ˈ)shē\ *pron* : that female one

sheaf \'shēf\ *n, pl* **sheaves** \'shēvz\ : bundle esp. of grain stalks

shear \'shir\ *vb* **sheared**; **sheared** *or* **shorn** \'shȯrn\; **shear·ing 1** : trim wool from **2** : cut off with scissorlike action

shears \'shirz\ *n pl* : cutting tool with 2 blades fastened so that the edges slide by each other

sheath \'shēth\ *n, pl* **sheaths** \'shēthz, 'shēths\ : covering (as for a blade)

sheathe \'shēth\ *vb* **sheathed**; **sheath·ing** : put into a sheath

shed \'shed\ *vb* **shed**; **shed·ding 1** : give off (as tears or hair) **2** : cause to flow or diffuse ~ *n* : small storage building

sheen \'shēn\ *n* : subdued luster

sheep \'shēp\ *n, pl* **sheep** : domesti-

cated mammal covered with wool
—**sheep-skin** *n*

sheep-ish \'shēpish\ *adj* : embarrassed by awareness of a fault

sheer \'shir\ *adj* 1 : pure 2 : very steep 3 : very thin or transparent —**sheer** *adv*

sheet \'shēt\ *n* : broad flat piece (as of cloth or paper)

sheikh, sheik \'shēk, 'shāk\ *n* : Arab chief —**sheikh-dom, sheik-dom** \-dəm\ *n*

shelf \'shelf\ *n, pl* **shelves** \'shelvz\ 1 : flat narrow structure used for storage or display 2 : sandbank or rock ledge

shell \'shel\ *n* 1 : hard or tough outer covering 2 : case holding explosive powder and projectile for a weapon 3 : light racing boat with oars ~ *vb* 1 : remove the shell of 2 : bombard —**shelled** \'sheld\ *adj* —**shell-er** *n*

shel-lac \shə'lak\ *n* : varnish ~ *vb* -**lacked; -lack-ing** 1 : coat with shellac 2 : defeat —**shel-lack-ing** *n*

shell-fish *n* : water animal with a shell

shel-ter \'sheltər\ *n* : something that gives protection ~ *vb* : give refuge to

shelve \'shelv\ *vb* **shelved; shelv-ing** 1 : place or store on shelves 2 : dismiss or put aside

she-nan-i-gans \shə'nanigənz\ *n pl* : mischievous or deceitful conduct

shep-herd \'shepərd\ *n* : one that tends sheep ~ *vb* : act as a shepherd or guardian —**shep-herd-ess** \-əs\ *n*

sher-bet \'shərbət\, **sher-bert** \-bərt\ *n* : fruit-flavored frozen dessert

sher-iff \'sherəf\ *n* : county law officer

sher-ry \'sherē\ *n, pl* -**ries** : type of wine

shield \'shēld\ *n* 1 : broad piece of armor carried on the arm 2 : something that protects —**shield** *vb*

shier *comparative of* SHY

shiest *superlative of* SHY

shift \'shift\ *vb* 1 : change place, position, or direction 2 : get by ~ *n* 1 : transfer 2 : scheduled work period 3 : loose-fitting dress

shift-less \'shif(t)ləs\ *adj* : lazy —**shift-less-ness** *n*

shifty \'shiftē\ *adj* **shift-i-er; -est** : tricky or untrustworthy

shil-le-lagh \shə'lālē\ *n* : club or stick

shil-ling \'shiliŋ\ *n* : former British coin

shil-ly-shally \'shilē,shalē\ *vb* -**shallied; -shally-ing** 1 : hesitate 2 : dawdle

shim-mer \'shimər\ *vb or n* : glimmer

shin \'shin\ *n* : front part of the leg

below the knee ~ *vb* -**nn-** : climb by sliding the body close along

shine \'shīn\ *vb* **shone** \-shōn\ *or* **shined; shin-ing** 1 : give off or cause to give off light 2 : be outstanding 3 : polish ~ *n* : brilliance

shin-gle \'shiŋgəl\ *n* 1 : small thin piece used in covering roofs or exterior walls ~ *vb* -**gled; -gling** : cover with shingles

shin-gles \'shiŋgəlz\ *n pl* : acute inflammation of spinal nerves

shin-ny \'shinē\ *vb* -**nied; -ny-ing** : shin

shiny \'shīnē\ *adj* **shin-i-er; -est** : bright or polished

ship \'ship\ *n* 1 : large craft for navigation 2 : aircraft or spacecraft ~ *vb* -**pp-** 1 : put on a ship 2 : transport by carrier —**ship-board** *n* —**ship-build-er** *n* —**ship-per** *n* —**ship-yard** *n*

-**ship** \,ship\ *n suffix* 1 : state, condition, or quality 2 : rank or profession 3 : skill 4 : something showing a state or quality

ship-ment \-mənt\ *n* : goods shipped

ship-ping \'shipiŋ\ *n* 1 : ships 2 : transportation of goods

ship-shape *adj* : tidy

ship-wreck *n* : destruction or loss of a ship —**shipwreck** *vb*

shire \'shī(ə)r, in place-name compounds ,shiər, shər\ *n* : British county

shirk \'shərk\ *vb* : evade —**shirk-er** *n*

shirr \'shər\ *vb* 1 : gather (cloth) by drawing up parallel lines of stitches 2 : bake (eggs) in a dish

shirt \'shərt\ *n* : garment for covering the torso —**shirt-less** *adj*

shiv-er \'shivər\ *vb* : tremble —**shiver** *n*

shoal \'shōl\ *n* : shallow place (as in a river)

¹**shock** \'shäk\ *n* : pile of sheaves set up in the field

²**shock** *n* 1 : forceful impact 2 : violent mental or emotional disturbance 3 : effect of a charge of electricity 4 : depression of the vital bodily processes ~ *vb* 1 : strike with surprise, horror, or disgust 2 : subject to an electrical shock —**shock-proof** *adj*

³**shock** *n* : bushy mass (as of hair)

shod-dy \'shädē\ *adj* -**di-er; -est** : cheaply or poorly made or done —**shod-di-ly** \'shäd²lē\ *adv* —**shod-di-ness** *n*

shoe \'shü\ *n* 1 : covering for the human foot 2 : horseshoe ~ *vb* **shod** \'shäd\; **shoe-ing** : put horseshoes on —**shoe-lace** *n* —**shoe-mak-er** *n*

shone *past of* SHINE

shook *past of* SHAKE

shoot \shüt\ *vb* **shot** \shät\; **shoot·ing** **1** : propel (as an arrow or bullet) **2** : wound or kill with a missile **3** : discharge (a weapon) **4** : drive (as a ball) at a goal **5** : photograph ~ *n* : new plant growth —**shoot·er** *n*

shop \shäp\ *n* : place where things are made or sold ~ *vb* -**pp**- : visit stores —**shop·keep·er** *n* —**shop·per** *n*

shop·lift *vb* : steal goods from a store —**shop·lift·er** \-,liftər\ *n*

1shore \shōr\ *n* : land along the edge of water —**shore·less** *adj*

2shore *vb* **shored; shor·ing** : prop up ~ *n* : something that props

shore·bird *n* : bird of the seashore

shorn *past part of* SHEAR

short \shȯrt\ *adj* **1** : not long or tall or extending far **2** : brief in time **3** : curt **4** : not having or being enough ~ *adv* : curtly ~ *n* **1** *pl* : short drawers or trousers **2** : short circuit —**short·en** \-ᵊn\ *vb* —**short·ly** *adv* —**short·ness** *n*

short·age \shȯrtij\ *n* : deficiency

short·cake *n* : dessert of biscuit with sweetened fruit

short·change *vb* : cheat esp. by giving too little change

short circuit *n* : abnormal electric connection —**short-circuit** *vb*

short·com·ing *n* : failing

short·cut \-,kət\ *n* **1** : more direct route than that usu. taken **2** : quicker way of doing something

short·hand *n* : method of speed writing

short-lived \shȯrt'līvd, -,līvd\ *adj* : of short life or duration

short·sight·ed *adj* : lacking foresight

shot \shät\ *n* **1** : act of shooting **2** : attempt (as at making a goal) **3** : small pellets forming a charge **4** : range or reach **5** : photograph **6** : injection of medicine **7** : portion (as of liquor) taken at one time —**shot·gun** *n*

should \shəd, (')shud\ *past of* SHALL —used as an auxiliary to express condition, obligation, or probability

shoul·der \shōldər\ *n* **1** : part of the body where the arm joins the trunk **2** : part that projects or lies to the side ~ *vb* : push with or take upon the shoulder

shoulder blade *n* : the flat triangular bone at the back of the shoulder

shout \shaut\ *vb* : give voice loudly —**shout** *n*

shove \shəv\ *vb* **shoved; shov·ing** : push along, aside, or away —**shove** *n*

shov·el \shəvəl\ *n* : broad tool for digging or lifting ~ *vb* -**eled** *or* -**elled; -el·ing** *or* -**el·ling** : take up or dig with a shovel

show \shō\ *vb* **showed** \shōd\; **shown** \shōn\ *or* **showed; show·ing** **1** : present to view **2** : reveal or demonstrate **3** : indicate **4** : conduct or escort **5** : act in (a specified manner) **6** : appear or be noticeable ~ *n* **1** : demonstrative display **2** : spectacle **3** : theatrical, radio, or television program —**show·case** *n* —**show off** *vb* **1** : display proudly **2** : act so as to attract attention —**show up** *vb* : arrive

show·down *n* : final settlement of a contested issue

show·er \shau(ə)r\ *n* **1** : brief fall of rain **2** : bath in which water sprinkles down on the person **3** : party at which someone gets gifts ~ *vb* **1** : fall in a shower **2** : bathe in a shower —**show·ery** *adj*

showy \shōē\ *adj* **show·i·er; -est** : very noticeable or overly elaborate —**show·i·ly** *adv* —**show·i·ness** *n*

shrap·nel \shrapnᵊl\ *n, pl* **shrapnel** : metal fragments of a bomb

shred \shred\ *n* : narrow strip cut or torn off ~ *vb* -**dd**- : cut or tear into shreds

shrew \shrü\ *n* **1** : scolding woman **2** : mouselike mammal —**shrew·ish** \-ish\ *adj*

shrewd \shrüd\ *adj* : showing cleverness or good judgment —**shrewd·ly** *adv* —**shrewd·ness** *n*

shriek \shrēk\ *n* : shrill cry —**shriek** *vb*

shrill \shril\ *adj* : piercing and high-pitched —**shril·ly** *adv*

shrimp \shrimp\ *n* : small sea crustacean

shrine \shrīn\ *n* **1** : tomb of a saint **2** : hallowed place

shrink \shriŋk\ *vb* **shrank** \shraŋk\; **shrunk** *or* **shrunk·en** \shrəŋkən\ **1** : draw back or away **2** : become smaller —**shrink·able** *adj*

shrink·age \shriŋkij\ *n* : amount something shrinks

shriv·el \shrivᵊl\ *vb* -**eled** *or* -**elled; -el·ing** *or* -**el·ling** : shrink or wither into wrinkles

shroud \shraud\ *n* **1** : cloth put over a corpse **2** : cover or screen ~ *vb* : veil or screen from view

shrub \shrəb\ *n* : low woody plant —**shrub·by** *adj*

shrub·bery \shrəb(ə)rē\ *n, pl* -**ber·ies** : growth of shrubs

shrug \shrəg\ *vb* -**gg**- : hunch the shoulders up in doubt, indifference, or dislike —**shrug** *n*

shuck \'shək\ *n* : strip of a shell or husk —**shuck** *vb*

shud·der \'shədər\ *vb* : tremble —**shudder** *n*

shuf·fle \'shəfəl\ *vb* -**fled; -fling 1** : mix together **2** : walk with a sliding movement —**shuffle** *n*

shuf·fle·board \'shəfəl,bōrd\ *n* : game of sliding disks into a scoring area

shun \'shən\ *vb* -**nn-** : keep away from

shunt \'shənt\ *vb* : turn off to one side

shut \'shət\ *vb* **shut; shut·ting 1** : bar passage into or through (as by moving a lid or door) **2** : suspend activity —**shut out** : exclude —**shut up** : stop or cause to stop talking

shut-in *n* : invalid

shut·ter \'shətər\ *n* **1** : movable cover for a window **2** : camera part that exposes film

shut·tle \'shət°l\ *n* **1** : part of a weaving machine that carries thread back and forth **2** : vehicle traveling back and forth over a short route ~ *vb* -**tled; -tling** : move back and forth frequently

shut·tle·cock \'shət°l,käk\ *n* : feathered object in badminton

shy \'shī\ *adj* **shi·er** *or* **shy·er** \'shī(ə)r\; **shi·est** *or* **shy·est** \'shīəst\ **1** : sensitive and hesitant in dealing with others **2** : wary **3** : lacking ~ *vb* **shied; shy·ing** : move back from fright —**shy·ly** *adv* —**shy·ness** *n*

sib·i·lant \'sibələnt\ *adj* : having the sound of the *s* or the *sh* in *sash* —**sibilant** *n*

sib·ling \'sibliŋ\ *n* : brother or sister

sick \'sik\ *adj* **1** : not in good health **2** : nauseated **3** : relating to or meant for the sick —**sick·bed** *n* —**sick·en** \-ən\ *vb* —**sick·ly** *adv* —**sick·ness** *n*

sick·le \'sikəl\ *n* : curved short-handled blade

side \'sīd\ *n* **1** : part to left or right of an object or the torso **2** : edge or surface away from the center or at an angle to top and bottom or ends **3** : contrasting or opposing position or group —**sid·ed** *adj*

side·board *n* : piece of dining-room furniture for table service

side·burns \-,bərnz\ *n pl* : whiskers in front of the ears

side·long \'sīd,lȯŋ\ *adv or adj* : to or along the side

si·de·re·al \sī'direəl, sə-\ *adj* : measured by the apparent motion of fixed stars

side·show *n* : minor show at a circus

side·step *vb* **1** : step aside **2** : avoid

side·swipe \-,swīp\ *vb* : strike with a glancing blow —**sideswipe** *n*

side·track *vb* : lead aside or astray

side·walk *n* : paved walk at the side of a road

side·ways \-,wāz\ *adv or adj* **1** : to or from the side **2** : with one side to the front

sid·ing \'sīdiŋ\ *n* **1** : short railroad track **2** : material for covering the outside of a building

si·dle \'sīd°l\ *vb* -**dled; -dling** : move sideways or unobtrusively

siege \'sēj\ *n* : persistent attack (as on a fortified place)

si·es·ta \sē'estə\ *n* : midday nap

sieve \'siv\ *n* : utensil with holes to separate particles

sift \'sift\ *vb* **1** : pass through a sieve **2** : examine carefully —**sift·er** *n*

sigh \'sī\ *n* : audible release of the breath (as to express weariness) —**sigh** *vb*

sight \'sīt\ *n* **1** : something seen or worth seeing **2** : process, power, or range of seeing **3** : device used in aiming **4** : view or glimpse ~ *vb* : get sight of —**sight·ed** *adj* —**sight·less** *adj* —**sight-see·ing** *adj* —**sight-seer** \-,sēər\ *n*

sign \'sīn\ *n* **1** : symbol **2** : gesture expressing a command or thought **3** : public notice to advertise or warn **4** : trace ~ *vb* **1** : mark with or make a sign **2** : write one's name on —**sign·er** *n*

sig·nal \'sign°l\ *n* **1** : sign of command or warning **2** : electronic transmission ~ *vb* -**naled** *or* -**nalled; -nal·ing** *or* -**nal·ling** : communicate or notify by signals

sig·na·to·ry \'signə,tōrē\ *n, pl* -**ries** : person or government that signs jointly with others

sig·na·ture \'signə,chùr\ *n* : one's name written by oneself

sig·net \'signət\ *n* : small seal

sig·nif·i·cance \sig'nifikəns\ *n* **1** : meaning **2** : importance —**sig·nif·i·cant** \-kənt\ *adj* —**sig·nif·i·cant·ly** *adv*

sig·ni·fy \'signə,fī\ *vb* -**fied; -fy·ing 1** : show by a sign **2** : mean —**sig·ni·fi·ca·tion** \,signəfə'kāshən\ *n*

si·lence \'sīləns\ *n* : state of being without sound ~ *vb* -**lenced; -lenc·ing** : keep from making noise or sound —**si·lenc·er** *n*

si·lent \'sīlənt\ *adj* : having or producing no sound —**si·lent·ly** *adv*

sil·hou·ette \,silə'wet\ *n* : outline filled

in usu. with black ~ **-ett·ed; -ett·ing** : represent by a silhouette

sil·i·ca \'silikə\ n : mineral found as quartz and opal

sil·i·con \'silikən, 'silə,kän\ n : nonmetallic chemical element

silk \'silk\ n 1 : fine strong lustrous protein fiber from moth larvae (**silkworms** \-,wərmz\) 2 : thread or cloth made from silk —**silk·en** \'silkən\ adj —**silky** adj

sill \'sil\ n : bottom part of a window frame or a doorway

sil·ly \'silē\ adj **sil·li·er; -est** : foolish or stupid —**sil·li·ness** n

si·lo \'sīlō\ n, pl **-los** : building for storing animal feed

silt \'silt\ n : fine earth carried by rivers ~ vb : obstruct or cover with silt

sil·ver \'silvər\ n 1 : white ductile metallic chemical element 2 : silverware ~ adj : having the color of silver —**sil·very** adj

sil·ver·ware \-,waər\ n : utensils of silver, silver-plated metal, or stainless steel

sim·i·lar \'simələr\ adj : resembling each other in some ways —**sim·i·lar·i·ty** \,simə'larətē\ n —**sim·i·lar·ly** \'simələrlē\ adv

sim·i·le \'simə(,)lē\ n : comparison of unlike things using like or as

si·mil·i·tude \sə'milə,t(y)üd\ n : likeness

sim·mer \'simər\ vb : stew gently

sim·per \'simpər\ vb : give a silly smile —**simper** n

sim·ple \'simpəl\ adj **-pler; -plest** 1 : not combined 2 : not other than 3 : not complex or fancy 4 : naive —**sim·ple·ness** n —**sim·ply** \-plē\ adv

sim·ple·ton \'simpəltən\ n : fool

sim·plic·i·ty \sim'plisətē\ n : state or fact of being simple

sim·pli·fy \'simplə,fī\ vb **-fied; -fy·ing** : make easier —**sim·pli·fi·ca·tion** \,simpləfə'kāshən\ n

sim·u·late \'simyə,lāt\ vb **-lat·ed; -lat·ing** : create the effect or appearance of —**sim·u·la·tion** \,simyə'lāshən\ n

si·mul·ta·ne·ous \,sīməl'tānēəs, ,siməl-\ adj : occurring or operating at the same time —**si·mul·ta·ne·ous·ly** adv —**si·mul·ta·ne·ous·ness** n

sin \'sin\ n : offense against God ~ vb **-nn-** : commit a sin —**sin·ful** \-fəl\ adj —**sin·less** adj —**sin·ner** n

since \'sins\ adv 1 : from a past time until now 2 : backward in time ~ prep 1 : in the period after 2 : continuously from ~ conj 1 : from the time when 2 : because

sin·cere \sin'siər\ adj : genuine or honest —**sin·cere·ly** adv —**sin·cer·i·ty** \-'serətē\ n

si·ne·cure \'sīni,kyůər, 'sini-\ n : well-paid job that requires little work

sin·ew \'sinyü\ n 1 : tendon 2 : physical strength —**sin·ewy** adj

sing \'sin\ vb **sang** \'san\ or **sung** \'sən\; **sung; sing·ing** : produce musical tones with the voice —**sing·er** n

singe \'sinj\ vb **singed; singe·ing** : scorch lightly

sin·gle \'singəl\ adj 1 : one only 2 : unmarried ~ n : separate one —**sin·gle·ness** n —**sin·gly** \-glē\ adv —**single out** vb : select or set aside

sin·gu·lar \'singyələr\ adj 1 : relating to a word form denoting one 2 : outstanding or superior 3 : queer —**singular** n —**sin·gu·lar·i·ty** \,singyə'larətē\ n —**sin·gu·lar·ly** \'singyələrlē\ adv

sin·is·ter \'sinəstər\ adj : threatening evil

sink \'sink\ vb **sank** \'sank\ or **sunk** \'sənk\; **sunk; sink·ing** 1 : submerge or descend 2 : grow worse 3 : make by digging or boring 4 : invest ~ n : basin with a drain

sink·er \'sinkər\ n : weight to sink a fishing line

sin·u·ous \'sinyəwəs\ adj : winding in and out —**sin·u·os·i·ty** \,sinyə'wäsətē\ n —**sin·u·ous·ly** adv

si·nus \'sīnəs\ n : skull cavity connecting with the nostrils

sip \'sip\ vb **-pp-** : drink in small quantities —**sip** n

si·phon \'sīfən\ n : bent tube through which a liquid is drawn by suction —**siphon** vb

sir \(')sər\ n 1 —used before the first name of a knight or baronet 2 —used in addressing a man without using his name

sire \'sīr\ n : father ~ vb **sired; sir·ing** : beget

si·ren \'sīrən\ n 1 : seductive woman 2 : wailing warning whistle —**siren** adj

sir·loin \'sər,lóin\ n : cut of beef

sirup var of SYRUP

si·sal \'sīsəl, -zəl\ n : strong rope fiber

sis·sy \'sisē\ n, pl **-sies** : timid or effeminate boy

sis·ter \'sistər\ n : female sharing one or both parents with another person —**sis·ter·hood** \-,hůd\ n —**sis·ter·ly** adj

sis·ter-in-law \'sist(ə)rən,lò\ n, pl **sis·ters-in-law** \-tərzən-\ : sister of one's husband or wife or wife of one's brother

sit \'sit\ *vb* **sat** \'sat\; **sit·ting 1** : rest on the buttocks or haunches **2** : roost **3** : hold a session **4** : pose for a portrait **5** : have a location **6** : rest or fix in place —**sit·ter** *n*

site \'sīt\ *n* : place

sit·u·at·ed \'sicha,wātəd\ *adj* : located

sit·u·a·tion \,sicha'wāshən\ *n* **1** : location **2** : condition **3** : job

six \'siks\ *n* : one more than 5 —**six** *adj or pron* —**sixth** \'siksth\ *adj or adv or n*

six·teen \siks'tēn\ *n* : one more than 15 —**sixteen** *adj or pron* —**six·teenth** \-'tēnth\ *adj or n*

six·ty \'sikstē\ *n, pl* **sixties** : 6 times 10 —**six·ti·eth** \-əth\ *adj or n* —**sixty** *adj or pron*

siz·able, size·able \'sīzabəl\ *adj* : quite large —**siz·ably** \-blē\ *adv*

size \'sīz\ *n* : measurement of the amount of space something takes up ∼ *vb* : grade according to size

siz·zle \'sizəl\ *vb* **-zled; -zling** : fry with a hissing sound —**sizzle** *n*

skate \'skāt\ *n* **1** : metal runner on a shoe for gliding over ice **2** : roller skate —**skate** *vb* —**skat·er** *n*

skein \'skān\ *n* : loosely twisted quantity (as of yarn)

skel·e·ton \'skelət³n\ *n* : bony framework —**skel·e·tal** \-ət³l\ *adj*

skep·tic \'skeptik\ *n* : one who is critical or doubting —**skep·ti·cal** \-tikəl\ *adj* —**skep·ti·cism** \-tə,sizəm\ *n*

sketch \'skech\ *n* **1** : rough drawing **2** : small story or essay —**sketch** *vb* —**sketchy** *adj*

skew·er \'skyūər\ *n* : pin for holding roasting meat —**skewer** *vb*

ski \'skē\ *n, pl* **skis** : long strip bound to the shoe for gliding over snow or water —**ski** *vb* —**ski·er** *n*

skid \'skid\ *n* **1** : plank for supporting something or on which it slides **2** : act of skidding ∼ *vb* **-dd-** : slide sideways

skiff \'skif\ *n* : small open boat

skill \'skil\ *n* : developed or learned ability —**skilled** \'skild\ *adj* —**skill·ful** \-fəl\ *adj* —**skill·ful·ly** *adv* —**skill·ful·ness** *n*

skil·let \'skilət\ *n* : pan for frying

skim \'skim\ *vb* **-mm- 1** : take off from the top of a liquid **2** : read or move over swiftly **3** : having the cream removed —**skim·mer** *n*

skimp \'skimp\ *vb* : give too little of something —**skimpy** *adj*

skin \'skin\ *n* **1** : outer layer of an animal body **2** : rind ∼ *vb* **-nn-** : take the skin from —**skin·less** *adj* —**skinned** *adj* —**skin-tight** *adj*

skin-flint \'skin,flint\ *n* : stingy person

skin-ny \'skinē\ *adj* **-ni·er; -est** : very thin

skip \'skip\ *vb* **-pp- 1** : move with leaps **2** : read past or ignore —**skip** *n*

skip·per \'skipər\ *n* : ship's master —**skipper** *vb*

skir·mish \'skərmish\ *n* : minor combat —**skirmish** *vb*

skirt \'skərt\ *n* : garment or part of a garment that hangs below the waist ∼ *vb* : pass around the edge of

skit \'skit\ *n* : brief usu. humorous play

skit·tish \'skitish\ *adj* : easily frightened

skulk \'skəlk\ *vb* : move furtively

skull \'skəl\ *n* : bony case that protects the brain

skunk \'skəŋk\ *n* : mammal that can forcibly eject an ill-smelling fluid

sky \'skī\ *n, pl* **skies 1** : upper air **2** : heaven —**sky·ey** \'skīē\ *adj* —**sky·line** *n* —**sky·ward** \-wərd\ *adv or adj*

sky·lark \'skī,lärk\ *n* : European lark noted for its song

sky·light *n* : window in a roof or ceiling

sky·rock·et *n* : shooting firework ∼ *vb* : rise suddenly

sky·scrap·er \-,skrāpər\ *n* : very tall building

slab \'slab\ *n* : thick slice

slack \'slak\ *adj* **1** : careless **2** : not taut **3** : not busy ∼ *n* **1** : part hanging loose **2** *pl* : casual trousers —**slack·ly** *adv* —**slack·ness** *n*

slag \'slag\ *n* : waste from melting of ores

slain *past part of* SLAY

slake \'slāk\ *vb* **slaked; slak·ing** : quench

slam \'slam\ *n* : heavy jarring impact ∼ *vb* **-mm-** : shut, strike, or throw violently and loudly

slan·der \'slandər\ *n* : malicious gossip ∼ *vb* : hurt (someone) with slander —**slan·der·er** *n* —**slan·der·ous** *adj*

slang \'slaŋ\ *n* : informal nonstandard vocabulary —**slangy** *adj*

slant \'slant\ *vb* **1** : slope **2** : present with a special viewpoint ∼ *n* : sloping direction, line, or plane

slap \'slap\ *vb* **-pp-** : strike sharply with the open hand —**slap** *n*

slash \'slash\ *vb* **1** : cut with sweeping strokes **2** : reduce sharply ∼ *n* : gash

slat \'slat\ *n* : thin narrow flat strip

slate \'slāt\ *n* **1** : dense fine-grained

297 slated · sloths

layered rock 2 : roofing tile or writing tablet of slate 3 : list of candidates ~ vb **slat·ed; slat·ing** : designate

slat·tern \'slatərn\ n : untidy woman —**slat·tern·ly** adv or adj

slaugh·ter \'slȯtər\ n 1 : butchering of livestock for market 2 : great and cruel destruction of lives ~ vb : commit slaughter upon —**slaugh·ter·house** n

slave \'slāv\ n : one owned and forced into service by another ~ vb **slaved; slav·ing** : work as or like a slave —**slave** adj —**slav·ery** \'slāv(ə)rē\ n

sla·ver \'slavər, 'slāv-\ vb or n : slobber

slav·ish \'slāvish\ adj : of or like a slave —**slav·ish·ly** adv

slay \'slā\ vb **slew** \'slü\; **slain** \'slān\; **slay·ing** : kill —**slay·er** n

slea·zy \'slēzē, 'slā-\ adj **-zi·er; -est** : shabby or shoddy

sled \'sled\ n : vehicle on runners —**sled** vb

¹sledge \'slej\ n : sledgehammer

²sledge n : heavy sled

sledge·ham·mer n : heavy long-handled hammer —**sledgehammer** adj or vb

sleek \'slēk\ adj : smooth or glossy —**sleek** vb

sleep \'slēp\ n : natural suspension of consciousness ~ vb **slept** \'slept\; **sleep·ing** : rest in a state of sleep —**sleep·er** n —**sleep·less** adj

sleep·walk·er n : one who walks during sleep

sleepy \'slēpē\ adj **sleep·i·er; -est** 1 : ready for sleep 2 : quietly inactive —**sleep·i·ly** \'slēpəlē\ adv —**sleep·i·ness** \-pēnəs\ n

sleet \'slēt\ n : partly frozen rain —**sleet** vb —**sleety** adj

sleeve \'slēv\ n : part of a garment for the arm —**sleeve·less** adj

sleigh \'slā\ n : horse-drawn sled with seats ~ vb : drive or ride in a sleigh

sleight of hand \'slīt-\ : skillful manual manipulation or a trick requiring it

slen·der \'slendər\ adj 1 : thin esp. in physique 2 : scanty

sleuth \'slüth\ n : detective

slew \'slü\ past of SLAY

slice \'slīs\ n : thin flat piece ~ vb **sliced; slic·ing** : cut a slice from

slick \'slik\ adj 1 : very smooth 2 : clever —**slick** vb

slick·er \'slikər\ n : waterproof raincoat

slide \'slīd\ vb **slid** \'slid\; **slid·ing** \'slīdiŋ\ : move smoothly along or down a surface ~ n 1 : act of sliding

2 : surface on which something slides 3 : transparent picture for projection

slier comparative of SLY

sliest superlative of SLY

slight \'slīt\ adj 1 : slender 2 : frail 3 : small in degree ~ vb 1 : ignore or treat as unimportant —**slight** n —**slight·ly** adv

slim \'slim\ adj **-mm-** 1 : slender 2 : scanty ~ vb **-mm-** : make or become slender

slime \'slīm\ n : dirty slippery film (as on water) —**slimy** adj

sling \'sliŋ\ vb **slung** \'sləŋ\; **sling·ing** : hurl with or as if with a sling ~ n 1 : strap for swinging and hurling stones 2 : looped strap or bandage to lift or support

sling·shot n : forked stick with elastic bands for shooting small stones or shot

slink \'sliŋk\ vb **slunk** \'sləŋk\; **slink·ing** : move stealthily or sinuously —**slinky** adj

¹slip \'slip\ vb **-pp-** 1 : escape quietly or secretly 2 : slide along smoothly 3 : make a mistake 4 : to pass without being noticed or done 5 : fall off from a standard ~ n 1 : ship's berth 2 : sudden mishap 3 : mistake 4 : woman's undergarment

²slip n : plant shoot 2 : small strip (as of paper)

slip·per \'slipər\ n : shoe that slips on easily

slip·pery \'slip(ə)rē\ adj **-peri·er; -est** 1 : slick enough to slide on 2 : tricky —**slip·peri·ness** n

slip·shod \'slip'shäd\ adj : careless

slit \'slit\ vb **slit; slit·ting** : make a slit in ~ n : long narrow cut

slith·er \'slithər\ vb : glide along like a snake —**slith·ery** adj

sliv·er \'slivər\ n : splinter

slob \'släb\ n : untidy person

slob·ber \'släbər\ vb : dribble saliva —**slobber** n

slo·gan \'slōgən\ n : word or phrase expressing the aim of a cause

sloop \'slüp\ n : sailing boat with one mast

slop \'släp\ n : food waste for animal feed ~ vb **-pp-** : spill

slope \'slōp\ vb **sloped; slop·ing** : deviate from the vertical or horizontal ~ n : upward or downward slant

slop·py \'släpē\ adj **-pi·er; -est** 1 : muddy 2 : untidy

slot \'slät\ n : narrow opening

sloth \'slȯth, 'slōth\ n, pl **sloths** \with ths or thz\ 1 : laziness 2 : slow-moving mammal —**sloth·ful** adj

slouch \'slaůch\ *n* **1** : drooping posture **2** : lazy or incompetent person ~ *vb* : walk or stand with a slouch

¹slough \'slü\ *n* : swamp or muddy place

²slough \'sləf\, **sluff** *vb* : cast off (a skin)

slov·en·ly \'sləvənlē\ *adj* : untidy

slow \'slō\ *adj* **1** : sluggish or stupid **2** : moving, working, or happening at less than the usual speed ~ *vb* **1** : make slow **2** : go slower —**slow** *adv* —**slow·ly** *adv* —**slow·ness** *n*

sludge \'sləj\ *n* : slushy mass (as of treated sewage)

slug \'sləg\ *n* **1** : mollusk related to the snails **2** : bullet **3** : metal disk ~ *vb* **-gg-** : strike forcibly —**slug·ger** *n*

slug·gish \'sləgish\ *adj* : slow in movement or flow —**slug·gish·ly** *adv* —**slug·gish·ness** *n*

sluice \'slüs\ *n* : channel for water ~ *vb* **sluiced; sluic·ing** : wash in running water

slum \'sləm\ *n* : thickly populated area marked by poverty

slum·ber \'sləmbər\ *vb or n* : sleep

slump \'sləmp\ *vb* **1** : sink suddenly **2** : slouch —**slump** *n*

slung *past of* SLING

slunk *past of* SLINK

¹slur \'slər\ *vb* **-rr-** : run (words or notes) together —**slur** *n*

²slur *n* : malicious or insulting remark —**slur** *vb*

slurp \'slərp\ *vb* : eat or drink noisily —**slurp** *n*

slush \'sləsh\ *n* : partly melted snow —**slushy** *adj*

slut \'slət\ *n* **1** : untidy woman **2** : prostitute —**slut·tish** \'slətish\ *adj*

sly \'slī\ *adj* **sli·er** \'slī(ə)r\; **sli·est** \'slīəst\ : given to or showing secrecy and deception —**sly·ly** *adv* —**sly·ness** *n*

¹smack \'smak\ *n* : characteristic flavor ~ *vb* : have a taste or hint

²smack *vb* **1** : move (the lips) so as to make a sharp noise **2** : kiss or slap with a loud noise ~ *n* **1** : sharp noise made by the lips **2** : noisy slap

³smack *adv* : squarely and sharply

⁴smack *n* : fishing ship

small \'smȯl\ *adj* **1** : little in size or amount **2** : few in number **3** : trivial —**small·ish** *adj* —**small·ness** *n*

small·pox \'smȯl.päks\ *n* : contagious virus disease marked by fever and eruption

smart \'smärt\ *vb* **1** : cause or feel stinging pain **2** : endure distress ~ *adj* **1** : intelligent or resourceful **2**

: stylish —**smart** *n* —**smart·ly** *adv* —**smart·ness** *n*

smash \'smash\ *vb* : break or be broken into pieces ~ *n* **1** : smashing blow **2** : act or sound of smashing

smat·ter·ing \'smatəriŋ\ *n* **1** : superficial knowledge **2** : small scattered number or amount

smear \'smir\ *n* : greasy stain ~ *vb* **1** : spread (something sticky) **2** : smudge **3** : slander

smell \'smel\ *vb* **smelled** \'smeld\ *or* **smelt** \'smelt\; **smell·ing** **1** : perceive the odor of **2** : have or give off an odor ~ *n* **1** : special sense by which one perceives odor **2** : odor —**smelly** *adj*

¹smelt \'smelt\ *n, pl* **smelts** *or* **smelt** : small food fish

²smelt *vb* : melt or fuse (ore) in order to separate the metal —**smelt·er** *n*

smile \'smīl\ *n* : facial expression with the mouth turned up usu. to show pleasure —**smile** *vb*

smirk \'smərk\ *vb* : wear a conceited smile —**smirk** *n*

smite \'smīt\ *vb* **smote** \'smōt\; **smit·ten** \'smit²n\ *or* **smote**; **smit·ing** \'smītiŋ\ **1** : strike heavily or kill **2** : affect strongly

smith \'smith\ *n* : worker in metals and esp. a blacksmith

smithy \'smithē\ *n, pl* **smith·ies** : a smith's workshop

smock \'smäk\ *n* : loose dress or protective coat

smog \'smäg, 'smȯg\ *n* : fog and smoke —**smog·gy** *adj*

smoke \'smōk\ *n* : sooty gas from burning ~ *vb* **smoked; smok·ing** **1** : give off smoke **2** : inhale and exhale the fumes of burning tobacco **3** : cure (as meat) with smoke —**smoke·less** *adj* —**smok·er** *n* —**smoky** *adj*

smoke·stack *n* : chimney through which smoke is discharged

smol·der, smoul·der \'smōldər\ *vb* **1** : burn and smoke without flame **2** : be suppressed but active —**smolder** *n*

smooth \'smüth\ *adj* **1** : having a surface without bends, curves, or irregularities **2** : not jarring or jolting ~ *vb* : make smooth —**smooth·ly** *adv* —**smooth·ness** *n*

smor·gas·bord \'smȯrgəs.bȯrd\ *n* : buffet consisting of many foods

smoth·er \'sməthər\ *vb* **1** : kill by depriving of air **2** : cover thickly

smudge \'sməj\ *vb* **smudged; smudg·ing** : soil or blur by rubbing ~ *n* **1** : thick smoke **2** : dirty spot

smug \'sməg\ *adj* **-gg-** : content in one's own virtue or accomplishment —**smug·ly** *adv* —**smug·ness** *n*

smug·gle \'sməgəl\ *vb* **-gled; -gling** : import or export secretly or illegally —**smug·gler** \'sməglər\ *n*

smut \'smət\ *n* **1** : something that smudges **2** : indecent language or matter **3** : fungous disease of plants —**smut·ty** *adj*

snack \'snak\ *n* : light meal

snag \'snag\ *n* : unexpected difficulty ~ *vb* **-gg-** : become caught on something that sticks out

snail \'snāl\ *n* : small mollusk with a spiral shell

snake \'snāk\ *n* : long-bodied limbless crawling reptile —**snake·bite** *n*

snap \'snap\ *vb* **-pp-** **1** : bite at something **2** : utter angry words **3** : break suddenly with a sharp sound ~ *n* **1** : act or sound of snapping **2** : fastening that closes with a click **3** : something easy to do —**snap·per** *n* —**snap·pish** *adj* —**snap·py** *adj*

snap·drag·on *n* : garden plant with spikes of showy flowers

snap·shot \'snap,shät\ *n* : casual photograph

snare \'snaər\ *n* : trap for catching game ~ *vb* : capture or hold with or as if with a snare

¹snarl \'snärl\ *n* : tangle ~ *vb* : cause to become knotted

²snarl *vb or n* : growl

snatch \'snach\ *vb* **1** : try to grab something suddenly **2** : seize and take away suddenly ~ *n* **1** : act of snatching **2** : something brief or fragmentary

sneak \'snēk\ *vb* : move or take in a furtive manner ~ *n* : one who acts in a furtive manner —**sneak·ing·ly** *adv* —**sneaky** *adj*

sneak·er \'snēkər\ *n* : sports shoe

sneer \'sniər\ *vb* : smile scornfully —**sneer** *n*

sneeze \'snēz\ *vb* **sneezed; sneez·ing** : force the breath out with sudden and involuntary violence —**sneeze** *n*

snick·er \'snikər\ *n* : partly suppressed laugh —**snicker** *vb*

snide \'snīd\ *adj* : subtly ridiculing

sniff \'snif\ *vb* **1** : draw air audibly up the nose **2** : detect by smelling —**sniff** *n*

snip \'snip\ *n* : fragment snipped off ~ *vb* **-pp-** : cut off by bits

¹snipe \'snīp\ *n, pl* **snipes** *or* **snipe** : bird of marshy areas

²snipe *vb* **sniped; snip·ing** : shoot at an enemy from a concealed position —**snip·er** *n*

snips \'snips\ *n pl* : scissorslike tool

sniv·el \'sniv-əl\ *vb* **-eled** *or* **-elled; -eling** *or* **-el·ling** **1** : have a running nose **2** : whine —**snivel** *n*

snob \'snäb\ *n* : one who acts superior to others —**snob·bery** \-(ə)rē\ *n* —**snob·bish** *adj* —**snob·bish·ly** *adv* —**snob·bish·ness** *n*

snoop \'snüp\ *vb* : pry in a furtive way ~ *n* : prying person

snooze \'snüz\ *vb* **snoozed; snooz·ing** : take a nap —**snooze** *n*

snore \'snōr\ *vb* **snored; snor·ing** : breathe with a hoarse noise while sleeping —**snore** *n*

snort \'snȯrt\ *vb* : force air noisily through the nose —**snort** *n*

snout \'snaůt\ *n* : long projecting muzzle (as of a swine)

snow \'snō\ *n* : crystals formed from water vapor ~ *vb* : fall as snow —**snow·ball** *n* —**snow·bank** *n* —**snow·drift** *n* —**snow·fall** *n* —**snow·plow** *n* —**snow·storm** *n* —**snowy** *adj*

snow·shoe *n* : frame of wood strung with thongs used for walking on snow

snub \'snəb\ *vb* **-bb-** : ignore or avoid through disdain —**snub** *n*

¹snuff \'snəf\ *vb* : put out (a candle) —**snuff·er** *n*

²snuff *vb* : draw forcibly into the nose ~ *n* : pulverized tobacco

snug \'snəg\ *adj* **-gg-** **1** : warm, secure, and comfortable **2** : fitting closely —**snug·ly** *adv* —**snug·ness** *n*

snug·gle \'snəgəl\ *vb* **-gled; -gling** : curl up comfortably

so \(')sō\ *adv* **1** : in the manner or to the extent indicated **2** : in the same way **3** : therefore **4** : finally **5** : thus ~ *conj* : for that reason

soak \'sōk\ *vb* **1** : lie in a liquid **2** : absorb ~ *n* : act of soaking

soap \'sōp\ *n* : cleaning substance —**soap** *vb* —**soapy** *adj*

soar \'sōr\ *vb* : fly upward on or as if on wings

sob \'säb\ *vb* **-bb-** : weep with convulsive heavings of the chest —**sob** *n*

so·ber \'sōbər\ *adj* **1** : not drunk **2** : serious or solemn —**so·ber·ly** *adv*

so·bri·ety \sə'brīətē, sō-\ *n* : quality or state of being sober

soc·cer \'säkər\ *n* : game played by kicking a ball

so·cia·ble \'sōshəbəl\ *adj* : friendly —**so·cia·bil·i·ty** \,sōshə'bilətē\ *n* —**so·cia·bly** \'sōshəblē\ *adv*

so·cial \'sōshəl\ *adj* **1** : relating to pleasant companionship **2** : naturally living or growing in groups **3** : relating to human society ~ n : social gathering —so·cial·ly adv

so·cial·ism \'sōshə,lizəm\ n : social organization based on government control of the production and distribution of goods —so·cial·ist \'sōsh(ə)ləst\ n or adj —so·cial·is·tic \,sōshə'listik\ adj

so·cial·ize \'sōshə,līz\ vb -ized; -iz·ing 1 : regulate by socialism 2 : adapt to social needs 3 : participate in a social gathering —so·cial·iza·tion \,sōsh(ə)lə'zāshən\ n

social work n : services concerned with aiding the poor and socially maladjusted —social worker n

so·ci·e·ty \sə'sīətē\ n, pl -et·ies 1 : companionship 2 : community life 3 : rich or fashionable class 4 : voluntary group

so·ci·ol·o·gy \,sōsē'äləjē\ n : study of social relationships —so·ci·o·log·i·cal \-ə'läjikəl\ adj —so·ci·ol·o·gist \-'äləjəst\ n

¹sock \'säk\ n, pl socks or sox : short stocking

²sock vb or n : punch

sock·et \'säkət\ n : hollow part that holds something

sod \'säd\ n : turf ~ vb -dd- : cover with sod

so·da \'sōdə\ n 1 : carbonated water or a soft drink 2 : ice cream drink made with soda

sod·den \'säd⁰n\ adj 1 : lacking spirit 2 : soaked or soggy

so·di·um \'sōdēəm\ n : soft waxy silver white metallic chemical element

so·fa \'sōfə\ n : wide padded chair

soft \'sȯft\ adj 1 : not hard, rough, or harsh 2 : nonalcoholic —soft·ly adv —soft·ness \'sȯf(t)nəs\ n

soft·ball n : game like baseball

soft·en \'sȯfən\ vb : make or become soft —soft·en·er \-(ə)nər\ n

sog·gy \'sägē\ adj -gier; -est : heavy with moisture —sog·gi·ness \-ēnəs\ n

¹soil \'sȯil\ vb : make or become dirty ~ n : embedded dirt

²soil n : loose surface material of the earth

so·journ \'sō,jərn, sō'jərn\ vb : reside temporarily ~ n —so·journ n

so·lace \'säləs\ n or vb : comfort

so·lar \'sōlər\ adj : relating to the sun or the energy in sunlight

sold past of SELL

sol·der \'sädər, 'sȯd-\ n : metallic alloy melted to join metallic surfaces ~ vb : cement with solder

sol·dier \'sōljər\ n : person in military

service ~ vb : serve as a soldier —sol·dier·ly adj or adv

¹sole \'sōl\ n : bottom of the foot or a shoe —soled adj

²sole n : flatfish caught for food

³sole adj : single or only —sole·ly \'sō(l)lē\ adv

sol·emn \'säləm\ adj 1 : dignified and ceremonial 2 : highly serious 3 : of great importance or responsibility —so·lem·ni·ty \sə'lemnətē\ n —sol·emn·ly adv —sol·emn·ness n

so·lic·it \sə'lisət\ vb : ask for —so·lic·i·ta·tion \-,lisə'tāshən\ n

so·lic·i·tor \sə'lisətər\ n 1 : one that solicits 2 : lawyer

so·lic·i·tous \sə'lisətəs\ adj : showing or expressing concern —so·lic·i·tous·ly adv —so·lic·i·tude \sə'lisə,t(y)üd\ n

sol·id \'säləd\ adj 1 : not hollow 2 : having 3 dimensions 3 : hard 4 : of good quality 5 : of one character ~ n 1 : 3-dimensional figure 2 : substance in solid form —solid adv —so·lid·i·ty \sə'lidətē\ n —sol·id·ly adv —sol·id·ness n

sol·i·dar·i·ty \,sälə'darətē\ n : unity of purpose

so·lid·i·fy \sə'lidə,fī\ vb -fied; -fy·ing : make or become solid —so·lid·i·fi·ca·tion \-,lidəfə'kāshən\ n

sol·il·o·quy \sə'liləkwē\ n, pl -quies : dramatic monologue —so·lil·o·quize \-,kwīz\ vb

sol·i·taire \'sälə,taər\ n 1 : solitary gem 2 : card game for one person

sol·i·tary \-,terē\ adj 1 : alone 2 : secluded 3 : single

sol·i·tude \-,t(y)üd\ n : state of being alone

so·lo \'sōlō\ n, pl -los : performance by only one person ~ adv : alone ~ adj or vb —so·lo·ist n

sol·stice \'sälstəs\ n : time of the year when the sun is farthest north or south of the equator

sol·u·ble \'sälyəbəl\ adj 1 : capable of being dissolved 2 : capable of being solved —sol·u·bil·i·ty \,sälyə'bilətē\ n

so·lu·tion \sə'lüshən\ n 1 : answer to a problem 2 : homogeneous liquid mixture

solve \'sälv\ vb solved; solv·ing : find a solution for —solv·able adj

sol·vent \'sälvənt\ adj 1 : able to pay all debts 2 : dissolving or able to dissolve ~ n : substance that dissolves or disperses another substance —sol·ven·cy \-vənsē\ n

som·ber, som·bre \'sämbər\ *adj* **1** : dark **2** : grave —**som·ber·ly** *adv*

som·bre·ro \səm'bre(ə)rō\ *n, pl* **-ros** : broad-brimmed hat

some \(')səm\ *adj* **1** : one unspecified **2** : unspecified or indefinite number of **3** : at least a few or a little ~ \'səm\ *pron* : a certain number or amount

-some \səm\ *adj suffix* : characterized by a thing, quality, state, or action

some·body \'səm,bädē, -bəd-\ *pron* : some person

some·day \'səm,dā\ *adv* : at some future time

some·how \-,haù\ *adv* : by some means

some·one \-(,)wən\ *pron* : some person

som·er·sault \'səmər,sȯlt\ *n* : body flip —**somersault** *vb*

some·thing \'səmthiŋ\ *pron* : some undetermined or unspecified thing

some·time \'səm,tīm\ *adv* : at a future, unknown, or unnamed time

some·times \-,tīmz\ *adv* : occasionally

some·what \-,hwät, -,hwət\ *adv* : in some degree

some·where \-,hwear\ *adv* : in, at, or to an unknown or unnamed place

som·no·lent \'sämnələnt\ *adj* : sleepy —**som·no·lence** \-ləns\ *n*

son \'sən\ *n* : male offspring

so·nar \'sō,när\ *n* : apparatus that locates underwater objects by reflected vibrations

so·na·ta \sə'nätə\ *n* : instrumental composition

song \'sȯŋ\ *n* : music and words to be sung

song·bird *n* : bird with musical tones

son·ic \'sänik\ *adj* : relating to sound waves or the speed of sound

son-in-law *n, pl* **sons-in-law** : husband of one's daughter

son·net \'sänət\ *n* : poem of 14 lines

so·no·rous \sə'nōrəs, 'sänərəs\ *adj* **1** : loud, deep, or rich in sound **2** : impressive —**so·nor·i·ty** \sə'nȯrətē\ *n*

soon \'sün\ *adv* **1** : before long **2** : promptly **3** : early

soot \'sùt, 'sət, 'süt\ *n* : fine black substance formed by combustion —**sooty** *adj*

soothe \'süth\ *vb* **soothed; sooth·ing** : calm or comfort —**sooth·er** *n*

sooth·say·er \'süth,sāər\ *n* : prophet —**sooth·say·ing** \-iŋ\ *n*

sop \'säp\ *n* : conciliatory bribe, gift, or concession ~ *vb* **-pp-** **1** : dip in a liquid **2** : soak **3** : mop up

so·phis·ti·cat·ed \sə'fistə,kātəd, sə-\ *adj* **1** : complex **2** : wise, cultured, or shrewd in human affairs —**so·phis·ti·ca·tion** \-,fistə'kāshən\ *n*

soph·ist·ry \'säfəstrē\ *n* : subtly fallacious reasoning or argument —**soph·ist** \'säfəst\ *n* —**so·phis·tic** \sə'fistik, sä-\, **so·phis·ti·cal** \-tikəl\ *adj*

soph·o·more \'säf,ō,mȯr, 'säf,mȯr\ *n* : 2d-year student

so·po·rif·ic \,säpə'rifik, ,sōp-\ *adj* : causing sleep or drowsiness

so·pra·no \sə'pranō\ *n, pl* **-nos** : highest singing voice

sor·cery \'sȯrs(ə)rē\ *n* : witchcraft —**sor·cer·er** \-rər\ *n* —**sor·cer·ess** \-rəs\ *n*

sor·did \'sȯrdəd\ *adj* : vulgar, degrading, or corrupt —**sor·did·ly** *adv* —**sor·did·ness** *n*

sore \'sȯr\ *adj* **sor·er; sor·est** **1** : causing pain or distress **2** : severe or intense **3** : angry ~ *n* : sore usu. infected spot on the body —**sore·ly** *adv* —**sore·ness** *n*

sor·ghum \'sȯrgəm\ *n* : forage grass

so·ror·i·ty \sə'rȯrətē\ *n, pl* **-ties** : club usu. for college women

sor·rel \'sȯrəl\ *n* : herb with sour juice

sor·row \'särō\ *n* : deep distress and regret or a cause of this —**sor·row·ful** \-fəl\ *adj* —**sor·row·ful·ly** \-f(ə)lē\ *adv*

sor·ry \'särē\ *adj* **-ri·er; -est** **1** : feeling sorrow, regret, or penitence **2** : dismal

sort \'sȯrt\ *n* **1** : kind **2** : nature ~ *vb* : classify —**out of sorts** : grouchy

sor·tie \'sȯrtē, sȯr'tē\ *n* : military attack esp. against besiegers

SOS \,es(,)ō'es\ *n* : call for help

so-so \'sō'sō\ *adj or adv* : barely acceptable

sot \'sät\ *n* : drunkard —**sot·tish** *adj*

souf·flé \sü'flā\ *n* : baked dish made light with beaten egg whites

sought *past of* SEEK

soul \'sōl\ *n* **1** : immaterial essence of an individual life **2** : essential nature **3** : person

soul·ful \'sōlfəl\ *adj* : full of or expressing deep feeling —**soul·ful·ly** *adv*

¹sound \'saùnd\ *adj* **1** : free from fault, error, or illness **2** : firm or hard **3** : showing good judgment —**sound·ly** *adv* —**sound·ness** *n*

²sound *n* **1** : sensation experienced by hearing **2** : noise ~ *vb* **1** : make or cause to make a noise **2** : seem —**sound·proof** *adj or vb*

³sound *n* : wide strait ~ *vb* **1** : measure the depth of (water) **2** : investigate

soup \'süp\ *n* : broth usu. containing pieces of solid food —**soupy** *adj*

sour \'saù(ə)r\ *adj* **1** : having an acid or tart taste **2** : disagreeable ~ *vb*

: become or make sour —**sour·ish** *adj*
—**sour·ly** *adv* —**sour·ness** *n*

source \'sōrs\ *n* **1** : point of origin **2**
: one that provides something needed

souse \'saus\ *vb* **soused; sous·ing** **1**
: pickle **2** : plunge into a liquid **3**
: intoxicate ~ *n* **1** : something pickled **2** : drunkard

south \'sauth\ *adv* : to or toward the
south ~ *adj* : situated toward, at, or
coming from the south ~ *n* **1** : direction to the right of sunrise **2** *cap* : regions to the south —**south·er·ly**
\'səthərlē\ *adv or adj* —**south·ern**
\'səthərn\ *adj* —**South·ern·er** *n*
—**south·ern·most** \-,mōst\ *adj*
—**south·ward** \'sauthwərd\ *adv or*
adj —**south·wards** \-wərdz\ *adv*

south·east \sauth'ēst, *naut* sau'ēst\ *n* **1**
: direction between south and east **2**
cap : regions to the southeast
—**southeast** *adj or adv* —**south·east-**
er·ly *adv or adj* —**south·east·ern**
\-ərn\ *adj*

south pole *n* : the southernmost point
of the earth

south·west \sauth'west, *naut* sau'west\
n **1** : direction between south and
west **2** *cap* : regions to the southwest
—**southwest** *adj or adv* —**south·west-**
er·ly *adv or adj* —**south·west·ern**
\-ərn\ *adj*

sou·ve·nir \,süvə,nir\ *n* : something
that is a reminder of a place or event

sov·er·eign \'säv(ə)rən\ *n* **1** : supreme
ruler **2** : gold coin of the United
Kingdom ~ *adj* **1** : supreme **2** : independent —**sov·er·eign·ty** \-tē\ *n*

1sow \'saü\ *n* : female swine

2sow \'sō\ *vb* **sowed; sown** \'sōn\ *or*
sowed, sow·ing **1** : plant or strew
with seed **2** : scatter abroad —**sow·er**
\'sō(ə)r\ *n*

sox *pl of* SOCK

soy·bean \'sòi'bēn, -,bēn\ *n* : legume
with edible seeds

spa \'spä\ *n* : resort at a mineral spring

space \'spās\ *n* **1** : period of time **2**
: area in, around, or between **3** : region beyond earth's atmosphere **4**
: accommodations ~ *vb* **spaced; spac-**
ing : separate —**space·craft** *n*
—**space·flight** *n* —**space·ship** *n*

spa·cious \'spāshəs\ *adj* : large or
roomy —**spa·cious·ly** *adv* —**spa-**
cious·ness *n*

1spade \'spād\ *n* : shovel with a flat
blade ~ *vb* **spad·ed; spad·ing** : dig
with a spade —**spade·ful** *n*

2spade *n* : playing card of a suit
marked with a black figure like an
inverted heart

spa·ghet·ti \spə'getē\ *n* : pasta strings

span \'span\ *n* **1** : amount of time **2**
: distance between supports ~ *vb*
-nn- : extend across

span·gle \'spangəl\ *n* : small disk of
shining metal —**spangle** *vb*

span·iel \'spanyəl\ *n* : small dog with
drooping ears

spank \'spaŋk\ *vb* : strike the buttocks
with the open hand

1spar \'spär\ *n* : pole or boom

2spar *vb* **-rr-** : practice boxing

spare \'spaər\ *adj* **1** : held in reserve **2**
: thin or scanty ~ *vb* **spared; spar·ing**
1 : reserve or avoid using **2** : avoid
punishing or killing —**spare** *n*

spar·ing \'spaəriŋ\ *adj* : thrifty
—**spar·ing·ly** *adv*

spark \'spärk\ *n* **1** : tiny hot and glowing particle **2** : smallest beginning or
germ **3** : visible electrical discharge
~ *vb* **1** : emit or produce sparks **2**
: stir to activity

spar·kle \'spärkəl\ *vb* **-kled; -kling** **1**
: flash **2** : effervesce ~ *n* : gleam
—**spark·ler** \-k(ə)lər\ *n*

spar·row \'sparō\ *n* : small singing bird

sparse \'spärs\ *adj* **spars·er; spars·est**
: thinly scattered —**sparse·ly** *adv*

spasm \'spazəm\ *n* **1** : involuntary
muscular contraction **2** : sudden, violent, and temporary effort or feeling
—**spas·mod·ic** \spaz'mädik\ *adj*

spas·tic \'spastik\ *adj* : relating to or
marked by muscular spasm —**spastic**
n

1spat \'spat\ *past of* SPIT

2spat *n* : petty dispute

spa·tial \'spāshəl\ *adj* : relating to
space —**spa·tial·ly** \-ē\ *adv*

spat·ter \'spatər\ *vb* : splash with
drops of liquid —**spatter** *n*

spat·u·la \'spachələ\ *n* : flexible knife-
like utensil

spawn \'spòn\ *vb* **1** : produce eggs or
offspring **2** : bring forth ~ *n* : egg
cluster

spay \'spā\ *vb* : remove the ovaries
from (an animal)

speak \'spēk\ *vb* **spoke** \'spōk\; **spo-**
ken \'spōkən\; **speak·ing** **1** : utter
words **2** : express orally **3** : address
an audience **4** : use (a language) in
speaking —**speak·er** *n*

spear \'spir\ *n* : long pointed weapon
~ *vb* : strike or pierce with a spear

spear·head *n* : leading force, element,
or influence —**spearhead** *vb*

spear·mint *n* : aromatic garden mint

spe·cial \'speshəl\ *adj* **1** : unusual or
unique **2** : particularly favored **3** : set

aside for a particular use —**special** *n*
—**spe·cial·ly** *adv*

spe·cial·ist \'spesh(ə)ləst\ *n* **1** : one devoted to a branch of learning or activity **2** : any of four enlisted ranks in the army corresponding to the grades of corporal through sergeant first class

spe·cial·ize \'speshə,līz\ *vb* **-ized; -iz·ing** : concentrate one's efforts —**spe·cial·iza·tion** \,speshələ'zāshən\ *n*

spe·cial·ty \'speshəltē\ *n, pl* **-ties** : area or field in which one specializes

spe·cie \'spēshē, -sē\ *n* : money in coin

spe·cies \'spēshēz, -sēz\ *n, pl* **species** : biological grouping of closely related organisms

spe·cif·ic \spi'sifik\ *adj* : definite or exact —**spe·cif·i·cal·ly** \-ik(ə)lē\ *adv*

spec·i·fi·ca·tion \,spesəfə'kāshən\ *n* **1** : item specified **2** : detailed description of work to be done —usu. pl.

spec·i·fy \'spesə,fī\ *vb* **-fied; -fy·ing** : mention precisely or by name

spec·i·men \-əmən\ *n* : typical example

spe·cious \'spēshəs\ *adj* : apparently but not really genuine or correct

speck \'spek\ *n* : tiny particle or blemish —**speck** *vb*

speck·led \'spekəld\ *adj* : marked with spots

spec·ta·cle \'spektikəl\ *n* **1** : impressive public display **2** *pl* : eyeglasses

spec·tac·u·lar \spek'takyələr\ *adj* : sensational or showy

spec·ta·tor \'spek,tātər\ *n* : one who looks on

spec·ter, spec·tre \'spektər\ *n* **1** : ghost **2** : haunting vision

spec·tral \'spektrəl\ *adj* : relating to or resembling a specter or spectrum

spec·trum \'spektrəm\ *n, pl* **-tra** \-trə\ *or* **-trums** : series of colors formed when white light is dispersed into its components

spec·u·late \'spekyə,lāt\ *vb* **-lat·ed; -lat·ing** **1** : think about things yet unknown **2** : risk money in a business deal in hope of high profit —**spec·u·la·tion** \,spekyə'lāshən\ *n* —**spec·u·la·tive** \'spekyə,lātiv\ *adj* —**spec·u·la·tor** \-,lātər\ *n*

speech \'spēch\ *n* **1** : power, act, or manner of speaking **2** : talk given to an audience —**speech·less** *adj*

speed \'spēd\ *n* **1** : quality of being fast **2** : rate of motion or performance ~ *vb* **sped** \'sped\ *or* **speed·ed; speed·ing** : go at a great or excessive rate of speed —**speed·boat** *n* —**speed·er** *n* —**speed·i·ly** \'spēdəlē\ *adv* —**speed·up** \-,əp\ *n* —**speedy** *adj*

speed·om·e·ter \spi'dämətər\ *n* : instrument for indicating speed

¹spell \'spel\ *n* : influence of or like magic

²spell *vb* **1** : name, write, or print the letters of (a word) **2** : mean —**spell·er** *n*

³spell *vb* : substitute for or relieve (someone) ~ *n* **1** : turn at work **2** : period of time

spell·bound *adj* : held by a spell

spend \'spend\ *vb* **spent** \'spent\; **spend·ing** **1** : pay out **2** : occupy oneself during (a period of time) —**spend·er** *n*

spend·thrift \'spen(d),thrift\ *n* : wasteful person

sperm \'spərm\ *n, pl* **sperm** *or* **sperms** : semen or a germ cell in it

spew \'spyü\ *vb* : gush out in a stream

sphere \'sfiər\ *n* **1** : figure with every point on its surface at an equal distance from the center **2** : round body **3** : range of action or influence —**spher·i·cal** \'sfirikəl, 'sfer-\ *adj*

spher·oid \'sfi(ə)r,ȯid, 'sfe(ə)r-\ *n* : spherelike figure

spice \'spīs\ *n* **1** : aromatic plant product for seasoning food **2** : interesting quality —**spice** *vb* —**spicy** *adj*

spi·der \'spīdər\ *n* : small insectlike animal with 8 legs —**spi·dery** *adj*

spig·ot \'spigət, 'spikət\ *n* : faucet

spike \'spīk\ *n* : very large nail ~ *vb* **spiked; spik·ing** : fasten or pierce with a spike —**spiked** \'spīkt\ *adj*

spill \'spil\ *vb* : cause or allow unintentionally to fall, flow, or run out ~ *n* **1** : act of spilling **2** : something spilled —**spill·able** *adj*

spill·way *n* : passage for surplus water

spin \'spin\ *vb* **spun** \'spən\; **spin·ning** **1** : draw out fiber and twist into thread **2** : form thread from a sticky body fluid **3** : revolve or cause to revolve extremely fast ~ *n* : rapid rotating motion —**spin·ner** *n*

spin·ach \'spinich\ *n* : garden herb with edible leaves

spi·nal \'spīn³l\ *adj* : relating to the backbone —**spi·nal·ly** *adv*

spinal cord *n* : thick strand of nervous tissue that extends from the brain along the back within the backbone

spin·dle \'spind³l\ *n* **1** : stick used for spinning thread **2** : shaft around which something turns

spin·dly \'spin(d)lē\ *adj* : tall and slender

spine \'spīn\ *n* **1** : backbone **2** : stiff sharp projection on a plant or animal —**spine·less** *adj* —**spiny** *adj*

spin·et \'spinət\ *n* : small piano

spin·ster \'spinstər\ *n* : woman who never married

spi·ral \'spīrəl\ *adj* : circling or winding around a single point or line —**spiral** *n or vb* —**spi·ral·ly** *adv*

spire \'spī(ə)r\ *n* : steeple —**spiry** *adj*

spir·it \'spirət\ *n* 1 : life-giving force 2 *cap* : presence of God 3 : ghost 4 : mood 5 : vivacity or enthusiasm 6 *pl* : alcoholic liquor ~ *vb* : carry off secretly —**spir·it·ed** *adj* —**spir·it·less** *adj*

spir·i·tu·al \'spirich(əw)əl\ *adj* 1 : relating to the spirit or sacred matters 2 : deeply religious ~ *n* : religious folk song —**spir·i·tu·al·i·ty** \,spirichə'walətē\ *n* —**spir·i·tu·al·ly** *adv*

spir·i·tu·al·ism \'spirich(əw)ə,lizəm\ *n* : belief that spirits communicate with the living —**spir·i·tu·al·ist** \-ləst\ *n* —**spir·i·tu·al·is·tic** \-,spirich(əw)ə-'listik\ *adj*

¹spit \'spit\ *n* 1 : rod for holding and turning meat over a fire 2 : point of land that runs into the water

²spit *vb* **spit** *or* **spat** \'spat\; **spit·ting** 1 : eject saliva from the mouth ~ *n* 1 : saliva 2 : perfect likeness

spite \'spīt\ *n* : grudge with a wish to injure ~ *vb* **spit·ed; spit·ing** : treat insultingly —**spite·ful** \-fəl\ *adj* —**spite·ful·ly** *adv* —**in spite of** : in defiance or contempt of

spit·tle \'spit⁹l\ *n* : saliva

spit·toon \spi'tün\ *n* : receptacle for spit

splash \'splash\ *vb* : scatter a liquid on —**splash** *n*

splat·ter \'splatər\ *vb* : spatter —**splatter** *n*

splay \'splā\ *vb* 1 : spread out 2 : slope or slant outward —**splay** *n or adj*

spleen \'splēn\ *n* 1 : organ for maintenance of the blood 2 : spite or anger

splen·did \'splendəd\ *adj* 1 : impressive in beauty or brilliance 2 : outstanding —**splen·did·ly** *adv*

splen·dor \'splendər\ *n* 1 : brilliance 2 : magnificence

splice \'splīs\ *vb* **spliced; splic·ing** : join (2 things) end to end —**splice** *n*

splint \'splint\, **splent** \'splent\ *n* 1 : thin strip of wood 2 : something that keeps an injured body part in place

splin·ter \'splintər\ *n* : thin needlike piece ~ *vb* : break into splinters

split \'split\ *vb* **split, split·ting** : divide lengthwise or along a grain —**split** *n*

splotch \'spläch\ *n* : blotch

splurge \'splərj\ *vb* **splurged; splurg·ing** : indulge oneself —**splurge** *n*

splut·ter \'splətər\ *n* : sputter —**splutter** *vb*

spoil \'spóil\ *n* : plunder ~ *vb* **spoiled** \'spóild, 'spóilt\ *or* **spoilt** \'spóilt\; **spoil·ing** 1 : pillage 2 : ruin 3 : rot —**spoil·age** \'spóilij\ *n* —**spoil·er** *n*

¹spoke \'spōk\ *past of* SPEAK

²spoke *n* : rod from the hub to the rim of a wheel

spo·ken *past part of* SPEAK

spokes·man \'spōksmən\ *n* : one who speaks for others —**spokes·wom·an** \-,wumən\ *n*

sponge \'spənj\ *n* 1 : porous mass that forms the skeleton of some marine animals 2 : spongelike material used for wiping ~ *vb* **sponged; spong·ing** 1 : wipe with a sponge 2 : live at another's expense —**spongy** \'spənjē\ *adj*

spon·sor \'spänsər\ *n* : one who assumes responsibility for another or who provides financial support —**sponsor** *vb* —**spon·sor·ship** *n*

spon·ta·ne·ous \spän'tānēəs\ *adj* : done, produced, or occurring naturally or without planning —**spon·ta·ne·i·ty** \,späntən'ēətē\ *n* —**spon·ta·ne·ous·ly** \spän'tānēəslē\ *adv*

spoof \'spüf\ *vb* : make good-natured fun of —**spoof** *n*

spook \'spük\ *n* : ghost ~ *vb* : frighten —**spooky** *adj*

spool \'spül\ *n* : cylinder on which something is wound

spoon \'spün\ *n* : utensil consisting of a shallow bowl with a handle —**spoon** *vb* —**spoon·ful** \-,fùl\ *n*

spoor \'spùr, 'spōr\ *n* : track or trail esp. of a wild animal

spo·rad·ic \spə'radik\ *adj* : occasional —**spo·rad·i·cal·ly** \-ik(ə)lē\ *adv*

spore \'spōr\ *n* : primitive usu. one-celled reproductive body

sport \'sport\ *vb* 1 : frolic 2 : wear or display ostentatiously ~ *n* 1 : physical activity engaged in for pleasure 2 : jest 3 : likable person 4 : one showing mutation —**sport·ive** \-iv\ *adj* —**sporty** *adj*

sports·cast \'sports,kast\ *n* : broadcast of a sports event —**sports·cast·er** \-,kastər\ *n*

sports·man \-mən\ *n* : one who enjoys hunting and fishing

sports·man·ship \-mən,ship\ *n* : ability to be gracious in winning or losing

spot \'spät\ *n* 1 : blemish 2 : distinctive small part 3 : location ~ *vb* **-tt-** 1 : mark with spots 2 : see or recognize ~ *adj* : made at random or in limited numbers —**spot·less** *adj* —**spot·less·ly** *adv*

spot·light *n* **1** : intense beam of light **2** : center of public interest —**spotlight** *vb*

spot·ty \'spätē\ *adj* **-ti·er; -est** : uneven in quality

spouse \'spaüs\ *n* : one's husband or wife

spout \'spaüt\ *vb* **1** : shoot forth in a stream **2** : say pompously ~ *n* **1** : opening through which liquid spouts **2** : jet of liquid

sprain \'sprān\ *n* : twisting injury to a joint ~ *vb* : injure with a sprain

sprat \'sprat\ *n* : small or young herring

sprawl \'sprȯl\ *vb* : lie or sit with limbs spread out —**sprawl** *n*

¹spray \'sprā\ *n* : branch or arrangement of flowers

²spray *n* **1** : mist **2** : device that discharges liquid as a mist —**spray** *vb* —**spray·er** *n*

spread \'spred\ *vb* **spread; spread·ing** **1** : open up or unfold **2** : scatter or smear over a surface **3** : cause to be known or to exist over a wide area ~ *n* **1** : extent to which something is spread **2** : cloth cover **3** : something intended to be spread —**spread·er** *n*

spree \'sprē\ *n* : burst of indulging in something

sprig \'sprig\ *n* : small shoot or twig

spright·ly \'sprītlē\ *adj* **-li·er; -est** : lively —**spright·li·ness** *n*

spring \'spriŋ\ *vb* **sprang** \'spraŋ\ *or* **sprung** \'sprəŋ\; **sprung, spring·ing** **1** : move or shoot up quickly or by elastic force **2** : make known suddenly ~ *n* **1** : source **2** : flow of water from underground **3** : season between winter and summer **4** : elastic body or device (as a coil of wire) **5** : leap **6** : elastic power —**springy** *adj*

sprin·kle \'spriŋkəl\ *vb* **-kled; -kling** : scatter in small drops or particles ~ *n* : light rainfall —**sprin·kler** \-k(ə)lər\ *n*

sprint \'sprint\ *n* : short run at top speed —**sprint** *vb* —**sprint·er** *n*

sprite \'sprīt\ *n* : elf or elfish person

sprock·et \'spräkət\ *n* : tooth on a wheel (**sprocket wheel**) shaped so as to interlock with a chain

sprout \'spraüt\ *vb* : send out new growth ~ *n* : plant shoot

¹spruce \'sprüs\ *n* : conical evergreen tree

²spruce *adj* **spruc·er; spruc·est** : neat and stylish in appearance ~ *vb* **spruced; spruc·ing** : make or become neat

spry \'sprī\ *adj* **spri·er** *or* **spry·er** \'sprī(ə)r\; **spri·est** *or* **spry·est** \'sprīəst\ : agile and active

spume \'spyüm\ *n* : froth

spun *past of* SPIN

spunk \'spəŋk\ *n* : courage —**spunky** *adj*

spur \'spər\ *n* **1** : pointed device used to urge on a horse **2** : something that urges to action **3** : projecting part ~ *vb* **-rr-** : urge on —**spurred** *adj*

spu·ri·ous \'spyùrēəs\ *adj* : not genuine

spurn \'spərn\ *vb* : reject

¹spurt \'spərt\ *n* : burst of effort, speed, or activity ~ *vb* : make a spurt

²spurt *vb* : gush out ~ *n* : sudden gush

sput·ter \'spətər\ *vb* **1** : talk hastily and indistinctly in excitement **2** : make popping sounds —**sputter** *n*

spu·tum \'spyütəm\ *n, pl* **-ta** \-ə\ : expectorated saliva and mucus

spy \'spī\ *vb* **spied; spy·ing** : watch or try to gather information about someone secretly —**spy** *n*

squab \'skwäb\ *n, pl* **squabs** *or* **squab** : young pigeon

squab·ble \'skwäbəl\ *n or vb* : dispute

squad \'skwäd\ *n* : small group

squad·ron \'skwädrən\ *n* : small military unit

squal·id \'skwäləd\ *adj* : filthy or wretched

squall \'skwȯl\ *n* : sudden violent brief storm —**squally** *adj*

squa·lor \'skwälər\ *n* : quality or state of being squalid

squan·der \'skwändər\ *vb* : waste

square \'skwaər\ *n* **1** : instrument for measuring right angles **2** : flat figure that has 4 equal sides and 4 right angles **3** : open area in a city **4** : product of number multiplied by itself ~ *adj* **squar·er; squar·est** **1** : being a square in form **2** : having sides meet at right angles **3** : multiplied by itself **4** : being a square unit of area **5** : honest **6** : even or tied ~ *vb* **squared; squar·ing** **1** : form into a square **2** : multiply a number by itself **3** : conform **4** : settle —**square·ly** *adv*

¹squash \'skwäsh, 'skwȯsh\ *vb* **1** : press flat **2** : suppress

²squash *n, pl* **squash·es** *or* **squash** : garden vegetable

squat \'skwät\ *vb* **-tt-** **1** : stoop or sit on one's heels **2** : settle on land one does not own ~ *n* : act or posture of squatting ~ *adj* **squat·ter, squat·test** : short and thick in stature —**squatter** *n*

squaw \'skwȯ\ *n* : Indian woman

squawk \'skwȯk\ *n* : harsh loud cry —**squawk** *vb*

squeak \'skwēk\ *vb* : make a thin high-pitched sound —**squeak** *n* —**squeaky** *adj*

squeal \'skwēl\ *vb* 1 : make a shrill sound or cry 2 : protest —**squeal** *n*

squea·mish \'skwēmish\ *adj* : easily nauseated or disgusted

squeeze \'skwēz\ *vb* **squeezed; squeez·ing** 1 : apply pressure to 2 : extract by pressure —**squeeze** *n* —**squeez·er** *n*

squelch \'skwelch\ *vb* : suppress (as with a retort) —**squelch** *n*

squid \'skwid\ *n, pl* **squid** *or* **squids** : 10-armed long-bodied sea mollusk

squint \'skwint\ *vb* : look with the eyes partly closed —**squint** *n or adj*

squire \'skwī(ə)r\ *n* 1 : knight's aide 2 : country landholder 3 : lady's devoted escort ~ *vb* **squired; squir·ing** : escort

squirm \'skwərm\ *vb* : wriggle

squir·rel \'skwər(ə)l\ *n* : rodent with a long bushy tail

squirt \'skwərt\ *vb* : eject liquid in a spurt —**squirt** *n*

stab \'stab\ *n* 1 : wound given by a pointed weapon 2 : quick thrust 3 : attempt ~ *vb* **-bb-** : pierce or wound with or as if with a pointed weapon

¹**sta·ble** \'stābəl\ *n* : building for livestock ~ *vb* **-bled; -bling** : keep in a stable

²**stable** *adj* **sta·bler; sta·blest** 1 : firmly established 2 : mentally well-balanced 3 : steady —**sta·bil·i·ty** \stə'bilətē\ *n* —**sta·bil·iza·tion** \ˌstābələ'zāshən\ *n* —**sta·bi·lize** \'stābə͵līz\ *vb* —**sta·bi·liz·er** *n*

stac·ca·to \stə'kätō\ *adj* : disconnected

stack \'stak\ *n* : large pile ~ *vb* : pile up

sta·di·um \'stādēəm\ *n* : outdoor sports arena

staff \'staf\ *n, pl* **staffs** \'stafs, stavz\ *or* **staves** \'stavz, 'stāvz\ 1 : rod or supporting cane 2 : people assisting a leader 3 : 5 horizontal lines on which music is written ~ *vb* : supply with workers —**staff·er** *n*

staff sergeant *n* : noncommissioned officer ranking in the army next below a sergeant first class, in the air force next below a technical sergeant, and in the marine corps next below a gunnery sergeant

stag \'stag\ *n, pl* **stags** *or* **stag** : male deer — *adj* : only for men — *adv* : without a date

stage \'stāj\ *n* 1 : raised platform for a speaker or performers 2 : theater 3 : step in a process ~ *vb* **staged; stag·ing** : produce (a play) —**stagy** \'stājē\ *adj*

stage·coach *n* : passenger coach

stag·ger \'stagər\ *vb* 1 : reel or cause to reel from side to side 2 : overlap or alternate —**stagger** *n* —**stag·ger·ing·ly** *adv*

stag·nant \'stagnənt\ *adj* : not moving or active —**stag·nate** \-͵nāt\ *vb* —**stag·na·tion** \stag'nāshən\ *n*

¹**staid** \'stād\ *adj* : sedate

²**staid** *past of* STAY

stain \'stān\ *vb* 1 : discolor 2 : dye (as wood) 3 : disgrace ~ *n* 1 : discolored area 2 : dishonor 3 : coloring preparation —**stain·less** *adj*

stair \'staar\ *n* 1 : step in a series for going from one level to another 2 *pl* : flight of steps —**stair·way** *n*

stair·case *n* : series of steps with their framework

stake \'stāk\ *n* 1 : small post driven into the ground 2 : bet 3 : prize in a contest ~ *vb* **staked; stak·ing** 1 : mark or secure with a stake 2 : place as a bet

sta·lac·tite \stə'lak͵tīt\ *n* : icicle-shaped deposit hanging in a cavern

sta·lag·mite \stə'lag͵mīt\ *n* : icicle-shaped deposit on the floor of a cavern

stale \'stāl\ *adj* **stal·er; stal·est** : not fresh —**stale** *n*

stale·mate \'stāl͵māt\ *n* : deadlock —**stalemate** *vb*

¹**stalk** \'stȯk\ *vb* 1 : walk stiffly or haughtily 2 : to approach (game) stealthily

²**stalk** *n* : plant stem —**stalked** \'stȯkt\ *adj*

¹**stall** \'stȯl\ *n* 1 : compartment in a stable 2 : booth where articles are sold

²**stall** *vb* : bring or come to a stand-still unintentionally

³**stall** *vb* : delay, evade, or keep a situation going to gain advantage or time

stal·lion \'stalyən\ *n* : male horse

stal·wart \'stȯlwərt\ *adj* : strong or brave

sta·men \'stāmən\ *n* : flower organ that produces pollen

stam·i·na \'stamənə\ *n* : endurance

stam·mer \'stamər\ *vb* : hesitate in speaking —**stammer** *n*

stamp \'stamp *also* 'stämp *or* 'stòmp\ *vb* **1** : pound with the sole of the foot or a heavy implement **2** : impress with a mark **3** : cut out with a die **4** : attach a postage stamp to ~ *n* **1** : device for stamping **2** : act of stamping **3** : government seal showing a tax or fee has been paid

stam·pede \stam'pēd\ *n* : headlong rush of frightened animals ~ *vb* **-ped·ed; -ped·ing** : flee in panic

stance \'stans\ *n* : way of standing

stan·chion \'stanchən\ *n* : upright support

¹**stanch** \'stònch, 'stänch\ *vb* : stop the flow of (as blood)

²**stanch** *var of* STAUNCH

stan·chion \'stanchən\ *n* : upright support

stand \'stand\ *vb* **stood** \'stùd\; **stand·ing 1** : be at rest in or assume an upright position **2** : remain unchanged **3** : be steadfast **4** : maintain a relative position or rank **5** : set upright **6** : undergo or endure ~ *n* **1** : act or place of standing, staying, or resisting **2** : sales booth **3** : structure for holding something upright **4** : group of plants growing together **5** *pl* : tiered seats **6** : opinion or viewpoint

stan·dard \'standərd\ *n* **1** : symbolic figure or flag **2** : model, rule, or guide **3** : upright support —**standard** *adj* —**stan·dard·iza·tion** \,standərdə'zāshən\ *n* —**stan·dard·ize** \'standərd,īz\ *vb*

standard time *n* : time established over a region or country

stand·ing \'standiŋ\ *n* **1** : relative position or rank **2** : duration

stand·still *n* : state of rest

stank *past of* STINK

stan·za \'stanzə\ *n* : division of a poem

¹**sta·ple** \'stāpəl\ *n* : U-shaped wire fastener —**staple** *vb* —**sta·pler** \-p(ə)lər\ *n*

²**staple** *n* : chief commodity or item —**staple** *adj*

star \'stär\ *n* **1** : celestial body visible as a point of light **2** : 5- or 6-pointed figure representing a star **3** : leading performer ~ *vb* **-rr- 1** : mark with a star **2** : play the leading role —**star·dom** \'stärdəm\ *n* —**star·less** *adj* —**star·light** *n* —**star·ry** *adj*

star·board \'stärbərd\ *n* : right side of a ship or airplane looking forward —**starboard** *adj*

starch \'stärch\ *n* : nourishing carbohydrate from plants also used in ad-

hesives and laundering ~ *vb* : stiffen with starch —**starchy** *adj*

stare \'staor\ *vb* **stared; star·ing** : look intently with wide-open eyes —**stare** *n* —**star·er** *n*

stark \'stärk\ *adj* **1** : absolute **2** : severe or bleak —**stark** *adv* —**stark·ly** *adv*

star·ling \'stärliŋ\ *n* : bird related to the crows

start \'stärt\ *vb* **1** : twitch or jerk (as from surprise) **2** : perform or show performance of the first part of an action or process ~ *n* **1** : sudden involuntary motion **2** : beginning —**start·er** *n*

star·tle \'stärt⁰l\ *vb* **-tled; -tling** : frighten or surprise suddenly

starve \'stärv\ *vb* **starved; starv·ing 1** : suffer or die from hunger **2** : kill with hunger —**star·va·tion** \stär'vāshən\ *n*

state \'stāt\ *n* **1** : condition of being **2** : condition of mind **3** : nation or a political unit within it ~ *vb* **stat·ed; stat·ing 1** : express in words **2** : establish —**state·hood** \-,hùd\ *n*

state·ly \'stātlē\ *adj* **-li·er; -est** : having impressive dignity —**state·li·ness** *n*

state·ment \'stātmənt\ *n* **1** : something stated **2** : financial summary

state·room *n* : private room on a ship

states·man \'stātsmən\ *n* : one skilled in government or diplomacy —**states·man·like** *adj* —**states·man·ship** *n*

stat·ic \'statik\ *adj* **1** : relating to bodies or forces at rest **2** : not moving **3** : relating to stationary charges of electricity ~ *n* : noise on radio or television from electrical disturbances

sta·tion \'stāshən\ *n* **1** : place of duty **2** : regular stopping place on a transportation route **3** : social standing **4** : place where radio or television programs originate ~ *vb* : assign to a station

sta·tion·ary \'stāshə,nerē\ *adj* **1** : not moving or not movable **2** : not changing

sta·tio·nery \'stāshə,nerē\ *n* : letter paper with envelopes

sta·tis·tic \stə'tistik\ *n* : single item of statistics

sta·tis·tics \-tiks\ *n pl* : numerical facts collected for study —**sta·tis·ti·cal** \-tikəl\ *adj* —**sta·tis·ti·cal·ly** *adv* —**stat·is·ti·cian** \,statə'stishən\ *n*

stat·u·ary \'stachə,werē\ *n, pl* **-ar·ies** : collection of statues

stat·ue \'stachü\ *n* : sculptured likeness of a being —**stat·u·ette** \ˌstachəˈwet\ n

stat·u·esque \ˌstachəˈwesk\ adj : well-proportioned or of dignified bearing

stat·ure \ˈstachər\ n 1 : height 2 : status gained by achievement

sta·tus \ˈstātəs, ˈstat-\ n : relative situation or condition

sta·tus quo \-ˈkwō\ n : existing state of affairs

stat·ute \ˈstachüt\ n : law —**stat·u·to·ry** \ˈstachəˌtōrē\ adj

staunch \ˈstónch\ adj : steadfast —**staunch·ly** adv

stave \ˈstāv\ n : narrow strip of wood ~ vb **staved** or **stove** \ˈstōv\; **stav·ing** 1 : break a hole in 2 : drive away

staves pl of STAFF

¹**stay** \ˈstā\ n : support ~ vb **stayed**; **stay·ing** 1 : prop up 2 : satisfy for a time

²**stay** vb **stayed** or **staid** \ˈstād\; **stay·ing** 1 : pause 2 : lodge 3 : remain 4 : stop or postpone ~ n : a staying

stead \ˈsted\ n : one's place, job, or function —**in good stead** : to advantage

stead·fast \-ˌfast\ adj : faithful or determined —**stead·fast·ly** adv —**stead·fast·ness** n

steady \ˈstedē\ adj **steadi·er; -est** 1 : firm in position or sure in movement 2 : calm or reliable 3 : constant 4 : regular ~ vb **stead·ied; steady·ing** : make or become steady —**stead·i·ly** \ˈstedᵊlē\ adv —**steadi·ness** n —**steady** adv

steak \ˈstāk\ n : thick slice of meat

steal \ˈstēl\ vb **stole** \ˈstōl\; **sto·len** \ˈstōlən\; **steal·ing** 1 : take and carry away wrongfully and with intent to keep 2 : move secretly or slowly

stealth \ˈstelth\ n : secret or underhand procedure —**stealth·i·ly** \-thəlē\ adv —**stealthy** adj

steam \ˈstēm\ n : vapor of boiling water ~ vb : give off steam —**steam·boat** n —**steam·ship** n —**steamy** adj

steed \ˈstēd\ n : horse

steel \ˈstēl\ n : tough carbon-containing iron ~ vb : make able to resist —**steel** adj —**steely** adj

¹**steep** \ˈstēp\ adj : having a very sharp slope or great elevation —**steep·ly** adv —**steep·ness** n

²**steep** vb : soak in a liquid

stee·ple \ˈstēpəl\ n : usu. tapering church tower

stee·ple·chase \-ˌchās\ n : race over hurdles

¹**steer** \ˈstiər\ n : castrated ox

²**steer** vb 1 : direct the course of (as a ship or car) 2 : guide

steer·age \ˈsti(ə)rij\ n : section in a ship for passengers paying the lowest fares

stein \ˈstīn\ n : mug

stel·lar \ˈstelər\ adj : relating to stars or resembling a star

¹**stem** \ˈstem\ n : main upright part of a plant ~ vb **-mm-** 1 : derive 2 : make progress against —**stem·less** adj —**stemmed** adj

²**stem** vb **-mm-** : stop the flow of

stench \ˈstench\ n : stink

sten·cil \ˈstensəl\ n : printing sheet cut with letters to let ink pass through —**stencil** vb

ste·nog·ra·phy \stəˈnägrəfē\ n : art or process of writing in shorthand —**ste·nog·ra·pher** \-fər\ n —**steno·graph·ic** \ˌstenəˈgrafik\ adj

sten·to·ri·an \sten'tōrēən\ adj : extremely loud

step \ˈstep\ n 1 : single action of a leg in walking or running 2 : rest for the foot in going up or down 3 : degree, rank, or stage 4 : way of walking ~ vb **-pp-** 1 : move by steps 2 : press with the foot

step- \ˈstep-\ comb form : related by a remarriage (as of a parent) and not by blood

step·lad·der \-ˌ\ n : light portable set of steps in a hinged frame

steppe \ˈstep\ n : dry grassy land esp. of Asia

-ster \stər\ n suffix 1 : one that does, makes, or uses 2 : one that is associated with or takes part in 3 : one that is

ste·reo \ˈsterēˌō, ˈstir-\ n, pl **-reos** : stereophonic sound system —**stereo** adj

ste·reo·phon·ic \ˌsterēəˈfänik, ˌstir-\ adj : relating to a 3-dimensional effect of reproduced sound

ste·reo·typed \ˈsterēəˌtīp, ˈstir-\ adj : represented as lacking originality or creativity

ster·ile \ˈsterəl\ adj 1 : unable to bear fruit, crops, or offspring 2 : free from disease germs —**ste·ril·i·ty** \stəˈrilətē\ n —**ster·il·iza·tion** \ˌsterələˈzāshən\ n —**ster·il·ize** \ˈsterəˌlīz\ vb —**ster·il·iz·er** n

ster·ling \ˈstərliŋ\ adj 1 : having a fixed standard of purity represented by an alloy of 925 parts of silver with 75 parts of copper 2 : made of sterling silver 3 : excellent

¹**stern** \ˈstərn\ adj : severe —**stern·ly** adv —**stern·ness** n

²**stern** n : back end of a boat

ster·num \'stərnəm\ *n, pl* **-nums** *or* **-na** \-nə\ : long flat chest bone joining the 2 sets of ribs

stetho·scope \'stethə,skōp\ *n* : instrument used for listening to sounds in the chest

ste·ve·dore \'stēvə,dōr\ *n* : worker who loads and unloads ships

stew \'st(y)ü\ *n* : dish of boiled meat and vegetables —**stew** *vb*

stew·ard \'st(y)üərd\ *n* **1** : manager of an estate or an organization **2** : person on a ship or airliner who looks after passenger comfort —**stew·ard·ess** \-əs\ *n* —**stew·ard·ship** *n*

¹stick \'stik\ *n* **1** : cut or broken branch **2** : long thin piece of wood or something resembling it

²stick *vb* **stuck** \'stək\; **stick·ing** **1** : stab **2** : thrust or project **3** : hold fast to something **4** : attach **5** : become jammed or fixed

stick·er \'stikər\ *n* : gummed label

stick·ler \'stik(ə)lər\ *n* : one who insists on exactness or completeness

sticky \'stikē\ *adj* **stick·i·er; -est 1** : adhesive **2** : gluey

stiff \'stif\ *adj* **1** : not bending easily **2** : tense **3** : formal **4** : strong **5** : severe —**stiff·ly** *adv* —**stiff·ness** *n*

stiff·en \'stifən\ *vb* : make or become stiff —**stiff·en·er** \-(ə)nər\ *n*

sti·fle \'stifəl\ *vb* **-fled; -fling 1** : smother or suffocate **2** : suppress

stig·ma \'stigmə\ *n, pl* **-ma·ta** \'stig'mätə, 'stigmətə\ *or* **-mas** : mark of disgrace —**stig·ma·tize** \'stigmə,tīz\ *vb*

stile \'stīl\ *n* : steps for crossing a fence

sti·let·to \stə'letō\ *n, pl* **-tos** *or* **-toes** : slender dagger

¹still \'stil\ *adj* **1** : motionless **2** : silent ~ *vb* : make or become still ~ *adv* **1** : without motion **2** : up to and during this time **3** : in spite of that ~ *n* : silence —**still·ness** *n*

²still *n* : apparatus used in distillation

still·born *adj* : born dead —**still·birth** *n*

stilt \'stilt\ *n* : one of a pair of poles for walking

stilt·ed \'stiltəd\ *adj* : pompous

stim·u·lant \'stimyələnt\ *n* : substance that temporarily increases the activity of an organism —**stimulant** *adj*

stim·u·late \-,lāt\ *vb* **-lat·ed; -lat·ing** : make active —**stim·u·la·tion** \,stimyə'lāshən\ *n*

stim·u·lus \'stimyələs\ *n, pl* **-li** \-,lī\ : something that stimulates

sting \'stin\ *vb* **stung** \'stən\; **sting·ing 1** : prick painfully **2** : hurt with an intense burning pain ~ *n* : act of stinging —**sting·er** *n*

stin·gy \'stinjē\ *adj* **stin·gi·er; -est** : not generous —**stin·gi·ness** *n*

stink \'stink\ *vb* **stank** \'stank\ *or* **stunk** \'stənk\; **stunk; stink·ing** : have a strong offensive odor —**stink** *n* —**stink·er** *n*

stint \'stint\ *vb* : be sparing or stingy ~ *n* **1** : restraint **2** : quantity or period of work

sti·pend \'stī,pend, -pənd\ *n* : money paid periodically

stip·ple \'stipəl\ *vb* **-pled; -pling** : engrave, paint, or draw with dots instead of lines —**stipple** *n*

stip·u·late \'stipyə,lāt\ *vb* **-lat·ed; -lat·ing** : demand as a condition —**stip·u·la·tion** \,stipyə'lāshən\ *n*

stir \'stər\ *vb* **-rr- 1** : move slightly **2** : prod or push into activity **3** : mix by continued circular movement ~ *n* : act or result of stirring

stir·rup \'stərəp\ *n* : saddle loop for the foot

stitch \'stich\ *n* **1** : loop formed by a needle in sewing **2** : sudden sharp pain ~ *vb* **1** : fasten or decorate with stitches **2** : sew

stock \'stäk\ *n* **1** : block or part of wood **2** : original from which others derive **3** : farm animals **4** : supply of goods kept by a merchant **5** : money invested in a large business **6** *pl* : instrument of punishment like a pillory but having holes for the feet or feet and hands ~ *vb* : provide with stock

stock·ade \stä'kād\ *n* : defensive or confining enclosure

stock·ing \'stäkin\ *n* : close-fitting covering for the foot and leg

stock·pile *n* : reserve supply —**stockpile** *vb*

stock·yard *n* : yard for livestock to be slaughtered or shipped

stocky \'stäkē\ *adj* **stock·i·er; -est** : short and relatively thick

stodgy \'stäjē\ *adj* **stodg·i·er; -est** : dull

sto·ic \'stōik\, **sto·i·cal** \-ikəl\ *adj* : showing indifference to pain —**stoic** *n* —**sto·i·cal·ly** \-ik(ə)lē\ *adv* —**sto·icism** \'stōə,sizəm\ *n*

stoke \'stōk\ *vb* **stoked; stok·ing** : stir up a fire or supply fuel to a furnace —**stok·er** *n*

¹stole \'stōl\ *past of* STEAL

²stole *n* : long wide scarf

stolen *past part of* STEAL

stol·id \'stäləd\ *adj* : having or showing little or no emotion —**sto·lid·i·ty** \stä'lidətē\ *n* —**stol·id·ly** \'stälədlē\ *adv*

stom·ach \'stəmək, -ik\ *n* 1 : saclike digestive organ 2 : abdomen 3 : appetite or desire —**stom·ach·ache** *n*

stomp \'stämp, 'stömp\ *vb* : stamp

stone \'stōn\ *n* 1 : hardened earth or mineral matter 2 : small piece of rock 3 : seed that is hard or has a hard covering ~ *vb* **stoned; ston·ing** : pelt or kill with stones —**stony** *adj*

stood *past of* STAND

stool \'stül\ *n* 1 : seat usu. without back or arms 2 : footstool 3 : discharge of feces

¹stoop \'stüp\ *vb* 1 : bend over 2 : lower oneself ~ *n* 1 : act of bending over 2 : bent position of shoulders

²stoop *n* : small porch at a house door

stop \'stäp\ *vb* **-pp-** 1 : block a hole or opening 2 : end or cause to end 3 : pause for rest or a visit in a journey ~ *n* 1 : plug 2 : act or place of stopping 3 : delay in a journey —**stop·light** —**stop·page** \-ij\ *n* —**stop·per** *n*

stop-gap *n* : temporary measure or thing

stor·age \'stōrij\ *n* : safekeeping of goods (as in a warehouse)

store \'stōr\ *vb* **stored; stor·ing** : put aside for future use ~ *n* 1 : something stored 2 : retail business establishment —**store·house** *n* —**store·keep·er** *n* —**store·room** *n*

stork \'stórk\ *n* : large wading bird

storm \'stórm\ *n* 1 : heavy fall of rain or snow 2 : violent outbreak ~ *vb* 1 : rain or snow heavily 2 : rage 3 : make an attack against —**stormy** *adj*

¹sto·ry \'stōrē\ *n, pl* **-ries** 1 : narrative 2 : report —**sto·ry·tell·er** *n* —**sto·ry·tell·ing** *adj or n*

²story *n, pl* **-ries** : floor of a building

stout \'staút\ *adj* 1 : firm or strong 2 : thick or bulky —**stout·ly** *adv* —**stout·ness** *n*

stove \'stōv\ *n* : apparatus for providing heat (as for cooking or heating)

²stove *past of* STAVE

stow \'stō\ *vb* 1 : pack in a compact mass 2 : put or hide away

strad·dle \'strad°l\ *vb* **-dled; -dling** : stand over or sit on with legs on opposite sides —**straddle** *n*

strafe \'strāf\ *vb* **strafed; straf·ing** : fire upon with machine guns from a low-flying airplane

strag·gle \'stragəl\ *vb* **-gled; -gling** : wander or become separated from others —**strag·gler** \-(ə)lər\ *n*

straight \'strāt\ *adj* 1 : having no bends, turns, or twists 2 : just,

proper, or honest 2 : neat and orderly ~ *adv* : in a straight manner

straight·en \'strāt°n\ *vb* : make or become straight

straight·for·ward \strāt'fórwərd\ *adj* : frank or honest

straight·way *adv* : immediately

¹strain \'strān\ *n* 1 : lineage 2 : trace

²strain *vb* 1 : exert to the utmost 2 : filter or remove by filtering 3 : injure by improper use ~ *n* 1 : excessive tension or exertion 2 : bodily injury from excessive effort —**strain·er** *n*

strait \'strāt\ *n* 1 : narrow channel connecting 2 bodies of water 2 *pl* : distress

strait·en \'strāt°n\ *vb* 1 : hem in 2 : make distressing or difficult

¹strand \'strand\ *vb* 1 : drive or cast upon the shore 2 : leave helpless

²strand *n* 1 : twisted fiber of a rope 2 : length of something ropelike

strange \'strānj\ *adj* **strang·er; strang·est** 1 : unusual or queer 2 : new —**strange·ly** *adv* —**strange·ness** *n*

strang·er \'strānjər\ *n* : person with whom one is not acquainted

stran·gle \'strangəl\ *vb* **-gled; -gling** : choke to death —**stran·gler** \-g(ə)lər\ *n*

stran·gu·la·tion \,strangyə'lāshən\ *n* : act or process of strangling

strap \'strap\ *n* : narrow strip of flexible material used esp. for fastening ~ *vb* 1 : secure with a strap 2 : beat with a strap —**strap·less** *n*

strap·ping \'strapin\ *adj* : large

strat·a·gem \'stratəjəm, -,jem\ *n* : deceptive scheme or maneuver

strat·e·gy \'stratəjē\ *n, pl* **-gies** : carefully worked out plan of action —**stra·te·gic** \strə'tējik\ *adj* —**strat·e·gist** \'stratəjist\ *n*

strat·i·fy \'stratə,fī\ *vb* **-fied; -fy·ing** : form or arrange in layers —**strat·i·fi·ca·tion** \,stratəfə'kāshən\ *n*

strato·sphere \'stratə,sfiər\ *n* : earth's atmosphere from about 7 to 37 miles above the earth's surface —**strato·spher·ic** \,stratə'sfi(ə)rik, -'sfer-\ *adj*

stra·tum \'strātəm, 'strat-\ *n, pl* **-ta** \'strātə, 'strat-\ : layer

straw \'stró\ *n* 1 : grass stems after grain is removed 2 : tube for drinking ~ *adj* : made of straw

straw·ber·ry \'stró,berē, -b(ə)rē\ *n* : red pulpy fruit

stray \'strā\ *vb* : wander from a course or herd ~ *n* : person or animal that strays ~ *adj* : separated from or not related to anything close by

streak \'strēk\ *n* **1** : mark of a different color **2** : narrow band of light **3** : trace **4** : run (as of luck) or series ~ *vb* **1** : form streaks in or on **2** : move fast

stream \'strēm\ *n* **1** : flow of water on land **2** : steady flow (as of water or air) ~ *vb* **1** : flow in a stream **2** : pour out streams

stream·er \'strēmər\ *n* : long ribbon or ribbonlike flag

stream·lined \-,līnd, -'līnd\ *adj* **1** : made with contours to reduce air or water resistance **2** : simplified **3** : modernized —**streamline** *vb*

street \'strēt\ *n* : thoroughfare esp. in a city or town

street·car *n* : passenger vehicle running on rails in the streets

strength \'streŋth\ *n* **1** : quality of being strong **2** : toughness **3** : intensity

strength·en \'streŋthən\ *vb* : make, grow, or become stronger —**strength·en·er** \'streŋth(ə)nər\ *n*

stren·u·ous \'strenyəwəs\ *adj* : requiring or showing energetic effort —**stren·u·ous·ly** *adv*

stress \'stres\ *n* **1** : pressure or strain that tends to distort a body **2** : relative prominence or importance given to one thing among others **3** : state of physical or mental tension or something inducing it ~ *vb* : put stress on

stretch \'strech\ *vb* **1** : spread or reach out **2** : draw out in length or breadth **3** : make taut **4** : exaggerate **5** : become extended without breaking ~ *n* : act of extending beyond normal limits

stretch·er \'strechər\ *n* : cot with handles for carrying a disabled person

strew \'strü\ *vb* **strewed**; **strewed** *or* **strewn** \'strün\; **strew·ing 1** : scatter **2** : cover by scattering something over

strick·en \'strikən\ *adj* : afflicted with disease

strict \'strikt\ *adj* **1** : severe and unyielding **2** : precise —**strict·ly** *adv* —**strict·ness** *n*

stric·ture \'strikchər\ *n* : hostile criticism

stride \'strīd\ *vb* **strode** \'strōd\; **strid·den** \'strid⁰n\; **strid·ing** \'strīdiŋ\ : walk or run with long steps ~ *n* **1** : long step **2** : manner of striding

stri·dent \'strīd⁰nt\ *adj* : loud and harsh

strife \'strīf\ *n* : conflict

strike \'strīk\ *vb* **struck** \'strək\; **struck**; **strik·ing** \'strīkiŋ\ **1** : hit sharply **2** : delete **3** : produce by impressing **4** : cause to sound **5** : afflict **6** : occur to or impress **7** : cause (a match) to ignite by rubbing **8** : refrain from working **9** : find **10** : take on (as a pose) ~ *n* **1** : act or instance of striking **2** : work stoppage **3** : military attack —**strik·er** *n* —**strike out** *vb* : start out vigorously —**strike up** *vb* : start

strik·ing \'strīkiŋ\ *adj* : very noticeable —**strik·ing·ly** *adv*

string \'striŋ\ *n* **1** : line usu. of twisted threads **2** : series **3** *pl* : stringed instruments ~ *vb* **strung** \'strəŋ\; **string·ing 1** : thread on or with a string **2** : hang or fasten by a string

stringed \'striŋd\ *adj* : having strings

strin·gent \'strinjənt\ *adj* : severe

stringy \'striŋē\ *adj* **string·i·er**; **-est** : tough or fibrous

¹strip \'strip\ *vb* **-pp- 1** : take the covering or clothing from **2** : undress —**strip·per** *n*

²strip *n* : long narrow flat piece

stripe \'strīp\ *n* : distinctive line or long narrow section ~ *vb* **striped** \'strīpt\; **strip·ing** : make stripes on

striped \'strīpt, 'strīpəd\ *adj* : having stripes or streaks

strive \'strīv\ *vb* **strove** \'strōv\; **striv·en** \'strivən\ *or* **strived**; **striv·ing** \'strīviŋ\ **1** : struggle **2** : try hard

strode *past of* STRIDE

stroke \'strōk\ *vb* **stroked**; **strok·ing** : rub gently ~ *n* **1** : act of swinging or striking **2** : sudden action

stroll \'strōl\ *vb* : walk leisurely —**stroll** *n* —**stroll·er** *n*

strong \'stróŋ\ *adj* **1** : capable of exerting great force or of withstanding stress or violence **2** : healthy **3** : zealous —**strong·ly** *adv*

strong·hold *n* : fortified place

stron·tium \'stränch(ē)əm, 'sträntēəm\ *n* : soft malleable metallic chemical element

struck *past of* STRIKE

struc·ture \'strəkchər\ *n* **1** : building **2** : arrangement of elements ~ *vb* **-tured; -tur·ing** : make into a structure —**struc·tur·al** \-chərəl, -shrəl\ *adj*

strug·gle \'strəgəl\ *vb* **-gled; -gling 1** : make strenuous efforts to overcome an adversary **2** : proceed with great effort ~ *n* **1** : strenuous effort **2** : intense competition for superiority

strum \'strəm\ *vb* **-mm-** : play (a musical instrument) by brushing the strings with the fingers

strum·pet \'strəmpət\ *n* : prostitute

strung past of STRING

strut \'strət\ vb -tt- : walk in a proud or showy manner ~ n 1 : proud walk 2 : supporting bar or rod

strych·nine \'strik,nīn, -nən, -,nēn\ n : bitter poisonous substance

stub \'stəb\ n : short end or section ~ vb -bb- : strike against something

stub·ble \'stəbəl\ n : short growth left after cutting —**stub·bly** adj

stub·born \'stəbərn\ adj 1 : unreasonably determined not to yield 2 : hard to control —**stub·born·ly** adv —**stub·born·ness** n

stub·by \'stəbē\ adj : short, blunt, and thick

stuc·co \'stəkō\ n, pl -cos or -coes : plaster for coating outside walls ~ vb : coat with stucco

stuck past of STICK

stuck-up \'stək'əp\ adj : conceited

¹stud \'stəd\ n : male horse kept for breeding

²stud n 1 : upright wall support 2 : projecting nail, pin, or rod ~ vb -dd- : supply or dot with studs

stu·dent \'st(y)üd°nt\ n : one who studies

stud·ied \'stədēd\ adj : premeditated

stu·dio \'st(y)üdē,ō\ n, pl -dios 1 : artist's workroom 2 : place where movies are made or television or radio shows are broadcast

stu·di·ous \'st(y)üdēəs\ adj : devoted to study —**stu·di·ous·ly** adv

study \'stədē\ n, pl stud·ies 1 : act or process of learning about something 2 : branch of learning 3 : careful examination 4 : room for reading or studying ~ vb stud·ied; study·ing : apply the attention and mind to a subject

stuff \'stəf\ n 1 : personal property 2 : raw or fundamental material 3 : unspecified often worthless material or things ~ vb : fill esp. by packing tightly —**stuff·ing** n

stuffy \'stəfē\ adj stuff·i·er; -est 1 : lacking fresh air 2 : unimaginative or pompous

stul·ti·fy \'stəltə,fī\ vb -fied; -fy·ing : cause to appear foolish —**stul·ti·fi·ca·tion** \,stəltəfə'kāshən\ n

stum·ble \'stəmbəl\ vb -bled; -bling 1 : lose one's balance or fall in walking or running 2 : speak or act clumsily 3 : come by chance —**stumble** n

stump \'stəmp\ n : part left when something is cut off ~ vb : confuse —**stumpy** adj

stun \'stən\ vb -nn- 1 : make senseless or dizzy by or as if by a blow 2 : bewilder

stung past of STING

stunk past of STINK

stun·ning \'stəniŋ\ adj : strikingly beautiful —**stun·ning·ly** adv

¹stunt \'stənt\ vb : hinder the normal growth of

²stunt n : spectacular feat

stu·pe·fy \'st(y)üpə,fī\ vb -fied; -fy·ing 1 : make insensible by or as if by drugs 2 : amaze —**stu·pe·fac·tion** \,st(y)üpə'fakshən\ n

stu·pen·dous \st(y)ü'pendəs\ adj : very big or impressive —**stu·pen·dous·ly** adv

stu·pid \'st(y)üpəd\ adj : not sensible or intelligent —**stu·pid·i·ty** \st(y)ü'pidətē\ n —**stu·pid·ly** adv

stu·por \'st(y)üpər\ n : state of being conscious but not aware or sensible —**stu·por·ous** adj

stur·dy \'stərdē\ adj -di·er; -est : strong —**stur·di·ly** \'stərd°lē\ adv —**stur·di·ness** n

stur·geon \'stərjən\ n : fish whose roe is caviar

stut·ter \'stətər\ vb or n : stammer

¹sty \'stī\ n, pl sties : pig pen

²sty, stye \'stī\ n, pl sties or styes : inflamed swelling on the edge of an eyelid

style \'stīl\ n 1 : distinctive way of speaking, writing, or acting 2 : elegant or fashionable way of living ~ vb styled; styl·ing 1 : name 2 : give a particular design or style to —**styl·ish** \'stīlish\ adj —**styl·ish·ly** adv —**styl·ish·ness** n —**styl·ist** \-əst\ n —**styl·ize** \'stī(ə)l,īz\ vb

sty·lus \'stīləs\ n, pl -li \'stī(ə)l,ī\ 1 : pointed writing tool 2 : phonograph needle

sty·mie \'stīmē\ -mied; -mie·ing : block or frustrate

suave \'swäv\ adj : well-mannered and gracious —**suave·ly** adv

¹sub \'səb\ n or vb : substitute

²sub n : submarine

sub- \,səb, 'səb, səb\ prefix 1 : under or beneath 2 : subordinate or secondary 3 : subordinate portion of 4 : with repetition of a process so as to form, stress, or deal with subordinate parts or relations 5 : somewhat 6 : nearly

subacute	subaverage
subagency	subbase
subagent	subbasement
subarctic	subbranch
subarea	subcabinet
subatmospheric	subcategory

subclass
subclassification
subclassify
subcommission
subcommunity
subcomponent
subconcept
subcontract
subcontractor
subculture
subdean
subdepartment
subdistrict
subentry
subequatorial
subfamily
subfreezing
subgroup
subhead
subheading
subhuman
subindex
subindustry
sublease
sublethal
sublevel
subliterate
subnetwork

suboceanic
suborder
subpar
subpart
subplot
subpolar
subprincipal
subprocess
subprogram
subproject
subregion
subsea
subsection
subsense
subspecialty
subspecies
substage
subsurface
subsystem
subteen
subtemperate
subtheme
subtopic
subtotal
subtreasury
subtype
subunit

sub·con·scious \ˌsəb'känchəs, 'səb-\ *adj* : existing without conscious awareness ~ *n* : part of the mind concerned with subconscious activities —**sub·con·scious·ly** *adv* —**sub·con·scious·ness** *n*

sub·di·vide \'səbdə'vīd, 'səbdə,vīd\ *vb* **1** : divide into several parts **2** : divide (a tract of land) into building lots —**sub·di·vi·sion** \-'vizhən, -,vizh-\ *n*

sub·due \səb'd(y)ü\ *vb* **-dued; -du·ing 1** : bring under control **2** : reduce the intensity of

sub·ject \'səbjikt\ *n* **1** : person under the authority of another **2** : something being discussed or studied **3** : word or word group about which something is said in a sentence ~ *adj* **1** : being under one's authority **2** : prone **3** : dependent on some condition or act ~ \səb'jekt\ *vb* **1** : bring under control **2** : cause to undergo —**sub·jec·tion** \-'jekshən\ *n*

sub·jec·tive \(,)səb'jektiv\ *adj* : deriving from an individual viewpoint or bias —**sub·jec·tive·ly** *adv* —**sub·jec·tiv·i·ty** \-jek'tivətē\ *n*

sub·ju·gate \'səbji,gāt\ *vb* **-gat·ed; -gat·ing** : bring under one's control —**sub·ju·ga·tion** \,səbji'gāshən\ *n*

sub·junc·tive \səb'jəŋktiv\ *adj* : relating to a verb form which expresses

possibility or contingency —**subjunctive** *n*

sub·let \'səb'let\ *vb* **-let; -let·ting** : rent (a property) from a lessee

sub·lime \sə'blīm\ *adj* : splendid —**sub·lim·i·ty** \-'blimətē\ *n*

sub·ma·rine \'səbmə,rēn, ,səbmə'-\ *adj* : existing, acting, or growing under the sea ~ *n* : underwater boat

sub·merge \səb'mərj\ *vb* **-merged; -merg·ing** : put or plunge under the surface of water —**sub·mer·gence** \-'mərjəns\ *n* —**sub·mers·ible** \səb'mərsəbəl\ *adj* —**sub·mer·sion** \-'mərzhən\ *n*

sub·mit \səb'mit\ *vb* **-tt- 1** : yield **2** : give or offer —**sub·mis·sion** \-'mishən\ *n* —**sub·mis·sive** \-'misiv\ *adj*

sub·nor·mal \ˌsəb'nórməl\ *adj* : falling below what is normal

sub·or·di·nate \sə'bórdnət, -ʘnət\ *adj* : lower in rank ~ *n* : one that is subordinate ~ \sə'bórdʘn,āt\ *vb* **-nat·ed; -nat·ing** : place in a lower rank or class —**sub·or·di·na·tion** \-,bórdʘn'āshən\ *n*

sub·poe·na \sə'pēnə\ *n* : summons to appear in court ~ *vb* **-naed; -na·ing** : summon with a subpoena

sub·scribe \səb'skrīb\ *vb* **-scribed; -scrib·ing 1** : give consent or approval **2** : agree to support or to receive and pay for —**sub·scrib·er** *n*

sub·scrip·tion \səb'skripshən\ *n* : order for regular receipt of a publication

sub·se·quent \'səbsikwənt, -sə,kwent\ *adj* : following after —**sub·se·quent·ly** \-,kwentlē, -kwənt-\ *adv*

sub·ser·vi·ence \səb'sərvēəns\ *n* : obsequious submission —**sub·ser·vi·en·cy** \-ənsē\ *n* —**sub·ser·vi·ent** \-ənt\ *adj*

sub·side \səb'sīd\ *vb* **-sid·ed; -sid·ing** : die down in intensity

sub·sid·iary \səb'sidē,erē\ *adj* **1** : furnishing support **2** : controlled by a main company —**subsidiary** *n*

sub·si·dize \'səbsə,dīz\ *vb* **-dized; -diz·ing** : aid with a subsidy

sub·si·dy \'səbsədē\ *n, pl* **-dies** : gift of supporting funds

sub·sist \səb'sist\ *vb* : acquire the necessities of life —**sub·sis·tence** \-'sistəns\ *n*

sub·stance \'səbstəns\ *n* **1** : essence or essential part **2** : physical material **3** : wealth

sub·stan·dard \ˌsəb'standərd, 'səb-\ *adj* : falling short of a standard or norm

sub·stan·tial \səb'stanchəl\ *adj* **1** : plentiful **2** : considerable —**sub·stan·tial·ly** *adv*

sub·stan·ti·ate \səb'stanchē,āt\ *vb* **-at·ed; -at·ing 1** : verify —**sub·stan·ti·a·tion** \-,stanchē'āshən\ *n*

sub·sti·tute \'səbstə,t(y)üt\ *n* : replacement ~ *vb* **-tut·ed; -tut·ing** : put or serve in place of another —**substitute** *adj* —**sub·sti·tu·tion** \,səbstə't(y)üshən\ *n*

sub·ter·fuge \'səbtər,fyüj\ *n* : deceptive trick

sub·ter·ra·nean \,səbtə'rānēən\, **sub·ter·ra·neous** \-nēəs\ *adj* : lying or being underground

sub·ti·tle \'səb,tīt²l\ *n* : movie caption

sub·tle \'sət²l\ *adj* **-tler** \'sətlər, -²l·ər\; **-tlest** \-ləst, -²l·əst\ **1** : hardly noticeable **2** : clever —**sub·tle·ty** \-tē\ *n* —**sub·tly** \-lē, -²l·ē\ *adv*

sub·tract \səb'trakt\ *vb* : take away (as one number from another) —**sub·trac·tion** \-'trakshən\ *n*

sub·urb \'səb,ərb\ *n* : residential area adjacent to a city —**sub·ur·ban** \sə'bərbən\ *adj or n* —**sub·ur·ban·ite** \-bə,nīt\ *n*

sub·vert \səb'vərt\ *vb* : overthrow or ruin —**sub·ver·sion** \-'vərzhən\ *n* —**sub·ver·sive** \-'vərsiv\ *adj*

sub·way \'səb,wā\ *n* : underground electric railway

suc·ceed \sək'sēd\ *vb* **1** : follow (someone) in a job, role, or title **2** : attain a desired object or end

suc·cess \-'ses\ *n* **1** : satisfactory completion of something **2** : gaining of wealth and fame **3** : one that succeeds —**suc·cess·ful** \-fəl\ *adj* —**suc·cess·ful·ly** *adv*

suc·ces·sion \sək'seshən\ *n* **1** : order, act, or right of succeeding **2** : series

suc·ces·sive \-'sesiv\ *adj* : following in order —**suc·ces·sive·ly** *adv*

suc·ces·sor \-'sesər\ *n* : one that succeeds another

suc·cinct \(,)sək'siŋkt, sə'siŋkt\ *adj* : brief —**suc·cinct·ly** *adv* —**suc·cinct·ness** *n*

suc·cor \'səkər\ *n or vb* : help

suc·co·tash \'səkə,tash\ *n* : beans and corn cooked together

suc·cu·lent \'səkyələnt\ *adj* : juicy —**suc·cu·lence** \-ləns\ *n* —**succulent** *n*

suc·cumb \sə'kəm\ *vb* **1** : give up **2** : die

such \'səch, (,)sich\ *adj* **1** : of this or that kind **2** : having a specified quality —**such** *pron or adv*

suck \'sək\ *vb* **1** : draw in liquid with

the mouth **2** : draw liquid from by or as if by mouth —**suck** *n*

suck·er \'səkər\ *n* **1** : one that sucks or clings **2** : shoot from the roots or lower part of a plant **3** : easily deceived person

suck·le \'səkəl\ *vb* **-led; -ling** : give or draw milk from the breast or udder

suck·ling \'səkliŋ\ *n* : young unweaned mammal

su·crose \'sü,krōs, -,krōz\ *n* : cane or beet sugar

suc·tion \'səkshən\ *n* **1** : act of sucking **2** : act or process of drawing in by partially exhausting the air

sud·den \'səd²n\ *adj* **1** : happening quickly or unexpectedly **2** : steep **3** : hasty —**sud·den·ly** *adv* —**sud·den·ness** *n*

suds \'sədz\ *n pl* : soapy water esp. when frothy —**sudsy** \'sədzē\ *adj*

sue \'sü\ *vb* **sued; su·ing 1** : petition **2** : bring legal action against

suede, suède \'swād\ *n* : leather with a napped surface

su·et \'süət\ *n* : hard beef fat

suf·fer \'səfər\ *vb* **1** : experience pain, loss, or hardship **2** : permit —**suf·fer·er** *n*

suf·fer·ing \-(ə)riŋ\ *n* : pain or hardship

suf·fice \sə'fīs\ *vb* **-ficed; -fic·ing** : be sufficient

suf·fi·cient \sə'fishənt\ *adj* : adequate —**suf·fi·cien·cy** \-ənsē\ *n* —**suf·fi·cient·ly** *adv*

suf·fix \'səf,iks\ *n* : letters added at the end of a word —**suffix** \'səfiks, (,)sə'fiks\ *vb* —**suf·fix·a·tion** \,səf,ik'sāshən\ *n*

suf·fo·cate \'səfə,kāt\ *vb* **-cat·ed; -cat·ing** : suffer or die or cause to die from lack of air —**suf·fo·cat·ing·ly** *adv* —**suf·fo·ca·tion** \,səfə'kāshən\ *n*

suf·frage \'səfrij\ *n* : right to vote

suf·fuse \sə'fyüz\ *vb* **-fused; -fus·ing** : spread over or through

sug·ar \'shögər\ *n* : sweet substance ~ *vb* : mix, cover, or sprinkle with sugar —**sug·ar·cane** *n* —**sug·ary** *adj*

sug·gest \sə(g)'jest\ *vb* **1** : put into someone's mind **2** : remind one by association of ideas —**sug·gest·ible** \-'jestəbəl\ *adj* —**sug·ges·tion** \-'jeschən\ *n*

sug·ges·tive \-'jestiv\ *adj* : suggesting something improper —**sug·ges·tive·ly** *adv* —**sug·ges·tive·ness** *n*

sui·cide \'süə,sīd\ *n* **1** : act of killing oneself purposely **2** : one who commits suicide —**su·i·cid·al** \,süə'sīd²l\ *adj*

suit \'süt\ n **1** : action in court to recover a right or claim **2** : number of things used or worn together **3** : one of the 4 sets of playing cards ~ vb **1** : be appropriate or becoming to **2** : meet the needs of —**suit·abil·i·ty** \₁sütə'bilətē\ n —**suit·able** \'sütəbəl\ adj —**suit·ably** adv

suit·case n : flat rectangular traveling bag

suite \'swēt, for 2 also \'süt\ n **1** : group of rooms **2** : set of matched furniture

suit·or \'sütər\ n : one who seeks to marry a woman

sul·fur, sul·phur \'səlfər\ n : nonmetallic yellow chemical element —**sul·fu·re·ous** \₁səl'fyürēəs\ adj —**sul·fu·ric** \-'fyürik\ adj —**sul·fu·rous** \-'fyürəs, 'səlf(y)ərəs\ adj

sulk \'səlk\ vb : be moodily silent —**sulk** n

sulky \'səlkē\ adj : inclined to sulk ~ n : light 2-wheeled cart —**sulk·i·ly** \'səlkəlē\ adv —**sulk·i·ness** \-kēnəs\ n

sul·len \'sələn\ adj **1** : gloomily silent **2** : dismal —**sul·len·ly** adv —**sul·len·ness** n

sul·ly \'səlē\ vb -**lied; -ly·ing** : cast doubt or disgrace on

sul·tan \'səlt²n\ n : sovereign of a Muslim state —**sul·tan·ate** \-₁āt\ n

sul·try \'səltrē\ adj -**tri·er; -est** : very hot and moist

sum \'səm\ n **1** : amount **2** : gist **3** : result of addition ~ vb -**mm-** : find the sum of

su·mac, su·mach \'s(h)ü₁mak\ n : shrub with spikes of berries

sum·ma·ry \'səmərē\ adj **1** : concise **2** : done without delay or formality ~ n, pl -**ries** : concise statement —**sum·mar·i·ly** \(₁)sə'merəlē, 'səmərəlē\ adv —**sum·ma·rize** \'səmə₁rīz\ vb

sum·ma·tion \(₁)sə'māshən\ n : a summing up esp. in court

sum·mer \'səmər\ n : season in which the sun shines most directly —**sum·mery** adj

sum·mit \'səmət\ n : highest point

sum·mon \'səmən\ vb **1** : send for or call together **2** : order to appear in court —**sum·mon·er** n

sum·mons \'səmənz\ n, pl **sum·mons·es** : an order to answer charges in court

sump·tu·ous \'səmpchə(wə)s\ adj : lavish

sun \'sən\ n **1** : shining celestial body around which the planets revolve **2** : light of the sun ~ vb -**nn-** : expose to the sun —**sun·beam** n —**sun·burn** n —**sun·glass·es** n pl —**sun·light** n

—**sun·ny** adj —**sun·rise** n —**sun·set** n —**sun·shine** n —**sun·tan** n

sun·dae \'səndē\ n : ice cream with topping

Sun·day \'səndē\ n : 1st day of the week

sun·di·al \-₁dī(ə)l\ n : device for showing time by the sun's shadow

sun·dries \'səndrēz\ n, pl : various small articles

sun·dry \-drē\ adj : several

sun·fish n : perchlike freshwater fish

sun·flow·er n : tall plant grown for its oil-rich seeds

sung past of SING

sunk past of SINK

sunk·en \'səŋkən\ adj **1** : submerged **2** : fallen in

sun·spot n : dark spot on the sun

sun·stroke n : heatstroke from the sun

sup \'səp\ vb -**pp-** : eat the evening meal

su·per \'süpər\ adj : very fine

super- \₁süpər, 'sü-\ prefix **1** : higher in quantity, quality, or degree than **2** : in addition **3** : exceeding a norm **4** : in excessive degree or intensity **5** : surpassing others of its kind **6** : situated above, on, or at the top of **7** : more inclusive than **8** : superior in status or position

superabundance	supermodern
superabundant	superpatriot
superambitious	superpatriotic
superathlete	superpatriotism
superbomb	superplane
superclean	superpolite
supercold	superport
supercolossal	superpowerful
superconvenient	superrefined
supercop	superrich
superdense	supersalesman
supereffective	superscout
superefficiency	supersecrecy
superefficient	supersecret
superenthusiasm	supersensitive
superenthusiastic	supership
superfast	supersize
supergood	supersized
supergovernment	superslick
supergroup	supersmooth
superhard	supersoft
superhero	superspecial
superheroine	superspecialist
superhuman	superspy
superintellectual	superstar
superintelligence	superstate
superintelligent	superstrength
superman	superstrong
	supersuccessful
	supersystem

supertanker	supertough
superthick	superweak
superthin	superweapon
supertight	superwoman

su·perb \su̇'pərb\ *adj* : outstanding —**su·perb·ly** *adv*

su·per·cil·i·ous \ˌsüpər'silēəs\ *adj* : haughtily contemptuous

su·per·fi·cial \ˌsüpər'fishəl\ *adj* : relating to what is only apparent —**su·per·fi·ci·al·i·ty** \-ˌfishē'alətē\ *n* —**su·per·fi·cial·ly** *adv*

su·per·flu·ous \su̇'pərflüəwəs\ *adj* : more than necessary —**su·per·flu·i·ty** \ˌsüpər'flüətē\ *n*

su·per·im·pose \ˌsüpərim'pōz\ *vb* : lay over and above something

su·per·in·tend \ˌsüp(ə)rin'tend\ *vb* : have charge and oversight of —**su·per·in·ten·dence** \-'tendəns\ *n* —**su·per·in·ten·den·cy** \-dənsē\ *n* —**su·per·in·ten·dent** \-dənt\ *n*

su·pe·ri·or \su̇'pirēər\ *adj* **1** : higher, better, or more important **2** : haughty —**superior** *n* —**su·pe·ri·or·i·ty** \-ˌpirē'örətē\ *n*

su·per·la·tive \su̇'pərlətiv\ *adj* **1** : relating to or being an adjective or adverb form that denotes an extreme level **2** : surpassing others —**superlative** *n* —**su·per·la·tive·ly** *adv*

su·per·mar·ket \'süpərˌmärkət\ *n* : self-service grocery store

su·per·nat·u·ral \ˌsüpər'nach(ə)rəl\ *adj* : beyond the observable physical world —**su·per·nat·u·ral·ly** *adv*

su·per·sede \ˌsüpər'sēd\ *vb* **-sed·ed; -sed·ing** : take the place of

su·per·son·ic \-'sänik\ *adj* : relating to speeds 1 to 5 times the speed of sound

su·per·sti·tion \ˌsüpər'stishən\ *n* : beliefs based on ignorance, fear of the unknown, or trust in magic —**su·per·sti·tious** \-əs\ *adj*

su·per·struc·ture \'süpərˌstrəkchər\ *n* : something built on a base or as a vertical extension

su·per·vene \ˌsüpər'vēn\ *vb* **-vened; -ven·ing** : occur unexpectedly —**su·per·ve·nient** \-'vēnyənt\ *adj*

su·per·vise \'süpərˌvīz\ *vb* **-vised; -vis·ing** : have charge of —**su·per·vi·sion** \ˌsüpər'vizhən\ *n* —**su·per·vi·sor** \'süpərˌvīzər\ *n* —**su·per·vi·so·ry** \ˌsüpər'vīz(ə)rē\ *adj*

su·pine \su̇'pīn\ *adj* **1** : lying on the back **2** : indifferent or abject

sup·per \'səpər\ *n* : evening meal

sup·plant \sə'plant\ *vb* : take the place of

sup·ple \'səpəl\ *adj* **-pler; -plest** : able to bend easily

sup·ple·ment \'səpləmənt\ *n* : something that adds to or makes up for a lack —**supplement** *vb* —**sup·ple·men·tal** \ˌsəplə'mentᵊl\ *adj* —**sup·ple·men·ta·ry** \-'ment(ə)rē\ *adj*

sup·pli·ant \'səplēənt\ *n* : one who supplicates

sup·pli·cate \'səpləˌkāt\ *vb* **-cat·ed; -cat·ing** **1** : pray to God **2** : ask earnestly and humbly —**sup·pli·cant** \-likənt\ *n* —**sup·pli·ca·tion** \ˌsəplə'kāshən\ *n*

sup·ply \sə'plī\ *vb* **-plied; -ply·ing** : furnish ∼ *n, pl* **-plies 1** : amount needed or available **2** *pl* : provisions —**sup·pli·er** \-'plī(ə)r\ *n*

sup·port \sə'pōrt\ *vb* **1** : take sides with **2** : provide with food, clothing, and shelter **3** : hold up or serve as a foundation for —**support** *n* —**sup·port·able** *adj* —**sup·port·er** *n*

sup·pose \sə'pōz\ *vb* **-posed; -pos·ing 1** : assume to be true **2** : expect **3** : think probable —**sup·po·si·tion** \ˌsəpə'zishən\ *n*

sup·pos·i·to·ry \sə'päzəˌtōrē\ *n, pl* **-ries** : medicated material for insertion (as into the rectum)

sup·press \sə'pres\ *vb* **1** : put an end to by authority **2** : keep from being known —**sup·pres·sion** \-'preshən\ *n*

sup·pu·rate \'səpyəˌrāt\ *vb* **-rat·ed; -rat·ing** : form or give off pus —**sup·pu·ra·tion** \ˌsəpyə'rāshən\ *n*

su·prem·a·cy \su̇'preməsē\ *n, pl* **-cies** : supreme power or authority

su·preme \su̇'prēm\ *adj* **1** : highest in rank or authority **2** : greatest possible —**su·preme·ly** *adv*

Supreme Being *n* : God

sur·charge \'sərˌchärj\ *n* **1** : excessive load or burden **2** : extra fee or cost

sure \'shu̇r\ *adj* **sur·er; sur·est 1** : confident **2** : reliable **3** : not to be disputed **4** : bound to happen ∼ *adv* : surely —**sure·ly** *adv* —**sure·ness** *n*

sure·ty \'shu̇rətē\ *n, pl* **-ties 1** : guarantee **2** : one who gives a guarantee for another person

surf \'sərf\ *n* : waves that break on the shore ∼ *vb* : ride the surf —**surf·board** *n* —**surf·er** *n* —**surf·ing** *n*

sur·face \'sərfəs\ *n* **1** : the outside of an object or body **2** : outward aspect ∼ *vb* **-faced; -fac·ing** **1** : rise to the surface

sur·feit \'sərfət\ *n* **1** : excess **2** : excessive indulgence (as in food or drink) **3** : disgust caused by excess ∼ *vb*

: feed, supply, or indulge to the point of surfeit

surge \'sərj\ *vb* **surged; surg·ing** : rise and fall in or as if in waves ∼ *n* : sudden increase

sur·geon \'sərjən\ *n* : physician who specializes in surgery

sur·gery \'sərj(ə)rē\ *n, pl* **-ger·ies** : medical treatment involving cutting open the body

sur·gi·cal \'sərjikəl\ *adj* : relating to surgeons or surgery —**sur·gi·cal·ly** *adv*

sur·ly \'sərlē\ *adj* **-li·er; -est** : cross —**sur·li·ness** *n*

sur·mise \sər'mīz\ *vb* **-mised; -mis·ing** : guess —**surmise** *n*

sur·mount \-'maúnt\ *vb* **1** : defeat **2** : get to or be the top of

sur·name \'sər,nām\ *n* : family name

sur·pass \sər'pas\ *vb* : go beyond or exceed —**sur·pass·ing·ly** *adv*

sur·plice \'sərpləs\ *n* : loose white outer ecclesiastical vestment

sur·plus \'sər,pləs\ *n* : quantity left over

sur·prise \sə(r)'prīz\ *vb* **-prised; -pris·ing 1** : come upon or affect unexpectedly **2** : amaze —**surprise** *n* —**sur·pris·ing** *adj* —**sur·pris·ing·ly** *adv*

sur·ren·der \sə'rendər\ *vb* : give up oneself or a possession to another ∼ *n* : act of surrendering

sur·rep·ti·tious \,sərəp'tishəs\ *adj* : done, made, or acquired by stealth —**sur·rep·ti·tious·ly** *adv*

sur·rey \'sərē\ *n, pl* **-reys** : horse-drawn carriage

sur·round \sə'raúnd\ *vb* : enclose on all sides

sur·round·ings \sə'raúndiŋz\ *n pl* : objects, conditions, or area around something

sur·veil·lance \sər'vāləns, -'vālyəns, -'vāəns\ *n* : careful watch

sur·vey \sər'vā\ *vb* **-veyed; -vey·ing 1** : look over and examine closely **2** : make a survey of (as a tract of land) ∼ \'sər,-\ *n, pl* **-veys** : inspection **2** : process of measuring (as land) —**sur·vey·or** \-ər\ *n*

sur·vive \sər'vīv\ *vb* **-vived; -viv·ing 1** : remain alive or in existence **2** : outlive or outlast —**sur·viv·al** *n* —**sur·vi·vor** \-'vīvər\ *n*

sus·cep·ti·ble \sə'septəbəl\ *adj* : likely to allow or be affected by something —**sus·cep·ti·bil·i·ty** \-,septə'bilətē\ *n*

sus·pect \'səs,pekt, sə'spekt\ *adj* : regarded with suspicion ∼ \'səs,pekt\ *n* : one who is suspected (as of a crime) ∼ \sə'spekt\ *vb* **1** : have

doubts of **2** : believe guilty without proof **3** : guess

sus·pend \sə'spend\ *vb* **1** : temporarily stop or keep from a function or job **2** : withhold (judgment) temporarily **3** : hang

sus·pend·er \sə'spendər\ *n* : one of 2 supporting straps for trousers which pass over the shoulders

sus·pense \sə'spens\ *n* : excitement and uncertainty as to outcome —**suspense·ful** *adj*

sus·pen·sion \sə'spenchən\ *n* : act of suspending or the state or period of being suspended

sus·pi·cion \sə'spishən\ *n* : act of suspecting something **2** : trace

sus·pi·cious \-əs\ *adj* **1** : arousing suspicion **2** : inclined to suspect —**sus·pi·cious·ly** *adv*

sus·tain \sə'stān\ *vb* **1** : provide with nourishment **2** : keep going **3** : hold up **4** : suffer **5** : support or prove

sus·te·nance \'səstənəns\ *n* **1** : nourishment **2** : something that sustains or supports

swab \'swäb\ *n* **1** : mop **2** : wad of absorbent material for applying medicine ∼ *vb* **-bb-** : use a swab on

swad·dle \'swäd'l\ *vb* **-dled; -dling** \'swädliŋ, -²liŋ\ : bind (an infant) in bands of cloth

swag·ger \'swagər\ *vb* **-gered; -ger·ing 1** : walk with a conceited swing **2** : boast —**swagger** *n*

[1]swal·low \'swälō\ *n* : small migratory bird

[2]swallow *vb* **1** : take into the stomach through the throat **2** : envelop or take in **3** : accept too easily **4** : endure **5** : retract or repress —**swallow** *n*

swam *past of* SWIM

swamp \'swämp\ *n* : wet spongy land ∼ *vb* : deluge (as with water) —**swampy** *adj*

swan \'swän\ *n* : white long-necked swimming bird

swap \'swäp\ *vb* **-pp-** : trade —**swap** *n*

swarm \'swórm\ *n* **1** : mass of honeybees leaving a hive to start a new colony **2** : large crowd moving together ∼ *vb* : gather in a swarm

swar·thy \'swórthē, -thē\ *adj* **-thi·er; -est** : dark in complexion

swash·buck·ler \'swäsh,bəklər\ *n* : boasting blustering soldier or daredevil —**swash·buck·ling** \-,bək(ə)liŋ\ *adj*

swat \'swät\ *vb* **-tt-** : hit sharply —**swat** *n* —**swat·ter** *n*

swatch \'swäch\ *n* : sample piece (as of fabric)

swath \'swäth, 'swȯth\, **swathe** \'swäth, 'swȯth, 'swāth\ *n* : row or path cut (as through grass)

swathe \'swäth, 'swȯth, 'swāth\ *vb* **swathed; swath·ing** : wrap with or as if with a bandage

sway \'swā\ *vb* 1 : swing gently from side to side 2 : influence ~ *n* 1 : gentle swinging from side to side 2 : controlling power or influence

swear \'swaȯr\ *vb* **swore** \'swōr\, **sworn** \'swōrn\; **swear·ing** 1 : make or cause to make a solemn statement or promise under oath 2 : use profane language —**swear·er** *n* —**swear·ing** *n*

sweat \'swet\ *vb* **sweat** *or* **sweat·ed; sweat·ing** 1 : excrete salty moisture from glands of the skin 2 : form drops of moisture on the surface 3 : work or cause to work hard ~ *n* 1 : liquid exuded through pores from glands (**sweat glands**) of the skin 2 : moisture gathering on a surface in drops —**sweaty** *adj*

sweat·er \'swetər\ *n* : knitted jacket or pullover

sweep \'swēp\ *vb* **swept** \'swept\; **sweep·ing** 1 : remove or clean by a brush or a single forceful wipe (as of the hand) 2 : move over with speed and force (as of the hand) 3 : move or extend in a wide curve ~ *n* 1 : a clearing off or away 2 : single forceful wipe or swinging movement 3 : scope —**sweep·er** *n* —**sweep·ing** *adj*

sweep·stakes \'swēp,stāks\ *n, pl* **sweep·stakes** : contest in which the entire prize may go to the winner

sweet \'swēt\ *adj* 1 : being or causing the pleasing taste typical of sugar 2 : not stale or spoiled 3 : not salted 4 : pleasant 5 : regarded with love or fondness ~ *n* : something sweet —**sweet·ly** *adv* —**sweet·ness** *n*

sweet·en \'swēt⁰n\ *vb* : make sweet —**sweet·en·er** \'swētnər, -⁰nər\ *n*

sweet·heart *n* : person one loves

sweet potato *n* : sweet yellow edible root of a tropical vine

swell \'swel\ *vb* **swelled; swelled** *or* **swol·len** \'swōlən\; **swell·ing** 1 : enlarge 2 : bulge 3 : fill or be filled with emotion ~ *n* 1 : increase 2 : long crestless wave

swel·ter \'sweltər\ *vb* : be uncomfortable from excessive heat

swept *past of* SWEEP

swerve \'swərv\ *vb* **swerved; swerv·ing**

: move abruptly aside from a course —**swerve** *n*

¹swift \'swift\ *adj* 1 : moving with great speed 2 : occurring suddenly —**swift·ly** *adv* —**swift·ness** *n*

²swift *n* : small insect-eating bird

swig \'swig\ *vb* **-gg-** : drink in gulps —**swig** *n*

swill \'swil\ *vb* : swallow greedily ~ *n* 1 : animal food of refuse and liquid 2 : garbage

swim \'swim\ *vb* **swam** \'swam\; **swum** \'swəm\; **swim·ming** 1 : propel oneself in water 2 : float in or be surrounded with a liquid 3 : have a sensation of dizziness ~ *n* : act or period of swimming —**swim·mer** *n*

swin·dle \'swind⁰l\ *vb* **-dled; -dling** \-(d)liŋ, -d⁰liŋ\ : cheat (someone) of money or property —**swindle** *n* —**swin·dler** \-(d)lər, -d⁰lər\ *n*

swine \'swīn\ *n, pl* **swine** : short-legged hoofed mammal with a snout —**swin·ish** \'swīnish\ *adj*

swing \'swiŋ\ *vb* **swung** \'swəŋ\; **swing·ing** 1 : move rapidly in an arc 2 : sway or cause to sway back and forth 3 : hang so as to sway or sag 4 : turn on a hinge or pivot 5 : accomplish through effort or influence ~ *n* 1 : act or instance of swinging 2 : swinging movement (as in trying to hit something) 3 : suspended seat for swinging —**swing** *adj* —**swing·er** *n*

swipe \'swīp\ *n* : strong sweeping blow ~ *vb* **swiped; swip·ing** 1 : strike or wipe with a sweeping motion 2 : steal esp. with a quick movement

swirl \'swərl\ *vb* : eddy —**swirl** *n*

swish \'swish\ *n* : hissing, sweeping, or brushing sound —**swish** *vb*

switch \'swich\ *n* 1 : slender flexible whip or twig 2 : blow with a switch 3 : shift, change, or reversal 4 : device that opens or closes an electrical circuit ~ *vb* 1 : punish or urge on with a switch 2 : change or reverse roles, positions, or subjects 3 : operate a switch of

switch·board *n* : panel of switches to control electrical circuits

swiv·el \'swivəl\ *vb* **-eled** *or* **-elled; -el·ling** *or* **-el·ing** : swing or turn on a pivot —**swivel** *n*

swollen *past part of* SWELL

swoon \'swün\ *n* : faint —**swoon** *vb*

swoop \'swüp\ *vb* : make a swift diving attack —**swoop** *n*

sword \'sōrd\ *n* : sharp cutting weapon with a long blade

sword-fish n : large ocean fish with a long swordlike projection

swore past of SWEAR

sworn past part of SWEAR

swum past part of SWIM

swung past of SWING

syc-a-more \'sikə,mōr\ n : shade tree

sy-co-phant \'sikəfənt\ n : servile flatterer —**syc-o-phan-tic** \,sikə'fantik\ adj

syl-la-ble \'siləbəl\ n : unit of a spoken word —**syl-lab-ic** \sə'labik\ adj

syl-la-bus \'siləbəs\ n, pl -**bi** \-,bī\ or -**bus-es** : summary of main topics (as of a course of study)

syl-van \'silvən\ adj 1 : living or located in a wooded area 2 : abounding in woods

sym-bol \'simbəl\ n : something that represents or suggests another thing —**sym-bol-ic** \sim'bälik\, **sym-bol-i-cal** \-ikəl\ adj —**sym-bol-i-cal-ly** adv

sym-bol-ism \'simbə,lizəm\ n : representation of meanings with symbols

sym-bol-ize \'simbə,līz\ vb -ized; -iz-ing : serve as a symbol of —**sym-bol-iza-tion** \,simbələ'zāshən\ n

sym-me-try \'simətrē\ n, pl -tries : regularity and balance in the arrangement of parts —**sym-met-ri-cal** \sə'metrikəl\ adj —**sym-met-ri-cal-ly** \-k(ə)lē\ adv

sym-pa-thize \'simpə,thīz\ vb -thized; -thiz-ing : feel or show sympathy —**sym-pa-thiz-er** n

sym-pa-thy \'simpəthē\ n, pl -thies 1 : ability to understand or share the feelings or interests of another 2 : expression of sorrow for another's misfortune —**sym-pa-thet-ic** \,simpə'thetik\ adj —**sym-pa-thet-i-cal-ly** \-ik(ə)lē\ adv

sym-pho-ny \'simfənē\ n, pl -nies : composition for an orchestra or the orchestra itself —**sym-phon-ic** \sim'fänik\ adj

sym-po-sium \sim'pōzēəm\ n, pl -sia \-zēə\ or -siums : conference at which a topic is discussed

symp-tom \'simptəm\ n : unusual feeling or reaction that is a sign of disease —**symp-tom-at-ic** \,simptə'matik\ adj

syn-a-gogue, syn-a-gog \'sinə,gäg\ n : Jewish house of worship

syn-chro-nize \'siŋkrə,nīz, 'sin-\ vb -nized; -niz-ing 1 : occur or cause to occur at the same instant 2 : cause to agree in time —**syn-chro-ni-za-tion** \,siŋkrənə'zāshən, ,sin-\ n

syn-co-pa-tion \,siŋkə'pāshən, ,sin-\ n : shifting of the regular musical accent to the weak beat —**syn-co-pate** \'siŋkə,pāt, 'sin-\ vb

syn-di-cate \'sindikət\ n : business association ~ \-də,kāt\ vb -cat-ed; -cat-ing 1 : form a syndicate 2 : publish through a syndicate

syn-drome \'sin,drōm\ n : particular group of symptoms

syn-onym \'sinə,nim\ n : word with the same meaning as another —**syn-on-y-mous** \sə'nänəməs\ adj —**syn-on-y-my** \-mē\ n

syn-op-sis \sə'näpsəs\ n, pl -op-ses \-,sēz\ : condensed statement or outline

syn-tax \'sin,taks\ n : way in which words are put together —**syn-tac-tic** \sin'taktik\ adj —**syn-tac-ti-cal** \-tikəl\ adj

syn-the-sis \'sinthəsəs\ n, pl -the-ses \-,sēz\ : combination of parts or elements into a whole —**syn-the-size** \-,sīz\ vb

syn-thet-ic \sin'thetik\ adj : artificially made —synthetic —**syn-thet-i-cal-ly** \-ik(ə)lē\ adv

syph-i-lis \'sif(ə)ləs\ n : venereal disease —**syph-i-lit-ic** \,sifə'litik\ adj or n

sy-ringe \sə'rinj, 'sirinj\ n : plunger device for injecting or withdrawing liquids

syr-up \'sərəp, 'sirəp\ n : thick sticky sweet liquid —**syr-upy** adj

sys-tem \'sistəm\ n 1 : arrangement of units that function together 2 : regular order —**sys-tem-at-ic** \,sistə'matik\, **sys-tem-at-i-cal** \-ikəl\ adj —**sys-tem-at-i-cal-ly** adv —**sys-tem-atize** \'sistəmə,tīz\ vb

sys-tem-ic \sis'temik\ adj : relating to the whole body

T

t \'tē\ *n, pl* **t's, ts** \'tēz\ : 20th letter of the alphabet

tab \'tab\ *n* **1** : short projecting flap 2 *pl* : careful watch

tab-by \'tabē\ *n, pl* **-bies** : domestic cat

tab-er-na-cle \'tabər,nakəl\ *n* : house of worship

ta-ble \'tābəl\ *n* **1** : piece of furniture having a smooth slab fixed on legs 2 : supply of food 3 : condensed list —**ta-ble-cloth** *n* —**ta-ble-top** *n* —**ble-ware** *n* —**tab-u-lar** \'tabyələr\ *adj*

tab-leau \'tab,lō\ *n, pl* **-leaux** \-,lōz\ *also* **-leaus** *n* : graphic description 2 : depiction of a scene by people in costume

ta-ble-spoon *n* **1** : large serving spoon 2 : measuring spoon holding ½ fluidounce —**ta-ble-spoon-ful** \-,fül\ *n*

tab-let \'tablət\ *n* **1** : flat slab suited for an inscription 2 : collection of sheets of paper glued together at one edge 3 : disk-shaped pill

tab-loid \'tab,lóid\ *n* : newspaper of small page size

ta-boo \tə'bü, ta-\ *adj* : banned esp. as immoral or dangerous —**taboo** *n or vb*

tab-u-late \'tabyə,lāt\ *vb* **-lat-ed; -lat-ing** : put in the form of a table —**tab-u-la-tion** \,tabyə'lāshən\ *n* —**tab-u-la-tor** \'tabyə,lātər\ *n*

tac-it \'tasət\ *adj* : implied but not expressed —**tac-it-ly** *adv* —**tac-it-ness** *n*

tac-i-turn \'tasə,tərn\ *adj* : not inclined to talk —**tac-i-tur-ni-ty** \,tasə'tərnətē\ *n*

tack \'tak\ *n* **1** : small sharp nail 2 : course of action ~ *vb* **1** : fasten with tacks 2 : add on

tack-le \'takəl, *naut often* 'tāk-\ *n* **1** : equipment 2 : arrangement of ropes and pulleys 3 : act of tackling ~ *vb* **-led; -ling** **1** : seize or throw down 2 : start dealing with

¹tacky \'takē\ *adj* **tack-i-er; -est** : sticky to the touch

²tacky *adj* **tack-i-er; -est** : cheap or gaudy

tact \'takt\ *n* : sense of the proper thing to say or do —**tact-ful** \-fəl\ *adj* —**tact-ful-ly** *adv* —**tact-less** *adj* —**tact-less-ly** *adv*

tac-tic \'taktik\ *n* : action as part of a plan

tac-tics \'taktiks\ *n sing or pl* **1** : science of maneuvering forces in com-

bat 2 : skill of using available means to reach an end —**tac-ti-cal** \-tikəl\ *adj* —**tac-ti-cian** \tak'tishən\ *n*

tac-tile \'taktəl, -,tīl\ *adj* : relating to or perceptible through the sense of touch

tad-pole \'tad,pōl\ *n* : larval frog or toad with tail and gills

taf-fe-ta \'tafətə\ *n* : crisp lustrous fabric (as of silk)

taf-fy \'tafē\ *n, pl* **-fies** : candy stretched until porous

¹tag \'tag\ *n* **1** : piece of hanging or attached material ~ *vb* **-gg- 1** : provide or mark with a tag 2 : follow closely

²tag *n* : children's game of trying to catch one another ~ *vb* : touch a person in tag

tail \'tāl\ *n* **1** : rear end or a growth extending from the rear end of an animal 2 : back or last part 3 : the reverse of a coin ~ *vb* : follow —**tailed** \'tāld\ *adj* —**tail-less** *adj*

tail-light *n* : red warning light at the back of a vehicle

tai-lor \'tālər\ *n* : one who makes or alters garments ~ *vb* **1** : fashion or alter (clothes) 2 : make or adapt for a special purpose

tail-spin *n* : spiral dive by an airplane

taint \'tānt\ *vb* : affect or become affected with something bad and esp. decay ~ *n* : trace of decay or corruption

take \'tāk\ *vb* **took** \'tůk\, **tak-en** \'tākən\; **tak-ing 1** : get into one's possession 2 : become affected by 3 : receive into one's body (as by eating) 4 : pick out or remove 5 : use for transportation 6 : need or make use of 7 : lead, carry, or cause to go to another place 8 : undertake and do, make, or perform ~ *n* : amount taken —**tak-er** *n* —**take advantage of** : profit by —**take exception** : object —**take off** *vb* **1** : remove 2 : go away 3 : mimic 4 : begin flight —**take over** *vb* : assume control or possession of or responsibility for —**take-over** *n*

take-off *n* : act or instance of taking off

talc \'talk\ *n* : soft mineral used in making toilet powder (**tal-cum pow-der** \'talkəm-\)

tale \'tāl\ *n* **1** : story or anecdote 2 : falsehood

tal-ent \'talənt\ *n* : natural mental, creative, or artistic ability —**tal·ent·ed** adj

tal·is·man \'taləsmən, -əz-\ n, pl **-mans** : object thought to act as a charm

talk \'tȯk\ vb 1 : express one's thoughts in speech 2 : discuss 3 : influence to a position or course of action by talking ~ n 1 : act of talking 2 : formal discussion 3 : rumor 4 : informal lecture —**talk·ative** \-ətiv\ adj —**talk·er** n

tall \'tȯl\ adj : extending to a great or specified height —**tall·ness** n

tal·low \'talō\ n : hard white animal fat used esp. in soap and lubricants

tal·ly \'talē\ n, pl **-lies** : recorded amount ~ vb **-lied; -ly·ing** 1 : add or count up 2 : match

tal·on \'talən\ n : bird's claw

tam \'tam\ n : tam-o'-shanter

tam·bou·rine \ˌtambə'rēn\ n : small drum with loose disks at the sides

tame \'tām\ adj **tam·er; tam·est** 1 : changed from being wild to being controllable by man 2 : docile 3 : dull ~ vb **tamed; tam·ing** : make or become tame —**tam·able, tame·able** adj —**tame·ly** adv —**tame·ness** n —**tam·er** n

tam·o'-shan·ter \'taməˌshantər\ n : Scottish woolen cap with a wide flat circular crown

tamp \'tamp\ vb : drive down or in by a series of light blows

tam·per \'tampər\ vb : interfere so as to change for the worse

tan \'tan\ vb **-nn-** 1 : change (hide) into leather esp. by soaking in a liquid containing tannin 2 : make or become brown (as by exposure to the sun) ~ n 1 : brown skin color induced by the sun 2 : light yellowish brown —**tan·ner** n —**tan·nery** \'tan(ə)rē\ n

tan·dem \'tandəm\ adv : one behind another

tang \'taŋ\ n : sharp distinctive flavor —**tangy** adj

tan·gent \'tanjənt\ adj : touching a curve or surface ~ n 1 : tangent line, curve, or surface 2 : abrupt change of course —**tan·gen·tial** \tan'jenchəl\ adj

tan·ger·ine \'tanjəˌrēn, ˌtanjə'-\ n : deep orange citrus fruit

tan·gi·ble \'tanjəbəl\ adj 1 : able to be touched 2 : substantially real —**tan·gi·bil·i·ty** \ˌtanjə'bilətē\ n —**tan·gi·bly** adv

tan·gle \'taŋgəl\ vb **-gled; -gling** : unite

in intricate confusion ~ n : tangled twisted mass

tan·go \'taŋgō\ n, pl **-gos** : dance of Spanish-American origin —**tango** vb

tank \'taŋk\ n : large artificial receptacle for liquids 2 : armored military vehicle —**tank·ful** n

tan·kard \'taŋkərd\ n : tall one-handled drinking vessel

tank·er \'taŋkər\ n : vehicle or vessel with tanks for transporting a liquid

tan·nin \'tanən\ n : substance of plant origin used in tanning and dyeing

tan·ta·lize \'tant°lˌīz\ vb **-lized; -liz·ing** : tease or torment by keeping something desirable just out of reach —**tan·ta·liz·er** n —**tan·ta·liz·ing·ly** adv

tan·ta·mount \'tantəˌmaȯnt\ adj : equivalent in value or meaning

tan·trum \'tantrəm\ n : fit of bad temper

1tap \'tap\ n 1 : faucet 2 : act of tapping ~ vb **-pp-** 1 : pierce so as to draw off fluid 2 : connect into —**tap·per** n

2tap vb **-pp-** 1 : rap lightly 2 : make (as a hole) by repeated light blows ~ n 1 : light stroke or its sound

tape \'tāp\ n 1 : narrow flexible strip (as of cloth, plastic, or metal) 2 : tape measure ~ vb **taped; tap·ing** 1 : fasten with tape 2 : record on tape

tape measure n : strip of tape marked in units for use in measuring

ta·per \'tāpər\ n 1 : slender wax candle 2 : gradual lessening of width in a long object ~ vb 1 : make or become smaller toward one end 2 : diminish gradually

tap·es·try \'tapəstrē\ n, pl **-tries** : heavy handwoven ruglike wall hanging

tape·worm n : long flat intestinal worm

tap·i·o·ca \ˌtapē'ōkə\ n : a granular starch used esp. in puddings

tar \'tär\ n 1 : thick dark sticky liquid distilled (as from coal) ~ vb **-rr-** : treat or smear with tar

ta·ran·tu·la \tə'ranch(ə)lə, -'rant°lə\ n : large hairy usu. harmless spider

tar·dy \'tärdē\ adj **-di·er; -est** : late —**tar·di·ly** \'tärd°lē\ adv —**tar·di·ness** n

tar·get \'tärgət\ n 1 : mark to shoot at 2 : goal to be achieved ~ vb 1 : make a target of 2 : establish as a goal

tar·iff \'tarəf\ n 1 : duty or rate of duty imposed on imported goods 2 : schedule of tariffs, rates, or charges

tar·nish \'tärnish\ vb : make or become dull or discolored —**tarnish** n

tar·pau·lin \tär'pȯlən, 'tärpə-\ n : waterproof protective covering

tar·ry \'tarē\ vb -ried; -ry·ing : be slow in leaving

¹tart \'tärt\ adj 1 : pleasantly sharp to the taste 2 : caustic —**tart·ly** adv —**tart·ness** n

²tart n : small pie

tar·tan \'tärt°n\ n : woolen fabric with a plaid design

tar·tar \'tärtər\ n : hard crust on the teeth —**tar·tar·ic** \tär'tarik\ adj

task \'task\ n : assigned work

task·mas·ter n : one that burdens another with labor

tas·sel \'tasəl, 'täs-\ n : hanging ornament made of a bunch of cords fastened at one end

taste \'tāst\ vb tast·ed; tast·ing 1 : try or determine the flavor of 2 : eat or drink in small quantities 3 : have a specific flavor ∼ n 1 : small amount tasted 2 : bit 3 : special sense that identifies sweet, sour, bitter, or salty qualities 4 : individual preference 5 : critical appreciation of quality —**taste·ful** \-fəl\ adj —**taste·ful·ly** adv —**taste·less** adj —**taste·less·ly** adv —**tast·er** n —**tasty** adj

tat·ter \'tatər\ n 1 : part torn and left hanging 2 pl : tattered clothing ∼ vb : make or become ragged

tat·tle \'tat°l\ vb -tled; -tling : inform on someone —**tat·tler** \'tatlər, -°lər\ n

tat·tle·tale n : one that tattles

tat·too \ta'tü\ vb : mark the skin with indelible designs or figures —**tattoo** n

taught past of TEACH

taunt \'tȯnt\ n : sarcastic challenge or insult —**taunt** vb —**taunt·er** n

taut \'tȯt\ adj : tightly drawn —**taut·ly** adv —**taut·ness** n

tav·ern \'tavərn\ n : establishment where liquors are sold to be drunk on the premises

taw·dry \'tȯdrē\ adj -dri·er; -est : cheap and gaudy

taw·ny \'tȯnē\ adj -ni·er; -est : brownish orange

tax \'taks\ vb 1 : impose a tax on 2 : charge 3 : put under stress ∼ n 1 : charge by authority for public purposes 2 : strain —**tax·able** adj —**tax·a·tion** \tak'sāshən\ n —**tax·pay·er** n —**tax·pay·ing** adj

taxi \'taksē\ n, pl **tax·is** \-sēz\ : automobile transporting passengers for a fare ∼ vb **tax·ied; taxi·ing** or **taxy·ing; tax·is** or **tax·ies** 1 : transport or go by taxi 2 : move along the ground before takeoff or after landing

taxi·cab \'taksē,kab\ n : taxi

taxi·der·my \'taksə,dərmē\ n : art of stuffing and mounting animal skins —**taxi·der·mist** \-məst\ n

tea \'tē\ n : cured leaves of an oriental shrub or a drink made from these —**tea·cup** n —**tea·pot** n

teach \'tēch\ vb **taught** \'tȯt\; **teach·ing** 1 : tell or show the fundamentals or skills of something 2 : cause to know the consequences 3 : impart knowledge of —**teach·able** adj —**teach·er** n —**teach·ing** n

teak \'tēk\ n : East Indian timber tree or its wood

tea·ket·tle \'tē,ket°l, -,kit-\ n : covered kettle with a handle and spout for boiling water

teal \'tēl\ n, pl **teal** or **teals** : small short-necked wild duck

team \'tēm\ n 1 : draft animals harnessed together 2 : number of people organized for a game or work ∼ vb : form or work together as a team —**team** adj —**team·mate** n —**team·work** n

team·ster \'tēmstər\ n : one that drives a team or truck

¹tear \'tiər\ n : drop of salty liquid that moistens the eye —**tear·ful** \-fəl\ adj —**tear·ful·ly** adv

²tear \'taər\ vb **tore** \'tōr\; **torn** \'tōrn\; **tear·ing** 1 : separate or pull apart by force 2 : move or act with violence or haste ∼ n : act or result of tearing

tease \'tēz\ vb **teased; teas·ing** : annoy by goading, coaxing, or tantalizing ∼ n 1 : act of teasing or state of being teased 2 : one that teases

tea·spoon \'tē,spün\ n 1 : small spoon for stirring or sipping 2 : measuring spoon holding ⅙ fluidounce —**tea·spoon·ful** \-,fûl\ n

teat \'tit, 'tēt\ n : protuberance through which milk is drawn from an udder or breast

tech·ni·cal \'teknikəl\ adj 1 : having or relating to special mechanical or scientific knowledge 2 : by strict interpretation of rules —**tech·ni·cal·ly** \-k(ə)lē\ adv

tech·ni·cal·i·ty \,teknə'kalətē\ n, pl -ties : detail meaningful only to a specialist

technical sergeant n : noncommissioned officer in the air force ranking next below a master sergeant

tech·ni·cian \tek'nishən\ n : person with the technique of a specialized skill

tech·nique \tek'nēk\ *n* : manner of accomplishing something

tech·nol·o·gy \tek'nälajē\ *n, pl* **-gies** : applied science —**tech·no·log·i·cal** \,teknə'läjikəl\ *adj*

te·dious \'tēdēəs, 'tējəs\ *adj* : wearisome from length or dullness —**te·dious·ly** *adv* —**te·dious·ness** *n*

te·di·um \'tēdēəm\ *n* : tedious state or quality

tee \'tē\ *n* : mound or peg on which a golf ball is placed before beginning play —**tee** *vb*

teem \'tēm\ *vb* : become filled to overflowing

teen·age \'tēn,āj\, **teen·aged** \-,ājd\ *adj* : relating to people in their teens —**teen·ag·er** \-,ājər\ *n*

teens \'tēnz\ *n pl* : years 13 to 19 in a person's life

tee·pee *var of* TEPEE

tee·ter \'tētər\ *vb* 1 : move unsteadily 2 : seesaw —**teeter** *n*

teeth *pl of* TOOTH

teethe \'tēth\ *vb* **teethed; teeth·ing** : grow teeth

tele·cast \'teli,kast\ *vb* **-cast; -cast·ing** : broadcast by television —**telecast** *n* —**tele·cast·er** *n*

tele·gram \'telə,gram\ *n* : message sent by telegraph

tele·graph \-,graf\ *n* : system for communication by electrical transmission of coded signals ~ *vb* : send by telegraph —**te·leg·ra·pher** \tə'legrəfər\ *n* —**te·leg·ra·phist** \-fəst\ *n*

te·lep·a·thy \tə'lepəthē\ *n* : apparent communication without known sensory means —**tele·path·ic** \,telə'pathik\ *adj* —**tele·path·i·cal·ly** \-ik(ə)lē\ *adv*

tele·phone \'telə,fōn\ *n* : instrument or system for electrical transmission of spoken words ~ *vb* **-phoned; -phon·ing** : communicate with by telephone —**tele·phon·er** *n*

tele·scope \-,skōp\ *n* : tube-shaped optical instrument for viewing distant objects ~ *vb* **-scoped; -scop·ing** : slide or cause to slide inside another similar section —**tele·scop·ic** \,telə'skäpik\ *adj*

tele·vise \'telə,vīz\ *vb* **-vised; -vis·ing** : broadcast by television

tele·vi·sion \-,vizhən\ *n* : transmission and reproduction of images by radio waves

tell \'tel\ *vb* **told** \'tōld\; **tell·ing** 1 : count 2 : relate in detail 3 : reveal 4 : give information or an order to 5 : determine

tell·er \'telər\ *n* 1 : one that relates or counts 2 : bank employee handling money

te·mer·i·ty \tə'merətē\ *n, pl* **-ties** : boldness

tem·per \'tempər\ *vb* 1 : dilute or soften 2 : toughen ~ *n* 1 : characteristic attitude or feeling 2 : toughness 3 : disposition or control over one's emotions

tem·per·a·ment \'temp(ə)rəmənt\ *n* : characteristic frame of mind —**tem·per·a·men·tal** \,temp(ə)rə'ment³l\ *adj*

tem·per·ance \'temp(ə)rəns\ *n* : moderation in or abstinence from indulgence and esp. the use of intoxicating drink

tem·per·ate \'temp(ə)rət\ *adj* : moderate

tem·per·a·ture \'tempər,chùr, -p(ə)rə,chùr, -chər\ *n* 1 : degree of hotness or coldness 2 : fever

tem·pest \'tempəst\ *n* : violent storm —**tem·pes·tu·ous** \tem'peschəwəs\ *adj*

¹**tem·ple** \'tempəl\ *n* : place of worship

²**temple** *n* : flattened space on each side of the forehead

tem·po \'tempō\ *n, pl* **-pi** \-(,)pē\ *or* **-pos** : rate of speed

tem·po·ral \'temp(ə)rəl\ *adj* : relating to time or to secular concerns

tem·po·rary \'tempə,rerē\ *adj* : lasting for a short time only —**tem·po·rar·i·ly** \,tempə'rerəlē\ *adv*

tempt \'tempt\ *vb* 1 : coax or persuade to do wrong 2 : attract or provoke —**tempt·er** *n* —**tempt·ing·ly** *adv* —**tempt·ress** \'temptrəs\ *n*

temp·ta·tion \temp'tāshən\ *n* 1 : act of tempting 2 : something that tempts

ten \'ten\ *n* 1 : one more than 9 2 : 10th in a set or series 3 : thing having 10 units —**ten** *adj or pron* —**tenth** \'tenth\ *n or adj or adv*

ten·a·ble \'tenəbəl\ *adj* : capable of being held or defended —**ten·a·bil·i·ty** \,tenə'bilətē\ *n*

te·na·cious \tə'nāshəs\ *adj* 1 : holding fast 2 : retentive —**te·na·cious·ly** *adv* —**te·nac·i·ty** \tə'nasətē\ *n*

ten·ant \'tenənt\ *n* : one who occupies a rented dwelling —**ten·an·cy** \-ənsē\ *n*

¹**tend** \'tend\ *vb* : take care of or supervise something

²**tend** *vb* 1 : move in a particular direction 2 : show a tendency

ten·den·cy \'tendənsē\ *n, pl* **-cies** : likelihood to move, think, or act in a particular way

¹ten·der \'tendər\ *adj* **1** : soft or delicate **2** : expressing or responsive to love or sympathy **3** : sensitive (as to touch) — **ten·der·ly** *adv* — **ten·der·ness** *n*

²tend·er \'tendər\ *n* **1** : one that tends **2** : vehicle attached to a locomotive **3** : transport to a larger ship

³ten·der *n* **1** : offer of a bid for a contract **2** : something that may be offered in payment — **tender** *vb*

ten·der·ize \'tendə,rīz\ *vb* **-ized; -iz·ing** : make (meat) tender — **ten·der·iz·er** \'tendə,rīzər\ *n*

ten·der·loin \'tendər,lȯin\ *n* : tender beef or pork strip from near the backbone

ten·don \'tendən\ *n* : cord of tissue attaching muscle to bone — **ten·di·nous** \-dənəs\ *adj*

ten·dril \'tendrəl\ *n* : slender coiling growth of some climbing plants

ten·e·ment \'tenəmənt\ *n* **1** : house divided into apartments **2** : shabby dwelling

te·net \'tenət\ *n* : principle of belief

ten·nis \'tenəs\ *n* : racket-and-ball game played across a net

ten·or \'tenər\ *n* **1** : general drift or meaning **2** : highest natural adult male voice

ten·pin \'ten,pin\ *n* : bottle-shaped pin bowled at in a game (**tenpins**)

¹tense \'tens\ *n* : distinct verb form that indicates time

²tense *adj* **tens·er; tens·est** **1** : stretched tight **2** : marked by nervous tension — **tense** *vb* — **tense·ly** *adv* — **tense·ness** *n* — **ten·si·ty** \'tensətē\ *n*

ten·sile \'tensəl, -,sīl\ *adj* : relating to tension

ten·sion \'tenchən\ *n* **1** : tense condition **2** : state of mental unrest or of potential hostility or opposition

tent \'tent\ *n* : collapsible shelter

ten·ta·cle \'tentikəl\ *n* : long flexible projection of an insect or mollusk — **ten·ta·cled** \-kəld\ *adj* — **ten·tac·u·lar** \ten'takyələr\ *adj*

ten·ta·tive \'tentətiv\ *adj* : subject to change or discussion — **ten·ta·tive·ly** *adv*

ten·u·ous \'tenyəwəs\ *adj* **1** : not dense or thick **2** : flimsy or weak — **te·nu·i·ty** \te'n(y)üətē, tə-\ *n* — **ten·u·ous·ly** *adv* — **ten·u·ous·ness** *n*

ten·ure \'tenyər\ *n* : act, right, manner, or period of holding something — **ten·ured** \-yərd\ *adj*

te·pee \'tē(,)pē\ *n* : conical tent

tep·id \'tepəd\ *adj* : moderately warm

term \'tərm\ *n* **1** : period of time **2** : mathematical expression **3** : special word or phrase **4** *pl* : conditions **5** *pl* : relations ~ *vb* : name

ter·mi·nal \'tərmən°l\ *n* **1** : end **2** : device for making an electrical connection **3** : station at end of a transportation line — **terminal** *adj*

ter·mi·nate \'tərmə,nāt\ *vb* **-nat·ed; -nat·ing** : bring or come to an end — **ter·mi·na·ble** \-nəbəl\ *adj* — **ter·mi·na·tion** \,tərmə'nāshən\ *n*

ter·mi·nol·o·gy \,tərmə'näləjē\ *n* : terms used in a particular subject

ter·mi·nus \'tərmənəs\ *n, pl* **-ni** \-,nī\ *or* **-nus·es** **1** : end **2** : end of a transportation line

ter·mite \'tər,mīt\ *n* : wood-eating insect

tern \'tərn\ *n* : small sea gull

ter·race \'terəs\ *n* **1** : balcony or patio **2** : bank with a flat top ~ *vb* **-raced; -rac·ing** : landscape in a series of banks

ter·ra-cot·ta \,terə'kätə\ *n* : reddish brown earthenware

ter·rain \tə'rān\ *n* : features of the land

ter·ra·pin \'terəpən\ *n* : No. American turtle

ter·rar·i·um \tə'rareəm\ *n, pl* **-ia** \-ēə\ *or* **-i·ums** : container for keeping plants or animals

ter·res·tri·al \tə'rest(r)ēəl\ *adj* **1** : relating to the earth or its inhabitants **2** : living or growing on land

ter·ri·ble \'terəbəl\ *adj* **1** : exciting terror **2** : distressing **3** : intense **4** : of very poor quality — **ter·ri·bly** \-blē\ *adv*

ter·ri·er \'terēər\ *n* : small dog

ter·rif·ic \tə'rifik\ *adj* **1** : exciting terror **2** : extraordinary

ter·ri·fy \'terə,fī\ *vb* **-fied; -fy·ing** : fill with terror — **ter·ri·fy·ing·ly** *adv*

ter·ri·to·ry \'terə,tōrē\ *n, pl* **-ries** : particular geographical region — **ter·ri·to·ri·al** \,terə'tōrēəl\ *adj*

ter·ror \'terər\ *n* : intense fear and panic or a cause of it

ter·ror·ism \-,izəm\ *n* : systematic covert warfare to produce terror for political coercion — **ter·ror·ist** \-əst\ *adj or n*

ter·ror·ize \-,īz\ *vb* **-ized; -iz·ing** **1** : fill with terror **2** : coerce by threat or violence

ter·ry \'terē\ *n, pl* **-ries** : absorbent fabric with a loose pile of uncut loops

terse \'tərs\ *adj* **ters·er; ters·est** : concise — **terse·ly** *adv* — **terse·ness** *n*

ter·tia·ry \'tərshē,erē\ *adj* : of 3d rank, importance, or value

test \\'test\\ *n* : examination or evaluation ~ *vb* : examine by a test — **test·er** *n*

tes·ta·ment \\'testəmənt\\ *n* 1 *cap* : division of the Bible 2 : will — **tes·ta·men·ta·ry** \\,testə'ment(ə)rē\\ *adj*

tes·ti·cle \\'testikəl\\ *n* : testis

tes·ti·fy \\'testə,fī\\ *vb* -**fied; -fy·ing** 1 : give testimony 2 : serve as evidence

tes·ti·mo·ni·al \\,testə'mōnēəl\\ *n* 1 : favorable recommendation 2 : tribute — **testimonial** *adj*

tes·ti·mo·ny \\'testə,mōnē\\ *n, pl* -**nies** : statement given as evidence in court

tes·tis \\'testəs\\ *n, pl* -**tes** \\-,tēz\\ : male reproductive gland

tes·ty \\'testē\\ *adj* -**ti·er; -est** : easily annoyed

tet·a·nus \\'tet°nəs\\ *n* : bacterial disease producing violent muscular spasm — **tet·a·nal** \\-°l\\ *adj*

tête-à-tête \\,tātə'tāt\\ *adv* : privately ~ *n* : private conversation ~ *adj* : private

teth·er \\'tethər\\ *n* : leash ~ *vb* : restrain with a leash

text \\'tekst\\ *n* 1 : author's words 2 : main body of printed or written matter on a page 3 : textbook 4 : scriptural passage used as the theme of a sermon 5 : topic — **tex·tu·al** \\'tekschə(wə)l\\ *adj*

text·book \\'teks(t),bùk\\ *n* : book on a school subject

tex·tile \\'tek,stīl, 'tekst°l\\ *n* : fabric

tex·ture \\'tekschər\\ *n* 1 : feel and appearance of something 2 : structure

than \\thən, (')than\\ *conj or prep* —used in comparisons

thank \\'thaŋk\\ *vb* : express gratitude to

thank·ful \\-fəl\\ *adj* : giving thanks — **thank·ful·ly** *adv* — **thank·ful·ness** *n*

thank·less *adj* : not appreciated

thanks \\'thaŋks\\ *n pl* : expression of gratitude

Thanks·giv·ing \\thaŋks'giviŋ\\ *n* : 4th Thursday in November observed as a legal holiday for giving thanks for divine goodness

that \\(,)that\\ *pron, pl* **those** \\(')thōz\\ 1 : something indicated or understood 2 : the one farther away ~ *adj, pl* **those** : being the one mentioned or understood or farther away ~ \\that, (,)that\\ *conj or pron* —used to introduce a clause ~ \\'that\\ *adv* : to such an extent

thatch \\'thach\\ *vb* : cover with thatch ~ *n* : covering of matted straw

thaw \\'thò\\ *vb* : melt or cause to melt — **thaw** *n*

the \\thə, *before vowel sounds usu* thē\\ *definite article* : that particular one ~ *adv* —used before a comparative or superlative

the·ater, the·atre \\'thēətər\\ *n* 1 : building or room for viewing a play or movie 2 : dramatic arts

the·at·ri·cal \\thē'atrikəl\\ *adj* 1 : relating to the theater 2 : involving exaggerated emotion

thee \\'thē\\ *pron, obejctive case of* THOU

theft \\'theft\\ *n* : act of stealing

their \\thər, (,)theər\\ *adj* : relating to them

theirs \\'theərz\\ *pron* : their one or ones

the·ism \\'thē,izəm\\ *n* : belief in the existence of a god or gods — **the·ist** \\-əst\\ *n or adj* — **the·is·tic** \\thē'istik\\ *adj*

them \\(th)əm, (')them\\ *pron, objective case of* THEY

theme \\'thēm\\ *n* 1 : subject matter 2 : essay 3 : melody developed in a piece of music — **the·mat·ic** \\thi'matik\\ *adj*

them·selves \\thəm'selvz, them-\\ *pron pl* : they, them —used reflexively or for emphasis

then \\'then\\ *adv* 1 : at that time 2 : soon after that 3 : in addition 4 : in that case 5 : consequently ~ \\'then\\ *n* : that time ~ *adj* : existing at that time

thence \\'thens, 'thens\\ *adv* : from that place or fact

the·oc·ra·cy \\thē'äkrəsē\\ *n, pl* -**cies** : government by officials regarded as divinely inspired — **the·o·crat·ic** \\,thēə'kratik\\ *adj*

the·ol·o·gy \\thē'äləjē\\ *n, pl* -**gies** : study of religion — **the·o·lo·gian** \\,thēə'lōjən\\ *n* — **the·o·log·i·cal** \\-'läjikəl\\ *adj*

the·o·rem \\'thēərəm, 'thirəm\\ *n* : provable statement of truth

the·o·ret·i·cal \\,thēə'retikəl\\ *adj* : relating to or being theory — **the·o·ret·i·cal·ly** *adv*

the·o·rize \\'thēə,rīz\\ *vb* -**rized; -riz·ing** : put forth theories — **the·o·rist** *n*

the·o·ry \\'thēərē, 'thirē\\ *n, pl* -**ries** 1 : general principles of a subject 2 : plausible or scientifically acceptable explanation 3 : judgment, guess, or opinion

ther·a·peu·tic \\,therə'pyütik\\ *adj* : offering or relating to remedy — **ther·a·peu·ti·cal·ly** \\-ik(ə)lē\\ *adv*

ther·a·py \\'therəpē\\ *n, pl* -**pies** : treatment for mental or physical disorder — **ther·a·pist** \\-pəst\\ *n*

there \\'thaər, 'theər\\ *adv* **1** : in, at, or to that place **2** : in that respect ~ \\(,)tha(ə)r, (,)the(ə)r, thər\\ *pron* —used to introduce a sentence or clause ~ \\'thaər, 'theər\\ *n* : that place or point

there·abouts, **there·about** \\,tharə'baút(s), 'tharə,-, ,therə-, 'therə,-\\ *adv* : near that place, time, number, or quantity

there·af·ter \\thar'aftər, ther-\\ *adv* : after that

there·by \\tha(ə)r'bī, the(ə)r-, 'tha(ə)r,bī, 'the(ə)r,bī\\ *adv* **1** : by that **2** : connected with or with reference to that

there·fore \\'tha(ə)r,fōr, 'the(ə)r-\\ *adv* : for that reason

there·in \\thar'in, ther-\\ *adv* **1** : in or into that place, time, or thing **2** : in that respect

there·of \\-'əv, -'av\\ *adv* **1** : of that or it **2** : from that

there·upon \\,tharə'pòn, 'ther-, -,pän; ,therə'pòn, -'pän, 'ther-\\ *adv* **1** : on that matter **2** : therefore **3** : immediately after that

there·with \\tha(ə)r'with, the(ə)r-, -'with\\ *adv* : with that

ther·mal \\'thərməl\\ *adj* : relating to, caused by, or conserving heat —**ther·mal·ly** *adv*

ther·mo·dy·nam·ics \\,thərmə·dī'namiks\\ *n* : physics of heat

ther·mom·e·ter \\tha(r)'mämətər\\ *n* : instrument for measuring temperature —**ther·mo·met·ric** \\,thərmə'metrik\\ *adj* —**ther·mo·met·ri·cal·ly** \\-rik(ə)lē\\ *adv*

ther·mos \\'thərməs\\ *n* : double-walled bottle used to keep liquids hot or cold

ther·mo·stat \\'thərmə,stat\\ *n* : automatic temperature control —**ther·mo·stat·ic** \\,thərmə'statik\\ *adj* —**ther·mo·stat·i·cal·ly** \\-ik(ə)lē\\ *adv*

the·sau·rus \\thi'sòrəs\\ *n, pl* **-sau·ri** \\-'sòr,ī\\ *or* **-sau·rus·es** \\-'sòrəsəz\\ : book of words and esp. synonyms

these *pl of* THIS

the·sis \\'thēsəs\\ *n, pl* **the·ses** \\'thē,sēz\\ **1** : proposition to be argued for **2** : essay embodying results of original research

thes·pi·an \\'thespēən\\ *adj* : dramatic ~ *n* : actor

they \\(')thā\\ *pron* **1** : those ones **2** : people in general

thi·a·mine \\'thīəmən, -,mēn\\ *also* **thi·a·min** \\-mən\\ *n* : essential vitamin

thick \\'thik\\ *adj* **1** : having relatively great mass from front to top

to bottom **2** : viscous ~ *n* : most crowded or thickest part —**thick·ly** *adv* —**thick·ness** *n*

thick·en \\'thikən\\ *vb* : make or become thick —**thick·en·er** \\-(ə)nər\\ *n*

thick·et \\'thikət\\ *n* : dense growth of bushes or small trees

thick-skinned \\-'skind\\ *adj* : insensitive to criticism

thief \\'thēf\\ *n, pl* **thieves** \\'thēvz\\ : one that steals

thieve \\'thēv\\ *vb* **thieved**; **thiev·ing** : steal —**thiev·ery** *n*

thigh \\'thī\\ *n* : upper part of the leg

thigh·bone \\'thī'bōn, -,bōn\\ *n* : femur

thim·ble \\'thimbəl\\ *n* : protective cap for the finger in sewing —**thim·ble·ful** *n*

thin \\'thin\\ *adj* **-nn-** **1** : having relatively little mass from front to back or top to bottom **2** : not closely set or placed **3** : relatively free flowing **4** : lacking substance, fullness, or strength ~ *vb* **-nn-** : make or become thin —**thin·ly** *adv* —**thin·ness** *n*

thing \\'thiŋ\\ *n* **1** : matter of concern **2** : event or act **3** : object **4** *pl* : possessions

think \\'thiŋk\\ *vb* **thought** \\'thòt\\; **think·ing** **1** : form or have in the mind **2** : have as an opinion **3** : ponder **4** : devise by thinking **5** : imagine —**think·er** *n*

thin-skinned *adj* : extremely sensitive to criticism

third \\'thərd\\ *adj* : being number 3 in a countable series ~ *n* **1** : one that is third **2** : one of 3 equal parts —**third**, **third·ly** *adv*

third dimension *n* : thickness or depth —**third-dimensional** *adj*

thirst \\'thərst\\ *n* **1** : dryness in mouth and throat **2** : intense desire ~ *vb* : feel thirst —**thirsty** *adj*

thir·teen \\,thər'tēn, 'thər-\\ *n* : one more than 12 —**thirteen** *adj or pron* —**thir·teenth** \\-'tēnth\\ *adj or n*

thir·ty \\'thərtē\\ *n, pl* **thirties** : 3 times 10 —**thir·ti·eth** \\-ēəth\\ *adj or n* —**thirty** *adj or pron*

this \\(')this\\ *pron, pl* **these** \\(')thēz\\ : something close or under immediate discussion ~ *adj, pl* **these** : being the one near, present, just mentioned, or more immediately under observation ~ \\'this\\ *adv* : to such an extent or degree

this·tle \\'thisəl\\ *n* : tall prickly herb

thith·er \\'thithər\\ *adv* : to that place

thong \\'thòŋ\\ *n* : strip of leather or hide

tho·rax \\'thōr,aks\ *n, pl* **-rax·es** *or* **-ra·ces** \\'thōr,sēz\ **1** : part of the body between neck and abdomen **2** : middle of 3 divisions of an insect body —**tho·rac·ic** \tho'rasik\ *adj*

thorn \\'thòrn\ *n* : sharp spike on a plant or a plant bearing these —**thorny** *adj*

thor·ough \\'thərō\ *adj* : omitting or overlooking nothing —**thor·ough·ly** *adv* —**thor·ough·ness** *n*

thor·ough·bred \\'thərə,bred\ *n* **1** *cap* : light speedy racing horse **2** : one of excellent quality —**thoroughbred** *adj*

thor·ough·fare \\'thərə,faər\ *n* : public road

those *pl of* THAT

thou \\(')thaủ\ *pron, archaic* : you

though \\'thō\ *adv* : however ~ \\(,)thō\ *conj* **1** : despite the fact that **2** : granting that

thought \\'thòt\ *past of* THINK ~ *n* **1** : process of thinking **2** : serious consideration **3** : idea

thought·ful \-fəl\ *adj* **1** : absorbed in or showing thought **2** : considerate of others —**thought·ful·ly** *adv* —**thought·ful·ness** *n*

thought·less \-ləs\ *adj* **1** : careless or reckless **2** : lacking concern for others —**thought·less·ly** *adv* —**thought·less·ness** *n*

thou·sand \\'thauz²nd\ *n, pl* **-sands** *or* **-sand 1** : 10 times 100 —**thousand** *adj* —**thou·sandth** \-²nth\ *adj or n*

thrash \\'thrash\ *vb* **1** : thresh **2** : beat **3** : move about violently —**thrash·er** *n*

thread \\'thred\ *n* **1** : fine line of fibers **2** : train of thought **3** : ridge around a screw ~ *vb* **1** : pass thread through **2** : put together on a thread **3** : make one's way through or between

thread·bare *adj* **1** : worn so that the thread shows **2** : trite

threat \\'thret\ *n* **1** : expression of intention to harm **2** : thing that threatens

threat·en \\'thret²n\ *vb* **1** : utter threats **2** : show signs of being near or impending —**threat·en·ing·ly** *adv*

three \\'thrē\ *n* **1** : one more than 2 **2** : 3d in a set or series —**three** *adj or pron*

three·fold \\'thrē,fōld, -'fōld\ *adj* : triple —**three·fold** \-'fōld\ *adv*

three·score *adj* : being 3 times 20

thresh \\'thrash, 'thresh\ *vb* : beat to separate grain —**thresh·er** *n*

thresh·old \\'thresh,ōld\ *n* **1** : sill of a door **2** : beginning stage

threw *past of* THROW

thrice \\'thrīs\ *adv* : 3 times

thrift \\'thrift\ *n* : careful management or saving of money —**thrift·i·ly** \\'thriftəlē\ *adv* —**thrift·less** *adj* —**thrifty** *adj*

thrill \\'thril\ *vb* **1** : have or cause to have a sudden sharp feeling of excitement **2** : tremble —**thrill** *n* —**thrill·er** *n* —**thrill·ing·ly** *adv*

thrive \\'thrīv\ *vb* **throve** \\'thrōv\ *or* **thrived; thriv·en** \\'thrivən\ **1** : grow vigorously **2** : prosper

throat \\'thrōt\ *n* **1** : front part of the neck **2** : passage to the stomach —**throat·ed** *adj* —**throaty** *adj*

throb \\'thräb\ *vb* **-bb-** : pulsate —**throb** *n*

throe \\'thrō\ *n* **1** : pang or spasm **2** *pl* : hard or painful struggle

throne \\'thrōn\ *n* : chair representing power or sovereignty

throng \\'thròng\ *n or vb* : crowd

throt·tle \\'thrät²l\ *vb* **-tled; -tling** : choke ~ *n* : valve regulating volume of fuel and air delivered to engine cylinders

through \\(')thrü\ *prep* **1** : into at one side and out at the other side of **2** : by way of **3** : among, between, or all around **4** : because of **5** : throughout the time of ~ \\'thrü\ *adv* **1** : from one end or side to the other **2** : from beginning to end **3** : to the core **4** : into the open ~ \\'thrü\ *adj* **1** : going directly from origin to destination **2** : finished

through·out \thrü'aủt\ *adv* **1** : everywhere **2** : from beginning to end ~ *prep* **1** : in or to every part of **2** : during the whole of

throve *past of* THRIVE

throw \\'thrō\ *vb* **threw** \\'thrü\; **thrown** \\'thrōn\, **throw·ing 1** : propel through the air **2** : cause to fall or fall off **3** : put suddenly in a certain position or condition **4** : move quickly as if throwing **5** : put on or off hastily —**throw** *n* —**throw·er** \\'thrō(ə)r\ *n* —**throw up** *vb* : vomit

thrush \\'thrash\ *n* : songbird

thrust \\'thrəst\ *vb* **thrust; thrust·ing 1** : shove forward **2** : stab or pierce —**thrust** *n*

thud \\'thəd\ *n* : dull sound of something falling —**thud** *vb*

thug \\'thəg\ *n* : ruffian or gangster

thumb \\'thəm\ *n* **1** : short thick division of the hand opposing the fingers **2** : glove part for the thumb ~ *vb* : leaf through with the thumb —**thumb·nail** *n*

thump \\'thəmp\ *vb* : strike with something thick or heavy causing a dull heavy sound —**thump** n

thun·der \'thəndər\ n : sound following lightning —**thunder** vb —**thun·der·clap** n —**thun·der·ous** \'thənd(ə)rəs\ adj —**thun·der·ous·ly** adv

thun·der·bolt \-,bōlt\ n : discharge of lightning with thunder

thun·der·show·er \'thəndər,shau̇(ə)r\ n : shower with thunder and lightning

thun·der·storm n : storm with thunder and lightning

Thurs·day \'thərzdē\ n : 5th day of the week

thus \'thəs\ adv 1 : in this or that way 2 : to this degree or extent 3 : because of this or that

thwart \'thwȯrt\ vb : block or defeat

thy \(,)thī\ adj, archaic : your

thyme \'tīm, 'thīm\ n : cooking herb

thy·roid \'thī,rȯid\, **thy·roi·dal** \thī'rȯid⁰l\ adj : relating to a large endocrine gland (**thyroid gland**)

thy·self \thī'self\ pron, archaic : yourself

ti·ara \tē'arə, -'er-, -'är-\ n : decorative formal headband

tib·ia \'tibēə\ n, pl -i·ae \-ē,ē\ : bone between the knee and ankle

tic \'tik\ n : twitching of facial muscles

¹**tick** \'tik\ n : small 8-legged blood-sucking animal

²**tick** n 1 : light rhythmic tap or beat 2 : check mark ~ vb 1 : make ticks 2 : mark with a tick 3 : operate

tick·er \'tikər\ n 1 : something (as a watch) that ticks 2 : telegraph instrument that prints on paper tape

tick·et \'tikət\ n 1 : tag showing price, payment of a fee or fare, or a traffic offense 2 : list of candidates ~ vb : put a ticket on

tick·ing \'tikiŋ\ n : fabric covering of a mattress

tick·le \'tikəl\ vb -led; -ling 1 : please or amuse 2 : touch lightly causing uneasiness, laughter, or spasmodic movements —**tickle** n

tick·lish \'tik(ə)lish\ adj 1 : sensitive to tickling 2 : requiring delicate handling —**tick·lish·ly** adv —**tick·lish·ness** n

tid·al wave \,tīd⁰l-\ n : high sea wave following an earthquake

tid·bit \'tid,bit\ n : choice morsel

tide \'tīd\ n : alternate rising and falling of the sea ~ vb **tid·ed; tid·ing** : be enough to allow (one) to get by for a time —**tid·al** \'tīd⁰l\ adj —**tide·wa·ter** n

tid·ings \'tīdiŋz\ n pl : news or message

ti·dy \'tīdē\ adj -di·er; -est 1 : well ordered and cared for 2 : large or substantial —**ti·di·ness** n —**tidy** vb

tie \'tī\ n 1 : line or ribbon for fastening, uniting, or closing 2 : cross support to which railroad rails are fastened 3 : uniting force 4 : equality in score or tally or a deadlocked contest 5 : necktie ~ vb **tied; ty·ing** or **tie·ing** 1 : fasten or close by wrapping and knotting a tie 2 : form a knot in 3 : gain the same score or tally as an opponent

tier \'tiar\ n : one of a steplike series of rows

tiff \'tif\ n : petty quarrel —**tiff** vb

ti·ger \'tīgər\ n : large black-striped flesh-eating mammal —**ti·ger·ish** \-g(ə)rish\ adj —**ti·gress** \-grəs\ n

tight \'tīt\ adj 1 : fitting close together esp. so as not to allow air or water to enter 2 : held very firmly 3 : taut 4 : fitting too snugly 5 : difficult 6 : stingy 7 : evenly contested 8 : low in supply —**tight** adv —**tight·en** \-⁰n\ vb —**tight·ly** adv —**tight·ness** n

tights \'tīts\ n pl : skintight garments

tight·wad \'tīt,wäd\ n : stingy person

tile \'tīl\ n : thin piece of stone or fired clay used on roofs, floors, or walls ~ vb : cover with tiles —**til·ing** \-iŋ\ n

¹**till** \(,)til\ prep or conj : until

²**till** \'til\ vb : cultivate (soil) —**till·able** adj

³**till** \'til\ n : money drawer

til·ler \'tilər\ n : lever for turning a boat's rudder

tilt \'tilt\ vb : cause to incline ~ n : slant

tim·ber \'timbər\ n 1 : cut wood for building 2 : large squared piece of wood 3 : wooded land or trees for timber ~ vb : cover, frame, or support with timbers —**tim·bered** adj —**tim·ber·land** \-,land\ n

tim·bre \'tambər, 'tim-\ n : sound quality

time \'tīm\ n 1 : period during which something exists or continues or can be accomplished 2 : point at which something happens 3 : customary hour 4 : age 5 : tempo 6 : moment, hour, day, or year as indicated by a clock or calendar 7 : one's experience during a particular period ~ vb **timed; tim·ing** 1 : arrange or set the time of 2 : determine or record the time, duration, or rate of —**time·keep·er** n —**time·less** adj —**time·less·ness** n —**time·li·ness** n —**time·ly** adv —**tim·er** n

time·piece n : device to show time

times \ˌtīmz\ *prep* : multiplied by

time·ta·ble \ˈtīm.ˌtābəl\ *n* : table of departure and arrival times

tim·id \ˈtiməd\ *adj* : lacking in courage or self-confidence —ti·mid·i·ty \təˈmidətē\ *n* —tim·id·ly *adv*

tim·o·rous \ˈtim(ə)rəs\ *adj* : fearful —tim·o·rous·ly *adv* —tim·o·rous·ness *n*

tim·pa·ni \ˈtimpənē\ *n pl* : set of kettledrums —tim·pa·nist \-nəst\ *n*

tin \ˈtin\ *n* 1 : soft white metallic chemical element 2 : metal food can

tinc·ture \ˈtiŋkchər\ *n* : alcoholic solution of a medicine

tin·der \ˈtindər\ *n* : substance used to kindle a fire

tine \ˈtīn\ *n* : one of the points of a fork

tin·foil \ˈtin.ˌfȯil\ *n* : thin metal sheeting

tinge \ˈtinj\ *vb* tinged; tinge·ing *or* ting·ing \ˈtinjiŋ\ 1 : color slightly 2 : affect with a slight odor ~ *n* : slight coloring or flavor

tin·gle \ˈtiŋgəl\ *vb* -gled; -gling : feel a ringing, stinging, or thrilling sensation —tingle *n*

tin·ker \ˈtiŋkər\ *vb* : experiment in repairing something —tin·ker·er *n*

tin·kle \ˈtiŋkəl\ *vb* -kled; -kling : make or cause to make a high ringing sound —tinkle *n*

tin·sel \ˈtinsəl\ *n* : decorative thread or strip of glittering metal or paper

tint \ˈtint\ *n* 1 : slight or pale coloration 2 : color shade ~ *vb* : give a tint to

ti·ny \ˈtīnē\ *adj* -ni·er; -est : very small

¹tip \ˈtip\ *n* : pointed end of something ~ *vb* -pp- 1 : furnish with a tip 2 : cover the tip of

²tip *vb* -pp- 1 : overturn 2 : lean ~ *n* : act or state of tipping

³tip *n* : small sum given for a service performed ~ *vb* : give a tip to

⁴tip *n* : piece of confidential information ~ *vb* -pp- : give confidential information to

tip-off \ˈtip.ˌȯf\ *n* : indication

tip·ple \ˈtipəl\ *vb* -pled; -pling : drink intoxicating liquor esp. habitually or excessively —tip·pler \-(ə)lər\ *n*

tip·sy \ˈtipsē\ *adj* -si·er; -est : unsteady or foolish from alcohol

tip·toe \ˈtip.ˌtō\ *n* : the toes of the feet ~ *adv or adj* : supported on tiptoe ~ *vb* -toed; -toe·ing : walk quietly or on tiptoe

tip-top *n* : highest point ~ *adj* : excellent

ti·rade \ˈtī.ˌrād, ˈtī.-\ *n* : prolonged speech of abuse

¹tire \ˈtī(ə)r\ *vb* tired; tir·ing 1 : make or become weary 2 : wear out the patience of —tire·less *adj* —tire·less·ly *adv* —tire·less·ness *n* —tire·some \-səm\ *adj* —tire·some·ly *adv* —tire·some·ness *n*

²tire *n* : rubber cushion encircling a car wheel

tired \ˈtī(ə)rd\ *adj* : weary

tis·sue \ˈtishü\ *n* 1 : soft absorbent paper 2 : layer of cells forming a basic structural element of an animal or plant body

ti·tan·ic \tīˈtanik, tə-\ *adj* : gigantic

ti·ta·ni·um \tīˈtānēəm, tə-\ *n* : gray light strong metallic chemical element

tithe \ˈtīth\ *n* : tenth part paid or given esp. for the support of a church —tithe *vb* —tith·er *n*

tit·il·late \ˈtit²l.ˌāt\ *vb* -lat·ed; -lat·ing : excite pleasurably —tit·il·la·tion \ˌtit²lˈāshən\ *n*

ti·tle \ˈtīt²l\ *n* 1 : legal ownership 2 : distinguishing name 3 : designation of honor, rank, or office 4 : championship —ti·tled *adj*

tit·ter \ˈtitər\ *n* : nervous or affected laugh —titter *vb*

tit·u·lar \ˈtich(ə)lər\ *adj* 1 : existing in title only 2 : relating to or bearing a title

TNT \ˌtē.ˌenˈtē\ *n* : high explosive

to \tə, (ˈ)tü\ *prep* 1 : in the direction of 2 : at, on, or near 3 : resulting in 4 : before or until 5 —used to show a relationship or object of a verb 6 —used with an infinitive ~ \ˈtü\ *adv* 1 : forward 2 : to a state of consciousness

toad \ˈtōd\ *n* : tailless leaping amphibian

toad·stool \-.ˌstül\ *n* : mushroom esp. when inedible or poisonous

toady \ˈtōdē\ *n, pl* toad·ies : one who flatters to gain favors —toady *vb*

toast \ˈtōst\ *vb* 1 : make (as a slice of bread) crisp and brown 2 : drink in honor of someone or something 3 : warm ~ *n* 1 : toasted sliced bread 2 : act of drinking in honor of someone —toast·er *n*

to·bac·co \təˈbakō\ *n, pl* -cos : broadleaved herb or its leaves prepared for smoking or chewing

to·bog·gan \təˈbägən\ *n* : long flat-bottomed light sled ~ *vb* : coast on a toboggan

to·day \təˈdā\ *adv* 1 : on or for this day

2 : at the present time ~ *n* : present day or time

tod·dle \'täd[ᵊ]l\ *vb* **-dled; -dling** : walk with tottering steps like a young child —**toddle** *n* —**tod·dler** \'tädlər, -[ᵊ]lər\ *n*

to-do \tə'dü\ *n, pl* **to-dos** \-'düz\ : disturbance or fuss

toe \'tō\ *n* : one of the 5 end divisions of the foot —**toe·nail** *n*

to·ga \'tōgə\ *n* : loose outer garment of ancient Rome

to-geth-er \tə'geth̷ər\ *adv* **1** : in or into one place or group **2** : in or into contact or association **3** : at one time **4** : as a group —**to·geth·er·ness** *n*

toil \'tȯil\ *vb* : work hard and long —**toil** *n* —**toil·er** *n* —**toil·some** *adj*

toi·let \'tȯilət\ *n* **1** : dressing and grooming oneself **2** : bathroom **3** : water basin to urinate and defecate in

toils \'tȯilz\ *n pl* : net or trap

to·ken \'tōkən\ *n* **1** : outward sign or expression of something **2** : small part representing the whole **3** : piece resembling a coin

told *past of* TELL

tol·er·a·ble \'täl(ə)rəbəl\ *adj* **1** : capable of being endured **2** : moderately good —**tol·er·a·bly** \-blē\ *adv*

tol·er·ance \'täl(ə)rəns\ *n* **1** : lack of opposition for beliefs or practices differing from one's own **2** : capacity for enduring **3** : allowable deviation —**tol·er·ant** *adj* —**tol·er·ant·ly** *adv*

tol·er·ate \'tälə,rāt\ *vb* **-at·ed; -at·ing** **1** : allow to be or to be done without opposition **2** : endure or resist the action of —**tol·er·a·tion** \,tälə'rāshən\ *n*

¹toll \'tōl\ *n* **1** : fee paid for a privilege or service **2** : cost of achievement in loss or suffering —**toll·booth** *n* —**toll·gate** *n*

²toll *vb* **1** : cause the sounding of (a bell) **2** : sound with slow measured strokes ~ *n* : sound of a tolling bell

tom·a·hawk \'tämi,hȯk\ *n* : light ax used as a weapon by Indians

to·ma·to \tə'mātō, -'māt-\ *n, pl* **-toes** : tropical American herb or its fruit

tomb \'tüm\ *n* : house, vault, or grave for burial

tom·boy \'täm,bȯi\ *n* : girl with boyish behavior

tomb·stone *n* : stone marking a grave

tom·cat \'täm,kat\ *n* : male cat

tome \'tōm\ *n* : large or weighty book

to·mor·row \tə'märō\ *adv* : on or for the day after today —**tomorrow** *n*

tom-tom \'täm,täm\ *n* : small-headed drum beaten with the hands

ton \'tən\ *n* : unit of weight equal to 2000 pounds

tone \'tōn\ *n* **1** : vocal or musical sound **2** : sound of definite pitch **3** : manner of speaking that expresses an emotion or attitude **4** : color quality **5** : healthy condition **6** : general character or quality —**tone down** *vb* : soften or muffle —**ton·al** \-[ᵊ]l\ *adj* —**to·nal·i·ty** \tō'nalətē\ *n*

tongs \'täŋz, 'tȯŋz\ *n pl* : grasping device of 2 joined or hinged pieces

tongue \'təŋ\ *n* **1** : fleshy movable organ of the mouth **2** : language **3** : something long and flat and fastened at one end —**tongued** \'təŋd\ *adj* —**tongue·less** *adj*

ton·ic \'tänik\ *n* : something (as a drug) that invigorates or restores health —**tonic** *adj*

to·night \tə'nīt\ *adv* : on this night ~ *n* : present or coming night

ton·sil \'tänsəl\ *n* : either of a pair of oval masses in the throat —**ton·sil·lec·to·my** \,tänsə'lektəmē\ *n* —**ton·sil·li·tis** \-'lītəs\ *n*

too \(')tü\ *adv* **1** : in addition **2** : excessively

took *past of* TAKE

tool \'tül\ *n* : hand implement used when working with the hands ~ *vb* : shape or finish with a tool

toot \'tüt\ *vb* : sound or cause to sound esp. in short blasts —**toot** *n*

tooth \'tüth\ *n, pl* **teeth** \'tēth\ **1** : one of the hard structures in the jaws for chewing **2** : one of the projections on the edge of a gear wheel —**tooth·ache** *n* —**tooth·brush** *n* —**toothed** \'tütht\ *adj* —**tooth·less** *adj* —**tooth·paste** *n* —**tooth·pick** *n*

tooth·some \'tüthsəm\ *adj* **1** : delicious **2** : attractive

¹top \'täp\ *n* **1** : highest part or level of something **2** : lid or covering ~ *vb* **-pp-** **1** : cover with a top **2** : surpass **3** : go over the top of ~ *adj* : being at the top —**topped** *adj*

²top *n* : spinning toy

to·paz \'tō,paz\ *n* : hard gem

top·coat *n* : lightweight overcoat

top·ic \'täpik\ *n* : subject for discussion or study

top·i·cal \-ikəl\ *adj* **1** : relating to or arranged by topics **2** : relating to current or local events —**top·i·cal·ly** \-k(ə)lē\ *adv*

top·most \'täp,mōst\ *adj* : highest of all

top-notch \-'näch\ *adj* : of the highest quality

to·pog·ra·phy \tə'pägrəfē\ *n* 1 : art of mapping the physical features of a place 2 : outline of the form of a place —**to·pog·ra·pher** \-fər\ *n* —**top·o·graph·ic** \,täpə'grafik\, **top·o·graph·i·cal** \-ikəl\ *adj*

top·ple \'täpəl\ *vb* -**pled**; -**pling** : fall or cause to fall

top·sy-tur·vy \,täpsē'tərvē\ *adv or adj* 1 : upside down 2 : in utter confusion

torch \'tórch\ *n* : flaming light —**torch-bear·er** \-,bərər\ *n* —**torch-light** *n*

tore *past of* TEAR

tor·ment \'tór,ment\ *n* : extreme pain or anguish or a source of this ~ *vb* 1 : cause severe anguish to 2 : harass —**tor·men·tor** \-ər\ *n*

torn *past part of* TEAR

tor·na·do \tór'nādō\ *n, pl* -**does** *or* -**dos** : violent destructive whirling wind

tor·pe·do \tór'pēdō\ *n, pl* -**does** : self-propelling explosive submarine missile ~ *vb* : hit with a torpedo

tor·pid \'tórpəd\ *adj* 1 : having lost motion or the power of exertion 2 : lacking vigor —**tor·pid·i·ty** \-'pidətē\ *n*

tor·por \'tórpər\ *n* : extreme sluggishness or lethargy

torque \'tórk\ *n* : turning force

tor·rent \'tórənt\ *n* 1 : rushing stream 2 : tumultuous outburst

tor·ren·tial \tó'renchəl, tə-\ *adj* : relating to or like a torrent

tor·rid \'tórəd\ *adj* 1 : parched with heat 2 : impassioned

tor·sion \'tórshən\ *n* : a twisting or being twisted —**tor·sion·al** \'tórsh(ə)nəl\ *adj* —**tor·sion·al·ly** *adv*

tor·so \'tórsō\ *n, pl* -**sos** *or* -**si** \-,sē\ : trunk of the human body

tor·til·la \tór'tē(y)ə\ *n* : round flat cornmeal bread

tor·toise \'tórtəs\ *n* : sea turtle

tor·tu·ous \'tórch(ə)wəs\ *adj* 1 : winding 2 : tricky

tor·ture \'tórchər\ *n* 1 : use of pain to punish or force 2 : agony ~ *vb* -**tured**; -**tur·ing** : inflict torture on —**tor·tur·er** *n*

toss \'tós, 'täs\ *vb* 1 : move to and fro or up and down violently 2 : throw with a quick light motion 3 : move restlessly —**toss** *n*

toss-up *n* 1 : a deciding by flipping a coin 2 : even chance

tot \'tät\ *n* : small child

to·tal \'tōt°l\ *n* : entire amount ~ *vb* -**taled** *or* -**talled**; -**tal·ing** *or* -**tal·ling** 1 : add up 2 : amount to —**total** *adj* —**to·tal·ly** *adv*

to·tal·i·tar·i·an \tō,talə'terēən\ *adj* : relating to a political regime based on subordination of the individual to the state and strict control of all aspects of life —**totalitarian** *n* —**to·tal·i·tar·i·an·ism** \-,izəm\ *n*

to·tal·i·ty \tō'talətē\ *n, pl* -**ties** : whole amount or entirety

tote \'tōt\ *vb* **toted**; **tot·ing** : carry

to·tem \'tōtəm\ *n* : often carved figure used as a family or tribe emblem

tot·ter \'tätər\ *vb* 1 : sway as if about to fall 2 : stagger

touch \'təch\ *vb* 1 : make contact with so as to feel 2 : be or cause to be in contact 3 : take into the hands or mouth 4 : treat or mention a subject 5 : relate or concern 6 : move to sympathetic feeling ~ *n* 1 : light stroke 2 : act or fact of touching or being touched 3 : sense of feeling 4 : trace 5 : state of being in contact

touch-down \'təch,daún\ *n* : scoring of 6 points in football

touch-stone *n* : test or criterion of genuineness or quality

touchy \'təchē\ *adj* **touch·i·er**; -**est** 1 : easily offended 2 : requiring tact

tough \'təf\ *adj* 1 : strong but elastic 2 : not easily chewed 3 : severe or disciplined 4 : difficult to influence or overcome ~ *n* : rowdy or belligerent person —**tough·ly** *adv* —**tough·ness** *n*

tough·en \'təfən\ *vb* : make or become tough

tou·pee \tü'pā\ *n* : small wig for a bald spot

tour \'túr, 1 *is also* 'taú(ə)r\ *n* 1 : period of time spent at work or on an assignment 2 : journey with a return to the starting point ~ *vb* : travel over to see the sights —**tour·ist** \'túrəst\ *n*

tour·na·ment \'túrnəmənt, 'tər-\ *n* 1 : medieval jousting competition 2 : championship series of games

tour·ney \-nē\ *n, pl* -**neys** : tournament

tour·ni·quet \'túrnikət, 'tər-\ *n* : twisted bandage for stopping blood flow

tou·sle \'taúzəl\ *vb* -**sled**; -**sling** : dishevel (as someone's hair)

tout \'taút, 'tüt\ *vb* : praise or publicize loudly

tow \'tō\ *vb* : pull along behind —**tow** *n*

to·ward, **to·wards** \(')tō(ə)rd(z), tə'wórd(z)\ *prep* 1 : in the direction of 2 : with respect to 3 : in part payment on

tow·el \'taú(ə)l\ *n* : absorbent cloth or paper for wiping or drying

tow·er \'taú(ə)r\ *n* : tall structure ~ *vb* : rise to a great height —**tow·ered** \'taú(ə)rd\ *adj* —**tow·er·ing** *adj*

tow·head \'tō,hed\ *n* : person having white or light blond hair —**tow·head·ed** \-,hedəd\ *adj*

town \'taún\ *n* **1** : small residential area **2** : city —**towns·peo·ple** \'taúnz,pēpəl\ *n pl*

town·ship \'taún,ship\ *n* **1** : unit of local government **2** : 36 square miles of U.S. public land

tox·ic \'täksik\ *adj* : poisonous —**tox·ic·i·ty** \täk'sisətē\ *n*

tox·in \'täksən\ *n* : poison produced by an organism

toy \'tói\ *n* : something for a child to play with ~ *vb* : amuse oneself or play with something — *adj* **1** : designed as a toy **2** : very small

¹trace \'trās\ *vb* **traced; trac·ing 1** : mark over the lines of (a drawing) **2** : follow the trail or the development of ~ *n* **1** : track **2** : tiny amount or residue —**trace·able** *adj* —**trac·er** *n*

²trace *n* : line of a harness

tra·chea \'trākēə\ *n, pl* **-che·ae** \-kē,ē\ : windpipe —**tra·che·al** \-kēəl\ *adj*

track \'trak\ *n* **1** : trail left by wheels or footprints **2** : racing course **3** : train rails **4** : awareness of a progression **5** : looped belts propelling a vehicle ~ *vb* **1** : follow the tracks of **2** : make tracks on —**track·er** *n*

track-and-field *adj* : relating to athletic contests of running, jumping, and throwing events

¹tract \'trakt\ *n* : pamphlet of propaganda

²tract *n* **1** : stretch of land **2** : system of body organs

trac·ta·ble \'traktəbəl\ *adj* : easily controlled

trac·tion \'trakshən\ *n* : gripping power to permit movement —**trac·tion·al** \-sh(ə)nəl\ *adj* —**trac·tive** \'traktiv\ *adj*

trac·tor \'traktər\ *n* **1** : farm vehicle used esp. for pulling **2** : truck for hauling a trailer

trade \'trād\ *n* **1** : one's regular business **2** : occupation requiring skill **3** : the buying and selling of goods **4** : act of trading ~ *vb* **trad·ed; trad·ing 1** : give in exchange for other goods **2** : buy and sell goods **3** : be a regular customer —**trades·peo·ple** \'trādz,pēpəl\ *n pl*

trade·mark \'trād,märk\ *n* : word or mark identifying a manufacturer —**trademark** *vb*

trades·man \'trādzmən\ *n* : shopkeeper

tra·di·tion \trə'dishən\ *n* : belief or custom passed from generation to generation —**tra·di·tion·al** \-'dish(ə)nəl\ *adj* —**tra·di·tion·al·ly** *adv*

tra·duce \trə'd(y)üs\ *vb* **-duced; -duc·ing** : lower the reputation of —**tra·duc·er** *n*

traf·fic \'trafik\ *n* **1** : business dealings **2** : movement along a route ~ *vb* : do business —**traf·fick·er** *n* —**traffic light** *n*

trag·e·dy \'trajədē\ *n, pl* **-dies 1** : serious drama describing a conflict and having a sad end **2** : disastrous event

trag·ic \'trajik\ *adj* : being a tragedy —**trag·i·cal·ly** \-ik(ə)lē\ *adv*

trail \'trāl\ *vb* **1** : hang down and drag along the ground **2** : draw along behind **3** : follow the track of **4** : dwindle ~ *n* **1** : something that trails **2** : path or evidence left by something

trail·er \'trālər\ *n* : vehicle intended to be hauled

train \'trān\ *n* **1** : trailing part of a gown **2** : retinue or procession **3** : connected series **4** : group of railroad cars moving together ~ *vb* **1** : cause to grow as desired **2** : make or become prepared or skilled **3** : point —**train·ee** *n* —**train·er** *n* —**train·load** \-,lōd\ *n* —**train·man** \-mən\ *n*

trait \'trāt\ *n* : distinguishing quality

trai·tor \'trātər\ *n* : one who betrays a trust or commits treason —**trai·tor·ous** *adj* —**trai·tress** \'trātrəs\ *n*

tra·jec·to·ry \trə'jekt(ə)rē\ *n, pl* **-ries** : curving path of something moving through air or space

tram·mel \'traməl\ *vb* **-meled** *or* **-melled; -mel·ing** *or* **-mel·ling** \-(ə)liŋ\ : impede —**trammel** *n*

tramp \'tramp, *2 is also* 'trämp, 'trömp\ *vb* **1** : walk or hike **2** : tread on ~ *n* : beggar or vagrant

tram·ple \'trampəl\ *vb* **-pled; -pling** : walk or step on so as to bruise or crush —**trample** *n* —**tram·pler** \-p(ə)lər\ *n*

tram·po·line \,trampə'lēn, 'trampə,-\ *n* : resilient canvas-and-springs surface used for bouncing —**tram·po·lin·er** *n* —**tram·po·lin·ist** \-əst\ *n*

trance \'trans\ *n* **1** : sleeplike condition **2** : state of mystical absorption

tran·quil \'traŋkwəl, 'tran-\ *adj* : quiet and undisturbed —**tran·quil·ize, tran·quil·lize** \-kwə,līz\ *vb* —**tran·quil·iz·er** *n* —**tran·quil·li·ty, tran-**

quil·i·ty \tran'kwilətē, tran-\ *n* —**tran·quil·ly** *adv*

trans·act \trans'akt, tranz-\ *vb* : conduct (business)

trans·ac·tion \-'akshən\ *n* **1** : business deal **2** *pl* : records of proceedings

tran·scend \trans'end\ *vb* : rise above or surpass —**tran·scen·dent** \-'endənt\ *adj* —**tran·scen·den·tal** \,trans,en'dent²l, -ən-\ *adj*

tran·scribe \trans'krīb\ *vb* -**scribed**; -**scrib·ing** : make a copy, arrangement, or recording of —**tran·scrip·tion** \trans'kripshən\ *n*

tran·script \'trans,kript\ *n* : official copy

tran·sept \'trans,ept\ *n* : part of a church that crosses the nave at right angles

trans·fer \trans'fər, 'trans,fər\ *vb* -**rr-** **1** : move from one person, place, or situation to another **2** : convey ownership of **3** : print or copy by contact **4** : change to another vehicle or transportation line ~ \'trans,fər\ *n* **1** : act or process of transferring **2** : one that transfers or is transferred **3** : ticket permitting one to transfer —**trans·fer·able** \trans'fərəbəl\ *adj* —**trans·fer·al** \-əl\ *n* —**trans·fer·ence** \-əns\ *n*

trans·fig·ure \trans'figyər\ *vb* -**ured**; -**ur·ing** **1** : change the form or appearance of **2** : glorify —**trans·fig·u·ra·tion** \,trans,fig)ə'rāshən\ *n*

trans·fix \trans'fiks\ *vb* **1** : pierce through **2** : hold motionless

trans·form \-'fórm\ *vb* **1** : change in structure, appearance, or character **2** : change (an electric current) in potential or type —**trans·for·ma·tion** \,transfər'māshən\ *n* —**trans·form·er** \trans'fórmər\ *n*

trans·fuse \trans'fyüz\ *vb* -**fused**; -**fus·ing** **1** : diffuse into or through **2** : transfer (as blood) into a vein —**trans·fu·sion** \-'fyüzhən\ *n*

trans·gress \trans'gres, tranz-\ *vb* : sin —**trans·gres·sion** \-'greshən\ *n* —**trans·gres·sor** \-'gresər\ *n*

tran·sient \'tranchənt\ *adj* : not lasting or staying long —**transient** *n* —**tran·sient·ly** *adv*

tran·sis·tor \tranz'istər, trans-\ *n* : small semiconductor —**tran·sis·tor·ize** \-tə,rīz\ *vb*

tran·sit \'transət, 'tranz-\ *n* **1** : movement over, across, or through **2** : local and esp. public transportation **3** : surveyor's instrument

tran·si·tion \trans'ishən, tranz-\ *n* : passage from one state, stage, or

subject to another —**tran·si·tion·al** \-'ish(ə)nəl\ *adj*

tran·si·to·ry \'transə,tōrē, 'tranz-\ *adj* : of brief duration

trans·late \trans'lāt, tranz-\ *vb* -**lat·ed**; -**lat·ing** : change into another language —**trans·lat·able** *adj* **trans·la·tion** \-'lāshən\ *n* —**trans·la·tor** \-'lātər\ *n*

trans·lu·cent \trans'lüs²nt, tranz-\ *adj* : diffusing light so that objects beyond cannot be distinguished —**trans·lu·cence** \-²ns\ *n* —**trans·lu·cen·cy** \-²nsē\ *n* —**trans·lu·cent·ly** *adv*

trans·mis·sion \-'mishən\ *n* **1** : act or process of transmitting **2** : system of gears between a car engine and drive wheels

trans·mit \-'mit\ *vb* -**tt-** **1** : transfer from one person or place to another **2** : pass on by inheritance **3** : broadcast —**trans·mis·si·ble** \-'misəbəl\ *adj* —**trans·mit·ta·ble** \-'mitəbəl\ *adj* —**trans·mit·tal** \-'mit²l\ *n* —**trans·mit·ter** *n*

tran·som \'transəm\ *n* : window above a door

trans·par·ent \trans'parənt\ *adj* **1** : clear enough to see through **2** : obvious —**trans·par·en·cy** \-ənsē\ *n* —**trans·par·ent·ly** *adv*

tran·spire \trans'pī(ə)r\ *vb* -**spired**; -**spir·ing** : take place —**tran·spi·ra·tion** \,transpə'rāshən\ *n*

trans·plant \trans'plant\ *vb* **1** : dig and move to another place **2** : transfer from one body part or person to another —**transplant** \'trans,-\ *n* —**trans·plan·ta·tion** \,trans,plan'tāshən\ *n*

trans·port \trans'pōrt\ *vb* **1** : carry or deliver to another place **2** : carry away by emotion ~ \'trans,-\ *n* **1** : act of transporting **2** : rapture **3** : ship or plane for carrying troops or supplies —**trans·por·ta·tion** \,transpər'tāshən\ *n* —**trans·port·er** *n*

trans·pose \trans'pōz\ *vb* -**posed**; -**pos·ing** : change the position, sequence, or key —**trans·po·si·tion** \,transpə'zishən\ *n*

trans·ship \tran(ch)'ship, trans-\ *vb* : transfer from one mode of transportation to another —**trans·ship·ment** *n*

trans·verse \trans'vərs, tranz-\ *adj* : lying across —**trans·verse** \'trans,vərs, 'tranz-\ *n* —**trans·verse·ly** *adv*

trap \'trap\ *n* **1** : device for catching animals **2** : something by which one is caught unawares **3** : device to allow one thing to pass through while keeping other things out ~ *vb* **-pp-** : catch in a trap —**trap·per** *n*

trap-door \'trap-\ *n* : door in a floor or roof

tra·peze \tra'pēz\ *n* : suspended bar used by acrobats

trap·e·zoid \'trapǝ,zòid\ *n* : plane 4-sided figure with 2 parallel sides —**trap·e·zoi·dal** \,trapǝ'zòid³l\ *adj*

trap·pings \'trapiņz\ *n pl* **1** : ornamental covering **2** : outward decoration or dress

trash \'trash\ *n* : something that is no good —**trashy** *adj*

trau·ma \'traùmǝ, 'tró-\ *n, pl* **-ma·ta** \-mǝtǝ\ *or* **-mas** : bodily or mental injury —**trau·mat·ic** \trǝ'matik, tro-, traù-\ *adj*

tra·vail \trǝ'vāl, 'trav,āl\ *n* : painful work or exertion ~ *vb* : labor hard

trav·el \'travǝl\ *vb* **-eled** *or* **-elled; -el·ing** *or* **-el·ling 1** : take a trip or tour **2** : move or be carried from point to point ~ *n* : journey —often pl. —**trav·el·er, trav·el·ler** *n*

tra·verse \trǝ'vǝrs, tra'vǝrs, 'travǝrs\ *vb* **-versed; -vers·ing** : go or extend across or over —**tra·verse** \'travǝrs\ *n*

trav·es·ty \'travǝstē\ *n, pl* **-ties** : terrible distortion or imitation of something —**travesty** *vb*

trawl \'tròl\ *vb* : fish or catch with a trawl ~ *n* : large cone-shaped net —**trawl·er** *n*

tray \'trā\ *n* : shallow flat-bottomed receptacle for holding or carrying something

treach·er·ous \'trech(ǝ)rǝs\ *adj* : disloyal or dangerous —**treach·er·ous·ly** *adv*

treach·ery \'trech(ǝ)rē\ *n, pl* **-er·ies** : betrayal of a trust

tread \'tred\ *vb* **trod** \'träd\; **trod·den** \'träd³n\ *or* **trod; tread·ing 1** : step on or over **2** : walk **3** : press or crush with the feet ~ *n* **1** : way of walking **2** : sound made in walking **3** : part on which a thing runs

trea·dle \'tred³l\ *n* : foot pedal operating a machine

tread·mill *n* **1** : mill worked by walking persons or animals **2** : wearisome routine

trea·son \'trēz³n\ *n* : attempt to overthrow the government —**trea·son·able** \'trēznǝbǝl, -³nǝbǝl\ *adj* —**trea·son·ous** \-nǝs, -³nǝs\ *adj*

trea·sure \'trezh-, 'trāzh-\ *n* **1** : wealth stored up **2** : something of

great value ~ *vb* **-sured; -sur·ing** : keep as precious

trea·sur·er \'trezhrǝr, 'trezhǝrǝr, 'träzh-\ *n* : officer who handles funds

trea·sury \'trezh(ǝ)rē, 'träzh-\ *n, pl* **-sur·ies** : place or office for keeping and distributing funds

treat \'trēt\ *vb* **1** : have as a topic **2** : pay for the food or entertainment of **3** : act toward or regard in a certain way **4** : give medical care for ~ *n* **1** : food or entertainment paid for by another **2** : something special and enjoyable —**treat·ment** \-mǝnt\ *n*

trea·tise \'trētǝs\ *n* : systematic written exposition or argument

trea·ty \'trētē\ *n, pl* **-ties** : agreement between governments

tre·ble \'trebǝl\ *n* **1** : highest part in music **2** : upper half of the musical range ~ *adj* : triple in number or amount ~ *vb* **-bled; -bling** : make triple —**tre·bly** *adv*

tree \'trē\ *n* : tall woody plant ~ *vb* **treed; tree·ing** : force up a tree —**tree·less** *adj*

trek \'trek\ *n* : difficult trip ~ *vb* **-kk-** : make a trek

trel·lis \'trelǝs\ *n* : structure of crossed strips

trem·ble \'trembǝl\ *vb* **-bled; -bling 1** : shake from fear or cold **2** : move or sound as if shaken

tre·men·dous \tri'mendǝs\ *adj* : amazingly large, powerful, or excellent —**tre·men·dous·ly** *adv*

trem·or \'tremǝr\ *n* : a trembling

trem·u·lous \'tremyǝlǝs\ *adj* : trembling or quaking —**trem·u·lous·ly** *adv*

trench \'trench\ *n* : long narrow cut in land

tren·chant \'trenchǝnt\ *adj* : sharply perceptive

trend \'trend\ *n* : prevailing tendency, direction, or style

trep·i·da·tion \,trepǝ'dāshǝn\ *n* : nervous apprehension

tres·pass \'trespǝs, -,pas\ *n* **1** : sin **2** : unauthorized entry onto someone's property ~ *vb* **1** : sin **2** : enter illegally —**tres·pass·er** *n*

tress \'tres\ *n* : long lock of hair

tres·tle \'tresǝl\ *n* **1** : support with a horizontal piece and spreading legs **2** : framework bridge

tri·ad \'trī,ad, -ǝd\ *n* : union of 3

tri·al \'trī(ǝ)l\ *n* **1** : hearing and judgment of a matter in court **2** : source of great annoyance **3** : test use or experimental effort —**trial** *adj*

tri·an·gle \'trī,aņgǝl\ *n* : plane figure with 3 sides and 3 angles —**tri·an·gu-**

lar \'trī'angyələr\ *adj* —**tri·an·gu·lar·ly** *adv*

tribe \'trīb\ *n* : social group of numerous families —**trib·al** \'trībəl\ *adj* —**tribes·man** \'trībzmən\ *n*

trib·u·la·tion \,tribyə'lāshən\ *n* : suffering from oppression

tri·bu·nal \trī'byünᵊl, trib'yün-\ *n* 1 : court 2 : something that decides

trib·u·tary \'tribyə,terē\ *n, pl* -**tar·ies** : stream that flows into a river or lake

trib·ute \'trib(,)yüt, -yət\ *n* 1 : payment to acknowledge submission 2 : tax 3 : gift or act showing respect

trick \'trik\ *n* 1 : scheme to deceive 2 : prank 3 : deceptive or ingenious feat 4 : mannerism 5 : knack 6 : tour of duty ~ *vb* : deceive by cunning —**trick·ery** \-(ə)rē\ *n* —**trick·ster** \-stər\ *n*

trick·le \'trikəl\ *vb* -**led**; -**ling** : run in drops or a thin stream —**trickle** *n*

tricky \'trikē\ *adj* **trick·i·er**; -**est** 1 : inclined to trickery 2 : requiring skill or caution

tri·cy·cle \'trī,sikəl\ *n* : 3-wheeled bicycle

tri·dent \'trīdᵊnt\ *n* : 3-pronged spear

tri·en·ni·al \trī'enēəl\ *adj* : lasting, occurring, or done every 3 years —**triennial** *n*

tri·fle \'trīfəl\ *n* : something of little value or importance ~ *vb* -**fled**; -**fling** 1 : speak or act in a playful or flirting way 2 : toy —**tri·fler** *n*

tri·fling \'trīfliŋ\ *adj* : trivial

trig·ger \'trigər\ *n* : finger-piece of a firearm lock that releases the hammer ~ *vb* : set into motion —**trigger** *adj* —**trig·gered** \-ərd\ *adj*

trig·o·nom·e·try \,trigə'nämətrē\ *n* : mathematics dealing with triangular measurement —**trig·o·no·met·ric** \-nə'metrik\, **trig·o·no·met·ri·cal** \-rikəl\ *adj*

trill \'tril\ *n* 1 : rapid alternation between 2 adjacent tones 2 : rapid vibration in speaking ~ *vb* : utter in or with a trill

tril·lion \'trilyən\ *n* : 1000 billions —**trillion** *adj* —**tril·lionth** \-yənth\ *adj or n*

tril·o·gy \'triləjē\ *n, pl* -**gies** : 3-part literary or musical composition

trim \'trim\ *vb* -**mm**- 1 : decorate 2 : make neat or reduce by cutting ~ *adj* -**mm**- : neat and compact ~ *n* 1 : state or condition 2 : ornaments —**trim·ly** *adv* —**trim·mer** *n* —**trim·ness** *n*

trim·ming \'trimiŋ\ *n* 1 : something

that ornaments or completes 2 *pl* : scraps left after cutting

Trin·i·ty \'trinətē\ *n* : divine unity of Father, Son, and Holy Spirit

trin·ket \'triŋkət\ *n* : small ornament

trio \'trēō\ *n, pl* **tri·os** 1 : music for 3 performers 2 : group of 3

trip \'trip\ *vb* -**pp**- 1 : step lightly 2 : stumble or cause to stumble 3 : make or cause to make a mistake 4 : release (as a spring or switch) ~ *n* 1 : journey 2 : stumble 3 : drug-induced experience

tri·par·tite \trī'pär,tīt\ *adj* : having 3 parts or parties

tripe \'trīp\ *n* 1 : animal's stomach used as food 2 : trash

tri·ple \'tripəl\ *vb* -**pled**; -**pling** : make 3 times as great ~ *n* : group of 3 ~ *adj* 1 : having 3 units 2 : being 3 times as great or as many

trip·let \'triplət\ *n* 1 : group of 3 2 : one of 3 offspring born together

trip·li·cate \'triplikət\ *adj* : made in 3 identical copies ~ *n* : one of 3 copies

tri·pod \'trī,päd\ *n* : a stand with 3 legs —**tripod**, **tri·po·dal** \'tripədᵊl, 'trī,päd-\ *adj*

tri·sect \'trī,sekt, trī'-\ *vb* : divide into 3 usu. equal parts —**tri·sec·tion** \'trī,sekshən\ *n*

trite \'trīt\ *adj* **trit·er**; **trit·est** : too much used

tri·umph \'trīəmf\ *n, pl* -**umphs** \-əmfs, -əm(p)s\ : victory or great success ~ *vb* : obtain or celebrate victory —**tri·um·phal** \trī'əmfəl\ *adj* —**tri·um·phant** \-fənt\ *adj* —**tri·um·phant·ly** *adv*

tri·um·vi·rate \trī'əmvərət\ *n* : ruling body of 3 persons

triv·et \'trivət\ *n* 1 : 3-legged stand 2 : stand to hold a hot dish

triv·ia \'trivēə\ *n sing or pl* : unimportant details

triv·i·al \'trivēəl\ *adj* : of little importance —**triv·i·al·i·ty** \,trivē'alətē\ *n*

trod *past of* TREAD

trod·den *past part of* TREAD

troll \'trōl\ *n* : dwarf or giant of folklore inhabiting caves or hills

trol·ley, trol·ly \'trälē\ *n, pl* -**leys** or -**lies** : streetcar run by overhead electric wires

trol·lop \'träləp\ *n* : untidy or immoral woman

trom·bone \träm'bōn, 'träm,-\ *n* : musical instrument with a long sliding tube —**trom·bon·ist** \-'bōnəst, -,bō-\ *n*

troop \'trüp\ *n* 1 : cavalry unit 2 *pl* : soldiers 3 : collection of people or things ~ vb : move or gather in crowds

troop·er \\'trüpər\ n 1 : cavalry soldier 2 : policeman on horseback or state policeman

tro·phy \\'trōfē\ n, pl **-phies** : prize gained by a victory

trop·ic \\'träpik\ n 1 : either of the 2 parallels of latitude one 23½ degrees north of the equator (**tropic of Cancer** \\-'kansər\) and one 23½ degrees south of the equator (**tropic of Cap·ri·corn** \\-'kaprə,kȯrn\) 2 pl : region lying between the tropics —**tropic, trop·i·cal** \\-ikal\ adj

trot \\'trät\ n 1 : moderately fast gait esp. of a horse with diagonally paired legs moving together ~ vb **-tt-** : go at a trot —**trot·ter** n

troth \\'träth, 'trȯth, 'trōth\ n 1 : pledged faithfulness 2 : betrothal

trou·ba·dour \\'trüba,dȯr\ n : medieval lyric poet

trou·ble \\'trəbəl\ vb **-bled; -bling** 1 : disturb 2 : afflict 3 : make an effort ~ n 1 : cause of mental or physical distress 2 : effort —**trou·ble·mak·er** n —**trou·ble·some** adj —**trou·ble·some·ly** adv

trough \\'trȯf, 'trȯth, by bakers often 'trō\ n, pl **troughs** \\'trȯfs, 'trȯvz; 'trȯths, 'trȯ(th)z; 'trȯz\ 1 : narrow container for animal feed or water 2 : long channel or depression (as between waves)

trounce \\'traúns\ vb **trounced; trouncing** : thrash, punish, or defeat severely

troupe \\'trüp\ n : group of stage performers —**troup·er** n

trou·sers \\'traúzərz\ n pl : long pants for men or boys —**trouser** adj

trous·seau \\'trüsō, trü'sō\ n, pl **-seaux** \\-sōz, -'sōz\ or **-seaus** : bride's collection of clothing and personal items

trout \\'traút\ n, pl **trout** : freshwater food and game fish

trow·el \\'traú(ə)l\ n 1 : tool for spreading or smoothing 2 : garden scoop —**trowel** vb

troy \\'trȯi\ n : system of weights based on a pound of 12 ounces

tru·ant \\'trüənt\ n 1 : one who shirks duty 2 : one absent from school without permission —**tru·an·cy** \\-ənsē\ n —**truant** adj

truce \\'trüs\ n : agreement to halt fighting

truck \\'trək\ n 1 : wheeled frame for moving heavy objects 2 : automotive vehicle for transporting heavy loads

~ vb : transport on a truck —**truck·er** n —**truck·load** n

truck·le \\'trəkəl\ vb **-led; -ling** : yield slavishly to another

tru·cu·lent \\'trəkyələnt\ adj : aggressively self-assertive —**truc·u·lence** \\-ləns\ n —**truc·u·len·cy** \\-lənsē\ n —**tru·cu·lent·ly** adv

trudge \\'trəj\ vb **trudged; trudg·ing** : walk or march steadily and with difficulty

true \\'trü\ adj **tru·er; tru·est** 1 : loyal 2 : in agreement with fact or reality 3 : genuine ~ adv 1 : truthfully 2 : accurately —**tru·ly** adv

true-blue adj : loyal

truf·fle \\'trəfəl, 'trüf-\ n : edible fruit of an underground fungus

tru·ism \\'trü,izəm\ n : obvious truth

trump \\'trəmp\ n : card of a designated suit any of whose cards will win over other cards ~ vb : take with a trump

trumped-up \\' 'trəm(p)t'əp\ adj : made-up

trum·pet \\'trəmpət\ n : tubular brass wind instrument with a flaring end ~ vb 1 : blow a trumpet 2 : proclaim loudly —**trum·pet·er** n

trun·cate \\'trəŋ,kāt, 'trən-\ vb **-cat·ed; -cat·ing** : cut short —**trun·ca·tion** \\,trəŋ'kāshən\ n

trun·dle \\'trəndəl\ vb **-dled; -dling** : roll along

trunk \\'trəŋk\ n 1 : main part (as of a body or tree) 2 : long muscular nose of an elephant 3 : storage chest 4 : storage space in a car 5 pl : shorts

truss \\'trəs\ vb : bind tightly ~ n 1 : set of structural parts forming a framework 2 : appliance worn to hold a hernia in place

trust \\'trəst\ n 1 : reliance on another 2 : assured hope 3 : credit 4 : property held or managed in behalf of another 5 : combination of firms that reduces competition 6 : something entrusted to another's care 7 : custody ~ vb 1 : depend 2 : hope 3 : entrust 4 : have faith in —**trust·ful** \\-fəl\ adj —**trust·ful·ly** adv —**trust·ful·ness** n —**trust·worth·i·ness** n —**trust·wor·thy** adj

trust·ee \\,trəs'tē\ n : person holding property in trust —**trust·ee·ship** n

trusty \\'trəstē\ adj **trust·i·er; -est** : dependable

truth \\'trüth\ n, pl **truths** \\'trüthz, 'trüths\ 1 : real state of things 2 : true or accepted statement 3 : agreement with fact or reality —**truth·ful** \\-fəl\ adj —**truth·ful·ly** adv —**truth·ful·ness** n

try \'trī\ *vb* **tried; try·ing 1** : conduct the trial of **2** : put to a test **3** : strain **4** : make an effort at ~ *n, pl* **tries** : act of trying

try·out *n* : competitive test of performance esp. for athletes or actors —**try out** *vb*

tryst \'trist, ,trīst\ *n* : secret rendezvous of lovers

tsar \'zär, 't)sär\ *var of* CZAR

T-shirt \'tē,shərt\ *n* : collarless pullover shirt with short sleeves

tub \'təb\ *n* **1** : wide bucketlike vessel **2** : bathtub

tu·ba \'t(y)übə\ *n* : large low-pitched brass wind instrument

tube \'t(y)üb\ *n* **1** : hollow cylinder **2** : round container from which a substance can be squeezed **3** : airtight circular tube of rubber inside a tire **4** : device with a space through which electricity is conducted esp. in radio —**tubed** \'t(y)übd\ *adj* —**tube·less** *adj*

tu·ber \'t(y)übər\ *n* : fleshy underground growth (as of a potato) —**tu·ber·ous** \-rəs\ *adj*

tu·ber·cu·lo·sis \t(y)ü,bərkyə'lōsəs\ *n, pl* **-lo·ses** \-,sēz\ : bacterial disease esp. of the lungs —**tu·ber·cu·lar** \-'bərkyələr\ *adj* —**tu·ber·cu·lous** \-ləs\ *adj*

tub·ing \'t(y)übiŋ\ *n* : series or arrangement of tubes

tu·bu·lar \'t(y)übyələr\ *adj* : of or like a tube

tuck \'tək\ *vb* **1** : pull up into a fold **2** : put into a snug often concealing place **3** : make snug in preparing —with *in* ~ *n* : fold in a cloth

tuck·er \'təkər\ *vb* : fatigue

Tues·day \'t(y)üzdē\ *n* : 3d day of the week

tuft \'təft\ *n* : clump (as of hair or feathers) —**tuft·ed** \'təftəd\ *adj*

tug \'təg\ *vb* -**gg- 1** : pull hard **2** : move by pulling ~ *n* **1** : act of tugging **2** : tugboat

tug·boat *n* : boat for towing or pushing ships through a harbor

tug-of-war \,təgə(v)'wȯr\ *n, pl* **tugs-of-war** : pulling contest between 2 teams

tu·ition \t(y)ü'ishən\ *n* : cost of instruction

tu·lip \'t(y)üləp\ *n* : herb with cup-shaped flowers

tum·ble \'təmbəl\ *vb* -**bled; -bling 1** : perform gymnastic feats of rolling and turning **2** : fall or cause to fall suddenly **3** : toss ~ *n* : act of tumbling

tum·bler \'təmblər\ *n* **1** : acrobat **2** : drinking glass **3** : obstruction in a lock that can be moved (as by a key)

tu·mid \'t(y)üməd\ *adj* : turgid —**tu·mid·i·ty** \t(y)ü'midətē\ *n*

tum·my \'təmē\ *n, pl* -**mies** : belly

tu·mor \'t(y)ümər\ *n* : abnormal and useless growth of tissue —**tu·mor·ous** *adj*

tu·mult \'t(y)ü,məlt\ *n* **1** : confusion of loud noise and movement **2** : violent agitation of mind or feelings —**tu·mul·tu·ous** \t(y)ü'məlch(ə)wəs, -'məlchəs\ *adj*

tun \'tən\ *n* : large cask

tu·na \'t(y)ünə\ *n, pl* -**na, -nas** : large sea food fish

tun·dra \'təndrə\ *n* : treeless arctic plain

tune \'t(y)ün\ *n* **1** : melody **2** : correct musical pitch **3** : harmonious relationship ~ *vb* **tuned; tun·ing 1** : bring or come into harmony **2** : adjust in musical pitch **3** : adjust a receiver so as to receive a broadcast **4** : put in first-class working order —**tune·ful** \-fəl\ *adj* —**tun·er** *n*

tung·sten \'təŋstən\ *n* : metallic element used for electrical purposes and in hardening alloys (as steel)

tu·nic \'t(y)ünik\ *n* **1** : ancient knee-length garment **2** : hip-length blouse or jacket

tun·nel \'tən°l\ *n* : underground passageway ~ *vb* -**neled** *or* -**nelled; -nel·ing** *or* -**nel·ling** : make a tunnel through or under something

tur·ban \'tərbən\ *n* : wound headdress worn esp. by Muslims

tur·bid \'tərbəd\ *adj* **1** : dark with stirred-up sediment **2** : confused —**tur·bid·i·ty** \,tər'bidətē\ *n* —**tur·bid·ly** \'tərbədlē\ *adv* —**tur·bid·ness** *n*

tur·bine \'tərbən, -,bīn\ *n* : engine turned by the force of gas or water on fan blades

tur·bo·jet \'tərbō,jet\ *n* : airplane powered by a jet engine having a turbine-driven air compressor

tur·bo·prop \'tərbō,präp\ *n* : airplane powered by a propeller turned by a jet engine-driven turbine

tur·bu·lent \'tərbyələnt\ *adj* **1** : causing violence or disturbance **2** : marked by agitation or tumult —**tur·bu·lence** \-ləns\ *n* —**tur·bu·lent·ly** *adv*

tu·reen \tə'rēn, tyü-\ *n* : deep bowl for serving soup

turf \'tərf\ *n, pl* **turfs** \'tərfs\ *or* **turves** \'tərvz\ : upper layer of soil bound by grass and roots

tur·gid \'tərjəd\ *adj* 1 : swollen 2 : too highly embellished in style —**tur·gid·i·ty** \,tər'jidətē\ *n*

tur·key \'tərkē\ *n, pl* -keys : large American bird raised for food

tur·moil \'tər,móil\ *n* : extremely agitated condition

turn \'tərn\ *vb* 1 : move or cause to move around an axis 2 : twist (a mechanical part) to operate 3 : wrench 4 : cause to face or move in a different direction 5 : reverse the sides or surfaces of 6 : upset 7 : go around 8 : become or cause to become 9 : seek aid from a source ~ *n* 1 : act or instance of turning : change 3 : place at which something turns 4 : place, time, or opportunity to do something in order —**turn down** : decline to accept —**turn in** 1 : deliver or report to authorities 2 : go to bed —**turn off** : stop the functioning of —**turn out** 1 : expel 2 : produce 3 : come together 4 : prove to be in the end —**turn up** 1 : discover or appear 2 : happen unexpectedly

turn·coat *n* : traitor

tur·nip \'tərnəp\ *n* : edible root of an herb

turn·out \'tərn,aút\ *n* 1 : gathering of people for a special purpose 2 : size of a gathering

turn·over *n* 1 : upset or reversal 2 : filled pastry 3 : volume of business 4 : movement (as of goods or people) into, through, and out of a place

turn·pike \'tərn,pīk\ *n* : expressway on which tolls are charged

turn·stile \-,stīl\ *n* : post with arms pivoted on the top that allows people to pass one by one

turn·ta·ble *n* : platform that turns a phonograph record

tur·pen·tine \'tərpən,tīn\ *n* : oil used as a solvent and in paint that is distilled from pine trees

tur·pi·tude \'tərpə,t(y)üd\ *n* : inherent baseness

tur·quoise \'tər,k(w)óiz\ *n* : blue or greenish gray gemstone

tur·ret \'tərət\ *n* 1 : little tower on a building 2 : revolving tool holder or gun housing

tur·tle \'tərt³l\ *n* : reptile with the trunk enclosed in a bony shell

tur·tle·dove *n* : wild pigeon

tur·tle·neck *n* : high close-fitting collar that can be turned over or a sweater with this collar

turves *pl of* TURF

tusk \'təsk\ *n* : long protruding tooth

(as of an elephant) —**tusked** \'təskt\ *adj*

tus·sle \'təsəl\ *n or vb* : struggle

tu·te·lage \'t(y)üt³lij\ *n* 1 : act of protecting 2 : instruction esp. of an individual

tu·tor \'t(y)ütər\ *n* : private teacher ~ *vb* : teach usu. individually

tux·e·do \,tək'sēdō\ *n, pl* -dos *or* -does : semiformal evening clothes for a man

TV \'tē'vē\ *n* : television

twain \'twān\ *n* : two

twang \'twaŋ\ *n* 1 : harsh sound like that of a plucked bowstring 2 : nasal speech or resonance ~ *vb* : sound or speak with a twang

tweak \'twēk\ *vb* : pinch and pull playfully —**tweak** *n*

tweed \'twēd\ *n* 1 : rough woolen fabric 2 *pl* : tweed clothing

tweet \'twēt\ *n* : chirping note —**tweet** *vb*

twee·zers \'twēzərz\ *n pl* : small pincerlike tool

twelve \'twelv\ *n* 1 : one more than 11 2 : 12th in a set or series 3 : something having 12 units —**twelfth** \'twelfth\ *adj or n* —**twelve** *adj or pron*

twen·ty \'twentē\ *n, pl* -ties : 2 times 10 —**twen·ti·eth** \-ēəth\ *adj or n* —**twenty** *adj or pron*

twice \'twīs\ *adv* 1 : on 2 occasions 2 : 2 times

twig \'twig\ *n* : small branch —**twig·gy** *adj*

twi·light \'twī,līt\ *n* : light from the sky at dusk or dawn —**twilight** *adj*

twill \'twil\ *n* : fabric with a weave that gives an appearance of diagonal lines in the fabric

twilled \'twild\ *adj* : made with a twill weave

twin \'twin\ *adj* 1 : born with one another or as a pair at one birth 2 : made up of 2 similar parts ~ *n* : either of 2 offspring born together

twine \'twīn\ *n* : strong twisted thread ~ *vb* twined; twin·ing 1 : twist together 2 : coil about a support —**twin·er** *n* —**twiny** *adj*

twinge \'twinj\ *vb* twinged; twing·ing *or* twinge·ing : affect with or feel a sudden sharp pain ~ *n* : sudden sharp stab (as of pain)

twin·kle \'twiŋkəl\ *vb* -kled; -kling : shine with a flickering light ~ *n* 1 : wink 2 : intermittent shining —**twin·kler** \-k(ə)lər\ *n*

twirl \'twərl\ *vb* : whirl round ~ *n* 1 : act of twirling 2 : coil —**twirl·er** *n*

twist \\'twist\\ *vb* **1** : unite by winding (threads) together **2** : wrench **3** : move in or have a spiral shape **4** : follow a winding course ~ *n* **1** : act or result of twisting **2** : unexpected development

twist·er \\'twistər\\ *n* : tornado

twit \\'twit\\ *vb* -**tt**- : taunt

twitch \\'twich\\ *vb* : move or pull with a sudden motion ~ *n* : act of twitching

twit·ter \\'twitər\\ *vb* : make chirping noises ~ *n* : small intermittent noise

two \\'tü\\ *n, pl* **twos** **1** : one more than one **2** : the 2d in a set or series **3** : something having two units —**two** *adj or pron*

two·fold \\'tü,föld, -'föld\\ *adj* : double —**two·fold** \\-'föld\\ *adv*

two·some \\'tüsəm\\ *n* : couple

-**ty** *n suffix* : quality, condition, or degree

ty·coon \\tī'kün\\ *n* : powerful and successful businessman

tying *pres part of* TIE

tyke \\'tīk\\ *n* : small child

tym·pa·num \\'timpənəm\\ *n, pl* -**na** \\-nə\\ : eardrum or the cavity which it closes externally —**tym·pan·ic** \\tim'panik\\ *adj*

type \\'tīp\\ *n* **1** : class, kind, or group set apart by common characteristics **2** : special design of printed letters ~ *vb* **typed; typ·ing 1** : produce on a typewriter **2** : identify or classify as a particular type

type·writ·er *n* : keyboard machine that produces printed material by striking with raised letters through an inked ribbon —**type·write** *vb*

ty·phoid \\'tī,fòid, tī'-\\ *adj* : relating to or being a communicable bacterial disease **(typhoid fever)**

ty·phoon \\tī'fün\\ *n* : hurricane of the western Pacific ocean

ty·phus \\'tīfəs\\ *n* : severe disease with fever, delirium, and rash

typ·i·cal \\'tipikəl\\ *adj* : having the essential characteristics of a group —**typ·i·cal·ly** *adv* —**typ·i·cal·ness** *n*

typ·i·fy \\'tipə,fī\\ *vb* -**fied; -fy·ing** : be typical of

typ·ist \\'tīpəst\\ *n* : one who operates a typewriter

ty·pog·ra·phy \\tī'pägrəfē\\ *n* **1** : art of printing with type **2** : style, arrangement, or appearance of matter printed from type —**ty·po·graph·ic** \\,tīpə'grafik\\, **ty·po·graph·i·cal** \\-ikəl\\ *adj* —**ty·po·graph·i·cal·ly** *adv*

ty·ran·ni·cal \\tə'ranikəl, tī-\\ *adj* : relating to a tyrant —**ty·ran·ni·cal·ly** *adv*

ty·ran·nize \\'tirə,nīz\\ *vb* -**nized; -niz·ing** : rule or deal with in the manner of a tyrant —**tyr·an·niz·er** *n*

tyr·an·ny \\'tirənē\\ *n, pl* -**nies** : unjust use of absolute governmental power

ty·rant \\'tīrənt\\ *n* : harsh ruler having absolute power

ty·ro \\'tīrō\\ *n, pl* -**ros** : beginner

tzar \\'zär, '(t)sär\\ *var of* CZAR

U

u \\'yü\\ *n, pl* **u's** *or* **us** \\'yüz\\ : 21st letter of the alphabet

ubiq·ui·tous \\yü'bikwətəs\\ *adj* : ever-present —**ubiq·ui·tous·ly** *adv* —**ubiq·ui·ty** \\-wətē\\ *n*

ud·der \\'ədər\\ *n* : animal sac containing milk glands and nipples

ug·ly \\'əglē\\ *adj* **ug·li·er; -est 1** : offensive to look at **2** : mean or quarrelsome —**ug·li·ness** *n*

uku·le·le \\,yükə'lālē\\ *n* : small 4-string guitar

ul·cer \\'əlsər\\ *n* : eroded sore —**ul·cer·ous** *adj*

ul·cer·ate \\'əlsə,rāt\\ *vb* -**at·ed; -at·ing** : cause or become affected with an ulcer —**ul·cer·a·tion** \\,əlsə'rāshən\\ *n* —**ul·cer·a·tive** \\'əlsə,rātiv\\ *adj*

ul·na \\'əlnə\\ *n* : inner bone of the forearm

ul·te·ri·or \\,əl'tirēər\\ *adj* : not revealed

ul·ti·mate \\'əltəmət\\ *adj* : final, maximum, or extreme —**ultimate** *n* —**ul·ti·mate·ly** *adv*

ul·ti·ma·tum \\,əltə'mātəm, -'mät-\\ *n, pl* -**tums** *or* -**ta** \\-ə\\ : final proposition or demand carrying or implying a threat

ul·tra·vi·o·let \\,əltrə'vīələt\\ *adj* : having a wavelength shorter than visible light

um·bil·i·cus \\,əmbə'likəs, ,əm'bili-\\ *n, pl* -**li·ci** \\-bə'lī,kī, -,sī; -'bili,kī, -,kē\\ *or* -**li·cus·es** : small depression on the abdominal wall marking the site of the cord **(umbilical cord)** that joins the unborn fetus to its mother —**um·bil·i·cal** \\,əm'bilikəl\\ *adj*

um·brage \\'əmbrij\\ *n* : resentment

um·brel·la \\,əm'brelə\\ *n* : collapsible fabric device to protect from sun or rain

um·pire \\'əm₁pī(ə)r\\ *n* 1 : arbitrator 2 : sport official —**umpire** *vb*

ump·teen \\'əmp'tēn\\ *adj* : very numerous —**umpteenth** \\-'tēnth\\ *adj*

un- \\₁ən, 'ən\\ *prefix* 1 : not 2 : opposite of

unable	uncontrolled	unforgiving	unneighborly
unabridged	unconventional	unfulfilled	unnoticeable
unacceptable	unconventionally	unfurnished	unnoticed
unaccompanied	unconverted	ungenerous	unobjectionable
unaccounted	uncooked	ungentlemanly	unobservable
unacquainted	uncooperative	ungraceful	unobservant
unaddressed	uncoordinated	ungrammatical	unobtainable
unadorned	uncovered	unharmed	unobtrusive
unadulterated	uncultivated	unhealthful	unobtrusively
unafraid	undamaged	unhurt	unofficial
unaided	undated	unidentified	unopened
unalike	undeclared	unimaginable	unopposed
unambiguous	undefeated	unimaginative	unorganized
unambitious	undemocratic	unimportant	unoriginal
unannounced	undependable	unimpressed	unorthodox
unanswered	undeserving	uninformed	unpaid
unanticipated	undesirable	uninhabited	unpardonable
unappetizing	undetected	uninjured	unpatriotic
unappreciated	undetermined	uninsured	unpaved
unapproved	undeveloped	unintelligent	unpleasant
unassisted	undeviating	unintelligible	unpleasantly
unattended	undignified	unintelligibly	unpleasantness
unattractive	undisturbed	unintended	unpopular
unauthorized	undivided	unintentional	unpopularity
unavailable	undomesticated	unintentionally	unposed
unavoidable	undrinkable	uninterested	unpredictable
unbearable	unearned	uninteresting	unpredictably
unbelievable	uneducated	uninterrupted	unprejudiced
unbelievably	unemotional	uninvited	unprepared
unbiased	unending	unjust	unpretentious
unbranded	unendurable	unjustifiable	unproductive
unbreakable	unenforceable	unjustified	unprofitable
uncensored	unenlightened	unjustly	unprotected
unchallenged	unethical	unknowing	unproved
unchangeable	unexcitable	unknowingly	unproven
unchanged	unexciting	unknown	unprovoked
unchanging	unexpected	unleavened	unpunished
uncharacteristic	unexpectedly	unlicensed	unqualified
uncharged	unexplainable	unlikable	unquenchable
unchaste	unexplored	unlike	unquestioning
uncivilized	unfair	unlikelihood	unreachable
unclaimed	unfairly	unlikely	unreadable
unclear	unfairness	unlikeness	unready
uncleared	unfavorable	unlimited	unrealistic
unclothed	unfavorably	unlovable	unreasonable
uncluttered	unfeigned	unmanageable	unreasonably
uncombed	unfilled	unmarked	unrefined
uncomfortable	unfinished	unmarried	unrelated
uncomfortably	unflattering	unmerciful	unreliable
uncomplimentary	unforeseeable	unmercifully	unremembered
unconfirmed	unforeseen	unmerited	unrepentant
uncontested	unforgivable	unmolested	unrequited
		unmotivated	unresolved
		unmoving	unresponsive
		unnamed	unrestrained
		unnavigable	unrestricted
		unnecessarily	unrewarding
		unnecessary	unripe
		unneeded	unsafe

unsalted
unsanitary
unsatisfactory
unsatisfied
unsatisfying
unscented
unscheduled
unseasoned
unseen
unselfish
unselfishly
unselfishness
unshaped
unshaved
unshaven
unskillful
unskillfully
unsolicited
unsolved
unsophisticated
unsound
unsoundly
unsoundness
unspecified
unspoiled
unsteadily
unsteadiness
unsteady
unstructured
unsubstantiated
unsuccessful
unsuitable
unsuitably
unsuited
unsupervised
unsupported

unsure
unsuspecting
unsweetened
unsympathetic
untamed
untanned
unthankful
untidy
untouched
untrained
untreated
untrue
untrustworthy
untruthful
unusable
unusual
unvarying
unverified
unwanted
unwarranted
unwary
unwavering
unweaned
unwed
unwelcome
unwholesome
unwilling
unwillingly
unwillingness
unwise
unwisely
unworkable
unworthily
unworthiness
unworthy
unyielding

un·ac·cus·tomed \ˌən-\ *adj* 1 : not customary 2 : not accustomed

un·af·fect·ed \ˌən-\ *adj* 1 : not influenced or changed by something 2 : natural and sincere —**un·af·fect·ed·ly** *adv*

unan·i·mous \yu̇ˈnanəməs\ *adj* 1 : showing no disagreement 2 : formed with the agreement of all —**una·nim·i·ty** \ˌyünəˈnimətē\ *n* —**unan·i·mous·ly** *adv*

un·armed \ˌən-\ *adj* : not armed or armored

un·as·sum·ing \ˌən-\ *adj* : not bold or arrogant

un·at·tached \ˌən-\ *adj* 1 : not attached 2 : not married or engaged

un·aware \ˌən-\ *adv* : unawares ~ *adj* : not aware

un·awares \ˌənəˈwaərz\ *adv* 1 : without warning 2 : unintentionally

un·bal·anced \ˌən-\ *adj* 1 : not balanced 2 : mentally unstable

un·beat·en \ˌən-\ *adj* : not beaten

un·be·com·ing \ˌən-\ *adj* : not proper or suitable —**un·be·com·ing·ly** *adv*

un·bend \ˌən-\ *vb* -**bent**; -**bend·ing** : make or become more relaxed and friendly

un·bend·ing \ˌən-\ *adj* : formal and inflexible

un·bind \ˌən-\ *vb* -**bound**; -**bind·ing** 1 : remove bindings from 2 : release

un·bolt \ˌən-, ˈən-\ *vb* : open or unfasten by withdrawing a bolt

un·born \ˌən-, ˈən-\ *adj* : not yet born

un·bo·som \ˌən-, ˈən-\ *vb* : disclose thoughts or feelings

un·bowed \ˌənˈbau̇d, ˈən-\ *adj* : not defeated or subdued

un·bri·dled \ˌənˈbrīdᵊld, ˈən-\ *adj* : unrestrained

un·bro·ken \ˌən-, ˈən-\ *adj* 1 : not damaged 2 : not interrupted

un·buck·le \ˌən-, ˈən-\ *vb* : unfasten the buckle of

un·bur·den \ˌən-, ˈən-\ *vb* : relieve (oneself) of anxieties

un·but·ton \ˌən-, ˈən-\ *vb* : unfasten the buttons of

un·called-for \ˌən-\ *adj* : too harsh or rude for the occasion

un·can·ny \ˌənˈkanē\ *adj* 1 : weird 2 : suggesting superhuman powers —**un·can·ni·ly** \-ˈkanᵊlē\ *adv*

un·ceas·ing \ˌən-\ *adj* : never ceasing —**un·ceas·ing·ly** *adv*

un·cer·e·mo·ni·ous \ˌən-\ *adj* : acting without ordinary courtesy —**un·cer·e·mo·ni·ous·ly** *adv*

un·cer·tain \ˌən-\ *adj* 1 : not determined, sure, or definitely known 2 : subject to chance or change —**un·cer·tain·ly** *adv* —**un·cer·tain·ty** *n*

un·chris·tian \ˌən-, ˈən-\ *adj* : not consistent with Christian teachings

un·cle \ˈəŋkəl\ *n* 1 : brother of one's father or mother 2 : husband of one's aunt

un·clean \ˌən-, ˈən-\ *adj* : not clean or pure —**un·clean·ness** *n*

un·clog \ˌən-, ˈən-\ *vb* : remove an obstruction from

un·coil \ˌən-, ˈən-\ *vb* : release or become released from a coiled state

un·com·mit·ted \ˌən-\ *adj* : not pledged to a particular allegiance or course of action

un·com·mon \ˌən-, ˈən-\ *adj* 1 : rare 2 : superior —**un·com·mon·ly** *adv*

un·com·pro·mis·ing \ˌən-\ *adj* : not making or accepting a compromise

un·con·cerned \ˌən-\ adj 1 : disinterested 2 : not anxious —**un·con·cern·ed·ly** adv

un·con·di·tion·al \ˌən-\ adj : not limited in any way —**un·con·di·tion·al·ly** adv

un·con·scio·na·ble \ˌən-, ˈən-\ adj : shockingly unjust or unscrupulous —**un·con·scio·na·bly** adv

un·con·scious \ˌən-, ˈən-\ adj 1 : not awake or aware of one's surroundings 2 : not consciously done ~ n : part of one's mental life that one is not aware of —**un·con·scious·ly** adv —**un·con·scious·ness** n

un·con·sti·tu·tion·al \ˌən-\ adj : not according to or consistent with a constitution

un·con·trol·la·ble \ˌən-\ adj : incapable of being controlled —**un·con·trol·la·bly** adv

un·count·ed \ˌən-\ adj : countless

un·couth \ˌən-ˈküth, ˈən-\ adj : rude and vulgar

un·cov·er \ˌən-, ˈən-\ vb 1 : reveal 2 : expose by removing a covering

unc·tion \ˈəŋkshən\ n 1 : rite of anointing 2 : exaggerated or insincere earnestness

unc·tu·ous \ˈəŋkchə(wə)s\ adj 1 : oily 2 : excessively or insincerely ingratiating —**unc·tu·ous·ly** adv

un·cut \ˌən-, ˈən-\ adj 1 : not cut down, into, off, or apart 2 : not shaped by cutting 3 : not abridged

un·daunt·ed \ˌən-, ˈən-\ adj : not discouraged —**un·daunt·ed·ly** adv

un·de·cid·ed \ˌən-\ adj 1 : not settled 2 : not having made up one's mind

un·de·ni·able \ˌən-\ adj : plainly true —**un·de·ni·ably** adv

un·der \ˈəndər\ adv : below or beneath something ~ \ˌəndər, ˈəndər\ prep 1 : lower than and sheltered by 2 : below the surface of 3 : covered or concealed by 4 : subject to the authority of 5 : less than ~ \ˈəndər\ adj 1 : lying below or beneath 2 : subordinate 3 : less than usual, proper, or desired

un·der·brush \ˈəndər,brəsh\ n : shrubs and small trees growing beneath large trees

un·der·clothes \ˈəndər,klō(th)z\ n pl : underwear

un·der·cloth·ing \-,klōthiŋ\ n : underwear

un·der·cov·er \ˌəndər-\ adj : employed or engaged in secret investigation

un·der·cur·rent \ˈəndər-\ n : hidden tendency or opinion

un·der·cut \ˌəndər-\ vb -**cut**; -**cut·ting** : offer to sell or to work at a lower rate than

un·der·de·vel·oped \ˌəndər-\ adj : not normally or adequately developed esp. economically

un·der·dog \ˈəndər-\ n : contestant given least chance of winning

un·der·done \ˌəndər-\ adj : not thoroughly done or cooked

un·der·es·ti·mate \ˌəndər-\ vb : estimate too low

un·der·ex·pose \ˌəndər-\ vb : give less than normal exposure to —**un·der·ex·po·sure** n

un·der·feed \ˌəndər-\ vb -**fed**; -**feed·ing** : feed inadequately

un·der·foot \ˌəndər-\ adv 1 : under the feet 2 : in the way of another

un·der·gar·ment \ˈəndər-\ n : garment to be worn under another

un·der·go \ˌəndər-\ vb -**went** \-ˈwent\; -**gone**; -**go·ing** 1 : endure 2 : pass through (as an experience)

un·der·grad·u·ate \ˌəndər-\ n : university or college student

un·der·ground \ˌəndər-\ adv 1 : beneath the surface of the earth 2 : in secret ~ \ˈəndər-\ adj 1 : being or growing under the surface of the ground 2 : secret ~ \ˈəndər-\ n : secret political movement or group

un·der·growth \ˈəndər-\ n : low growth on the floor of a forest

un·der·hand \ˈəndər-\ adv or adj 1 : with secrecy and deception 2 : with the hand kept below the waist

un·der·hand·ed \ˌəndər-\ adj or adv : underhand —**un·der·hand·ed·ly** adv —**un·der·hand·ed·ness** n

un·der·line \ˈəndər-\ vb 1 : draw a line under 2 : stress —**underline** n

un·der·ling \ˈəndərliŋ\ n : inferior

un·der·ly·ing \ˌəndər-ˈlīiŋ\ adj : basic

un·der·mine \ˌəndər-\ vb 1 : excavate beneath 2 : weaken or wear away secretly or gradually

un·der·neath \ˌəndər-ˈnēth\ prep : directly under ~ adv 1 : below a surface or object 2 : on the lower side

un·der·nour·ished \ˌəndər-\ adj : insufficiently nourished —**un·der·nour·ish·ment** n

un·der·pants \ˈəndər,pants\ n pl : pants worn as underwear

un·der·pass \-,pas\ n : passage underneath

un·der·pin·ning \ˈəndər,piniŋ\ n : support

un·der·priv·i·leged \ˌəndər-\ adj : poor

un·der·rate \ˌəndə(r)ˈrāt\ vb : rate or value too low

343

un·der·score \'əndər-\ *vb or n* : underline

un·der·sea \,əndər,sē\ *adj* : being, carried on, or used beneath the surface of the sea ~ \,əndər'sē\ *adv* — **un·der·seas** \-'sēz\ *adv* : beneath the surface of the sea

un·der·sec·re·tary \,əndər-\ *n* : deputy secretary

un·der·sell \,əndər-\ *vb* -**sold**; -**sell·ing** : sell articles cheaper than

un·der·shirt \'əndər,shərt\ *n* : shirt worn as underwear

un·der·shorts \'əndər,shȯrts\ *n pl* : short underpants

un·der·side \'əndər,sīd, ,əndər'sīd\ *n* : side or surface lying underneath

un·der·sized \,əndər'sīzd\ *adj* : unusually small

un·der·stand \,əndər'stand\ *vb* -**stood** \-'stu̇d\; -**stand·ing** 1 : be aware of the meaning of 2 : deduce 3 : have a sympathetic attitude — **un·der·stand·able** \-'standəbəl\ *adj* — **un·der·stand·ably** \-blē\ *adv*

un·der·stand·ing \,əndər'standiŋ\ *n* 1 : intelligence 2 : ability to comprehend and judge 3 : mutual agreement ~ *adj* : sympathetic

un·der·state \,əndər-\ *vb* 1 : represent as less than is the case 2 : state with restraint — **un·der·state·ment** *n*

un·der·stood \,əndər'stu̇d\ *adj* 1 : agreed upon 2 : implicit

un·der·study \'əndər-, ,əndər-\ *vb* : study another actor's part in order to substitute — **understudy** \'əndər-\ *n*

un·der·take \,əndər-\ *vb* -**took**; -**tak·en**; -**tak·ing** 1 : attempt (a task) or assume (a responsibility) 2 : guarantee

un·der·tak·er \'əndər,tākər\ *n* : one in the funeral business

un·der·tak·ing \'əndər-, ,əndər-\ *n* 1 : something (as work) that is undertaken 2 : promise

under-the-counter *adj* : illicit

un·der·tone \'əndər-\ *n* : low or subdued tone or utterance

un·der·tow \-,tō\ *n* : current beneath the waves that flows seaward

un·der·val·ue \,əndər-\ *vb* : value too low

un·der·wa·ter \,əndər-\ *adj* : being or used below the surface of the water — **underwater** *adv*

under way *adv* : in motion or in progress

un·der·wear \'əndər-\ *n* : clothing worn next to the skin and under ordinary clothes

un·der·world \'əndər-\ *n* 1 : place of departed souls 2 : world of organized crime

un·der·write \'əndər(r)-, ,əndər-\ *vb* -**wrote**; -**writ·ten**; -**writ·ing** \-,rītiŋ, -'rīt-\ 1 : provide insurance for 2 : guarantee financial support of — **un·der·writ·er** *n*

un·dies \'əndēz\ *n pl* : underwear

un·do \,ən-, 'ən-\ *vb* -**did**; -**done**; -**do·ing** 1 : unfasten 2 : reverse 3 : ruin — **un·do·ing** *n*

un·doubt·ed \,ən-\ *adj* : certain — **un·doubt·ed·ly** *adv*

un·dress \,ən-, 'ən-\ *vb* : remove one's clothes

un·due \,ən-\ *adj* : excessive — **un·du·ly** *adv*

un·du·late \'ənjə,lāt\ *vb* -**lat·ed**; -**lat·ing** : rise and fall regularly

un·dy·ing \,ən-, 'ən-\ *adj* : immortal or perpetual

un·earth \,ən-, 'ən-\ *vb* : dig up or discover

un·earth·ly \,ən-, 'ən-\ *adj* : supernatural

un·easy \'ən-\ *adj* 1 : awkward or embarrassing 2 : disturbed or worried — **un·eas·i·ly** *adv* — **un·eas·i·ness** *n*

un·em·ployed \,ən-\ *adj* : not having a job — **un·em·ploy·ment** *n*

un·equal \,ən-, 'ən-\ *adj* : not equal or uniform — **un·equal·ly** *adv*

un·equaled \,ən-, 'ən-\ *adj* : having no equal

un·equiv·o·cal \,ən-\ *adj* : leaving no doubt — **un·equiv·o·cal·ly** *adv*

un·err·ing \,ən-, 'ən-\ *adj* : infallible — **un·err·ing·ly** *adv*

un·even \,ən-, 'ən-\ *adj* 1 : not smooth 2 : not regular or consistent — **un·even·ly** *adv* — **un·even·ness** *n*

un·event·ful \,ən-\ *adj* : lacking interesting or noteworthy incidents

un·fail·ing \,ən-, 'ən-\ *adj* : steadfast — **un·fail·ing·ly** *adv*

un·faith·ful \,ən-, 'ən-\ *adj* : not loyal — **un·faith·ful·ly** *adv* — **un·faith·ful·ness** *n*

un·fa·mil·iar \,ən-\ *adj* 1 : not well known 2 : not acquainted — **un·fa·mil·iar·i·ty** *n*

un·fas·ten \,ən-, 'ən-\ *vb* : release a catch or lock

un·feel·ing \,ən-, 'ən-\ *adj* : lacking feeling or compassion — **un·feel·ing·ly** *adv*

un·fit \,ən-\ *adj* : not suitable — **un·fit·ness** *n*

un·flap·pa·ble \,ən'flapəbəl, 'ən-\ *adj* : not easily upset or panicked

un·fold \\ˌən-, 'ən-\ *vb* **1** : open the folds of **2** : reveal **3** : develop

un·for·get·ta·ble \\ˌən-\ *adj* : memorable —**un·for·get·ta·bly** *adv*

un·for·tu·nate \\ˌən-\ *adj* **1** : not lucky or successful **2** : deplorable —**unfortunate** *n* —**un·for·tu·nate·ly** *adv*

un·found·ed \\ˌən-, 'ən-\ *adj* : lacking a sound basis

un·freeze \\ˌən-, 'ən-\ *vb* : —**froze; fro·zen; -freez·ing** : thaw

un·friend·ly \\ˌən-, 'ən-\ *adj* : not friendly or kind —**un·friend·li·ness** *n*

un·furl \\ˌən-, 'ən-\ *vb* : unfold or unroll

un·gain·ly \\ˌən-, 'ən-\ *adj* : clumsy —**un·gain·li·ness** *n*

un·god·ly \\ˌən'gädlē, -'gŏd-, 'ən-\ *adj* : wicked —**un·god·li·ness** *n*

un·grate·ful \\ˌən-, 'ən-\ *adj* : not thankful for favors —**un·grate·ful·ly** \-ē\ *adv* —**un·grate·ful·ness** *n*

un·guent \'əngwənt, 'ən-\ *n* : ointment

un·hand \\ˌən-, 'ən-\ *vb* : let go

un·hap·py \\ˌən-, 'ən-\ *adj* **1** : unfortunate **2** : sad —**un·hap·pi·ly** *adv* —**un·hap·pi·ness** *n*

un·healthy \\ˌən-, 'ən-\ *adj* **1** : not wholesome **2** : not well

un·heard-of \\ˌən'hərdəv, 'ən-, -ˌäv\ *adj* : unprecedented

un·hinge \\ˌən'hinj, 'ən-\ *vb* **1** : take from the hinges **2** : make unstable (as one's mind)

un·hitch \\ˌən-, 'ən-\ *vb* : unfasten (something hitched)

un·ho·ly \\ˌən-, 'ən-\ *adj* : sinister or shocking —**un·ho·li·ness** *n*

un·hook \\ˌən-, 'ən-\ *vb* : release from a hook

uni·cel·lu·lar \\ˌyüni'selyələr\ *adj* : of or having a single cell

uni·corn \'yüniˌkȯrn\ *n* : legendary animal with one horn in the middle of the forehead

uni·cy·cle \'yüniˌsīkəl\ *n* : pedal-powered vehicle with only a single wheel

uni·di·rec·tion·al \\ˌyünidə'reksh(ə)nəl, -dī-\ *adj* : working in only a single direction

uni·form \'yünəˌfȯrm\ *adj* : not changing or showing any variation ~ *n* : distinctive dress worn by members of a particular group —**uni·for·mi·ty** \ˌyünə'fȯrmətē\ *n* —**uni·form·ly** *adv*

uni·fy \'yünəˌfī\ *vb* -**fied; -fy·ing** : make into a coherent whole —**uni·fi·ca·tion** \ˌyünəfə'kāshən\ *n*

uni·lat·er·al \ˌyünə'lat(ə)rəl\ *adj* : hav-

ing, affecting, or done by one side only —**uni·lat·er·al·ly** *adv*

un·im·peach·able \\ˌən-\ *adj* **1** : blameless **2** : not to be doubted

un·in·hib·it·ed \\ˌən-\ *adj* : free of restraint —**un·in·hib·it·ed·ly** *adv*

union \'yünyən\ *n* **1** : act or instance of joining 2 or more things into one or the state of being so joined **2** : confederation of nations or states **3** : organization of workers (**labor union, trade union**)

union·ize \'yünyəˌnīz\ *vb* -**ized; -iz·ing** : form into a labor union —**union·iza·tion** \ˌyünyənə'zāshən\ *n*

unique \yu̇'nēk\ *adj* **1** : being the only one of its kind **2** : very unusual —**unique·ly** *adv* —**unique·ness** *n*

uni·son \'yünəsən, -nəzən\ *n* **1** : sameness in pitch **2** : exact agreement

unit \'yünət\ *n* **1** : smallest whole number **2** : definite amount or quantity used as a standard of measurement **3** : single part of a whole —**unit** *adj*

unite \yu̇'nīt\ *vb* **unit·ed; unit·ing** : put or join together

uni·ty \'yünətē\ *n, pl* -**ties 1** : quality or state of being united or a unit **2** : harmony

uni·ver·sal \ˌyünə'vərsəl\ *adj* **1** : relating to or affecting everyone or everything **2** : present or occurring everywhere —**uni·ver·sal·ly** *adv*

uni·verse \'yünəˌvərs\ *n* : the complete system of all things that exist

uni·ver·si·ty \ˌyünə'vərs(ə)tē\ *n, pl* -**ties** : institution of higher learning

un·kempt \ˌən-, 'ən-\ *adj* : not neat or combed

un·kind \ˌən-, 'ən-\ *adj* : mean or severe —**un·kind·ly** *adv* —**un·kind·ness** *n*

un·law·ful \ˌən-, 'ən-\ *adj* : illegal —**un·law·ful·ly** *adv*

un·leash \ˌən-, 'ən-\ *vb* : free from control or restraint

un·less \ən ̩les, 'ən-\ *conj* : except on condition that

un·load \ˌən-, 'ən-\ *vb* **1** : take (cargo) from a vehicle, vessel, or plane **2** : take a load from **3** : discard

un·lock \ˌən-, 'ən-\ *vb* **1** : unfasten through release of a lock **2** : release or reveal

un·lucky \ˌən-, 'ən-\ *adj* **1** : experiencing bad luck **2** : likely to bring misfortune —**un·luck·i·ly** *adv*

un·mis·tak·able \ˌən-\ *adj* : not capable of being mistaken or misunderstood —**un·mis·tak·ably** *adv*

un·moved \ˌən-\ *adj* **1** : not emotionally affected **2** : remaining in the same place or position

un·nat·u·ral \,ən-, 'ən-\ *adj* **1** : not natural or spontaneous **2** : abnormal —**un·nat·u·ral·ly** *adv* —**un·nat·u·ral·ness** *n*

un·nerve \,ən-, 'ən-\ *vb* : deprive of courage

un·oc·cu·pied \,ən-, 'ən-\ *adj* **1** : not busy **2** : not occupied

un·pack \,ən-, 'ən-\ *vb* **1** : remove (things packed) from a container **2** : remove the contents of (a package)

un·par·al·leled \,ən-, 'ən-\ *adj* : having no equal

un·plug \,ən-, 'ən-\ *vb* **1** : unclog **2** : disconnect from an electric circuit by removing a plug

un·prec·e·dent·ed \,ən-, 'ən-\ *adj* : unlike or superior to anything known before

un·prin·ci·pled \,ən-, 'ən-\ *adj* : unscrupulous

un·ques·tion·able \,ən-, 'ən-\ *adj* : acknowledged as beyond doubt —**un·ques·tion·ably** *adv*

un·rav·el \,ən-, 'ən-\ *vb* **1** : separate the threads of **2** : solve

un·re·al \,ən-, 'ən-\ *adj* : not real or genuine —**un·re·al·i·ty** \,ən-\ *n*

un·rea·son·ing \,ən-, 'ən-\ *adj* : not using or being guided by reason

un·re·lent·ing \,ən-, 'ən-\ *adj* : not yielding or easing —**un·re·lent·ing·ly** *adv*

un·rest \,ən-, 'ən-\ *n* : turmoil

un·ri·valed \,ən-, **un·ri·valled** \,ən-\ *adj* : having no rival

un·roll \,ən-, 'ən-\ *vb* **1** : unwind a roll of **2** : become unrolled

un·ruf·fled \,ən-, 'ən-\ *adj* : not agitated or upset

un·ruly \,ən-'rülē, -\ *adj* : not readily controlled or disciplined —**un·rul·i·ness** *n*

un·scathed \,ən'skāthd, 'ən-\ *adj* : unharmed

un·sci·en·tif·ic \,ən-, 'ən-\ *adj* : not in accord with the principles and methods of science

un·screw \,ən-, 'ən-\ *vb* : loosen or remove by withdrawing screws or by turning

un·scru·pu·lous \,ən-, 'ən-\ *adj* : being or acting in total disregard of conscience, ethical principles, or rights of others —**un·scru·pu·lous·ly** *adv* —**un·scru·pu·lous·ness** *n*

un·seal \,ən-, 'ən-\ *vb* : break or remove the seal of

un·sea·son·able \,ən-, 'ən-\ *adj* : not appropriate or usual for the season —**un·sea·son·ably** *adv*

un·seem·ly \,ən'sēmlē, 'ən-\ *adj* : not polite or in good taste

un·set·tle \,ən-, 'ən-\ *vb* : disturb —**un·set·tled** *adj*

un·skilled \,ən-, 'ən-\ *adj* : not having or requiring a particular skill

un·snap \,ən-, 'ən-\ *vb* : loosen by undoing a snap

un·speak·able \,ən'spēkəbəl, 'ən-\ *adj* : extremely bad —**un·speak·ably** \-blē\ *adv*

un·sta·ble \,ən-, 'ən-\ *adj* **1** : not mentally or physically balanced **2** : tending to change

un·stop \,ən-, 'ən-\ *vb* **1** : unclog **2** : remove a stopper from

un·strung \,ən-, 'ən-\ *adj* : nervously tired or anxious

un·sung \,ən'səŋ, 'ən-\ *adj* : not celebrated in song or verse

un·tan·gle \,ən-, 'ən-\ *vb* **1** : free from a state of being tangled **2** : find a solution to

un·think·able \,ən'thiŋkəbəl, 'ən-\ *adj* : not to be thought of or considered possible

un·think·ing \,ən-, 'ən-\ *adj* : careless —**un·think·ing·ly** *adv*

un·tie \,ən-, 'ən-\ *vb* **-tied**; **-ty·ing** *or* **-tie·ing** : open by releasing ties

un·til \,ən,til\ *prep* : up to the time of ~ *conj* : to the time that

un·time·ly \,ən-, 'ən-\ *adj* **1** : premature **2** : coming at an unfortunate time

un·to \,əntə, 'ən(,)tü\ *prep* : to

un·told \,ən-, 'ən-\ *adj* **1** : not told **2** : too numerous to count

un·to·ward \,ən'tō(ə)rd, \ *adj* : difficult to manage **2** : inconvenient

un·truth \,ən-, 'ən-\ *n* **1** : lack of truthfulness **2** : lie

un·used *adj* **1** \,ən'yüst, 'ən-, -'yüzd\ : not accustomed **2** \-'yüzd\ : not used

un·well \,ən-, 'ən-\ *adj* : sick

un·wieldy \,ən'wēldē, 'ən-\ *adj* : too big or awkward to manage easily

un·wind \,ən-, 'ən-\ *vb* **-wound**; **-winding 1** : undo something that is wound **2** : become unwound **3** : relax

un·wit·ting \,ən-, 'ən-\ *adj* **1** : not intended **2** : not knowing —**un·wit·ting·ly** *adv*

un·wont·ed \,ən-, 'ən-\ *adj* **1** : unusual **2** : not accustomed by experience

un·wrap \,ən-, 'ən-\ *vb* : remove the wrappings from

un·writ·ten \,ən-, 'ən-\ *adj* : made or passed on only in speech or through tradition

un·zip \,ən-, 'ən-\ *vb* : zip open

up \\'əp\ *adv* **1** : in or to a higher position or level **2** : from beneath a surface or level **3** : in or into an upright position **4** : out of bed **5** : to or with greater intensity **6** : into existence, evidence, or knowledge **7** : away **8** —used to indicate a degree of success, completion, or finality **9** : in or into parts ~ *adj* **1** : in the state of having risen **2** : raised to or at a higher level **3** : moving, inclining, or directed upward **4** : in a state of greater intensity **5** : at an end ~ *vb* **upped** *or in 1* **up**; **upping**; **ups** *or in 1* **up 1** : act abruptly **2** : move or cause to move upward ~ *prep* **1** : to, toward, or at a higher point of **2** : along or toward the beginning of

up·braid \\,əp'brād\ *vb* : criticize or scold

up·bring·ing \\'əp-,-\ *n* : process of bringing up and training

up·com·ing \\,əp,kəmiŋ\ *adj* : approaching

up·date \\,əp'dāt\ *vb* : bring up to date —**update** \\'əp,dāt\ *n*

up·end \\,əp-\ *vb* : stand or rise on end

up·grade \\'əp,grād\ *n* **1** : upward slope **2** : increase \\'əp,-, ,əp'-\ ~ *vb* : raise to a higher position

up·heav·al \\,əp'hēvəl\ *n* **1** : a heaving up (as of part of the earth's crust) **2** : violent change

up·hill \\'əp'hil\ *adv* : upward on a hill or incline ~ \\'əp,-\ *adj* : going up **2** : difficult

up·hold \\,əp-\ *vb* -**held**; -**holding** : support or defend —**up·hold·er** *n*

up·hol·ster \\,əp'hōlstər\ *vb* : cover (furniture) with padding and fabric (**up·hol·stery** \\-st(ə)rē\) —**up·hol·ster·er** *n*

up·keep \\'əp,kēp\ *n* : act or cost of keeping up or maintaining

up·land \\'əpland, -,land\ *n* : high land —**upland** *adj*

up·lift \\,əp'lift\ *vb* **1** : lift up **2** : improve the condition or spirits of —**up·lift** \\'əp,-\ *n*

up·on \\ə'pȯn, -'pȧn\ *prep* : on

up·per \\'əpər\ *adj* : higher in position, rank, or order ~ *n* : top part of a shoe

up·per·most \\'əpər,mōst\ *adv* : in or into the highest or most prominent position —**uppermost** *adj*

up·right \\'əp,rīt\ *adj* **1** : vertical **2** : erect in posture **3** : morally correct ~ *n* : something in an upright position —**upright** *adv* —**up·right·ly** *adv* —**up·right·ness** *n*

up·ris·ing \\'əp,rīziŋ\ *n* : revolt

up·roar \\'əp,rōr\ *n* : state of commotion or violent disturbance

up·roar·i·ous \\,əp'rōrēəs\ *adj* **1** : marked by uproar **2** : extremely funny —**up·roar·i·ous·ly** *adv*

up·root \\,əp-\ *vb* : remove by or as if by pulling up by the roots

up·set \\,əp'set\ *vb* -**set**; -**set·ting 1** : force or be forced out of the usual position **2** : disturb emotionally or physically ~ \\'əp,-\ *n* **1** : act of throwing into disorder **2** : minor physical disorder

up·shot \\'əp,shät\ *n* : final result

up·side down \\,əp,sīd'daún\ *adv* **1** : turned so that the upper and lower parts are reversed **2** : in or into confusion or disorder —**upside-down** *adj*

up·stairs \\'əp-\ *adv* : up the stairs or to the next floor ~ *adj* : situated on the floor above ~ *n sing or pl* : part of a building above the ground floor

up·stand·ing \\,əp'standiŋ, 'əp,-\ *adj* : honest

up·start \\'əp,stärt\ *n* : one who claims more personal importance than is warranted —**upstart** \\,əp-\ *adj*

up·swing \\'əp,swiŋ\ *n* : marked increase (as in activity)

up·tight \\'əp'tīt\ *adj* **1** : tense **2** : angry **3** : rigidly conventional

up-to-date *adj* : current —**up-to-date·ness** *n*

up·town \\'əp-\ *adv* : toward, to, or in the upper part of town —**up·town** *adj*

up·ward \\'əpwərd\, **up·wards** \\-wərdz\ *adv* **1** : in a direction from lower to higher **2** : toward a higher or greater state or number ~ *adj* : directed toward or situated in a higher place

up·wind \\'əp'wind\ *adv or adj* : in the direction from which the wind is blowing

ura·ni·um \\yú'rānēəm\ *n* : metallic radioactive chemical element

ur·ban \\'ərbən\ *adj* : characteristic of a city

ur·bane \\,ər'bān\ *adj* : polished in manner —**ur·ban·i·ty** \\,ər'banətē\ *n*

ur·chin \\'ərchən\ *n* : mischievous youngster

-ure *n suffix* : act or process

ure·thra \\yú'rēthrə\ *n*, *pl* -**thras** *or* -**thrae** \\-(,)thrē\ : canal that carries off urine from the bladder —**ure·thral** \\-thrəl\ *adj*

urge \\'ərj\ *vb* **urged**; **urging 1** : earnestly plead for or insist on (an action) **2** : try to persuade **3** : impel to a course of activity ~ *n* : force or impulse that moves one to action

ur·gent \'ərjənt\ *adj* 1 : calling for immediate attention 2 : urging insistently —**ur·gen·cy** \-jənsē\ *n* —**urgent·ly** *adv*

uri·nal \'yurənᵊl\ *n* : receptacle to urinate in

uri·nate \'yurə,nāt\ *vb* -**nat·ed**; -**nat·ing** : discharge urine —**uri·na·tion** \,yurə'nāshən\ *n*

urine \'yurən\ *n* : liquid waste material from the kidneys —**uri·nary** \-ə,nerē\ *adj*

urn \'ərn\ *n* 1 : vaselike or cuplike vessel on a pedestal 2 : large coffee pot

us \(')əs\ *pron, objective case of* WE

us·able \'yüzəbəl\ *adj* : suitable or fit for use —**us·abil·i·ty** \,yüzə'bilətē\ *n*

us·age \'yüsij, -zij\ *n* 1 : customary practice 2 : way of doing or of using something

use \'yüs\ *n* 1 : act or practice of putting something into action 2 : state of being used 3 : way of using 4 : privilege, ability, or power to use something 5 : utility or function 6 : occasion or need to use ~ \'yüz\ *vb* **used** \'yüzd\ *"used to" usu* 'yüstə\; **us·ing** \'yüzin\ 1 : accustom 2 : put into action or service 3 : consume 4 : behave toward 5 —used in the past tense with *to* to indicate a former practice —**use·ful** \'yüsfəl\ *adj* —**use·ful·ly** *adv* —**use·ful·ness** *n* —**use·less** \'yüsləs\ *adj* —**use·less·ly** *adv* —**use·less·ness** *n* —**us·er** *n*

used \'yüzd\ *adj* : not new

ush·er \'əshər\ *n* : one who escorts people to their seats ~ *vb* : conduct

to a place —**ush·er·ette** \,əshə'ret\ *n*

usu·al \'yüzhə(wə)l\ *adj* : being what is expected according to custom or habit —**usu·al·ly** \'yüzh(ə)wəlē, 'yüzh(ə)lē\ *adv*

usurp \yu'sərp, -'zərp\ *vb* : seize and hold by force or without right —**usur·pa·tion** \,yüsər'pāshən, -zər-\ *n* —**usurp·er** *n*

usu·ry \'yüzh(ə)rē\ *n, pl* -ries 1 : lending of money at excessive interest or the rate or amount of such interest —**usur·er** \-zhərər\ *n* —**usu·ri·ous** \yu'zhurēəs\ *adj*

uten·sil \yu'tensəl\ *n* 1 : eating or cooking tool 2 : useful article

uter·us \'yütərəs\ *n, pl* uteri \-,rī\ : organ for containing and nourishing an unborn offspring —**uter·ine** \-,rīn, -rən\ *adj*

util·i·tar·i·an \ yü,tilə'terēən\ *adj* : being or meant to be useful rather than beautiful

util·i·ty \yü'tilətē\ *n, pl* -ties 1 : usefulness 2 : regulated business providing a public service (as electricity)

uti·lize \'yütᵊl,īz\ *vb* -lized; -liz·ing : make use of —**uti·li·za·tion** \,yütᵊlə'zāshən\ *n*

ut·most \'ət,mōst\ *adj* 1 : most distant 2 : of the greatest or highest degree or amount —**utmost** *n*

uto·pia \yu'tōpēə\ *n* : place of ideal perfection —**uto·pi·an** \-pēən\ *adj or n*

ut·ter \'ətər\ *adj* : absolute ~ *vb* : express with the voice —**ut·ter·ly** *adv*

ut·ter·ance \'ətərəns, 'ətrəns\ *n* : what one says

V

v \'vē\ *n, pl* **v's** *or* **vs** \'vēz\ : 22d letter of the alphabet

va·can·cy \'vākənsē\ *n, pl* -cies 1 : state of being vacant 2 : unused or unoccupied place or office

va·cant \-kənt\ *adj* 1 : not occupied, filled, or in use 2 : foolish or without expression —**va·cant·ly** *adv*

va·cate \-,kāt\ *vb* -cat·ed; -cat·ing 1 : annul 2 : leave unfilled or unoccupied

va·ca·tion \vā'kāshən, və-\ *n* : extended period of rest from routine —**vacation** *vb* —**va·ca·tion·er** *n*

vac·ci·nate \'vaksə,nāt\ *vb* -nat·ed; -nat·ing : inoculate

vac·ci·na·tion \,vaksə'nāshən\ *n* : act of or the scar left by vaccinating

vac·cine \vak'sēn, 'vak,-\ *n* : substance to induce immunity to a disease —**vaccine** *adj*

vac·il·late \'vasə,lāt\ *vb* -lat·ed; -lat·ing : waver between courses or opinions —**vac·il·la·tion** \,vasə'lāshən\ *n*

vac·u·ous \'vakyəwəs\ *adj* 1 : empty 2 : dull or inane —**va·cu·ity** \va'kyüətē, və-\ *n* —**vac·u·ous·ly** *adv* —**vac·u·ous·ness** *n*

vac·u·um \'vak-,yüm, -yəm\ *n, pl* **vac·u·ums** *or* **vac·ua** \-yəwə\ : empty space with no air ~ *vb* : clean with a vacuum cleaner

vac·uum clean·er \n : appliance that cleans by suction

vag·a·bond \'vagə,bänd\ n : wanderer with no home —**vagabond** adj

va·ga·ry \'vāgərē, və'ge(ə)rē\ n, pl -ries : whim

va·gi·na \və'jīnə\ n, pl -**nae** \-(,)nē\ or -**nas** : canal that leads out from the uterus —**vag·i·nal** \'vajən²l\ adj

va·grant \'vāgrənt\ n : person with no home and no job —**va·gran·cy** \-grənsē\ n —**vagrant** adj

vague \'vāg\ adj **vagu·er; vagu·est** : not clear, definite, or distinct —**vague·ly** adv —**vague·ness** n

vain \'vān\ adj **1** : of no value **2** : unsuccessful **3** : conceited —**vain·ly** adv —**in vain** : without result or success

va·lance \'valəns, 'vāl-\ n : border drapery

vale \'vāl\ n : valley

vale·dic·to·ri·an \,valə,dik'tōrēən\ n : student giving the farewell address at commencement

vale·dic·to·ry \-'diktə(ə)rē\ adj : bidding farewell —**valedictory** n

va·lence \'vāləns\ n : degree of combining power of a chemical element

val·en·tine \'valən,tīn\ n : sweetheart or a card sent to a sweetheart or friend on St. Valentine's Day

va·let \'valət, 'val(,)ā, va'lā\ n : male personal servant

va·liant \'valyənt\ adj : brave or heroic —**val·iant·ly** adv

val·id \'valəd\ adj **1** : proper and legally binding **2** : founded on truth or fact —**va·lid·i·ty** \və'lidətē, va-\ n —**val·id·ly** adv —**val·id·ness** n

val·i·date \'valə,dāt\ vb -**dat·ed; -dat·ing** : establish as valid —**val·i·da·tion** \,valə'dāshən\ n

va·lise \və'lēs\ n : bag for a traveler's clothing and personal articles

val·ley \'valē\ n, pl -**leys** : long depression between ranges of hills

val·or \'valər\ n : bravery or heroism —**val·or·ous** \'valərəs\ adj

valu·able \'valyə(wə)bəl\ adj **1** : worth a lot of money **2** : being of great importance or use —**valuable** n

val·u·a·tion \,valyə'wāshən\ n **1** : act or process of valuing **2** : market value of a thing

val·ue \'valyü\ n **1** : fair return or equivalent for something exchanged **2** : how much something is worth **3** : distinctive quality (as of a color or sound) **4** : guiding principle or ideal—usu. pl. ~ vb **val·ued; val·u·ing 1** : estimate the worth of **2** : appreci-

ate the importance of —**valued** adj —**val·ue·less** adj —**val·u·er** n

valve \'valv\ n : structure or device to control flow of a liquid or gas —**valved** \'valvd\ adj —**valve·less** adj

vam·pire \'vam,pī(ə)r\ n **1** : legendary night-wandering dead body that sucks human blood **2** : bat that feeds on the blood of animals

¹van \'van\ n : vanguard

²van n : enclosed truck

va·na·di·um \və'nādēəm\ n : soft ductile metallic chemical element

van·dal \'vand²l\ n : one who willfully defaces or destroys property —**van·dal·ism** \-,izəm\ n —**van·dal·ize** \-,īz\ vb

vane \'vān\ n : bladelike device designed to be moved by force of the air or water

van·guard \'van,gärd\ n **1** : troops moving at the front of an army **2** : forefront of an action or movement

va·nil·la \və'nilə\ n : tropical orchid with pods yielding a flavoring substance

van·ish \'vanish\ vb : disappear suddenly

van·i·ty \'vanətē\ n, pl -**ties 1** : futility or something that is futile **2** : undue pride in oneself **3** : makeup table

van·quish \'vaŋkwish, 'van-\ vb **1** : overcome in battle or in a contest **2** : gain mastery over

van·tage \'vantij\ n : position of advantage or perspective

va·pid \'vapəd, 'vāpəd\ adj : lacking spirit, liveliness, or zest —**va·pid·i·ty** \va'pidətē\ n —**va·pid·ly** \'vapədlē\ adv —**vap·id·ness** n

va·por \'vāpər\ n **1** : fine separated particles floating in and clouding the air **2** : gaseous form of an ordinarily liquid substance ~ vb : give off vapor —**va·por·ish** \-p(ə)rish\ adj —**va·po·rous** \-p(ə)rəs\ adj

va·por·ize \'vāpə,rīz\ vb -**ized; -iz·ing** : convert into vapor —**va·por·iza·tion** \,vāpərə'zāshən\ n —**va·por·iz·er** n

vari·able \'verēəbəl\ adj : apt to vary —**vari·abil·i·ty** \,verēə'bilətē\ n —**variable** n —**vari·able·ness** n —**vari·ably** adv

vari·ance \'verēəns\ n **1** : instance or degree of variation **2** : legal permission to build contrary to a zoning law

vari·ant \-ənt\ n : something that differs from others of its kind —**variant** adj

vari·a·tion \,verē'āshən\ n : instance or extent of varying

var·i·cose \'varə,kōs\ *adj* : abnormally swollen

var·ied \'verēd\ *adj* : showing variety —**var·ied·ly** *adv*

var·ie·gate \'verē,gāt, 'veri,gāt\ *vb* **-gat·ed; -gat·ing** : diversify in appearance esp. with different colors —**var·ie·gat·ed** *adj* —**var·ie·ga·tion** \,verē'gāshən, ,veri'gā-\ *n*

va·ri·ety \və'rīətē\ *n, pl* **-et·ies 1** : state of being different **2** : collection of different things **3** : something that differs from others of its kind

var·i·ous \'verēəs\ *adj* : being many and unlike —**var·i·ous·ly** *adv*

var·nish \'värnish\ *n* : liquid that dries to a hard glossy protective coating ~ *vb* : cover with varnish

var·si·ty \'värsətē, -stē\ *n, pl* **-ties** : principal team representing a school

vary \'verē\ *vb* **var·ied; vary·ing 1** : alter **2** : make or be of different kinds

vas·cu·lar \'vaskyələr\ *adj* : relating to a channel for the conveyance of a body fluid (as blood or sap)

vase \'vās, 'vāz\ *n* : tall usu. ornamental container to hold flowers and water

vas·sal \'vasəl\ *n* **1** : one acknowledging another as feudal lord **2** : one in a dependent position —**vas·sal·age** \-əlij\ *n*

vast \'vast\ *adj* : very great in size, extent, or amount —**vast·ly** *adv* —**vast·ness** *n*

vat \'vat\ *n* : large tub- or barrel-shaped container

vaude·ville \'vȯd(ə)vəl, 'väd-, 'vȯd-, -(ə),vil\ *n* : stage entertainment of unrelated acts

¹vault \'vȯlt\ *n* **1** : masonry arch **2** : usu. underground storage or burial room ~ *vb* : form or cover with a vault —**vault·ed** *adj* —**vaulty** *adj*

²vault *vb* : spring over esp. with the help of the hands or a pole ~ *n* : act of vaulting —**vault·er** *n* —**vault·ing** *adj*

vaunt \'vȯnt\ *vb* : boast —**vaunt** *n*

veal \'vēl\ *n* : flesh of a young calf

veer \'viər\ *vb* : change course esp. gradually —**veer** *n*

veg·e·ta·ble \'vej(ə)təbəl\ *adj* **1** : relating to or obtained from plants **2** : like that of a plant ~ *n* **1** : plant **2** : plant grown for food

veg·e·tar·i·an \,vejə'terēən\ *n* : person who eats no meat —**vegetarian** *adj* —**veg·e·tar·i·an·ism** \-ēə,nizəm\ *n*

veg·e·tate \'vejə,tāt\ *vb* **-tat·ed; -tat·ing** : lead a dull inert life

veg·e·ta·tion \,vejə'tāshən\ *n* : plant life —**veg·e·ta·tion·al** \-sh(ə)nəl\ *adj*

ve·he·ment \'vēəmənt\ *adj* : showing strong esp. violent feeling —**ve·he·mence** \-məns\ *n* —**ve·he·ment·ly** *adv*

ve·hi·cle \'vē,(h)ikəl, 'vēəkəl\ *n* **1** : medium through which something is expressed, applied, or administered **2** : structure for transporting something esp. on wheels —**ve·hic·u·lar** \vē'hikyələr\ *adj*

veil \'vāl\ *n* **1** : sheer material to hide something or to cover the face and head **2** : something that hides ~ *vb* : cover with a veil

vein \'vān\ *n* **1** : rock fissure filled with deposited mineral matter **2** : vessel that carries blood toward the heart **3** : sap-carrying tube in a leaf **4** : distinctive nature or mode of expression —**veined** \'vānd\ *adj*

ve·loc·i·ty \və'läs(ə)tē\ *n, pl* **-ties** : speed

ve·lour, ve·lours \və'lùr\ *n, pl* **velours** \-'lùrz\ : fabric with a velvetlike pile

vel·vet \'velvət\ *n* : fabric with a short soft pile —**velvet** *adj* —**velvety** *adj*

ve·nal \'vēnᵊl\ *adj* : capable of being corrupted esp. by money —**ve·nal·i·ty** \vi'nalətē\ *n* —**ve·nal·ly** *adv*

vend \'vend\ *vb* : sell —**vend·ible** *adj* —**ven·dor** \'vendər\ *n*

ven·det·ta \ven'detə\ *n* : feud between clans

ve·neer \və'niər\ *n* **1** : thin layer of fine wood glued over a cheaper wood **2** : superficial display ~ *vb* : overlay with a veneer

ven·er·a·ble \'venər(ə)bəl, 'venrəbəl\ *adj* : deserving of respect

ven·er·ate \'venə,rāt\ *vb* **-at·ed; -at·ing** : respect esp. with reverence —**ven·er·a·tion** \,venə'rāshən\ *n*

venereal disease \və,nirēəl-\ *n* : contagious disease spread through copulation

ven·geance \'venjəns\ *n* : punishment in retaliation for an injury or offense

venge·ful \'venjfəl\ *adj* : filled with a desire for revenge —**venge·ful·ly** *adv*

ve·nial \'vēnēəl, -nyəl\ *adj* : capable of being forgiven

ven·i·son \'venəsən, -zən\ *n* : deer meat

ven·om \'venəm\ *n* **1** : poison secreted by certain animals **2** : ill will —**ven·om·ous** \-məs\ *adj*

vent \'vent\ *vb* **1** : provide with or let out at a vent **2** : give expression to ~ *n* : opening for passage or for relieving pressure

ven·ti·late \'vent³l̩,āt\ *vb* **-lat·ed; -lat·ing** : allow fresh air to circulate through **—ven·ti·la·tion** \,vent³l'āshən\ *n* **—ven·ti·la·tor** \'vent³l,ātər\ *n*

ven·tri·cle \'ventrikəl\ *n* : heart chamber that pumps blood into the arteries of the brain

ven·tril·o·quist \ven'trilə,kwəst\ *n* : one who can make the voice appear to come from another source **—ven·tril·o·quism** \-,kwizəm\ *n* **—ven·tril·o·quy** \-kwē\ *n*

ven·ture \'venchər\ *vb* **-tured; -tur·ing** **1** : risk or take a chance on **2** : put forward (an opinion) ~ *n* : speculative business enterprise

ven·ture·some \-səm\ *adj* : brave or daring **—ven·ture·some·ly** *adv* **—ven·ture·some·ness** *n*

ven·ue \'venyü\ *n* : scene of an action or event

ve·rac·i·ty \və'rasətē\ *n, pl* **-ties** : truthfulness or accuracy **—ve·ra·cious** \-'rāshəs\ *adj*

ve·ran·da, ve·ran·dah \və'randə\ *n* : large open porch

verb \'vərb\ *n* : word that expresses action or existence

ver·bal \'vərbəl\ *adj* **1** : having to do with or expressed in words **2** : oral **3** : relating to or formed from a verb **—ver·bal·ize** \,vərbəl'zāshən\ *n* **—ver·bal·ize** \'vərbə,līz\ *vb* **—ver·bal·ly** \-ē\ *adv*

verbal auxiliary *n* : auxiliary verb

ver·ba·tim \(,)vər'bātəm\ *adv or adj* : using the same words

ver·biage \'vərbēij\ *n* : excess of words

ver·bose \(,)vər'bōs\ *adj* : using more words than are needed **—ver·bos·i·ty** \-'bäsətē\ *n*

ver·dant \'vərd³nt\ *adj* : green with growing plants **—ver·dant·ly** *adv*

ver·dict \'vər,dikt\ *n* : decision of a jury

ver·dure \'vərjər\ *n* : green growing vegetation or its color

verge \'vərj\ *vb* **verged; verg·ing** : be almost on the point of happening or doing something ~ *n* **1** : edge **2** : threshold

ver·i·fy \'verə,fī\ *vb* **-fied; -fy·ing** : establish the truth, accuracy, or reality of **—ver·i·fi·able** *adj* **—ver·i·fi·ca·tion** \,verəfə'kāshən\ *n*

ver·i·ly \'verəlē\ *adv* : truly or confidently

ver·i·ta·ble \'verətəbəl\ *adj* : actual —often used to suggest the aptness of a metaphor **—ver·i·ta·bly** *adv*

ver·i·ty \'verətē\ *n, pl* **-ties** : truth

ver·mi·cel·li \,vərmə'chelē, -'sel-\ *n* : thin spaghetti

ver·min \'vərmən\ *n, pl* **vermin** : small animal pest

ver·nac·u·lar \və(r)'nakyələr\ *adj* : relating to a native language or dialect and esp. its normal spoken form ~ *n* : vernacular language

ver·nal \'vərn³l\ *adj* : relating to spring

ver·sa·tile \'vərsət³l\ *adj* : having many abilities or uses **—ver·sa·til·i·ty** \,vərsə'tilətē\ *n*

verse \'vərs\ *n* **1** : line or stanza of poetry **2** : poetry **3** : short division of a chapter in the Bible

versed \'vərst\ *adj* : familiar from experience, study, or practice

ver·sion \'vərzhən\ *n* **1** : translation of the Bible **2** : account or description from a particular point of view

ver·sus \'vərsəs\ *prep* : opposed to or against

ver·te·bra \'vərtəbrə\ *n, pl* **-brae** \-,brā, -(,)brē\ *or* **-bras** : segment of the backbone **—ver·te·bral** \(,)vər'tēbrəl, 'vərtə-\ *adj*

ver·te·brate \'vərtəbrət, -,brāt\ *n* : animal with a backbone **—vertebrate** *adj*

ver·tex \'vər,teks\ *n, pl* **ver·tex·es** *or* **ver·ti·ces** \'vərtə,sēz\ **1** : point of intersection of lines or surfaces **2** : highest point

ver·ti·cal \'vərtikəl\ *adj* : rising straight up from a level surface **—vertical** *n* **—ver·ti·cal·ly** *adv* **—ver·ti·cal·ness** *n*

ver·ti·go \'vərti,gō\ *n, pl* **-goes** *or* **-gos** : dizziness

verve \'vərv\ *n* : liveliness or vividness

very \'verē\ *adj* **veri·er; -est 1** : exact **2** : exactly suitable **3** : precisely the same ~ *adv* : to a high degree

ves·i·cle \'vesikəl\ *n* : membranous cavity **—ve·sic·u·lar** \və'sikyələr\ *adj*

ves·pers \'vespərz\ *n pl* : late afternoon or evening worship service

ves·sel \'vesəl\ *n* **1** : a container (as a barrel, bottle, pan, or cup) for a liquid **2** : craft for navigation esp. on water **3** : tube in which a body fluid is circulated

¹vest \'vest\ *vb* **1** : give a particular authority, right, or property to **2** : clothe with or as if with a garment

²vest *n* : sleeveless garment worn under a suit coat

ves·ti·bule \'vestə,byül\ *n* : enclosed entrance **—ves·tib·u·lar** \ve'stibyələr\ *adj*

ves·tige \'vestij\ n : visible trace or remains —**ves·ti·gial** \ve'stijēəl\ adj —**ves·ti·gial·ly** adv

vest·ment \'ves(t)mənt\ n : clergyman's garment

ves·try \'vestrē\ n, pl **-tries** : church storage room for garments and articles

vet·er·an \'vet(ə)rən\ n 1 : former member of the armed forces 2 : person with long experience —**veteran** adj

Veterans Day n : 4th Monday in October or formerly November 11 observed as a legal holiday in commemoration of the end of war in 1918 and 1945

vet·er·i·nar·i·an \‚vet(ə)rən'erēən, ‚vetᵊn-\ n : doctor of animals —**vet·er·i·nary** \'vet(ə)rən‚erē, 'vetᵊn-\ adj

ve·to \'vētō\ n, pl **-toes** 1 : power to forbid and esp. the power of a chief executive to prevent a bill from becoming law 2 : exercise of the veto ~ vb 1 : forbid 2 : reject a legislative bill

vex \'veks\ vb **vexed**; **vex·ing** : trouble, distress, or annoy —**vex·a·tion** \vek'sāshən\ n —**vex·a·tious** \-shəs\ adj

via \'vīə, 'vēə\ prep : by way of

vi·a·ble \'vīəbəl\ adj 1 : capable of surviving or growing 2 : practical or workable —**vi·a·bil·i·ty** \‚vīə'bilətē\ n —**vi·a·bly** \'vīəblē\ adv

via·duct \'vīə‚dəkt\ n : high road or railway bridge

vi·al \'vī(ə)l\ n : small bottle

vi·brant \'vībrənt\ adj 1 : vibrating 2 : pulsing with vigor or activity 3 : sounding from vibration —**vi·bran·cy** \-brənsē\ n

vi·brate \'vī‚brāt\ vb **-brat·ed**; **-brat·ing** 1 : move or cause to move quickly back and forth or side to side 2 : respond sympathetically —**vi·bra·tion** \vī'brāshən\ n —**vi·bra·tor** \'vī‚brātər\ n —**vi·bra·tory** \'vībrə‚tōrē\ adj

vic·ar \'vikər\ n : parish clergyman —**vi·car·i·al** \vī'karēəl\ adj —**vi·car·i·ate** \-ēət\ n

vi·car·i·ous \vī'kerēəs, -'kar-\ adj : experienced imaginatively or sympathetically —**vi·car·i·ous·ly** adv —**vi·car·i·ous·ness** n

vice \'vīs\ n 1 : immoral habit 2 : depravity

vice- \(')vīs, ‚vīs\ prefix : one that takes the place of

vice–chairman
vice–chairmanship
vice–chancellor
vice–chancellorship
vice–consul
vice–mayor
vice–premier
vice–presidency
vice–president
vice–presidential
vice–principal
vice–regent

vice admiral n : commissioned officer in the navy or coast guard ranking above a rear admiral

vice·roy \'vīs‚roi\ n : provincial governor who represents the sovereign

vice ver·sa \‚vīsi'vərsə, (')vīs'vər-\ adv : with the order reversed

vi·cin·i·ty \və'sinətē\ n, pl **-ties** : surrounding area

vi·cious \'vishəs\ adj 1 : wicked 2 : savage 3 : malicious —**vi·cious·ly** adv —**vi·cious·ness** n

vi·cis·si·tude \və'sisə‚t(y)üd, vī-\ n : irregular, unexpected, or surprising change —usu. used in pl.

vic·tim \'viktəm\ n : person killed, hurt, or abused

vic·tim·ize \'viktə‚mīz\ vb **-ized**; **-iz·ing** : make a victim of —**vic·tim·iza·tion** \‚viktəmə'zāshən\ n —**vic·tim·iz·er** \'viktə‚mīzər\ n

vic·tor \'viktər\ n : winner

Vic·to·ri·an \vik'tōrēən\ adj : relating to the reign of Queen Victoria of England or the art, taste, or standards of her time ~ n : one of the Victorian period

vic·to·ri·ous \vik'tōrēəs\ adj : having won a victory —**vic·to·ri·ous·ly** adv

vic·to·ry \'vikt(ə)rē\ n, pl **-ries** : success in defeating an enemy or opponent or in overcoming difficulties

vict·uals \'vitᵊlz\ n pl : food

vid·eo \'vidē‚ō\ adj : relating to the television image

vid·eo·tape \'vidēō‚tāp\ vb : make a recording of (a television production) on special tape —**video·tape** n

vie \'vī\ vb **vied**; **vy·ing** : contend —**vi·er** \'vī(ə)r\ n

view \'vyü\ n 1 : process of seeing or examining 2 : opinion 3 : area of landscape that can be seen 4 : range of vision 5 : purpose or object ~ vb 1 : look at 2 : think about or consider

view·point n : position from which something is considered

vig·il \'vijəl\ n 1 : day of devotion before a religious feast 2 : act or time of keeping awake 3 : long period of keeping watch (as over a sick or dying person)

vig·i·lant \'vijələnt\ adj : alert esp. to

avoid danger —**vig·i·lance** \-ləns\ *n* —**vig·i·lant·ly** *adv*

vig·i·lan·te \ˌvijəˈlantē\ *n* : one of a group independent of the law working to suppress crime

vi·gnette \vinˈyet\ *n* : short descriptive literary piece

vig·or \ˈvigər\ *n* **1** : energy or strength **2** : intensity or force —**vig·or·ous** \ˈvig(ə)rəs\ *adj* —**vig·or·ous·ly** *adv* —**vig·or·ous·ness** *n*

vile \ˈvīl\ *adj* **vil·er; vil·est** : thoroughly bad or contemptible —**vile·ly** *adv* —**vile·ness** *n*

vil·i·fy \ˈviləˌfī\ *vb* **-fied; -fy·ing** : speak evil of —**vil·i·fi·ca·tion** \ˌviləfəˈkāshən\ *n* —**vil·i·fi·er** \ˈviləˌfī(ə)r\ *n*

vil·la \ˈvilə\ *n* : country estate

vil·lage \ˈvilij\ *n* : small country town —**vil·lag·er** *n*

vil·lain \ˈvilən\ *n* : bad person —**vil·lain·ess** \-ənəs\ *n* —**vil·lainy** *n*

vil·lain·ous \-ənəs\ *adj* : evil or corrupt —**vil·lain·ous·ly** *adv* —**vil·lain·ous·ness** *n*

vim \ˈvim\ *n* : energy

vin·di·cate \ˈvindəˌkāt\ *vb* **-cat·ed; -cat·ing** **1** : avenge **2** : exonerate **3** : justify —**vin·di·ca·tion** \ˌvindəˈkāshən\ *n* —**vin·di·ca·tor** \ˈvindəˌkātər\ *n*

vin·dic·tive \vinˈdiktiv\ *adj* : seeking or meant for revenge —**vin·dic·tive·ly** *adv* —**vin·dic·tive·ness** *n*

vine \ˈvīn\ *n* : climbing or trailing plant

vin·e·gar \ˈvinigər\ *n* : acidic liquid obtained by fermentation —**vin·e·gary** \-g(ə)rē\ *adj*

vine·yard \ˈvinyərd\ *n* : plantation of grapevines

vin·tage \ˈvintij\ *n* **1** : season's yield of grapes or wine **2** : period of origin ~ *adj* : of enduring interest

vi·nyl \ˈvīnᵊl\ *n* : strong plastic

vi·o·la \vēˈōlə\ *n* : instrument of the violin family tuned lower than the violin —**vi·o·list** \-ləst\ *n*

vi·o·late \ˈvīəˌlāt\ *vb* **-lat·ed; -lat·ing** **1** : act with disrespect or disregard of **2** : rape **3** : desecrate —**vi·o·la·tion** \ˌvīəˈlāshən\ *n* —**vi·o·la·tor** \ˈvīəˌlātər\ *n*

vi·o·lence \ˈvīələns\ *n* : intense physical force that causes or is intended to cause injury or destruction —**vi·o·lent** \-lənt\ *adj* —**vi·o·lent·ly** *adv*

vi·o·let \ˈvīələt\ *n* **1** : small flowering plant **2** : reddish blue —**violet** *adj*

vi·o·lin \ˌvīəˈlin\ *n* : bowed stringed instrument —**vi·o·lin·ist** \-əst\ *n*

VIP \ˌvē⸳īˈpē\ *n, pl* **VIPs** \-ˈpēz\ : very important person

vi·per \ˈvīpər\ *n* **1** : venomous snake **2** : treacherous or malignant person

vi·ra·go \vəˈrägō, -ˈrä-; ˈvirəˌgō\ *n, pl* **-goes** *or* **-gos** : shrew

vi·ral \ˈvīrəl\ *adj* : relating to or caused by a virus

vir·gin \ˈvərjən\ *n* : unmarried or chaste woman ~ *adj* **1** : chaste **2** : natural and unspoiled —**vir·gin·al** \-əl\ *adj* —**vir·gin·al·ly** *adv* —**vir·gin·i·ty** \vərˈjinətē\ *n*

vir·gule \ˈvərgyül\ *n* : mark / used esp. to denote "or" or "per"

vir·ile \ˈvirəl\ *adj* : masculine —**vi·ril·i·ty** \vəˈrilətē\ *n*

vir·tu·al \ˈvərchə(wə)l\ *adj* : being almost the same —**vir·tu·al·ly** *adv*

vir·tue \ˈvərchü\ *n* **1** : moral excellence **2** : effective or commendable quality **3** : chastity

vir·tu·os·i·ty \ˌvərchəˈwäsətē\ *n, pl* **-ties** : great skill (as in music)

vir·tu·o·so \ˌvərchəˈwōsō, -zō\ *n, pl* **-sos** *or* **-si** \-sē, -zē\ : highly skilled performer esp. of music —**virtuoso** *adj*

vir·tu·ous \ˈvərch(ə)wəs\ *adj* **1** : morally good **2** : chaste —**vir·tu·ous·ly** *adv*

vir·u·lent \ˈvir(y)ələnt\ *adj* **1** : bitterly hostile **2** : extremely severe or infectious —**vir·u·lence** \-ləns\ *n* —**vir·u·len·cy** \-lənsē\ *n* —**vir·u·lent·ly** *adv*

vi·rus \ˈvīrəs\ *n* : tiny disease-causing agent

vi·sa \ˈvēzə, -sə\ *n* : authorization to enter a foreign country

vis·age \ˈvizij\ *n* : face

vis·cera \ˈvisərə\ *n pl* : internal bodily organs esp. of the trunk

vis·cer·al \ˈvisərəl\ *adj* **1** : bodily **2** : instinctive **3** : deeply or crudely emotional —**vis·cer·al·ly** *adv*

vis·cid \ˈvisəd\ *adj* : viscous —**vis·cid·i·ty** \visˈidətē\ *n* —**vis·cid·ly** *adv*

vis·cos·i·ty \visˈkäsətē\ *n, pl* **-ties** : quality of being viscous

vis·count \ˈvīˌkaůnt\ *n* : British nobleman ranking below an earl and above a baron —**vis·count·ess** \-əs\ *n*

vis·cous \ˈviskəs\ *adj* : having a thick or sticky consistency

vise \ˈvīs\ *n* : device for clamping something being worked on

vis·i·bil·i·ty \ˌvizəˈbilətē\ *n, pl* **-ties** : degree or range to which something can be seen

vis·i·ble \ˈvizəbəl\ *adj* **1** : capable of

being seen **2** : manifest —**vis·i·bly** adv

vi·sion \'vizhən\ n **1** : vivid picture seen in a dream or trance or in the imagination **2** : foresight **3** : power of seeing ~ vb : imagine

vi·sion·ary \'vizhə,nerē\ adj **1** : given to dreaming or imagining **2** : illusory **3** : not practical ~ n : one with great dreams or projects

vis·it \'vizət\ vb **1** : go or come to see **2** : stay with for a time as a guest **3** : cause or be a reward, affliction, or punishment ~ n : short stay as a guest —**vis·it·able** adj —**vis·i·tor** \-ər\ n

vis·i·ta·tion \,vizə'tāshən\ n **1** : official visit **2** : divine punishment or favor **3** : severe trial

vi·sor \'vīzər\ n **1** : front piece of a helmet **2** : part (as on a cap or car windshield) that shades the eyes

vis·ta \'vistə\ n : distant view

vi·su·al \'vizh(əw)əl\ adj **1** : relating to sight **2** : visible —**vi·su·al·ly** adv

vi·su·al·ize \'vizh(ə)wə,līz\ vb -ized; -iz·ing : form a mental image of —**vi·su·al·i·za·tion** \,vizhə(wə)lə'zāshən\ n —**vi·su·al·iz·er** \'vizh(ə)wə,līzər\ n

vi·tal \'vītᵊl\ adj **1** : relating to or characteristic of life **2** : full of life and vigor **3** : basic **4** : very important —**vi·tal·ly** adv

vi·tal·i·ty \vī'talətē\ n, pl -ties **1** : life force **2** : energy

vi·ta·min \'vītəmən\ n : natural organic substance essential to health

vi·ti·ate \'vishē,āt\ vb -at·ed; -at·ing **1** : spoil or impair **2** : invalidate —**vi·ti·a·tion** \,vishē'āshən\ n —**vi·ti·a·tor** \'vishē,ātər\ n

vit·re·ous \'vitrēəs\ adj : relating to or resembling glass

vit·ri·fy \'vitrə,fī\ vb -fied; -fy·ing : change into a glassy substance by heat and fusion —**vit·ri·fi·ca·tion** \,vitrəfə'kāshən\ n

vit·ri·ol \'vitrēəl\ n : something caustic, corrosive, or biting —**vit·ri·ol·ic** \,vitrē'älik\ adj

vi·tu·per·ate \vī't(y)üpə,rāt, və-\ vb -at·ed; -at·ing : abuse in words —**vi·tu·per·a·tion** \-,t(y)üpə'rāshən\ n —**vi·tu·per·a·tive** \-'t(y)üp(ə)rətiv, -pə,rāt-\ adj —**vi·tu·per·a·tive·ly** adv

vi·va·cious \vəvāshəs, vī-\ adj : lively —**vi·va·cious·ly** adv —**vi·va·cious·ness** n —**vi·vac·i·ty** \-'vasətē\ n

viv·id \'vivəd\ adj **1** : lively **2** : brilliant **3** : intense or sharp —**viv·id·ly** adv —**viv·id·ness** n

viv·i·fy \'vivə,fī\ vb -fied; -fy·ing : give life or vividness to

vivi·sec·tion \,vivə'sekshən, 'vivə,-\ n : experimental operation on a living animal

vix·en \'viksən\ n **1** : female fox **2** : scolding woman

vo·cab·u·lary \vō'kabyə,lerē\ n, pl -lar·ies **1** : list or collection of words **2** : terminology of a person or subject

vo·cal \'vōkəl\ adj **1** : relating to or produced by or for the voice **2** : speaking out freely and usu. emphatically

vocal cords n pl : membranous folds in the larynx that are important in making vocal sounds

vo·cal·ist \'vōkələst\ n : singer

vo·cal·ize \-,līz\ vb -ized; -iz·ing : give vocal expression to

vo·ca·tion \vō'kāshən\ n : regular employment —**vo·ca·tion·al** \-sh(ə)nəl\ adj

vo·cif·er·ous \vō'sif(ə)rəs\ adj : noisy and insistent —**vo·cif·er·ous·ly** adv

vod·ka \'vädkə\ n : colorless distilled grain liquor

vogue \'vōg\ n : brief but intense popularity

voice \'vȯis\ n **1** : sound produced through the mouth by humans and many animals **2** : power of speaking **3** : right of choice or opinion ~ vb voiced; voic·ing : express in words —**voiced** \'vȯist\ adj

void \'vȯid\ adj **1** : containing nothing **2** : lacking —with of **3** : not legally binding ~ n **1** : empty space **2** : feeling of hollowness ~ vb **1** : discharge (as body waste) **2** : make (as a contract) void —**void·able** adj —**void·er** n

vol·a·tile \'välətᵊl\ adj **1** : readily vaporizing at a relatively low temperature **2** : explosive or easily stirred to violence **3** : changeable —**vol·a·til·i·ty** \,välə'tilətē\ n —**vol·a·til·ize** \'välət²l,īz\ vb

vol·ca·no \väl'kānō\ n, pl -noes or -nos : opening in the earth's crust from which molten rock and steam come out —**vol·ca·nic** \-'kanik\ adj

vo·li·tion \vō'lishən\ n : free will —**vo·li·tion·al** \-'lish(ə)nəl\ adj

vol·ley \'välē\ n, pl -leys **1** : flight of missiles (as arrows or bullets) **2** : simultaneous shooting of many weapons

vol·ley·ball n : game of batting a large ball over a net

vol·plane \'väl,plān\ vb -planed; -plan·ing : glide in an airplane

volt \'vōlt\ *n* : unit for measuring the force that moves an electric current

volt-age \'vōltij\ *n* : measure of volts

vol-u-ble \'välyəbəl\ *adj* : fluent and smooth in speech —**vol-u-bil-i-ty** \ˌvälyə'bilətē\ *n* —**vol-u-bly** \'välyəblē\ *adv*

vol-ume \'välyəm\ *n* **1** : book **2** : space occupied as measured by cubic units **3** : amount **4** : intensity of a sound

vo-lu-mi-nous \və'lümənəs\ *adj* : large or bulky

vol-un-tary \'välənˌterē\ *adj* **1** : done, made, or given freely and without expecting compensation **2** : relating to or controlled by the will —**vol-un-tari-ly** *adv*

vol-un-teer \ˌvälən'tiər\ *n* : person who offers to help or work without expecting payment or reward ∼ *vb* **1** : offer or give voluntarily **2** : offer oneself as a volunteer

vo-lup-tuous \və'ləpchə(wə)s\ *adj* **1** : luxurious **2** : having a full and sexually attractive figure —**vo-lup-tuous-ly** *adv* —**vo-lup-tuous-ness** *n*

vom-it \'vämət\ *vb* : throw up the contents of the stomach —**vomit** *n*

voo-doo \'vüdü\ *n, pl* **voodoos 1** : religion derived from African ancestor worship and involving sorcery **2** : one who practices voodoo **3** : charm or fetish used in voodoo —**voodoo** *adj* —**voo-doo-ism** \ˌizəm\ *n*

vo-ra-cious \vó'rāshəs, və-\ *adj* : greedy or exceedingly hungry —**vo-ra-cious-ly** *adv* —**vo-ra-cious-ness** *n* —**vo-rac-i-ty** \-'rasətē\ *n*

vor-tex \'vórˌteks\ *n, pl* **vor-ti-ces** \'vórtəˌsēz\ : whirling liquid

vo-ta-ry \'vōtərē\ *n, pl* **-ries 1** : devoted participant, adherent, admirer, or worshiper

vote \'vōt\ *n* **1** : individual expression of preference in choosing or reaching a decision **2** : right to indicate one's preference or the preference expressed ∼ *vb* **vot-ed; vot-ing 1** : cast a vote **2** : choose or defeat by vote —**vote-less** *adj* —**vot-er** *n*

vo-tive \'vōtiv\ *adj* : offered or performed in fulfillment of a vow or in petition, gratitude, or devotion

vouch \'vauch\ *vb* : give a guarantee or personal assurance

vouch-er \'vauchər\ *n* : written record or receipt that serves as proof of a transaction

vouch-safe \vauch'sāf\ *vb* **-safed; -saf-ing** : grant

vow \'vau\ *n* : solemn promise to do something or to live or act a certain way —**vow** *vb*

vow-el \'vau(ə)l\ *n* **1** : speech sound produced without obstruction or friction in the mouth **2** : letter representing such a sound

voy-age \'vóij\ *n* : long journey esp. by water or through space ∼ *vb* **-aged; -ag-ing** : make a voyage —**voy-ag-er** *n*

vul-ca-nize \'vəlkəˌnīz\ *vb* **-nized; -niz-ing** : treat (as rubber) to make more elastic or stronger —**vul-ca-ni-za-tion** \ˌvəlkənə'zāshən\ *n*

vul-gar \'vəlgər\ *adj* **1** : relating to the common people **2** : lacking refinement **3** : offensive in manner or language —**vul-gar-ism** \-ˌrizəm\ *n* —**vul-gar-ize** \-ˌrīz\ *vb* —**vul-gar-ly** *adv*

vul-gar-i-ty \ˌvəl'garətē\ *n, pl* **-ties 1** : state of being vulgar **2** : vulgar language or act

vul-ner-a-ble \'vəln(ə)rəbəl\ *adj* : susceptible to attack or damage —**vul-ner-a-bil-i-ty** \ˌvəln(ə)rə'bilətē\ *n* —**vul-ner-a-bly** *adv*

vul-ture \'vəlchər\ *n* : large flesh-eating bird

vul-va \'vəlvə\ *n, pl* **-vae** \-ˌvē, -ˌvī\ : external genital parts of the female

vying *pres part of* VIE

W

w \'dəbəl(ˌ)yü\ *n* : 23d letter of the alphabet

wab-ble \'wäbəl\ *var of* WOBBLE

wad \'wäd\ *n* **1** : little mass **2** : soft mass of fibrous material **3** : pliable plug to retain a powder charge ∼ *vb* **1** : form into a wad **2** : stuff with a wad

wad-dle \'wäd'l\ *vb* **-dled; -dling** : walk with short steps swaying from side to side —**waddle** *n*

wade \'wād\ *vb* **wad-ed; wad-ing 1** : step in or through (as water) **2** : move with difficulty —**wade** *n* —**wad-er** *n*

wa-fer \'wāfər\ *n* **1** : thin crisp cake or cracker **2** : waferlike thing

waf-fle \'wäfəl\ *n* : crisped cake of batter cooked in a hinged utensil (**waffle iron**)

waft \\'wäft, 'waft\\ *vb* : cause to move lightly by wind or waves —**waft** *n*

wag \\'wag\\ *vb* -**gg**- : sway or swing from side to side or to and fro ~ *n* 1 : wit 2 : act of wagging —**wag·gish** *adj*

wage \\'wāj\\ *vb* **waged; wag·ing** : engage in ~ *n* 1 : payment for labor or services 2 : compensation

wa·ger \\'wājər\\ *n or vb* : bet

wag·gle \\'wagəl\\ *vb* -**gled; -gling** ~ —**waggle** *n*

wag·on \\'wagən\\ *n* 1 : 4-wheeled vehicle drawn by animals 2 : child's 4-wheeled cart

waif \\'wāf\\ *n* : homeless child

wail \\'wāl\\ *vb* 1 : mourn 2 : make a sound like a mournful cry —**wail** *n*

wain·scot \\'wānskət, -ˌskōt, -ˌskät\\ *n* : usu. paneled wooden lining of an interior wall —**wainscot** *vb*

waist \\'wāst\\ *n* 1 : narrowed part of the body between chest and hips 2 : waistlike part —**waist·line** *n*

wait \\'wāt\\ *vb* 1 : remain in readiness or expectation 2 : delay 3 : attend as a waiter ~ *n* 1 : concealment 2 : act or period of waiting

wait·er \\'wātər\\ *n* : man who waits on tables

wait·ress \\'wātrəs\\ *n* : woman who waits on tables

waive \\'wāv\\ *vb* **waived; waiv·ing** : give up claim to

waiv·er \\'wāvər\\ *n* : act of waiving right, claim, or privilege

1wake \\'wāk\\ *vb* **waked** \\'wākt\\ *or* **woke** \\'wōk\\ **waked** *or* **wo·ken** \\'wōkən\\ *or* **woke; wak·ing** 1 : keep watch 2 : bring or come back to consciousness after sleep ~ *n* 1 : state of being awake 2 : watch held over a dead body

2wake *n* : track left by a ship

wake·ful \\'wākfəl\\ *adj* : not sleeping or able to sleep —**wake·ful·ness** *n*

wak·en \\'wākən\\ *vb* : wake

wale \\'wāl\\ *n* 1 : streak or ridge made on the skin 2 : ridge on cloth

walk \\'wȯk\\ *vb* 1 : move or cause to move on foot 2 : pass over, through, or along by walking ~ *n* 1 : a going on foot 2 : place or path for walking 3 : distance to be walked 4 : way of living 5 : way of walking 6 : slow 4-beat gait of a horse —**walk·er** *n*

wall \\'wȯl\\ *n* 1 : structure for defense or for enclosing something 2 : upright enclosing part of a building or room 3 : something like a wall ~ *vb*

: provide, separate, surround, or close with a wall —**walled** \\'wȯld\\ *adj*

wal·la·by \\'wäləbē\\ *n, pl* -**bies** : small or medium-sized kangaroo

wal·let \\'wälət\\ *n* : pocketbook with compartments

wall·flow·er *n* 1 : mustardlike plant with showy fragrant flowers 2 : one who remains on the sidelines of social activity

wal·lop \\'wäləp\\ *n* 1 : powerful blow 2 : ability to hit hard ~ *vb* 1 : defeat soundly 2 : hit hard

wal·low \\'wälō\\ *vb* 1 : roll about in deep mud 2 : live with excessive pleasure ~ *n* : place for wallowing

wall·pa·per *n* : decorative paper for walls —**wallpaper** *vb*

wal·nut \\'wȯl(ˌ)nət\\ *n* 1 : edible nut with a furrowed shell and adherent husk 2 : tree on which this nut grows or its brown wood 3 : hickory nut or tree

wal·rus \\'wȯlrəs, 'wäl-\\ *n, pl* -**rus** *or* -**rus·es** : large seallike mammal of northern seas

waltz \\'wȯlts\\ *n* : gliding dance to music having 3 beats to the measure or the music —**waltz** *vb*

wam·pum \\'wämpəm\\ *n* : strung shell beads used by No. American Indians as money

wan \\'wän\\ *adj* -**nn**- : sickly or pale —**wan·ly** *adv* —**wan·ness** *n*

wand \\'wänd\\ *n* : slender staff

wan·der \\'wändər\\ *vb* 1 : move about aimlessly 2 : stray 3 : become delirious —**wan·der·er** *n*

wan·der·lust \\'wändərˌləst\\ *n* : strong urge to wander

wane \\'wān\\ *vb* **waned; wan·ing** 1 : grow smaller or less 2 : lose power, prosperity, or influence —**wane** *n*

wan·gle \\'wangəl\\ *vb* -**gled; -gling** : obtain by sly or indirect means

want \\'wȯnt\\ *vb* 1 : lack 2 : need 3 : desire earnestly ~ *n* 1 : deficiency 2 : dire need 3 : something wanted

want·ing \\-iŋ\\ *adj* 1 : not present or in evidence 2 : falling below standards 3 : lacking in ability ~ *prep* 1 : lacking 2 : diminished by

wan·ton \\'wȯntᵊn\\ *adj* 1 : excessively merry 2 : lewd 3 : having no regard for justice or for others' feelings, rights, or safety ~ *n* : lewd or immoral person ~ *vb* : be wanton —**wan·ton·ly** *adv* —**wan·ton·ness** *n*

wa·pi·ti \\'wäpətē\\ *n, pl* -**ti** *or* -**tis** : elk

war \\'wȯr\\ *n* 1 : armed fighting between nations 2 : state of hostility or conflict 3 : struggle between opposing forces or for a particular end ~ *vb* -rr- : engage in warfare —war·less \-ləs\ *adj* —war·time *n*

war·ble \'wȯrbəl\ *n* 1 : melodious succession of low pleasing sounds 2 : musical trill ~ *vb* -bled; -bling : sing or utter in a trilling way

war·bler \'wȯrblər\ *n* 1 : small thrushlike singing bird 2 : small bright-colored insect-eating bird

ward \'wȯrd\ *n* 1 : a guarding or being under guard or guardianship 2 : division of a prison or hospital 3 : electoral or administrative division of a city 4 : person under protection of a guardian or a law court ~ *vb* : turn aside —ward·ship *n*

1.ward \wȯrd\ *adj suffix* 1 : that moves, tends, faces, or is directed toward 2 : that occurs or is situated in the direction of

2.ward, -wards *adv suffix* 1 : in a (specified) direction 2 : toward a (specified) point, position, or area

war·den \'wȯrdᵊn\ *n* 1 : guardian 2 : official charged with supervisory duties or enforcement of laws 3 : official in charge of a prison

ward·er \'wȯrdər\ *n* : watchman or warden

ward·robe \'wȯrd,rōb\ *n* 1 : clothes closet 2 : collection of wearing apparel

ware \waər\ *n* 1 : articles for sale —often pl. 2 : items of fired clay

ware·house \-,haůs\ *n* : place for storage of merchandise —warehouse *vb* —ware·house·man \-mən\ *n* —warehous·er \-haůzər, -sər\ *n*

war·fare \'wȯr,faər\ *n* 1 : military operations between enemies 2 : struggle

war·head \-,hed\ *n* : part of a missile (as a bomb) holding the charge

war·like *adj* : fond of or threatening war

warm \'wȯrm\ *adj* 1 : having or giving out moderate or adequate heat 2 : serving to retain heat 3 : showing strong feeling 4 : giving a pleasant impression of warmth, cheerfulness, or friendliness ~ *vb* 1 : make or become warm 2 : give warmth or energy to 3 : become increasingly ardent, interested, or competent —warm·er *n* —warm·ly *adv*

war·mon·ger \'wȯr,məŋgər, -,mäŋ-\ *n* : one who attempts to stir up war

warmth \'wȯrmth\ *n* 1 : quality or state of being warm 2 : enthusiasm

warn \'wȯrn\ *vb* 1 : put on guard 2

: notify in advance —warn·ing \-iŋ\ *n or adj*

warp \'wȯrp\ *n* 1 : lengthwise threads in a woven fabric 2 : twist ~ *vb* 1 : twist out of shape 2 : lead astray 3 : distort

war·rant \'wȯrənt, 'wär-\ *n* 1 : authorization 2 : legal writ authorizing action ~ *vb* 1 : declare or maintain positively 2 : guarantee 3 : approve 4 : justify

warrant officer *n* 1 : officer in the armed forces ranking next below a commissioned officer 2 : commissioned officer in the navy or coast guard ranking below an ensign

war·ran·ty \'wȯrəntē, 'wär-\ *n, pl* -ties : guarantee of the integrity of a product

war·ren \'wȯrən, 'wär-\ *n* : area for the keeping of small game as rabbits

war·rior \'wȯryər, 'wȯrēər; 'wärē-, 'wäryər\ *n* : man engaged or experienced in warfare

war·ship \'wȯr,ship\ *n* : armed military ship

wart \'wȯrt\ *n* 1 : small projection on the skin caused by a virus 2 : wartlike protuberance

wary \'wa(ə)rē\ *adj* war·i·er; -est : careful in guarding against danger or deception

was *past 1st & 3d sing of* BE

wash \'wȯsh, 'wäsh\ *vb* 1 : cleanse with or as if with a liquid (as water) 2 : wet thoroughly with liquid 3 : flow along the border of 4 : flow in a stream 5 : move or remove by or as if by the action of water 6 : cover or daub lightly with a liquid 7 : undergo laundering ~ *n* : act of washing or being washed 2 : articles to be washed 3 : surging action of water or disturbed air

wash·able \-əbəl\ *adj* : capable of being washed without damage

wash·board *n* : grooved board to scrub clothes on

wash·bowl *n* : large bowl for water for washing hands and face

wash·cloth *n* : cloth used for washing one's face and body

wash·er \'wȯshər, 'wäsh-\ *n* 1 : machine for washing 2 : ring used around a bolt or screw to ensure tightness or relieve friction

wash·ing \'wȯshiŋ, 'wäsh-\ *n* : articles to be washed

Washington's Birthday *n* : the 3d Monday in February or formerly February 22 observed as a legal holiday

wash·out *n* 1 : washing out or away of

earth 2 : place where earth is washed away 3 : failure

wash-room *n* : room with washing and toilet facilities

wasp \'wäsp, 'wosp\ *n* : slender-bodied winged insect related to the bees and having a formidable sting

wasp-ish \'wäspish, 'wos-\ *adj* : irritable

was-sail \'wäsəl, wä'säl\ *n* 1 : toast to someone's health 2 : liquor drunk on festive occasions 3 : riotous drinking —**wassail** *vb*

waste \'wäst\ *n* 1 : sparsely settled or barren region 2 : act or an instance of wasting 3 : refuse (as garbage or rubbish) 4 : material (as feces) produced but not used by a living body ~ *vb* **wast-ed; wast-ing** 1 : ruin 2 : spend or use carelessly 3 : lose substance or energy ~ *adj* : wild and uninhabited 2 : being of no further use —**wast-er** *n* —**waste-ful** \-fəl\ *adj* —**waste-ful-ly** *adv* —**waste-ful-ness** *n*

waste-bas-ket \'wās(t),baskət\ *n* : receptacle for refuse

waste-land \'wāstland, -lənd\ *n* : barren uncultivated land

wast-rel \'wāstrəl, 'wāstrəl\ *n* : one who wastes

watch \'wäch, 'woch\ *vb* 1 : be or stay awake intentionally 2 : be on the lookout for danger 3 : observe 4 : keep oneself informed about ~ *n* 1 : act of keeping awake to guard 2 : close observation 3 : one that watches 4 : period of duty on a ship or those on duty during this period 5 : timepiece carried on the person —**watch-er** *n*

watch-dog *n* 1 : dog kept to guard property 2 : one that protects

watch-ful \-fəl\ *adj* : steadily attentive —**watch-ful-ly** *adv* —**watch-ful-ness** *n*

watch-man \-mən\ *n* : person assigned to watch

watch-word *n* 1 : secret word used as a signal 2 : slogan

wa-ter \'wotər, 'wät-\ *n* 1 : liquid that descends as rain and forms rivers, lakes, and seas 2 : liquid containing or resembling water ~ *vb* 1 : supply with or get water 2 : dilute with or as if with water 3 : form or secrete watery matter

water buffalo *n* : common oxlike often domesticated Asian buffalo

wa-ter-col-or *n* 1 : paint whose liquid part is water 2 : picture made with watercolors

wa-ter-course *n* : stream of water

wa-ter-cress \-,kres\ *n* : perennial salad plant found chiefly in clear running water

wa-ter-fall *n* : steep descent of the water of a stream

wa-ter-fowl *n* 1 : bird that frequents the water 2 *pl* : swimming game birds

wa-ter-front *n* : land fronting a body of water

water lily *n* : aquatic plant with floating leaves and showy flowers

wa-ter-logged \-,lógd, -,lägd\ *adj* : filled or soaked with water

wa-ter-mark *n* 1 : mark showing how high water has risen 2 : a marking in paper visible under light ~ *vb* : mark (paper) with a watermark

wa-ter-mel-on *n* : large fruit with sweet juicy usu. red pulp

water moccasin *n* : venomous snake of the southern U.S.

wa-ter-pow-er *n* : power of moving water used to run machinery

wa-ter-proof *adj* : not letting water through ~ *vb* : make waterproof —**wa-ter-proof-ing** *n*

wa-ter-shed \-,shed\ *n* : dividing ridge between two drainage areas or one of these areas

water ski *n* : ski used on water when the wearer is towed —**wa-ter-ski** *vb* —**wa-ter-ski-er** *n*

wa-ter-spout *n* 1 : pipe from which water is spouted 2 : tornado over a body of water

wa-ter-tight *adj* 1 : so tight as not to let water in 2 : so worded that its meaning cannot be misunderstood or its purpose defeated

wa-ter-way *n* : navigable body of water

wa-ter-works *n pl* : system by which water is supplied (as to a city)

wa-tery \'wotərē, 'wät-\ *adj* 1 : relating to water 2 : containing, full of, or giving out water 3 : being like water 4 : soft and soggy

watt \'wät\ *n* : unit of electric power —**watt-age** \'wätij\ *n*

wat-tle \'wät[?]l\ *n* 1 : framework of flexible branches used for fencing 2 : fleshy process hanging usu. about the head or neck (as of a bird) —**wat-tled** \-[?]ld\ *adj*

wave \'wāv\ *vb* **waved; wav-ing** 1 : flutter 2 : signal with the hands 3 : wave to and fro with the hand 4 : curve up and down like a wave ~ *n* 1 : moving swell on the surface of water 2 : wavelike shape 3 : waving motion 4 : surge 5 : disturbance that transfers energy from point to point —**wave-let** \-lət\ *n* —**wave-like** *adj* —**wavy** *adj*

wave·length \'wāv,leŋth\ n : distance from crest to crest in the line of advance of a wave

wa·ver \'wāvər\ vb 1 : fluctuate in opinion, allegiance, or direction 2 : flicker 3 : falter —waver n —wa·ver·er n —wa·ver·ing·ly adv

¹wax \'waks\ n 1 : yellowish plastic substance secreted by bees 2 : substance resembling beeswax ~ vb : treat or rub with wax esp. for polishing

²wax vb 1 : grow larger 2 : become

wax·en \'waksən\ adj : made of or resembling wax

waxy \'waksē\ adj wax·i·er; -est : made of, full of, or resembling wax

way \'wā\ n 1 : thoroughfare for travel or passage 2 : route 3 : course of action 4 : method 5 : detail 6 : usual or characteristic state of affairs 7 : condition 8 : distance 9 : progress along a course —by way of 1 : for the purpose of 2 : by the route through —out of the way : remote —under way : in motion or progress

way·bill n : paper that accompanies a shipment and gives details of goods, route, and charges

way·far·er \'wā,farər\ n : traveler esp. on foot —way·far·ing \-,farin\ adj

way·lay \'wā,lā\ vb -laid \-,lād\; -lay·ing 1 : lie in wait for 2 : stop (someone) to converse

way·side n : side of a road

way·ward \'wāword\ adj 1 : disobedient 2 : unpredictable 3 : opposite to what is desired

we \(')wē\ pron —used of a group that includes the speaker or writer

weak \'wēk\ adj 1 : lacking strength or vigor 2 : deficient in vigor of mind or character 3 : deficient in the usual ingredients 4 : not having or exerting authority —weak·en \'wēkən\ vb —weak·ly adv

weak·ling \-liŋ\ n : person who is physically, mentally, or morally weak

weak·ly \'wēklē\ adj : feeble

weak·ness \-nəs\ n 1 : quality or state of being weak 2 : fault 3 : object of special liking

wealth \'welth\ n 1 : abundant possessions or resources 2 : profusion

wealthy \'welthē\ adj wealth·i·er; -est : having wealth

wean \'wēn\ vb 1 : accustom (a young mammal) to take food otherwise than by nursing 2 : free from dependence

weap·on \'wepən\ n 1 : something (as a gun) that may be used to fight with 2

: means by which one contends against another

wear \'waər\ vb wore \'wōr\; worn \'wōrn\; wear·ing 1 : use as an article of clothing or adornment 2 : carry on the person 3 : show an appearance of 4 : decay by use or by scraping 5 : lessen the strength of 6 : endure use ~ n 1 : act of wearing 2 : clothing 3 : lasting quality 4 : result of use —wear·able \'warəbəl\ adj —wear·er n —wear out vb 1 : make or become useless by wear 2 : tire

wea·ri·some \'wirēsəm\ adj : causing weariness

wea·ry \'wi(ə)rē\ adj -ri·er; -est 1 : worn out in strength, freshness, or patience 2 : expressing or characteristic of weariness ~ vb -ried; -ry·ing : make or become weary —wea·ri·ly adv —wea·ri·ness n

wea·sel \'wēzəl\ n : small slender flesh-eating mammals

weath·er \'wethər\ n : condition of the atmosphere ~ vb 1 : expose to or endure the action of weather 2 : endure

weath·er-beat·en adj : altered by exposure to the weather

weath·er·man \-,man\ n : one who forecasts and reports the weather

weath·er·proof adj : able to withstand exposure to weather —weather-proof vb

weather vane n : movable device that shows the way the wind blows

weave \'wēv\ vb wove \'wōv\ or weaved; wo·ven \'wōvən\ or weaved; weav·ing 1 : form by interlacing strands of material 2 : contrive 3 : make a coherent whole 4 : follow a winding course ~ n : pattern or method of weaving —weav·er n

web \'web\ n 1 : cobweb 2 : animal or plant membrane 3 : network ~ vb -bb- : cover or provide with a web

webbed \'webd\ adj : having or being toes or fingers united by a web

web·bing \'webiŋ\ n : strong closely woven tape

wed \'wed\ vb -dd- 1 : marry 2 : unite

wed·ding \'wediŋ\ n : marriage ceremony and celebration

wedge \'wej\ n : V-shaped object used for splitting, raising, forcing open, or tightening ~ vb wedged; wedg·ing 1 : tighten or split with a wedge 2 : force into a narrow space

wed·lock \'wed,läk\ n : marriage

Wednes·day \'wenzdē\ n : 4th day of the week

wee \'wē\ *adj* : very small

weed \'wēd\ *n* 1 : unwanted plant ~ *vb* : remove weeds or other unwanted items —**weed-er** *n* —**weedy** *adj*

weeds *n pl* : mourning clothes

week \'wēk\ *n* 1 : 7 successive days 2 : calendar period of 7 days beginning with Sunday and ending with Saturday 3 : the working or school days of the calendar week

week-day \'wēk,dā\ *n* : any day except Sunday and often Saturday

week-end \-,end\ *n* : Saturday and Sunday ~ *vb* : spend the weekend

week-ly \'wēklē\ *adj* : occurring, done, produced, or issued every week ~ *adv* : once a week ~ *n*, *pl* **-lies** : weekly publication —**weekly** *adv*

weep \'wēp\ *vb* **wept** \'wept\; **weep-ing** : shed tears —**weep-er** *n* —**weepy** *adj*

wee-vil \'wēval\ *n* : small injurious beetle with a long head usu. curved into a snout —**wee-vily**, **wee-vil-ly** \'wēv(ə)lē\ *adj*

weft \'weft\ *n* : woof

weigh \'wā\ *vb* 1 : determine the heaviness of 2 : have a specified weight 3 : consider carefully 4 : heave up (an anchor) 5 : press down or burden

weight \'wāt\ *n* 1 : amount that something weighs 2 : relative heaviness 3 : heavy object 4 : burden or pressure 5 : importance ~ *vb* 1 : load with a weight 2 : oppress —**weight-less** \-ləs\ *adj* —**weight-less-ness** *n* —**weighty** \'wātē\ *adj*

weird \'wiərd\ *adj* 1 : unearthly or mysterious 2 : strange —**weird-ly** *adv* —**weird-ness** *n*

wel-come \'welkəm\ *vb* **-comed; -coming** : accept or greet cordially ~ *adj* : received or permitted gladly ~ *n* : cordial greeting or reception

weld \'weld\ *vb* : unite by heating, hammering, or pressing ~ *n* : union by welding —**weld-er** *n*

wel-fare \'wel,faər\ *n* 1 : prosperity 2 : relief

¹**well** \'wel\ *n* 1 : spring 2 : hole sunk in the earth to obtain a natural deposit (as of oil) 3 : source of supply 4 : open space extending vertically through floors ~ *vb* : flow forth

²**well** *adv* **bet-ter** \'betər\; **best** \'best\ 1 : in a good or proper manner 2 : satisfactorily 3 : fully 4 : considerably ~ *adj* 1 : satisfactory 2 : prosperous 3 : desirable 4 : healthy

well-ad-vised \,welad'vīzd\ *adj* : prudent

well-be-ing \'wel'bēiŋ\ *n* : state of being happy, healthy, or prosperous

well-bred \-'bred\ *adj* : having good manners

well-done *adj* 1 : properly performed 2 : cooked thoroughly

well-heeled \-'hēld\ *adj* : financially well-off

well-mean-ing *adj* : having good intentions

well-nigh *adv* : nearly

well-off *adj* : being in good condition esp. financially

well-read \-'red\ *adj* : well informed through reading

well-round-ed \-'raúndəd\ *adj* : broadly developed

well-spring *n* : source

well-to-do \,weltə'dü\ *adj* : prosperous

well-worn \-'wōrn\ *adj* 1 : worn by much use 2 : trite

welsh \'welsh, 'welch\ *vb* : default dishonorably

Welsh rabbit *n* : melted often seasoned cheese poured over toast or crackers

Welsh rare-bit \-'raərbət\ *n* : Welsh rabbit

welt \'welt\ *n* 1 : narrow strip of leather between a shoe upper and sole 2 : ridge raised on the skin usu. by a blow ~ *vb* : hit hard

wel-ter \'weltər\ *vb* 1 : toss about 2 : wallow ~ *n* : confused jumble

wen \'wen\ *n* : cyst formed by blockage of a skin gland

wench \'wench\ *n* : young woman

wend \'wend\ *vb* : direct one's course

went *past of* GO

wept *past of* WEEP

were *past 2d sing, past pl, or past subjunctive of* BE

were-wolf \'wiər,wùlf, 'wər-, 'wear-\ *n*, *pl* **-wolves** \-,wùlvz\ : person held to be able to change into a wolf

west \'west\ *adv* : to or toward the west ~ *adj* : situated toward or at or coming from the west ~ *n* 1 : direction of sunset 2 *cap* : regions to the west —**west-er-ly** \'westərlē\ *adv or adj* —**west-ward** \-wərd\ *adv or adj* —**west-wards** \-wərdz\ *adv*

west-ern \'westərn\ *adj* 1 *cap* : of a region designated West 2 : lying toward or coming from the west —**West-ern-er** *n*

wet \'wet\ *adj* **-tt-** 1 : consisting of or covered or soaked with liquid 2 : not dry ~ *n* : moisture ~ *vb* **-tt-** : make or become moist —**wet-ly** *adv* —**wet-ness** *n*

whack \'hwak\ *vb* : strike sharply ~ *n* 1 : sharp blow 2 : proper working order 3 : chance 4 : try

¹whale \'hwāl\ *n, pl* **whales** *or* **whale** : large marine mammal ~ *vb* **whaled; whal·ing** : hunt for whales —**whale·boat** *n* —**whal·er** *n*

²whale *vb* **whaled; whal·ing** : strike or hit vigorously

whale·bone *n* : horny substance attached to the upper jaw of some large whales (**whalebone whales**)

wharf \'hworf\ *n, pl* **wharves** \'hworvz\ : structure alongside which boats lie to load or unload

what \('')hwät\ *pron* **1** —used to inquire the identity or nature of something **2** : that which **3** : whatever ~ *adv* : to what degree or in what respect ~ *adj* **1** —used to inquire about the identity or nature of something **2** : how remarkable or surprising **3** : whatever

what-ev·er \hwät'evər\ *pron* **1** : anything or everything that **2** : no matter what ~ *adj* : of any kind at all

what·so·ev·er \,hwätsə'wevər\ *pron or adj* : whatever

wheal \'hwēl\ *n* : a wale or welt on the skin

wheat \'hwēt\ *n* : cereal grain that yields flour —**wheat·en** *adj*

whee·dle \'hwēd²l\ *vb* -**dled; -dling** : coax or tempt by flattery

wheel \'hwēl\ *n* **1** : disk or circular frame capable of turning on a central axis **2** : device of which the main part is a wheel ~ *vb* **1** : convey or move on wheels or a wheeled vehicle **2** : rotate **3** : turn so as to change direction —**wheeled** *adj* —**wheel·er** *n* —**wheel·less** *adj*

wheel·bar·row \-,barō\ *n* : one-wheeled vehicle for carrying small loads

wheel·base *n* : distance in inches between the front and rear axles of an automotive vehicle

wheel·chair *n* : chair mounted on wheels esp. for the use of invalids

wheeze \'hwēz\ *vb* **wheezed; wheez·ing** : breathe with difficulty and with a whistling sound —**wheeze** *n* —**wheezy** *adj*

whelk \'hwelk\ *n* : large sea snail

whelp \'hwelp\ *n* : one of the young of various carnivorous mammals (as a dog) ~ *vb* : bring forth whelps

when \('')hwen, hwən\ *adv* —used to inquire about or designate a particular time ~ *conj* **1** : at or during the time that **2** : every time that **3** : if **4** : although ~ \,hwen\ *pron* : what time

whence \('')hwens\ *adv* **1** : from what

place, source, or cause **2** : from or out of which

when·ev·er \hwen'evər, hwən-\ *conj or adv* : at whatever time

where \('')hwear\ *adv* **1** : at, in, or to what place **2** : at, in, or to what situation, position, direction, circumstances, or respect ~ *conj* **1** : at, in, or to what place, position, or circumstance **2** : at, in, or to which place ~ \'hwear\ *n* **1** : place **2** : what place

where·abouts \-ə,baúts\ *adv* : about where ~ *n sing or pl* : place where a person or thing is

where·as \hwer'az\ *conj* **1** : because **2** : while on the contrary

where·by *conj* : by, through, or in accordance with which

where·fore \'hwear,fōr\ *adv* **1** : why **2** : therefore ~ *n* : cause

where·in \hwer'in\ *adv* : in what respect

where·of \-'əv, -äv\ *conj* : of what, which, or whom

where·up·on \'hwerə,pön, -,pän\ *conj* —used to introduce a result or consequence

wher·ev·er \hwer'evər\ *adv* : where ~ *conj* : at, in, or to whatever place or circumstance

where·with·al \'hwerwith,öl, -with-\ *n* : resources and esp. money

whet \'hwet\ *vb* -**tt-** **1** : sharpen by rubbing (as with a stone) **2** : stimulate —**whet·stone** *n*

whether \'hwethər\ *conj* **1** : if it is or was true that **2** : if it is or was better **3** : whichever is the case

whey \'hwā\ *n* : watery part of sour milk

which \('')hwich\ *adj* **1** : being what one or ones of a group **2** : whichever ~ *pron* **1** : which one or ones **2** : whichever

which·ev·er \hwich'evər\ *pron or adj* : no matter what one

whiff \'hwif\ *n* **1** : slight gust **2** : inhalation of odor, gas, or smoke **3** : slight trace ~ *vb* : inhale an odor

while \'hwīl\ *n* **1** : period of time **2** : time and effort used ~ \('')hwīl\ *conj* **1** : during the time that **2** : as long as **3** : although ~ \'hwīl\ *vb* **whiled; whil·ing** : cause to pass esp. pleasantly

whim \'hwim\ *n* : sudden or brief idea or wish

whim·per \'hwimpər\ *vb* : cry softly —**whimper** *n*

whim·si·cal \'hwimzikəl\ *adj* **1** : full of whims **2** : erratic —**whim·si·cal·i·ty**

\\ˌhwimzə'kalətē\ n —**whim·si·cal·ly** adv

whim·sy, whim·sey \'hwimzē\ n, pl **-sies** or **-seys** 1 : whim 2 : fanciful creation

whine \'hwīn\ vb whined; whin·ing 1 : utter a usu. high-pitched plaintive or distressed cry 2 : complain —**whine** n

whin·ny \'hwinē\ vb **-nied; -ny·ing** : neigh —**whinny** n

whip \'hwip\ vb **-pp-** 1 : move quickly 2 : strike with something slender and flexible 3 : defeat 4 : incite 5 : beat into a froth ~ n 1 : flexible device used for whipping 2 : party leader responsible for discipline 3 : thrashing motion —**whip·per** n

whip·cord n 1 : thin tough cord 2 : cloth made of hard-twisted yarns

whip·lash n : injury from a sudden sharp movement of the neck and head

whip·per·snap·per \'hwipər₁snapər\ n : small, insignificant, or presumptuous person

whip·pet \'hwipət\ n : small swift dog often used for racing

whip·poor·will \'hwipər₁wil\ n : American nocturnal bird

whir \'hwər\ vb **-rr-** : move, fly, or revolve with a whizzing sound ~ n : continuous fluttering or vibratory sound

whirl \'hwərl\ vb 1 : move or drive in a circle 2 : spin 3 : move or turn quickly 4 : reel ~ n 1 : rapid circular movement 2 : state of commotion or confusion

whirl·pool n : whirling mass of water having a depression in the center

whirl·wind n : whirling wind storm

whisk \'hwisk\ n 1 : quick light sweeping or brushing motion 2 : usu. wire kitchen implement for beating ~ vb 1 : move or convey briskly 2 : beat 3 : brush lightly

whisk broom n : small broom

whis·ker \'hwiskər\ n 1 pl : beard 2 : long bristle or hair near an animal's mouth —**whis·kered** \-kərd\ adj

whis·key, whis·ky \'hwiskē\ n, pl **-keys** or **-kies** : liquor distilled from a fermented mash of grain

whis·per \'hwispər\ vb 1 : speak softly 2 : tell by whispering ~ n 1 : soft low sound 2 : rumor

whist \'hwist\ n : card game

whis·tle \'hwisəl\ n 1 : device by which a shrill sound is produced 2 : shrill clear sound made by a whistle or through the lips ~ vb **-tled; -tling** 1

: make or utter a whistle 2 : signal or call by a whistle 3 : produce by whistling —**whis·tler** n

whis·tle-stop n 1 : small community 2 : brief political appearance

whit \'hwit\ n : bit

white \'hwīt\ adj whit·er; -est 1 : free from color 2 : of the color of new snow or milk 3 : having light skin ~ n 1 : color of maximum lightness 2 : white part or thing 3 : person who is light-skinned —**white·ness** n

white-bait \'hwīt₁bāt\ n : young of a herring

white blood cell n : blood cell that does not contain hemoglobin

white·cap \'hwīt₁kap\ n : wave crest breaking into foam

white-col·lar adj : relating to salaried employees with duties not requiring protective or work clothing

white elephant n : unwanted often useless item

white·fish \'hwīt₁fish\ n : freshwater food fish

whit·en \'hwītᵊn\ vb : make or become white —**whit·en·er** \'hwītnər, -ᵊnər\ n

white slave n : woman or girl held unwillingly for purposes of prostitution —**white slavery** n

white-tail \'hwīt₁tāl\ n : No. American deer

white·wash vb 1 : whiten with a composition (as of lime and water) 2 : gloss over or cover up faults or wrongdoing —**whitewash** n

whith·er \'hwithər\ adv 1 : to what place 2 : to what situation, position, degree, or end

¹**whit·ing** \'hwītiŋ\ n : usu. light or silvery food fish

²**whiting** n : pulverized chalk or limestone

whit·ish \'hwītish\ adj : somewhat white

whit·tle \'hwitᵊl\ vb **-tled; -tling** 1 : pare 2 : shape by paring 3 : reduce gradually

whiz, whizz \'hwiz\ vb **-zz-** : make a sound like a speeding object —**whiz, whizz** n

who \('\)hü\ pron 1 —used to inquire the identity of an indicated person or group 2 : person or persons that 3 \(₁\)hü, ü\ —used to introduce a relative clause

who·dun·it \hü'dənət\ n : detective or mystery story

who·ev·er \hü'evər\ pron : no matter who

whole \'hōl\ adj 1 : being in healthy or

sound condition **2** : having all its parts or elements **3** : constituting the total sum of ~ *n* **1** : complete amount or sum **2** : coherent complex system —**on the whole 1** : considering all circumstances **2** : in general —**whole·ness** *n*

whole·heart·ed \'hōl'härtəd\ *adj* : sincere

whole number *n* : integer

whole·sale *n* : sale of goods in quantity usu. for resale by a retail merchant ~ *adj* **1** : of or relating to wholesaling **2** : performed on a large scale ~ *vb* **-saled; -sal·ing** : sell at wholesale —**wholesale** *adv* —**whole·sal·er** *n*

whole·some \-səm\ *adj* **1** : promoting mental, spiritual, or bodily health **2** : healthy —**whole·some·ness** *n*

whole wheat *adj* : made of ground entire wheat kernels

whol·ly \'hōl(l)ē\ *adv* **1** : totally **2** : solely

whom \(')hüm\ *pron, objective case of* WHO

whom·ev·er \hüm'evər\ *pron, objective case of* WHOEVER

whoop \'h(w)üp, 'h(w)üp\ *vb* : shout loudly ~ *n* : shout

whooping cough *n* : infectious disease marked by convulsive coughing fits

whop·per \'hwäpər\ *n* **1** : something unusually large or extreme of its kind **2** : monstrous lie

whop·ping \'hwäpiŋ\ *adj* : extremely large

whore \'hōr\ *n* : prostitute

whorl \'hwȯrl, 'hwərl\ *n* : spiral —**whorled** *adj*

whose \(')hüz\ *adj* : of or relating to whom or which ~ *pron* : whose one or ones

who·so·ev·er \ˌhüsə'wevər\ *pron* : whoever

why \(')hwī\ *adv* : for what reason, cause, or purpose ~ *conj* **1** : reason for which **2** : for which ~ \'hwī\ *n, pl* **whys** : reason ~ *interj* \(ˌ)wī, (ˌ)hwī\ —used esp. to express surprise

wick \'wik\ *n* : cord that draws up oil, tallow, or wax to be burned

wick·ed \'wikəd\ *adj* **1** : morally bad **2** : harmful or troublesome **3** : very unpleasant **4** : mischievous —**wicked·ly** *adv* —**wick·ed·ness** *n*

wick·er \'wikər\ *n* **1** : small pliant branch **2** : wickerwork —**wicker** *adj*

wick·er·work *n* : work made of wickers

wick·et \'wikət\ *n* **1** : small gate, door, or window **2** : frame in cricket or arch in croquet

wide \'wīd\ *adj* **wid·er; wid·est 1** : covering a vast area **2** : measured at right angles to the length **3** : having extension from side to side **4** : opened fully **5** : far from the goal ~ *adv* **wid·er; wid·est 1** : over a great distance **2** : so as to leave considerable space between **3** : fully **4** : astray —**wide·ly** *adv* —**wid·en** \'wīdən\ *vb*

wide-awake *adj* : alert

wide-eyed *adj* **1** : having the eyes wide open **2** : amazed **3** : naive

wide·spread *adj* : widely extended

wid·ow \'widō\ *n* : woman who has lost her husband by death and has not married again ~ *vb* : cause to become a widow —**wid·ow·hood** *n*

wid·ow·er \'widəwər\ *n* : man who has lost his wife by death and has not married again

width \'width\ *n* **1** : distance from side to side **2** : largeness of extent **3** : measured and cut piece of material

wield \'wēld\ *vb* **1** : use or handle esp. effectively **2** : exert —**wield·er** *n*

wie·ner \'wēnər\ *n* : frankfurter

wife \'wīf\ *n, pl* **wives** \'wīvz\ : married woman —**wife·hood** *n* —**wife·less** *adj* —**wife·ly** *adj*

wig \'wig\ *n* : manufactured covering of hair for the head

wig·gle \'wigəl\ *vb* **-gled; -gling 1** : move with quick jerky or shaking movements **2** : wriggle —**wiggle** *n* —**wiggler** *n*

wig·gly \-(ə)lē\ *adj* **1** : tending to wiggle **2** : wavy

wig·wag \'wig,wag\ *vb* : signal by a flag or light waved according to a code or by the hand or arm

wig·wam \'wig,wäm\ *n* : American Indian hut consisting of a framework of poles overlaid with bark, rush mats, or hides

wild \'wīld\ *adj* **1** : living or being in a state of nature and not domesticated or cultivated **2** : unrestrained **3** : turbulent **4** : crazy **5** : uncivilized **6** : erratic ~ *n* **1** : wilderness **2** : undomesticated state ~ *adv* : without control —**wild·ly** *adv* —**wild·ness** *n*

wild·cat \'wīld(,)kat\ *n* **1** : any of various undomesticated cats (as a lynx) **2** : oil or gas well drilled in an area not known to be productive ~ *adj* **1** : not sound or safe **2** : unauthorized ~ *vb* **-tt-** : drill a wildcat oil or gas well

wil·der·ness \'wildərnəs\ *n* : uncultivated and uninhabited region

wild·fire \'wīl(d)ₜfī(ə)r\ *n* : sweeping and destructive fire

wild·fowl *n* : game waterfowl

wild·life \'wīl(d)ₜlīf\ *n* : undomesticated animals

wile \'wīl\ *n* : trick to snare or deceive ~ *vb* **wiled; wil·ing** : lure

will \wəl, (ə)l, (ˈ)wil\ *vb, past* **would** \wəd, (ə)d, (ˈ)wud\; *pres sing & pl* **will** 1 : wish 2 —used as an auxiliary verb to express (1) desire or willingness (2) customary action (3) simple future time (4) capability (5) determination (6) probability (7) inevitability or (8) a command 3 \'wil\ : dispose of by a will — \'wil\ *n* 1 : often determined wish 2 : act, process, or experience of willing 3 : power of controlling one's actions or emotions 4 : legal document disposing of property after death

will·ful, wil·ful \'wilfəl\ *adj* 1 : governed by will without regard to reason 2 : intentional — **will·ful·ly** *adv*

will·ing \'wiliŋ\ *adj* 1 : inclined or favorably disposed in mind 2 : prompt to act 3 : done, borne, or accepted voluntarily or without reluctance — **will·ing·ly** *adv* — **will·ing·ness** *n*

will-o'-the-wisp \ₜwiləⁱthə'wisp\ *n* 1 : light that appears at night over marshy grounds 2 : misleading or elusive goal or hope

wil·low \'wilō\ *n* : quick-growing shrub or tree with flexible shoots

wil·lowy \'wilōwē\ *adj* : gracefully tall and slender

will·pow·er \'wil,paú(ə)r\ *n* : energetic determination

wil·ly-nil·ly \ₜwilē'nilē\ *adv or adj* : without regard to one's choice

wilt \'wilt\ *vb* 1 : lose or cause to lose freshness and become limp 2 : grow weak

wily \'wīlē\ *adj* **wil·i·er; -est** : full of craftiness — **wil·i·ness** *n*

win \'win\ *vb* **won** \'wən\; **win·ning** 1 : gain victory in a contest 2 : get possession of esp. by effort 3 : gain in battle or contest 4 : make friendly or favorable ~ *n* : victory

wince \'wins\ *vb* **winced; winc·ing** : shrink back involuntarily — **wince** *n*

winch \'winch\ *n* : hand- or power-operated machine for hoisting or pulling with a drum around which rope is wound — **winch** *vb*

¹wind \'wind\ *n* 1 : movement of the air 2 : breath 3 : gas in the stomach or intestines 4 : air carrying a scent 5 : intimation ~ *vb* 1 : get a scent of 2 : cause to be out of breath

²wind \'wīnd\ *vb* **wound** \'waúnd\; **wind·ing** 1 : have or follow a winding course 2 : move or lie to encircle 3 : encircle or cover with something pliable 4 : tighten the spring of 5 : turn ~ *n* : turn or coil — **wind·er** *n*

wind·break *n* : trees and shrubs to break the force of the wind

wind·fall \'win(d)ₜfȯl\ *n* 1 : thing blown down by wind 2 : unexpected benefit

wind instrument *n* : musical instrument (as a flute or horn) sounded by wind and esp. by the breath

wind·lass \'windləs\ *n* : winch esp. for hoisting anchor

wind·mill \'win(d)ₜmil\ *n* : machine worked by the wind turning radiating vanes

win·dow \'windō\ *n* 1 : opening in the wall of a building to let in light and air 2 : pane in a window — **win·dow·less** *adj*

win·dow-shop *vb* : look at the displays in store windows — **win·dow-shop·per** *n*

wind·pipe \'win(d)ₜpīp\ *n* : passage for the breath from the larynx to the lungs

wind·shield \'win(d)ₜshēld\ *n* : transparent screen in front of the occupants of a vehicle

wind-up \'wīnₜdəp\ *n* : end — **wind up** \(ˈ)wīn'dəp\ *vb*

wind·ward \'win(d)wərd\ *adj* : moving toward or situated on the side toward the direction from which the wind is blowing ~ *n* : direction from which the wind is blowing

windy \'windē\ *adj* **wind·i·er; -est** 1 : having wind 2 : indulging in useless talk

wine \'wīn\ *n* 1 : fermented grape juice 2 : usu. fermented juice of a plant product (as fruit) used as a beverage ~ *vb* : treat to or drink wine

wing \'wiŋ\ *n* 1 : movable paired appendage for flying 2 : winglike thing 3 : projecting part of a building 4 *pl* : area at the side of the stage out of sight 5 : faction ~ *vb* 1 : fly 2 : let fly — **winged** *adj* — **wing-less** *adj* — **on the wing** : in flight — **under one's wing** : in one's charge or care

wink \'wiŋk\ *vb* 1 : close and open the eyes quickly 2 : avoid seeing or noticing something 3 : twinkle 4 : close and open one eye quickly as a signal or hint ~ *n* 1 : brief sleep 2 : act of winking 3 : instant — **wink·er** *n*

win·ner \'winər\ *n* : one that wins

win·ning \'-iŋ\ *n* 1 : victory 2 : money

won at gambling ~ *adj* **1** : victorious **2** : charming

win·now \'winō\ *vb* **1** : remove (as chaff from grain) by a current of air **2** : get rid of something unwanted or separate something

win·some \'winsəm\ *adj* **1** : causing joy **2** : cheerful or gay —**win·some·ly** *adv* —**win·some·ness** *n*

win·ter \'wintər\ *n* : season between autumn and spring ~ *adj* : sown in autumn for harvest the next spring or summer ~ *vb* : pass the winter —**win·ter·time** *n*

win·ter·green \'wintər‚grēn\ *n* : low heathlike evergreen plant with red berries

win·try \'wintrē\, **win·tery** \'wint(ə)rē\ *adj* **win·tri·er**, **-est 1** : characteristic of winter **2** : cold in feeling

wipe \'wīp\ *vb* **wiped**; **wip·ing 1** : clean or dry by rubbing **2** : remove by rubbing or cleaning **3** : erase completely **4** : destroy **5** : pass (as a cloth) over a surface ~ *n* : act or instance of wiping —**wip·er** *n*

wire \'wī(ə)r\ *n* **1** : thread of metal **2** : work made of wire **3** : telegram or cablegram ~ *vb* **1** : provide with wire **2** : bind or mount with wire **3** : telegraph

wire·less \-ləs\ *n* : system for communicating by code signals and radio waves and without connecting wires —**wireless** *adj or vb*

wire·tap *vb* : connect into a telephone or telegraph wire to get information —**wiretap** *n* —**wire·tap·per** *n*

wir·ing \'wī(ə)riŋ\ *n* : system of wires esp. for distributing electricity through a building

wiry \'wī(ə)rē\ *adj* **wir·i·er** \'wīrēər\, **-est 1** : resembling wire **2** : slender yet strong and sinewy —**wir·i·ness** *n*

wis·dom \'wizdəm\ *n* **1** : accumulated learning **2** : good sense

wisdom tooth *n* : last tooth on each half of each jaw in man

¹wise \'wīz\ *n* : manner

²wise *adj* **wis·er**; **wis·est 1** : having or showing wisdom, good sense, or good judgment **2** : aware of what is going on —**wise·ly** *adv*

wise·crack *n* : clever, smart, or flippant remark ~ *vb* : make a wisecrack

wish \'wish\ *vb* **1** : have a desire **2** : express a wish concerning **3** : request ~ *n* **1** : a wishing or desire **2** : expressed will or desire

wish·bone *n* : forked bone in front of the breastbone in most birds

wish·ful \-fəl\ *adj* **1** : expressive of a wish **2** : according with wishes rather than fact

wishy-washy \'wishē‚wȯshē, -ı‚wäsh-\ *adj* : weak or insipid

wisp \'wisp\ *n* **1** : small bunch of hay or straw **2** : thin strand, strip, fragment, or streak **3** : something frail, slight, or fleeting —**wispy** *adj*

wis·te·ria \wis'tirēə\ *n* : pealike woody vine with long clusters of flowers

wist·ful \'wistfəl\ *adj* : full of longing —**wist·ful·ly** *adv* —**wist·ful·ness** *n*

wit \'wit\ *n* **1** : reasoning power **2** : mental soundness —usu. pl. **3** : quickness and cleverness in handling words and ideas **4** : talent for clever remarks or one noted for witty remarks —**wit·less** *adj* —**wit·less·ly** *adv* —**wit·less·ness** *n* —**wit·ted** *adj*

witch \'wich\ *n* **1** : person believed to have magic power **2** : ugly old woman ~ *vb* : bewitch —**witch·craft** *n*

witch·ery \'wich(ə)rē\ *n, pl* **-er·ies 1** : witchcraft **2** : charm

witch ha·zel \'wich‚hāzəl\ *n* **1** : shrub having small yellow flowers in fall **2** : alcoholic solution of material from witch hazel bark used as a lotion

witch-hunt *n* **1** : searching out and persecution of supposed witches **2** : harassment of those with unpopular views

witch·ing \'wichiŋ\ *adj* : bewitching

with \(')with, (')with\ *prep* **1** : against, to, or toward **2** : in support of **3** : because of **4** : in the company of **5** : having **6** : despite **7** : containing **8** : by means of

with·draw \with'drȯ, with-\ *vb* **-drew** \-'drü\; **-drawn** \-'drȯn\; **-draw·ing** \-'drȯiŋ\ **1** : take back or away **2** : call back or retract **3** : go away **4** : terminate one's participation in or use of —**with·draw·al** \-'drȯ(ə)l\ *n*

with·drawn \with'drȯn\ *adj* : socially detached and unresponsive

with·er \'withər\ *vb* **1** : shrivel **2** : lose or cause to lose energy, force, or freshness

with·ers \'withərz\ *n pl* : ridge between the shoulder bones of a horse

with·hold \with'hōld, with-\ *vb* **-held** \-'held\; **-hold·ing 1** : hold back **2** : refrain from giving

with·in \with'in, with-\ *adv* **1** : in or into the interior **2** : inside oneself ~ *prep* **1** : in or to the inner part of **2** : in the limits or compass of ~ *n* : inner place or area

with·out \with'aut, with-\ *prep* **1** : outside 2 : lacking 3 : unaccompanied or unmarked by **—without** *adv*

with·stand \with'stand, with-\ *vb* **-stood** \-'stud\; **-stand·ing** : oppose successfully

wit·ness \'witnəs\ *n* 1 : testimony 2 : one who testifies 3 : one present at a transaction to testify that it has taken place 4 : one who has personal knowledge or experience 5 : something serving as proof ~ *vb* 1 : bear witness 2 : act as legal witness of 3 : furnish proof of 4 : be a witness of 5 : be the scene of

wit·ti·cism \'witə,sizəm\ *n* : witty saying or phrase

wit·ting \'witiŋ\ *adj* : intentional **—wit·ting·ly** *adv*

wit·ty \'witē\ *adj* **-ti·er; -est** : marked by or full of wit **—wit·ti·ly** \'witᵊlē\ *adv* **—wit·ti·ness** *n*

wives *pl of* WIFE

wiz·ard \'wizərd\ *n* 1 : magician 2 : very clever person **—wiz·ard·ry** \-ə(r)drē\ *n*

wiz·ened \'wiz²nd\ *adj* : dried up

wob·ble \'wäbəl\ *vb* **-bled; -bling** 1 : move or cause to move with an irregular rocking motion 2 : tremble 3 : waver **—wobble** *n* **—wob·bly** \'wäb(ə)lē\ *adj*

woe \'wō\ *n* 1 : deep suffering 2 : misfortune

woe·be·gone \'wōbi,gòn\ *adj* : exhibiting woe, sorrow, or misery

woe·ful \'wōfəl\ *adj* 1 : full of woe 2 : bringing woe **—woe·ful·ly** *adv*

woke *past of* WAKE

woken *past part of* WAKE

wolf \'wùlf\ *n, pl* **wolves** \'wùlvz\ : large doglike predatory mammal ~ *vb* : eat greedily **—wolf·ish** *adj*

wol·fram \'wùlfrəm\ *n* : tungsten

wol·ver·ine \,wùlvə'rēn\ *n, pl* **-ines** : flesh-eating mammal related to the sables

wom·an \'wùmən\ *n, pl* **wom·en** \'wimən\ 1 : adult female person 2 : womankind 3 : feminine nature **—wom·an·hood** \-,hùd\ *n* **—wom·an·ish** *adj*

wom·an·kind \-,kīnd\ *n* : females of the human race

wom·an·ly \-lē\ *adj* : having qualities characteristic of a woman **—wom·an·li·ness** \-lēnəs\ *n*

womb \'wüm\ *n* : uterus

won *past of* WIN

won·der \'wəndər\ *n* 1 : cause of astonishment or surprise 2 : feeling (as of astonishment) aroused by something extraordinary ~ *vb* 1 : feel surprise 2 : feel curiosity or doubt

won·der·ful \'wəndərfəl\ *adj* 1 : exciting wonder 2 : unusually good **—won·der·ful·ly** \-f(ə)lē\ *adv* **—won·der·ful·ness** *n*

won·der·land \-,land, -lənd\ *n* 1 : fairylike imaginary realm 2 : place that excites admiration or wonder

won·der·ment \-mənt\ *n* : wonder

won·drous \'wəndrəs\ *adj* : wonderful **—won·drous·ly** *adv* **—won·drous·ness** *n*

wont \'wònt, 'wōnt\ *adj* : accustomed ~ *n* : habit **—wont·ed** *adj*

woo \'wü\ *vb* : try to gain the love or favor of **—woo·er** *n*

wood \'wùd\ *n* 1 : dense growth of trees usu. smaller than a forest —often *pl.* 2 : hard fibrous substance of trees and shrubs beneath the bark 3 : wood prepared for some use (as burning) ~ *adj* 1 : wooden 2 : suitable for working with wood 3 or **woods** \wùdz\ : living or growing in woods **—wood·chop·per** *n* **—wood·pile** *n* **—wood·shed** *n*

wood·bine \'wùd,bīn\ *n* : climbing vine

wood·chuck \-,chək\ *n* : thick-bodied grizzled animal of No. America

wood·craft *n* 1 : skill and practice in matters relating to the woods 2 : skill in making articles from wood

wood·cut \-,kət\ *n* 1 : relief printing surface engraved on wood 2 : print from a woodcut

wood·ed \'wùdəd\ *adj* : covered with woods

wood·en \'wùd²n\ *adj* 1 : made of wood 2 : lacking resilience 3 : lacking ease, liveliness or interest **—wood·en·ly** *adv* **—wood·en·ness** *n*

wood·land \-lənd, -,land\ *n* : land covered with trees

wood·peck·er \'wùd,pekər\ *n* : brightly marked bird with a hard bill for drilling into trees

woods·man \'wùdzmən\ *n* : one who works in the woods

wood·wind \'wùd,wind\ *n* : one of a group of wind instruments (as a flute or oboe)

wood·work *n* : work (as interior house fittings) made of wood

woody \'wùdē\ *adj* **wood·i·er; -est** 1 : abounding with woods 2 : of, containing, or like wood fibers **—wood·i·ness** *n*

woof \'wùf\ *n* : threads in a woven fabric that cross the warp

wool \'wùl\ *n* 1 : soft hair of some

mammals and esp. the sheep **2** : something (as a textile) made of wool **—wooled** \'wùld\ *adj*

wool·en, wool·len \'wùlən\ *adj* **1** : made of wool **2** : relating to the manufacture of woolen products ~ *n* **1** : woolen fabric **2** : woolen garments —usu. pl.

wool·gath·er·ing *n* : act of indulging in idle daydreaming

wool·ly \'wùlē\ *adj* **-li·er; -est 1** : of, relating to, or bearing wool **2** : consisting of or resembling wool **3** : confused or turbulent

woo·zy \'wüzē\ *adj* **-zi·er; -est 1** : confused **2** : somewhat dizzy, nauseated, or weak **—woo·zi·ness** *n*

word \'wərd\ *n* **1** : brief remark **2** : speech sound or series of speech sounds that communicates a meaning **3** : written representation of a word **4** : order **5** : news **6** : promise **7** *pl* : dispute ~ *vb* : express in words **—word·less** *adj*

word·ing \'wərdiŋ\ *n* : verbal expression

wordy \'wərdē\ *adj* **word·i·er; -est** : using many words **—word·i·ness** *n*

wore *past of* WEAR

work \'wərk\ *n* **1** : labor **2** : employment **3** : task **4** : something (as an artistic production) produced by mental effort or physical labor **5** *pl* : buildings, grounds, and machinery of a factory **6** *pl* : moving parts of a mechanism **7** : workmanship ~ *adj* **1** : suitable for wear while working **2** : used for work ~ *vb* **worked** \'wərkt\ *or* **wrought** \'ròt\, **work·ing 1** : bring to pass **2** : create by expending labor upon **3** : bring or get into a form or condition **4** : set or keep in operation **5** : solve **6** : cause to labor **7** : arrange **8** : excite **9** : labor **10** : perform work regularly for wages **11** : function according to plan or design **12** : produce a desired effect **—work·bag** *n* **—work·bas·ket** *n* **—work·bench** *n* **—work·man** \-mən\ *n* **—work·room** *n* **—in the works** : in preparation

work·able \'wərkəbəl\ *adj* **1** : capable of being worked **2** : feasible **—work·able·ness** *n*

work·a·day \'wərkə,dā\ *adj* **1** : relating to or suited for working days **2** : ordinary

work·er \'wərkər\ *n* : person who works esp. for wages

work·horse *n* **1** : horse used chiefly for labor **2** : person who undertakes difficult labor

work·house *n* : place of confinement for persons who have committed minor offenses

work·ing \'wərkiŋ\ *adj* **1** : adequate to allow work to be done **2** : adopted or assumed to help further work or activity ~ *n* : operation

work·ing·man \'wərkiŋ,man\ *n* : one who works for wages usu. at manual labor

work·man \'wərkmən\ *n* **1** : worker **2** : artisan

work·man·like \-,līk\ *adj* : worthy of a good workman

work·man·ship \-,ship\ *n* **1** : art or skill of a workman **2** : quality imparted to a piece of work

work·out \'wərk,aút\ *n* : exercise to improve one's fitness

work·shop *n* **1** : small establishment for manufacturing or handicrafts **2** : seminar emphasizing exchange of ideas and practical methods

world \'wərld\ *n* **1** : universe **2** : earth with its inhabitants and all things upon it **3** : people in general **4** : great number or quantity **5** : class of persons or their sphere of interest

world·ly \'wərldlē\ *adj* **1** : devoted to this world and its pursuits rather than to religion **2** : sophisticated **—world·li·ness** *n*

world·ly-wise *adj* : possessing understanding of human affairs

world·wide *adj* : extended throughout the entire world

worm \'wərm\ *n* **1** : earthworm or a similar animal **2** *pl* : disorder caused by parasitic worms ~ *vb* **1** : move or cause to move in a slow and indirect way **2** : to free from worms **—wormy** *adj*

worm·wood \'wərm,wùd\ *n* **1** : aromatic woody herb related to the daisies **2** : something bitter or grievous

worn *past part of* WEAR

worn-out \'wòrn'aút\ *adj* : exhausted or used up by or as if by wear

wor·ri·some \'wərēsəm\ *adj* **1** : causing distress **2** : inclined to worry

wor·ry \'wərē\ *vb* **-ried; -ry·ing 1** : shake and mangle with the teeth **2** : disturb **3** : feel or express anxiety ~ *n*, *pl* **-ries 1** : anxiety **2** : cause of anxiety **—wor·ri·er** *n*

worse \'wərs\ *adj, comparative of* BAD *or of* ILL **1** : bad or evil in a greater degree **2** : more unwell ~ *n* **1** : one that is worse **2** : greater degree of badness ~ *adv, comparative of* BAD *or of* ILL : in a worse manner

wors·en \'wərsən\ *vb* : make or become worse

wor·ship \'wərshəp\ *n* **1** : reverence

toward a divine being or supernatural power 2 : expression of reverence 3 : extravagant respect or devotion ~ *vb* -**shiped** *or* -**shipped**; -**ship-ing** *or* -**ship-ping** 1 : honor or reverence 2 : perform or take part in worship —**wor-ship-er, wor-ship-per** *n*

worst \'wərst\ *adj, superlative of* BAD *or of* ILL 1 : most bad, evil, ill, or corrupt 2 : most unfavorable, unpleasant, or painful ~ *n* 1 : one that is worst 2 : greatest degree of badness ~ *adv, superlative of* ILL *or of* BAD *or* BADLY : to the extreme degree of badness ~ *vb* : defeat

wor-sted \'wu̇stəd, 'wərstəd\ *n* : smooth compact wool yarn or fabric made from such yarn

worth \'wərth\ *prep* 1 : equal in value to 2 : deserving of ~ *n* 1 : monetary value 2 : value of something measured by its qualities or by the esteem in which it is held 3 : moral merit

worth-less \-ləs\ *adj* 1 : lacking worth 2 : useless —**worth-less-ness** *n*

worth-while \-'hwīl\ *adj* : being worth the time or effort spent

wor-thy \'wərthē\ *adj* -**thi-er; -est** 1 : having worth or value 2 : having sufficient worth ~ *n, pl* -**thies** : worthy person —**wor-thi-ly** *adv* —**wor-thi-ness** *n*

would \wəd, əd, d, (')wu̇d\ *past of* WILL —used to express (1) preference (2) intent (3) habitual action (4) contingency (5) probability or (6) a request

would-be \,wu̇d,bē\ *adj* : desiring or professing to be

¹wound \'wu̇nd\ *n* 1 : injury in which the skin is broken 2 : mental hurt ~ *vb* : inflict a wound to or in

²wound \'wau̇nd\ *past of* WIND

wove *past of* WEAVE

woven *past part of* WEAVE

wrack \'rak\ *n* : ruin

wraith \'rāth\ *n, pl* **wraiths** \'rāths, 'rā͟t͟hz\ 1 : ghost 2 : insubstantial appearance

wran-gle \'raŋgəl\ *vb or n* : quarrel —**wran-gler** *n*

¹wrap \'rap\ *vb* -**pp-** 1 : cover esp. by winding or folding 2 : envelop and secure for transportation or storage 3 : enclose, surround, or conceal wholly 4 : coil, fold, draw, or twine about something ~ *n* 1 : wrapper or wrapping 2 : outer garment (as a shawl)

wrap-per \'rapər\ *n* 1 : that in which something is wrapped 2 : one that wraps

wrap-ping *n* : something used to wrap an object

wrath \'rath\ *n* : violent anger —**wrath-ful** \-fəl\ *adj*

wreak \'rēk\ *vb* : inflict

wreath \'rēth\ *n, pl* **wreaths** \'rēthz, 'rēths\ : something (as boughs) intertwined into a circular shape

wreathe \'rē͟t͟h\ *vb* **wreathed; wreath-ing** 1 : shape into or take on the shape of a wreath 2 : surround

wreck \'rek\ *n* 1 : broken remains (as of a ship or vehicle) after heavy damage 2 : something disabled or in a state of ruin 3 : an individual who has become weak or infirm 4 : action of breaking up or destroying something ~ *vb* : ruin or damage by breaking up

wreck-age \'rekij\ *n* 1 : act of wrecking 2 : remains of a wreck

wreck-er \-ər\ *n* 1 : one that wrecks or tears down and removes buildings 2 : automotive vehicle for removing disabled cars

wren \'ren\ *n* : small mostly brown singing bird

wrench \'rench\ *vb* 1 : pull with violent twisting or force 2 : injure or disable by a violent twisting or straining ~ *n* 1 : forcible twisting 2 : tool for exerting a twisting force

wrest \'rest\ *vb* 1 : pull or move by a forcible twisting movement 2 : gain with difficulty ~ *n* : forcible twist

wres-tle \'resəl, 'ras-\ *vb* -**tled; -tling** 1 : scuffle with an opponent in attempt to throw him down 2 : contend against in wrestling 3 : struggle (as with a problem) ~ *n* : action or an instance of wrestling —**wres-tler** \'reslər, 'ras-\ *n*

wres-tling \'resliŋ\ *n* : sport in which 2 opponents try to throw and pin each other

wretch \'rech\ *n* 1 : miserable unhappy person 2 : vile person

wretch-ed \'rechəd\ *adj* 1 : deeply afflicted, dejected, or distressed 2 : grievous 3 : inferior —**wretch-ed-ness** *n*

wrig-gle \'rigəl\ *vb* -**gled; -gling** 1 : twist and turn restlessly 2 : move or advance by twisting and turning —**wriggle** *n* —**wrig-gler** \'rig(ə)lər\ *n*

wring \'riŋ\ *vb* **wrung** \'rəŋ\; **wring-ing** 1 : squeeze or twist out moisture 2 : get by or as if by forcible exertion 3 : twist together in anguish 4 : pain —**wring-er** *n*

wrin-kle \'riŋkəl\ *n* : crease or small fold on a surface (as in the skin or in cloth) ~ vb -**kled; -kling** : develop or cause to develop wrinkles —**wrin-kly** \-kəlē\ adj

wrist \'rist\ n : joint or region between the hand and the arm

writ \'rit\ n 1 : something written 2 : legal order in writing

write \'rīt\ vb **wrote** \'rōt\; **writ-ten** \'rit²n\; **writ-ing** \'rītiŋ\ 1 : form letters or words on a surface 2 : form the letters or the words of (as on paper) 3 : make up and set down for others to read 4 : write a letter to —**write off** vb : cancel

writ-er \'rītər\ n : one that writes esp. as a business or occupation

writhe \'rīth\ vb **writhed; writh-ing** : move or proceed with twists and turns

writ-ing \'rītiŋ\ n 1 : act of one that writes 2 : handwriting 3 : something written or printed

wrong \'rȯŋ\ n 1 : unfair or unjust act 2 : something that is contrary to justice 3 : state of being or doing wrong

~ adj **wrong-er** \'rȯŋər\; **wrong-est** \'rȯŋəst\ 1 : sinful 2 : not right according to a standard 3 : unsuitable 4 : incorrect ~ adv 1 : in a wrong direction or manner 2 : incorrectly ~ vb **wronged; wrong-ing** 1 : do wrong to 2 : treat unjustly —**wrong-ly** adv

wrong-do-er \-'düər\ n : one who does wrong —**wrong-do-ing** \-'düiŋ\ n

wrong-ful \-fəl\ adj 1 : wrong 2 : illegal —**wrong-ful-ly** adv —**wrong-ful-ness** n

wrong-head-ed \'rȯŋ'hedəd\ adj : obstinately wrong —**wrong-head-ed-ly** adv —**wrong-head-ed-ness** n

wrote past of WRITE

wrought \'rȯt\ adj 1 : formed 2 : hammered into shape 3 : deeply stirred

wrung past of WRING

wry \'rī\ adj **wri-er** \'rī(ə)r\; **wri-est** \'rīəst\ 1 : turned abnormally to one side 2 : twisted 3 : cleverly and often ironically humorous —**wry-ly** adv —**wry-ness** n

X

x \'eks\ n, pl **x's** or **xs** \'eksəz\ 1 : 24th letter of the alphabet 2 : unknown quantity ~ vb **x-ed; x-ing** or **x'ing** : cancel with a series of x's—usu. with **out**

xe-non \'zē,nän,'zen,än\ n : heavy gaseous chemical element

xe-no-pho-bia \,zenə'fōbēə, ,zēn-\ n : fear and hatred of foreign people and things —**xe-no-phobe** \'zenə,fōb, 'zēn-\ n

Xmas \'krisməs also 'eksməs\ n : Christmas

x-ra-di-a-tion n 1 : exposure to X rays 2 : radiation consisting of X rays

x-ray \'eks,rā\ vb : examine, treat, or photograph with X rays

X ray n 1 : radiation of short wavelength that is able to penetrate solids 2 : photograph taken with X rays

xy-lo-phone \'zīlə,fōn\ n : musical instrument with wooden bars that are struck —**xy-lo-phon-ist** \-,fōnəst\ n

Y

y \'wī\ n, pl **y's** or **ys** \'wīz\ 1 : 25th letter of the alphabet

¹-y, -ey \ē\ adj suffix 1 : composed or full of 2 : like 3 : performing or apt to perform an action 4 : somewhat

²-y \ē\ n suffix, pl **-ies** 1 : state, condition, or quality 2 : activity, place of business, or goods dealt with 3 : whole group

yacht \'yät\ n : luxurious pleasure boat ~ vb : race or cruise in a yacht

ya-hoo \'yähü, 'yä-\ n, pl **-hoos** : uncouth or rowdy person

yak \'yak\ n : big hairy Asian ox

yam \'yam\ n 1 : edible root of a tropi-

cal vine 2 : deep orange sweet potato

yam-mer \'yamər\ vb 1 : whimper 2 : chatter —**yammer** n

yank \'yaŋk\ n : strong sudden pull —**yank** vb

Yank \'yaŋk\ n : Yankee

Yan-kee \'yaŋkē\ n : native or inhabitant of New England, the northern U.S., or the U.S. —**Yankee** adj

yap \'yap\ vb **-pp-** 1 : yelp 2 : chatter —**yap** n

¹yard \'yärd\ n 1 : 3 feet 2 : long spar for supporting and extending a sail —**yard-age** \-ij\ n

²yard n 1 : enclosed roofless area 2

: grounds of a building **3** : work area

yard-arm \\'yärd,ärm\\ *n* : end of the yard of a square-rigged ship

yard-stick *n* **1** : measuring stick 3 feet long **2** : standard for judging

yarn \\'yärn\\ *n* **1** : spun fiber for weaving or knitting **2** : tale

yaw \\'yò\\ *vb* : deviate erratically from a course —**yaw** *n*

yawl \\'yòl\\ *n* **1** : ship's small boat **2** : sailboat with 2 masts and one or more jibs

yawn \\'yòn\\ *vb* : open the mouth wide ~ *n* : deep breath through a wide open mouth —**yawn-er** *n*

ye \\'yē\\ *pron* : you

yea \\'yā\\ *adv* **1** : yes **2** : truly ~ *n* : affirmative vote

year \\'yiər\\ *n* **1** : period of about 365 days **2** *pl* : age

year-book *n* : annual report of the year's events

year-ling \\'yiərliŋ, 'yərlən\\ *n* : one that is or is rated as a year old

year-ly \\'yiərlē\\ *adj* : annual —**yearly** *adv*

yearn \\'yərn\\ *vb* **1** : feel desire esp. for what one cannot have **2** : feel tenderness or compassion

yearn-ing \\-iŋ\\ *n* : tender or urgent desire

yeast \\'yēst\\ *n* : froth or sediment in sugary liquids containing a tiny fungus and used in making alcoholic liquors and as a leaven in baking —**yeasty** *adj*

yell \\'yel\\ *vb* : utter a loud cry —**yell** *n*

yel-low \\'yelō\\ *adj* **1** : of the color yellow **2** : sensational **3** : cowardly ~ *vb* : make or turn yellow ~ *n* **1** : color of lemons **2** : yolk of an egg —**yellow-ish** \\'yeləwish\\ *adj*

yellow fever *n* : virus disease marked by prostration, jaundice, fever, and often hemorrhage

yellow jacket *n* : wasp with yellow stripes

yelp \\'yelp\\ *vb* : utter a sharp quick shrill cry —**yelp** *n*

yen \\'yen\\ *n* : strong desire

yeo-man \\'yōmən\\ *n* **1** : attendant or officer in a royal or noble household **2** : small farmer **3** : naval petty officer with clerical duties —**yeo-man-ry** \\-rē\\ *n*

-yer —see ER

yes \\'yes\\ *adv* —used to express consent or agreement ~ *n* : affirmative answer

yes-man \\'yes,man\\ *n* : toady

yes-ter-day \\'yestərdē\\ *adv* **1** : on the day preceding today **2** : only a short

time ago ~ *n* **1** : day last past **2** : time not long past

yet \\(')yet\\ *adv* **1** : in addition **2** : up to now **3** : so soon as now **4** : nevertheless ~ *conj* : but

yew \\'yü\\ *n* : evergreen tree or shrubs with dark stiff poisonous needles

yield \\'yēld\\ *vb* **1** : surrender **2** : grant **3** : bear as a crop **4** : produce **5** : cease opposition or resistance ~ *n* : quantity produced or returned

yo-del \\'yōdᵊl\\ *vb* **-deled** *or* **-delled; -del-ing** *or* **-del-ling** : sing by abruptly alternating between chest voice and falsetto —**yodel** *n* —**yo-del-er** \\'yōdlər, ᵊlɔr\\ *n*

yo-ga \\'yōgə\\ *n* : system of exercises for attaining bodily or mental control and well-being

yo-gi \\'yōgē\\, **yo-gin** \\-gən, -₁gin\\ *n* : person who practices yoga

yo-gurt, yo-ghurt \\'yōgərt\\ *n* : fermented slightly acid soft nearly fluid food made from milk

yoke \\'yōk\\ *n* **1** : neck frame for coupling draft animals or for carrying loads **2** : clamp **3** : slavery **4** : tie or link **5** : piece of a garment esp. at the shoulder ~ *vb* **yoked; yok-ing 1** : couple with a yoke **2** : join

yo-kel \\'yōkəl\\ *n* : bumpkin

yolk \\'yō(l)k\\ *n* : yellow part of an egg —**yolked** \\'yō(l)kt\\ *adj*

Yom Kip-pur \\₁yōmᵊkipər, -ki'púr\\ *n* : Jewish holiday observed in September or October with fasting and prayer as a day of atonement

yon \\'yän\\ *adj or adv* : YONDER

yon-der \\'yändər\\ *adv* : at or to that place ~ *adj* : distant

yore \\'yòr\\ *n* : time long past

you \\(')yü, yə\\ *pron* **1** : person or persons addressed **2** : person in general

young \\'yəŋ\\ *adj* **youn-ger** \\'yəŋgər\\; **young-est** \\'yəŋgəst\\ **1** : being in the first or an early stage of life, growth, or development **2** : recently come into being **3** : having the qualities (as vigor) of youth ~ *n, pl* **young** : persons or lower animals that are young —**young-ish** \\-ish\\ *adj*

young-ster \\-stər\\ *n* **1** : young person **2** : child

your \\yər, (')yúr, (')yòr\\ *adj* : relating to you or yourself

yours \\'yúrz, 'yòrz\\ *pron* : the ones belonging to you

your-self \\yər'self\\ *pron, pl* **yourselves** \\-'selvz\\ : you —used reflexively or for emphasis

youth \\'yüth\\ *n, pl* **youths** \\'yüthz,

'yūths\ 1 : period between childhood and maturity **2** : young man **3** : young persons **4** : state or quality of being young, fresh, or vigorous

youth-ful \'yüthfəl\ *adj* **1** : relating to or appropriate to youth **2** : young **3** : vigorous —**youth-ful-ly** *adv* —**youth-ful-ness** *n*

yowl \'yaůl\ *vb* : utter a loud long mournful cry —**yowl** *n*

yo-yo \'yō(,)yō\ *n, pl* **-yos** : toy that falls from or rises to the hand as it unwinds and rewinds on a string

yuc-ca \'yəkə\ *n* : any of several plants related to the lilies that grow in dry regions

Yule \'yül\ *n* : Christmas —**Yule-tide** \-,tīd\ *n*

yum-my \'yəmē\ *adj* **-mi-er; -est** : highly attractive or pleasing

Z

z \'zē\ *n, pl* **z's** *or* **zs** : 26th letter of the alphabet

za-ny \'zānē\ *n, pl* **-nies** **1** : clown **2** : silly person ~ *adj* **-ni-er; -est** : crazy or foolish —**za-ni-ly** *adv* —**za-ni-ness** *n*

zeal \'zēl\ *n* : enthusiasm

zeal-ot \'zelət\ *n* : fanatical partisan

zeal-ous \'zeləs\ *adj* : filled with zeal —**zeal-ous-ly** *adv* —**zeal-ous-ness** *n*

ze-bra \'zēbrə\ *n* : horselike African mammal marked with light and dark stripes

zeit-geist \'tsīt,gīst, 'zīt-\ *n* : general spirit of an era

ze-nith \'zēnəth\ *n* : highest point —**ze-nith-al** \-əl\ *adj*

zeph-yr \'zefər\ *n* : gentle breeze

zep-pe-lin \'zep(ə)lən\ *n* : cylindrical balloonlike rigid airship

ze-ro \'zērō\ *n, pl* **-ros** **1** : number represented by the symbol 0 or the symbol itself **2** : starting point **3** : lowest point ~ *adj* : having no size or quantity

zest \'zest\ *n* **1** : quality of enhancing enjoyment **2** : keen enjoyment —**zest-ful** \-fəl\ *adj* —**zest-ful-ly** *adv* —**zest-ful-ness** *n*

zig-zag \'zig,zag\ *n* : one of a series of short sharp turns or angles ~ *adj* : having zigzags ~ *adv* : in or by a zigzag path ~ *vb* **-gg-** : proceed along a zigzag path

zil-lion \'zilyən\ *n* : large indeterminate number

zinc \'ziŋk\ *n* : bluish white crystalline metallic chemical element

zing \'ziŋ\ *n* **1** : shrill humming noise **2** : energy —**zing** *vb*

zin-nia \'zēnēə, 'zēnyə\ *n* : American herb widely grown for its showy flowers

¹zip \'zip\ *vb* **-pp-** : move or act with speed ~ *n* : energy

²zip *vb* **-pp-** : close or open with a zipper

zip code *n* : 5-digit number that identifies a U.S. postal delivery area

zip-per \'zipər\ *n* : fastener consisting of 2 rows of interlocking teeth

zip-py \'zipē\ *adj* **-pi-er; -est** : brisk

zir-con \'zər,kän\ *n* : zirconium-containing mineral sometimes used in jewelry

zir-co-ni-um \,zər'kōnēəm\ *n* : heat-resistant and corrosion-resistant metallic element

zith-er \'zithər, 'zith-\ *n* : stringed musical instrument played by plucking

zo-di-ac \'zōdē,ak\ *n* : imaginary belt in the heavens encompassing the paths of the planets and divided into 12 signs used in astrology —**zo-di-a-cal** \zō'dīəkəl\ *adj*

zom-bie \'zämbē\ *n* : supernatural power held to enter a dead body and bring it back to life

zon-al \'zōn²l\ *adj* : of, relating to, or having the form of a zone —**zon-al-ly** *adv*

zone \'zōn\ *n* **1** : division of the earth's surface based on latitude and climate **2** : distinctive area ~ *vb* **zoned; zon-ing 1** : mark off into zones **2** : reserve for special purposes —**zo-na-tion** \zō'nāshən\ *n*

zoo \'zü\ *n, pl* **zoos** : collection of living animals usu. for public display

zo-ol-o-gy \zō'äləjē\ *n* : science of animals —**zo-o-log-i-cal** \,zōə'läjikəl\ *adj* —**zo-ol-o-gist** \zō'äləjəst\ *n*

zoom \'züm\ *vb* **1** : move with a loud hum or buzz **2** : move or increase with great speed —**zoom** *n*

zuc-chi-ni \zü'kēnē\ *n, pl* **-ni** *or* **-nis** : summer squash with smooth cylindrical dark green fruits

zwie-back \'swēbak, 'swī-, 'zwē, 'zwī-\ *n* : biscuit of baked, sliced, and toasted bread

zy-gote \'zī,gōt\ *n* : cell formed by the union of 2 sexual cells —**zy-got-ic** \zī'gätik\ *adj*

Abbreviations

Most of these abbreviations have been given in one form. Variation in use of periods, in type, and in capitalization is frequent and widespread (as *mph, MPH, m.p.h., Mph*).

abbr abbreviation
AC alternating current
acad academic, academy
AD in the year of our Lord
adj adjective
adv adverb, advertisement
AF air force, audio frequency
agric agricultural, agriculture
AK Alaska
aka also known as
AL, Ala Alabama
alg algebra
Alta Alberta
a.m., AM before noon
Am, Amer America, American
amp ampere
amt amount
anc ancient
anon anonymous
ans answer
ant antonym
APO army post office
approx approximate, approximately
Apr April
apt apartment, aptitude
AR Arkansas
arith arithmetic
Ariz Arizona
Ark Arkansas
art article, artificial
assn association
asst assistant
att attached, attention, attorney
attn attention
atty attorney
Aug August
auth authentic, author, authorized
aux, auxil auxiliary
av avoirdupois
AV audiovisual
ave avenue
avg average
AZ Arizona
bal balance
bar barrel
bbl barrel, barrels

BC before Christ, British Columbia
bet between
biog biographer, biographical, biography
biol biologic, biological, biologist, biology
bldg building
blvd boulevard
Brit Britain, British
bro brother, brothers
bu bureau, bushel
c carat, cent, centimeter, century, chapter, circa, cup
C Celsius, centigrade
ca circa
CA, Cal, Calif California
Can, Canad Canada, Canadian
cap capacity, capital, capitalize, capitalized
Capt captain
CB citizens band
CDT Central daylight time
cen central
cert certificate, certification, certified, certify
cf compare
chap chapter
chem chemistry
cir circle, circuit, circular, circumference
civ civil, civilian
cm centimeter
co company, county
CO Colorado
c/o care of
COD cash on delivery, collect on delivery
col colonial, colony, color, colored, column, counsel
Col colonel, Colorado
Colo Colorado
comp comparative, compensation, compiled, compiler, composition, compound
cong congress, congressional
conj conjunction
Conn Connecticut

cont continued
contr contract, contraction
corp corporal, corporation
corr corrected, correction
cp compare, coupon
cr credit, creditor
CSA Confederate States of America
CST Central standard time
ct carat, cent, count, court
CT Central time, certified teacher, Connecticut
cu cubic
cur currency, current
CZ Canal Zone
d penny
DA district attorney
dag dekagram
dal dekaliter
dam dekameter
dbl double
DC direct current, District of Columbia
DDS doctor of dental science, doctor of dental surgery
DE Delaware
dec deceased, decrease
Dec December
deg degree
Del Delaware
Dem Democrat, Democratic
dept department
det detached, detachment, detail, determine
dg decigram
dia, diam diameter
diag diagonal, diagram
dict dictionary
dif, diff difference
dim dimension, diminished
dir director
disc discount
dist distance, district
div divided, dividend, division, divorced
dkg dekagram
dkl dekaliter
dkm dekameter
dks dekastere
dl deciliter
dm decimeter
DMD doctor of dental medicine
doz dozen
DP data processing
dr dram, drive, drum
Dr doctor
DST daylight saving time
dz dozen
E east, eastern, excellent
ea each
ecol ecological, ecology
econ economics, economist, economy
EDT Eastern daylight time
e.g. for example
elec electric, electrical, electricity
elem elementary
eng engine, engineer, engineering
Eng England, English
esp especially
EST Eastern standard time
ET eastern time
et al and others
etc et cetera
exec executive
f false, female, feminine
F, Fah, Fahr Fahrenheit
Feb February
fed federal, federation
fem female, feminine
FL, Fla Florida
FPO fleet post office
fr father, friar, from
Fri Friday
ft feet, foot, fort
fut future
g gram
G good
Ga, GA Georgia
gal gallery, gallon
gen general
geog geographic, geographical, geography
geol geologic, geological, geology
geom geometric, geometrical, geometry
gm gram
GMT Greenwich mean time
GOP Grand Old Party (Republican)
gov government, governor
GP general practice, general practitioner
gr grade, grain, gram
gram grammar, grammatical
gt great
GU Guam
hd head
hf half
hgt height
HI Hawaii
hist historian, historical, history
hon honor, honorable, honorary
hr here, hour
HS high school
ht height
HT Hawaiian time
hwy highway
I intransitive, island, isle
Ia, IA Iowa
ID Idaho, identification
i.e. that is
IL, Ill Illinois

imp imperative, imperfect
in inch
IN Indiana
inc incomplete, incorporated
ind independent
Ind Indian, Indiana
inf infinitive
int interest
interj interjection
ital italic, italicized
Jan January
JD juvenile delinquent
jour journal, journeyman
JP justice of the peace
jr, jun junior
JV junior varsity
Kans Kansas
kg kilogram
km kilometer
KS Kansas
kw kilowatt
Ky, KY Kentucky
l late, left, liter, long
L large
La, LA Louisiana
lb pound
lg large, long
lib liberal, librarian, library
m male, masculine, meter, mile
M medium
MA Massachusetts
Man Manitoba
Mar March
masc masculine
Mass Massachusetts
math mathematical, mathematician
max maximum
Md Maryland
MD doctor of medicine, Maryland
MDT Mountain daylight time
Me, ME Maine
med medium
mg milligram
mgr manager
MI, Mich Michigan
mid middle
min minimum, minor, minute
Minn Minnesota
misc miscellaneous
Miss Mississippi
ml milliliter
mm millimeter
MN Minnesota
mo month
Mo, MO Missouri
Mon Monday
Mont Montana
mpg miles per gallon
mph miles per hour
MS Mississippi

MST Mountain standard time
mt mount, mountain
MT Montana, Mountain time
n neuter, noun
N north, northern
NA North America, not applicable
nat national, native, natural
naut nautical
NB New Brunswick
NC North Carolina
ND, N Dak North Dakota
NE, Neb, Nebr Nebraska
neg negative
neut neuter
Nev Nevada
Nfld Newfoundland
NH New Hampshire
NJ New Jersey
NM, N Mex New Mexico
no north, number
Nov November
NS Nova Scotia
NV Nevada
NWT Northwest Territories
NY New York
NYC New York City
O Ohio
obj object, objective
occas occasionally
Oct October
off office, officer, official
OH Ohio
OK, Okla Oklahoma
Ont Ontario
opp opposite
OR, Ore, Oreg Oregon
orig original, originally
oz ounce, ounces
p page
Pa Pennsylvania
PA Pennsylvania, public address
par paragraph, parallel
part participle, particular
pass passenger, passive
pat patent
pc percent, piece, postcard
pd paid
PD police department
PDT Pacific daylight time
PEI Prince Edward Island
Penn, Penna Pennsylvania
pg page
pk park, peak, peck
pkg package
pl place, plural
p.m., PM afternoon
PO post office
Port Portugal, Portuguese
pos position, positive
poss possessive
pp pages

PQ Province of Quebec
pr pair, price, printed
PR public relations, Puerto Rico
prep preposition
pres present, president
prob probable, probably, problem
prof professor
pron pronoun
prov province
PS postscript, public school
PST Pacific standard time
psych psychology
pt part, payment, pint, point
PT Pacific time
pvt private
qr quarter
qt quantity, quart
Que Quebec
quot quotation
r right, river
rd road, rod, round
recd received
reg region, register, registered, regular, regulation
rel relating, relative, religion
rep report, reporter, representative, republic
Rep Republican
res residence
rev reverse, review, revised, revision, revolution
Rev reverend
RFD rural free delivery
RI Rhode Island
rm room
rpm revolutions per minute
RR railroad, rural route
RSVP please reply
rt right
rte route
S small, south, southern
SA South America
Sask Saskatchewan
Sat Saturday
SC South Carolina
sci science, scientific
SD, S Dak South Dakota
secy secretary
sen senior
Sept, Sep September
sing singular
sm small
so south, southern
soph sophomore
sp spelling
spec special, specifically
sq square

sr senior
Sr sister
SSR Soviet Socialist Republic
st street
St saint
std standard
subj subject
Sun Sunday
supt superintendent
syn synonym
t teaspoon, temperature, ton, transitive, troy, true
T tablespoon
tbs, tbsp tablespoon
TD touchdown
tech technical, technician, technology
Tenn Tennessee
terr territory
Tex Texas
Th, Thu, Thur, Thurs Thursday
TN Tennessee
trans translated, translation, translator
tsp teaspoon
Tues, Tu, Tue Tuesday
TX Texas
UN United Nations
univ universal, university
US United States
USA United States of America
USSR Union of Soviet Socialist Republics
usu usual, usually
UT Utah
v verb, versus
Va, VA Virginia
var variant
vb verb
VG very good
VI Virgin Islands
vol volume, volunteer
VP vice-president
vs versus
Vt, VT Vermont
W west, western
WA, Wash Washington
Wed Wednesday
WI, Wis, Wisc Wisconsin
wk week, work
wt weight
WV, W Va West Virginia
WY, Wyo Wyoming
XL extra large, extra long
yd yard
yr year, younger, your
YT Yukon Territory

Handbook of Style

Punctuation

The English writing system uses punctuation marks to separate groups of words for meaning and emphasis; to convey an idea of the variations of pitch, volume, pauses, and intonations of speech; and to help avoid ambiguity. English punctuation marks, together with general rules and bracketed examples of their use, follow.

APOSTROPHE '

1. **indicates the possessive case of nouns and indefinite pronouns** ⟨the boy's mother⟩ ⟨the boys' mothers⟩ ⟨It is anyone's guess.⟩
2. **marks omissions in contracted words** ⟨didn't⟩ ⟨o'clock⟩
3. **often forms plurals of letters, figures, and words referred to as words** ⟨You should dot your *i*'s and cross your *t*'s.⟩ ⟨several 8's⟩ ⟨She has trouble pronouncing her *the*'s.⟩

BRACKETS [ ]

1. **set off extraneous data such as editorial additions esp. within quoted material** ⟨wrote that the author was "trying to dazzle his readers with phrases like *jeu de mots* [play on words]"⟩
2. **function as parentheses within parentheses** ⟨Bowman Act (22 Stat., ch. 4, § [or sec.] 4, p. 50)⟩

COLON :

1. **introduces word, clause, or phrase that explains, illustrates, amplifies, or restates what has gone before** ⟨The sentence was poorly constructed: it lacked both unity and coherence.⟩
2. **introduces a series** ⟨Three countries were represented: England, France, and Belgium.⟩
3. **introduces lengthy quoted material set off from the rest of a text by indentation but not by quotation marks** ⟨I quote from the text of Chapter One:⟩
4. **separates data in time-telling and data in bibliographic and biblical references** ⟨8:30 a.m.⟩ ⟨New York: Smith Publishing Co.⟩ ⟨John 4:10⟩
5. **separates titles and subtitles (as of books)** ⟨*The Tragic Dynasty: A History of the Romanovs*⟩
6. **follows the salutation in formal correspondence** ⟨Dear Sir:⟩ ⟨Gentlemen:⟩

COMMA ,

1. **separates main clauses joined by a coordinating conjunction (as *and, but, or, nor,* or *for*) and very short clauses not so joined** ⟨She knew very little about him, and he volunteered nothing.⟩ ⟨I came, I saw, I conquered.⟩
2. **sets off an adverbial clause (or a long phrase) that precedes the main clause** ⟨When she found that her friends had deserted her, she sat down and cried.⟩
3. **sets off from the rest of the sentence transitional words and expressions (as *on the contrary, on the other hand*), conjunctive adverbs (as *consequently, furthermore, however*), and expressions that introduce an illustration or example (as *namely, for example*)** ⟨Your second question, on the other hand, remains open.⟩ ⟨The mystery, however, remains

unsolved.⟩ ⟨She expects to travel through two countries, namely, France and England.⟩

4. **separates words, phrases, or clauses in series and coordinate adjectives modifying a noun** ⟨Men, women, and children crowded into the square.⟩ ⟨The harsh, cold wind was strong.⟩

5. **sets off from the rest of the sentence parenthetic elements (as nonrestrictive modifiers)** ⟨Our guide, who wore a blue beret, was an experienced traveler.⟩ ⟨We visited Gettysburg, the site of a famous battle.⟩

6. **introduces a direct quotation, terminates a direct quotation that is neither a question nor an exclamation, and encloses split quotations** ⟨John said, "I am leaving."⟩ ⟨"I am leaving," John said.⟩ ⟨"I am leaving," John said with determination, "even if you want me to stay."⟩

7. **sets off words in direct address, absolute phrases, and mild interjections** ⟨You may go, Mary, if you wish.⟩ ⟨I fear the encounter, his temper being what it is.⟩ ⟨Ah, that's my idea of an excellent dinner.⟩

8. **separates a question from the rest of the sentence which it ends** ⟨It's a fine day, isn't it?⟩

9. **indicates the omission of a word or words, and esp. a word or words used earlier in the sentence** ⟨Common stocks are preferred by some investors; bonds, by others.⟩

10. **is used to avoid ambiguity** ⟨To Mary, Jane was someone special.⟩

11. **is used to group numbers into units of three in separating thousands, millions, etc.; however, it is generally not used in numbers of four figures, in page numbers, in dates, or in street numbers** ⟨Smithville, pop. 100,000⟩ *but* ⟨3600 rpm⟩ ⟨the year 1973⟩ ⟨page 1411⟩ ⟨4507 Smith Street⟩

12. **punctuates an inverted name** ⟨Smith, John W., Jr.⟩

13. **separates a proper name from a following academic, honorary, governmental, or military title** ⟨John Smith, M.D.⟩

14. **sets off geographical names (as state or country from city), items in dates, and addresses from the rest of a text** ⟨Shreveport, Louisiana, is the site of a large air base.⟩ ⟨On Sunday, June 23, 1940, he was wounded.⟩ ⟨Number 10 Downing Street, London, is a famous address.⟩

15. **follows the salutation in informal correspondence and follows the closing line of a formal or informal letter** ⟨Dear Mary,⟩ ⟨Affectionately,⟩ ⟨Very truly yours,⟩

DASH —

1. **usu. marks an abrupt change or break in the continuity of a sentence** ⟨When in 1960 the stockpile was sold off—dumped as surplus—natural-rubber sales were hard hit.—Barry Commoner⟩

2. **introduces a summary statement after a series** ⟨Oil, steel, and wheat—these are the sinews of industrialization.⟩

3. **often precedes the attribution of a quotation** ⟨My foot is on my native heath . . . . .—Sir Walter Scott⟩

ELLIPSIS . . .   .

1. **indicates the omission of one or more words within a quoted passage** ⟨The head is not more native to the heart . . . than is the throne of Denmark to thy father.—Shakespeare⟩

2. **indicates halting speech or an unfinished sentence in dialogue** ⟨"I'd like to . . . that is . . . if you don't mind . . . ." He faltered and then stopped speaking.⟩

3. **indicates the omission of one or more sentences within a quoted passage or the omission of words at the end of a sentence by using four spaced dots the last of which represents the period** ⟨That recovering

the manuscripts would be worth almost any effort is without question.
... The monetary value of a body of Shakespeare's manuscripts would
be almost incalculable—Charlton Ogburn⟩

4. **usu. indicates omission of one or more lines of poetry when ellipsis is
   extended the length of the line**

⟨Thus driven

By the bright shadow of that lovely dream,

....

He fled.

—P. B. Shelley⟩

EXCLAMATION POINT !

1. **terminates an emphatic phrase or sentence** ⟨Get out of here!⟩
2. **terminates an emphatic interjection** ⟨Encore!⟩

HYPHEN -

1. **marks separation or division of a word at the end of a line** ⟨mill-[end
   of line]stone⟩ ⟨pas-[end of line]sion⟩
2. **is used between some prefix and word combinations, as prefix + proper
   name;** ⟨pre-Renaissance⟩ **prefix ending with a vowel + word beginning often with the same vowel** ⟨co-opted⟩ ⟨re-ink⟩; **stressed prefix
   + word, esp. when this combination is similar to a different one** ⟨re=
   cover a sofa *but* ⟨recover from an illness⟩
3. **is used in some compounds, esp. those containing prepositions** ⟨pres-
   ident-elect⟩ ⟨sister-in-law⟩
4. **is often used between elements of a unit modifier in attributive position
   in order to avoid ambiguity** ⟨He is a small-business man.⟩ ⟨She has
   gray-green eyes.⟩
5. **suspends the first part of a hyphened compound when used with another
   hyphened compound** ⟨a six- or eight-cylinder engine⟩
6. **is used in writing out compound numbers between 21 and 99** ⟨thirty=
   four⟩ ⟨one hundred twenty-eight⟩
7. **is used between the numerator and the denominator in writing out
   fractions esp. when they are used as modifiers** ⟨a two-thirds majority
   of the vote⟩
8. **serves instead of the phrase "(up) to and including" between numbers
   and dates** ⟨pages 40-98⟩ ⟨the decade 1960-69⟩

HYPHEN, DOUBLE =

**is used in the end-of-line division of a hyphened compound to indicate that
the compound is hyphened and not closed** ⟨self-[end of line]seeker *but*
⟨self-[end of line]same⟩

PARENTHESES ( )

1. **set off supplementary, parenthetic, or explanatory material when the
   interruption is more marked than that usu. indicated by commas**
   ⟨Three old destroyers (all now out of commission) will be scrapped.⟩
   ⟨He is hoping (as we all are) that this time he will succeed.⟩
2. **enclose numerals which confirm a written number in a text** ⟨Delivery
   will be made in thirty (30) days.⟩
3. **enclose numbers or letters in a series** ⟨We must set forth (1) our
   long-term goals, (2) our immediate objectives, and (3) the means at our
   disposal.⟩

PERIOD

1. **terminates sentences or sentence fragments that are neither interrogatory nor exclamatory** ⟨Obey the law.⟩ ⟨He obeyed the law.⟩
2. **follows some abbreviations and contractions** ⟨Dr.⟩ ⟨Jr.⟩ ⟨etc.⟩ ⟨cont.⟩

QUESTION MARK ?

1. **terminates a direct question** ⟨Who threw the bomb?⟩ ⟨"Who threw the bomb?" he asked.⟩ ⟨To ask the question Who threw the bomb? is unnecessary.⟩
2. **indicates the writer's ignorance or uncertainty** ⟨Omar Khayyám, Persian poet (?–?1123)⟩

QUOTATION MARKS, DOUBLE " "

1. **enclose direct quotations in conventional usage** ⟨He said, "I am leaving."⟩
2. **enclose words or phrases borrowed from others, words used in a special way, and often slang when it is introduced into formal writing** ⟨He called himself "emperor," but he was really just a dictator.⟩ ⟨He was arrested for smuggling "smack."⟩
3. **enclose titles of short poems, short stories, articles, lectures, chapters of books, songs, short musical compositions, and radio and TV programs** ⟨Robert Frost's "Dust of Snow"⟩ ⟨Pushkin's "Queen of Spades"⟩ ⟨The third chapter of *Treasure Island* is entitled "The Black Spot."⟩ ⟨"America the Beautiful"⟩ ⟨Ravel's "Bolero"⟩ ⟨NBC's "Today Show"⟩
4. **are used with other punctuation marks in the following ways: the period and the comma fall *within* the quotation marks** ⟨"I am leaving," he said.⟩ ⟨His camera was described as "waterproof," but "moisture-resistant" would have been a better description.⟩ **the semicolon falls *outside* the quotation marks** ⟨He spoke of his "little cottage in the country"; he might have called it a mansion.⟩ **the dash, the question mark, and the exclamation point fall *within* the quotation marks when they refer to the quoted matter only; they fall *outside* when they refer to the whole sentence** ⟨He asked, "When did you leave?"⟩ ⟨What is the meaning of "the open door"?⟩ ⟨The sergeant shouted, "Halt!"⟩ ⟨Save us from his "mercy"!⟩

QUOTATION MARKS, SINGLE ' '

enclose a quotation within a quotation in conventional usage ⟨The witness said, "I distinctly heard him say, 'Don't be late,' and then I heard the door close."⟩

SEMICOLON ;

1. **links main clauses not joined by coordinating conjunctions** ⟨Some people have the ability to write well; others do not.⟩
2. **links main clauses joined by conjunctive adverbs (as *consequently, furthermore, however*)** ⟨Speeding is illegal; furthermore, it is very dangerous.⟩
3. **links clauses which themselves contain commas even when such clauses are joined by coordinating conjunctions** ⟨Mr. King, whom you met yesterday, will be our representative on the committee; but you should follow the proceedings carefully yourself, because they are vitally important to us.⟩

VIRGULE /

1. **separates alternatives** ⟨. . . designs intended for high-heat and/or high-speed applications—F. S. Badger, Jr.⟩
2. **separates successive divisions (as months or years) of an extended period of time** ⟨the fiscal year 1972/73⟩
3. **serves as a dividing line between run-in lines of poetry** ⟨Say, sages, what's the charm on earth/Can turn death's dart aside?—Robert Burns⟩
4. **often represents** *per* **in abbreviations** ⟨9 ft/sec⟩ ⟨20 km/hr⟩

Italicization

The following are usually italicized in print and underlined in manuscript:

1. **titles of books, magazines, newspapers, plays, movies, works of art, and longer musical compositions** ⟨Eliot's *The Waste Land*⟩ ⟨*Saturday Review*⟩ ⟨*Christian Science Monitor*⟩ ⟨Shakespeare's *Othello*⟩ ⟨the movie *Gone With the Wind*⟩ ⟨Gainsborough's *Blue Boy*⟩ ⟨Mozart's *Don Giovanni*⟩
2. **names of ships and aircraft, and often spacecraft** ⟨M.V. *West Star*⟩ ⟨Lindbergh's *Spirit of St. Louis*⟩ ⟨*Apollo 13*⟩
3. **words, letters, and figures when referred to as words, letters, and figures** ⟨The word *receive* is often misspelled.⟩ ⟨The *g* in *align* is silent.⟩ ⟨The first *2* and the last *0* in the address are barely legible.⟩
4. **foreign words and phrases that have not been naturalized in English** ⟨*che sarà, sarà*⟩ ⟨*ich dien*⟩
5. **New Latin scientific names of genera, species, subspecies, and varieties (but not groups of higher rank) in botanical and zoological names** ⟨a thick-shelled American clam (*Mercenaria mercenaria*)⟩

Capitalization

Capitals are used for two broad purposes in English: they mark a beginning (as of a sentence) and they signal a proper noun or adjective.

1. **The first word of a sentence or sentence fragment is capitalized.** ⟨The play lasted nearly three hours.⟩ ⟨How are you feeling?⟩ ⟨Bravo!⟩
2. **The first word of a direct quotation is capitalized.** ⟨And God said, Let there be light.—Gen 1:3⟩ ⟨He replied, "We can stay only a few minutes."⟩
3. **The first word of a direct question within a sentence is capitalized.** ⟨That question is this: Is man an ape or an angel?—Benjamin Disraeli⟩
4. **The first word of a line of poetry is conventionally capitalized.** ⟨The best lack all conviction, while the worst / Are full of passionate intensity.—W. B. Yeats⟩
5. **Words in titles are capitalized with the exception of internal conjunctions, prepositions, and articles.** ⟨*The Way of the World*⟩ ⟨*Of Mice and Men*⟩
6. **The first word of the salutation of a letter and the first word of the closing line are capitalized.** ⟨Dear Mary⟩ ⟨My dear Mrs. Smith⟩ ⟨Sincerely yours⟩
7. **The names of persons and places, of organizations and their members, of congresses and councils, and of historical periods and events are capitalized.** ⟨Noah Webster⟩ ⟨Rome⟩ ⟨Texas⟩ ⟨England⟩ ⟨Rotary International⟩ ⟨Baptists⟩ ⟨the Atomic Energy Commission⟩ ⟨the Yalta Conference⟩ ⟨the Middle Ages⟩ ⟨World War II⟩

8. The names of ships, aircraft, and spacecraft are capitalized. ⟨Lindbergh's *Spirit of St. Louis*⟩

9. Words designating peoples and languages are capitalized. ⟨Canadians⟩ ⟨Iroquois⟩ ⟨Latin⟩

10. Derivatives of proper names are capitalized when used in their primary sense. ⟨Roman customs⟩ ⟨Shakespearean comedies⟩ ⟨the Edwardian era⟩

11. Words designating family relationship preceding the name of a person are capitalized. ⟨Uncle George⟩

12. Titles preceding the name of a person and epithets used instead of a name are capitalized. ⟨President Roosevelt⟩ ⟨Professor Harris⟩ ⟨Pope Paul⟩ ⟨Old Hickory⟩ ⟨the Iron Chancellor⟩

13. The pronoun *I* is capitalized. ⟨only I know the real story⟩

14. Words designating the Deity (and pronouns referring thereto) are often capitalized. ⟨God⟩ ⟨Jehovah⟩ ⟨Allah⟩ ⟨the Supreme Being in His great wisdom⟩

15. Personifications are capitalized. ⟨She dwells with Beauty—John Keats⟩

16. The days of the week, the months of the year, and holidays and holy days are capitalized. ⟨Tuesday⟩ ⟨June⟩ ⟨Thanksgiving⟩ ⟨Yom Kippur⟩

17. Names of specific courts of law are capitalized. ⟨the United States Court of Appeals for the Second Circuit⟩

18. Names of treaties are capitalized. ⟨Treaty of Versailles⟩ ⟨Kellogg-Briand Pact⟩

19. Registered trademarks and other registered marks are capitalized. ⟨Orlon⟩ ⟨Air Express⟩

20. Geological eras, periods, epochs, strata, and names of prehistoric divisions are capitalized. ⟨Silurian period⟩ ⟨Age of Reptiles⟩ ⟨Neolithic age⟩

21. Planets, constellations, asteroids, stars, and groups of stars are capitalized; however, sun, earth, and moon are not capitalized unless they are listed with other capitalized astronomical names. ⟨Venus⟩ ⟨Big Dipper⟩ ⟨Sirius⟩

22. Genera in scientific names in zoology and botany are capitalized; names of species are not. ⟨a cabbage butterfly (*Pieris rapae*)⟩

Plurals

The plurals of English words are regularly formed by the addition of the suffix *-s* or *-es* to the singular, as

⟨dog → dogs⟩ ⟨race → races⟩ ⟨guy → guys⟩ ⟨monarch → monarchs⟩ ⟨grass → grasses⟩ ⟨dish → dishes⟩ ⟨buzz → buzzes⟩ ⟨branch → branches⟩

The plurals of words that follow other patterns, as

⟨army → armies⟩ ⟨duo → duos⟩ ⟨ox → oxen⟩ ⟨foot → feet⟩ ⟨p. → pp.⟩ ⟨sheep → sheep⟩ ⟨phenomenon → phenomena *or* phenomenons⟩ ⟨libretto → librettos *or* libretti⟩ ⟨curriculum → curricula⟩ ⟨alga → algae⟩ ⟨corpus → corpora⟩ ⟨sergeant major → sergeants major *or* sergeant majors⟩ are given at the appropriate entries in the main body of the dictionary.